CORPORATION LAW

By

Franklin A. Gevurtz

Professor of Law
University of the Pacific, McGeorge School of Law,
Sacramento, California

HORNBOOK SERIES®

WEST
GROUP

ST. PAUL, MINN., 2000

Hornbook Series, WESTLAW, and the West Group symbol
are registered trademarks used herein under license.

COPYRIGHT © 2000 By WEST GROUP
          610 Opperman Drive
          P.O. Box 64526
          St. Paul, MN 55164–0526
          1–800–328–9352

ISBN 0–314–21191–8

 TEXT IS PRINTED ON 10% POST CONSUMER RECYCLED PAPER

To Carmen, Sara, Marvin and Manya

*

Preface

This book is intended for several audiences. As with all books in the "hornbook" series, a primary audience is law students; in this instance, students taking courses variously labeled Corporations or Business Associations. The book corresponds to the advice I give to students who ask for recommendations on secondary reading. This advice is to go beyond sources which simply provide pithy recitals of rules, and seek a source which provides a careful explanation of what the rules mean, the context and policies out of which the rules arise, and how the rules might apply to different situations. Otherwise, the result all too often is an examination answer consisting of recitals of rules, followed by sentences which demonstrate that the student has little idea as to the meaning of what he or she just said, much less how to apply the rules to analyze the problem at hand. Keeping in mind that the goal of this book is to clarify rather than simply recite, the text pays particular attention to correcting common misconceptions I have found among students of corporations law over the years. In addition, consistent with the notion that one cannot comprehend the law without understanding leading and illustrative cases in which courts have developed and applied various rules, the text spends considerable time discussing and critiquing court opinions found in most of the Corporations casebooks.

A second audience consists of members of the practicing bar; particularly those who only encounter corporations law problems on an occasional basis. A work of this size cannot hope to duplicate the sort of jurisdiction-specific research found in a multi-volume treatise. Instead, the goal of this book is to meet the type of request made by practitioners who have contacted me from time to time and explained that they had read all of the relevant cases on the particular issue facing them, but, lacking an overall context, they were not sure how the cases fit together.

In addition, I hope this treatise might be of interest to courts and commentators in seeking the appropriate resolution of issues of corporations law. In teaching corporations law for almost two decades, I confess that I have developed some strong opinions as to what the law is and what the law should be. In several areas, I already had expressed my viewpoint in law review articles, from which this book draws. In numerous other areas, I have taken advantage of the opportunity of writing this book to provide a more efficient forum for setting out my views.

At this point, word or two about style might be appropriate. I have deliberately adopted a conversational style; indeed, occasionally a light-hearted one. To be candid, it made the book more enjoyable for me to write (the utility of which is not to be underestimated in a four year project). I hope it also makes for a more accessible—or, to use the marketing cliche, "user friendly"—product. In order to maximize the space available for explanation and discussion, I deliberately have kept citations to a minimum; just enough to keep me honest and to provide the interested reader with a stepping stone for additional research.

Finally, a few words of thanks are called for. My colleague, Michael Malloy—who, being the author of West's hornbook on banking law, has some experience with this sort of work—graciously gave his time to review the manuscript for this book. My research assistants, Ryan Herrick and Anne Sherlock spent long hours cite checking the manuscript. Not to sound like a PBS commercial, but this work was made possible by generous financial support from the McGeorge School of Law. My wife, Carmen, deserves credit for her encouragement when it seemed like this project would never finish. Even my daughter, Sara, lent a hand by typing in all of the internal cross references.

WESTLAW® Overview

Corporation Law offers a detailed and comprehensive treatment of basic rules, principles and issues relating to the law of corporations. To supplement the information contained in this book, you can access Westlaw, a computer–assisted legal research service of West Group. For information on subscribing to Westlaw, call 1–800–762–5272. Westlaw contains a broad array of legal resources, including case law, statutes, expert commentary, current developments and various other types of information.

Learning how to use these materials effectively will enhance your legal research abilities. To help you coordinate the information in the book with your Westlaw research, this volume contains an appendix listing Westlaw databases, search techniques and sample problems.

THE PUBLISHER

Summary of Contents

*

Table of Contents

───────

CORPORATION
LAW

*

Chapter I

FORMATION

[Research References]

AmJur 2d, Corporations §§ 98–272

CJS, Corporations §§ 19–66

ALR Index: Articles of Incorporation; Disregard of Corporate Entity; Piercing Corporate Veil

ALR Digest: Corporations §§ 5–14.5

Am Jur Legal Forms 2d, Corporations §§ 74:141–74:1306

Am Jur Pleading and Practice Forms (Rev), Corporations §§ 41–56, 243–253.6

45 POF3d 1, Grounds for Disregarding the Corporate Entity and Piercing the Corporate Veil

This chapter explores a variety of topics unified by two themes. The first, as evident from the title of this chapter, is that these topics generally relate to the formation of corporations. This includes considering the "why," "where" and "how" persons go about forming corporations. A second theme involves the principle reason persons traditionally have for choosing to do business in the corporate form—this being to obtain limited liability for the business' owners. In these materials, we shall explore both the history and policy behind limited liability, and a number of circumstances in which owners will not obtain the limited liability they sought.

§ 1.1 Why Corporations Exist

Odds are that corporations own most of the businesses which any of us come into contact with on any given day. Almost all large businesses—the big chain stores, the producers of brand name merchandise, and the like—operate through corporations. While smaller businesses are more diverse in their forms, use of corporations is extremely common there too. We begin our study of corporate law by asking why is this the case.

Corporations exist by virtue of two decisions. The more immediate is a choice by private parties. Persons who plan to start a business, or who already are in business, decide they should operate this business through a corporation. Commonly, they reach this decision upon the advice of their attorney.

The second decision is one of public policy. State governments decided to establish the legal entity we call a corporation as a form in which to conduct businesses. Legislative and judicial developments over the years have removed impediments to the use of business corporations, while granting corporations various features desired by those choosing between business forms. The most significant of these features is limiting the shareholders' liability for the debts of the business.

These two decisions provide the road map for our discussion in this section.

1.1.1 Private Perspective [I]: Available Choices of Business Form

One or more individuals arrive at an attorney's office for help in setting up a business. They must choose what form the business organization will take. Alternately, perhaps the individuals already are in business and wish to reconsider its form as they reach a different stage in the business' development. In either event, they have several options:

a. Sole proprietorship

The sole proprietorship is the simplest form of business. One individual is the owner. If he or she needs help in operating the business, he or she hires employees or contracts the work out. To obtain property needed in the business, the owner buys or leases the property. If the business requires more capital (money) than the owner has, the owner must borrow. The owner is personally responsible to repay whatever he or she borrows and to pay for whatever he or she rents or buys (including under contracts entered on the owner's behalf by his or her employees or other agents acting within their actual or apparent authority). The owner is also vicariously liable for any torts committed by his or her employees in the scope of their employment. If any revenue produced by the business is left over after payment of the business' expenses (in other words, there is a profit), the owner gets it. The owner is entirely in charge of the business. This is the way Tveye conducted his milk business in the shtetl in Russia, to take an example from literature.

b. Partnership

Individuals who supply services, capital or property to a business often agree to share the profits from, and control over, the venture. The result is, instead of having one owner, we now have a number of co-owners. Barring affirmative steps to establish another form of business, this is a partnership—an association of persons carrying on, as co-owners, a business for profit.[1] Traditionally, most law firms with more than one lawyer have been partnerships.

The first thing to note about a partnership is that, as traditionally understood at common law, it is a label for a relationship between participants in a business. If two or more individuals agree to be in effect co-owners of a business, they are, by definition, partners. This is true

§ 1.1
1. *E.g.*, Uniform Partnership Act § 6(1).

even if they did not realize they were partners.[2] Notice that this creates the potential for litigation over who is a partner or co-owner. Generally, this entails having a share in profits and control;[3] albeit, many partners, in fact, may exercise little control over the business, and it is possible to share in a business' profits without being a partner.[4]

Because common law courts conceived of a partnership simply as a group of individuals who entered into a relationship with each other, a number of legal rules seemed to follow as logical corollaries. The most significant is that the individual partners have unlimited personal liability for debts incurred in the business. After all, this is simply a group of people who became joint parties to a contract or vicariously liable for a tort. As such, the creditor can force each member of the group to pay.

While the common law recognized and created rules for partnerships, almost every state has enacted the Uniform Partnership Act (or the recent Revised Uniform Partnership Act). The Uniform Act sometimes codifies and sometimes alters common law rules regarding partnerships. It does not change, however, the basic rule of unlimited personal liability for partners.[5]

c. *Limited partnership*

Dissatisfaction with the unlimited liability of partners and sole proprietors has been a primary impetus for the development of other business forms. One of these, the limited partnership, derives its genesis from the *societe en commandite* of continental Europe. The idea is that passive investors should not be liable for the debts of the business. After all, they did not have control over either the creation of the debts or the activities of the business which resulted in the firm being unable to pay its bills.

Starting in New York in 1822, legislatures adopted this idea by enacting statutes creating an entity called the limited partnership. Almost every state now has enacted the Uniform Limited Partnership Act as revised in 1976 and 1985. A limited partnership has two types of partners. There are general partners, for whom the ordinary rules of partnership, including unlimited personal liability, apply.[6] Then there are limited partners. For the limited partners, the statutes historically imposed a tradeoff: Abstain from controlling the business, and the statute will limit your liability to loss of your investment in the business.[7] By virtue of this tradeoff, individuals can invest in a business in return for a share of the profits—something which might otherwise result in courts considering the investors to be partners—and still avoid personal liability for the firm's debts.

---

2. *E.g.*, Minute Maid Corp. v. United Foods, Inc., 291 F.2d 577 (5th Cir.1961).

3. *See, e.g.*, Martin v. Peyton, 246 N.Y. 213, 158 N.E. 77 (1927).

4. *See, e.g.*, Uniform Partnership Act § 7(4).

5. Uniform Partnership Act § 15; Revised Uniform Partnership Act § 306(a).

6. *E.g.*, Uniform Limited Partnership Act § 403.

7. *E.g.*, Uniform Limited Partnership Act (1916) § 7.

Because limited partnerships, unlike partnerships and sole proprietorships, only exist by virtue of statutes, their formation requires complying with the statute. This essentially means filing a document with the state.[8]

d. Corporation

Like limited partnerships, corporations exist by virtue of statutes. Yet, the underlying idea behind the corporation is historically different than the notion behind the limited partnership. Traditionally, the key concept regarding the corporation has been that it is a legal entity separate and distinct from its owners. This entity has its own rights and obligations. Notice how this idea of a separate entity with its own obligations can provide a very different rationalization for limited liability than the "no control" rationale underlying the limited partnership statutes.

Interestingly enough, however, as we shall discuss later, owners of corporations often did not enjoy limited liability during the early history of business corporations. Other attributes of separate entity status still made this form useful. For example, since the corporation had a life of its own, owners could come and go by transferring their interests, without impact on the entity. By contrast, since the law traditionally conceived of a partnership as a specific group of individuals, departure of any partner meant the end of the existing partnership. Furthering this difference, fungible shares (or "stock") came to represent ownership interests in the corporation (hence, the reference to the corporation's owners as stockholders or shareholders). This means that the division of profits and power in a corporation results from the distribution, at any given moment, of these transferable instruments representing tiny shares in the company. This facilitates the development of active trading markets in corporate stock. By comparison, normally an initial agreement among partners, alterable only by unanimous consent, governs the allocation of profits and power in a partnership or limited partnership.

Moreover, the corporation developed around different management principles than the partnership or limited partnership. Presumably drawing from ideas of republican government, control over the corporation resides in a board (the board of directors) elected annually by the shareholders. The board then appoints officers to carry out day-to-day management. The directors and officers, as agents, have no personal liability for the debts of the business. This stands in contrast to the traditional partnership scheme of direct governance by the owners (the partners), or the traditional limited partnership scheme of a group of partners having permanent management responsibilities by virtue of their willingness to accept unlimited personal liability.

e. Limited liability company and limited liability partnership

One other corollary to conceiving of the corporation as a legal entity separate from its owners is the treatment of corporations as separate

---

8. *E.g.,* Uniform Limited Partnership Act § 201.

taxpayers under federal and state income tax laws. For reasons we shall outline shortly, this tax treatment often results in paying more taxes.

The limited liability company and limited liability partnership are new business forms which state legislatures developed in response to tax concerns. The idea is to have a business form which federal income tax authorities will treat like a partnership, thereby avoiding the tax disadvantages of the corporation's separate entity treatment. At the same time, the owners of these firms enjoy limited liability, just like shareholders in a corporation. Moreover, unlike a limited partnership, all the owners of the limited liability company or limited liability partnership enjoy limited liability regardless of their participation in control.

Wyoming enacted the first limited liability company statute in 1977. Following a favorable pronouncement by the Internal Revenue Service in 1988 as to the tax treatment of such firms, legislation establishing limited liability companies quickly spread to every state. The governing statutes contain a blend of provisions borrowed from the laws of partnerships, limited partnerships and corporations, with a heavy emphasis on establishing features (such as direct owner management, non-transferable ownership interests, and dissolution of the entity upon owner departure) which would lead the IRS to tax such entities as partnerships despite limited liability for the owners. Recently, however, the Internal Revenue Service generously announced that it will allow owners of unincorporated businesses simply to request tax treatment as partnerships or corporations without regard to such factors (a so-called check-the-box approach).[9]

Limited liability partnerships are an even more recent invention. Generally, they allow either professional firms or all businesses—depending upon the statute in the state—to continue to operate under the law of ordinary partnership, except that the partners enjoy limited liability. Under many statutes, this limited liability is only for tort claims against the partnership and not contract debts.

As creatures of statute, the formation of limited liability companies and limited liability partnerships requires compliance with statutory requirements[10]—much like limited partnerships and corporations.

1.1.2 Private Perspective [II]: Factors in Selecting Between Business Forms

Having set out the generally available forms for conducting business, we can now explore the major factors the parties and their attorney should consider in selecting which form to use.

a. Limited liability

The discussion above emphasized limited liability, because of the impact this factor has had on the historic evolution of business entities.

---

9. Treas. Reg. §§ 7701–1–7701–3.

10. *E.g.*, Cal. Corp. Code §§ 16953, 17050.

Yet, an attorney advising specific clients must be more discerning in weighing how significant limited liability is in a particular case. For example, say a recent graduate from a culinary academy approaches an attorney for help in setting up a restaurant business in which this chef will be the only owner or investor. It might be useful for the attorney to inquire into the chef's financial situation before launching into a long dissertation on the various entities which offer limited liability. After all, it may turn out that the chef must, as a practical matter, put all of his or her meager assets into starting the business, meaning he or she stands to lose everything if the business fails, regardless of limited liability.

Assuming, however, that the owner(s) of the business have sufficient assets to make limited liability worthwhile, the question then becomes where does this factor lead the attorney and his or her clients in terms of choice of business form. As we discussed earlier, sole proprietors and partners are, as a general proposition, personally liable for contract and tort debts incurred in the business. One question about this arises in the partnership context: How much of the firm's debt is each partner responsible for? For example, if there are five partners, is each only liable for one-fifth of the debt?

To answer this question, one must distinguish between the rights of the partners as between themselves, and the liability of partners to third party creditors. With respect to the rights of the partners inter se, the partnership agreement (or the Uniform Partnership Act in the absence of agreement) dictates how much of the business' losses each partner is supposed to suffer.[11] Outside creditors, however, are not parties to the partnership agreement. Instead, each creditor has the right to seek payment of the entire debt from any partner.[12] The partner who pays the debt may then have a claim for indemnity against his or her fellow partners, but keep in mind that this claim is only as good as the solvency of one's partners. What this means is that each partner is at risk for potentially the entire amount of the partnership's debts.

This fact explains in large part why there are very few publicly held partnerships—in other words, partnerships with numerous, even thousands, of scattered owners—as there are corporations. With more owners, any given owner receives a smaller percentage of the business' profits and has less control over the business to protect one's interest. Yet, each owner theoretically could face liability for the entire debt of the business. The result is that risk grows disproportionately to return with more partners.

---

11. Uniform Partnership Act § 18; Revised Uniform Partnership Act §§ 103, 401.

12. *E.g.,* Uniform Partnership Act § 15; Revised Uniform Partnership Act § 306(a). Under the Uniform Partnership Act, partners are jointly liable to contract creditors. This means the creditor must name and serve all partners as defendants, but does not prevent a single solvent partner ending up paying the entire debt. The Revised Uniform Act, following the lead of a number of states, makes partners jointly and severally liable to contract, as well as tort, creditors. Under joint and several liability, a creditor can selectively sue only some of the partners.

Yet, the notion of unlimited liability for the sole proprietor or partner is somewhat oversimplified. It is possible to achieve a degree of protection even in these business forms. For example, if the business has assets which can serve as collateral for loans, some creditors might be willing to make a "non-recourse" loan. This is a loan in which the creditor agrees only to look to the collateral, and not the borrower's other assets, for repayment. To protect from tort claims, owners can purchase liability insurance. While it is true that tort damages sometimes exceed insurance policy limits, this is a risk which all of us accept every time we drive, since auto insurance policies invariably have limits.

Conversely, we suggested earlier that owners of corporations (stockholders) have limited liability. It is important to understand precisely what this means. It means that stockholders have no liability for the corporation's debts simply by virtue of being stockholders.[13] Hence, all they stand to lose by virtue of being stockholders if the corporation goes under is whatever they paid to purchase their stock. This is why it is often said that stockholders' liability is limited to their investment. We also noted that those who manage the corporation (the directors and officers) do not have personal liability for the corporation's debts simply by virtue of managing the company.[14]

Understanding the meaning of limited liability leads one to recognize its important gaps. While stockholders and managers are not liable for the *corporation's* debts by reason of their status, they are liable for any contracts to which they agree to become a party personally, or for any torts they personally commit. For example, suppose an attorney forms a corporation to provide legal services (which he or she will perform in the role of an employee for the corporation). If the attorney commits malpractice, the attorney is liable for his or her own tort. The fact that the attorney, as shareholder, does not need to pay for the corporation's vicarious liability is irrelevant.[15] This is because vicarious liability adds another defendant; it does not relieve the employee of liability. Of more frequent significance, creditors dealing with small corporations commonly demand that the shareholders give personal guarantees for the corporation's performance. This puts the shareholder on the hook based upon his or her own contract.

Moreover, we shall see in later portions of this book exceptions to the general rule of limited liability for a corporation's shareholders and managers. For example, this chapter closes with a look at the doctrine of piercing the corporate veil. This doctrine enables courts, "for reasons of justice," to make shareholders personally liable for the corporation's debts. We shall see that courts apply this doctrine with such frequency and freakishness that shareholders of closely held corporations can never really consider themselves entirely safe.

---

13. *E.g.*, Model Business Corporation Act § 6.22.

14. For an extended exploration of the liabilities of directors and officers, see §§ 4.1–4.2 *infra*.

15. *E.g.*, Michaelis v. Benavides, 61 Cal. App.4th 681, 71 Cal.Rptr.2d 776 (Cal.App. 1998).

Assuming, given all the above, the attorney and clients still desire a form of business which provides limited liability, they have a number of options besides the corporation. For example, we discussed earlier the limited partnership. The obvious problem lies in the traditional requirement that control remains in the hands of one or more general partners who will have unlimited personal liability. This creates two problems.

To begin with, individuals wishing limited liability must be willing to give up control. In fact, however, the Uniform Limited Partnership Act, as revised in 1976 and especially 1985, dramatically waters down this requirement. It contains a laundry list of powers which limited partners can exercise without being considered to have impermissible control.[16] This includes, under the 1985 revision, voting on anything the partnership agreement empowers the limited partners to approve or disapprove. Moreover, under the act as revised in 1985, limited partners who exercise control only face liability to creditors (or, at least, only to contract creditors) who, because of the control, mistakenly thought that the limited partner was, in fact, a general partner.[17]

Even if limited partners are satisfied with limited control, there is a second problem. There must be at least one general partner willing to face unlimited liability. Lest one look for a "street person" to fill this role, keep in mind that the general partner(s) manage the limited partnership. One common response has been to have a corporation act as general partner. Of course, you might then ask why not just have the corporation without the limited partnership. The answer lies in tax concerns. Even this answer is now obsolete (and so may be the limited partnership) given the rise of the limited liability company.

As we noted earlier, the limited liability company provides the same limited liability to its owners and managers as a corporation does to its shareholders and managers.[18] Accordingly, from a limited liability standpoint, neither form of business should have an advantage over the other. By contrast, in some jurisdictions, the limited liability partnership only provides protection from tort claims and not contract debts.[19] In other jurisdictions, however, a limited liability partnership provides the partners protection from both tort and contract claims.[20]

b. Exit rules

We briefly discussed earlier the traditionally perceived advantages of the corporation over the partnership in terms of perpetual existence (the

---

16. Uniform Limited Partnership Act § 303(b).

17. Uniform Limited Partnership Act § 303(a). The reference in Section 303(a) to a limited partner's liability to persons who "transact business with the limited partnership" is ambiguous. One way to read this language is that the caveat about creditor reliance is only relevant to contract creditors, and, hence, tort claimants can recover from limited partners who exercise impermissible control without showing confusion as to the status of the limited part-

ner. An alternate reading, however, is that tort claimants cannot recover from limited partners, regardless of the limited partners' control.

18. See, e.g., Robert B. Thompson, *The Limits of Liability in the New Limited Liability Entities,* 32 Wake Forest L. Rev. 1 (1997).

19. E.g., Texas Revised Partnership Act § 3.08.

20. E.g., Cal. Corp. Code § 16306(c).

corporation continues to exist despite departure of a shareholder)[21] and transferability of interests (stockholders may sell their shares representing interests in both profits and control).[22] In fact, while many writers refer to these two factors as separate considerations to weigh in choosing between business forms,[23] they are really flip sides of the same question: What happens when an owner departs the firm, either because he or she decides to sell, or because of death, or because creditors force the sale of the owner's property in a personal bankruptcy—in other words, what are the exit rules?

If there is only one owner, it generally does not matter whether we have a sole proprietorship or a corporation. If the owner decides to sell, or dies, or goes bankrupt, he or she must sell the entire business or pass it on to his or her heirs.

The presence of more than one owner, however, introduces several models for handling an owner's death, bankruptcy or desire to sell. One possibility is a "buy-out" model. Under this approach, if the other owners wish to continue the business, they must buy out the interest of the owner who dies, goes bankrupt or desires to sell. Another approach is the "free transfer" model. Here, one owner's death, bankruptcy or desire to sell does not affect the legal right of the other owners to continue the business. Instead, if an owner wishes to sell his or her interest, the owner has the right to sell the interest to any buyer. If an owner dies, the deceased owner's interest passes to his or her heirs. If an owner goes bankrupt, his or her creditors can force the sale of the bankrupt owner's interest. The buyer or heir then picks up all the rights to profits and control which the departing owner had by virtue of the ownership interest. Finally, we can have a "lock-in" model. The owner who wishes to sell has no right either to do so or to force the other owners to buy him or her out. Of course, a lock-in cannot prevent a transfer to somebody in the case of death or bankruptcy.

The different business forms follow different models. As we already saw, corporations follow the free transfer model. Partnerships, limited partnerships and limited liability companies follow the buy-out model. The mechanics of the buy-out, however, vary between these different forms.

The partnership buy-out scheme is rather complicated. Under the Uniform Partnership Act, each partner (barring other agreement) has the right to dissolve the partnership at any time.[24] Any partner's death or bankruptcy also causes dissolution of the partnership.[25] It is erroneous to think of dissolution, however, as akin to Dorothy's pouring water

---

21. *See, e.g.,* Model Business Corporation Act § 3.02.

22. *See, e.g.,* Model Business Corporation Act § 6.27.

23. *E.g.,* Thomas Hazen, *The Decision to Incorporate,* 58 Neb. L. Rev. 627 (1979).

24. Uniform Partnership Act § 31(1)(b); Revised Uniform Partnership Act § 801(1).

25. Uniform Partnership Act § 31(4), (5). Under the Revised Act, however, a partner's death or bankruptcy causes a "dissociation," but not necessarily a dissolution. Revised Uniform Partnership Act § 601(6)(I), (7)(I), 801.

on the "Wicked Witch of the West." Dissolution of the partnership does not terminate the business. True, upon dissolution, each partner, who has not breached the agreement, has the right to demand the sale of the business' assets, payment of its debts and distribution of the remaining proceeds to the partners (often referred to as liquidation).[26] Yet, one might accomplish this by selling the entire business as a going concern. Moreover, the partners can agree to some other outcome to follow dissolution.[27] What this means is that the partners who want to continue the venture either can attempt to purchase the business in the liquidation sale or else reach an agreement with the departing partner (or the representative of his or her estate) to buy out the departing partner's interest in lieu of liquidation. In other words, if the remaining partners wish to continue the business, they must buy out the departing partner.[28] Partners can change the ability to dissolve at will by agreeing to a partnership for a term. Yet, this will not alter the situation upon death or bankruptcy. Moreover, even with a term, a partner can depart at any time and force a buy-out—but at a much less favorable price and with the possibility of no payment until expiration of the term.[29]

Suppose, however, a partner seeks to sell his or her ownership interest to another person (or pass it to an heir upon the partner's death). Unless the partners agree otherwise, the Uniform Partnership Act provides that the recipient only obtains the partner's interest in profit distributions. The recipient will not become a new partner with any rights to participate in controlling the firm (or even the right to look at the partnership's financial records) unless the other partners unanimously agree.[30] This typically makes the transferred interest much less valuable.

Under the Uniform Limited Partnership Act, limited partnerships also follow a buy-out model, albeit under a somewhat different scheme. A general partner's departure—by virtue of death, bankruptcy, a decision to withdraw, or the like—triggers dissolution and liquidation barring other agreement or consent of the partners to continue without dissolution.[31] A limited partner's departure, however, does not trigger dissolution.[32] In lieu of the right to demand liquidation of the firm, the Uniform Act gives general partners (or their estate) the right to demand that the limited partnership pay them the fair value of their interest when their departure does not result in dissolution, and gives limited partners the right to withdraw and receive similar payment from the limited partner-

---

26. Uniform Partnership Act § 38(1); Revised Uniform Partnership Act § 807(a).

27. Uniform Partnership Act § 38(1); Revised Uniform Partnership Act § 802(b).

28. The Revised Act contains provisions for such a buy-out when there is a dissociation which does not lead to dissolution. Revised Uniform Partnership Act § 701.

29. Uniform Partnership Act §§ 31(2), 38(2); Revised Uniform Partnership Act §§ 602, 701(c), (h).

30. Uniform Partnership Act §§ 18(g), 27(1); Revised Uniform Partnership Act §§ 401(I), 503.

31. Uniform Limited Partnership Act § 801(4).

32. *See* Uniform Limited Partnership Act § 801.

ship upon six months notice.[33] This is subject to other agreement, which might provide departing partners more or less favorable price and terms.[34] Rights to transfer interests follow the same rules as a partnership.[35]

Limited liability company statutes vary as to exit rules. Most follow a limited partnership style buy-out scheme.[36] As with the withdrawal of a general partner from a limited partnership, departure of an owner (typically referred to as a "member") from a limited liability company—because of death, bankruptcy, a desire to withdraw, or the like—triggers dissolution unless there is a contrary agreement, or the remaining members consent to continue the company without dissolution. If there is no dissolution, then, in most states, members can withdraw and demand the company buy them out. Many states require the withdrawing member to give six months notice, much like a withdrawing limited partner. Members, under most limited liability company statutes, can alter these rules by agreement. Most limited liability company statutes follow the same rules for transfer of interests as partnerships and limited partnerships. One should note, however, that, up until recently, a primary reason limited liability company statutes followed partnership and limited partnership style exit rules was to ensure tax treatment as a partnership. This is no longer necessary under the Internal Revenue Services' "check-the-box" regulation. Hence, some states may change the exit rules in their limited liability company statutes.

These exit rules for the different forms of business, however, are not immutable. Rather, they are mostly default rules; in other words, the owners generally can alter these rules by agreement. For example, shareholders could change their corporation from the free transfer to the buy-out model. All this takes is their advance agreement that, if a shareholder dies, goes bankrupt, or wants to sell, the other shareholders or the corporation must purchase, instead of the shares going to an outsider. Alternately, shareholders might agree simply to not sell their shares without the consent of the other stockholders, thereby moving to the lock-in model (albeit, this may be an impermissible restraint on alienation). We shall examine such agreements in a later chapter of this book.

Owners can also change partnerships, limited partnerships or limited liability companies to follow a free transfer model. The governing agreement between the partners or members could provide that upon a partner's or member's departure, the remaining partners or members have the right to continue the business without buying out the interest of the departing partner or member. The agreement also could state that the departing partner or member, not only can transfer his or her

---

33. Uniform Limited Partnership Act §§ 603, 604.

34. Uniform Limited Partnership Act § 604.

35. Uniform Limited Partnership Act §§ 401, 702, 704(a).

36. For citations to the relevant provisions in various state limited liability company statutes see Franklin A. Gevurtz, *Freeze-outs and Squeeze-outs in Limited Liability Companies*, 73 Wash. U. L. Q. 497, 513–514 (1995).

interest in the firm's profits, but can substitute (without the need for consent from the remaining partners or members) the buyer or heir as a new partner or member in the firm with all the rights of the seller.

Where then does this take us as far as choice of business form? It turns out that exit rules are probably not a particularly important factor in choosing the form in which to conduct the closely held business (in other words, one with few owners). Actually, none of these three approaches is without problems in the closely held business. The buy-out model creates a liquidity problem for the continuing owners, who must be prepared to come up with funds to make the purchase. The other models, however, probably are even worse. Free transfer creates the problem of a stranger, with whom the existing owners may not be able to get along, entering into a close working relationship. Moreover, free transfer is often illusory because there is rarely an outside buyer for a minority interest in a closely held business. This turns free transfer into a de facto lock-in. The problems of locking individuals into relationships which have soured can be seen daily in the nation's family law courts (and soured business relationships can be every bit as nasty as a soured marriage). Assuming, based upon this, a decision to follow a buy-out approach, all the various forms give the parties the ability to do this with a modicum of planning.

On the other hand, free transfer works very nicely in the widely held business; as exemplified by the activities of stock exchanges every day. Corporate law follows the free transfer approach as its basic model. As stated above, partnerships, limited partnerships and limited liability companies could follow this approach by specially drafted agreements. Indeed, a number of limited partnerships have done so. Still, there are problems. Most significantly, consider the effect unlimited personal liability will have on the practical, if not legal, transferability of ordinary partnership interests. The buyer who becomes a new partner must be prepared to accept unlimited liability for all future debts of the business. At the same time, barring the creditors' agreement to a novation, the seller remains on the hook for all of the debts already incurred by the partnership.[37]

c. *Governance*

We noted earlier that corporate law provides for a sort of republican (in other words, representative) style of governance. Stockholders elect a board of directors, who are in overall charge of the corporation. Directors, in turn, appoint officers to handle day-to-day management. Certain fundamental decisions may require a vote of the shareholders. Shareholders normally vote, either to elect directors or on fundamental decisions, in proportion to their stock ownership. Director and shareholder decisions typically are by majority vote. This, of course, is a highly

---

37. *E.g.,* Uniform Partnership Act § 36.

simplified description and we shall spend time refining it later in this book.[38]

By contrast, the Uniform Partnership Act[39] and most state limited liability company statutes[40] provide, unless otherwise agreed, for a sort of direct democratic governance. All owners participate in management. For ordinary matters, the majority rules. Under the Uniform Partnership Act, the partners each have an equal vote, even if their contributions or interests in profits are unequal. Limited liability company statutes vary in terms of the voting power of members. Some follow the partnership scheme of one-owner-one-vote. Others follow a more corporate model of voting in proportion to contributions or interests in profits. Unlike the corporate scheme of majority rule, fundamental decisions in the partnership and under many limited liability company statutes require a unanimous vote.

We have already discussed the limited partnership governance scheme. The general partners manage the business under the same rules, as between themselves, as partners in an ordinary partnership. Limited partners are, for the most part, supposed to be passive. Unlike the corporate governance model, the owners of a limited partnership do not annually elect the general partners to run the company. Instead, the agreement initially entered between the partners normally specifies who are the general partners.

What is the significance of these different governance arrangements as far as choosing a business form? Notice how the corporate model seems to work for a business with numerous scattered owners with freely transferable interests. Here, direct management by all of the owners, and requirements for unanimous votes even on fundamental decisions, are likely to be impractical. By contrast, the direct governance scheme of the partnership likely corresponds with the desires of most owners of closely held businesses. If there are only a few owners, each with a major stake in the venture, most, if not all, of them are likely to want to participate in managing the business. They are also often likely to demand a veto on extraordinary decisions.

Does this mean that one should choose corporations for widely held businesses and partnerships or limited liability companies for closely held businesses? The answer is not necessarily. Again, as in the case of exit rules, these governance rules are not immutable. For example, the governance rules of the Uniform Partnership Act and almost all limited liability company statutes allow the owners to follow any model of management to which they agree. Hence, if a firm's partners or members wish management to reside in an annually elected board, they could provide this in their governing agreement. In fact, many large partnerships have managing committees instead of direct governance by all the

38. See § 3.1 *infra.*

39. Uniform Partnership Act § 18(e), (h); Revised Uniform Partnership Act § 401(f), (j).

40. See Gevurtz, *supra* Note 36 at 506–507.

partners. Conversely, we shall explore in a later chapter various methods by which owners of closely held corporations can follow a partnership style of governance. We shall see that this is extremely common.

So, is governance irrelevant to choice of business form? Not entirely. For example, while partners can agree as between themselves on any style of management, third party rights occasionally might undermine the effectiveness of this agreement. Under the Uniform Partnership Act, all partners have authority to bind the partnership to some transactions, despite the partnership agreement. Specifically, a partner can bind the firm to a transaction with a party who is unaware of the limits on the partner's actual authority, when the transaction is apparently for carrying on the partnership business "in the usual way."[41] Yet, this may not be as worrisome as it first seems. After all, in a partnership with numerous partners and a well established tradition of management by only some partners, a third party might have a difficult time with showing that the third party did not know of the limits on the individual partner's power or that the conduct of the partner who purported to act for the firm constituted carrying on the business in the usual way.

Many limited liability company statutes solve the partnership law problem of all owners having apparent authority to bind the firm. These statutes allow the owners to state, often in the public document filed to create the company, that "managers," rather than all members, will run the company. Doing so cuts off the authority of members who are not managers.[42]

Conversely, we will see that many courts historically were reluctant to allow shareholders in closely held corporations to follow partnership style management.[43] At one point, this might have suggested that parties desiring partnership style governance should not use the corporate form. Now, however, parties exercising a modicum of legal skill should be able to avoid falling victim to this judicial attitude, to the extent it still exists.

d. Cost, acceptance and coherence

What we have seen so far is that the factors often suggested as the basis for choosing between corporations and other business forms are, for the most part, things which owners can obtain regardless of which form they use. Contracting can dictate governance, exit rules and even to a great extent limited liability, despite the form chosen. Perhaps choice of business form is irrelevant.

Before dismissing all of our previous discussion of choice of business form, however, one should consider the impact of contracting itself. Altering the rules normally prescribed by the law for a business form entails a number of costs. One obvious cost is the attorney's fees for drafting the necessary contracts. This is not to say well advised parties

---

41. Uniform Partnership Act § 9; Revised Uniform Partnership Act § 301.

42. *E.g.*, Cal. Corp. Code § 17157(a), (b).

43. See § 5.2.2.*a infra*.

can avoid the need for custom contracting by their choice of business form. Rather, it is a matter of degree. The more the parties choose a business form with the intention of drafting around its norms, the more drafting their attorney must do. For example, recall we earlier discussed how partners or proprietors could gain limited liability if their creditors agree to non-recourse contracts. Making such contracts, however, can entail significant negotiating and drafting, especially with respect to the collateral. It can be far easier to have the creditors deal with a corporation.

Two other costs of contracting around statutory norms are more subtle. The first is the burden of convincing the participants in the venture and those doing business with it to accept unconventional arrangements. A study of "Silicon Valley" start-up companies by Professor Joseph Bankman provides an illustration.[44] Generally, participants in these high technology start-up ventures have organized them as corporations, despite the fact that this has meant the loss of significant tax savings. Professor Bankman interviewed the participants to find out why. One common answer was this allowed managers in these ventures to receive stock options as compensation. Yet, one can structure partnership interests to provide the economic equivalent to stock options. The reason various interviewees gave Professor Bankman for not doing so was that it would be too difficult to convince the managers that the partnership interests, in fact, gave the equivalent of stock options. If convincing sophisticated individuals in face-to-face dealings to accept an unconventional arrangement is difficult, one can imagine how challenging it is to market to widely scattered investors a different sort of ownership than the corporate stocks and bonds they are used to.

At this point the reader might wonder what kind of bureaucratic mind-set one must deal with in the business world, when individuals have such an irrational aversion to change. In fact, however, this is not as irrational as it might seem. This is because there is one other cost to consider: The cost of contracting mistakes and omissions. Specifically, the more parties choose a form for their business with the intention of contracting around the statutory norms, arguably the greater the potential for unintended and undesirable consequences.

To understand why, it is useful to introduce the concept of "coherence," by which we mean that all the terms governing the business venture work together in a sensible fashion.[45] To illustrate, return to the fact that corporations normally follow a free transfer model to deal with departure of owners. This norm, in turn, makes possible active trading markets in corporate stock. The liquidity provided by such markets encourages investment in the publicly held corporation. Why has this not

44. Joseph Bankman, *The Structure of Silicon Valley Start–Ups*, 41 U.C.LA. L. Rev. 1737 (1994).

45. For a development of this concept see Larry E. Ribstein, *Statutory Forms for* *Closely Held Firms: Theories and Evidence from LLCs,* 73 Wash. U. L. Q. 369, 381–382 (1995).

happened to anywhere near the same extent for partnerships and other non-corporate forms?

The answer is not that partnerships and other non-corporate forms legally cannot follow a free transfer model. On the contrary, we saw earlier that partnerships and other forms could provide this by contract. Rather, the answer is that the practicality of free transfer depends on a lot more than simply the exit rules. We already noted one example: Unlimited personal liability will put a damper on trading ownership interests which would make the purchaser a partner.

Governance also plays a role. The republican model of corporate governance in which shareholders elect directors by voting in proportion to their stockholding is well suited to the firm with free transfer of ownership. Because stockholders, as such, do not directly participate in managing the corporation, they can trade their stock without disrupting the running of the company. At the same time, the liquidity from being able to sell in an active trading market makes the shareholders more willing not to participate directly in management. On the other hand, the fact stock carries proportionate voting rights gives the purchaser of a majority of the stock the power to replace management. The fact that the purchaser of a majority of the stock also gets most of the economic worth of the corporation gives the purchaser an incentive for responsible action in selecting management. This creates some discipline over those in charge of the corporation.

Finally, the fact that corporate law both assumes the norm of, and provides for, ownership interests based upon fungible shares of stock encourages active trading. Purchasers can buy in small quantities. Current shareholders can sell portions of their holdings. There is no need to amend, or even for the buyer to read, any agreement setting out the profit shares or management rights of all the owners of the corporation. The bottom line is that a variety of corporate law rules work together to make public ownership and trading in corporate shares attractive.

By contrast, unlimited personal liability is likely to make partners particularly insistent on being able to protect themselves through a direct role in management and by having the right to veto extraordinary decisions. This, in turn, suggests the desirability of following a buy-out, rather than a free-transfer, approach to owner departure, since free transfer can lead to problems when there is direct management by, and a veto for, all owners. On the other hand, the availability of a buy-out makes direct management and veto powers more tolerable than if there was no exit for dissatisfied partners. Also, as we shall see later in this book, it is much more straightforward and less prone to unintended consequences for a few owners to specify their economic and management rights expressly in a contract, than it is to attempt to achieve the same results by playing with the distribution of stock. Hence, partnership rules also interrelate.

These interrelationships create the hazard that parties and their attorneys will underestimate the impact of deviations from statutory norms. Often more dangerous, parties risk overlooking some of the terms they should agree to in order to achieve coherence when they choose a form of business organization which the legislature established with a very different type of ownership in mind.

For example, later in this book, we will look at situations in which the majority owner(s) of a closely held corporation squeeze a minority shareholder out from sharing in the profits of the business.[46] This is a frequent problem in closely held corporations, but rarely comes up in partnerships. Why? Because various provisions in partnership law work together to prevent the phenomenon. Corporations statutes, drafted with the widely held business in mind, have different provisions. Unfortunately, many times, neither the parties putting together a closely held corporation, nor their attorney, recognize the significance of all of the different provisions until after a problem arises and it is too late for contracting.

e. Taxes

As we mentioned earlier, saving taxes is often an important consideration in choosing between forms in which to conduct a business. The details are complex and well beyond the scope of this book. For our purposes, it is sufficient to understand the broad outline.

The Internal Revenue Code treats a corporation as a taxpaying entity separate from its shareholders. This means the corporation pays tax on its income.[47] The corporation's stockholders do not recognize the corporation's earnings as part of their taxable income. On the other hand, when the corporation pays a dividend—in other words, distributes profits—to its shareholders, the shareholders must recognize, as taxable income, the dividend they receive.[48] This dividend does not provide a deduction for the corporation; that is to say, the corporation cannot subtract the amount of the dividend from its earnings in computing the income on which it must pay tax.

By contrast, a partnership is not a taxpaying entity. When the partnership makes income, it pays no tax. Instead, each partner treats his or her share of the partnership's earnings as part of the partner's taxable income.[49] This is true whether the partnership distributes the earnings to the partners or keeps the earnings to reinvest in the business. Unlike dividends paid by a corporation to its shareholders, partners generally do not recognize as taxable income any money distributed by the partnership to them.[50] This is because the partners already paid a tax on this income when the partnership earned it. A sole proprietorship reaches the same result. The income of the business is simply the proprietor's taxable income, and it is his or her money to use.

46. See § 5.1.1 infra.
47. I.R.C. § 11.
48. I.R.C. § 61(a)(7).

49. I.R.C. §§ 701, 702.
50. I.R.C. §§ 705(a), 731.

So, which treatment saves taxes? The answer depends upon a number of variables. To begin with, the tax rates paid by corporations on their income (in other words, the percentage of income which the taxpayer pays as tax) are different than the tax rates paid by individuals on their income.[51] This difference depends upon the amount of earnings made. For some levels of earnings, corporations pay tax at a higher tax rate than an individual making the same amount of money. For some levels of income (particularly higher levels) corporate rates are lower. To add to the complexity, Congress keeps changing the rates as it passes various "tax reform" and deficit reduction bills. The upshot is that at some levels of income a corporation will pay more taxes, and at some levels it will pay less taxes, than would partners or proprietors whose partnership or proprietorship made the same amount of money.

Some business owners may be tempted to choose their form of business based upon how this rate comparison will play out for a business with the earnings they expect to have. This is shortsighted. The owners need to ask themselves how they are going to see any benefit from the money their business earns. As we noted above, when a corporation pays a dividend to its shareholders, the shareholders must recognize the dividend as taxable income. This means that the government gets two bites at taxing a corporation's earnings—once when the corporation earns the money and a second time when the corporation pays a dividend to its shareholders. Writers often refer to this as the double taxation of corporate earnings. By contrast, the government gets only one bite at taxing the earnings of a partnership or proprietorship— when the business makes the money. The owners' withdrawal of the money from the business for personal use is tax free.

Does this double taxation of corporate earnings mean that a corporation is always at a tax disadvantage relative to a partnership or sole proprietorship? Not necessarily. Owners of a corporation can avoid the double tax by having the corporation *not* pay dividends. For example, suppose the corporation hires its shareholders as employees and pays them a salary for their work. Reasonable salaries are deductible; in other words, the corporation can subtract the amount paid as a reasonable salary from its earnings in computing its taxable income.[52] This means the government will tax this amount only once (salaries are taxable income for the employee shareholder). Needless to say, there are limits to this approach. The Internal Revenue Service can, and frequently does, challenge salaries as being in excess of reasonable compensation, and so not fully deductible.

Another approach to avoiding the payment of taxable dividends is simply to have the corporation accumulate the earnings. There are penalty taxes, however, for corporations caught engaging in this sort of tactic for the purpose of preventing the double tax.[53] More fundamentally, what then is the point of having the business earn money? Presum-

---

51. I.R.C. §§ 1, 11.
52. I.R.C. § 162(a)(1).

53. I.R.C. §§ 531–537.

ably, the shareholders will see the value of their stock rise in reflection of the corporation's retained earnings. Yet, any profit the shareholders make on selling their stock is taxable income; which brings us back to the double tax. Perhaps, in some cases, deferring tax until an owner sells his or her stock—particularly if the gain on the sale of stock qualifies for the often favorable rates on capital gains income—will substantially mitigate the double tax from this strategy. Determining whether this will be so in a given case can require complex calculations. Best of all (from a standpoint of saving taxes), the shareholder can die. This will allow his or her heirs to sell the stock without paying any tax on the pre-death increase in the stock's value.[54]

So far, we have been looking at the tax impact for a business which is earning money. Suppose we expect the business to lose money. In fact, many new ventures expect to go through a period of losses (often for years in the case of some high technology firms) before they reach profitability. These losses can generate deductions. A corporation, being a separate taxpaying entity, can subtract these deductions from its earnings in computing its taxable income. Unfortunately, if the corporation has no earnings (or less earnings than deductible losses), then all the company can do is wait and hope that in some future year it will have earnings against which it can subtract its accumulated unused deductions. Many times, however, this hope is forlorn and no one ever gets the benefit of the deductions. Even if the corporation eventually achieves profits against which to offset the deductions, the delay in the deductions' use makes the deductions less valuable (because of the time value of money).

By contrast, not only does the tax code treat the income of a partnership or proprietorship as the taxable income of the partners or proprietor, but deductions from the business also flow through to the partners or proprietor. What this means is that, in computing their taxable income for the year, partners and proprietors can subtract all (for a proprietor), or each partner's share (for a partnership), of the deductions generated by the business from earnings partners or proprietors made during the year in other ventures or activities. This creates what is known as a tax shelter. Congress has enacted highly complex rules limiting the ability of taxpayers to use deductions from one business to offset (or "shelter") income from other activities.[55] Nevertheless, these rules do not prevent all such use. The upshot is that the use of partnerships and proprietorships, rather than the corporate form, often allows the owners of a business, which is expected to incur losses, to save significant taxes.

Subchapter S of the Internal Revenue Code[56] provides an additional wrinkle on this discussion. It allows certain corporations to elect tax treatment along the same lines as a partnership. Corporations which so elect are known as "S corporations." There are a number of require-

54. *See* I.R.C. § 1014.

55. *E.g.,* I.R.C. §§ 465, 469.

56. I.R.C. §§ 1361–1379.

ments for electing to be an S corporation; most especially, that the corporation issue only one class (type) of stock. Moreover, S corporations do not follow all of the same tax rules as partnerships. The result is that partnerships have significantly more tax savings potential in many situations than S corporations.

Finally, this all becomes much simpler in the widely held business. In that context, the tax code imposes separate taxpaying entity treatment regardless of the form chosen. Corporations can have no more than 75 shareholders if they wish to make an S election. The code taxes publicly traded partnerships as a corporation.[57] Hence, in the widely held context, one may as well form a corporation and obtain limited liability, as well as exit and governance rules designed for widely held firms.

1.1.3 Public Perspective [I]: Historical Development of Corporate Law

So far, we have looked at the considerations which presently might lead an attorney to recommend, and his or her clients to decide, to conduct business through a corporation. Now let us take a look at how the corporation reached this stage. There were four critical developments.

a. From special chartering to general incorporation laws

As in so many other areas, the antecedents of American corporate law lie in England. Under English law at the time of the American revolution, corporations came into existence by a special act of government. Following the revolution, the individual states continued this approach. What this meant was that if any persons wished to form a corporation to carry out a venture, they needed to go to the state legislature and persuade it to pass a special bill granting them a charter creating the corporation.

Needless to say, if this had remained the law, corporations would not be anywhere near as prevalent as they are today. Indeed, over the history of special chartering, the English government created remarkably few corporations. As a result, the dominant form for large businesses in England up until the middle of the 19th Century was the "joint stock company." In fact, these were essentially partnerships, but with legal title to the assets of the business held by trustees and with the partners owning transferable shares. This history helps explain why English attorneys would refer to subject matter of this book as "company law" rather corporate law.

The various state legislatures in the United States were far more willing to grant special charters than the English government. Still, the number of corporations formed by this route was not extremely large. During the 1800s, this system gave way as state legislatures enacted general incorporation statutes. Under these statutes, individuals can form a corporation, without a special bill, simply by complying with the

57. I.R.C. § 7704.

statute. We shall discuss what these requirements are under modern statutes later in this chapter. New York enacted the first general incorporation statute in 1811, but it took decades before these statutes supplanted special chartering. The early general incorporation laws were often highly restrictive, and, thus, many individuals desiring to establish a corporation still went to the legislature for a special charter. Ultimately, the combined effect of liberalized general incorporation statutes, and the enactment of state constitutional provisions curbing the legislature's power to grant special charters, forced the changeover.

What led legislatures to make this change? There were several factors. To begin with, the demand for new corporations grew with the young American economy. This made special chartering an increasingly unmanageable burden on the legislatures. In addition, consider the incentives created by a system in which individuals must lobby legislators for private bills (even before the era of multi-million dollar election campaigns). Not surprisingly, there were scandals. Moreover, while examples of corruption provided ammunition, there was a broader reform agenda at work as well. As part of the ideas of Jacksonian democracy, the notion grew that corporate privileges should be available to all, rather than just bestowed upon a favored few.[58]

b. The decline of size, duration and purpose limits

19th Century democratic or populist notions were a two-edged sword as far as the growth of corporations. An overarching goal was to prevent the concentration of economic power. Making the corporate form widely available through enactment of general incorporation laws was one means toward this goal. So, however, was imposing various limits on corporations.

Early 19th Century corporate laws attempted to limit the size of corporations. Statutes often set a maximum capital which the corporation could raise. For example, New York's statute started with limits of between $50,000 and $100,000, depending upon the type of business. The corporation laws also limited the length of the company's existence. 20, 30 and 50 years were common maximums. Most significant in terms of the development of corporate doctrine is the fact that statutes and court opinions imposed limits on the activities in which a given corporation could engage.

To understand the mechanism for this last limit, we need to go back to special chartering. Individuals desiring to form a corporation did not go to the legislature and ask the legislature to charter a corporation which could do anything the individuals felt, from time to time, would make money. Instead, they requested a corporate charter to carry out a particular venture: Build a barge canal; Open a bank; Establish a textile mill. Indeed, initially the notion was that the corporation would carry

58. For further discussion of the evolution from special chartering to general incorporation laws see J. Willard Hurst, The Legitimacy of the Business Corporation in the Law of the United States, 1780–1970 (1970); Lawrence Friedman, A History of American Law, 188–198 (2d ed. 1985).

out some public function, like providing transportation or banking services. Along these lines, corporate charters often gave the corporation quasi government powers (such as the right of eminent domain) or a legal monopoly (such as the right to operate the sole turnpike through a given route) much like a public utility. It was not long, however, before states were chartering manufacturing corporations with no particular public function.

Early general incorporation laws picked up from this tradition. They required individuals forming a corporation to specify in their governing document the corporation's purpose. A flippant statement like "To make money" was not what the statutes had in mind. Rather, the founders had to set out the specific business venture in which the corporation would engage. Suppose, however, those in charge of the corporation decided to have the company engage in activities which went beyond furthering the specified business: What happened then? This brings us to the judicially created doctrine of ultra vires.

We shall spend some time looking at what current significance is left of this doctrine later in the book.[59] For now, however, it is sufficient to introduce the broad concept. Ultra vires roughly translates as "beyond one's powers." The notion was that the corporation owed its existence to, and received its powers from, the state. Since the state had created the corporation only to further the purpose specified in its charter, the corporation lacked the power to engage in activities which went beyond furthering that purpose. Applying this doctrine, courts could enjoin and void activities not directed toward the company's purpose. Thus, if a corporation, chartered to build a railroad, started to operate a general store, courts could void any contracts made on behalf of the corporation to build and supply the store. Not only did charters and the ultra vires doctrine confine the activities which the corporations carried on directly, but courts also held it was ultra vires for corporations to own stock in other corporations. Needless to say, if these limits remained in effect today, then precisely those large, diversified firms which we most associate with corporations would not be able to operate in the corporate form.

In the latter part of the 19th and early 20th centuries, all of this changed. Legislatures repealed maximum limits on corporate capital and on the length of corporate existence. Courts and legislatures chipped away at the limits on corporate activities. Courts became more expansive in their interpretations of what activities furthered a given corporate purpose. With a little imagination, a court could conclude that operating a hotel along the route furthered the purpose of running a railroad.[60] Moreover, courts reduced the penalties attached to engaging in ultra vires conduct. For example, they refused to unwind already executed contracts, even if this allowed the corporation to get away with ultra vires conduct.[61]

---

59. See § 3.1.4 *infra.*

60. *See, e.g.,* Jacksonville, M., P. Ry. & Nav. Co. v. Hooper, 160 U.S. 514, 16 S.Ct. 379 (1896).

61. *E.g.,* Whitney Arms Co. v. Barlow, 63 N.Y. 62 (1875).

More significantly, legislatures allowed increasingly broad statements of purpose in the corporation's governing document. A critical step in this evolution occurred when the legislatures allowed the document to list any number of purposes, including activities which the corporation's founders had no plans for the company to pursue. This, in turn, led to the practice of including laundry lists specifying every possible activity of which one could conceive. Other than providing an amusing drafting exercise, there was now little purpose (pun intended) to requiring specific purposes in the corporation's governing document. Legislatures then took the inevitable next step of allowing the document simply to state the corporation's purpose to be "any lawful business." Legislatures also added provisions to corporation statutes which expressly gave corporations powers, such as the power to hold stock in other corporations, which courts had held to be ultra vires.

What caused these changes? To begin with, there were changing attitudes toward large businesses. After the civil war, many opinion makers were inclined to see economic concentration as both inevitable and desirable—a source of economic prosperity, rather than something to be feared. In addition, there was competition between states to encourage corporations to form in each state. We shall look at this competition in greater detail later in this chapter. For now, however, it is sufficient to note that as one state changed its law to remove various constraints on corporations, other states felt pressure to follow suit for fear corporations otherwise would flock to reincorporate in the "liberalizing" state.[62]

c.   *The growth of management and majority prerogatives*

Closely linked to the decline in the use of corporate law to limit the power of the corporation vis-a-vis society, is the growth in the ability of both the corporation's managers, and the owner(s) of a majority of the corporation's stock, to have their way over the objections of minority stockholders. Many of the same doctrines (ultra vires) and the same forces for change (different attitudes toward concentration, as well as competition between states) which we discussed above played a role here as well.

Early norms of corporate governance contained marked differences from the governance model we looked at in discussing choice of business form. To begin with, partnership law was influential in early thinking about corporate governance. Drawing from the concept that the power to manage a partnership normally resides with the partners, many early courts viewed the shareholders as having the ultimate power to manage the corporation. What then was the role of directors? Much as partners might hire agents to manage day-to-day affairs, under this view, directors were the agents of the shareholders to manage the ordinary

---

62. For more extended discussions of the removal of various constraints on corporate size and activities see Morton J. Horwitz, Santa Clara *Revisited: The Develop-* *ment of Corporate Theory*, 88 W. Va. L. Rev. 173 (1985); Joel Seligman, *A Brief History of Delaware's General Corporation Law of 1899,* 1 Del. J. Corp. L. 249 (1976).

business of the corporation. The practical impact of this sort of thinking was that directors lacked authority to make decisions outside of ordinary business affairs. Moreover, even as to ordinary business, shareholders had the power to command the directors as to what to do.

Another corollary which followed from looking to partnership rules was that even a majority of the shareholders lacked the power to make decisions outside of ordinary business. Rather, such decisions required unanimous agreement of the shareholders. A second line of reasoning reinforced this view. This line of reasoning involves viewing the corporate charter as a contract.

The idea that the corporate charter constitutes a contract finds one of its most famous expressions in the United States Supreme Court's *Dartmouth College* decision.[63] There, the court held that New Hampshire could not change the college corporation's governance structure as established under its charter, since to do so would violate the Constitutional prohibition on a state impairing the obligations of a contract.

Viewing the corporate charter as a contract suggests a majority of the shareholders cannot alter the charter over the objections of a minority. After all, the basic rule in contract law is all parties must agree to modify a contract. The practical impact is that all of the shareholders would have to agree to any action which would effectively alter the corporation's charter (say by merging with another corporation). Notice, as well, how this provides an additional basis for the ultra vires doctrine. Since the contract to which all the shareholders subscribed—the charter—sets out the purpose of the venture, any action beyond furthering the purpose breached the contract unless all the shareholders agreed to the alteration.

Here too, changing attitudes toward concentration, and competition between the states, led to changes in the law. The requirement of unanimous shareholder approval was an impediment to the late 19th Century drive toward consolidating different companies under one ownership. Those desiring such consolidation pressured state legislatures for change, and, once one state succumbed, others followed.

The idea of the corporate charter as a contract, however, created a barrier. Given the Supreme Court's decision in *Dartmouth College*, could a state constitutionally allow the majority of stockholders to change an objecting minority's rights under the charter? In fact, the concept of charter as contract provides a road map for doing just this. Contracts are normally not alterable over the objection of any party to the contract. Yet, this does not apply if the contract, itself, allows alteration with less than unanimous consent. Hence, if the charter allowed amendment by the majority, the minority could have no constitutional objection to such action—or at least not an objection based upon impairment of contract. Moreover, a legislature might state in the general incorporation statute that all of the statute's provisions will be considered part of the govern-

---

63. Trustees of Dartmouth College v. Woodward, 17 U.S. 518 (1819).

ing document of all corporations formed under the statute. Then, if individuals choose to incorporate under this statute, the statute's terms would be part of their contract. Indeed, even in the absence of such a statement in the statute, courts have held that incorporation under a given statute implicitly makes all the provisions of the statute part of the contract.[64] In either event, what this means is that a statute which allows alteration of the charter by less than universal consent becomes part of the charter. Further along this line, if the statute (or state constitution) at the time of incorporation indicated that later changes in the statute were part of the contract (a so-called reservation clause, since it reserves to the state the power to amend the statute and apply the amendment to existing corporations), then applying changes in the statute to existing corporations would also not run afoul of *Dartmouth College*.[65]

Nevertheless, legislatures were not entirely convinced of their constitutional power to allow the majority to alter the corporation over the minority's objection. So, just to be sure, legislatures came up with a quid pro quo. In lieu of having the right to veto a merger or other fundamental change in corporate direction, objecting minority shareholders would have the right to demand that the corporation cash them out at a fair price, set, if necessary, by appraisal.[66]

Corporation statutes began to provide that corporations could change their charter, merge, sell substantially all of their assets, or dissolve by vote of the directors and the holders of two-thirds or even just a majority of the outstanding shares. Objecting shareholders received appraisal rights. These statutory changes had another impact. Courts began to read these provisions as setting out the exclusive list of corporate decisions upon which shareholders were entitled to vote.

This, in turn, became part of a broader revision in judicial and legislative views as to the role of the directors. No longer were they agents who derived their power, and potentially instructions, from the shareholders. Instead, courts deemed the power of the directors to manage the corporation as coming from the corporation's statute itself. This sort of thinking relegated the shareholders' role largely to electing directors and voting on those items expressly listed in the statute. We alluded to one impact of such thinking when discussing governance as a factor in choosing between forms in which to conduct one's business. Some courts have held that attempts by shareholders to manage closely held corporations directly like a partnership ran afoul of statutes placing management in the hands of the board of directors.[67]

These changes produced the governance model we discussed earlier, which makes the corporate form more desirable for widely held firms with freely transferable ownership interests. Yet, these changes create

64. *See, e.g.,* Weinberg v. Baltimore Brick Co., 114 A.2d 812 (Del.1955).

65. *E.g.,* Bove v. Community Hotel Corp., 105 R.I. 36, 249 A.2d 89 (1969).

66. See § 7.2.1a *infra.*

67. See § 5.2.2.a *infra.*

problems as well. Greater powers to directors and majority shareholders provide the opportunity for abuse at the expense of minority shareholders. The history of the corporation shows, all too often, directors and majority shareholders have not ignored this opportunity for abuse. We shall have repeated occasions throughout this book to return to the tensions this produces.[68]

d. Limited liability

We tend to think today of limited liability as probably the most important feature of the corporation. In fact, however, during its early history, the corporation, as often as not, exposed its owners to liability. This took two forms: Corporate creditors could sue shareholders directly for unpaid debts of the corporation, and the corporation's management could impose a levy (sometimes called a levitation) upon the shareholders to raise the funds to pay the company's debts.

As we discussed above, early corporations both in England and the United States came into existence by virtue of special charters. Many times, these charters addressed the liability of the corporation's shareholders. Some charters expressly made the shareholders personally liable for the corporation's debts. Other charters contained express provisions to the contrary. Very often, however, the charter was silent on the question. What then was the rule? In England, the rule became that the shareholders were not liable if the charter was silent on the issue. As in much of English legal history, it is somewhat murky when this became the rule, with estimates varying between the end of the 16th and 18th Centuries.

Actually, the significant history of limited liability in England does not involve specially chartered corporations. As we noted earlier, there were very few of those. Instead, the significant history involves the joint stock companies. Since these were essentially partnerships, their owners faced unlimited personal liability. This produced a couple of interesting results. For one thing, the owners of the joint stock companies attempted to create limited liability by contract. This started with insurance companies. They issued policies which stated that the insured agreed to look only to the capital of the company, and not the owners personally, in satisfaction of any claim. English courts upheld these provisions, and the idea of using similar non-recourse contracts spread to joint stock companies in other fields. To further their efforts toward limited liability by contract, many joint stock companies placed the term "limited" in their names, presumably figuring this would support the argument that the creditors agreed to limited liability. A second interesting result involved the practicality of actually suing all of the owners of a widely held joint stock company in order to collect on a debt owed by the company. Attempting both to bring an action, and collect a judgment, against numerous (and changing) owners turned out to be an extraordi-

---

68. For more extended discussions of this growth in the power of managers and majority shareholders see Horwitz, *supra* note 62; Seligman, *supra* note 62; Lynne I. Dallas, *The Control and Conflict-of-Interest Voting Systems,* 71 N.C. L. Rev. 1 (1992).

narily difficult undertaking. As a result, creditors apparently did not attempt this very often.

Still, despite considerable limited liability by virtue of contract, as well as procedural barriers, the idea of granting companies limited liability by statute set off much debate in England during the first half of the 19th Century. Finally, in 1855, the English Parliament enacted the Limited Liability Act. This allowed existing and new companies to register under the act and receive limited liability.

In the United States also the question came up as to whether or not there was limited liability when a corporate charter did not address the issue. A number of courts held there was no personal liability unless the charter or corporations statute expressly so stated. It is easy to overstate the practical importance of these decisions, however. As one of the rationales for holding that silence meant no liability, these courts pointed to the prevalence of charters which expressly imposed personal liability upon the shareholders. This was particularly true of manufacturing corporations. By contrast, public utility (such as transportation) and financial (banks, insurance companies) corporations more often received charters providing limited liability.

Ultimately, if corporations in the United States were to provide limited liability, it was up to the state legislatures. The ground breaking New York general incorporation statute of 1811 allowed the incorporation of manufacturing corporations, with double liability for the shareholders. Double liability means, if the corporation cannot pay its debts, creditors can require the shareholders to kick in an amount equal to the price for which the corporation originally sold the shares. In other words, the shareholders risk two times their original investment, but no more than this.

Limited liability statutes spread to New England, starting with New Hampshire in 1816. Interestingly, the two most industrialized New England states, Massachusetts and Rhode Island, did not adopt limited liability statutes for their corporations until 1830 and 1847, respectively. Their legislatures finally did so in response to arguments that the other New England states with limited liability were getting an advantage in attracting capital investment. Curiously, the failure of Massachusetts and Rhode Island to have limited liability as soon as their neighbors does not, in hindsight, appear to have impeded their industrial growth. Indeed, there was no significant increase in the number of Massachusetts corporations formed after the enactment of limited liability in the state in 1830.

Double liability statutes, like New York's 1811 act, remained common in the United States throughout the 19th Century. Eventually, they gave way to limited liability as we know it today for most corporations. Banks were a different story. Double liability for bank shareholders— under statutory provisions enacted to protect depositors—remained common until after the depression of the 1930s. The bank failures in the depression convinced Congress and state legislatures to substitute deposit insurance for double liability.

California provided the most interesting holdout. California law imposed pro-rata liability—in other words, liability proportionate to the percentage of stock each shareholder owned—upon shareholders for unpaid debts. This applied to California corporations for debts incurred anywhere, and to non-California corporations for debts incurred in California. California only repealed this law in 1931, over 100 years after Massachusetts had switched to limited liability. Much like Massachusetts before it, California had been able to maintain significant economic growth despite being a laggard in adopting limited liability.[69]

1.1.4   Public Perspective [II]: The Policy Behind Limited Liability

The policy issues raised by the four developments in corporate law outlined above vary in their significance. No one (save perhaps some political fund raisers) sheds a tear anymore over the replacement of special chartering with general incorporation laws. While concerns with economic concentration remain salient for many, the locus for these concerns now lies with the federal antitrust laws, rather than state corporate law. On the other hand, we shall return repeatedly in this book to the issues raised by the power of corporate directors and majority shareholders versus the minority shareholder. For now, however, it is useful to examine the policy behind the factor which, when all is said and done, is the primary consideration most individuals look to when they choose to do business using the corporate form—this being limited liability.

As we noted when exploring the history of limited liability, particularly in England, the decision to grant corporations limited liability by statute was highly controversial. In the historical debates, three views found common expression.[70] Proponents of limited liability argued it would increase investment in business. Opponents argued it would transfer risks of the business to the creditors—which might both be unfair and make it more difficult for corporations to get needed credit. A third view asserted that limited liability by statute did not make any difference.

The third view seems counterintuitive, but, in fact, has a great deal of merit. We already have seen part of the reason why. Business owners and creditors can contract for the liability rule they want regardless of the statute. For example, suppose states had never created the corporation or any other business form with limited liability. In this case, if proprietors or partners want limited liability, they can seek agreement

---

69. For a more detailed discussion of the historical development of limited liability see Phillip I. Blumberg, *Limited Liability and Corporate Groups*, 11 J. Corp. L. 573 (1986).

70. For a discussion of these views see Paul Halpern, Michael Trebilcock & Stuart Turnbull, *An Economic Analysis of Limited Liability in Corporation Law*, 30 U. Toronto L.J. 117 (1980).

from their creditors to non-recourse loans. In fact, joint stock companies commonly did this before the enactment of the Limited Liability Act in England. Conversely, creditors of corporations can obtain unlimited personal liability of the owners despite the owners' operating through a corporation. All they need to do is demand a personal guarantee by the owners. Indeed, this is so commonly done when large creditors deal with small business borrowers, that it significantly undercuts the supposed advantage in doing business in the corporate form.

Moreover, there is another way in which creditors can respond to the liability rule. If creditors do business with an entity whose owners have no personal liability, the creditors face a greater risk of not getting paid than they face if the owners are personally liable. To compensate for this higher risk, presumably creditors will demand higher interest on loans (or a higher price on goods or services supplied on credit). Ultimately, creditors and owners will bargain, trading off interest rates versus liability rules, until they reach a result both sides are satisfied with. All told, since owners and creditors can bargain over the liability rule, and since owners must pay creditors for any shifting of the risk of business failure from owners to creditors, this suggests there is nothing unfair about providing limited liability for corporations. Nor, under this analysis, would limited liability by statute provide any great boon to investment.

The view that providing limited liability through the corporate form is irrelevant, however, overlooks another factor we discussed earlier. This is the cost of contracting. If owners who want limited liability must go out and negotiate non-recourse loans with all of the business' creditors, they may need to spend more money on attorneys, not to mention spending extra time dickering with each creditor. Making limited liability available through the corporate form allows owners to save this time and money. Hence, providing limited liability through the corporate form seems socially useful, if not earth shattering in its importance.

Yet, perhaps things are not this simple. After all, with the corporate form, now the burden of contracting around limited liability is on the creditor, who must ask for personal guarantees. So, have we really accomplished anything? To figure this out, we need to address several questions.

To begin with, will either regime allow society to save net contracting costs? For example, suppose in ninety percent of the contracts between owners and creditors, we can predict that the parties will agree to limited liability. In this event, it would seem to save costs if the law provided for limited liability and let the ten percent of the parties who want something different contract around the rule. Conversely, if we predict only ten percent of the parties will agree to limited liability, then it would seem to save costs for the law to provide personal liability and leave the ten percent to make non-recourse loans.

So, is there any way to make this prediction? Numerous writers have attempted to do so by asking which regime is more efficient: In other words, would rational, wealth maximizing owners and creditors prefer limited or unlimited liability?[71] At first glance, one may be tempted to respond that rational owners will always prefer limited liability, while rational creditors will always prefer personal liability. Hence, it is impossible to answer the question. This view, however, ignores the fact that creditors presumably will charge higher interest if they agree to greater risk by accepting limited liability. This means owners will only bargain for limited liability if the extra interest they must pay is less than the value they place on reducing their risk from unlimited personal liability.

Are we back then to the proposition that the rule does not matter? After all, if creditors must assume whatever risks the owners avoid by virtue of limited liability, and the creditors will charge owners an interest rate equal to the value of assuming those risks, then will not the parties be neutral as to which regime they pick? This will be true if there is perfect symmetry in the risks, and any other costs, which creditors and owners face depending on the liability rule. By perfect symmetry, we mean that the dollar value of the risks and other costs which owners will avoid with limited liability equals precisely the dollar value of the added risks and other costs this regime creates for creditors. But suppose there was an asymmetry in impacts of the liability rule; say, owners could avoid more risk or save more other costs by having limited liability than creditors will face under such a regime. In this event, we would expect parties to agree to limited liability, since creditors will charge less in extra interest than the value of limited liability to owners.

A number of writers have argued such asymmetry exists for the widely held business. We have already encountered some of the reasons. For instance, recall that procedural difficulties confronted creditors in England who attempted to collect from owners of widely held joint stock companies. Even assuming some of the English problems reflected archaic rules of civil procedure, it will remain true today that the more individuals a creditor must track down and sue, the greater the costs of collecting on the debt. This means the amount of money which widely scattered owners end up paying with personal liability is inevitably more than what creditors end up collecting; an asymmetry favoring limited liability, where the creditor sues only one debtor.

Yet, perhaps creditors might respond by suing just the wealthiest owners. Assuming the applicable rules of civil procedure allow this— which gets into the question of joint versus joint and several liability and what is a necessary party to a lawsuit—there are still problems. There is the added expense for the creditors in investigating the wealth of the individual owners. Moreover, the wealthiest owners might then sue other owners for indemnity, thereby resulting in more litigation costs. This means we still end up with potentially much higher total payments by the owners than what the creditors actually recover.

71. *E.g.*, Halpern, et al., *supra* note 70; Frank H. Easterbrook & Daniel R. Fischel, *Limited Liability and the Corporation,* 52 U. Chi. L. Rev. 89 (1985).

Moreover, this only looks at the situation after the business fails. Parties contemplating business dealings commonly want to assess their risks before entering the transaction. Notice that the risk to both creditors and owners under a personal liability regime depends on the wealth of individual owners. Wealthy owners make it easier for creditors to collect. Wide disparities in owner wealth expose the wealthiest owners to greater risk of creditors singling them out. (After all, judgment proof owners will not be able either to pay the creditors or to reimburse other owners who pay creditors.) This means both creditors and owners have an incentive to investigate the wealth of all the individual owners under a personal liability regime. This can add considerably to the costs of both creditors deciding to extend credit and owners deciding to invest. By contrast, with limited liability, the wealth of individual owners is irrelevant. Hence, limited liability saves all parties these investigation costs.

Of course, the more important determinant of risk for both creditors and owners is not the wealth levels of the owners, but rather the prospects of the business. After all, if the parties expected the transaction to end in a collection suit, they would not have agreed to the loan to start with. Here, too, writers have argued limited liability may save net costs. To understand why, return to the advantages we noted of the corporate governance model for the business with widely held, freely traded ownership. In this situation, owners cannot run the venture; managers do.

When managers run the business, evaluating and limiting the risks of business failure can require monitoring the managers—in other words, keeping an eye on the honesty, diligence and capability of the firm's managers. If owners have unlimited personal liability, they have a stronger incentive to engage in such monitoring than they would have if all they stand to lose is their investment. At first glance, one might say such an incentive is good; it will help prevent business failures. Yet, there can be too much of a good thing. Monitoring of managers by owners in a widely held company can be very inefficient, since there would be a large number of owners duplicating each others' efforts. By contrast, large creditors may be able to monitor managers with much less duplication of effort (and also with greater expertise in many cases than possessed by small investors). This again creates an asymmetry in the costs which personal liability imposes on owners versus creditors.

We can find yet another asymmetry based upon our earlier discussion of the liquidity advantages of the corporate form. As we noted then, the ability to sell one's interest in active trading markets helps make it desirable to own stock in widely held corporations. We also noted that unlimited personal liability could put a significant damper on such trading. This is a substantial value which owners of a widely held business will attach to limited liability. By contrast, creditors do not lose any liquidity for their interest by agreeing to limited liability. This is because creditors, like stockholders with limited liability, stand at worst to lose only their investment (the amount of the loan) if the business fails. Hence, there is no uncapped downside potential to deter potential purchasers to whom creditors can assign rights to repayment. Indeed, there is active trading in corporate debt (bonds).

Along similar lines, investors might gain a significant advantage by diversifying their investments. In this manner, they can offset bad results from one company or industry with good results in other companies or industries. Diversifying ownership of companies in an unlimited personal liability regime, however, is a dangerous strategy, since each investment creates the potential of financially wiping out the owner. Hence, owners who desire to diversify will attach value to limited liability. By contrast, limited liability for owners will not upset lenders' abilities to diversify by limiting the size of their loans to any one borrower.

All these asymmetries mean owners in the widely held company lose more under a regime of unlimited personal liability than creditors will gain. This suggests both sides will be happy with an agreement giving owners limited liability in exchange for extra interest to creditors.

So far, we have focused our attention on the widely held business. What about the venture in which there are only a few owners? The advantages of limited liability discussed above largely disappear. There are no great extra expenditures collecting from a large number of owners, nor is there the need to investigate the wealth of large numbers of owners. Creditors no longer have an advantage over the duplicative efforts of numerous owners when it comes to monitoring managers. Indeed, in the closely held business, the owners are likely to be the managers. There typically is no active trading market for ownership in closely held firms. Hence, personal liability will not disrupt a trading market. Owners of a closely held firm are usually not diversifying their investment (since this ownership commonly ties up a substantial amount of the owners' worth).

Does this mean rational creditors and owners should be neutral regarding the tradeoff between limited liability and an additional interest charge in the closely held business? Perhaps not. Some writers have argued that limited liability in the closely held context may actually impose asymmetric risks upon creditors. The problem comes from the incentive structure created by limited liability when owners are in charge of the venture.

A simple example illustrates the problem. Suppose one could borrow money under an agreement wherein if the borrower makes money with the funds, he or she will repay the lender with fixed interest and keep the rest of earnings, but if the borrower loses all the money, he or she will bear no personal responsibility. The borrower could invest the funds conservatively, say buying some rental property. On the other hand, consider the incentives with such a loan to take the money and head to Las Vegas.

Creditors might react to this risk in several ways. They might attempt to control what owners can do with borrowed funds. Yet, this creates added contracting and monitoring costs and can undercut the need of a business' owners for flexibility. Besides, if the creditor wanted to be in charge of the business, why not become an owner? Creditors might demand the owners put some of the owners' funds at risk, if not through unlimited personal liability, then at least through some minimum investment by the owners in the business. Still, risks in excess of the owners' investment create the same potential for skewed incentives. Ultimately, creditors will charge more interest to offset the risk from skewed incentives. Notice this extra interest to offset the risk that some owners will gamble with borrowed money falls upon all owners. This is because the creditors will not know in advance which owners will succumb to the skewed incentives and which will not. This, in turn, means that owners who intend not to incur excessive risks simply because they are using borrowed money in their business can end up paying more in interest than the value they receive from limited liability.

Under these circumstances, one might expect that owners and creditors would tend to agree to personal liability. Creditors avoid the skewed incentive problem. Owners who did not intend to engage in excessive risk-taking avoid paying interest based upon the actions of other owners who do have this intent. The main owners who then hold out for limited liability would be those who planned to misbehave. These, of course, are the owners who, once identified, creditors would not wish to give limited liability to. This analysis may explain the prevalence of personal guarantees in the closely held corporation context.

Why does this skewed incentive problem not also work against limited liability in the widely held firm? The answer is that the owners are not in control; managers are. While managers wish to make profits for owners, managers have limited incentives to engage in excessive risk-taking in order to do so. After all, a main goal of managers is typically to keep their jobs. Driving the corporation into bankruptcy in a gamble to make money for someone else is inconsistent with that goal.

At this point, we might conclude that the law could minimize the need for special contracting by providing limited liability for owners in widely held businesses (barring other agreement) and personal liability for owners of closely held businesses (again, barring other agreement). This, however, only minimizes transactions costs (the costs of parties entering contracts) if we assume that the cost of contracting around the statutory rule is always the same. Suppose, however, that it is easier (and therefore cheaper) to prepare a personal guarantee than it is to draft a non-recourse loan (where one must deal with collateral). If this is so, then it may save net transactions costs to provide for limited liability, barring other agreement, even when most parties will contract around this rule by use of personal guarantees. Also, contracting costs increase with the number of parties involved. Hence, it may be more expensive to contract around the statutory rule when dealing with the widely held business than when dealing with the firm having few owners. This, in turn, means that if the law must have the same liability rule for widely held and closely held firms—perhaps to avoid line drawing problems and strategic behavior[72]—it could be better to focus on what makes the most sense for widely held firms and let those dealing with closely held businesses contract around the rule.

There is another approach one could take to all this. Instead of trying to figure out which regime is more efficient, and, therefore, desired by rational parties, why not simply provide choices? Indeed, this is what the law has done by providing different forms of business organization with different liability rules. One problem with this approach occurs, however, if unrelated factors, such as differing tax treatment, constrain parties from choosing a business form which they believe provides a more efficient liability rule.

Thus far, we have discussed liability to contract creditors, where the statutory liability rule does not so much allocate the risks of non-payment, as it does the burdens of contracting to the result desired by the parties. Things change when we start talking about tort victims. Now, parties can no longer avoid the statutory liability rule by use of personal guarantees or non-recourse loans. Moreover, tort victims cannot obtain compensation for the increased risk of non-payment due to limited liability by demanding extra interest up front. Accordingly, extending limited liability for tort claims forces us to confront how the law should allocate the costs of personal injury and property damage resulting from business activities.

To address this question, it is useful to start by recalling that limited liability refers to the absence of personal liability for the corporation's debts, not for the obligations of the owner him- or herself. Hence, if the owner personally commits a tort, he or she remains responsible to pay for the consequences. What sort of tort claims then will the owner avoid by virtue of limited liability? The answer is those which he or she would otherwise face by virtue of vicarious liability—in other words, torts committed by employees, or by other owners, in the scope of their employment—and those based upon strict liability (primarily defective products claims). This, in turn, requires us to weigh the policies behind vicarious and products liability against the impacts of providing limited liability.

A detailed exploration of the policy behind vicarious and products liability is well beyond the scope of this book. Oversimplifying quite a bit, the modern justification for these doctrines largely rests on the notion of internalizing the cost of accidents into the price of the goods or services whose production and use led to those accidents. In other words, if a business' employee, for example, injures someone in the course of carrying out the employee's job, the business should pay for the injury and pass the cost of doing so (or, more realistically, of buying insurance to do so) onto the business' customers. In this manner, the business has an economic incentive to take cost effective accident avoidance steps. Moreover, forcing consumers to pay for accidents which it is not cost

---

72. For example, some parties might introduce a number of small owners into their   business in order to fit into the widely held rule.

effective to avoid allows the market to determine whether producing the good or service in question justified the risks of injuries which that activity created.

To the extent limited liability leaves tort victims uncompensated, it undercuts the goal of vicarious and products liabilities. Two factors, however, mitigate this effect. To begin with, recall the various advantages limited liability creates for owners in a widely held business. It facilitates diversification and the development of active trading markets, and avoids the incentive for excessive monitoring of managers and of the wealth levels of other owners. As a result, limited liability encourages the formation of larger firms with widespread ownership. Because such firms aggregate together large amounts of capital, they may be better able to pay tort claimants than the sort of firms which might predominate if limited liability were unavailable. Moreover, the cost of going after large numbers of scattered owners to recover unpaid claims might substantially undercut the utility of unlimited personal liability in favor of tort claimants, just as it does for contract creditors.

The other mitigating factor is insurance. If the law conditions limited liability upon the maintenance of liability insurance sufficient to meet foreseeable levels of tort damages, then we achieve the cost internalization purpose of vicarious and products liabilities. Later in this chapter when we discuss piercing the corporate veil, we shall see how that doctrine can provide a tool for courts to create this quid pro quo.

§ 1.2   State of Incorporation and Governing Law

As we discussed above, corporations exist by virtue of state statutes. These general incorporation laws both enable persons to form a corporation and provide rules concerning this entity. This, in turn, raises the question of which state's law fills this role. A simple-minded answer might be the state within which the corporation does business. Alternately, perhaps we could look to the law of the state in which most of the corporation's owners reside. As we shall see, however, neither of these simple-minded solutions are the rule. Instead, persons forming a corporation can choose which state's law will establish the corporation and will provide rules governing the company's internal affairs, and this choice is largely unfettered by limitations based upon where the participants in the venture actually intend to conduct business or even where most or any of the participants reside. This provides an important planning tool for the attorney and clients forming a corporation. It also raises troubling policy questions. We shall explore both aspects in the following discussion.

1.2.1   The Internal Affairs Doctrine

When a corporation does business in a state, it must observe the state's laws generally applicable to persons doing business there. These laws deal with such issues as worker safety, consumer protection, pollution, and so forth. Hence, a Delaware corporation cannot claim that it only need follow Delaware's, rather than California's, environmental regulations when conducting operations in California.

By contrast, courts generally have taken a different approach when it comes to the rules governing the so-called internal affairs of a corporation. Broadly speaking, "corporate internal affairs" refers to the powers and obligations of a corporation's managers vis-a-vis the corporation and its shareholders, and the rights and duties of the corporation's shareholders vis-a-vis the corporation, its management and the other shareholders. Put differently, corporate internal affairs pretty much encompass the subject matter of those state laws typically referred to as corporate law. In dealing with a corporation's internal affairs, courts, for the most part, have looked to the law of the state of incorporation for the governing rule.[1] Courts often refer to this choice of law principle as the "internal affairs doctrine."

What gives the internal affairs doctrine its practical impact is that corporation statutes typically allow persons to form a corporation pursuant to the statute (in other words, incorporate in the state) without regard to the residence of those who intend to participate in the venture and without regard to where the parties intend to conduct business.[2] For example, one can form a Delaware corporation and have Delaware corporate law govern the corporation's internal affairs even if the only tangible contacts the corporation will have with Delaware are the presence of an agent for service of process and an in-state "office"[3] (both of which the corporation might obtain for a fee from one of the firms which sell this service to thousands of other corporations). What this means is that parties forming a corporation simply can select which state's law they wish to govern their corporation's internal affairs.

We saw earlier, in discussing the development of corporate law in the United States, one result of this freedom to choose the applicable law. State legislatures have removed various restrictions from their corporation laws often for fear that, if they did not, persons would simply form corporations in other states whose laws did not create the restriction. We shall explore later the continuing policy debate set off by this state of affairs. For now, however, it is useful to ask what alternatives exist to the internal affairs doctrine.

One extreme would be to prohibit out-of-state corporations from doing business in a state. Rather, if parties wished to do business in a state, they would need to incorporate there. With some historic exceptions,[4] states have not done this. Instead, the overwhelming approach to dealing with out-of-state, or "foreign," corporations simply is to require that they "qualify" in order to do business within a state.

§ 1.2

1. *See, e.g.,* Restatement (Second) of Conflict of Laws § 302; Model Business Corporations Act § 15.05 Official Comment.

2. *See, e.g.,* Model Business Corporations Act § 3.02(10).

3. Del. Gen. Corp. Law §§ 101(a), 102(a)(2).

4. *See, e.g.,* Railway Express Agency, Inc. v. Virginia, 282 U.S. 440, 51 S.Ct. 201 (1931).

Qualification normally requires filing a document (typically, a copy of the document filed to form the corporation in its state of incorporation) with a state official (typically, the same official with whom one would file to form a corporation within the state).[5] By and large, states have not used the requirement of qualifying as a tool to control the internal affairs of foreign corporations which do business within the state. Rather, the practical significance of qualification lies in the requirements that the foreign corporation appoint a local agent for service of process (thereby facilitating local lawsuits against out-of-state corporations) and that the foreign corporation pay a fee or tax for the privilege of qualifying. Still, it turns out that these two requirements have, in a sort of round about way, curbed some of the potential of the internal affairs doctrine. As we will discuss shortly, corporations which do business solely in one state tend to incorporate in that state in order to avoid the added expense of paying fees and taxes both to the state of incorporation and the state in which they are doing business, as well the potential added burden of being subject to suit in two different states.

Several states, especially California and New York, have attacked the internal affairs doctrine more directly. They have sought to impose portions of their corporations laws upon out-of-state corporations which have substantial connections with the state. For example, Section 2115 of the California Corporations Code establishes a multi-part test to see whether a corporation's dominant relationship is with California. Specifically, the section calls for examining whether over 50 percent of a corporation's property, sales and payroll, as well as the residence of the owners of over 50 percent of the outstanding voting stock, are in California. If so, the section states that numerous specified provisions of the California Corporations Code will apply to the corporation (unless the corporation's stock is traded on a national securities exchange).[6]

Provisions such as these raise the question as to whether the United States Constitution constrains states which choose not to follow the internal affairs doctrine. The answer is highly uncertain and would require an understanding of constitutional law doctrines which are well beyond the scope of this book. Several points are reasonably clear, however. Early in its history, the United States Supreme Court settled that corporations are not citizens for purposes of the Privileges and Immunities Clause, thereby removing the most direct possible prohibition on states either excluding foreign corporations from doing business within the state or else admitting them subject to conditions.[7] This leaves the interstate commerce clause as the primary restraint on a state's efforts to govern out-of-state corporations. Numerous cases have established a basic dividing line here: States can exclude or admit subject to conditions corporations which wish to do business within a state, but

5. *E.g.,* Model Business Corporations Act § 15.01(a).

6. New York's statute is less demanding than California's as far as the required contacts with New York, but also less aggressive in the extent of New York statutory provisions which will apply. N.Y. Bus. Corp. Law §§ 1317–1320.

7. *E.g.,* Bank of Augusta v. Earle, 38 U.S. 519 (1839).

the clause prohibits states from excluding or requiring qualification of a corporation which does no business within a state and whose sole connection with the state is entirely through interstate transactions.[8] Needless to say, this can lead to difficult questions as to what activities constitute doing business within a state, rather than simply interstate commerce.[9]

More recently, the Supreme Court handed down an opinion which contains language some writers have interpreted as suggesting the commerce clause compels states to follow the internal affairs doctrine (at least as to corporations with widely traded stock). The opinion is *CTS Corp. v. Dynamics Corp. of America,*[10] in which the court upheld Indiana's anti-corporate-takeover legislation against various constitutional challenges, including one based upon the commerce clause.[11] In rejecting this challenge, the court wrote a brief paean to the internal affairs doctrine:

> Large corporations that are listed on national exchanges, or even regional exchanges, will have shareholders in many States and shares that are traded frequently. The markets that facilitate this national and international participation in ownership of corporations are essential for providing capital not only for new enterprises but also for established companies that need to expand their businesses. This beneficial free market system depends at its core upon the fact that a corporation—except in the rarest situations—is organized under, and governed by, the law of a single jurisdiction, traditionally the corporate law of the State of its incorporation.[12]

Still, the issue of whether the commerce clause compels states to follow the internal affairs doctrine was not before the court in *CTS*. Moreover, it is one thing to note the obvious problem that would occur if states were to impose inconsistent regulations upon the internal affairs of a corporation with shareholders in more than one state. (Imagine what a shareholder meeting would look like of one state required a scheme of shareholder voting which another state prohibited.) Yet, it is quite a different question as to whether, in case of conflict, the law of the state of incorporation should trump the law of a state with far more tangible contacts.

Three other alternatives exist which would limit the impact of the internal affairs doctrine. If states were to adopt uniform corporate laws, then the doctrine would lose much of its bite. Indeed, the widespread adoption of the Uniform Partnership and Uniform Limited Partnership Acts, mentioned earlier, has done much to reduce choice of law concerns in the partnership context. There was an attempt in the 1920s to promulgate a uniform corporations act, but it was ultimately not success-

---

8. *E.g.,* Crutcher v. Kentucky, 141 U.S. 47, 11 S.Ct. 851 (1891).

9. *See, e.g.,* Eli Lilly & Co. v. Sav–On– Drugs, Inc., 366 U.S. 276, 81 S.Ct. 1316 (1961).

10. 481 U.S. 69, 107 S.Ct. 1637 (1987).

11. For a discussion of the constitutionality of state anti-takeover legislation, see § 7.3.3 *infra.*

12. 481 U.S. at 90.

ful. In 1950, the Committee on Corporate Laws of the American Bar Association came out with a Model Business Corporations Act. Since then, the Model Act has undergone a couple of major revisions, most recently in 1984. A large number of states base their corporations statutes on the Model Act. However, highly important jurisdictions— such as Delaware (the state of incorporation for many of the largest corporations in the United States) and California (the largest state)— have not.

State securities laws sometimes provide a backdoor check on the internal affairs doctrine. We shall briefly discuss these laws later in this book.[13] Under some of these statutes, the state may forbid the sale of stock within the state unless the corporation agrees to give the stockholders various rights which the law of the state of incorporation did not require.

Finally, some critics of the internal affairs doctrine have proposed that the federal government regulate the internal affairs of corporations engaged in interstate business (in other words, have federally chartered corporations).[14] By and large, this has not happened. We shall see later, however, that federal securities laws have become a significant component of corporate law.

1.2.2 *Private Perspective: Selecting the State of Incorporation*

As mentioned above, small corporations which do all of their business in one state tend to incorporate in the state in which they are doing business. Otherwise, they will face the added expense of paying taxes and fees both to the state in which they incorporate and to the state in which they do business. There is also the added expense of paying for an "office" in the state of incorporation (which typically means paying a fee to a corporation service company which provides its office for this purpose). A further consideration is that incorporating in a jurisdiction other than where one intends to conduct business subjects the corporation to suit in two jurisdictions—where it does business and where it is incorporated. Defending a suit in the latter location could be very inconvenient for the small company.

For corporations with more resources and revenues, these added costs become less significant. Besides, for a corporation which conducts business in more than one state, it will face the need to pay fees and taxes to, as well as maintain offices and be subject to suit in, multiple states regardless of where it chooses to incorporate. Hence, for larger corporations, choice of the state of incorporation basically comes down to picking a law to regulate the corporation's internal affairs.

How can parties forming a corporation, and their attorney, decide which state's law would be better to regulate a corporation's internal

---

13. See § 6.2.1 *infra.*

14. *E.g.,* Ralph Nader, Mark Green & Joel Seligman, Taming the Giant Corporation (1976).

affairs? Attorney's often look to four criteria. To begin with, there is flexibility. Specifically, parties generally want a state which will not prevent them from governing the corporation in the manner they desire. Recall that early corporations laws contained significant restrictions on the activities and governance of corporations. These fell by the wayside as parties chose to incorporate in jurisdictions whose laws did not contain the restrictions, in other words, jurisdictions whose laws allowed greater flexibility.

If flexibility was the only criterion, attorneys would look for a corporations law which contains no rules at all (other than that parties can form corporations and have limited liability). Yet, attorneys would probably not advise their clients to incorporate in a state with such a law. This is because much of corporations law consists of gap-filling, or default, rules to address issues upon which the parties did not expressly contract. Hence, a second criterion for choosing a state's law is to see which state provides default rules that more closely resemble what the parties would provide if they expressly contracted on the question. Notice, in this regard, that the best statute may not be the one that provides the most freedom of action for directors and majority shareholders. Rather, if the parties had sat down and considered what rules to provide, perhaps they would have desired rules to protect minority shareholders. Unfortunately, it may be more difficult to pick a jurisdiction based upon desirable default rules than it is to pick a jurisdiction based upon flexibility. After all, default rules address issues the parties overlook. If the parties forming a corporation, and their attorney, have time to compare how various statutes react to problems which could come up, perhaps they may as well go ahead and draft an agreement addressing the issues.

A third criterion is predictability: Specifically, to what extent are judicial or other authoritative interpretations of the state's corporations statute available? A well developed body of corporate case-law gives parties planning various corporate transactions confidence in knowing what the law requires and allows. This is highly valuable for parties planning corporate transactions and for the attorneys who advise them. Notice, the more companies which incorporate in a given state, the more corporate litigation the state's courts are likely to hear, and, in turn, the more this state's courts can produce a well developed body of corporate law. This suggests a significant advantage in incorporating in the same state as many other corporations. Indeed, this factor may explain much of the reason why Delaware remains so attractive for larger corporations despite other states' adoptions of corporations laws which are at least as flexible as Delaware's.

Finally, a little discussed factor is the attorney's own familiarity with a state's corporations law. For smaller corporations employing locally oriented attorneys, this is often the law of the state in which the attorneys and their clients reside.

1.2.3 *Public Perspective: The "Race to the Bottom" Thesis*

Justice Brandeis' dissent in *Louis K. Liggett Co. v. Lee*[15] contains an often quoted lament regarding what he labeled a "race of laxity." Specifically, he noted how a number of smaller states had enacted less restrictive corporations laws in order to attract persons desiring to incorporate. These states sought thereby to gain revenues from incorporation fees and franchise taxes. New Jersey was a pioneer in this endeavor, but when it retrenched under the reform leadership of then-governor Woodrow Wilson, Delaware became the leading state in attracting incorporation through so-called liberal corporation laws. Leading industrial states, like New York, in turn, felt forced to remove various restrictions from their corporations statutes. After all, the result of retaining unpopular restrictions would be to lose incorporation fees and any control over corporate internal affairs at all, since corporations would simply circumvent restrictions by incorporating out-of-state.

The focus of Justice Brandeis' dissent was on the demise of corporate size and activity limits—an evolution we discussed earlier, and one which is now the concern of antitrust rather than corporate law. The more recent criticism of competition between states for incorporations has concentrated on another resulting evolution in corporate law, which we also outlined earlier. This is the growth in the prerogatives of management and majority shareholders to take actions over the objections of minority shareholders.

To understand this concern, it is useful to start by asking who actually decides where to incorporate. The answer, as a practical matter, is that individuals who anticipate the role of managers (and often majority shareholders) of the new corporation typically decide where to incorporate.[16] Such individuals presumably would prefer a corporations

---

15. 288 U.S. 517, 548–565, 53 S.Ct. 481 (1933).

16. At the founding of a closely held corporation, it is possible that all of those who anticipate being shareholders might be involved in the decision as to where to incorporate. As discussed earlier, however, the state of incorporation for such a company tends to be the state in which the company is doing business anyway. The race to the bottom thesis largely focuses on widely held corporations, which select the state of incorporation based upon differences in corporate law, and which have substantial numbers of minority shareholders. Here, those who anticipate the role of manager almost always make the decision as to the state of incorporation.

Actually, the state of incorporation for publicly held corporations commonly results from a reincorporation. For example, a smaller corporation, when it is first going to sell shares to the general public, often will reincorporate in a new state which it desires to become its state of incorporation.

Technically, a reincorporation entails forming a new corporation in the desired state and then transferring the existing corporation's operations to the new corporation through a sale of assets or merger. The existing corporation's directors initiate this process (and, in any event, they must initiate the transfer of the operations to the new corporation). While the shareholders of the existing corporation must approve the merger or asset sale, if the corporation is preparing to issue the first shares to the public, those anticipating the role of manager will have most or all of the shares at the time of the shareholder approval. Even if the corporation already has minority public shareholders, many times they can be enticed into voting for a reincorporation by hinging some action desired by the shareholders (like an increase in dividends) to favorable action on the reincorporation. *See, e.g.,* Lucian A. Bebchuk, *Federalism and the Corporation: The Desirable Limits on State Competition in Corporate Law,* 105 Harv. L. Rev. 1435 (1992).

law which contains the least constraints on their freedom to take actions to which minority shareholders might object. In an ideal world, legislatures would balance the minority's need for protection versus the management's and majority's need for flexibility. If a state is small enough, however, gaining revenues from incorporation fees and taxes arguably can become a more important consideration than balancing the interests of minority shareholders—relatively few of whom will live in the state anyway. If such states kowtow to prospective managers and majority shareholders (who ordinarily decide where to incorporate), larger states cannot achieve their desired balance in protecting minority interests, since this will simply lead to incorporations in other states. The result, under this view, is a "race to the bottom" with a continual watering down of the protections accorded by corporate law to minority shareholders.[17]

A number of writers have attacked this "race to the bottom" thesis. For example, to the extent Delaware has gained an advantage over other states in attracting corporations by virtue of already having numerous companies incorporated there and, accordingly, having a well-developed corporate law, it need not kowtow to prospective managers and majority shareholders in order to encourage Delaware incorporation. Moreover, some cynics have suggested that Delaware has an interest in providing minority shareholder protections, because the resulting litigation and extra planning creates work for the state's corporate bar.[18] Most significantly, however, many writers have argued that competition between states for incorporations leads to the best, rather than the worst, rules as far as protecting shareholder (including minority shareholder) interests.[19] In other words, there is a "race to the top," rather than to the bottom.

This "race to the top" thesis argues that if Delaware, or any other state, adopts corporate law rules which are against the financial interests of minority shareholders, prospective minority shareholders will respond by paying less for the stock of companies incorporated in Delaware, or other such states, than they would pay if the companies incorporated in states with better protections of minority shareholder interests. This, the argument runs, would place Delaware corporations at a disadvantage in raising capital relative to corporations formed under the laws of more protective states. This disadvantage, in turn, provides a check on efforts by prospective managers, majority shareholders and small state legislatures to ignore the interests of minority stockholders. Moreover, it might also provide an empirical way to ascertain whether Delaware corporate law has undermined minority shareholder interests. One can see whether share prices declined after any publicly traded corporations an-

17. For a classic article expounding this theory see William Cary, *Federalism and Corporate Law: Reflections Upon Delaware,* 83 Yale L.J. 663 (1974).

18. Jonathan R. Macey & Geoffrey P. Miller, *Toward an Interest–Group Theory of*

Delaware Corporate Law, 65 Tex. L. Rev. 469 (1987).

19. *E.g.,* Ralph K. Winter, Jr., *State Law, Shareholder Protection, and the Theory of the Corporation,* 6 J. Legal Studies 251 (1977).

nounced their intentions to reincorporate in Delaware (which corporations do from time to time). In fact, several studies of share price reactions to reincorporation announcements have found little effect one way or the other.[20]

Nevertheless, it is difficult to say what such studies prove. For example, the perceived advantage enjoyed by Delaware in having a well-developed corporate law might be enough to offset, in investors' minds, the disadvantage of any lesser protections for minority shareholders. Also, to the extent other states already have knuckled under to the competitive pressure for relaxed protections of minority interests (or even to the extent investors think states inevitably will do so), investors will not think much one way or the other about a reincorporation in Delaware.[21]

More broadly, even if investors pay somewhat less for shares of corporations formed under laws which are less protective of minority shareholder interests, it is difficult to say how much deterrence this will provide. Corporations might simply respond by issuing a larger amount of new shares when they must raise capital. Besides, most capital for corporations comes from retaining earnings rather than issuing shares.

§ 1.3 Promoters' Contracts

Over the years, the term promoter sometimes has had an unsavory connotation. Yet, all the term refers to in the corporate law context is someone putting together a new business. A new business typically needs capital, services and property. Hence, an individual putting together a new venture will want to contract with prospective investors, lenders, employees, independent contractors and those who might sell or lease property to the venture. The most straightforward way to do this is to first take the legal steps necessary to form a corporation and then have the corporation enter the various contracts. After all, much of the idea of doing business through a corporation is to have the corporation incur the liability.

Often, however, the promoter enters the contract before forming the corporation. Many times, this results from a mistake. The promoter thought the corporation already existed, yet some glitch has delayed its formation. Alternately, the promoter might be acting deceitfully. Aware

20. *See, e.g.,* Peter Dodd & Richard Leftwich, *The Market for Corporate Charters: "Unhealthy Competition" versus Federal Regulation,* 53 J. Bus. 259 (1980).

21. Or perhaps sophisticated investors have already discounted the price they will pay for a non-Delaware corporation's stock to take into account the prospect that the corporation might reincorporate in Delaware at an opportune moment. In any event, a study of stock price reactions to seven major corporate law decisions by the Delaware Supreme Court casts some doubt on the utility of this whole line of inquiry. This study found that these seven decisions, many of which substantially changed at least the perceived Delaware law on important corporate law issues affecting the rights of minority shareholders, caused no significant impact on the prices of Delaware corporation stocks. Elliot J. Weiss & Lawrence J. White, *Of Econometrics and Indeterminacy: A Study of Investors' Reactions to "Changes" in Corporate Law,* 75 Cal. L. Rev. 551 (1987).

that no corporation yet exists, the promoter figures he or she will simply tell the party he or she is dealing with that it does. We shall examine the results in these sort of cases in a later section of this chapter. Notice for now, however, what they both have in common is that the party the promoter deals with (whom we will refer to as the "third party") thinks a corporation exists at the time this party enters the deal.

Our focus in this section is when there is no mistake or deception, but, instead, both parties are aware there is not yet a corporation and decide to enter the contract anyway. In this case, why the contract before the corporation? In some circumstances, there is simply no alternative. If the promoter needs assistance from an attorney in actually forming the corporation, the promoter must deal with the attorney before the corporation exists. In other situations, the question is one of practicality, rather than necessity. Perhaps there is some reason to rush, so the promoter feels he or she should not delay entering the contract until completion of the incorporation process. Often, the venture may not be viable without certain funds, property or services. Under those circumstances, the promoter may not wish to spend (and potentially waste) money on incorporating until he or she has a commitment that the corporation will receive the needed funds, property or services. As a result of these concerns, the promoter may decide to contract before incorporating and to be up-front with the third party about this. One should note, however, that incorporation has become much quicker and cheaper over the years. As a result, better advice increasingly may be to form the corporation first. Otherwise, we end up with the legal issues to which we now turn

1.3.1 Rights and Obligations of the Corporation

Corporations, being fictitious entities, cannot enter contracts for themselves. Instead, the only way for corporations to enter contracts is through the actions of persons who have authority. This common sense and commonly understood notion sometimes might confuse individuals into thinking that the promoter can enter a contract binding on a planned corporation. In fact, this is not the case.

Later in this book, we will discuss in detail the management of corporations, including who has authority to bind the corporation to a contract. It is unnecessary, however, to know any of that in order to understand why a promoter lacks authority to bind a planned corporation. Instead, the reason the promoter cannot bind the planned corporation stems from a simple rule of agency law: Without a principal in existence at the time the purported agent acts, there can be no authority. Accordingly, the promoter lacks authority to bind the corporation to any transaction entered before the corporation existed.[1]

§ 1.3

1. *See, e.g.,* Clifton v. Tomb, 21 F.2d 893 (4th Cir.1927).

Of course, one might object to the sort of legal formalism represented by mechanically applying the rule of "no principal, no authority" to promoters' contracts. Is there some policy reason for not treating the corporation as bound once it comes into existence? Perhaps the best answer lies in the difficulty of otherwise figuring out when the self-appointed promoter's actions should bind the new corporation. We might find a sympathetic case for binding the corporation when the promoter becomes its sole owner and manager after incorporation. Yet, what will happen in the common scenario in which other individuals—who may not have approved, or even been aware of, the promoter's actions—participate in the corporate endeavor? So long as we feel the "no principal, no authority" rule will not unfairly surprise most individuals, perhaps there is something to be said for its simplicity.

As we discussed above, the reason the promoter entered the contract was to gain the benefit of the deal for the corporation. So, after the corporation comes into existence, what can those now in charge of the company—who include, as often as not, the former promoter(s)—do to gain this benefit for the company? The answer is simple: They can have the corporation adopt the contract.[2] What this means is that the corporation agrees to abide by the deal. Sometimes, courts refer to the corporation "ratifying" the contract; ratification being the term commonly used to denote the principal's acceptance of commitments made by an agent who acted without authority. Persnickety writers and courts, however, insist on using the term "adopt" in a situation, as here, in which not only did the agent lack authority, he or she even lacked an existing principal at the time he or she acted.[3]

How does the corporation adopt the contract? Most of the time, those with the authority to run the company (this being the board of directors) vote to do so. Of course, not only does adoption give the corporation the benefit of the deal, such action also makes the corporation liable upon the contract.

So far, simple enough. Where then can problems arise? There are two possibilities. First, those in charge of the new corporation might decide they do not like the deal made by the promoter. Perhaps the promoter lacks influence among the individuals who are now in charge of the corporation. Alternately, perhaps circumstances have changed so the deal made by the promoter no longer looks good even to the promoter. The second possibility is a change of heart by the third party. Perhaps the third party wants out of the deal.

---

2. *But see* Framingham Savings Bank v. Szabo, 617 F.2d 897 (1st Cir.1980) (Massachusetts does not allow the corporation to adopt a pre-incorporation contract; but the company can enter a new contract).

3. *E.g.*, McArthur v. Times Printing Co., 48 Minn. 319, 51 N.W. 216 (1892). Beyond terminology, a practical significance of the difference lies in courts treating an adoption as making the contract at the time of the adoption, while ratification relates back in time to deem the contract made when the agent acted. In *McArthur*, this difference saved the contract from coming within the statute of frauds, since the contract was to last more than one year from the time of the promoter's action, but less than one year after the corporation adopted.

Since the corporation is not bound unless the company adopts the pre-incorporation contract, the refusal of those in charge of the corporation to adopt the deal prevents liability for the company.[4] Thus, a clear and immediate rejection of the deal keeps things simple. Sometimes, however, there is not a clear and immediate rejection. Under such circumstances, the third party might argue that the attempted rejection came too late, because the corporation had already adopted the contract by the company's actions.

McArthur v. Times Printing Co.[5] provides an illustration. There, a promoter made a contract employing the plaintiff to work one year as an advertising solicitor for a planned newspaper corporation. After the corporation was formed, its board took no formal action to adopt this contract. Nevertheless, the plaintiff began working for the corporation. All of the corporation's shareholders, directors and officers were aware of the pre-incorporation deal, yet there was no effort to repudiate the deal or negotiate a new one, until, half way through the one-year employment period, those in charge of the company fired the plaintiff. The court held that those in charge of the corporation impliedly adopted the contract by accepting the plaintiff's services while knowing of the pre-incorporation contract.

Notice the utility of finding an implied adoption when the corporation accepts the benefits of a promoter's contract. This can avoid the most serious injustices resulting from adherence to the "no principal, no authority" rule. Still, there are limits to finding an implied adoption. For example, in *Kridelbaugh v. Aldrehn Theatres Co.*,[6] the court refused to find that the corporation's simply coming into existence constituted an implied adoption of a contract to pay an attorney to form the corporation. The court pointed out that the corporation had no choice about accepting the benefit of the attorney's services. After all, the corporation could not very well refuse to come into existence when the attorney filed the necessary documents for incorporation. Instead, the court in *Kridelbaugh* found an adoption in the initial board of directors' requesting further work by the attorney so that the corporation could raise funds to pay him.

Suppose it is the third party who wants to get out of the deal. Once the corporation adopts the contract, the third party is bound.[7] Can the third party, however, avoid the contract before the corporation adopts? This depends upon whether the third party has a contract with the promoter—the subject to which we next turn.

1.3.2 *Liability of the Promoter to the Third Party*

Usually, the planned corporation comes into existence, adopts contracts made on its behalf by the promoter, performs its end of the

4. An exception might exist if the third party can state a claim against the corporation for unjust enrichment or the like. *See, e.g.,* David v. Southern Import Wine Co., 171 So. 180 (La. App. 1936).

5. 48 Minn. 319, 51 N.W. 216 (1892).

6. 195 Iowa 147, 191 N.W. 803 (1923).

7. *E.g.,* K & J Clayton Holding Corp. v. Keuffel & Esser Co., 113 N.J.Super. 50, 272 A.2d 565 (1971).

bargain, and the third party is content. Occasionally, however, the planned corporation, for one reason or another, never comes into existence. Sometimes, as we saw above, those in charge of a new corporation refuse to adopt a contract made before the corporation came into existence. Another possibility reflects the failure rate among new businesses: The new corporation not infrequently will go broke before it can perform. If, for any of these reasons, the corporation does not carry out the contract, the third party commonly responds by suing the promoter.

In dealing with these sort of claims, courts generally recite the "rule" that promoters are liable on contracts they enter before the corporation exists even though the contract is to benefit the future corporation. Normally, courts also state an "exception" to this rule: The promoter is not liable when the third party only intended to look to the planned corporation and did not intend to bind the promoter to the contract.[8]

Unfortunately, as is often the case when courts and writers attempt to reduce the law to broad rules, the "rule" for promoter liability can confuse instead of clarify. For example, focusing on the so-called general rule sometimes can tempt litigants and courts into resolving issues of liability by asking who is a promoter.[9] Anyone succumbing to this temptation does not understand the rule.

It is not the status as a "promoter" which creates liability; rather the issue is one of intent. If the parties intended to bind an individual making pre-incorporation deals to a contract, this party will be liable; if not, then he or she is not liable. This follows from the fact that we are dealing with contractual liability here, in other words, liability based upon the agreement of the parties to be bound. In fact, the traditional recitation of the rule of promoter liability is upside down. The so-called exception—which tells us this is all a question of intent—is really the general rule. By contrast, the so-called general rule—that the promoter is liable—is simply a default provision. It tells us that if the court cannot figure out what the parties intended, then the court will assume the parties intended to bind the individual making pre-incorporation deals.

Okay, so we have identified the question as one of intent. This, however, does not end our analysis. Rather, it raises three further questions: (1) What specifically are the options the parties might have intended? (2) What evidence can we use to ascertain the parties' intent? (3) Why have courts chosen as the default rule one which makes the promoter liable on the contract if the corporation does not perform?

Let us start with the question of what the parties might intend. The traditional statement of the rule of promoter liability, and its exception,

8. *E.g.*, Goodman v. Darden, Doman & Stafford Associates, 100 Wash. 2d 476, 670 P.2d 648 (1983).

9. *See, e.g.*, McDaniel v. Service Feed & Supply, Inc., 271 Md. 371, 316 A.2d 800 (Md.Ct.App.1974).

suggest that there are two possibilities. In fact, however, there are at least four realistic choices:[10]

One alternative is that the parties intended no present agreement between the promoter and the third party. Notice, since the corporation does not yet exist, this means the third party has not contracted with anyone. Put another way, there is no contract. What then do we have? We have the terms for a contract which, as we saw above, the corporation can adopt after it comes into existence. In other words, we have something in the nature of an offer from the third party to the future corporation. Since this is simply a naked offer, the third party can withdraw it before the corporation adopts.

The second possibility (which is the default rule) is that the contract is between the third party and the promoter. After it comes into existence, the corporation might adopt the contract, thereby both demanding the benefit of the contract and agreeing to perform the promoter's obligations under the contract. If, for any reason, the corporation does not fully perform, then, since it was ultimately the promoter's contract, the promoter is liable.

A third alternative exists between the extremes of no contract or a contract which leaves the promoter on the hook until and unless the corporation fully performs. Suppose the promoter agrees to be bound to the contract with the third party. If the corporation comes into existence and adopts the contract, the third party then could accept the corporation's commitment as a novation of the promoter's obligation (in other words, the third party agrees to let the promoter off the hook in exchange for the corporation's promise to perform). Moreover, what the third party could do when the corporation adopts, the third party can promise to do when forming the contract. This provides the basis for the third alternative: The parties might intend a present contract between the third party and the promoter; yet this contract is subject to the understanding that if the corporation comes into existence and adopts the contract, the promoter will be off the hook even if the corporation later does not perform. In other words, the contract between the third party and the promoter is subject to an advance agreement by the third party to accept the corporation's promise as a novation of the promoter's obligation.

Yet a fourth possibility goes back to the idea that the third party could be making an offer to the future corporation. The promoter could turn this from a revocable offer into an option contract by providing the third party with some consideration in exchange for the third party's promise to keep the offer open. What might constitute such consideration? Cash obviously would do nicely. Another idea might be the promoter's promise to use his or her's best efforts both to form the corporation and to have the company adopt the contract.

10. *See, e.g.,* Restatement (Second) of Agency § 326 Comment b.

Armed with knowledge of these possibilities, an attorney representing a promoter can aid the promoter in negotiating the most desirable arrangement. For reasons we shall discuss shortly, from the promoter's standpoint, the most desirable arrangement normally would be the third or fourth alternatives. Once there is agreement, it should not be too difficult to write up a contract clearly expressing whichever choice the parties made. Unfortunately, many times promoters act without the aid of an attorney (or, more embarrassing, sometimes the promoter's attorney does not understand this area of law or is unable to draft clearly). In such cases, the contract between the promoter and third party may be ambiguous as to which arrangement the parties agreed. In these cases, what can courts look to in order to determine the parties' intent?

The obvious place to start in searching for the parties' intent is with whatever language the parties used in the contract. Often, the only potentially relevant language is the way the promoter signed the contract. For example, it is quite common for the promoter to sign the contract as "President" (or some other position) "of a corporation to be formed" (perhaps giving the name planned for the corporation). Sometimes, the signature block will refer to the promoter as "President" (or some other position) of the corporation (giving its planned name), as if the corporation presently exists, even though both parties are aware that the promoter has not yet formed the corporation. Typically, the promoter will point to either of these signature forms as showing the parties' intent that the promoter was not bound. After all, in a situation in which the corporation exists, a signature form identifying the signer as an agent would be normally enough to show an intent to bind the company and not the agent personally.

Courts' reactions to this sort of language in the promoter context have been decidedly mixed. In *Goodman v. Darden, Doman & Stafford Associates*,[11] the Washington Supreme Court held that such language (the defendant signed the contract as "President" of a corporation "in formation") simply raised the question as to what the parties intended, but was not enough to rebut the presumption created by the default rule that the promoter is liable. A Tennessee appellate court reached a very different result in *Company Stores Development Corp. v. Pottery Warehouse, Inc.*[12] There, the court found an intent not to bind the defendant personally to a contract he signed as "President" for a corporation "to be formed." One potentially important factor in this might be who drafted the contract and suggested the signature form. In *Quaker Hill, Inc. v. Parr*,[13] the plaintiff had drafted the promissory note naming a corporation (even though not yet formed) as the debtor and providing for the defendant to sign as the corporation's president. The court found an intent not to bind the defendant personally. While the court did not invoke the principle, the old saw about resolving contractual ambiguities against the drafter would seem to apply.

---

11. 100 Wash. 2d 476, 670 P.2d 648 (1983).

12. 733 S.W.2d 886 (Tenn.App.1987).

13. 148 Colo. 45, 364 P.2d 1056 (1961).

Perhaps one could clarify things if the promoter signs the contract as an "agent for a corporation to be formed who will be the obligor." This is what the defendant thought in *Stanley J. How & Associates, Inc. v. Boss.*[14] Nevertheless, the court held that this language, while showing an intent to bind the planned corporation, was not inconsistent with the intent that the promoter also would be bound.

In addition to the language of the contract, various extrinsic circumstances might shed light on the parties' intent. For example, if the contract calls for some performance before the parties expect the corporation will come into existence, this suggests an agreement on the part of the promoter to be a party to the contract.[15] Otherwise, we would have parties starting to carry out a non-existent contract. This inference is especially strong if the promoter must perform in order to meet the contract schedule; albeit, it is difficult to imagine many third parties agreeing to start their own performance before there is a contract. On the other hand, courts may read less into the third party's acceptance of initial corporate performance.[16] After all, a third party is unlikely to refuse such performance even if the parties agreed that the promoter would be liable in the event the corporation did not fully perform.

Various conversations between the parties might also shed light upon their intent. In *Stewart Realty Co. v. Keller*,[17] the defendant promoter expressly refused to sign any contract naming him as a party individually. The court found no intent to bind the promoter to the contract. In *Sherwood & Roberts–Oregon, Inc. v. Alexander*,[18] the plaintiff had insisted on doing business with a corporation, rather than with the defendants as individuals (in order to avoid usury problems). The court found an intent not to bind the promoters.

Suppose, after all the evidence is in, the court just cannot figure out what the parties intended. As stated above, this triggers the default rule that the promoter is liable. Yet, why is this the default rule? After all, does not the promoter want to avoid liability? Why assume the third party was able to demand it?

In selecting a default rule, courts generally are seeking to determine what parties would have agreed to had they considered the issue when they originally contracted. If the parties' interests at the outset are diametrically opposed on an issue, this could be tricky. On the other hand, if a particular interpretation usually would be against both parties' interests as viewed at the outset, then a default rule should assume they would not have agreed to it. In fact, this explains why the default rule on promoter liability rejects the alternative that there is no contract at all between the promoter and third party.

14. 222 F.Supp. 936 (S.D.Iowa 1963).

15. *E.g.,*Stanley J. How & Associates, Inc. v. Boss, 222 F.Supp. 936 (S.D.Iowa 1963).

16. *E.g.,* Goodman v. Darden, Doman & Stafford Associates, 100 Wash. 2d 476, 670 P.2d 648 (1983).

17. 118 Ohio App. 49, 193 N.E.2d 179 (1962).

18. 269 Or. 389, 525 P.2d 135 (1974).

It is easy to see why the third party typically would oppose the no contract alternative, but why is it not in the promoter's interest? The answer lies in going back to the discussion at the beginning of this section as to why promoters might want to contract with third parties before forming the corporation. Various reasons—the need for help in establishing the corporation or the importance of rushing or getting a commitment to critical inputs for the business—can lead the promoter to wish to lock in the third party. Yet, if there is no contract between the third party and the promoter, then not only is the promoter not bound, but the third party is not bound either.

Of course, it is possible that the promoter went through the effort of preparing and executing a contract-like document with no desire to bind the third party until the corporation actually adopts the contract. Possible, but unlikely. If all that the promoter really desired was to get a head start on drafting by having an offer ready for the corporation, why did the parties feel the promoter should also sign it? It is also possible that the promoter was confused as to the law and thought that the third party would be bound even if the promoter was not a party to any contract. The third party obviously denies thinking this, or we would have evidence of no intent to bind the promoter. Hence, the default rule must ask what agreement usually would result if the promoter, as well as the third party, had understood the law. While some promoters might feel avoiding liability would be more important than locking in the third party, the efforts expended to make the pre-incorporation deal suggest that most promoters place greater value on committing the third party. Even if not, how sympathetic can we be to parties who assume the law allows them to "have their cake and eat it too" by making one party contracts?

Now we see why courts presume the parties intend some contract between the promoter and the third party. It is more difficult, however, to decide which of the various possible permutations this should take. Specifically, why assume the parties agreed to a contract under which the promoter remains liable until and unless the corporation fully performs, rather than a contract in which the promoter's liability ends once the corporation adopts the deal, or an option contract where the promoter's only obligation is to use best efforts toward forming the corporation and having the company accept the offer?

The option contract seems unlikely. In these cases, we are dealing with a situation in which the contract identifies no specific consideration from the promoter (or else there would not be the ambiguity). Hence, we are forced to hypothesize that the third party agreed to give the planned corporation the option to enter a contract (or not enter it if the company later finds a better deal elsewhere) in exchange only for some ill-defined promise of good faith effort by the promoter. Moreover, an option contract normally has a time limit for its exercise, which seems absent in the typical promoter's contract. All told, had the parties intended an option contract, one suspects there would be greater specificity and a more tangible benefit to the third party.

To choose between the unlimited obligation on the promoter and the obligation subject to an advance agreement for a novation, it may be useful to consider the risks facing the third party. As mentioned earlier, there can be three reasons for corporate non-performance: (1) failure of the corporation to come into existence; (2) refusal of the corporation to adopt the contract; (3) financial inability of the corporation to perform or else pay damages. The first and second risks are inherent in the fact that the parties are dealing before the corporation exists. Notice that the novation arrangement eliminates these two risks for the third party. By contrast, the third risk is present when dealing with an existing corporation. Anyone willing to deal with a corporation accepts the risk that the corporation will not have the money to pay. Accordingly, the novation arrangement seems to eliminate the added risks to the third party of dealing with a non-existent corporation, without going beyond this to give the sort of personal guarantee which corporate creditors must specially demand, and so seems a logical choice as to what the parties would have agreed.[19] One rebuttal, however, is that when dealing with an existing corporation, the third party would have some ability to check out the company's current financial status. The third party cannot do this when entering a transaction before the corporation exists. Based upon this fact, one might argue that only the contract which leaves the promoter bound until complete performance removes the additional risks the third party faces in the pre-incorporation contract situation.

1.3.3 *Obligations of the Promoters to the Corporation and to Each Other*

In the cases we have discussed so far, the promoter seeks to have the corporation gain the direct benefit of the third party's performance under the contract. For example, if the third party owns property useful for the corporation, the deal between the promoter and the third party allows the corporation to adopt the contract and purchase the property directly from the third party. Often, however, the promoter, him- or herself, will purchase the desired property from the third party and then turn around and resell the property to the corporation after the company is formed. This avoids the questions we considered above about who is liable to the third party on the contract. It can lead to other problems, however.

Little controversy is likely to arise if the promoter resells the property to the corporation at the same price the promoter paid for it (at least if the promoter bought the property from a stranger). Often, however, the promoter will resell the property to the corporation at a higher price than the promoter paid. For example, in the classic *Old Dominion* cases,[20] two promoters bought mining properties for around $1 million. They then organized a new corporation and sold the mining

19. *See, e.g.,* 2 Williston on Contracts § 306 (3d ed. 1959).

20. Old Dominion Copper Mining & Smelting Co. v. Lewisohn, 210 U.S. 206, 28 S.Ct. 634 (1908); Old Dominion Copper Mining & Smelting Co. v. Bigelow, 203 Mass. 159, 89 N.E. 193 (1909), *aff'd,* 225 U.S. 111, 32 S.Ct. 641 (1912).

properties to the corporation for stock in the new corporation with a par value—the legal minimum sales price—of over $3 million.

In dealing with these sort of cases, courts sometimes speak of a fiduciary duty which promoters owe to the corporation (or to other promoters or to future investors in the corporation).[21] Introducing a fiduciary duty specifically for promoters in these cases, however, is usually unnecessary and distracting.

To begin with, we are dealing here with a conflict-of-interest transaction—in other words, a transaction between the corporation and one or more of its directors or officers—since normally the promoters will assume such roles after forming the corporation. We shall spend significant time later in this book examining how the law seeks to protect the corporation from managers abusing their control through transactions in which they stand at both ends. For example, we will ask what impact shareholder approval has on such a transaction. Indeed, the impact of shareholder approval was the issue in the *Old Dominion* cases. Specifically, the promoters there were the only shareholders of the corporation at the time of the transaction. The question of whether there can be either a breach of duty or fraud toward a corporation when all of the existing shareholders approve a conflict-of-interest transaction caused the United States Supreme Court and the Supreme Court of Massachusetts—in actions brought separately against the two promoters—to reach different results in the two *Old Dominion* cases.

In addition to the simple conflict-of-interest aspect, consider the fact that the promoters in the *Old Dominion* cases received stock in the new corporation. Indeed, promoters typically will be among the first to buy shares from the new corporation. This may introduce concerns beyond those of the garden variety conflict-of-interest transaction. Specifically, we must ask what the promoters accomplished by placing an inflated value on the mining property. This did not increase the real worth of the shares the promoters received for the property. Perhaps what was going on here was an attempt to fool future investors into thinking the corporation as a whole was worth more than it really was. In other words, there is an attempt to defraud future shareholders and creditors. We shall return to this subject later both when we explore financing the corporation and securities fraud.

In some contexts, however, it may be useful to think in terms of the obligations of promoters as such. Specifically, if promoters are dealing among themselves prior to forming a corporation in which they all plan to participate, then we might need to ask what contractual and fiduciary obligations the promoters owe to each other.

For example, suppose several individuals agree to go into business together. They decide to form a corporation. Each will supply some money, property or services to the venture in exchange for stock in the corporation. Under the analysis we discussed earlier, they cannot make a

---

21. *E.g.,* Frick v. Howard, 23 Wis.2d 86, 126 N.W.2d 619 (1964).

binding contract with the corporation to buy the stock (sometimes referred to as a subscription) before the company legally exists. What then is to prevent one of the individuals from pulling out of the deal before the corporation adopts? Much as when dealing with third parties, one answer is for these promoters to make a contract among themselves. Each would promise to buy the stock in exchange for the other promoters' promises to do the same. Many statutes, however, create another alternative.[22] These statutes allow the parties to make pre-incorporation subscriptions the equivalent of irrevocable offers to the corporation for a certain period of time (typically six months) without any special consideration for holding the offer open—in other words, they create the equivalent of one party contracts.

§ 1.4 Incorporation

1.4.1 How to Incorporate

Each state's corporations statute sets out the requirements for incorporating in that state. Hence, the short answer to the question "How does one incorporate?" is "Read the statute." In fact, incorporation under most modern statutes is a fairly simple process.

The key to this process is the preparation and filing of a document. Most statutes refer to this document either as the articles or certificate of incorporation, or, occasionally, the charter—different words used by different states for the same basic document. For simplicity, we shall use the term articles of incorporation or just articles. One bit of different terminology existed under the pre–1984 Model Business Corporation Act. It used the term articles of incorporation to refer to the document prepared and filed to form a corporation—nothing special there. However, the old Model Act used the term certificate of incorporation to refer to a document issued by the state agency receiving the articles to indicate that the corporation existed.

What do the articles contain? Again, the answer comes from the statute. Broadly speaking, statutes refer to two types of provisions in articles. There are mandatory provisions, which the statute requires the articles to contain in order to form the corporation. We shall discuss these in a moment. There are also optional provisions, which the statute states may be in the articles. We shall not address these now. Rather, we shall have the opportunity in a number of places throughout this book to discuss various optional provisions which parties may decide to place in the corporation's articles. It is worth noting, however, that these optional provisions themselves fall into two camps. Some provisions are optional both in the sense that parties may omit such provisions from the articles because they do not wish to have such provisions govern the corporation at all and also in the sense that parties who wish to have such provisions can place them in another document (such as the corporation's bylaws). For example, in Delaware, either articles or bylaws can provide, if so desired, for board members to serve staggered

---

22. *E.g.*, Del. Gen. Corp. Law § 165; M.B.C.A. § 6.20(a).

terms (like the United States Senate).[1] Other provisions are only optional in the sense that the articles may omit them if the parties do not wish these provisions to apply to the corporation. If, however, parties wish this second type of provision to apply to their corporation, the statute requires the provision to be in the articles. An example of such a provision in Delaware would be one limiting the liability of directors for breach of their duty of care. Such a limitation, if desired at all, must be in the articles.[2] Accordingly, it is important in drafting articles to carefully consider what optional provisions the articles should contain.

Now let us look at the required provisions. We can use the Revised Model Business Corporations Act and Delaware's corporations law as typical of modern statutes. They specify four or five mandatory items:[3]

(1) The corporation's name

There are a couple of items of note here. Statutes require the name to contain a term like incorporated (or "inc."), corporation (or "corp."), company (or "co."), or the like, to indicate this is a corporation. Also, the name must be distinguishable from names already taken by companies incorporated or doing business in the state. In other words, a new company cannot incorporate under the name General Motors Corporation. The state agency which accepts filings of articles of incorporation maintains a list of names already taken. Some states require that the name not be deceptively similar to a name already in use.[4] "Deceptively similar" is a term of art from the law of trademark and unfair competition. It prohibits use of a name that may be different from another name (in other words, distinguishable), but nevertheless is close enough to cause consumer confusion. In many states, it may be possible to reserve a name for a short period of time before actually incorporating.

(2) The name of the corporation's registered agent, and the address of its registered office, in the state

This is so public records show where one can serve the corporation with legal documents (such as a summons and complaint from a litigant or tax notices from the state). This does not need to be, and in many instances it is not, the place at which the corporation does business. An attorney's office, or the office of a corporation service company (especially if one incorporates in a state in which the corporation undertakes no activities), are common choices.

(3) The purpose of the corporation

This is a relic remaining from the historical development of corporate law. As we discussed earlier,[5] states originally granted corporate charters in order to carry out particular businesses. Moreover, there was the hope, ultimately forlorn, of preventing the concentration of economic

---

§ 1.4

1. Del. Gen. Corp. Law § 141(d).
2. Del. Gen. Corp. Law § 102(b)(7).
3. M.B.C.A. § 2.02(a); Del. Gen. Corp. Law § 102(a).

4. This was the approach under the pre–1984 Model Act.
5. See § 1.1.3*b supra*.

power by curbing the activities in which a given corporation could engage. Once it became permissible to make purpose clauses consist of "laundry lists" containing every endeavor one could conceive of, the exercise became pointless. Modern statutes, like Delaware's, allow one to state simply that the purpose will be to engage in any lawful business (or like language). An even more modern approach, found in the Revised Model Act, says do not bother to include a purpose clause at all (unless, for some strange reason, the drafters of the articles want to constrain future corporate activities through an article provision).

(4) Authorized stock

This provision is important. The articles specify the total number of shares of stock the corporation can issue. If the corporation will be able to issue different types (classes) of stock, the articles specify the rights of each class. In many jurisdictions, the articles also specify something called "par value" for the stock. We shall discuss all this in detail later when we discuss financing the corporation.

(5) The name and address of the incorporators

Technically, these are the folks who form the corporation. Actually, all that the incorporators must do (besides include their names and addresses in the articles) is sign the articles. Some states require the signature be notarized. Given this limited role, sometimes an attorney for the parties desiring a corporation will serve as the incorporator. Modern statutes, like the Revised Model Act and Delaware's law, allow any person (including corporations), no matter where a resident, to act as an incorporator. They also require no more than one incorporator.[6] When the articles do not name the initial directors, the incorporators have another task, which we shall address shortly.

Some states may require the articles to contain other provisions beyond the five items listed above. For example, some states require the articles to specify the length of corporate existence.[7] In this event, normally the statute allows, and the articles provide, for perpetual existence.

To form the corporation, statutes require filing the articles with a designated state agency.[8] Typically, this is the office of the particular state's secretary of state (which seems strange to those used to thinking of the role of the United States' Secretary of State as the nation's top diplomat). Naturally, there will be a fee for filing. The degree of scrutiny which the secretary of state's office gives to ensure the articles comply with the corporations statute varies from state to state, depending on both the authority granted the office by the state's corporations statute and the practices adopted by the office. A few states also require filing with county recorders' offices or publication of the articles.[9]

6. M.B.C.A. § 2.01; Del. Gen. Corp. Law § 101(a).

7. This was the rule under the pre–1984 Model Act.

8. *E.g.*, M.B.C.A. § 2.01; Del. Gen. Corp. Law § 101(a).

9. Delaware requires filing a copy of the articles with the county recorder where the registered office will be (Del. Gen. Corp.

Under a statute like Delaware's or the Revised Model Act, corporate existence begins upon filing the articles.[10] Yet, it is one thing to say that a legally recognized entity exists, it is quite another matter to have a functioning corporation. After all, at this point, we do not have any owners of the corporation (shareholders) or anyone who normally has the authority to run the corporation (directors and officers). The only individuals we have identified so far are the incorporators. Here, we have a bit of a "chicken or the egg" problem. Normally, shareholders elect directors; yet directors must decide to issue stock in order for there to be shareholders.[11] Statutes generally provide two ways to break the impasse. Articles may (or, in some states, must[12]) contain a provision specifying who are the corporation's initial directors.[13] Otherwise, incorporators have the authority to appoint the initial directors. Before appointing the initial directors, incorporators also have authority under many statutes to take various actions for the corporation, such as adopt initial bylaws.[14]

Typically, statutes call for the incorporators or the initial directors (if specified in the articles) to hold an organizational meeting (albeit, under some statutes, it may be permissible to carry out this exercise by unanimous written consent instead of actually holding a meeting).[15] At this meeting, the incorporators appoint the initial directors (unless the articles already specified the initial directors). In addition, this meeting typically accomplishes a variety of other tasks. The incorporators or initial directors usually adopt bylaws. They normally approve a corporate seal (a suitably pretentious design one can stamp on various corporate documents to make them look official) and a form for stock certificates (also suitably pretentious looking). Actually, one can purchase seals and stock certificate forms in kits (which also often include fancy leather binders in which to keep corporate minutes and other documents). The corporation can take this opportunity to adopt pre-incorporation contracts made by the promoters. It would be nice to approve the establishment of a corporate bank account. This is a convenient time to appoint officers for the corporation. An important step by the initial directors is to issue stock, thereby establishing the corporation's first group of stockholders and giving the corporation some beginning capital. Indeed, many states used to require the corporation have a specified minimum amount of capital before conducting any business. We shall discuss this later when we address financing the corporation.

As just stated, one of the early tasks of incorporators or initial directors is to adopt bylaws for the corporation. Many, if not most, organizations—be they a club or a community service group, or a

Law § 103(c)(5)); albeit failure to do so does not prevent the existence of a corporation.

10. M.B.C.A. § 2.03; Del. Gen. Corp. Law § 106.

11. See § 2.1.2a infra.

12. This was the case under the pre–1984 Model Act.

13. E.g., M.B.C.A. § 2.02(b)(1); Del. Gen. Corp. Law § 102(a)(6).

14. E.g., M.B.C.A. § 2.05(a)(2), 2.06(a); Del. Gen. Corp. Law § 107.

15. E.g., M.B.C.A. § 2.05; Del. Gen. Corp. Law § 108.

corporation—adopt bylaws. These are simply a set of rules for running the organization. They answer basic questions, such as: When and where are regular meetings, who can call special meetings, and what notice and quorum is necessary to hold a meeting? If there is a governing board, how many members will it have, with what requirements for membership, and how are vacancies filled? What officers will the organization have, with what duties, and how appointed? Corporate bylaws answer the same sort of questions with respect to shareholders and directors meetings, the composition of the board of directors, and the responsibilities and appointment of corporate officers. They also often contain provisions dealing with keeping records of share ownership and transfer. They may cover a variety of other matters as well. We shall have occasion to address bylaws more when we discuss corporate management later in this book. Unlike articles, there is no requirement to file bylaws with any state office.

1.4.2 Consequences of Defective Incorporation

Whenever there are formal requirements, some people, through inadvertence or otherwise, fail to comply. So it is not surprising that cases arise in which parties undertake business purportedly as a corporation despite having failed to meet all of the statutory requirements to form a corporation. A common example occurs when a person charged with the job of filing articles of incorporation with the appropriate state official forgets to do so. Sometimes, the forgetful individual is the parties' attorney.

Failure to comply with the requirements for incorporation can have a number of consequences. Perhaps the noncompliance is trivial (say, some minor mistake in the articles). If so, courts might deem there to be substantial compliance with the statute and a legally valid corporation exists.[16] Courts often refer to a legally valid corporation as a "de jure corporation."

Otherwise, there can be problems. For example, parties with whom the defective "corporation" purportedly contracted may attempt to disavow any obligation on the ground that, without a corporation in existence, there could be no contract.[17] Alternately, parties in charge of the company might decide to have the corporation, after it does come into existence, disclaim liability on contracts ostensibly made on its behalf after a defective attempt at formation.[18] The most common problem, however, occurs if the business fails. Disappointed creditors may seize upon the defective attempt to incorporate as an opening to seek payment of their claims from various participants in the venture.

Why exactly might a defective attempt to incorporate lead to liability of various participants in the venture? After all, a defective attempt to

---

16. *E.g.,* People v. Ford, 294 Ill. 319, 128 N.E. 479 (1920) (failure to have a seal on a statement of incorporation did not preclude de jure status).

17. *See, e.g.,* Southern–Gulf Marine Co. No. 9, Inc. v. Camcraft, Inc., 410 So.2d 1181 (La.App.1982).

18. *See, e.g.,* Peterson v. Baloun, 715 F.Supp. 212 (N.D.Ill.1989).

incorporate does not, in and of itself, create liability for anyone. There are three theories.

The first theory stems from agency law. As we saw earlier in discussing promoters' contracts,[19] no one has authority to bind a corporation to a contract before the corporation comes into existence. This lack of authority applies, not only to promoters, but also to a person who purports to bind a "corporation" to a contract, when, in fact, failure to comply with the statute meant the "corporation" did not exist. There is an important difference, however, between the defective corporation situation and the situation with promoters' contracts. When we spoke of promoters' contracts, we were referring to the situation in which the third party, or creditor, is aware that the corporation does not exist. Under this circumstance, promoter liability depends on the intent of the parties. If the creditor only intended to look to the later-formed corporation for performance, then the promoter is off the hook. In the defective incorporation case, the creditor only intended to look to the corporation for performance. Nevertheless, in this instance, this intent does not preclude liability beyond the corporation. The reason is that the person purporting to represent the corporation has misled the creditor as to the existence of the corporation, and, in turn, the power of this individual to bind the corporation.

Misleading the creditor provides the basis for a possible claim. If the person dealing with the creditor knowingly misinformed the creditor (in other words, this person knew the corporation had not been validly formed), then the creditor has a claim against the individual involved for misrepresentation (fraud). Suppose, however, as is commonly the case, the person dealing with the creditor thinks the corporation exists. Even so, there is liability for misrepresenting one's authority.[20] In this case, there is no fraud (knowing falsity). Rather, the claim is that the individual has breached an implied warranty that he or she had the authority he or she purported to have.

There are several corollaries worth noting about this approach. To begin with, liability depends upon who actually dealt with a given creditor. This could produce some rather freakish results. Different participants in the business might be liable to different creditors depending on the happenstance of who picked up the telephone to take or place a given order or enter any other transaction. Also, one might logically argue that there should be no liability under this approach if either the corporation adopted the contract after coming into existence or the business failure meant that the company could never have paid the creditor in question. After all, in these cases, the creditor would have been no better off if the party it dealt with actually had the authority to bind the corporation.[21] Finally, this theory of liability presumably would not work for tort claimants.

19. See § 1.3.1 *supra.*

20. *E.g.,* Conway v. Samet, 59 Misc.2d 666, 300 N.Y.S.2d 243 (1969).

21. One way to avoid this conclusion is to assert that the participant is liable on the contract, rather than simply for misrep-

A second theory has a broader reach. If the participants failed to establish a corporation, one must ask in what legal form are the participants carrying out their business. After all, unlike the promoter contract situation, here the creditor intended to contract with a presently existing business entity. If not a corporation, what is it? Assuming we have more than one participant, then the answer is that we have an association of two or more persons carrying on, as co-owners, a business for profit. This is the definition of a partnership.[22] There are no statutory formalities to create a partnership. On the contrary, a partnership is the default form of co-owned business when the participants do not establish any other type of entity. As pointed out earlier,[23] all partners have personal liability for the debts of the partnership. Of course, if there is only one participant, we could not have a partnership. In this event, presumably there would be a sole proprietorship and still personal liability. Notice that this theory will pick up tort claimants as well as contract creditors.

The theory that persons participating in a defectively formed "corporation" can be personally liable as partners creates a question, however, as to who are the partners. The problem arises because individuals might take the roles of "shareholder," "director" or "officer" in what they thought was a corporation. When the participant acts as both a "shareholder" (in other words, he or she will be entitled to share in the profits of the business), and as an "officer" or "director" (in other words, he or she takes a role in managing the venture), then there is little problem treating this individual as a co-owner and hence a partner.[24] Difficulties come up, however, if the participant is only an "officer" or "director" (in other words, the individual participates in management, but does not claim any interest in the profits of the venture). Here, one might conclude that a person cannot be a co-owner of a business if he or she is not entitled to any profits.[25] Instead, this person is really just an employee and hence bears no liability as a partner. Less easy to resolve is the situation in which the participant thought he or she was just a shareholder and took no role in management. The conventional view is that shareholders are the owners of a corporation. Moreover, a share in the profits (which our ostensible shareholder would have) is prima facie evidence of being a partner,[26] and many partnerships exist under agreements which cut off the right of some partners to participate in management. Even so, some courts have been reluctant to

resenting or breaching a warranty of authority. While there is authority for the proposition that an agent for a non-existent principal becomes liable on the contract, this applies when the third party knows that no principal exists (in other words, the promoters' contract situation). Restatement (Second) of Agency § 326. By contrast, the third party's mistaken view that a principal exists precludes saying that the third party intended to bind the agent personally to the contract.

22. *E.g.,* Uniform Partnership Act § 6 (1914).

23. See § 1.1.2a *supra.*

24. *See, e.g.,* Gazette Publ'g Co. v. Brady, 204 Ark. 396, 162 S.W.2d 494 (1942).

25. *See, e.g.,* State ex rel. Carlton v. Triplett, 213 Kan. 381, 517 P.2d 136 (1973).

26. *E.g.,* Uniform Partnership Act § 7(4) (1914).

treat passive investors in defectively formed "corporations" as partners.[27]

The third theory of liability is the most straightforward. Liability exists because the corporations statutes in many jurisdictions so provide. Traditionally, corporations statutes did not specify the consequences which a defective attempt to incorporate had on participant liability. Hence, the development of the common law theories set out above. This is still the case in many of the leading states, such as Delaware.[28] Starting with its first version in 1950, however, the drafters of the Model Business Corporations Act decided to address the question. Through various incarnations, the Model Act has imposed joint and several liability upon persons who assume or purport to act as or on behalf of a defectively formed "corporation" for the resulting debts.[29] As we shall discuss later, the most recent version limits this liability to those who knew the corporation did not exist.

As with the common law theories, statutory liability under the Model Act leads to questions regarding who exactly it will reach. For example, one way to read the language making individuals who purport "to act as or on behalf of a corporation" liable for debts "created while so acting" is that each person purporting to bind the non-existent corporation is liable just on the contracts he or she made. This would do little more than codify the agency theory.[30] If, however, the Model Act makes individuals who purport to act as a corporation liable for all the firm's debts, regardless of who made the particular contract, then the question becomes whether individuals purporting "to act as a corporation" include those who thought they were passive shareholders.

The Oregon Supreme Court addressed these possible interpretations in *Timberline Equip. Co. v. Davenport*.[31] There, a failure of the originally filed articles to conform to the statute had delayed the formation of the corporation until after execution of a rental contract on the company's

---

27. *See, e.g.,* Rutherford v. Hill, 22 Or. 218, 29 P. 546 (1892).

28. A study of defective incorporation cases in the years between 1952 and 1989 found that courts resolved most of them by using common law doctrines, rather than statutory provisions specifically addressing the consequences of a defective attempt to incorporate. Comment, *An Empirical Study of Defective Incorporation,* 39 Emory L.J. 523 (1990).

The Delaware corporations statute does address one impact of defective attempts to incorporate. Section 329 of the Delaware General Corporation Law prevents either the corporation or a third party from using the defect as an excuse to get out of a contract entered into between a defective corporation and a third party.

29. This provision was Section 139 of the 1950 version; moved to Section 146 of

the 1969 revision; and now is Section 2.04 of the 1984 Revised Model Business Corporations Act.

30. Such a limited impact could especially be the case under pre–1984 versions of the Model Act. The language in the pre–1984 versions made individuals who "assumed to act as a corporation without authority" of a certificate of incorporation liable for all debts and obligations "incurred or arising as a result thereof." While the "result thereof" language might refer to all debts incurred by assuming to act as a corporation, this language could just refer to those debts (in other words, liability for damages) which result from the lack of authority. Under the narrower interpretation, liability under the Model Act would be co-extensive with liability for breach of a warranty of authority under agency law

31. 267 Or. 64, 514 P.2d 1109 (1973).

behalf. When the corporation later failed to pay the rent due, the creditor sued. Among the defendants was an individual who was both a shareholder and director in the venture, but who evidently was not the person that acted for the corporation in entering the rental agreement. Oregon had enacted the Model Act's provision creating statutory liability in defective corporation situations. The Oregon Supreme Court refused to read this provision as only creating liability for debts made by the particular defendant. This, the court felt, would lead to liability based upon the chance of who dealt with a particular creditor—which is the freakish quality we noted earlier about the agency theory. On the other hand, apparently influenced by the result of some the partnership theory cases, the court in *Timberline* stated that it would not read the Model Act provision as reaching those who were merely passive investors. Since the defendant was not just a passive investor, but took a role in management, the court found liability.

1.4.3 *De facto Corporations, Estoppel and Other Defenses*

Most courts and legal writers dealing with the liability of participants following a defective attempt to incorporate have not focused on the theories of liability discussed above. Instead, they mostly focus on two doctrines: de facto corporations and estoppel. Indeed, so great has been the emphasis on these two doctrines, that some writers refer to these two doctrines as governing liability in the defective corporation situation.[32] They do not. Rather, these two doctrines are potential defenses to liability under the theories discussed above.

The reason for their prominence is because they raise the two fundamental policy questions involved in this area: (1) To what extent should courts forgive innocent mistakes? and (2) Should courts prevent creditors from obtaining windfall recoveries from parties whom creditors never originally intended to hold responsible?

a. *De facto corporations*

Let us start with so-called de facto corporations. What is this all about? Simply, the court is saying that it will treat the venture as if it was a corporation for purposes of determining the rights and liabilities of private parties, despite the failure to comply with the statutory requirements for incorporation. This means that the participants will not face liability under the agency or partnership theories set out above. It could also prevent both third parties and later formed corporations from using a defective attempt to incorporate as grounds to avoid contractual obligations. Because courts treat de facto corporations as existing only for the purpose of determining rights between private parties, the state can still challenge (in what historically was referred to as a quo warranto proceeding) the existence of what would otherwise be a de facto corporation.

---

32. *E.g.,* Alexander H. Frey, *Legal Anal-*   Pa. L. Rev. 1153 (1952).
ysis and the "De Facto" Doctrine, 100 U.

What does it take for a court to treat a venture as a "de facto" corporation? Typically, courts list three requirements: (1) the existence of a statute allowing incorporation of the venture; (2) a colorable or good faith attempt to incorporate under the statute; and (3) some action as a purported corporation.[33] Since every state has a corporations statute, and since the participants were acting as a corporation or we would not be discussing this whole problem, the only real requirement is a colorable or good faith attempt to comply with the statute. In essence, the de facto corporation doctrine is just an involved way of saying that the court is willing to overlook relatively minor technical mistakes of someone who tried to incorporate, even if those mistakes go beyond the de minimis level and so there is no de jure corporation. Simply put, one who tried and got pretty close should not be liable.

If the general idea behind the de facto corporation doctrine is not difficult, the same cannot be said as to the application of the doctrine. The problem is to figure out how much of a try is enough, or, put another way, how minor must the mistake be.

Cantor v. Sunshine Greenery, Inc.,[34] illustrates the sort of mistake that courts might forgive under the de facto corporation doctrine. The incorporators prepared and mailed a certificate of incorporation to the Secretary of State, but, perhaps because a mistake in the address, the certificate was not considered officially filed with the state until two days after the defendant had entered a lease on the company's behalf with the plaintiff. The defendant had waited thirteen days after the mailing before executing the lease. The court held this was enough of a bona fide effort to incorporate before entering contracts on the corporation's behalf in order to apply the de facto label.

By contrast, in *Ratner v. Central Nat'l Bank of Miami,*[35] the court refused find a de facto corporation. There, the participants had not even attempted to file articles of incorporation until eight months after the defendant had entered the contract in question upon the purported corporation's behalf.

Between *Cantor* and *Ratner* there is much room for difficult cases. Moreover, the simplification of the incorporation process over the years has rendered the mistakes in many of the early de facto corporation cases no longer relevant.

b. Estoppel

The concept behind estoppel is very different. It has nothing to do with the defendant making a good try. Instead, the concept behind estoppel in general lies with injustices created when one party seeks to gain an advantage by changing his or her story as to the existence of a fact or legal relationship. Hence, if a speaker makes a misrepresentation

---

33. *E.g.,* Robertson v. Levy, 197 A.2d 443 (D.C.App.1964).

34. 165 N.J.Super. 411, 398 A.2d 571 (1979).

35. 414 So.2d 210 (Fla.Dist.Ct.App. 1982).

upon which a listener reasonably relies to the listener's detriment, a court can later estop the speaker from asserting the true facts in litigation against the listener.

This sort of estoppel works simply enough in one circumstance which occasionally arises following a defective attempt to incorporate. As stated earlier, sometimes the participants in the venture point to the defective incorporation in an effort to have the later formed corporation escape liability on a contract. Here, the court will have little difficulty in estopping the participants from asserting that the corporation did not exist at the time they entered the contract purportedly on its behalf.[36]

More problematic, however, is the situation in which the participants in the venture ask the court to estop a party they dealt with from denying the existence of the corporation. This could occur when such a party seeks to escape from a contract with the company by arguing the corporation did not exist when the "contract" was executed. More commonly, participants often try to employ estoppel as a defense to personal liability in the defective incorporation situation.

At first glance, this seems to be a sympathetic situation for estoppel. The third party agreed to deal with a corporation. This party then seeks to use a delay in forming the corporation, which typically did not impact the third party, as an excuse to either escape from an obligation upon an agreement or to obtain recovery from individuals the third party never expected to look to in entering the deal. In either event, there appears to be a windfall.

Nevertheless, there are a couple problems with estoppel here. Normally, courts estop the party who made a misrepresentation or created a false impression from later asserting the truth. In the defective incorporation situation, however, the parties who made the false statements are the participants, who told the third party that they were acting on behalf of a corporation, when, in fact, no corporation yet existed. Hence, here, the parties who made the misrepresentation are trying to estop the party they misled from later pointing out the truth. This seems to be something of an "upside-down" estoppel.

More practically, if individuals can gain the advantage of corporate limited liability by simply telling third parties that they are dealing with a corporation—which then estops the third parties from later denying the existence of the corporation—perhaps people would lose their incentive to even try to meet incorporation requirements.

As a result of these concerns, many courts have refused to apply estoppel to protect participants from liability in the defective corporation context[37] (albeit, courts seem to have less reticence to use this upside-

---

36.　*See, e.g., In re* Gold Depository Unlimited of America, 106 Misc.2d 992, 436 N.Y.S.2d 794 (1980).

37.　*E.g.,* Harrill v. Davis, 168 F. 187 (8th Cir.1909).

down estoppel when the third party is seeking to escape liability upon a contract entered after a defective attempt at incorporation[38]).

c. Two defenses or one?

The discussion thus far suggests two distinct potential defenses to liability in the defective incorporation situation: de facto corporation, which focuses on the efforts of the defendants, and estoppel, which focuses on the windfall to the plaintiff. Indeed, some judicial opinions have taken pains to point out the distinct nature of these two defenses. For example, in *Cranson v. I.B.M. Corp.*,[39] an attorney forgot to file a certificate of incorporation for seven months after its preparation (during which time, the so-called corporation bought typewriters it later did not pay for). While conceding this delay might be too much of a mistake to find a de facto corporation, the court nevertheless estopped the plaintiff—who had been content to rely on the supposed corporation's credit—from using its later discovery of the defect as an opportunity to go after a participant in the venture.

Yet, for every case like *Cranson*, there are numerous others in which courts talk as if de facto corporation and estoppel are part of the same defense.[40] Is this just sloppy opinion writing or is something more significant going on here? A noted study of defective incorporation cases up to 1952 by Professor Alexander Frey[41] suggests the latter. This study found that tort claimants were almost invariably successful in imposing liability upon participants in defective incorporation cases. Yet, if the de facto corporation doctrine calls for forgiving relatively minor mistakes, one would have expected at least some of these cases to go the other way. Conversely, in the contract creditor context, the percentage of success for creditors in holding participants liable depended upon the severity of noncompliance. For example, failure to meet requirements to file copies of incorporation papers in the county recorder's office rarely led to liability, whereas failure to file articles of incorporation with the appropriate state official yielded about an even chance at liability. Yet, if estoppel were an independent defense, why did it not always apply in cases in which the plaintiff had agreed to look only to what it thought was a corporation?

One possible interpretation of this study is that courts are using a conjunctive approach. Under this approach, courts are normally only willing to forgive participants who made a defective attempt to incorporate when there will be some windfall to the plaintiff (in other words, the plaintiff is a contract creditor who had been willing to look to a corporation's credit, rather than a tort claimant). Even then, the willingness to forgive depends on how excusable the court finds the participants' mistake. In other words, it takes elements of both estoppel and de

---

38. *See, e.g.,* Walker v. Joanna M. Knox & Associates, Inc., 132 Ga.App. 12, 207 S.E.2d 570 (1974).

39. 234 Md. 477, 200 A.2d 33 (1964).

40. Indeed, the court in *Cranson* sought to disavow prior Maryland cases which had done this.

41. Frey, *supra* note 32.

facto corporation for the defendant to get off the hook.[42] Even *Cranson* may be consistent with this. After all, perhaps we should not completely blame the participant for the attorney's mistake.

d. The Impact of the Model Act

We discussed earlier how the drafters of the Model Act decided to address the impact of a defective attempt to incorporate on participant liability. One of the motivations for their doing so came from dissatisfaction with the de facto corporation doctrine. The drafters criticized the de facto corporation doctrine as "fuzzy"—presumably a reference to the difficulty under the doctrine in deciding what mistakes are too serious for forgiveness. The Model Act's drafters also felt that they had simplified the process of incorporation such that there was little room left for the sort of technical mistakes which the de facto corporation doctrine often had covered up. Therefore, the drafters decided to have the Model Act abolish the doctrine.

The Model Act's drafters, however, eschewed the direct approach. No provision in the statute comes out and says that courts cannot apply the de facto corporation doctrine. Instead, one discovers the intent to abolish the doctrine by reading this goal in the official comments to provisions in the Model Act.

This sort of drafting can lead to questions. To begin with, what section in the statute actually abolishes the doctrine? The obvious candidate is the section we discussed earlier which creates statutory liability for those who assume to act for a defectively formed corporation. Not surprisingly, the official comment to this provision in the 1969 version of the Model Act sets out the justification outlined above for abolishing the de facto corporation doctrine. There is just one problem. This is not the only official comment suggesting that the Model Act abolishes de facto corporations. The 1950 and 1969 versions of the Model Act also contain a section which states that issuance of a certificate of incorporation begins the existence of a corporation.[43] The official comment to this provision (especially in the 1969 version) suggests that, by defining the moment of initial corporate existence, this section precludes the possibility of de facto corporations.[44] Still, this question would be rather academic, but for one fact: Only a minority of the states have adopted the Model Act provision creating liability for those assuming to act for a defectively formed corporation, while a larger number of states have adopted provisions, such as proposed by the Model Act, defining when corporate existence begins. Did this broader group of states there-

---

42. For an attempt to demonstrate this through a statistical analysis, see Fred S. McChesney, *Doctrinal Analysis and Statistical Modeling in Law: The Case of Defective Incorporation*, 71 Wash. U. L. Q. 493 (1993).

43. This was Section 50 in the 1950 version of the Model Act and Section 56 in the 1969 version. Section 2.03 of the 1984

Revised Model Act provides that corporate existence begins upon the filing of the articles.

44. The official comment under Section 2.03 is less explicit. In contrast to the 1969 version—in which the comment stated "a de facto corporation cannot exist under the Model Act"—the new comment never expressly refers to de facto corporations.

by abolish the de facto corporation defense even though they did not adopt the Model Act's statutory liability provision? There is little authority to this effect.

Even when it is clear that the Model Act abolishes de facto corporations, there is a second ambiguity. What about the estoppel defense? The official comments to the 1950 and 1969 versions of the Model Act did not address estoppel. Nevertheless, a number of courts held that the Model Act precludes it.

For example, the situation in *Robertson v. Levy*[45] presented a sympathetic case for estoppel. The plaintiff had agreed to sell his business to a corporation to be formed by the defendant. The defendant filed articles, but the Superintendent of Corporations rejected them, resulting in a fifteen day delay in forming the corporation. During this delay, the defendant executed, on behalf of the corporation, a contract to purchase the plaintiff's business in exchange for an installment note. After the corporation later defaulted on the note, the plaintiff took advantage of the defect in incorporation to sue the defendant personally. Despite an obvious effort to get something the plaintiff never bargained for—especially given that the plaintiff knew he would be dealing with a newly formed corporation—the court held that the Model Act's statutory liability provision trumped, not only the de facto corporation defense, but also estoppel.

One rationale for this result would be that de facto corporations and estoppel are really just part of the same defense. If so, one can conclude that the elimination of de facto corporations leaves nothing left for estoppel. This was not the rationale in *Robertson*, however. Instead, the court appeared to recognize the possibility of a separate estoppel defense, but held that it too must fall to the intent of the statute to set clear-cut lines as to liability.

Other courts have left open the possibility of an estoppel defense despite the Model Act. For example, the *Timberline* court refused to decide whether the statute ended the defense, because estoppel turned out to be inapplicable to the situation there (as there was evidence that the plaintiff did not realize it was dealing with a supposed corporation).

The effect of the 1950 and 1969 versions of the Model Act was to make it more likely that participants in a defective incorporation situation would face liability. The Model Act took a dramatic U-turn in 1984. Instead of continuing to condemn the de facto corporation defense, the Model Act's 1984 revision effectively goes the defense one better. Specifically, the 1984 revision significantly changed the provision creating statutory liability in case of defective incorporation. Now, those who purport to act as or for a defectively formed corporation are only liable if they know the corporation does not exist.

Notice how this knowledge requirement would have saved the defendant in a case like *Cantor* in which the court found a de facto corpora-

---

45. 197 A.2d 443 (D.C.App.1964).

tion. Indeed, it also would have saved the defendant in a situation like *Cranson* in which the mistake may have been too serious to qualify under the de facto corporation doctrine. Moreover, unlike estoppel, this new knowledge element can protect participants from liability to torts claimants. This latter impact illustrates how much the new Model Act would have altered the results of the cases in Professor Frey's 1952 study.

What then is the effect of the new Model Act provision upon the various common law doctrines dealing with liability following a defective attempt to incorporate? At first glance, it still seems to preclude the de facto corporation defense, albeit now for a different reason. Specifically, under the new Model Act, there is no need for this defense to statutory liability if the defendant is not aware of the problem, and courts generally would not find a de facto corporation anyway when the defendant was aware there was no corporation.

The official comment to Section 2.04 addresses estoppel. This comment suggests that estoppel could exist in a situation in which the third party is aware that there is no corporation. This, however, is the promoter contract situation and Section 2.04 should not apply altogether.[46] Otherwise, the official comment rules out estoppel as a defense to statutory liability. This may have limited impact, however. It is questionable how many courts, regardless of the Model Act, would apply estoppel in favor of a defendant who knew there was no corporation.

On the other hand, by substantially narrowing the scope of statutory liability in the defective incorporation situation, the revised Model Act raises a new question concerning the continuance of earlier judicial doctrines: Can creditors still assert the agency or partnership theories of liability? Since these doctrines do not require knowledge for liability, they have renewed desirability for creditors. Analytically, this question is somewhat different than the issue facing the court in cases such as *Robertson*. It is one thing to say that a statutory provision creating liability is not subject to common law defenses. It is quite a different matter to answer whether the legislature intended a statutory liability provision to supplement or supplant existing common law theories of liability. Unfortunately, the Model Act's official comments do not expressly address the question. At least one appellate court has held that the statute precludes common law theories of liability.[47] No doubt more courts will address the issue in the future. Moreover, if any courts decide that common law liability theories remain available as an alternative to

---

46. *E.g.,* Sherwood & Roberts–Oregon, Inc. v. Alexander, 269 Or. 389, 525 P.2d 135 (1974). *But see* Heintze Corp. v. Northwest Tech–Manuals, Inc., 7 Wash. App. 759, 502 P.2d 486 (1972).

47. Steve's Equipment Service, Inc. v. Riebrandt, 121 Ill.App.3d 66, 76 Ill.Dec. 612, 459 N.E.2d 21 (1984). There, the court interpreted the pre–1984 Model Act provision to only apply to those who knew the corporation did not exist (in this case, not because of defective formation, but rather because of dissolution for failing to pay franchise taxes). The court rejected the plaintiff's attempt to assert liability upon an agency theory, holding that the statute provided the exclusive remedy. The court gave little explanation as to why it found the statute to be exclusive.

statutory liability, then the question will arise as to whether the de facto corporation or estoppel defenses remain available in response to those theories. Ultimately, the end result of allowing common law liability theories and defenses could be to render the statutory liability provision of little practical relevance. For this reason, one suspects courts will interpret the new Model Act provision to preempt common law liability theories.

1.4.4 Post-incorporation filing and franchise tax requirements

States typically impose a periodic (usually annual) obligation on companies incorporated in the state to pay a tax for the privilege (franchise taxes). Sometimes, a reporting requirement accompanies this. Various sanctions attend failure to meet such obligations. This often includes suspension of the corporate privilege or even dissolution of the corporation.[48] In the former case, payment of the taxes can end the suspension, while dissolution means that one would need to form a new corporation. Statutes vary as to whether suspension or dissolution results automatically from non-performance, or whether state officials must act to suspend or dissolve the company.[49]

Suspension or dissolution of the corporation for failing to pay franchise taxes can raise the same sort of problems as does a defective attempt to incorporate. For instance, third parties might point to the suspension or dissolution in an effort to escape from obligations to the corporation. Typically, suspension will prevent the corporation from being able to sue upon its contracts. Indeed, in some jurisdictions, a corporation which has not paid its franchise taxes cannot even defend itself in court.[50] Less certain is whether the contract entered into during a suspension is void, so that the corporation could not enforce the contract even after ending the suspension.[51]

Also, third parties might seek to use the suspension or dissolution as grounds for recovery from various participants in the venture if the company is unable to pay. The same three theories of liability outlined above for defective incorporation might apply to the suspended or dissolved corporation.[52]

§ 1.5 Piercing the Corporate Veil

Limited liability means leaving creditors of failed corporations unpaid. A common response by such unpaid creditors is to sue one or more

---

48. *See, e.g.,* Note, *Dissolution and Suspension as Remedies for Corporate Franchise Tax Delinquency: A Comparative Analysis,* 41 N.Y.U. L. Rev. 602 (1966).

49. *See, e.g.,* Bryant Constr. Co. v. Cook Constr. Co., 518 So.2d 625 (Miss.1987).

50. *See, e.g.,* Brown v. Superior Court, 242 Cal.App.2d 519, 51 Cal.Rptr. 633 (1966).

51. *See, e.g.,* Bryant Construction Co. v. Cook Construction Co., 518 So.2d 625 (Miss.1987).

52. *See, e.g.,* Richmond Wholesale Meat Co. v. Hughes, 625 F.Supp. 584 (N.D.Ill. 1985) (applying statutory liability under a Model Act type of provision).

of the shareholders of the failed corporation, arguing that the court should extend liability beyond the corporate entity, or, in the more colorful phrasing, "pierce the corporate veil." If the creditor is successful in this argument, the court will impose liability upon one or more of the corporation's shareholders for the company's debt to the creditor.[1]

Given the high mortality rate among small businesses, it should not surprise one to learn that piercing claims constitute the single most litigated area in corporate law.[2] It is probably also the area of corporation law which the attorney seeking to avoid corporate practice is most likely to confront. It is therefore especially unfortunate that, despite hundreds of opportunities to get it right, judicial opinions in this area have made it one of the most befuddled. In the following discussion, we will attempt to pierce some of the veil of confusion surrounding this area.

1.5.1 Sources of Confusion

Courts in piercing cases almost invariably begin at the same point of departure: Piercing is an equitable remedy the court can impose in order to avoid injustice.[3] Fair enough. The problem, of course, is to go beyond this broad generality and determine what specific facts establish such an injustice, and why. Unfortunately, here one confronts three judicial foibles which have gone a long way to make this area such a mess.

To begin with, many writers have criticized the courts' tendency in this area to reason by pejorative.[4] For example, courts often explain their decision to pierce by announcing that the corporation was a mere "sham" or "shell" or the defendant's "alter ego" or "instrumentality." At best, such terms are unhelpful. All too often, they confuse the issue.

Terms like "sham" and "shell" seem to convey a lack of substance to the corporation. To the extent this refers to inadequate capitalization, it would be clearer to state this and discuss whether inadequate capitalization should provide grounds to pierce in the situation at hand. Otherwise, it is easy for the court and litigants to start wandering off looking for additional ways in which a corporation can lack substance. For instance, this can lead to a focus on the non-observance of rituals or "corporate formalities," which, as discussed later, rarely has much to do with the equities of piercing in a given situation.

---

§ 1.5

1. Occasionally, courts pierce the corporate veil to impose liability for a corporation's debts upon parties who are not shareholders. This might include an individual controlling a corporation, but who never became a shareholder because the corporation never issued shares, or corporations under common control with the debtor corporation. Also, courts may disregard the separate entity status of a corporation for reasons other than to extend liabilities for the corporation's unpaid debts. We shall address these possibilities later.

2. Robert B. Thompson, *Piercing the Corporate Veil: An Empirical Study*, 76 Cornell L. Rev. 1036 (1991).

3. *E.g.*, DeWitt Truck Brokers v. W. Ray Flemming Fruit Co., 540 F.2d 681 (4th Cir. 1976).

4. *E.g.*, Phillip I. Blumberg, The Law of Corporate Groups: Procedural Problems in the Law of Parent and Subsidiary Corporations 8 (1983).

Worse, terms such as these sometimes lead into a search of the defendant's purpose for establishing the corporation. This, in turn, can convey the impression that creating a corporation for the purpose of enjoying the benefits of owning a business while, at the same time, avoiding personal liability, should be grounds to pierce. This cannot be correct. Most corporations exist for the purpose of achieving limited liability for their owners. It would be perverse to grant limited liability to anyone who did not care about it and deny it to everyone who sought it.[5]

A relatively recent case, *Kinney Shoe Corp. v. Polan*[6], provides an illustration of this sort of confusion. The defendant established two corporations to undertake his venture. One, a leasing corporation with no assets, leased premises from the plaintiff, and, in turn, subleased the premises to the second company, a manufacturing corporation. The defendant intended to use the manufacturing corporation to conduct a manufacturing operation on the site. In deciding to pierce, the court labeled the leasing corporation a "transparent shell." Sounds bad, but what exactly does this term mean and how does it justify piercing? The inadequate capitalization of the leasing company bothered the court. To rely solely on this fact, however, would have forced the court to address the defendant's argument that the plaintiff was a voluntary creditor who could have checked on the leasing company's financial status. Instead of coming to grips with this argument, the court pointed to the defendant's failure to follow corporate formalities and his establishment of the leasing corporation apparently for the purpose of insulating the manufacturing corporation from liability on the lease. So? The court never explains how the lack of formalities prejudiced the plaintiff nor how the use of the leasing corporation was unfair to a party that could have insisted on contracting with the manufacturing corporation.

A second foible is to follow what one might call a "template" approach. Under this approach, a court either quotes or constructs a list of facts, which, in prior cases, accompanied decisions to pierce the corporate veil. The court then compares the list with the facts in the situation at hand and pierces if enough of the facts present fit the list.

The court's opinion in *DeWitt Truck Brokers v. W. Ray Flemming Fruit Co.*[7] provides an example of this sort of reasoning. The defendant was the ninety percent shareholder of a corporation engaged in selling fruit on commission for growers. The company defaulted on obligations to pay the plaintiff for transportation services—despite having collected sums to cover those costs from the growers—and the plaintiff sought to pierce. The court set up its evaluation of the plaintiff's claim by listing the following factors which prior cases had pointed to in deciding to pierce the corporate veil:

---

5. The bulk of courts recognize there is nothing wrong with incorporating for the purpose of limiting liability. *E.g.*, Walkovszky v. Carlton, 18 N.Y.2d 414, 223 N.E.2d 6, 276 N.Y.S.2d 585 (1966).

6. 939 F.2d 209 (4th Cir.1991).

7. 540 F.2d 681 (4th Cir.1976).

1) Undercapitalization

2) Failure to observe corporate formalities

3) Non-payment of dividends

4) Insolvency of the corporation "at the time" (what time, the court does not say)

5) Siphoning of corporate funds by the dominant shareholder

6) Non-functioning of other officers and directors besides the defendant

7) Absence of corporate records

8) Non-participation in corporate affairs by the shareholders other than the defendant[8]

The template approach is a godsend to students, litigants and courts who recognize the weakness of reasoning by pejorative, but still wish to remain aloof from analysis based on policy. Unfortunately, it leads to difficulties. To begin with, listing facts from prior opinions without an evaluation of why these facts should or should not lead to piercing inevitably introduces facts into this sort of list, which, upon reflection, seem of questionable significance. For example, the list in *DeWitt* included, as many such lists do, the non-payment of dividends. It is hard to understand why a creditor should complain about the *non*-payment of dividends, which, after all, are payments from the corporation to its shareholders and leave less money in the company for its creditors. In fact, loan agreements and corporations statutes commonly limit dividends for the protection of creditors.

A second difficulty with the template approach is that the relevance of some facts in the list, even when present in a given case, may depend upon the circumstances. Again, *DeWitt* provides an example. The court's list included undercapitalization, and the court dutifully matched this item to the existence of a lack of capital in the case before it. Ignored in this is the question of whether undercapitalization, which, as we shall see, should be of significance in dealing with tort claimants, should be relevant to the claim of a contract creditor, as in *DeWitt*, who might have checked the financial status of the corporation before dealing with it.

Finally, this sort of multi-factor approach carries tremendous indeterminacy. Must all factors on the list be present? Is the presence of any one factor enough? If the answer to these two questions is, as seems to be the rule from the opinions, no[9], then how many factors does one need and which factors are more important than the others? The opinions provide little guidance. Actually, there were ample grounds to hold the defendant liable in *DeWitt* based upon his promise personally to pay the

---

8. There are longer lists. *E.g.*, Laya v. Erin Homes, Inc., 177 W.Va. 343, 352 S.E.2d 93 (W.Va.1986)(listing nineteen factors).

9. *See, e.g.*, Secon Service System, Inc. v. St. Joseph Bank & Trust Co., 855 F.2d 406, 414 (7th Cir.1988) (the multi-factor approach requires the court "to balance many imponderables, all important but none determinative").

plaintiff if the corporation did not, as well as for the sort of abusive dealings with the corporation's assets which we will discuss later. The invocation of multiple factors simply confused the situation and will confuse those who look to the case for precedent.

The third foible is to employ a character test. Consciously or subconsciously, many courts in piercing cases appear to engage in a sort of general review of the defendant's business ethics: Is this an honest business person who simply suffered misfortune, or is this some sort of "sharp operator"? A stark illustration in a recent case is the court's pointing to the defendant's tax fraud as among the facts leading to piercing.[10] The problem, of course, is that the defendant's tax fraud in this case had absolutely nothing to do with the plaintiff's (who was a private creditor) claim. We might all agree that tax or other fraud is wrong, but to allow recovery by parties who were not the victims creates a windfall. In any event, if courts are going to turn a piercing case into the corporate equivalent of standing before the pearly gates for the weighing of all one's sins, perhaps the defendant similarly ought to able to point to unrelated business misdeeds by the plaintiff creditor.

1.5.2 *Tort Claimants versus Contract Creditors*

Innumerable writers over the years have argued that courts should draw a distinction between piercing claims asserted by voluntary (or contract) creditors of the corporation and involuntary (or tort) claimants against the corporation.[11] The basic notion is that contract creditors deserve less sympathy from a court when asking it to pierce. After all, they chose to do business with an entity whose owners have, as a rule, limited liability. If the contract creditor wanted to look to the owner for repayment, it could have negotiated for a personal guarantee. Hence, piercing in favor of a contract creditor gives the creditor something more than it bargained for and thus is a windfall. By contrast, the tort victim generally did not choose to deal with a corporation and accept the consequences of limited liability.

This rationale, in turn, has led to a conventional wisdom often recited by students of corporate law. It has become common to state that courts are more likely to pierce in favor of a tort than a contract creditor of the corporation.[12] In fact, this conventional wisdom is wrong. An important study conducted by Professor Robert Thompson surveyed every reported piercing decision through 1985 contained in the Westlaw database (totaling around 1600 decisions). This study found that courts pierced about forty percent of the time in contract claims and only about thirty percent of the time when dealing with tort victims.[13]

10. Sea–Land Services, Inc. v. Pepper Source, 993 F.2d 1309 (7th Cir.1993).

11. *E.g.*, Robert W. Hamilton, *The Corporate Entity*, 49 Tex. L. Rev. 979, 984–85 (1971).

12. *E.g.*, Frank H. Easterbrook & Daniel R. Fischel, *Limited Liability and the Corporation*, 52 U. Chi. L. Rev. 89, 112 (1985).

13. Thompson, *supra* note 2 at 1058.

Perhaps this result simply illustrates how badly the courts have been handling piercing cases. Indeed, long before Professor Thompson's work, other writers had condemned the courts for not perceiving the need to distinguish between contracts and torts claimants.[14] There is another explanation, however. The insight of various writers that there is a need to distinguish between contracts and torts claimants in evaluating piercing claims is fundamentally correct. The notion that courts should treat torts plaintiffs more sympathetically than contracts plaintiffs, however, is oversimplified. The question is not what sort of creditor more deserves piercing in the abstract. Rather, the question is what specific facts justify piercing in favor of either type of creditor. The utility of the torts versus contracts distinction is that the facts which should justify piercing may be different when dealing with the different types of claimants. The probability of the courts piercing then becomes a question, not of who is a more sympathetic type of plaintiff, but whether the sort of conduct that justifies piercing for a contract creditor is more or less common than the conduct that justifies piercing for a tort victim.

When dealing with a piercing claim by a contract creditor, it is important to start by asking why, in the absence of piercing, the corporation is liable and its shareholders are not. The answer is simple: This is what the parties agreed. By choosing to do business in the corporate form, the owners have in effect asked creditors to agree to limited liability. By doing business with the corporation and not demanding a personal guarantee, the creditors have in effect agreed to this request. The fundamental issue posed in a piercing case brought by a contract creditor, therefore, is what grounds can justify letting the contract creditor out of its agreement to look only to the corporation for recovery. Well, what sort of grounds does contracts law provide for parties to get out of their agreements?

One common ground for voiding an agreement is fraud. Hence, as we will see, if the creditor can show that the defendant induced the creditor to do business with the corporation by making misrepresentations, this will be grounds to pierce. Another basis for relief from a contractual obligation is to show a material breach by the other side. Can this provide the underpinning for a piercing claim? Of course, the corporation has failed to perform its end of the contract or we would not have a contract creditor seeking to pierce. But this is not the nonperformance we are talking about, since insulation from such claims is the whole idea of limited liability. The question is can the creditor point to nonperformance by the defendant shareholder of some personal obligation which was a quid pro quo for the creditor's agreement to limited liability.

A non-corporate example may help clarify the rationale. Suppose a bank agrees to make a non-recourse loan, which the borrower will use to purchase property that will serve as collateral for the loan. The agreement commonly will impose upon the borrower obligations to protect the

14. *E.g.*, Hamilton, *supra* note 11 at 985.

collateral. If the borrower fails to perform those obligations and the collateral is destroyed, the borrower should hardly be in a position to default on the loan and claim the advantage of the contract's non-recourse provision.[15] Similarly, we might assert that the agreement to do business on a limited liability basis by contracting with a corporation carries with it certain implicit obligations for the controlling owners of the corporation in how they deal with the "collateral" (that is, the corporation's assets). What those obligations are we shall return to later.

By contrast, it makes little sense to talk about fraud (at least in the narrow sense of a misrepresentation), or the failure to perform implicit contractual obligations, when facing piercing claims by tort victims. Instead, we again need to go back and look at the underlying reasons for the corporation to be liable and, in the absence of piercing, its shareholders not to be. Corporate tort liability largely arises from the doctrines of vicarious liability (making the corporation liable for the torts of its employees committed in the scope of their employment) and products liability (making the corporation liable for defects in the products it produces). The modern justification for these doctrines lies in internalizing the cost of accidents so as to become part of the cost of the goods or services that created those accidents. In this manner, producers of goods or services have an incentive to adopt cost-justified accident prevention measures. Moreover, consumers called upon to pay a price reflecting the cost of accidents which it would not be cost-effective to avoid, will see the total resources (including accident losses) used in the production of the good or service in question. Allowing limited liability for tort claims inevitably undercuts this cost internalization. Presumably, certain societal benefits from limited liability justify this result. Even if this is true as a general proposition—a question on which there has been considerable debate[16]—there may be specific cases in which the externalization of costs because of limited liability is particularly egregious, while the societal gains from limited liability are especially slight. These cases, examples of which we shall discuss later, are appropriate for judicial piercing in favor of torts claimants.

Having identified the different theoretical bases for piercing in favor of contracts and torts claimants, we can now evaluate the various specific grounds often mentioned as the reasons for piercing.

1.5.3   *Control or Domination*

One frequently mentioned factor in piercing cases is the defendant's domination or control over the corporation.[17] Courts commonly get into this factor by invoking one of two multi-part tests often said to provide

---

15. *Cf* Cornelison v. Kornbluth, 15 Cal.3d 590, 542 P.2d 981, 125 Cal.Rptr. 557 (1975) (a mortgagor who, in bad faith, damages the property subject to the mortgage, is personally liable for the damage despite California's anti-deficiency legislation).

16. See § 1.1.4 *supra*.

17. Professor Thompson found this factor mentioned in 551 of the approximately 1600 piercing decisions surveyed in his study. Thompson, *supra* note 2 at 1063.

the elements of a successful piercing claim. One is a three-part test. To pierce, under this formulation, there must be:

> (1) Control, "not merely majority or complete stock control, but complete domination, not only of finances but of policy and business practice in respect to the transaction attacked so that the corporation had at the time no separate mind, will or existence of its own;"

> (2) The defendant used the control "to commit fraud or wrong, to perpetrate the violation of a statutory or other positive legal duty, or dishonest and unjust act in contravention of plaintiff's legal rights;" and

> (3) The fraud or wrong "proximately" caused injury to the plaintiff.[18]

The alternate is a two-pronged test: First, there must be such "unity of interest and ownership that the separate personalities of the corporation and the individual no longer exist," and second, adherence to the corporate fiction under the circumstances would "sanction a fraud or promote injustice."[19]

The second element in both formulations—that there be some fraud, wrong or injustice—seems to be nothing more than a restatement of the basic starting point that piercing is an equitable remedy used to prevent injustice. The notion that there ought to be some causal relationship between the fraud or wrong of the defendant, and harm to the plaintiff, is sound, yet, as we have seen above, often forgotten by the courts in piercing cases. What does the first element, control or unity of interest, add?

At first glance, this element seems to add very little. After all, the typical defendant in a piercing case is the majority, or even sole, shareholder of the corporate debtor. One would expect it to be quite rare for a majority (and especially a sole) shareholder of a corporation not to exercise control over the business. If this is grounds to pierce, few closely held corporations would provide limited liability.

Perhaps this would not be a bad result. A number of economics writers have argued that limited liability is generally inefficient for a closely held business because of the incentives for excessive risk taking and the lack of offsetting gains from promoting securities markets.[20] Indeed, historically, the notion that abstention from control was the quid pro quo for limited liability provided the basis for the enactment of limited partnership acts.[21] Nevertheless, given well-established legislative and judicial permission for closely held and even single shareholder

---

18. For a detailed discussion of the history of this test see Cathy S. Krendl & James R. Krendl, *Piercing the Corporate Veil: Focusing the Inquiry*, 55 Denver L. Rev. 1 (1978).

19. For a discussion of the two-pronged formulation see Phillip I. Blumberg, The

Law of Corporate Groups: Tort, Contract, and Other Common Law Problems in the Substantive Law of Parent and Subsidiary Corporations 111 (1987).

20. See § 1.1.4 *supra*.

21. See § 1.1.1c *supra*.

corporations,[22] it is far too late in the day to make an ex post judicial change through piercing decisions. Indeed, the legislative trend is away from any rule that suggests liability must follow control. For example, statutory provisions sanctioning greater direct shareholder control over closely held corporations[23] make little sense if shareholder control meant the loss of limited liability. Similarly, the Revised Uniform Limited Partnership Act dramatically watered down the prohibition on limited partners participating in control.[24] Finally, we have the rapid spread of legislation creating new entities (the limited liability company and limited liability partnership) in which limited liability expressly can co-exist with direct owner control.[25]

Given this, courts generally do not pierce simply because one or more shareholders exercise control over the corporation.[26] Many courts attempt to arrive at this result doctrinally by explaining that the impermissible "control" referred to in the formulations for piercing goes beyond "mere" control, to "domination," in which the corporation "has no mind of its own."[27] This distinction is silly. No corporation in the world has a mind of its own; they are fictitious entities. People control corporations. True, in a large corporation, decisionmaking may occur in differing levels of managers leading up to a chief executive officer and the board of directors. As there are less participants in the corporation, inevitably there are fewer decisionmakers, until, in the corporation with a majority or sole owner, normally that party will decide what the corporation is to do.

Implicitly recognizing this, many courts start throwing in other factors as part of the test for impermissible domination or control. For example, in *Sea-Land Services, Inc. v. Pepper Source,*[28] the court examined four factors to determine if the case met the "shared control/ unity of interest and ownership" element for piercing: (1) failure to maintain

22. *See, e.g.,* Salomon v. A. Salomon & Co., Ltd., [1897] A.C. 22. For a discussion of how many individuals are required under modern statutes to form a corporation see § 1.4.1 *supra.* For a discussion of the statutory minimum number of directors see 3.1.2a *infra.*

23. For a discussion of statutory close corporation provisions allowing shareholder control over the corporation, including by dispensing with a board of directors, see § 5.2.2.b *infra.*

24. Revised Uniform Limited Partnership Act § 303 (1985) (creating an extensive list of actions which limited partners can take without losing limited liability, and allowing limited partners to participate in control without losing limited liability except to a party transacting business with the limited partnership, who, because of the limited partner's exercising control, reasonably thought that the limited partner was, in fact, a general partner).

25. Limited liability company and limited liability partnership statutes allow owners of such entities to enjoy limited liability despite the fact that these statutes generally call, barring other agreement, for direct management of such entities by their owners. *See, e.g.,* Franklin A. Gevurtz, *California's New Limited Liability Company Act: A Look at the Good, the Bad, and the Ambiguous,* 27 Pac. L.J. 261, 263 (1996).

26. *See, e.g.,* Secon Service System, Inc. v. St. Joseph Bank & Trust Co., 855 F.2d 406, 415 (7th Cir.1988) (something more than control is required to pierce in contract cases). Professor Thompson's study found that those courts which expressly noted the presence of domination and control still refused to pierce over forty percent of the time. Thompson, *supra* note 2 at 1063.

27. *E.g.,* Craig v. Lake Asbestos, 843 F.2d 145 (3d Cir.1988).

28. 941 F.2d 519 (7th Cir.1991).

corporate records and comply with corporate formalities; (2) comingling of funds or assets; (3) undercapitalization; and (4) treating the assets of the corporation as the defendant's own (albeit, this seems to be somewhat the same as comingling).

As we shall see, many of these factors can provide grounds to pierce. To evaluate them as a template for proving impermissible domination or control, however, simply creates confusion. *Sea-Land* itself provides an illustration. The appellate court upheld the finding of impermissible "control," based largely upon the defendant's misuse of corporate assets (such as paying personal expenses with corporate funds). Nevertheless, the court remanded the case for determination of the element of wrong or injustice. This necessitated a trial and second appeal, the end result of which—other than to increase litigation costs—was to pierce based largely upon the defendant's misuse of the corporation's assets.[29] How did the court get itself into ordering such a pointless exercise?

The formulation of the test for piercing speaks of "control" and "wrong" in the conjunctive. Hence, the *Sea-Land* court was correct that, under the formulation, a finding of control or "unity of interest" did not alone justify piercing. The problem resulted from trying to beef up the control test by adding factors picked because they suggest the court should pierce. If these factors are persuasive, however, it is because they are the sort of wrongs or injustices which the second element identifies as the reason for piercing. Hence, using them to distinguish "ordinary" control from impermissible domination and control does little but create a potentially confusing redundancy.

One alternative is to change the test into a disjunctive one: "control" or "wrong" leads to piercing. In fact, a few recent opinions state that meeting the impermissible domination and control element can, in itself, justify piercing.[30] This avoids the *Sea-Land* result, but carries its own risks. Discussing factors such as the misuse of corporate assets in the context of whether they create an injustice at least gives a hint that one must consider the effect of such facts on the creditor. Using these facts instead as a sort of proxy to show the defendant's domination or control creates the danger of a court occasionally piercing simply because the defendant shareholder controls the corporation. After all, why look at the proxy when we can determine the reality? More broadly, listing facts to prove a test—"domination or control"—which does not mean what it says, simply encourages the template approach where courts compare facts against lists with no idea of why these facts should matter.

Given this, is there anything to be said for looking at control in a piercing case? The answer is yes. In the first place, requiring control screens out piercing against the shareholders of a publicly traded corporation, who, as a practical matter, do not exercise control. This provides a doctrinal underpinning to explain the fact that there never has been a

29. Sea–Land Services, Inc. v. Pepper Source, 993 F.2d 1309 (7th Cir.1993).

30. *E.g.*, Wm. Passalacqua Builders, Inc. v. Resnick Developers South, Inc., 933 F.2d 131 (2d Cir.1991).

case in which the court pierced to hold shareholders in a public corporation liable for the company's debts.[31] Moreover, economic policy supports this result, since it is in the public corporation that limited liability produces efficiencies.

Control also has a role to play in the closely held corporation context. We may find a situation in which one shareholder (or a group of shareholders) is in control of the corporation, while one or more minority shareholders are (voluntarily or not) passive. Assuming some fraud or injustice creates grounds to pierce, the controlling shareholders, who presumably committed the fraud or created the unjust situation, should be liable, while the passive shareholders, unless they did something wrong, should not.[32] In other words, there is wisdom in the traditional conjunctive formulation. The "fraud or injustice" element tells the court when to pierce, the control element tells it against whom.

1.5.4 Disregard of Corporate Formalities

Among the bramble which has grown up around the doctrine of piercing the corporate veil is the notion that a major factor in the courts' decisions is the non-observance of so-called corporate formalities.[33] Attorneys dutifully warn their small business clients to carefully observe corporate formalities lest the bogeyman of piercing get them. Many small business clients predictably ignore such warnings. Thereafter, if the business fails, litigants and courts in a piercing case spend time evaluating how many corporate formalities the defendant had the corporation follow.

In fact, the notion that corporate formalities are a major determinant in piercing cases may be the legal equivalent of an "old wives' tale." Professor Thompson's study of piercing decisions found that courts mentioned the failure to follow formalities in only a small fraction of the cases in which the courts pierced (twenty percent of the contract cases and eleven percent of the tort cases).[34] While it is true that courts pierced two-thirds of the time in which the opinion mentions the lack of formalities, the question is whether this is causal or coincidental. Reading "between the lines" of judicial opinions is, by definition, a speculative undertaking; still, one gets the impression reading piercing decisions that the invocation of the defendant's failure to observe corporate formalities is often a make-weight recited in support of a decision reached on other grounds. For example, while the courts in *Kinney Shoe*, *DeWitt* and *Sea-Land* discussed the defendants' failure to observe corporate formalities, one suspects that the lack of formalities would not have led the courts to pierce had the defendants not undercapitalized the

---

31. Thompson, *supra* note 2 at 1047.

32. *See, e.g.*, K.C. Roofing Center v. On Top Roofing, Inc., 807 S.W.2d 545 (Mo.App. 1991) (held husband, but not wife, shareholder liable, because there was no evidence the wife was an active participant in the wrongful conduct). The study by Professor Thompson found that courts almost never hold passive shareholders liable in piercing cases. Thompson, *supra* note 2 at 1056.

33. *E.g.*, Hamilton, *supra* note 11 at 989–990.

34. Thompson, *supra* note 2 at 1067.

corporation, appropriated corporate assets or made assurances to creditors. Conversely, one suspects that had the defendants in these three cases scrupulously observed corporate formalities, then *Kinney Shoe*, *DeWitt* and *Sea-Land* might have provided three more decisions for Professor Thompson's study in which the court pierced despite not finding an absence of formalities.

In any event, if the significance of corporate formalities is not merely an old wives' tale, it should be. To understand why, it useful to start by asking what one means by corporate formalities. In fact, the initial problem in this area is that courts, litigants and writers use this term to lump together conduct whose logical significance to a piercing decision should be quite different.

Among conduct said to constitute the non-observance of corporate formalities we find: (1) failure to issue stock;[35] (2) failure to have shareholder meetings to elect directors, or to hold director meetings, or to prepare minutes of such meetings;[36] and (3) failure to formally approve or carefully document transactions between the corporation and its shareholder(s) or with related corporations.[37]

The failure to issue stock might prejudice creditors. The reason, however, has nothing to do with adherence to formalities. Issuance of stock is normally how a corporation obtains capital from its owners. Hence, the real concern here is whether the corporation is undercapitalized, and, if so, whether this should provide the grounds to pierce in favor of the particular creditor. Listing the failure to issue stock as a failure to follow formalities only distracts from these questions. One other impact of not issuing stock is the corporation then has no shareholders. It is therefore amusing to see a court referring to the defendant as a shareholder in an opinion in which the court notes that the corporation never issued stock.[38] Presumably, this reflects implicit recognition that it would be poor policy to allow a party, who used his or her control over a corporation to engage in conduct which justifies piercing, to avoid liability because he or she never formerly became a shareholder.[39]

Like the failure to issue stock, the failure to formally approve or carefully document transactions between the corporation and its owner is really only a piece of a larger problem, whose significance is not a matter of formalities. The real concern is unfair self-dealing between the shareholder and the corporation, which results in the removal of assets from the reach of the corporation's creditors. The lack of formal approval may be some evidence of unfairness of various transactions. More

35. *E.g.*, Kinney Shoe Corp. v. Polan, 939 F.2d 209 (4th Cir.1991).

36. *E.g.*, Sea–Land Services, Inc. v. Pepper Source, 941 F.2d 519 (7th Cir.1991).

37. *E.g.*, DeWitt Truck Brokers v. W. Ray Flemming Fruit Co., 540 F.2d 681 (4th Cir.1976).

38. *E.g.*, Kinney Shoe Corp. v. Polan, 939 F.2d 209 (4th Cir.1991).

39. For an opinion explicitly deciding to pierce against an individual who never became a shareholder see Minton v. Cavaney, 56 Cal.2d 576, 15 Cal.Rptr. 641, 364 P.2d 473 (1961).

significantly, lack of documentation may justify a remedy, as in piercing, which goes beyond unwinding specific transfers from the corporation to the defendant. We shall develop these points in more detail later. What is important for now is to note how treating this problem simply as a failure to follow corporate formalities clouds the issue.

Often, reference to the non-observance of corporate formalities brings up the failure to hold, or have minutes of, shareholder and director meetings. Why this should have any bearing on a decision to pierce is a mystery. Typically, the answer one gets is some sort of quid pro quo argument. One variation of this argument is to state that if the defendant is not going to respect the corporation, then the court also need not respect the corporation.[40] Such statements substitute rhetoric for policy. One must identify the precise manner in which the defendant did not "respect" the corporation and then ask what practical significance does the defendant's conduct have when weighed against the reasons for limited liability.

When dealing with contract creditors, this brings us to ask whether the non-observance of formalities involving shareholder and director meetings should be grounds to let the creditor out of the creditor's agreement to look solely to the corporation for recovery. Does this mislead the creditor or fail to live up to implied obligations on the controlling shareholder? Not unless the non-observance of such meeting formalities would be material to the reasonable creditor. It is difficult to see how the non-observance of such formalities could be material. About the only possible impact that the failure to hold shareholder and director meetings might have on a creditor is to raise questions about the authority of the party dealing with the creditor to bind the corporation to the transaction in question. If the creditor had been worried about authority, however, it could always have insisted on seeing a board resolution. In any event, in the cases in which a contract creditor seeks to pierce the corporate veil, the corporation typically does not try to disown the company's obligations. Why should the company; it is broke. Hence, even if anyone were to point out the possible lack of authority to bind the corporation, it would not matter when the corporation could not perform anyway.

With respect to torts claimants, the observance of formalities regarding shareholders and directors meeting is equally irrelevant to the policies behind limited liability. Insisting that such meetings take place will hardly help internalize the costs of accidents in order to achieve the purposes of vicarious and products liability. Moreover, even in corporations which have annual shareholder and regular director meetings, it is rare to use such meetings to consider accident avoidance measures.

The alternate formulation of the quid pro quo argument is to state that if one wishes to gain the advantage of what corporate statutes

40. *See, e.g.,* Victoria Elevator Co. v.   1979).
Meriden Grain Co., 283 N.W.2d 509 (Minn.

provide, limited liability, one must observe what formalities the corporate statutes require.[41] Corporations statutes typically require annual shareholders meetings to elect directors.[42] They also state that the corporation shall be managed by or under the direction of the board of directors, who normally act through meetings.[43] Yet, before treating such provisions as legislative requirements for limited liability, it is important to ask what their purpose is. Corporations statutes contain a host of terms designed to achieve a variety of purposes. Many are simply default rules designed to fill in gaps in agreements by participants in the corporate venture. Others may be mandatory. Of the mandatory rules, some, such as limits on dividends, are intended to protect creditors. Many, such as the requirement of an annual meeting to elect directors, however, are intended to protect shareholders. Unless the legislature designed the rule to protect creditors—something which does not appear to be the case with meetings formalities—there is no logical reason to treat compliance with the rule as a quid pro quo for limited liability.[44]

Having spent considerable time seeking to debunk some of the mythology surrounding piercing, we now can turn to the critical factors which should lead to shareholder liability.

1.5.5 Defendant's Wrongful Dealings with the Creditor

Numerous piercing decisions find their most persuasive justification in various dealings between the defendant and the plaintiff creditor. In the *DeWitt* case discussed earlier, the defendant gave personal assurances to the plaintiff that, if the corporation did not pay, the defendant would. In *Western Rock Co. v. Davis*[45], the court pierced in favor of owners of property damaged by a corporation's blasting activities. In fact, the defendants ordered the blasting, knowing it was damaging the plaintiffs' properties. The most common example of this factor, however, involves statements or actions by the defendant which misled the creditor into doing business with the corporation.

Technically, these cases do not involve piercing at all, at least if by piercing one means holding the shareholder liable for the debt of the corporation. The reason is that in each of these cases, the plaintiff has a tort or contract cause of action against the shareholder. The personal assurance, if enforceable, makes the shareholder a party to his or her own contract with the creditor. If the shareholder committed the tort damaging the plaintiff, as in *Western Rock*, then the shareholder is liable for his or her own tort. The vicarious liability of the corporation for the tort does not change this. And, of course, the party who is the victim of

41. *See, e.g.*, Labadie Coal Co. v. Black, 672 F.2d 92 (D.C.Cir.1982).

42. See § 3.1.2a *infra*.

43. See § 3.1.2b *infra*.

44. A number of courts have shown greater sophistication by expressly refusing to give any weight to a failure to follow formalities when that failure did not impact the plaintiff. *E.g.*, Preston Farm & Ranch Supply, Inc. v. Bio–Zyme Enterprises, 615 S.W.2d 258 (Tex.Civ.App.1981). Texas recently amended its corporations statute to state that failure to observe statutory formalities for running a corporation was not grounds to pierce. Tex. Rev. Civ. Stat. Ann. art. 2.21(A)(3) (West. Supp. 1995).

45. 432 S.W.2d 555 (Tex.Civ.App.1968).

fraud can sue the party who committed the fraud. Hence, in none of these cases is it really necessary to make the shareholder liable for the debt of the corporation. Still, the end result should be the same whether one labels the defendant's liability as the result of piercing or as direct liability for the defendant's own tort or contract. The measure of damages on these sorts of claims generally ought to equal the creditor's unpaid judgment against the corporation. Accordingly, one cannot complain too much if the court wants to label this piercing—at least so long as the court avoids some of the foibles which arise in piercing cases.

In any event, it has become customary among both courts and commentators to state that fraud provides grounds to pierce.[46] The important question is what constitutes fraud. There are three types of representations which often arise in piercing cases.

The first are representations concerning the corporation's financial status. Prospective creditors, naturally, often request financial information about corporations which seek credit with them. It is tempting for the controlling owner of a company in trouble to dissemble in response to such requests. There is little question that any material dissembling ought to lead to liability for such an owner. Sometimes, moreover, misrepresentations as to the corporation's financial health may be subtle. For example, meeting corporate obligations through short-term shareholder loans could constitute fraud if designed to give the corporation a misleading credit history.[47]

A much more difficult question arises if the prospective creditor does not request financial information from the company. Is there any duty to inform such a creditor of an unusually weak corporate financial condition? In fact, this is another way to view the question of whether contracts creditors should be able to assert inadequate capitalization as grounds to pierce. We will return to the broad question later. For now, however, it is useful to note that no court is likely to pierce based upon inadequate capitalization in favor of a creditor who was fully informed of the corporation's financial condition and chose to do business solely on the corporation's credit. Hence, piercing based upon inadequate capitalization in favor of contracts creditors is, in effect, a statement that controlling shareholders of financially weak corporations have a duty to inform prospective creditors of the corporation's financial situation. Put another way, such a result makes non-disclosure of financial weakness a fraud.

---

46. *E.g.*, DeWitt Truck Brokers v. W. Ray Flemming Fruit Co., 540 F.2d 681 (4th Cir.1976) (fraud is a common but not exclusive ground for piercing); Richard A. Posner, *The Rights of Creditors of Affiliated Corporations*, 43 U. Chi. L. Rev. 499, 521–522 (1976) (arguing fraud constitutes the exclusive ground). Professor Thompson's study identified 169 piercing cases in which courts mentioned the presence of misrepre-

sentations. The courts pierced in 159 of these cases. The courts noted a lack of misrepresentations in 391 piercing cases. They refused to pierce in 361 of these cases. Thompson, *supra* note 2 at 1063–1064.

47. *See, e.g.,* Linco Services, Inc. v. DuPont, 239 Cal.App.2d 841, 49 Cal.Rptr. 196 (1966).

Closely related to this problem is the possibility of finding fraud in statements made by the defendant in promising corporate performance. In fact, this is likely to be an extremely common, if not always appreciated, phenomenon in piercing cases involving contracts creditors. One can imagine that owners of struggling corporations are often on the phone desperately trying to obtain further extensions of credit from the companies' suppliers. Under such circumstances, statements that the creditor has nothing to worry about, "the check is as good as in the mail," and the like, flow trippingly to tongue. Indeed, the world might be more sensible if attorneys of small corporate clients spent less time urging compliance with corporate formalities, and more time suggesting care and candor in communicating with creditors.

The key issue in cases involving statements promising corporate performance is whether there is fraud by the controlling shareholder, or just a breach of contract by the corporation. The fact that the corporation does not perform does not turn the promise into fraud, or else all breaches of contract would create a claim for fraud, and there could never be limited liability with respect to contracts creditors. On the other hand, there is fraud if, at the time of the promise, the controlling shareholder intended to have the company default. This follows from a well-established doctrine in the common law of fraud and deceit. This doctrine is that promises contain within them an implied statement as to the speaker's present intention with respect to performance. If the speaker never intended to perform, then this implied statement is false.

The situation uncovered by the court on remand in the *Sea-Land* case discussed earlier provides a nice example. The trial court found that the controlling shareholder made assurances that the corporation would pay the plaintiff if the company had sufficient funds. At the same time the defendant was making these assurances, the trial court found he had already formed the intent to manipulate funds between various companies he owned in order to ensure the debtor corporation lacked the money to pay.

This sort of result always raises the question: How does the court know what the defendant secretly intended? Barring some confession, one can only draw inferences based upon the objective circumstances. It is important to keep in mind, however, that owners of small corporations typically are an optimistic lot, and the human capacity for self delusion is large. Hence, it should not be enough to find fraud merely because an objective observer in the defendant's position would have known the corporation was not going to be able to perform. At some point, however, the situation becomes so bleak that a finder of fact can say even a foolish defendant knew his or her promises were hollow. Inferences to this effect become particularly strong if, at the same time the defendant is busy trying to beg for corporate credit, he or she is bailing assets out of the corporation.[48]

---

48. *See, e.g.,* Victoria Elevator Co. v. Meriden Grain Co., 283 N.W.2d 509 (Minn. 1979) (shortly after the defendant persuaded the plaintiff to continue dealing with his

Incidentally, this sort of false promise fraud is not limited to explicit statements seeking to calm creditors' fears as to future corporate performance. Merely entering new corporate obligations at a time the controlling owner knows the corporation will never perform creates the same problem.[49]

The third common problem area involves representations and other actions which lead the creditor to believe that someone, other than the corporation it is seeking to pierce, stands behind the debt. This might be either the controlling shareholder or a related corporation. If such representations meet the requirements to constitute a binding contract, then there is no need to discuss piercing. Many times, however, the representations or conduct will not be sufficient to create a contract. For example, the attempt to cast oral assurances as a personal guarantee faces a problem under the statute of frauds. Alternately, the parole evidence rule might prevent an attempt to argue that a written contract naming the corporation as a party really constituted a contract between the creditor and the controlling shareholder. Many times, such as the situation in which related corporations share an office and have similar names, or when an owner simply refers to the creditor as "dealing with me," the communication may be too ambiguous to set up a persuasive argument in contract. In such an event, can the creditor pierce based upon fraud?

Answering this question requires resolving three issues: To begin with, will allowing such a piercing claim circumvent the policies behind the statute of frauds or the parole evidence rule? Courts have reached differing assessments of this concern.[50] Much depends upon how sympathetic one is toward the advantages of the statute of frauds or parole evidence rule in creating legal certainty; a subject for a contracts treatise. Next, should the existence of ambiguity or confusion as to who is the obligor be enough to pierce, or must the creditor be able to point to some clear statement which led the creditor to believe that someone other than the corporation was bound? Closely related to this question is whether the defendant must have intended to mislead or confuse the creditor. To the extent the defendant intended to fool or confuse the creditor, the answer to the question concerning ambiguity or confusion should favor the plaintiff. On the other hand, if this was not the defendant's intent, the question becomes, between two sloppy parties, who should bear the risk of loss from unintended misunderstandings: the party who created a potentially misleading or confusing situation, or

corporation by promising the corporation would perform, the defendant had the corporation transfer its principal property to him and his wife).

49. *See, e.g.,* K.C. Roofing Center v. On Top Roofing, Inc., 807 S.W.2d 545 (Mo.App. 1991) (the trial court found that the defendant's corporation purchased substantial supplies from the plaintiff on credit at a time the corporation owed between $75,000 and $100,000 to previous suppliers which it

was unable to pay; in addition, the defendant had a pattern of ceasing to do business in one corporate entity when that corporation was unable to pay its bills, only to start up the business in a new corporate entity).

50. *Compare* DeWitt Truck Brokers v. W. Ray Flemming Fruit Co., 540 F.2d 681 (4th Cir.1976), *with* Wagner v. Manufacturers. Trust Co., 237 App.Div. 175, 261 N.Y.S. 136 (1932), *aff'd mem.,* 261 N.Y. 699, 185 N.E. 799 (1933).

the party who could have checked more carefully. An efficiency analysis might suggest that the defendant was generally in a position to have more cheaply prevented the confusion and hence ought to bear its consequences.

1.5.6 Defendant's Wrongful Dealings with the Corporation's Assets

We have already confronted a couple of decisions, *DeWitt* and *Sea-Land*, in which abusive dealings between a controlling shareholder and his corporation provided much or all of the real grounds to pierce. In fact, after one strips away all the flak about formalities and domination, many piercing cases come down to a problem of self-dealing.[51] Often, courts refer to "siphoning" or "commingling" as labels for this phenomenon.[52]

Understanding why unfair self-dealing should be grounds for shareholder liability is not difficult. On a superficial level, one might note that, in a variety of contexts, courts have labeled unfair self-dealing as "fraud."[53] Indeed, we shall see later that many of the self-dealing transactions which provide grounds for piercing could also be attacked as fraudulent conveyances. Accordingly, such conduct can constitute "fraud," and courts commonly state that fraud provides grounds to pierce.

Beyond such semantic arguments, one can look at underlying policy. When dealing with contracts creditors, we saw earlier how the defendant's failure to live up to the implied terms under which the creditor agreed to do business on the corporation's credit can justify piercing. Principal among terms which one would imply is that the controlling shareholder of the corporation will not be free to do whatever he or she wants with corporate assets. Otherwise, the owner could have the corporation borrow, take out all the money, and leave the creditor unpaid. In essence, the loan then becomes one which says to the owner "pay back if you feel like it," with no sanction for non-payment other than the possible loss of future loans. This is not the sort of loan we expect persons in a commercial relationship to make. Consistent with this expectation, large loan agreements with corporations often contain explicit limits on dividends, salaries, and other mechanisms by which owners might take money out of the corporation. Implied terms can create similar protection for smaller extensions of credit, thereby saving the cost of negotiating and drafting to deal with every future contingency.

There is one caveat to this analysis. Suppose, at the time the creditor chooses to do business with the corporation, the creditor is aware of conduct which might constitute unfair self-dealing. In this

51. *See, e.g.,* Robert C. Clark, *Duties of the Corporate Debtor to its Creditors,* 90 Harv. L. Rev. 505, 542 (1977).

52. *See, e.g.,* DeWitt Truck Brokers v. W. Ray Flemming Fruit Co., 540 F.2d 681 (4th Cir.1976).

53. See § 4.3.5 *infra.*

event, the creditor should not expect sympathy if it complains about such self-dealing later.

This could explain the otherwise puzzling decision of the New York Court of Appeals in *Bartle v. Home Owners Cooperative*.[54] This was an action seeking to hold a parent cooperative corporation liable for debts of its subsidiary. The cooperative had formed the subsidiary to build houses for the members of the cooperative. The members were veterans (which some might speculate explains the result). The subsidiary sold the houses to the members at or below cost. Such favorable prices are not what one typically finds in an arms-length transaction and may account for the subsidiary's financial failure. Nevertheless, the court refused to pierce. The key line in the opinion may be the statement that the creditors "were in no wise misled." This would be true, and the decision defensible, if, as seems probable, the subsidiary's creditors knew that its function was to build houses to sell at bargain prices to the cooperative's members.

Abusive self-dealing might also provide grounds to pierce in favor of tort victims. It undercuts the goal of internalizing the costs of accidents. Viewed *ex post*, if the controlling shareholder has yanked assets out of the corporation, there is less for tort victims to collect. More important, viewed *ex ante*, if the controlling shareholder knows he or she can yank assets out of the corporation before tort victims can get or enforce a judgment, there is less incentive to insure and to make sure the costs of the corporation's goods or services fully reflect the likely costs of accidents. At the same time, allowing controlling shareholders untrammeled rights to take corporate property hardly seems necessary in order to achieve the societal goals behind limited liability.

On the other hand, one might argue that if a corporation lacks adequate insurance to cover foreseeable levels of damages, courts should pierce based upon inadequate capitalization. The fact that abusive self-dealing may have partially motivated the controlling shareholder to under-insure is besides the point. Conversely, if the corporation is adequately insured, the abusive self-dealing did not cause a failure to internalize accident costs and again seems irrelevant. Yet, many times the situation will not be this cut-and-dry. There often is some insurance, but the fact a tort claimant seeks to pierce means that the insurance coverage fell short. Hence, the question becomes whether the company had insured to the level of reasonably foreseeable damages. Given the incentive discussed above, it might be reasonable to deny the controlling shareholder who engages in abusive self-dealing the benefit of the doubt on this question.

In any event, not all self-dealing transactions between the corporation and its controlling shareholder should provide grounds to pierce. A closely held corporation often will purchase or rent important assets from its controlling shareholder. The controlling shareholder typically works for the company and legitimately is entitled to compensation.

54. 309 N.Y. 103, 127 N.E.2d 832 (1955).

Should there be profits, the shareholders expect to get some distribution of them. To say that some self-dealing is sufficiently abusive or unfair to justify piercing, therefore, forces one to define a standard for determining when this occurs.

Fortunately, one does not need to undertake such an analysis from scratch. Corporations statutes contain limits on dividends or similar distributions from the corporation to its shareholders. Typically, such statutes prohibit a distribution when the corporation is, or the distribution will render the corporation, insolvent in either the bankruptcy sense (assets less than liabilities) or equitable sense (unable to pay its bills as due).[55] Cases in which shareholders alleged directors breached their fiduciary duty to the corporation provide a well-developed jurisprudence on when compensation, or any exchange between a corporation and one in control of it, is unfair. By and large, these cases look to see if the corporation received a fair equivalent to what it gave in the sense that this was the sort of exchange the company would have made if dealing with an outsider.[56] Fraudulent conveyance acts employ concepts from both sources. Among transfers constituting a fraudulent conveyance is one made when the debtor is (or thereby becomes) insolvent and without the transferor receiving fair consideration in exchange. Transfers intended to hinder creditor collection are also fraudulent conveyances.[57]

These rules give us a fair proxy of the terms we might infer that the typical creditor expects from the controlling shareholder of a corporate borrower. They are also a judgment as to what conduct society does not find necessary to allow in order to obtain the policy goals sought in granting limited liability from tort claims. The presence of these rules, however, raises another question: Why pierce, rather than simply rely on these statutes and judicial doctrines to provide a remedy?

Later, we shall explore these statutes and judicial doctrines in more depth. For now, however, it is important to note two related differences between piercing and these alternate theories. The first is that these alternate theories require careful evaluation of specific transactions: What did the corporation transfer? What is the defendant's justification for the transfer? How does this measure up against the specific tests of fairness or solvency imposed by the relevant statute or judicial doctrine? By contrast, one does not find this same sort of careful transaction-by-transaction scrutiny in piercing cases. The second difference is in remedy. These alternate approaches lead to the return of the property taken in the transaction under challenge (or the monetary equivalent). Piercing, in comparison, creates liability measured by the debt the corporation owes to the plaintiff creditor (which could be much greater than what the defendant took from the company). Hence, while we discussed earlier why abusive self-dealing should lead to liability, this did not entirely

---

55. For a discussion of statutory limits on dividends see § 2.3.2 *infra*.

56. For a discussion of conflict-of-interest transactions see § 4.2.1–4.2.5 *infra*.

57. *E.g.*, Uniform Fraudulent Conveyance Act §§ 3, 4, 7.

answer why liability should take the form of piercing. More precisely, what, if anything, justifies these differences in both the manner of scrutiny and the measure of damages?

The difference in damages might reflect a policy of deterrence. Merely forcing the return of property does not deter its taking. Yet, this simply forces one to ask why deterrence is more important in the context of piercing cases than in situations in which the only remedy is return. There are several possible answers. Consider first the situation in which a party receives property from a debtor who is an individual rather than a corporation. Here, there can be no piercing claim against the transferee, but only a fraudulent conveyance action to force return of the property. Yet, in this situation, the transferee cannot have the complete control over the debtor who is an individual, which a controlling shareholder can have over a corporation. After all, real people do have minds of their own. When the transferee is not the person who decided to make the fraudulent conveyance, there seems less need to deter the transferee by making him or her liable for the entire debt. There also may be greater need for the measure of damages to deter unfair self-dealing in a piercing context than in the normal breach of fiduciary duty context. Piercing invariably involves a terminal relationship between owner and creditor. By contrast, the continued power of the shareholders to sack directors provides (at least in theory) an ongoing deterrent to director self-dealing. Of course, the difference in remedy could be accidental. In these other contexts, there is not a natural measure of compensatory damages, as there is in the piercing context, aside from return of the property.

Alternately, perhaps the need to deal with uncertainties can explain both the differences in remedy and in scrutiny. For example, one can never be sure the corporation received fair consideration in any transaction with its controlling shareholder. After all, we are speculating on what the result would have been had there been an arms-length exchange in a situation in which there was no such exchange. Also, merely forcing the return of assets risks under-compensating the creditor because of uncertainties. Are we sure the creditor has been able to identify every transaction in which the controlling shareholder obtained assets from the corporation? Can we be sure that, if the corporation had use of the property taken, it would not have been able to avoid failure altogether and thereby have paid the plaintiff? Piercing places the burden of these uncertainties on the controlling shareholder.

Here then is where the notion of formalities has a grain of merit—albeit one obscured by the focus on holding regular shareholder and director meetings for their own sake. Failure to make contemporaneous records of all transactions between the corporation and its controlling shareholder—including precisely what the corporation transferred, what, if anything, it received in exchange, what was the rationale for the transaction, and what steps the controlling shareholder took to evaluate whether there was either equivalence in the exchange or the corporation was solvent at the time—makes the court suspicious. While contemporaneous documentation is no guarantee against abusive self-dealing, the lack of such documentation, and the resultant need for an after-the-fact reconstruction, contributes to the uncertainties. Indeed, in the most extreme situation, the absence of financial records, combined with a pattern of commingling shareholder and corporate funds, could make it impossible even to figure out what funds belong to the debtor corporation. It is not surprising that courts resolve such uncertainties against the party who caused them, the controlling shareholder.

The *DeWitt* case, discussed earlier, illustrates this sort of approach. The controlling shareholder made withdrawals of between $15,000 and $25,000 per year from the corporation. In condemning these payments by listing them as a factor for piercing, the court spent no time trying to measure the payments against any justification. While the defendant testified that the payments represented a salary, the lack of any contemporaneous formal approval, and especially the fact that the defendant set the size of the payment by the amount of money available to the corporation, was enough to make them irretrievably suspect.

Our discussion so far has focused on intentional misconduct by the controlling shareholder in dealing with his or her corporation. What about negligent misconduct? Specifically, suppose, instead of dishonestly transferring assets into his or her own pocket, the controlling shareholder causes the corporation to fritter away its assets through negligent business decisions?

This sort of negligent mismanagement does not appear to be a significant factor in piercing decisions. For example, the study by Professor Thompson does not list it among the common factors courts recite in such decisions. Moreover, there is a policy hazard to venturing down this track. Piercing decisions involve failed businesses. Typically, a post mortem of a business failure can identify mistakes made by those in charge. This, in turn, may make it too easy for those who look at the business wreck in "twenty-twenty hindsight" to find negligence. Therefore, making such negligence grounds for piercing could potentially destroy limited liability.

Besides, later we shall discuss actions which may allow recovery against those in charge of a corporation specifically for negligent mismanagement.[58] At that point, we will consider curbs on such actions in order to prevent the "twenty-twenty hindsight" problem. We shall also consider the extent to which creditors should be the beneficiaries of such actions. Admittedly, the existence of alternate remedies did not prevent us from using abusive self-dealing as grounds to pierce. Yet, when dealing with negligence instead of intentional misconduct, there is neither the same moral culpability or need for deterrence. More significantly, there is more risk of confusing decisions which turn out badly, with legally culpable decisions. Hence, it may make more sense to confine a negligence theory to claims for damages suffered because of specific

---

58. See § 4.1 *infra.*

negligent business decisions, rather than allowing it to become the basis for a loosely applied piercing remedy.

1.5.7 Inadequate Capitalization

a. Should it be grounds to pierce?

In contrast to fraud and unfair self-dealing, which may explain far more piercing decisions than reading the literature on the subject would lead one to believe, inadequate capitalization may explain far fewer. In fact, Professor Thompson's study found inadequate capitalization mentioned in only nineteen percent of the torts and thirteen percent of the contracts opinions in which courts pierced.[59]

Still, even if inadequate capitalization is not the most prevalent grounds for piercing, we must address how significant this fact should be when it is present. The issue is sufficiently complex to require a longer discussion than necessary with the more common factors considered so far. To begin with, Professor Thompson's study suggests some judicial ambivalence. Courts pierced between seventy and seventy-five percent of the time when they found inadequate capitalization, and refused to do so in twenty-five to thirty percent of the cases (depending on whether the case involved a tort or contract creditor). These statistics are consistent with the impression one gets from reading a sampling of cases.

Some court opinions have held that inadequate capitalization leads to piercing. In *Minton v. Cavaney*[60], the California Supreme Court dealt with a claim brought on behalf of a girl who drowned while swimming in a pool operated by a corporation with no assets. The corporation leased the pool and had never issued stock. Pointing to the lack of capital, the court pierced.[61]

At the other extreme (and, coincidentally, at the other coast) one has the often discussed New York Court of Appeals' opinion in *Walkovszky v. Carlton*.[62] A taxicab operated by a corporation struck the plaintiff. The corporation's assets consisted of a couple of cabs, its non-transferable license to operate cabs in New York, and a liability insurance policy in the minimum amount required to drive a vehicle in New York. The situation is confusing because of the plaintiff's mixing together three potentially separate concerns in seeking to pierce. One is his allegation that the shareholder defendant, Carlton, had broken up Carlton's taxicab business into ten corporations, each owning one or two cabs, apparently for the purpose of limiting the loss which would result in case of an accident. For reasons we shall explore later, the court treated this as irrelevant to the plaintiff's right to pursue Carlton, as opposed to stating a claim against the other nine cab companies. There was also an allegation that Carlton was taking assets out of the corporation. What is

---

59. Thompson, *supra* note 2 at 1066.

60. 56 Cal.2d 576, 15 Cal.Rptr. 641, 364 P.2d 473 (1961).

61. The court remanded, however, in order to give the defendant an opportunity to show that the corporation should not have been held liable for negligence.

62. 18 N.Y.2d 414, 276 N.Y.S.2d 585, 223 N.E.2d 6 (1966).

important for present purposes is the allegation that the corporation was undercapitalized. The Court of Appeals held that this was insufficient to state a cause of action.[63] The scope of this holding, however, is not entirely clear. One reading is to reject the argument that inadequate capitalization provides grounds to pierce. On the other hand, the court's opinion placed much weight on the corporation possessing the minimum liability insurance required to operate a vehicle. This might allow a role for inadequate capitalization in a case where no minimum insurance statute applies.

Most courts have avoided following a broad reading of either *Minton* or *Walkovszky*. Instead, the tendency has been to exploit the indeterminacy of a multi-factor approach to piercing by stating that inadequate capitalization is a factor for the court to consider.[64] This dodge is not very satisfactory. Once we concede that inadequate capitalization is a factor toward piercing, the inevitable question becomes whether it alone can be enough to pierce.

A number of courts (including, surprisingly in light of *Minton*, several intermediate appellate courts in California) have held that the answer to this question is no.[65] Perhaps some of these courts simply meant that one must look at the nature of the plaintiff and defendant in deciding whether to pierce based upon inadequate capitalization. This is reasonable. As we shall discuss in more detail shortly, inadequate capitalization should not be grounds to pierce in favor of many contracts creditors who could have checked into the corporation's financial posture. Also, we should ask if the particular defendant was in sufficient control of the corporation so as to bear responsibility for its undertaking operations without adequate capital. Alternately, perhaps some of these courts recognized that, in some cases, inadequate capitalization will not be relevant on its own, but will provide part of the basis for a claim of fraud or abusive self-dealing. We shall explore this in detail shortly. Unfortunately, however, some courts, in holding that inadequate capitalization is not enough to pierce on its own, seem to have factors such as a failure to follow formalities in mind for what else may be necessary.[66] For example, one could point to the corporation's failure to issue stock in *Minton*. Yet, the *Minton* court was too sophisticated to rely on this sort of irrelevancy, and it would be hard to justify a different outcome simply because a corporation issues stock for some token amount.

This then brings us squarely to the question of whether courts should pierce, at least in some cases, based upon inadequate capitaliza-

---

63. The court gave the plaintiff an opportunity to amend his complaint. Two years later, the Court of Appeals held that the plaintiff's amended complaint alleged grounds for piercing, albeit the court never explained precisely how the amended complaint differed from the one it earlier found inadequate. Walkovszky v. Carlton, 23 N.Y.2d 714, 296 N.Y.S.2d 362, 244 N.E.2d 55 (1968).

64. *E.g.*, DeWitt Truck Brokers v. W. Ray Flemming Fruit Co., 540 F.2d 681 (4th Cir.1976).

65. *E.g.*, Harris v. Curtis, 8 Cal.App.3d 837, 87 Cal.Rptr. 614 (1970).

66. *E.g.*, Consumer's Co-op. v. Olsen, 142 Wis.2d 465, 419 N.W.2d 211 (1988).

tion. At the outset, the court's opinion in *Walkovszky* raises a legislative interpretation question: Will piercing based upon a lack of capital contravene legislation which either imposes financial requirements the corporation met or imposes no financial requirements on the corporation? The court in *Walkovszky* thought so, although there the particular insurance requirement had nothing to do with corporate law. It was a minimum insurance requirement for anybody to drive in the state. Hence, it is unlikely that the legislature, in enacting the requirement, gave any thought to its impact on piercing doctrine.

Historically, many corporations statutes required a certain amount of paid-in capital (often $500 or $1000) before a corporation could commence business.[67] Such requirements have faded from the scene. Does either the existence of such requirements or their disappearance tell us anything about legislative views of piercing for inadequate capital? The answer is probably no. The problem with legislative minimum capitalization requirements is that different businesses have different capital needs. Hence, the old statutes set a token sum suitable for the smallest venture. This is hardly a legislative determination as to what is adequate capital for any corporation, no matter what its business. The repeal of these provisions simply recognizes the futility of attempting to attack the adequate capital question through across-the-board legislative requirements. Case-by-case judicial evaluation through piercing decisions is a different matter.

Looking at the question as one of policy, we again must divide our analysis between contract and tort plaintiffs. In fact, it is in dealing with claims of inadequate capitalization that a number of courts have drawn the distinction between tort claimants and contract creditors, often speaking of "waiver" or "estoppel" of the contract creditor to complain of inadequate capital.[68] This focused lack of sympathy for contract creditors complaining about inadequate capital is fairly consistent with the lower overall percentage of piercing in torts as opposed to contracts cases found by Professor Thompson's study, once we recognize how fraud (which should only help contract creditors) and unfair self-dealing are more prevalent in piercing cases than is inadequate capitalization.

As we saw earlier, piercing an underfinanced corporation in favor of contract creditors is as much about nondisclosure as it is about inadequate capitalization. After all, had the controlling shareholder fully disclosed the financial status of the corporation, and the creditor still agreed to do business solely on the company's credit, a court presumably would not, and it should not, pierce based upon inadequate capitalization.[69] Moreover, had the creditor requested financial information, and the controlling shareholder lied in response, there would be fraud and grounds to pierce without the need to discuss capital in itself. Hence, the

67. See § 2.1.2a *infra*.

68. *E.g.*, Consumer's Co-op. v. Olsen, 142 Wis.2d 465, 419 N.W.2d 211 (1988).

69. *See, e.g.,* O'Hazza v. Executive Credit Corp., 246 Va. 111, 431 S.E.2d 318 (1993).

question becomes should the law protect creditors who neglect to protect themselves by demanding financial information before doing business.

To answer this question, it is useful to ask another: Why did the creditor not demand financial data before doing business? There are three possible answers to this question: First, the creditor is dumb. Alternately, the creditor rationally concluded that other information is more probative of the risks than is financial data. Finally, the creditor rationally concluded that the size of this transaction did not make it worth the added costs of demanding and analyzing financial information. Piercing based upon inadequate capitalization in favor of contracts creditors often leads into a discussion of the relative frequency and policy significance of these three possibilities. For example, some writers draw a distinction between creditors engaging in large negotiated transactions with the corporation—where, presumably, the failure to demand the data reflects either the first or second possibilities and where the court should therefore not pierce—and those engaging in small short-term transactions (such as the trade creditor who ships with an invoice giving thirty days to pay). These writers suggest the latter sort of creditor should be able to pierce, since it would not be fair or efficient to require such a creditor to incur the transaction costs of investigating the financial status of every corporation it does business with.[70]

This model of the trade creditor who could not reasonably expend the effort to investigate, however, may be divorced from the reality of piercing plaintiffs. The reason is simple. A lawsuit seeking to pierce is not an inexpensive proposition. Hence, a fairly sizable bill is involved or the creditor would not have brought the action. Given this, why did the creditor not deem it worthwhile to demand financial data to start with? Perhaps the prospect of being stiffed on any given short-term bill is so rare that even transactions large enough to provoke a piercing action are not worth an advance investigation into the corporation's finances. Alternately, perhaps other data (especially credit history) is usually more predictive of problems in most short-term credit transactions. If either of these two suppositions is true, this raises the question of whether financial data showing inadequate capitalization is simply not material to those extending short-term credit and hence its non-disclosure does not constitute fraud. Put another way, might the only result of piercing in favor of short-term contracts creditors based upon undisclosed undercapitalization be to encourage the pro forma transmittal of financial information which such creditors will ignore?

Perhaps not, since we might argue that the very act of stepping forward to warn the creditor about the corporation's financial health would serve as a flag to the creditor that in this case financial information is worth paying more attention to. If we assume that creditors face a "lemons problem"—there are a few undercapitalized corporations which it is not worthwhile to search for before extending short-term credit—and that the owners of those corporations know their companies are the

70. *E.g.,* Easterbrook & Fischel, *supra* note 12 at 113.

"lemons," it might make sense to force those owners to identify themselves. Yet, this works if only those owners whose corporations present extraordinary short-term credit risks come forward. If, instead, the owners of every muddling-through small business issue warnings, the creditors will not know which warnings to pay attention to. What this means is that the critical information to the creditor is not financial data at all. Instead, it is the owner's realization that the corporation is in serious enough trouble that the company will probably be unable to pay even short-term credit. Once we have reached this point, however, we have come back to false promise fraud. The owner who promises corporate performance knowing, at the time, the corporation will never be able to perform, has obtained limited liability by fraud. Under this analysis, inadequate capitalization no longer provides the grounds to pierce, but serves simply as evidence of the defendant's scienter.

The notion that inadequate capitalization might play a supporting role as part of another theory for piercing is not limited to fraud. It might also apply to abusive self-dealing. Recall, we earlier identified abusive transfers from the corporation to its owners by looking to the standards encompassed within the rules on dividends, conflict-of-interest transactions and fraudulent conveyances. Under this approach, the owner can receive corporate assets in exchange for fair consideration. Alternately, the owner can receive property from his or her corporation when the corporation is not insolvent or rendered insolvent by the transfer. Interestingly, the fraudulent conveyance statutes also proscribe transfers without fair consideration when the transferor is left with unreasonably small capital in light of the business the transferor expects to do.[71] Hence, in cases like *DeWitt* and *Sea-Land*, the problem is not just the gratuitous taking of assets. The problem is that the defendant took the assets without fair consideration from a financially imperiled corporation. To this extent, proof of inadequate capitalization may help prove that the defendant's self-dealing was abusive.

Turning to tort victims, the direct relevance of inadequate capitalization is much easier to see. Inadequate capitalization externalizes the costs of accidents. This is not simply a matter that, after the accident, the undercapitalized corporation finds itself unable to pay the victim. The more important problem arises before the accident. If a corporation insures to cover foreseeable accidents, it pays premiums. Lower premiums can reward cost effective accident prevention measures (such as a taxi company hiring drivers with better safety records). As the company incorporates the premiums into the price of its goods or services, the consumer, who must chose, say, between taking a cab, the subway, driving one's own car, or walking, makes this choice based upon a price which includes, among many other things, the relative accident risks of these various means of transportation. If, however, one can operate a corporation with insurance which will not cover foreseeable risks, the corporation's premium costs are lower. Its incentives to take premium

---

71. *E.g.*, Uniform Fraudulent Conveyance Act § 5.

reducing accident prevention measures are, in turn, less, and the consumers of its products receive a subsidy from accident victims.

This sort of externalization of accident costs is not what limited liability should achieve. Viewed both historically, and in terms of economic efficiency, limited liability is principally for the protection of shareholders in a widely held corporation. It is acceptable for closely held corporations dealing with contracts creditors since, in this context, parties could always contract in or out of a limited liability regime regardless of corporations law. Limited liability is even acceptable for the closely held corporation which faces tort liability that its owners did not reasonably foresee. After all, without a limited liability regime, one presumably would not have insured against unforeseeably large claims. Hence, the firm's goods or services would not have reflected those costs anyway. The use of limited liability by owners of a closely held business to deliberately externalize foreseeable accident costs, however, simply undercuts the goals of tort law.[72]

b. What is inadequate capitalization?

Thus far, we have been discussing "inadequate capitalization" without defining what we mean by the term. The reason for this organization is because defining the term "inadequate capitalization" sensibly requires evaluating why this factor might lead to piercing. In fact, it turns out that once we start to determine inadequate capitalization with reference to the policies discussed above, we might reject much of the conventional wisdom recited by commentators and courts on how to measure this factor.

Addressing whether a corporation is adequately capitalized requires answering three questions: (1) What is "capital" (in other words, what are we measuring); (2) How much capital is enough; and (3) When do we measure the amount of capital?

In a number of cases, such as *Kinney Shoe* and *Minton*, courts are able to blow past all three questions because the corporation never had any assets at all. Once we get past such stark facts, opinions on what counts as capital become confused. Some courts look to all of the corporation's assets.[73] Most, however, focus on assets that came from the shareholder(s).[74] This works simply enough when shareholders put money into the corporation in exchange for stock. It creates a difficult issue, however, when, as is common, shareholders put much or all of their contribution into the corporation in the form of loans, or guarantees of

---

72. This point is distinguishable from the earlier observation that there is nothing wrong with incorporating a business for the purpose of limiting liability in general. The corporation allows its owner to offer to deal on a limited liability basis with contracts creditors, who are free to reject this offer. It also protects its owner from tort liabilities in excess of reasonable insurance policy limits. After all, virtually no one buys liability insurance with unlimited coverage even when one faces personal liability. Accordingly, limited liability remains an important reason to incorporate even for those who plan on having the business maintain adequate insurance.

73. *See, e.g.,* Auer v. Frank, 227 Cal. App.2d 396, 38 Cal.Rptr. 684 (1964).

74. *See, e.g.,* Baatz v. Arrow Bar, 452 N.W.2d 138 (S.D.1990).

third party loans. Opinions on whether to treat such transactions as capital for purposes of determining if the corporation is undercapitalized are in hopeless conflict.[75]

Court opinions also supply little guidance on how much of whatever assets count as capital is enough. *Minton* referred to capital which was "trifling compared with the business to be done and the risks of loss" as insufficient. The notion that one must measure needed capital by the nature and risks of the business is reasonable enough, but how small is "trifling"?

The rule for when to measure capital, at least, appears clear. Most courts and commentators agree one measures this at the inception of the venture.[76] A possible exception exists if the corporation expands the size and risks of its business.[77]

We started the discussion of what is inadequate capitalization with the concept that a sensible definition should follow from the reasons one thinks this factor ought to lead to piercing. Let us see how the views just outlined do under this approach. Notice that the focus of most courts and commentators seems to be on the shareholders' initial investment in the corporation. At first glance, this seems strange. After all, whatever the shareholders put into the company is gone or we would not have unpaid creditors seeking to pierce. The creditors are concerned with what the corporation has to pay them now. The notion could not be that the shareholders are supposed to invest up front enough money to cover all the corporation's future debts, or else limited liability would be rather meaningless. Indeed, why would a corporation ever incur debt if its shareholders had put in all necessary funds for its operations at the start?

In fact, the focus on the shareholders' initial investment is only indirectly, if at all, concerned with making sure creditors get paid. Rather, the idea is that shareholders should be forced to put some of their own funds at risk. There are a couple of rationales for this. Some writers and courts have viewed the question as one of fairness or quid pro quos. If a party wants the advantage of engaging in a business on a limited liability basis, that party ought to be willing to risk at least some of his or her own money, rather than shifting the entire risk of the venture onto others.[78] The second rationale looks to economic incentives. A party with none of his or her own funds at risk has an incentive to engage in uneconomically risky investments.

75. *Compare* Arnold v. Browne, 27 Cal. App.3d 386, 103 Cal.Rptr. 775 (1972), *with* Nilsson, Robbins, Dalgarn, Berliner, Carson & Wurst v. Louisiana Hydrolec, 854 F.2d 1538 (9th Cir.1988).

76. *E.g.*, Consumer's Co-op. v. Olsen, 142 Wis.2d 465, 419 N.W.2d 211 (1988); William P. Hackney & Tracy G. Benson, *Shareholder Liability for Inadequate Capital*, 43 U. Pitt. L. Rev. 837, 898 (1982). *But*

see DeWitt Truck Brokers v. W. Ray Flemming Fruit Co., 540 F.2d 681 (4th Cir. 1976).

77. *See, e.g.*, Consumer's Co-op. v. Olsen, 142 Wis.2d 465, 419 N.W.2d 211 (1988).

78. *E.g.*, Elvin R. Latty, Subsidiaries and Affiliated Corporations 120–121 (1936).

If we accept this as the reason for looking at inadequate capitalization, we can answer some of the questions upon which courts seem confused. As far as what to look at, consideration paid for stock clearly counts. Courts have had difficulty with loans and guarantees because they have attempted to treat this as an all-or-nothing proposition. Shareholder loans and guarantees put the shareholder's money at risk and provide an incentive for responsible decisionmaking. On the other hand, the risk is not quite the same as a purchase of stock. Barring subordination, which we shall discuss later,[79] a shareholder loan, or the loan the shareholder guarantees, may receive some payment after the failure of the business—assuming, of course, the corporation has any assets—even if all the creditors do not get fully paid. Hence, shareholder loans and guarantees should count as capital under this rationale, but perhaps at some discounted rate.

As far as how much capital is enough, it is a mistake to say that the standard is enough to cover the foreseeable needs or debts of the business. Otherwise, the mere fact of corporate borrowing for anything other than an unforeseen contingency would show a lack of capital. Yet, even the most financially sound public corporations engage in long-term borrowing as part of their capitalization.[80] Instead, one is looking for enough capital for the shareholders to meet a "fair" share of the risks of business failure, or, to be more results oriented, enough capital to create an incentive for the controlling owners to make reasonable business decisions. Rather than speculate on this amount, we might examine the practices used by sophisticated lenders in assessing whether to make business loans.

The discerning reader may have noticed that the idea of requiring capital in order to achieve a "fair" sharing of risks, or to provide an incentive for reasonable business decisions, came out of our discussion of the traditional definition of inadequate capitalization. None of this appeared in our consideration of when and why inadequate capitalization should lead to piercing. The reason is simple—this has little to do with why the courts should pierce.

The traditional view reflects a notion that limited liability is a privilege made available through the granting of corporate status and that courts can condition this privilege based on the courts' views of fairness or efficiency. We have already seen, however, with respect to contracts creditors, that limited liability fundamentally exists because this is what the owners and creditors agreed. It is rather presumptuous for a court to trash this agreement simply because the court thinks the parties have agreed to an unfair or inefficient allocation of risks. Accord-

79. See § 2.2.3 *infra.*

80. Along this line, the suggestion of some writers that the shareholders ought to provide enough capital to give the corporation a "reasonable chance of success" fails to provide a workable guideline as to what should be the shareholders' initial investment. Admittedly, potentially viable start-up businesses may fail if they lack access to sufficient cash to get through the development and early marketing phases and reach profitability. Yet, there is no inherent reason that this investment must come from the initial shareholders' equity, rather than borrowing or later investors.

ingly, while creditors making long-term larger loans to a corporation often are concerned about making sure the shareholders have a sufficient stake in the company to avoid excessive risk-taking, such creditors are fully able to protect against inadequate initial capitalization by investigating this fact.

This is not a case, as with abusive self-dealing, in which we might imply terms, rather than require creditors to set everything out in a contract. Addressing abusive self-dealing in a contract requires anticipating and negotiating over variations of future conduct which normally will not come to pass. Implied terms save parties this often wasted effort. Moreover, decades of judicial and legislative experience have created a set of general guidelines which we might reasonably assume are the minimum any creditor would demand. Application of either these or contractually tailored guidelines to specific conduct requires, in any case, an ex post judicial decision. Hence, recognizing and enforcing implied terms regarding self-dealing through piercing decisions is efficient. By contrast, the shareholders' initial investment in the corporation is a present fact that any prospective creditor can establish, without elaborate negotiation and drafting, by simply requesting information from the corporation. Each long-term creditor is at least as capable as the courts to evaluate whether this level of investment is adequate to ensure proper incentives. There does not presently exist any long-developed judicial or legislative standards as to what initial investment is enough. Nor, unlike the situation with abusive self-dealing, does an after-the-fact evaluation of conduct provide an efficient mechanism for the evolution of standards, since one can never be sure that the subsequent failure of the business resulted from a lack of incentives. This is also not a situation in which, if the creditor attempted self-protection, we would end up with a judicial evaluation of later events in any case. Accordingly, establishing that the shareholders' initial investment is satisfactory to the long-term creditor is something long-term creditors can most efficiently do for themselves. If the long-term creditors do not find this effort worth their while, neither should the courts.

What about smaller short-term extensions of credit? Here, as we discussed earlier, one might argue that owners of inadequately capitalized corporations ought to inform creditors of this status. Yet, then we must ask what are the critical financial facts short-term creditors want to know. It is extremely unlikely that short-term creditors want to know about the shareholders' initial investment in the corporation. After all, the question of whether the shareholders originally had an incentive to make responsible business decisions is rather academic to one only concerned about payment in the next thirty days.

If the shareholders' initial investment should not be the relevant criteria for inadequate capitalization as far as short-term creditors, then what should? Such creditors are concerned with the corporation's near-term ability to pay its bills. This suggests a focus on current resources and liabilities (in other words, the company's working capital), as well, perhaps, as its cash flow. Recall, however, we earlier speculated that short-term creditors may not be interested in any raw financial data at all, because it would generally not be efficient to spend the effort digesting such information. What such creditors might find more efficient to know is the owner's expectations as to their payment. Under this analysis, the relevant measure of capital is the corporation's ability to pay its short-term bills as incurred, and particularly any financial facts which suggest that the owner knew the corporation was unlikely to pay.

The notion that limited liability exists by legislative grace has validity for torts claims. Here, as we discussed before, piercing for inadequate capitalization based upon judicial views of fairness or efficiency (or, to be more precise, about the trade-offs between internalizing the costs of accidents and allowing limited liability) is appropriate. Yet, once we focus on the goal of internalizing the costs of accidents, the concept of measuring inadequate capitalization by the shareholder's initial investment still makes little sense. We do not expect corporations to pay for accident costs out of what the shareholders invested for their stock. We expect them to buy insurance (albeit, large firms might self-insure). Hence, the relevant measure is how much insurance the corporation has, not how much the shareholders invested.[81]

In rebuttal, one might argue that the shareholder's investment remains relevant because it gives the controlling shareholder an incentive to make sure the corporation has adequate insurance. This is true, but not determinative. To see why, assume we have a corporation with negligible shareholder investment, but which maintains insurance adequate to meet reasonably foreseeable levels of damages. Little would be served in this case by piercing for lack of shareholder investment if the purpose for looking to shareholder investment is to provide an incentive for adequate insurance. Conversely, suppose there was a corporation with substantial shareholder investment, but which has unreasonably small insurance coverage. The large shareholder investment should not distract the court from piercing. Of course, this discussion is somewhat unrealistic in its assumption that determining what are reasonably foreseeable damages is free from doubt. Accordingly, perhaps in a case when there is a borderline insurance policy (*Walkovszky*) one might look to the size of the shareholder investment to see if it gave the shareholder enough incentive to adequately insure. On the other hand, what is an adequate shareholder investment is itself as much or more uncertain as what are reasonably foreseeable damages. Thus, about the best one can say is that an unarguable case of inadequate shareholder investment (the shareholder has no equity at all in the corporation) could provide some indirect evidence that a borderline insurance policy is inadequate.

This discussion suggests that the conventional wisdom not only measures the wrong thing, it also looks at the wrong time. If the

81. For a recent opinion which recognized this point see Radaszewski v. Telecom Corp., 981 F.2d 305 (8th Cir.1992).

corporation has allowed its insurance to lapse, the fact that it had a policy at the outset should not preclude piercing. The question is did the company internalize the risk of accidents into the cost of the goods or services which led to the accident; in other words, did it have insurance in effect for the activity which resulted in the injury. Similarly, the short-term trade creditor wants to know about the corporation's current financial picture. Along the same lines, if we are using inadequate capitalization to show the abusiveness of gratuitous transfers from the corporation to the defendant, we need to look to the corporation's financial state at the time of the transfer.

The commonly stated rationale for the measure-at-the-inception rule is that otherwise limited liability becomes illusory because obviously the corporation was inadequately capitalized when it failed. This rationale becomes inapropos once we reframe the inadequate capitalization issue for contracts creditors as a disclosure concern (or as a matter of not making gratuitous withdrawals of corporate assets), and reframe the issue for tort victims as one of maintaining insurance. The law should not require the shareholders to treat their corporation as a black hole into which they are obligated to put unlimited funds. If, however, the corporation cannot get needed supplies, services or other items on credit from fully informed parties, or maintain insurance policies for foreseeable injuries, it should close its doors.

Finally, the policies discussed earlier also provide a benchmark for how much "capital" is adequate. Insurance ought to cover foreseeable risks. One way to measure this is to ask how much insurance would a reasonable person seeking to protect his or her own assets from the potential tort liabilities of this business have purchased. Seen in this light, the *Walkovszky* court was not completely wrong to look at the insurance requirement in the vehicle code, even though the insurance requirement did not relate to any legislative policy on piercing. If the $10,000 requirement reflected a legislative assessment as to the likely extent of damages in the vast majority of auto accidents, then the court's end result could be correct. Of course, this is a big "if", and it would be useful to know more about how the legislature reached this figure and whether most of the auto policies sold in New York at this time had only this amount of coverage. Moreover, one should ask if cabs present significantly greater risks of going over the policy limit. Probably not, because, even if cabs might get into more accidents, it is difficult to say that they get into worse ones than other vehicles.

We might also use a reasonable person standard in the contracts creditor context: Specifically, would a reasonable creditor have found the state of the corporation's working capital important in deciding to extend the credit at issue (in other words, was this information material)? The problem here, however, is that we are dealing with a situation in which the creditor did not ask about working capital. If we are basing our analysis on fraud, it really comes from the misrepresentation as to the controlling shareholder's intent to perform.

More fundamentally, our rationale for looking to adequate capital in the contracts creditor context was to force owners, who knew that the corporation's financial situation made short-term credit unusually dangerous, to step forward and point this out to the creditor. If the owner did not perceive the extraordinary danger, we cannot ask him or her to point it out. True, the owner may have been unreasonable in failing to perceive the danger, and thereby negligent. Yet, we noted earlier the importance of not encouraging every muddling-through small business to drown short-term creditors in data. Otherwise, such creditors will ignore the warnings they should heed. Hence, an approach which penalizes non-disclosure when a reasonable person would have seen the danger, even though the defendant did not, may well be counterproductive. Following this logic, capital is inadequate when the finder of fact infers from the corporation's financial position that the controlling shareholder knew the corporation was not likely to perform contracts it was entering. As far when inadequate capital makes gratuitous transfers of corporate assets to the controlling shareholder grounds for piercing, one can look to the financial tests developed under the dividend and fraudulent conveyance statutes.

Finally, understanding what one means by inadequate capitalization, and why it might lead to piercing, helps clear up a question sometimes raised by writers in this area. Why should the defendant pay the entire debt owed to the plaintiff, rather than the amount by which the corporation was undercapitalized?[82] To the extent inadequate capitalization refers to the lack of an initial investment by the shareholder, and the rationale is to require a "fair" sharing of risks, then the only reason for going beyond requiring the shareholder belatedly to put in adequate capital would be to punish the shareholder (perhaps for the sake of deterrence). On the other hand, if the rationale for focusing on the shareholder's initial investment is to ensure incentives for reasonable business decisions, then one can justify going beyond making up the shortfall in initial investment on the grounds that the poor incentive structure may have contributed to the ultimate corporate failure. If the real problem is a failure to disclose the lack of capital, then the creditor can argue it would not have extended the corporation credit had it known the truth. Failure to have insurance coverage for reasonably foreseeable levels of damages logically leads to liability to the extent of the plaintiff's unpaid judgment, unless the plaintiff's recovery goes beyond a foreseeable level. In that case, the only way to justify liability beyond the extent of insurance the corporation should have carried would be to invoke some sort of punitive or deterrence rationale.

1.5.8 Multiple Corporations

Many piercing cases involve more than one corporation. To begin with, the controlling shareholder of the debtor corporation might be another corporation, instead of an individual. In other words, we are

---

82. *See* Clark, *supra* note 51 at 547.

dealing with parent and subsidiary corporations. Alternately, we have the situation found in *Kinney Shoe*, *Sea-Land* and *Walkovszky*. In each of these cases, one individual owned a controlling interest in a number of corporations which engaged in related activities. These are sometimes referred to as "brother-sister" corporations. What, if any, impact will the presence of multiple corporations have on piercing?

Let us start with the situation in which the controlling shareholder is a corporation rather than an individual (the parent-subsidiary situation). As a first approximation, we might assume that this should not make any difference at all. Rather, one can employ the same analysis for piercing against controlling shareholders regardless if such shareholders are individuals or corporations.

Some writers have asserted, however, that courts should be more willing to pierce against a corporation than an individual.[83] The argument is that no real people face the risk of unlimited liability when the defendant shareholder is another corporation. Yet, the Thompson study found that courts actually pierced in a somewhat higher percentage of cases against individuals as opposed to corporate defendants.[84] Moreover, courts in piercing cases tend to cite and apply prior opinions interchangeably regardless of whether the cases were against individual or corporate shareholder defendants. Hence, whatever the merits of the argument that courts should pierce more against corporate as opposed to individual defendants, it seems to have fallen on deaf ears.

So, who has it right? Let us go back to our basic analysis for contract and tort creditors. The reason that the subsidiary is liable to contract creditors, and, in the absence of piercing, the parent is not, remains because this is what the parties agreed. If this agreement resulted from fraud (including perhaps undisclosed inadequate capitalization), or the parent has engaged in abusive self-dealing with the subsidiary, then there can be grounds to pierce, just as when dealing with an individual shareholder. Suppose there is no fraud or abusive self-dealing. Why should the fact that the defendant is another corporation, rather than an individual, allow the creditor to get out of the agreement to limited liability?

What about tort claims? Here, the key to our analysis has been maintaining adequate insurance to cover a foreseeable extent of damage. If a corporation owned by an individual did not have adequate insurance, the court should pierce. Suppose a subsidiary corporation does have insurance sufficient to meet foreseeable levels of liability, but faces liability for a mass tort (Bopal) which it did not foresee. Should the court pierce simply because the liability would flow to a parent corporation rather than an individual? It is difficult to see why. If the extent of damage exceeded what the parent would have insured for even if it had

83. Easterbrook & Fischel, *supra* note 12 at 110–111.

84. Courts pierced around 43% of the time against individuals, versus around 37% of the time when dealing with a corporation as the defendant. Thompson, *supra* note 2 at 1056.

faced the liability in the first instance, then piercing does not advance the purposes of internalizing the costs of accidents.

Our discussion so far suggests no reason to distinguish between corporate and individual controlling shareholders. What then might explain the fact that courts actually pierce less often against parent corporations? One possibility is that there is greater sophistication among management of parent corporations. This, in turn, might lead such managers to avoid quite the degree of misleading communications and abusive self-dealing as found in the small business context (or, at least, to have better documentation to meet later challenges).

There is another possibility, however, which returns us to the element of control. Unlike an individual who is a controlling shareholder, a parent corporation can only act through its personnel. Hence, it may be a difficult question in some cases as to whether personnel of the parent undertook fraudulent or abusive conduct in the scope of their employment for the parent, so as to make the parent responsible for the conduct. The problem arises because the personnel in question can be directors, officers or employees of both the parent and the subsidiary.

Craig v. Lake Asbestos[85] provides an illustrative case. *Craig* involved an attempt to hold an investment corporation (Charter Consolidated) liable for default judgments against another corporation (Cape Industries) in which the investment company held two-thirds of the stock. The district court found fraud or injustice based upon the activities of Cape Industries to avoid liability on asbestos claims. These claims arose out of the activities of Cape's wholly owned United States subsidiary. Cape dissolved the subsidiary and allowed American courts to enter default judgments against itself in various suits arising out of the United States subsidiary's asbestos sales. The plaintiffs were unable to get the English courts to enforce these judgments against Cape. Evidently, Charter Consolidated had assets in the United States and so the plaintiffs attempted to pierce.

The court of appeals did not challenge the district court's finding of fraud or injustice. Instead, it reversed due to the failure to show that Charter had the requisite control over Cape. The facts of the opinion provide limited detail regarding who made the decision to dissolve the subsidiary and not to defend the suits in American courts. The district court found that Charter's three nominees on Cape's board were aware of the scheme to avoid liability prior to the meeting of Cape's board which approved the subsidiary's dissolution. Moreover, Cape's chairman, who one supposes may have had some input into this plan, was also a director of Charter. This said, however, it is still difficult to conclude that the evidence showed Charter's personnel, in the course of their employment for Charter rather than Cape, hatched the scheme to engage in the conduct the court condemned. In any event, the court of appeals avoided even trying to parse out this question. Instead, it wandered off into the question of whether Charter' control over Cape reached the

---

85.   843 F.2d 145 (3d Cir.1988).

level of "domination." Noting that "Charter" did not intrude into the day-to-day management of Cape, and that the two corporations maintained separate records, offices and staffs, the court of appeals concluded that there was no such domination. Well, this at least shows the advantage of rote application of labels as a way to avoid difficult factual questions.

Now, let us turn to the brother-sister corporation context. We have two questions to consider: First, will this add anything to our analysis as to when and why courts should pierce? In addition, who should be liable if courts pierce when dealing with brother-sister corporations?

With respect to contract creditors, we can adhere to our analysis that creditors who choose to do business on one corporation's credit cannot, barring fraud or abusive self-dealing, go beyond that company for repayment. Nevertheless, while not altering the basic grounds for piercing, the presence of brother-sister corporations creates additional prospects for fraud or self-dealing. For example, in *Sea-Land*, not only did the controlling shareholder withdraw funds from the debtor corporation for his personal use, he also transferred funds between various corporations he owned. In *Zaist v. Olson*[86], the plaintiff agreed to clear and grade land. He also agreed to look to one of the controlling shareholder's corporations for payment. It turned out, however, that another of the defendant's corporations actually owned the land which the plaintiff cleared and graded, and the debtor corporation lacked the funds to pay for the work (presumably because the debtor corporation gained no benefit from this undertaking). Not surprisingly, given this self-dealing, the court pierced.

The situation in which a number of corporations share a common office and telephone lines, or have similar sounding names, may mislead a creditor as to which company it is extending credit to. This problem could exist as well in the parent-subsidiary situation. Perhaps this could apply to the two corporations in *Kinney Shoe*, since the leasing corporation had a similar name to the manufacturing corporation. If the plaintiff had been confused into leasing to a corporation with no assets, rather than to the manufacturing corporation, this could explain the court's complaint about the defendant's establishing the two corporations. The problem in *Kinney Shoe* is that nowhere does the court refer to any claim, much less any evidence, that the creditor was, in fact, confused. The mere possibility of confusion should not result in piercing in favor of creditors who were not misled.

Walkovszky brings us to consider the significance of brother-sister corporations to piercing in favor of torts claimants. Carlton was following what one might refer to as a "Titanic" strategy. Much as the designers of the famous ocean liner had divided the ship into eight watertight compartments, any two of which could flood without sinking the ship, Carlton broke up his taxicab venture into ten separate corporations so that accident liability would not sink the whole business. The

---

86. 154 Conn. 563, 227 A.2d 552 (1967).

court decided this was irrelevant to the issue before it. Specifically, the appeal in the case arose from the trial court's granting the motion to dismiss the action against Carlton. Evidently, in what was probably a tactical decision to create a more sympathetic situation for Carlton, the other nine cab corporations (who Walkovszky had also named as defendants) did not move to dismiss the action against themselves. The court, while it did not need to reach the issue, seemed to feel that breaking up the venture in this manner provided grounds for piercing to make the other corporations liable, but held that this did not state a claim against Carlton.

In suggesting that all ten cab companies can be liable for the tort claim against one, the court followed the urging of some writers to disregard artificial divisions between separate corporate entities of what is, in effect, one enterprise or business.[87] We have already addressed whether this should matter for contracts creditors. At first glance, we might find it persuasive grounds to pierce in favor of torts claimants. After all, there seems to be an attempt to avoid internalizing the costs of accidents, with little offsetting social utility (save extra filing fees from forming more corporations).

A practical problem, however, is to decide when there is an artificial division of one business. Consider the situation in *Walkovszky* for example. There are cab companies throughout the world who only operate one or two cabs and whose owner does not have any other cab companies. Hence, can we say that the debtor corporation in *Walkovszky* was just an artificially created fragment of a larger business? On the other hand, it would be interesting to know whether small cab companies often operate out of a common garage (and presumably with a common dispatcher) with other independently owned companies.

A broader problem, however, may be that we have wandered off from what we should be attempting to accomplish when piercing in favor of torts creditors. After all, forcing the sale of the twenty cabs owned by Carlton's companies is not going to help much either Walkovzsky's cause or to internalize accident costs. What was needed was more insurance. Hence, if the debtor corporation was unreasonably underinsured, the court should have pierced for inadequate capitalization against Carlton. If the corporation had reasonable insurance, then so what if Carlton artificially divided one business?

Yet, this discussion assumes no uncertainty as to what is adequate insurance; a point we have noted before in considering the relevance of abusive self-dealing and shareholder investment to piercing for tort plaintiffs. Indeed, the court may have been too eager to compartmentalize Walkovszky's three arguments. Both the siphoning and the artificial division of the business reduced Carlton's incentive to purchase more insurance. In a case in which one can say with confidence that $10,000 of

87. *E.g.*, Adolf A. Berle, *The Theory of* (1947).
Enterprise Entity, 47 Colum. L. Rev. 343

coverage is, or is not, enough, this would not have mattered. In a case in which we are not sure, Carlton's conduct—particularly the division of his cabs into ten companies—is strong evidence that Carlton himself did not view the insurance as adequate for the risks of the business. This suggests that the *Walkovszky* court had it upside down. It should have pierced against Carlton and left the other nine cab companies alone.

This, in turn, brings us to the broader question of determining who is the appropriate defendant when dealing with an abuse involving brother-sister corporations. The *Walkovszky* court appears to have felt that if the wrong involved using multiple corporations, the logical remedy was to make the other corporations liable. This may have misconstrued the wrong in the situation there. In a case in which the controlling shareholder misleads the creditor as to which corporation will be liable, or engages in abusive transactions between the brother-sister corporations, however, making the other corporation(s) liable may rectify the precise harm complained of. Should the court go beyond this to hold the controlling shareholder personally liable? The controlling shareholder cannot complain too much if, as in *Zaist*, the court does, since he or she misled the creditor or caused the abusive transactions. While holding the controlling shareholder personally responsible goes beyond undoing the wrong in these cases, perhaps this is justified to achieve deterrence.

Yet, we need to ask a further question about holding brother-sister corporations liable for each others' debts. Notice, in this case, we are not piercing against a shareholder (individual or corporate). Should this matter? Recall from our discussion of the relevance of control to piercing that our goal in looking to control is to point the finger at the party who committed the fraud or wrongful act which led the court to pierce. In fact, this is typically the controlling shareholder of the brother-sister corporations, rather than the non-debtor corporations. One could argue perhaps in some cases that the controlling shareholder committed the fraud or abusive self-dealing in the scope of his or her employment for the non-debtor corporation(s). Better, one can often avoid getting into such a subtle inquiry by noting it may not matter. Among the controlling shareholder's assets are his or her stock in the brother-sister corporations. Hence, if the court pierces against the controlling shareholder, his or her stock in the other corporations can be available to satisfy the plaintiff's claim. If there is only one stockholder and no other creditors, then the other corporations could be dissolved or sold to pay the judgment against the controlling shareholder. Thus, there is little practical impact if, instead, the other corporations simply pay off the plaintiff's claim.

The problem arises, however, when the brother-sister corporations have other creditors or shareholders. Making the other corporations directly liable to the plaintiff grants the plaintiff a priority over the other shareholders, and places the plaintiff on a par with the other corporations' unsecured creditors, neither of which would be the case with a levy on the controlling shareholder's stock.

Sea-Land provides an illustration. Among the corporations held liable for the plaintiff's claim was Tie–Net. The individual defendant only owned half the stock of Tie–Net; an apparently passive investor owned the other half. While Tie–Net evidently engaged in questionable dealings with the its brother-sister corporations, there was no evidence that Tie–Net had come out ahead from the debtor corporation. Moreover, in piercing, Tie–Net became liable for the entire debt, rather than just whatever unfair excess it might have received from the debtor corporation. The court's rationale was to point to the controlling shareholder's abuse of Tie–Net. In other words, the fact that the controlling shareholder had already victimized the passive shareholder justified somehow the further injury of allowing collection by another corporation's creditor. Perhaps the court felt no sympathy because of the other shareholder's neglect of the situation. We do not know, because the court never explores why the other shareholder remained passive, or whether this breached any sort of duty. Indeed, the court never seems to see the real issue.

Of course, piercing also can impact innocent shareholders and creditors in the parent-subsidiary situation. Indeed, it can impact the personal creditors of a controlling shareholder who is an individual. Hence, in a multi-corporation bankruptcy, the court might attempt to analyze the situation in terms of the relative equities of competing groups of claimants.[88] One should not get too carried away with this approach, however. After all, a debtor, be it a corporation or individual, can always do things which expose the debtor to further liability and thereby prejudice the position of its unsecured creditors in a bankruptcy.

1.5.9 *Whose Law and Who Decides?*

Recall that the law of the state of incorporation governs the internal affairs of a corporation.[89] Does this apply to piercing? By and large, judicial opinions have given little attention to this question. For one thing, courts have often cited and applied the same general principles regarding piercing without clear delineations between different states. In addition, piercing claims typically have involved small corporations incorporated in the same state in which they are doing business and incurring liability. Still, the issue arises from time-to-time. When this has happened, courts usually have chosen to follow the law of the state of incorporation.[90]

To determine what approach courts should follow, it is useful to go back to the rationales for the internal affairs rule. One rationale is shareholder choice. If shareholders do not like the laws of the state of incorporation, they do not have to invest in this corporation (or, to be more sophisticated, they can discount the price they are willing to pay for the stock to offset the added risks they face from inferior state law

---

88. *See, e.g.,* Stone v. Eacho, 127 F.2d 284 (4th Cir.1942).

89. See § 1.2.1 *supra.*

90. *E.g.,* Realmark Investment Co. v. American Financial Corp., 171 Bankr. Rptr. 692 (Bankr. N.D. Ga. 1994).

protections). The second rationale is the practicality problem created if corporations must comply with potentially inconsistent state law rules for their internal governance. Do these rationales apply to piercing?

The shareholder choice rationale does not. Instead, because piercing involves the rights of creditors, it creates the potential for states to compete for corporate charters by establishing rules whose costs are not born either by the individuals selecting where to incorporate or by those investing in the company. Contracts creditors might adjust the interest rates they charge to compensate for risks of dealing with corporations from different states with varying willingness to pierce. Yet, this ability might be more theoretical than practical. Moreover, tort victims cannot make such adjustments. This strongly suggests that the internal affairs rule is inappropriate for piercing.

What about concerns over imposing inconsistent state rules for corporate governance? Here, one must look at the specific grounds for piercing. For example, to the extent the ground involves dealings between the controlling shareholder and the creditor (fraud), there seems little objection to inconsistent standards. Each state ought to be able to control specific business transactions within the state. A more persuasive case for a single standard exists for piercing based upon abusive self-dealing, inadequate capitalization or (if one insists) failure to follow formalities. Even here, however, we will not be dealing with a situation (which might exist for some other issues in corporate governance) in which one state could command actions that another prohibits.

Another problem in choice of law occurs when the piercing claim involves liability under a federal statute. This problem has arisen with greater frequency in recent years, especially for liability imposed under the Comprehensive Environmental Response, Compensation and Liability Act (CERCLA). In dealing with federal statutes, it is useful to start by separating out the question of who the statute imposes direct liability upon, from the question of whether to pierce in order to extend one corporation's liability to its controlling shareholder. For example, CERCLA imposes liability upon an "operator" of a facility releasing hazardous substances. The United States Supreme Court has interpreted the term "operator" to include a person (including a parent corporation) who controls the facility in question.[91] By contrast, courts have held that liability under CERCLA as an "owner" of a facility releasing hazardous substances rests only with the corporation owning the facility—unless their are general grounds to pierce the corporate veil.[92]

Piercing the corporate veil for CERCLA or for liability under other federal statutes, in turn, creates the question of whether to look to state law piercing standards or to develop a federal approach. Generally, the federal courts have opted for the latter.[93] This seems appropriate if, as

---

91. United States v. Bestfoods, 524 U.S. 51, 118 S.Ct. 1876 (1998).

92. *E.g.*, Lansford–Coaldale Joint Water Authority v. Tonolli Corp., 4 F.3d 1209 (3d Cir.1993).

93. *E.g.*, United States v. Pisani, 646

discussed earlier, piercing should depend upon the underlying policies behind the type of liability.

Beyond the question of whose law to apply, there is the question of who decides whether the grounds exist to pierce. Specifically, is this a factual issue for a jury to resolve or an equitable evaluation for the trial court judge? Courts in different jurisdictions are in disagreement on this question.[94] There are obvious reasons for discomfort with leaving the matter to a jury when piercing results from the application of multiple factors of indeterminate weight or from some intuitive sense of inequitable conduct—albeit one might question whether trial court judges are going to do much better. On the other hand, if piercing should result from some relatively specific conduct—fraud, abusive self-dealing, inadequate insurance to meet foreseeable tort recovery—then there is no reason the jury cannot find the specific factual predicates which would justify piercing (such as whether the defendant knew the corporation could never perform a contract when it entered it).

1.5.10 *Piercing in other Contexts*

Most piercing cases involve disregarding the separate entity status of a corporation in order to impose liability for the company's debts on its shareholders. Sometimes, however, courts must decide whether to disregard the separate entity status of a corporation for other purposes.

One common context in which this occurs is when a party forms a corporation with the hope of gaining an advantage under a statute or contract, which the party would not gain if he or she acted as an individual. For example, suppose an individual enters a covenant not to compete. Can the individual set up a corporation and have the corporation go into competition against the beneficiary of the covenant?[95]

This general sort of issue arises frequently in dealing with tax and employee benefit statutes. It is sometimes the case that individuals who are employees will qualify under statutory social welfare schemes (such as unemployment compensation, social security retirement and disability benefits) or for tax advantaged fringe benefits (such as retirement plans and health insurance) which would not be available, or available to the same extent, for those who are self employed. Hence, it is tempting to set up a corporation whose principal employee is its owner.[96] Alternately, the existence of a progressive income tax rate structure might lead an owner to conduct a business through a number of corporations in order to split up income and thereby have more income taxed at the lower rates.

These sort of cases explain why some formulations of the criteria for piercing speak of "fraud, wrong or violation of a statutory or other legal

---

F.2d 83 (3d Cir.1981).

94. *Compare* Castleberry v. Branscum, 721 S.W.2d 270 (Tex.1986), *with* Kinney Shoe Corp. v. Polan, 939 F.2d 209 (4th Cir.1991).

95. *See, e.g.,* Hirsh v. Miller, 167 So.2d 539 (La.App.1964).

96. *See, e.g.,* Stark v. Flemming, 283 F.2d 410 (9th Cir.1960).

duty." Nevertheless, the factors we examined for piercing in the liability context are not particularly relevant in these statutory and contractual contexts. Instead, a better analysis might focus on interpreting whether the statute or contract is meant to cover the situation at hand. Ultimately, as experience shows the potential for unintended use of the corporate form, legislatures have redrafted statutes, and parties have drafted contracts, to clarify their application to corporations in potentially abusive situations.[97]

Another problem regarding the separate entity status of corporations involves jurisdiction. Will the activities of subsidiary corporations in a state give the state a basis for asserting personal jurisdiction over the parent corporation?[98] We shall leave this question to works on civil procedure.

Finally, sometimes it is the shareholder (or a creditor of the shareholder) who seeks to have the court disregard the separate entity status of a corporation. For example, in one case,[99] a husband and wife placed their farm in a corporation. After both the corporation and the couple suffered a judgment against them, the couple sought to claim a homestead exemption in the farm. Since only individuals were entitled to such an exemption, this meant disregarding the fact that the couple owned a corporation which owned the farm. This is sometimes referred to as "reverse piercing." In this particular case the court was willing to reverse pierce. Nevertheless, courts are often not sympathetic to individuals who seek the advantages of corporate status and then to ask the court to disregard the corporation when the choice turns out to be a mistake.[100]

97. *See, e.g.,* Internal Revenue Code §§ 1561, 1563 (preventing income splitting at the lowest marginal rates between corporations under common ownership).

98. *See, e.g.,* Quarles v. Fuqua Indus., 504 F.2d 1358 (10th Cir.1974).

99. Cargill, Inc. v. Hedge, 375 N.W.2d 477 (Minn.1985).

100. *E.g.,* Gregory S. Crespi, *The Reverse Pierce Doctrine: Applying Appropriate Standards,* 16 J. Corp. L. 33 (1990).

Chapter II

FINANCIAL STRUCTURE

[Research References]

AmJur 2d, Corporations §§ 423–577

CJS, Corporations §§ 122–216

ALR Index: Capital Stock; Common Stock; Corporate Bonds and Bondholders; Corporate Stock and Stockholders; Uniform Stock Transfer Act

ALR Digest: Corporations §§ 174–220

Am Jur Legal Forms 2d, Corporations §§ 74:1941–74:2592

Am Jur Pleading and Practice Forms (Rev), Corporations §§ 57–125

47 POF3d 138, Liability of Shareholder for Wrongfully Transferring or Assigning Corporate Common Stock Shares to Third Party; 22 POF3d 559, Legal Malpractice in a Securities Offering

22 POF2d 593, Wrongful Failure of Corporate Directors to Declare Dividend; 11 POF2d 271, Failure to Disclose Material Facts to Stock Purchaser

---

In dealing with corporate formation in Chapter I, much of our focus was on the owners' hope to avoid personal liability for debts incurred in the venture. Yet, if parties embarking on a business venture expect the venture to end in failure under a pile of debt, they normally would not start the enterprise in the first place. Rather, parties generally embark upon a business venture because they expect it to make money. As the old saying goes, however, in order to make money, one must spend money. Hence, this chapter looks at the financial structure of the corporation, both in terms of acquiring the capital needed to make money and in terms of distributing the rewards of the venture to its owners.

§ 2.1 Issuing Stock

When a corporation "issues" (in other words sells) stock, two things happen: The corporation obtains money, property or whatever other consideration the buyers pay to the corporation for the stock, and the buyers become the owners of the corporation, known as stockholders or shareholders. This section looks at these two impacts. Following a chronological order, we start by looking at how the articles of incorporation define the ownership rights of the stock. Then, looking at the issuance itself, we will explore the legal rules governing the consideration which the corporation must receive for its shares. Finally, we turn to the situation in which the corporation has issued some stock and proposes to issue more. Specifically, we will look at the protections which the existing shareholders have against prejudice to their interest through the issuance of additional stock.

2.1.1 *Specifying the Rights of Shares*

a. The utility of creating classes of stock with different rights

Owners of any business must agree in some manner as to how they will divide among themselves the basic incidents of ownership, these being the right to obtain the wealth of the business and the right to exercise control over the venture. There are two ways to conceptualize dividing the right to obtain the wealth of the business. The bottom line question is what claims the various owners will have to any given distribution of money or property from the business, either during the ongoing course of the venture (which is often referred to as a current distribution), or upon the venture's termination (which is generally referred to as a liquidating distribution). Generally speaking, the two ultimate sources of these distributions are the profits made by the business, and the capital which the owners invested in the business.[1] Hence, owners often think in terms of how they will divide the business' profits, as well as their relative rights to the return of their invested capital.[2] With respect to control over the venture, the questions include what subjects will various owners have a voice in, and, in the event of disagreement among the owners, what vote by the owners is required for action and what is the relative voting power of the owners vis-a-vis each other.

In a partnership (or in various other non-corporate business forms, such as a limited partnership or limited liability company), the owners can answer questions about the allocation of wealth and power directly in a contract among themselves (typically called a partnership or limited partnership agreement or a limited liability company operating agreement). The agreement can specify what portion of the profits and distributions each owner is entitled to and what voting rights the various owners have. (If the agreement contains gaps, state statutes provide default rules.) Corporations work differently.

Traditionally in a corporation, there is no contract directly among the owners which expressly states which owner is entitled to what proportion of any distributions from the business and has what control.[3] Instead, in a corporation, the allocation of wealth and power flows from the ownership of stock. The basic idea behind stock is to create fungible

---

§ 2.1

1. In addition, a firm might borrow in order to fund a distribution. If the firm has the money to pay back such a loan, then the distribution ultimately comes from profits or the capital invested by the owners.

2. Specifying the relative rights to the return of invested capital allocates among the owners the burdens of bearing losses of the business, since the owner who stands last in line to receive the return of the owner's invested capital bears the risk of the first losses incurred by the business.

3. Owners of many closely held corporations attempt to deviate from this traditional norm and set out their rights in a contract among themselves. We shall discuss such shareholder agreements in a later chapter.

units of ownership, each one of which has the right to receive the same amount of distributions, and has the same voting power, as each other one of these fungible units. Under this scheme, the rights of specific owners to receive distributions, and the voting power of specific owners, depends simply on the relative holdings of these fungible units called shares or stock. Hence, if a corporation had three stockholders, each of whom owned one-third of the outstanding stock, each stockholder would be entitled to one-third of any distribution from the corporation, and each would have one-third of the voting power on any matter put before the stockholders for a vote (such as the election of directors to manage the company). Notice that the absolute number of shares owned by the stockholders does not matter; only their relative proportions. In other words, no rights hinge upon whether the three equal shareholders each own 100 shares, 1000 shares or 1 million shares.

As noted when discussing choice of business form in the beginning of this book, this scheme of specifying the rights of owners through their relative ownership of fungible units of stock is very useful in a firm with a large and constantly changing group of owners. It avoids both the need for owners to read an agreement to determine their rights, as well as the need to amend an agreement each time an owner transfers his or her interest (or any part of it) to someone else. Nevertheless, this scheme as presented so far has a serious weakness. It bundles different incidents of ownership together into a package to produce a result which often will be inconsistent with the desired agreement of the corporation's owners.

To illustrate this bundling problem it helps to look at several simple examples. To start with, assume two parties form a corporation to market some software. They agree that one party will contribute the software, which he has developed, while the other party will contribute $500,000 in cash to get the venture going. If the two parties decide that the software and the cash are equally important to the success of the business, they are likely to agree to share equally the profits from the venture. Moreover, they might conclude that there is no reason for one party to have a greater voice over running the business than the other party, and so agree to an equal division of voting power. This may lead them to agree to have the corporation issue the same number of shares to both parties—the cash contributor paying $500,000 for her shares, and the software developer contributing the software in exchange for his stock. Suppose, however, something happens soon after the parties start the venture (before the corporation has spent much of the $500,000) which causes the parties to decide to abandon the enterprise—say another company has beaten them to the punch with better software than they were planning to market (rendering the software in their corporation worthless). If both parties own an equal number of shares, and all shares have the same right to distributions from the corporation as all other shares, then the result is that each party is entitled to half of whatever is left over from the $500,000 which the cash contributor put into the venture. This is not likely to be what the cash contributor had in mind. The problem is that by having shares which are all the same, the parties have bundled together the allocation of their voting power, and their rights to distributions, regardless of whether the distributions reflect profits or a return of invested capital. By contrast, had the parties separately addressed these issues in a partnership, or limited liability company operating, agreement, they might have taken into account the different natures of their contributions in deciding how to allocate distributions which reflect a return of invested capital.

As another illustration of the problems from bundling, assume that there is a corporation with two owners—Constance and Lotto. Constance wants a steady flow of income from the corporation (which, say, is her sole source of income). Lotto is less concerned about achieving a steady flow of income from this investment (presumably because he has other sources of income), but instead wants to make a big killing. If the parties' business plan leads them to anticipate seven lean years and seven fat years, they might be inclined to make a trade between themselves. Lotto might offer to give Constance first crack at a set amount of current distributions from the corporation (so that Constance can get something during the lean years) in exchange for Constance giving Lotto most or all of the distributions above a certain level (so that Lotto gets a larger proportion of the income from the fat years). If all shares of stock have the same rights as all other shares of stock, Lotto and Constance would need to incorporate such a trade in a separate contract between themselves. Yet, if instead of having one person who wanted constant income and another more interested in a big killing, the corporation's shareholders consisted of many such parties, and if there is constant trading of the corporation's shares, then forcing parties to encapsulate their trade of distribution rights in separate contracts destroys the advantage of fungible units.

Finally, consider a corporation with two owners, Braveheart and Tremble, each of whom agrees to invest $500,000 in the venture. Assume that Tremble is much more afraid of losing his money than is Braveheart. Again, the two parties might agree to a trade. Braveheart might propose to Tremble that if the company loses money, the losses will come out of Braveheart's investment before they come out of Tremble's—or, put differently, Tremble will be entitled to distributions from the corporation which return Tremble's $500,000 before Braveheart is entitled to distributions from the company which return any of Braveheart's $500,-000. Naturally, Braveheart would want something in return for this agreement, such as a greater share of the income made by the corporation. Once again, if all shares of stock have the same rights as all other shares of stock, Braveheart and Tremble would need to encapsulate their trade in a separate contract between themselves—which would be a pain if the corporation had numerous stockholders like Braveheart and Tremble and constant trading of stock.

These three examples illustrate the utility of deviating from the idea that all shares should have the same rights as all other shares, and, instead, creating different types or "classes" of stock. The notion is that all shares of a class would have the same rights as all other shares of this class, but that different classes of stock would have different rights to distributions, or different voting power, from other classes. One governing document can specify the differing rights between these classes, with the result that the company can accommodate desired tradeoffs between owners in terms of distribution and voting rights, and, at the same time, not lose the advantage of free trading which comes from fungible units of ownership.

b. Drafting articles to define the rights of classes of stock

The basic default rule governing the relative rights of stock is that all shares have the same rights as all other shares unless the articles of incorporation create classes of stock, in which case the articles specify the rights of the classes vis-a-vis the other classes.[4] Hence, defining the rights of different classes of shares is a matter of drafting (and, if unfortunately necessary, interpreting) the articles.[5]

In addressing the right to obtain the wealth of the business, corporate articles focus on the bottom line question of the relative claims to current and liquidating distributions from the corporation, rather than directly allocate profits and the right to return of invested capital. "Dividends" is the traditional term for current distributions from a corporation. A very simple example of differing dividend rights would be for a corporation's articles to authorize two classes of shares, and entitle shares of one class to receive twice (or some other multiple) as much per share of any dividend as shares of the other class. (In other words, if the board votes to have the corporation pay a dividend of $1 per share for the disfavored class, the corporation must pay $2 per share for the favored class.) Of course, one could achieve the same effect using only one class of stock by giving some shareholders twice as many shares. Hence, creating a class of stock which is merely entitled to some greater multiple of any dividend than shares of another class is generally not useful or often done.

Far more useful, and frequently found, is to create one or more classes of stock which have the right to receive a certain amount of dividends before the company may distribute any dividend to shareholders of other classes. For example the articles may authorize two classes of stock and entitle one class to receive a dividend of $5 per share before the board can vote to have the corporation pay a dividend for the other

---

4. *See, e.g.*, M.B.C.A. § 6.01; Del. Gen. Corp. Law §§ 102(a)(4).

5. An exception to specifying the rights of shares in the articles exists by virtue of statutes which provide that the articles can contain what is sometimes referred to as a blank check stock authorization. Under a blank check term, the articles authorize the corporation to issue a class of stock, but the articles do not specify the rights of the class (or the articles specify some, but not other, rights). The blank check provision then authorizes the board of directors to specify the rights of the stock at the time the board votes to have the corporation sell the shares. Moreover, the blank check provision normally authorizes the board to create subdivisions within the class—typically called "series"—which will have different rights from shares within other series. The idea is to give the board flexibility to set different rights of shares in order to react to changing market conditions at the time the corporation needs to issue additional stock.

class. The right to receive dividends before another class of stock typically is referred to as a dividend preference, and, accordingly, shares having such a right usually are called "preferred." (Shares without a preference generally are known as "common"—as in ordinary. Hence, if the articles do not create multiple classes of stock, then all shares are common.) Notice how in the illustration above involving Constance, who desired a steady source of income, and Lotto, who was more interested in a big killing, use of stock with a dividend preference could enable the parties to carry out their desired trade. Specifically, Constance could obtain stock with a dividend preference—which means that she will get the first crack at any distributions from the corporation during either the lean or fat years—while Lotto can receive common stock which would entitle him to receive most of the corporate dividends during the fat years.

Drafting a dividend preference in the articles requires answering a number of questions. The most obvious is what is the amount of the preference. The example above referred to a preference of $5 per share. (Sometimes, the articles specify the amount as a percentage of par value. This is simply another way of giving a dollar amount.) Yet, simply specifying a dollar amount begs a fundamental question: Is this the actual sum payable each time the corporation pays a dividend before the common shares may receive any money? If so, the relative claims of the preferred shares to corporate earnings vis-a-vis the common would be radically different depending upon whether the board voted to have the corporation pay a dividend every quarter, yearly, or only once in several years. For this reason, articles often specify the preference as an amount accruing over a period of time (such as $5 per year). Taking this step raises further issues for the drafter to address. Suppose the corporation has no earnings (or insufficient earnings to cover the preference amount) during the period specified. Does the sum still accrue?[6] Closely related to this question is the question of what happens if the board declares a dividend less often than the accrual period—in other words, if it skips dividends. This could occur either because the corporation lacked earnings to cover the dividend, or because the directors chose to reinvest earnings rather than have the corporation pay a dividend. If the articles state that the preferred stock is "cumulative," this means that the articles require the corporation to distribute all of the arrearage (the accumulated skipped dividends) before paying any dividends on the junior shares. If the articles state that the preferred is non-cumulative, skipped dividends are lost, and the company need only pay the preference amount for the present period before declaring a dividend for the other shares.[7] Notice the conflict-of-interest between the classes created

---

6. *See, e.g.,* Fawkes v. Farm Lands Co., 112 Cal.App. 374, 297 P. 47 (1931) (holding that dividends accrue even if the corporation has no earnings, so long as the preferred is cumulative and the articles say nothing to the contrary).

7. *E.g.,* Guttman v. Illinois Central R. Co., 189 F.2d 927 (2d Cir.1951). In *Sanders v. Cuba Railroad Co.,* 21 N.J. 78, 120 A.2d 849 (1956), however, the New Jersey Supreme Court interpreted non-cumulative preferred to still be entitled to skipped divi-

by issuing non-cumulative preferred shares. The directors can increase the proportion of corporate earnings going to the common shares by omitting dividends. For example, if directors have the corporation pay an annual dividend, then, in 10 years, stock with a dividend preference of $5 per share will have received a total of $50 per share before the corporation could pay dividends to the common. If, however, the directors only declare one dividend in 10 years, then each share of $5 non-cumulative preferred will have received only $5 in preferred dividends during the 10 year period, leaving way more money to pay dividends to the common shareholders. This conflict-of-interest problem is compounded if the non-cumulative preferred shares lack the right to vote for directors and thereby influence the board's decision. Given this problem, it is not surprising that most courts interpret ambiguous article provisions as making the preferred cumulative.[8]

Having specified the preference amount, one question remains regarding the preferred's rights to dividends. This is whether the preferred is entitled to any further distribution after it receives the preference amount. If the articles give the stock no right to receive dividends beyond the stated preference, the preferred stock often is called "non-participating". "Participating" preferred is entitled to receive additional dividends under terms specified by the articles. These provisions sometimes call for a certain amount of money to go to the common before the common and participating preferred stock share any additional dividends. Moreover, each share could receive an equal amount of additional dividends, or the articles may give shares of some classes a greater proportion than others. If the articles are silent, courts disagree as to whether or not preferred shares participate in further dividends.[9] Essentially, courts in this instance must choose between the view that all shares are entitled to the same rights unless the articles specify a difference—in which case, silence leads to participation in further dividends—and the view that the normal tradeoff for preferred dividends is to give up participation in dividends beyond the preference amount.

Articles also may differentiate between classes of shares in terms of their rights to liquidating distributions. As discussed with dividend rights, the articles simply could entitle some shares to receive a greater proportion per share of any liquidating distribution than other shares (for instance, $2 per share for one class, for every dollar received per share by the other class). Again, however, this generally does not do much that giving some parties additional shares would not accomplish. Much more useful, and frequently found, are provisions entitling a class

dends from the years when the corporation had earnings sufficient to pay the dividend, unless the articles clearly disavowed any such right. The impact of the New Jersey court's interpretation is to create an equivalent result to articles which provide for cumulative preferred dividends, but do not have the preferred dividends accrue unless the corporation has the earnings to fund the dividends. Such an article provision is sometimes referred to as "cumulative if earned."

8. *See, e.g.,* Hazel Atlas Glass Co. v. Van Dyk & Reeves, 8 F.2d 716 (2d Cir.1925).

9. *Compare* Englander v. Osborne, 261 Pa. 366, 104 A. 614 (1918), *with* St. Louis Southwestern Railway Co. v. Loeb, 318 S.W.2d 246 (Mo.1958).

of shares to receive a certain amount of money from the corporation upon liquidation before the company may pay anything to other shares. This is known as a liquidation preference, and, accordingly, such shares again are referred to as "preferred". (Keep in mind, however, that preferred shares can possess a liquidation preference and no dividend preference, or vice versa.)

Liquidation preferences can serve three purposes. The first purpose is to disconnect the right to return of invested capital from the division of profit (and even from voting control). Recall the example earlier of where a party contributing cash to a corporation agreed to share profits and control equally with a party contributing software (the value of which is highly speculative) to the corporation. For the reason illustrated by that example, it could make sense for the parties to agree that, upon liquidation, the corporation will return the cash contributor's investment before the software contributor receives anything. Issuing the cash provider stock with a liquidation preference equal to its issue price can accomplish this objective. The parties can then divide the common stock in order to achieve their desired equal sharing of profit and control. This is also handy when some parties contribute services to the corporation, while other parties contribute cash.

The second goal achieved by liquidation preferences involves the allocation of losses. Recall in the example involving Tremble and Braveheart, how Braveheart might propose to assume greater risk of loss in exchange for a larger share of profits. To accomplish this objective, the corporation could issue to Tremble shares having a liquidation preference equal to the $500,000 Tremble will pay for his shares, while Braveheart will receive common shares in exchange for her $500,000. In this manner, the first losses will use up Braveheart's contribution (since the first $500,000 of whatever is left in the business after a business failure will go to Tremble). At the same time, by adjusting the number of the common versus preferred shares issued to the two parties, or the rights to dividends of the two classes, Braveheart can receive a greater share of the dividends.

The third objective of a liquidation preference is to allocate profits. Even successful corporations may eventually dissolve (perhaps after selling their assets to a bigger company). Much, if not most, of the dissolved corporation's assets will represent the accumulation of retained earnings which the directors reinvested in the business rather than distributed as dividends. At this point, it is important to recognize a relationship between dividend and liquidation rights. With only one class of stock, each share will obtain its pro-rata amount of all profits made by the corporation, whether paid as dividends or retained until liquidation. Suppose, however, the parties introduce a class of stock with a dividend preference (even one that is cumulative), but no preference on liquidation. In this event, earnings which would go to the preferred holders if paid as dividends, the common will share if the company skipped dividends and retained the earnings until its liquidation.[10] Beyond the evident problem of fairness, one practical difficulty which this shift in earnings creates is that it may tempt the board to liquidate the company—perhaps after selling the company's assets to a shell corporation set up just for this purpose—in order to favor one class over the other. For these reasons, corporate articles normally try to coordinate dividend and liquidation preferences so that each share's claim against earnings remains the same regardless of whether distributed as dividends or in liquidation. Hence, preferred stock with cumulative dividend rights typically will have a liquidation preference (beyond return of its issue price) for an amount equal to any dividends in arrears. Incidentally, it is only with respect to this third objective (profit allocation) that there is any logical necessity for preferred stock to possess both a dividend and a liquidation preference.

With these goals in mind, the drafter of a liquidation preference can answer analogous questions to those raised when specifying a dividend preference. Again, the first question is what is the amount of the preference. This relates to its purpose. If the purpose is either to sever the connection between the profit division and the right to return of invested capital, or to allocate losses, then the preference amount is normally the issue price of the stock. If the purpose is to ensure the allocation of profits in conformity with a dividend preference, then an amount equal to any arrearage seems sensible. Of course, both these purposes often overlap, in which case one can simply add the two sums together. Having set the preference amount, one must consider again whether the shares can participate in any further distribution. This may logically call for parallel treatment to that provided for dividend distributions, lest the board be tempted to liquidate in order to shift income between classes. (First, however, one may wish to return to the common holders the issue price of the common, since only after this is done do the remaining sums represent retained earnings.) As in the case of dividends, failure to specify whether the preferred participates in liquidating distributions beyond the preference amount can lead to litigation.[11] Another question which can lead to dispute is when is there a "liquidation" within the meaning of the articles. For example, does a merger in which all shareholders receive cash for their shares equal a liquidation for purposes of triggering a liquidation preference?[12]

We will consider the uses of differing voting rights between classes of shares at several points in this book. For example, we shall see that the use of shares classified by different voting rights can be helpful to ensure that minority shareholders retain representation on the board of a closely held corporation. For present purposes, it is sufficient to point

10. *See, e.g.,* Wouk v. Merin, 283 App. Div. 522, 128 N.Y.S.2d 727 (1954).

11. *See, e.g.,* Mohawk Carpet Mills, Inc. v. Delaware Rayon Co., 35 Del.Ch. 51, 110 A.2d 305 (Ch. 1954) (denying participation when not stated).

12. *See, e.g.,* Rothschild Intl. Corp. v. Liggett Group, Inc., 474 A.2d 133 (Del. 1984) (holding that a merger did not equal a liquidation for purposes of triggering a liquidation preference).

out some possible relationships between dividend preferences and voting rights. Articles often deny preferred shares the right to vote; albeit there is no legal requirement that preferred be non-voting, and if the articles are silent they can vote.[13] Also, statutes may require the vote of the holders of preferred stock, even if otherwise non-voting, to approve certain fundamental changes (such as amending the articles, or mergers), particularly if the change prejudices the preferred shareholders' rights as a class.[14] Articles frequently draw one connection between dividend preferences and voting rights which may be logical if the preferred are otherwise non-voting. This is to provide contingent voting rights if the corporation skips a certain number of dividends. Such contingent rights might range from exclusive power to elect the entire board, to a right to elect just some directors, to simply a right to have one vote per share like the common.

Articles sometimes make preferred shares convertible into shares of another class (typically common). A convertible share allows its owner to exchange the share for shares of another class of corporate stock. By having preferred convertible into common, the holder may claim the advantage of the dividend preference to obtain a greater portion of a low level of corporate earnings (and even decrease his or her risk of loss through a liquidation preference should things go badly), yet, if the corporation does very well, he or she can convert the stock into common and enjoy a greater share of higher levels of corporate earnings. Notice, however, one could accomplish roughly the same objective by issuing participating (rather than convertible) preferred. While the normal pattern of convertible stock is to go from preferred to common, holders of common stock might desire a right to convert to preferred if things go poorly. Many statutes, however, prohibit such upstream conversion.[15]

The articles which authorize convertible preferred normally specify when and how owners may exercise their conversion rights—in other words, when is the first and last time the owner can convert (assuming the right does not run from date of issuance until liquidation), and what type of notice must the owner give to do so. Of critical importance, the articles specify the conversion ratio—i.e. how many shares of common (or whatever other class the conversion is into) does the owner receive for each share of preferred surrendered. In this regard, problems result when the articles neglect to address what happens if the number of common increases due to stock splits, stock dividends, or other additional issuances.[16]

---

13. *E.g.*, M.B.C.A. § 7.21(a). The rationale for denying preferred shareholders voting rights is that, because they have less risk, and, if non-participating, less potential for gain, the owners of preferred do not have as much incentive to maximize the corporation's fortunes as do the common holders.

14. *E.g.*, M.B.C.A. §§ 10.04, 11.03(f).

15. *E.g.*, N.Y. Bus. Corp. Law § 519(a)(1). *But see* Del. Gen. Corp. Law. § 151(b),(e); M.B.C.A. § 6.01(c)(2).

16. *See, e.g.*, Pratt v. American Bell Tel. Co., 141 Mass. 225, 5 N.E. 307 (1886) (the court refused to increase the number of shares which a convertible security holder would receive, in order to offset a stock split, when the conversion right did not

Turning from the rights of the preferred stockholders, to the rights of the corporation vis-a-vis the preferred stockholders, many articles authorizing preferred give the company the option to redeem the shares (in other words, buy the shares back) at a certain price.[17] There are a number of reasons to give a corporation the option to repurchase its shares. Many of these reasons have to do with problems attendant upon share transfers in a closely held corporation, and, accordingly, will be explored in a later chapter of this book dealing with the special problems of closely held corporations. With respect to redeemable preferred, redeemability serves to put something of a cap on the amount of the corporation's profits going to those holding the redeemable stock. For example, the corporation might choose to redeem the preferred when the corporation can raise money at a lesser claim against its profits, for example by issuing new stock with a smaller dividend preference. This is analogous to the reason individuals refinance their mortgage.

The terms of a redemption provision sometimes can raise questions. For example, when can the corporation exercise its right to redeem?[18] Also, what notice must the company give?[19] This notice is especially important if the shareholders have conversion rights which they could exercise in lieu of redemption. Of obvious importance is the redemption price. At a minimum, this will equal the issue price, plus, for reasons analogous to those discussed when dealing with liquidation preferences, any arrearage in dividends. Typically, there is some premium above this sum as well. If the company wishes flexibility to redeem less than the entire class, the question arises as to how the corporation will choose (for example, by lot) which shares to redeem.[20] Finally, what rights (particularly if the shares are convertible) do the stockholders have between the time the company announces that it will redeem and the surrender of the shares?[21] Incidentally, many statutes authorize the issuance of shares redeemable at the owner's (rather than the corporation's) option.[22] Also to benefit owners of redeemable stock, some articles contain provisions

specifically provide this protection against dilution).

17. Articles granting a company the option to redeem common are rare, and they may not be valid under some state corporation statutes. *See, e.g.,* Starring v. American Hair & Felt Co., 21 Del.Ch. 380, 191 A. 887 (1937), *aff'd,* 21 Del.Ch. 431, 2 A.2d 249. *But see* Cal. Corp. Code § 402 (allowing redeemable common if another class of common is not redeemable); M.B.C.A. § 6.01(c)(2) (not drawing a distinction between redeemable common and preferred). As discussed in a later chapter of this book, however, corporations might enter into side contracts with the purchasers of common (or preferred), giving the company the option to repurchase the stock upon certain circumstances.

18. *See, e.g.,* Thompson v. Fairleigh, 300 Ky. 144, 187 S.W.2d 812 (1945) (when the

articles specified the initial, but not the final, time the corporation had the right to redeem, the court held that the corporation must redeem, if at all, within a reasonable time after the option became available).

19. *See, e.g.,* Van Gemert v. Boeing Co., 520 F.2d 1373 (2d Cir.1975) (dealing with convertible debentures).

20. *See, e.g.,* State v. Miller–Wohl Co., 42 Del. 73, 28 A.2d 148 (1942) (dispute over how to interpret a provision which called for selection of shares to redeem "by lot, pro-rata or otherwise, as determined by the directors").

21. *See, e.g.,* M.B.C.A. § 7.21(d) (not allowing redeemed shares to vote after the company mails notice and deposits funds to cover redemption).

22. *E.g.,* M.B.C.A. § 6.01(c)(2).

requiring the corporation to set aside periodically a certain amount of money to fund redemptions of the preferred—a so-called sinking fund.

2.1.2 *Consideration for Shares*

For many years, rules governing the consideration which corporations must receive in exchange for issuing stock occupied an important role in corporate law. There are a couple of reasons for this. To begin with, given the principle that the shareholders' liability for corporate debts ordinarily only extends to the loss of whatever the shareholders paid for their stock, it seemed natural to create rules governing the amount which shareholders must pay in order to purchase stock from the corporation. In addition, the history of corporations is strewn with cases in which persons in control of a corporation had the company issue to themselves large quantities of stock, while paying little or nothing for the stock. The temptation for such conduct is especially strong since issuing stock is a little like printing money, in that, other than the impact on the value of other shares of stock, issuing stock generally does not cost the corporation anything. The traditional approach to address these concerns has been to establish limits on the acceptable type and amount of consideration which a corporation must receive for its stock. Over time, the importance of these limits has receded substantially as the law increasingly has looked to other approaches to deal with concerns once addressed by rules governing acceptable consideration for shares. For example, earlier in this book, we explored protecting corporate creditors by piercing the corporate veil based upon inadequate capitalization. Later in this book, we shall examine fiduciary duty constraints on conflict-of-interest transactions, and securities law requirements for full and honest disclosure to future investors, both of which can deal with the issuance of cheap stock to those in control of the corporation. Still, despite the decline in utility of rules governing consideration for stock, corporate attorneys must be aware of these limits.

a. *Permissible consideration*

The basic rule found in most corporation statutes is that a corporation can issue stock in exchange for whatever consideration the board of directors decides (or for whatever consideration the shareholders decide if the articles empower the shareholders, rather than the board, to decide upon the terms for issuing stock).[23] The statutes, however, traditionally have imposed two constraints upon this authority.

Traditionally, corporations statutes (or, in some cases, state constitutions) have limited the types of consideration for which a corporation can issue its stock. Money is always okay. Property, and even services, once the services have been rendered, are also generally acceptable.[24]

---

23. *E.g.*, M.B.C.A. § 6.21; Del. Gen. Corp. Law § 153.

24. This, of course, assumes that the services were rendered for the benefit of the corporation. *E.g.*, Clark v. Cowart, 445

So.2d 884 (Ala.1984). Some uncertainty exists when the past services consist of the efforts of promoters on behalf of a corporation prior to its formation. *See, e.g.*, Lofland v. Cahall, 118 A. 1 (Del.1922). The logical

Traditionally unacceptable, however, have been promises to pay the corporation for the stock in the future (in other words, a promissory note) and promises to perform services for the corporation in the future.[25]

One possible rationale for prohibiting the issuance of stock for future services or promissory notes is that such consideration does not provide anything for creditors of the corporation to seize if the company fails. This rationale is rather silly. Issuing stock for services already performed, or even for money to the extent that the corporation then spends the funds, also commonly leaves nothing for creditors of a failed company. (Actually, the issuance of stock for a promissory note may be more likely to leave something for creditors than issuing stock for cash, since the creditors might latch onto the corporation's right to enforce the note, whereas the corporation could already have spent the cash.) Another possible concern with issuing stock for promissory notes or promises of future services is that those in control of the corporation can thereby acquire large quantities of stock without any immediate payment. One might worry that this could prejudice the other shareholders. Yet, in many cases, it may be in the interest of the corporation and all of its shareholders to issue stock for promissory notes or future services; for example, issuing stock for future services can allow a new company to obtain critical services without having to pay cash. Overall, given the questionable rationales behind the prohibition on issuing shares for promissory notes and future services, it is not surprising that the 1984 revision of the Model Business Corporations Act dropped this restriction and allows the issuance of stock for any type of consideration.[26]

The limitation on acceptable types of consideration for issuing stock can lead to questions when individuals transfer various items of intangible "property"—such as business plans, third party loan commitments, and technical know-how—to the company. Given both the intangible nature of such items, as well as the fact that such items might simply reflect a euphemism for future services or promissory notes,[27] there

---

answer here is that if the corporation benefited sufficiently from these preincorporation services to justify the corporation's paying cash to the promoter (despite the lack of a contractual obligation to do so), there seems little reason why the corporation should be unable to issue stock for such services.

25. *E.g.*, Cal. Corp. Code § 409(a). Many statutes express this limit only in an oblique manner. These statutes refer to stock issued for money, property or labor done as "fully paid and nonassessable." *E.g.*, Del. Gen. Corp. Law § 152. By negative implication, shares issued for promissory notes or promises of future services are not fully paid and nonassessable. *E.g.*, Scully v. Automobile Fin. Co., 109 A. 49 (Del. 1920). *But see* Petrishen v. Westmoreland

Fin. Corp., 394 Pa. 552, 147 A.2d 392 (Pa. 1959). At first glance, one might say that this "fully paid and nonassessable" language is a tautology, rather than a prohibition on issuing stock for promissory notes and future services. After all, stock issued for a promissory note or a promise of future services is, in a very real sense, not yet paid for. As we shall see, however, the impact of stock not being fully paid and nonassessable goes beyond simply giving the corporation a right to collect upon the promissory note, or the promise of future services, which the company received for the shares.

26. M.B.C.A. § 6.21(b).

27. For instance, reference to know-how could refer, in reality, to the transferor's future efforts to use this know-how on behalf of the corporation.

often can occur litigation over whether such items, in fact, represent property within the meaning of the corporation statute.[28]

An easy method to circumvent restrictions on acceptable types of consideration for stock is for the corporation to issue shares at a very low price, paid in cash. This, in turn, brings us to the second constraint traditionally imposed upon the power of the board (or the shareholders) to set the consideration which the corporation will receive for issuing stock. This constraint deals with the amount of consideration which a corporation must receive for its shares. There are several aspects to this constraint. To begin with, implicit in the statutes empowering the board to specify the consideration which the corporation will receive for its stock is the notion that the corporation must receive some consideration for stock. In other words, the board cannot vote to have the corporation simply give away stock.[29] (Stock given for no consideration is sometimes referred to as bonus stock.)

A more involved aspect of the constraint on the amount of consideration which a corporation must receive for its stock arises from the concept of par value. We encountered par value earlier in discussing the mechanics of incorporation. Historically, corporation statutes required the articles of incorporation to specify a par value for the corporation's shares. Par value is simply a dollar amount per share which the drafters include as part of the provision in the corporation's articles describing the stock which the corporation is authorized to issue (or, if the articles authorize the corporation to issue more than one class of stock, the articles will contain such a dollar amount as the par for each class of stock which the corporation can issue). The drafters can make this dollar amount large (say $1000 per share); they can make this dollar amount small (say $.01 per share); there is no legal rule as to what this amount must be. There are several impacts to this amount. One impact of practical note is that some states have imposed a tax on firms incorporated in the state based upon the par value of the corporation's authorized shares—the higher the par, the greater the tax. A second impact is that par value serves as a measuring device to constrain the ability of a corporation's directors to declare dividends which would represent a refund of the shareholders' investment rather than a distribution of the company's earnings. We shall discuss this later in this chapter. What is important about par value for present purposes is that the amount which the articles state to be par constitutes the minimum price for which the corporation legally can issue its shares. In other words, if the par value of stock set by the articles is $1000 per share, corporation statutes forbid the corporation from issuing its stock for less than $1000 per share; if the par value is $.01 per share, the corporation cannot issue

28. *E.g.*, Trotta v. Metalmold Corp., 139 Conn. 668, 96 A.2d 798 (1953) (unpatented ideas held not to constitute property that was acceptable consideration for shares).

29. *E.g.*, Andrews v. Chase, 89 Utah 51, 49 P.2d 938 (Utah 1935). Note, however, that common shares issued as a bonus to induce the purchase of other corporate securities seemingly have consideration for their issuance. *E.g.*, In re Associated Oil Co., 289 F. 693 (6th Cir.1923). *But see* Hopper v. Brodie, 134 Md. 290, 106 A. 700 (Md. 1919).

the shares for less than $.01 per share.[30] (Stock issued at a price less than par is sometimes referred to as discount stock.) It is important to keep in mind that par value only constitutes a minimum price; the directors are free to have the corporation charge any greater amount. Moreover, par value only constrains the price which the corporation must charge in issuing its stock; it has no impact at all on the price for which shareholders can resell their stock.

The notion that a corporation's articles should specify a minimum price which future directors must charge for a corporation's stock, when the drafters of the articles essentially select this amount out of thin air, and especially when the directors have discretion to charge any greater sum for the stock, seems strange. After all, what does it accomplish when, as is commonly done, articles can specify a low par (such as $.01 per share) for stock which the directors plan to sell at $10 per share? Accordingly, it is not surprising that corporations statutes some time ago came to allow articles to state that the corporation's shares are without par value—in other words, no-par shares. The directors can issue no-par shares for whatever amount of consideration (as long as there is some consideration) the directors think appropriate.[31] More recently, starting in California, and spreading to the Model Act, statutes have moved to abolish the whole concept of par value. Such statutes do not call for the articles either to specify a par value for stock or to state that the shares have no par value, and these statutes do not impose a legal minimum price on the issuance of stock (other that there be some consideration).[32]

If par value represents a rather strange and increasingly archaic limit on the quantity of consideration which a corporation must receive for its stock, the same is not true of the concept that the corporation, in fact, should receive the consideration for which the directors issued the stock. In other words, if directors vote to issue stock for $100 per share,

---

30. *E.g.*, Del. Corp. Code § 153(a). *See also* Rickerson Roller–Mill Co. v. Farrell Foundry & Mach. Co., 75 F. 554 (6th Cir. 1896) (holding that directors cannot have the corporation issue shares at less than par even in the absence of a statute stating that par is the minimum price at which a corporation can issue its shares). *But see* Handley v. Stutz, 139 U.S. 417, 11 S.Ct. 530 (1891) (holding that in the absence of a statute forbidding the corporation from issuing shares at less than par, directors may have a corporation, which is conducting an ongoing business, and which is in disparate need of more funds, issue stock at less than par when this is the best price available). Because corporation statutes typically state that par value is the minimum price at which a corporation can "issue" its shares, courts generally hold that this limitation does not apply to the corporation's sale of "treasury shares"—in other words, stock which the corporation issued and then

bought back and now seeks to resell. *E.g.*, Henderson v. Plymouth Oil Co., 141 A. 197 (Del.1928).

31. *E.g.*, Del. Gen. Corp. Code § 153(b). Because many of the states which taxed corporations based upon the par value of the corporation's stock deemed no-par shares to have a fairly high par for purposes of this tax, use of no-par shares turned out to be less popular than one might have expected. Instead, drafters of articles in such states often set extremely low par values for the corporation's stock in order, in part, to minimize such taxes.

32. *E.g.*, Cal. Corp. Code § 409; M.B.C.A. § 6.21. These statutes do not forbid drafters from stating a par value in the corporation's articles; instead, these statutes remove from such a statement the traditional significance which corporate law attached to par value.

the corporation, in fact, should sell the stock for $100 per share.[33] This works simply enough when the consideration for stock constitutes cash. A difficulty can arise, however, when the directors vote to have the corporation issue shares in exchange for non-cash consideration, such as property. The problem is that both conventional practice, as well as many traditional corporation statutes, call for directors to place a value on the property or other non-cash consideration which a corporation receives for issuing stock.[34] This raises the question as to what the consequences are if the property or other non-cash consideration, in fact, turns out to be worth less than the value the directors specified. (No one ever complains if the consideration turns out to be worth more than the directors specified. Shares issued for overvalued property or other over-valued non-cash consideration are often referred to as watered stock—albeit, the term watered stock might refer also to bonus or discount shares.[35])

Deciding upon an appropriate resolution of the problem of over-valued non-cash consideration for shares presents a couple of difficulties. From a purely analytical standpoint, one might ask if the corporation received the consideration for which the directors issued the stock. In one sense, the corporation clearly did, so long as the company actually received the property or other non-cash consideration. Yet, in another sense, the corporation did not receive the consideration specified for the shares, since it did not receive property or other non-cash consideration worth what the directors stated the corporation would receive for the shares. More fundamentally, from a practical standpoint, the problem of overvalued consideration presents a serious tension. On the one hand, overvaluation of property received for shares creates a much more realistic prospect for prejudice to later corporate creditors and sharehold-ers than does the corporation's receipt of cash consideration which is less than par. The reason is that the valuation set by the board for the property will appear on the corporation's financial statements, making the corporation's assets appear to be worth more than they are. This might convince parties to extend credit to, or purchase shares from, the corporation on terms to which these parties otherwise would not have agreed. Indeed, the suspicion is strong that this is the reason why the directors set a high value on the property received by the corporation. On the other hand, valuation of property or other non-cash consideration is generally more of an art than a science. Hence, penalizing parties when directors set a value with which a court later disagrees could make life unreasonably dangerous for directors who approve the issuance of stock for any consideration other than cash, and for parties who ex-change property for stock.

33. *See, e.g.,* M.B.C.A. § 6.22(a).

34. *E.g.,* Cal. Corp. Code § 409(e). *But see* M.B.C.A. § 6.21(c) (not requiring the directors to value the noncash consideration received for shares).

35. The term watered stock apparently originated as a metaphor from the practice of having cattle drink lots of water, in order increase their weight, right before the cattle were weighed for sale.

Some time ago, there were a few courts who applied what is known as the strict value rule to the problem of overvalued non-cash consideration received for stock. Under this approach, shares constituted improperly issued watered stock if the court later found that the directors overvalued the consideration which the corporation received for the shares, regardless of whether the directors knew that the value was (at least in the court's later view) inflated.[36] This strict approach, however, has passed into history. The contemporary approach in many jurisdictions comes from statutes which state that the board of directors' determination as to the value of consideration received for stock is conclusive in the absence of fraud.[37] Fraud generally refers to a knowing or intentional overvaluation.[38]

These "conclusive absent fraud" statutes create a couple of problems. To begin with, how can a court know whether the directors knowingly or intentionally overvalued the consideration? Unless the directors foolishly admit that they did not really believe in the accuracy of the valuation they specified, the court must infer the directors' state of mind based upon the objective circumstances. Hence, even though the absence of fraud approach is essentially subjective, evidence as to the consideration's objective value might, in gross cases, show knowing overvaluation.

A second problem with the "conclusive absent fraud" statutes lies in determining their impact upon possible challenges against the directors based upon general fiduciary duties. A later chapter of this book will explore the duties of care and loyalty of corporate directors. For now, it is sufficient to note that a decision by the board of directors to purchase property for the corporation could breach the directors' duty of care if the directors, for example, were grossly negligent in investigating the worth of the property before agreeing to the purchase price.[39] Moreover, if the transaction involves a conflict-of-interest—for instance, the directors vote to have the corporation purchase property from the directors themselves—then the directors will breach their duty of loyalty unless the transaction receives disinterested approval or the directors prove

36. *E.g.*, William E. Dee Co. v. Proviso Coal Co., 290 Ill. 252, 125 N.E. 24 (Ill. 1919). Many other courts, however, have upheld the directors' valuation so long as the directors acted in good faith. *E.g.*, Coit v. North Carolina Gold Amalgamating Co., 119 U.S. 343, 7 S.Ct. 231 (1886).

37. *E.g.*, Del. Corp. Code § 152. The revised Model Act makes the directors' decision as to the adequacy of consideration received for stock conclusive for purposes of determining whether the shares are validly issued and nonassessable, without any express caveat for fraud. M.B.C.A. § 6.21(c). This evidently reflects the notion that since the new Model Act does not call for the directors to value the consideration which

the corporation receives for shares, there is no reason for the provision which deals with share issuance to address fraudulent overvaluation of non-cash consideration for stock. Since this provision only concerns whether the shares are validly issued and nonassessable, it presumably would not protect directors, who knowingly inflate the value shown for corporate assets on the corporate financial statements, from liability for fraud.

38. *E.g.*, Diamond State Brewery, Inc. v. De La Rigaudiere, 17 A.2d 313 (Del.Ch. 1941).

39. See § 4.1.2 *infra*.

that the transaction is fair to the corporation.[40] A simple-minded reading of the conclusive absent fraud statutes might suggest that these rules involving the duties of care and loyalty, which would apply if the directors have the corporation purchase property for cash, will not apply if the directors have the corporation purchase property for stock—in which event, all that the directors must do is to avoid fraud. Yet, it makes little sense to water down the directors' fiduciary duties because a transaction involves paying in stock, rather than in cash. Hence, it is not surprising that courts have rejected the argument that these statutes trump the normal rules of director fiduciary duty.[41]

One interesting aspect of these various rules regarding the amount of consideration for shares is that they do not require the corporation to receive any amount of capital at all. In other words, if the corporation issues few, if any, shares, at little or no par value, the corporation can comply with these statutes and still end up with virtually no capital investment from its owners. If legislatures were concerned with assuring some level of shareholder investment for the protection of the corporation's creditors, this seems to be a strange way of going about it. At one time, a large number of state statutes took a more direct approach. They required a corporation to have a minimum amount of paid in capital before undertaking business.[42] The amounts set by these statutes were typically modest: $1000 was a common minimum. These statutes, with a few exceptions, have disappeared—presumably based upon the recognition that it is impossible to specify one minimum level of capital which will not be unnecessarily large for corporations conducting very small operations, but not ridiculously small for corporations conducting more substantial ventures.

b. Consequences of issuing stock for improper consideration

The potential impact of issuing stock for improper consideration depends upon whether the corporation is a failure. If the corporation is a

---

40. See § 4.2.1 *infra.*

41. *E.g.*, Pipelife Corp. v. Bedford, 145 A.2d 206 (Del.Ch.1958) (holding that the court can rescind the directors' purchase of stock from the corporation, when the directors fail to prove that the transaction is fair, despite an absence of fraud in valuing the consideration received by the corporation for the stock). One might also reach this result by interpreting the term "fraud" to encompass a breach of fiduciary duty. Indeed, occasionally courts will refer to unfair conflict-of-interest transactions as constituting "fraud" or "constructive fraud." See § 4.3.5 *infra.* This linguistic method of reconciling the "absence of fraud" statutes with the normal rules of fiduciary duty becomes more difficult, however, if the statute in question makes the directors' judgment as to the value of consideration received for stock conclusive in the absence of "actual

fraud." The revised Model Act is somewhat better written to avoid this issue. It states that the judgment of the directors is conclusive for purposes of determining if the stock is validly issued, fully paid and nonassessable. This leaves open challenges for other purposes, such as liability for breach of fiduciary duty (assuming, of course, that breach of fiduciary duty does not render the shares invalidly issued within the meaning of the Model Act).

42. *E.g.*, M.B.C.A. (1966 revision) § 51. Authorities have differed as to whether the failure to comply with these minimum capital statutes results in personal liability for the entire amount of the corporation's debts, or liability just up to the amount of minimum capital required by the statute. *Compare* M.B.C.A. (1966 revision) § 43, *with* Tri–State Developers, Inc. v. Moore, 343 S.W.2d 812 (Ky.1961).

failure, creditors of the corporation may seize upon the improper issuance in an attempt to impose personal liability upon the individuals who received the stock (or upon the directors who voted to issue the shares). If the corporation is not a failure, other shareholders may point to the improper issuance in an effort to have the court cancel the stock, thereby keeping a larger portion of ownership for themselves.

Over the years, a number of theories have evolved under which shareholders (or directors) might become liable to creditors due to improper consideration for stock. A simple theory of liability exists for shareholders who obtain stock in exchange for a promissory note, or who fail to pay the agreed consideration for the shares. This is to sue the shareholders upon the contract under which they bought the stock. While this claim belongs to the corporation, rather than to its creditors, a trustee in bankruptcy can pursue the claim as part of the trustee's efforts to gather the company's assets in order to pay the company's debts. Most of the time, however, this simple contract theory will be of little help to creditors. For example, if the shareholder has paid what he or she agreed, even though this is less than the par value of the shares, or has delivered the agreed non-cash consideration, to which the parties gave an inflated valuation, or received the shares in exchange for a promise of future services, which the shareholder remains willing to carry out, then a claim to enforce the contract under which the shareholder received the shares will produce no recovery.[43]

A theory developed early in the history of American corporate law to impose liability upon shareholders who received bonus, discount or watered stock is known as the trust fund theory. This theory postulated that the money (or other permissible consideration) which, under corporation law, the shareholders should have paid for their stock—in other words, a sum at least equal to the par value of the shares—constitutes a trust fund for the protection of creditors of the corporation. Just as one who misappropriates money from a trust fund must put the misappropriated money back, so, under the trust fund theory, the shareholders who received discount, bonus or watered stock must make good on the money (or other permissible consideration) which the shareholders should have put into the trust.[44]

The trust fund theory for the most part has disappeared.[45] A problem with the theory from a doctrinal standpoint is that it is difficult

43. In the case of overvalued non-cash consideration, however, one might argue that the shareholder did not pay the agreed consideration when the shareholder did not actually give property of the value specified. *See* G. Loewus & Co. v. Highland Queen Packing Co., 125 N.J. Eq. 534, 6 A.2d 545 (N.J.Ch.1939) (rejecting the argument). Problems can arise with a contract claim even when the shareholder gave a promissory note in exchange for his or her shares. For example, the shareholder might attempt to assert as a setoff money owed to him or her by the corporation. Moreover, those in charge of the corporation might agree to compromise the corporation's claim to recovery on the note to the prejudice of the corporation's creditors.

44. *E.g.,* Sawyer v. Hoag, 84 U.S. 610 (1873).

45. *But see* Cargill, Inc. v. American Pork Producers, Inc., 426 F.Supp. 499 (D.S.D.1977).

to speak of a trust fund when there is no fund. Indeed, the trust fund theory appears to have originated in cases in which the shareholders received distributions from the corporation, which effectively returned the shareholders' initial investment before the corporation paid off all of its creditors.[46] In the distribution context, it might make a certain amount of sense to speak of the shareholders' investment as a trust fund for the protection of creditors, and to demand that the shareholders put back the distributed funds. This is different, however, than describing money, which was never in a fund to start with, as a trust fund. Still, courts have not been shy about creating fictitious or constructive trusts when it makes policy sense to do so.

An influential opinion by the Minnesota Supreme Court in *Hospes v. Northwestern Manufacturing & Car Co.*,[47] announced a replacement for the trust fund theory. This is known as the fraud theory. The fraud theory has become the dominant common law theory for imposing liability upon shareholders who receive bonus, discount or watered stock. At its core, the fraud theory works from unassailable legal premise: If issuing bonus, discount or watered stock misrepresents the state of the corporation's finances to creditors who agree to do business with the corporation on the strength of this misrepresentation, then the creditors should have a remedy against the persons committing the fraud. Unfortunately, while the legal premise behind the misrepresentation theory is unassailable, its factual premise is shaky.

The factual problem with the fraud theory is that, by and large, creditors are not misled as to the corporation's credit worthiness by the issuance of bonus or discount stock. Short-term trade creditors are typically unaware of, and unconcerned about, the purported paid-in capital of a corporation. After all, what difference does the size of the shareholders' initial investment make to a creditor who is only concerned about whether the corporation will pay a bill due in the next 30 days? Such creditors are interested in the corporation's reputation for paying its bills. Creditors making long-term loans may well be concerned about the size of the shareholders' equity in the corporation (because of the impact of such equity on the incentives for responsible management of the corporation). Yet, the issuance of bonus or discount stock is not going to fool such creditors. This is because the issuance of bonus or discount stock does not provide anything to increase the asset side of the corporation's balance sheet.[48] Given this reality, it would seem that

---

46. *E.g.*, Wood v. Dummer, 30 Fed. Cas. 435 (C.C.D. Me. 1824).

47. 48 Minn. 174, 50 N.W. 1117 (Minn. 1892).

48. The court in *Hospes* seemed to be under the impression that those controlling a corporation obtained credit for the company, at least at the beginning of the company's operations, by going around and telling prospective lenders what the total par value was of the corporation's outstanding

stock. Perhaps at some point in the dim history of corporate practices, this may have been true. If so, this has not been the case for some time. Instead, prospective creditors, who care about the shareholders' equity in the corporation, ask to see the corporation's balance sheet. Admittedly, a balance sheet may show the total par value of the corporation's outstanding stock as an entry within the section commonly labeled "shareholder's equity." For example, if the corporation issued 1000 shares of par $100

shareholders who received bonus or discount stock almost always should be able to defeat claims under the fraud theory simply by asking the creditor whether the creditor's officials relied on, or were even aware of, the corporation's capitalization. The expected negative answer establishes that there was no reliance and, therefore, no actionable fraud.[49]

Anticipating the reliance problem, the court in *Hospes* stated that it would presume reliance by a creditor who dealt with the corporation after the corporation improperly issued the stock, and who did not know of the impropriety. (Even the *Hospes* court recognized that the creditor who dealt with the corporation before the stock was issued, or one who knew that the stock had been improperly issued, could not have relied on the capital represented by those shares.) The rationale behind this presumption of reliance is somewhat similar to the "fraud on the market theory" employed in securities fraud cases.[50] The court felt that creditors who never became aware of the corporation's purported capital nevertheless indirectly relied on this fact, because the parties controlling the corporation had used the purported capitalization of the corporation to convince the company's first creditors to do business with the corporation and thereby established the corporation's general reputation. This rationale sounds nice, and perhaps might even have corresponded to 19th Century business practices. It does not correspond to the realities of how even the first creditor would investigate a corporation today.

When dealing with watered stock, there is a more realistic potential for fraud. This is because the issuance of watered stock entails giving inflated values to assets appearing on the corporation's balance sheet. Still, it questionable how many creditors are going to accept at face value the worth shown on the corporation's balance sheet for the company's assets. It is more likely that this sort of balance sheet inflation is aimed at unsophisticated potential investors, as opposed to sophisticated lenders.

In any event, if there is fraud, the question becomes who is liable for the fraud: the directors who voted to issue the bonus, discount or watered stock, or the shareholders who received the stock? Since these

stock, the balance sheet might show an entry equal to $100,000, which may be labeled "capital," and will appear under the broader heading of shareholder's equity. Yet, if the corporation simply gave away this stock, there will not be an offsetting entry on the asset side of the balance sheet resulting from the issuance of this stock. (Or, if the corporation sold the stock in this example for cash at less than par, the offsetting entry on the asset side of the balance sheet will be less than $100,000.) Hence, the total equity of the corporation—which, by definition, equals assets less liabilities—cannot increase by $100,000 in this example if the corporation issued bonus or discount stock. Accordingly, if the corporation did not receive $100,000 for issuing the stock in this example, the equity section of the balance sheet will need a deficit item to offset the capital item, or else the balance sheet will not balance. The end result is that the balance sheet will quickly inform the reader that the present equity of the corporation does not equal the total par value of the outstanding stock, and hence there is no misrepresentation.

49. *E.g.*, Bing Crosby Minute Maid Corp. v. Eaton, 297 P.2d 5, 46 Cal.2d 484 (1956).

50. See § 6.3.1e *infra*.

are often the same persons, courts commonly have been spared the need to answer this question.[51]

The final theory of liability is probably the most sensible. Since the corporation statutes establish the constraints on acceptable consideration for shares, it would be nice if the statutes also set out the consequences when parties do not follow these constraints. Many states' corporation statutes do just this. For example, Section 162 of Delaware's General Corporation Law provides that, when the corporation cannot pay its debts, the corporation's stockholders are liable for the "unpaid balance of the consideration for which such shares were issued."[52] Unfortunately, these statutory liability provisions often contain a number of ambiguities. For instance, what is the "unpaid balance of the consideration for which such shares were issued" in a situation in which the directors violated the statute by voting to issue shares at below par? Presumably, the unpaid balance should be an amount sufficient to meet the statutory minimum price of par—since otherwise the statute seems pretty pointless—but Section 162 could be clearer in stating this. Similarly, if the directors issue stock for either overvalued or impermissible non-cash consideration, is the amount of liability under a statute such as Delaware's Section 162 measured by the par value of the shares or by the dollar value which the directors placed upon the non-cash consideration (which is commonly greater than par)? Moreover, if the directors issue the shares for future services, can the shareholder insist on paying the unpaid balance of the consideration by performing the services?

The alternate impact of issuing shares for improper consideration is that other stockholders may sue to have the shares canceled on the ground that the improper consideration rendered the issuance of the shares void.[53] In this regard, notice that the impact of stock not being fully paid and nonassessable can go beyond simply having to pay for the stock. In some instances, the shareholders who seek to have the stock canceled knew about, or were involved in, the issuance of the stock for improper consideration—as, for instance, when two individuals agree to form a corporation in which one individual will invest cash while the other individual will provide future services in exchange for stock, and, after the corporation is successful, the cash contributor seeks to have the service provider's stock canceled. In this event, a court might well decide

---

51. Complexity arises, however, if the original shareholders transfer their stock to persons who were unaware of the improper consideration. In this event, most courts hold that the original shareholders who participated in the impropriety, and not the ignorant transferees, are liable to the defrauded creditors. *E.g.*, Palmer v. Scheftel, 194 A.D. 682, 186 N.Y.S. 84 (1921), *aff'd*, 236 N.Y. 511, 142 N.E. 263 (1923).

52. Sections 162 and 325 of Delaware's statute work together to give creditors, who have sought unsuccessfully to execute upon a judgment against a corporation, the right to bring an action against the shareholders

to collect the unpaid balance of the consideration due on the shares. Section 162 excludes from liability, however, good faith transferees who did not know about the failure to fully pay for the stock.

53. *E.g.*, Frankowski v. Palermo, 47 App. Div. 2d 579, 363 N.Y.S.2d 159 (1975). Occasionally, the shareholders who received the stock for improper consideration have argued that the issuance was void, with the hope of thereby avoiding liability to creditors. *E.g.*, Belt v. Belt, 106 Idaho 426, 679 P.2d 1144 (Idaho Ct.App.1984) (rejecting the argument).

that it would be inequitable to cancel the improperly issued stock.[54] Also, some statutes allow directors to issue partially paid stock[55]—which might save at least some of the unpaid for shares from cancellation.[56]

2.1.3 *Preemptive Rights and Other Protections for Existing Shareholders*

Issuing stock can have two adverse impacts upon the existing shareholders who do not purchase further shares. The impact which often first comes to mind is the reduction of the non-purchasing shareholders' percentage of voting control. Normally, however, either the non-purchasing shareholders lacked control even before the additional share issuance, or else the non-purchasing shareholders had been willing to see their control weakened—otherwise, shareholders who had control presumably would have blocked the additional share issuance. Hence, the more frequent concern is the potential dilution of the economic worth of the existing shares. With one class of stock, such dilution is a function of price. If the corporation issues new shares for less than the worth of the existing stock, the result is to transfer wealth from the non-purchasing shareholders to those who buy the new stock. To illustrate, suppose a corporation has one million shares of stock outstanding, and the net worth of the company is $10 million. If the corporation were to issue an additional one million shares at $5 per share, the value of the existing shares will decline from $10 per share ($10 million divided by one million shares) to $7.50 per share ($10 million plus $5 million from the sale of the new shares, divided by the now two million shares outstanding).[57] By contrast, if the new shares sell for the worth of the existing stock, there is no such effect (the existing non-purchasing shareholders own a smaller percentage of a proportionately larger pie). Indeed, if the corporation sells the new shares for more than the worth of the existing stock, the result is to enrich the non-purchasing shareholders at the expense of the buyers of the new stock.[58] With multiple classes of stock,

54. *E.g.,* Frasier v. Trans–Western Land Corp., 210 Neb. 681, 316 N.W.2d 612 (Neb. 1982).

55. *E.g.,* Del. Gen. Corp. Law § 156.

56. In the absence of statutorily authorized partially paid shares, courts differ as to whether they will cancel all of the shares issued for insufficient consideration, or just enough of the shares to bring the price per share up to where it should have been. *Compare* Frankowski v. Palermo, 47 A.D.2d 579, 363 N.Y.S.2d 159 (1975), *with* Belt v. Belt, 106 Idaho 426, 679 P.2d 1144 (Idaho Ct.App.1984).

57. This highly simplified example ignores the obvious difficulty in determining the net worth of a corporation. It also assumes that additional investment in a corporation increases the worth of the corporation on a dollar for dollar basis. In fact, the impact of additional investment on the

worth of a corporation depends on the effectiveness with which the management uses the additional money, since the value of a going business generally is a function of its earning generating potential.

58. The buyers of the new stock, however, have a defense against this dilution, which not available to the existing shareholders: Prospective buyers of newly issued stock can refuse to purchase the shares if the price is too high. Hence, much of the focus of the law as far as protecting new buyers against dilution has been to ensure that the prospective buyers are fully informed so that the buyers can exercise this self-defense. (Some state laws, however, have taken a more paternalistic approach toward new buyers by seeking to prevent the sale of securities in which the buyers will suffer unfair dilution.) We shall explore this subject in a later chapter dealing with laws regulating the sale of securities.

the effect is more complicated because of the need to consider differing rights of the shares.

What protections do the existing shareholders have against the dilution of their economic interests (or the occasionally significant involuntary undercutting of their voting power) through the issuance of new stock? The first possible defense lies in the fact that the corporation only can issue as many shares as the corporation's articles authorize. Specifically, corporation statutes normally require a company's articles, even if the articles contain nothing else about the corporation's stock, to state the number of shares which the corporation is authorized to issue.[59] (To put this into the traditional parlance, the number appearing in the articles represents the corporation's "authorized stock." By comparison, the number of shares "outstanding" generally refers total number of shares which the corporation has "issued"—in other words sold—and not repurchased.) The statutes explicitly or implicitly forbid the corporation's directors or shareholders from having the corporation issue shares which would make the number of shares outstanding exceed the number of authorized shares.[60]

It turns out, however, that the rule preventing the corporation from issuing more shares than authorized by the company's articles generally does little to protect the existing stockholders. This is because drafters of corporate articles usually have the articles authorize the corporation to issue a far greater number of shares than there is any plan for the company actually to issue. There are a couple of reasons for this practice. To begin with, it gives the board of directors flexibility to issue more shares when this might be advantageous, without going through the effort of amending the articles. Besides, limiting the number of authorized shares to the number which the corporation's founders plan to have the corporation issue will generally fail to protect minority shareholders anyway. After all, the majority owners can always amend the articles to increase the number of authorized shares.

The rules we discussed earlier regarding consideration for shares also might be rationalized as a means of protecting the existing shareholders against the dilution of their interest. For example, at one time in corporate practice, par value may have been used as a way of attempting to have all persons pay the same price (par) for their stock. This no longer worked after the practice of using low par and no par shares became the norm. Besides, having a constant price for the corporation's issuance of stock is no guarantee against dilution. Quite the contrary. Since the value of a corporation's stock constantly changes with the fortunes of the company, always issuing stock at the same price is a prescription for diluting either the existing shareholders' or the new buyers' interests.

Another approach to protecting the existing shareholders against prejudice from the issuance of more stock is to guarantee each existing

59. *E.g.,* Del. Gen. Corp. Law § 102(a)(4).   **60.** *E.g.,* M.B.C.A. § 6.03(a)

stockholder the right to buy his or her pro-rata share of any newly issued stock. For example, if the corporation plans to issue 100,000 new shares at $5 per share, a ten percent shareholder could have the right to buy 10,000 of the shares at this price. In this way, the corporation might raise further funds without diluting the voting or economic interests of any shareholder. Such a guarantee is referred to as a preemptive right.

At common law, preemptive rights existed as a matter of course.[61] Statutes now generally make this subject controlled by the corporation's articles. Specifically, some statutes provide that preemptive rights exist unless the articles expressly exclude them.[62] Most statutes exclude preemptive rights unless the articles expressly provide them.[63]

Preemptive rights have several shortcomings. Such rights do not help the shareholder who lacks either the funds or the willingness to take advantage of the right by purchasing more shares. Another problem is that preemptive rights may complicate efforts to raise money from outside sources (such as through a public offering).[64]

Providing preemptive rights also can raise a number of interpretation questions (unless the particular corporation's articles carefully define the rights). For example, suppose a corporation wishes to issue shares in exchange for property (such as the assets of another firm). If preemptive rights apply and some of the shareholders exercise them, it becomes more difficult for the corporation accomplish this objective.[65] Presumably for this reason, court opinions and statutes tend not to call for preemptive rights (in the absence of express provision in the articles to the contrary) when the corporation issues shares in exchange for property.[66] A similar analysis applies if the corporation seeks to issue shares as part of compensation to its employees.[67]

Since the notion of preemptive rights is to allow existing stockholders to purchase their pro-rata share of any additional issuances of stock, the question can arise as to when the issuance of stock becomes an additional sale to which the rights apply, rather than part of the original issuance that decides who has the rights. For example, suppose A, B and C each purchase one-third of the shares of a corporation. If, three months later, A and B wish the corporation to sell shares to D, can C assert preemptive rights? Traditionally, many courts answered this question simply by looking at whether the later-issued shares already had been authorized in the articles or whether the articles needed to be

61. *E.g.,* Stokes v. Continental Trust Co., 186 N.Y. 285, 78 N.E. 1090 (1906).

62. *E.g.,* N.Y. Bus. Corp. Law § 622 (for corporations formed before 1997).

63. *E.g.,* Del. Gen. Corp. Law § 102(b)(3); M.B.C.A. § 6.30(A).

64. For example, the marketability of an initial public offering may depend upon the corporation issuing enough shares to the general public—rather than to insiders who exercise preemptive rights—to create a trading market for the corporation's stock.

65. For instance, if the owners of half of the shares exercise preemptive rights, the corporation would need to issue twice as many shares in order both to acquire the property and satisfy the preemptive rights.

66. *E.g.,* M.B.C.A. § 6.30(b)(3)(iv); Thom v. Baltimore Trust Co., 158 Md. 352, 148 A. 234 (1930).

67. *See, e.g.,* M.B.C.A. § 6.30(b)(3)(I), (ii).

amended to authorize the shares.[68] A more sophisticated answer, however, might look both at the time which has lapsed between the sales,[69] and at whether the sales were all part of a preexisting plan.[70] Otherwise, given the typical practice of drafting the articles to authorize far more shares than the corporation plans to issue, if courts confined preemptive rights only to newly authorized shares, preemptive rights would rarely serve their purpose. In any event, the answer usually is more clear-cut if the corporation proposes to resell treasury stock (in other words, stock the corporation once issued and repurchased). Here, the general rule (in the absence of express provision in the articles to the contrary) is that preemptive rights do not apply;[71] which is rather curious since the sale of treasury shares can prejudice the existing shareholders as much as the original issuance of shares.

The question of whether preemptive rights apply can become very complex when more than one class of stock is involved. Specifically, when do shares of one class possess preemptive rights to buy shares of another class?[72] A rational approach to this question would start by asking if the rights of the two classes are such that issuing new shares of one class will have an impact on the voting power or economic rights of the other class. For example, issuing additional common will not impact the owners of non-voting, non-participating preferred shares, while issuing additional preferred shares would impact the interest of the owners of common. Hence, there is no need for the non-voting, non-participating preferred stockholders to have preemptive rights in the former situation, but such rights can be useful in the latter. Notice, however, that this analysis might lead to the conclusion that holders of more than one class of stock will have preemptive rights—in which event, figuring out how much stock each holder has a preemptive right to purchase becomes tricky. For this reason, one can understand why some authorities take a narrow view of preemptive rights between classes.[73]

What usually protects the existing shareholders' interests from the adverse consequences of the issuance of additional shares, however, is none of the above. Instead, it is the simple fact that the board of directors normally would not wish to sell shares at a price which dilutes the existing shareholders' economic interests. After all, the shareholders elect the board, and the directors are probably substantial shareholders themselves. This protection breaks down, however, in a situation in which the directors are the purchasers.[74]

68. *See, e.g.,* Dunlay v. Avenue M Garage & Repair Co., 253 N.Y. 274, 170 N.E. 917 (1930).

69. *See, e.g.,* M.B.C.A. § 6.30(b)(3)(iii) (no preemptive rights to purchase shares issued within six months of incorporation).

70. *E.g.,* Yasik v. Wachtel, 25 Del.Ch. 247, 17 A.2d 309 (Ch. 1941).

71. *E.g.,* Borg v. International Silver Co., 11 F.2d 147 (2d Cir.1925).

72. *See, e.g.,* Thomas Branch & Co. v. Riverside & Dan River Cotton Mills, Inc., 139 Va. 291, 123 S.E. 542 (1924) (held that preferred shareholders had a preemptive right to buy a new issue of common).

73. *See, e.g.,* M.B.C.A. § 6.30(b)(4), (5).

74. One situation in which the protection of the directors' self interest may break down even though the directors are not the purchasers is when the directors issue stock to a friendly party in order to prevent a

When the directors purchase stock from the corporation, the existing shareholders might challenge the transaction as a breach of the directors' fiduciary duty. We shall explore the fiduciary duties of corporate directors in a later chapter. For now, it is useful to note that when dealing with a conflict-of-interest transaction—as would be the case if the directors, or even persons who control the directors, purchase shares from the corporation—the general rule is that either the transaction must receive disinterested approval, or the directors must prove that the transaction is fair to the corporation.[75] A price sufficiently low to dilute the existing shareholders' interests presumably does not qualify as fair.[76] Hence, the general rules of fiduciary duty normally should work reasonably well to protect the existing shareholders from the directors having the corporation issue to themselves shares under terms which dilute the existing shareholders' interest.[77] Still, situations occasionally arise in which the corporation's issuing shares to its directors creates issues beyond those encountered in the run-of-the-mill conflict-of-interest transaction.

One such situation occurs if directors have the corporation sell shares to themselves in order to upset a balance of power within the corporation. *Schwartz v. Marien*,[78] provides an example. *Schwartz* involved a feud between two families. Each family had owned half of the outstanding shares of the corporation, and each family had occupied two of the four seats on the board. When one director died, the other family found itself in temporary control of the board (because two out of the remaining three directors were able to fill the vacancy on the board with another member of their family). To cement this control, the three directors of the family in control voted to have the company sell to themselves several treasury shares held by the corporation. (These were shares which the company had issued to the third founder of the firm, and had repurchased upon this founder's death.) In a situation such as in *Schwartz*, simply reviewing to see if the price charged for the stock was fair to the corporation can be inadequate to protect the non-purchasing shareholders, since the real concern is with a shift in control. The court in *Schwartz* responded by forcing the defendant directors to show a corporate purpose for the sale.[79]

Katzowitz v. Sidler,[80] illustrates another potential issue. The defendant directors in *Katzowitz* voted to have the corporation offer to sell shares to all of its stockholders at a bargain price. The corporation had

hostile takeover of the corporation. We shall consider this situation when discussing corporate takeovers later in this book.

75. See § 4.2.1 *infra*.

76. An exception could be if the bargain sale was to compensate the directors for their services to the corporation.

77. Since dilution depends upon the corporation selling shares at less than the shares' value, it is worth keeping in mind that the valuation of a given stock is a subject upon which reasonable persons often disagree.

78. 37 N.Y.2d 487, 373 N.Y.S.2d 122, 335 N.E.2d 334 (1975).

79. Some courts have been more reluctant to prevent sales which shift control. *E.g.*, Tallant v. Executive Equities, Inc., 232 Ga. 807, 209 S.E.2d 159 (1974).

80. 24 N.Y.2d 512, 301 N.Y.S.2d 470, 249 N.E.2d 359 (1969).

three equal shareholders—the plaintiff and the two defendants—all of whom were also the directors. The defendants bought the bargain shares, but the plaintiff declined. Given the conflict-of-interest in the defendants' vote, the bargain price normally would render the decision, without any argument, unfair and a breach of fiduciary duty. The defendants, however, asserted that the transaction was fair because the plaintiff had the same opportunity to make a bargain purchase as they did. The court, quite appropriately, rejected this claim. The court held that unless there was some business purpose for the bargain sale, shareholders should not be placed in a position where they must invest or face dilution of their interest.

§ 2.2 Debt as Part of The Corporate Capital Structure

It is hardly surprising that corporations borrow money. After all, as discussed in Chapter I, the primary purpose for conducting a business in the corporate form most often is to limit the owners' personal liability for debts incurred in the business. Corporate borrowing is not limited to emergencies, or to situations in which the corporation could not have obtained more money by selling stock. Rather, even the largest and richest corporations borrow. In fact, both lenders and those in charge of corporations consider long-term loans to be part of the company's "capital"—using this term in an economic, rather than an accounting, or legal, sense, as money which the lender has invested in the corporation for the company to employ in making money. This, in turn, leads one to ask why corporations borrow to raise capital, rather than raising capital by selling more stock. After answering this question, we can look at a couple of the more unique issues raised by corporate debt.

2.2.1 Why Have Debt?

There are a number of reasons why corporations borrow, rather than issue more stock, to raise capital. One reason harkens back to the discussion earlier in this chapter regarding the purposes for issuing preferred stock. A basic rule of corporate law is that, upon dissolution, a corporation must repay any outstanding debts prior to making liquidating distributions to the corporation's shareholders.[1] Hence, when a corporation borrows money, the effect for purposes of liquidation is much the same as issuing a class of stock with a liquidation preference over all other classes of stock. Such a priority to payment on liquidation can allow the more risk averse investors to shift a greater share of the danger of losing one's investment to those investors more willing to take that risk (presumably in exchange for a higher possible return). One difference, however, between debt and even preferred stock is that debt normally requires repayment before liquidation. Hence, debt entails a more temporary investment. Of course, some loans are quite long-term, and corporations often finance the repayment of long-term debt through

<hr/>

§ 2.2

1. See § 7.2.2*b infra.*

new long-term loans. Moreover, as discussed later in this chapter, corporations can, and often do, repurchase stock prior to liquidation.

Debt also has an impact on the right to receive current distributions from the corporation. Debt ordinarily entitles the lender to receive interest. To some extent, this creates an impact like a preferred stock dividend in that interest represents a priority claim on the corporation's current distributions. Yet, the impact of interest goes beyond the impact of a dividend preference. A dividend preference simply requires the corporation to pay the preference amount before the corporation can pay dividends to junior classes of stock, but a dividend preference does not require the corporation to pay any dividends to any shares at all. By contrast, interest normally represents a fixed obligation of the firm— payable regardless of whether the firm has earnings. This means that interest gives the lender greater certainty of income than preferred stock (subject only to the practical limit of the company running out of money to pay the interest). Moreover, while some preferred stock has the right to participate in further dividends beyond the preference amount, the amount of interest due on debt is normally the same no matter what the business earns. Accordingly, should the company do very well, the lender, like a nonparticipating preferred stockholder, gets no extra return. All told, debt creates an investment for those who place a greater value on receiving a steady return than on the possibility of making a killing.

From the standpoint of those holding stock, the effect of debt on current distributions is the opposite of debt's impact for the lender. Should the business do poorly, the shareholders face a greater risk of receiving nothing (should earnings not exceed interest), or, worse, having their investment depleted to make interest payments, than the stockholders would have faced had the corporation raised money by selling more stock rather than borrowing. On the other hand, should the business do very well, those with stock gain a greater share of the rewards if the corporation borrows at fixed interest rather than raising money by selling more stock.[2] This impact is often referred to as leverage. Like a lever, debt magnifies both the rewards which the owners of the corporation gain if the company prospers and the risk the owners face if the company flounders.

---

2. To illustrate, suppose Initial Owner holds all of the outstanding stock of a corporation, and the corporation needs $100,-000. Initial Owner has two offers to supply the money: Lender offers to loan the corporation the money in exchange for an annual interest of ten percent; Added Owner offers to pay the corporation $100,000 in exchange for an amount of stock equal to Initial Owner. If the corporation thereafter earns $10,000 per year (excluding the cost of obtaining the $100,000), then, if Initial Owner accepted Lender's offer, Lender will receive all of the corporation's income and Initial Owner will own all of a corporation which makes no profits, whereas if Initial Owner accepted Added Owner's proposal, then Initial Owner will still own half of a corporation which makes $10,000 per year. By contrast, if the corporation makes $50,-000 per year (excluding the cost of the $100,000), Initial Owner will own 100% of a corporation making $40,000 a year if Initial Owner accepted Lender's offer, but will own only half of a corporation making $50,-000 per year if Initial Owner accepted Added Owner's offer.

There has been considerable controversy over the years about the desirability of leverage. Traditionally, the notion has been that a certain amount of leverage is useful to increase returns to the corporation's shareholders; but prudent corporations should not overdo it. After all, obligating a corporation to meet a fixed interest expense near the outer limits of the company's near-term predicted revenues is a prescription for bankruptcy if the slightest setback occurs in the business.

Some financial economists have argued that the traditional wisdom about leverage is wrong. They assert that the mix of debt and equity is fundamentally irrelevant to the worth of the business.[3] Specifically, one can view a business as a vehicle for producing a stream of revenue. Lenders and stockholders are simply different claimants for a share of the revenue from this stream. If the firm borrows so much that lenders claim almost all of this stream, there is less left for the stockholders, but this does not reduce the amount of revenues generated by the business. Moreover, if the lenders' claims exceed the stream of income, then the stockholders may lose their claim to any future money from the firm, and the lenders may need to readjust their claims to the reality of how much income the venture can generate. This is what happens in a bankruptcy reorganization. Yet, the revenue generating capability of the firm is not changed; simply who has what claim. Moreover, under this view, corporations gain little advantage in raising capital by offering a different mix of investments. True, different investors have different preferences in terms of their desire for a steady return versus a larger, but more speculative, gain. Hence, at first glance, one might assume that a corporation could lower its cost of capital by attracting more investors with a mix of investments having different trade-offs between risk and return. Yet, given the different investments available in the market generally, as well as the ability of investors to use a portfolio of equities and risk-free investments (government bonds) to meet their particular risk-return desires, it is not clear that corporations should be able to lower their overall cost of capital by offering a mix of investments.

One problem with this agnostic view of leverage, however, is that it ignores the legal and other costs of going through a bankruptcy reorganization. More fundamentally, this view ignores impact of leverage on the decisions of those in charge of the business. For example, as the claims of debt holders approach the entire worth of the business, the risk of business reverses falls almost entirely on the debt holders (since the shareholders have little left to lose). Under this circumstance, the interest of the shareholders—who elect the directors—calls for taking risks even if the prospective loss for the business as a whole, multiplied by the probability of the loss occurring, exceeds the prospective gain for the business as a whole, multiplied by the probability of the gain occurring; in other words, even if the risk is unreasonable when looked at terms of the interests of all the claimants in the corporation. Hence, excessive leverage can lead to unreasonable business decisions.

3. *E.g.*, Modigliani & Miller, *The Cost of Capital, Corporation Finance and the Theo-* *ry of Investment*, 48 Am. Econ. Rev. 261 (1958).

By contrast, some writers have claimed that leverage actually increases the quality of business decisions.[4] The notion is that the directors of publicly held corporations are often likely to retain and waste corporate earnings, rather than have the corporation pay an optimal level of dividends. We shall develop the reasoning behind this notion later in this chapter when we address the subject of dividends. Because directors do not have the discretion over making interest payments as they do over declaring dividends, a large level of corporate debt, the argument goes, serves as a discipline to prevent the directors from retaining and wasting corporate earnings.

In addition to allowing stockholders to leverage their potential economic gains, borrowing rather than selling more stock allows stockholders to leverage their control over the corporation. Specifically, debt holders traditionally do not have any vote on who will be the directors of the corporation. Hence, borrowing can avoid the dilution of voting power which would attend issuing additional voting stock.

In many instances, however, the most significant advantage of raising capital through borrowing rather than issuing stock has nothing to do with financial economics or preserving control. Instead, the advantage lies in the different treatment under the income tax law of corporate payments to debt holders versus to shareholders. Interest payments generally constitute a deductible expense for the corporation,[5] whereas dividend payments do not.[6]

2.2.2 Corporate Bonds

Corporate borrowing is primarily a matter of contract law, much as any other lender-debtor relationship. The primary corporate law rule, which we have examined elsewhere, is limited liability for the corporation's owners. Nevertheless, another aspect of corporate debt often introduces issues different from the run-of-the-mill loan. Instead of going to a lending institution, such as a bank, large corporations (like government entities) often borrow by issuing bonds. Essentially, what this means is that the corporation (or government entity) is borrowing a large amount of money by having numerous persons make relatively small loans to the corporation on the same terms. The IOUs which these

4. *E.g.*, Jensen, *The Takeover Controversy: Analysis and Evidence*, Midland Corp. Fin. J. 4 (Summer 1986).

5. I.R.C. § 163(a).

6. Normally, the recipient of either dividends or interest payments must recognize the dividend or interest payment as ordinary income. I.R.C. § 61(a). *But see* I.R.C. § 243 (a shareholder, who itself is a corporation, need not recognize as part of its taxable income most or all of the dividends it receives). Hence, corporate earnings distributed as dividends generally are taxed twice—once when the corporation makes the money and again when the shareholders receive the dividends. By contrast, corporate revenues paid as interest are taxed only once—when the debt holder recognizes the interest as income. This difference often leads shareholders in closely held corporations to make much of their investment in the corporation nominally in the form of loans rather than purchases of stock. This practice has led to repeated litigation in which the Internal Revenue Service has argued that what the corporation and its owners labeled a loan was, in fact, an equity (stock) investment. *E.g.*, Bauer v. Commissioner, 748 F.2d 1365 (9th Cir.1984).

numerous lenders receive from the corporation commonly are called bonds—albeit, to be more precise, the term "bonds" traditionally refers only to such multiple IOUs when the corporation pledges some of its property as collateral to secure the loan. "Debentures" is the traditional term to describe multiple IOUs for unsecured long-term loans to a corporation.

The use of multiple IOUs with the same terms introduces several concerns which do not exist when dealing with one large lender and an individually negotiated loan. The first concern is mechanical. It is not very efficient for numerous small lenders to enforce compliance with the terms of the loans. Enforcing compliance is not simply a matter of suing if payments stop. In addition, lending agreements often contain numerous promises by the borrower designed to avoid conduct which endangers repayment. Lenders often monitor compliance by the borrower with such terms. This is not practical when an individual loans a few thousand dollars to a major corporation at the other end of the country. The solution to this problem is to appoint a trustee to represent the interest of all of the bond holders. The trustee, which itself is often a large institution, can monitor the borrower's compliance with the lending agreements and can take action in the event of default. The document appointing the trustee is known as the trust indenture. In addition to appointing the trustee, the trust indenture serves as a central governing document containing all of the detailed promises by the borrowing corporation, and specifying the rights of enforcement of the trustee and the lenders. By placing all of this detail in the trust indenture, the bonds themselves can contain just the essential terms of the loan: the interest rate, maturity date, and the like.

Introduction of a trustee, in turn, can create new issues. For example, the trustee may be subject to conflicts of interest. This might occur because the trustee itself has loaned money to the corporation, and so the trustee's interest as a lender could diverge from the bond holders' interests in a situation in which the corporation will not be able to pay back all of the corporation's debts.[7] Also, through neglect or debatable judgment, the trustee may fail to protect the bond holders, leading the bond holders to argue that the trustee has breached a duty of care.[8] Trustees often seek to protect themselves against such claims by placing exculpatory language in the trust indenture. Moreover, if bond holders individually seek to enforce terms in the indenture against the borrowing corporation, the purpose for having central administration of the loans may be frustrated. Hence, trust indentures often limit the bond holders' rights to seek individual relief.[9] The law governing these issues is a combination of the terms of the trust indenture, common law rules

---

7. *E.g.*, United States Trust Co. v. First Natl. City Bk., 57 App. Div. 2d 285, 394 N.Y.S.2d 653 (1977), *aff'd*, 45 N.Y.2d 869, 382 N.E.2d 1355, 410 N.Y.S.2d 580 (1978).

8. *See, e.g.*, Elliott Assoc. v. J. Henry Schroder Bk. & Tr. Co., 838 F.2d 66 (2d Cir.1988).

9. *E.g.*, Simons v. Cogan, 549 A.2d 300 (Del.1988).

concerning the fiduciary obligations of trustees, and a federal statute—the Trust Indenture Act of 1939.

Bonds and trust indentures, like other contracts, often contain ambiguities calling for judicial interpretation. Such interpretation involves much of the same analysis employed in interpreting contracts generally. There are, however, a couple of new twists when interpreting bonds and trust indentures. To begin with, courts have placed a premium on achieving a uniform interpretation of so-called boilerplate terms in bonds and trust indentures.[10] Boilerplate is a legal slang expression for the standard form terms used in numerous similar contracts. It is no secret that lawyers rarely draft all of the terms of a contract from scratch, but, instead, copy language for common terms from various forms. The American Bar Foundation's Commentaries on Model Debenture Indenture Provisions has been a frequently used form for terms in trust indentures. Bonds are commonly traded in public trading markets, and few bond holders actually bother to read the boilerplate in the trust indenture. Under these circumstances, it is very useful for courts to consistently interpret boilerplate terms, rather than try to figure out what a particular corporation and the specific bond holders had in mind. For one thing, it is questionable whether the particular corporation, and especially its bond holders, had anything in mind for terms they never read. More fundamentally, by having a uniform interpretation, the trading market, influenced by professionals who have looked at the contract terms, can take into account the terms of the trust indenture in the price of the bonds.[11] This will not work if different courts interpret inconsistently the same boilerplate language in trust indentures—since then professionals cannot be sure as to the meaning of the terms in the trust indenture. The desire for a uniform interpretation means that courts will defer to the first court which interprets a provision, even though the later court might have reached a different interpretation.[12]

One principle of contract interpretation which seems to receive less emphasis in interpreting trust indentures than perhaps in some other contexts is the old saw about interpreting ambiguities against the drafter. Perhaps this is because it is somewhat difficult to say where this principle should lead in the case of ambiguous trust indentures. The bond holders did not draft the indenture and therefore will claim the advantage of the rule. Yet, the corporation often did not entirely draft the indenture either. Rather, an underwriter—in other words, an investment banking firm whose role is to market the bonds—often plays an active role in putting together the indenture. It is difficult to say which side the underwriter represents. Courts sometimes assert that the underwriter represents the future bond holders.[13] After all, if the terms of

---

10. *E.g.,* Sharon Steel Corp. v. Chase Manhattan Bk., 691 F.2d 1039 (2d Cir. 1982).

11. This is a variation on the efficient market hypothesis for stock traded in pub-lic markets, which we shall examine later in this book.

12. *See, e.g.,* Morgan Stanley & Co. v. Archer Daniels Midland Co., 570 F.Supp. 1529 (S.D.N.Y.1983).

13. *Id.*

the bonds are not favorable to the bond holders, it will be difficult for the underwriter to sell the bonds. Yet, it is the corporation who selects the underwriter. Hence, underwriters cannot afford to be too antagonistic toward the corporation who selected them (and may have occasion to select an underwriter for more offerings in the future).

Another problem occasioned by the mass lender nature of bonds concerns modifications to the bonds or trust indenture. Often a borrower might request the lender to agree to a modification of the terms of a loan. Sometimes this happens because the borrower is in financial difficulties and so the borrower and lender attempt to reach some accommodation to prevent a default and bankruptcy. Other times, the restrictive provisions in a loan agreement might prevent a borrower from undertaking a transaction which would be advantageous to the borrower and would not prejudice the lender. If there is one lender, negotiating such a modification is straightforward. What happens, however, when the borrower is a corporation and the lenders consist of numerous bond holders? If every bond holder had to approve any modification, the result is that modifications would be rare. Some bond holders might be unreasonable or just unreachable. Accordingly, bond agreements and trust indentures often allow amendments by majority vote of the bond holders.

Unfortunately, provisions allowing amendment of bond agreements and trust indentures by majority vote are subject to abuse. For example, suppose shareholders of the corporation also own most of the bonds. In this event, these bond owning shareholders might vote to amend the bond agreement to delay payments or reduce interest, thereby improving their position as shareholders.[14] To prevent abuse, the Trust Indenture Act limits the ability of trust indentures to allow amendment of interest and payment terms, and limits the voting power of those bond holders who also own a controlling interest in the corporation.[15]

Alternately, sometimes the corporation may attempt to induce an amendment to the trust indenture in a manner which is arguably coercive. For example, in *Katz v. Oak Indus., Inc.*,[16] a corporation in financial trouble made an offer to its bond holders to pay cash in exchange for their bonds. The problem was that the amount offered was less than the principal amount of the bonds—albeit, the amount was in excess of the bond's current price on the trading market.[17] Under the offer, any bond holder tendering his or her bond to the company had to agree to give the corporation a consent to remove various protective provisions in the trust indenture. The plaintiff bond holder argued that this was a coercive tactic designed to force bond holders to give up their bonds for less than the bonds' principal amount. Essentially, the theory is that bond holders who did not wish to tender their bonds would do so

14. *See, e.g.,* Aladdin Hotel Co. v. Bloom, 200 F.2d 627 (8th Cir.1953).

15. Trust Indenture Act of 1939 § 316 (as amended in 1990).

16. 508 A.2d 873 (Del.Ch.1986).

17. The low trading price for the bonds presumably reflected the company's poor health.

anyway out of fear about the removal of the financial protections.[18] In refusing to grant a preliminary injunction against the offer, the court concluded that the plaintiff was unlikely to succeed on the merits. One justification for this result in *Katz* is that a small number of institutional investors held most of the bonds. Hence, there probably was no coercion in this case, since these institutions could have coordinated a rejection of the tender if they felt it was not in their interest. Moreover, the corporation's offer was part of a transaction in which a third party was infusing cash into the corporation, without which the company appeared to be doomed.

In *Katz*, the plaintiff could not point to a literal breach of any term in the bond or trust indenture. This raises the question of whether bond holders are entitled to protections beyond the express terms of the contract. One such protection recognized under contract law is to invoke an implied covenant of good faith and fair dealing. By and large, courts have not been sympathetic to bond holders who argue that the corporation's conduct toward them breaches such an implied obligation—the general attitude seeming to be that bond holders are sophisticated investors and ought to look to express contract terms for their protection.[19] Alternately, bond holders might argue that corporate directors owe fiduciary duties to the bond holders, just as directors owe such duties to the stockholders. We shall explore this argument more in dealing with the duties of directors in a later chapter.

One final difference between corporate bonds and run of the mill debt is that sometimes bond holders have the right to convert their bonds into stock in the corporation. This is similar to the right to convert convertible preferred into common stock, which we discussed earlier in this chapter. To some extent, such a convertible bond gives its owner the best of both worlds—a lower risk-more assured income investment in the bond, but the ability to share in the greater wealth by converting to stock should the corporation's fortunes really take off. Of course, there is a cost to this attempt to "have one's cake and eat it too" in that convertible bonds typically pay an interest rate less than the rate paid by non-convertible bonds with similar risks.

Convertible bonds raise very complex doctrinal and practical questions regarding to whom the corporation's directors owe a duty. The doctrinal problem is that even if courts hold, as a general proposition, that directors owe a duty to stockholders and not bond holders, in which camp do convertible bond holders fall prior to their conversion? The practical problem—which prevents one from ignoring the doctrinal question—is that the conversion option can create significant conflicts of

---

18. Of course, if the holders of most of the bonds refuse to tender, then the corporation would receive insufficient consents to amend the trust indenture, and there would be no problem. Yet, unless the bond holders can coordinate their response, each must would worry that the other bond holders might tender if, for no other reason, then because the other bond holders have the same worry.

19. *See, e.g.,* Metropolitan Life Ins. Co. v. RJR Nabisco, Inc., 716 F.Supp. 1504 (S.D.N.Y.1989). *But see* Van Gemert v. Boeing Co., 520 F.2d 1373 (2d Cir.1975).

interest between the shareholders and the convertible bond holders. For example, convertible security holders typically will prefer the corporation to retain earnings for expansion, whereas common owners might prefer more current dividends.[20] The law in this area is not well defined.

2.2.3 *Subordination of Shareholder Loans*

Often, the persons loaning money to a corporation are also shareholders of the company. This practice sometimes creates an issue as to whether a court should treat a loan from the corporation's shareholders the same as any other debt incurred by the company. Specifically, if the corporation goes bankrupt, outside creditors might argue that the bankruptcy court should subordinate the loans from the shareholders to the loans of the creditors who are not shareholders. Subordinating a debt means only paying the debt if there is money left after paying the company's unsubordinated debt(s)—which, in bankruptcy, commonly means not paying the subordinated loan at all.

This raises the question as to why a court might subordinate loans made by shareholders. One uncontroversial reason for subordination exists if a lender agreed to subordinate his or her loan to other loans. Such voluntary subordination is not our concern in this discussion. Rather, our concern here is whether, and when, courts might involuntarily subordinate a shareholder's loan. Perhaps one might argue that loans by shareholders should always be subordinate to debt owed to non-shareholders. The notion could be that it is an abuse for shareholders to cast some of their investment in the form of debt in order to circumvent the rule that shareholders receive return of their investment only after the corporation pays its debts. This idea, however, is not the law. Rather, the general rule is that shareholders can make some of their investment to a corporation in the form of loans, and such loans normally are entitled to the same treatment in the event of corporate failure as loans to the corporation from outsiders.[21]

There are several reasons for rejecting a rule which would make shareholder loans always subordinate to outsider loans. In part, it is not necessarily desirable to deter shareholders from making loans to their corporation. After all, shareholders might provide better terms for the corporation than would a lender with no other stake in the corporation, and, indeed, in some situations, the shareholders might be the only source for a loan.[22] Moreover, a rule which subordinated any corporate debt held by a shareholder could present administrative problems when dealing with corporations with publicly traded stocks and bonds (and

---

20. *See, e.g.,* Harff v. Kerkorian, 347 A.2d 133 (Del.1975) (convertible bond holders challenged dividend declaration).

21. *See, e.g.,* Obre v. Alban Tractor Co., 228 Md. 291, 179 A.2d 861 (1962).

22. There is, however, little empirical evidence on the extent to which shareholders provide companies with funds through favorable loans that the corporations could not have obtained from outsiders (and that the shareholders would not otherwise have provided in the form of subordinated debt, or even as stock purchases).

especially with publicly traded convertible bonds).[23] Most fundamentally, it is not clear what policy a rule which automatically subordinated shareholder loans would achieve. For example, a contract creditor who cares about the form of the shareholders' investment in the corporation can check before doing business with the company. Then, if the contract creditor is upset that the shareholders made their investment in the form of loans as well as stock purchases, the creditor can always demand that the shareholders agree to subordinate the shareholder loans to the creditor's loan. If contract creditors do not demand such protection for themselves, then why should the court automatically provide it for the creditors?[24] Turning from contract creditors to tort victims, as discussed when dealing with piercing the corporate veil, the primary concern with respect to corporate capital and tort victims is to achieve adequate insurance. Hence, so long as the corporation has adequate insurance for foreseeable tort damages, why should the court automatically subordinate shareholder loans to the claims of tort victims whose damages exceeded reasonably foreseeable levels?

If shareholder loans are not automatically subordinate to outsider loans, then when, if ever, will a court subordinate such loans? Several courts have recited a three-part test: (1) the shareholder engaged in inequitable conduct; (2) this conduct resulted in injury to other creditors or an unfair advantage to the shareholder; and (3) subordination would not be contrary to the Bankruptcy Code.[25] Actually, as is commonly true of such multi part tests, this test sounds like more than it is. The final element lacks significance, because the Bankruptcy Code expressly authorizes equitable subordination.[26] In the end, the test comes down to inequitable conduct. Unfortunately, what is inequitable conduct needs considerable definition in order to be a useful standard.

To understand when it might make sense to subordinate shareholder loans, it helps to look at a couple of leading Supreme Court decisions. Equitable subordination is often referred to as the "Deep Rock" doctrine, after the name of the debtor corporation involved in *Taylor v. Standard Gas & Electric Co.*[27] Standard Gas & Electric was the controlling shareholder of the Deep Rock Oil Corp. (by virtue of owning the common stock). Standard used its control to engage in a series of abusive transactions with the subsidiary. These included having Deep Rock pay

23. One might avoid this problem by only subordinating loans made by controlling shareholders; albeit this raises line drawing questions.

24. One might argue that such self-defense is too much to expect of trade creditors. After all, checking the nature of the shareholders' investment is rather burdensome for a party who simply sells goods on an invoice giving 30 days to pay. Yet, as discussed in dealing with piercing the corporate veil, a creditor only concerned with getting paid in the next 30 days generally is not interested in the nature of the shareholders' investment anyway. An exception to this conclusion when dealing with shareholder loans arises in the situation in which the shareholder(s) make short-term loans to the corporation, which corporation then uses to pay enough bills to create a misleading credit history. This prospect, however, does not call for subordination of all shareholder loans.

25. *E.g.*, Benjamin v. Diamond, 563 F.2d 692 (5th Cir.1977).

26. Bankruptcy Code § 510(c).

27. 306 U.S. 307, 59 S.Ct. 543 (1939)

hefty management fees and lease payments to other Standard subsidiaries, and to declare dividends Deep Rock could barely afford to pay. Deep Rock ended up deeply in debt to Standard (small wonder) on an open account—many of the items of which may have been fraudulent, and on which Standard charged a high interest. After Deep Rock entered bankruptcy, the Supreme Court held that Deep Rock's open account debt to Standard should be subordinated to Deep Rock's other creditors, and also, interestingly enough, subordinated to the claims of the holders of Deep Rock's publicly traded preferred stock.

Along the same lines, the Supreme Court, in an often-quoted opinion by Justice Douglas, subordinated debt owed to the sole shareholder of a bankrupt corporation in *Pepper v. Litton*.[28] Litton was the sole shareholder of the Dixie Split Coal Company. After Pepper brought suit against the coal company for unpaid royalties, it suddenly occurred to Litton that the corporation owed him unpaid salary which he had not collected for years. Litton then not only decided to claim his back salary, but rushed to have the corporation confess a judgment to him. After Pepper also obtained a judgment against Dixie Split, Litton executed upon the judgment for the back wages, bought Dixie Split's assets in the resulting execution sale, and had the corporation file for bankruptcy. Litton thereafter even had the chutzpa to file a claim in the bankruptcy proceeding based upon unpaid amounts of Litton's judgment. Citing *Taylor*, and pointing out (in an often quoted passage) the fiduciary obligation of directors and controlling shareholders to deal fairly with their corporation, the court held that Litton's claim should be subordinated to Pepper's.

What *Taylor* and *Pepper* have in common is the sort of abusive transactions between a corporation and its controlling shareholder, which, in an earlier chapter, we saw can justify piercing the corporate veil. Equitable subordination serves simply as a milder remedy, since it does not involve personal liability of the controlling shareholder for the corporation's debts.[29]

In contrast to cases in which the shareholder-lender took unfair advantage of the corporation and the other creditors, suppose a shareholder-lender gives the corporation better terms than would an outside lender. In this event, it would seem rather bizarre to subordinate the shareholder loan on the ground that it did not correspond to the deal the corporation would have made in an arms-length transaction. After all, as suggested above, one reason not to subordinate shareholder loans automatically is because shareholders might give to their corporation better

28. 308 U.S. 295, 60 S.Ct. 238 (1939).

29. The abusive transactions in *Taylor* and *Pepper* were fairly easy to see. In other cases, the question of whether there were abusive dealings is less clear-cut. For example, in *Gannett Company v. Larry*, 221 F.2d 269 (2d Cir.1955), a parent corporation, which was a newspaper conglomerate, loaned money to its subsidiary in order to fund the subsidiary's conversion from a newspaper publisher into a supplier of newsprint to the parent. After the subsidiary went bankrupt, the court, evidently viewing the attempt to use the subsidiary as a captive supplier to be unfair, subordinated the parent's loan.

terms in a loan than would a stranger. Nevertheless, some courts have subordinated shareholder loans based upon a theory which could make the shareholder's generosity to the corporation grounds for subordination. The theory is that shareholder loans made on terms better than an outside lender would have given (or, even more so, shareholder loans made in situations in which an outside lender would not have loaned money to the corporation at all) are not really loans. Instead, such so-called loans, in fact, constitute an equity investment in the corporation, and, as such, fall under the rule that debt must receive repayment in bankruptcy before anything goes to return the shareholders' equity investment.[30]

This sort of substance over form analysis owes much to tax law. Because of the tax advantages of debt versus equity investments in a corporation, numerous court opinions involve cases in which the Internal Revenue Service has argued that so-called loans made by shareholders to their corporations really constitute equity. In the tax context, it may make sense to ask whether the corporation is getting so-called loans from its shareholders which the company could not obtain from outsiders. After all, if the company gets a loan from shareholders which the company could just as well have obtained from a stranger, then denying the corporation an interest deduction might achieve nothing more than to force corporations next time to borrow from strangers. If, however, shareholders make "loans" which outsiders would not, then perhaps money paid as "interest" on such "loans" constitutes the sort of return on risk capital which Congress thought did not deserve to generate a deduction for the corporation. This sort of tax policy, however, has nothing to do with the policy behind subordination of some debts in bankruptcy.

One factor mentioned in a number of equitable subordination cases straddles both the "inequitable conduct" and "is it really a loan?" approaches to subordination. This factor is inadequate capitalization. As in some opinions involving piercing the corporate veil, a number of courts have held that inadequate capital is not grounds by itself to subordinate a shareholder loan.[31] Other courts have seen things differently. *Costello v. Fazio*[32] is one of the leading cases in which a court subordinated shareholder loans based upon inadequate capital.

The corporation in *Costello* began life when three individuals, who operated a plumbing supply business, decided to change the form of the business from a partnership to a corporation. At the time of the change, the three partners' capital accounts—in other words, the amount of money each partner was entitled to receive if the partnership liquidated at that moment by selling its assets at the assets' book values—stood at $43,169 for Fazio, $6451 for Ambrose, and $2000 for Leonard. As part of the incorporation, the three individuals had the partnership issue IOUs

---

30. *E.g.*, Fett Roofing & Sheet Metal Co. v. Moore, 438 F.Supp. 726 (E.D.Va. 1977).

31. *E.g.*, Branding Iron Steak House v. Richmond, 536 F.2d 299 (9th. Cir.1976).

32. 256 F.2d 903 (9th Cir.1958).

to Fazio for $41,169, and to Ambrose for $4451, bringing each of their capital accounts down to $2000. The new corporation then issued 200 shares of stock to each of the three individuals in exchange for their interests in the partnership, and assumed all of the partnership's debts, including the $41,169 owed to Fazio and the $4451 owed to Ambrose. A couple years later, the corporation went bankrupt. Fazio and Ambrose filed claims against the bankruptcy estate as creditors of the corporation. The trustee in bankruptcy (Costello) argued that the court should subordinate these claims to the claims of the corporation's other creditors. Pointing to the inadequate capital of the corporation, which was only "two jumps ahead of the wolf," the court subordinated Fazio's and Ambrose' claims.

We encountered inadequate capitalization as arguably inequitable conduct before in dealing with piercing the corporate veil, but how might a lack of capital suggest to a court that a shareholder loan is really equity and not a loan? In fact, courts in numerous tax cases have pointed to "thin capitalization"—in other words, a high ratio of corporate debt to equity—as a significant factor in deciding to recharacterize so-called shareholder loans as really equity.[33] There are a couple of possible reasons for this conclusion. To begin with, a thinly capitalized corporation likely could not have received the same loans from an outside lender as it obtained from its shareholders—after all, an outside lender would be concerned about the incentives created when the shareholders have so little of their own money at risk. Moreover, there may be simply an attack on tax piggishness involved in the focus on thin capitalization in the tax cases. If shareholders can capitalize the corporation with very little equity, and huge amounts of shareholder debt, the result could be to allow shareholders to completely circumvent the double-tax regime of dividend distributions which Congress created.

There may also be a certain amount of piggishness involved if shareholders cast much of their investment in the corporation in the form of loans, rather than stock purchases, with the idea that the shareholders then can share on a par with outside lenders in the event of corporate failure. Yet, outside lenders have a defense against such piggishness not available to the Internal Revenue Service: Outside lenders can refuse to do business with the corporation if they do not like the capital structure. Actually, however, shareholder debt may not be all that objectionable to lenders. True, unsecured lenders will not, without subordination, have the priority in bankruptcy over shareholder loans as the lenders would have over the right of shareholders, as shareholders, to receive liquidating distributions. Yet, the concern of lenders with shareholder investment typically has less to do with having someone beneath the lenders in bankruptcy, than it does with avoiding bankruptcy altogether. Specifically, the lenders want the shareholders to have money at risk in order to give the shareholders an incentive for responsi-

33. *E.g.*, Dobkin v. Commissioner of Internal Revenue, 15 T.C. 31 (1950), *aff'd* 192   F.2d 392 (2d Cir.1951).

ble management. Shareholder loans, while not having quite the same degree of risk as shareholder payments for stock, still place the shareholders' money at risk of business failure. Indeed, in the piercing context, there is both some logic and some authority for the proposition that shareholder loans count as part of the corporation's capital in deciding if the company is undercapitalized.[34] Moreover, the size and form of the shareholders' investment is not all that relevant to trade creditors and tort victims—the former being concerned with the corporation's working capital or cash flow, and the later being concerned with insurance.

This analysis suggests that the *Costello* court's concern about inadequate capitalization was misplaced. There was nothing inequitable about what the three owners did. The court's principal concern was that the three owners recharacterized sums, which the business needed to function, as debt rather than equity. Had this occurred after the corporation borrowed from outside lenders, then this sort of bait and switch would be a legitimate concern—since the lenders may have relied on the original capital structure in deciding to loan. The critical fact in *Costello*—which the court expressly disregarded—however, was that the corporation's outside debts all came after the owners converted the former equity into debt. Of course, the business' historic need for all of the sums the three owners invested shows that the business could not function solely on the amounts that the shareholders invested for their stock. Yet, if shareholder loans are inequitable simply because they supply capital essential to the business, then courts could end up subordinating virtually all shareholder loans. After all, corporations typically do not borrow if the company does not have some need for the money.[35]

§ 2.3 Distributions to Stockholders

So far in this chapter, we have looked at the financial structure of the corporation in terms of inflows of capital to the corporation, either as the corporation issues stock or as the corporation borrows money. Now, we turn to the subject of outflows of money or property from the corporation to the shareholders by virtue of their position as shareholders.

34. See § 1.5.7b *supra*.

35. Actually, it is interesting to ask why the three owners in *Costello* structured the capitalization of their corporation in the manner in which they did. In fact, apparently what they wanted to do was to unbundle their liquidation priorities from their interests in profit and control so that their rights vis-a-vis each other in the corporation remained what they had been in the partnership. Specifically, in the partnership—unless the three partners made a contrary agreement not mentioned in the opinion—each of the three owners had equal profit shares and equal management rights, despite their unequal capital accounts. The disparate capital accounts meant, however, that they had different rights to liquidating distributions. By equalizing the amount each paid for stock, while recharacterizing as debt the amounts by which Ambrose's and Fazio's capital accounts exceeded Leonard's, the three owners preserved their prior profit, management and liquidating rights despite the incorporation. The fact that this arrangement also, but for the court's decision to subordinate the debts, would have improved Ambrose' and Fazio's position vis-a-vis the outside creditors upon the company's bankruptcy, was probably just an incidental, and maybe unintended, outcome.

2.3.1 *The Directors' Discretion Over Dividends*

"Dividends" is the common term for distributions from a corporation to its shareholders by virtue of their position as shareholders.[1] Normally, it is within the board of director's discretion to decide at any given time whether the corporation will pay a dividend to its shareholders, and, if so, what amount of dividend the corporation will pay.[2] There are, however, a number of limitations on this discretion.

To begin with, there can be contractual or quasi-contractual restrictions. The contractual restrictions generally come from lending agreements, which often contain terms restricting how much dividends a corporation can pay to its shareholders.[3] In addition, articles of incorporation commonly contain provisions governing dividends, which courts and writers often view as somewhat contractual in nature. For example, as discussed earlier in this chapter, articles often authorize the corporation to issue classes of stock with the right to receive a dividend before the board can have the corporation pay dividends to other classes. Yet, such a dividend preference does not force the directors to pay anything if the directors choose not to declare a dividend for any shares.[4] A company's articles, however, not only can give one class of stock a preference to dividends, when and if declared, but also could require the directors to declare for the class a certain amount of dividends at stated intervals.[5]

§ 2.3

1. This assumes that the distribution is neither in exchange for the shareholder's stock, nor in liquidation of the company. We shall address distributions to shareholders in exchange for their stock later in this section; we shall consider liquidating distributions (sometimes also referred to as liquidating dividends) in a later chapter.

Incidentally, since shareholders receive dividends by virtue of their ownership of stock, the question could arise as to who is entitled to dividends when shares change hands between the time the directors decide to have the corporation pay a dividend, and the actual payment. To solve this problem, directors, when they declare a dividend, typically fix a "record date." The person who owns the stock on this date is the person entitled to the dividend.

2. *E.g.*, Dodge v. Ford Motor Co., 204 Mich. 459, 170 N.W. 668 (1919). The directors' discretion ends once they declare a dividend; in other words, once the directors vote to have the corporation pay a certain dividend, they cannot change their minds and cancel the dividend. *See, e.g.*, Cole Real Estate Corp. v. Peoples Bank & Trust Co., 160 Ind.App. 88, 310 N.E.2d 275 (Ind.Ct. App.1974). *But see* Ford v. Easthampton Rubber Thread Co., 158 Mass. 84, 32 N.E. 1036 (1893) (directors can revoke a dividend declaration prior to its announcement to the shareholders or the public).

3. Another source of contractual restrictions on the board's discretion over dividends comes from agreements sometimes made among shareholders in closely held corporations. Such agreements occasionally contain terms which seek to require the board to declare a certain level of dividends. The attempt of shareholders to curb the board's discretion by virtue of such contracts raises legal and policy questions considered in a later chapter dealing with the special problems of closely held corporations.

4. *E.g.*, Field v. Lamson & Goodnow Mfg. Co., 162 Mass. 388, 38 N.E. 1126 (1894).

5. *E.g.*, Crocker v. Waltham Watch Co., 315 Mass. 397, 53 N.E.2d 230 (1944). As discussed in the next subsection, state statutes prevent a corporation from legally paying dividends unless a certain minimum amount of funds are available. Hence, a provision requiring the directors to pay dividends must condition, expressly or implicitly, the requirement upon the availability of legally adequate funds.

In addition to these contractual or quasi-contractual constraints, there are statutory limits on permissible dividends. These limits are fairly involved and we shall explore them in a separate subsection.

Finally, minority shareholders might bring a lawsuit against the directors, arguing that the board abused its discretion either in declaring, or in refusing to declare, dividends. Occasionally, a court will find that the board abused its discretion and order the corporation pay, or not pay, a dividend. For example, in its famous decision in *Dodge v. Ford Motor Company*,[6] the Michigan Supreme Court ordered the Ford Motor Company to pay additional dividends. By and large, however, courts have been hesitant to find an abuse of discretion in the absence of fairly extraordinary facts. Indeed, in *Dodge*, the court only ordered a dividend because Ford Motor Company was making money faster than the company's directors had plans to spend it, even if the company paid the dividend.[7] By comparison, so long as directors can identify some arguable corporate need to retain funds, courts generally will not second guess the board's judgment.[8] True, in some cases, courts have stated that they will find an abuse of discretion if directors withhold dividends in bad faith to force minority shareholders to sell out. Yet it is often difficult to come up with convincing evidence to prove such bad faith.[9]

It is easy to understand why courts would be reluctant to second guess directors' decisions to declare or withhold dividends. The decision to withhold or declare a dividend involves an inherent trade-off between allowing the owners to enjoy the fruits of the venture, versus reinvesting the business' profits with the hope of obtaining even more profits in the future. Since different shareholders often place differing utilities upon receiving immediate income (a dollar today) as opposed to receiving greater amounts in the future (two dollars tomorrow), the directors' decision about dividends is never going to please all of the shareholders. Moreover, the efficacy of reinvesting corporate earnings involves predictions as to future returns. A court is unlikely to view either itself, or a minority shareholder, as better able to make this prediction than the directors. In any event, since the shareholders elect the directors, and since the directors are often substantial shareholders themselves, one might suppose that the directors have every incentive to declare dividends when consistent with maximizing shareholder wealth.

6. 204 Mich. 459, 170 N.W. 668 (1919).

7. Ford Motor Company was literally making money hand over fist. It had a surplus of almost $112 million, cash and marketable securities of nearly $54 million, and was making over $60 million per year. The company had been paying a regular dividend of $1.2 million per year—which meant that each shareholder was getting back every year an amount greater than the shareholder's entire original investment. On top of this, Ford Motor had been paying huge special dividends. Henry Ford had the board stop paying the special dividends in order to reinvest the funds in a dramatic expansion of the company. The Dodge brothers—who owned 10 percent of the outstanding stock in Ford Motor, and who were using their share of the dividends to develop their own auto company—sued to compel more dividends.

8. *E.g.*, Zidell v. Zidell, Inc., 277 Or. 413, 560 P.2d 1086 (Or. 1977). *But see* Miller v. Magline, Inc., 76 Mich.App. 284, 256 N.W.2d 761 (1977).

9. *E.g.*, Gottfried v. Gottfried, 73 N.Y.S.2d 692 (1947).

Unfortunately, the supposition that directors have every incentive to declare dividends when consistent with maximizing shareholder wealth turns out to be highly questionable. The reasons differ somewhat depending upon whether one is dealing with a closely held or publicly held corporation.

In a closely held corporation, the refusal to declare dividends can alter the relative shares of profit received by the company's various owners—instead of simply postponing all of the owners' enjoyment of the income. The directors of a closely held corporation, who are typically also the majority shareholders of the company, commonly receive money from the company through mechanisms besides dividends. For example, the majority shareholders and directors may loan money to the corporation and receive interest payments from the corporation in return, or they may have the corporation make interest-free loans to themselves. They might also have the corporation repurchase some of their stock. Most especially, they will have the corporation pay to themselves salaries for their management of the company. By comparison, minority shareholders (particularly those not employed by the company) may receive nothing but dividends. Hence, lowering dividends and increasing these other payouts can shift the rewards of corporate ownership almost entirely to the majority shareholders.

In a publicly held corporation, directors also might have incentives to declare less than an optimal amount of dividends. Often, the directors of a public corporation will not own enough stock to benefit substantially from larger dividends. By contrast, retaining money for corporate expansion can produce a variety of personal benefits for directors and corporate management. A larger company often justifies larger compensation for the corporation's officers and directors. A larger and more diversified corporation might be less likely to get into financial trouble so as to endanger the jobs of the company's officers and directors. Perhaps most significant, however, is the psychological satisfaction of being a director or officer of a bigger rather than smaller company. By contrast, shareholders of a publicly traded corporation might obtain less advantage from corporate expansion than they would through greater dividends. While corporate growth should produce greater dividend paying capacity in the future, the shareholders might have been able to take the immediate dividends and put the money into investments with a better rate of return for the level of risk.[10]

---

10. Implicit in this statement is the assumption that the shareholders do not have any immediate plans to spend the dividends on consumption, but rather would reinvest the money. Under this assumption, the optimal dividend policy depends upon whether the corporation can reinvest its earnings at a higher rate of return for a given level of risk than can its shareholders. What about the shareholder who wants to spend on consumption? In a publicly traded corporation, such a shareholder can obtain a self-

help dividend by selling some of his or her stock. On the other hand, once one accepts the notion that shareholders of publicly traded corporations always can obtain a self-help dividend by selling some of their shares, one might ask why a shareholder, who thinks that he or she can more effectively invest retained earnings, also cannot employ this approach. The problem is that, if the corporation is not investing its retained earnings to obtain a return commensurate with other uses for the funds, the

Multiple classes of stock and convertible bonds also undercut the rationale that one can trust the directors to seek the optimal level of dividends. The problem is that such a multi-level capital structure often makes the optimal level of dividends different for the holders of different types of securities. We confronted one example of this phenomenon earlier in this chapter: Skipping dividends effectively transfers a share of earnings from the holders of non-cumulative preferred stock to the holders of common stock. Hence, an optimal level of dividends from the standpoint of the common is not an optimal level from the standpoint of the non-cumulative preferred. Another example comes when dealing with convertible securities. Because the value of a conversion feature for convertible preferred stock or convertible bonds depends upon growth in the value of the common stock into which the owner of the convertible security can convert, the convertible security holder benefits by having the corporation pay little immediate dividends to the common, and, instead, reinvest most or all of the corporation's earnings into growth. By contrast, the existing common stockholder, who faces the prospect of dilution of his or her interest by virtue of the exercise of the conversion rights, might figure that he or she just as soon would have the corporation pay the most dividends up-front. The common holder then can use the dividends to buy other investments which he or she will not have to share with convertible security holders.

From a doctrinal standpoint, these subtle conflicts lead one to question whether courts have been too deferential to directors in reviewing decisions regarding dividends. In fact, in some circumstances, courts have shown a willingness to subject dividend decisions to greater scrutiny. For example, courts might apply more rigorous scrutiny to a dividend decision which favors one class of stock over another if the directors themselves own a substantial amount of the favored class (or if the directors are under the control of a shareholder owning a substantial amount of the favored class).[11] In addition, we shall see later in discussing the special problems of closely held corporations that there is some authority for a more careful review of dividend denials in the closely held corporation context when the effect of the denial is to squeeze minority shareholders out of any reward from their ownership in the corporation.[12] Still, despite the various subtle conflicts, practical concerns dictate a general standard of deference to the board. After all, any other approach could degenerate into the court making the fundamental decisions of whether and to what extent the corporation should expand, rather than the board making those decisions.

market presumably will discount the price of the corporation's stock to take into account this fact. Put differently, the next buyer will discount the shares our dissatisfied shareholder wants to unload to bring the return up to that of competitive investments. One should note, however, that the tax law favors the corporation retaining and reinvesting the company's earnings, since dividends are normally taxable to the recipient.

11. *E.g.*, Burton v. Exxon Corp., 583 F.Supp. 405 (S.D.N.Y.1984).

12. See § 5.1.1 *infra*.

2.3.2 *Statutory Limits on Dividends*

In an ordinary partnership, creditors are unconcerned for the most part about distributions of money from the firm to its owners, because the owners have unlimited personal liability. Once one introduces limited liability, this changes. If those with no personal liability could legally withdraw their original investment at any time, they could deprive creditors of the cushion provided by this invested capital, which the creditors may have relied upon in advancing money to the business. Worse, the unscrupulous might take advantage of such a regime by withdrawing money representing not only their investment, but also that obtained through borrowing by the firm. For this reason, corporation statutes impose restrictions upon dividends paid by corporations to their shareholders. These dividend rules vary among the different state statutes.

a. *Traditional balance sheet statutes*

The most traditional approach to statutory dividend limits is often referred to as the balance sheet test.[13] Delaware's corporation statute provides a good illustration of this approach. Under Delaware's statute, dividends generally cannot exceed the amount of the corporation's "surplus."[14] "Surplus" is not any segregated stash of money. Rather, it is a term of art, meaning the difference between the corporation's "net assets," and its "capital."[15] "Net assets," in turn, is the amount arrived at by subtracting the company's total liabilities from its total assets. The difference between total assets and total liabilities is the amount commonly referred to as "equity" or "net worth" on a balance sheet, and one can now see why this approach often is called the balance sheet test.

As just stated, to determine surplus, one must subtract "capital" from net assets. If one assumes (incorrectly as it turns out) that capital equals what the shareholders paid for their stock, one can see how a statute like Delaware's might protect creditors against both the dangers of dividends which leave the corporation with insufficient funds to pay its debts, and dividends which return to the shareholders the money that the shareholders invested for their stock. Specifically, if capital equaled what the shareholders paid for their stock, then limiting dividends to the amount of surplus would mean that the assets left in the corporation after the dividend would at least equal the combined amount of the corporation's liabilities and the shareholders' investment.[16]

---

13. Another label for the approach followed by these statutes is the impairment of capital test.

14. Del. Gen. Corp. Law § 170(a).

15. Del. Gen. Corp. Law § 154.

16. To illustrate, assume that a corporation has assets of $1 million, debts of $500,000, and "capital" of $200,000. The corporation's surplus would equal $300,000 ($1 million in assets, minus $500,000 in debts, minus $200,000 of capital). Paying the maximum permissible dividend of $300,000 would leave the corporation with assets of $700,000, which equals the amount of its debts and capital. Hence, if the $200,000 capital in this example equaled what the shareholders paid for their stock, the result of the traditional balance sheet approach is to prevent the shareholders withdrawing their investment through dividends.

It turns out, however, that such a potentially sensible approach is not what Delaware's law, or other balance sheet approach statutes, provide. The problem is found in the definition of capital. Under Delaware's statute, and balance sheet statutes generally, "capital," does not equal what the shareholders paid for their stock. Instead, capital is largely whatever sum directors (and shareholders) choose to call capital. Specifically, under Delaware's statute, capital initially represents that portion of the consideration the company received in exchange for its shares which the directors, at the time the company sold the shares, decided to designate as capital.[17] This could be the entire purchase price, or any fraction of it, so long as the amount is no less than the aggregate par value of those shares sold which have a par value (in other words, par value multiplied by the number of shares sold which have this par).[18]

To illustrate, assume that a corporation sold 1000 shares of $1 par stock for $10 per share. In this event, the directors upon the issuance of the stock could designate all of the $10,000 received by the corporation to be capital. Or, the directors could designate only $1000—$1 par multiplied by 1000 shares sold—of the $10,000 received to be capital. Or the directors could pick as capital any sum between $1000 and $10,000. If, instead of having a par of $1, the 1000 shares were no-par stock, then the directors can pick any number between $10,000 and zero to be capital. If the directors neglect to set any amount, then, under Delaware's statute, capital equals the aggregate par value of shares with par, and the entire sum received for shares without par.

Directors, by resolution, can increase capital. This does not involve actually transferring any funds; the company simply increases the number shown for capital on its balance sheet, and decreases, by the same amount, the number shown for surplus (since surplus, by definition, is the difference between net assets and capital).

Far more significantly, directors (with, in some cases, the necessary cooperation of shareholders) can reduce capital. Canceling repurchased shares provides one mechanism to reduce capital. We shall examine this later when considering share repurchases. In addition, Delaware's corporation law gives the board the power, by simple resolution, to decrease capital until the capital equals the aggregate par value of the outstanding stock.[19] Moreover, even the aggregate par value of the outstanding stock is not an immutable barrier below which the company cannot reduce its capital. The directors and shareholders can vote to amend the corporation's articles to lower par value (or change the stock into no-par shares).[20] The amendment of the articles, in itself, might not lower

---

17. Del. Gen. Corp. Law § 154.

18. As explained earlier in this chapter, par simply represents a dollar amount per share which the articles of incorporation state to be the par value for the corporation's authorized stock (or for a particular class of the corporation's authorized stock). The drafters of the articles simply select this amount out of thin air. While corporations cannot legally issue shares at a price less than par, corporations can, and commonly do, issue shares at a price greater than par.

19. Del. Gen. Corp. Law § 244(a).

20. Del. Gen. Corp. Law § 242(a)(3).

capital; but it clears the way for a board resolution which does. Statutes sometimes contain restrictions upon reductions in capital. For instance, Delaware's law provides that no capital reduction can occur unless the assets remaining are sufficient to pay the corporation's debts.[21] Actually, this limit is rather meaningless, since, in and of itself, reducing capital does not reduce assets—it is simply a paper transaction. More fundamentally, a reduction in capital cannot create a surplus—thereby allowing a distribution of assets—if assets are less than liabilities.

All told, the traditional balance sheet approach typified by Delaware's statute is something of a joke. It purports to prevent the shareholders from receiving dividends which represent a return of the shareholder's invested capital. Yet, by allowing directors to designate as capital sums which are less than what the corporation received for its stock, the statute undercuts this idea at the outset.[22] Perhaps one might argue that creditors are on notice of this possibility, because the corporation's balance sheet should show what the directors labeled as capital. Yet, even this rationalization fails given the power of the board and shareholders to reduce capital to nothing.[23] Of course, creditors who are knowledgeable of the law should realize that the statute is no protection against the reduction of capital. But then what is the point of the whole exercise of designating capital to begin with?

In addition to prejudicing creditors who relied upon a level of shareholder investment in deciding to do business with the corporation, the ability to declare dividends which represent the return of invested capital, rather than earnings, may prejudice some shareholders to favor others. Specifically, as discussed earlier in this chapter, articles often create classes of stock with a liquidation preference in the amount of the share's issue price. The purpose of such a preference is to ensure that the owners of the preferred get back from the corporation the money they invested, before the owners of the common shares receive back their investment. Allowing the common holders to receive dividends which represent the money invested by the preferred holders circumvents this purpose. Unfortunately, traditional balance sheet statutes such as Delaware's might only protect against this outcome indirectly and incompletely through the prohibition on dividends which invade capital as defined by the statute. If the corporation issues the preferred shares at a price above par, the "capital" contributed to the balance sheet by the preferred shares can be less than the amount of the share's issue price. The result is to create an immediate surplus available to pay dividends despite leaving insufficient assets to cover a liquidation preference equal to the preferred's issue price. Alternately, as we saw above, corporations may be able under the traditional statutes to reduce their capital for

21. Del. Gen. Corp. Law § 244(b).

22. Hence, if a corporation issues stock for $10,000, but the directors only designate $1000 as capital, the corporation has an immediate $9000 surplus which it could use to pay dividends.

23. Once the directors and shareholders have reduced the corporation's "capital" to nothing, then the corporation can pay dividends until the remaining assets equal the corporation's debts, thereby leaving no shareholder investment in the company.

purposes of the statute. Some traditional balance sheet statutes, however, contain additional limits designed specifically to protect shares with liquidation preferences.[24]

To complete the discussion, it is useful to point out a couple of wrinkles on the basic balance sheet approach. To begin with, it is possible for a corporation to have a surplus, yet still be insolvent in the sense that it lacks sufficient liquid or current assets (cash and the like) to pay its current or soon to be due bills. (The inability to pay bills as they become due is commonly referred to as "equitable insolvency;" by comparison, "bankruptcy insolvency" is the term for being insolvent in the sense that one's assets are less than one's debts.) Some balance sheet statutes contain provisions prohibiting dividends either when the corporation is insolvent, or when paying the dividend would render the company insolvent, in the sense of being unable to pay its bills as due.[25] A dividend under such circumstances might also violate fraudulent conveyance statutes.[26]

On the other hand, Delaware and some other states allow a corporation to declare a dividend, even though it has no surplus, so long as the dividend does not exceed the company's net earnings for the present or preceding year (or the combined earnings for both years).[27] This is often referred to as a "nimble" dividend, because the directors must act relatively quickly to declare it.[28]

b. *The earned surplus approach*

The pre–1980 Model Business Corporation Act employed another test for permissible dividends, which a number of states have followed. Like the traditional balance sheet approach, this test starts at a seemingly sensible point, and then degenerates. Under the pre–1980 Model Act, a corporation may pay dividends out of its "earned surplus."[29] As with the concept of surplus under the traditional balance sheet approach, "earned

---

24. *See, e.g.,* N.Y. Bus. Corp. Law §§ 506(b) (preventing the allocation to surplus, rather than to capital, of any amount received for no-par shares, unless the amount allocated to surplus is in excess of the shares' liquidation preference), 806(b)(3) (a corporation cannot, by amending its certificate, reduce its capital to an amount below the aggregate liquidation preferences payable upon involuntary liquidation).

25. *E.g.,* N.Y. Bus. Corp. Law §§ 102(a)(8), 510(a).

26. *E.g.,* Wells Fargo Bank v. Desert View Building Supplies, Inc., 475 F.Supp. 693 (D.Nev.1978), *aff'd. without opinion*, 633 F.2d 221 (9th Cir.1980).

27. *E.g.,* Del. Gen. Corp. Law § 170(a).

28. At first glance, one might wonder why a year's earnings would not produce a surplus to allow dividends under the general balance sheet test, making nimble dividends irrelevant. If, at the start of the year in question, the corporation's assets at least equaled the company's debts and capital, then the net income for the year would increase surplus by the amount of the year's net income. The problem is that the corporation could have been losing money in prior years, so that the company's assets are now less than its debts and capital—in other words, instead of having a surplus on the balance sheet, there is a deficit. Without a statute allowing for nimble dividends, the corporation would need to cure the deficit before declaring a dividend. A rationale for allowing a dividend from current earnings, rather than demanding that the corporation cure the deficit first, is that the dividend will not make the situation worse than it was before the corporation made the current income.

29. M.B.C.A. (1969) § 45.

surplus'' under the old Model Act is a term of art rather than a stash of money. Specifically, earned surplus, for the most part, refers to the sum of the corporation's income, net profits and gains over the years, less the company's losses, and less prior distributions to the shareholders.[30]

The concept of earned surplus differs from the concept of surplus under the balance sheet approach in two ways—one presumably not significant, while the other is potentially significant. The first difference goes to the accounting document at which the test seemingly looks. Instead of looking to the balance sheet, as under Delaware's statute, the old Model Act apparently keys to the corporation's income statements. In other words, the old Model Act's definition of earned surplus suggests that one should go back through all of the corporation's income statements since the inception of the company, total all of the income, subtract the losses incurred in the years in which the corporation lost rather than made money, and subtract the total of prior distributions to the shareholders. Actually, however, this difference from the balance sheet test is probably more apparent than real. The reason is that, under basic principles of accounting, the balance sheet should reflect the total of earnings over the years, less losses and distributions. After all, if the balance sheet shows that the assets of the corporation are greater than the sum of the corporation's debts and the amount the shareholders invested for their stock, then where else could this increase in assets have come from but earnings accumulated over the years? Indeed, the item on the balance sheet which shows the difference between the amount of assets, and the amount of debts and shareholder investment, typically is called "retained earnings."[31]

The second difference between earned surplus under the old Model Act, and surplus as defined under a statute like Delaware's, is potentially very significant. Generally speaking, earned surplus only comes from the corporation's income over the years; whereas we saw above that surplus under Delaware's statute not only comes from earnings, but also comes from any amounts which the shareholders pay for their stock which are greater than what the directors and shareholders choose, from time to time, to call capital. Hence, if the old Model Act actually limited dividends to earned surplus, it would have prevented dividends which returned to the shareholders their invested capital.

It turns out, however, that the old Model Act, and many (albeit not all) of the states which copied this approach, contain provisions which undercut the limitation of dividends to earned surplus. Most significantly, the old Model Act recognizes a category of "surplus" called "capital surplus." Capital surplus is the difference between the corporation's "surplus"—defined the same way as under the balance sheet test—and

30. *Id* at § 2(1).

31. In addition to preparing a balance sheet and an income statement at the end of the relevant financial period, accountants commonly prepare a statement which reconciles the income statement with the balance sheet by showing how the income (or loss) for the period, less any distributions to the shareholders, led to the difference in retained earnings between the most recent balance sheet and the prior balance sheet of the corporation.

the corporation's earned surplus.[32] Since capital under the old Model Act, like capital under the traditional balance sheet statutes, need equal no more than aggregate par value of the corporation's outstanding stock,[33] the corporation's issuance of stock at a price exceeding the share's par value, or the issuance of no-par shares, can create a paid-in capital surplus. Moreover, the old Model Act allows the directors, with the cooperation of the shareholders, to reduce capital to virtually nothing,[34] just as directors and shareholders could do under the traditional balance sheet statutes. The added surplus created by a reduction in capital (sometimes referred to as a reduction surplus) increases capital surplus. The old Model Act allows a corporation to pay dividends out of capital surplus if so authorized by the company's articles, or if each class of shareholders votes to allow such a dividend, or to pay cumulative preferred dividends.[35] The upshot is to give the shareholders the power to withdraw their investment through dividends, despite the possible reliance by creditors upon the shareholder's investment.[36]

c. Modern approaches

The end result of the traditional statutes has been to pretend to provide more protection than the statutes actually deliver. Specifically, the traditional statutes, whether based on the balance sheet test, or on earned, coupled with capital, surplus, generally do not prevent dividends which reflect a return of the shareholders' original investment. More recent corporation statutes have responded to this phenomenon in different ways.

The current Model Business Corporation Act reacts by giving up. Specifically, the current Model Act eliminates the concept of capital as a limit on corporate distributions. Instead, so long as the corporation is solvent in the equitable sense (the company can pay its bills as due), a corporation can declare a dividend up to the amount by which its assets exceed its liabilities (or, if the corporation has outstanding stock with liquidation preferences, the amount by which the company's assets exceed the combination of its liabilities and the liquidation preferences of its outstanding shares).[37] Paying a dividend equal to the amount by which the corporation's assets exceed its liabilities will leave no shareholders' equity to cushion the company's creditors.

California takes another tack. California's corporations statute attempts to retain an equity cushion for creditors by the use of a numerical test. Specifically, the California Corporations Code allows a dividend

---

32. M.B.C.A. (1969) § 2(k), (m).

33. Id at § 2(j).

34. Id at §§ 58, 69.

35. Id at § 46. In addition, the old Model Act allows the corporation to "transfer" funds from capital surplus to earned surplus in order to wipe out a deficit in earned surplus. Id at § 70.

36. It is worth noting, however, that both through its requirements for share-

holder votes, and by limiting dividends out of capital surplus when the corporation's assets would be less than the company's debts and any liquidation preferences, the old Model Act provides more protection to preferred shareholders than did a statute like Delaware's.

37. M.B.C.A. § 6.40(c).

under either of two conditions: (1) the company may distribute a sum not in excess of the amount of the corporation's retained earnings; or (2) if there are insufficient retained earnings, the company can distribute a sum which leaves the corporation with total assets in excess of 1 1/4 times the company's total liabilities and current assets greater than its current liabilities (or greater than 1 1/4 times its current liabilities if the company did not manage to earn more than its interest expense the prior two years).[38]

Both the current Model Act and California's statute mark an improvement over the traditional dividend limits in that neither the current Model Act nor California's statute pretends to provide more protection than it actually delivers. Yet, the two statutes embody very different policy choices. The current Model Act contents itself with making transparent the result which the preexisting law largely had reached. California attempts to improve upon the protections accorded by prior law. Choosing between these approaches forces one to ask whether the law should attempt to limit the ability of the shareholders to withdraw their invested capital. After all, under the Model Act, the corporation still must have sufficient assets to pay all of its debts despite the dividend.

To evaluate this difference in approach, it is useful to begin by considering the role which shareholder equity plays in protecting creditors. One aspect is to provide a cushion against downturns in the business. Far more significant, however, is the impact on incentives. If the owners of a business have neither any personal liability, nor any money of their own invested in the business, they have an incentive to undertake what may be unreasonably risky undertakings. As discussed earlier in this chapter, few states attempt to address this problem any more by requiring a minimum amount of capital for a corporation— presumably because of the difficulty of setting a minimum capital which could sensibly apply to corporations engaged in a multitude of differing businesses. The problem of inadequate shareholder investment, however, becomes potentially both more dangerous and more subject to remedy if one focuses solely on the withdrawal of money which shareholders invested in the corporation. This situation is more dangerous because it is changing the incentive structure, after creditors decided to deal with the company, to one which may have been unacceptable had it been in place before. This situation is also more subject to remedy because it does not require figuring out what should be the minimum capital, but rather involves simply limiting the withdrawal of money once put in.

Of course, one could respond to this analysis by pointing out that creditors might create protections for themselves by contractually limit-

---

38. Cal. Corp. Code § 500. Current assets generally are cash and assets likely to be turned into cash within a year, while current liabilities generally are liabilities due within a year. In addition to this basic limit, California's statute forbids a dividend if the company is, or paying the dividend will make the company, insolvent (in the sense of being unable to pay one's bills as due), or if the corporation's net assets after paying a dividend to junior shares will be less than the liquidation priorities of the company's outstanding stock with liquidation preferences. *Id* at §§ 501, 502.

ing dividends. Yet, the logical extension of this argument is to eliminate all restrictions on dividends. The fact that legislatures have chosen to make any restrictions presumably reflects a notion that creditors should not be put to the added transaction costs of always needing to specify limits on dividends.

If we conclude that the shareholders should not be able to withdraw all of their investment through dividends, then we must ask whether the shareholders should be able to withdraw any of their investment through dividends, and, if so, how much. Limiting dividends to retained earnings would prevent the shareholders from withdrawing any of their invested capital through dividends. Why not stick with this limit? The answer presumably is that such a rule would curb too severely the flexibility of the shareholders to withdraw capital no longer needed in the business, or the flexibility of the board to dip into invested capital in order to smooth over ups and downs in earnings and maintain the steady dividends desired by some shareholders. In fact, such a limit might go beyond what creditors demand in negotiated loan agreements with corporate borrowers. Seen in this light, the California statute makes a reasonable attempt to craft a compromise between allowing shareholders to withdraw some of their invested funds, and protecting creditors against excessive removal of equity.

d. Accounting questions

Common to the various statutory dividend limits which we have been discussing is the need to put a dollar amount on the corporation's total assets, and, under some tests, a dollar amount on the corporation's earnings. Specifically, the greater the dollar value of the corporation's assets, the larger the dividend which the corporation legally can declare under the traditional balance sheet test, under both the old and the current Model Act, and under California's statute. Under statutes which look to earned surplus, or retained earnings, or which allow nimble dividends, the greater the income of the corporation for the relevant period, the larger the dividend the corporation legally can pay. Unfortunately, it turns out that placing a dollar value on a corporation's assets, or even stating the amount of a corporation's earnings during a period of time, is not a straightforward matter.

Conventional accounting practice generally uses the cost of an asset, less depreciation, as the amount placed on the books for the value of each asset. Suppose, however, a corporation's directors wish to declare a larger dividend than this practice would allow: Can the directors argue that some assets have, in fact, appreciated in value since their purchase? Decisions under the traditional statutes are divided.

In the leading case, *Randall v. Bailey*,[39] the trustee of a bankrupt corporation claimed that the corporation's directors had violated the state's dividend statute by declaring dividends when the corporation did not have a surplus. While the corporation's balance sheet showed a

---

39. 288 N.Y. 280, 43 N.E.2d 43 (1942).

surplus, this reflected writing up the value of the company's land to almost six times the land's purchase price.[40] The New York court held that this was permissible. Courts in some other states, however, have stated that the directors, in determining the permissibility of a dividend, should not take into account any appreciation in the value of the corporation's assets until the corporation actually realizes this appreciation by selling the assets.[41]

The provisions of the recent statutes echo the disagreement among the courts. The current Model Act is explicitly permissive. The Act allows directors to base their determination of the legality of a dividend upon financial statements prepared on the basis of accounting practices which are "reasonable in the circumstances," or on a "fair valuation," or any other method that is "reasonable."[42] California, in contrast, mandates that corporations follow generally accepted accounting principles in determining the dollar amount of the companies' assets.[43] Generally accepted accounting principles generally preclude revaluing assets at greater than the assets' initial costs.

The divergence of authority on the subject of allowing dividends based upon upward revaluations of a corporation's assets stems from the fact that the appropriate answer is not obvious. Historic costs less depreciation, more often than not, do not equal the present values of a firm's assets. On the other hand, prior to realizing a profit upon actual disposition of an asset, any upward revision is inherently speculative. Moreover, there is always a temptation for those desiring to declare a dividend to error on the side of more rather than less in any upward revaluation.[44]

A variety of accounting choices can impact the earnings recognized by a corporation during a given period of time. As stated above, California's dividend test uses the corporation's "retained earnings" as one measure for permissible dividends. Retained earnings is a commonly used accounting term, and California's corporation code essentially demands that corporations follow generally accepted accounting principles in computing this sum. By contrast, the old Model Act's reference to "earned surplus" is ambiguous as to what principles companies' must

---

40. The write up was based upon an assessment of the property for tax purposes.

41. *E.g.,* Kingston v. Home Life Ins. Co., 11 Del.Ch. 258, 101 A. 898 (1917), *aff'd,* 104 A. 25 (Del.1918). *But see* Klang v. Smith's Food & Drug Centers, Inc., 702 A.2d 150 (Del.1997). Both *Randall,* as well as courts which have been hesitant to allow dividends based upon upward revaluations of the corporation's assets, have suggested that the directors, in determining whether to pay a dividend, should revalue the company's assets downward if circumstances suggest that the company's assets are worth less than the value on the company's books. *See, e.g.,* Vogtman v. Merchants'

Mortgage & Credit Co., 20 Del.Ch. 364, 178 A. 99 (1935). Generally accepted accounting principles also call for downward revaluations of certain types of assets, such as inventory. The asymmetry reflects the fact that downward revaluations do not present the same danger of natural optimism blinding one's better judgment as do upward revaluations.

42. M.B.C.A. § 6.40(d).

43. *See* Cal. Corp. Code § 114.

44. The fact that the corporation in *Randall* ended up in bankruptcy might provide at least some evidence of this danger.

follow in computing earned surplus. Part of the problem is that the old act's definition of earned surplus refers to "income," "net profits," and "gains and loses," in a manner which is totally confusing. For example, it is not clear what, if anything, is the difference between income and net profits. Most folks might assume that these terms mean the same thing, but that would mean that the definition of earned surplus contains redundant language—which is contrary to the normal assumption that all words in a statute should have some significance.[45]

e. Remedies for improper declaration of dividends

Two parties might face liability when a corporation pays a dividend in violation of statutory dividend limits: the directors who voted to declare the dividend, and the shareholders who received the dividend. This liability might exist by virtue of express liability provisions in corporation statutes, by virtue of common law, or by virtue of provisions in creditor protection laws of general applicability (such as the fraudulent conveyance acts). An important issue is whether this liability exists without respect to fault. After all, directors may have acted in reliance upon corporate financial statements when declaring an illegal dividend, while shareholders (especially in a publicly held corporation) might have little idea as to whether the corporation's financial status renders a dividend impermissible.

Corporations statutes typically contain provisions which expressly impose liability upon directors who vote to declare a dividend in violation of the statutory dividend limits.[46] Generally, these statutes do not impose liability without respect to fault, but, instead, condition liability on negligence or bad faith.[47] Statutes vary as to whether they impose liability solely in favor of the corporation—thereby leaving creditors to recover only through the efforts of a trustee in bankruptcy—or whether the statute also allows actions by creditors against the directors.[48]

Shareholders who receive impermissible dividends face more diverse liabilities. Corporation statutes often contain provisions imposing liabili-

---

45. Some states' statutes expressly sanction one deviation from both generally accepted accounting principles and a realistic attempt to determine either the value of the corporation's assets or the corporation's earnings. Normally, as a firm uses up property—either because the property wears out with use, or because the property consists of a consumable resource—the company should take this depreciation or depletion into account in determining its earnings and the value of its assets. Some statutes, however, allow so-called wasting-asset corporations—in other words, a corporation in the business of exploiting a non-replenishable asset, like a mine—not to take depletion of its key asset into account in determining permissible dividends. *E.g.*, Del. Gen. Corp. Law § 170(b) (a wasting asset corporation can ignore depletion in deter-

mining profits for purposes of nimble dividends). The rationale for this exception is not obvious.

46. *E.g.*, M.B.C.A. § 8.33.

47. The Model Act follows one scheme for conditioning liability on fault, which is to cross reference the standards governing the general conduct of the directors. Other statutes contain requirements of fault which are specific to liability for an improper dividend declaration. *E.g.*, Del. Gen. Corp. Law § 174(a) (violation must be "willful or negligent"). Statutes also commonly protect directors from liability if they acted in a good faith and reasonable reliance on corporate financial records and reports. *E.g.*, Del. Gen. Corp. Law § 172.

48. *Compare* M.B.C.A. § 8.33, *with* Del. Gen. Corp. Law § 174(a).

ty upon shareholders who receive impermissible dividends. Some statutes require shareholders to return improper dividends to the corporation.[49] Most statutes, however, simply allow the directors, who were liable for an impermissible dividend, to seek a contribution from the shareholders who received the illegal dividend.[50] Generally, either type of statute only makes shareholders liable if the shareholders knew that the dividend was improper.

Given the narrow reach of the typical corporation statute as far as shareholder liability—in that the typical statute only creates liability for shareholders if, first, a director is found liable, and then the director pursues the shareholders for contribution—creditors may seek to come up with other theories of liability against the shareholders. Under the common law, courts required shareholders to return improper dividends. There is a critical difference under the common law depending upon whether the impropriety involved the corporation being insolvent when it paid the dividend, or whether the dividend violated the statute because the dividend exceeded the corporation's surplus. In the case of insolvency, courts hold that shareholders are liable without regard to fault, whereas in the situation of exceeding surplus, courts generally came to hold that the shareholder would be liable only if he or she knew that the dividend was improper.[51] One rationale for this distinction is that liability without regard to knowledge in the case of insolvency is consistent with the law of fraudulent conveyances—and, indeed, the fraudulent conveyance statutes might provide an independent basis for suing the shareholders who receive a dividend from an insolvent corporation.[52]

One issue created by attempting to impose liability on shareholders under common law or under fraudulent conveyance statutes is whether the corporation code provisions dealing with liability for impermissible dividends preempt such common law, or general creditor protection law, remedies. It is difficult to imagine that the legislature intended a statute to preempt the entire field of shareholder liability for receipt of illegal dividends, when the statute only addresses shareholder liability in terms of a right of directors to seek contribution. Hence, it is not surprising to see courts reject a preemption claim, at least for the typical narrow shareholder liability statute.[53]

2.3.3   *Repurchases of Stock*

Corporation statutes typically contain express authorization for companies to repurchase or redeem their own shares.[54] Repurchases of

---

49. *E.g.*, Cal. Corp. Code § 506(a).

50. *E.g.*, M.B.C.A. § 8.33(b)(2).

51. *E.g.*, Wood v. National City Bank, 24 F.2d 661 (2d Cir.1928).

52. One reason for allowing shareholder liability without fault, even when the law requires fault to impose liability upon directors, is that shareholder liability for impermissible dividends simply returns the shareholders to where they were before they received the dividend.

53. *E.g.*, Reilly v. Segert, 31 Ill.2d 297, 201 N.E.2d 444 (1964).

54. *E.g.*, M.B.C.A. § 6.31(a). These statutes remove the question which had existed under a number of old court opinions as to whether a corporation had the power to repurchase its stock. *See, e.g.*, Pace v. Pace Bros. Co., 91 Utah 132, 59 P.2d 1 (1936).

shares by the corporation can serve a variety of purposes. Share repurchases by a closely held corporation can provide an important source of liquidity to stockholders who lack the trading market available to shareholders of a publicly held corporation. Publicly held corporations sometimes justify their repurchases by saying the stock was at a bargain price. Share repurchases often have been used either to facilitate or to foil an insider's or an outsider's purchase of control of the corporation. Unfortunately, share repurchases are subject to a number of abuses, and, hence, raise a number of legal issues.

a. Stockholder concerns

Three groups of stockholders might complain about a corporation's acquisition of its own shares. To begin with, shareholders left out of the purchase might raise objections. The most straightforward objection occurs when the directors cause the company to repurchase shares from the directors themselves. This constitutes an interested director transaction, and the directors must validate the transaction by showing disinterested approval or proof that the transaction is fair to the corporation.[55]

An alternate claim arises when the corporation purchases shares of a stockholder who challenges the board's control. We shall explore the law's reaction to such "greenmail" when considering defenses to hostile takeovers in the last chapter of this book.

The most far reaching challenge is to argue that the corporation must give all of its stockholders an equal opportunity to sell back their shares whenever the company repurchases stock from any shareholder— a sort of reverse preemptive right. The rationale behind this argument begins with the fact that corporate repurchases of stock result in money flowing from the corporation to its shareholders, much as is true of a dividend. A corporation cannot discriminate among the owners of the same class of stock and pay a dividend to some and not to other such owners. Therefore, the argument concludes, why can a corporation discriminate among its shareholders by distributing money to some shareholders and not others in repurchasing stock?

This logic would be unassailable if share repurchases, like dividends, had no other impact than to take money from the corporation and give it to the shareholders. This, however, is not the case. Rather, with a share repurchase, there is another impact: the selling shareholder gives up some or all of his or her stock and thereby gives up some or all of his or her claim to future distributions from the corporation. As a result, the non-selling shareholders end up with a larger claim to future distribu-

---

English courts had held that corporations lack the power to repurchase their stock, and, accordingly, the position that corporations lack the power to repurchase their stock is sometimes referred to as the English rule. Incidentally, some writers use the term "redemption" to refer to acquisitions by the corporation of its outstanding stock pursuant to an option in the articles, and the term "repurchase" to refer to other acquisitions by the corporation of its own stock. The tax code, by comparison, generally refers to all purchases by a company of its own shares as a "redemption." I.R.C. § 317(b).

55. See § 4.2.1 *infra*.

tions from the corporation. Moreover, once one views the repurchase as a two-way exchange, rather than simply a one-way distribution, the repurchase comes to look like all kinds of other transactions which corporations might have with their shareholders. For example, corporations commonly employ individuals who are also shareholders of the company—which means that these employee-shareholders receive money from the corporation which other shareholders do not. Would a rule that the corporation cannot discriminate between shareholders mean that all shareholders must receive an opportunity to work for the company in proportion to their stock ownership? On the other hand, one difference between share repurchases, and other exchanges between a corporation and an individual who happens to be a shareholder, is that, in the case of a share repurchase, the shareholder's position as a shareholder is central to his or her eligibility to make the exchange, rather than irrelevant. Moreover, even if repurchases equal an exchange rather than a distribution, the opportunity to engage in this exchange is itself an item of value which the corporation, in a selective repurchase, does not distribute pro-rata to all of the shareholders of the relevant class.

In the end, perhaps the most important factor in deciding whether to allow repurchases which are not equally open to all shareholders is a practical concern: Do share repurchases from only some stockholders serve worthwhile corporate purposes? If so, then courts presumably should not frustrate the corporation's ability to achieve these purposes by adopting a rule giving all shareholders an equal opportunity to sell whenever the company repurchases some of its stock. If not, then perhaps the potential mischief of selective share repurchases calls for a rule of equal opportunity. Rather than speculate about such purposes in the abstract, perhaps the appropriate rule would be one which requires directors to show a business purpose for any share repurchases not to be open to all shareholders.[56]

In any event, by and large, courts have rejected arguments that shareholders are entitled to an equal opportunity to be among the sellers whenever a corporation repurchases its stock from any shareholder.[57] Some courts, however, have held that the rule is different when a closely-held corporation repurchases stock from a controlling shareholder. *Donahue v. Rodd Electrotype Co.*[58] is the leading case adopting this view. *Donahue's* rationale is based upon the notion of a special fiduciary duty between shareholders in closely held corporations. Hence, we shall delay consideration of *Donahue* until a later chapter which explores the special problems of closely held corporations. For now, it is sufficient to note that a number of other courts have rejected an equal opportunity rule even for repurchases from controlling shareholders in closely held

---

56. Since the corporation cannot repurchase all of its outstanding shares, a requirement of equal opportunity presumably should mean only that the corporation must offer to buy from each stockholder a pro-rata share of the total amount of the stock which the corporation wants.

57. *E.g.*, Karfunkel v. USLIFE Corp., 116 Misc.2d 841, 455 N.Y.S.2d 937 (1982).

58. 367 Mass. 578, 328 N.E.2d 505 (1975).

corporations—at least if the corporation has a business purpose for the selective repurchase.[59]

The second group of stockholders who might challenge a corporate repurchase are those who sell back their shares. Often, such shareholders will come to regret their decision to sell and then claim that the corporation (or its managers or controlling shareholders) misled the sellers into selling their shares.[60] Making false or misleading statements to a seller of stock not only might create claims based upon state law, but also can violate federal securities law—particularly Rule 10b–5 promulgated by the Securities Exchange Commission pursuant to Section 10(b) of the 1934 Securities Exchange Act.[61] While mere nondisclosure of material facts by a purchaser of stock to a seller generally violates Rule 10b–5 only if a fiduciary relationship exists between the buyer and seller, such a relationship presumably exists between the company repurchasing its own shares and its stockholders.[62]

Many times, the nature of the transaction precludes the selling stockholders from having an individual choice as to whether to give up their shares. This is often referred to as a "freeze-out." The most straightforward mechanism to force a sale of shares back to the corporation is for the company to exercise its option under a provision in the articles giving the corporation the right to redeem a class of shares. It is difficult to be all that sympathetic to shareholders who complain about a corporate redemption of their shares pursuant to a provision in the corporation's articles. After all, when these shareholders bought the stock, they essentially agreed to give the company this option. The shareholders might argue that it is somehow unfair for the corporation to exercise the option for the benefit of the non-redeemed shares.[63] Yet, what other purpose could giving the corporation an option to redeem shares have besides to benefit the non-redeemed shares? If the purpose of the redemption provision was to benefit the redeemed shares, presumably the articles would have given those shareholders the option to force the corporation to buy their shares, rather than the other way around.

The situation is potentially different, however, when the mechanism for freezing out shareholders is not the exercise of an article provision which expressly gives the corporation an option to redeem a class of shares. Without such a provision, it is more difficult to conclude that the complaining shareholders agreed to the later sale when they acquired their stock. Moreover, in the freeze-out cases involving nonredeemable stock, the shareholders forced to sell typically own the same class of stock as held by the shareholders who will remain—thereby raising questions about the corporation discriminating in its treatment between

59. *E.g.*, Toner v. Baltimore Envelope Co., 304 Md. 256, 498 A.2d 642 (1985).

60. *See, e.g.*, Rochez Bros., Inc. v. Rhoades, 491 F.2d 402 (3d Cir.1973).

61. We shall explore Rule 10b–5 and the 1934 Securities Exchange Act in detail in a later chapter.

62. *See, e.g.*, Staffin v. Greenberg, 672 F.2d 1196 (3d Cir.1982). *But see* American General Ins. Co. v. Equitable General Corp., 493 F.Supp. 721 (E.D.Va.1980).

63. *See, e.g.*, Zahn v. Transamerica Corp., 162 F.2d 36 (3d Cir.1947).

holders of the same class of shares. We shall explore both the mechanisms for such freeze-outs, and the challenges available to the frozen out shareholders, in the final chapter of this book.

In between the selling shareholders who complain that they were misled, and those who complain that they were given no choice about whether to sell, are those who might complain that they were subject to unfair pressure to sell. Concerns about unfair pressures to sell stock lie at the heart of the Williams Act, which amended the 1934 Securities Exchange Act to add provisions regulating tender offers and substantial acquisitions of shares. We shall explore both the potentially coercive aspects of tender offers, and the Williams Act, in the final chapter of this book. For now, it is useful to note that the Williams Act exempts repurchases by the issuer from most of its general provisions regulating tender offers and purchases creating over five percent ownership.[64] Instead, Section 13(e)(1) of the Securities Exchange Act, as amended by the Williams Act, grants the Securities Exchange Commission authority to make rules governing issuer repurchases. This authority extends only to corporations with securities requested pursuant to Section 12 of the 1934 Act (and to registered investment companies). Pursuant to this authority, the SEC has regulated three types of repurchases which have the potential for undue pressure. Rule 13e–1 requires specified disclosures by the issuer who seeks to repurchase its shares during a tender offer by another person. Rule 13e–4 regulates tender offers by the issuer. The rule imposes disclosure requirements, and substantive regulations on the manner and terms of the offer, along the lines imposed by the Williams Act on tender offers by non-issuers. One substantive requirement of note, in view of the earlier discussion regarding selective repurchases under state law, is that Rule 13e–4(f)(8)(I) requires an issuer tender offer to be open to all holders of the sought after class of shares. Finally, Rule 13e–3—there is no Rule 13e–2—regulates going private transactions. This encompasses purchases or tender offers by the issuer (or an affiliate of the issuer), or mergers, recapitalizations, sales of assets, or the like, which result in a company ceasing to be registered under the 1934 Act, or ceasing to be listed on an exchange or traded on the NASD interdealer quotation system.[65] The issuer (or its affiliate) making the purchase must provide specified disclosures to its stockholders. Most significantly, these disclosures call for a discussion of whether and why the issuer or its affiliate considers the purchase fair to its shareholders—which sets up a possible securities fraud claim by disgruntled stockholders who can argue the company did not really believe the transaction was fair, or left out material facts in its discussion of fairness.

64. Sec. Exch. Act §§ 13(d)(6)(C), 14(d)(8)(B). *But see* Sec. Exch. Act § 14(e) (prohibiting false, deceptive or manipulative practices in connection with any tender offer by any person).

65. Repurchases of outstanding stock by the issuing corporation can result in the stock exchanges delisting the company's stock if the repurchase leaves too few remaining shareholders. Delisting renders the stock much less liquid. Fear of being stuck with illiquid shares could lead shareholders to sell their stock back to the corporation, even though they do not like the offer.

The third group of stockholders who might complain about corporate repurchases are persons who bought shares at about the same time as the corporation engaged in repurchasing some of its stock. Members of this group may complain that the corporate repurchases artificially raised the price which they paid for their stock.[66]

Several provisions in the 1934 Securities Exchange Act, and in the rules promulgated pursuant to the Act, are relevant to issuer repurchases designed to prop up the price of stock. Section 9(a)(2) prohibits a series of transactions in securities registered on a national exchange if those transactions (among other things) raise the price of the shares for the purpose of inducing their purchase. Section 9(a)(6) gives the SEC authority to promulgate rules limiting transactions in shares registered on a national exchange made for the purpose of stabilizing the price of the stock. Section 10(b) gives the SEC broad authority to make rules against manipulative or deceptive conduct in connection with the purchase or sale of securities (whether registered or not). In addition to Rule 10b–5, the Commission has created several rules under the mandate of Section 10(b) which can impact repurchases. These include: Rule 10b–6 (prohibiting issuers and others involved in the distribution of a security from bidding for or buying, subject to certain exceptions, shares of the same class as they are distributing); Rules 10b–7 and 10b–8 (allowing certain purchases for the purpose of stabilizing at market levels (but not higher) the price of shares undergoing a distribution); and Rule 10b–18 (creating a safe harbor, under which the Commission will not deem

---

66. Actually, the question of whether a corporation can raise the price of its outstanding stock by repurchasing shares is more complicated than it would first appear. Superficially, it would seem that by creating more demand (or less supply), corporate repurchases should increase price. Yet, the effect of corporate repurchases is also to decrease the corporation's assets, making the company worth less. If the corporation repurchases shares at their value, presumably these two impacts ought to offset each other and the end result should be a wash. Only if the corporation can repurchase stock at less than its value should the price of the remaining shares go up. Assuming that the corporation's shares are traded in a fully informed, efficient trading market, it is questionable whether corporate repurchases on the market will be below the shares' value. Of course, the key assumption here is that the market is fully informed and efficient; an ill-informed market might undervalue the corporation's stock. In this event, however, one must wonder whether corporations should take advantage of their uninformed shareholders. In any event, this is not the complaint of the person who buys shares while the corporation is also buying. Rather, the question is whether corporation repurchas-

es can artificially raise the price above the shares' value. Again, the key is information. If those in the market know that the corporation is repurchasing its shares, corporate repurchases at above the market price should not increase the price, since the market will take into account the reduced assets of the corporation. (An exception could exist if market participants assume that corporate repurchases reflect undisclosed information possessed by the corporation, or if the market has been discounting the corporation's stock because of a negative reaction to the corporation's inefficient reinvestment rather than distribution of its earnings.) On the other hand, if the corporation can repurchase shares in such a manner as to keep its identity as the purchaser secret, then perhaps it could artificially raise the price. Even here, however, it is not certain that corporate repurchases will lead to this result, since modern financial theory has suggested that stock prices may not be all that sensitive to demand. *See, e.g.,* R. Brealey & S. Myers, Principles of Corporate Finance 296 (3d ed. 1988). *But see* Lynn A. Stout, *Are Takeover Premiums Really Premiums? Market Price, Fair Value, and Corporate Law,* 99 Yale L. J. 1235 (1990).

issuer repurchases to be manipulative, if they meet certain guidelines as to their timing during the day, their price, and their volume). Notice these prohibitions generally come into play for issuer repurchases only when the corporation is buying its shares at the same time it, or others on its behalf, are trying to sell its stock.

b. Creditor concerns

From the standpoint of creditors, corporate distributions to repurchase shares present the same hazard as dividends. Accordingly, state corporations statutes impose limitations on stock repurchases analogous (but not necessarily identical) to those they place upon dividends.

California and the current Model Act take the simplest approach. These statutes place limitations upon "distributions", which the acts define to include cash or property paid to shareholders either as a dividend or in exchange for selling back their stock.[67]

More traditional statutes, such as in Delaware, contain separate provisions governing repurchases.[68] At first glance, these sections seem to track the state's dividend restrictions. For example, Delaware's law generally precludes repurchases when the company's capital is impaired, or when the repurchase will cause the capital to become impaired; put another way, when the amount paid in the repurchase exceeds the amount of the corporation's surplus.[69]

It turns out, however, that the traditional statutes allow repurchases to come indirectly out of capital in such a way as to do a complete end run around any protection against shareholders withdrawing their investment before the company pays its debts. This phenomenon stems from the question of how to treat the repurchased shares. Such shares, if not "canceled," are referred to as treasury stock. If the company treats treasury stock just as any other asset, then the repurchase will have no effect upon the corporation's surplus. (The acquisition of a new asset, treasury stock, offsets the decrease of an existing asset, cash, so nothing else on the balance sheet changes.) Since the company still has its surplus under such an approach, it can continue to buy back its shares until it dissipates all its other assets. This result illustrates that treasury stock is really not an asset at all. (The company whose only "asset" consists of stock in itself is worth nothing.) Statutes like Delaware's implicitly recognize treasury stock is not an asset; otherwise it would make no sense to talk about the purchase impairing capital (purchase of an asset can never impair capital) or coming out of surplus. Hence, the repurchase of stock lowers the firm's net assets by the amount paid out.

---

67. Cal. Corp. Code §§ 166, 500–503; M.B.C.A. §§ 1.40(b), 6.40(c). California, however, relaxes the rules for the redemption of a deceased or disabled stockholder's shares, if the company uses insurance proceeds. Cal. Corp. Code §§ 503.1, 503.2.

68. On the other hand, while the standard for improper repurchases is in a differ-

ent section, the provision in Delaware's statute imposing liability upon directors and shareholders in the case of impermissible declarations of dividends also provides the sanction for impermissible repurchases of stock. Del. Gen. Corp. Law § 174.

69. Del. Gen. Corp. Law § 160(a)(1).

The real question lies in whether the effect of this decrease in net assets shows up in a reduction of surplus, of capital, or of both. If one were to parallel dividend treatment, the repurchase should leave capital unchanged, and, accordingly, reduce surplus (which is, by definition, the difference between net assets and capital). This would give creditors and senior stockholders an equivalent protection in either type of distribution. From the company's standpoint, such a rule would limit total repurchases to the extent of its surplus. On the other hand, with share repurchases, less stock remains in the hands of the shareholders, and, if capital represents money the company received for outstanding stock, perhaps the repurchase should correspondingly reduce capital as it reduces outstanding stock. Traditional statutes leave the question of whether to reflect share repurchases by reducing surplus, or by reducing capital, substantially to the discretion of the directors. New York's law, for example, provides that repurchases do not decrease capital—and hence must reduce surplus—if the company retains the shares as treasury stock.[70] However, the directors may cancel the stock (in which case the stock reverts to the status of unissued shares). In this event, the company's total stated capital decreases by the amount the canceled shares represented (in other words, by the aggregate par value of the canceled shares, or whatever greater amount the board fixed as stated capital when the company issued those shares).[71] Delaware's statute goes even further. It allows the directors to reduce the corporation's capital by all or part of the capital represented by the repurchased shares, whether or not the board cancels them.[72] Notice, by reducing capital, the corporation increases surplus (since surplus equals the difference between net assets and capital). The company, in turn, can use the surplus to repurchase more shares, and repeat the procedure until it has no more capital or surplus (in other words, its remaining assets equal its debts).[73]

Many times, corporations will not immediately pay cash for the repurchased shares, but, instead, will give the seller an IOU—put differently, the corporation plans to pay for the repurchased shares in installments. This complicates the determination of whether the corporation's repurchase violates the statutory financial limits. Specifically, giving an IOU for repurchased shares raises the question as to when to measure the repurchase against the statutory financial limits—at the time the corporation obtains the shares back in exchange for its promise to pay; at the time the corporation actually makes each installment payment; or at both times. Further complicating this inquiry is the fact that there are typically two financial limits on share repurchases (just as

70. N.Y. Bus. Corp. Law § 515(c).

71. *Id* at § 515(b), (d), (e).

72. Del. Gen. Corp. Law § 244(a).

73. California and the current Model Act avoid the whole problem of whether to reduce capital or surplus upon the repurchase of stock by not basing their distribu-
tion limits on any notion of capital. Moreover, California and the current Model Act abolish the concept of treasury shares by providing that repurchased shares return to the status of unissued stock. Cal. Corp. Code § 510(a); M.B.C.A. § 6.31(a).

there are on dividends): a surplus (or other balance sheet) test, and a requirement of equitable solvency.

Court opinions are all over the map as to when to measure the corporation's finances for purposes of assessing the permissibility of share repurchases. Most courts apply the equitable insolvency test at the time of each payment on the IOU—either exclusively,[74] or as part of a test which requires solvency both when the corporation issues the IOU and at the time of each payment.[75] A few court opinions only look to whether the corporation was solvent at the time the company issued the IOU.[76] Courts also disagree on when to apply a surplus test—albeit, in this instance, the courts are more evenly divided between those which look to the time of payment and those which look at the time the company issued the IOU.[77]

The rationales used by the courts also vary. Some courts focus on interpreting the words "payment" or "purchase," since the statutes commonly refer to the test as involving the permissibility of payments made by the corporation in exchange for purchasing its stock.[78] Under this approach, the questions become whether an IOU constitutes payment, or whether payments on the IOU constitute payment, and whether a purchase takes place when the corporation acquires stock for an IOU or whether the purchase takes place when the corporation pays for the stock by paying off the IOU. More pragmatic approaches, however, are possible. A focus on creditor protection suggests a time of each installment measure, since, until the corporation actually pays out cash, the creditors are not impacted. By contrast, the interests of the bought out shareholders, and of promoting certainty in transactions, might suggest a the desirability of measuring the corporation's finances when the corporation issues the IOU. This was the position taken by the court in *Neimark v. Mel Kramer Sales, Inc.*[79]

Neimark involved an agreement made between a closely held corporation and its shareholders, which, in the event of a shareholder's death, obligated the estate of the stockholder to sell, and the corporation to buy, the decedent's shares. After the majority shareholder died, his widow had second thoughts about this arrangement. She argued that the

---

74. *E.g.*, Robinson v. Wangemann, 75 F.2d 756 (5th Cir.1935).

75. *E.g.*, Neimark v. Mel Kramer Sales, Inc., 102 Wis.2d 282, 306 N.W.2d 278 (1981).

76. *E.g.*, Williams v. Nevelow, 513 S.W.2d 535 (Tex.1974).

77. *Compare* Neimark v. Mel Kramer Sales, Inc., 102 Wis.2d 282, 306 N.W.2d 278 (1981) (test at the issuance of the note), *with* Mountain State Steel Foundries, Inc. v. Commissioner, 284 F.2d 737 (4th Cir. 1960) (test at the time of payment), *and with* McConnell v. Estate of Butler, 402 F.2d 362 (9th Cir.1968) (test at both times). Yet, further variation exists if the selling shareholder obtains a security interest in

corporate assets in order to secure the IOU. *Compare* In re National Tile & Terrazzo Co., 537 F.2d 329 (9th Cir.1976) (held that the mortgage survives if the corporation had an adequate surplus when it created the debt, even though the debt became unenforceable because of insolvency at time of payment), *with* Reiner v. Washington Plate Glass Co., 711 F.2d 414 (D.C.Cir. 1983) (held that the security interest fails with the underlying obligation).

78. *E.g.*, Williams v. Nevelow, 513 S.W.2d 535 (Tex.1974).

79. 102 Wis.2d 282, 306 N.W.2d 278 (App. 1981).

agreement could not be carried out because it would violate the statutory financial limits on share repurchases. In deciding to apply the surplus limit at the time the corporation issued the IOU, the court listed a variety of practical disadvantages for the bought out shareholder of the measure at each installment approach. For example, a corporation, in order to torpedo its ability to pay an installment, might, right before the installment is due, pay out dividends using up all of the company's surplus. In this event, it will be difficult to come up with an appropriate remedy. Return of all of the shares to the selling stockholder would be excessive if the corporation had already paid for some of the repurchased shares before the default. Yet, return of less than all of the shares might not be adequate if this leaves the selling shareholder with a significantly less powerful block. On the other hand, *Neimark* itself illustrates one practical problem with the measure when the corporation issues the IOU approach. Measuring all at once the impact of a substantial purchase created the potential failure to meet the surplus limit in *Neimark*. Such a result is not unexpected; after all, the reason for installment payments is presumably because an immediate disbursement poses too great a burden on the company.

A number of state statutes address the question of when to apply the financial limits to share repurchases. Like the courts, these statutes take a variety of approaches. California, for example, specifies that the time to measure the corporation's finances against both California's insolvency test, and California's basic numerical test, is at the point of actual payment.[80] One exception exists to this rule. The California statute applies the tests at the time of purchase if the company issues a negotiable instrument (within the meaning of U.C.C. § 8–102) as evidence of its promise to pay. Delaware goes in the other direction. Delaware's statute indicates that corporate obligations exchanged for stock, which do not invade capital when issued, are valid regardless of the situation when paid.[81] The current Model Act takes yet a different approach. It essentially allows the parties structuring the repurchase to elect which timing they wish to follow. Specifically, much like the Delaware law, the current Model Act generally measures the effect of the repurchase at the time the corporation issues the IOU. The Model Act allows the parties, however, to avoid an immediate test by providing that the debt issued for the stock is not payable unless a distribution at the time of each payment would be legal.[82]

2.3.4   Stock Dividends and Stock Splits

A corporation can issue additional shares to its stockholders, without receiving consideration in return, in transactions commonly referred

---

80. Cal. Corp. Code § 166. Moreover, in determining the company's retained earnings or liabilities in order to measure the permissibility of each payment, the California test disregards the company's remaining liability from repurchasing the shares. Cal. Corp. Code §§ 500(b), 502, 503.

81. Del. Gen. Corp. Law § 160.

82. M.B.C.A. § 6.40(e)(1), (g).

to as stock dividends and stock splits.[83] Such share distributions can achieve a number of objectives. To begin with, consider the simplest situation: A corporation, which has only one class of stock outstanding, distributes additional shares of this class pro-rata among its stockholders. Fundamentally, this transaction seems meaningless. Each stockholder may have more certificates, or a larger number printed on his or her certificate, but his or her entitlement to dividends, to liquidating distributions, or to voting power remains unchanged. Nevertheless, there can be some utility for such a distribution. It lowers the value of each individual share, and thus can facilitate their trading. In addition, some empirical studies have suggested a further effect in companies with widely held shares. The price per share may not decline proportionately to the increased outstanding stock (thus actually enriching the recipient shareholders).[84] In part, this may be a function of increased marketability at lower prices. It may also reflect assumptions about the prospects for the corporation, as often companies distribute stock dividends or make stock splits when they expect increased earnings. Stock dividends which consist of distributing shares of a different class than held by the recipients (for example, distributing preferred shares among to the holder of common stock) have a variety of purposes. For example, the distribution of preferred in a closely held corporation might facilitate estate planning.[85]

The traditional theory behind a stock dividend is that it constitutes a dividend like any other, except paid in shares of the corporation's own stock. This means complying with a mix of the statutory requirements for both stock issuances and dividends. As with all issuances of stock, the articles must authorize the shares the company proposes to distribute. The authority of directors to declare dividends of cash or property (such as the corporation's own shares) substitutes for the normal requirement that the company receive consideration in exchange for issuing its stock.[86] In states adhering to traditional concepts of stated capital, the corporation must increase the capital shown on its books to reflect the issuance of additional shares as a dividend (just as it must increase capital if it sold further shares).[87] How much should this increase be? Consistent with the latitude traditional statutes give to directors to set how much of the sale price of stock constitutes capital, the Delaware statute allows the board, in the case of a stock dividend, to increase capital by any amount the board desires so long as the amount is not less than the aggregate par value of the shares distributed as a dividend.[88] Of course, if the company increases its capital, it must decrease its surplus by an equivalent amount (since surplus, by definition, equals the differ-

83. *E.g.*, M.B.C.A. § 6.23(a).

84. *E.g.*, Lewellen, The Cost of Capital 113 (1978) (1969). *But see* E. Brigham, Financial Management Theory and Practice 481–85 (5th ed. 1988).

85. Some statutes, however, restrict stock dividends to shares generally of the same class. *E.g.*, N.Y. Bus. Corp. Law § 511(a)(3); M.B.C.A. § 6.23(b).

86. *See, e.g.*, Del. Gen. Corp. Law § 173.

87. *But see* N.Y. Bus. Corp Law § 511(b) (allowing distribution of treasury shares without the need to increase capital).

88. Del. Gen. Corp. Law § 173.

ence between net assets and capital). This places the same limit on stock dividends as exists on dividends generally; that is, the amount of the dividend (as presumably measured by the amount capital increases) cannot exceed the amount of a corporation's surplus.[89]

The traditional view of a stock split, in contrast, is it constitutes a form of recapitalization—in other words, an exchange of existing stock for new stock. Carrying out a stock split may require amendment of the articles to increase the number of authorized shares and to lower the par value of the shares. Then, through article amendment (or possibly just an exchange offer), the corporation gives each shareholder of the class affected the right to obtain a greater number of shares for each share owned.[90] Under traditional stated capital statutes, the central difference between a stock split and a stock dividend is that the split need not increase capital.[91] Hence, a company can engage in a stock split even if it does not have any surplus.

A number of agencies have been concerned with investors possibly misunderstanding stock dividends and stock splits. This could be particularly the case in situations when the company makes only a small increase in the number of shares outstanding, and, therefore, the price may not change to fully reflect the dilution. One response has been to require corporations to characterize as a dividend, rather than a split, distributions equal to less than 25 percent of the number of already outstanding shares, and, in the case of a stock dividend, to add to capital an amount equal to the fair market value of the distributed stock, rather than just the shares' par value.[92] At the same time, these authorities have sought to discourage companies from referring to any distribution in which the firm does not capitalize fair market value as a dividend, rather than a stock split.

Moving in opposite direction are those statutes which have done away with the concept of stated capital. Under such statutes, no real distinction may remain between share distributions through stock splits or stock dividends. Also, with these statutes, the limitations applicable to distributions of cash or other property do not apply to distributions of the company's own shares, regardless of how characterized.[93]

89. *E.g.*, Northern Bank & Trust Co. v. Day, 83 Wash. 296, 145 P. 182 (1915).

90. *See, e.g.*, Cal. Corp. Code § 1188 (stock split affected by article amendment). In a reverse stock split, the directors and shareholders amend the articles to reduce the number of authorized shares and thereby force each stockholder to exchange his or her stock for a lower number of shares. *E.g.*, Lerner v. Lerner, 306 Md. 771, 511 A.2d 501 (1986).)

91. *E.g.*, Del. Gen. Corp. Law § 173. This is why the corporation may need to amend its articles to decrease par value if it undertakes a stock split.

92. Accounting Research Bulletin No. 43 Ch 7b (1953); N.Y.S.E. Listed Company Manual pp. 7–13—7–16 (1983); Sec. Exch. Act Rel. No. 8268.

93. *See* Cal. Corp. Code §§ 166, 409(a)(2); M.B.C.A. §§ 1.40 (b); 6.23.

Chapter III

GOVERNANCE

[Research References]

AmJur 2d, Corporations §§ 310–332, 728–1167

CJS, Corporations §§ 112–121, 305–432

ALR Index: Bylaws; Corporate Bonds and Bondholders; Corporate Stock and Stockholders; Ultra Vires

ALR Digest: Corporations §§ 224–322.5

Am Jur Legal Forms 2d, Corporations §§ 74:1791–74:1938

Am Jur Pleading and Practice Forms (Rev), Corporations §§ 143–232

38 POF3d 279, Self–Dealing by Trustee

37 POF2d 739, Principal's Repudiation of Agent's Unauthorized Act; 24 POF2d 71, Proper Purpose for Shareholder's Inspection of Corporate Books and Records

---

Stripped to the fundamentals, participants in a business organization are concerned about two things—wealth and power. The previous chapter looked at the means by which corporate law allocates wealth among the venture's owners. This chapter looks at how corporate law allocates power.

§ 3.1   The Division of Power Under State Law

To understand the basic model of corporate governance, it is helpful to draw upon some introductory civics class concepts of democratic government. As outlined in beginning of Chapter I, partnerships follow what a civics class might refer to as the Athenian, or direct, democracy model of governance. All of the partners participate in making business decisions. By contrast, corporations follow the republican, or representative, model of governance. Under the basic model of corporate governance, the owners of the corporation (the shareholders) elect a body of individuals (the board of directors) to be in charge of the corporation. The board of directors makes decisions; it normally does not carry them out. In this sense, the board occupies a role analogous to the legislature. The corporation's officers, such as the company's president, perform the executive function of carrying out the board's policies.[1]

§ 3.1

1. The basic model of corporate governance calls for nothing approximating a judicial branch.

Actually, the simple civics class model of the roles of the electorate, and of the legislative and the executive branches of government, fails to present an entirely realistic portrait of federal or state governments. Similarly, the basic model of corporate governance is not all that realistic a portrait of how corporations operate. Still, it provides a convenient road map to start our discussion as we work our way up the chain of authority from officers to directors to the shareholders.

3.1.1 Officers

a. Who are the corporation's officers?

Many corporation statutes require a corporation to have certain officers—typically a president, secretary, treasurer and sometimes a vice president—and, in addition, allow a corporation to have any other officers which the company's bylaws specify or which the company's board of directors appoints.[2] Many other statutes, such as Delaware's[3] and the current Model Act,[4] simply call for the corporation to have whatever officers the company's bylaws or its board of directors specify— albeit, there must be an officer responsible for taking minutes of shareholders' and directors' meetings. Ultimately, the question of what officers a given corporation will have is largely a business, not a legal, question. A smaller business might get by with a principle executive officer with the title of president, possibly coupled with a single financial officer with the title of treasurer, and some person designated to serve as secretary to take notes at directors' and shareholders' meetings. Larger businesses may see the need for both a chief executive and a chief operating officer (the former perhaps given the title of chairman of the board, while the later receives the title of president) and a host of senior and junior vice presidents, and assistant treasurers and secretaries. Indeed, in some companies it seems as if everyone above the lowest level employees is a vice president. This proliferation of titles illustrates that there is no fixed demarcation separating what is a corporate officer from what is simply an executive employee. This fact, in turn, occasionally creates a problem when a corporate statute or rule refers to corporate "officers."[5] About the best the court can do when a rule or statute requires the court to determine which corporate executives are, or which are not, "officers," is to make this assessment in light of the purposes of the particular statute or rule in question.

For the most part, corporation statutes do not impose any limits on who is qualified to hold corporate office, and the statutes generally allow one person to hold more than one office at the same time.[6] The statutes

---

2. *E.g.*, Cal. Corp. Code § 312(a).

3. Del. Gen. Corp. Law § 142(a).

4. M.B.C.A. § 8.40(a).

5. *E.g.*, Merrill Lynch, Pierce, Fenner & Smith, Inc. v. Livingston, 566 F.2d 1119 (9th Cir.1978) (interpreting whether a vice president in a brokerage firm was an officer for purposes of Section 16(b) of the Securities Exchange Act).

6. *E.g.*, M.B.C.A. § 8.40. A few statutes historically would not allow the same person to hold at the same time the position of president and vice president (presumably based upon the notion that the role of the vice president is to fill in in the absence of

commonly call for the appointment of officers as provided in the bylaws or by the board of directors.[7] Normally, the board of directors appoints the corporation's senior officers, who then appoint more junior officers and so on.[8] Occasionally, a corporation will provide in its bylaws (or articles) for the election of certain officers by the shareholders.

A corollary of the board's power to appoint officers is the board's power to fire officers with or without cause.[9] Sometimes, a corporation will have entered into an employment contract with an officer, which contract contains terms limiting the corporation's right to fire the officer. Reconciling such contract terms with the board's authority to fire officers can generate confusion. The simple answer is that the board has the power to fire the officer despite the contract, but the corporation might become liable under the contract for damages.[10] In other words, a board of directors has the same power to have the corporation fire an officer, who is subject to an employment contract, as a sole proprietor would have to fire an employee covered by such an agreement—no more and no less. After all, there is no reason to treat the board's power to have the corporation enter or breach an employment contract any differently than the board's power to have the company enter or breach any other contract.

b. What authority do the officers possess?

Disputes over whether a corporate officer possessed the authority to bind his or her company to a particular transaction often produce litigation. Resolution of such disputes entails the application of basic rules of agency law to the corporate setting. For the most part, agents have the power to bind their principals based upon either actual or apparent authority.[11] Actual authority involves the agent doing what the principal gave the agent permission to do. If the principal explicitly granted the agent permission to perform the act, then the actual authority is express. Often times, agents attempt to determine what the principal desires of them based upon a previous course of dealing, the nature of the agent's job, what is necessary to carry out express instructions, and the like. If the agent is reasonable in inferring the existence of

---

the president), or the role of president and secretary (based upon the notion that there should two separate persons to sign corporate documents).

7. *E.g.,* Del. Gen. Corp. Law § 142(b).

8. *See, e.g.,* M.B.C.A. § 8.40(b).

9. *E.g.,* M.B.C.A. § 8.43(b). Under a statute like the Model Act, corporate bylaws which specify a term in office for certain corporate officers seem not to change the board's power to remove the officer even before the expiration of his or her term.

10. *E.g.,* M.B.C.A. § 8.44(b).

11. *E.g.,* Restatement (Second) of Agency § 140. After-the-fact actions by the principal, which affirm an agent's unauthorized conduct, also can result in the principal being bound. The name for this is ratification. *Id.* at § 82. In addition, Section 8A of the Second Restatement of Agency, and some courts, have referred to a concept called "inherent agency power" as an alternate source of an agent's power to bind his or her principal. In practice, the concept of inherent agency power so often overlaps with either implied actual authority or apparent authority—at least when the situation involves a principal whose existence is known to the party dealing with the agent—as to generate more confusion than clarity.

such unspoken permission, then the agent has implied actual authority.[12] Many times, agents act beyond the scope of their actual authority, as, for instance, if the agent is doing something which the principal told the agent not to do, or when the agent is not reasonable in believing that he or she has the implied permission to act. Nevertheless, the principal still can be bound by the agent's action if: (1) the principal in some manner communicated to the party with whom the agent dealt that the agent has the authority to act, and (2) based upon this communication, the party with whom the agent dealt reasonably believes that the agent has such authority. This is known as apparent authority.[13] Notice that both actual authority and apparent authority stem from communication by the principal—the difference is that actual authority comes from communication from the principal to the agent, while apparent authority comes from communication from the principal to the party with whom the agent dealt. Just as implied actual authority stems from unspoken communication by the principal, so apparent authority often comes from unspoken communication by the principal. A previous course of conduct by the principal or the position in which the principal places the agent can lead a party with whom the agent deals to develop a reasonable belief that the agent has certain authority.

When considering the authority of corporate officials, a complication arises because a corporation is not an individual who can speak for him- or herself. How then can a corporation give an agent permission to act? The answer is that corporations can grant their officials express authority through provisions in the bylaws (or the articles), or by resolution of the board of directors, or by the actions of superior officials (assuming that the superior official, him- or herself, has the authority to grant permission to the junior official).[14]

Frequently, corporate officials, like most all agents, act in situations in which they have no express instruction from their principal. In this event, the issue becomes whether the official had implied actual, or apparent, authority. To the extent that the argument for the existence of either implied actual or apparent authority is based upon facts such as a prior course of dealing, or what was necessary to carry out express instructions, or the like, then each case must stand upon its own facts. Many times, however, the argument for the existence of implied actual authority, apparent authority, or both, is based upon the official's position with the corporation. It is not difficult to understand why. In appointing someone to a position and giving that person a title, the appointed individual, barring instructions to the contrary, might reasonably assume that he or she has permission to do those acts which other individuals who have occupied this sort of position with this title customarily have done. Similarly, parties dealing with the official might reasonably assume that the official has the authority to do those acts

12. *See, e.g.,* Restatement (Second) of Agency §§ 26, 33.

13. *Id.* at § 27.

14. *E.g.,* Missouri Valley Steel Co. v. New Amsterdam Casualty Co., 275 Minn. 433, 148 N.W.2d 126 (1966).

which other persons with such positions and title customarily have done. In other words, the position and title itself serves as communication from the corporation which can form the basis for both implied actual and apparent authority.

The notion that the official's position and title, itself, can create either, or both, implied actual or apparent authority has played out in a number of cases involving individuals who held the position of corporate president. For example, in *Lee v. Jenkins Brothers*,[15] the court considered whether the president of a corporation had the authority to promise the plaintiff that, if the plaintiff came to work for the corporation, the plaintiff would receive a pension at age 60 even if the plaintiff did not continue to work for the corporation until age 60. There was no evidence of any provision in the bylaws, or a board resolution, granting the president express authority to promise the pension, nor was there any evidence of a previous course of dealing by the corporation's president, with the board's acquiescence, upon which to base a claim of implied authority for this action. Hence, the question was whether holding the position of president, in itself, was sufficient to clothe the president with apparent authority to promise the pension.[16] Surveying the case law on the apparent authority of corporate presidents, the court in *Lee* noted that the rule which emerged was that the president had apparent authority to bind the company to contracts arising in the ordinary course of business, but not to extraordinary contracts. Unfortunately, the *Lee* court found that, while the basic rule was widely accepted, judicial opinions differed on what contracts fit within the ordinary course of business, and what contracts were extraordinary.

Ultimately, the court in *Lee* rejected the argument that, as a matter of law, the president lacked apparent authority to enter the pension agreement in the case—a result which, at least today, seems totally unsurprising given the rather modest amount of money at stake in the pension. What is more interesting about the court's opinion is its recognition that courts must apply the ordinary versus extraordinary contract line in light of common expectations and business custom— which have seen corporate presidents increasingly exercise authority without specific board approval. After all, when dealing with apparent authority, the question is not whether a contract fits some notion of ordinary versus extraordinary in the abstract, but whether the party dealing with a corporation's president reasonably believed that the president had the authority to make the contract. Such a reasonable belief depends largely upon accepted practice. This suggests that determining which side of the ordinary versus extraordinary line a given contract falls should be more a matter of empirical, than legal, research.

---

15. 268 F.2d 357 (2d Cir.1959).

16. While the court only considered apparent authority—since this was all that was necessary to sustain the plaintiff's claim that the corporation would be bound to grant the pension—a similar analysis might also lead (in the absence of any contrary instructions from the board) to a finding of implied actual authority. The existence of actual, rather than just apparent, authority would be important if the corporation sued the president for exceeding his actual authority.

In other words, the question should be whether presidents of corporations of a similar size and type submit this type and size of contract to the board for approval, not whether some older court opinion labeled a similar contract as extraordinary.

Still, while the ultimate test for a president's apparent authority should call for an empirical assessment of business practice, there are some general factors which suggest what the practice is likely to be. An obvious factor noted by the court's opinion in *Lee* is the impact of the contract, as measured by its reasonableness and its size relative to the size of the corporation. Current practice also seems to be that changes in corporate financial structure (in other words, dealings with long-term corporate debt and corporate stock), changes in control over the corporation, and significant changes in what lines of business the corporation conducts, normally go before the board for approval.[17] In addition, bringing corporate resources to bear on one side of an intra-corporate control dispute—for instance, by having the corporation file suit against a major shareholder or directors of the corporation—would appear beyond the authority of the president.[18] There would not seem to be any apparent authority involved for the president to file such a lawsuit, because there is no uninformed outside party relying upon the president's appearance of authority. Nor would it seem reasonable for the president to infer that he or she was hired to take sides in disputes between directors or shareholders.

Moreover, one should keep in mind that the relationship between court opinions dealing with the authority of a corporate president, and customary business practice, goes two ways. While courts should look at customary practice to decide if a transaction is extraordinary and, therefore, beyond the president's authority, to the extent that court opinions hold a particular type of transaction is extraordinary, then legal advisors will counsel their clients to obtain formal approval by the board of directors. This, in turn, will establish a custom that such transactions require board approval. In addition, statutory provisions remove certain matters from the president's implied or apparent authority, regardless of custom. Specifically, if the statute expressly commits a decision to the board of directors—as, for example, setting the consideration for which the corporation will issue stock—or the statute requires board approval for a transaction (as with a merger), then the president lacks authority to bind the company.

One source of confusion in determining the scope of a corporate president's implied or apparent authority is that corporations have made inconsistent and evolving use of the title "president." At one time, many corporations used the term president simply as the title for the official who would preside at shareholders' and directors' meetings. The person who was in charge of the corporation's day-to-day operations often had

17. *E.g.* Principles of Corporate Governance § 3.01 Reporter's Note.

18. *E.g.*, Keogh Corp. v. Howard, Weil, Labouisse, Friedrichs, Inc., 827 F.Supp. 269 (S.D.N.Y.1993).

the title "general manager." This fact may help explain some, mostly older, court opinions which hold that the title of president confers no apparent authority.[19] More recently, title inflation has occurred at many corporations. At a number of large corporations, the title of president is no longer good enough for the primary executive officer, who instead obtains the title of "chief executive officer" or "chairman of the board" (or both). Because the title "chairman of the board" can have a number of different meanings—in some corporations it refers to the chief executive officer, in other corporations it may refer to a semi-retired former chief executive officer who plays an advisory role, and yet in other corporations it simply may refer to the individual who presides at board of directors meetings—this title, in itself, may not create any well defined apparent authority.[20] The title "chief executive officer" is rather new, with the result that there is little case law on what implied or apparent authority this title conveys.

If a party dealing with a corporation decides that the transaction involved is sufficiently significant to require approval by the board of directors, how does this party know that the board, in fact, approved the transaction? Unless the contracting party personally attends the meeting of the board of directors (to which this person may well not be invited), the contracting party must rely on minutes of the meeting, or a copy of the resolution, as establishing the board's action. The corporation's officer in charge of making such minutes, and certifying the authenticity of corporate documents, commonly has the title of "secretary" (which should not be confused with a secretary who types, answers telephones, and the like). Suppose, however, the corporation's secretary shows the contracting party a bogus set of minutes that purport to show a board resolution approving a transaction, which, in fact, the board never approved. This is pretty much what happened in *In re Drive–In Development Corp.*[21] This case involved a loan made by a bank to Drive–In's parent company. The bank insisted that Drive–In guarantee the loan, and, recognizing the unusual nature of the transaction, the bank requested a resolution by Drive–In's board of directors approving the guarantee. Drive–In's secretary gave the bank what purported to be a copy of such a resolution, which the secretary certified with Drive–In's corporate seal. In fact, however, the actual corporate minutes did not contain any such resolution. Nevertheless, the court held that Drive–In was bound. This result is pretty easy to justify. After all, what is a party dealing with a corporation supposed to do if the party cannot rely upon the apparent authority of a corporation's secretary to produce a copy of a resolution of the board?

While the title and position of president generally conveys significant implied and apparent authority, and the title and position of secretary conveys apparent authority for one potentially critical action,

---

19. *E.g.*, Federal Services Finance Corp. v. Bishop Natl. Bk. of Hawaii, 190 F.2d 442 (9th Cir.1951).

20. *See, e.g.*, American Express Co. v. Lopez, 72 Misc.2d 648, 340 N.Y.S.2d 82 (Civ. Ct. 1973).

21. 371 F.2d 215 (7th Cir.1966).

the titles and positions of treasurer or vice president, in and of themselves, generally seem to convey little implied or apparent authority. Since the normal responsibility of the treasurer is to receive and keep corporate funds, and to disburse funds as directed by the president or the board, the treasurer has negligible implied or apparent authority to commit the corporation to contracts.[22] In some corporations, a vice president is a senior position with substantial responsibility. By contrast, other companies hand out the title vice president willy-nilly. As a result of this disparate use, the title vice president, itself, conveys little authority.[23]

3.1.2 Directors

a. Composition of the board

Normally, the corporation's bylaws or articles specify how many directors will be on the board;[24] albeit the articles might specify a maximum and minimum size for the board and leave the actual size to the bylaws; or the articles or bylaws might specify a range of permissible board sizes and leave the actual number to the shareholders or directors to set from time to time.[25] At one time, corporation statutes typically required a minimum of three directors—which could create some problems when there was only one shareholder. Most statutes now, however, allow a one-person board of directors.[26]

At one time, it was also common for corporation statutes to set certain qualifications for who could serve as a director—especially requiring that directors also be shareholders. The requirement that directors must be shareholders lead to the common practice of selling a token share to individuals who were going to act as directors. Contempo-

---

22. *E.g.*, Ideal Foods, Inc. v. Action Leasing Corp., 413 So.2d 416 (Fla.App. 1982) (involving person who held positions of both secretary and treasurer). If a particular corporation's bylaws grant the company's treasurer greater authority (such as to execute promissory notes), or the company's course of dealing had been to allow its treasurer to make contracts (such as loan agreements) on the corporation's behalf, then the treasurer could have broader express, implied or perhaps apparent authority. *See, e.g.*, General Overseas Films, Ltd. v. Robin Int'l., Inc., 542 F.Supp. 684 (S.D.N.Y. 1982) (but not finding the authority of a person who was both treasurer and vice-president extended to entering contracts which were not for the corporation's benefit). This, however, would not be authority which stemmed from the title, or the general position, of treasurer itself.

23. *E.g.*, Royal Mfg. Co. v. Denard & Moore Constr. Co., 137 Ga.App. 650, 224 S.E.2d 770 (1976). Since the traditional function of a vice president is to act as president if the president becomes incapacitated, the sole vice president of a corporation may have both actual and apparent authority to perform any act which the corporation's president could, in the event that the company's president becomes incapacitated. *See, e.g.*, Anderson v. Campbell, 176 Minn. 411, 223 N.W. 624 (1929). Moreover, while the title of vice president, itself, normally conveys little authority, the practices of a specific corporation often create significant express, implied and apparent authority for its vice president(s). *E.g.*, First Interstate Bank of Texas v. First National Bank of Jefferson, 928 F.2d 153 (5th Cir.1991).

24. *E.g.*, Del. Gen. Corp. Law § 141(b).

25. *E.g.*, M.B.C.A. § 8.03(b), (c).

26. *E.g.*, M.B.C.A. § 8.03(a). A number of states only allow less than three directors if the corporation has less than three shareholders. *E.g.* Cal. Corp. Code § 212(a).

rary statutes tend not to impose any qualifications on who can serve on the board, leaving any such limits to the articles or bylaws.[27]

Shareholders normally vote for directors in an at-large election. What this means is that shareholders do not vote for an individual to fill a particular slot on the board—as in a legislative race—but rather shareholders simply vote for as many individuals to be directors as there are open positions on the board. Then, the number of individuals receiving the largest number of votes, up to the number of positions to be filled, are elected to the board.[28] A variation on this scheme, called cumulative voting, allows a shareholder, instead of voting for as many individuals as there are positions to fill, to concentrate the shareholder's votes on a smaller number of individuals.[29] We shall explore cumulative voting in more detail in a later chapter dealing with closely held corporations.

Directors normally serve one-year terms, with an election held at each annual shareholders' meeting to fill the entire board.[30] Most state corporation statutes, however, allow corporations, by provision in their articles[31] (or, under some statutes, by a provision in the articles or bylaws[32]) to adopt what are called staggered terms. The United States Senate provides an example of staggered terms. Senators have six year terms, with one-third of the senators up for re-election every two years. Similarly, if a corporation has a board of directors with staggered terms, the directors could have three year terms in office, with one-third of director positions open at each annual shareholders' meeting (or the directors could have two year terms in office, with half of the board up for reelection at each annual meeting). The ostensible rationale for staggered terms is to maintain continuity of experience on the board. However, given that director elections are rarely contested, one suspects that the real reasons corporations employ staggered terms largely have been either as a device to frustrate the effectiveness of cumulative voting, or as a defensive tactic against hostile corporate takeovers in which the purchaser of a majority of the stock wants to replace the board. Hence, we shall look at staggered terms again when we consider

---

27. *E.g.,* M.B.C.A. § 8.02. One exception, however, is that corporation statutes generally require a director to be an individual, rather than another corporation or other legal person. *Id.* at § 8.03(a). For a case in which a corporation's articles contained rather demanding qualifications for who could be the corporation's directors, see Stroud v. Grace, 606 A.2d 75 (Del.1992) (the court held that a provision in the corporation's articles, which required directors to meet qualifications based upon general executive experience, share holdings in the corporation, or having a position as a corporate officer—and a complimentary bylaw provision for pre-screening nominees

against those requirements—did not inequitably disenfranchise the shareholders).

28. *See, e.g.,* M.B.C.A. § 7.28(a).

29. *E.g.,* Del. Gen. Corp. Law § 214.

30. *E.g.,* M.B.C.A. § 8.05. If, however, new directors are not elected at the annual shareholders' meeting—as might occur if two opposing factions each own half of the outstanding shares—then the existing directors continue in office until their successors are elected. Directors appointed to fill a vacancy only serve the remainder of the term unless reelected.

31. *E.g.,* M.B.C.A. § 8.06.

32. *E.g.,* Del. Gen. Corp. Law § 141(d).

cumulative voting in dealing with closely held corporations, and when we examine hostile takeovers.

Not surprisingly, attempts to remove directors prior to the expiration of their term have lead to controversy and litigation. The common law, drawing an analogy to elected public officials, took a narrow view toward the removal of directors: Under the common law, the shareholders possessed the inherent power to remove a director, but only for cause.[33] Intra corporate power struggles or policy disputes are not cause.[34] Rather, cause generally entails some sort of breach of duty by the director.[35] Courts have applied due process notions to removal for cause—for example, requiring that the director(s) involved receive notice of the charges and the opportunity to present to the shareholders a defense.[36]

In contrast to the limited common law view of director removal, many contemporary corporation statutes allow the shareholders to remove directors with or without cause.[37] By allowing the shareholders to replace the directors and thereby force a change in corporate management and operation—often following the sale of most shares to a new owner—such statutes generally promote the efficient use of corporate resources. After all, why should the shareholders, who normally have the most at stake, and who ultimately will be able to elect new directors anyway, need to wait for part of a year before changing corporate direction? Still, there are some limits on the statutory power to remove directors without cause. To begin with, this power may be subject to contrary provision in the articles.[38] Moreover, if a director owes his or her position on the board to the votes of a minority of the outstanding shares—as can occur if the corporation allows cumulative voting or if the corporation's articles give different classes of shares the right to elect a certain number of directors—then the statutes allowing removal without cause temper this power in order to prevent the majority turning around and removing directors elected by the minority. For example, the statute might allow only the class of shares entitled to vote to elect the director to vote on his or her removal, or the statute might require that, if the corporation allows cumulative voting, a director cannot be removed without cause if the number of votes against removal would have been sufficient to ensure his or her election under cumulative voting.[39]

33. *E.g.*, Frank v. Anthony, 107 So.2d 136 (Fla.Dist.Ct.App.1958). While a bylaw or article provision might alter the common law approach and allow the shareholders to remove directors without cause (*e.g.*, Everett v. Transnation Development Corp., 267 A.2d 627 (Del.Ch.1970), such a provision might not apply to directors elected before the provision's adoption. *E.g.*, Pilat v. Broach Systems, Inc., 108 N.J.Super. 88, 260 A.2d 13 (1969).

34. *E.g.*, Campbell v. Loew's, Inc., 36 Del.Ch. 563, 134 A.2d 852 (1957).

35. *E.g.*, Eckhaus v. Ma, 635 F.Supp. 873 (S.D.N.Y.1986).

36. *E.g.*, Campbell v. Loew's, Inc., 36 Del.Ch. 563, 134 A.2d 852 (1957).

37. *E.g.*, M.B.C.A. § 8.08(a).

38. *Id.* Under some statutes, a staggered term provision renders directors only removable for cause. Del. Gen. Corp. Law § 141(k). In other words, a staggered term provision constitutes an implicit article (or bylaw) provision preventing removal without cause.

39. *E.g.*, M.B.C.A. § 8.08(b), (c).

While, at common law, directors lacked the power to remove a fellow member of the board even for cause,[40] some statutes now allow the board to remove a member for specified grounds.[41] Some statutes now also allow courts (upon the petition of the owners of a specified percentage of stock) to remove a director for cause.[42] By comparison, courts applying the common law have been divided as to whether the court has the power to remove a director.[43]

Removal of a director will create a vacancy on the board. More frequently, vacancies on the board occur because a director inconveniently dies in office, or, for whatever reason, resigns from the board. The corporation could wait until the next annual shareholders' meeting to fill the vacancy—but waiting might create problems if a number of vacancies occur (thereby endangering the board's ability to have a quorum for a meeting). Alternately, the corporation might call a special meeting of shareholders to fill the vacancy—but this could be a hassle, especially in a publicly held corporation. Hence, statutes often empower the board to fill vacancies, unless provided to the contrary in the articles or bylaws.[44] Unfortunately, if the board has the power both to increase its own size, and to fill the vacancies thereby created, the potential exists for a corporate parallel to Franklin Roosevelt's famous court packing scheme.[45] Some statutes limit the degree to which the board can expand its own size, or, under an older approach, might limit the ability of the board to fill openings created by expanding its size, in order to avoid this sort of tactic.[46]

40. *E.g.,* Bruch v. National Guarantee Credit Corp., 13 Del.Ch. 180, 116 A. 738 (1922).

41. *E.g.,* Cal. Corp. Code § 302. Since a misbehaving majority of the directors are not going to vote to remove themselves, and since individual directors, who might be subject to removal by the majority, lack any power to act for the corporation, it is uncertain how much protection is provided to the corporation by granting a majority of the board the power to remove a director for cause.

42. *E.g.,* M.B.C.A. § 8.09.

43. *Compare* Webber v. Webber Oil Co., 495 A.2d 1215 (Me.1985), *with* Brown v. North Ventura Road Dev. Co., 216 Cal. App.2d 227, 30 Cal.Rptr. 568 (1963). Judicial removal for cause adds a prophylactic remedy which could compliment the after-the-fact remedies available in case of a corporate director's breach of fiduciary duty. On the other hand, the need for judicial, rather than shareholder, action to remove the wrongdoing director(s) suggests that the impetus for wrongful action might have originated with the majority shareholder(s). If so, even if the court forbids the expelled wrongdoers from seeking reelection, the court may not be able to prevent the election of new wrongdoers to the board.

44. *E.g.,* M.B.C.A. § 8.10 (the board can fill a vacancy unless the articles are to the contrary). Just in case too many vacancies occur before the board acts, statutes even allow the board to fill vacancies when the remaining directors are too few to constitute a quorum.

45. When FDR sought to expand the size of the United States Supreme Court in order to appoint a majority of justices who would uphold New Deal legislation.

46. *E.g.,* M.B.C.A. § 8.03(b) (limiting the board's ability to expand its own size more than 30 percent). Since a faction would need already to control a majority of the board in order to carry out this tactic, it would be a somewhat unusual state of affairs in which this tactic actually would have any significant impact on control over the company. *Blasius Indus. v. Atlas Corp.,* 564 A.2d 651 (Del.Ch.1988), provides an example of such an unusual situation. Blasius Industries, a shareholder in Atlas Corp., sought to wrest control of Atlas away from its current board. To accomplish this, Blasius sought consent from the holders of a majority of Atlas stock to an amendment of Atlas's bylaws—which amendment would increase the board from seven to fifteen

b. Exercise of the board's authority

Unlike officers, the board of directors obtains its authority from the corporation statute. Specifically, corporation statutes invariably contain a provision which states, in the traditional formulation, that the corporation will be managed by the board of directors, or, in the formulation which is now prevalent, that the corporation will be managed by, or under the direction of, the board of directors.[47] The idea behind the "under the direction of" language is to reflect the fact that, while the board of directors has the ultimate responsibility for the management of the corporation, the board is not expected to operate as the hands-on managers of the company—that role normally falls to the officers. We shall explore later in of this chapter the rather controversial question of just exactly what it is that the board is supposed to do.

For now, let us focus on the mechanical question of how the board exercises its authority. The critical concept to keep in mind is that the directors operate as a board, not as individuals. In other words, even though the board of directors, as a body, has vast authority over the corporation, the authority of the individual directors on their own is virtually nil. A number of corollaries derive from this basic concept.

To begin with, since directors only have authority for actions taken as a board, directors normally must take actions at a meeting of the board. Once one introduces the requirement that actions take place at a meeting, however, questions arise about various formalities which go with decision making meetings. For example, we need to introduce the idea of a quorum. A quorum refers to a minimum number of the group who must be present at the meeting in order to take valid action. The need for setting a quorum comes from the fact that typically it is too much to expect every member of any group will be able to attend every meeting of the group; yet the group generally would not want a small number of the members making decisions at a meeting many members missed and which the absent members oppose. Corporation statutes commonly set a quorum for a meeting of the board of directors as a majority of the members.[48] Modern statutes usually allow, however, the

members. Blasius also sought consent from the shareholders for the election of eight persons selected by Blasius to fill the new positions. Atlas' board responded by amending the bylaws before Blasius could. The board's amendment increased the size of the board to nine members. The current board then filled the two new positions. Because Atlas' articles set a maximum size of fifteen on the board, the current directors' action guaranteed their continued control—a result which the court set aside as inequitable.

47. *E.g.*, Del. Gen. Corp. Law § 141(a). *See also* M.B.C.A. § 8.01(b).

48. *E.g.*, M.B.C.A. § 8.24. Ambiguities sometimes can occur as to how and when to measure the quorum. Most statutes seem reasonably clear that if there are vacancies on the board, the quorum generally is measured against the number of positions authorized, rather than the number of directors presently serving—albeit, there is less clarity when the size of the board is not fixed, and when openings exist on the board due to newly created positions. *See, e.g.*, Rocket Mining Corp. v. Gill, 25 Utah 2d 434, 483 P.2d 897 (1971) (not counting unfilled newly created positions). The Model Act indicates that the quorum must be present at the time the directors vote on an action, not just at the start of the meeting; but there are statutes to the contrary. *E.g.*, Cal. Corp. Code § 307(a)(8).

articles or bylaws (or, under some statutes, just the articles[49]) to contain a provision setting a greater quorum;[50] and many statutes also allow the articles or bylaws to set a smaller quorum (but typically no less than one-third of the directors).[51]

Even though the requirement of a quorum normally means that most board members must be present to take action, minority members might still be upset if they missed the meeting because they never knew about it. This brings up the requirement of notice. Presumably, board members should not need notice of regularly scheduled meetings—in other words, meetings which take place at stated intervals at a location and time set by the bylaws, articles, board resolutions or customary practice. By contrast, without notice, some members will not be aware of a specially called meeting. Many corporation statutes follow this logic—requiring notice of special meetings, but not regularly scheduled ones (unless the corporation's bylaws or articles provide to the contrary).[52] Corporation bylaws commonly provide details about how far in advance of the meeting the notice should be, how the corporation will provide the notice, and what the notice must contain—otherwise, statutory or common law default rules come into play.[53] Since the notice requirement exists for the benefit of the directors, each director can waive the notice to him- or herself.[54] Moreover, since the purpose of the notice is to let directors know about the time and place of the meeting, showing up at the meeting can waive the notice requirement (at least if the director does not promptly object and refuse to participate).[55]

In the absence of a valid contrary provision in the corporation's articles or bylaws, it takes a majority vote of the directors present (not a majority of the whole board) to approve an action.[56] Directors normally cannot vote by proxy[57]—albeit modern statutes typically allow directors to be present at the meeting by telephone conference call or such medium.[58]

Suppose directors seek to take action without a formal meeting; what happens then? Many modern statutes allow directors to act without a meeting if the board members give unanimous written consent to the proposed action.[59] This seems to be a sensible approach. After all, if the

---

49. *E.g.*, New York Bus. Corp. Law § 709.

50. *E.g.*, M.B.C.A. § 8.24.

51. *E.g.*, M.B.C.A. § 8.24(b).

52. *E.g.*, M.B.C.A. § 8.22.

53. *E.g.*, M.B.C.A. § 8.22(b) (unless otherwise provided in the articles or bylaws, two-day notice of the time and place of a special directors' meeting is required, but the notice need not describe the purpose of the meeting); Harding v. Vandewater, 40 Cal. 77 (1870) (requiring personal notice to directors unless otherwise provided).

54. *E.g.*, M.B.C.A. § 8.23(a) (can waive notice either before or after the meeting).

55. *E.g.*, M.B.C.A. § 8.23(b).

56. *E.g.*, M.B.C.A. § 8.24(c). We shall explore the validity of supermajority voting requirements for actions by the board of directors in a later chapter dealing with the special problems of closely held corporations (where such supermajority voting requirements are likely to be found).

57. *E.g.*, Greenberg v. Harrison, 143 Conn. 519, 124 A.2d 216 (1956).

58. *E.g.*, M.B.C.A. § 8.20(b).

59. *E.g.*, M.B.C.A. § 8.21. These statutory provisions typically allow corporate articles or bylaws to deprive the board of the option to act by unanimous written consent.

directors agree to an action, why should they go to the hassle of meeting just to meet? One question, however, about these statutes is why the statutes require the consent to be unanimous—put differently, why should the consent of a majority of the board not be enough?[60] Admittedly, the majority of directors ultimately will have their way. Yet, the requirement of a meeting whenever there is dissent among the directors to a proposed action serves a valid purpose. It is not at all unusual for one or more individuals to sway their fellows away from a proposed course of action originally favored by most of the group.

In jurisdictions which lack a statute allowing board action by unanimous written consent, or in situations in which there was no formal written consent, or the consent came only from a majority of the directors, the issue can arise as to whether the corporation is nonetheless bound by approval from most of the directors, despite the fact that this approval occurred without a valid meeting. The traditional answer was that the corporation is not bound. For example, in *Baldwin v. Canfield*,[61] the owner of all of the stock in a corporation made a deal for the corporation to sell its real property (a fairgrounds) to Canfield. The owner had all of the directors of the corporation execute a deed conveying the property to Canfield, but the directors never met as a group to approve the sale. Instead, the directors executed the deed individually at various times and places. The owner then disappeared with the sales proceeds. In an action by Baldwin—who had a lien on the owner's stock, and who obtained the shares after the owner defaulted on a loan—the court canceled the deed. The court explained that directors only can bind the corporation through decisions taken at a meeting, not individually.

Over time, however, courts in a number of situations have been willing to hold a corporation bound by the informal actions of the company's directors. The most sympathetic case for such a result occurs in the closely held corporation context when all of the shareholders and all of the directors concur in an action relied upon by an outside party.[62] After all, in such a case, there are no dissenting directors who would have tried to change minds at a meeting; the shareholders (for whose benefit the board acts) all concur in the informal action; as a practical matter, owners of closely held corporations often make decisions through informal processes; and it seems unfair to allow persons to take advantage of their own informal practices in order to have their company weasel out of a deal with a third party who relied upon the action.

Once we get beyond the situation in which all of the directors and all of the shareholders concur in an action relied upon by an outside party, the question of whether to avoid the traditional rule becomes more difficult. For example, suppose the informally-approved contract is not with an outside party, but with the corporation's directors. In this

60. The requirement for the consent to be in writing presumably serves an evidentiary function of avoiding later disputes about whether there was consent.

61. 26 Minn. 43, 1 N.W. 261 (1879).

62. *E.g.*, Gerard v. Empire Square Realty Co., 195 App.Div. 244, 187 N.Y.S. 306 (1921).

event, the court might not be all that sympathetic to persons who participated in the failure to obtain formal approval.[63] Moreover, suppose not all of the shareholders were aware of, and concurred in, the proposed informal action. Then, one might argue that the non-concurring shareholders are entitled to the protection of adherence to deliberative board processes.[64] Indeed, *Baldwin* might fit somewhat within the camp of cases in which the action received informal approval by all of the directors, but not concurrence by all of the shareholders. This is because the owner of all of the corporation's stock had pledged the shares to a party who was ignorant of the challenged deal.

Baldwin took place before the advent of statutes allowing action by unanimous written consent—which otherwise might have validated the directors' action in that case. In jurisdictions with such statutes, the only problem with directors acting without a meeting would be if the consent was not in writing (for instance, if the consent was oral, or if the consent involved the directors' knowing acquiescence in the transaction, rather than express approval), or if the consent came from a majority, rather than all, of the directors. In a number of cases, courts, based upon the equities of the situation rather than unanimous written consent statutes, have held that the corporation was bound by unanimous concurrence by the directors, even when some or all of the directors did not express such concurrence in writing.[65] In a number of other cases, acquiescence by the owners of all (or even just a majority) of the outstanding shares, either in the challenged transaction,[66] or in the practice of informal board action,[67] has been sufficient to persuade the court to hold the corporation bound to actions agreed to without a meeting by a majority, but not all, of the directors. The continued validity of such opinions in the face unanimous written consent statutes, however, raises serious questions. If non-written or non-unanimous director concurrence in an action without a meeting is adequate to bind the company, then why did the legislature need to enact the unanimous written consent provisions? Perhaps it was simply to provide a safe harbor within which such action was clearly valid and outside of which courts could do what they wanted based upon the equities; but this is not the only interpretation of the statutes.[68]

Ultimately, the fundamental question is whether upholding informal board action which falls short of unanimous written consent will frustrate the policies served by requiring that director consent to actions without a meeting be in writing, and that the consent be unanimous. If

---

63. *See, e.g.,* Fradkin v. Ernst, 571 F.Supp. 829 (N.D.Ohio 1983).

64. *Id.*

65. *E.g.,* Juergens v. Venture Capital Corp., 1 Mass.App.Ct. 274, 295 N.E.2d 398 (1973).

66. *E.g.,* Phillips Petroleum Co. v. Rock Creek Mining Co., 449 F.2d 664 (9th Cir. 1971).

67. *E.g.,* Holy Cross Gold Mining & Milling Co. v. Goodwin, 74 Colo. 532, 223 P. 58 (1924).

68. *E.g.,* Village of Brown Deer v. City of Milwaukee, 16 Wis.2d 206, 114 N.W.2d 493 (1962) (holding that the unanimous written consent statute preempted informal director concurrence, which did not comply with the statute, from binding the corporation).

the court is confident that all of the directors did, in fact, at least tacitly concur in the challenged action, then the evidentiary function of the writing requirement seems satisfied. On the other hand, the requirement that the consent be unanimous appears to reflect a legislative judgment that, for reasons discussed above, dissenting directors are entitled to a meeting before the board can take action. To the extent that the corporation's shareholders are the intended beneficiaries of this deliberative process, then allowing all of the shareholders to waive the defect by their concurrence does not seem to flout the legislative judgment. By contrast, it is much more problematic for the court to allow a majority of shareholders and a majority of directors to deprive non-concurring shareholders of the protections accorded by the requirement that dissenting directors have the opportunity to express their views. In this regard, it is useful to keep in mind that the whole problem normally only arises if the transaction involved is beyond the increasingly broad scope of the implied and apparent authority of the corporation's president—which, itself, should put the outside party on notice of the need for a formal board resolution.

There are a couple of final caveats to the concept that directors act as a board. To begin with, corporation statutes commonly empower the board to establish committees of board members to which the board as a whole delegates some of its decisions.[69] Some common examples of board committees include: nominating committees (charged with the task of selecting nominees for election to the board at the next annual shareholders' meeting); audit committees (charged with the task of reviewing the corporation's finances with the company's outside accounting firm); compensation committees (charged with task of setting compensation for the corporation's senior executives); and executive committees (empowered to act for the board on matters requiring director approval which come up between meetings of the whole board).[70] Corporation statutes, however, often restrict the board from delegating certain decisions—such as declaring dividends, issuing or repurchasing stock, approving fundamental transactions like mergers and amendments of the articles or bylaws, and filling vacancies—to a committee.[71]

A second caveat to the concept that directors operate as a board is that individual members have certain rights necessary to carry out their role as directors. For example, each director has the right obtain information about the corporation through the inspection of corporate books, records and the like. Courts differ as to whether the director loses this right to information if the director has an improper motive; or whether

---

69. *E.g.*, M.B.C.A. § 8.25. These statutes commonly require that a majority of the whole board, rather than just a majority of the directors present at the meeting, vote to establish the committee.

70. Later, in discussing derivative suits, we shall explore the use of committees of

directors (commonly referred to a special litigation committees) to consider the corporation's interest in pursuing legal action against some of its directors.

71. *E.g.*, M.B.C.A. § 8.25(d).

the only remedy for improper use of information by a director is an after-the-fact suit for breach of fiduciary duty.[72]

3.1.3 Shareholders

a. The shareholders' role in governance

As stated earlier, the role of the shareholders under the basic model of corporate governance is not to manage the corporation; rather, it is to elect the directors, who will have the ultimate responsibility for managing the company. In addition, shareholders may be called upon to vote on certain corporate actions, such as amendment of the articles, mergers, sales of substantially all assets, and dissolving the corporation. We shall explore article amendments, mergers and asset sales, and corporate dissolution in the final chapter of this book. For now, it is useful to make a couple of broad observations concerning the requirement that shareholders vote on approving such transactions.

To begin with, there seems to be no entirely coherent rationale distinguishing the corporate actions which the law requires the directors to submit for shareholder approval, from the corporate actions which do not require such approval. It is common to state that the law requires shareholder approval of "fundamental" transactions. Yet, the law typically requires a shareholder vote in order to amend the corporation's articles, even though the amendment (say, changing the par value of the corporation's stock) might have only a trivial impact upon the company or the shareholders; while directors might completely restructure the nature of a corporation's business and the shareholders' risk (say, changing from a telephone company into a financial services company through a series of corporate acquisitions or internal expansions) without putting the change to a shareholder vote.[73]

---

72. *Compare* Cohen v. Cocoline Products, Inc., 309 N.Y. 119, 127 N.E.2d 906 (1955), *with* State v. Seiberling Rubber Co., 53 Del. 295, 168 A.2d 310 (1961). A proposed amendment to the Model Business Corporation Act (adding Section 16.05) seeks to reach a balance between the two practical concerns which make it difficult to resolve whether directors should have an absolute right to inspection. The proposed section limits the directors' inspection right to a proper purpose—thereby avoiding the problem of attempting to rectify the foreseen misuse of information after the misuse occurs. The proposed section, however, also calls for judicial disposition of inspection disputes on an expedited basis—in order to mitigate the danger that corporate officials might use a proper purpose requirement as a tool to stall appropriate investigation by directors.

73. For a comprehensive discussion of various attempts to rationalize what subjects should require shareholder approval,

see Lynne L. Dallas, *The Control and Conflict-of-interest Voting Systems*, 71 N.C. L. Rev. 1 (1992). Among criteria suggested by various writers for when the law should require shareholder approval are: (i) whether the decision involves investment expertise (which the shareholders possess) versus business expertise (which the board has) (Melvin A. Eisenberg, The Structure of the Corporation 14–16 (1976)); (ii) the size of the transaction (shareholders will pay attention to larger transactions) (Frank H. Easterbrook & Daniel R. Fischel, *Voting in Corporate Law*, 26 J. L. & Econ. 395, 416 (1983)); and (iii) whether the transaction involves a termination in the relationship between the board and the shareholders (in which event, the shareholders cannot trust the board as much to look out for their interests) (Ronald J. Gilson, The Law and Finance of Corporate Acquisitions 578–579 (1986)). None of these suggestions, however, satisfactorily explain how the existing statutes divide the decisions which require

The second observation about the requirement for a shareholder vote on certain transactions is that this does not give the shareholders the power to make decisions; rather, it gives the shareholders the power to veto decisions made by the board.[74] In other words, shareholders cannot initiate, for instance, a merger or sale of all assets; they cannot negotiate the terms of such a merger or asset sale; they cannot order the board to make such a deal, or set in advance the parameters of the deal the board should make (unlike how directors might instruct corporate officers to carry out the board's decisions); all that the shareholders can do is to vote up or down a merger or asset sale negotiated by the board.

We should be careful, however, not to overstate the practical significance of the legal inability of shareholders, as shareholders, to command corporate action. After all, it normally would be difficult, as a practical matter, to get the numerous scattered shareholders of a publicly held corporation to command the directors to take a specific action—even if it were legally permissible. Of course, the difficulty of getting numerous scattered shareholders to focus on specific corporate decisions is not usually a practical barrier to shareholder governance in a closely held corporation. Still, in the closely held corporation context, shareholders are also often directors, and so generally can act in their capacity as directors to make decisions.[75] In any event, the threat of replacement seemingly should give the directors reason to listen to shareholder suggestions, even if the suggestions do not rise to the level of legally binding commands. Yet, despite these practical factors, there are a number of reported court opinions in which shareholders became sufficiently irate to unite behind a command to the board, and then found, probably to their surprise, that courts struck down the shareholders' efforts to command action from reluctant directors.[76]

One common exception to the reactive nature of shareholder voting involves the power to amend the bylaws. State statutes typically allow the shareholders to amend the bylaws on the shareholders' own initiative, rather than simply approving amendments proposed by the board.[77]

shareholder approval from those which do not, and it is unclear whether any of them provide a workable boundary.

74. *But see* Cal. Corp. Code § 1900(a) (allowing the holders of 50 percent of the shares to dissolve a corporation, without action from the board); Mass. Ann. Laws ch. 156 § 42 (not stating that directors must initiate a shareholder vote to amend the articles).

75. The one problem with shareholders in a closely held corporation carrying out their wishes through their role as directors occurs if the shareholders seek to bind themselves in advance by shareholder agreement to make certain business decisions. We shall examine the validity of such contracts in a later chapter dealing with the special problems of closely held corporations.

76. *E.g.*, Charlestown Boot & Shoe Co. v. Dunsmore, 60 N.H. 85 (1880). Moreover, experience with state ballot initiatives shows in a different context the possibility, if not the wisdom, of obtaining specific action from widely scattered voters.

77. *E.g.*, M.B.C.A. § 10.20(a). Interestingly, under the language of the Model Act and similar statutes, the shareholders' power to amend the bylaws seems not to be subject to contrary provision in the bylaws or articles. Under many statutes, the board may have concurrent power (depending upon the articles) to amend the bylaws, so that either the board or the shareholders could make such an amendment without the involvement of the other body. The existence of concurrent power to amend the bylaws in both the shareholders and di-

Why the shareholders should have this power over the bylaws, but not over amending the articles (where the board typically must propose the amendment) is not entirely clear. In any event, bylaws normally deal with the structure or mechanics of corporate decision making—setting out the responsibilities of corporate officers, the size of the board, the mechanics of directors' and shareholders' meetings, and the like. Hence, at first glance, the shareholders' power to initiate bylaw amendments would not appear to give the shareholders much direct power over corporate decisions. Yet, what is to stop the shareholders from using bylaw amendments in a more aggressive manner to control corporate decisions?

In a potentially important recent decision—*International Brotherhood of Teamsters General Fund v. Fleming Companies, Inc.*[78]—the Supreme Court of Oklahoma upheld an aggressive use by shareholders of their power over the bylaws. The Teamsters fund owned some stock in Fleming Companies. Fleming Companies had, as do many corporations, a "poison-pill" plan in effect.[79] Fleming's plan was due to expire in 1996, and the Teamsters had Fleming include, in Fleming's proxy solicitation materials for the 1996 annual shareholders' meeting, a proposal to recommend that the corporation redeem the poison pill options.[80] The Teamsters' 1996 proposal passed, but the directors disregarded the recommendation. As a result, the Teamsters switched from pushing a recommendation, to instead seeking a command. Specifically, the Teamsters demanded that Fleming include, in Fleming's 1997 proxy solicitation, a proposal to amend Fleming's bylaws. The proposed amendment added to Fleming's bylaws a provision requiring the board to seek shareholder approval before issuing poison-pill options, and also requiring the company to redeem the existing options. Fleming's board refused to put this proposal in the company's 1997 solicitation, and the matter ended up in federal court.[81]

Fleming's board argued that the proposal was not a proper matter for shareholder action, because the corporation statute of Oklahoma (Fleming's state of incorporation) expressly gave the board of directors the power to have the corporation issue stock options. Since this raised a

rectors raises an intriguing prospect for a cartoon-like exchange of amendment and counter-amendment. How the law would resolve such an exchange is unclear.

78. 975 P.2d 907 (Okla.1999).

79. We shall look at poison-pills in more detail in the final chapter of this book. For now, it is sufficient to state that under a poison-pill plan, as used by Fleming, the corporation issues a sort of stock option to the corporation's shareholders. What makes this stock option into a "poison-pill" is that the terms of this stock option cause it to be prohibitively expensive to acquire control of the corporation over the opposition of the existing board.

80. As we shall discuss later in this chapter, federal law requires a public corporation to include, in the company's proxy solicitation materials, proposals which shareholders wish to submit to a vote at the annual stockholders' meeting. However, the corporation does not need to include the proposal if the proposal is not a proper subject for shareholder action under state law or falls within certain other exceptions.

81. The federal district court held that the matter was a proper subject for shareholder action under Oklahoma law, and ordered Fleming to include the proposal. During the course of the board's appeal, Fleming's shareholders enacted the proposed bylaw amendment.

question of Oklahoma law, the federal court of appeals certified the question to the Oklahoma Supreme Court. The Oklahoma court held that a corporate bylaw could restrict the directors' power to issue options—despite the statutory provision empowering the board to have the corporation issue options—and hence this was a proper shareholder action. The implications of the decision are profound. If shareholders can enact a bylaw which not only requires the board to obtain shareholder approval before issuing new poison pill options, but also commands the board to redeem the outstanding options, why cannot shareholders enact a bylaw commanding the board to carry out any business decision the shareholders think best?

From a normative standpoint, the *Fleming* decision raises a couple of questions. To begin with, there is a question of legislative intent: Specifically, did the Oklahoma legislature, in granting directors the power to have the corporation issue stock options, intend to make this power immune from any shareholder action through the bylaws? The court's negative answer is probably correct. In all likelihood, the legislature was simply concerned with the ability of corporations to issue stock options, and never considered whether the shareholders should be able to assert a veto over this decision. Actually, to the extent that the legislature intended to preclude a voice for the shareholders, the legislature probably expressed this intent in the general corporate statutory provision which grants directors the power to manage the corporation. This, in turn, raises the broader policy question as to whether shareholders should be able to command the board to take specific actions (or forbid the board from taking specific actions) regarding options or any other matter. Shareholders in a public corporation may be a less informed decision making body than the board. Offsetting this handicap, however, is the fact that shareholders might have less conflicts of interest than directors. For example, poison pill options are designed to prevent takeovers which could oust the current directors from power.[82]

b.   *The mechanics of shareholder action*

Shareholders normally exercise their voice through voting—whether on electing directors or on approving various transactions. This fact returns us to the subject of the mechanics of meetings—a subject we confronted when dealing with decision making by the board of directors.

Many of the issues involved with shareholders' meetings are the same as the issues we examined in exploring directors' meetings. For example, there are, not surprisingly, requirements for notice of, and a quorum to be present at, shareholders' meetings. A number of specific differences exist, however, in the rules governing notice and quorum for shareholders' meetings as opposed to directors' meetings.

---

82. One must be wary of a certain amount of hypocrisy on this issue. To the extent that a board questions the competence of the shareholders to make corporate decisions through enacting bylaws, does this same distrust extend to shareholder approval of charter amendments which, say, insulate the board from liability?

For instance, unlike the norm for directors, most statutes entitle shareholders to notice of regular, and not just special, meetings.[83] (This reflects different expectations on directors versus shareholders to keep track of regularly scheduled meetings on their own calendar.) Moreover, while corporation statutes often do not require the directors to receive notice of the purpose for a special board meeting (just notice of its time and place), the same statutes often require shareholders receive notice not only of the time and place of a special meeting, but also notice of what the meeting is all about.[84] (Perhaps the notion here is that shareholders do not have the duty of directors to attend meetings which do not interest them, and, hence, shareholders need to know what the meeting will be about. Since shareholders presumably should know that the primary purpose of the annual meeting is to elect directors, state statutes generally do not require the notice of an annual meeting to include its purpose.[85]) Corporate articles, bylaws, or acts of the board often fill in the details of notice—for example, with respect to how far in advance of the meeting the company will send out the notice—but corporation statutes (presumably concerned about abuse of the shareholders) typically contain more constraints on corporations making up their own rules for notice to the shareholders than is the case for notice to directors.[86] Nevertheless, shareholders, like directors, individually can waive the notice, either before or after the meeting, and showing up at the meeting without objection waives notice.[87]

There also can be differences in statutory requirements for a quorum between shareholders' and directors' meetings. While some statutes indicate that the quorum of directors must remain present at the time the board acts on a particular matter in order for the particular action to be valid, the same statute might indicate that the quorum for a shareholders' meeting simply must be present at the start of the meeting, but that the departure of shareholders will not break the quorum for the meeting.[88] (This might reflect different practicalities with respect to adjourning and reconvening a meeting of shareholders, as opposed to directors, when it becomes inconvenient for some participants to stay.) Moreover, the existence of multiple classes of shares with different voting rights can create issues, which do not exist for directors' meetings, as far as measuring the quorum—specifically, does one measure the quorum against separate classes, or against all voting shares?[89] In any

---

83. *E.g.*, M.B.C.A. § 7.05(a). When a meeting is adjourned to reconvene at a time and place announced at the adjourned meeting, then the shareholders might not be entitled to new notice, so long as the corporation does not set a new record date (*id.* at § 7.05(e)), or if the time before the reconvened meeting is short enough. *E.g.*, Cal. Corp. Code § 601.

84. *E.g.*, M.B.C.A. § 7.05(c).

85. If, however, the directors will ask the shareholders to approve certain significant transactions (such as amendment of the articles) at the annual meeting, then corporation statutes often require the notice to specify that the transaction will be voted upon at the meeting. *E.g.*, M.B.C.A. § 10.03(d).

86. *Compare* M.B.C.A. § 7.05 *with* § 8.22.

87. *E.g.*, M.B.C.A. § 7.06.

88. *E.g.*, M.B.C.A. § 7.25(b).

89. *See, e.g.*, M.B.C.A. § 7.25(a) (depends if entitled to vote as a separate class on an issue).

event, as with directors, the normal statutory quorum for a shareholders' meeting is a majority (in this case, of the relevant shares); but statutes commonly allow articles to set higher or lower quorums.[90]

As with directors, once one has a quorum at a shareholders' meeting, the question becomes what vote is required to take action. As discussed earlier, election of directors is normally by a plurality of the votes cast. On matters put before the shareholders for an up or down vote, the required shareholder vote typically is a majority of the shares present at the meeting (so long as there is a quorum), rather than a majority of all shares.[91] Many corporation statutes, however, change this rule for approval of certain transactions, such as mergers, and require that the transaction receive an affirmative vote from a majority of all shares entitled to vote on the matter. Indeed, under some statutes, major transactions like mergers might require a two-thirds vote. We shall explore this when considering mergers and such transactions in the final chapter of this book. The current Model Act contains an interesting wrinkle on the required shareholder vote. Instead of a majority of the shares present, the Model Act requirement is only for a majority of the shares voting.[92] This does away with the normal presumption—which is to treat abstentions as effectively a "no" vote—and, instead, ignores abstentions. As is the case when dealing with directors, corporation statutes commonly allow the articles (or, under some statutes, the articles or bylaws[93]) to require a greater vote for shareholder action.[94]

While the issues of notice, quorum and required vote are common to both directors' and shareholders' meetings—even if some of the specific rules are different—shareholders' meetings present several issues which generally are not a concern with directors' meetings. These include:

(1) Control over the timing of the meeting

Litigation over when to call a meeting of the board of directors is quite rare. By contrast, a number of cases have arisen over the timing of shareholders' meetings. This should not be surprising. After all, the primary purpose of most shareholders' meetings is to elect directors. Accordingly, some incumbent directors might succumb to the temptation to act like the government of a "banana republic," and postpone elections they might lose, or otherwise juggle the timing of a corporate election in order to gain an advantage over challengers.

A number of constraints exist on the ability of an incumbent board to dictate in an abusive manner when shareholders will meet. To begin with, corporations statutes invariably mandate that corporations hold annual meetings of their shareholders in order to elect directors, and often empower the courts, upon the petition of a shareholder, to order

---

90. *Id.* As with directors' meetings, many statutes do not allow the corporation to set the quorum for a shareholders' meeting at less than one-third (in this case, of the relevant shares). Del. Gen. Corp. Law § 216.

91. *E.g.*, Del. Gen. Corp. Law § 216(2).

92. M.B.C.A. § 7.25(c).

93. *E.g.*, Del. Gen. Corp. Law § 216.

94. *E.g.*, M.B.C.A. § 7.27.

the holding of an annual meeting if a corporation does not do so within a specified period of time.[95] This rules out a corporate putsch in which directors cancel all elections in order to retain power.

Sometimes, however, shareholders do not wish to wait until the next annual meeting in order to act—for example, to remove directors. Corporate bylaws (or occasionally the articles) commonly contain a provision stating who can call a special meeting of the shareholders.[96] This might not do much good if only the directors, or perhaps the corporation's president, have the power to call a special shareholders' meeting. In *Auer v. Dressel*,[97] however, the corporation's bylaws contained a provision requiring the corporation's president to call a shareholders' meeting whenever requested by the holders of a majority of the stock. After the president refused to call a meeting in response to such a request, the shareholders went to court and obtained an order forcing the president to call the special meeting.[98] More broadly, some statutes empower a certain percentage of the shareholders (ten percent under the current Model Act) to call a special shareholders' meeting.[99] This reflects a balance in favor of enabling the owners of a substantial percentage of the shares to force an issue without waiting until the next annual meeting; albeit, it risks enabling a substantial minority shareholder to call a meeting which even most shareholders oppose.

Occasionally, instead of trying to postpone the inevitable by refusing to call a shareholders' meeting, incumbent directors seek to time the meeting in order to obtain a maximum advantage. In *Schnell v. Chris-Craft Industries, Inc.*,[100] Chris-Craft's board amended the corporation's bylaws to advance the date of the annual meeting by approximately a month. The board acted after it learned that a dissident group of shareholders intended to solicit proxies for an alternate slate of directors. The effect of moving the meeting forward—at the same time the board stalled access by the dissident group to the corporation's list of shareholders (without which the dissidents did not know who to solicit for proxies)—was to dramatically undercut the challengers' chances of unseating the incumbents at the annual meeting. The Delaware Supreme Court canceled the change in meeting date.

Significantly, the court in *Schnell* explained that even though the corporation's bylaws and Delaware's corporation statute allowed the directors to change the meeting date, this did not insulate from judicial

---

95. *E.g.*, M.B.C.A. §§ 7.01(a); 7.03.

96. *See, e.g.*, M.B.C.A. § 7.02(a)(1) (empowering the board of directors, or the person(s) authorized by the company's articles or bylaws, to call a special meeting of the shareholders).

97. 306 N.Y. 427, 118 N.E.2d 590 (1954).

98. The president argued that the meeting was requested for improper purposes— including removing several directors for cause, recommending to the board the reinstatement of the corporation's former president, and amending the bylaws and articles. The court held that the shareholders had the inherent power to remove directors for cause, and were entitled to vote on recommendations to the board (which the directors could ignore at the incumbent directors' peril in the next election).

99. *E.g.*, M.B.C.A. § 7.02(a)(2).

100. 285 A.2d 437 (Del.1971).

scrutiny a change which gave the directors an inequitable advantage in the election. *Schnell* thus becomes a highly important decision beyond the question of the timing of shareholders' meetings. The court's decision is the foundation for a series of Delaware court opinions which have subjected to strict scrutiny, and set aside, actions by directors to frustrate the practical effectiveness of the shareholders' voting rights.[101]

(2) Who is entitled to attend and vote?

Barring a dispute concerning the outcome of a contested election for directors, there should not be any question about who is entitled to receive notice of, and show up and vote at, a directors' meeting. The same is not true of shareholders' meetings. There are several reasons for this. To begin with, as discussed in the previous chapter when exploring the issuance of stock, a corporation may issue different classes of stock with different voting rights. Hence, the holders of some stock may not be entitled to vote (or otherwise may have different voting power) on the matters before the shareholders at the meeting in question.[102] As explained in the earlier discussion, such differential voting rights depend upon the articles, since, in the absence of special provision in the articles, each share has the same voting rights (which means that the rule is one-share, one-vote, rather than one-shareholder, one-vote).[103]

Beyond the issue of what stock has what right to vote, other issues with respect to shareholder voting rights stem from the mechanics of how the corporation knows who owns its stock. It would be a nightmare if, before every meeting, a corporation could find itself in the middle of disputes between various parties regarding who actually owns some stock; nor is it any way to run an election involving potentially large number of voters, if there is no convenient list of who is eligible to vote. For these reasons, corporations statutes typically instruct the corporation to prepare a list of shareholders eligible to vote before each meeting.[104] In preparing this list, corporations largely are entitled to rely upon the company's records of who owns how many shares.[105] What sort of records will the corporation have as to who owns its stock? The corporation presumably knows who originally bought stock from the company. Thereafter, it is up to transferees of stock to supply the corporation with satisfactory indicia of the transfer (typically, the stock certificate(s) endorsed by the transferring shareholder) so that the corporation will record the change of ownership in the company's rec-

---

101. *E.g.*, Blasius Indus., Inc. v. Atlas Corp., 564 A.2d 651 (Del.Ch.1988). *But see* Stroud v. Grace, 606 A.2d 75 (Del.1992) (*Schnell* and *Blasius* do not apply to actions voted in favor of by a fully-informed majority of shareholders; only to unilateral board actions to frustrate the vote of the shareholders).

102. *See, e.g.*, Providence & Worcester Co. v. Baker, 378 A.2d 121 (Del.1977) (upheld an article provision which stated that

each holder of common stock could vote one vote per share for the first 50 shares owned, but only one vote for each 20 shares for all shares owned more than 50).

103. *E.g.*, M.B.C.A. § 7.21(a).

104. *E.g.*, M.B.C.A. § 7.20.

105. *E.g.*, Schott v. Climax Molybdenum Co., 38 Del.Ch. 450, 154 A.2d 221 (1959).

ords (variously referred to as the stock transfer books, share register or stock ledger).[106]

Even if the corporation is entitled to rely on its records in showing who owns how much stock, a practical problem arises from the fact that shares in a publicly traded corporation are constantly changing hands. Waiting until the moment of the vote to construct a list of who actually can cast how many votes would make it extraordinarily difficult to vote by proxy, and, in any event, could lead to total chaos at the shareholders' meeting. The common contemporary solution is for the directors or the bylaws to set a given date before the meeting as the "record date." The persons who own the shares on that date are the persons entitled to notice of, and to vote at, the meeting.[107] Recall from the previous chapter that corporations use this same solution to deal with the problems of shares changing hands before a corporation pays a dividend.[108]

In order to facilitate the frequent transfer of shares, it is common for buyers of publicly traded stock not to contact the corporation in order to become the owner shown in the corporation's records, and not to insist that the corporation issue share certificates in the new owner's name. Instead, the owner shown in the corporation's records, and the holder of the stock certificate, is a brokerage firm (or a depository company maintained by a group of brokerage firms). This is often referred to as holding stock in "street name." The record owner has the right to vote the shares, but the record owner also has a fiduciary obligation to vote as instructed by the actual owners.[109]

When a corporation repurchases some of its outstanding stock, the corporation may not cancel the shares, but instead could hold them as so-called treasury stock. If the corporation could then vote the treasury stock, the directors (who would decide how the corporation will vote the stock) could perpetuate themselves in power despite the wishes of the real owners of the corporation. For this reason, corporations cannot vote treasury stock.[110] Suppose, however, one corporation owns a controlling

---

106. So-called transfer agents commonly handle for the corporation the actual mechanics of recording the transfer and issuing a new certificate to the transferee.

107. *E.g.*, M.B.C.A. § 7.07. Statutes often limit how far in advance of the meeting the record date can be, thereby preventing abusive efforts to stack the electorate.

108. Before the common use of record dates, corporations would close their transfer books—and refuse to change record ownership—a certain period of time before the meeting. The practical problem with this approach is that it created a backlog of unrecorded transfers to clean up. In any event, a purchaser after the record date, who really cares about an upcoming election (as, for instance, a purchaser in a tender offer seeking control) might always demand a proxy from the selling shareholder.

There is also some authority which suggests that if the shareholder who sells after the record date goes ahead and votes the shares, the selling shareholder might have a duty not to vote in a manner which injures the buyer. In re Giant Portland Cement Co., 26 Del.Ch. 32, 21 A.2d 697 (1941).

109. *E.g.*, Gim v. Jan Chin, Inc., 117 R.I. 39, 362 A.2d 143 (1976). Federal proxy rules discussed later in this chapter provide mechanisms to ensure that the beneficial owners of stock in public corporations receive information concerning the matters subject to a shareholder vote and can instruct the record owners as to how to vote their shares.

110. *E.g.*, Atterbury v. Consolidated Coppermines Corp., 26 Del.Ch. 1, 20 A.2d 743 (1941).

amount of stock in another corporation—in other words, we have a parent and a subsidiary corporation. A parent corporation can vote stock in its subsidiary in the manner in which the parent's board decides. This, of course, is how a parent can control a subsidiary. Yet, what happens if the subsidiary purchases stock in the parent? Allowing the subsidiary to vote its stock in the parent could enable the subsidiary's board—who the parent's board selected—to decide who will be on the parent's board. This could give the parent's directors the ability to perpetuate themselves in power despite the wishes of the real owners of the parent corporation. For this reason, corporation statutes often provide that subsidiaries cannot vote stock the subsidiary owns in the parent.[111]

(3) Concerns created by allowing shareholders to vote by proxy rather than in person

Voting by proxy simply means that a person, who is entitled to vote, authorizes another person to cast the vote.[112] As stated earlier, directors normally cannot vote by proxy, and, at common law, the same was true for shareholders. Corporations statutes changed this rule and allow shareholders to vote by proxy.[113] While one might attempt to rationalize the resulting divergence between shareholders and directors as based upon different duties and expectations of the two groups, the easiest justification lies in fundamental practicalities: Without allowing shareholders to vote by proxy, few shareholders in a public corporation would vote at all. Proxy voting, however, creates a number of additional issues for shareholders' meetings, which are not a concern in directors' meetings.

To begin with, proxy voting further complicates the question of deciding who is entitled to cast votes at the shareholders' meeting. Now, in addition to the question of who owns what stock, we must ask, "who did the owners of the stock authorize to vote their shares?"[114] This is more than just a matter of demanding satisfactory evidence of the proxy.[115] There is also the fact that, in a contested election, it is not at all

---

111. *E.g.*, M.B.C.A. § 7.21(b). This creates a potentially amusing dilemma when two corporations each own a majority of each other's stock.

112. People often use the term "proxy" in several different ways: It can refer to the person who votes for another person; the relationship between the person entitled to vote and the person who actually votes; the authority one person gives to another person to vote on the grantor's behalf; or a written document which contains permission for one person to vote for another.

113. *E.g.*, M.B.C.A. § 7.22.

114. Since proxy voting makes it likely that questions will arise during the course of a shareholders' meeting in a public corporation as to whom shareholders granted a proxy, there needs to be a mechanism by

which to resolve such questions without the meeting coming to a grinding halt. To provide such a mechanism, corporation statutes commonly call for the appointment of election inspectors. *E.g.*, Del. Gen. Corp. Law § 231. While the losing side might always challenge the election inspector's determination in court, presumably a court will defer to a good faith decision by the inspector. *See, e.g.*, M.B.C.A. § 7.24.

115. In order to avoid questions about the existence of a proxy, statutes commonly require a written authorization signed by the shareholder, instead of allowing oral proxies. *E.g.*, M.B.C.A. § 7.22(b). Modern technology, however, has complicated the question of assuring the authenticity of proxies. *See, e.g.*, Parshalle v. Roy, 567 A.2d 19 (Del.Ch.1989) (holding that datagrams

uncommon for some shareholders to be fickle and grant more than one person a proxy to vote the same shares. The basic rule in this event is that the last grant of authority trumps all that came before.[116]

The rule that the last proxy trumps follows from the principle that a proxy is a species of agency (as was implicit in the earlier description of a proxy as a grant of authority from one person to another). As a general proposition under agency law, a party granting authority retains the power to terminate the authority at any time. This is certainly true if, as is normal in proxy voting in a public corporation, the party granting the authority made no promise not to terminate the authority—in which event, the party granting the authority retains both the power and the right to terminate the authority. Even, however, if the party granting the proxy or other authority promised not to revoke it, the party generally retains the power, if not the right, to revoke.[117] To lose both the power and right to revoke a proxy, there must not only be a promise not to revoke, but also the proxy must be "coupled with an interest," or, under some statutes, granted pursuant to a valid shareholders agreement.[118] We shall return to this subject in discussing the special problems of closely held corporations in a later chapter. For the present, it is sufficient to see how the general rule leads to the conclusion that the final proxy trumps earlier ones. The notion is that granting a later proxy shows an implicit intent to terminate any earlier proxies covering the same shares.

For a shareholder who does not terminate the proxy (either expressly or by granting a new one), how long will the proxy last? The document granting the proxy should indicate its duration in the absence of earlier termination. If not, corporation statutes commonly contain default limits.[119]

Occasionally, as with all matters of authority, questions may arise over the scope of the proxy holder's power to vote for the shareholder.[120] Such questions are particularly likely to arise when issues come to a vote at the shareholders' meeting about which the shareholder granting the proxy was unaware at the time of the grant. In addition to normal rules relevant to interpreting grants of authority, courts, when faced with a potential misuse of a proxy, might keep in mind that, as a species of agent, a proxy holder owes a fiduciary duty to the shareholder who gave

and telecopied proxies did not have sufficient indicia of authenticity to receive a presumption of validity). Some corporation statutes have added specific provisions in response to concerns about the authenticity of electronically transmitted proxies. *E.g.*, Del. Gen. Corp. Law § 212(c).

116. *E.g.*, Schott v. Climax Molybdenum Co., 38 Del.Ch. 450, 154 A.2d 221 (1959).

117. In other words, the party can terminate the proxy or authority, but may need to pay damages for breach of contract.

118. *E.g.*, M.B.C.A. § 7.22(d).

119. *E.g.*, M.B.C.A. § 7.22(c) (11 months, unless the proxy specifies a longer period); Del. Gen. Corp. Law § 212(b) (3 years, unless the proxy specifies a longer period).

120. *See, e.g.*, Gottlieb v. McKee, 34 Del.Ch. 537, 107 A.2d 240 (1954) (proxy holder voted to ratify gift of corporate assets to directors).

him or her the proxy.[121]

An issue of practical importance raised by proxy voting is who pays to solicit proxies from shareholders in a public corporation. The importance of the issue lies in the fact that contacting numerous scattered shareholders to obtain their proxies can get quite expensive. As a result, persons soliciting proxies might seek to have the corporation pay for the solicitation. The law in this area is unsettled to a remarkable extent.

One reason that the law in this area remains unsettled in important particulars is that, in the vast majority of cases, proxy solicitations involve uncontested elections in which the only party seeking proxies is the existing board. Under this circumstance, there appears little dispute about the propriety of the corporation paying for the proxy solicitation. After all, as discussed above, the corporation must give notice to the shareholders of the meeting. Hence, the corporation is going to incur the expense of mailing material to all of the shareholders anyway. Moreover, there is a corporate purpose served by going beyond just giving notice, and also including a proxy solicitation in the corporation's mailing. Without obtaining proxies from the owners of most of the shares, there will probably not be a quorum to hold the shareholders' meeting. Having gone this far, the corporation's mailing may as well solicit proxies to vote for the individuals who are running unopposed for positions on the board (in other words, the incumbents, sometimes coupled with other persons recommended by the existing board to fill expected openings). Otherwise, we end up with the strange result that most of the shares present at the meeting (through proxies) will end up not voting at all.

The problem occurs when there is a contest between competing slates of candidates for the board. The leading case dealing with corporate reimbursement of proxy solicitation expenses in the context of a contested election is the New York Court of Appeals' decision in *Rosenfeld v. Fairchild Engine & Airplane Corp.*[122] *Rosenfeld* arose out of a proxy contest in which an insurgent group was able to defeat Fairchild's incumbent directors and elect a new slate of directors to the board. Prior to their defeat, the incumbents had the corporation spend around $106,000 on their campaign. This was more than just mailing costs, but included hiring public relations consultants and proxy solicitors. The insurgents spent over $127,000 on their successful campaign, and, upon their victory, had the corporation reimburse these expenditures. Feeling magnanimous toward the losers, the insurgents even had the corporation reimburse the incumbents for an additional $28,000 which the corporation had not previously covered. While a majority of the shareholders voted (evidently as part of the proxy contest) to have the corporation reimburse the insurgents, Rosenfeld, who owned a few shares (and who happened to be an attorney) brought a lawsuit challenging this use of corporate funds.

---

121. *E.g.*, Rice & Hutchins, Inc. v. Triplex Shoe Co., 16 Del.Ch. 298, 147 A. 317 (1929), *aff'd*, 17 Del.Ch. 356, 152 A. 342 (Del. 1930).

122. 309 N.Y. 168, 128 N.E.2d 291 (1955).

Unfortunately, the result of the *Rosenfeld* decision is to leave the issue more muddled than before. This occurred because a majority of the court could not agree on a single position. Three of the seven judges held that the corporation could legitimately make these expenditures, because the proxy contest involved a dispute over "policy," and there is a corporate interest served by seeking to persuade the shareholders to back policies believed to be in the best interest of the corporation. By contrast, had the contest been a "purely personal power contest" then use of corporate funds seemingly would have been inappropriate. Significantly, under this approach, not only can incumbent directors have the corporation pay their solicitation expenses, but the corporation can reimburse insurgents in such a policy oriented contest—at least, if the insurgents are successful,[123] and if the shareholders vote to approve this reimbursement.[124]

While *Rosenfeld* is often cited as standing for this "policy versus personality" rule,[125] most of the judges did not accept this approach. Three of the judges would have invalidated the vast bulk of the corporate reimbursement. Under the view of these three dissenters, the corporation could only pay the expenses incurred by the incumbent board to "fully and fairly inform the stockholders of corporate affairs," and, in no event, could the company cover the insurgents' costs. The swing vote simply concluded that the plaintiff should lose for failing to prove how much of the expenditures were for legitimate notice to the shareholders, and how much went beyond that.

Perhaps surprisingly, the passage of time since *Rosenfeld* has not seen later courts fully resolve the issue. For example, in *Heineman v. Datapoint Corp.*,[126] the Delaware Supreme Court allowed a plaintiff shareholder to go forward with a complaint, which, among other things, challenged corporate payments to reimburse the proxy contest expenses of successful insurgents. The court made the unsurprising observation that such payments constituted self-dealing—in other words, a conflict-of-interest transaction. However, as we shall address in a later chapter, to say that payments made by a corporation for the benefit of the

---

123. The need for insurgents to be successful in order to obtain corporate reimbursement is as much a practical as it is a legal requirement. If the insurgents do not obtain control over the board, then it is unlikely that the victorious incumbents will vote to have the corporation pay the reimbursement. In this event, to obtain reimbursement, the insurgents would need to convince a court to order such payment over the board's opposition—something few courts would do, even when the courts would have upheld a voluntary payment by the corporation. Indeed, in a case in which a dissident shareholder defeated a management proposal in a proxy contest (which did not involve election of directors), a court held that the courts lack the power to order a corporation to reimburse a shareholder's

proxy solicitation expenses. Grodetsky v. McCrory Corp., 49 Misc.2d 322, 267 N.Y.S.2d 356 (Sup. Ct.), *aff'd.*, 27 A.D.2d 646, 276 N.Y.S.2d 841 (1966). Notice the asymmetry this creates between insurgents (who must gain control of the board to recover their expenses) and incumbents (who, even if they lose, could have had the corporation pay most of their costs before the election).

124. The opinion of the three judges also states that, even if the proxy contest involves policy, the amount reimbursed by the corporation must be reasonable.

125. *E.g.*, Johnson v. Tago, Inc., 188 Cal.App.3d 507, 233 Cal.Rptr. 503 (1986).

126. 611 A.2d 950 (Del.1992).

directors involve a conflict-of-interest does not mean that the payments are inappropriate—the question is whether the payment produces a benefit to the corporation proportionate to what the corporation paid.[127]

So, what should be the rule with respect to the corporation reimbursing proxy contest expenses? The policy versus personality distinction has produced well deserved skepticism as being unrealistic. As political campaigns illustrate, one person's mud-slinging personal attack is another individual's policy difference. Besides, sophisticated investors often recognize that perhaps the largest determinate of a firm's profitability is the capability and integrity of its management. Hence, the shareholders might be better served by information about the personal strengths and weaknesses of competing candidates, than about whether the corporation should expand into the field of widget production. Indeed, the so-called policy dispute in *Rosenfeld* involved charges of excessive compensation paid to an officer and director of the corporation.

There are also problems with a rule which would deny corporate payment for any expenses other than giving the shareholders notice of the meeting, and a "full and fair" (neutral?) explanation concerning the issues (and persons?) upon which the shareholders will vote. One might be concerned that well-financed insurgents, with shady plans or credentials, could oust incumbent directors who are unwilling to spend their own money to retain moderately compensated positions on a board. Conversely, individuals who could provide better corporate leadership might not wish to spend their own money to gain election, when the benefits of improved leadership will be dispersed among all of the shareholders. Moreover, the asymmetry suggested in the *Rosenfeld* dissent—under which insurgents can never have corporate reimbursement, while the incumbents might at least have the corporation cover costs of simply "informing" the shareholders—is a prescription for preserving incumbents and deterring challengers.

Perhaps the rule could be that the corporation will reimburse the winning side, but not the losers. One difficulty with such a rule is the incentive it might create to make large expenditures, because the only way to get reimbursed is to win. Alternately, fear of unreimbursed expenditures if one's side loses could deter incumbents or challengers from making the effort. On the other hand, a rule which reimbursed losing insurgents could pave the way to spurious challenges made just for the heck of it (as long as someone else is paying). In the end, perhaps the reason that the law remains underdeveloped in this area is that it is difficult to figure out what the appropriate rule should be.

Having looked at three areas in which shareholders' meetings present different issues than confronted when dealing with meetings of

---

127. See § 4.2.2 *infra.* In this regard, the significance in *Rosenfeld* of the new directors voting to have the corporation reimburse the losing incumbents, or of the shareholders voting to have the corporation reimburse the insurgents, presumably lies in altering the scrutiny which the court will apply in reviewing a conflict-of-interest transaction; it should not, however, alter the fundamental question of determining whether the expenses produced a corporate benefit.

directors, we can now turn back to an issue which directors and shareholders have in common: What happens when action is taken without a meeting? Once again, the basic rule is that the action is invalid.[128] For shareholders, like directors, however, corporation statutes sanction an exception. Corporation statutes typically allow shareholders to take action without a meeting if there is written consent by the shareholders to such action.

As with directors, under most corporation statutes, shareholders can act through written consent without a meeting only if the consent is unanimous.[129] The practical impact of this is to restrict the utility of such provisions to closely held corporations. Some states, however, including such important jurisdictions as Delaware,[130] do not require that the consent by shareholders be unanimous. Rather, it is enough if there is written consent from the owners of a majority of the shares entitled to vote (or from whatever greater percentage of stock might be required for the action in question if all shares were present at a meeting).

Statutes like Delaware's raise the question of why written consent from the owners of a majority of the shares can be adequate for shareholder action, but, as discussed earlier, even in Delaware it takes unanimous consent of the directors to act without a meeting. The answer is that the requirement of unanimous consent might not serve the same purpose for shareholder action as it does for director action. With respect to director action, dissenters might be able to turn the vote around if they have the opportunity to present their views at a meeting of the board. Proxy voting renders this in apropos to a shareholder meeting. On the other hand, one might argue that allowing shareholder consent without unanimity creates the potential for a stealth campaign to gather consents—which gives dissenters no time to try and convince shareholders not to give written consent—whereas dissenters might campaign against the solicitation of proxies for a meeting they know is coming. While statutes like Delaware's require that non-consenting shareholders receive prompt notice of action taken by the other shareholders through written consent, this is a little late for dissenting shareholders to prevent the action. Still, it is difficult to say how often, as a practical matter, anyone could conduct a stealth consent campaign in a public corporation.[131] Moreover, even if such a campaign could get a head start in stealth, consents, like proxies, are revocable.[132]

One problem posed by shareholder consent, which does not exist for director consent, is figuring out who owns how many shares in order to give the consent when, in a public corporation, shares constantly change

128. *E.g.*, Stott v. Stott, 258 Mich. 547, 242 N.W. 747 (1932). *But see* Philadelphia Life Insurance Co. v. Crosland–Cullen Co., 234 F.2d 780 (4th Cir.1956) (upholding informal shareholder action when no minority shareholders were prejudiced).

129. *E.g.*, M.B.C.A. § 7.04.

130. Del. Gen. Corp. Law § 228.

131. As we shall see later, one could not conduct much of a stealth consent campaign in a public corporation subject to federal proxy rules.

132. Calumet Indus., Inc. v. MacClure, 464 F.Supp. 19 (N.D.Ill.1978).

hands. Recall that this same problem exists for voting at shareholders' meetings. The solution is the same: directors can set a record date.[133] Both the Delaware corporation statute and case law limit the directors' ability to use the board's power over the record date simply as a tactic to delay action by consent.[134]

c. *Shareholder information rights*

We generally take it as a given that voters are more likely to vote intelligently if they are fully informed. Presumably, this applies to shareholders in the corporate context. Moreover, as the owners of the corporation, one would suppose that shareholders are entitled to information about their company for purposes beyond making decisions as to how to vote (as, for example, deciding whether to retain their investment). The law takes two broad approaches toward providing shareholders with information about their corporation. The first is to grant shareholders the right to inspect corporate records. A more far reaching approach is to impose obligations upon the corporation to make disclosures to shareholders, without waiting for the shareholders to affirmatively request information.

The right of shareholders to inspect corporate records exists both by virtue of court opinions applying the common law,[135] and by provisions in the corporation statutes of most states.[136] An unfettered application of

---

133. *E.g.*, Del. Gen. Corp. Law § 213(b). If the board does not set a record date, Section 213(b) sets the record date as the day the first consent is delivered to the corporation.

134. *E.g.*, Datapoint Corp. v. Plaza Securities Co., 496 A.2d 1031 (Del.1985). Cases like *Datapoint* illustrate the danger which the ability of the holder(s) of a majority of the stock to act by consent can pose to a board threatened with a hostile takeover: The consent procedure can allow a party seeking control to change directors without even a special shareholders' meeting. As a result, many corporations have taken advantage of the optional nature of the statute by amending their articles to require that shareholder consent be unanimous.

135. *E.g.*, Albee v. Lamson & Hubbard Corp., 320 Mass. 421, 69 N.E.2d 811 (1946).

136. *E.g.*, M.B.C.A. §§ 7.20, 16.01–16.04. One of the primary impetuses for legislation dealing with shareholder inspection rights came, not from dissatisfaction with the common law's delineation of the substantive right of inspection, but rather from problems with enforcing the right under the common law. Specifically, while courts, in a mandamus proceeding, could order recalcitrant corporate officials to allow inspection, corporate officials had an incentive to deny inspection requests from shareholders, and force the shareholder to

go to court for an order. In this manner, the corporate officials could impose cost and delay upon the requesting shareholder—who might be seeking to challenge the incumbents in the next election—with little downside for the officials themselves. To combat such tactics, statutes often contain penalties for denying inspection rights without an appropriate basis. *See, e.g., id.* at § 16.04(c) (empowering the court to order reimbursement of the shareholder's costs, including attorneys fees, unless denial of inspection was in good faith and with a reasonable basis).

Statutes in some states are fairly narrow in their reach, either in terms of what records they cover or what shareholders can take advantage of the statutory right. In this event, the question arises as to whether the statute eliminates, or merely supplements, the common law right of inspection. Generally, courts have held that the common law right of inspection survives the statutes. *E.g.*, Tucson Gas & Electric Co. v. Schantz, 5 Ariz.App. 511, 428 P.2d 686 (1967). *But see* Caspary v. Louisiana Land & Exploration Co., 707 F.2d 785 (4th Cir. 1983).

Under either common, or statutory, law, the shareholders' inspection rights might be subject to reasonable regulations, but not abrogation, by provisions in bylaws or arti-

a right to inspect corporate records, however, might impose two burdens upon the corporation. The first is simply the hassle of making records physically available to the requesting shareholder. So long as the shareholder must go to the corporation's office to see the records (rather than being able to demand that the corporation bring the requested records to the shareholder),[137] the significance of this hassle factor may depend largely upon the quantity of requested materials, and where and how the corporation maintains the requested records.[138] A potentially more significant burden involves the possible misuse of the corporate records. An obvious example would be if a shareholder of Coca Cola demands to see the secret formula for the famous beverage with the goal of starting up a competing soft drink company. The law with respect to shareholder inspection rights has taken three principal approaches to deal with these burdens.

The most traditional approach focuses on the shareholder's purpose for demanding inspection. While courts have held that shareholders, as the owners of the corporation, have a common law right to inspect corporate records, the courts also have held that this common law right only exists if the shareholder has a proper purpose for the inspection.[139] This proper purpose requirement also exists under many of the statutory provisions which provide for inspection rights.[140]

The existence of a proper purpose requirement, in turn, raises the question as to what is a proper, and what is an improper, purpose for inspection. Some purposes are obviously improper. As suggested by the example above, seeking trade secrets in order to become, or to aid, a competitor is a no-no.[141] Nor is it appropriate to seek a list of shareholders in order to generate an advertising list.[142] Idle curiosity, or the desire to burden corporate officials with the need to respond to requests for inspection, also do not count as proper purposes.[143]

cles. *E.g.*, State ex rel. Cochran v. Penn–Beaver Oil Co., 34 Del. 81, 143 A. 257 (1926). *See also* Cal. Corp. Code § 1601(b).

137. *E.g.*, M.B.C.A. § 16.02(b) (right to inspection at a reasonable location specified by the corporation during regular business hours).

138. Obnoxious parties on either side can always turn any inspection of records into a hassle. To provide guidance on matters where shareholders and corporate officials can get into fights, statutes often contain provisions dealing with such issues as copying records and who the shareholder might bring to aid in the inspection. *E.g.*, M.B.C.A. § 16.03.

139. *E.g.*, Albee v. Lamson & Hubbard Corp., 320 Mass. 421, 69 N.E.2d 811 (1946).

140. *E.g.*, Del. Gen. Corp. Law § 220(b); M.B.C.A. § 16.02(c). Some statutes do not refer to a proper purpose requirement, in which event the question arises as to

whether the statute deviates from the common law rule of requiring a proper purpose. Most courts have interpreted ambiguous statutes as retaining the proper purpose requirement—albeit, perhaps with the burden on the corporation to show that the shareholder did not have a proper purpose, rather than on the shareholder to show that he or she has a proper purpose. *E.g.*, Crane Co. v. Anaconda Co., 39 N.Y.2d 14, 382 N.Y.S.2d 707, 346 N.E.2d 507 (1976). *But see* Riser v. Genuine Parts Co., 150 Ga.App. 502, 258 S.E.2d 184 (1979). Some statutes, however, indicate a clear intent to eliminate the proper purpose requirement, at least for certain types of records. *E.g.*, M.B.C.A. § 16.02(a), (c).

141. *E.g.*, Morton v. Rogers, 20 Ariz. App. 581, 514 P.2d 752 (1973).

142. *See, e.g.*, Theile v. Cities Service Co., 31 Del. 514, 115 A. 773 (1922).

143. *E.g.*, Carpenter v. Texas Air Corp., 1985 WL 11548 (Del.Ch.).

By contrast, classic proper purposes would seem to include obtaining the list of shareholders in order to communicate with one's fellow owners about the election of directors or other matters upon which the shareholders might act, and investigating possible management wrongdoing for the purpose of bringing an action on behalf of the corporation or the shareholders against the wrongdoers. Just to prove that little in the law is ever simple, however, it turns out that both of these purposes have produced court opinions which suggest that such objectives might not always be appropriate.

The Minnesota Supreme Court's opinion in *State ex rel Pillsbury v. Honeywell, Inc.*[144] provides an illustration. Honeywell manufactured anti-personnel fragmentation bombs used by the United States during the Vietnam War. Pillsbury was an individual who was opposed to the Vietnam War and use of such weapons in the war. He purchased a small amount of Honeywell stock admittedly for the sole purpose of attempting to change corporate policy against continuing the production of such munitions. He requested to see the list of Honeywell shareholders—ostensibly in order to solicit proxies to elect a slate of directors to the board of Honeywell who would affect the desired change in corporate policy—and also requested to see corporate records related to munitions production. After Honeywell refused both requests, Pillsbury brought an action to force inspection. In response, the Minnesota Supreme Court held that Pillsbury did not have a proper purpose for the inspection.[145] In doing so, the court rejected the contention that the desire to communicate with other shareholders about matters concerning the corporation was, per se, a proper purpose. The court explained that a different case would be presented if Pillsbury had invested in Honeywell for economic reasons and was concerned about the economic impact of munitions production on Honeywell.

The *Pillsbury* decision is probably best understood as a reflection of the strong passions raised on both sides by the Vietnam War and the protests over that war. The Delaware Supreme Court subsequently criticized the decision,[146] while the Delaware Chancery Court, in one case,[147] flatly refused to follow the decision, and, in other case,[148] seized upon the *Pillsbury* court's caveat about adverse economic impact in order allow inspection of the shareholder list by a party who bought a few shares in Chevron Corporation in order to stop Chevron doing business with the Marxist government in Angola. The tactic of the Chevron shareholder—claiming that Chevron's dealings in Angola ex-

144. 291 Minn. 322, 191 N.W.2d 406 (1971).

145. Because Honeywell was a Delaware corporation doing business in Minnesota, there was some question as to whether Minnesota or Delaware law applied to shareholder inspection rights. The court decided that the result was the same under either law.

146. Credit Bureau Reports, Inc. v. Credit Bureau of St. Paul, Inc., 290 A.2d 691 (Del.1972).

147. Food & Allied Service Trades Dept. v. Wal–Mart Stores, Inc., 18 Del. J. Corp. L. 651 (Del. Ch. 1992).

148. Conservative Caucus Research, Analysis & Educ. Found., Inc. v. Chevron Corp., 525 A.2d 569 (Del.Ch.1987).

posed the company to certain economic risks—indicates one weakness in the *Pillsbury* decision: its possible circumvention by parties willing to make up an economic rationale. More fundamentally, the *Pillsbury* decision rests upon the questionable value judgment that it is inappropriate for an individual to seek to change corporate management based upon political, rather than economic, goals. No doubt, shareholders, by and large, invest for economic reasons. Accordingly, the Honeywell shareholders almost certainly would have rebuffed Pillsbury's effort to change the board in order to further political ends. Yet, what would have been the harm in letting Pillsbury work within the corporate governance system in a quixotic effort to change corporate actions?

Suppose a shareholder wishes to inspect the shareholder list, not to solicit proxies from other shareholders, but rather to invite other shareholders to participate in litigation arising out of purported management wrongdoing. If the proposed litigation consists of a derivative action on behalf of the corporation, then viewing the shareholder list in order to contact shareholders for support is a proper purpose.[149] On the other hand, viewing the shareholder list in order to invite other stockholders to join a securities fraud action against the corporation raises a more difficult question. After all, increasing the number of plaintiffs suing the corporation hardly seems to be in the corporation's interest. Nevertheless, in *Compaq Computer Corp. v. Horton*,[150] the Delaware Supreme Court held that inviting other shareholders to join a securities fraud action against the corporation was a proper purpose.[151] The court reasoned that, while the impact of disclosing the list could be to increase the amount of damages which the corporation ultimately would pay in the securities fraud action—albeit, the company might then obtain indemnity from its wrongfully acting management—this still was a demand based upon protecting the legitimate interests of the shareholders both in terms of addressing past misconduct and in preventing future wrongs.

In *Security First Corp. v. United States Die Casting & Development Co.*,[152] the Delaware Supreme Court faced the question of the extent to which investigating whether there has been management wrongdoing constitutes a proper purpose. U.S. Die Casting was a shareholder in Security First. U.S. Die Casting became upset when a merger deal involving Security First fell apart, resulting in a significant decline in the price of Security First stock. Suspecting the worst, U.S. Die Casting demanded to see all of Security First's books and records relating to the merger and its termination. When Security First refused, U.S. Die Casting went to court.

At first glance, investigating possible management misdeeds would seem to be the epitome of a proper purpose for a shareholder inspection

149. *E.g.*, Baker v. MacFadden Pub., Inc., 300 N.Y. 325, 90 N.E.2d 876 (1950).

150. 631 A.2d 1 (Del.1993).

151. The inspection demand in this case came from a shareholder of Compaq Computer, who had brought a securities fraud action against the company alleging that Compaq misled the public as to the value of Compaq stock at a time when members of management were selling their shares.

152. 687 A.2d 563 (Del.1997).

of corporate records. After all, as the owners of the corporation—who are dependant upon the integrity of corporate management, and who annually vote to elect directors—shareholders have an obvious interest in keeping tabs on management diligence and honesty. Yet, it could unreasonably burden the corporation if every shareholder has a license to fish through all corporate records on the off chance that the shareholder might turn up something wrong. Accordingly, the Delaware Supreme Court sought a balance. It held that the shareholder seeking corporate records in order to investigate for mismanagement must show, by a preponderance of evidence, that a credible basis exists to find probable wrongdoing—albeit, the shareholder does not actually need to prove wrongdoing. Moreover, even if the shareholder establishes a credible basis to find probable wrongdoing, the shareholder must justify each category of requested records. In essence, the court seems as to have created a sort of a search warrant approach to inspection requests based upon suspected wrongdoing—the shareholder needs to have something approximating probable cause.

Suppose the shareholder has both a legitimate and an illegitimate purpose for inspection. In *General Time Corp. v. Talley Indus., Inc.*,[153] the Delaware Supreme Court stated that if the shareholder's primary purpose for seeing the shareholder list is proper, any further or secondary purpose is irrelevant. At least one subsequent Delaware Chancery Court opinion has gone even further and stated that, if the shareholder has a proper purpose for requesting to see the shareholder list (as opposed to other corporate records), the court will not allow litigation over whether this purpose is primary or secondary to another improper purpose.[154] Given the minimal burden for the corporation to allow an inspection of the shareholder list, the Chancery Court's desire to avoid parsing out secondary versus primary purposes is understandable.

Of course, the mere fact that a shareholder professes a proper purpose does not entitle the shareholder to inspection if the court finds that the real motive for inspection is something else—in other words, there is a difference between a shareholder having more than one purpose for inspection, and a shareholder disguising an improper real purpose with an appropriate sounding rationale. For example, in *Thomas & Betts Corp. v. Leviton Mfg. Co.*,[155] the court disallowed an inspection request purportedly to investigate for management wrongdoing, when the court found, based upon the lack of credibility of the shareholder's witnesses, that the real motivation was to exert pressure on the corporation's controlling shareholder to sell out.

Assuming, however, that a shareholder has a bona fide proper purpose combined with an improper goal, one possible approach is to grant disclosure, subject to an injunction against making improper use of

---

153. 43 Del.Ch. 531, 240 A.2d 755 (Sup. Ct. 1968).

154. *E.g.,* Mite Corp. v. Heli–Coil Corp., 256 A.2d 855 (Del.Ch.1969).

155. 681 A.2d 1026 (Del.1996).

the information.[156] Of course, this solution raises concerns about the practical enforceability of the injunction against improper use. Also, the court might more tightly restrict what documents the court will allow the shareholder to inspect, when the court finds such mixed motives.[157]

Uncertainty over the real motives of the shareholder seeking inspection seemingly might make the allocation of the burden of proof on the issue important. Courts applying the common law disagree over who has the burden: the shareholder to show a proper purpose, or the corporation to show an improper purpose.[158] Statutes also reflect ambivalence on who has the burden of proof on the issue of proper purpose.[159] Worry about the burden of proof exposes the principal weakness of the proper purpose test: It can produce fairly extensive court proceedings looking into the shareholder's purpose for demanding inspection. One wonders in many cases whether the burden on the corporation of simply allowing the inspection would have been all that much greater than the burden on the corporation (not to mention the shareholder) of employing attorneys to litigate over the shareholder's purpose.

A second approach to avoid placing undue burdens upon the corporation from shareholder inspection demands is to limit the shareholders who can make such demands. The intuition behind this approach is evident in the *Pillsbury* court's reaction to demands from a shareholder who had owned only a few shares for a short period of time. Perhaps if the shareholder had a much more significant economic stake in the company, the *Pillsbury* court would have been sympathetic to his desire to solicit other shareholders in order to change corporate policies—even if the motive for the change was political, rather than economic.

Several corporation statutes have adopted the idea that shareholders with a greater economic stake in the corporation should have more right to inspection. New York had provided the most prominent example. Former Section 624(b) of New York's Business Corporation Law provided inspection rights to owners of at least five percent of the outstanding shares of any class of stock in the corporation, or to persons who owned their stock for at least six months. The pre–1984 version of the Model Act contained similar provisions. Since courts interpreted former 624(b) not to allow inspection for an improper purpose, and since the common law right of inspection remained for any shareholder in New York for a proper purpose,[160] about all the quantity and holding requirements did

156. *E.g.*, Tatko v. Tatko Bros. Slate Co., 173 App. Div. 2d 917, 569 N.Y.S.2d 783 (1991).

157. In *Thomas & Betts*, the court allowed the shareholder to inspect some financial records for the legitimate purpose of valuing the shareholder's stock, but, given the presence of abusive motives, the court placed greater limits than the court otherwise might have on which financial documents the shareholder could see.

158. *Compare* N V F Co. v. Sharon Steel Corp., 294 F.Supp. 1091 (W.D.Pa.1969),

with Weigel v. J. W. O'Connor, 57 Ill. App.3d 1017, 373 N.E.2d 421 (1978).

159. *See, e.g.*, Del. Gen. Corp. Law § 220(c) (the burden of proof on the issue of purpose shifts depending on the type of record requested).

160. Crane Co. v. Anaconda Co., 39 N.Y.2d 14, 382 N.Y.S.2d 707, 346 N.E.2d 507 (1976).

was to shift the burden of proof on the issue of proper purpose. Recently, New York amended Section 624 to abandon the effort to treat more than five percent or six month shareholders differently from any other shareholder. California, however, continues to use the five percent idea in a manner which has real impact. Such stockholders have an absolute right to inspect the corporation's shareholder list.[161]

While the statutes which treat shareholder inspection rights differently depending upon the size of one's holding may offend egalitarian instincts, there is a degree of merit in the idea—at least to deal with certain problems posed by inspection rights. For example, as discussed above, shareholder inspection in order to check on possible management misdeeds would seem to be, not only appropriate, but also extraordinarily useful. Hence, it would be nice if the law could encourage such inspections, rather than putting up roadblocks to them. Seen in this light, it is unfortunate that the Delaware Supreme Court in *Security First* felt compelled to require that shareholders establish probable wrongdoing before allowing inspection. This limitation is an understandable reaction to the fear (whether or not realistic) that hundreds of shareholders would go snooping through corporate files. Granting the right to inspect for wrongdoing, without establishing probable misdeeds, to shareholders who own, say, at least five or ten percent of the outstanding stock, would not pose the same problem.[162]

The third approach to mitigate the potential burden of shareholder inspection rights is to draw distinctions based upon the type of document requested. The rationale behind this approach becomes evident if one compares both the legitimate utility to the shareholders, and the dangers to the corporation, of a request to see the corporation's articles or bylaws, on the one hand, versus a request to see the secret formula for the corporation's unpatented product, on the other hand.

A number of corporation statutes have picked up, to varying degrees, on this sort of distinction. For example, Delaware's statute shifts the burden of proof on the question of proper purpose, depending on whether the request is to see the shareholder list (in which event, the burden of proof is on the corporation resisting disclosure), or whether the request is to see other corporate records (in which event, the burden of proof is on the shareholder). The current Model Act divides records into three camps. In the first group are certain types of records which the Act gives a shareholder the right to see without regard to the

---

161. Cal. Corp. Code § 1600(a). The California statute also grants an absolute right to inspect the shareholder list to any holder of at least one percent of the outstanding stock who has filed, with the Securities Exchange Commission, materials to solicit proxies.

162. The fact that the inspection right belongs to "shareholders" of the corporation is itself a limitation which can sometimes create questions. For example, the practice discussed earlier of shareholders holding their stock in "street name" raises the issue as to whether the record owner, the actual owner, or both parties, have the right to inspect records. Some statutes contain provisions addressing such questions. *Compare* M.B.C.A. § 16.02(f) (beneficial owners are entitled to inspection rights), *with* Del. Gen. Corp. Law § 220(a) (only giving inspection rights to record owners).

shareholder's purpose.[163] In the next group are board meeting minutes, shareholder lists, and accounting records. These, the Model Act allows a shareholder to inspect for a proper purpose. All other corporate records are beyond the reach of the shareholder's inspection rights under the Act.[164]

Indeed, a sensible system of shareholder inspection rights might go further than these statutory distinctions. For example, why not give the shareholders an automatic right to see the shareholder list? The burden on the corporation to provide the list is slight.[165] Perhaps, as in *Pillsbury*, a shareholder might use the list to make politically oriented mailings, or (heaven forbid) use the list as a "sucker" list for direct mail advertisements. Yet, given the normal flow of junk mail to which everyone is subject, it is unlikely that a few more political or product mailings will make much difference to most shareholders. Accordingly, it seems rather a waste to litigate over the shareholder's motives for seeing the shareholder list.

By contrast, requests to see various business documents present much greater dangers. Hence, a court could well view Mr. Pillsbury's request to see Honeywell's records on munitions production with some skepticism (even if he was not a communist spy). In this instance, screening based upon the purpose for the request, and the extent of the shareholder's investment, is appropriate. Still, while shareholders, barring extraordinary circumstances, should not have access to trade se-

163. M.B.C.A. §§ 16.01(e), 16.02(a). The records to which the shareholder has this automatic right include the articles and by-laws, board designations of the rights of shares, minutes of shareholders' meetings, more recent communications to the shareholders, the names and addresses of the current directors and officers, and the most recent annual report delivered to the Secretary of State pursuant to the Model Act.

164. *Id.* at § 16.02(b). Shareholders, however, still may have common law rights to inspect other documents. *Id.* at § 16.02(e)(2).

165. As mentioned earlier, statutes typically command the corporation to prepare a shareholder voting list in advance of any shareholders' meeting. Shareholder inspection of this list obviously presents the least burden on the corporation, and, accordingly, statutes tend to provide the broadest, but still not an absolute, right to inspect the voting list prepared in advance of the meeting. *See, e.g.,* Del. Gen. Corp. Law § 219 (open for inspection for any purpose germane to the meeting); M.B.C.A. § 7.20 (automatic right to inspect, but copying of list must be for a proper purpose). Moving beyond the list prepared in advance of the meeting, allowing access to the corporation's stock ledger is also not that burdensome, especially in a computerized era.

One potential added burden might arise, however, from the fact that the corporation's books show the record owners of stock. As mentioned above, the record owners are often nominees for shares held in street name. Accordingly, a shareholder might request to see a list of the actual owners. If the corporation lacks this information, then the company should have no obligation. Federal proxy rules discussed later in this chapter, however, require record owners to provide public corporations who request with the names and addresses of the actual owners who do not object to such disclosure (so-called non-objecting beneficial owners, or "NOBOs"). Courts applying state corporation law, in turn, have required corporations, which have used the information from record owners to construct a list of the NOBOs, to allow stockholders (who have a proper purpose) access to the NOBO list, rather than just the record owner list. *E.g.,* Shamrock Assoc. v. Texas Am. Energy Corp., 517 A.2d 658 (Del. Ch.1986). Yet, suppose the corporation has not constructed an NOBO list. By and large, there is no obligation upon the corporation to construct an NOBO list for purposes of inspection if the company had not otherwise done so. *E.g.,* Parsons v. Jefferson–Pilot Corp., 333 N.C. 420, 426 S.E.2d 685 (1993); N. Y. Bus. Corp. Law § 624(b).

crets, the Model Act goes too far in not providing access to business documents beyond accounting records. The situation in *Security First* illustrates that examination of various memos and contracts might be quite appropriate in monitoring for probable management wrongdoing. Accordingly, the common law approach—under which courts, for good cause shown, can be quite expansive in terms of what records a shareholder can inspect[166]—makes sense.

Ultimately, despite all of the effort by courts and legislatures to provide for shareholder inspection rights, few shareholders become informed about corporate affairs by virtue of an inspection right—for the simple reason that few shareholders will expend the time or energy to undertake such an inspection. Indeed, the primary practical significance of the inspection right may lie in providing the shareholder list to dissident shareholders who wish to solicit proxies for a slate of directors running in opposition to the incumbents,[167] or else in allowing prospective derivative suit plaintiffs the rough equivalent of document discovery before filing their complaint (so that they might meet the heightened pleading requirements imposed upon derivative suit plaintiffs). Accordingly, if one's goal is to create an informed shareholder electorate, the law must go beyond passively allowing shareholder inspection, and must mandate affirmative action by the corporation to disclose.

In large part, the job of mandating affirmative disclosure has fallen to federal securities laws, which we shall discuss elsewhere. Some state corporation statutes, however, have imposed modest reporting requirements upon companies incorporated in the state. For example, the Model Act calls for corporations to furnish annual financial statements to their shareholders, and also to report to the shareholders any indemnification by the company of a director's litigation expenses, and any issuance of shares for promissory notes or futures services.[168]

In addition, a number of courts, most prominently led by the Delaware Supreme Court, have held that the directors owe the shareholders a duty of full disclosure whenever the board requests the shareholders to approve a transaction (such as a merger or the like).[169] In other words, it is not enough that directors avoid making knowingly false or misleading statements in the course of the soliciting proxies. Rather, as fiduciaries, directors have a duty to disclose to the solicited shareholders any material facts about the transaction.[170] This duty extends not only to directors, but also can extend to controlling share-

---

166. *E.g.* Kemp v. Sloss–Sheffield Steel & Iron Co., 128 N.J.L. 322, 26 A.2d 70 (1942).

167. This fact reinforces the notion that the right to see the shareholder list ought to be automatic. Still, even as an aid to proxy solicitation, the practical impact of inspection rights may be declining due to the growth in institutional investors, and the ability of dissidents to learn about the share holdings of institutions from public disclosure by the institutions themselves.

168. M.B.C.A. §§ 16.20, 16.21.

169. *E.g.*, Lynch v. Vickers Energy Corp., 383 A.2d 278 (Del.1977).

170. Delaware courts have adopted the definition of materiality used by the United States Supreme Court in interpreting the federal proxy rules. Rosenblatt v. Getty Oil Co., 493 A.2d 929 (Del.1985).

holders—albeit it does not extend to proxy solicitations by third parties who have no fiduciary relationship to the shareholders.[171]

Suppose, however, the directors do not solicit proxies for approval of a transaction: Do the directors nevertheless have a disclosure obligation under state common law? The Delaware Supreme Court has held that directors have an obligation to disclose material facts at the shareholders' meeting when a transaction is put to a vote,[172] or to disclose material facts if a transaction places the shareholders in a position in which the shareholders must decide whether to assert legal rights (such as the right of appraisal).[173] If, however, directors take action which does not entail any shareholder approval or other response, then it is not clear when, if ever, the directors still must disclose material facts concerning the transaction to the shareholders.[174]

One fact about the directors' common law duty of disclosure seems reasonably clear as a result of the Delaware Supreme Court's recent decision in *Malone v. Brincat*.[175] If the directors choose to communicate to shareholders—even in situations in which the directors did not have had any duty to do so—the directors have a duty not to make materially false or misleading statements. Unfortunately, if the duty of honest communication is clear, the consequences under Delaware law of breaching this duty are not clear. The facts in *Malone* illustrate the problem. The complaint in *Malone* alleged that the defendant directors of the Mercury Finance Company inflated the corporation's earnings in reports filed with the Securities Exchange Commission, and in communications to the shareholders of the corporation. The complaint also alleged that the accounting firm of KPMG Peat Marwick had aided and abetted the making of these false reports. Since these reports or communications did not request the shareholders to take any action, however, it is not entirely clear what damage the false earnings figures caused. The plaintiffs in *Malone* claimed that the corporation lost virtually all of its around $2 billion value, but the complaint did not contain allegations explaining how the false earnings reports caused this "loss"—particularly insofar as the true earnings of the company suggest that the company never had such a value to begin with. In the end, the court held that the complaint should be dismissed, but with leave to amend in order to allow the plaintiffs to state whether they were asserting a claim on the corporation's, or on their own, behalf; how exactly the false reports caused either individual or corporate damage; and what remedy is appropriate.

---

171. *See, e.g.,* Citron v. Fairchild Camera & Instrument Corp., 569 A.2d 53 (Del. 1989). Interestingly, Delaware courts have refused to consider the corporation, itself, to stand in a fiduciary relationship to its shareholders in order for the corporation, as opposed to the directors, to be liable for non-disclosure. *E.g.,* In re Dataproducts Corp. Shareholders Litig., 1991 WL 165301 (Del.Ch.1991).

172. *See, e.g.,* Stroud v. Grace, 606 A.2d 75 (Del.1992).

173. *E.g.,* Shell Petroleum, Inc. v. Smith, 606 A.2d 112 (Del.1992).

174. *Compare* Kahn v. Roberts, 1994 WL 70118 (Del.Ch.1994), *with* Bragger v. Budacz, 1994 WL 698609 (Del.Ch.1994).

175. 722 A.2d 5 (Del.1998).

3.1.4 The Ultra Vires Doctrine

So far, we have worked our way up the chain of authority from officers, to directors, to the shareholders. Is there any action which the board, with, if necessary, a vote of approval by the shareholders, lacks the power to undertake? The answer to this question brings us back to the ultra vires doctrine briefly introduced in Chapter I.

a. Powers and purposes

Ultra vires roughly translates as beyond one's power. The ultra vires doctrine refers to the notion that certain actions are beyond the power of a corporation to perform. As discussed when describing the development of corporate law in Chapter I, the ultra vires doctrine initially arose as a corollary to concept that a corporation exists only by virtue of an act of government—historically, the granting of a charter by the state legislature.[176] Since, under this concept, the corporation only exists by virtue of the grant of a charter, the corporation can have no more powers than the legislature bestowed upon the company in the charter. Any action by those in charge of the company beyond the grant in the charter is thus ultra vires and void. As discussed in Chapter I, this view of corporate power was not simply a matter of doctrinal logic, but also reflected an early effort to limit the concentration of economic power in corporations.

Notice that we have just referred to certain actions as beyond a corporation's "powers." The reader might recall, however, that the discussion in Chapter I focused on the purpose(s) set out in the corporation's articles as the traditional determinant of what actions were ultra vires. The difference and interrelationship between corporate powers and corporate purposes calls for a bit of explanation. When specifying permissible actions—whether one is dealing with the authority of an agent, or the powers of a corporation—one can take either, or both, of two basic approaches. The first is to focus on the type of action. For example, a principal might grant or deny his or her agent the power to sign checks, convey property, or enter contracts. Alternately, instead of focusing on "what" the agent or corporation is doing, the focus can be on "why" the agent or corporation is taking the action. An agent employed solely to purchase blackacre for his or her principal might have authority to spend money, but would lack authority to spend money if the purpose of the expenditure is not related toward buying blackacre.

Applying the "what" and "why" limits to corporate powers, we can see how the purposes clause of a corporation's articles traditionally served as a major determinant of which actions were ultra vires. A corporation formed for the purpose stated in the articles of, say, building and operating a railroad would lack the power to undertake activities for the purpose of silver mining. In other words, while there might be no dispute that a corporation has the power to perform a type of action such as contracting for the purchase of real property, whether a particular contract to purchase real property is beyond the power of the corpora-

176. This is often referred to as the concession theory of the corporation.

tion would depend upon whether, in the example above, the property was for a railroad or for a silver mine.

This is not to say, however, that the purpose of a corporate action was the only determinant of whether the action was ultra vires. Historically, courts also held that corporations lacked the power to perform certain types of actions, regardless of the action's purpose. Indeed, early corporate attorneys often feared that a court, which viewed corporate powers as stemming from the articles, could decide that the failure to specify a particular power in the articles deprived the corporation of the power. As a result of this fear, corporate attorneys would draft the proposed corporation's articles not only to list every imaginable purpose, but also to grant every conceivable power expressed in the broadest possible language. It is unclear, however, to what extent this practice really was needed, since courts have long held that a corporation possesses the implied power to undertake actions necessary or incidental to carrying out the company's purposes.[177] Still, in certain instances, courts held that specific actions were beyond corporate powers because of concerns about the consequences or abuse of those particular types of actions. For instance, concern about depriving the board of the final say over a corporation's business operations led a number of courts to state that corporations could not enter into partnerships.[178] Also probably reflecting an unspoken concern about abuse, a number of courts historically have held that corporations could not guarantee loans, at least without an express statement of such a power in the articles.[179]

In any event, as discussed in Chapter I, most of this focus on whether corporate actions are beyond the scope of specific corporate purposes and powers has long since faded into legal history. Legislative sanction for corporations to state their purpose to be "any lawful business" largely has ended disputes about whether a new business venture is ultra vires for a corporation which neglected to amend the purpose clause of its articles before pursuing the new venture. In situations in which courts refused to imply certain powers, legislatures have stepped in and added provisions to corporation statutes allowing companies to enter partnerships, guarantee loans, and the like.[180]

What then is left of the ultra vires doctrine once we reach the point that a corporation has the power to undertake any activities which are necessary or useful toward achieving the corporation's purpose of carrying out any lawful business? Presumably, all that potentially remains ultra vires are activities which are directed toward unlawful business (in other words, illegal activities), and activities which are not directed toward any business goal at all (in other words, activities which are not directed toward any sort of profit making).

---

177. *E.g.*, Jacksonville, M., P. Ry. & Nav. Co. v. Hooper, 160 U.S. 514, 16 S.Ct. 379 (1896).

178. *E.g.*, Whittenton Mills v. Upton, 76 Mass. 582 (1858).

179. *E.g.*, Brinson v. Mill Supply Co., 219 N.C. 498, 14 S.E.2d 505 (1941).

180. *E.g.*, M.B.C.A. § 3.02; Del. Gen. Corp. Law §§ 122, 123.

The notion that illegal activities might be ultra vires can serve as a doctrinal rationale for holding corporate directors, who have the corporation commit illegal acts, liable to the corporation. We shall explore this in a later chapter dealing with the duties of corporate directors. Another possible implication of concluding that illegal activities by a corporation are ultra vires involves the question of corporate liability for such conduct. If illegal activities are ultra vires and void, one might argue that the corporation cannot be guilty of such conduct. Whatever the logic of this sort of reasoning, its practical impact could be to undercut the deterrence of corporate criminal conduct.[181] Hence, both statutory and judicial authority allow corporations to be held liable for illegal acts.[182]

b. Gratuitous activities

As suggested by the discussion thus far, the predominant significance potentially remaining to the ultra vires doctrine involves activities which do not have any business purpose. Specifically, if a corporation simply gives away some of its assets, a shareholder might charge that the action is ultra vires. Such gifts largely arise in two contexts, which have elicited different legal responses.

One context involves corporate gifts to recognized charities (including within this term educational, philanthropic, civic and similar institutions). Indeed, one need only turn on a PBS television station in order to get a quick feel for the pervasiveness of corporate gifts to various charities and similar non-profit endeavors. By and large, courts have rejected challenges that such gifts are ultra vires. The opinion of the New Jersey Supreme Court in *A.P. Smith Mfg. Co. v. Barlow*[183] provides a tour through the three principal rationales for this result.

This opinion stemmed from a vote by the directors of the A.P. Smith Manufacturing Company to make an annual contribution of $1500 to Princeton University. After some shareholders objected, the corporation brought an action seeking a declaration that the gift was permissible. The court concluded that it was. The court began by noting how, after a period of some uncertainty, judicial opinions had traditionally sustained corporate charitable contributions by liberally finding that such contributions might advance corporate profit making objectives. For example, in the case in front of the court, there was testimony from corporate officials at trial that contributing to liberal arts colleges could serve the company's interest in assuring a flow of properly trained personnel for administrative and other corporate posts. Similarly, cynics might suggest that much of Public Television's corporate support has less to do with

181. Presumably, the individuals who made or carried out the decision to have the company engage in illegal behavior will themselves have broken the law and are subject to punishment. See § 4.1.6 *infra*. The need for an additional sanction upon the corporation in order to achieve an optimal level of deterrence raises questions more appropriate for a work on criminal law and is beyond the scope of this treatise.

182. *See, e.g.,* N.Y. Penal Law § 20.20; Commonwealth v. Fortner LP Gas Co., 610 S.W.2d 941 (Ky.App.1980).

183. 13 N.J. 145, 98 A.2d 581 (1953), *appeal dismissed,* 346 U.S. 861, 74 S.Ct. 107.

charity than it does with public relations advertising. The *A.P. Smith* court itself took this sort of approach to an extreme (which perhaps reflected the timing of this opinion at the height of the cold war). The court seems to suggest that without private colleges there could be no free enterprise with private corporations—as if it were but a short step from education at state universities to a communist nationalization of the A.P. Smith Manufacturing Company.

The court in *A.P. Smith* was not content, however, with this sort of often contrived search for a corporate profit making benefit from charitable giving. Instead, going beyond the approach of most previous judicial opinions, the court in *A.P. Smith* forthrightly decided to praise, rather than condemn, corporate charitable giving for charitable giving's own sake. Fundamentally, the court's rationale in this regard comes down to two propositions: (1) charitable contributions are good for society, and (2) corporations (to paraphrase Willy Sutton's famous reply when asked why he robbed banks) are where the money is for such contributions. Hence, why should corporations not be able to act like good citizens and contribute to charities and other worthwhile causes?

In addition to its narrower and broader common law rationales, the court in *A.P. Smith* pointed to a provision in New Jersey's corporation's statute which expressly empowers corporations to contribute reasonable sums to charitable and such institutions. Indeed, at first glance, the presence of such provisions in the corporation statutes of virtually every state[184] seemingly renders the common law rationales in *A.P. Smith* moot.[185] Such statutes, however, might not have quite this decisive an impact. The limitation lies in an ambiguity in the structure of most of these statutes. Typically, the provision in the corporation statute authorizing charitable contributions is part of a broader section which lists various powers of the corporation (such as the ability to bring a lawsuit, to own and convey property, and the like). As discussed above, the fact that a corporation possesses the power to perform a type of action, however, does not prevent the action from being ultra vires if the purpose for the action in a particular instance does not mesh with advancing the corporation's stated purpose. Hence, it is possible to interpret the provisions authorizing corporate charitable giving as only authorizing such giving when consistent with advancing the business purpose of the corporation. Essentially, such an interpretation would simply codify the rationale of the traditional cases discussed in *A.P. Smith*, and uphold corporate charitable gifts so long as the court can conjure up some profit making rationalization for the gift. On the other hand, one suspects that legislatures, not wanting to play Scrooge, had a broader agenda behind these provisions. Essentially, the legislatures, like the broader common law rationale in *A.P. Smith*, probably believed that

184. *E.g.*, M.B.C.A. § 3.02(13).

185. In fact, one might ask why the court in *A.P. Smith* did not just cite the statute and call it a day. The answer in *A.P. Smith* is that the objecting shareholders argued that the statute could not constitutionally apply to a corporation, like A.P. Smith Manufacturing, formed before the enactment of this provision.

corporate charitable giving is good and worthy of support for its own sake.

This then brings us to the nub of the question when considering whether the law should allow corporate charitable contributions. In many instances, no doubt corporate charitable contributions in fact achieve profit making objectives—such as promoting goodwill from prospective customers or from a citizenry whose representatives could decide to impose regulations upon the corporation—and reasonable persons could find that the value of what the corporation achieved from the contribution at least roughly approximated the amount of the contribution. If there is such a business purpose, and a rational relationship between the size of the contribution and the extent of corporate benefit, then the contribution poses no more ultra vires problem than any other corporate activity directed toward the company's ultimate profit making objective. In other instances, however, any serious look at the rationalization for the contribution would lead to the conclusion that the corporation gained nothing approximating the amount of the contribution, and, instead, the real reason that the corporation's management made the contribution was simply to support the charitable cause in question. In this event, should the law follow the broader common law rationale of the *A.P. Smith* opinion and allow the contribution? It is a good bet that most folks' answer would be that, of course, the law should allow corporate charitable giving for its own sake. Indeed, anyone who would answer otherwise seemingly deserves a Christmas Eve visit from Morley's ghost.

Still, one does not have to be a miser to raise questions about the propriety of corporate charitable giving for charity's own sake. For example, suppose the purpose for a contribution to Princeton is to support the maintenance of a Western Civilization oriented core curriculum which focuses on the works of dead white European male authors. Or, suppose the purpose for a contribution is to support the orientation of Princeton's curriculum toward multi cultural studies. In either event, a different group of shareholders might well oppose the gift. The moral is that the court in *A.P. Smith* overlooked a difficult issue when espousing its broader common law rationale in support of corporate charitable giving. We might all agree that it is desirable for persons to share their wealth with charitable causes. A problem with corporate charitable giving, however, is who decides what charitable causes to support. Allowing corporate charitable giving for its own sake enables directors to decide which charitable causes deserve support. Denying corporations the ability to make such contributions—unless there is some legitimate business purpose for the contribution—presumably means that the corporation can distribute the extra funds to the shareholders, who then can make their own choices as to which causes are more deserving.

One might respond to this concern by noting that shareholders elect the directors, and the nature of corporate governance is that the elected board constantly must make decisions on a variety of issues with which some shareholders will disagree. Hence, why should the fact that the board might choose to make a charitable contribution with which some shareholders disagree deprive the board of the power to make such a contribution, any more than would such a concern deprive the board of the power to make any business decision? Indeed, if the shareholders are so opposed to a particular contribution, they can seek to elect new directors or sell their stock. Yet, this suggests that shareholders should select among corporations in which to invest, and directors to elect, for the directors' proclivities with respect to charitable giving, rather than for the business acumen of the corporation's management. This seems to be an unnecessary mixing of apples and oranges. Moreover, there is an inherent necessity, if business ventures are to exist on a greater scale than possible with a single owner, to make choices between business strategies upon which multiple owners might disagree. There is much less reason that individuals cannot choose for themselves which charitable causes to support. In fact, to the extent that centralized administration of charitable funding provides efficiencies, there are organizations devoted to this (the United Way).

Still, in support of corporate charitable giving, one might point out that corporate charitable giving has a number of advantages over the corporation distributing funds to the shareholders (who then might contribute to charities). To begin with, corporate charitable giving will mean paying less taxes than would distributing the funds to the shareholders for the shareholders then to contribute as the shareholders see fit.[186] On the other hand, why is paying taxes to support the activities of government a less socially worthwhile use of funds than is supporting various private charities? In addition, the centralization of larger amounts of money in corporate coffers may make it easier for charities to raise money than would dispersal of funds among the shareholders. To the extent that this ease of collection reflects lower administrative costs from soliciting fewer donors, then it is a legitimate concern; albeit, many charities are able to raise substantial funds from numerous donors without excessive fundraising costs. One suspects, however, that often the advantage of raising funds from corporations stems from the greater willingness of corporate directors to part with money which is not their own. Yet, if the law seeks to promote greater funding for charitable endeavors than the real owners of the money voluntarily would choose to provide, perhaps the law should be up-front about this and enact a tax.

In any event, the court in *A.P. Smith* expressed a couple of caveats about corporate charitable giving. To begin with, the court suggested that the contribution could not be to a "pet charity" of the directors, or otherwise to further the personal ends of the board. Along this line, the

186. Corporate earnings used to make tax deductible charitable contributions will face no income tax, whereas if the corporation distributes earnings to the shareholders, who then use the distribution to make charitable contributions, the shareholders will have received money already subject to an income tax on the corporate level. The deduction which the shareholders obtain for making charitable contributions only offsets the taxable income which the shareholders otherwise would report upon having received dividends from the corporation, but not the corporation's payment of tax upon the income the company made.

New Jersey statute involved in *A.P. Smith* expressly prevented contributions to organizations owning over ten percent of the corporation's stock. In addition, following an express limitation in the New Jersey statute, the court in *A.P. Smith* stated that the contribution must be no more than a reasonable amount.

Interestingly, most state corporation statutes do not contain the sort of express limits on corporate charitable contributions found in the New Jersey act involved in *A.P. Smith*. Nevertheless, it is likely courts will hold that a statute silent on the point contains an implied limit under which corporate charitable contributions must be no more than a reasonable amount. It is less clear, however, whether other courts will be as sensitive as the *A.P. Smith* opinion and the New Jersey statute to guard against contributions which support pet charities, or reflect personal agendas of board members or dominant shareholders. For example, in *Theodora Holding Corp. v. Henderson*,[187] a Delaware Chancery Court judge held that, while there is an implied limit of reasonableness on the amount of charitable contributions authorized by Delaware's statute, extensive gifts to a charitable foundation organized and controlled by the majority shareholder of the corporation were acceptable. Such an incestuous relationship between a corporation and a charitable foundation, both controlled by the same director, epitomizes a pet charity and personal agenda.

Given the fairly universal view that corporate charitable contributions cannot exceed a reasonable sum, the question arises as to what is a reasonable sum. In *Theodora Holding*, the court used the deducibility of the contribution under the federal income tax law as one test of reasonableness. It is useful to keep in mind, however, that, while the income tax rules might provide some guidelines as to when a charitable contribution is reasonable, one should not be confused into thinking that the income tax deduction constitutes a business justification, in itself, for the contribution. This is because a charitable contribution deduction normally reduces tax payments by only a fraction of the amount contributed.[188]

In contrast to the cases involving contributions to recognized charities, are the sort of "charity begins at home" cases such as *Adams v. Smith*.[189] *Adams* held that corporate payments to the widows of former executives were ultra vires. We shall consider the problem posed in *Adams* when we examine executive compensation in a later chapter dealing with directors' duties. For now, it is sufficient to note that courts may be more skeptical of gratuitous payments which do not go to recognized charities and which raise concerns of self-dealing.

c. *The impact of being ultra vires*

So far, we considered what makes a corporate action ultra vires, but without carefully delineating what impact follows as a result. Over time,

---

187. 257 A.2d 398 (Del.Ch.1969).

188. An exception exists when the corporation gives to the charity surplus property the company planned to throw out anyway.

189. 275 Ala. 142, 153 So.2d 221 (1963).

the law has undergone a fair amount of evolution on this question. Modern corporate statutes, following a pattern established by the Model Act,[190] have reduced the impact to three basic consequences:

(1) An action by the attorney general to dissolve the corporation[191]

This is a vestige from the original rationale for the ultra vires doctrine. If the purpose of the ultra vires doctrine is to protect society from corporations usurping more power than the legislature chose to bestow upon the company, then it makes sense to allow the attorney general to prevent the usurpation, or even dissolve the offending corporation. Yet, no one really believes in the societal protection rationale for the ultra vires doctrine any more, and it is difficult to imagine a court dissolving a corporation simply because the company engaged in activities beyond the purpose stated in the corporation's articles. Fortunately, judicial attitudes in this regard are unlikely to be put to the test, not only because few corporate actions are now ultra vires, but also because attorney generals have better things to do than seeking to dissolve corporations engaged in ultra vires actions.[192]

(2) An action by or on behalf of the corporation against the directors or officers who ordered the ultra vires action

This follows from a basic rule of agency law. An agent who exceeds his or her actual authority is liable for any damages which the principal suffers as a result.[193] By definition, corporate directors or officers exceed their authority if they have the corporation engage in ultra vires actions. Hence, the directors or officers who ordered the ultra vires action can be liable to the corporation for any losses the company suffers.[194]

(3) An action by a shareholder to enjoin the ultra vires transaction

This remedy has reflected the most evolution in judicial attitudes toward the ultra vires doctrine. Originally, courts took a rigid approach toward ultra vires transactions. Since, the corporation lacked the power to undertake the transaction, any ultra vires contract entered by the corporation was void.[195] As a result, either party could get out of the contract. One suspects that in most cases in which the corporation or the other contracting party sought to void an ultra vires contract, the motivation for doing so had less to do with the contract being ultra vires than it did with the contract having turned out to be a bad deal.

---

190. *E.g.*, M.B.C.A. § 3.04.

191. Under some statutes, the attorney general has the option to sue either to enjoin the ultra vires action or to dissolve the corporation. *E.g.*, Del. Gen. Corp. Law § 124(3).

192. One intriguing exception follows from the notion, discussed earlier, that illegal actions by a corporation can be considered ultra vires. An aggressive attorney general, who wanted to exploit this notion, might threaten to dissolve a corporation caught engaging in illegal activity—a sort of capital punishment for wrongdoing corporations.

193. *See, e.g.*, Restatement (Second) of Agency § 383.

194. Some courts, however, have stated that the directors will only be liable if the directors were negligent in failing to realize that they were having the corporation engage in ultra vires actions. *E.g.*, Litwin v. Allen, 25 N.Y.S.2d 667 (Sup. Ct. 1940).

195. *E.g.*, Asbury Ry Carriage & Iron Co. v. Riche, 7 L.R. Eng. & Ir. App. 653, 33 L.T.R. 450 (1875).

The rigid rejection of ultra vires contracts did not last. A critical reason for its demise lies in a shift in the perceived rationale behind the ultra vires doctrine. With the rise of general incorporation laws, increased liberality in permissible purpose statements in corporate articles, and the ability of shareholders to amend the statement of corporate purposes in the articles, it becomes difficult to continue to view the ultra vires doctrine as protecting society from corporations gaining dangerous economic control by entering fields beyond what the legislature chose to allow. If the rationale for the ultra vires doctrine is not to confine corporations to their legislatively determined spheres, what then is the reason behind the doctrine? Looking to the idea that the corporation's articles embody a sort of contract among the future shareholders of the corporation, one can argue that the real reason for the ultra vires doctrine is to enforce an agreement among the shareholders as to what will be the purpose and scope of their business venture. In other words, the rationale behind the ultra vires doctrine now becomes protecting minority shareholders from those in charge of the corporation changing the business beyond the initial agreement.

Once one reaches the point that the ultra vires doctrine is really a protection for minority shareholders, it becomes logical to reject the position of some early court decisions that ultra vires transactions were void even if all of the shareholders approved. Instead, courts came to hold that unanimous shareholder approval would validate an ultra vires contract (at least in the absence of prejudice to creditors).[196] Suppose, however, shareholder approval of the ultra vires contract was less than unanimous. If the rationale behind the doctrine is to protect minority shareholders from those in charge of the corporation changing the agreed venture without the minority's consent, then it follows that less than unanimous shareholder approval would not save an ultra vires transaction. This certainly made sense at a time when state corporate laws required a unanimous shareholder vote to amend the articles. It becomes somewhat more difficult to sustain after state laws migrated toward allowing amendment of the articles with less than a unanimous vote. Still, to the extent that a corporate action is ultra vires because the action is beyond any permissible purpose (as potentially the case with gratuitous activities), then minority shareholder protection remains a viable rationale even in an era when it only takes a majority vote to amend a corporation's articles.

Given the shift in rationale to minority shareholder protection, one can see why corporation statutes contain a remedy allowing a shareholder to sue to enjoin an ultra vires transaction (and also why the statutes do not contain a provision allowing those in charge of the corporation to weasel out of a contract by using the ultra vires doctrine). On the other hand, if the purpose for the ultra vires doctrine is simply minority shareholder (rather than societal) protection, it becomes much easier to start thinking about the equities of the party on the other side of the

196. *E.g.*, Note, 83 U. Pa. L. Rev. 479, 488–92 (1935).

contract. True, articles of incorporation are public documents, and, hence, one might argue that a party dealing with a corporation at least has constructive notice of any ultra vires problem. Yet, it seems unrealistic to suggest that parties dealing with a corporation should always read the corporation's articles first.

The softening of the ultra vires doctrine to reflect competing equities is implicit in the refusal of courts to unwind already executed ultra vires contracts.[197] Before long, a majority of the courts refused to invalidate contracts which one side had performed, when the other side then sought to use the ultra vires doctrine to escape the still executory obligation.[198] Moreover, even the courts refusing to enforce an ultra vires contract, despite the performance of one side, often allowed the performing party to recover, on a quasi-contract theory, the value of any benefit bestowed on the other party by the performance.[199]

Modern statutes expressly empower the courts to apply the courts' sense of equity when it comes to enjoining an ultra vires contract at the behest of a complaining shareholder. The court can refuse to enjoin the transaction if such an injunction would be inequitable. For example, in *Goodman v. Ladd Estate Co.*,[200] the court refused to enjoin a gratuitous guarantee by the corporation of a personal loan to one of the corporation's directors. The court noted that the former owner of all of the corporation's stock had agreed to the guarantee in order to induce the loan, and the shareholders who brought the action to enjoin enforcement of the guarantee had purchased the former owner's stock while fully aware of the outstanding guarantee. In any event, if the court enjoins an ultra vires transaction, modern statutes empower the court to award damages in order to compensate either party for any losses suffered (except lost profits) by virtue of the court's blocking the transaction.

3.1.5 Problems with the Basic Governance Model

a. Descriptive failings

Our discussion of corporate governance so far has proceeded from a model which posits that shareholders select directors, who decide on corporate policy and select senior officers, who, in turn, carry out the board's will. The reality of corporate governance differs in subtle, but important, ways from this model. The nature of this difference depends upon whether one is dealing with a corporation with very few shareholders (a closely held corporation) or a corporation with very many shareholders (a publicly held corporation).

In the closely held corporation, reality diverges from the corporate governance model because the shareholders, directors and officers are the same people. In other words, instead of having a large group of

---

197. *See, e.g.,* Whitney Arms Co. v. Barlow, 63 N.Y. 62 (1875).

198. *E.g.,* Joseph Schlitz Brewing Co. v. Missouri Poultry & Game Co., 287 Mo. 400, 229 S.W. 813 (1921).

199. *E.g.,* Central Transportation Co. v. Pullman's Palace Car Co., 139 U.S. 24, 11 S.Ct. 478 (1891).

200. 246 Or. 621, 427 P.2d 102 (1967).

passive shareholders elect directors (who may or may not be shareholders) to manage the company, in a corporation with few shareholders, all or most of those shareholders will elect themselves as the directors of the company. Similarly, instead of having the board select officers who may or may not be directors and shareholders, in the closely held corporation, the shareholder-directors typically also will select themselves to be the officers. Under these circumstances, the owners often simply view themselves as running the business as owners—much as partners operate— and pay little attention to niceties concerning the role (officer, director or shareholder) in which technically they are acting. This confusion illustrates the point made when discussing choice of business form in Chapter I that the corporate governance model originated with the publicly held business in mind.

The divergence between the corporate governance model and reality in a publicly held corporation does not involve the melding of shareholders, directors and officers into the same few people, but, instead, involves the flow of power between these three groups. Specifically, the corporate governance model perceives power to flow from shareholders, who decide who will be the directors, to the directors, who decide corporate policy and who select the corporate officers, to the officers. In large measure, the reality in the publicly held corporation has been almost the reverse. The officers, particularly the chief executive officer, commonly have decided who will be the directors and what policies the corporation will pursue. To understand why this inversion has taken place, we need to examine the incentives which impact decision making at the shareholder level and at the director level.

Shareholders in the publicly held corporation typically are "rationally apathetic;" in other words, the rational shareholder in a publicly held corporation normally will conclude that it is not worthwhile to spend much time or effort worrying about control over the corporation. After all, the typical shareholder in the publicly held corporation has such a small percentage of ownership in the company that the shareholder's vote alone will not have much impact. Moreover, the shareholder will capture only a small proportion of the gain resulting from better management. The result is that the cost of trying to change corporate management is quite high—since the dissatisfied shareholder must seek support from numerous scattered other shareholders—while the rewards are relatively low, since the other shareholders will reap most of the gains. In economics lingo, there is a huge "free rider" problem. Of course, one might respond that the same problem exists when dealing with federal, state and local government elections. A significant difference, however, exists between the options open to dissatisfied shareholders and the options open to dissatisfied citizens. The shareholder who is displeased with management in a publicly held corporation can quickly and easily sell his or her shares. This self-help remedy of selling out is often referred to as following the "Wall Street rule." It is much less practical for the dissatisfied citizen to pack up and move out of the jurisdiction.

Compounding the rational apathy phenomenon is the incumbent directors' control over the corporate proxy machinery. As discussed earlier, the corporation will pay for the incumbent directors' (or their nominees') solicitation of proxies. This is certainly the case if the election is uncontested, and normally is the case even in a contested election. By contrast, challengers will need to foot their own solicitation expenses unless (at the very least) they win. This imbalance creates a significant financial disincentive for anyone to challenge the incumbent board. The end result is that, unlike federal, state and local government elections, elections of corporate directors rarely are contested. Notice how the rational apathy and proxy contest factors reinforce each other. Potential challengers recognize that the shareholder electorate inherently is stacked against a challenge—since dissatisfied shareholders will have followed the Wall Street rule and sold their shares, leaving only the more contented shareholders. At the same time, dissatisfied shareholders have an incentive to follow the Wall Street rule because they realize it is unlikely that anyone will mount a challenge, much less a successful challenge, to the existing board.

The observation that shareholders in publicly held corporations do not really control the corporation by selecting the directors is known as the "Berle–Means thesis" after the two professors who wrote a book in 1932 which recognized this phenomenon.[201] The discussion so far, however, only explains why shareholders do not control the composition of the board; it does not explain why the officers do. Nor have we explained why officers, rather than directors, control corporate decisions.

To understand why officers, rather than directors, control the public corporation, it useful to divide directors into two types: "inside" directors and "outside" directors. "Inside" directors refers to directors who also work full time for the corporation, in other words, directors who are also officers. "Outside" directors refers to directors who are not full time employees of the corporation.

A number of practical constraints traditionally have operated to curb the control which outside directors can exercise over the corporation. Some of these constraints are obvious. For example, outside directors have limited time to devote to the corporation. After all, these are individuals who, by definition, might have full time employment somewhere else.[202] Indeed, the typical board of a publicly held corporation meets less once a month, with meetings lasting only a few hours. Given this little time to devote to a large complex organization, not only is it impossible for the board to address more than a few specific business decisions, it is doubtful that the board even can engage in thoughtful overall (or strategic) planning for the corporation.

---

201. Adolph A. Berle & Gardiner C. Means, The Modern Corporation and Private Property (1932).

202. Among the sorts of individuals who commonly serve as outside directors on corporate boards are chief executive officers of other companies, bankers and lawyers. Even academics and former government officials who sometimes sit on boards have other things to do.

Closely related to the lack of time is the quality of information available to the outside directors in making corporate decisions. As a practical matter, the outside directors must rely on information presented to them by the corporation's officers when making decisions. True, as discussed earlier, directors have a legal right to inspect corporate records. Yet, time constraints generally render this right more theoretical than actual. Hence, directors typically must settle for whatever information the officers provide to the board prior to the meeting. Moreover, boards normally have no independent staff to evaluate the information the directors receive from the corporation's officers.

Given these constraints of time and information, the board hardly can initiate much of any corporate strategy or decisions. Instead, the board's role largely falls to approval of such strategies and decisions as are brought before the board by the officers. Even in the context of approving strategies and decisions made by the corporation's officers, however, the board's effective control tends to be marginal. This is so not only because most corporate decisions never come before the board, but also because a number of factors make it a rare case in which a board will veto an action proposed by the officers. A couple of these factors we have just seen: Lack of time and lack of independent information make it difficult for outside directors to second guess the corporation's officers.

In addition, there are various biases which work against the outside directors second guessing the corporation's officers. For example, if outside directors such as lawyers and bankers hope to obtain continued business from the corporation, they would not want to tick off the officers of the corporation who will decide in the future which attorneys or bankers the corporation will use. Outside directors who are chief executive officers of another corporation might take the attitude that they should treat the chief executive officer of this corporation the way in which they expect their outside directors to treat them.

Most fundamentally, however, inside directors, and particularly the chief executive officer, have controlled (at least until fairly recently) the corporate proxy machinery and decided who sat on the board. This may simply be the consequence of the normal tendency of those with the greater stake—in this event, the insiders whose jobs are on the line—to be more assertive in exercising control over the key levers of power. In any event, if the officers, especially the chief executive officer, pick directors, the normal human instinct will be to select directors who are likely to defer to the officers. While anecdotal accounts of board toadyism under the chief executive officer have long been going around, the best study documenting this phenomenon was done by Professor Mace of the Harvard Business School.[203]

What about the inside directors? Since they work full time for the corporation, presumably they do not face the same time or information constraints as the outside directors. Yet, in evaluating the ability of the

203. Myles L. Mace, Directors: Myth and Reality (1971).

inside directors to manage the corporation in their role as directors, we must take cognizance of the two inconsistent realms in which the inside directors operate. As board members, the inside directors operate in what is supposed to be a collegial decision making process among equals, with differences resolved, if necessary, by majority vote. As officers, however, the inside directors operate in a hierarchial setting in which the chief executive officer has the last word. Moreover, the chief executive officer traditionally has dictated the junior officers' prospects for retention and promotion. Ultimately, it is probably too much to expect that directors who are subordinate to the chief executive officer 29 or 30 days every month are suddenly going to switch gears and second guess the chief executive officer at the monthly board meeting. The end result is that, instead of the directors—insiders or outsiders—determining corporate policy, traditionally the chief executive officer has. While the junior officers of the corporation may have a significant voice in developing policy, this input comes in their role as subordinate officers rather than co-equal board members.

b. Normative implications

The divergence between the reality of corporate governance and the traditional model no doubt has significance for those interested in organizational theory. The reader whose interest is more narrowly focused on the law of corporations, however, might be tempted to ask "so what?" In fact, the gap between the corporate governance model and the way things work in the real world has a number of implications for corporate law. For example, courts and legislatures have made a number of adjustments to the rules applicable to closely held corporations in order to comport with the realities of how such corporations operate. We shall address this in a later chapter dealing with closely held corporations. For now, let us focus on the publicly held corporation.

Broadly speaking, three concerns arise when power in a publicly held corporation resides in a body of officers who are not realistically accountable to the directors or the shareholders. To begin with, this development raises an issue of legitimacy. As discussed in Chapter I, early corporate history featured a fear over the concentration of economic power in corporations. We now accept that a private organization (a corporation) can amass significant economic power. Still, one might ask by what right should a self perpetuating oligarchy control this economic power. After all, the general premise in a free enterprise system is that owners, rather than the state, are entitled to control business enterprises. Once we see that the nominal owners of the corporation, the shareholders, do not really control the company, what is the justification for not turning the whole organization over to the state?

Of course, few folks presently challenge the legitimacy of private corporations. Instead, the frequent worry is that managers might take advantage of their unchecked power over the corporation to act in ways which are contrary to the interests of the corporation's owners (the shareholders). Organizational theorists point out that managers have a number of incentives to act contrary to the interests of the owners.[204]

The first, and most obvious, incentive managers have to act contrary the owners' interests is the desire for self-enrichment which arises in the traditional conflict-of-interest transaction. To take a simple example, managers require compensation for their efforts on behalf of the venture. If the managers possess the power to set their own compensation, the amount is likely to be considerably higher than it will be if the managers must bargain with an owner.

Beyond self-enrichment, managers, like all agents, have an incentive to engage in "shirking." Shirking refers to the desire of agents not to work as hard as their principals would like. Actually, when it comes to senior managers, the significant shirking might not involve the sort of shortened work days and long lunches which one normally thinks of in using the term. Of greater impact can be mental shirking—a laziness of thinking in which senior managers are content to have both themselves and the company stay in well worn patterns, rather than adapt to changing circumstances.

Reinforcing the problem of shirking is the managers' incentive to maintain and enhance their positions. This entails not only the desire of managers to keep their jobs—or even get a promotion—but also the very human desire to avoid scrutiny and criticism. Notice that the managers' desire to maintain and enhance their positions not only protects those who consciously shirk, but also might protect and enhance the positions of managers who work as hard as they can, but, possibly as a result of the "Peter Principle,"[205] are not up to the job.

Perhaps one might dismiss this worry about managerial incentives as the shareholders' tough luck. If the shareholders do not find it worthwhile to protect their own interests, why should the law? Before dismissing this subject, however, we must consider a societal concern with economic efficiency. It is not a coincidence that the Berle–Means book appeared in 1932, at the height of the Great Depression. Managerial incentives toward shirking, maintaining their positions, and even self-enrichment, not only can prejudice the interests of the owners of a business, but also might undermine the health of the business and, in turn, the broader economy.[206]

204. *E.g.*, Michael C. Jensen & William H. Meckling, *Theory of the Firm: Managerial Behavior, Agency Costs & Ownership Structure*, 3 J. Fin. Econ. 305 (1976). The losses which the owners suffer as a result of these incentives are known as "agency costs."

205. This is the amusing notion that individuals, who perform competently in their existing positions, will receive promotions until they are placed in positions for which they are incompetent.

206. It is pretty evident why shirking, and the desire to maintain one's position despite shirking and ineptitude, could weaken a business and undermine economic efficiency. The impact of managerial incentives toward self-enrichment in conflict-of-interest transactions is more mixed. After all, unless the managers short-sightedly destroy the firm by robbing it blind, the impact of excessive compensation for managers might be simply to shift a greater share of the firm's revenues from the shareholders to the managers, but not to decrease the revenues of the firm. On the other hand, a

To give one example of the potential for economic inefficiency from managerial incentives, consider the incentives managers have to grow the business by acquiring other firms. Such acquisitions might feed the managers' interest in self-enrichment, because being an officer in a larger firm often is seen as justifying greater compensation. Growing the business by purchasing someone else's business might take less effort from managers inclined toward shirking than would growing the business by developing better products and services delivered at lower costs. Acquisitions which grow and diversify the corporation can serve the managers' interests in maintaining and enhancing their positions. Indeed, corporate diversification often provides greater job security for managers than it provides investment security for shareholders (since shareholders can obtain the advantage of diversification by purchasing stock in different corporations). Finally, managers often measure personal success by the size of their firm, rather than its profit margins. The result of these incentives is that managers may engage in corporate acquisitions which are inefficient—as witnessed by the constant stream of stories in the financial press about corporations who find themselves forced to divest one line of business or another "in order to concentrate on the company's core business;" in other words, corporations forced to undo earlier foolish acquisitions.

Not surprisingly, there are widely divergent ideas for corporate law rules to deal with the lack of effective shareholder and director control over the public corporation. Broadly speaking, these ideas fall into several basic camps:

(1) Reliance on market forces

A number of writers have argued that various market forces can constrain managerial disloyalty and inefficiency.[207] The most obvious market pressure on managers comes from the need for the corporation to compete with other producers of the products or services sold by the corporation. If the managers are too greedy or too inept, then the corporation will not be able to compete. Of course, there may be room for a fair amount of managerial self-enrichment and incompetence before the typical large publicly held corporation goes bankrupt—especially since the corporation often is competing against other corporations whose managers may succumb to the same incentives for disloyalty and inefficiency.

Another market force comes into play if circumstances tie the managers' personal rewards to profitable corporate performance. There are several ways in which this can occur. Corporations might link the compensation received by managers to corporate or stock performance.

---

decreased return on investment for shareholders because a greater share of corporate earnings goes to managers could result in a lower willingness of individuals to invest in corporations and, therefore, less capital for economic growth.

207. *E.g.*, Henry G. Manne, *Our Two Corporation Systems: Law and Economics*, 53 Va. L. Rev. 259 (1967). For a less sanguine view of the potential of market forces, see, *e.g.*, Melvin A. Eisenberg, *The Structure of Corporation Law*, 89 Colum. L. Rev. 1461 (1989).

For example, if part of the managers' compensation package consists of options to purchase stock in the corporation at a fixed price, managers have an incentive to take action which will increase the market price of the corporation's stock—since the options only pay off if the market price of the corporation's stock reaches an amount higher than the option price. In addition, managers might own stock in the corporation, which serves to align the interests of managers with that of the shareholders. Finally, managers operate in labor markets—internally for retention and promotion, and externally for management positions with other corporations—which gives managers an incentive to develop a record for good performance.

There are limits, however, on the extent to which these personal incentives fully align the managers' interests with the interests of the shareholders and corporate efficiency. For example, if managers engage in conflict-of-interest transactions which enrich themselves at the expense of the shareholders, the managers gain the whole value on one side of the transaction, while the impact of the other side of the transaction on the price of the corporation's stock is dispersed among all of the shareholders. As a result, the ownership by managers of stock in the corporation, or the manager's receipt of stock options, will not remove their temptation toward self-enrichment by unfair conflict-of-interest dealings with their corporation. Moreover, the relationship between the value of a corporation's stock and any one manager's shirking is attenuated. Hence, stock ownership or receipt of stock options only provides a limited incentive not to shirk. Perhaps more importantly, the manager with lazy thought patterns or who is simply incompetent might not even perceive his or her shortcomings, which means that stock ownership or receipt of stock options is unlikely to change his or her behavior. Finally, to the extent that success in the intra-corporation managerial labor market (in other words, retention and promotion within the corporation) depends, for senior officers, upon pleasing the chief executive, and to the extent that the chief executive officer often is beyond worry as far as either removal or promotion, than the labor market for managers might provide only limited incentives for efficiency.

A final market force comes from larger and more activist shareholders. There are several types of shareholders who can play this role. To begin with, many corporations do not fit within either of the extremes we focused on in examining the descriptive failings of the corporate governance model. These corporations are not closely held with only a few shareholders, but also do not have their shares so widely dispersed that no one shareholder owns more than a tiny fraction of the outstanding stock. Instead, many corporations have a combination of one large shareholder (or share holding group) and a large number of shareholders with very small holdings. In this event, the large shareholder (or group) typically will be in control of the corporation. Such a shareholder has incentives toward efficient management—albeit, such a shareholder might provide inefficient management because the shareholder is inept, and such a shareholder might act to enrich him- or herself at the expense of the small shareholders.

Institutional investors constitute a second type of larger and potentially active shareholder. Institutional investors include pension plans, mutual funds, insurance companies, various foundations, universities and charitable endowments, bank administered trust funds, brokerage firms investing for their own account, and the like. The amount of stock held by such investors, relative to individual investors, has grown dramatically in recent years. As a result, institutional investors now own a majority of the outstanding stock of the largest corporations.

Historically, institutions were passive investors, preferring to follow the Wall Street rule when dissatisfied with the management of one of their portfolio companies. Recently, a number of institutions have become quite active as shareholders. There are several reasons for this development. One reason is that, with larger holdings, it might become more difficult for dissatisfied institutions to dump their shares without the sale depressing the price of the stock.

Perhaps more significantly, there has been a growth in the ownership of shares by institutional investors who have less reason to be concerned about offending the management of the corporations in which they invest. In other words, one reason institutional investors traditionally have been passive shareholders is because many institutional investors have had reasons to stay on the good side of corporate management. Bankers might want corporate management to do business with their bank. Brokerage firms might not only want corporate business, but also information about the corporation. Management may have selected the party who administrators the pension plan set up by the corporation. By contrast, individuals charged with running pension plans not established by corporations—such as pension plans for state workers, university faculty or union members—have less reason to be inhibited when dealing with corporate management. Indeed, those in charge of a union or public employee pension plan might find it politically useful to throw their weight around as shareholders. Hence, it is not surprising that the shareholder who pushed through the bylaw amendment ending the poison pill plan in the *Fleming* case discussed earlier was the Teamsters union pension fund.

Activism by institutional investors is a fairly recent phenomenon, and it is too early to say to what extent this development will render the Berle–Means thesis obsolete. As the *Fleming* case exemplifies, there have been a number dramatic and successful efforts by institutional shareholders to assert some control over corporate governance. Moreover, there have been a number of well publicized instances in recent years in which boards of major corporations have fired the corporation's chief executive officer. While evidence is sketchy, it is widely believed that the presence of upset institutional investors may have stiffened the spines of these boards.

Perhaps the most significant type of large activist shareholder, however, are persons who buy controlling interests in corporations with the goal of replacing the existing management with individuals who can do a better job—in other words, parties who engage in hostile takeovers. In essence, such shareholders are one answer to a riddle posed by the Wall Street rule: If enough dissatisfied shareholders sell, who buys? Not only might the hostile takeover, itself, install more efficient management, but the threat of such takeovers provides an incentive for existing managements to act efficiently.

The efficacy of hostile takeovers at disciplining management depends, among other things, on how many barriers exist to such takeovers and how expensive such takeovers are to undertake: The more difficult and more expensive it is to undertake a takeover, the more slack existing managers have to act inefficiently. We shall explore the barriers to hostile takeovers in considerable detail in the last chapter of this book.

If one looks to market forces to solve the problem of unaccountable management, what is the role of corporate law? For the most part, writers who look to market based solutions assign corporate law a fairly passive role.

Primarily, under this view, corporate law should not, itself, become a barrier to market solutions. For example, federal proxy solicitation rules, which we will discuss later in this chapter, had for some time interfered with the ability of institutional investors to work together to assert greater control over the corporation. In 1992, the Securities Exchange Commission amended the rules to allow freer communication between institutional investors. The result appears to be greater corporate responsiveness to such investors. By contrast, a number of states have amended their corporation statutes to make hostile takeovers more difficult. The result, as we shall discuss later, can be to weaken the discipline which the threat of such takeovers imposes on existing managements.

The law can also affirmatively encourage actions which increase the effectiveness of market forces. For example, laws (such as tax laws) might encourage compensation schemes tied to corporate or stock performance.

(2) Structural changes

In contrast to market based solutions are the reform proposals made over the years to empower the shareholders or the board through changes in the structure or mechanics of corporate governance. In recent years, such proposals have moved beyond academic writing and have found proponents in official or quasi-official sources.

For example, in the late 1970s, the Securities Exchange Commission began using its influence to push for structural reform in the composition and operation of the boards of public corporations. The SEC's efforts in this regard took two tracks: One was to require public corporations to provide greater disclosure to their shareholders concerning the composition and operation of the board and its committees. The Commission's apparent hope was to embarrass corporations into reform. The second track took advantage of the opportunity created by a number of enforcement actions the SEC brought against corporations for failing to disclose illegal business practices. The agreements settling these actions negotiated between the SEC and the target corporations often called for structural reforms in board composition and operation.

More recently, the American Law Institute promulgated its so-called "Principles of Corporate Governance." In this project, the ALI decided to go beyond restating judicially created corporate law—which is why this work did not receive the typical ALI title of "Restatement." In addition to the more traditional black letter rules, the Principles include proposals for structural changes in corporate governance, some of which courts or legislatures might accomplish by adoption of legal requirements, and some of which corporations might adopt on their own as a matter of good practice.

The idea of instituting changes in board composition and operation through voluntary adherence to so-called good corporate practices has produced guidelines suggested by a number of other organizations. These include: the 1994 edition of the "Corporate Director's Guidebook" written by the American Bar Association Section on Business Law's Committee on Corporate Law; a 1997 report entitled "Director Professionalism" written by the National Association of Corporate Directors' "Blue Ribbon Commission;" and a 1997 "Statement on Corporate Governance" written by The Business Roundtable (a group composed of corporate counsel and chief executive officers). Some institutional investors have also started to push for the boards of their portfolio companies to institute various changes in composition and operation.

While the proposals made by these groups and others exhibit considerable variation, there are a number of recurrent themes. One of the most common themes is to change the composition of the board with the goal of increasing the board's independence from management. A simple-minded idea along this line is to have most or all of the board members be outside directors. In fact, such an evolution in board composition has occurred over the last couple decades. Today, publicly held corporations almost always have boards composed primarily of outside directors.

Still, for reasons discussed earlier, just because a director is an outsider does not mean that he or she is independent of management influence. An outside director may have financial or other ties which cause him or her to wish to remain on good terms with management, and, in any event, may owe his or her position on the board to management. To deal with this reality, many of the proposals suggest not only that boards be comprised mostly or entirely of outside directors, but that these outside directors not have personal or financial ties which would undermine their independence from management influence. Moreover, these proposals often call for a nominating committee composed of independent outside directors to pick all of the nominees for board positions who will appear in the corporation's proxy solicitation.

Even if we remove bias in the outside directors, what can we do about their lack of time and information? More radical approaches have called for the development of a cadre of professional directors—in other words, individuals who would do nothing but act as directors for corporations, and, accordingly, would have more time to spend.[208] Perhaps boards could have independent staffs to provide and evaluate information for the board. More common and less extreme proposals involve use of the committee system to improve board performance. For example, appointment of an audit committee to go over the firm's financial situation with the corporation's outside auditors might provide a way for directors to gain independent insights into corporate performance without unreasonable expenditures of time.

An increasingly common suggestion for addressing the time constraints on the board is to rethink what the board ought to be doing with its time. As mentioned earlier, changing the language of corporation statutes to state that the corporation will be managed "under the direction of" the board provides recognition that it is unrealistic for the board actually to manage the corporation. Yet, if the board does not actually manage the corporation, what does the board do? The traditional notion that the board sets broad policy—which, in the business context, presumably means strategic planning—also might be, as we saw above, unrealistic. Relegating the board to the role of approving so-called extraordinary corporate actions might serve the function of forcing officers to think through such actions (or, at least, their rationale) more carefully, but otherwise does little to ensure accountability—especially for actions *not* taken. Hence, a theme in the ALI's Principles and many of the other proposals is that the board assume a "monitoring function."

Of course, it is easy to assert that the board should perform a monitoring function; it is much more difficult to define what such monitoring would entail. Essentially, we must ask "what should the board monitor?" "how?" and "with what result?"

It is obvious that the board no more can monitor all of the activities within a large complex corporation than can the board make a myriad of specific business decisions for such an operation. Presumably, there must be some focus—most likely on bottom line financial performance of the overall corporation and perhaps on the financial performance of the major corporate divisions. It is also common to hear suggestions that boards should monitor overall efforts to ensure corporate compliance with various laws.[209] One danger here, however, is that this can quickly degenerate into a lot of special interest pleading for the board's attention—in other words, claims that the board should make special efforts

208. Ronald J. Gilson & Reinier Kraakman, *Reinventing the Outside Director: An Agenda for Institutional Investors*, 43 Stan. L. Rev. 863 (1991).

209. See § 4.1.1 *infra*.

to monitor corporate environmental compliance, workforce diversity, transactions involving financial derivatives, dealing with new technologies, or whatever else happens to be the issue of the day.

In any event, to say that the board should monitor cannot mean that the board is supposed to go out on its own and investigate corporate performance. Presumably, the point is for the board to establish systems to collect the pertinent information. This explains the importance attached to the audit committee in various reform proposals.

Okay, so suppose the board selects areas of corporate performance to monitor and establishes systems within the corporation to collect information regularly on those areas; what is the board supposed to do with the results? Hopefully, the mere existence of someone looking over their shoulder might improve the performance of corporate officers. Still, monitoring seems somewhat pointless if the board will not do anything in the event of continual unsatisfactory performance. Perhaps the answer is to put reality into the model that the board selects the officers, particularly, given the hierarchical structure of corporate management, the chief executive officer. Specifically, instead of trying to do too much, boards might gain more effective control by concentrating their energy on doing one task right—this being hiring and, if necessary, firing the chief executive officer. Up until recently, boards, for the most part, in reality selected the chief executive officer only when the existing chief executive officer unexpectedly departed without grooming a successor, and boards would not fire a chief executive officer unless the corporation was near bankruptcy. As mentioned above, recent firings of chief executive officers at corporations which were not in financial trouble, but were under-performing, is a sign of potentially important change.

(3) Vigorous enforcement of fiduciary duties

The final approach to create accountability is the one which often first occurs to lawyers: lawsuits! We shall devote the next chapter of this book to looking at the fiduciary duties of corporate directors, the breach of which can lead to such lawsuits. For now, what is useful to recognize is that the less which market forces or corporate structure provide accountability, the greater is the justification for vigorous enforcement of duties of care and loyalty for corporate directors and officers; while the more which market forces or corporate structure provide accountability, the less justification there is for incurring the expense and burden of lawsuits charging breaches of fiduciary duty.

§ 3.2   Federal Proxy Rules

As discussed in Chapter I, corporate law, for better or worse, is for the most part a matter of state law. Accordingly, the prior section of this chapter dealt with the division of power over the corporation under state statutes and state common law. In several areas, however, federal statutes and rules have made inroads into the normally state domain of corporate law. One inroad of relevance to the structure of corporate governance is the federal regulation of proxy solicitations involving public corporations.

3.2.1 *Overview*

a. *The statute*

Federal proxy regulation stems from Section 14(a) of the 1934 Securities Exchange Act. The 1934 Securities Exchange Act contains a hodgepodge of provisions, some of which we will encounter in later chapters of this book. Congress enacted the 1934 Securities Exchange Act, as well as an earlier statute (the 1933 Securities Act), as part of the New Deal legislation. The goal of these two statutes was to combat certain abuses which Congress believed had led to the 1929 stock market crash and the subsequent Great Depression.

Section 14(a) of the 1934 Securities Exchange Act makes it unlawful to violate Securities Exchange Commission rules when using the mails or any means or instrumentalities of interstate commerce to solicit proxies, consents or authorizations regarding securities registered under the Act. There are a number of points to note about Section 14(a).

To begin with, one might ask what proxy solicitations had to do with the stock market crash and the Great Depression. It is not a coincidence that Congress enacted Section 14(a) two years after the publication by Professors Berle and Means of a book setting out the thesis discussed earlier in this chapter that shareholders in publicly held corporations lacked the ultimate control over such corporations. As outlined in the earlier discussion, economic inefficiencies can result when corporate governance lies with managers who are, as a practical matter, unaccountable to the owners of the business. Since proxies are the means by which shareholders in a publicly held corporation exercise power, Congress responded to the notion that unaccountable management was producing some of the nation's economic woes by including Section 14(a) in the 1934 Act. Of course, if the reason for unaccountable management lies in rational shareholder apathy, rather than lack of informed proxy voting or management abuse of the proxy system, then it is unclear how much good federal proxy regulations will do.

In any event, one little problem with federal proxy regulation is that nothing in the United States Constitution expressly authorizes Congress to establish federal regulation of corporate proxy solicitations. This explains why Section 14(a) only makes it unlawful to violate the rules governing proxy solicitations through the use of the mails or through means or instrumentalities of interstate commerce—which are subjects Congress has the Constitutional authority to regulate.[1] Still, since it would be extraordinarily difficult to solicit proxies from shareholders of a publicly held corporation without using the mails or means or instrumentalities of interstate commerce, the jurisdictional limitation in Section 14(a) will rarely have any practical consequence.

§ **3.2**

1. Section 14(a) also refers to the use of a national securities exchange, the regulation of which presumably falls within the power to regulate interstate commerce.

Significantly, in and of itself, Section 14(a) neither prohibits nor commands any action with respect to proxy solicitations. Instead, the Section states that it is unlawful to solicit proxies in violation of rules prescribed by the Securities Exchange Commission (an executive agency of the federal government established by the 1934 Securities Exchange Act). In other words, Section 14(a) is a delegation of authority by Congress to the Securities Exchange Commission to make up rules regulating the solicitation of proxies. Beyond the criteria that the rules be "necessary or appropriate in the public interest or for the protection of investors"—which covers the universe of desirable regulation—Section 14(a) gives no guidance as to what sort of rules the Commission is supposed to make up.

Ultimately then, the only limitation on the Commission's rulemaking authority under Section 14(a) is that the rules involve the solicitation of proxies, consents or authorizations with respect to securities registered under Section 12 of the Securities Exchange Act. As we shall discuss in a later chapter, Section 12 of the Securities Exchange Act requires corporations with shares traded on a national exchange (such as the New York Stock Exchange), or which have over 500 holders of a class of stock and over $10 million in assets, to register with the Securities Exchange Commission and file periodic reports. Hence, the federal proxy rules reach only publicly held corporations (and not even all publicly held corporations).

While the line with respect to which corporations are subject to federal proxy rules is clear-cut, the question of what constitutes a solicitation of a proxy, consent or authorization sometimes can be more difficult to answer. A pair of court opinions illustrate some of the problems.

In *Studebaker Corp. v. Gittlin*,[2] Gittlin, a shareholder of Studebaker Corporation, wanted to inspect the corporation's shareholder list with the goal of soliciting proxies for the upcoming annual shareholders' meeting. In order to come within a state corporations statute which granted inspection rights to the holders of over five percent of the outstanding stock, Gittlin had obtained written authority from 42 other shareholders to demand inspection. Studebaker sued in federal court to block Gittlin's use of the written authority from the other shareholders on the ground that Gittlin had not complied with the federal regulations governing proxy solicitations. The court held that Gittlin's solicitation fell within Section 14(a).

Literally, Gittlin did ask for, in other words "solicit," "authorizations" from the 42 other shareholders, and, hence, his actions came with the language of Section 14(a). The court, however, declined to follow the suggestion of the Securities Exchange Commission to interpret Section 14(a) literally. Instead, the court decided the case upon the narrower ground that making requests of other shareholders, such as done by Gittlin, comes within Section 14(a) when undertaken as part of a plan

2.   360 F.2d 692 (2d Cir.1966).

that will culminate in a proxy solicitation. The court left unanswered the question of whether the solicitation of authorizations not aimed at a proxy contest might nevertheless come within the proxy rules.

In *Studebaker*, it was undisputed that the defendant had solicited shareholders; the question seemingly was whether *what* the defendant had solicited from shareholders fell within the reach of a "proxy, consent or authorization" as meant by Congress in enacting Section 14(a). The court's use of a test geared to the ultimate goal of the defendant's action, however, came from a case[3] which had a different concern: When is a communication to shareholders, which does not come out and ask for a proxy (or consent or authorization), nevertheless a "solicitation?"

The question of what is a solicitation more recently faced the Second Circuit in *Long Island Lighting Co. v. Barbash*.[4] Long Island Lighting brought this action against a local citizens' committee and a politician, after the citizens' committee took out several advertisements criticizing the company's management and urging the replacement of the company's franchise with service provided with a municipally owned power company. The politician, at the same time, sought to accomplish the goal of changing power suppliers through a proxy contest for control over Long Island Lighting (in which the politician had purchased some shares). The district court threw out the suit, holding that communications to shareholders through general and indirect publications can in no circumstances constitute a "solicitation" of proxies within the meaning of Section 14(a). The court of appeals reversed, holding that even indirect or general communications can constitute a solicitation if "reasonably calculated" to influence shareholder votes in a corporate election.[5]

From a simple statutory construction context, *Studebaker* and *Long Island Lighting* are unexceptional. The shareholder's action in *Studebaker* fell within the literal language of the statute. Moreover, the courts in both *Studebaker* and *Long Island Lighting* understandably were concerned that an interpretation which limited the meaning of "solicitation" to communications that come out and request a proxy could allow parties to circumvent the federal proxy rules by issuing communications which soften up the shareholders for a later explicit request, but do not yet include any request of the shareholders, or else request the shareholders to undertake some action other than giving a proxy.[6]

Nevertheless, both opinions raise concerns. The advertisements in *Long Island Lighting* occurred in the middle of a local election campaign in which replacement of Long Island Lighting with a municipal utility

---

3. SEC v. Okin, 132 F.2d 784 (2d Cir. 1943).

4. 779 F.2d 793 (2d Cir.1985).

5. Other courts, however, have not been as expansive in treating any communication which might impact an ultimate shareholder vote as constituting a solicitation. *E.g.*,

Brown v. Chicago Rock Island & Pacific RR., 328 F.2d 122 (7th Cir.1964).

6. In this light, notice how Gittlin's soliciting the 42 other shareholders to join in his inspection request also would serve to predispose the 42 other shareholders to later give Gittlin their proxies.

was an issue. Hence, subjecting the ads to scrutiny under the federal proxy rules, because the ads might impact shareholder decisions with respect to a later proxy solicitation, raises serious free speech issues under the First Amendment. Indeed, the result of *Long Island Lighting* can be to force individuals seeking to change corporate behavior based upon political or social concerns to choose between generating external pressure on the corporation, or endeavoring to work within the corporation to alter the attitudes of shareholders or management (since working within the corporation can subject external efforts to potentially burdensome proxy regulations).

Studebaker carries the potential to impact more explicitly corporate governance. If informal communications among a group of shareholders, which ultimately leads to a proxy contest, can constitute a solicitation triggering the proxy rules, then it may become more difficult for shareholders to organize an effective challenge to management. The result can be to undercut the ability of institutional and other large investors to serve as a check on under-performing or disloyal managers.

Still, even if communications along the lines of what occurred in *Studebaker* and *Long Island Lighting* constitute proxy solicitations within the meaning of Section 14(a), this simply means that the Securities Exchange Commission can subject such communications to its proxy solicitation rules; it does not mean the Commission must subject such communications to rules which impede either communication among large shareholders or the exercise of First Amendment rights, or, indeed, that the Commission must subject such communications to any proxy rules at all. In other words, it is up the SEC to justify the courts' broad interpretation of Section 14(a) by showing a little self-restraint in exercising the Commission's rulemaking authority.

b. The rules

The Securities Exchange Commission has promulgated a series of rules pursuant to Section 14(a)—which conveniently all have the label "Rule 14a-" followed by a number. Rule 14a–1 contains definitions, the most important of which, in light of the previous discussion, are the definitions of the terms "proxy" and "solicitation."

Rule 14a–1(f) defines "proxy" as co-extensive with whatever is a proxy, consent or authorization under Section 14(a). Given the uncertainty left by *Studebaker* as to what is an "authorization" within the meaning of Section 14(a) for any context other than a situation in which a party ultimately solicits proxies, the failure of the rules to provide guidance on this question is unfortunate.

Rule 14a–1(*l*) defines "solicitation" to include not only requests for proxies, but also, in language relied upon by the court in *Long Island Lighting*, any "communication to security holders under circumstances reasonably calculated to result in the procurement, withholding or revocation of a proxy." Notice how this definition of solicitation not only can pick up the advertising involved in *Long Island Lighting*, but also could include the grumbling among shareholders which presumably proceeded the granting of the authorizations in *Studebaker*, and even could reach critiques of corporate management by those who themselves will neither actually request a proxy or, as alleged in *Long Island Lighting*, work in cahoots with those requesting proxies. Recognizing the overbreadth in this definition, the SEC, among other actions in 1992, amended Rule 14a–1(*l*) to exclude, from the definition of a solicitation, announcements by security holders (who otherwise do not engage in a proxy solicitation) of how the security holders intend to vote in an upcoming election.

Having provided a broad definition of the term solicitation in Rule 14a–1, Rule 14a–2 carves out a series of exceptions. A couple of these exceptions attempt to deal with the concern we discussed above that the *Studebaker* holding could extend proxy regulation to grumbling among a small group of shareholders who decide to engage in a proxy contest. Rule 14a–2(b)(2) exempts, from most of the proxy regulations,[7] solicitations which are not on behalf of the corporation so long as the solicitation is made to no more than ten persons. The growth of institutional shareholder activism, however, caused the SEC to question the sufficiency of the ten person exception, since discussions among institutions upset with management might easily exceed ten participants. To prevent the proxy rules from impeding the efforts of institutional investors to monitor management and communicate among themselves, the SEC, in 1992, amended Rule 14a–2 to add a new exemption from most of the proxy rules: Rule 14a–2(b)(1). Rule 14a–2(b)(1) provides an exemption for solicitations by persons who do not seek an actual proxy. This exemption will not cover, however, solicitations by the corporation, its officers or directors, nominees to the board, groups seeking control of the company who must file under the Williams Act, or persons having a substantial interest different from that of the other shareholders in the matter subject to the shareholder vote. In other words, this exemption allows discussions among shareholders who do not have an axe to grind other than as shareholders. Other exemptions in Rule 14a–2 cover specified communications between beneficial owners of stock and persons holding record title to the beneficial owners' shares, and advice in the ordinary course of business by investment advisors to their clients.

The substantive requirements of the proxy regulations begin in Rule 14a–3. This rule requires anyone who solicits proxies, to furnish the solicited shareholders with a so-called proxy statement containing the information called for in Schedule 14A (which is found at the end of the proxy rules). The notion is that shareholders are more likely to vote intelligently if they are fully informed. The precise information required varies depending upon whether the solicitation occurs on behalf of corporate management, or on behalf of those challenging management, and upon the subject matter of the vote. Proxy statements for all

---

7. Rule 14a–2(b) does not exempt solicitations from Rule 14a–9's prohibition on   false or misleading statements.

solicitations must give information about the meeting, the voting rights of shareholders, and about the person(s) soliciting the proxies.[8] In a proxy solicitation seeking authority to vote for the management nominated directors at the upcoming annual shareholders' meeting, the proxy statement also must give information about the nominees, about board structure and operation, about conflicts of interest of board members, and about management compensation. Notice that by focusing particular attention upon disclosing board structure and operation, director conflicts of interest, and management compensation, the proxy rules may create some pressure on corporations with respect to the companies' substantive practices in these areas. The corporation's proxy statement for the annual shareholders' meeting to elect directors also must be accompanied by an annual report containing the corporation's financial statements. In addition to financial statements, corporations commonly include in the annual report an upbeat narrative and nifty pictures bound together in a glossy booklet (which, of course, is not required by the proxy rules).

Rule 14a–4 contains guidelines for the proxy form—that is to say the written document which grants authority to vote on behalf of the shareholder. Among these guidelines is the requirement that the proxy form give the solicited shareholder the option to instruct the proxy holder to vote the shares either for or against the matters identified as being up for a shareholder vote at the meeting.[9] Notice that by requiring the proxy form to give shareholders the option to vote for or against various proposals, Rule 14a–4 can end up actually forcing the proxy holder to cast votes contrary to the position for which the proxy holder was soliciting proxies. The result is to turn the proxy into something of a ballot. Along similar lines, Rule 14a–4 requires the proxy form to give the solicited shareholder the ability to withhold authority to vote for any or all of the nominees for election to the board listed by the party soliciting the proxy. The analogy to a ballot in a democratic election is not complete, however, since the proxy form need not contain the names of all individuals known to be seeking election to the board, but only those nominees supported by the party seeking the proxy.[10] (By only

---

8. In a rough analogy to political campaign finance laws, there also must be disclosure concerning any "participant" (defined as anyone who contributes at least $500) in a proxy contest.

9. Rule 14a–4 requires that the proxy form list each "separate matter" intended to be acted upon and allow the shareholders the option of voting for or against each "separate matter." This seemingly precludes the proxy form from attempting to force the solicited shareholders to vote for or against proposals as a group. The problem with such grouping of proposals is that it can allow the directors to obtain shareholder approval of proposals which the shareholders do not like, by combining the proposal with another action desired by the shareholders. Still, while directors cannot deprive the shareholders of the ability to vote separately on action items, directors might be able to condition the effectiveness of one action item on the adoption of another item.

10. Indeed, Rule 14a–4 generally prohibits the proxy form from listing persons as nominees who did not consent to the proxy listing their names. A 1992 amendment to the proxy rules modifies this restriction, however, to allow parties who seek to elect only a minority of the directors to place on their proxy form the names of nominees appearing on the corporation's solicitation.

listing one side's nominees, the proxy form resembles a ballot from the old Soviet Union, in which the voter only had the option of voting yes or no on the Communist Party's nominated candidate for the position in question. The critical difference from the old Soviet elections is that other candidates in a corporate election always may solicit their own proxies.) Reinforcing a ballot-like approach to the proxy, Rule 14a–4 limits the ability of the proxy to grant discretionary authority upon the proxy's holder. Rule 14a–4 also requires a place for dating the proxy and limits the proxy's effectiveness to the next shareholders' meeting.

Rule 14a–5 is designed to ensure clear and readable presentation of the material in the proxy statement. Rule 14a–6 requires the filing of the proxy statement, proxy form and other soliciting materials with the Securities Exchange Commission. This filing occurs in two stages: If the solicitation involves something more than the corporation's routine seeking of proxies for the annual meeting, then the party undertaking a solicitation must file a preliminary proxy statement and form of proxy at least ten days before the distribution of these materials. This gives the Commission an opportunity to review the documents for problems. Thereafter, a party soliciting proxies (even for a routine annual meeting) must file with the SEC the final proxy statement, form of proxy, plus copies of all other soliciting materials (advertisements and the like) no later than when this party sends solicitation materials to the shareholders.

Rule 14a–7 requires the corporation, which has or will make a proxy solicitation, either to give a shareholder, who appropriately requests, a copy of the shareholder list, or else mail the requesting shareholder's proxy solicitation materials to the other shareholders. In order to be eligible to make such a request, the shareholder must be undertaking a proxy solicitation regarding the same subject matter (such as election of directors) as the corporation's solicitation. Generally, it is the corporation's (in other word's management's) option to choose between giving the list or making the mailing. Since the shareholder must pay for the mailing, corporate management typically elects the option of mailing the materials rather than giving up the shareholder list. In this manner, management might hope to hamper any efforts by the dissident shareholder to contact other shareholders personally, and also can respond simultaneously to the dissident's materials (which management will peek at before mailing). The end result is that demanding the shareholder list pursuant to state law inspection rights typically provides a better avenue than Rule 14a–7 for the shareholder attempting to wage a proxy contest.

Rule 14a–8 deals with shareholder proposals, while Rule 14a–9 prohibits false or misleading statements in soliciting proxies. These two rules have produced most of the litigation under the federal proxy solicitation rules, and, accordingly, we shall discuss them soon in considerable detail.

Rule 14a–10 prohibits soliciting undated and post-dated proxies. It compliments Rule 14a–4's provisions limiting the length of time for which a proxy can be effective, and also avoids questions about which proxy came last in the event that a shareholder gives more than one person a proxy to vote the same shares.[11]

Rule 14a–11 contains special provisions involving the timing of disclosure by those undertaking a proxy contest against the management's slate of directors. Sometimes, a shareholder may be spurred into undertaking a proxy contest against the management's slate of directors at the last minute (perhaps because the shareholder was surprised by who the corporation's proxy solicitation listed as nominees for the board). Under these circumstances, the dissident shareholder would be at a serious disadvantage if he or she must prepare a full-fledged proxy statement and wait ten days for SEC review before beginning efforts to dissuade the other shareholders from supporting management's slate. Rule 14a–11 meets this problem by allowing such opposition solicitations, if not accompanied by a proxy form, to occur prior to furnishing the solicited shareholders with a proxy statement (which then must be sent to the solicited shareholders at the earliest possible date). Rule 14a–12 provides a similar solution for those who decide, with little time left, to try to dissuade shareholders from granting proxies in favor of a proposed action such as a merger or the like.

Finally, Rule 14a–13 is designed to ensure receipt of the corporation's proxy statements and annual reports by the beneficial owners of stock held in street name (in other words, when the corporation's records show title to the shares in the name of brokers, depository companies and other nominees, rather than the actual owners). Under the Rule, corporations must provide parties holding stock in street name with sufficient copies of the corporation's proxy statement and annual report, plus funds to cover mailing expenses, in order for the record owners to send these materials to the beneficial owners. This raises the question of what ensures that the record owners will pass on the proxy materials to the beneficial owners. The answer comes from Section 14(b) of the 1934 Securities Exchange Act, and Rules 14b–1 and 14b–2 promulgated by the Securities Exchange Commission under the Act. Section 14(b) authorizes the SEC to issue rules governing the giving or refusing of proxies, or proxy statements, by brokers and others holding stock in street name. Pursuant to this authority, Rules 14b–1 and 14b–2 require brokers and banks, respectively, to forward proxy materials to the beneficial owners of stock held in street name.

Rules 14a–13, 14b–1 and 14b–2 contain an alternate scheme which the corporation can opt for to distribute the annual report to the beneficial owners of stock held in street name. The corporation can demand that the record owners provide the company with the names and addresses of the beneficial owners who do not object to disclosure of their identity. The corporation then can mail the annual report directly

11. As discussed earlier, in the event of such multiple proxies for the same shares,   the last proxy trumps. See § 3.1.3*b supra*.

to the non-objecting beneficial owners (and let the record owners just mail the report to those beneficial owners who objected to release of their identities to the corporation).

c. *Dissemination of annual reports and information without a proxy solicitation*

As discussed above, one of the principal goals of the proxy rules is to provide shareholders with information in order for shareholders intelligently to make decisions in granting a proxy. It is fairly easy to see how requiring financial statements in the annual report fits into this goal. The annual report goes to shareholders solicited to give proxies for the annual election of directors, and, of course, information as to the corporation's financial performance is relevant to a decision as to whether the existing board members ought to keep their positions.

Corporate financial statements, however, might be relevant to shareholders for purposes beyond the decision as to whether to grant a proxy. For example, the information from financial statements might play into a shareholder's decision as to whether to retain or sell his or her stock. Yet, Section 14(a)—which only authorizes regulation of proxy solicitations—does not provide the SEC with the power to force corporations to distribute annual statements to the shareholders if the corporations do not solicit proxies from the shareholders. While publicly held corporations usually must solicit proxies (or else there will not be a quorum present at the shareholders' meeting), some publicly held corporations do not solicit proxies. This may occur when the corporation has a majority shareholder whose presence and voting at the shareholders' meeting is sufficient for purposes of a quorum. To fill this gap, Congress amended the Securities Exchange Act in 1964 to add Section 14(c). Section 14(c) authorizes the SEC to force corporations, which do not make proxy solicitations for their annual shareholders' meetings, to provide their shareholders with the same disclosure materials which the corporation would have had the company made such a solicitation.

3.2.2 *False and Misleading Solicitations*

Throughout this chapter, we have made a number of comparisons between corporate governance, including corporate elections, and federal, state and local governments and elections. One of the most striking contrasts between the federal proxy rules, and the laws governing federal, state and local government election campaigns, involves the treatment of false and misleading statements. In federal, state and local government election campaigns, charges and countercharges between candidates, and for and against various ballot propositions, which, if not outright false, are at least misleading, seem to be the norm. The only remedy is to respond with denials (as in the famous "War Room" of the 1992 presidential campaign) and perhaps by hurling more scurrilous charges at one's opponent in retaliation. By contrast, Rule 14a–9 of the federal proxy rules prohibits solicitations which contain any false or misleading statements as to material facts, or which omit material facts that make statements in the solicitation misleading or no longer correct.

This difference in law reflects a difference in philosophy as to the appropriateness of courts acting as a sort of truth squad to police statements made in campaigning for votes. From a doctrinal standpoint, such a role for the courts in a federal, state or local election campaign presumably intrudes upon First Amendment protections of free speech. The fact that corporate elections ultimately come down to matters of money seems to trigger the lesser First Amendment protections accorded to commercial speech. Policy justifications reinforce this distinction. There are obvious problems with judges and juries deciding if election charges are true or false. After all, judges are appointed by elected officials (if not elected themselves), and both judges and jurors normally are not free from personally-held political views. By contrast, judges and juries presumably have no personal stake or pre-existing view in a corporate proxy contest. Moreover, the remedy of response and counter-attack by the other side commonly exists in the political campaign. In contrast, there often will be little organized opposition to a management proxy solicitation. Without such organized opposition, there is no one who will spend the money to alert the other shareholders to any misleading or false statements made by the board.[12]

In any event, litigation under Rule 14a–9 revolves around several possible issues:

a.   *False or misleading statement of fact or omission*

The language in Rule 14a–9 identifies three types of falsity: (1) a false or misleading statement of fact; (2) an omission of fact which makes a statement misleading (a so-called half-truth); and (3) the failure to correct a statement which subsequent events have rendered false or misleading, when the matter has not yet come to a shareholder vote.

From a legal (as opposed to a factual) standpoint, the most straight-forward statement to deal with is one which simply contains wrong facts: for instance, the proxy statement asserts that a corporation had revenues of $200 million last year, when, in fact, the corporation's revenues were $100 million. As a casual observation of general election campaigns illustrates, however, statements which are outright false are relatively rare. Far more common is the statement which is literally true, but misleading—often because of the failure to disclose certain facts. For example, a presidential candidate during the New Hampshire primary might deny that he had an extended extramarital affair with a woman, while neglecting to disclose that he had a "one night stand" with the woman in question. Similarly, a proxy statement in support of a cash-out

---

12.   At first glance, it seems strange that management would make a false or misleading solicitation when there was no organized opposition. In fact, however, the most significant Rule 14a–9 cases have involved false or misleading statements made in support of mergers to which there was little organized opposition. Presumably, the goal for the misrepresentations in these cases was to prevent such opposition from developing.

merger can be misleading in asserting that the minority shareholders will receive a premium price over book value, when the statement neglects to point out that if one takes into account the appreciated value of the corporation's real estate there will not be premium price.[13]

In some cases, the problem is not whether the statement is false or misleading; rather, the question is whether the challenged language constitutes a statement of fact at all. The United States Supreme Court faced this issue *Virginia Bankshares, Inc. v. Sandberg.*[14] *Virginia Bankshares* involved a freeze-out merger under which the minority stockholders of a Virginia bank received $42 per share for their stock, and a bank holding company went from owning 85 percent of the Virginia bank's outstanding stock to owning 100 percent. Even though the holding company had more than enough votes by itself to force through the merger, the directors of the Virginia bank decided to solicit the minority shareholders for proxies in favor of the proposal. In their solicitation, the directors asserted that they had approved the merger because of the opportunity which the transaction gave the minority shareholders to obtain a "high" value for the minority shareholders' stock. The directors also described $42 per share as a "fair" price for the minority's stock. A minority shareholder named Sandberg refused to give her proxy in favor of the merger, and sued claiming that the directors' statements violated Rule 14a–9. After a jury found for the plaintiff, the defendants appealed.

The defendants argued that their statements about "high" value and "fair" price were merely expressions of opinion which could not constitute misrepresentations of fact violating Rule 14a–9. This argument draws upon the traditional reticence of courts, in common law fraud and deceit cases, to treat statements such as "this is a great deal," or "this is the best widget on the market," as the basis for an action.[15] Doctrinally, courts often explain that such language constitutes statements of opinion rather than statements of fact, and, hence, such language cannot constitute a misrepresentation of fact. Courts, in these common law fraud and deceit cases, also often seem to feel that the plaintiff should have more sense than to give any credence to such sales talk or "puffing." Perhaps the best justification, however, for the traditional reluctance to treat the sort language quoted above as a basis for a claim of fraud is the difficulty of trying to establish the truth or falsity of statements about whether a particular transaction is a "good" deal or a particular product is the "best" or the like. After all, there is typically room for persons to disagree about the truth of these sort of statements (in part because it is often not clear what exactly the statement really means). Still, courts applying the common law of fraud or deceit sometimes recognize a claim in the case of challenged opinions. This might occur when the defendant was an expert regarding the matter on which

13. Virginia Bankshares, Inc. v. Sandberg, 501 U.S. 1083, 111 S.Ct. 2749 (1991).

14. 501 U.S. 1083, 111 S.Ct. 2749 (1991).

15. See § 6.1.1 *infra.*

the defendant spoke, while the plaintiff was not, and so the plaintiff might reasonably rely on the opinion.

In any event, the court in *Virginia Bankshares* seemed unconcerned with this common law background. Ultimately, the court held that allegations the directors misrepresented their state of mind—in other words, the directors lied when they stated that their purpose for approving the transaction was to obtain a high price for the minority, or the directors did not really believe that $42 per share was a fair price—would not alone state a claim under Rule 14a–9. The court conceded that assertions as to the directors' state of mind were statements of fact and that the directors' motives or beliefs could be material to shareholders in deciding how to vote; but the court worried that proving the directors' state of mind one way or the other would be too difficult and this evidentiary problem might allow frivolous suits to proceed through discovery. (On the other hand, if proof of state of mind is so difficult, one wonders how all of the criminal cases which turn on state of mind manage to go through the court system every day.)

Having refused to allow Rule 14a–9 claims solely based upon misrepresentations as to motives or beliefs, the court in *Virginia Bankshares* turned around and recognized a claim based upon the notion that statements about "high" value or "fair" price could be false if the value is not "high" or the price is not "fair" (at least if the directors did not believe the statements). The court rejected the contention that such terms were too indefinite to be true or false, concluding instead that such terms in the commercial context are understood to rest on a factual basis. Hence, the truth of such statements depended upon whether provable facts as to a company's assets and operations justified the assertion that $42 per share was "fair" or "high" under recognized methods of valuation.

The court in *Virginia Bankshares* is correct that there are methods of valuing corporate stock, and that it is common in both business and legal contexts to speak about whether a given price for stock is "fair" in light of these methods of valuation. Indeed, we will see later in this book that minority shareholders in a cash-out merger commonly have rights under state law to go to court and argue that they did not receive a fair price for their stock.[16] Hence, courts have experience deciding whether the price paid for stock is "fair," and, accordingly, courts presumably can decide whether the assertion that the price paid is "fair" is true or false. The fact that state courts engage in this determination, however, points out a potential problem with the *Virginia Bankshares* holding. Allowing shareholders to assert that proxy statements are false because they describe a transaction as fair,[17] when, in fact, the transaction is not fair, enables shareholders to make a federal case out of the sort of fair price disputes ordinarily tried in state courts. Perhaps there is nothing

16. See § 7.4.1c *infra*.

17. Proxy statements are hardly going to describe a transaction for which the soliciting party seeks support as unfair.

wrong with this result. Yet, we shall see in another context that the Supreme Court has attempted to resist the tide of turning federal securities laws into a tool for making the federal courts the arbiters of normally state corporate law issues.[18]

b. Materiality

In order to violate Rule 14a–9 it is not enough that a proxy solicitation includes false or misleading statements or omissions. In addition, the facts misstated or omitted must be material. The requirement that the falsely stated or omitted facts be material comes not only from the language of Rule 14a–9, but also from the traditional elements of common law fraud, and, indeed, from common sense. After all, there is no point rewarding parties who bring lawsuits complaining about misstatements or omissions of facts when the misstated or omitted facts were trivial in any event.

The Supreme Court defined materiality under Rule 14a–9 in *TSC Industries, Inc. v. Northway, Inc.*[19] The court stated that a fact is material "if there is a substantial likelihood that a reasonable shareholder would consider it important in deciding how to vote."[20] Curiously, the Supreme Court granted review in *TSC* to decide the issue of whether the standard for materiality requires that a reasonable shareholder *would* consider the fact important, or whether the standard was that a reasonable shareholder *might* consider the fact important—which issue seems to have all the relevance of a medieval debate about how many angels can fit on the head of a pin.[21] In any event, the Supreme Court counted the angels and decided that the standard is "would" rather than "might." Of more practical use, the *TSC* opinion elaborated on what this standard means and what policy the standard seeks to achieve. Critically, the court explained that the standard does not require proof of a substantial likelihood that a reasonable shareholder would have changed his or her vote had he or she known the full truth. Instead, the fact simply must be one that would have assumed a significant, even if not ultimately decisive, role in a reasonable shareholder's deliberations on how to vote. In terms of policy, what the court sought to achieve was a balance between ensuring adequate disclosure, but without burying the shareholders under a pile of trivial information.

Notice that the standard for materiality refers to what a reasonable shareholder, not the plaintiff shareholder, would consider important. What this mythical person would find significant in deciding how to vote ultimately depends upon the facts of each case. Nevertheless, several areas often create recurring materiality issues in Rule 14a–9 cases.

One common materiality problem in Rule 14a–9 cases involves facts concerning ethically questionable practices. For example, suppose a

18. See § 6.3.3 *infra*.

19. 426 U.S. 438, 96 S.Ct. 2126 (1976).

20. *Id* at 449.

21. Indeed, the reason for the confusion was that the Supreme Court had used the terms would and might interchangeably in prior opinions dealing with materiality under Rule 14a–9.

candidate for election to the board of directors fails to disclose that he is the subject of a grand jury investigation into bribery and tax evasion charges in his role as a corporate officer,[22] or that his sister has sued him for an alleged breach of fiduciary duty in managing family assets.[23] These sort of facts would seem important to a reasonable shareholder in voting on directors, because they raise questions as to whether the candidate can be trusted to have power over the shareholders' money. True, the fact that an individual may have breached a fiduciary duty owed toward a sibling does not mean that the individual will breach a duty owed toward the corporation and its shareholders. Similarly, the willingness of an individual to sanction illegal actions by the corporation in order to achieve greater profits for the company might not show a danger that this person would engage in illegal actions for personal benefit at the expense of the corporation.[24] Still, it is not unreasonable to suppose that an individual's willingness to cross the line in one context might raise concerns about his or her willingness to engage in misconduct in other contexts. On the other hand, if the charges of misconduct are not yet established, a court might be less willing to treat them as material—after all, we do not know that the individual has crossed any lines into unethical conduct.

The problem of how to evaluate ethics charges which are pending, but not yet proved, brings us to a second common materiality problem. This involves facts whose relevance is clear should they occur, but whether they will occur is in substantial doubt. For example, a proposed merger which the board asks the shareholders to approve might create a risk of exposing the corporation to future products liability claims. The Supreme Court's approach to this sort of problem bears a vague resemblance to half of the famous "Learned Hand" formula for negligence. The materiality of uncertain facts depends upon their probability of occurring and their importance if they do occur: the more important the fact will be if it occurs, the lower the probability of occurrence which is necessary in order to find materiality; the greater the probability of occurrence, the less impact the fact must have if it occurs in order for it's possibility to be material.[25]

A third common materiality problem involves the situation in which the defendant argues that omitted or misstated facts were not material because facts disclosed elsewhere undercut the significance of the misstatement or omission. The Supreme Court in *TSC* applied this sort of

22. *See* United States v. Matthews, 787 F.2d 38 (2d Cir.1986).

23. *See* GAF Corp. v. Heyman, 724 F.2d 727 (2d Cir.1983).

24. *See, e.g.,* Gaines v. Haughton, 645 F.2d 761 (9th Cir.1981). A candidate's prior decisions to engage in illegal actions on behalf of the corporation raises a couple of other arguments as to materiality. The risk of fines or other consequences to the corporation from such conduct, should the

corporation get caught, may be material in itself—albeit, forcing the corporation to disclose in proxy statements that it is engaging in illegal conduct will ensure that the corporation does get caught. Also, shareholders might have moral qualms about investing in a company which engages in illegal or unethical conduct, even if such conduct is generally profitable.

25. For a further discussion of this sort of materiality issue, see § 6.3.1*b infra.*

reasoning in dealing with a board's failure to disclose in its proxy statement that the other party to the transaction for which the board sought approval controlled the board. Since the proxy statement disclosed that the other party owned 34 percent of the corporation's outstanding shares, and that five of the ten directors were nominees of this party, the court held that the failure to state explicitly that the other party controlled the board was not material. On the other hand, the Supreme Court in *Virginia Bankshares* noted some important limitations on this sort of context argument. The Supreme Court explained that the significance of the corrective information on the misleading statement had to be readily apparent in order to preclude materiality—in other words, if it would take a financial analyst to figure out how the facts disclosed elsewhere corrected the misleading statements, then the misstatements or omissions are material. Moreover, the court in *Virginia Bankshares* refused to find that other portions of the proxy statement rendered the misstatements or omissions in the case immaterial when the other portions themselves were half-truths. Finally, courts have rejected this sort of context argument when the corrective information is found in a document other than the document containing the misstatement or omission.[26] After all, one cannot expect shareholders to cross-check all corporate filings and documents for inconsistencies when deciding how to vote their proxies.

c. Fault

Rule 14a–9 flatly states that proxy solicitations shall not be made by proxy statements or other materials which contain false or misleading statements of fact. The Rule does not say that this prohibition only applies when defendant knows the statement is false, or, if the defendant thought he or she was speaking the truth, only when the defendant was reckless or even negligent in making the mistake. Does this mean that anyone who makes a false statement in soliciting proxies is strictly liable no matter how innocent the mistake? A literal reading of Rule 14a–9 suggests this result. On the other hand, it is possible to interpret Rule 14a–9's silence concerning fault as showing merely that the Securities Exchange Commission overlooked the issue, thereby leaving the Rule open for judicial interpretation.

While the Supreme Court has yet to resolve what standard of culpability exists for a Rule 14a–9 violation, several United States Court of Appeals decisions have addressed the question. In *Shidler v. All American Life & Financial Corp.*,[27] the Eighth Circuit declined to impose strict liability under Rule 14a–9 upon parties who misstated or omitted facts in soliciting proxies. On the other hand, in *Gerstle v. Gamble–Skogmo, Inc.*,[28] the Second Circuit refused to require a showing that the defendant knew the statement was false, or was reckless as to truth or falsity, in order to impose liability under Rule 14a–9. Instead, the court

---

26. *E.g.*, United Paperworkers International Union v. Specialty Paperboard, Inc., 999 F.2d 51 (2d Cir.1993).

27. 775 F.2d 917 (8th Cir.1985).

28. 478 F.2d 1281 (2d Cir.1973).

held that negligence in ascertaining the facts before speaking was sufficient. While several other opinions have followed *Gerstle*,[29] an opinion from the Sixth Circuit concluded that knowledge of falsity or recklessness should be required under Rule 14a–9—at least in an action to impose monetary damages upon the corporation's outside accountants.[30]

From a policy standpoint, perhaps the appropriate level of fault should depend upon the relief sought in the lawsuit. If the plaintiff seeks to enjoin the use of proxies gathered through a false or misleading solicitation, then strict liability might well be appropriate. After all, even if the mistake was innocent, why not give the shareholders a chance to consider whether they still wish to grant the proxies in light of the true facts? Monetary damages, however, are a different story. To begin with, nothing in Rule 14a–9 speaks of awarding monetary damages in a private cause of action; as we shall see shortly, this is a judicial invention. Hence, there is nothing wrong with the courts making up the ground rules for such a private cause of action based upon judicial notions of fairness or policy. In terms of fairness, it seems harsh to impose financial liability without fault upon parties who make false or misleading statements in soliciting proxies; after all, everyone makes mistaken statements.[31] In terms of policy, the question may be how much deterrence is enough when it comes to accidental misstatements in a proxy solicitation. Precluding liability unless the defendant knows the statement is false, or at least is reckless as to the statement's truth or falsity, creates little incentive to investigate one's facts before speaking. Liability based upon negligence creates an incentive for a reasonable investigation, as does strict liability—the difference between negligence and strict liability being who suffers the loss from mistakes which could not be avoided with reasonable investigation. While creating incentives for a reasonable investigation before one speaks seems to be a worthwhile objective, notice that parties might react to a negligence or strict liability regime, not by investigating, but rather by not speaking at all. To the extent that the object of the exercise is to provide the fullest possible information to shareholders when deciding how to cast their proxies, discouraging discourse might not be such a good idea.

d. *Private cause of action*

Not only is Rule 14a–9 silent with respect to the issue of fault, the Rule also does not state what happens if a person makes a false or misleading statement in soliciting a proxy. Likewise, Section 14(a) of the 1934 Securities Exchange Act states that it is unlawful to violate Securities Exchange Commission rules in soliciting proxies, but does not state the consequences of such a violation. Several other provisions of the 1934 Securities Exchange Act address consequences. Section 21

29. *E.g.*, Gould v. American–Hawaiian Steamship Co., 535 F.2d 761 (3d Cir.1976).

30. Adams v. Standard Knitting Mills, Inc., 623 F.2d 422 (6th Cir.1980).

31. Even law professors.

grants the Securities Exchange Commission authority to bring civil actions to enjoin violations of the Act, while Section 32 creates criminal liability for those who willfully violate the statute. However, no provision either in the Securities Exchange Act, or in the proxy rules, expressly creates a cause of action specifically in favor of private parties who are injured in any manner by virtue of a false or misleading statement in a proxy solicitation.[32]

The existence of a private cause of action for violations of Rule 14a–9 is the result of the Supreme Court's decision in *J.I. Case Co. v. Borak*.[33] In *Borak*, the Supreme Court allowed a shareholder to sue directors who violated Rule 14a–9 in soliciting proxies in support of a merger. The court gave three rationales for this result.

The court pointed to Section 27 of the Securities Exchange Act, which gives the federal courts exclusive jurisdiction over lawsuits to enforce the statute. This is a rather bogus argument, however, since Section 27 simply addresses which courts should hear lawsuits under the Act (such as lawsuits by the SEC authorized by Section 21). Section 27 does not even hint that Congress intended to allow private claims to enforce Section 14(a).

A second rationale stems from a stated objective for rules under Section 14(a), this being "the protection of investors." Since shareholders were a class of persons who the law intended to protect, it seemed logical to the court that shareholders should have a cause of action against those who violate the Rule. This sort of reasoning is similar to that found in torts cases in which the court must decide whether violation of a statute creates a claim of negligence per se.

Finally, the court pointed to the enforcement advantage of allowing a private cause of action. Specifically, the court noted that the SEC lacked the resources to investigate and go after everyone who might make a false or misleading statement in a proxy solicitation. Hence, it would help to ensure compliance with Rule 14a–9 if private parties could sue in case of violation. This argument is often referred to as the private attorney general rationale.

One problem, however, with the rationales employed by *Borak* is that they seem to make violations of all provisions in the 1934 Securities Exchange Act, or, indeed, all provisions in all of the federal securities laws, the subject of a private cause of action. By the 1970s, the Supreme Court had second thoughts about this. As a result, the court has become much less willing to find a private cause of action for those injured by the violation of a federal statute, unless the statute itself states that such a cause of action exists.[34] *Borak*, however, remains the law for Rule 14a–9 claims.

32. Section 18 of the 1934 Securities Exchange Act creates a cause of action for persons who purchase or sell securities in reliance upon a false statement contained in any document filed with the Securities Exchange Commission. Proxy statements, however, are normally not documents upon which persons rely in purchasing or selling stock.

33. 377 U.S. 426, 84 S.Ct. 1555 (1964).

34. *E.g.*, Touche Ross Co. v. Redington, 442 U.S. 560, 99 S.Ct. 2479 (1979).

Having recognized a private cause of action for violations of Rule 14a–9, the question becomes who can bring such an action. The obvious candidate would be a shareholder who claims that he or she granted a proxy based upon the false or misleading solicitation. Recall, however, that the plaintiff in *Virginia Bankshares* refused to give a proxy in support of the cash-out merger. This fact might lead one to ask how a shareholder, who was not fooled into granting a proxy, can complain about false or misleading statements in the solicitation. The answer is that such a shareholder might complain that other, presumably dumber, shareholders did grant proxies because of the false or misleading solicitation, with the result that the vote went the wrong way (at least from the plaintiff's perspective).

Indeed, in *Borak*, the court suggested that the claim might not be the individual shareholder's at all. Rather, the court held that the plaintiff shareholder in *Borak* could bring what is called a derivative action on behalf of the corporation. We shall explore derivative actions in a later chapter of this book, at which time we will look at the sometimes difficult question of when an action by a shareholder against the corporation's directors must be a derivative action seeking recovery on behalf of the corporation, and when the shareholder might have a personal (or direct) claim for recovery against the directors. For now, it is sufficient to note that allowing shareholders to bring 14a–9 claims as derivative suits may be more a matter of expediency than it is a logical application of the nature of derivative versus direct suits. After all, it is the shareholders to whom the defendants lied. Moreover, it seems to be the shareholders, not the corporation, who suffer injury when the shareholders, as in *Borak*, are fooled into approving a merger. This becomes most apparent in a case like *Virginia Bankshares* in which the underlying harm is that the shareholders did not receive enough money from the corporation for their stock. Perhaps the *Borak* court felt that the derivative suit would be more practical than having a host of individual shareholders sue for personal recovery (albeit, a class action could have provided a solution to such practicality concerns).

e. *Causation*

One corollary to the discussion just completed is that proving a false or misleading proxy solicitation caused harm to the plaintiff presents a very different problem than proof of causation in the conventional common law fraud or deceit action. In the conventional fraud or deceit action, the plaintiff proves a causal link between the false statement and his or her damages by showing that he or she relied upon the false statement in deciding to take an action which the plaintiff now regrets. Notice that the most direct evidence of such reliance normally is the testimony of the plaintiff. When dealing with proxy solicitations, it is not the plaintiff's reliance which usually matters—indeed, in *Virginia Bankshares*, the plaintiff refused to give the defendants her proxy. Rather, the critical reliance comes from the actions of shareholders who together have sufficient votes to have decided the election. This fact, in turn, creates a practical evidentiary problem: Is the plaintiff supposed to haul hundreds or even thousands of shareholders into court to ask them whether they relied upon the false statements in the proxy solicitation?

In *Mills v. Electric Auto–Lite Co.*,[35] the Supreme Court decided to give Rule 14a–9 plaintiffs a significant break. *Mills*, like *Borak* and *Virginia Bankshares*, involved a merger. One party to the merger already owned 54 percent of the corporation's outstanding shares, but it took a two-thirds vote to approve the merger. Hence, it was necessary to solicit proxies from minority shareholders in order to get the necessary votes to approve the deal. The plaintiff claimed that the proxy statement in support of the proposed merger was misleading in its failure to disclose that the corporation's directors who approved the merger were controlled by the other party to the transaction. The causation question was whether disclosure of this fact would have led enough shareholders to vote against the merger to change the outcome.[36]

The District Court, the Court of Appeals, and the Supreme Court in *Mills* all rejected as impractical the notion that the plaintiffs must prove causation by testimony from enough shareholders to have changed the result that these shareholders would have voted differently had they known all the facts. Having rejected direct testimony of reliance, the Court of Appeals came up with the idea of using the fairness of the merger as the means to test causation. Specifically, if the merger terms were fair, then presumably the shareholders would have voted for the deal even if they had received full disclosure; if the deal was unfair, then presumably the shareholders would have voted against the transaction had they not been bamboozled by the misleading solicitation. One problem with the Court of Appeals' approach, as noted by the Supreme Court, is it is simply not true that shareholders will vote to accept any fair offer to merge the corporation; on the contrary, the shareholders may figure that even though an offer is fair, it is not the best deal they can get. More fundamentally, the Supreme Court felt that the Court of Appeals' idea effectively substituted a judicial review of substantive fairness for a fully-informed shareholder vote, which is contrary to the whole idea behind Section 14(a) and the proxy rules. Accordingly, the Supreme Court refused to follow the Court of Appeals' fairness approach to proving causation.

Having rejected requiring direct testimony of reliance, or using the fairness of the deal as a guide to likely action by fully informed shareholders, the Supreme Court in *Mills* decided to base causation simply on the materiality of the false or misleading statements or omissions, combined with the fact that the proxy solicitation was an "essential link" in completing the transaction. In other words, if the

---

35.   396 U.S. 375, 90 S.Ct. 616 (1970).

36.   The plaintiffs actually filed suit the day before the shareholder vote on the merger took place. At that point, rather than speculate on what the shareholders would do if presented with all the facts, the court could have enjoined the exercise of the proxies and forced a resolicitation. Perhaps because of the shortness of time, however, the plaintiffs did not seek a temporary restraining order and the vote took place.

defendants needed to solicit proxies in order to approve the transaction in question, and if the defendants made material misrepresentations or omissions in soliciting the proxies, the court will presume that enough shareholders would have voted differently had they known the full truth to have changed the outcome. To appreciate how generous this approach is to the plaintiff, recall that the test for materiality is not that a reasonable shareholder necessarily would have voted differently in the absence of the false or misleading statement, but only that a reasonable shareholder would have considered the true or omitted facts significant in deciding how to vote.

While *Mills* dramatically eases the plaintiff's burden of establishing causation in a Rule 14a–9 action, a plaintiff still can run into problems proving that a misleading proxy solicitation caused him or her damages. To begin with, *Mills* only deals with establishing what is sometimes referred to as "transaction causation"—in other words, that the vote on the challenged transaction (for example, a merger) would have come out differently had the material misstatements or omissions not occurred. Transaction causation, however, does not establish that the plaintiff suffered any monetary damages, much less the amount of any damages. For instance, a proposed merger such as in *Borak, Mills* or *Virginia Bankshares* might, in fact, be in the best interest of all of the shareholders.

In a situation in which the court resolves the lawsuit quickly, the failure to show monetary damages might not matter. The court can enjoin the voting of the proxies (if the court is able to act before the actual vote), or the court can order the transaction unwound (if the court acts after the vote). Such relief can allow the shareholders to decide if they really want to vote for the transaction after they are fully and accurately informed. Often, however, the court will not be able to resolve the matter expeditiously. For example, in *Mills*, the challenged vote took place in 1963, the Supreme Court issued its opinion in 1970, and it was not until 1977 that the case was finally resolved—a pace of litigation which seems inspired by Charles Dickens' *Bleak House*. In this event, equitable relief commonly becomes impractical, if, for no other reason, because numerous parties will have acted in reliance on the transaction over the years.

When it is too late for equitable relief, all the plaintiff has left is to seek damages. Establishing such damages in the case of a merger, however, requires showing that the transaction did not give a good deal to the shareholders—put differently, that the transaction terms were unfair. Interestingly, this meant that the Court of Appeals had the last laugh in *Mills*. After the Supreme Court reversed the Court of Appeals' effort to decide transaction causation based upon the fairness of the merger, the matter went back to the lower courts to consider the remedy. The lower courts decided it was too late to unwind the merger, and the Court of Appeals held that, because the merger was fair, the plaintiffs were not entitled to damages.[37]

In *Mills*, the fact that the proponent of the merger needed to solicit proxies in order to obtain sufficient votes to approve the deal established transaction causation. Suppose, however, the merger's proponent owns enough shares to force the deal through even if all of the other shareholders vote in opposition. If, for whatever strange reason, the corporation nevertheless solicits proxies with materials that violate Rule 14a–9, can there still be transaction causation in this case? The Supreme Court faced this question in *Virginia Bankshares*.

At first glance, there seems to be no way to establish a causal connection between any misrepresentation in soliciting proxies, and damage to the plaintiff, in a situation in which the defendant(s) had the votes to push through the transaction without any proxies. Nevertheless, the plaintiff in *Virginia Bankshares* asserted two alternate theories in her attempt to establish a causal link. Both theories ask why it is the defendant went to the trouble of making a misrepresentation in seeking proxies if the defendant had the votes anyway (or, indeed, why even bother to solicit proxies).

The first theory is often referred to as the "shame facts" theory. The notion is that the defendant made misrepresentations in soliciting proxies because the defendant would be embarrassed if the true facts came out as to how badly the defendant was treating the minority shareholders. Of course, so far this only shows that honest disclosure would have embarrassed the defendant, not that it would have helped the plaintiff (at least in economic, as opposed to emotional, terms). The bridge to transaction causation under the shame facts theory is either to assume, or attempt to prove, that the defendant would be so concerned to avoid embarrassment that the defendant would have abandoned the transaction rather than face the scorn of honest disclosure. The majority of the court in *Virginia Bankshares*, however, was neither willing to make such an assumption, nor to open such psychological issues to evidentiary inquiry.

The second theory is generally referred to as the "sue facts" theory. Here, the notion is that the defendant made the misrepresentations in the proxy solicitation in order to avoid lawsuits by minority shareholders under state corporate laws, or, in the event of such suits, to improve the defendant's litigation position. For example, perhaps false assurances that the minority shareholders were receiving a fair price for the minority shareholders' stock would prevent the minority shareholders from dissenting from the merger and timely asserting any appraisal

---

37. The irony is that this resulted in a judicial review of substantive fairness substituting for a properly informed shareholder vote—which is precisely the outcome the Supreme Court seemingly had sought to avoid in *Mills*. What then did the Supreme Court's opinion in *Mills* accomplish, besides adding seven years to the lawsuit? Perhaps the only practical impact came from the Supreme Court's ordering the corporation to pay interim attorneys fees to the plaintiffs' attorneys based upon the plaintiffs' success in establishing a violation of Rule 14a–9. Maybe this was the whole point—enlisting private attorneys at corporate expense to act as bounty hunters to police for misleading proxies.

rights under state law. The court in *Virginia Bankshares* left open the question of whether this sort of theory would establish a causal relationship between a Rule 14a–9 violation and injury to a shareholder who lost state law rights. The majority in *Virginia Bankshares*, however, did not find that the particular facts before the court supported this sort of theory. The plaintiff argued that the defendants had sought shareholder approval in order to improve their legal position in the event a state court reviewed the merger as a conflict-of-interest transaction.[38] The majority of the court responded, however, that such an impact would not exist under state law if the defendants had not given full and honest disclosure of the facts concerning the transaction when seeking minority shareholder approval. Hence, the defendants did not improve their own legal position, or weaken the minority shareholders' claim under state law, by the Rule 14a–9 violation; accordingly, the violation caused no harm.

So far, we have been discussing causation when the proxy solicitation relates to one discrete transaction, such as a merger. The problem becomes considerably more complex if the Rule 14a–9 violation occurs in soliciting proxies for the election of directors at the annual shareholders' meeting. In this instance, showing harm to the shareholders might entail both establishing that there would have been a different outcome in the director election, and also that different directors would have made different decisions for the corporation. Actually, finding these two steps might be possible if the Rule 14a–9 violation occurs in the course of a proxy contest between two competing slates of candidates where the insurgents have a specific agenda (say, sale of the corporation to a hostile acquirer). Yet, if the misrepresentation occurs during an uncontested election, then it would seem impossible to establish what difference an honest disclosure would have made. After all, who else would have gained election to the board if no one else was running and what would such hypothetical alternate directors have done differently? Accordingly, courts have refused to find any causation of harm in a number of cases in which corporations have left embarrassing facts (such as the corporation paying bribes or engaging in other illegal practices) out of the annual report or proxy statement.[39]

38. As we will discuss in a later chapter, disinterested shareholder approval of a transaction in which directors or controlling shareholders have a conflict-of-interest can lessen the judicial scrutiny to which the transaction is subject when challenged as a breach of fiduciary duty.

39. *See, e.g.,* Abbey v. Control Data Corp., 603 F.2d 724 (8th Cir.1979). Here again, however, a plaintiff might argue a variation on the shame facts theory of causation: if those in charge of the corporation knew they had to disclose the embarrassing practices, then they would not have had the company engage in them. While this theory has had no more success than did the shame facts theory in *Virginia Bankshares*, there may be a critical distinction. To the extent one is dealing with disclosure of illegal practices, such as bribery, then the deterrence created by disclosure goes beyond simply the psychological desire to avoid embarrassment. After all, it would not make much sense to engage in bribery or other illegal practices if one knows one will get caught because one must publicly disclose one's conduct.

3.2.3 *Shareholder Proposals*

As indicated in the earlier description of the federal proxy rules, Rule 14a–8 has produced considerable litigation over the years. This rule allows a shareholder to demand that the corporation include, in both the company's proxy statement and form of proxy, a proposal which the shareholder wishes to put before his or her fellow shareholders for a vote at the annual stockholders' meeting.

Rule 14a–8 originated out of an incident involving the Bethlehem Steel Corporation. The corporation's directors had received notice from a shareholder of his intent to present a motion at the upcoming annual shareholders' meeting. After the directors refused to disclose this fact in the corporation's proxy statement, the shareholder complained to the Securities Exchange Commission. The Commission agreed with the shareholder that this omission rendered the corporation's proxy statement misleading. Thereafter, the SEC added to the proxy rules a provision explicitly requiring disclosure whenever a party making a proxy solicitation is aware that any other person plans to make a proposal at a stockholders' meeting. Taking this step, however, raised a series of questions: Is it enough simply to disclose the existence of the proposal, or should the disclosure also set out the rationale behind the proposal? If the latter, would it not make more sense for the proponent, rather than an opponent, to write up the rationale? Finally, what point will disclosure serve unless the proxy solicitation provides the shareholders with the ability to react to the proposal through the proxy? These questions led the SEC in 1942 to adopt what is now Rule 14a–8.

Rule 14a–8 goes beyond simply requiring the corporation to disclose that a shareholder notified the company of his or her intent to make a proposal at the annual meeting. It also allows the shareholder to submit a statement in support of the proposal, which the corporation must include along with the proposal in the corporation's proxy statement. In addition, the proxy form must give the solicited stockholders the option to instruct the corporation to vote their shares for or against the proposal. Implicit in these provisions is a shift from simply avoiding a misleading failure to disclose the company's knowledge about issues that will arise at the stockholders' meeting, to a broader goal of facilitating shareholder decision making through the proxy process. Specifically, Rule 14a–8 allows a shareholder to conduct a limited proxy campaign in favor of a proposal without having to spend his or her own money sending out proxy solicitations.

This impact of Rule 14a–8 raises the question of why the corporation should subsidize a shareholder's attempt to gain adoption of his or her proposal by the stockholders as a whole. There are several possible rationales. To begin with, Rule 14a–8 might be fairly cost efficient. Since the Rule only applies when the corporation is sending out proxy statements and forms anyway, the added cost to the corporation of including shareholder proposals is not large. By contrast, if the shareholder must conduct his or her own proxy solicitation, the shareholder will face significant out of pocket expenses. Moreover, the expense of undertaking one's own solicitation will deter shareholders from making a proposal even when the proposal might be worthwhile for the stockholders as a whole. After all, the proponent shareholder will bear all of the expense of the campaign, while the other stockholders will reap the vast bulk of the benefit—in other words, there is a huge free-rider problem. Rule 14a–8 is one way to avoid this problem. In addition, Rule 14a–8 may serve to return the balance of power between shareholders and directors to what it might have been in an earlier era. Specifically, before geographic dispersion of stockholders rendered personal attendance at shareholder meetings impractical in the widely held corporation, shareholders could bring their proposals before their fellow stockholders in person at the annual meeting. Rule 14a–8 creates a rough equivalent for a era in which shareholders vote overwhelmingly through proxies.

In any event, shareholder proposals pursuant to Rule 14a–8 largely have fallen into two types. The first type—which predominated in the early years of the Rule (including the proposal at Bethlehem Steel which triggered the whole matter)—concern corporate governance issues. An example would be a motion to amend the bylaws to have the shareholders, rather than directors, select the corporation's outside auditors. Many of these proposals came from two brothers, the Gilberts, who were on something of a crusade to make directors more accountable to the shareholders. The second type—which hit their zenith in the 1970s—are proposals motivated by social and political concerns. The most famous of these were the so-called "Campaign GM" proposals, which sought to have General Motors shareholders adopt various resolutions designed to make General Motors operate in a more socially responsible (at least from the proponents' standpoint) fashion.

As pointed out by critics of Rule 14a–8,[40] shareholder proposals under the Rule, until fairly recently, have served more to stir up litigation, than to accomplish anything else. With extraordinarily rare exceptions, stockholders voted against Rule 14a–8 proposals by overwhelming margins.[41] This changed with the rise of institutional shareholder activism in the late 1980s. A new wave of corporate governance oriented proposals—often addressing the directors' ability to resist hostile takeovers—have garnered significant support from institutional investors. The result is that in a number of cases the proposals have passed (or directors have preemptively adopted reforms to prevent the proposal's passage).

So far, we have not explained why Rule 14a–8 has produced litigation. The litigation arises from a variety of restrictions which the Rule places on a shareholder's right to demand that the corporation include a proposal in its proxy statement.

---

40. *E.g.*, George Dent, *SEC Rule 14a–8: A Study in Regulatory Failure*, 30 N.Y.L. Sch. L. Rev. 1 (1985).

41. This, however, raises an interesting question as to why a corporation's management would spend any time or money resisting the inclusion of shareholder proposals in the corporation's proxy materials.

Many of the restrictions in Rule 14a–8 are straightforward and have not caused significant problems. For example, the Rule limits the shareholders who are eligible to make a proposal. The shareholder must have owned at least one percent or $2000 in market value (whichever is less) of the outstanding voting stock in the corporation for at least one year before submitting the proposal, and must continue to hold the stock through the date of the stockholders' meeting at which the shareholder will make the proposal. This limit is designed to avoid those who lack a real economic interest in the corporation from purchasing a token share in order to make a proposal.[42] To give the corporation ample opportunity either to include or to object to a proposal, the Rule requires delivery to the corporation of the proposal a minimum time in advance of the meeting.[43] In order to prevent the corporation's proxy statement from drowning in proposals and supporting arguments, each shareholder has the right to submit only one proposal at a time, with a supporting statement no longer than 500 words.

The source of dispute lies in a series of grounds listed by Rule 14a–8 under which the corporation can refuse to include the proposal. Actually, many of these grounds have not caused much controversy either in their policy or application. For example, the corporation can omit a proposal which would require the company to violate a law, or where the proposal or supporting statement itself violates the proxy rules, particularly by containing false or misleading statements. The company can omit a proposal which simply pursues a personal grievance (such as one seeking reinstatement of an employee-shareholder to his or her job), or is otherwise simply seeking a personal benefit not shared by the stockholders at large. The corporation also can omit proposals which are beyond the power of the company to effectuate, which have been rendered moot, or which substantially duplicate another shareholder proposal already slated for inclusion in the company's proxy materials.

Several of the exclusions in Rule 14a–8(c) have not resulted in much litigation, but raise policy questions. For example, several exclusions speak to situations in which the shareholder's legitimate interest in making the proposal seems most evident. These include proposals which relate to the specific amount of dividends (like asking for more), which relate to an election for office (such as by listing a slate of candidates for election to the board), and which would be counter to a proposal the company is making to the shareholders. The exclusion of proposals relating to a specific amount of dividends presumably stems from a concern as to the powers of directors versus shareholders—a concern to which we will return shortly. The exclusion of proposals relating to election to office is a corollary to the rule we discussed earlier which does

---

42. The reader may recall a similar concern in the *Pillsbury* case (discussed earlier in this chapter), in which an individual, who sought to change corporate policy for social reasons, purchased a token amount of stock in order to obtain access to the shareholder list. See § 3.1.3c *supra*.

43. The due date for submitting proposals depends upon when the corporation released its proxy statement for the previous year's annual meeting.

not require proxy forms to include the names of candidates for director beyond those nominated by the party soliciting the proxy. A shareholder making a proposal contrary to management's proposal presumably is not worrying about bringing the issue to a shareholder vote—since this is going to happen anyway. Rather, this party no doubt wants the opportunity to make a 500 word argument against the management proposal. While these last two exclusions have not produced much litigation, they do undercut the potential which Rule 14a–8 otherwise might have had to level somewhat the playing field between management and shareholders when it comes to the election of directors and the approval of matters requiring a shareholder vote. Oh well.

An exclusion which generated some criticism from fans of quixotic efforts is the one which allows the corporation to omit proposals that are substantially the same as prior proposals the shareholders have already soundly defeated. This exclusion lists a series of percentages, which increase depending upon how many times the shareholders already have voted down a substantially similar proposal. If the prior similar proposals have not received the specified percentage of votes, the corporation can exclude the new effort.

An exclusion whose rationale is straightforward, but whose application can, at times, be difficult, covers proposals which would not be proper subjects for shareholder action under state law. This exclusion reflects the notion that Rule 14a–8 (and, indeed, Section 14(a)) is designed to facilitate the exercise by shareholders of their rights under state corporate law, but not to alter the fundamental division of power over the corporation under state law. We encountered this exclusion earlier in this chapter when discussing the recent *Fleming* decision dealing with the power of the shareholders to command action from the board through bylaw amendments.[44] As the discussion of *Fleming* indicates, most of the time the question of whether a proposal is a proper subject for shareholder action stems from the proposed action's intrusion on the statutory power of the board of directors. A common way to avoid this problem (as suggested in Rule 14a–8 itself) is to cast the resolution as a request to the board, rather than a command. As the New York Court of Appeals pointed out in the *Auer* decision discussed earlier in this chapter,[45] shareholders always can pass resolutions making requests of the board, even when the state corporation statute gives the board ultimate authority on the matter.

In *SEC v. Transamerica Corp.*,[46] the court confronted a different sort of problem in applying the "not a proper subject" exclusion—this being procedural rather than substantive impediments to the proposed shareholder action. This case arose out of the refusal by Transamerica Corporation to include in its proxy statement several proposals received from one of the Gilbert brothers. Primarily, Gilbert wanted to amend Transamerica's bylaws to require that the shareholders rather than

44. See § 3.1.3a *supra.*
45. See § 3.1.3b *supra.*
46. 163 F.2d 511 (3d Cir.1947).

directors would select the company's auditors. Transamerica's bylaws provided that the shareholders could amend the bylaws by majority vote at any shareholders' meeting, but only if the notice of the meeting contained notice of the proposed amendment. Transamerica's directors refused to include notice of Gilbert's proposed amendment in the notice of the meeting, and then used their refusal to give notice as the basis to argue that Gilbert's proposed amendment was not a proper subject for shareholder action.

Not surprisingly, the court rejected the overly cute argument made by Transamerica's directors. What is interesting is the court's rationale for doing so. The court stated that the proposals were proper subjects for stockholder action, since they were "subjects in respect to which stockholders have the right to act" under the corporation statute of Delaware (Transamerica's state of incorporation). It is not clear what the court meant by this. Perhaps the court meant that under state law, as the court understood it, directors could not deprive shareholders of the power to amend the bylaws by refusing to give notice—either because state courts would reject such an action as an abuse of the directors' discretion, because such action was contrary to Delaware's statutory provision dealing with amendment of the bylaws, or because the Transamerica bylaw provision in question did not intend to give the directors discretion to leave out notice. Alternately, perhaps the court meant that the only issue under Rule 14a–8 is whether the substantive subject matter of the proposal was within the shareholders' power, and that any procedural requirements for shareholder action (such as notice and the like) were not relevant in considering the "not a proper subject" exclusion. (On the other hand, the court noted that Gilbert did not intend to deny the shareholders notice of his proposal, which would be beside the point under this interpretation of Rule 14a–8.) More dramatically, the court went on to assert that Section 14(a) preempted a corporate bylaw from giving directors the discretion to cut off shareholder proposals by refusing to give notice. At the very least, this alternate holding appears to establish that corporations cannot simply opt out of Rule 14a–8 by bylaw (or article) provisions denying shareholders the right to make motions which the state law would not otherwise prohibit. More broadly, this holding might suggest that federal courts can use Rule 14a–8 to invalidate corporate bylaw provisions which the court finds to create too great a burden on the shareholders' ability to make proposals.[47]

47. It is not entirely clear whether this alternate holding survived a subsequent amendment to Rule 14a–8. Specifically, at the time the court decided *Transamerica*, the Rule referred to whether the proposal was a proper subject for shareholder action, without mentioning state law (albeit, an SEC interpretative release concerning the Rule did refer to state law). Hence, the court may have felt at liberty to decide whether a proposal was a proper subject for shareholder action based upon a mix of state law and the policies behind Section 14(a) and Rule 14a–8. A subsequent amendment to Rule 14a–8 clarified that the not a proper subject exclusion refers to whether the proposal is a proper subject under state law. Accordingly, after the amendment, presumably the only inquiry is whether state law allows the proposal. In the release announcing the amendment, however, the SEC said that it viewed the amendment as consistent with *Transamerica*.

The most difficult exclusions, both in terms of policy and application, are the "ordinary business" and the "not significantly related to the corporation's business" exclusions. Specifically, Rule 14a–8 allows the corporation to exclude proposals which relate to the conduct of the corporation's ordinary business operations, and proposals which relate to operations which account for less than five percent of the corporation's assets and income and are "not otherwise significantly related to the corporation's business."

The stated rationale behind the ordinary business exclusion is to correspond with the basic division of power under state corporate law—this being that directors and officers control matters of ordinary business, while shareholders concern themselves with the selection of directors and with corporate decisions which are not ordinary business. Still, to the extent a shareholder proposal impermissibly intrudes on the board's power to manage the corporation's business (ordinary or otherwise), then the not a proper subject exclusion already deals with the proposal. To the extent that state law would allow shareholders to vote on a matter (of ordinary business or otherwise), then why should the proxy rules screen out such proposals from taking advantage of Rule 14a–8? Perhaps the only rationale would be to prevent the clutter of proxy materials with matters which are too mundane to warrant the space the proposal would take.

The "not significantly related to the corporation's business" exclusion stems from the SEC's attempt to deal with shareholder proposals whose primary concern is political or social. An earlier exclusion had allowed the corporation to omit proposals submitted "primarily for the purpose of promoting general economic, political, racial, religious, social or similar causes." The change in language is an effort to shift the test from focusing on what motivated the proposal or what it addresses (political, social and such causes) to what the proposal does not address (matters significantly related to the corporation's business).[48] In either event, the idea is that shareholder proposals are supposed to be a forum for matters relating to the corporation, not general causes. The problem, of course, is that there is often an inevitable overlap between matters related to the corporation's business, and general social and political causes.

For example, in *Medical Committee for Human Rights v. SEC*,[49] the District of Columbia Circuit faced the question of what to do with a

48. In addition, the SEC sought through a five percent test to create a more objective standard for deciding if a proposal significantly relates to the corporation's business. The effort at quantitative objectivity ultimately has proven illusory, however, because Rule 14a–8 still allows proposals, despite the proposal's not relating to at least five percent of the corporation's assets or income, if the proposal is "otherwise significantly related" to the corporation's business. *See, e.g.,* Lovenheim v. Iroquois

Brands, Ltd., 618 F.Supp. 554 (D.D.C.1985) (the court held that a proposal concerning the forced feeding of geese raised to make pate was "otherwise significantly related" to the corporation's business due to the societal implications of the proposal, despite the fact that goose liver pate sales accounted for less than .05 percent of the company's revenues).

49. 432 F.2d 659 (D.C.Cir.1970).

shareholder proposal to stop Dow Chemical from manufacturing napalm.[50] Dow refused to include the proposal, arguing somewhat inconsistently that the decision to manufacture napalm was a matter of ordinary business and also that the proposal was primarily for the purpose of promoting general political, social and such causes. The court remanded the case in order for the SEC to reconsider the Commission's rather cursory refusal to force Dow to include the proposal. Since the proposal related to a business activity of Dow—the production of napalm—the court suggested that it was appropriate for the shareholders to consider whether the company should continue this activity, even if the motive for abandoning production would be political or social. In this regard, the court anticipated the change in focus—from looking at whether the shareholder had political motives, to looking at the relationship of the proposal to the corporation's business—later adopted, as discussed above, by the SEC. Moreover, the Medical Committee was fortunate because of an unusual position taken by Dow's management. In various public statements, Dow's management claimed to be manufacturing napalm as the company's patriotic duty, despite making little money by selling napalm and despite the impairment of the corporation's college recruitment efforts due to campus opposition to the use of napalm in the Vietnam War. Hence, it appeared to the court that it was the corporation's management which was acting primarily for political reasons. Under these circumstances, it becomes even more difficult to exclude proposals based upon the notion that it is the shareholder who is acting out of political or social motives.

In *Medical Committee*, the court rather curtly dismissed the argument regarding the ordinary business exclusion. Taking its cue from the stated rationale behind the exclusion, the court equated the ordinary business exclusion with what issues were inappropriate subjects for shareholder action under state law (thereby rendering the ordinary business exclusion redundant of the not a proper subject exclusion). Having recast the ordinary business exclusion into a question of shareholder power under state law, it became easy for the court to suggest that the amendment of a corporation's articles to limit the company's permissible lines of business fell outside of the ordinary business exclusion. More recent cases, however, have suggested that the ordinary business exclusion has a greater role to play in dealing with politically or socially motivated proposals.

In *Roosevelt v. E.I. Du Pont de Nemours & Co.*,[51] the District of Columbia Circuit once again dealt with a shareholder proposal concerning political or social issues—in this instance, a proposal asking the directors of Du Pont both to accelerate the company's plan for phasing out the production of chlorofluorocarbons, and to make a presentation to the shareholders detailing the company's efforts to develop and market

---

50. More precisely, the proposal requested that the directors consider initiating an amendment to Dow's articles which would limit the permissible purposes of the corporation to exclude the production of napalm. Napalm is a jellied gasoline used in bombs.

51. 958 F.2d 416 (D.C.Cir.1992).

environmentally sound alternates.[52] The court concluded that this proposal fell within the ordinary business exclusion. In doing so, the court emphasized that the issue posed by the resolution was not whether to phase out chlorofluorocarbons—since Du Pont had decided to do this. Rather, the difference between the shareholder proposal and the policy of Du Pont's management involved a one-year difference in the phase-out period. Moreover, the court concluded that the request to report to the shareholders was likewise within the ordinary business exception, since the subject matter of the report involved merely arrangements to implement a policy on which the management and the shareholder were agreed.

Probably the most controversial recent use of the ordinary business exclusion in the context of political or social proposals did not occur in a judicial opinion. Rather it occurred in the Securities Exchange Commission's "no action" letter written to Cracker Barrel Old Country Store, Inc. In this letter, the SEC announced that the Commission would not take action against Cracker Barrel for omitting a shareholder proposal requesting the directors to halt the corporation's practice of firing employees for being homosexual. What made the letter particularly significant was its statement abandoning the Commission's prior view that some employment matters fell outside of the ordinary business exclusion because of their social policy implications. Not only did this mean that the SEC viewed all employment issues, including employment discrimination, as beyond the reach of shareholder proposals under Rule 14a–8, it also suggested a critical change in the Commission's view of the relationship between social issues and the ordinary business exclusion generally. Specifically, in the Release explaining the 1976 amendments to Rule 14a–8, the SEC had stated that matters which would otherwise be simply ordinary business could fall outside of this exclusion because of the broader social implications of the business practice at issue. If this approach no longer applied to employment issues, why should it apply anyplace?[53] Recently, the SEC switched positions again, and stated that it was abandoning the position it took in the Cracker Barrel matter. Such flip-flopping by the Commission has led some to question whether the ordinary business, and the "not significantly related to the corporation's business," exclusions grant too much discretion to the Commission to guess at what subjects are worthwhile enough to present to the shareholders.[54]

Before leaving Rule 14a–8, it is useful to note the different litigation contexts involved in *Transamerica*, *Medical Committee*, and *Roosevelt*. *Transamerica* is the most straight-forward. This was an action by the SEC pursuant to its express statutory authority to bring suits to enjoin

---

52. Chlorofluorocarbons are used in aerosol sprays, but endanger the ozone layer in the earth's atmosphere.

53. The effort by the SEC in the Cracker Barrel letter to alter the position the agency took in the 1976 Release raised problems under the Administrative Procedure Act. NYCERS v. SEC, 45 F.3d 7 (2d Cir.1995).

54. *See, e.g.,* Alan R. Palmiter, *The Shareholder Proposal Rule: A Failed Experiment in Merit Regulation,* 45 Ala. L. Rev. 879 (1994).

violations of the Securities Exchange Act. In order to allow the Commission to bring such actions in a timely manner, Rule 14a–8 requires corporations to notify the Commission of their refusal to include any shareholder proposal in the corporation's proxy statement and the justification for this refusal. Suppose, however, the Commission decides not to object to a corporation's refusal to include a proposal—as in the Cracker Barrel no-action letter. In *Medical Committee*, the shareholder brought a proceeding against the SEC in the District of Columbia Circuit Court to challenge the agency's decision.[55] While the court held that it had jurisdiction to hear the case, this result is not free from doubt.[56] In *Roosevelt*, the shareholder sued the corporation for refusing to include her proposal. The court decided to apply *Borak* and recognized a private cause of action by a shareholder to force the company to include his or her proposal.

55. The Administrative Procedure Act allows affected persons to challenge, under certain circumstances, the actions of federal agencies in the District of Columbia Circuit Court.

56. The Supreme Court granted certiorari to consider the issue, but dismissed the case as moot after Dow went ahead and included the shareholder's proposal in its next proxy statement.

Chapter IV

DUTIES OF DIRECTORS
AND OFFICERS

[Research References]

AmJur 2d, Corporations §§ 1684–1989

CJS, Corporations §§ 460–553

ALR Index: Corporate Officers, Directors, and Agents; Corporate Opportunity; Corporate Responsibility Doctrine; Derivative Actions

ALR Digest: Corporations §§ 114–158

Am Jur Legal Forms 2d, Corporations §§ 74:1531–74:1785

Am Jur Pleading and Practice Forms (Rev), Corporations §§ 257–311

29 POF3d 133, Liability Of A Director To A Corporation For Mismanagement; 16 POF3d 583, Corporate Director's Breach of Fiduciary Duty to Creditors

30 POF2d 291, Corporate Opportunity Doctrine–Fairness of Corporate Official's Acquisition of Business Opportunity; 9 POF2d 57, Corporate Officer or Director as Alter Ego of Corporation

---

In the previous chapter, we looked at the powers of corporate directors and officers. With power often goes responsibility. Hence, in this chapter, we look at the duties of directors and officers. From time to time as corporate law evolved, courts and writers have spent some effort discussing whether directors and officers of a corporation are more analogous to a trustee or to an agent when it comes to the determining what duties directors and officers owe to the corporation.[1] Such discussions have long since ceased, perhaps based upon the recognition that it really does not matter. Like both trustees and agents, directors and officers act for the benefit of another, in this case the corporation. As such, just as trustees have a fiduciary duty to their beneficiaries, and agents have a fiduciary duty to their principals, directors and officers have a fiduciary duty to the corporation. This fiduciary duty, in turn, encompasses two more specific duties: A duty to exercise care in avoiding harm to the corporation, and a duty of loyally placing the corporation's interests ahead of one's own. These two duties are the subject of the first two sections of this chapter. Later sections of this chapter shall consider the primary mechanism for enforcing these duties, and explore some

1. *See, e.g.,* Harry G. Henn & John R. Alexander, Laws of Corporations and Other Business Enterprises § 235 (3d ed. 1983).

means of mitigating the consequences to directors and officers of possible breaches of their duties.

§ 4.1   Duty of Care

We begin our discussion of the duties of corporate directors and officers with an examination of their duty of care. The concept of a duty of care is a notion with which the reader should be familiar. It is the underpinning of the tort of negligence. Hence, we say that lawyers have a duty of care to their clients, doctors have a duty of care to their patients, drivers and other individuals throughout society have a duty of care to persons who foreseeably might suffer personal injury or property damage by virtue of unreasonable conduct. The idea is that persons, who engage in conduct which creates a risk of harm to others, have, as a general proposition, a duty to act as a reasonably prudent person would act under the same circumstances to avoid such harm.

At first glance, then, the duty of care of directors and officers to their corporation should involve nothing more than an application of tort law principles to this particular context. In some situations, this is true. In other situations, however, we shall see that courts have altered the rules governing the duty of care of directors and officers from what we might expect if we were simply applying general tort law principles.

4.1.1   Inattention

One common type of claim against directors or officers for violating their duty of care involves the allegation that the directors or officers were essentially "asleep at the switch" while subordinates harmed the corporation. *Francis v. United Jersey Bank*[1] provides a classic illustration.

In *Francis*, Mrs. Pritchard and her two sons were the shareholders and directors of a corporation which conducted a reinsurance brokerage business. As part of this business, the corporation collected premiums owed by insurance companies to reinsurance companies, and collected payouts owed by reinsurance companies to insurance companies. This meant that, at any given time, the corporation held large amounts of money owed to its clients. A few years before his death, Mrs. Pritchard's husband turned over control of the business to the couple's two sons. Upon her husband's death, Mrs. Pritchard inherited 48 percent of the corporation's outstanding stock, while the two sons ended up with 52 percent. Despite being a director both before and after her husband's death, Mrs. Pritchard paid virtually no attention to the business. Indeed, after her husband's death, Mrs. Pritchard became listless and began to drink heavily. Unfortunately for Mrs. Pritchard, her neglect as a director combined with her possible failings as a parent. After taking control of the business, the two sons gradually looted the company. Specifically, the two sons "borrowed" ever increasing amounts of money from the company, which they could not repay. Ultimately, this led to the corporation

§ 4.1

1.   87 N.J. 15, 432 A.2d 814 (1981).

going bankrupt while owing considerable amounts to its clients. The trustee in bankruptcy sued Mrs. Pritchard. The court held that Mrs. Pritchard had breached her duty of care to the corporation.

In reaching its result, the court in *Francis* largely applied tort law principles in an unsurprising manner. The court stated that to find Mrs. Pritchard liable, she must have a duty, breach this duty, and the breach must be the proximate cause of the plaintiff's damage. The court found the standard of care in the state's corporation statute. The statute stated that directors must discharge their responsibilities with the degree of diligence, care and skill which ordinarily prudent men would exercise under similar circumstances in like positions. Similar provisions exist in most states' corporation statutes.[2] This standard appears to be nothing more than a restatement of the reasonably prudent person test familiar to all students of tort law. Indeed, the court noted that the statutory standard was the same as courts had applied to director liability for beaching one's duty of care, even before the statute.

To apply this standard, one must figure out what a reasonably prudent person would do when he or she is a corporate director. The court in *Francis* stated that, as a general rule, a director should acquire at least a rudimentary understanding of the business of the corporation. In addition, the court explained, directors are under a continuing obligation to keep informed about the activities of the corporation. As part of keeping informed, directors should make it a practice to attend board meetings, even if they cannot attend every meeting. Directors should also keep informed by regular review of corporate financial statements.

In setting out these expectations for corporate directors, the *Francis* court accepted the view that directors have at least some obligation to monitor corporate affairs. In contrast to this holding, a few courts have exonerated directors because the directors were simply figureheads.[3] The vast majority of opinions, however, are consistent with *Francis* in demanding that directors pay some attention to their role.[4] Having held that directors must pay at least some attention, it was easy to find a breach of duty in *Francis*. Mrs. Pritchard apparently was utterly oblivious to corporate affairs. Needless to say, many cases of inattention are not this straightforward.

The *Francis* opinion provides useful guidance for dealing with more difficult cases. The court took pains to note that the demands of a director's duty of care depend upon the circumstances. This is entirely consistent with the tort law principle which measures negligence based upon what a reasonable person would do in the same situation. What sort of circumstances, then, will courts look at in deciding what efforts a

2. *E.g.*, Cal. Corp. Code § 309(a).

3. *E.g.*, Allied Freightways, Inc. v. Cholfin, 325 Mass. 630, 91 N.E.2d 765 (Mass. 1950).

4. For a listing of cases finding directors liable for breaching their duty of care, see

Norwood P. Beveridge, Jr., *The Corporate Director's Duty of Care: Riddles Wisely Expounded*, 24 Suffolk U. L. Rev. 923, 947–949 n.129 (1990).

reasonably prudent director would expend in monitoring corporate affairs?

One factor noted in *Francis* is the nature of the business conducted by the corporation. The court found it significant that the corporation in *Francis* conducted a reinsurance brokerage business, which required the corporation to act as a fiduciary for its clients and to hold large amounts of the clients' money. Similarly, numerous court opinions have drawn a distinction between the expectations imposed on directors of banking corporations, which hold large amounts of money received from depositors, versus the directors of non-banking corporations. Traditionally, courts seemingly have been much more willing to find a breach of the directors' duty of care when dealing with bank directors than with directors of corporations engaged in non-financial businesses.[5] While courts often have not articulated a coherent rationale for this distinction, presumably one basis is the assumption that there is a greater likelihood for dishonesty by corporate personnel in the absence of monitoring when dealing with a business with more liquid assets.

Another factor to consider is the role of the defendant in the corporation. For example, courts may expect more of a full-time corporate executive than of an outside director. The court's opinion in *Bates v. Dresser*[6] illustrates this distinction. In *Bates*, the plaintiff sued the president and directors of a bank for failing to detect and stop embezzlement by the bank's bookkeeper. The court held the president liable, but not the bank's directors. The court felt that the directors had no reason to suspect a problem. The bookkeeper had covered up the embezzlement by the rather novel (at the time) devise understating the bank's deposits rather than overstating the bank's assets. By virtue of being on the scene, however, the bank's president had come across a number of circumstances which should have alerted him to the bookkeeper's dishonesty.

Another factor is the size of the corporation. The court in *Francis* suggested that directors of a closely held corporation—at least if the corporation does not handle large amounts of money as a fiduciary— might reasonably be more casual with their monitoring of corporate affairs, than should directors of a publicly traded corporation. Perhaps the notion is that the typical active involvement of the shareholders in running a closely held corporation makes a formal monitoring role for directors less necessary than in a corporation in which the managers do not have their own dollars at stake.

On the other hand, the large size of a corporation poses a limit on what the law reasonably cam expect of directors. The Delaware Supreme Court's opinion in *Graham v. Allis–Chalmers Mfg. Co.*[7] illustrates the problem. This suit stemmed from Allis–Chalmers and four of its employ-

---

5. *Compare* Medford Trust Co. v. McKnight, 292 Mass. 1, 197 N.E. 649 (Mass. 1935), *with* Uccello v. Gold'n Foods, Inc., 325 Mass. 319, 90 N.E.2d 530 (Mass. 1950).

6. 251 U.S. 524, 40 S.Ct. 247 (1920).

7. 41 Del.Ch. 78, 188 A.2d 125 (1963).

ees pleading guilty to price fixing in violation of federal antitrust law. A shareholder claimed that Allis–Chalmers' directors breached their duty of care by not preventing this law violation. The Delaware Supreme Court rejected this claim. The court pointed to the size of Allis–Chalmers' operations—the company had over 30,000 employees conducting business at establishments spread over a large geographic area. This meant that the board, of necessity, had to confine the board's control to broad policy decisions, rather than attempt to supervise the corporation's day-to-day activities (such as setting prices).

Many writers have criticized the *Graham* decision.[8] The concern about the directors' ability personally to supervise corporate activities, such as pricing decisions, was really something of a "red herring." The plaintiff's argument was not that the directors personally should have undertaken this activity, but, rather, that the board should have created a system to monitor pricing decisions—presumably even if someone other than the directors themselves performed the monitoring—to ensure compliance with antitrust laws. In rejecting this argument, the court made some rather overbroad statements. Specifically, the court stated that directors are entitled to rely on the honesty and integrity of corporate employees until something happens to create suspicion.

It is doubtful if the court intended this statement about reliance on employee honesty to be taken in its broadest interpretation. Otherwise, directors of a bank might decide that the bank should not have any controls to prevent tellers from embezzling funds—such as comparing cash to records of transactions—unless and until a specific teller gives reasons to suspect his or her honesty. It is unlikely that any court would find such an action by bank directors to be reasonable.

Presumably, what the court meant was that directors need not automatically assume that all employees are crooks. Indeed, a large business could not function without reposing a substantial degree of trust in its personnel. Corporation statutes often codify this point. Numerous states, such as Delaware, have a provision in their corporation statute protecting directors who reasonably and in good faith rely upon records and reports of subordinates.[9] At some point, however, trust would not be reasonable. This could be because the conduct of a particular employee—such as the bookkeeper in *Bates* visibly living beyond his salary—raises suspicion. Alternately, it could be because the context (such as with bank tellers) is one in which historical experience and an understanding of human nature show the need for some monitoring against temptation. Ultimately, the question is whether the frequency of the particular dishonest conduct in the circumstances, coupled with the consequences of such conduct for the corporation, justify the costs of monitoring to deter the conduct's occurrence. Hence, to the extent the plaintiff in *Graham* produced little evidence that price fixing was a

8. *E.g.,* William L. Cary, *Federalism and Corporate Law: Reflections Upon Delaware,* 83 Yale L.J. 663, 683–84 (1974).

9. *E.g.,* Del. Gen. Corp. Law § 141(e); M.B.C.A. § 8.30(b).

frequent problem in the industry (other than an old consent decree against Allis–Chalmers), or that price fixing was likely to produce calamitous consequences for the corporation, the court's result in *Graham* was correct, even if its language was overbroad.[10]

There are a couple of factors the court in *Francis* refused to consider. Mrs. Pritchard received no slack from the court because she was depressed over her husband's death and took to heavy drinking.[11] Also, the court stated that the reference to "shareholder loans" on the corporation's balance sheet should have alerted Mrs. Pritchard to the misappropriations by her sons, if she only had bothered to look at the corporation's financial statements. The court never inquired, however, whether Mrs. Pritchard understood anything about accounting or balance sheets, or, whether, without such an understanding, she would have recognized the significance which the court saw in the reference to shareholder loans. In fact, this lack of sympathy is entirely consistent with the objective nature of the reasonable prudent person test in tort law. Drinking, depression, and ignorance would not be an excuse for someone while driving, and presumably should not be an excuse for someone while acting as a corporate officer or director. After all, presumably no one forced Mrs. Pritchard to take the job.

4.1.2 Business Decisions and the "Business Judgment Rule"

So far, in looking at cases in which the complaint is that the directors were not paying attention, we have seen courts generally apply the reasonable prudent person test in manner familiar to students of tort law. Things change when the complaint is not that the directors were inattentive, but, rather, that the directors made a business decision for the corporation which turned out poorly, or which the plaintiff asserts was otherwise a poor decision. For example, suppose the board of directors of a corporation votes to have the corporation merge with another company under a deal which gives the existing stockholders $55 in cash per share for each share of stock in the corporation a stockholder owns.[12] A shareholder might allege that the directors breached their duty of care in that they should have held out for more money. Such a complaint causes courts to turn to something known as the "business judgment rule."

The business judgment rule traces its roots back around 170 years.[13] The idea underlying the rule is that courts should exercise restraint in

---

10. Federal criminal sentencing guidelines issued by the United States Sentencing Commission have increased the reason for corporations to monitor against illegal conduct. Under the guidelines, corporations which have an "effective compliance program" face significantly less sanctions for illegal conduct than do corporations without such a program. Typically, such compliance programs entail promulgating and making sure employees have read a code of ethical conduct, and installing a system to monitor and audit for criminal conduct by employees (including by establishing a mechanism for employees to report violations without fear of retaliation).

11. *But see* Briggs v. Spaulding, 141 U.S. 132, 11 S.Ct. 924 (1891)(taking into account the old age and ill health of the directors).

12. This is what occurred in the famous case of *Smith v. Van Gorkom*, 488 A.2d 858 (Del.1985), which we shall discuss shortly.

13. *See* Percy v. Millaudon, 8 Mart. (N.S.) 68 (La.1829).

holding directors liable for (or otherwise second guessing) business decisions which produce poor results or with which reasonable minds might disagree. This seems to be a sensible notion. After all, business decisions typically involve taking calculated risks. As a result, even the most reasonable business decision, viewed at the time it was made, often ends up not panning out. Also, directors frequently must make business decisions in situations in which, no matter what decision the directors make, someone is going to disagree with what the directors did.

A difficulty with the business judgment rule occurs, however, when courts and writers go beyond the general concept of judicial restraint and attempt to inject specific content into the rule. Immediately, a lack of consensus emerges as to exactly what the business judgment rule really is. An example of this difficulty occurred during the drafting of the 1984 revision of the Model Business Corporation Act. The drafters of the 1984 revision initially thought it would be a good idea to include the rule as part of the Act. This process broke down, however, when the drafters could not reach a consensus on a formulation of the rule.[14] As one of the participants explained, "we are saying that there is a business judgment rule, that we know what it is and when it should be applied, but we can't define it."[15]

Much of the difficulty confounding efforts to define the business judgment rule stems from beginning with a faulty premise. This premise is that there is *a* business judgment rule. In fact, there is no single rule. Instead, the phrase "the business judgment rule" has a number of different, and conflicting, meanings:

a.   *The business judgment rule as a tautological statement*

A quotation from the opinion of the court in *Miller v. American Telephone & Telegraph Co.*,[16] provides a good illustration of the first common usage of the phrase "the business judgment rule." In bringing up the rule, the court explained:

> The sound business judgment rule ... expresses the unanimous decision of American courts to eschew intervention in corporate decision-making if the judgment of directors and officers i[s] uninfluenced by personal considerations and is exercised in good faith.... Underlying the rule is the assumption that reasonable

---

14. In the end, the Model Act simply punted by including the following apologia in the Official Comment to the section of the Act (Section 8:30) which sets out the directors' duty of care:

The elements of the business judgment rule and the circumstances for its application are continuing to be developed by the courts,. In view of that continuing judicial development, section 8.30 does not try to codify the business judgment rule or to delineate the differences, if any, between that rule and the standards of director conduct set forth in this section.

That is a task left to the courts and possibly to later revisions of this Model Act.

More recently, the drafters of the Model Act decided to add a new Section 8.31 to the Act dealing with director liability. Even here, however, the drafters disclaimed any intent to codify the business judgment rule.

15. Robert Hamilton, Corporations: Including Partnerships and Limited Partnerships: Cases and Materials, 703 (4th ed. 1990).

16. 507 F.2d 759, 762 (3d Cir.1974).

diligence has been used in reaching the decision which the rule is invoked to justify.

A moment's reflection establishes that this statement really does not say much of anything. Stating that courts will not interfere with the decisions of corporate directors so long as the directors act with reasonable diligence, are not in a conflict-of-interest, and act in good faith, is simply saying that directors will not be liable for their decisions unless there is a reason for holding the directors liable—specifically, that the directors breached their duties of care or, as we shall discuss later, loyalty. This is hardly an earth-shattering proposition. No one expects directors to act as insurers that all their decisions work out and please everyone.

There are a number of variations on this use of the phrase. For example, some sources point out that the rule only applies to business judgments—in other words, the challenge must involve a decision the directors made, rather than the directors simply having been inattentive.[17] This explains why the court in *Francis* did not mention the rule. Other sources add assorted items, such as the absence of fraud or illegality,[18] to the prerequisites for the rule's protection. These additions may be marginally useful for those desiring a handy checklist of ways in which directors can breach their duties of care or loyalty, but there still is not much real significance to this "rule." Another common variation on this theme is to state the "rule" as containing a rebuttable presumption. The presumption is that the directors have not violated their duties—in other words, the directors did not have a conflict-of-interest, act in bad faith, or act without due care—in making their decision.[19] Here too there is less substance then meets the eye. This "presumption" entails nothing more than saying that the plaintiff who challenges a decision of the board has the burden of proving the directors breached one of their duties. Yet, the proposition that the plaintiff, in any context, has the burden of proving his or her prima facie case is a rule with which every first year law student should be familiar.

b. The business judgment rule as consistent with the norm of liability for ordinary negligence

Given the not surprising conclusion that directors are only liable if the plaintiff proves a breach of the directors' duties, the question then becomes whether the business judgment rule says anything significant about what it takes to prove a breach, particularly of the duty of care. For many courts and writers the answer is really no. These courts and writers apply concepts of ordinary negligence to identify conduct which breaches the directors' duty of care even in cases of business decisions. For example, in one of the most often quoted reconciliations of the

17. *E.g.*, Aronson v. Lewis, 473 A.2d 805 (Del.1984).

18. *E.g.*, Shlensky v. Wrigley, 95 Ill. App.2d 173, 237 N.E.2d 776 (1968).

19. *E.g.*, Aronson v. Lewis, 473 A.2d 805 (Del.1984).

business judgment rule with the law of negligence, a New York trial court explained:

> The question is frequently asked, how does the operation of the so-called "business judgment rule" tie in with the concept of negligence? There is no conflict between the two. When courts say that they will not interfere in matters of business judgment, it is presupposed that judgment—reasonable diligence—has in fact been exercised.[20]

Probably the most widely cited case actually applying an ordinary negligence standard to find directors liable for a business decision is *Litwin v. Allen*.[21] In *Litwin*, a New York trial court held the directors of Guaranty Trust Company liable for their decision to purchase three million dollars of debentures. The problem, as the court saw it, was not simply that the debentures declined in value, causing Guaranty Trust to incur a loss. Rather, the problem with the directors' action was that the purchase agreement gave the seller the option to repurchase the debentures at the sale price within six months. This meant that, while Guaranty Trust faced the risk of loss if the debentures declined in value, Guaranty Trust did not obtain the corresponding potential for gain, since, if the debentures appreciated, the seller presumably could exercise its option to repurchase. The court concluded:

> There is more here than a question of business judgment as to which men might well differ. The directors plainly failed in this instance to bestow the care which the situation demanded. Unless we are to do away entirely with the doctrine that directors of a bank are liable for negligence in administering its affairs liability should be imposed in connection with this transaction.[22]

The court gave its view of the business judgment rule when it explained: "In other words, directors are liable for negligence in the performance of their duties. Not being insurers, directors are not liable for errors of judgment or for mistakes while acting with reasonable skill and prudence."[23]

This version of the business judgment rule continues the type of broad tautological statement quoted earlier to an unexceptional conclusion: Directors are not liable unless they breach their duties of loyalty or care, and the duty of care is that of reasonable skill and prudence—which is to say the same standard as is the norm throughout the law of torts. About the only thing the "rule" adds are a couple of cautionary notes: Decisions over which reasonable minds might differ are not negligent; nor does an "error in judgment" or a mistake—in the sense a decision does not turn out as one hoped—automatically equal negligence. These same cautions could be sounded for doctors, lawyers or automobile drivers sued for their mistakes.

20. Casey v. Woodruff, 49 N.Y.S.2d 625, 643 (Sup. Ct. 1944).

21. 25 N.Y.S.2d 667 (Sup. Ct. 1940).

22. *Id*. at 699.

23. *Id*. at 678.

In fact, while no one speaks of a "medical," "legal" or "vehicle operator judgment rule," there is a similar cautionary "rule" sometimes invoked, especially in the medical malpractice field. This is the "honest error in judgment rule." A typical expression of the honest error in judgment rule runs along the following lines: "A [physician] is not a guarantor of a cure or a good result from his treatment and he is not responsible for an honest error in judgment in choosing between accepted methods of treatment."[24] The parallel between this language and the language in *Litwin* and in numerous similar invocations of the business judgment rule is evident.

c.   *The business judgment rule as protecting directors from liability so long as they act in good faith*

Other interpretations of the business judgment rule are far more significant than what we have encountered so far. Numerous courts and writers view the business judgment rule as providing a special standard of culpability against which to assess whether directors breached their duty of care. Unfortunately, these courts and commentators disagree on what this special standard is or should be. Worse still, several factors complicate any effort to delineate the respective views. For one thing, judicial opinions in this area are replete with imprecise and inconsistent use of language.[25] The result is that some opinions sound as if they are employing different standards, when, in fact, the courts really mean the same thing.[26] Alternately, some formulations may sound the same, but, in fact, embody quite different standards.[27] In addition, the different standards in this area range along a continuum, rather than representing discreet splits of authority. Nevertheless, it is possible to discern three major viewpoints which go a long way to define this spectrum. What ties them all together is that each holds that director liability under the business judgment rule requires greater fault than ordinary negligence.[28]

The most extreme view of the protection accorded by the business judgment rule comes from a number of courts and writers who consider the business judgment rule to command a largely subjective approach. The New York trial court's opinion in *Kamin v. American Express Company*[29] provides a good example of this position.[30] *Kamin* involved a

---

24. Ouellette v. Subak, 391 N.W.2d 810, 813 (Minn.1986).

25. *E.g.*, Meyers v. Moody, 693 F.2d 1196, 1209–1211 (5th Cir.1982) (referring interchangeably to negligence and gross negligence).

26. *See, e.g.*, Aronson v. Lewis, 473 A.2d 805, 812 n. 6 (1984) (listing different terms used by Delaware cases to embody a gross negligence standard).

27. *Compare* Aronson v. Lewis, 473 A.2d 805, 812 (1984) (referring to gross negligence as a less exacting standard of care than simple negligence), *with* Wallace v. Lincoln Savings Bank, 89 Tenn. 630,

652–53, 15 S.W. 448, 454 (1891) (referring to gross negligence as the failure to exercise ordinary care).

28. One other source of confusion is whether this special standard of liability applies to corporate officers as well as directors. *Compare* Platt v. Richardson, [1989–1990 Transfer Binder] Fed. Sec. L. Rep. (CCH) ¶ 94,786 (M.D. Pa. 1989), *with* Massaro v. Vernitron Corp., 559 F.Supp. 1068 (D.Mass.1983).

29. 86 Misc.2d 809, 383 N.Y.S.2d 807 (1976).

shareholders' derivative complaint against directors of American Express Company who approved distributing an in-kind dividend. This dividend consisted of shares of stock in another company, which American Express had purchased some years before as an investment and which had declined substantially in value. The plaintiffs contended that the directors should have sold the shares at a loss, rather then distributing them to the stockholders. In this manner, American Express could have obtained a capital loss deduction which would have saved American Express around eight million dollars in taxes.[31] The court dismissed the complaint as not stating a cause of action. In doing so, the court set out a standard of liability which, from all appearances, disclaims any objective review of the directors' decision:

> Section 720(a)(1)(A) of the Business Corporation Law permits an action against directors for "the neglect of, or failure to perform, or other violation of his duties in the management and disposition of corporate assets committed to his charge." This does not mean that a director is chargeable with ordinary negligence for having made an improper decision, or having acted imprudently. The "neglect" referred to in the statute is neglect of duties (i.e., malfeasance or nonfeasance) and not misjudgment. To allege that a director "negligently permitted the declaration and payment" of a dividend without alleging fraud, dishonesty or nonfeasance, is to state merely that a decision was taken with which one disagrees.[32]

In other words, unless the complaint alleged nonfeasance (inattention), the directors are off the hook barring fraud or dishonesty. What this means is that the court's review of a challenged decision focuses largely, if not exclusively, upon the subjective motivations for the action. While courts use a variety of terms to identify the pertinent inquiry—

---

30. The reader, recalling the earlier discussion of *Litwin*, may wonder how New York court opinions could provide such extremely different views of the business judgment rule. This illustrates that attempting to use the business judgment rule as a standard for breach of duty of care liability has produced as much or more intrajurisdictional confusion as it has interjurisdictional divisions of authority. *See also* Gearhart Indus., Inc. v. Smith International, Inc., 741 F.2d 707, 721 (5th Cir.1984) (discussing inconsistencies in Texas court interpretations of the business judgment rule).

31. From a tax planning standpoint, the board's decision made no sense. The American Express shareholders received a basis (the sum used in computing gain or loss for tax purposes on the disposition of property) equal to no more than the current fair market value of the stock at the time the shareholders received the dividend. Hence the dividend destroyed the potential for anyone obtaining the loss deduction on the

stock's pre-distribution decline in value. Nor apparently was the dividend tax-free to the recipient shareholders (as there is no indication that American Express owned enough shares in this other company for a tax-free spin-off). The board's rationale for the in-kind dividend evidently was to avoid recognizing a loss on the corporation's income statement, which might depress the price of American Express stock. This seems like the ostrich which sticks its head in the sand in order to pretend there is no danger. After all, the plaintiffs knew about the loss American Express suffered on this investment. Thus, it was unlikely that avoiding recognizing the loss on the corporation's financial statements kept the loss a secret. Besides, how legitimate is it for directors to attempt to bamboozle investors in the stock market (or avoid embarrassing the directors) by covering up bad investments? Accordingly, this decision seems no more reasonable than the action condemned in *Litwin*.

32. 383 N.Y.S.2d at 811.

such as the presence or absence of good faith, honesty or fraud—the heart of the matter is whether or not the directors believed what they were doing was in the best interest of the corporation.[33] Excluded from the inquiry for the most part is any review of the objective reasonableness of such a belief. Under this extreme interpretation, the result of the business judgment rule is to effectively abolish the duty of care for any situation in which the plaintiff challenges an action by the board. Instead, all that remains of the duty under this view is to avoid the sort of inattention and inactivity typified by cases such as *Francis*.

Actually, however, as stated earlier, views of the business judgment rule as a standard for duty of care liability form a continuum, rather than precisely defined positions. The cases following a good faith approach illustrate this point. Few unequivocally rule out any review of objective reasonableness. Instead, after proclaiming that directors' decisions are unassailable in the absence of bad faith, dishonestly or fraud, such opinions often fuzzy the picture by backpedaling in varying degrees. Some opinions, like *Kamin*, will supplement their holding limiting claims to fraud or bad faith with an alternate holding finding the directors' decision objectively reasonable (or, at least, finding that the plaintiff had not shown the decision was unreasonable).[34] Other opinions adhering to a largely subjective approach expressly leave the door open to finding liability in a truly egregious case despite good motives.[35]

d. The business judgment rule as establishing a gross negligence standard

One middle ground between ordinary negligence and the "good faith only" standard is found in Delaware. The Delaware Supreme Court has settled, at least since the mid–1980's, on the notion that the business judgment rule embodies a standard of gross negligence. Delaware's Supreme Court announced this position in *Aronson v. Lewis* by stating that: "While the Delaware cases use a variety of terms to describe the applicable standard of care, our analysis satisfies us that under the business judgment rule director liability is predicated upon concepts of gross negligence."[36] The Delaware Supreme Court subsequently reaffirmed this standard in *Smith v. Van Gorkom*.[37] While Delaware thus provides the clearest and most important expression of this approach, the gross negligence standard extends well beyond the Delaware courts.[38]

33. *See, e.g.*, Stern v. General Electric Co., 924 F.2d 472, 478 n. 8 (2d Cir.1991) (equating bad faith with an improper purpose).

34. *See also* Shlensky v. Wrigley, 95 Ill. App.2d 173, 237 N.E.2d 776 (1968)(the court held that the plaintiff had to allege that the directors' decision not to install lights in Wrigley Stadium at least "bordered on" fraud, illegality or a conflict-of-interest in order to state a cause of action against the directors; but the court then stated that the plaintiff's allegation that all the other major league baseball stadiums had lights for night games did not show the directors' decision was "negligent").

35. *E.g.*, Fielding v. Allen, 99 F.Supp. 137, 142 (S.D.N.Y.1951).

36. 473 A.2d 805, 812 (Del.1984).

37. 488 A.2d 858 (Del.1985).

38. *E.g.*, Deal v. Johnson, 362 So.2d 214 (Ala.1978).

This leaves the related questions of what exactly the gross negligence standard means and how is this different from ordinary negligence. One Delaware court opinion explained that "In the corporate area, gross negligence would appear to mean, 'reckless indifference to or a deliberate disregard of the stockholders' ... or actions which are 'without the bounds of reason.' "[39] The reader may be forgiven for finding such a definition less than entirely helpful. In fact, it is difficult to pin a precise meaning upon the term gross negligence. This has led some to suggest the term has no significance, or, put another way, gross negligence is "the same thing [as negligence] with the addition of a vituperative epithet."[40] Reinforcing this skepticism is the fact that it is not easy to find cases applying the gross negligence standard to directors' actions in which use of this standard, rather than an ordinary negligence test, unquestionably made a critical difference to the outcome.

A good example of the uncertain impact of the gross negligence standard lies in the Delaware Supreme Court's decision in *Van Gorkom*. Van Gorkom was the CEO of Trans Union Corporation. Shortly before he was due to retire, Van Gorkom negotiated a deal on his own to sell Trans Union to a company controlled by financier, Jay Pritzker. The deal took the form of a merger between Trans Union and a company controlled by Pritzker. The merger agreement gave each Trans Union shareholder $55 in cash for each share of stock in Trans Union owned before the merger. The merger required the approval of both Trans Union's directors and shareholders. The court found the directors of Trans Union Corporation liable for approving this transaction after only a two hour meeting, at which the directors relied upon a 20 minute oral presentation by Van Gorkom concerning the transaction and did not read the merger agreement or inquire into the basis for the agreed price. While the majority of the court found this to be gross negligence, a pointed dissent raises questions which lead one to wonder whether there was even ordinary negligence here. The Trans Union directors were highly sophisticated in business—for example, one director had been the dean of the University of Chicago business school, while other outside directors were CEOs of various corporations—and they were thoroughly familiar with the company. Hence, it is questionable whether the directors really needed additional time or advice to assess whether the offered price was a good one, especially when the price represented a substantial premium over the market price of Trans Union stock at the time (around $38 per share) and when the stockholders could always vote the deal down. In any event, regardless of who is right or wrong as to the result in *Van Gorkom*, this dispute makes it evident that the gross rather than ordinary negligence label had little impact upon the result.

Still, one should not dismiss the term gross negligence too quickly. Even if not amenable to precise definition, most individuals would have no trouble identifying the concept that gross negligence entails some

39. Rabkin v. Philip A. Hunt Chemical Corp., 547 A.2d 963, 970 (Del.Ch.1986).

40. Wilson v. Brett, 152 Eng. Rep. 737, 739 (1843).

worse level of dereliction than ordinary negligence. Actually, from a practical standpoint, the significance of a gross negligence test may be more a matter of altering statistical probabilities than of changing the results in any specific case. If enough fact finders in enough close cases are instructed they must find gross rather than ordinary negligence, there will be in all likelihood a greater number of defense verdicts.[41]

e. *The business judgment rule as creating a distinction between the review of process versus substance*

In thinking about the cases discussed so far, the reader might have noticed that there are two ways in which a plaintiff can attempt to show that directors breached their duty of care in making a business decision (or, put differently, there are two aspects of a decision which a court might review in examining whether the directors breached their duty of care): In *Litwin*, the challenge went to the substantive merits of the decision. The court found the decision itself unreasonable, because the purchase of the debentures exposed the corporation to risk without (due to the by-back provision) any offsetting prospect of reward. In other words, to put the matter crudely, the court thought this was an extraordinarily stupid agreement for the board to make. Note that we have very little idea in *Litwin* how the directors went about deciding upon this course of action. By contrast, in *Van Gorkom*, the plaintiff's focus was on the process the directors used to make their decision. The court condemns the directors for being grossly negligent in deciding to sell the corporation after only a two hour meeting in which the directors had not read the agreement, asked important questions or investigated the value of the company. In fact, however, we do not know whether $55 per share was a good price for Trans Union's stock; the court in *Van Gorkom* remands for a determination of this issue.[42]

This focus in *Litwin* and in *Van Gorkom* resulted from the way in which each plaintiff chose to prove the plaintiff's case. For example, the plaintiff in *Van Gorkom*, having discovered the sloppy manner in which the directors went about making their decision, presumably chose to emphasize the process, rather than argue the merits of a $55 per share deal. There is nothing, however, in either opinion which suggests the standard for the court's review would have been different had the issue involved the decision making process (in *Litwin*) or the substantive merits of the decision (in *Van Gorkom*). In fact, the gross negligence standard in Delaware comes originally from cases dealing with chal-

---

41. In fact, recent litigation concerning the liability of directors of failed financial institutions suggests there may be more significance to the gross negligence label than some critics thought. Otherwise, one would be hard pressed to explain the plethora of reported decisions involving the question of whether the FDIC may assert state law claims sounding in ordinary negli-

gence against directors of failed banks, or whether federal legislation limits such claims to gross negligence. *E.g.*, Atherton v. FDIC, 519 U.S. 213, 117 S.Ct. 666 (1997).

42. If $55 was a good price, there would be a breach of the duty of care, but no damages.

lenges to the substantive merits of director decisions, rather than to the process the directors used to make their decisions.[43]

Nevertheless, a number of courts and writers have come up with yet another interpretation of the business judgment rule, which focuses on these two ways in which plaintiffs might attempt to prove a breach of the directors' duty of care. This approach draws a distinction between the level of judicial scrutiny of the directors' decision itself, versus the scrutiny the court will apply in reviewing the process the directors used to arrive at the decision.

The American Law Institute's Principles of Corporate Governance provides an example of this approach. For the business judgment rule to protect a director from liability under the American Law Institute's Principles, the director must be "informed with respect to the subject of the business judgment to the extent the director ... *reasonably* believes to be appropriate under the circumstances," but the director must only "*rationally* believe ... that the business judgment is in the best interests of the corporation."[44] The distinction between "reasonable" and "rational" in the Principles is deliberate. The Comment which accompanies this section of the Principles explains that the rationally believes test gives greater protection to directors than would a reasonableness test. In essence, then, the American Law Institute's approach focuses the protective thrust of the business judgment rule on limiting judicial scrutiny of the substance of the directors' decision. As far as the process the directors use to reach their decision, or, more specifically, whether directors acted after gathering adequate information, the American Law Institute's formulation uses a standard of reasonable belief. This would appear consistent with the norm of ordinary negligence. When it comes to the substance of the directors' decision, however, the American Law Institute's proposed version of the business judgment rule lowers the standard of care to a rational belief. The American Law Institute's comments suggest this rational belief standard may be similar to an absence of gross negligence.[45]

There are a number of variations on this process versus substance theme. All have in common, however, the notion that the business judgment rule calls for less judicial scrutiny of the merits of the directors' decision than of the process the directors used in arriving at the determination. One obvious extreme is to conclude that the business

43. Specifically, the cases cited by the court in *Aronson* as embodying a gross negligence test looked to see if terms in the transactions approved by directors involved "gross overreaching" or the like. This presumably is why the court in *Van Gorkom* felt it necessary to state that gross negligence was "also" the appropriate standard to use under the business judgment rule in determining if the directors were adequately informed.

44. Principles of Corporate Governance § 401(c)(emphasis added).

45. The American Law Institute states in the comment dealing with its proposed version of the business judgment rule that the rational belief test is similar to the approach used by a number of cases applying Delaware law. As explained earlier, Delaware apparently employs a gross negligence standard both as to process and result. *E.g.*, Rabkin v. Philip A. Hunt Chemical Corp., 547 A.2d 963, 970 (Del.Ch. 1986). *But see* In re J.P. Stevens & Co., 542 A.2d 770, 780–81 (Del.Ch.1988).

judgment rule precludes any review at all of the substance of the decision. The opinion of the New York Court of Appeals in *Auerbach v. Bennett* [46] provides an example of this extreme.

Auerbach involved the decision of a "special litigation committee." Specifically, shareholders of General Telephone & Electronics Corporation brought a derivative suit against directors of the company and its outside accountants. The complaint alleged breaches of fiduciary duty in connection with so-called questionable payments made by the company to overseas public officials and political parties. In response, the board of GTE appointed a committee of three directors, who were not defendants in the derivative action, to determine what position the company should take regarding the suit. The committee, after some investigation, concluded the derivative suit was not in the best interest of the corporation and the corporation moved to dismiss. The Court of Appeals decided the appropriate response to such a motion was to apply the business judgment rule to the committee's recommendation. In dealing with derivative suits later in this book, we shall explore the issues raised by this approach to deal with the recommendation of these sort of committees. What is significant to the present discussion is how the court then interpreted the business judgment rule. The court held that the rule precluded any review of the substance of the committee's decision. The court explained:

> We turn then to the action of the special litigation committee itself which comprised two components. First, there was the selection of procedures appropriate to the pursuit of its charge, and second, there was the ultimate substantive decision, predicated on the procedures chosen and the data produced thereby, not to pursue the claims advanced in the shareholders' derivative actions. The latter, substantive decision falls squarely within the embrace of the business judgment doctrine, involving as it did the weighing and balancing of legal, ethical, commercial, promotional, public relations, fiscal and other factors familiar to the resolution of many if not most corporate problems. To this extent the conclusion reached by the special litigation committee is outside the scope of our review. Thus, the courts cannot inquire as to which factors were considered by that committee or the relative weight accorded them in reaching that substantive decision. . . . [47]

Instead, under the court's holding, the only review allowed—other than as to subjective good faith—was to the adequacy and appropriateness of the committee's investigative procedures and methodologies.

4.1.3   Why a Special Rule for Decisions by Directors?

We have just seen that a number of interpretations of the business judgment rule create a discontinuity between the treatment of corporate directors and the treatment of other individuals charged with breaching

---

46. 47 N.Y.2d 619, 393 N.E.2d 994, 419 N.Y.S.2d 920 (1979).

47. 47 N.Y.2d at 633, 393 N.E.2d at 1002, 419 N.Y.S.2d at 928.

their duty of care. If for no other reason than jealousy, it is useful to ask what policy justifies such a distinction. Why should directors not face liability for ordinary negligence just like everyone else? Over the years, numerous courts and writers have recited a variety of justifications for the business judgment rule insulating directors from liability for ordinary negligence. These rationales fall into four broad camps.

a. *Difficulties with after-the-fact review of business decisions*

The most traditional arguments for insulating directors from liability for ordinary negligence center upon the difficulties which can attend after-the-fact judicial review of business decisions.[48] These arguments often begin with the observation that business decisions involve taking risks, which inevitably means many decisions by directors end up producing a loss for the company. Yet, this observation is not inconsistent with the premises underlying the negligence standard. Specifically, the mere fact a decision involves taking risks or ultimately results in a loss does not make the decision negligent. Spinning off from Judge Hand's famous formula,[49] if the magnitude of gain expected from a board decision, multiplied by the probability measured ex ante of achieving the gain, exceeds the magnitude of loss risked by the directors' decision, multiplied by the probability of the loss, than the board's decision presumably is reasonable.[50] Accordingly, a negligence standard should neither deter directors from taking desirable risks nor punish simply bad results.

The problem, however, is that this sort of formula is easier to recite than actually to apply in an after-the-fact judicial proceeding. Such a proceeding is neither infallible nor cost-free. Rather, there is always the concern that a fact finder, with the benefit of hindsight, will confuse bad results with an unreasonable decision. Moreover, even if the defendant prevails, victory may come only after expensive litigation. Accordingly, without protection from liability for ordinary negligence, directors have

---

48. *E.g.*, Joy v. North, 692 F.2d 880 (2d Cir.1982); Melvin A. Eisenberg, *The Duty of Care of Corporate Directors and Officers*, 51 U. Pitt. L. Rev. 945, 963–4 (1990).

49. United States v. Carroll Towing Co., 159 F.2d 169 (2d Cir.1947)(liability depends upon whether the burden of prevention is less than the probability of the accident multiplied by the severity of the injury).

50. Put algebraically: if $Pg \times Mg > Pl \times Ml$ then the decision is reasonable (where Pg = probability of gain; Mg = magnitude of gain; Pl = probability of loss; and Ml = magnitude of loss). More realistically, there can be a number of potential outcomes from a business decision. In that case, the formula becomes: if $(Pg_1 \times Mg_1) + (Pg_2 \times Mg_2) + \ldots + (Pg_n \times Mg_n) > (Pl_1 \times Ml_1) + (Pl_2 \times Ml_2) + \ldots + (Pl_n \times Ml_n)$ then the decision is reasonable (where Pg_1 through Pl_n and Mg_1 through Ml_n are the probabilities and magnitudes of the various possible outcomes). This approach is perhaps simplistic because it treats any decision yielding a positive net expected return as reasonable without regard to how the expected return would compare with other investments of similar risk. Still, the point remains that there is nothing presumptively negligent about taking risks. One might also note that the Hand formula actually works better when dealing business risks than with accidents. With business risks, there is no need to put a dollar figure on the magnitude of loss from personal injury nor to consider whether one party's cost savings from neglecting accident prevention should constitute a socially acceptable excuse for injuring another party without paying compensation.

an incentive to avoid potentially more desirable higher risk activities in favor of less profitable but more sure fire undertakings.

Yet, does this argument distinguish business decisions from medicine, law or a myriad of other undertakings to which the standard of ordinary negligence applies? In fact, this line of reasoning is part of complaints by doctors and various other groups of prospective defendants, who assert the high cost of even a successful defense, as well as the propensity of fact finders to confuse bad results with negligence, have created a "malpractice crisis" and a need to reform the tort system. Hence, if one is to defend a business judgment rule which embodies a different standard of liability for directors, one must point to ways in which after-the-fact judicial review of business decisions poses greater difficulty than found in other areas. Specifically, we must ask whether there is a greater prospect for error in assessing the reasonableness of a business decision, and whether incentives to avoid risk create some greater harm when dealing with business decisions, then true in medicine, law or other activities subject to the standard of ordinary negligence.

Let us start by asking if there is a greater prospect that finders of fact will erroneously label a reasonable business decision as negligent, than there is that a finder of fact will make such an error in reviewing a medical or other decision subject to the standard of ordinary negligence. Defenders of an expansive business judgment rule like to point out that judges and juries generally are not business experts. Yet, judges and juries are not medical experts, or experts in innumerable other fields in which they must decide if a defendant was negligent—this is what expert witnesses are for.

If judicial expertise cannot justify different treatment, perhaps there is something about the nature of business decisions which renders review more problematic. A number of courts and writers have made the argument that business decisions are each unique, heavily intuitive and judgmental, which both undermines the accuracy of after-the-fact review and is not true of other fields.

There are a couple of difficulties with this argument. First and foremost, it is factually questionable. For one thing, the very existence of extensive formal business education would seem to be at odds with the notion that no norms guide the making of business decisions. Moreover, it would be a myth to suppose that medical or other professional decisions have been routinized down to the scientific application of accepted protocols. For example, most doctors will admit that significant percentage of their patients are "not in the book," by which doctors mean the patients' complaints and symptoms do not fall into any familiar categories of diagnosis and treatment. As far as the legal profession, one of the primary goals of law school is to prepare students to deal in situations where there is substantial uncertainty. Even in accounting, the California Supreme Court noted, not long ago, how auditing is a complex process requiring discretion and judgment at every stage.[51] In fact, law, medicine, business and other professions may be largely alike in that they involve a substantial degree of what one author has labeled "knowing in action," in other words, undertaking actions in unique situations based upon intuition and experience and without being able to articulate exactly why or how the professional is doing what he or she is doing.[52] To the extent this sort of intuitive "knowing in action" does not lend itself to an accurate after-the-fact judicial assessment of reasonableness, then perhaps there is a need to rethink the standards of malpractice generally. Be this as it may, the important point for present purposes is that business decisions do not represent a distinctly intuitive field in a way which renders them particularly inappropriate for judicial review; on the contrary, business decisions are very similar in this regard to decisions by other professionals.

Yet, even if it was true that business decisions are more judgmental and have less guidance for later reviewers than found in other fields, would this justify directors receiving added insulation from liability for ordinary negligence? To answer this question, it is useful to consider the area of legal malpractice. One part of legal practice which is especially intuitive and judgmental is trial strategy. What prospective jurors to excuse, what witnesses to call, what questions to ask (or not ask), what objections to forgo, what areas to emphasize in opening and closing, indeed what overall theory of the case to pursue, are all subjects upon which the attorney must exercise judgment guided in large part by intuition and experience (and often with little or no time for reflection). If, in fact, highly judgmental areas are particularly prone to judicial second guessing which confuses bad results with negligence, then one would expect such trial decisions to be the grist for innumerable legal malpractice suits. This is especially true given that trials inevitably produce losers, thereby providing a steady stream of prospective malpractice plaintiffs. Yet, challenges to trial decisions do not constitute the predominant source of legal malpractice claims and are rarely successful. It is not difficult to deduce why. The more judgmental and less subject to consensus a given decision is, the more difficult it is for the plaintiff to prove a given decision was unreasonable, much less that a different decision would have produced a better result.

The moral is to flag an important point missed by those who worry that a lack of accepted protocols or guidelines for business decisions will leave directors too much at risk under an ordinary negligence standard. This point is that a lack of guidelines for determining the reasonableness of actions hurts most the party with the burden of proof. This is the plaintiff. The experience with trial attorneys also suggests that an ordinary negligence standard would not mean directors will face a lawsuit every time they make a decision.

51. Bily v. Arthur Young & Co., 3 Cal.4th 370, 834 P.2d 745, 11 Cal.Rptr.2d 51 (1992).

52. Donald A. Schon, The Reflective Practitioner: How Professionals Think in Action 49–50 (1983).

Now, let us take a look at the impact of deterring directors from taking risks. After all, risk taking is important in business. Perhaps the harm resulting from deterring directors from taking risks is greater than the harm which occurs when the threat of malpractice liability deters doctors, lawyers or other prospective defendants from taking risks. Put differently, perhaps it is more important to encourage risk taking in the business context, than in these other fields. Be careful before making such an assertion in front of your doctor! In fact, anyone who has been through the experience of discussing surgery in a doctor's office comes to realize that medical treatment inherently involves taking calculated risks.[53] The same is true when deciding litigation and trial strategy and throughout much of the practice of law. Indeed, the concern that liability for ordinary negligence will deter directors from taking worthwhile risks sounds remarkably like the lament of doctors who complain that the threat of malpractice suits has forced them to engage in "defensive medicine" with the result of unnecessary increased costs and the avoidance of worthwhile but more risky medical treatments. Similar laments can be heard coming from lawyers and other professionals faced with liability for negligence. The concern about director liability and risk taking may well be valid. It is questionable, however, whether this problem is unique to directors.

b. Nature of the damages

A second group of arguments made in favor of a special standard of liability for directors focuses on the damages suffered by the corporation. Specifically, unlike medical malpractice or many other torts, which cause physical injuries, director gaffes cause only monetary loss. In addition, the potentially huge dollar losses which a director's decision could cause might deter individuals from serving on the board.

Yet, directors are hardly unique among prospective tort defendants in that their negligence is likely to cause economic loss rather than physical injury. To name one obvious group, the same could be said of attorneys. Neither is the concern about the size of damage awards unique to directors. Doctors and other professionals have repeatedly expressed similar concerns about the size of awards against them. Moreover, the threat that large awards will drive individuals from service on boards of directors finds its parallel among like claims that the cost of malpractice suits is driving individuals away from certain areas of medical practice or many small accounting firms out of auditing.

In any event, if draconian potential damage awards are the problem, the logical solution does not lie in fiddling with the standard of liability. Instead, it would be to put a limit on the amount of recovery. This, in fact, has been an approach followed by a number of states when dealing

---

53. While the ultimate decision as to treatment lies with the patient, typically the patient expects a recommendation from the doctor. Hence, it is unlikely that doctors normally can avoid exercising judgment through the device of giving their patients mini-courses in medicine and passing off the decisions.

with the concerns of doctors. We shall discuss later such caps on damages applied to directors.

c. Nature of the plaintiff

A third group of arguments in favor of less liability for directors centers on the nature of the plaintiff in a derivative suit. Several factors generally make the shareholder who brings such a suit into a less than sympathetic victim of any director negligence. To begin with, normally the shareholder voluntarily entered into the relationship with the directors. After all, no one forced the shareholder to buy his or her stock, and the stockholders as a whole were the people who elected the board. Accordingly, if shareholders do not like the way the directors manage their company, a solution is either to elect someone else or sell out. Further, according to currently popular financial theory, shareholders should protect themselves against the risks of mismanagement in any one company by holding a diversified portfolio of stock. Finally, as we shall explore later in dealing with derivative suits, the plaintiff in such a lawsuit often is a fairly nominal shareholder who is serving primarily as a front for an attorney pursuing the action for the sake of fees. This fact, in turn, raises suspicions that plaintiffs may bring actions alleging a breach of the duty of care on only a slender basis and when the suit is not in the best interest of the corporation.

Each of these arguments, however, has a number of shortcomings. The fact that shareholders entered into a voluntary relationship with the directors is not different from most situations involving malpractice claims. The same is generally true of patient with doctor, client with attorney, or in a host of other situations out of which negligence actions may arise. Indeed, in a number of contexts, such as law or accounting, privity (in other words, a voluntary contractual relationship) remains an important, if not necessary, factor in establishing any duty of care at all.

The argument regarding diversification is more sophisticated, but may not be more persuasive. To begin with, owning a portfolio of stocks only dilutes, but does not eliminate, the effects of mismanagement on the individual shareholder.[54] In addition, the ability to protect oneself from director negligence by diversification is not entirely unique. Medical and disability insurance cushion the financial risk from personal injury much as diversification cushions the loss from bad investments. Moreover, not every investor can or will hold an efficiently diversified portfolio of stocks. This is particularly the case when dealing with closely held corporations, when it is quite common for shareholders to tie up a substantial percentage of their wealth in the stock of one company. Besides, whatever one thinks of the acumen of numerous investors who

---

54. Diversification can only provide full protection against bad results from a director decision which had a net positive expected return (in other words, a decision which should not be considered negligent). In that case, the positive actual returns from those decisions which pan out should eventually more than offset the losses from those which, because of bad luck, fail. On the other hand, if directors negligently make decisions with a net negative expected return (as in *Litwin*), diversification can at best dilute the losses.

do not diversify, it seems questionable whether courts should gear rules of law to demand individuals follow a particular investment strategy. Most fundamentally, however, perhaps the diversification argument proves too much. Holding diversified portfolios also dilutes the individual stockholder's risk from any given company becoming the victim of breaches of contract by those the company does business with, of illegal trade practices by the firm's competitors, of tortious activities by those outside the firm, or of a host of other conduct which might harm and create a cause of action in favor of a corporation. Does anyone suggest the law abolish the ability of corporations to bring lawsuits, since their stockholders could always diversify to minimize such risks?

Finally, it is important to keep in mind that the business judgment rule can impact actions which are not shareholder derivative suits, such as when a trustee in bankruptcy (as in *Francis*) or even the corporation's elected management decide to sue. Accordingly, if there is a problem with abuse of shareholder derivative suits, maybe the answer lies in attacking the problem directly. We shall return to this prospect when we explore derivative suits later in this chapter.

d. *Utility of compensation or deterrence*

The final series of arguments made in favor of limiting the liability of directors for negligence—even, according to some writers, to the point of abolishing any claim for breach of the duty of care[55]—involves an analysis of the economic utility served by liability in this context. This analysis takes as a given the two goals often expressed for tort recovery: compensation and deterrence.

A number of writers have argued that director liability for negligence serves poorly the goal of compensating corporations injured by such negligence.[56] As a factual matter, recovery rarely comes from the negligent directors themselves. Rather, if there is a settlement, the corporation might seek to indemnify the directors. In this case, all one has accomplished is for money to go in a circle—from director to corporation and back to director. As we shall discuss later when exploring indemnity of directors, however, the answer here is not to have silly laws which allow corporations to indemnify directors for the very sums which directors agree to pay to the corporation. Alternately, liability insurance purchased by the corporation for its directors and officers commonly funds the payment directors must make to the corporation for breaching their duty of care. Yet, insurance—whose premiums come from the fees charged to patients or clients—commonly funds the payment of malpractice liability by doctors, lawyers and other professionals. Perhaps, it is wasteful for corporations, patients or clients to pay the extra transactions costs of a system which depends upon litigation and liability insurance to cover medical costs, legal problems and business

55. *E.g.*, Kenneth E. Scott, *Corporation Law and the American Law Institute Corporate Governance Project*, 35 Stan. L. Rev. 927, 937 (1983).

56. *E.g.*, Alfred F. Conard, *A Behavioral Analysis of Directors' Liability for Negligence*, 1972 Duke L.J. 895, 909–12.

reverses. Perhaps, it would be more efficient simply to rely on first party insurance. This is the idea behind various no-fault automobile accident compensation schemes. In any event, the problem with director liability in this regard is little different from criticisms raised about the fault system in general.

Other writers have questioned the necessity of director liability to deter directors from careless conduct.[57] They argue that a number of economic incentives other than fear of liability exist for directors to make careful and reasonable decisions. These incentives include stock ownership by directors in the corporation, compensation schemes which tie financial rewards to corporate performance, the desire of officers and directors to develop and preserve their reputations for business acumen so as to advance their individual careers, and the fear that poor decisions will make the corporation a takeover target and result in the current directors losing their positions.

Some writers have questioned the efficacy of these incentives.[58] For example, many of these incentives depend upon poor director decisions impacting the market price for the corporation's stock. Such a drop, in turn, lowers the value of shares owned by the directors, decreases the financial rewards under the common compensation schemes, such as stock options, which tie rewards to stock performance, and makes the corporation vulnerable to a takeover. This linkage might be absent in privately held corporations, where there is no active market for the company's shares. More broadly, the link between specific board decisions and stock prices in many instances might be sufficiently attenuated so as to undercut the efficacy of these incentives. Cynics might also suggest that career advancement within the corporate world depends in many instances upon a whole host of factors other than making good business decisions.[59]

In any event, the argument about other incentives for directors to make good decisions does not distinguish director liability from other contexts in which similar assertions could be made. For example, professionals often face market incentives for good performance. This may be most visible for trial attorneys, whose reputations often hinge upon winning. Another example may hit even closer to home for most readers. Consider the incentives automobile drivers have to drive carefully. While these lack the ring of "the market for corporate control," they would seem nevertheless powerful. Most significant could be simply the risk to the driver's personal safety of an accident. The sad truth, however, is that such incentives seem to be unable to eliminate either professional malpractice or reckless driving. There may be little reason to expect

57. *E.g.*, David M. Phillips, *Principles of Corporate Governance: A Critique of Part IV*, 52 Geo. Wash. L. Rev. 653, 673–682 (1984).

58. *E.g.*, Dierdre A. Burgman & Paul N. Cox, *Corporate Directors, Corporate Realities and Deliberative Process: An Analysis of*

the Trans Union Case, 11 J. Corp. L. 311, 355–57 (1986).

59. For a more extended discussion of market discipline on corporate management, see § 3.1.5*b supra*.

market incentives to fare better in eliminating careless director decisions.

e. *Testing the justifications in specific situations*

Perhaps the ultimate test of the various justifications of a special liability standard for directors is to examine whether they would be persuasive in distinguishing between directors and other defendants in specific contexts. Consider first the situation in *Van Gorkom*. One aspect of the case relevant here is the guidance the directors of Trans Union received from an outside counsel brought in to advise them on the proposed sale of the company. The attorney evidently did not warn the directors they were about to breach their duty of care by acting on the limited information before them. On the contrary, he purportedly advised the board they did not need an investment banker's fairness opinion regarding the proposed sale and, what is more, he stated they might be sued if they voted not to sell.[60]

These facts lead one to wonder what would have happened had either the directors or the shareholders sued this attorney for malpractice.[61] The standard against which the court would have measured the attorney's advice presumably would be the skill and care ordinarily possessed and exercised by attorneys in the locality. No court has ever suggested the business judgment rule would provide a defense for a corporation's outside counsel.[62] In contrast, the Delaware Supreme Court held that, under the business judgment rule, the directors of Trans Union could not be liable unless they were grossly negligent. Why the difference? Can any of the previously discussed justifications explain such a result?

To begin with, would after-the-fact judicial review of the attorney's advice pose any lesser problem here than did review of the directors' decision? The decision of what and how much legal advice to give is a question of judgment. In *Van Gorkom*, the attorney had to weigh the risk (ultimately realized) that he would fail to warn the directors of an action which would lead to their liability, versus the risk that by urging too much caution upon the directors they could lose the opportunity for a

---

60. The court characterized the attorney's purported advice as literally true. This was being too kind. Whether or not the advice was literally true, the failure to warn the directors that they were about to breach their duty by acting on inadequate information clearly raises the issue of malpractice.

61. Whether the appropriate plaintiffs would be the directors, the shareholders, or both raises the question of who the corporate counsel's duty runs to. For present purposes, however, it is unnecessary to resolve which party should sue, since the concern here lies with the standard for liability to anyone.

62. *Cf* Holland v. Stenhouse, 1991 WL 30138 (N.D.Ill.). In this case, the trustee for a bankrupt insurance company sued the former directors for breach of their duty of care. The trustee also sued the insurance company's attorney for legal malpractice for, among other things, failing to advise the directors on their duty. The directors moved to dismiss based upon Delaware's business judgment rule. There is no indication any party considered the business judgment rule at all relevant to the claim against the attorney.

highly desirable sale.[63] This substantially parallels the judgment the directors of Trans Union had to make. Indeed, it is difficult to see—especially given the narrow margin by which the directors lost this case,[64] as well as the general uncertainty in this whole area of law—how the attorney's decision would be much less intuitive and judgmental than the directors'. Litigation over whether the attorney negligently advised the Trans Union board would risk the fact finder confusing bad results (the board was held liable) with negligence, and would be expensive even if the attorney won. This prospect, in turn, creates an incentive for attorneys to avoid the risk of liability for themselves by always warning the client of any potential hazard.[65] The result of such a practice, however, is to undermine the utility of the attorney's advice to the client, who is left to figure out what warnings to take seriously. About the only thing one could say is that judges (at least in Delaware) might have some expertise in providing legal advice to corporate boards. Yet, expertise cannot explain a different standard here, witness the fact that had the board received poor advice from a professional other than an attorney—such as an opinion on valuation from an investment banker—the standard in a malpractice suit presumably still would not have been the business judgment rule.

If problems of after-the-fact judicial review would not justify different treatment of the lawyer in *Van Gorkom*, neither could the nature of the damages or the plaintiff. The damages faced by the attorney presumably would have been the same as faced by the directors he advised. Similarly, if the shareholders of Trans Union sued the attorney, there would be no difference in the plaintiff to explain the difference in standard applied.

Is there any difference in terms of the economic utility of compensation or deterrence? In a suit against either the directors or the attorney, compensation would come largely from insurance. While the attorney's policy would not have been purchased directly by the corporation, as were the directors', the corporation (along with the law firm's other clients) paid for the attorney's policy through the fees the attorney charges.[66] As far as deterrence, the attorney, like the directors, faces

---

63. The directors were meeting on Saturday; the offer expired Monday morning.

64. The Delaware Supreme Court's decision was 3–2.

65. This fear may, in part, explain why the attorney in *Van Gorkom* apparently gave the board the unfortunate advice that they might be sued if they voted not to sell.

66. Some writers have argued that directors are poorer "loss avoiders" than outside attorneys or accountants, because directors do not spread the loss over a large base of clients. *E.g.,* John Coffee, *Litigation and Corporate Governance: An Essay on Steering Between Scylla and Charybdis,* 52 Geo. Wash. L. Rev. 789, 802 (1984). Why

this makes any difference is obscure. Either director and officer, or legal malpractice, insurance spreads the loss. In either case, there is some "social accounting." In other words, the consumers, here the corporations, will pay for the injuries which may occur to themselves by virtue of the legal or managerial services they are buying—either through higher fees to cover the legal malpractice insurance or by directly paying for the directors' liability policy. Hence, in both cases, liability serves the same function of avoiding overconsumption of services which do not reflect their full cost. Moreover, liability for negligence has never been limited to enterprises able to disperse insurance

market incentives. After all, the mergers and acquisitions field is one in which a reputation for good results can dictate economic success for a lawyer. Conversely, one might suspect boards would be leery of hiring an attorney who previously led his clients into a well publicized fiasco.[67]

As a second test of these justifications, consider the following hypothetical. Suppose a corporation operates oil tankers. Due to a decision by one of the company's captains as to speed, course, or whatever, his ship runs aground resulting in an oil spill. If coastal property owners damaged by the spill sue the corporation, the issue will be whether the captain's decision was negligent. The corporation would hardly get anywhere by arguing for a "nautical judgment rule" under which it could avoid liability unless the captain acted in bad faith, or with gross rather than ordinary negligence, or which confined the fact finder to focusing exclusively or primarily upon the methodology by which the captain reached his decision rather than upon the decision itself.

Now suppose the corporation sued its captain to indemnify it for any judgment it paid the property owners or even for loss of the ship and cargo.[68] Again, the standard upon which the captain's liability will hinge is simple negligence. There appears to be little or no authority for applying the business judgment rule to accidents caused by corporate employees below top management.

To introduce the business judgment rule, let us add to the facts of the hypothetical. Assume that had the tanker possessed a double hull, it would have survived the grounding without a spill. Further, let us suppose the corporation's board of directors made the decision to purchase single rather than double hulled oil tankers. This is a business decision in which the board must balance the protective advantages of double hulled tankers against their added costs and lower cargo carrying capabilities. What will be the result if the damaged coastal property owners base their suit against the corporation on an allegation of negligence in not having double hull tankers? Again, the standard for liability would be simple negligence, not the business judgment rule. The same would be true if the damaged property owners sued the directors personally: Directors, as any other agent, are liable for their own torts, and courts do not apply the business judgment rule to suits by third parties against directors whose decisions have caused injury.[69]

Now, however, consider what would happen if the corporation sues the directors who decided against double hulls, either to indemnify it for

---

costs in the price of goods or services charged to a wide customer base.

67. The problem is not simply that the directors were liable. Business clients may appreciate attorneys willing to propose an aggressive position to achieve the clients' aims even though there is some risk of liability. Probably no one, however, appreciates being blindsided by facing liability without any warning.

68. *See* Gaffner v. Johnson, 39 Wash. 437, 81 P. 859 (1905)(the owner of a steamship sued the ship's captain he employed after the captain negligently collided with another vessel).

69. *E.g.*, Frances T. v. Village Green Owners Ass'n, 42 Cal.3d 490, 723 P.2d 573, 229 Cal.Rptr. 456, 465–466 (1986).

any payment to the injured property owners or for loss of the ship and cargo. This seems to call for application of the business judgment rule. The incongruities are striking. The same board decision about double hulls which a court would have no trouble scrutinizing under an ordinary negligence standard in a suit brought by third parties—either against the corporation or against the directors personally—suddenly demands the lesser scrutiny of the business judgment rule when the corporation brings the suit. Moreover, any qualms about the corporation suing those acting on its behalf fades immediately if the suit is against the captain rather than the directors.[70]

f. Reconciling the business judgment rule with statutory duty of care standards

Recall from our earlier discussion of *Francis* how the court found the applicable standard of care in the state's corporation statute. Numerous states have similar statutory provisions. For example, up until recently, Section 8.30 of the Model Business Corporation Act required a director to act "with the care an ordinarily prudent person in a like position would exercise under similar circumstances," and Section 8.30 still requires a director to act "in a manner the director reasonably believes to be in the best interests of the corporation." As we noted in discussing *Francis*, such language to the common lawyer's understanding is synonymous with the standard for ordinary negligence. This creates an apparent conflict when courts apply the business judgment rule to preclude director liability for ordinary negligence.

Courts and writers who interpret the business judgment rule to insulate directors from liability for ordinary negligence have dealt with this seeming contradiction in a couple of ways (other than just by ignoring it). One way is to interpret the statute as imposing a lower duty on directors. For example, a few judicial decisions have made their point of departure the fact that some duty of care statutes speak of the care of an ordinary prudent person "in similar circumstances," while other statutes speak of the care of an ordinary prudent person "in his own affairs." This has led these courts to conclude that a statute which speaks of care "in similar circumstances" does not create the same duty of ordinary care which the statute would if it spoke of an ordinary

70. The situation facing the Massachusetts Supreme Court in *Uccello v. Gold'n Foods, Inc.*, 325 Mass. 319, 90 N.E.2d 530 (1950), came tantalizingly close to creating such a paradox. Uccello, a minority shareholder in Gold'N Foods, sued the directors for mismanagement. Gold'N Foods manufactured salad dressing. Due to use of poor ingredients, Gold'N Foods suffered numerous complains and returns of spoiled dressing and ultimately went out of business. The directors knew of the problem but continued manufacturing without solving it. The court applied a gross negligence standard under its interpretation of the business judgment rule and exonerated the directors. Fortunately, the spoilage did not create a health hazard. Had the spoilage done so, then the Massachusetts court would have confronted the situation in which the same board decision would face review either under a gross or under an ordinary negligence standard—this case having arisen before strict products liability—depending upon who brought the action. Moreover, had an ordinary employee's negligence caused the spoilage, the business judgment rule presumably would not apply even to an action by the company against the employee.

prudent person "in his own affairs."[68] Specifically, under this view, a statute which requires the care of an ordinary prudent person "in his own affairs" creates liability for ordinary negligence, but a statute which refers to an ordinary prudent person "in similar circumstances" only creates liability for gross negligence.

There are a couple of problems with this distinction. To begin with, the notion behind finding a higher duty when the statute refers to the director's own affairs appears to be the rather strange idea that the ordinary prudent person should be less careful with other people's money than with his or her own. Moreover, to view the "in similar circumstances" language as somehow abrogating an ordinary negligence standard ignores the fact that such language, as we discussed when dealing with *Francis*, is an integral part of the reasonable person test, not a contradiction of it. Given these weaknesses in logic, it is not surprising that few, if any, recent decisions rely on this distinction.[69]

This has led to an alternate approach for many years alluded to in the Official Comment to Section 8.30 of the Model Business Corporation Act. The notion is that the corporation statute sets out the directors' duty of care, but does not address what impact breach of this duty will create. This omission, in turn, the argument runs, allows the courts to decide the rules for imposing liability. Hence, the courts can, consistently with the statute, apply a business judgment rule which insulates directors from liability despite the directors having fallen below the statutory mandate of reasonable care.

It is, of course, possible for legislatures to enact statutes setting out the duties of corporate directors with the expectation that courts will refuse to impose liability on directors who fail to carry out those duties. This would seem to be a rather queer and pointless exercise, however.

Apparently not satisfied with the result that the Act should set out standards with no consequence for their breach, the drafters of the Model Act recently embarked upon a new approach. To begin with, to get away from tort law terminology, the drafters amended Section 8.30 to remove language about an "ordinary prudent person." Instead, the standard of care in becoming informed or performing oversight is simply that of "a person in like position." Other than vaguely expressing the notion that the directors' duty of care differs from traditional negligence standards, it is not clear precisely what this change means. Specifically, in tort law, the ordinary prudent person concept encapsulates the idea that the law of negligence generally does not take into account the particular limitations of the defendant's mental capabilities. In other words, it is irrelevant that the defendant was too dumb to recognize the danger in his or her conduct, if an ordinary prudent person would

---

68. *E.g.*, Selheimer v. Manganese Corp. of America, 423 Pa. 563, 224 A.2d 634, 640–41 (1966).

69. *See, e.g.*, Keyser v. Com. Nat. Financial Corp., 675 F.Supp. 238, 255–58

(M.D.Pa.1987)(interpreting Pennsylvania statute using "under similar circumstances" language to create liability for ordinary negligence).

recognize the danger. If removal of the ordinary prudent person language from Section 8.30 is supposed to change this, then the result seemingly could be to alter cases like *Francis*, in which the defendant's attorney unsuccessfully asked the court to take into account that the defendant director was a depressed, drunk old lady. It is doubtful, however, the drafters of the Model Act intended such a result.[70]

Of more relevance to business judgment, Section 8.30 retains the requirement that directors must "reasonably" believe their actions are in the best interest of the corporation, and the Official Comment emphasizes that the requirement of a reasonable belief involves an objective standard—i.e. could "a reasonable person" believe that the action was in the best interest of the company. Moreover, the drafters have added a new Section 8.31 which states that directors can be liable for conduct which the director did not "reasonably believe" to be in the best interests of the corporation, or as to which the director was not informed to an extent the director "reasonably" believed appropriate in the circumstances. Hence, it now would appear that the Model Act addresses both standards of conduct and standards for imposing liability—and that both standards appear to call for a review of objective reasonableness. Nevertheless, the Official Comment to Section 8.31 retains the escape clause that the Act does not "automatically" establish liability for breach of the standard of reasonableness, and thus there is still room for the courts to apply the business judgment rule.

4.1.4 Causation and Damages

So far, we have discussed what it takes to show that directors or officers breached their duty of care. Liability, however, does not result simply from such a breach. Instead, we earlier saw how the court in *Francis*, applying familiar tort law principles, recognized that such a breach must be the cause of damage in order for there to be liability. In *Barnes v. Andrews*,[71] Judge Learned Hand—no stranger to students of tort law—applied this principle.

Barnes involved a corporation formed to manufacture engine starters. The corporation went bankrupt after squabbling among its managers delayed starting production. The defendant, Andrews, was a director of the corporation—something Andrews agreed to do as a favor to the corporation's president, who was Andrew's friend. Much like Mrs. Pritchard in *Francis*, Andrews paid little attention to the corporation, and the court held that Andrews breached his duty of care. Nevertheless, the court refused to find Andrews liable for the corporation's failure. The problem, in the court's view, was that the plaintiff produced no evidence that the corporation would have succeeded had Andrews recognized the

70. *See* M.B.C.A. § 8.30 Official Comment (Section 8.30(b)'s language does "not excuse a director lacking business experience or particular expertise from exercising the basic director attributes of common sense, practical wisdom, and informed judgment.").

71. 298 F. 614 (S.D.N.Y.1924).

company's problems and attempted to do something about them—in other words, the plaintiff did not prove causation.

More recently, the Delaware Supreme Court, in *Cede & Co. v. Technicolor, Inc.*,[72] took a very different approach. The facts in *Cede* are reminiscent of *Van Gorkom*. A dominant CEO pushed a compliant board to merge the corporation with little investigation. The trial court felt that the directors may well have violated their duty of care in so acting, but nevertheless gave judgment for the defendants. The reason was that the plaintiffs had not proven injury from the directors' action; in other words, the plaintiffs had not proven that, with more investigation, the directors would have rejected the deal or gotten a better one. The Delaware Supreme Court reversed this judgment. In doing so, the court employed a rather curious rationale. The Delaware Supreme Court expressly rejected the approach in *Barnes* as involving tort rather than corporate law principles. Instead, the court turned to the business judgment rule for guidance. As we discussed earlier, under any interpretation of the business judgment rule, directors are not liable for decisions unless the directors either breached their duty of care or were in a conflict-of-interest. As we shall see later, however, directors do not automatically face liability for entering a transaction in which the directors have a conflict-of-interest. Rather, the law generally requires the directors to prove that a conflict-of-interest transaction is fair to the corporation.[73] The court in *Cede* extrapolated from this approach to conflict-of-interest transactions that whenever the business judgment rule does not apply—either because of a conflict-of-interest or due to a breach of the directors' duty of care—to avoid liability, the directors must prove that their decision was fair to the corporation.

So, which court, *Barnes* or *Cede*, has it correct? Perhaps neither. The *Cede* court's rejection of tort law causation principles, in favor of a sort of reverse application of the business judgment rule, seems bizarre. Indeed, it appears to illustrate the power of the so-called business judgment rule to confuse courts. As we saw at the outset of this section, the concept of a duty of care comes from tort law. The causation element in torts reflects the common-sense notion that even parties who commit wrongful acts need compensate only parties actually damaged by the wrongful acts. As we discussed earlier, the business judgment rule in the eyes of many courts requires plaintiffs, for reasons of policy, to show more than ordinary negligence in order to prove that directors breached the duty of care. This, however, has nothing to do with proving causation. The *Cede* court focused on the so-called presumption entailed in the business judgment rule. As we discussed earlier, this "presumption" is nothing more than a statement that the plaintiff has the burden to prove either breach of the directors' duty of care or a conflict-of-interest— something we knew anyway. It does not logically follow that if the plaintiff rebuts the so-called presumption—in other words, proves breach

---

72. 634 A.2d 345 (Del.1993).   **73.** See §§ 4.2.1, 4.2.2 *infra*.

of the duty of care—the burden of proof on all other issues should shift to the directors.

What about the fact that the existence of a conflict-of-interest shifts the burden to the directors to prove the transaction is fair? As we shall discuss when considering conflict-of-interest transactions later, the concern with a conflict-of-interest transaction is that directors with such a conflict may take advantage of their positions to give themselves good terms at the expense of the corporation. Hence, a judicial review to see if the deal is fair to the corporation makes sense, and shifting the burden of proof on the issue to the directors provides a worthwhile protection for the corporation. By contrast, it seems somewhat strange to review the "fairness" of a transaction in a case in which the directors have no conflict-of-interest. We shall see later that courts generally determine "fairness" in the conflict-of-interest context by asking what terms a disinterested board would have approved. Yet, by this definition, we already know the transaction is "fair" when dealing with a duty of care challenge to action taken by a disinterested board. Alternately, we shall see later that "fairness" is supposed to create a more demanding standard than the business judgment rule. If so, then any transaction which flunked the business judgment rule for lack of care presumably should automatically flunk the fairness test.

Given the illogic in *Cede*, it is not surprising that a recent amendment to the Model Business Corporation Act expressly states that the plaintiff, in an action seeking damages against directors for breaching their duty of care, has the burden to prove that the directors' conduct was the "proximate cause" of the damage.[74]

On the other hand, the opinion in *Barnes* may be inconsistent with modern tort law notions, if not in the court's result, at least in some of its language. The problem becomes visible by asking exactly what the court wanted the plaintiff to prove. There are several reasons why, even if Andrews had paid attention, it might not have made any difference: As the court points out, he might not "have prevailed upon his fellows" (in other words, since Andrews was only one member of the board, the board might have disregarded his suggestion that the board do something). Alternately, Andrews and the board might not have been able to figure out a way to stop the delays in entering into production. Finally, even if the corporation solved the production problems, perhaps it would found an insufficient market for its starters.

Judge Hand makes a mistake in suggesting that the plaintiff, to show causation, must prove the defendant director would have been able to prevail upon the board to take action. Otherwise, each negligent director avoids liability by pointing to his or her fellow directors' negligence, and arguing that, as just one director, his or her breach of duty did not change the outcome. In fact, this is much like the classic tort case in which two defendants negligently cause two separate fires, each one of which spreads and alone would have burned down the

---

74. M.B.C.A. § 8.31(b)(1).

plaintiff's house. Under these circumstances, courts will not allow each defendant to avoid liability by pointing out that, even if he or she had not been negligent, the other defendant's negligence still would have caused the plaintiff to lose his house.

It is more difficult to say whether Judge Hand is too demanding in requiring the plaintiff to show that, had the whole board acted reasonably, the corporation would have been a success. After all, the defendant's negligence made this impossible to prove. Indeed, courts have relieved plaintiffs from the burden of proving causation in many tort cases in which the defendant's negligence has rendered proof of causation impossible.[75] Hence, there may be something to be said for the court's holding (if not its reasoning) in *Cede*. Maybe, negligent directors should have the burden to prove their carelessness did not change the end result.

The causation problem in *Francis* was somewhat different. The two dishonest sons were both the majority of the directors and owned a majority of the stock. Under these circumstances, what is a director (or a mother) to do? The court speculates that a protest would have deterred the sons. This, however, is pure conjecture. If Mrs. Pritchard resigned, what difference would that have made? Ultimately, the only sure way to stop the sons would be to sue. Yet, notice that the corporation conducted a personal service business dependant on the trust of its clients. Under these circumstances, legal action by Mrs. Pritchard against the sons presumably would have killed the business. After all, who would want to entrust money to persons under such a cloud? In effect, Mrs. Pritchard's choice was to destroy the corporation in order to save it. So, how did Mrs. Pritchard's inaction cause harm? The answer forces us to consider more carefully to whom does the corporate director's duty of care run.

4.1.5 To Whom Do Directors Owe a Duty?

Normally, we speak of directors owing a duty to the corporation.[76] This is a convenient conceptualization which produces the appropriate result in the large majority of cases. Essentially, what this means is that the directors should be seeking to maximize the profits of the corporation.[77] After all, the objective of a for-profit corporation seemingly is to make profits. Hence, in *Litwin*, the court found the directors negligent for exposing the corporation to a risk of loss in purchasing the debentures, without the corporation receiving the potential of profiting on the appreciation of the debentures to compensate the corporation for taking this risk.

---

75. *See, e.g.,* Haft v. Lone Palm Hotel, 3 Cal.3d 756, 478 P.2d 465, 91 Cal.Rptr. 745 (1970) (the court shifted the burden of proof on causation to the defendant, when a father and son drowned in the defendant motel's swimming pool, which lacked either a lifeguard or a warning sign).

76. *See, e.g.,* M.B.C.A. § 8.30(a) (requiring directors to discharge their duties in a manner they reasonably believe to be "in the best interest of the corporation").

77. *E.g.,* Principles of Corporate Governance § 2.01(a).

Occasionally, directors must make decisions in a context in which it is no longer adequate to speak of the directors owing their duty simply to the corporation. For example, in *Van Gorkom*, the directors faced the decision of whether or not to approve a merger of Trans Union under an agreement which would cash out the existing shareholders. It is difficult to say whether this would have increased or decreased Trans Union's future profits—this may have depended on the quality of whatever management Pritzker, the buyer in the deal, chose to install. Neither the directors nor the court evidently felt this was particularly relevant. Rather, in a transaction which essentially amounted to selling all of the existing shareholders' stock for cash, the question, as both the directors and the court in this case saw it, was whether this was a good deal for the shareholders—in other words, would the shareholders be better off receiving $55 now for each of their shares, or would the shareholders be better off by rejecting the offer in the hope of making more money by staying as shareholders? In order to accommodate this sort of analysis, courts typically expand the statement of the directors' duty to say that directors owe their duty to the corporation and its shareholders.[78]

Francis illustrates how even this expanded statement of the directors' duty may be inadequate in some cases. Actually, as the corporation's trustee in bankruptcy, the plaintiff was asserting the corporation's claim against Mrs. Pritchard. Yet, it is difficult to say that Mrs. Pritchard's inaction caused the corporation to go bankrupt. After all, as we discussed earlier, the corporation's business may have been pretty well doomed no matter what Mrs. Pritchard did. Moreover, the only shareholders were the two dishonest sons and Mrs. Pritchard herself. These facts led the court to hold that Mrs. Pritchard had a duty to the corporation's clients (whose losses she could have reduced).

The result in *Francis* forces us to ask when, if ever, should directors have a duty other than to maximize the profits of the corporation or to look out for the economic interests of the corporation's shareholders. Put differently, when should directors consider the interests of the corporation's creditors, customers, employees or the community in which the company operates? It has become common to refer to these other groups as "other constituencies." It turns out that this question has provoked some of the most long-standing debates in corporate law.[79] It also turns out that this is not really one question, but, rather, involves two inquires: (1) Do directors have a legally enforceable duty to these other constituencies? (2) If directors do not have a legally enforceable duty to these other constituencies, will directors breach their duty to the shareholders if the directors act in the interests of these other constituencies at the expense of the interest of the shareholders?

78. *E.g.,* Katz v. Oak Indus., Inc., 508 A.2d 873 (Del.Ch.1986).

79. *See, e.g.,* E. Merrick Dodd, *For Whom Are Corporate Managers Trustees?,* 45 Harv. L. Rev. 1145 (1932); A.A. Berle, Jr., *For Whom Corporate Managers are Trustees: A Note,* 45 Harv. L. Rev. 1365 (1932).

a. Do directors have a legally enforceable duty to other constituencies?

In *Francis*, the court held that Mrs. Pritchard had a duty to the corporation's clients. In finding such a duty, however, the court emphasized the unusual nature of the corporation's business. As a reinsurance broker, the corporation had a fiduciary duty to its clients, who entrusted the corporation with their money. Under these circumstances, it is not unprecedented to suggest that the company's fiduciary obligation to its clients carries through to create individual duties on the part of the company's officials, including its directors, to the clients. After all, in a law firm, one normally assumes that all of the individual attorneys employed by the firm (whether or not specifically assigned to represent a particular client) have a personal obligation to all of the firm's clients.

Normally, however, courts have refused to recognize that directors have fiduciary obligations to the corporation's creditors (or to other constituent groups beyond the shareholders). For example, in *Metropolitan Life Ins. Co. v. RJR Nabisco, Inc.*,[80] bondholders in RJR Nabisco sued to block a leveraged buy-out of RJR Nabisco. A leveraged buy-out involves using borrowed money to purchase the outstanding stock of a corporation. As we shall discuss later in this book,[81] it is possible to structure such a transaction in a manner in which the corporation itself becomes obligated to repay the loans used to fund the purchase. This is the transaction to which the board of RJR Nabisco—in record breaking transaction which became the basis for the book *Barbarians at the Gate*—agreed. The transaction dramatically increased the total debt owed by RJR Nabisco, thereby lowering the credit worthiness of RJR Nabisco's preexisting debt (including the bonds held by the plaintiffs). This, in turn, decreased the market value of the preexisting bonds. Among other claims, the bondholders argued that this transaction breached "something approaching a fiduciary duty." The court, however, rejected the notion that RJR Nabisco (or presumably its directors) owed the bondholders any fiduciary duty.

Why should directors not have an enforceable duty toward creditors and other constituent groups of the corporation? The answer which immediately pops into mind is that directors would then be unable to take actions in numerous cases without the fear that members of some constituent group will sue the directors, claiming the action prejudiced their group.[82] An attempt to raise prices presumably harms the corporation's customers. An attempt to trim wages or increase productivity might be contrary to the interest of the employees. Refinancing loans when interest rates fall is contrary to the interests of the creditors whose loans the corporation pre-pays. On the other hand, not doing these things may harm the shareholders.

80. 716 F.Supp. 1504 (S.D.N.Y.1989).

81. See § 7.2.1*b infra.*

82. American Bar Association Committee on Corporate Laws, *Other Constituen-cies Statutes: Potential for Confusion*, 45 Bus. Law. 2253, 2270 (1990).

A second rationale is that groups like creditors, employees and customers can protect their own interests by contract. Alternately, communities can protect their own interests (or the interests of employees, consumers and creditors) by regulating corporate conduct. Critics point out, however, that no contract (or regulation) can anticipate all of events which might occur during the course of a long-term relationship, such as exists between the corporation and its employees, between the corporation and its long-term creditors (such as bondholders), and even between the corporation and some of the corporation's customers.[83] Indeed, many writers have argued that the primary purpose of courts recognizing fiduciary duties is to avoid imposing on parties in long-term relationships the need to make impossible attempts at contracting for every contingency. Otherwise, why not insist that shareholders must protect themselves by contract, rather than looking to fiduciary duty?

In one circumstance, which may also fit *Francis*, however, courts have recognized a duty of directors toward creditors, rather than just toward the shareholders. This is when the corporation is insolvent (or even just closely approaching insolvency). Chancellor Allen, in *Credit Lyonnais Bank Nederland, N.V. v. Pathe Communications Corp.*,[84] gave the rationale for such a duty. He explained how the interests of the shareholders, and the maximization of wealth for the whole enterprise, diverge in this situation. The reason is not difficult to see. If the corporation is insolvent, in the sense that its assets are less than or equal to its debts, then losing further money essentially only harms the creditors and not the shareholders. On the other hand, any earnings in excess of the debts will go to the shareholders. Under this circumstance, high risk investments (like bets at a roulette wheel) make sense from the shareholders' standpoint. This will be true even though such investments have a net negative value (in that the magnitude of the possible loss from the investment, multiplied by the probability of the loss, exceeds the magnitude of the possible gain from the investment, multiplied by the probability of the gain). Hence, failing to recognize a duty to creditors here produces socially undesirable economic decisions. On the other hand, in the near insolvent situation, the creditors' interest is not entirely optimal either. Chancellor Allen noted how creditors might sacrifice worthwhile decisions in this situation to avoid a risk of non-payment, where the upside will go to the shareholders. Chancellor Allen's suggested solution is to view the directors' duty as running to the corporate enterprise—which brings us back full circle to where we started this discussion.[85]

83. Morey W. McDaniel, *Stockholders and Stakeholders*, 21 Stetson L. Rev. 121, 156–157 (1991).

84. 1991 WL 277613 (Del.Ch.1991).

85. We noted earlier one additional circumstance in which corporate directors or officers have a duty of care to persons other than the corporation or its shareholders. Corporate directors and officers have the same duty to avoid creating unreasonable risks of physical injury or property damage from their actions (including actions on behalf of the corporation) to foreseeable victims as does any other individual.

b.   To what extent can directors take the interests of other constituencies into account?

Just because the directors have no legal obligation to take the interests of other constituencies into account does not mean that the directors might not voluntarily do so. This raises the question of whether directors have the discretion to take into account the interests of other constituencies at the potential expense of the shareholders. *Dodge v. Ford Motor Co.*[86] is the classic case addressing this question.

The Dodge brothers were minority shareholders in Ford Motor Co. Henry Ford owned a majority of the outstanding stock and apparently dominated the board. Ford Motor Co. at this time was unbelievably successful. The corporation had huge cash reserves and was making money hand over fist. The board was declaring a generous regular dividend, and also had been declaring special dividends. The Dodge brothers sued after Henry Ford announced that the corporation would not pay any more special dividends, but, instead, would retain the extra earnings for expansion. As discussed earlier in this book, so long as the board does not exceed statutory limits, courts leave the declaration of dividends largely to the discretion of the board. *Dodge* is one of the rare cases in which a court found an abuse of discretion—largely based upon the fact that the corporation was making money faster than the directors could spend it on expansion, even if the board declared more dividends.

What is important about the case for present purposes is a side discussion the court undertook regarding the corporation's expansion plans. Statements by Henry Ford, both in and out of court, suggest that his reason for expanding the business was not to maximize profits, but, rather, stemmed from his desire to implement his economic and social views. Specifically, Henry Ford expressed the view that the company should lower the price of its cars and expand its production, not to increase profits, but in order to enable more Americans to own a car and to provide employment for more persons. Cynics might wonder whether Henry Ford actually cut the dividend because the Dodge brothers were using the money to start their own car company. Biographers of Henry Ford suggest, however, his statements were sincere. At this point in his life (before he got into fights with his employees), Henry Ford evidently had developed a certain grand view of his mission in life as the person to bring industrial prosperity to America. The court took a different view of the permissible goals of a business corporation. Such a corporation (as opposed to a corporation organized as a non-profit corporation) exists, the court explained, "primarily for the profit of the shareholders." The directors have great discretion in choosing the means toward that end, but the directors breach their duty if they act to change the end objective itself from profiting the shareholders to seeking to benefit others.

Actually, until fairly recently, the issue raised by the court's statement in *Dodge* had figured far more prominently in academic debates (both in the classroom and in print) than it had in the practical workings

---

86. 204 Mich. 459, 170 N.W. 668 (1919).

of corporate law. The reason is found in the court's holding. The court ordered the payment of a special dividend; but this was only because Ford Motor Co. had plenty of money both to expand and to pay the dividend. The court refused, however, to block the corporation's expansion plans, despite what the court had to say concerning Henry Ford's express motivations for those plans. The court felt that the expansion plans might serve a business purpose and refused to substitute the court's judgment for the business expertise of the directors.

The court's opinion in *Shlensky v. Wrigley*[87] is similar. A minority shareholder in the corporation which operated the Chicago Cubs baseball team sued to compel the directors to install lights at Wrigley Field. The plaintiff alleged that the inability to play night baseball games at Wrigley Field lowered attendance and resulted in the corporation losing money. The plaintiff further alleged that the reason the directors refused to install lights was because the majority shareholder, Philip Wrigley, believed baseball is a daytime sport and because of Wrigley's concern regarding the possibly detrimental effect of night games on the surrounding neighborhood. The court dismissed the complaint as not stating a cause of action. In response to the plaintiff's allegations concerning Wrigley's motives, the court speculated that it might be in the corporation's best interest to look out for the neighborhood, since the company owned real estate (the ballpark) there and since patrons might not wish to attend games in a poor neighborhood.

The practical upshot of cases like *Dodge* and *Wrigley* is that, by and large, courts have not scrutinized business decisions to see whether directors sacrificed profit maximization to advance the interests of employees, creditors, customers and the community. Instead, the courts almost invariably accept some rationale as to how the business decisions were in the long range interest of the shareholders. Indeed, even in those few cases in which outspoken individuals (like Henry Ford or Philip Wrigley) might ignore legal advice and express "profit be damned" sentiments, courts seem willing, on the court's own, to conjure up profit maximizing rationalizations for the directors' actions.

Moreover, it is not simply business decisions—such whether to expand production or to install stadium lights—which courts effectively have immunized from allegations that the directors decided upon these actions to advance the interests of constituencies other than the shareholders. We saw earlier, in discussing complaints that corporate charitable giving was ultra vires, how courts could hypothesize long-range shareholder benefits from corporate charitable gifts.[88] In any event, we also saw in discussing the ultra vires issue with charitable gifts, how the state legislatures, not wishing to play "Grinch," enacted provisions in corporation statutes expressly empowering corporations to make charitable contributions.

87. 95 Ill.App.2d 173, 237 N.E.2d 776 (1968).

88. See § 3.1.4b *supra*.

The corporate takeover battles of the 1980s brought renewed attention to the question of whether directors can sacrifice maximum gain for the shareholders in order to look out for the interests of other constituencies. We can use the facts in *Van Gorkom* to illustrate why. Recall that the transaction in *Van Gorkom* essentially consisted of the existing stockholders in Trans Union selling their shares for cash. The focus of the directors' decision was on whether this was a good deal for the shareholders. The Trans Union directors apparently did not consider the impact of the deal on other constituencies. For example, the transaction evidently involved a leveraged buy-out. As we saw before in discussing *RJR Nabisco*, such a buy-out may impact the credit worthiness, and hence the market value, of the corporation's bonds, thereby harming the existing creditors. Also, perhaps the buyer, Pritzker, intended to lay off some of Trans Union's employees. Perhaps Pritzker also planned to make changes in Trans Union's operations which would impact detrimentally the company's customers and the communities in which the company did business. Could the directors of Trans Union have rejected the offer because of such concerns? Notice, in this event, it would be much more difficult to argue that protecting other constituencies is in the long-run best interest of the existing shareholders, since, under the deal, the shareholders are selling out.

In a couple of opinions, the Delaware Supreme Court addressed the question of whether directors breach their duty if they seek to prevent a corporate takeover in order to protect the interests of constituencies other than the shareholders. We shall have occasion to discuss these opinions in more detail when dealing with takeover defenses later in this book. The result of these opinions has been to leave Delaware law less than entirely clear. In *Unocal Corp. v. Mesa Petroleum Co.,*[89] the Delaware Supreme Court stated that, in deciding to oppose a takeover bid, the directors could consider the impact of the bid on constituencies other than the shareholders. This includes, according to the court, creditors, customers, employees, and "perhaps even the community generally."[90] Nine months later, however, in *Revlon, Inc. v. MacAndrews & Forbes Holdings, Inc.,*[91] the same court rejected the directors' other constituencies rationale for favoring one takeover bid over another. The board argued that the favored bid protected the holders of certain promissory notes issued by the corporation better than did the disfavored bid. In rejecting this rationale, the court qualified the statement in *Unocal* about considering other constituencies. This is permissible, according to the *Revlon* opinion, only to the extent there are rationally related benefits accruing to the shareholders. In other words, we are evidently back to the notion that one must rationalize looking out for other constituents as ultimately benefitting the shareholders. Needless to say, such a rationalization is impossible in a situation in which the directors are choosing between two buyers in auctioning off the company.

89. 493 A.2d 946 (Del.1985).   **91.** 506 A.2d 173 (Del.1985).

90. *Id.* at 955.

State legislatures also reacted to the impact which corporate take-overs can have on other constituencies. Numerous states enacted provisions empowering directors, in making decisions for the corporation, to take into account the interests of the corporation's employees, customers, creditors, suppliers and the communities in which the company has facilities.[92] Some statutes go beyond these obvious constituencies to allow directors to consider broader economic and social concerns. For the most part, these statutes simply grant the directors discretion to consider these other constituencies; albeit, at least one state's law requires the directors to consider such impacts. In any event, none of these statutes expressly grant members of these other constituencies a cause of action against directors who do not take the constituencies' interests into account. To forestall courts from interpreting these statutes consistently with the *Revlon* approach—in other words, taking the view that directors must justify concerns for other constituencies by finding long-range shareholder benefit—several of the statutes make it clear that directors need not give primacy to shareholder interests. While largely motivated by the impact of corporate takeovers, these statutes generally are not limited to that context.

Other jurisdictions have resisted this trend. Most notably, Delaware has not enacted such a provision, and the American Bar Association Committee on Corporate Law expressly rejected the idea of adding such a provision to the Model Business Corporation Act.

Why has there been such controversy over whether directors have discretion to consider the effects of corporate decisions on employees, customers, creditors and the community, even if this means not always maximizing profits for the shareholders? After all, opposing such discretion seems a little like opposing "mom and apple pie." As a society, we applaud the business which is good to its employees, its customers, its creditors and the community. By contrast, the businessperson who is concerned only with profits rates a Christmas eve visit from "Marley's ghost."

Many individuals might be tempted to respond to this position by arguing that the shareholders are the owners of the corporation. Hence, the directors should be working for the owners and not sacrificing the interests of the shareholders to the interests of others. Yet, the distinction between the so-called "owners" of the corporation, this is to say the shareholders, and "non-owners," such employees and creditors, may be inconsistent with modern economic theory. Rather, shareholders, employees, suppliers and creditors all contribute inputs (money, property, labor) to the enterprise and all make a claim against some of the corporation's earnings. In other words, each such party is a "stakeholder" or "claimant." The only difference is that the shareholders are the "residual claimants," in other words, shareholders get what earnings are

92. For a discussion of these statutes, see *Other Constituencies Statutes, supra* note 82.

left over after all the other claimants receive payment. Given this viewpoint, we must ask why should the status as residual claimants entitle the shareholders to demand that the directors make the shareholders' interests always trump the interests of other stakeholders or claimants. Why not, instead, allow directors to mediate between the competing stakeholders to come up with decisions which are fair to all?

One response is that the interest of the residual claimant is most consistent with the interest of wealth maximization for the overall enterprise.[93] In other words, since the shareholders stand last in line to obtain assets from the corporation, the first dollar of corporate loss comes out of their pockets. Also, since the shareholders get everything made by the corporation after paying the other claimants, the last dollar of profit goes into their pockets. Hence, looking out for the shareholders' interests forces the directors to focus on the effect of the directors' decisions at the margin—in other words, invest until the next possible dollar of gain multiplied by the probability of obtaining it is less than the next possible dollar of loss multiplied by the probability of incurring it—which, in turn, produces the wealth maximizing or efficient result for the whole venture.

In fact, however, it is not true that decisions in the shareholder's interest are necessarily in the interests of wealth maximizing for the whole endeavor.[94] For example, we discussed earlier how this would not be the case for the corporation near insolvency.

A more typical criticism made against a rule which would allow directors the discretion to take into account the interests of other constituencies is that such a rule makes directors less accountable to anyone for the directors' decisions. In other words, such a rule gives the directors an unwarranted second chance to save decisions which fail to pass muster when looked only from the standpoint of corporate and shareholder profit maximization. One suspects in many cases the argument that the directors made the decision in the interest of another constituency might be an after-the-fact rationalization for a decision made for other reasons all together. For example, directors who oppose a takeover because of concerns with their own positions can use the interests of employees or creditors as an excuse for opposing a takeover. Alternately, directors who just made a dumb mistake might point to the interests of other constituencies as an after-the-fact reconstruction of what they were attempting to achieve. Moreover, allowing the directors to sacrifice shareholder interests for the interests of other constituencies raises the inevitable and unanswerable question as to how much of such a sacrifice can the directors force the shareholders to make. Presumably, there should be some limit other than conscience of the directors. Yet, it is difficult to articulate any basis upon which to draw such a limit.

93. *E.g.*, Frank H. Easterbrook & Daniel R. Fischel, *Voting in Corporate Law*, 26 J.L. & Econ. 395 (1983).

94. *E.g.*, Jonathan R. Macey, *An Economic Analysis of the Various Rationales* *for Making Shareholders the Exclusive Beneficiaries of Corporate Fiduciary Duties*, 21 Stetson L. Rev. 23 (1991).

Still, as a practical matter, the concern with removing director accountability may be overblown. After all, we saw above how the business judgment rule in many jurisdictions results in a highly deferential review of director decisions in any event. Moreover, as *Dodge* and *Schlensky* show, generally directors can come up with shareholder interest rationalizations for looking out for other constituencies. Hence, it is difficult to say how much less accountability will result if the directors can be up-front in their willingness to consider the interests of other constituencies. Besides, directors are human beings. As such, we cannot expect them to check their consciences at the door when they enter the board room. Directors often are going to try to do the "right thing" vis-a-vis the corporation's employees, creditors, customers and the community, just as proprietors or partners often do. Thus, a rule which requires directors to act purely as profit maximizers is unenforceable.

4.1.6   *Illegal Actions*

The desire to protect various constituencies impacted by corporate action—particularly the community in general—leads us into the subject of director and officer liability for approving illegal corporate activities. After all, one way to protect groups impacted by corporations is by regulating corporate actions, rather than by placing broader boundaries on the directors' general duties.

We can start our discussion of this topic with two well-established propositions. To begin with, corporate directors and officers who violate laws, including by ordering the corporation to break the law, face the sanctions which the particular law imposes on those who violate it.[95] For example, if a corporate director or officer has the corporation enter a conspiracy to fix prices, the officer or director personally is subject to a fine or imprisonment for breaking the antitrust laws.

In addition, it is unheard of for a court to suggest that a director or officer could possibly breach his or her duty to the corporation by refusing to have the corporation engage in illegal activity. In other words, there may be situations in which, from a purely profit maximizing standpoint, it might make sense for a company to disobey a law. This would occur if the profits the corporation could make from engaging in the illegal conduct, multiplied by the probability of not getting caught, exceeded the sanctions the company would face under the law, multiplied by the probability of getting caught in the illegal conduct. Even so, it is difficult to conceive that a court would hold that directors or officers breached their duty to the corporation if they refuse to have the company go ahead and break the law.

Things get tricky, however, when a shareholder sues directors or officers, claiming that the directors or officers breached their duty to the corporation by ordering the company to engage in illegal conduct (or, as

---

95. *E.g.*, M.P.C. § 2.07(6)(a). Indeed, some states' criminal statutes contain express provisions which make it clear that a person who performs, or causes to be performed, a criminal act on behalf of a corporation is responsible to the same extent as if he or she engaged in the act on his or her own behalf. *E.g.*, N.Y. Penal Law § 20.25.

in *Graham*, by not preventing the corporation from engaging in such conduct). Should courts treat such a decision the same as any other decision made by directors or officers—in other words, should a plaintiff need to prove that the directors or officers did not reasonably investigate the decision or could not rationally believe that the decision was in the best interest of the corporation—or, does the mere fact that directors or officers decided to have the corporation engage in illegal conduct make the decision a violation of the directors' or officers' duty to the corporation?

In *Miller v. American Telephone & Telegraph Co.,*[96] the court held that authorizing illegal corporate conduct, in itself, could violate a director's fiduciary duty. *Miller* involved a complaint filed against the directors of AT & T. The complaint alleged that the directors breached their duty to AT & T by not having the corporation attempt to collect a $1.5 million unpaid telephone bill incurred by the Democratic National Committee.[97] The district court dismissed the complaint as precluded by the business judgment rule, but the court of appeals reversed. The complaint evidently did not contain any allegations of careless process in deciding not to pursue the bill; nor did the complaint allege the decision was irrational. Instead, the complaint alleged that the forgiveness of the debt constituted an illegal campaign contribution. The court of appeals held that this stated a cause of action. In other words, if the reason for not pursuing the debt was to aid the Democratic election campaign (which would violate campaign finance laws), rather than because the Democrats lacked sufficient assets to make a collection effort worthwhile, then the directors would have breached their duty to AT & T.

This, however, leads us to ask why should having the corporation engage in illegal activity, in and of itself, breach the directors' or officers' duty to the corporation. It may not be enough to answer that such conduct exposes the corporation to sanctions for breaking the law. After all, it may be that what the corporation could gain through the violation exceeds the loss the sanctions will entail, when discounted for the probability that the corporation will get caught.

In *Miller*, the court stated that Congress enacted the campaign finance statute involved in the case in part for the protection of shareholders (who might oppose a candidate to which their corporation contributed). Hence, a corporate remedy made sense in this particular case, but might not for most illegal acts. A broader reading of *Miller*, however, is possible. In support of its result, the court in *Miller* cited opinions in which New York courts held that directors or officers who had the corporation pay bribes,[98] or violate labor laws,[99] breached their duty to the corporation.

---

96.   507 F.2d 759 (3d Cir.1974).

97.   The bill was for telephone services at the infamous 1968 Democratic National Convention in Chicago.

98.   Roth v. Robertson, 64 Misc. 343, 118 N.Y.S. 351 (1909).

99.   Abrams v. Allen, 297 N.Y. 52, 74 N.E.2d 305 (1947).

One explanation for these results is to return to the ultra vires doctrine. Recall that the broadest statement of a corporate purpose would be to conduct "any lawful business." Accordingly, one could argue that an illegal activity would be ultra vires. As we discussed earlier in this book when dealing with the ultra vires doctrine, courts have long since rejected the notion that the law cannot hold a corporation responsible for an illegal act, since it was ultra vires for the corporation to do it.[100] Nevertheless, the notion that illegal acts are ultra vires could still apply for the purpose of holding corporate officials liable on the grounds that agents, who have a corporation engage in an ultra vires activity, are liable for any damages the corporation suffers as a result.

Still, this sort of formalistic reasoning might not be fully persuasive. The New York cases cited in *Miller* suggest that the reason for the result is found in public policy. It seems morally reprehensible for directors to defend having the corporation violate the law as simply a "business judgment." Also, allowing corporate recovery adds to deterrence. Yet, to sanction a corporate recovery for such conduct seems to be a bit of "piling on." After all, whatever criminal or regulatory statute the officers or directors had the corporation violate no doubt contains its own sanctions for both the corporation and the offending officers or directors. If this is not enough deterrence, perhaps the answer is to increase the sanctions in the statute, rather than to allow a corporate recovery from the directors or officers involved.

Perhaps we can find a more persuasive argument for corporate recovery against its officials who have the company engage in unlawful acts. To do so, let us turn upside down the policy argument that courts should allow recovery in order to increase deterrence. Suppose, instead, courts presume that legislatures know what they are doing and that, therefore, regulatory and criminal statutes provide sufficient penalties to deter reasonable individuals from violating the law. True, no matter how draconian the penalty, people break laws. This, however, might simply show that many persons are not reasonable, but, instead, make unrealistic assessments as to the likely risk of being caught. Once, a court makes the presumption that the legislature knew what is was doing in setting sanctions, it inevitably follows that any officer or director acts unreasonably in exposing the corporation to the risk of such sanctions, and, therefore, breaches his or her duty of care. Put another way, if the business judgment rule reflects the notion that courts should defer to the business expertise of directors, treating violations of law as a per se breach of the duty of care reflects deference to the sanction setting expertise of the legislature.

4.1.7 *Exoneration by Statute and Charter Provision*

The *Van Gorkom* decision we discussed above came as quite a shock to the corporate world. For a court to hold that distinguished business leaders breached their duty of care and could be liable for millions of

---

100. See § 3.1.4a *supra.*

dollars in damages was not something which had happened much before. At about the same time, insurance policies covering directors and officers for breaching their duty of care became more expensive and less available. In part, this may have reflected greater perceived risk as a result of the *Van Gorkom* decision; in part, it may have reflected other factors in the insurance industry. The upshot was to lead to pressure on state legislatures to enact statutes curbing the potential liability of directors for breaching their duty of care.

State legislatures enacted several types of statutes in response to this pressure for protection. The most common type first appeared in Delaware. The Delaware legislature amended Section 102 of the Delaware General Corporation Law, which deals with the contents of certificates of incorporation. The amendment (encompassed in Section 102(b)(7)) expressly allows certificates of incorporation to include provisions which limit the liability of directors for breaching the duty of care. Statutes such as Delaware's Section 102(b)(7) are sometimes referred to as charter option statutes.

There are several items worth noting about statutes such as Delaware's Section 102(b)(7). To begin with, Delaware's Section 102(b)(2) only allows the certificate to contain a provision limiting the directors' liability for monetary damages. It does not speak of limiting the ability of a court to grant equitable relief. Hence, shareholders, who act rapidly enough, still might be able to have a court block board action which the shareholders can show violated the directors' duty of care. Alternately, shareholders still might assert breaches of the directors' duty of care in lawsuits seeking to compel directors to undertake structural reforms (such as monitoring for price fixing, as the plaintiffs suggested in *Graham*).

Next, Delaware's Section 102(b)(7) only speaks of the liability of directors. It does not authorize provisions to limit the liability of corporate officers. This raises an interesting question when dealing with an individual who is both a corporate officer and director: Can this individual still be liable for actions taken in his or her role as an officer? The Delaware Supreme Court's answer is that liability can still exist for a person who is both a director and an officer, despite an article provision authorized by Section 102(b)(7), only if the person undertook the challenged action solely in his or her role as an officer and not also as a director.[101]

In addition, Delaware's Section 102(b)(7) only addresses liability to the corporation or its stockholders. To the extent a court is willing to find directors have a duty to creditors, which creditors can enforce in their own right, or if directors personally committed a tort damaging a third party, the directors might still be liable.

The most significant portion of Delaware's Section 102(b)(7), and similar statutes, however, is the list of claims which the statutes do not

101. Arnold v. Society for Savings Bancorp, Inc., 650 A.2d 1270 (Del.1994).

allow the certificate to waive. In fact, while the aim of these statutes generally is to curb duty of care claims, the statutes do not directly refer to the duty of care. Rather, the statutes start with a broad reach—allowing certificates to limit directors' liability for "breach of fiduciary duty," to use the language in Delaware's law. The statutes then list various claims which the certificate cannot waive. This includes, under Delaware Section 102(b)(7):

(1) breach of the duty of loyalty;

(2) actions not in good faith;

(3) intentional misconduct;

(4) knowing violation of law;

(5) declaring dividends in excess of statutory limits; and

(6) transactions in which directors received an improper personal benefit.

Given the significance of these exceptions, one might have expected an extra effort to be clear in drafting this list. Unfortunately, however, this list is rather sloppy. Specifically, what exactly is the difference between breaches of the duty of loyalty, actions not in good faith, intentional misconduct, and transactions in which directors receive an improper personal benefit? The normal rule of statutory interpretation calls for courts to give independent significance to each category. Yet, as we shall see later when discussing the duty of loyalty, the essence of breaching the duty of loyalty involves improperly gaining a personal benefit at the expense of the corporation. Actions improperly favoring one's own interests over the corporation's also show bad faith and are intentional.

It is also worth noting that, in some cases, courts have not been able to draw a bright line between violations of a director's duty of loyalty versus breaches of other fiduciary duties. This has been an especial problem when dealing with efforts by directors to maintain themselves in power by opposing a tender offer. Statutes such as Delaware's Section 102(b)(7) might force courts to resolve the issue they had heretofore successfully avoided: Do actions which impermissibly entrench the board constitute duty of care or duty of loyalty violations?[102]

The charter option provision in Section 2.02(b)(4) of the revised Model Act attempts to avoid some of the ambiguity resulting from the repetitive drafting in Delaware Section 102(b)(7). The Model Act provision is largely the same as Delaware's, except that the Model Act deletes the exceptions for duty of loyalty breaches and actions not in good faith. Since the financial benefit and intentional harm exceptions substantially overlap the duty of loyalty and good faith exceptions anyway, there is not too much substantive difference between Delaware Section 102(b)(7) and the Model Act.

---

102. Breaches of disclosure obligations might create similar problems in determining whether the claim involves the duty of loyalty or the duty of care. *E.g.*, Arnold v. Society for Savings Bancorp, Inc., 650 A.2d 1270 (Del.1994).

The basic policy reflected in charter option statutes is that the shareholders of a corporation ought to be able to agree to waive the liability of the corporation's directors for breaching the directors' duty of care. Actually, the idea of persons agreeing prospectively to waive their right to sue for negligence is neither a new idea nor an idea limited to corporate law. In confronting such negligence waivers in other contexts, courts have been concerned that the plaintiff, in fact, agreed to waive negligence claims,[103] and that the agreement did not reflect unacceptable coercion.[104] These same concerns are also the point of contention when debating the wisdom of charter option statutes. Critics of such statutes worry that shareholders might vote to limit director liability without understanding the impact of the vote (especially since it is typically not worthwhile for the small shareholder in a widely held company to spend much time delving into the proxy materials he or she receives).[105] Alternately, shareholders might be under some coercion to vote for the limitation (perhaps because the directors proposing the limitation packaged it in a combination with some action desired by the shareholders). Moreover, since the holders of a majority of the shares have the power to amend the corporation's articles or certificate, minority shareholders can lose the ability to assert claims, even though the minority shareholders voted against the limitation. This is especially troubling if many of those voting for the limitation have a side agenda for doing so (as would occur if the corporation's directors own a significant portion of the outstanding stock).

These concerns with shareholder consent are not limited, however, to charter provisions waiving duty of care liability. They can apply with equal force to shareholder approval of charter amendments, mergers, or other corporate actions which might waive or otherwise impact rights of shareholders. Hence, it is fair to ask why should the law single out duty of care liability as not subject to charter provision. Perhaps one difference is that it may be more difficult for shareholders to assess the significance of waiving future duty of care claims than it is to consider the impact of making present changes in financial or voting rights.

Actually, most of the shareholders likely to be affected by article provisions limiting the liability of directors probably never even will have had the opportunity to vote on the provision. Rather, most persons who are stockholders when the duty of care breach occurs, in all likelihood, will have purchased their stock after the adoption of the article provision. Given the constant turnover in shares in a publicly traded corporation, this is likely even when the limitation enters the articles by amendment, rather than upon the original corporate formation. For such later acquiring stockholders, one might argue that stockholders individually agreed to the waiver by virtue of purchasing their shares. Of course,

103. This might be a concern when the negligence waiver appears in fine print on the back of a claim ticket.

104. As, for instance, might exist when a hospital presents the waiver as part of the admitting documents to gain service at an emergency room.

105. *See, e.g.,* Melvin A. Eisenberg, *The Structure of Corporation Law,* 89 Colum. L. Rev. 1461, 1478 (1989).

most folks who buy stock never read the articles of incorporation. Assuming that securities markets are efficient, however, the price of stock should reflect the terms of the articles. Indeed, there is some evidence that investors have discounted the price they are willing to pay for stock in Delaware corporations which have amended their certificates along the lines allowed under Section 102(b)(7).[106]

Having gone this far, one might ask, why should there be any constraints in statutes such as Delaware's Section 102(b)(7) on the shareholders' ability to adopt charter provisions waiving liability. Why not let the articles or certificate contain any liability waivers the shareholders vote for?

One evident answer is to protect parties who do not get to vote. Hence, the statute only addresses liability to the shareholders and the corporation, not liability to creditors or other third parties. This rationale also seems to explain the exception for liability for excessive dividends, since the statutory limits on the declaration of dividends largely exist for the protection of creditors. Yet, one might then ask why do creditors, or at least voluntary creditors, deserve any more protection from charter provisions than do later purchasing or dissenting shareholders?

The restriction on waiving liability for illegal acts perhaps reflects a public policy objective of adding to deterrence. The restriction on waiving claims based upon duty of loyalty violations (or illegitimate personal gain) is more difficult to explain if the legislature really believed in shareholder choice. Perhaps this restriction reflects an underlying distrust as to how knowing and voluntary shareholder choice really is.

Perhaps most mysterious is that the statute addresses waiving the liability only of directors. Does this reflect the same sort of favored treatment of directors versus junior corporate employees as we saw embodied in many interpretations of the business judgment rule? Perhaps not. Normal contract law might allow the corporation to agree to waive negligence liability as part of employment contracts with its employees and officers.[107] Perhaps all the charter option statutes do is to allow the same waivers for directors, but through a mechanism (provision in the articles) which embodies shareholder acquiescence. This is useful, since there is no one in the corporation to negotiate an employment contract with the directors, as there is with officers and employees.

In contrast to the charter option statutes are two other types of statutes passed in a number of jurisdictions. One type requires that a high degree of culpability exist in order to impose liability upon directors. For example, Indiana requires a showing of "willful misconduct or recklessness" in order for directors to be liable for any action they

106. Michael Bradley & Cindy A. Schipiani, *The Relevance of the Duty of Care Standard in Corporate Governance*, 75 Iowa L. Rev. 1 (1989). Indeed, this study found that investors discounted the price of all Delaware corporations after the Delaware legislature enacted Section 102(b)(7).

107. *See, e.g.,* Restatement (Second) of Agency § 379 Comment a.

take as directors or for any failure to take action.[108] To some extent, this is just a codification of a highly protective version of the business judgment rule. One difference, however, is that such statutes may not be limited to business decisions, as is the business judgment rule. Rather, by referring to the failure to take action, a statute like Indiana's might also change the standard for cases of inattention as in *Francis*.

The other type of protective statute places a cap on the amount of damages for which directors can be liable. Virginia pioneered this approach. Virginia's statute limits director liability for actions which do not involve wilful misconduct to the greater of $100,000 or the amount of cash compensation received by the director from the corporation during the twelve months preceding the director's breach of duty.[109]

The policy rationale behind the statutes which increase the culpability required to impose liability, or limit the amount of damages, is very different from the rationale underlying the charter option statutes. Neither Indiana's nor Virginia's protective statute gives shareholders the option to impose greater liability upon directors. Hence, one cannot argue for these statutes simply as facilitating shareholder choice.

Still, the idea of codifying a standard for liability, as in Indiana, is hardly unprecedented. As we discussed earlier, many states' corporation statutes, as well as the Model Act, contain provisions codifying a duty of care for directors. The only difference is that Indiana's standard significantly departs from the norm of ordinary negligence. Hence, the wisdom of the Indiana statute depends on what one thinks of having a different standard for directors versus other persons who might be charged with breaching a duty of care. To the extent one cannot justify a different rule for directors, then Indiana's statute is symptomatic of the results which occur when legislatures adopt liability rules based upon pressure from one group of prospective defendants—be this directors or doctors—rather than considering tort law as a whole.

As we discussed earlier, one concern about director liability for breaching the duty of care is that the damages could turn out to be huge. One answer to this concern is to cap the amount of damages for which directors can be liable. Such damage caps are not confined to corporate law. A number of states have done this for doctors charged with malpractice. Hence, Virginia's approach has something to be said for it. In fact, the during the course of drafting its Principles of Corporate Governance, the American Law Institute toyed around with this idea. In the end, however, all the Principles of Corporate Governance does is to allow charter provisions to limit damages for certain duty of care breaches to no less than the amount of the director or officer's annual compensation.[110]

---

108. Ind. Code Ann. § 23–1–35(1)(e)(2).
109. Va. Code Ann. § 13.1–692.1

110. Principles of Corporate Governance § 7.19

§ 4.2 Duty of Loyalty

We depart now from cases in which the complaint is that directors or officers breached their duty of care—in other words, they were lazy or dumb. In this section, we consider complaints that directors or officers breached their duty of loyalty—in other words, they were greedy and put their own financial interests ahead of the interests of the corporation and its shareholders. This may occur in a number of contexts. The most obvious danger that directors or officers will favor themselves at the expense of the corporation exists when directors or officers enter into a contract with their corporation. A second common problem occurs when directors or officers learn of a business opportunity which may be of use to their corporation, but take the opportunity for themselves. We shall consider both of these types of situations, as well as variations on them, in this section.

4.2.1 Conflict-of-interest Transactions: The Basic Approach

Suppose one or more directors or officers of a corporation own property, or can supply services or capital, which could be of use to the company. They might enter a contract with the corporation under which they exchange the property, or services, or capital, for cash, or stock in the company, or some other consideration. Alternately, perhaps the corporation has some assets it no longer needs. It might enter into a contract to sell the assets to one or more of its directors or officers. The problem in such cases is that the corporation, itself, in reality, can neither negotiate the contract nor decide whether or not to make the deal. After all, a corporation is a fictitious entity which can only act through its directors, officers and other personnel. If the officers or directors who negotiate or approve the deal on behalf of the corporation are the parties on the other side of the transaction, they will face a clear conflict between their personal financial interest in obtaining the best terms for themselves and their obligation to seek the best bargain for the corporation. Given this conflict, how should the law handle such contracts if a shareholder objects to the deal?

We noted earlier that the business judgment rule does not apply to a transaction in which the directors have a conflict-of-interest (at least, as we shall discuss later, if there is no approval by directors who do not have any personal interest in the deal). Indeed, courts sometimes use the expression they "will apply the business judgment rule" as a short-hand way of saying that the case before them does *not* involve a conflict-of-interest and so the court will review the transaction solely in terms of the duty of care. For example, in *Sinclair Oil Corp. v. Levien,*[1] the court phrased the primary issue before it as whether to apply the "intrinsic fairness test" rather than the "business judgment standard" in reviewing the challenged actions. The court then explained that this choice depended on whether the challenged actions constituted "self-dealing" (in other words, conflict-of-interest transactions), in which case the business judgment standard, or rule, would not apply.

§ 4.2

1. 280 A.2d 717 (Del.1971).

It is pretty easy to see why virtually no one seriously advocates applying the business judgment rule to conflict-of-interest transactions (again, at least in the absence of approval by disinterested directors). The various rationales for the business judgment rule discussed earlier largely disappear when dealing with conflict-of-interest transactions. The idea that directors, with their expertise, are more likely to reach a better business decision than the courts presupposes a situation in which we can trust the directors to act in the best interest of the corporation. After all, what advantage is expertise if we cannot trust the directors to use their expertise in the company's best interest? Needless to say, when the directors have a personal financial interest in conflict with the corporation's, there is a reason not to trust the directors. Moreover, there seems little point to encourage (even if we do not prohibit) conflict-of-interest transactions. Hence, the rationale that we need the business judgment rule to promote necessary business risk-taking is in apropos. As we shall discuss later, the typical remedy with a conflict-of-interest transaction is to unwind the deal and force the directors to give back what they received. Accordingly, there is unlikely to be the sort of draconian damages which might exist when holding directors liable for business decisions which go awry. Also, since directors are personally profiting from a conflict-of-interest transaction, there is more need for deterrence through the legal system than when dealing simply with duty of care issues.

If a conflict-of-interest precludes application of the business judgment rule, then what? At one time (the late 1800s), a number of courts took a very simple minded approach: Any contract in which one or more directors had a conflict-of-interest was voidable if any shareholder objected.[2] Under this approach, it did not matter whether the corporation received a good deal in the transaction. Nor did it matter whether other directors, who had no personal stake in the transaction, approved the contract. Moreover, this absolutist approach not only applied to the situation in which a director had a personal financial stake in the contract. Courts also applied the rule when two corporations entered into a contract with each other and one or more of the same individuals sat on both corporations' boards of directors. In this situation, the conflict-of-interest is not between the personal advantage of the director versus his or her obligation to the corporation, but, rather, the problem comes from the conflicting obligations of the director to the two contracting corporations.

By the 20th Century, this sort of absolute prohibition faded away. This occurred in two stages. In the first, numerous courts began to uphold conflict-of-interest transactions so long as the transaction met both of two requirements: (1) directors, who had no personal financial

---

2. For a history of the judicial approach to conflict-of-interest transactions, see Harold Marsh, Jr., *Are Directors Trustees? Conflict-of-Interest and Corporate Morality*, 22 Bus. Law. 35 (1966). For an opposing view, which argues courts did not apply a rule of absolute voidability, see Norwood P. Beveridge, Jr., *The Corporate Director's Fiduciary Duty of Loyalty: Understanding the Self–Interested Director Transaction*, 41 DePaul L. Rev. 655 (1992).

stake in the deal ("disinterested directors"), approved the contract, and (2) the contract was fair to the corporation. The conjunctive requirement of approval by disinterested directors and a finding of fairness turned out to be only a way station before another approach. This is to forget about requiring disinterested director approval and simply demand that a conflict-of-interest contract be fair to the corporation. This remains a highly common, and arguably still the dominant, approach today.

Interestingly enough, there continue to be writers who lament the passing of the rule of absolute voidability.[3] This rule had the merit of simplicity. By contrast, the judicial scrutiny entailed in the fairness test means costly trials with uncertain outcomes. The indeterminacy of the fairness approach also means that occasionally directors may be able to get away with taking advantage of their corporations through contracts which the courts mistakenly conclude are fair or which shareholders decline to incur the expense of challenging.

The often expressed justification for abandoning the absolute voidability rule is that this rule prevents the corporation from entering advantageous contracts with its directors. It is an unexplored empirical question as to just how often corporations get deals from their directors which the company could not have received from someone else, and whether this prospect outweighs the advantages of having a simpler test. In fact, however, the real problem with the rule probably is not that it prevents the corporation getting good deals from its directors. Rather, a more fundamental problem may lie in the need to make exceptions in so many cases as to undermine the point of having an absolute rule.

The first necessary exception would involve compensating the directors for their work. After all, presumably if the corporation expects directors to spend significant time and effort, and certainly if the board will include among its members any full time executives of the corporation, then the corporation must contract with its directors with respect to their compensation. Such compensation contracts are the epitome of a conflict-of-interest transaction.

In addition, one would normally expect directors to own shares in the corporation. Indeed, most writers consider this to be desirable, since it aligns the interests of the directors with those of the shareholders. Yet, unless the directors are to purchase their shares only from other stockholders, or exclusively before they get on the board (but how would the initial directors get their shares?), board members will be contracting with the corporation to buy stock.

Related to the problem of stock purchases is the situation of essential inputs into a closely held business. For example, a person who owns some intellectual property (say, some software) might go into business with another individual who will provide capital to develop the property and market the resulting product. If the parties decide to conduct this business through a corporation, both are likely to want to be directors.

---

3. *E.g.*, Robert Clark, Corporate Law 180–189 (1986).

This means—barring some extraordinary machinations with temporary directors—that the transfer of the intellectual property and the capital to the corporation will entail conflict-of-interest transactions.

One could presumably still have a rule of absolute voidability, but with exceptions for compensation, stock purchases, and transfers involved in the establishment of a closely held business. In terms of the shear number of transactions involved, these exceptions may be larger than the rule. Moreover, there will always be the temptation to make exceptions for other transactions which seem especially necessary or desirable. Once courts go down this route, however, they are essentially back to the fairness test—upholding conflict-of-interest transactions if the court finds the deal was a good one for the corporation.

If judicially created doctrine was all we had to contend with, by and large we could end our discussion with an exploration of the fairness test. Most state legislatures, however, have enacted, as part of their corporations statutes, special provisions dealing with conflict-of-interest transactions. California, in 1931, was the first state to adopt such a special provision.[4] The idea spread to other corporations statutes, including Delaware's[5] and the Model Act.[6]

These conflict-of-interest statutes vary in a number of particulars, which we will discuss. Nevertheless, their overall approach follows the pattern set by the original California provision. Essentially, these statutes state that conflict-of-interest transactions—which, as we shall discuss later, the statutes define in greater or lesser detail—will not be void or voidable because of the conflict, so long as the transaction meets one of three conditions. These three options to save the transaction are:

(1) Approval by disinterested directors,

(2) Approval by the shareholders, or

(3) Proof that the transaction is fair.[7]

The third option, fairness, is the approach which judicial doctrine had evolved into using to deal with conflict-of-interest transactions. Courts had also looked to approval by disinterested directors at one point in the evolution of judicial doctrine. There is a critical difference, however, between the language of these statutes and this earlier judicial approach. The statutes refer to disinterested director approval as an *alternative* to fairness; whereas the earlier judicial approach had required *both* disinterested director approval and fairness to save the

4. California's current version is contained in Section 310 of the California Corporations Code.

5. Del. Gen. Corp. Law § 144.

6. The 1984 Revised Model Business Corporations Act contained its conflict-of-interest provision in Section 8.31. In 1988, however, the drafters of the Model Act proposed a new series of sections (Sections 8.60 through 8.63) dealing with director conflicts of interest to replace Section 8.31. So far, many of the states which base their statutes on the Model Act have not yet adopted the new sections.

7. In this regard, these statutes might remind one of a television game program in which the host asks the contestants whether they want the prize behind "door number one, door number two, or door number three."

transaction. The statutes also incorporate the alternative of shareholder approval. Prior judicial doctrine had been hazy on the impact of shareholder approval of a conflict-of-interest transaction.

While the three options in these statutes have judicial antecedents, there is a broader logic to the statutory approach. Keep in mind that the fundamental problem with conflict-of-interest transactions is that we do not trust individuals with a personal financial stake at odds with the corporation's to put the corporation's interest ahead of their own. If the problem is a lack of trust, one solution is to find someone we can trust to review the transaction. We can view each of the three options listed by the conflict-of-interest statutes as pointing to a different party who can fill this role. This party can be the disinterested directors, the shareholders or, under the fairness test, the court. In other words, under this concept, the fairness test, like the other two alternatives, is simply a mode of finding a trustworthy decision maker.

4.2.2   *The Fairness Test*

In thinking about various areas of law, one might notice that while fairness is often a goal of the law, rarely is it a legal standard in and of itself. Perhaps this is because fairness in many contexts is an amorphous concept too often only defined by the eye of the beholder. Still, while a review of cases applying the test of fairness to conflict-of-interest transactions does not completely dispel this concern, it does provide us a number of guidelines for making the test into something more analytical than the seven-year-old's classic complaint about parental action: "it ain't fair."

To begin with, much as we saw in discussing the business judgment rule,[8] the fairness test can involve looking at either the substance of the directors' decision—in this case, to have the corporation enter a contract in which some directors have an interest—or the process the directors used to reach this decision.[9]

When dealing with process and the business judgment rule, we saw how courts might examine the care with which the directors investigated the merits of the transaction, for example, looking at the extent the directors investigated whether $55 per share was a good price at which to sell Trans Union Corporation. This same concern with the directors' investigation of a deal's merits appears in a number of cases evaluating the fairness of conflict-of-interest transactions. For example, in *Lewis v. S.L. & E., Inc.*,[10] the court evaluated the fairness of a transaction which involved renting the corporation's principal asset, a commercial building, to a firm conducting a tire dealership on the premises. Several brothers owned the tire dealership, and were also directors of the corporation

8. See § 4.1.2 *supra.*

9. *See, e.g.,* Weinberger v. UOP, Inc., 457 A.2d 701 (Del.1983) (fairness entails fair dealing and fair price).

10. 629 F.2d 764 (2d Cir.1980).

owning the building.[11] In condemning the rental as unfair, the court noted that the defendant brothers had undertaken no effort at the time of the arrangement to determine if the rental the building corporation charged the tire company was fair to the building corporation. There were no appraisals, no efforts to sell or rent the property to third parties, and the defendants' only thought at the time apparently was to have the rent be sufficient to cover the expenses of maintaining the building.

Actually, however, the directors' care in investigating the merits of the deal tends not to be the typical process issue with conflict-of-interest transactions. Rather, the more frequent question concerns communications by the interested directors with the shareholders and any disinterested directors. Specifically, courts have held that fairness requires candor by the interested directors in their dealings with shareholders or disinterested directors. Exploring both the requirements for such candor, and the impact of its absence, gets into the question of what effect disinterested director or shareholder approval has on a conflict-of-interest transaction. Hence, we will defer this discussion until we return to the subject of such approvals.

We saw under the business judgment rule a greater emphasis by many courts on reviewing the decision making process than on second guessing the substantive merits of a transaction. When considering the fairness of a conflict-of-interest transaction, however, the emphasis is often the other way around, that is on considering the substantive merits of the deal. This, in turn, raises three questions: What should courts measure in assessing substantive fairness? When should they measure this? And against what criteria?

As far as what to measure, courts generally compare the value of what the corporation gave up in the transaction versus the value of what it received. For example, in *Lewis*, the court compared whether the rent which the corporation received equaled the value of the use of the building the company gave. This concept of fairness may seem obvious, yet it has an important corollary which is contrary to a commonly held intuitive notion about fairness. This corollary is that the defendants' profits on the deal are largely irrelevant to the deal's fairness. In other words, contrary to what might seem intuitively correct, the fact that directors make even huge profits in a transaction with their corporation does not make the transaction unfair.[12]

Fliegler v. Lawrence[13] provides an example of a case in which the court found a conflict-of-interest transaction to be fair to the corporation despite the fact one might say the directors "made out like bandits" in terms of the profits they obtained. In *Fliegler*, the president of a corporation ("Agau"), formed to look for gold and silver, received the

---

11. In what may have been a foolish piece of estate planning, a father, who had been the principal shareholder of both corporations, had several of his sons take over the tire business, while making these sons, as well as an apparently disfavored son and his daughters, shareholders of the building corporation.

12. Nor, as in *Lewis*, will a defendant's lack of large profits make a transaction fair.

13. 361 A.2d 218 (Del.1976).

opportunity to obtain property on which there might be another valuable mineral, antimony. Because Agau lacked the funds to exploit this opportunity, the president, along with various other Agau officers and directors, formed a new corporation ("USAC"), all the shares of which they purchased, to obtain and explore the property. The officers and directors, however, made a contract with Agau, which gave Agau the option to purchase all their shares in USAC for 800,000 shares of Agau. The parties based the 800,000 figure on an amount which, at the then price of Agau shares, would compensate the officers and directors for the sums they expected to put into USAC to explore the antimony property. The property turned out to contain antimony and the directors had Agau exercise the option.

A shareholder brought suit, complaining that the deal was unfair to Agau. It turned out that the officers and directors had made far more profit on the exercise of the option than originally envisioned. The price of Agau shares had skyrocketed upon word of the antimony discovery, making the 800,000 shares worth much more than their price at the time the parties made the option contract. Moreover, development of the antimony property had cost the officers and directors less than expected; in fact, it had cost them very little, since they had USAC borrow most of the money, and, after exercise of the option, Agau owned USAC. Nevertheless, the court found the transaction to be fair to Agau. After all, the critical question is not how much profit the officers and directors made, but, rather, whether the antimony property was worth 800,000 shares of Agau. The fact that investors bid up the price of Agau shares apparently in response to knowledge of the discovery and Agau's option to it strongly suggests that the property was worth the shares.

There is a caveat to this measure of fairness. To be fair, a transaction should serve a corporate purpose. In other words, it is not enough that the objective value of what the corporation receives in a transaction with its directors equals the value of what the corporation gave. If the transaction does nothing for the corporation—for example, the corporation, itself, has no use for what it received—then the transaction can still be unfair to the corporation.[14]

The next question is when one should measure the value of what the corporation gave versus what it received. *Fliegler* again illustrates the issue. At the time the directors had the corporation enter the option contract, the expected value of what the corporation would give under the option (the 800,000 shares), as well as the cost to the directors and officers to produce what the corporation would receive under the option, were very different from what they later turned out to be. It did not matter. As a general rule, the time of measurement is at the moment the directors have the corporation enter the contract.[15] After all, directors can only make a decision based upon the facts at the time they act.

---

14. *E.g.,* Fill Bldgs., Inc. v. Alexander Hamilton Life Ins. Co., 396 Mich. 453, 241 N.W.2d 466 (1976).

15. Many of the conflict-of-interest statutes explicitly state that fairness is measured based upon the facts at the time of approval. Incidentally, in *Fliegler,* there

Of course, this does not mean later events are irrelevant to assessing the fairness of a deal at the time the directors made it. If later events are ones the directors anticipated (or should have anticipated), they bear upon the fairness of the transaction at the time the corporation enters the contract. For example, in *Globe Woolen Co. v. Utica Gas & Electric Co.*,[16] a power company made a contract to supply electricity to mills operated by a wool company. The principal stockholder of the wool company was one of the power company's directors. The contract guaranteed that the wool company's total power costs under the contract would not exceed the wool company's power costs of prior years—no matter how much electricity the wool company used—or else the power company would not only provide the wool company with all its electricity free, but the power company would also pay liquidated damages to the wool company. Possibly reacting to the obvious incentive in the contract, the wool company changed the operations at its mills in a way which dramatically increased its overall energy usage. Ultimately, the power company was supplying the mills with huge quantities of electricity and, instead of receiving payment from the wool company, the power company was actually having to pay the wool company for the privilege. The court voided the contract, explaining that the director with the conflict-of-interest either anticipated or should have anticipated this result at the time the parties entered the contract.

Finally, having looked at what to measure in assessing substantive fairness and when to measure it, the question becomes against what criteria. The basic idea is that the corporation should receive value equivalent to what it gave up. Yet, how can one determine this in comparing different items—"apples versus oranges" so to speak? The test is whether this is the sort of bargain the corporation would have made if dealing with a stranger.[17] In other words, directors should not have the corporation give to themselves a better deal than the directors would have the corporation give to outsiders.

Unfortunately, this test may be easier to recite than actually to apply in many cases. If the transaction involves a standardized item which has a prevailing market price, then it is easy to see whether directors received a better deal than an outsider. Yet, the conflict-of-interest transactions which provoke challenges typically involve non-standardized consideration (a unique piece of property, the unique services of an officer or director, a large block of stock in the corporation) which does not have a market price one can simply go and look up. Hence, the fairness test asks what price an arms-length negotiation would produce in a situation in which there never was an arms-length negotiation by anybody. Needless to say, this is not an easy inquiry.

Also, one must be wary of expecting that courts will apply this sort of test with a blind eye to surrounding circumstances. *Cookies Food*

---

were two contracting times: the time of entering the option and the time the corporation chose to exercise the option.

16.   224 N.Y. 483, 121 N.E. 378 (1918).

17.   *E.g.*, Fliegler v. Lawrence, 361 A.2d 218 (Del.1976).

Products, Inc. v. Lakes Warehouse, Inc.,[18] provides a good illustration. *Cookies* involved a challenge to various contracts between a corporation and its dominant director (as well as majority shareholder), under which the director, and another company he owned, provided various services to distribute the corporation's product—barbecue and taco sauce, not cookies—and shared with the corporation the director's recipe for taco sauce. The minority shareholders, who challenged these contracts, produced evidence that one generally could obtain the sorts of services provided by the defendant for much less than the contracts gave the defendant. Nevertheless, the majority of the court found the contracts to be fair. Critical to this finding was that the corporation had been struggling before the defendant began his efforts to distribute its product and that, as a result of the defendant's efforts, the corporation had become highly successful. In other words, the majority felt that sometimes the best proof of value may be in the results.[19]

So far, we have examined what facts and circumstances the courts look at in ascertaining whether a conflict-of-interest transaction is fair to the corporation. Given the frequent indeterminacy of these facts and circumstances, however, a more important aspect of the fairness test actually lies in how it tells the courts to go about making this evaluation. Once again, a comparison with our previous discussion of the business judgment rule is instructive.

Running throughout all of the interpretations of the business judgment rule is a reticence by the courts to second-guess decisions of directors when there is no conflict-of-interest. By contrast, the fairness test is all about the court feeling free to second guess the board's decision. The courts in cases like *Lewis, Fliegler* and *Cookies* had no difficulty exercising their judgment as to whether the contracts were good for the corporation. This makes sense, since the purpose of the fairness test is to have the court act as a disinterested decision-maker.[20]

Coupled with this differing judicial willingness to make business judgments is another difference between the business judgment rule and the fairness test which is even more outcome determinative in many cases. This difference involves how the court deals with uncertainty. We saw earlier that the shareholder who challenges a decision of the board subject to the business judgment rule has the burden to prove breach of the duty of care (for instance, the existence of gross negligence). The general rule recited for conflict-of-interest transactions, however, is the burden shifts to the defendants to show that the challenged transaction is fair to the corporation.[21]

18. 430 N.W.2d 447 (Iowa 1988).

19. Similarly, in *Fliegler*, the fact that the corporation could go under if it did not obtain the antimony influenced the court in finding that the deal was fair.

20. The reader may notice that a parallel exists in Constitutional Law to this difference between the business judgment rule and the fairness test. Specifically, the business judgment rule might remind one of the rational basis standard for reviewing a challenged statute, while the fairness test might remind one of the strict scrutiny applied to statutes treading upon suspect categories.

21. *E.g.,* Lewis v. S. L. & E., Inc., 629 F.2d 764 (2d Cir.1980).

Yet, why is this shift in the burden of proof significant? After all, the issue arises in a civil trial in which the burden of proof is merely to show that a fact is more probable than not. The answer is that this shift is really part of a larger change in approach. In dealing with many, perhaps most, of the board decisions which provoke a shareholder suit, the court is likely to hear conflicting expert testimony and be left in substantial doubt as to the wisdom of the directors' decision. Under the business judgment rule, the court tends to resolve all such doubts in favor of the directors. Under the fairness test, however, the court tends to resolve doubts against the directors in a conflict-of-interest.[22]

Lewis again illustrates the point. The issue before the court was whether the rent paid during the period from 1966 to 1972 was fair to the building corporation. The defendant directors introduced evidence of lower rents on leases of two comparable properties in the area. The court dismissed this as not meeting the directors' burden of proof to show a fair rent from 1966 to 1972. One of the comparables involved a lease entered in 1961, while the other comparable involved rent paid in 1973 and 1974. Yet, if we know that fair rents in both 1961 and 1973 were below what the defendants agreed to pay to the corporation from 1966 to 1972, why cannot one draw the inference from the comparable leases that the defendants' tire company paid a fair rent? Presumably, there is more than a shift in the burden of proof going on here. Rather, the court is resolving doubts against the directors in a conflict-of-interest.

We can find a good contrast between the scrutiny under the business judgment rule and the scrutiny under the fairness test—because the same court in the same opinion had the opportunity when facing different challenged transactions to apply both tests—in *Sinclair Oil Corp. v. Levien.*[23] In *Sinclair*, a minority shareholder complained about two decisions by the directors of the corporation in which he owned shares: (1) to declare dividends so large that the corporation was unable to expand; and (2) not to enforce a contract which had required another company to buy a minimum quantity of oil from the corporation.[24] For reasons we will discuss later, the court treated the second decision as involving a conflict-of-interest and, therefore, subject to the fairness test, but the first decision did not and so came within the business judgment rule. Applying the business judgment rule to the dividend decision, the court dismissed the plaintiff's claim with little examination of the merits of the directors' action. By contrast, under the fairness test, the court rejected the defendant's rationale for not enforcing the oil supply contract. The defendant argued that the corporation could not have supplied the contract minimum quantities of oil anyway. In rejecting this argu-

---

22. For a development of this difference using fuzzy set theory, see Charles Yablon, *On the Allocation of Burdens of Proof in Corporate Law: An Essay on Fairness and Fuzzy Sets,* 13 Cardozo L. Rev. 497 (1991).

23. 280 A.2d 717 (Del.1971).

24. As we shall discuss later, the plaintiff claimed the directors made these deci-

sions to further the interests of the 97 percent majority shareholder, Sinclair Oil. He also complained that Sinclair Oil deprived its subsidiary of opportunities for expansion—a problem we will return to later when we discuss the corporate opportunity doctrine.

ment, the court stated that the defendant "has failed to prove that Sinven [the corporation involved] could not *possibly* have produced or *someway* have obtained the contract minimums."[25] In other words, under an approach which resolves doubts against those in a conflict-of-interest, mere possibilities that the contract is unfair doom the transaction.

This raises the question of why the courts resolve doubts against directors in a conflict-of-interest. One possible answer is that the directors normally will have better access to evidence as to the merits of a transaction than will a challenging shareholder. A more significant answer, however, lies in the incentive created by this approach. If directors in a conflict-of-interest know that the court will resolve any doubts as to the fairness of a conflict-of-interest transaction against upholding the transaction, the directors have an incentive to make sure the deal is a good one for the corporation—thereby removing doubt. This can serve to offset the natural instinct of directors in a conflict to pursue terms as favorable to themselves as they think they possibly can get away with. In other words, the threat of skeptical judicial review under the fairness standard serves as an invisible bargaining agent for the corporate interest, whether or not the matter ever reaches litigation.

4.2.3 *Disinterested Director Approval*

We earlier saw statutory provisions which state that disinterested director approval might save a conflict-of-interest transaction. These provisions raise a number of questions.

a. *Who is a disinterested director?*

Interestingly enough, most of the conflict-of-interest statutes, as for example Delaware's, do not explicitly define who is a disinterested director. These provisions state what transactions they cover. This includes contracts between the corporation and one or more of its directors. It also includes contracts between the corporation and another entity in which one or more of the corporation's directors have a financial stake or have the role of director or officer. At first glance, then, disinterested directors would seem to refer to directors who are not the ones transacting business with the corporation or who have a financial interest or management role in the firm transacting business with the corporation. Yet, suppose the director in question is a close relative (say a child or spouse)[26] or the personal attorney[27] of a director transacting business with the corporation. Is such an individual a "disinterested director?" Most of us would have trouble completely trusting such persons to be disinterested. Yet, once we start down the

---

25. 280 A.2d at 723 (emphasis added).

26. *See* Rocket Mining Corp. v. Gill, 25 Utah 2d 434, 483 P.2d 897 (1971)(holding that the spouse, father and brother of an interested director were disinterested directors).

27. *See* Sarner v. Fox Hill, Inc., 151 Conn. 437, 199 A.2d 6 (1964) (holding that the defendant director's attorney was not a disinterested director).

path of treating such individuals as not disinterested, where will we draw the line in the absence of any statutory definition?

The drafters of the Model Business Corporations Act, in revisions made in 1988, attempted to cure this problem. Instead of referring to approval by "disinterested directors," the Model Act revision refers to "qualified directors." This change in terminology obviously is not significant in itself. What is significant is that the Model Act then defines the term "qualified director."[28] This is a director who does not have a conflicting interest in the transaction—which, as we shall discuss later, the Act defines at some length. Also, to be a qualified director under the Model Act's new provisions, the director must not have a family, financial, professional or employment relationship with an interested director of such significance that one would reasonably expect the relationship to exert an influence on the qualified director's judgment.

b. How many disinterested votes are needed?

During the period when many courts required both disinterested director approval and fairness in order to save a conflict-of-interest transaction, they typically refused to allow interested directors to count as part of the quorum. This meant there had to be enough disinterested directors on the board to constitute a quorum (typically, a majority of the total board). Then, if enough disinterested directors showed up at the meeting to have a quorum, and a majority of the disinterested directors present voted to approve the transaction, it met the requirement for disinterested director approval.

Currently, the conflict-of-interest statutes vary in terms of their requirements for how many disinterested directors must vote in favor. The language in California's statute—which, since these statutes started in California, was originally the most common approach—refers to "a vote sufficient without counting the vote of the interested director or directors."[29] While not entirely free from ambiguity,[30] the most natural reading of this language is that the number of disinterested directors voting to approve the transaction must equal a majority of the directors who are present at the meeting. For example, suppose a corporation has a seven person board and enters a contract in which four of the directors have a financial interest, while the remaining three directors are disinterested. If the board unanimously votes to approve the contract at a meeting at which all seven directors are present, this vote would not meet the statutory language. This is because, if we only count the affirmative votes of the three disinterested directors, we do not have a majority of those present—that is to say, a majority of seven—voting for the transaction. By contrast, if only one or two of the interested directors showed up at the meeting (so, if all three disinterested directors were also at the meeting, we would have a quorum present), then the three

---

28. M.B.C.A. § 8.62(d) (1988).

29. Cal. Corp. Code § 310(a)(2).

30. For a discussion of possible interpretations of conflict-of-interest statutes,

see Kenneth Davis, Jr., *Approval by Disinterested Directors,* 20 J. Corp. L. 215 (1995).

votes of the disinterested directors would be a majority of those present, and so sufficient without counting any votes by the interested directors.

By contrast, Delaware's statute speaks of receiving the votes of a majority of the disinterested directors, even if they are less than a quorum.[31] While again not completely free from ambiguity, the most natural reading of this language is that, in order to satisfy the test, a majority of the total number of disinterested directors on the board must vote for the transaction. Hence, if a board had, say, five disinterested directors, but only two showed up at the meeting and voted for the conflict-of-interest transaction, the vote would not meet the disinterested director approval prong of Delaware's statute. On the other hand, in the earlier example of a seven person board only three of whose members are disinterested, the vote of three (or even two) disinterested directors in favor would meet the requirement, regardless of how many interested directors were at the meeting.

The recent version of the Model Act's conflict-of-interest provisions (as well as the 1984 version) basically follows Delaware's, rather than California's, approach to this issue.[32] The Model Act has one interesting difference from Delaware. Under Delaware's approach, if the board has only one disinterested director, this individual's lonely vote can meet the requirement for disinterested director approval. Presumably concerned about a solitary director's ability to hold out when reviewing a transaction with his or her colleagues on the board, the Model Act adds a requirement that at least two qualified directors must vote to approve the deal.

c. *When must the vote occur?*

Normally, we would expect disinterested directors to vote before the corporation enters the contract which involves a conflict-of-interest. Suppose, however, that individuals, who are both officers and directors in the corporation, use their authority as officers to have the company enter a contract in which they have a conflicting interest. After all, most contracts do not require board approval. If a shareholder should later object to this deal, can these officer-directors then take the matter to the board and have approval by disinterested directors cure the conflict? Or is it too late?

The answer varies depending upon the particular state's statute. For example, California's statute refers to authorization, approval or ratification by disinterested directors.[33] Referring to ratification pretty clearly means that an after-the-fact vote is acceptable. The latest revision of the Model Act is even more explicit in allowing the qualified director vote to

---

31. Del. Gen. Corp. Law § 144(a)(1).

32. M.B.C.A. §§ 8.31(c) (1984); 8.62(a) (1988). Poor drafting makes it possible to argue that the newest version of the Model Act only requires a majority of the qualified directors who actually vote. The official comment, however, states that the measure is the number of qualified directors on the whole board.

33. Cal. Corp. Code § 310(a)(2).

take place "at any time."[34] By comparison, Delaware's provision seems only to look to a pre-transaction vote. Specifically, in speaking of disinterested director approval, Delaware's statute refers only to authorization; whereas, in speaking to the fairness test, the statute refers to the transaction being fair at the time the board authorizes, approves or ratifies the deal.[35] The negative implication is that an after-the-fact ratification by disinterested directors will not cure the conflict.

Is there any policy reason, however, for not allowing after-the-fact disinterested director action to cure the conflict? Some writers argue there is.[36] Specifically, directors asked to review a transaction between the corporation and one or more of their colleagues often are going to feel some psychological pressure to give their colleagues what they want. It may be much easier to stand up to this pressure in voting before the transaction than when asked to ratify an already completed deal. After all, in the former case, a negative vote warns one's colleagues they should not do something; in the later case, a negative vote tells one's colleagues to unwind an already done deal or face a lawsuit.[37]

d.   What are the obligations of the interested directors in obtaining disinterested director approval?

So far, we have addressed questions regarding the disinterested directors. Now, let us ask if there are any rules which govern the conduct of the interested directors in obtaining disinterested director approval. Earlier, we mentioned the most important such rule. In discussing the fairness test, we noted that courts require the interested directors to be candid in their dealings with disinterested directors and shareholders.

In fact, this requirement of candor is little more than an application of fundamental tenets of agency law and fiduciary duty. Specifically, among the primary duties flowing from a fiduciary relationship is the obligation of full and truthful disclosure. After all, the very definition of a fiduciary relationship is a relationship of trust and confidence. When most of us place our trust and confidence in another person, we expect this other person will be forthcoming in disclosing any information we ought to know when dealing with this person. Conversely, if we must be on our guard to ask all the right questions, this is hardly what most of us expect out of a relationship of trust or confidence. Accordingly, agents, including corporate officers and directors, have an obligation of full disclosure when dealing with their principal.[38]

34. M.B.C.A. § 8.61(b)(1) (1988).

35. Del. Gen. Corp. Law § 144(a)(1), (3).

36. *E.g.,* Richard M. Buxbaum, *Conflict-of-Interest Statutes and the Need for a Demand on Directors in Derivative Actions,* 68 Cal. L. Rev. 1122 (1980).

37. The American Law Institute's Principles of Corporate Governance recommends recognizing disinterested director approval only if the disinterested directors authorize the conflict-of-interest transaction in advance, or if the interested director did not act unreasonably in failing to seek advance approval. § 5.02(a)(2)(B) and (C).

38. *See, e.g.,* Restatement (Second) of Agency § 389–392 (1957).

In the *Globe Woolen* case we discussed earlier, Judge Cardozo applied this sort of reasoning in reviewing a conflict-of-interest transaction under common law. In typically eloquent fashion, he declared that the director in the conflict had a duty to warn his fellow directors—indeed, to "protest"—of the dangerous incentives in the contract they were approving.

Globe Woolen involved the failure to disclose important facts about the merits of the conflict-of-interest transaction. Another frequent problem involves non-disclosure of the conflict-of-interest itself. In other words, a corporation will contract with another firm (say another corporation) in which one of its directors or officers has a financial interest or a management role. The director or officer might not inform those who approve the transaction of his or her interest in the other firm, and the persons who approve the transaction might not know about the interest. Courts invariably condemn such non-disclosure.[39]

The conflict-of-interest statutes carry forward the requirement of disclosure. In order to cure the conflict by disinterested director approval, the interested directors must disclose the conflict-of-interest to the disinterested directors. Most of these statutes also require the interested directors to disclose any material facts they know about the transaction itself; in other words, the interested directors must disclose any facts relevant to the deal, which they know and which the disinterested directors reasonably would want to know. Some conflict statutes, like New York's, however, only expressly require disclosure of the conflict-of-interest, but make no mention of disclosing other material facts about the transaction.[40] This suggests that, under a statute like New York's, the directors in a conflict need only disclose their conflict and then can keep their mouths shut. On the other hand, given the pre-existing common law, one suspects many courts might react to this sort of statute by holding that a director or officer, who fails to disclose material facts about the transaction, breaches his or her fiduciary duty (or commits fraud), even if the statute otherwise cures the conflict-of-interest itself.

Suppose then that the director with a conflict-of-interest fails to disclose. The indisputable result is that he or she cannot take advantage of approval by disinterested directors (unless the disinterested directors already knew the non-disclosed facts). There remains an issue, however, which has been the subject of some debate. Can the non-disclosing director still save the conflict-of-interest transaction by arguing that its terms are fair to the company?

The legal basis for this argument lies in the structure of the conflict-of-interest statutes. Under the conflict-of-interest statutes, a transaction is not void because of the conflict either if there is disinterested director approval following full disclosure or if the transaction is fair. Hence, one

39. *E.g.*, State ex rel. Hayes Oyster Co. v. Keypoint Oyster Co., 64 Wash. 2d 375, 391 P.2d 979 (1964).

40. N.Y. Bus. Corp. Law § 713(a)(1).

might assert that even though the lack of disclosure precludes reliance on disinterested director approval, it does not prevent the director from saving the deal by proving the terms are fair.

Authorities are divided on this argument. New York's statute, for example, expressly allows directors in a conflict to save a transaction by proving it to be fair despite their lack of disclosure.[41] In contrast, a number of courts have held that non-disclosure can itself render a conflict-of-interest transaction unfair.[42] The official comment to the Model Act's revised conflict-of-interest provisions supports the view that unfairness in the approval process, and specifically non-disclosure, can make the deal unfair regardless of its terms.[43]

This, however, raises the question, why is the fairness of the substantive terms not enough. Put differently, what is the point of demanding fairness of process (disclosure) if the court determines that, in fact, the corporation got a good deal? One answer is to deter non-disclosure. Moreover, we can never be sure, even if a court finds the terms of a contract are fair, that the corporation might not have received a better deal if the disinterested directors had known of the conflict, or whatever other material facts the interested director did not disclose.[44]

For example, let us assume that an interested director did not disclose his or her conflict-of-interest. Here, one might argue the deal equaled what an outsider have would received—the definition of substantive fairness—since, after all, the disinterested directors thought they were dealing with an outsider. Yet, had the disinterested directors known they were dealing with another director, they might have demanded a better bargain. Specifically, the disinterested directors might rationally figure that if a party with inside knowledge (knowledge from within the corporation) sees value in a deal, maybe there is more value to whatever the corporation is giving up than they thought. Indeed, the decision of the interested director to conceal his or her conflict reinforces this possibility. After all, the interested director presumably would have revealed the conflict if the interested director thought this would have given him or her an advantage.

In any event, conflict-of-interest statutes have removed a number of the common law constraints on the conduct of interested directors. The statutes typically allow interested directors to attend the meeting, count toward a quorum, and even vote on the transaction, without rendering the transaction void simply because the interested directors did so.[45]

41. *Id.* at § 713(b).

42. *E.g.,* State ex rel. Hayes Oyster Co. v. Keypoint Oyster Co., 64 Wash. 2d 375, 391 P.2d 979 (1964). *But see* Marciano v. Nakash, 535 A.2d 400 (Del.1987) (dicta suggesting that the court still could review fairness of a conflict-of-interest transaction despite non-disclosure).

43. The official comment suggests that the court should give the corporation the

option to rescind the contract after full disclosure, even though the terms as approved without such disclosure appear to be fair. M.B.C.A. § 8.61 Official Comment: Note on Fair Transaction.

44. *See, e.g.,* Principles of Corporate Governance, Comment to § 5.02(a).

45. The Model Act is ambiguous with respect to the impact of interested directors on a quorum. If a majority of the "quali-

e. What is the impact of the vote?

We have saved the most contentious issue regarding disinterested director approval for last. What impact does the vote have? To answer this question, we need to consider both the situation in which the action of the board satisfies the statutory requirements for disinterested director approval, and the situation in which the board's action does not satisfy these requirements.

Let us start with the situation in which the board does *not* satisfy the requirements for disinterested director approval. As we discussed above, this could result from an insufficient number of disinterested directors voting for the transaction, the vote occurring too late, or some problem with the conduct of the interested directors, most especially non-disclosure. At one time, when the common law required both fairness and disinterested director approval of a conflict-of-interest transaction, failure to obtain disinterested director approval would doom the transaction. The conflict-of-interest statutes, however, make fairness an alternative to disinterested director approval. Hence, as a general proposition, interested directors can still save the transaction, despite not obtaining disinterested director approval, by proving the deal is fair. Notice, this means that a conflict-of-interest transaction may be valid, even though most of the disinterested directors voted against the transaction, and the board only approved the transaction by virtue of the votes of the interested directors.[46]

There is one important caveat to this conclusion. Sometimes, the fact which prevented the disinterested director vote from meeting the requirements of the conflict-of-interest statute will also convince the court that the transaction is unfair—thus precluding reliance on the fairness prong as well. For example, we earlier pointed out that non-disclosure will not only prevent reliance on the disinterested director vote, but many courts also treat non-disclosure as an unfair process. Also, presumably a court would be highly dubious of the substantive merits of a conflict-of-interest transaction opposed by most of the disinterested directors.

Suppose the reason for not obtaining disinterested director approval is because the board never voted on the transaction. After all, most

---

fied" directors vote for the transaction, then the recent revision of the Act states that a quorum is present for purposes of action which complies with the conflict-of-interest provision. M.B.C.A. § 8.62(c) (1988). The 1984 version is similar. M.B.C.A. § 8.31(c). Does this mean that there is a quorum simply for curing the conflict, or is there also a quorum for purposes of valid corporate action regardless of the conflict? Presumably, the Model Act meant to change the earlier common law rule that interested directors could not count as part of the quorum, or else much of the purpose of the provision would be lost. After all, what is the point of curing the conflict, if the transaction fails for want of authority whenever most of the directors are interested and the transaction is of sufficient magnitude to require board approval?

46. It should go without saying, however, that if a majority of the board votes down the transaction, then the corporation is not bound regardless of whether the deal is fair. In other words, fairness only cures the conflict-of-interest, it does not create approval.

corporate contracts do not require board approval. Does the absence of any board approval prevent the court from upholding a conflict-of-interest transaction based upon fairness? It is difficult to see why it should. Yet, notice that the fairness prong of Delaware's statute refers to conflict-of-interest transactions being fair at the time the board or the shareholders authorize, approve or ratify the deal.[47] Probably all the legislature meant by this language was to codify the rule we saw earlier about when to measure fairness. Nevertheless, the Delaware Supreme Court in *Marciano v. Nakash*,[48] assumed that this language prevented the statute from applying when neither the directors (even if interested) nor the shareholders had approved the transaction. In *Marciano*, feuding between two fifty percent shareholder factions had precluded either director or shareholder approval of loans which one faction wished to make to the corporation. As a result, this faction, presumably using their authority as officers, agreed on behalf of the corporation to borrow the money.[49] Still, in the end, the court, after assuming the fairness prong of the statute could not apply, nevertheless applied the fairness test as a matter of common law to uphold the loans.

Now let us consider the situation in which the transaction receives disinterested director approval meeting the statutory guidelines. Here is where things get controversial. The point of contention is whether or not the court can still review the fairness of the transaction.

At first glance, the answer seems obvious under the basic pattern followed by most of these statutes. The statutes list disinterested director approval and fairness as alternate means of saving a conflict-of-interest transaction. Hence, if the transaction receives approval by disinterested directors, it should not be subject to judicial review for fairness.

Does this mean there will be no judicial review? The answer is no. Courts can still review transactions in which no directors or officers have a conflict-of-interest. The business judgment rule, however, limits the extent of review of director decisions when there is no conflict-of-interest. Under this analysis, then, disinterested director approval of a conflict-of-interest transaction should cause the court to treat the transaction as if it did not involve a conflict to start with—no better, no worse. Accordingly, judicial review of the transaction should follow the guidelines of the business judgment rule, rather than the fairness test.

Several Delaware court opinions have adhered to this approach. For example, in a footnote in *Marciano*, the court stated that had the transaction received disinterested director approval, the court would have reviewed the transaction under the business judgment rule.

---

47. Del. Gen. Corp. Law § 144(a)(3). By contrast, the new Model Act provisions and California's statute simply refer to measuring fairness at the time of approval or ratification, without stating who will approve or ratify. M.B.C.A. § 8.61(b)(3); Cal. Corp. Code § 310(a)(3).

48. 535 A.2d 400 (Del.1987).

49. This raises an interesting question about authority, but that is a different issue.

On the other hand, a number of courts have reviewed conflict-of-interest transactions for fairness despite compliance with the disinterested director (or, in some cases, shareholder) approval prongs of the conflict statutes. Two of the more cited cases are *Remillard Brick Co. v. Remillard–Dandini Co.*[50] and the *Fliegler* case we discussed earlier. These cases, however, involved situations in which the approval came from the shareholders, and the shareholder approval may only have passed by virtue of votes cast by those who had the conflict-of-interest. Hence, we shall return to the impact of these cases later when we take up shareholder approval of conflict-of-interest transactions. More recently, the Iowa Supreme Court, in the *Cookies* case we discussed earlier, stated that compliance with the disinterested approval prongs of Iowa's statute did not remove fairness as an issue.

This muddled state of judicial authority has led some state legislatures to add language seeking to address the issue. The conflict-of-interest provisions in a number of states now explicitly provide that fairness remains at issue despite disinterested director approval. For example, California's statute cures a conflict-of-interest if there is director approval by a vote sufficient without counting the votes of the interested directors *and* the transaction is "just and reasonable"[51] (different words for fair). Does this mean that California has gone back to the earlier common law approach of requiring both disinterested director approval and fairness? The answer is no, because California's statute also states that transactions not receiving disinterested approval can still be valid if proven to be just and reasonable (fair).[52]

In contrast, the recent Model Act conflict-of-interest provisions seem to contemplate no fairness review in case of qualified director approval. The official comment states that qualified director approval must comply with the good faith and due care provisions of the Model Act and that terms of the deal might be so unfavorable as to show bad faith.[53] Still, this is not the same thing as calling for the sort of intrusive judicial review we earlier saw entailed by the fairness test.

So, what approach should the law follow? To begin with, one might consider the appropriate judicial role in interpreting statutes. If a statute sets out a disjunctive test, it seems somewhat arrogant to ignore this because prior common law had always required a review of fairness. One often expressed rationale for continuing to use a fairness test, despite these statutes, points to the initial language in the statutes. This language essentially states that compliance with one of the three prongs will prevent a contract from being void or voidable "solely" because of the conflict-of-interest. In contrast, the court in voiding an *unfair* conflict-of-interest transaction is not voiding the transaction *solely* because of the conflict.

50. 109 Cal.App.2d 405, 241 P.2d 66 (1952).

51. Cal. Corp. Code § 310(a)(2).

52. *Id.* at (a)(3).

53. M.B.C.A. § 8.61 Official Comment.

Cute; but not totally persuasive. Admittedly, the three prongs of the conflict statutes do not immunize conflict transactions from all attack. If there is some problem with the deal under contract law (such as non-compliance with the statute of frauds) or under various provisions of corporate law (lack of authority, breach of the duty of care), then the transaction is subject to attack. Unfairness, however, is not grounds for voiding a transaction under general contract law, nor, in and of itself, under corporate law. Proof of fairness entered the picture as a way to save conflict-of-interest transactions from the earlier rule of voidability. Accordingly, if disinterested director approval prevents voiding a transaction because of a conflict-of-interest, there is no independent doctrinal basis for applying the fairness test to the deal.

California's current statute removes the disregard of statutory language problem, since it expressly calls for a fairness review despite disinterested director approval. Yet, this introduces a new question. What is the point of including reference to disinterested director approval if the court ends up going through the same fairness review as the court would conduct even if the transaction received no disinterested director approval? Perhaps disinterested director review shifts the burden of proof in the fairness inquiry back to the plaintiff to show the transaction is unfair; albeit, the statute does not state this explicitly.

Ultimately, the question of what the law should be comes down to an issue of trust: Do we trust disinterested directors to look out for the corporation in transacting business with their colleagues? Courts and writers who would apply the business judgment rule do; courts and writers who insist on still applying the fairness test do not.

At first glance, one might say why not trust the disinterested directors. After all, by definition, these are directors who have no personal financial stake in the deal. The response involves the political and psychological dynamics of a group like the board of directors. Often, the so-called disinterested directors owe their positions on the board to the directors whose contract with the corporation they must consider. Also, the psychology of getting along in a group creates pressure to approve a transaction involving a colleague.[54]

Still, approval by nominally disinterested directors might be worth something in terms of trusting the decision. Perhaps a compromise is in order: Not the highly deferential business judgment rule; but also not the exacting scrutiny of the fairness test. The American Law Institute's Principles of Corporate Governance takes this sort of approach. The American Law Institute recommends that courts review a conflict-of-interest transaction which receives approval by disinterested directors

---

54. *E.g.*, Note, *The Propriety of Judicial Deference to Corporate Boards of Directors*, 96 Harv. L. Rev. 1894 (1983). Various writers have attempted to look empirically at the willingness of nominally disinterested directors to challenge conflict-of-interest transactions. *E.g.*, Luara Lin, *The Effective-* *ness of Outside Directors as a Corporate Governance Mechanism: Theories and Evidence*, 90 Nw. U. L. Rev. 898 (1996); Victor Brudney, *The Independent Director—Heavenly City or Potemkin Village?*, 95 Harv. L. Rev. 597 (1982).

under an intermediate standard. The court would not need to find the transaction was actually fair—as it would for conflict-of-interest transactions which receive no disinterested director approval. Yet, it would not be adequate if the directors just rationally believed the transaction was in the best interest of the corporation—the American Law Institute's business judgment standard. Instead, the court would need to find that the directors reasonably could have concluded the transaction was fair.[55] Indeed, this sort of intermediate fairness review might well reflect what is really going on in those opinions in which courts continue to review conflict-of-interest transactions for fairness despite disinterested director approval.

4.2.4   *Shareholders and Conflicts of Interest*

Matters become even more complex once we introduce shareholders into the conflict-of-interest picture. On the potentially positive side, shareholders might review the merits of contracts in which directors have a conflict-of-interest. On the other hand, the party with a conflict-of-interest could be the owner of a majority (or at least a controlling block) of the corporation's voting stock.

a.   *Shareholder approval of director conflicts*

We saw earlier that statutes create three avenues for upholding transactions despite a conflict-of-interest by directors. So far, we have discussed fairness and disinterested director approval. The third option is approval by a shareholder vote. Indeed, even without the guidance of conflict-of-interest statutes, courts have taken shareholder approval into account when determining how carefully the court will scrutinize whether the terms of a conflict-of-interest transaction are fair, and in deciding whether the interested directors, or the party challenging the transaction, bears the burden of proof on fairness.[56] The questions we addressed in exploring disinterested director approval provide a useful road map for considering the issues raised by shareholder approval.

We began our discussion of disinterested director approval by asking who is disinterested. In the context of shareholder approval, we must begin with a related, but more fundamental, question: Does it matter if the shareholders voting to approve the transaction are disinterested? It sometimes happens that the directors in a conflict-of-interest own a substantial percentage, or even a majority, of a corporation's outstanding stock. If so, the votes of the shares owned by the interested directors might provide the margin of victory for a shareholder vote approving the conflict-of-interest transaction. In this event, can the interested directors still point to the shareholder vote as curing the conflict under the statute?

55. Principles of Corporate Governance § 5.02(a)(2)(B).

56. *E.g.,* Gottlieb v. Heyden Chemical Corp.,33 Del.Ch. 177, 91 A.2d 57 (Sup. Ct. 1952).

Some statutes—for example, California's[57] and both the 1984 and 1988 versions of the Model Act's conflict-of-interest provisions[58]—expressly provide that only the votes of shareholders without a conflict-of-interest count toward curing the conflict. Indeed, the recent revision of the Model Act's conflict provisions coins the term "qualified shares" to limit which shares count in a vote to approve a conflict-of-interest transaction. The definition of qualified shares excludes shares owned by the director(s) in a conflict-of-interest, by specified close relatives of such director(s), or by trusts and estates for the benefit of such individuals, or administered by such director(s).[59]

Many other conflict statutes—most notably Delaware's[60]—do not expressly address the question. The resulting need for statutory interpretation confronted the court in the *Fliegler* case we discussed earlier. In making this interpretation, we can begin with the structure of Delaware's and similar statutes. This structure suggests that the votes of the shares owned by interested directors count. Specifically, these statutes refer to votes by "disinterested" directors in discussing disinterested director approval, but do not use the term disinterested in referring to shareholder approval. The negative implication is that disinterest is not a qualifier on shareholder votes.

The language of Delaware's shareholder approval provision suggests a couple of responses to this line of reasoning. The provision refers to the shareholders "entitled to vote thereon." Perhaps one might argue that shares owned by the interested directors are not entitled to vote. Perhaps; but not promising. After all, if this language meant to exclude shares owned by the interested directors, the legislature chose an awfully obtuse way to express itself. More likely, the "entitled to vote" language refers to the fact that the corporation might have outstanding classes of shares which lack voting rights under the company's articles (such as non-voting preferred). A second response is to note that, under the provision, the shareholders must vote in "good faith." One might argue that a vote by interested directors of their shares would not be in good faith. Again, this is not terribly persuasive. The problem is that the disinterested director provision also requires the disinterested director vote to be in good faith. If any interested vote is automatically not in good faith, then why did the legislature find it necessary to refer to "disinterested" directors, rather than just a good faith vote by directors?

Still, it seems poor policy for shares voted by interested directors to immunize a conflict-of-interest transaction. Admittedly, as we shall discuss shortly, there is a traditional notion that shareholders generally lack a fiduciary duty and are entitled to "vote their pocketbooks" (in other words, to advance their personal financial interests). But this is

57. Cal. Corp. Code § 310(a)(1).

58. M.B.C.A. §§ 8.31(d) (1984), 8.63(a), (b) (1988).

59. Comparing this definition to the definition of qualified directors shows, however, that shares owned by individuals who might not be qualified directors for purposes of disinterested director approval, might nevertheless be qualified shares.

60. Del. Gen. Corp. Law § 144(a)(2).

different from saying that directors—who do have a fiduciary duty—can immunize breaches of their duty as directors so long as they own a majority of the outstanding shares. Moreover, if the point of looking to shareholder approval is to find someone we can trust to determine the corporate interest, this is not a shareholder in a conflict-of-interest.

Perhaps the *Fliegler* court simply should have been honest and said it could not believe the legislature intended to count the votes of interested shareholders, whatever the negative implications of the statutory structure.[61] The court did not do so. Instead, the court achieved the result it wanted with a judicial sleight of hand. Tacitly accepting the defendants' argument that interested shareholder votes count under the statute, the court then held, as we discussed earlier, that the statute did not preclude applying a fairness review. Looking to prior Delaware common law cases, the court decided it would apply such a review when the approval came through the votes of shares owned by interested directors.

Again, as with disinterested director approval, the next question—at least in those jurisdictions which do not count the votes of shares owned by interested directors—is how many votes are needed to cure the conflict. Statutes which do not allow the votes of shares owned by interested directors to count toward finding shareholder approval also tend to ignore these shares in determining how many votes are needed for such approval.[62] In other words, unlike the approach followed in some jurisdictions (such as California) when it comes to determining how many disinterested director votes are required for disinterested director approval, when it comes to disinterested shareholder approval, the statutes treat shares owned by parties in a conflict-of-interest as if the shares do not exist. This means that a conflict-of-interest transaction involving a majority shareholder could be cured by a vote of a majority of the minority-owned shares.

As far as the timing of shareholder approval, the statutory provisions follow the same breakdown seen before when discussing disinterested director approval. For example, California and the recent Model Act revisions allow after-the-fact ratification, while Delaware's statute is ambiguous as to whether such ratification will cure the conflict.

Shareholder approval entails the same requirements of disclosure (in this case, to the shareholders), and the same impact of non-disclosure (both on the adequacy of approval and on the fairness of the transaction), as we saw in discussing disinterested director approval.

Once again, as with disinterested director approval, the most difficult question concerns the impact of the shareholder vote. Indeed, some of the most cited judicial opinions holding that fairness remains at issue despite technical compliance with the approval prongs of the conflict-of-

61. *See* Woodstock Enterprises, Inc. v. International Moorings & Marine, Inc., 524 So.2d 1313 (La.Ct.App.1988) (holding that a Louisiana statute, with language similar to Delaware General Corp. Law Section 144, contemplated approval only from shareholders who were disinterested).

62. *See, e.g.,* Cal. Corp. Code § 112.

interest statutes—*Fliegler* and *Remillard*–involved shareholder approval. In fact, however, *Fliegler* and *Remillard* involved approval by a shareholder vote in which shares voted by the directors in a conflict-of-interest apparently provided the winning margin. If the shareholder vote is disinterested, the rule is different. Here, courts generally do not apply the fairness test to review the transaction; at least, not the highly intrusive fairness test as we described it earlier.

Actually, some confusion on this point exists because courts sometimes refer to the "fairness" of a conflict-of-interest transaction which received approval by disinterested shareholders. For example, in *Cohen v. Ayers*,[63] the court faced a challenge to the directors' decision to lower the exercise price of stock options issued to employees, including some of the corporation's directors.[64] The company's shareholders ratified the change in exercise price. The favorable vote was so large that it is unlikely the votes of any shares owned by the directors in a conflict provided the winning margin. Applying New York's conflict-of-interest statute, the court stated that the transaction still must be "fair," even with shareholder approval. Yet, not only did the court hold that shareholder ratification shifted the burden of proof to the plaintiff to show that the transaction was unfair, but the court also took a much more circumspect role in scrutinizing the transaction than normally entailed by the fairness test. There was no attempt by the court to examine what the corporation gained by reducing the option price, or to compare what one might expect in an arms-length transaction. Accordingly, while courts in cases such as *Cohen* often refer to "fairness," this does not mean they are applying the fairness test.

One exception to this may occur in transactions with majority or controlling shareholders. If such a transaction receives approval from most of the other shareholders—a so-called "majority of the minority"— some courts may shift the burden of proof to the objecting minority shareholder to show the transaction is unfair, but still may be willing to give the transaction a degree of scrutiny consistent with the fairness test, as opposed to the business judgment rule.[65] The basis for following this approach lies in the concern that minority shareholders might vote to approve a transaction desired by the majority shareholder, despite the minority's dislike of the transaction, simply out of fear of retaliation by the majority shareholder.

If courts are not going to apply the fairness test, then what, if any, test will apply to a conflict-of-interest transaction approved by a disinterested shareholder vote? One might be tempted to answer, the business judgment rule. Indeed, the Delaware Supreme Court in *Marciano* suggested this in a footnote. Yet, the business judgment rule is a standard for review of director decisions and is not exactly relevant to shareholder

---

63.   596 F.2d 733 (7th Cir.1979).

64.   Lowering the exercise price makes the option more valuable to the employee.

65.   *See, e.g.,* In re Wheelabrator Technologies, Inc. Shareholders Litigation, 663 A.2d 1194 (Del.Ch.1995) (explaining the distinction).

actions. The reason is not because of the various policies behind the business judgment rule—which may or may not seem apropos to shareholder action. Rather, the reason has to do with the duty of care. Even under the business judgment rule, directors have a duty of care which allows the court, at least in most jurisdictions, to examine the diligence used by the directors in making their decisions. By contrast, shareholders do not appear to have a duty of care in deciding how to vote. If a shareholder decides how to vote on an issue by pasting a proxy solicitation to the wall and throwing darts at it, he or she apparently would not be liable for doing so.[66] This appears to be the rule, if for no other reason, because any other rule would be impossible to administer.

Does this mean that a shareholder vote puts a transaction beyond any judicial challenge? The answer is no. Courts state that shareholder approval cannot save a transaction which amounts to "gift or waste."[67]

To understand the notion of gift or waste, we need to go back to the ultra vires doctrine. Recall that even the owners of a majority of the outstanding shares cannot approve, over the objections of a minority shareholder, a transaction which is ultra vires.[68] Generally speaking, since the purpose of a business corporation is to conduct business, giving away corporate assets for no business purpose is ultra vires. Hence, anything less than unanimous shareholder approval cannot save a transaction which simply gives away corporate assets. Suppose, however, the majority shareholder(s) seek to circumvent this rule by having the corporation receive token consideration (a "peppercorn") in the transaction? Even though the consideration might be adequate under contract law, the result under corporate law should be the same as with a gift. After all, what is the difference between the shareholders voting to give away $100 of corporate funds, versus voting to spend $101 of corporate funds on an item worth only $1? Following this logic, we see courts state that even the owners of a majority of the shares cannot simply make a "gift" of corporate assets or vote to approve a transaction which spends far more than the corporation receives in return (in other words, "wastes" corporate assets).[69]

On the other hand, it is often arguable whether the corporation received something in return that was worth what the corporation gave in a transaction. Under a fairness review, the court would carefully scrutinize the question of equivalence with doubts resolved against

---

66. *Cf* Ringling Bros.-Barnum & Bailey Combined Shows, Inc. v. Ringling, 29 Del. Ch. 610, 53 A.2d 441, 447 (Sup. Ct. 1947) ("it is not objectionable that [a shareholder's motives in voting his shares] may be for personal profit, or determined by whims or caprice . . .").

67. *E.g.,* Aronoff v. Albanese, 85 A.D.2d 3, 446 N.Y.S.2d 368 (1982).

68. See § 3.1.4c *supra.*

69. *E.g.,* Rogers v. Hill, 289 U.S. 582, 53 S.Ct. 731 (1933).

This analysis suggests unanimous shareholder approval can preclude a challenge that a transaction constituted waste or gift. As mentioned earlier in dealing with promoters' contracts, however, this conclusion becomes less certain when an initial group of shareholders ratify conflict-of-interest transactions involving themselves, and then have the corporation bring in innocent investors either as additional shareholders or creditors. See § 1.3.3 *supra.*

upholding the transaction. Determining whether a transaction amounts to gift or waste is much different. In looking at waste or gift, the burden is on the shareholder challenging the transaction to show that no reasonable person would conclude the corporation received the equivalent to what it gave in the deal.[70] In other words, the waste or gift standard entails a highly circumspect judicial review with doubts resolved in favor of upholding the transaction. In this regard, the waste or gift standard is similar to the business judgment rule (minus any review of the care used by shareholders in making their decision).[71]

Before leaving the impact of shareholder approval, we might ask whether even disinterested shareholders provide a good source for reviewing a conflict-of-interest transaction. Certainly, the shareholders' hearts should be in the right place, since it is ultimately their money at stake. There may be concern, however, at least in the widely-held corporation, with the shareholders' competence. Specifically, shareholders in a widely-held corporation are likely to be ill-informed decisionmakers. Even if they receive complete information as part of the solicitation of proxies to vote their shares, stockholders have limited incentives to expend the time reading and carefully considering the information. Still, it is not clear that this problem makes shareholder approval into a worse solution for dealing with conflict-of-interest transactions than is imposing the burden of judicial fairness review, relying on nominally disinterested directors, or going back to the old rule that conflict-of-interest transactions are void if any shareholder objects.

b. Dealings with majority or controlling shareholders.

As we saw above, the owner(s) of a majority (or even just a controlling block) of the outstanding stock might be the person(s) with a conflict-of-interest. The impact of a conflict-of-interest on the part of majority or controlling shareholders goes beyond the question of cleaning up director conflicts through shareholder approval. In addition, such a conflict on the shareholder level opens up further questions about fairness, disinterested director approval, and even what constitutes a conflict-of-interest transaction and who can be liable for it.

The *Sinclair* case encountered earlier illustrates many of these questions. Sinclair Oil Corp. owned 97% of the outstanding stock in Sinclair Venezuelan Oil Company ("Sinven"). A minority shareholder in Sinven sued Sinclair. Interestingly, no one spent much time arguing over whether Sinven's directors, who, after all, made the decisions challenged by the plaintiff, were themselves in a conflict-of-interest. Rather, the court devotes much of its opinion to determining whether these decisions constitute self-dealing (in other words, a conflict-of-interest transaction) between Sinclair and Sinven. We shall return to that question later. Now, however, we must ask a more fundamental question: Why should it

70. *E.g.,* Michelson v. Duncan, 407 A.2d 211 (Del.1979).

71. This may explain why the Delaware Supreme Court in *Marciano* seems to treat waste or gift and the business judgment rule as embodying the same test.

matter whether a majority shareholder—be this a parent company or an individual—engages in a conflict-of-interest transaction with the corporation?

The answer is not as simple as it might first appear. The corporation and its shareholders hire directors and officers to manage the firm. As a result, the directors and officers receive compensation to put the company's interest ahead of their own, in other words, for assuming a duty of loyalty. Moreover, a corporation can only act through its directors and officers. This fact gives directors and officers the power to enter transactions between themselves and the corporation, which might advance their financial interests at the company's expense. By contrast, no one pays shareholders, including a majority shareholder, to act on behalf of the corporation. On the contrary, persons pay to become shareholders in order to enjoy the benefits of owning stock. This is why courts sometimes say shareholders are entitled, in voting their stock, to "vote their pocketbooks" (in other words, for their own financial interests). Put differently, shareholders have some right to selfish ownership. Moreover, shareholders normally do not have the power to act for the corporation; officers and directors do.[72] Hence, even a majority shareholder, acting as a shareholder, generally cannot bind the corporation to a conflict-of-interest transaction. Instead, unless the majority shareholder is an officer or director, the majority shareholder must negotiate with individuals (the corporation's officers or directors) who have a duty to the company and all of its shareholders.

This suggests we must be more analytical in assessing the legal significance of a transaction between a corporation and its majority (or controlling) shareholder (or a transaction in which the majority or controlling shareholder otherwise has a personal financial interest at odds with the company's or even the minority shareholders'). *Sinclair* illustrates several possible lines of attack. To begin with, maybe we can find a conflict-of-interest on the part of the directors. If the majority shareholder is him-or herself a director, this will do. Yet, this will not be the case when, as in *Sinclair*, the majority shareholder is itself a corporation.

Alternately, a conflict-of-interest occurs not only when the officers or directors of a corporation enter a contract with the corporation. It also can occur when officers or directors of a corporation have a financial stake or a management role in another firm (such as another corporation) which enters a contract with the corporation. In *Sinclair*, the directors of Sinven were also officers, directors or employees of Sinclair or other subsidiaries of Sinclair. Hence, one or more of Sinven's directors may have had enough of a financial interest or a management role in Sinclair to bring the transactions between Sinven and Sinclair within the parameters of a director conflict-of-interest.

The court in *Sinclair*, however, took a different tack, which turns out to be the approach courts most often use. The trial court found as a

---

72. See § 3.1.3a *supra*.

fact, and, indeed, Sinclair conceded, the members of Sinven's board were not independent, but, rather, Sinclair dominated these individuals. Based upon this domination, the court in *Sinclair* held that the parent had a fiduciary duty in its dealings with the subsidiary.

The Third Circuit in *Zahn v. Transamerica Corp.*,[73] reached a similar result. There, a shareholder of a tobacco corporation (Axton–Fisher) alleged that the tobacco corporation's board of directors exercised the corporation's option to redeem a class of stock ("Class A"), some of which he owned, in order to benefit the shareholder who held stock of another class ("Class B"). He further alleged that the directors of the tobacco corporation were the instruments of this shareholder, Transamerica Corp., who owned most of the voting stock. In holding that this complaint stated a cause of action, the court explained, "there is a radical difference when a stockholder is voting strictly as a stockholder and when voting as a director."[74] Specifically, under the court's view, when voting as a shareholder, one may vote with a view to one's own benefits; but when voting as a director, one represents all the shareholders and cannot use the office for personal benefit. This result follows whether the shareholder is an individual who is a director, or, as alleged in Zahn's complaint, the directors do not exercise independent judgment, but, rather, act as mere agents or puppets of the shareholder. In other words, controlling shareholders pick up the directors' duty of loyalty when the controlling shareholders tell the directors what actions to take.

Looking at our analysis so far of transactions between a corporation and its controlling shareholder, there are a couple of points worth special focus. To begin with, each of the challenges outlined above depends upon the existence of action by the corporation's board. If all we have is action taken by a majority shareholder solely as a shareholder, then it is a much more difficult question as to whether and, if so, when, there is any fiduciary duty. We will consider this question elsewhere in this book.

The second point worth special focus when analyzing a transaction between a corporation and its controlling shareholder is that all of the challenges outlined above ultimately entail evaluating the independence of the directors who approved the transaction. This is obvious under the *Sinclair* and *Zahn* approach of recognizing a fiduciary duty of the majority shareholder who dominates the directors. Independence is also a critical inquiry under the approaches which seek to find a conflict-of-interest on the part of individual directors (such as when the majority shareholder is him-or herself a director, or individual directors have a financial interest or a management role in a parent corporation). The reason is because normally the board in such cases will have, among its members, directors who do not have any personal conflict-of-interest. If these directors are independent of the majority shareholder's control,

73.   162 F.2d 36 (3d Cir.1947).   **74.**   *Id.* at 44.

then they could provide disinterested director approval of a transaction between the corporation and the majority shareholder.

This, in turn, raises questions as to what courts mean when they say directors are "independent" versus "dominated" by a majority shareholder, and what facts establish such independence or domination. A simple approach might be to say that ownership of a majority of the voting stock equals domination. After all, a majority stockholder presumably selected the individuals who sit on the board, and, under most modern corporate statutes, a majority shareholder generally can remove directors at any time with or without cause.[75]

Still, it is possible, despite the manner of his or her selection, and the overhanging prospect of removal, that a given director may be sufficiently strong-willed to maintain objectivity in reviewing corporate dealings with a majority shareholder. The problem is that, without an extensive track record of bucking the majority shareholder, it would be difficult either to prove or disprove this independent temperament. Much, therefore, depends on whether the court presumes independence even in the face of majority ownership. Generally, courts appear to equate majority ownership with control over the board;[76] albeit, in at least some contexts, courts have stated that the presumption of independence remains even when there is a majority shareholder.[77]

More difficult are cases when the shareholder with a conflict-of-interest owns a large percentage, but not an outright majority, of the voting stock. For example, in *Puma v Marriott*,[78] the Marriott family sold real estate to the hotel corporation in which they owned 46% of the outstanding voting stock. Similarly, in *Aronson v. Lewis*[79]—which we will discuss in more detail later when exploring rules regarding derivative lawsuits—the corporation entered into a consulting contract with a 47% shareholder. In both cases, Delaware courts refused to accept claims of domination based upon the percentage of ownership, or even the fact the defendant shareholder(s) had selected the individuals who sat on the board. Yet, the conventional wisdom in the corporate world is that a large percentage of stock, even if not a majority, can yield working control over the board of a widely held corporation. Indeed, courts have operated upon this assumption in other contexts.[80]

Otherwise, cases like *Sinclair* seem to be looking for domination through relationships between the directors and the majority shareholder; in that case, the employment of Sinven's directors by the parent corporation or its other subsidiaries. Conversely, the director most likely to stand up to a majority shareholder would be one who has no outside

75. See § 3.1.2a *supra*.

76. *See, e.g.*, Ivanhoe Partners v. Newmont Mining Corp., 535 A.2d 1334, 1344 (Del.1987).

77. *See, e.g.*, Aronson v. Lewis, 473 A.2d 805 (Del.1984) (stating that ownership of even a majority of shares might not establish domination for purposes of excusing

demand on the board prior to bringing a derivative suit).

78. 283 A.2d 693 (Del.Ch.1971).

79. 473 A.2d 805 (Del.1984).

80. See § 7.1.1b *infra* (discussing sale of control).

economic ties to the shareholder and who receives no significant economic benefit from remaining a director.

So far, we have seen how transactions between the corporation and a majority shareholder force us to expand our notions of when directors might not be disinterested (because of domination by the majority shareholder) and when there is a conflict-of-interest transaction calling for fairness review (due to a financial interest by the majority shareholder, as opposed to a director). Moreover, *Sinclair* and *Zahn* show that majority shareholders, and not just directors, might personally be liable for an unfair conflict-of-interest transaction. A conflict-of-interest on the part of a controlling shareholder also can introduce additional complexity into determining the fairness of a corporate action.

Zahn provides a good illustration of this added complexity. There, Axton–Fisher's articles of incorporation entitled owners of Class A shares (the class owned by the plaintiff) to twice as much per share of any liquidating distribution as the amount received by owners of Class B shares (most of which, the defendant, Transamerica, owned). In other words, if Axton–Fisher called it quits and passed out to its shareholders all of its assets left after paying off the creditors, for each dollar per share which went to the owners of Class B shares, two dollars per share had to go to the owners of Class A shares. Axton–Fisher's articles, however, gave the directors the option to redeem the Class A shares (in other words, force the owners to sell the shares back to the corporation) at a fixed price. What precipitated the plaintiff's complaint was that Axton–Fisher's directors exercised this option at a time when this fixed price was much less than the shares would have received in the liquidation which the directors ordered shortly after the redemption. Indeed, the fixed redemption price was even less than the Class A shareholders would have received on liquidation had they exercised an option which Axton–Fisher's articles gave them to convert each one of their Class A shares into one Class B share. This meant the Class B shareholders (principally, Transamerica) received much more on the liquidation than they would have without the redemption of the Class A shares.

Was this fair? To begin with, the plaintiff did not argue about whether this was fair to the corporation. He seemed content that if it is more profitable for the shareholders to liquidate the company than to keep it running, there is nothing unfair about that. Instead, the issue was one of fairness between classes. Exercise of the option meant more money to the owners of Class B shares and less to the owners of Class A. On the other hand, failing to exercise the option would mean more to the owners of Class A and less to the owners of Class B. How can one say which alternative is fair? Notice, in this case, we are not dealing with a voluntary exchange, when one might compare values to see if they match what parties in an arms-length transaction would have agreed.

Perhaps the answer lies in why the articles granted Axton–Fisher the option to redeem the shares. The only reason to have such an option is to advantage the owners of shares not subject to the option; in other words, the option exists so that the directors can call the shares when it would be in the economic interest of the other shareholders to do so. After all, the corporation, itself, has no stake in buying back its shares. Moreover, if the option is to benefit the shares subject to the redemption, their owners presumably would get control on the exercise of the option. This means the court in *Zahn* goofed when it appears to suggest that the exercise of the option in order to advantage Transamerica was itself wrongful. In a later opinion dealing with the measure of damages, the court caught its mistake.[81] In this later opinion, the court decided to award damages measured, not by the amount the Class B holders would have received had Axton–Fisher not redeemed their shares, but, rather, by an amount equal to what the Class A shareholders would have received had they exercised the option which Axton–Fisher's articles gave them to convert their shares into Class B. In essence, the wrongful conduct did not consist of ordering the redemption. Rather, it lay in failing to fully inform the Class A shareholders of the reason for the redemption so they could protect themselves, at least somewhat, by converting their shares.

We shall have occasions elsewhere in this book to encounter other situations in which the question is whether actions taken by directors at the behest of a majority or controlling shareholder are fair to minority shareholders, rather than fair to the corporation.

4.2.5 What Is a Conflict-of-Interest?

Our discussion so far shows how the courts take very different approaches to reviewing decisions by corporate directors depending upon whether the directors have a conflict-of-interest: Without a conflict, the highly deferential business judgment rule applies; with a conflict, courts turn to the exacting scrutiny of the fairness test (at least in the absence of disinterested approval). This places a premium on deciding what is a conflict-of-interest. Unfortunately, what constitutes a conflict-of-interest is often not clear.

Most conflict-of-interest statutes, as, for example, Delaware's, suggest a simple definition of conflicts of interest. They refer to two types of conflicts of interest. First, there is a contract or transaction between the corporation and one or more of the corporation's directors (or officers[82]). Some sources refer to this as a "direct" conflict-of-interest.[83] Second, there is a contract or transaction between the corporation and another firm (such as another corporation) in which one or more of the corporation's directors (or officers) have an interest. This could be a financial interest, as when a corporation's director owns the company which the corporation is contracting with. Alternately, under many statutes such as Delaware's, the interest could be a role in managing the firm which

---

81. Speed v. Transamerica Corp., 235 F.2d 369 (3d Cir.1956).

82. Most of the conflict-of-interest statutes only refer to conflicts involving directors, and not officers. *E.g.*, M.B.C.A. § 8.31 (1984); M.B.C.A. § 8.60(1)(1988). In

this event, presumably general agency and corporate common law rules govern conflicts of interest involving officers.

83. *E.g.*, M.B.C.A. § 8.31 (1984).

the corporation is contracting with (as, for example, when one or more individuals are directors of both of the corporations entering a contract). In this last situation, the conflict is not between the interest of the corporation and the personal financial interest of the director or officer. Instead, the conflict lies in the competing duties the director or officer has to two adverse parties to a contract. This is the sort of conflict-of-interest problem which attorneys personally face all the time.[84] Some sources refer to the conflict-of-interest which arises from having an interest in an entity the corporation is contracting with as an "indirect" conflict.

Unfortunately, things are nowhere near as clear-cut as suggested by the simple-minded language of the typical conflict-of-interest statute. For example, let us start with one of the most frequent decisions made by the board of directors, this being to declare a dividend. Further, assume, as is typical, the directors own some stock in the corporation. This means that, in declaring a dividend, the directors, as stockholders, will receive money from the corporation. Is this a conflict-of-interest transaction? Literally, one might say there is something of a transaction between the corporation and its directors as recipients of the dividend, in other words, a direct conflict. Moreover, the directors have a personal financial interest in the decision; they might eagerly be awaiting the money. Does this mean every declaration of a dividend by directors who own stock should be subject to scrutiny under the fairness test? This would not seem to be very practical.

This was the issue which faced the Delaware Supreme Court in *Sinclair*. The plaintiff claimed that the parent corporation caused the board it dominated to declare excessive dividends because the parent corporation needed the cash. The trial court treated this as a conflict-of-interest and applied the fairness test. The Delaware Supreme Court reversed. This is not surprising. The Delaware Supreme Court must have realized the implications of treating this as a conflict-of-interest. Remove the added wrinkle that the dividend went to a parent corporation which controlled the individual directors, rather than personally to directors who owned stock, and the trial court's result was a prescription for applying a fairness test practically every time a board declares a dividend. The trick, however, is to come up with a principled test as to why this is not a conflict-of-interest transaction, or, as the Delaware Supreme Court phrased it, not "self-dealing."

The test the *Sinclair* court came up with for self-dealing is whether the parent corporation received something "to the exclusion of, and detriment to, the minority stockholders."[85] Unfortunately, this may not have been the best choice of words to express what the court what had in mind. Some writers and courts read too much into the word "detriment." They seem to treat the test as if finding self-dealing (a conflict-of-

84. Because this situation involves competing duties, rather than self-interest, some statutes provide more relaxed rules for dealing with this sort of conflict-of-interest. *See, e.g.,* Cal. Corp. Code § 310(b).

85. 280 A.2d at 720.

interest) almost demands showing the transaction was unfair.[86] This cannot be correct. The purpose of assessing whether there was self-dealing is to set the standard for the court's review of the merits of the transaction: Will the plaintiff need to prove gross negligence under the business judgment rule (in Delaware), or will the defendant need to prove the transaction was fair? It would be completely circular to require the court first to decide the merits of a transaction in order to determine what standard the court will use in reviewing the merits of the transaction.

So what did the *Sinclair* court mean? The answer lies in how the court applied the test to the two challenged decisions. The dividend decision did not entail self-dealing because the parent corporation received nothing to the exclusion of the minority shareholders. Rather, all of the shareholders received the same dividend per share. Hence, all of the shareholders faced roughly the same tradeoff inherent in every decision to declare dividends: Have the money now, or reinvest earnings in the corporation with hope of receiving even more money in the future. True, different shareholders may have differing needs for money today versus tomorrow. Yet, if courts treat such potentially differing needs as a conflict-of-interest, then almost every dividend decision would require fairness review. Indeed, there often are differences in the aversion to the risk of business failure between shareholders (for whom their shares in this corporation may only be one small investment in a diversified portfolio) and managers (who may be out of a job if the corporation goes under). Hence, if courts treat any differences in personal circumstances which might weigh upon a corporate decision as a conflict-of-interest, the result could be to make practically every business decision subject to fairness review.[87] In essence, then, not every personal interest in a transaction constitutes a conflict-of-interest. If the director's or controlling shareholder's interest is, for the most part, the same as the other shareholders' interest, this is not a conflict.

By contrast, the failure to enforce the oil supply contract in *Sinclair* was self-dealing (a conflict-of-interest). Here, the parent corporation, Sinclair, received something—avoiding liability on the part of another of its subsidiary corporations—which the other Sinven shareholders did not obtain. Since Sinven did not gain the benefit of enforcing the oil supply contract, this action potentially was detrimental to the minority shareholders. Keep in mind, however, at this point, the court does not know if, in fact, this was a bad deal for Sinven and its minority shareholders. It could be that insisting on full performance would expose Sinven itself to liability for breach of contract, because Sinven could not supply this quantity of oil. The reason for asking if this is self-dealing is to decide how carefully the court will scrutinize this rationale, and who will have

---

86. *See ,e.g.,* Chasin v. Gluck, 282 A.2d 188 (Del.Ch.1971); James D. Cox, Thomas Lee Hazen, & F. Hodge O'Neal, Corporations 253–254 (1997).

87. This explains, as well, why, in the *Van Gorkom* case discussed in dealing with

the duty of care (§ 4.1.2d *supra*), Van Gorkom's possible desire for a quick sale of his shares due to his impending retirement did not create a conflict-of-interest.

the burden of proof. Because all of the shareholders are not, more or less, in the same boat on this decision—Sinclair obtains something the other shareholders do not—there is reason not to fully trust Sinclair's rationale. So, the court applies the fairness test.

Sinclair illustrates how some financial interests of directors or controlling shareholders might not entail a conflict. Another common problem is to decide, even when the interest is potentially in conflict, whether the interest is significant enough to worry about. For example, suppose an airline corporation's director owns a few shares of stock in an aircraft manufacturing company. Technically, a purchase of planes by the airline corporation from the aircraft manufacturer involves a conflict-of-interest for this director. Yet, is the danger here serious enough to call for the burdens of fairness review? Some conflict-of-interest statutes attempt to deal with this problem by requiring that a financial interest in the other party to the contract be "material" in order to count as a conflict-of-interest.[88]

Cede & Co. v. Technicolor, Inc[89] illustrates some of the difficulty courts face in deciding what is a material financial interest. The plaintiffs in *Cede* claimed that the board of Technicolor breached both the directors' duty of care and the directors' duty of loyalty in voting to merge the company. In order to establish the duty of loyalty claim, the plaintiffs argued that various members of Technicolor's board had conflicts of interest. Specifically, one of Technicolor's directors would obtain a finder's fee if the merger went through, while several other directors of Technicolor might obtain increased compensation or otherwise improved job prospects with the corporation after the merger. The Delaware Supreme Court held that a director's financial interest in a transaction had to be material in order to trigger the fairness standard (even though Delaware's conflict-of-interest statute does not use the term "material").[90] The Delaware Supreme Court rejected, however, the trial court's use of a reasonable person standard in determining if a given director's self-interest in a transaction was material. On remand, the trial court judge interpreted this to require an "actual person" test of materiality; in other words, the test focuses on what effect the financial interest, in fact, had on the director in question.[91] This could require the court to look at evidence that the particular director involved was especially susceptible or immune to opportunities for self-enrichment, or evidence that the director, in fact, behaved differently in the transaction than one would expect from a reasonable person with the same self-interest. Applying this test, the trial court held the finder's fee was a conflict-of-interest, but the possibilities of increased compensation or improved job prospects after the merger were not tangible or large enough in this

88. *E.g.,* Cal. Corp. Code § 310(a).

89. 634 A.2d 345 (Del.1993).

90. The court also stated that one director's interest did not render the board interested, which is another way of expressing the concept that disinterested director approval can cure a conflict on the part of some directors.

91. Cinerama, Inc. v. Technicolor, Inc., 663 A.2d 1134 (Del.Ch.1994).

particular case to count. The Delaware Supreme Court affirmed this approach and result on appeal.[92]

In fact, however, the financial interests in *Technicolor* did not fit within the definition of even an indirect conflict-of-interest under the typical conflict-of-interest statute, such as Delaware's. The finder's fee, which the court found to present a material conflict for one director, was not a financial interest in the party Technicolor contracted to merge with. Rather, it was a financial interest in the transaction itself. The finder's fee gave the recipient director a monetary interest in the merger going through, albeit not necessarily an interest in giving favorable terms to the other party to the merger.[93] Nevertheless, both Delaware courts involved in *Technicolor* did not feel themselves limited in finding a conflict-of-interest to situations within Delaware's conflict-of-interest statute.

This illustrates that the statutory definition we started out with might be too narrow. Directors may have economic interests in a transaction which lead a court not to trust them, even though the transaction is not between the corporation and a director, or between the corporation and another firm in which the corporation's director has a financial interest or management role.

Once we go down this route, however, deciding if there is a conflict-of-interest can get even trickier. For example, directors generally have an economic interest in maintaining their positions as directors (and, for inside directors, maintaining their positions as officers). Does this mean that any steps directors take to prevent a corporate takeover present a conflict-of-interest? We shall return to this question when considering corporate acquisitions later in this book. Moreover, why should we limit conflicts just to the financial interests of the directors? For example, few would say that a director does not face a conflict in voting on a transaction between the corporation and his or her spouse—even if they are not in a community property state.[94] Yet, suppose the transaction (say, a loan from a bank) is with a party (say, a real estate developer) who has employed the son of the corporation's president;[95] is this a conflict-of-interest?

Perhaps the problem here is that we are attempting to treat conflicts of interest as an all or nothing proposition. This results from having two very different standards of review depend on whether or not there is a conflict. Suppose, in reality, personal interests of directors and officers, which might conflict with their responsibility to the corporation

---

92. Cinerama, Inc. v. Technicolor, Inc., 663 A.2d 1156 (Del.1995).

93. Courts commonly condemn such "secret commissions" paid to agents by the other party to a transaction. *E.g.,* Tarnowski v. Resop, 236 Minn. 33, 51 N.W.2d 801 (1952) (holding the principal can recover the secret commission from the agent even if the principal had already recovered compensation for any damages suffered in the transaction from the other party). In fact, such payments are really a bribe, which is an extreme form of a conflict-of-interest for the agent who receives the bribe.

94. *See, e.g.,* Bayer v. Beran, 49 N.Y.S.2d 2 (Sup. Ct. 1944).

95. *See* Joy v. North, 692 F.2d 880 (2d Cir.1982).

and its shareholders, exist in varying degrees throughout many decisions. If so, it might make more sense for courts to use intermediate levels of scrutiny in reviewing a transaction, depending on the degree the court thinks personal interests could have impacted the decision. Indeed, there is some reason to believe this is what many courts do. For example, later we will discuss an intermediate standard of review Delaware courts explicitly developed to deal with takeover defenses. Other times, the courts' employment of an intermediate standard is not explicit. For instance, many writers have noted that in most cases in which courts found directors breached their duty of care, there is at least some inkling of a conflict-of-interest.[96]

The *Litwin* decision,[97] which we discussed in exploring the duty of care, provides an example. The court there condemned directors of Guaranty Trust Company for buying debentures, which declined in value, under a contract which allowed the seller to obtain the profit if the debentures had appreciated. Some writers seek to explain the result by pointing out that the case involved something of a conflict-of-interest.[98] Specifically, these writers note that J. P. Morgan & Company owned a substantial block of stock both in Guaranty Trust and in the firm which sold Guaranty Trust the debentures. While J. P. Morgan & Company may not have dominated the board of Guaranty Trust, who can say that J. P. Morgan & Company's ownership had no influence on Guaranty Trust's directors?

Preferring predictability to realism, the drafters of the recent revisions to the Model Business Corporation Act's conflict-of-interest sections attempted to go in a different direction. The Model Act's drafters decided to adopt a "bright line" test for dealing with conflicts of interest. Specifically, the Model Act's conflict provisions, as recently revised, set out a fairly detailed definition of what is a conflict-of-interest.[99] The official comment to the Act then states this is supposed to preempt the field as far as challenges to a transaction because the transaction entails a conflict-of-interest.[100] Actually, however, the new Model Act provisions might be more of a general demarcation than a bright line.

The Model Act revisions identify a number of persons whose involvement in a transaction—either as a party, or because the person has some financial interest linked to the transaction—might create a conflict-of-interest. This includes the director, so-called related persons to a director (such as specified close relatives), and other entities in which the director is a director, general partner, agent or employee (but only if the transaction is significant enough to go before the board of directors). Transactions between the corporation and a director always constitute a conflict-of-interest under the Model Act. For other possible conflicts of

---

96. *E.g.,* Joseph W. Bishop, Jr., *Sitting Ducks and Decoy Ducks: New Trends in the Indemnification of Corporate Directors and Officers,* 77 Yale L. J. 1078 (1968).

97. Litwin v. Allen, 25 N.Y.S.2d 667 (Sup. Ct. 1940).

98. *E.g.,* Clark, *supra* note 3 at 127 (1986).

99. M.B.C.A. § 8.60(1)(1988).

100. M.B.C.A. § 8.60 Official Comment (1988).

interest, the Model Act creates an objective test to determine if there is a conflict. Under the Model Act's test, the director's or other covered person's interest in the transaction must be of such financial significance that one would reasonably expect the interest to influence the director's judgment. Actually, it might have been simpler just to collapse the whole conflict-of-interest definition into the question of whether one reasonably expects the interest involved to influence the director's judgment. In any event, the Model Act provision only addresses director conflicts. It leaves conflicts involving controlling shareholders to the common law.[101] It also only addresses conflict-of-interest "transactions." This may allow shareholders to claim directors had conflicting interests (which otherwise might not have met the Model Act's definition) in a wide variety of actions (such as takeover defenses) that do not constitute a transaction with the corporation.[102]

4.2.6 Executive Compensation

Probably the most frequent conflict-of-interest transaction is the corporation's payment of compensation to its managers. Interestingly enough, at one time, courts generally expected directors to serve without fees.[103] Indeed, individuals normally still serve without expecting fees on the governing boards of non-profit corporations (for example, as university regents, trustees of non-profit hospitals and religious congregations, and the like).[104] Moreover, large shareholders (as in a closely held corporation) often wish to be directors, even without fees, in order to protect their investment. Nevertheless, few persons today regard serving on the board of General Motors to be community service worthy of doing pro bono. Moreover, such widely held corporations are unlikely to have many shareholders with a large enough stake to motivate their serving as directors just to protect their investment. At the same time, as we discussed when dealing with the duty of care, the law expects directors to spend some time and effort on their tasks. Accordingly, widely held corporations now commonly pay their directors substantial fees. Most states' corporations statutes expressly empower the directors to set the directors' fees.[105]

Actually, however, directors' fees tend not to be the primary focus of controversy when dealing with compensation of a corporation's manag-

---

101. Id.

102. Recently, the drafters of the Model Act added to the soup by adopting a new provision (Section 8.31(a)(2)(iii)) addressing the liability of directors who do not have a conflict-of-interest themselves, but vote to approve a transaction in which the director lacks objectivity due to the director's family, financial, or business relationship with, or domination by, a person who does have a conflict-of-interest. Such directors can be liable unless they establish that they reasonably believed the transaction was in the best interests of the corporation.

103. See, e.g., Rocky Mountain Powder Co. v. Hamlin, 73 Nev. 87, 310 P.2d 404 (1957). Such an expectation was necessary in an era when courts treated conflict-of-interest transactions as void if any shareholder objected.

104. In fact, it is not unknown to invite wealthier individuals onto the boards of such institutions and then ask the individuals to make a donation to the institution.

105. E.g., M.B.C.A. § 8.11.

ers. While directors' fees in a public company may seem like a lot of money for most folks, they typically pale when compared to the sums received by the corporation's chief executive officer and other senior full time managers. These individuals receive compensation for serving as officers of the corporation. After all, even earlier courts did not expect individuals to work full time as officers of a corporation for nothing.[106]

Needless to say, a corporation's officers are interested in obtaining the most generous compensation package they can. This, however, is no different than any agent negotiating compensation with his or her principal. Generally, the board of directors decides what compensation the corporation is willing to give its senior officers. What creates the conflict-of-interest problem is that senior corporate officers are also commonly directors of the corporation.

The conflict-of-interest involved when the board sets compensation of its own members brings into play the various doctrines we discussed to deal with conflicts of interest generally. Specifically, while courts normally demand that directors prove the fairness of any compensation which the directors vote to have the corporation pay to themselves,[107] disinterested shareholder approval generally shifts the burden to the party challenging the compensation to prove gift or waste,[108] and approval by disinterested directors often leads courts to review the compensation under the business judgment rule (or, at least, under a more relaxed form of fairness review).[109]

In fact, it is fairly rare for a court to find compensation which received disinterested director or shareholder approval to be so outlandish as to flunk the business judgment rule or to constitute waste. One of the most noted cases doing so is *Rogers v. Hill*.[110] This case involved a bylaw adopted by the shareholders of the American Tobacco Company. The bylaw gave bonuses based upon a percentage of the company's profits to the company's officers. At first, these bonuses were reasonable enough, but when the corporation's profits began to skyrocket, the bonuses become huge (for the era). The Supreme Court held they had become so large that the plaintiff's complaint stated a claim of waste. One interesting aspect of this case is that the result seems to fly against the normal rule that one measures fairness at the time when the corporation enters a contract—here, the shareholders' adoption of the bylaw. At that time, there was no evidence (or, at least, none referred to by the court) that one should have expected the bonus amounts to get out of hand. *Rogers*, however, is the exception. Most courts confronted with disinterested director or shareholder approval make scant effort to determine if the compensation paid by the corporation is excessive.[111]

---

106. *See, e.g.,* Shaw v. Harding, 306 Mass. 441, 28 N.E.2d 469 (Mass. 1940).

107. *E.g.,* Wilderman v. Wilderman, 315 A.2d 610 (Del.Ch.1974).

108. *E.g.,* Michelson v. Duncan, 407 A.2d 211 (Del.1979).

109. *See, e.g.,* Beard v. Elster, 39 Del. Ch. 153, 160 A.2d 731 (Sup. Ct. 1960).

110. 289 U.S. 582, 53 S.Ct. 731 (1933).

111. *See, e.g.,* Beard v. Elster, 39 Del. Ch. 153, 160 A.2d 731 (Sup. Ct. 1960).

Indeed, in a later case involving American Tobacco's bonus plan, the court there refused to substitute its judgment for the vote by the shareholders as to what were appropriate rewards.[112]

By contrast, it is not at all unusual for a court to find compensation which received no disinterested approval to be unfair. For example, in *Wilderman v. Wilderman*,[113] the court held that the defendant failed to prove the fairness of the raises he voted to have the corporation pay to himself. The court focused on the defendant's failure to produce evidence as to what other executives in similar positions in the industry earned. It also attached considerable significance to the fact that the raises were disproportionate to the growth in the corporation's earnings—in other words, the court used the growth in corporate earnings as a measure of what increased value the defendant's management might have which would justify a raise. In addition, the court noted that the raises put the defendant's earnings in excess of what the Internal Revenue Service was willing to allow the corporation to deduct as reasonable compensation. This is consistent with a number of court opinions in duty of loyalty cases, which look for guidance from the well developed body of law dealing with the reasonableness of compensation for purposes of taking an income tax deduction.[114] The court also suggested that the defendant's compensation was high for the size of the business (only twenty employees).

This discussion suggests that disinterested director or shareholder approval can make a major difference in the likelihood of a court upholding a conflict-of-interest transaction involving compensation for directors. Suppose, however, all directors will receive compensation; is there any way to obtain disinterested director approval? Sometimes, boards attempt to achieve this by having a seriatim approval of the salaries of the individual members. In other words, if a board has three members—let us call them 'A', 'B' and 'C'—A and B will vote on C's salary, while A and C will vote on B's salary, and B and C will vote on A's salary. By and large, courts have refused to treat this as disinterested approval sufficient to avoid strict fairness review.[115] After all, the bias in the vote seems obvious. Still, given the continuing relationship among members of a board, one must wonder if the concern about mutual "back scratching" here only differs in degree, rather than in kind, from the situation with all "disinterested" director approvals. Interestingly enough, California's conflict-of-interest provision appears to treat such seriatim approvals as meeting the standard for disinterested director

---

112. Heller v. Boylan, 29 N.Y.S.2d 653 (Sup. Ct. 1941).

113. 315 A.2d 610 (Del.Ch.1974).

114. *E.g.*, Ruetz v. Topping, 453 S.W.2d 624 (Mo.App.1970). Section 162(a)(1) of the Internal Revenue Code allows an employer to deduct employee compensation to the extent the compensation is reasonable. Efforts by closely held corporations to funnel earnings to their owners through deductible salaries, rather than non-deductible dividends, have led to numerous court actions in which the Internal Revenue Service challenges the reasonableness of the compensation for which the corporation seeks a deduction.

115. *See, e.g.*, Stoiber v. Miller Brewing Co., 257 Wis. 13, 42 N.W.2d 144 (Wis. 1950).

approval;[116] but then California still requires fairness review even when there is disinterested director approval of a conflict-of-interest transaction.

In any event, courts face several problems in reviewing whether compensation paid to directors and senior executives is fair (or, if there was disinterested approval, constitutes waste or gift). To begin with, there is the problem of finding arms-length comparisons. True, there is a labor market for senior executives, so one might examine what other companies pay their officers and directors. Yet, to the extent the compensation one uses as a comparative also comes from a conflict-of-interest transaction, this does not tell the court what an arms-length transaction would produce.

In addition, there is the question as to how much the court wants to insist on an exact quid pro quo when reviewing compensation. With a salary, there is a direct quid pro quo: The officer works, the officer receives his or her salary. On the other hand, employers often provide various benefits, the entitlement to, or amount of, which the company may not directly tie to performance. The facts in *Adams v. Smith*[117] provide a stark illustration.

In *Adams*, a corporation's directors voted to have the company pay a pension to the widow of the company's recently-deceased president and to the widow of its deceased controller. A shareholder challenged the payments, and the court held them to be ultra vires. The problem in the court's view was that there was no consideration for the payments.

Unfortunately, the court confuses consideration in the contract sense, with the notion of gift under corporate law. Employers (corporate and otherwise) commonly pay Christmas bonuses, make gifts to retiring workers, and the like. Generally, there is no exchange of consideration for these payments in a contract sense. In other words, an employee who did not receive the bonus or parting gift would not likely have any cause of action for breach of contract. This does not mean a corporation engages in ultra vires conduct in paying such bonuses or making such gifts. The question is did the corporation gain any advantage in return, even if not part of a bargained for exchange. The typical answer is yes: The corporation will gain from improved employee morale. Moreover, this increase in morale might occur, in the case of retirement gifts or widows' pensions, among employees who did not receive the gift or pension. After all, employees often appreciate working for a company which "takes care of its own." Of course, one must balance the amount of expected gain from increased morale, against the size of the bonus or gift. Perhaps the pension in *Adams* so exceeded any possible gain to morale that the court's end result was correct. One never knows, because the court never sees the real question.

Stock option and similar plans create further problems in tying the amount of compensation to the corporation's benefit. Stock option plans

116. Cal. Corp. Code § 310(a).   **117.** 275 Ala. 142, 153 So.2d 221 (1963).

grant covered employees the right to purchase a certain number of shares in the corporation at a set price. If the option price is less than the market price for the stock, the employee benefits by exercising the option, buying the stock at the option price, and reselling the stock at the higher market price.[118] Where, however, is the benefit to the corporation? It is not in raising money by selling stock, since, if this is the goal, presumably the corporation could have sold the stock at the higher market price. Rather, these plans are a form of compensating employees.

If employees must work a certain length of time in order to gain the benefit of the options, the quid pro quo might seem little different than a salary. Indeed, in some court opinions, the validity of stock option plans has turned, at least in part, on whether the plan effectively requires some period of continued employment in order to gain the benefit. Thus, in *Kerbs v. California Eastern Airways, Inc.,*[119] the court invalidated stock options issued under a plan in which the employees could quit immediately after receiving options and could still exercise the options up to six months later. By contrast, in *Beard v. Elster,*[120] the court distinguished *Kerbs* by noting the plan in *Beard* immediately terminated the employee's ability to exercise the options at the moment he or she departed. This means the employee must stick around waiting for the market price of the stock to rise above the option price if he or she is to get the benefit of the options (assuming the option price was equal to or greater than the market price at the time the employee received the options).

Actually, the potentially more significant corporate benefit from these plans lies not in encouraging employees to stay with the corporation—especially when many of the covered individuals would not have left the company even without the plan. Rather, the principal benefit probably lies in the incentives such plans can create for corporate managers. Since the employee's benefit from the option depends upon the market price of the corporation's stock—the higher the price, the greater the employee's gain—these plans appear to give employees an incentive to take actions which will increase the market price of the corporation's stock. In other words, these plans give corporate officers an incentive to manage the corporation for the maximum benefit of its stockholders.

There is one problem, however, with this justification. All sorts of factors contribute to the market price of a corporation's stock. Hence, the magnitude of the reward which an employee obtains by virtue of

118. A further benefit of these plans for employees can lie in the tax treatment of such options, as compared with the tax treatment of a regular salary or a bonus. Plans meeting certain requirements may allow the recipients of the options to delay recognizing taxable income until they sell stock at a profit (instead of at the time they receive the options or exercise the options). Moreover, this income will be taxable at capital gains, rather than ordinary income, rates. An offsetting disadvantage is that the corporation does not obtain the deduction it otherwise would receive when paying compensation.

119. 33 Del.Ch. 69, 90 A.2d 652 (1952).

120. 39 Del.Ch. 153, 160 A.2d 731 (Sup. Ct. 1960).

stock options and similar compensation plans may have little relation to the quality of the individual recipient's efforts. For this reason, some courts have invalidated compensation plans which tie rewards to stock prices.[121] Most courts, however, ignore this concern.[122] After all, no compensation plan can create a perfect relationship between the utility of the employee's efforts and the amount of compensation.

4.2.7 Corporate Opportunities

So far, we have been examining the duty of loyalty problem which exists when directors or officers have the corporation enter into transactions in which the directors or officers (or even controlling shareholders) have a financial interest conflicting with the interest of the corporation. Now, we turn to a second major type of duty of loyalty problem. This is when directors or officers take for themselves business opportunities which could be of use to the corporation. Notice, here, there need be no transaction by the corporation with anybody.

The most frequently cited corporate opportunity case, *Guth v. Loft, Inc.,*[123] illustrates the typical scenario. Guth was the president of a corporation (Loft) which operated a candy store chain. The person in control of the company producing Pepsi–Cola informed Guth of the opportunity to buy the assets of the Pepsi–Cola company, which was then in bankruptcy. Shrewdly sensing that Pepsi would be "the taste of a new generation," Guth joined with this individual to start up a new company to buy the bankrupt Pepsi–Cola company's assets (essentially the formula for the syrup and the trademark), and to produce and market Pepsi. The problem was, instead of undertaking this activity for the candy store corporation, Guth bought into the new Pepsi company for himself. The court held this breached Guth's fiduciary duty to Loft and ordered him to transfer his stock in the new Pepsi company to Loft.

Does this mean directors and officers of a corporation can never take a business opportunity for themselves rather than give it to their corporation? As the court's opinion in *Guth* points out, the answer is no. The problem in this area, therefore, is to figure out when directors and officers must give the opportunity to the corporation and when they may keep it for themselves. Unfortunately, courts have been unable to come up with any clear tests for resolving this issue.

a. The judicial tests

The court's opinion in *Guth* typifies the difficulty courts have had in developing a clear test for what opportunities belong to the corporation and what opportunities directors and officers can take for themselves.

121. *E.g.*, Berkwitz v. Humphrey, 163 F.Supp. 78 (N.D.Ohio 1958). This case involved a so-called "phantom stock plan," rather than stock options. Such a plan essentially cuts out the steps of the employee buying the corporation's stock at the option price and reselling it at the higher market price. Instead, the corporation just gives the employee basically the profit he or she would have made on exercising the option and selling the stock.

122. *E.g.*, Lieberman v. Becker, 155 A.2d 596 (Del.1959).

123. 5 A.2d 503 (Del.1939).

The opinion contains a mishmash of the traditional formulations for what is a corporate opportunity:

(1) "Official" versus "individual" capacity

To start with, the court in *Guth* stated it was reasonable to infer that the person who brought the opportunity to Guth's attention originally approached Guth in Guth's role as president of Loft. In other words, this person, thinking a candy store company (rather than Guth personally) would be interested in Pepsi, went to an individual (Guth) the person figured could act for the candy store company. Did this fact make Pepsi into Loft's opportunity? In its general discussion of the law of corporate opportunity, the court in *Guth* seems to state that a corporate officer only can take opportunities (depending upon other factors) which come to him or her in his or her "individual" rather than "official capacity." In other words, a corporate officer can never take an opportunity which comes in his or her corporate capacity. Yet, if this is the law, why did the court, after drawing the inference that Guth first heard of the opportunity in his capacity as president of Loft, feel the need to continue discussing whether Pepsi was Loft's opportunity? Perhaps the court simply wanted to reinforce its holding, because there was some evidence that Guth did not, in fact, first hear of the opportunity in his role as president of Loft.

(2) "Line of business"

The court in *Guth* also held that the Pepsi opportunity was in Loft's "line of business." This holding has turned into the most noted aspect of the court's opinion. Later courts[124] and writers[125] generally have interpreted this holding as adopting what is known as the "line of business" test for corporate opportunities.

Under this test, a corporate official must turn over to the corporation any opportunity which is in the corporation's line of business, in other words, opportunities which relate to the business the corporation engages in.[126] Of course, this raises the question as to what is the scope of the business of the corporation claiming the opportunity.

Guth illustrates the quandary. Loft operated a chain of retail candy stores. Loft produced some of the candies sold at its stores, as well as various fountain syrups to supply the needs of its stores. Loft also sold some of the candy it made to other retailers. Loft's candy stores had soda fountains at which Loft dispensed soft drinks, including cola. Loft had been dispensing Coca Cola, but was dissatisfied with the price Coca Cola charged Loft for cola syrup. Pepsi, on the other hand, made and sold a syrup, which when mixed with carbonated water by bottlers or soda fountains, became Pepsi Cola. Is making such a syrup in Loft's line of business? It could depend on how one characterizes Loft's business. If we

---

124. *E.g.*, Miller v. Miller, 301 Minn. 207, 222 N.W.2d 71 (1974).

125. *E.g.*, Melvin A. Eisenberg, Cary & Eisenberg's Cases and Materials on Corporations, 732 (7th ed. 1995)

126. *See, e.g.*, Imperial Group (Texas), Inc. v. Scholnick, 709 S.W.2d 358 (Tex. Ct. App. 1986).

characterize Loft's business as a candy store chain, which also made and sold some candies to other stores, then manufacturing soft drink syrup to sell to bottlers and other retailers does not fit. On the other hand, if we more broadly characterize Loft's business as, say, manufacture and sale, on both the retail and wholesale level, of sweets or "junk food," then manufacturing Pepsi syrup for wholesale distribution does fit.

Perhaps to its credit, the court in *Guth* did not make its application of the line of business test turn on such semantic games. Instead, the court found Pepsi was in Loft's line of business because producing Pepsi syrup was a natural area for Loft's expansion, given Loft's resources and expertise. Specifically, because Loft already made some syrups, Loft was able to manufacture Pepsi Cola syrup (as it, in fact, did for a while for Guth's company). Indeed, this evidently made efficient use of Loft's manufacturing capacity. Notice that this sort of approach can turn the line of business test into a search for what business school types refer to as "synergies"—in other words, efficiencies from combining businesses. One problem with this approach, however, is that it can threaten to make practically every opportunity the corporation might desire, into an opportunity the officer or director must give to the corporation. After all, generally a corporation would not wish to take an opportunity unless the opportunity was in a natural area for the corporation's expansion given the company's existing resources and expertise.

In fact, however, the common assertion that the court in *Guth* adopted the line of business test is highly questionable. The court never said that finding Pepsi was in Loft's line of business was sufficient to make the opportunity belong to Loft. Instead, the court went on also to apply the alternate principal test traditionally recited in corporate opportunity cases. This is the "interest or expectancy" test.[127]

(3) "Interest or expectancy"

Unlike the phrase "line of business," the label "interest or expectancy" gives one little idea as to the meaning of the "interest or expectancy" test for what is a corporate opportunity. For instance, does "interest" simply mean the corporation would have been interested in taking the opportunity? Interestingly enough (pun intended), some court opinions contain statements which sound as if this is what the court thinks.[128] Yet, this cannot be correct. After all, if the test is whether or not the corporation would have been interested in taking the opportunity, then, unless the corporation is broke or already has considered and rejected the opportunity, pretty much any really good opportunities become corporate opportunities.

127. Over half a century later, the Delaware Supreme Court remains befuddled on the relationship between the line of business test and the interest or expectancy test. Specifically, in *Broz v. Cellular Information Systems, Inc.*, 673 A.2d 148 (Del. 1996), the court appears to treat line of business, and interest or expectancy, as conjunctive elements in the test for what is a corporate opportunity–which makes no sense at all.

128. *See, e.g.,* Broz v. Cellular Information Systems, Inc., 673 A.2d 148 (Del.1996).

Reading most cases in which courts purport to apply the interest or expectancy test shows that courts generally have something narrower in mind. Indeed, the court opinion which originally announced this test[129] applied it in a remarkably cramped manner. This case involved a stone quarry, a one-third interest in which the corporation owned, another one-third interest in which the corporation was leasing from a party who promised to sell the interest to the corporation as soon as the interest was clear of liens, and the final one-third interest in which the corporation unsuccessfully had attempted to buy. The court held that the defendant directors and officers breached their duty to the corporation by purchasing for themselves the one-third interest the corporation was leasing, but did not breach their duty in buying the one-third interest the corporation unsuccessfully had sought. The difference, according to the court, was that the lease and promise to sell gave the corporation an existing interest in the property, or an expectancy growing out of an existing right.

Most later cases have not applied the interest or expectancy test quite so narrowly. Instead, the concept of interest or expectancy has typically come to refer to opportunities the corporation already has some tentative claim to, or, at least, actively is seeking or negotiating for, even if the corporation does not yet have a contractual or property interest in the opportunity. In fact, this test, as employed by various courts, runs through a spectrum of possibilities. This ranges from the situation in which the corporation already has a contract to buy the opportunity in question[130] (a situation in which the corporation might even have an interference with contract claim against a non-fiduciary who takes the opportunity from it), to the situation in which the corporation has some property interest in the opportunity,[131] to the situation in which the corporation actively is seeking this particular opportunity,[132] to the situation in which the corporation simply is seeking this general type of opportunity.[133]

In addition, courts applying the interest or expectancy test typically include within its reach opportunities which are essential to the corporation. This does not simply mean the opportunity will make money for the corporation and the corporation needs money. Rather, the opportunity involves some property which the corporation needs in order to continue its operations; for example, a patent to the process used by the corporation to manufacture its product.[134]

129. Lagarde v. Anniston Lime & Stone Co., 126 Ala. 496, 28 So. 199 (1900).

130. *See, e.g.,* Irving Trust Co. v. Deutsch, 73 F.2d 121 (2d Cir.1934).

131. *E.g.,* Lagarde v. Anniston Lime & Stone Co., 126 Ala. 496, 28 So. 199 (1900).

132. *E.g.,* Southeast Consultants, Inc. v. McCrary Eng'g. Corp., 246 Ga. 503, 273 S.E.2d 112 (1980).

133. *But see* Johnston v. Greene, 35 Del.Ch. 479, 121 A.2d 919 (Sup. Ct. 1956) (holding that if the corporation is simply seeking general investments, this would not put all investment opportunities into the interest or expectancy test).

134. *See, e.g.,* Rapistan Corp. v. Michaels, 203 Mich.App. 301, 511 N.W.2d 918 (1994) (to be "essential" the opportunity must be "so indispensably necessary to the conduct of the business ... that the deprivation ... threatened the viability" of the corporation).

In any event, the interest or expectancy test is normally narrower than the line of business test.

(4) Other factors and "fairness"

Guth illustrates the elastic nature of both the line of business and interest or expectancy tests. For example, the court held that Loft had an interest or expectancy in Pepsi, because Loft needed an alternate source of supply for cola syrup after having decided to stop buying from Coca Cola. Yet, it is quite a leap from saying that Loft needed to find someone to sell Loft cola syrup, to saying that Loft needed to become a cola syrup producer. This, in turn, leads one to ask why the court in *Guth* took such an expansive approach. Perhaps this reflects a view that business opportunities generally ought to belong to corporations, rather than to their officers and directors. Perhaps, however, other factors, which did not fit precisely within the two tests, influenced the court. We already mentioned one such factor—the possibility that Guth originally received the opportunity as a representative of Loft. In addition, the court noted how Guth used considerable resources of Loft (funds, personnel and marketing) to develop Pepsi. The use of corporate resources to develop an opportunity often has been a factor influencing courts to characterize the opportunity as belonging to the corporation.[135]

This analysis of *Guth* suggests that whether an opportunity belongs to the corporation often depends on factors in addition to whether the defendant learned of the opportunity in his or her official capacity, whether the opportunity fits within the corporation's line of business, or whether the corporation has an existing interest or expectancy in the opportunity. Recognizing this fact, some courts have announced other tests for corporate opportunities.

For example, some courts have stated that the test is one of "fairness."[136] This is not the same as the fairness test courts apply to conflict-of-interest transactions. After all, we cannot really ask, in trying to define a corporate opportunity, whether the corporation received the equivalent value to what the company gave up as measured by what deal the company would have made with a stranger. Instead, courts applying this "fairness" test to corporate opportunities will look at a variety of factors similar to what we discussed so far—how the defendant learned of the opportunity; was it part of the defendant's job to acquire such opportunities for the corporation; how important was the opportunity to the corporation; whether the corporation was seeking the opportunity; whether defendant used the opportunity to compete with, or sold the opportunity to, the corporation; whether the corporation had the resources to develop the opportunity; and whether the defendant used corporate assets to develop the opportunity—to decide whether it was "fair" for the defendant to take the opportunity. Unfortunately, this

---

135. *E.g.,* Graham v. Mimms, 111 Ill. App.3d 751, 67 Ill.Dec. 313, 444 N.E.2d 549 (1982).

136. *E.g.,* Durfee v. Durfee & Canning, Inc., 323 Mass. 187, 80 N.E.2d 522 (1948).

does not provide much guidance as to when these factors will make an officer's or director's taking of the opportunity unfair.

There can be endless variations on these sorts of approaches. In *Miller v. Miller*,[137] the Minnesota Supreme Court created a two-step test: First, the court considered if the opportunity was in the corporation's line of business; if so, then the court asked if it was nevertheless fair for the defendant to take the opportunity. Based upon this approach, the Supreme Court in *Miller* upheld the trial court's finding that the defendants had not usurped corporate opportunities.[138]

b. *Triangulating corporate opportunities*

The discussion so far suggests that the various specific tests for what should be a corporate opportunity—"line of business," "interest or expectancy," "official capacity"—fail to encompass all of the factors which courts find relevant in deciding whether an opportunity should go to the corporation rather than to its officers or directors. Yet, to say the test is simply one of "fairness" fails to give much guidance. We need to step back and take a fresh look. One way to do so is to put aside the corporate opportunity cases and examine a classic court opinion which involved the same basic issue, but in the context of a joint venture (essentially, a partnership) rather than a corporation.

In *Meinhard v. Salmon*,[139] the court faced a situation in which Meinhard and Salmon had formed a joint venture in order to convert an old hotel into a building with offices and shops, which they then operated. The joint venture did not own the building, but, instead, leased the building for a term of twenty years. Meinhard contributed funds to the venture, but left the management to Salmon. Toward the end of the twenty year lease, the owner of the reversion approached Salmon with a proposal. This was to enter a new, much longer, lease. The new lease would encompass both the lot on which the old hotel building stood, as well as several adjoining lots. The idea was to tear down the old building, as well as the buildings on these other lots, and build a new, much larger, building. Salmon took this opportunity for himself without informing Meinhard. Upon learning what had happened, Meinhard sued.

---

137. 301 Minn. 207, 222 N.W.2d 71 (1974).

138. The defendants in *Miller* had developed various business enterprises through companies they owned, rather than through the corporation (Miller Waste) in which the plaintiff (their brother), along with the defendants, was a shareholder. The court found some of these ventures to be outside of Miller Waste's line of business. In other instances, the court felt that the new ventures may have been within the line of business, but the defendants did not act unfairly in taking the opportunities for themselves. Essentially, the court did not think the defendants were seeking to enrich themselves at corporate expense in acting

as they did. They had worked hard developing the business of Miller Waste and did not use its assets in developing these other ventures. More critically, the defendant's actions, in the court's view, benefitted, rather than harmed, Miller Waste, since the defendants had their new ventures purchase products sold by Miller Waste in such quantities that Miller Waste became the most successful company in its field. Also, the court felt that the defendants had fully disclosed their activities and the shareholders had acquiesced in the actions of the defendants.

139. 249 N.Y. 458, 164 N.E. 545 (1928).

In his majority opinion, Judge Cardozo held that Salmon had breached his duty in taking the opportunity for himself without informing Meinhard. This opinion is widely known for its eloquent language about fiduciaries being bound to act with a "punctilio of an honor." For our purposes, what is useful is to see precisely why the court concluded this opportunity was one Salmon could not take for himself. The court pointed to three factors. To begin with, there was the manner in which Salmon learned of the opportunity. The owner of the reversion presumably figured Salmon might be interested in the proposal because Salmon was managing the office building on the site. Evidently, the owner of the reversion was unaware of Meinhard, who was essentially a silent partner in the venture. Next, there was Salmon's position in the venture. He was not simply a partner in the venture; he was the managing partner. Finally, there was a nexus between the opportunity and the business of the joint venture. The opportunity was, in the court's view, an extension and enlargement of the subject matter of the prior lease.

It turns out that the three factors relied upon by the court in *Meinhard* provide a useful road map for evaluating whether something is an opportunity which should go to the corporation. Indeed, to understand what is a corporate opportunity, it helps to visualize a triangle into which these three factors will fit. At the three points of this "corporate opportunity triangle," are the three things which are present in every corporate opportunity case: at one point, there is the opportunity itself; at the second point, there is the corporation; at the third point, there is the person who took the opportunity. The three factors relied upon in *Meinhard* involve the three relationships between these three points. The court's invocation of how the defendant came to hear of the opportunity, involves the relationship between the opportunity and the person who took the opportunity. The court's noting that Salmon was not just a partner, but was the managing partner, involves the relationship between the corporation (or, in *Meinhard*, the joint venture) and the person who took the opportunity. Finally, the court's consideration of the nexus between the opportunity and the existing business of the venture, involves the relationship between the opportunity and the corporation (or, again, in *Meinhard*, the joint venture).

What is useful about this corporate opportunity triangle is not simply that it might provide a neat mnemonic device to spot the relevant facts in a corporate opportunity situation. It also explains the results in corporate opportunity cases much better than the traditional tests. The reason is because the results in the corporate opportunity cases often depend upon the interplay of these three relationships. Specifically, the more one relationship suggests a particular opportunity belongs to the corporation, the less the other relationships must provide grounds for finding the opportunity should go to the corporation. In some instances, one relationship is so decisive that it makes the opportunity one which belongs to the corporation, regardless of the other two relationships. In other instances, one relationship is sufficiently in favor of finding the opportunity belongs to the corporation that courts, consciously or unconsciously, apply broader tests vis-a-vis the other relationships for finding a corporate opportunity. Conversely, the weaker grounds one relationship gives for finding the opportunity should be the corporation's, the stronger the grounds which the other relationships must provide before the court will order the opportunity turned over to the corporation.

Let us start by looking at the relationship between the opportunity and the person who took it. The question here is how did this person learn of the opportunity. There are essentially four possibilities:

The first possibility would be if it was the individual's assignment to go out and look for this sort of opportunity for the corporation. Then, having found the opportunity while carrying out this assignment, the corporate agent proceeds to purchase the opportunity for him- or herself. An example would be if an oil company hired a geologist to search for oil, and, after finding oil under a piece of property, the geologist purchased the property for him- or herself. There seems little doubt that courts would find this breached the agent's duty.[140] Of course, this sort of opportunity presumably would be within the corporation's line of business, and a court might even say that the corporation had an interest or expectancy in an opportunity it was actively searching for. Yet, this is really besides the point. The critical fact is that the agent is taking for him- or herself the very opportunity he or she was hired to obtain for the corporation. A court almost does not need to talk about breaching a duty of loyalty here; the agent has breached his or her contract of employment with the corporation.

Guth involves a slightly weaker case. Loft's board evidently did not ask Guth to go out and look for cola syrup companies to buy. Nevertheless, the court inferred that the person who approached Guth about Pepsi, initially did so expecting Guth to act on behalf of Loft in obtaining the opportunity. The court treated this as involving an opportunity obtained in Guth's official, rather than individual, capacity. Moreover, the court appears to state that this fact alone makes the opportunity belong to the corporation, regardless of the opportunity's relationship to the corporation or, presumably, the agent's relation to the corporation. The American Law Institute's Principles of Corporate Governance takes the same approach: If a corporate official receives an opportunity from a party who originally expected the official to pass the opportunity on to the corporation, then it is the corporation's opportunity.[141]

It is not too difficult to understand why this should be the rule. A person who wants to present an opportunity to a corporation must communicate through the corporation's officials. After all, a corporation has no ears of its own. Given this reality, if corporate officials could take for themselves opportunities originally intended for the corporation,

140. *E.g.,* Restatement (Second) of Agency § 387 Illustration 5.

141. Principles of Corporate Governance § 5.05(b)(1)(A). *See also* Northeast Harbor Golf Club, Inc. v. Harris, 661 A.2d 1146 (Me.1995) (adopting the American Law Institute's approach, under which a corporation's president would be liable if she received an offer to buy real estate in her capacity as president, and then bought the real estate for herself without first offering the opportunity to the corporation).

corporations (and their shareholders) would be at a severe disadvantage. Essentially, the company might be able to pursue only the opportunities which its officials did not think were good enough to take for themselves. Moreover, since a corporation can only receive communications through its officials, it is reasonable to infer that part of every corporate official's job is to pass on messages he or she receives, which are intended for the corporation. Hence, in this case too, we can conclude that the official, in effect, is taking for him- or herself an opportunity which he or she was hired to obtain for the corporation. Besides, one might ask how it came to pass that an opportunity originally intended for the corporation ended up in the hands of the official who took it. Presumably, the official talked the third party into giving the opportunity to the official personally, rather than insisting that it go to the corporation. This seems to constitute competing with the corporation, which, as we shall discuss later, constitutes a breach of an agent's fiduciary duty.

Meinhard represents a much more difficult situation. The owner of the reversion did not originally approach Salmon in Salmon's role as managing partner. The owner did not know there was a joint venture. Nevertheless, Salmon presumably would not have obtained the opportunity but for his position with the joint venture. It was Salmon's managing the building, which made Salmon a logical person for the owner to contact. The variations on this pattern are endless. The corporation has not assigned the agent to search for the opportunity in question, nor did the person selling the opportunity present it originally to the agent for the agent to pass on to the corporation. Yet, being an agent for the corporation places the agent at the right place at the right time to learn of the opportunity. Often, somewhat as in *Meinhard*, the agent, while acting for the corporation, met and impressed the individual who has the opportunity to sell. Alternately, the experience gained working for the corporation has allowed the agent to recognize, and have the skill to exploit, a business opportunity.

Meinhard suggests that the fact the fiduciary would not have received the opportunity but for his or her role with the corporation (or joint venture) weighs in favor of finding the opportunity belongs to the corporation. Yet, it does not have the decisive weight accorded to opportunities received in one's official capacity. Rather, *Meinhard* also looked at the role of the agent in the venture and the nexus between the opportunity and the venture. Too weak a link on these other two relationships and Salmon could still have taken the opportunity, even though it was only because of the joint venture that he ever heard of the opportunity.

This approach seems consistent both with intuitive notions of fairness and the probable expectations of the parties. After all, the corporation reasonably can claim some entitlement when its agent never would have received an opportunity but for the employment. Yet, agents would be reticent to work for firms which asserted an absolute claim to any future business opportunities the agent would not have received but for the employment with the corporation. All careers are a case of building on one's experience. Hence, a compromise, under which the corporation's claim depends upon the relationships between the agent and the corporation, and the opportunity and the corporation, seems both fair, and might well approximate what we would expect most parties would have agreed to had they considered the issue at the time the corporation hired the agent.

In contrast with this approach, some writers argue for a corporate claim in this situation because the information about the opportunity is somehow corporate property.[142] If the agent learns of, or exploits, the opportunity by using corporate trade secrets, then the corporation certainly has a claim. This claim is for stealing trade secrets, rather than usurping a corporate opportunity. Problems arise when writers advocate treating information regarding an opportunity as corporate property simply because the agent would not have received the information but for his or her job. There is little support for this broad position in existing case law, and it would constitute a radical departure from the normal expectations of the parties in an employment relationship. One could water down this sort of corporate property rationale by stating that information which an agent would not have received but for his or her employment might *sometimes* be corporate property. This, however, makes the analysis hopelessly circular. Unless we have some theft of trade secrets, how is a court to say when information about an opportunity is corporate property; or is this not the same question as to what is a corporate opportunity?

Finally, we have the opportunity which the agent learns of completely independent of his or her role with the corporation. We can imagine a situation in which the agent hears of the opportunity from a relative or an old friend who is unaware of, or uninfluenced by, the agent's role with the corporation. In this situation, one or both of the other two relationships must point extremely strongly toward finding the opportunity to be a corporate one. Otherwise, the agent can take the opportunity for him- or herself.[143]

Now, let us look at the relationship between the agent and the corporation. The significance of this relationship depends on the answer to two questions. To begin with, there is the question as to how high up the agent is in the corporate hierarchy. The court in *Meinhard* found it important that Salmon was not just a partner, he was the managing partner. The notion seems to be that the greater the agent's management responsibilities (in other words, the higher up he or she is in the company hierarchy), the broader the scope of the opportunities which the agent must give to the corporation rather than keep for him- or herself.

Indeed, some writers have gone so far as to suggest that senior full-time executives in a widely-held corporation ought to be obligated to

142. *E.g.,* Victor Brudney & Robert C. Clark, *A New Look at Corporate Opportunities,* 94 Harv. L. Rev. 997, 999 (1981).

143. *See, e.g.,* Johnston v. Greene, 35 Del.Ch. 479, 121 A.2d 919 (Sup. Ct. 1956).

turn any opportunity over to the corporation.[144] This is presumably not a rule which even these writers would apply to lower level corporate employees. The American Law Institute's Principles of Corporate Governance does not go as far as these writers, but it does indicate a broad obligation for senior executives. Under the Principles, senior executives must turn over any opportunities the executives receive in their official capacity, any opportunities they obtain through the use of corporate information or property, or, and here is where things get somewhat broad, any opportunities which are closely related to the corporation's current or expected business (which may not be that dissimilar to the line of business test).[145] Presumably, the American Law Institute would not place an obligation to turn over every opportunity closely related to the corporation's business on every lower level corporate employee.

There is a certain intuitive appeal to the idea that the further up one is in the corporate hierarchy, the wider the scope of opportunities which one must give to the corporation. Perhaps the notion is that those higher up must devote all of their waking hours working for the corporation, leaving no time for pursuing opportunities on their own. A simpler explanation may be that senior executives get paid more and, therefore, should give more to the company.

The other question concerning the relationship of the agent to the corporation is whether the agent occupies a full time versus part time position. For example, the American Law Institute's Principles of Corporate Governance imposes a much narrower obligation on outside directors—in other words, directors who are not also full-time employees of the corporation—than it imposes on senior full time executives. Outside directors need only turn over opportunities if the director received the opportunity in his or her official capacity, or obtained the opportunity through the use of corporate information or property.[146] Outside directors, under the American Law Institute's approach, do not need to turn over the opportunity simply because the opportunity is closely related to the corporation's business.

Courts also have focused on the defendant's part time role in deciding if an opportunity belonged to the corporation. For instance, in *Johnston v. Greene,*[147] the court gave, among its reasons for finding that a director did not usurp a corporate opportunity, the fact that the director served on the boards of other corporations. Under this circumstance, the court noted, applying an expansive test for whether the opportunity in question should go to the corporation could have resulted in more than one corporation having a claim to the opportunity.

Burg v. Horn[148] also illustrates the significance courts attach to whether the defendant has a full-time, versus part-time, role in the corporation. The Burgs and the Horns were two couples, who formed a

---

144. Brudney & Clark, *supra* note 142 at 1024.

145. Principles of Corporate Governance § 5.05(b).

146. *Id.* at § 5.05(b)(1).

147. 35 Del.Ch. 479, 121 A.2d 919 (1956).

148. 380 F.2d 897 (2d Cir.1967).

corporation to own and operate low rent apartments in Brooklyn. After the Burgs moved to California,[149] there was a falling out, and Mrs. Burg sued the Horns.[150] She claimed that the Horns had taken corporate opportunities by purchasing for themselves, rather than the corporation, several other low rent Brooklyn apartment buildings. The court rejected this claim. In doing so, the court chose to follow the interest or expectancy test, rather than the line of business test. This choice, however, was not unequivocal. Rather, the court explained that the defendants might have had an obligation to give the corporation first crack at all opportunities in the company's line of business if they had been full-time employees of the corporation. Since, however, the defendants were managing this corporation simply as a sideline, and spent most of their time on their other ventures, the court applied the narrower interest or expectancy test. In other words, under *Burg*, the choice between using the interest or expectancy versus the line of business test may depend on full- versus part-time status.

The *Burg* court's opinion suggests why full- versus part-time status should be important. Especially significant to the court was that, before the defendants became involved with this corporation, they already owned other corporations operating low rent apartment buildings. The fact that the Horns already had other ventures in the same line of business is extremely strong evidence that the two families never intended the Horns to have an obligation to turn over to the new corporation all future opportunities in this line of business. More broadly, when a corporation employs someone on a part-time basis (for instance, solely as a director) it understands that the individual will have other business activities, and, accordingly, the corporation can expect this individual to pursue for him- or herself some opportunities which might be of use to the corporation. Hence, it will take a far stronger basis in one or both of the other two relationships to find a corporate opportunity for such a part-time agent.

Finally, we turn to the relationship addressed by both the interest or expectancy and line of business tests. This is the relationship between the opportunity and the corporation. Again, this relationship comes in a spectrum of varying strengths.

The strongest relationship between the opportunity and the corporation occurs when the opportunity is absolutely essential to the corporation's business. We saw earlier that courts often state, as the Delaware Supreme Court did in the *Guth*, that such an opportunity belongs to the corporation, seemingly without regard to how the agent obtained the opportunity or the agent's position with the corporation. This is no doubt overstated, since one would doubt that a court would compel a lower-level corporate employee to sell to the corporation some property rights the employee might have inherited, just because the corporation

149. Perhaps to follow their favorite baseball team.

150. While her husband handled accounting for the corporation, only Mrs. Burg actually was a shareholder, along with the Horns.

cannot continue its business without the property. Nevertheless, as a general proposition one might presume that is it probably contrary to the parties' original expectations (not to mention unseemly) for an agent to take for him- or herself the very opportunity which is essential for the survival of the principal's business.

A somewhat weaker relationship exists for opportunities in which the corporation has an interest or expectancy. As we saw in *Guth*, how broadly a court chooses to define the interest or expectancy test may depend upon the relationships between the opportunity and the agent, and the agent and the corporation.

There are several reasons why the existence of an interest or expectancy creates a strong claim for the corporation. To begin with, the existence of an interest or expectancy normally rebuts the possible concern that the corporation only became desirous of the opportunity after it turned out to be a success. Moreover, the existence of the interest or expectancy typically gives the agent more notice of the corporation's desire to obtain this particular opportunity than would be true if the agent seizes an opportunity having little, or only a more generalized, connection with the corporation's activities. Finally, the image throughout the situations in which courts find an interest or expectancy is one of the corporate official snatching away the opportunity right before the corporation can grab it. In these situations, it is highly probable that the corporation would have obtained the opportunity but for the interference of the agent. This distinguishes situations involving an interest or expectancy, from those situations in which the agent's taking the opportunity does not make the corporation any worse off—even if no better off—than if the agent had never been in the picture to start with.

The line of business test encompasses opportunities having an even weaker link to the corporation. *Horn* shows how getting a court to use this test may require strong relationships in one or both of the other two legs of the corporate opportunity triangle. Certainly few would advocate requiring all corporate employees to turn over to the corporation all opportunities in the corporation's line of business no matter how the employee learned of the opportunity or what the employee's position is with the company. Such a rule would probably be inconsistent with the typical expectations concerning employment. Moreover, it might produce anti-competitive consequences if corporations use this rule to prevent employees from starting new ventures in the corporation's field.

Beyond this, we reach the point at which the opportunity has little connection to the corporation. Here, the only way to find the opportunity belongs to the corporation is for one of the other two relationships completely to dictate the outcome—as, for example, when the agent originally received the opportunity in his or her official capacity to pass on to the corporation.

4.2.8 *Justifications for Taking a Corporate Opportunity*

There are several circumstances in which corporate officers, directors or other agents may avoid liability even though they take what otherwise would be a corporate opportunity. Often, courts lump these circumstances into their consideration of whether the opportunity falls within the various tests entitling the corporation to the opportunity.[151] The result is to further muddle an already difficult inquiry. We, therefore, shall consider these various circumstances as possible excuses or defenses for taking what is a corporate opportunity under the tests discussed above.

a. Corporate rejection

The most universally recognized justification for taking what otherwise would be a corporate opportunity is that those in charge of the corporation turned down the opportunity.[152] After all, if the corporation had a chance at the opportunity and did not want it, the company is hardly in a position to complain just because one or more of its personnel then took the opportunity.

This works simply enough when the person taking the opportunity is a lower level employee or officer. In this instance, senior officers, or, if necessary, the board of directors, can decide whether the corporation wants the opportunity. For many of the same reasons we discussed when dealing with disinterested director approval of conflict-of-interest transactions, corporate employees or officers must fully disclose all material facts they know when they present the opportunity to their superiors.[153] Also, when those in charge of the corporation neither have the company immediately seize, nor explicitly reject, the opportunity, disputes can arise over whether, in fact, there was a rejection.[154]

Things get tricky when directors take an opportunity after claiming that the corporation turned it down. In this case, the individuals who decided the corporation should reject the opportunity might be the very persons who then took the opportunity for themselves. Technically, this is not a transaction between the corporation and its directors. Hence, the conflict-of-interest statutes will not apply. Still, the conflict-of-interest which exists when directors vote to have the corporation turn down an opportunity, only to take it for themselves, seems little different from the conflict-of-interest which exists when directors contract with the corporation. Accordingly, it might make sense to look to disinterested director approval, shareholder approval, or proof of fairness in order to

---

151. *E.g.*, Broz v. Cellular Information Systems, Inc., 673 A.2d 148 (Del.1996).

152. *See, e.g.*, Abbott Redmont Thinlite Corp. v. Redmont, 475 F.2d 85 (2d Cir. 1973). Some courts have treated corporate rejections of the opportunity as showing the corporation does not have an "interest" in the opportunity for purposes of the interest or expectancy test. *E.g.*, Kaplan v. Fenton, 278 A.2d 834 (Del.1971). As discussed earlier, all this succeeds in doing is confusing

the meaning of the interest or expectancy test.

153. *E.g.*, Havlicek/Fleisher Enterprises, Inc. v. Bridgeman, 788 F.Supp. 389 (E.D.Wis.1992).

154. *Compare* Suburban Motors of Grafton, Inc. v. Forester, 134 Wis.2d 183, 396 N.W.2d 351 (Wis.Ct.App.1986), *with* CST, Inc. v. Mark, 360 Pa.Super. 303, 520 A.2d 469 (1987).

validate such a rejection. In fact, the American Law Institute's Principles of Corporate Governance takes this approach.[155]

Disinterested director or shareholder rejection of a corporate opportunity raises the same sort of issues we discussed when dealing with disinterested director or shareholder approval of conflict-of-interest transactions, albeit now with no statutory guidance. Similarly, proof of fairness of the rejection presumably should require the court to ask if this is the decision a disinterested board would have made for the corporation.[156]

Notice that this evaluation of fairness is very different from the fairness test sometimes employed in attempting to determine whether something is a corporate opportunity. The "fairness" test we discussed earlier as an alternative to the line of business or the interest or expectancy tests involved looking at multiple factors which essentially balance the equities favoring the corporation, versus the equities favoring its agent, in order to see whether "fairness" required the agent to give the corporation first crack at the opportunity. Having decided, however, that the corporation deserved first crack at the opportunity, the court, in assessing the fairness of a rejection, should look at things only from the standpoint of the best interest of the corporation.

The *Sinclair* opinion we discussed earlier has been the source of some confusion regarding the application of the fairness standard in dealing with opportunities in the parent-subsidiary context. The plaintiff in *Sinclair* complained that the parent corporation, Sinclair, developed oil fields around the world for Sinclair, or for Sinclair's other subsidiaries, but not for Sinven—the subsidiary in which the plaintiff owned shares. The court stated that the business judgment rule was the proper standard to evaluate Sinclair's expansion plans. Many writers have interpreted this statement to hold that the business judgment rule, rather than the fairness test, governs the allocation of opportunities between parent and subsidiary corporations.[157] This is a misunderstanding of the court's opinion. The court's invocation of the business judgment rule occurred in the context in which the plaintiff identified no opportunities which had come to Sinven and were then taken by Sinclair. In other words, this was not a situation in which Sinclair used its control over Sinven to force Sinven to reject opportunities which otherwise belonged to Sinven under the various tests we discussed above.[158] Under these circumstances, the courts invocation of the business judgment rule was actually generous to the plaintiff. Normally, only the decisions of Sinven's directors concerning expansion plans should be subject to judicial review, even under the business judgment rule, at the

---

155. Principles of Corporate Governance § 5.05(a).

156. *E.g.*, Johnston v. Greene, 35 Del. Ch. 479, 121 A.2d 919 (Sup. Ct. 1956).

157. *E.g.*, Brudney & Clark, *supra* note 142 at 1049.

158. The dual obligations of Sinven's directors—because they were also employees of Sinclair—would, as we discussed earlier, lead the court to apply narrower tests for whether Sinven (or even Sinclair) was entitled to opportunities of which these directors became aware.

behest of a shareholder of Sinven. Sinclair, in contrast, can do whatever it wants with opportunities which do not otherwise belong to Sinven. Otherwise, we end up with the rather strange result that a majority shareholder has a greater obligation than an officer or director to turn over opportunities.[159]

Determining whether it is fair to the corporation to reject an opportunity presents some differences from deciding if a conflict-of-interest transaction is fair to the corporation. To begin with, one might ask what the corporation gains from turning down an opportunity. Presumably, no one pays the corporation to reject the opportunity. Indeed, the lack of such payment might confuse one into thinking that corporate rejection constitutes waste and should require unanimous shareholder approval.[160] The gain to the corporation, however, lies in avoiding the risks and burdens of developing the opportunity. After all, business is all about making choices as to where to deploy resources in search of the most profits.

This suggests that the obvious reason to have the corporation reject an opportunity is because the decision maker does not think the opportunity will be profitable. Presumably, if anyone thinks it worthwhile to sue corporate officials for taking a corporate opportunity after the corporation turned it down, this pessimistic assessment of the opportunity must have turned out to be wrong. As discussed earlier, however, courts measure fairness based upon the situation at the time the directors acted. A more serious problem here is that directors who take an opportunity, after voting to have the corporation turn it down, lack credibility if they state they did not think the opportunity would be profitable. Therefore, directors in this situation must come up with another reason why they decided that the corporation should not pursue the opportunity. One common response is to say the corporation lacked the money.

b. *Financial inability*

One of the most frequent and controversial justifications for taking a corporate opportunity is the claim that the corporation lacked the money to take the opportunity for itself. Courts have responded to this claim in a variety of different ways.

At one extreme, we have the court's opinion in *Irving Trust Co. v. Deutsch*.[161] The corporation in this case (Acoustic) made radios and record players. Acoustic's board voted to enter a contract to acquire stock in another company—which was then in receivership—in order to obtain the right to use critical patented technology. At the time the board voted to enter this contract, Acoustic's president (Deutsch) in-

---

159. The American Law Institute's Principles of Corporate Governance attempts to create a special definition of corporate opportunities for controlling shareholders. Principles of Corporate Governance § 5.12(b). There is little support for this in the case law.

160. *See* Clark, *supra* note 3 at 249–250.

161. 73 F.2d 121 (2d Cir.1934).

formed the board that he had been unsuccessful in his efforts to seek
funds for Acoustic to make this purchase. Deutsch also told the board
that there were several individuals interested in buying the stock under
the proposed contract for themselves and, if these individuals did buy the
stock, they would be willing to give Acoustic the rights it needed to use
the patented technology. Shortly thereafter, when Acoustic evidently
lacked funds to pay for the stock under the contract, Deutsch and several
other individuals paid for and kept the stock themselves. These individuals were able to make a profit by selling this stock. Some time later,
Acoustic went bankrupt and the trustee in bankruptcy sued to collect
this profit for the corporation.

Naturally, the defendants asserted Acoustic's lack of funds as justification for their buying the stock. The court, however, rejected the
justification. The court noted that there was some question as to
whether Acoustic really could not obtain the money to make the purchase. Yet, the court refused to reverse the trial court's finding that
Acoustic lacked the funds. Instead, the court chose to follow a "rigid
rule" forbidding directors of a solvent corporation from taking over a
corporation's contract, even if the corporation is financially unable to
perform. While the court only addressed taking an opportunity which the
corporation had already contracted to buy, later courts and writers
generally interpret *Irving Trust* to stand for a broad rule that financial
inability is never a defense for taking any corporate opportunity.[162]

At the other extreme are statements in court opinions, including
Guth and *Miller*, which indicate that part of the very definition of a
corporate opportunity is the corporation's financial wherewithal to take
advantage of the opportunity. The practical impact of this view goes
beyond making the corporation's financial inability to obtain the opportunity a justification for officials taking the opportunity for themselves.
It also suggests the burden of proof on the issue of whether the
corporation can afford the opportunity is on the plaintiff, rather than on
those who took the opportunity. Actually, however, these statements in
Guth and *Miller* were essentially dicta.

In between these two extremes, there are a variety of judicial
viewpoints. For example, the court in *Klinicki v. Lundgren*[163] chose to
follow the approach recommended by the American Law Institute's
Principles of Corporate Governance. Under this approach, financial
inability of the corporation to take an opportunity is not a justification,
in itself, for an official personally taking the opportunity. Unlike the
broader interpretation of *Irving Trust*, however, this does not mean
financial inability can never be relevant. Instead, financial ability can
become relevant if the official offers the opportunity to the corporation,
the corporation turns down the opportunity, and then the plaintiff
challenges the decision to reject the opportunity. In that case, under the

162. *E.g.*, Klinicki v. Lundgren, 298 Or.
662, 695 P.2d 906 (1985); Note, *Corporate
Opportunity*, 74 Harv. L. Rev. 765, 773
(1961).

163. 298 Or. 662, 695 P.2d 906 (1985).

American Law Institute's approach, directors who vote to turn down an opportunity, and then take the opportunity for themselves, might attempt to prove that the rejection is in the best interest of the corporation—in other words, fair—because the corporation cannot afford the opportunity. In *Klinicki*, the defendant's failure to present the opportunity to the corporation meant, under this approach, he could not assert financial inability as a defense. After all, there is no sense talking about whether a lack of funds would have made a corporate rejection fair, when there never had been a corporate rejection.

Other courts accept corporate financial inability as a defense, regardless of any formal rejection, but place the burden on those asserting financial inability to prove the corporation could not come up with the funds.[164] Still other courts look at financial capacity without focusing on who has the burden of proof,[165] or else shift the burden of proof on the issue of financial capacity back and forth depending on the circumstances.[166]

So, what approach should the law follow? Placing the burden on the plaintiff to prove that the corporation can afford the opportunity is bizarre. This puts the burden on the party often with the poorest access to evidence concerning the corporation's financial capabilities (at least in the situation in which a minority shareholder brings a derivative action on behalf of the corporation). By contrast, if corporate officials assert corporate financial inability as a justification for taking an opportunity, they presumably have some knowledge of corporate finances to back this assertion up. If the party taking the opportunity does not have such knowledge (perhaps because he or she is a lower level employee) then this party should not have taken what was otherwise a corporate opportunity.

Poor access by potential plaintiffs to evidence concerning corporate finances is part of the rationale behind the *Irving Trust* rule. The concern is that, even if the burden of proof is on corporate officials, plaintiffs will be unable to rebut questionable claims of lack of funds. There is little hard data as to whether this will be true. A more persuasive reason for the *Irving Trust* rule lies in the incentives which otherwise might exist for corporate officials. If corporate officials can take desirable opportunities for themselves whenever the corporation cannot afford the opportunity, the officials might lose their incentive to do their absolute best to gain the necessary financing for the corporation. For example, in *Irving Trust*, Acoustic's president made no further efforts to obtain money for Acoustic to buy the stock after the board voted to enter the contract.

164. *See, e.g.,* CST, Inc. v. Mark, 360 Pa.Super. 303, 520 A.2d 469 (1987).

165. *E.g.,* Broz v. Cellular Information Systems, Inc., 673 A.2d 148 (Del.1996).

166. *See, e.g.,* Ellzey v. Fyr-Pruf, Inc., 376 So.2d 1328 (Miss.1979) (the court stated that the burden was on the plaintiff to show the corporation was financially able to take the opportunity, unless the plaintiff showed the financial inability stemmed from breach of fiduciary duty or non-payment of a debt owed to the corporation by the defendants).

Suppose, however, the board in *Irving Trust* had voted to allow Deutsch and his associates to buy the stock.[167] Do the concerns behind *Irving Trust's* prophylactic rule require the court to ignore the corporate rejection defense, because, in this instance, the reason for the rejection lies in the corporation's lack of funds? Such a rule could have highly undesirable consequences in a situation such as that facing Acoustics. Assuming Acoustics truly lacked funds, allowing the defendants to buy the stock may have been the only way for Acoustics to obtain access to the patented technology. Moreover, what will a court do if financial concerns are simply part of a mixture of motives which may have led the corporation to reject the opportunity? In any event, if corporate rejection is a defense except when the motivation is a lack of funds, the end result could be simply to lead directors to conjure up other rationalizations for rejecting the opportunity.

If courts remain willing to allow the corporate rejection defense despite the reason for the rejection being a lack of funds, they arrive at the position of the American Law Institute. Perhaps a rejection of the opportunity by disinterested directors or shareholders is sufficient to allay the concerns about access to information and poor incentives which underlie *Irving Trust's* prophylactic rule. Suppose, however, the directors who vote to have the corporation reject the opportunity, then take it for themselves. It is difficult to see how allowing directors to defend a rejection based on lack of funds, when the directors voting to reject the opportunity were the individuals who took the opportunity, avoids the concerns behind the *Irving Trust* rule. Yet, if courts were only to allow a rejection based upon a lack of funds if there is disinterested director or shareholder approval, the courts would be acting on an implicit assumption that judicial review under the fairness test is less likely to protect the corporate interest from overreaching directors than is disinterested director or shareholder approval. This seems contrary to the logic we developed when dealing with conflict-of-interest transactions.

Having gone as far as the American Law Institute's approach, why not simply let corporate officials prove lack of funds as a defense to taking an opportunity, even if the corporation does not formally reject the opportunity? Put differently, what did the court in *Klinicki* gain by refusing to consider the lack of money claim simply because the defendant did not first present the opportunity to the corporation? In a situation in which control of the corporation resides in disinterested decision makers, demanding that the corporate official present the opportunity to the company seems sensible. Independent directors or senior officers are in a better position than the court to consider initially whether the corporation can afford the opportunity.

---

167. It is possible that Acoustic's directors thought this is what they did. The problems are that there apparently was no express resolution stating that the individuals could buy the stock if the corporation could not afford to carry out the purchase, and Deutsch evidently did not disclose that he was among the individuals interested in buying the stock (thereby disclosing his conflict-of-interest).

Yet, in many cases, the party who takes the opportunity is in control of the corporation. This may have been the case in *Klinicki*, since the defendant, and another corporation owned by the defendant with members of his family, held 66 percent of the corporation's stock. Here, one might argue that it is pointless to force the defendant to present the opportunity to the corporation so that the defendant can decide to have the corporation turn down the opportunity for lack of funds. Still, there might be something said for the American Law Institute's approach. In a closely held corporation, such as in *Klinicki*, forcing the majority owner to seek corporate rejection often means forcing disclosure of the defendant's action to minority shareholders. A person who is confident that the corporation lacks funds should have no problem with a requirement of disclosure. Conversely, the secretive taking of an opportunity, such as occurred in *Klinicki*, may tell us that the defendant really does not believe the corporation lacks funds.

c.   *Third party unwillingness to do business with the corporation*

Sometimes, corporate officials seek to justify their seizing of an opportunity on the ground that the party who offered the opportunity absolutely refused to do business with the corporation. Judicial reactions to this excuse have been similar to the reactions we saw to the lack of money defense.

For example, in *Energy Resources Corp. v. Porter*,[168] the court took a position that it would not recognize a refusal to deal defense unless, before taking the opportunity, the corporate official disclosed all the facts to the corporation, and allowed the corporation a chance to convince the third party to do business with the corporation. Other court's, however, have held that, if the party with the opportunity is unwilling to deal with the corporation, the opportunity is not a corporate opportunity, and the corporate officials can take the opportunity without disclosure.[169]

At first glance, it seems reasonable to say that if the party with the opportunity will not sell it to the corporation, the company hardly can complain about officials taking the opportunity for themselves. The court in *Energy Resources* makes a persuasive point, however, that one never can be entirely sure that the third party would not have dealt with the corporation until the corporation had a chance to convince the third party. Besides, much as in the case of the financial inability defense, recognition of the refusal to deal defense creates perverse incentives. If courts recognize the refusal to deal defense, corporate officials lose their incentives to try to convince third parties to sell the opportunity to the corporation.

168. 14 Mass.App.Ct. 296, 438 N.E.2d 391 (1982).

169. *E.g.*, Science Accessories Corp. v. Summagraphics Corp., 425 A.2d 957 (Del. 1980).

d.   Ultra vires or other legal incapacity

Finally, corporate officials might argue that they can seize a corporate opportunity because it is ultra vires or it is otherwise legally impermissible for the corporation to take the opportunity. The ultra vires justification is not common. As we discussed before,[170] modern corporation articles typically do not limit the businesses in which the corporation may engage. Still, regulatory statutes may prohibit certain types of corporations from engaging in various activities—for example, banking laws traditionally have limited the non-banking activities of bank corporations. In any event, if an opportunity is ultra vires or prohibited by regulation, it typically would not fit within the various tests for a corporate opportunity anyway.

Judicial reactions have varied along predictable lines when courts have faced the argument that corporate officials can take what was otherwise be a corporate opportunity because the opportunity would have been ultra vires or illegal for the corporation to pursue. The court in *Miller* stated that it would not consider ultra vires as an excuse to allow corporate officials to take what would be otherwise a corporate opportunity. The court reasoned that shareholders might amend the articles if the opportunity was good enough. By contrast, other courts, ignoring this rather sensible point, have recognized ultra vires as an excuse for corporate officials to seize what would otherwise be a corporate opportunity.[171] By and large, courts have made their own evaluation of whether regulatory barriers, other than the corporation's articles, prevent the corporation from taking an opportunity.[172] After all, presumably the court is in a good position to assess what the law allows a corporation to do.

4.2.9 *Taking corporate property and competing with the corporation*

Corporate opportunity cases sometimes involve charges that the defendants took corporate property for use in developing the opportunity, or that the development of the opportunity placed the defendants in competition with the corporation. In fact, however, use of corporate property and competition with the corporation are distinct wrongs from usurping a corporate opportunity.

a.   Taking corporate property

Taking corporate property for personal use without consent is actually an extreme case of an unfair conflict-of-interest transaction.[173] The terms are unfair: The agent gets property (or its use) from the

---

170. See § 3.1.4*a supra*.

171. *E.g.,* Diedrick v. Helm, 217 Minn. 483, 14 N.W.2d 913 (1944).

172. *See, e.g.,* Goodman v. Perpetual Bldg. Assoc., 320 F.Supp. 20 (D.D.C. 1970).

173. *See* Principles of Corporate Governance § 5.04(a) (treating use of corporate property by directors and senior executives as a conflict-of-interest transaction requiring disinterested director approval, shareholder approval or proof of fairness).

corporation, while the corporation gets nothing. Also, the process is unfair; typically accomplished without disclosure, if not outright concealment. More simply, what we have here is conversion or theft.

Sometimes, there can be a question as to whether what the agent took was corporate property. This occurs when the so-called property consists of information which the corporation claims is a trade secret.[174] Other times, there may be a factual dispute over whether the corporation gave the employee express or implied consent to make personal use of some corporate assets. If so, then the use presumably constitutes a sort of compensation and implicates the issues discussed earlier when dealing with executive compensation.

When an agent makes unauthorized use of corporate property to develop a profitable opportunity, the extent of the remedy can become an issue. There is no dispute that the corporation is entitled to its property (or the property's value) back. Can the corporation go beyond this, however, to demand that the company obtain the entire opportunity developed with the property?

In *Guth*, the extensive use of Loft's resources to develop Pepsi Cola was a factor used by the court to justify finding that Guth should have presented the Pepsi opportunity to Loft. Other courts, as well, cite use of corporate property as a factor to weigh in deciding if an opportunity should go to the corporation.[175] Some writers advocate going beyond this. They would make use of corporate property, in and of itself, grounds for giving the opportunity to the corporation.[176] The American Law Institute's Principles of Corporate Governance follows this broader approach when a corporate official becomes aware of an opportunity by use of corporate property. The corporation is entitled to such an opportunity, without regard to other factors, so long as the official should reasonably expect the corporation would have wanted the opportunity.[177] On the other hand, the American Law Institute does not specifically address the remedy for using corporate property to develop (rather than discover) an opportunity.[178]

Why should use of corporate property turn what otherwise might not be a corporate opportunity into an opportunity the corporation can claim? The answer lies in the traditional equitable remedy of tracing. Tracing allows a victim of conversion, not only to obtain return of wrongfully taken property, but also to receive any profits made by the converter through the use of the property. A classic illustration would be if a thief used stolen money to buy a winning lottery ticket. The person whose money the thief stole would be entitled to the winnings. This avoids the thief profiting from his or her wrongdoing. Besides, the

174. *See, e.g.,* AMP, Inc. v. Fleischhacker, 823 F.2d 1199 (7th Cir.1987).
175. See note 135 *supra.*
176. Brudney & Clark, *supra* note 142 at 1006.
177. Principles of Corporate Governance § 5.05(b)(1)(B).
178. *See id.* at § 5.04(c).

victim's money was at risk, because the thief might lose, and, as a result, be unable to return the money.

This rationale works in a case like *Guth*, in which Guth's use of Loft's resources was massive, critical to Pepsi's success, and would have meant major losses for Loft if Pepsi had not succeeded. On the other hand, we should not expect courts mechanically to apply this approach any time a corporate employee uses any corporate property in a side venture. For example, suppose a corporate executive takes home a company "lap top" computer to draft a business plan for a new venture unrelated to anything involving the executive's work for the company. Should the corporation be entitled to the new venture simply by virtue of the use of the computer?

The court in *Rapistan Corp. v. Michaels*[179] recognized the need to avoid taking the tracing remedy to extremes. There, the court refused to find that the defendants' use of corporate property—including funds, facilities, personnel, and the defendants' compensated time—was sufficient to make an opportunity one which must go to the corporation. The court noted that the amount of corporate assets used was minimal, especially in comparison to the $29.5 million cost of the opportunity. Also, the court stated that there was not a "direct and substantial nexus or causal connection" between the use of corporate assets and the creation, acquisition or development of the opportunity. In other words, the court apparently looked, not only at how much corporate property the defendants used, but also at how critical the corporate property was to the discovery or development of the opportunity.

Does this mean the corporation should only be entitled to return of the property in a situation in which it is not entitled to claim the entire opportunity? Perhaps not. The court could still seek to award to the corporation the profits traceable to the use of the corporation's property. One way to do this might be to calculate the ratio of corporate versus non-corporate property used to develop the opportunity. Then, the court could award the corporation profits from, or even ownership of, the fraction of the opportunity which corresponds to this ratio.

b. *Competing with the corporation*

Competing with the corporation while employed by the company is also, as a general proposition, an elementary breach of an agent's duty of loyalty.[180] After all, competing with one's employer seems the very definition of disloyalty. On the other hand, employers occasionally agree to let their employees compete with them, at least in certain limited ways. If so, then this conduct will not breach the agent's duty of loyalty.[181]

179. 203 Mich.App. 301, 511 N.W.2d 918 (1994).

180. *E.g.*, Ritterpusch v. Lithographic Plate Service, Inc., 208 Md. 592, 119 A.2d 392 (1956).

181. *E.g.*, Principles of Corporate Governance § 5.06(a).

While the basic rule is that employees cannot compete with their employer, it is not only allowable, but socially desirable, for former employees to compete with their former employer.[182] Such competition promotes consumer choices. Because such competition is socially desirable, courts carefully scrutinize contracts by which employees agree not to compete with their employer following termination of employment (non-competition agreements or covenants not to compete). Such contracts are contrary to public policy and unenforceable unless limited in location and duration so as to be reasonable.[183]

There is an inherent tension between the rule that current employees cannot compete with their employer, and the rule that former employees can compete with their former employer. Typically, employees do not quit their job one day, wake up the next day, and then decide to go into competition with their former employer. Rather, the decision to go into competition with one's employer commonly occurs before one quits. Moreover, part of the process of making this decision often involves taking various steps to explore the viability of starting a competing venture. After all, it is highly embarrassing, not to mention economically disadvantageous, to find out after one quits that the competing venture is not feasible. Overlapping with steps to explore the viability of a competing enterprise, are steps to set up the competing business. In many instances, these constitute the same activities. For example, negotiating a lease for the new venture may serve both to give one an idea as to the venture's viability and to lay the groundwork to start the venture. Even if an activity is not necessary in order to decide to start the competing venture, the employee typically wants to do as much preparation as possible before quitting (after which, the employee might no longer receive a steady paycheck for a while).

Numerous courts have faced the question as to how far employees can go to prepare a competing venture without crossing the line and engaging in impermissible competition before the employee quits. Incorporating the new business and lining up its finances and facilities seem okay.[184] Soliciting the employer's customers is unacceptable.[185] Borderline questions involve soliciting one's fellow employees to leave and join the new venture,[186] and notifying customers of the employee's intentions without soliciting their business.[187] A practical problem here is that discussions with customers and fellow employees are often the most important activity the employee needs to undertake in order to decide whether he or she should leave and go into a competing venture.

182. *E.g.,* Maryland Metals, Inc. v. Metzner, 282 Md. 31, 382 A.2d 564 (Md. App.1978).

183. *E.g.,* Reed, Roberts Assoc., Inc. v. Strauman, 40 N.Y.2d 303, 386 N.Y.S.2d 677, 353 N.E.2d 590 (1976).

184. *E.g.,* Lawter Int'l, Inc. v. Carroll, 116 Ill.App.3d 717, 72 Ill.Dec. 15, 451 N.E.2d 1338 (1983).

185. *E.g.,* Smith–Shrader Co. v. Smith, 136 Ill.App.3d 571, 91 Ill.Dec. 1, 483 N.E.2d 283 (1985).

186. *See, e.g.,* Bancroft–Whitney Co. v. Glen, 64 Cal.2d 327, 411 P.2d 921, 49 Cal. Rptr. 825 (1966).

187. *See, e.g.,* Ellis & Marshall Associates, Inc. v. Marshall, 16 Ill.App.3d 398, 306 N.E.2d 712 (1973).

Courts also often condemn employees for concealing from, or misrepresenting to, their employers, the employees' intention to leave and set up a competing business.[188] This seems to follow as a corollary to the disclosure obligations of agents to their principals, which we discussed earlier. Still, there is a bit of unreality to expecting employees to disclose intentions which will prompt the employer to fire them. Indeed, one suspects this is an area in which there may be a substantial discontinuity between legal expectations and customary practice.

Once again, there is a question of remedy. Should impermissible predeparture competition turn a business which otherwise would not be a corporate opportunity into something which the former employee must hand over to the corporation? The court in *Lincoln Stores, Inc. v. Grant*[189] answered this question in the negative. The court in *Lincoln Stores* held that impermissible competition by corporate officers did not entitle the corporation to take the competing department store which the officers had purchased and run for themselves.

4.2.10 *Remedies for Duty of Loyalty Violations*

We already have alluded to the basic remedies for duty of loyalty violations. Unfair conflict-of-interest transactions are voidable. This means the corporation has the right to rescind the transaction and get back what the corporation paid. The remedy of rescission normally also requires the corporation to return what it received in the transaction. The usual remedy for usurping a corporate opportunity is to turn the opportunity over to the corporation.[190] Courts often refer to this as imposing a constructive trust on the opportunity in the corporation's favor. The corporation normally must reimburse the defendant for what the defendant paid to obtain the opportunity.

One problem with these recoveries is that they generally do not make the defendant any worse off than he or she would have been if he or she had not made an unfair conflict-of-interest transaction or usurped a corporate opportunity to start with. Hence, one might worry that the law does not deter directors and officers from trying to get away with duty of loyalty violations. Courts sometimes impose additional sanctions to avoid this problem. Punitive damages are one possibility.[191] Also, courts have occasionally ordered faithless corporate officials to repay to the corporation any salary the corporation paid them while they were breaching their duty.[192]

§ 4.3 Derivative Suits

We have seen that directors owe duties of care and loyalty to the corporation, the breach of which can produce a cause of action for the

188. *E.g.,* Bancroft–Whitney Co. v. Glen, 64 Cal.2d 327, 411 P.2d 921, 49 Cal. Rptr. 825 (1966).

189. 309 Mass. 417, 34 N.E.2d 704 (1941).

190. *E.g.,* Guth v. Loft, 23 Del.Ch. 255, 5 A.2d 503 (Sup. Ct. 1939).

191. *E.g.,* Goben v. Barry, 234 Kan. 721, 676 P.2d 90 (1984).

192. *E.g.,* American Timber & Trading Co. v. Niedermeyer, 276 Or. 1135, 558 P.2d 1211 (1976).

corporation against its directors. Who decides, however, whether the corporation will assert such potential claims against its directors? Normally, the board of directors, or officers acting under the board's control, decide whether a corporation will pursue a possible claim through litigation. This presents an obvious problem when the prospective lawsuit is against the directors themselves. If courts were to leave exclusive control over corporate litigation in the hands of the board, then enforcement of the directors' duties to the corporation would be confined to those relatively rare cases in which the corporation goes broke and a bankruptcy trustee asserts the claim, or else there is a change in management and the new directors decide the corporation should act.

To deal with this problem, courts devised the idea of the derivative suit. In such an action, an individual shareholder sues on behalf of the corporation. In other words, the cause of action asserted belongs to the corporation, and, with rare exceptions, any recovery must go to the corporation. The plaintiff shareholder serves merely as a self-appointed champion of the corporate right.

Unfortunately, such self-appointed champions sometimes turn out to be less than noble knights seeking only to advance the corporate interest. Concern about this phenomenon has led courts and legislatures over the years to adopt a variety of constraints on derivative actions. The result, as we shall explore in this section, is that derivative suits have become a procedural morass.

4.3.1   The Nature of a Derivative Suit

a.   Derivative versus direct suits

As just pointed out, the fundamental feature of a derivative suit is that the plaintiff shareholder is asserting the corporation's cause of action and seeking recovery for the corporation. Many times, however, a shareholder might prefer to argue that he or she is asserting his or her own cause of action. To use the common parlance, the shareholder would argue that he or she is asserting a "direct" rather than a derivative claim. One obvious advantage to asserting a direct claim is that the shareholder might then personally recover. Moreover, such a characterization of the suit can avoid the need to deal with the various procedural barriers confronting derivative suits.

Suppose directors of a corporation make grossly negligent decisions which cause the corporation to incur substantial losses. Or, suppose the directors have the corporation enter into unfair contracts with the directors, or usurp a valuable opportunity properly belonging to the corporation. In these instances, there is a corporate cause of action which can form the basis of a derivative suit. Yet, in these instances, the corporation's shareholders have also suffered harm, since the damage to the corporation will decrease the value of the shareholders' stock. Does this mean that the shareholders can assert claims on their own behalf against the directors? With certain limited exceptions, courts have held that shareholders cannot bring such actions on their own behalf. Instead, if the essence of the shareholder's claim is for damage the shareholder suffered by virtue of the directors' conduct harming the corporation and thereby lowering the value of the shareholder's stock, then the shareholder must bring the action as a derivative suit.[1]

Yet, why require shareholders to bring such actions only as a derivative suit? To say that the cause of action asserted belongs to the corporation is circular. If courts were to recognize shareholder claims for harm to the corporation which decreases the value of the shareholders' stock, then it would not be true that the only cause of action belonged to the corporation.

Courts have asserted several rationales for refusing to recognize personal claims based upon the argument that harm to the corporation lowers the value of the shareholders' stock.[2] To begin with, courts have expressed concern about the multiplicity of suits which could result from allowing such claims. Obviously, if individual shareholders must assert their own claims, there may be a lot of lawsuits. Moreover, shareholders who do not bring suit will be left out. In addition, courts have pointed to the interests of the corporation's creditors. After all, if the shareholders, rather than the corporation, recover for harm which reduced the worth of the corporation, the result might be to increase the risk that the corporation will be unable to pay its creditors.

To some extent, the law might deal with the concern about the multiplicity of actions from shareholders suing on their own behalf through the device of the class action. Yet, the class action presents many of the same problems of abuse which, as we shall discuss, have plagued the derivative suit. The concern about creditors illustrates a broader point: Harm to the corporation impacts more than just the shareholders. It impacts creditors, employees, those who do business with the corporation, and the community in which the corporation operates. If the law allows the shareholders to sue for indirect damages, why not allow all these other parties to sue for indirect damages? To ask this question is to illustrate why the law generally does not allow suits for indirect damages. Finally, it is no answer to say that the law can allow both derivative and direct claims in this context, since that would create the prospect of double recovery.

On the other hand, in circumstances in which these rationales do not apply, some courts have recognized an exception to the requirement that shareholders must bring claims for indirect injury as a derivative suit. This can occur in a closely held corporation. The classic example would be a corporation which has only two shareholders, say one owning 51 percent, and the other 49 percent, of the outstanding stock. If the 51 percent shareholder were to use his or her control to have the corporation lease property from him or her at an unfair rent, or pay to him or her an excessive management fee, this would normally call for a deriva-

§ 4.3

1. *E.g.,* Sax v. World Wide Press, Inc., 809 F.2d 610 (9th Cir.1987).

2. *E.g.,* Watson v. Button, 235 F.2d 235 (9th Cir.1956).

tive claim. Yet, assuming there are no corporate creditors prejudiced by a direct action, why force the 49 percent shareholder to go through the rigmarole of a derivative suit? Based upon this reasoning, some courts have allowed the shareholder in a situation such as this to bring the action as a direct suit.[3] The American Law Institute's Principles of Corporate Governance supports this approach.[4] Other courts, however, have refused to recognize an exception even in this circumstance.[5]

The mere fact that a shareholder sues directors, however, does not mean that the action involves derivative claims. To take a simple illustration, if a director strikes a shareholder while the director is driving a car negligently, the shareholder obviously has a direct tort claim against the director. Of more relevance to corporate law, if a majority shareholder breaches a shareholders' agreement, the minority shareholder has a direct cause of action for breach of contract, whether or not the majority shareholder's action also breached a duty to the corporation.[6] Similarly, if a director misleads a shareholder in order to induce the shareholder to buy or sell stock, the shareholder has a direct cause of action against the director for fraud.[7] These examples are easy because the plaintiff shareholder does not base his or her claim on rights he or she possesses as a shareholder.

Matters become less straightforward if the shareholder's claim is that the directors breached a duty which the directors owed to the shareholder by virtue of his or her status as a shareholder. For example, a shareholder might complain that actions by the directors interfere with the shareholder's voting rights. Alternately, a shareholder might complain about the failure of directors to declare dividends. A shareholder might also complain about decisions by directors either to accept or to oppose mergers and tender offers through which the shareholder will sell his or her stock. Even though the claim arises from the shareholder's status as a shareholder, these sort of claims generally are not derivative. The reason is that the shareholder is not complaining that harm to the corporation caused harm to him- or herself. Rather, the shareholder is stating that the board's actions directly undercut his or her rights as a shareholder, regardless of the action's impact on the corporation.

For example, in *Smith v. Van Gorkom*,[8] the plaintiff complained that the directors breached their duty by voting, without careful investigation, for a merger in which the existing shareholders would receive $55 in cash per share. As discussed earlier in this book,[9] it is difficult to say whether the directors' decision was good, bad or indifferent from the standpoint of future corporate profitability. That was not the concern; the concern was whether the shareholders could have received a higher

---

3. *E.g.*, Schumacher v. Schumacher, 469 N.W.2d 793 (N.D.1991).

4. Principles of Corporate Governance § 7.01(d).

5. *E.g.*, Bagdon v. Bridgestone/Firestone, Inc., 916 F.2d 379 (7th Cir.1990).

6. *E.g.*, Hikita v. Nichiro Gyogyo Kaisha, Ltd., 713 P.2d 1197 (Alaska 1986).

7. *E.g.*, Siegel v. Engelmann, 1 Misc.2d 447, 143 N.Y.S.2d 193 (Sup. Ct. 1955).

8. 488 A.2d 858 (Del.1985).

9. See § 4.1.5 *supra*.

price. Accordingly, the plaintiff brought this claim as a class action on behalf of the individual shareholders.

In *Eisenberg v. Flying Tiger Line, Inc.*,[10] the situation was more complex, but the outcome similar. The management of the original Flying Tiger corporation had the corporation engage in a merger, which resulted in the shareholders of the original Flying Tiger corporation becoming shareholders of a new holding company. The holding company, in turn, owned all of the stock of another new corporation, which carried out Flying Tiger's air freight business. The plaintiff's theory was that this was a scheme to decrease the shareholders' ability to control the air freight corporation. The court agreed with the plaintiff shareholder that this was a direct claim, and, hence, the plaintiff did not need to meet a security for expenses statute applicable to derivative suits. The key point for the court was that the claim involved an alleged dilution of the shareholders' governance rights, not an alleged harm to the corporation. The fact that the directors accomplished the alleged dilution by merging the corporation did not alter this point.

Some courts, however, have had a more difficult time differentiating between suits to vindicate shareholder rights, and suits based upon harm to the corporation. For example, one obstacle facing the *Eisenberg* court was the need to distinguish an opinion by the New York Court of Appeals, which held that an action t compel the payment of dividends was derivative.[11] This holding seems strange[12]—after all, it is generally hard to see how an action to compel the corporation to pay dividends is an action on behalf of the corporation—and the New York legislature changed New York's corporation statute effectively to overrule the case.[13] Still, this New York court decision is symptomatic of a number of court opinions which attempt to decide if an action is a derivative or a direct suit by asking whether the plaintiff shareholder has a claim "unique" from the other shareholders.[14] Sometimes, courts use a uniqueness test to allow direct claims for actions which otherwise would be derivative—for example to allow a party who pledged his stock to sue for mismanagement by directors installed by the pledgee.[15] In either case, this approach tends to distract courts from the central inquiry: Is the plaintiff shareholder simply complaining about harm which flowed to the shareholder by virtue of injury to the corporation?[16]

Perhaps the key to deciding more difficult characterization cases is to go back to the concerns which led courts to demand that shareholders

---

10. 451 F.2d 267 (2d Cir.1971).

11. Gordon v. Elliman, 306 N.Y. 456, 119 N.E.2d 331 (1954).

12. *See, e.g.,* Cowin v. Bresler, 741 F.2d 410 (D.C.Cir.1984) (holding that a suit to compel dividends was a direct suit).

13. Section 626 of New York's Business Corporation Law now states that an action is derivative only if the action seeks a judgment in the corporation's favor.

14. *E.g.,* In re Nuveen Fund Litigation, 855 F.Supp. 950 (D.C.Ill.1994).

15. Citibank, N.A. v. Data Lease Financial Corp., 828 F.2d 686 (11th Cir.1987).

16. A rare exception to this analysis would occur if the shareholder had an independent contractual basis to complain about the defendant's causing harm to the corporation. *See* Hikita v. Nichiro Gyogyo Kaisha, Ltd., 713 P.2d 1197 (Alaska 1986).

pursue corporate claims through derivative suits, rather than through individual suits for indirect injury. As we saw, a critical problem with suits for indirect injury would be limiting such actions to the shareholders, when other parties, such as creditors, could also make such claims. Put differently, recognizing the exclusive nature of the corporation's cause of action serves to protect the interests of all parties harmed by damage to the corporation. Actions by shareholders to vindicate voting or dividend rights directly impacted by a board decision do not raise this specter of a host of indirect injury claims.[17] Admittedly, one might argue that the corporation, itself, could benefit in some cases from protecting shareholder voting rights (which might theoretically lead to better management), or even from declaring dividends (which could facilitate greater shareholder willingness to invest). Yet, here it is the corporation which is the secondary victim of harm to the shareholders; not the other way around.[18]

Maybe the most difficult characterization cases occur in situations in which derivative and direct claims arguably coincide. For example, suppose the shareholder alleges, not just that a conflict-of-interest transaction was unfair to the corporation, but also that the shareholder vote to approve the transaction was invalid.[19] Alternately, a plaintiff may challenge the issuance of stock to directors, both on the ground that the corporation received inadequate consideration for the stock, and on the ground that the issuance undercut the shareholders' control or preemptive rights.[20] Courts sometimes have been willing to recognize direct suits in these sort of situations. Still, a danger here is that the plaintiff shareholder may be attempting to avoid derivative suit characterization by artful pleading.

b. Implications of seeking corporate recovery

The fact that a derivative suit seeks corporate recovery raises a number of questions. To begin with, is the corporation a party to the lawsuit? The answer is yes. Courts hold that the corporation is an indispensable party.[21] Otherwise, an action brought on behalf of the corporation would not be res judicata on the corporation, and another shareholder, or even the corporation itself, could bring the action again. Curiously enough, however, while the action seeks recovery for the corporation, the corporation is named as a defendant in the action. A

17. Of course, actions which lead the corporation into bankruptcy can impact the shareholders' voting and dividend rights. The rationale set out above for treating voting and dividend claims as direct actions involves cases in which the intended purpose or direct consequence of the challenged conduct is to undercut voting or dividend rights.

18. A different situation could exist if the plaintiff shareholder based his or her objection to the lack of dividends on a harm to the corporation—for example, the compa-

ny's incurring penalty taxes for accumulating income without declaring dividends. See Maul v. Kirkman, 270 N.J.Super. 596, 637 A.2d 928 (App. Div. 1994).

19. See Reifsnyder v. Pittsburgh Outdoor Advertising Co., 405 Pa. 142, 173 A.2d 319 (1961).

20. See, e.g., Bennett v. Breuil Petroleum Corp., 34 Del.Ch. 6, 99 A.2d 236 (1953).

21. E.g., Dean v. Kellogg, 294 Mich. 200, 292 N.W. 704 (1940).

rationalization for this is that a derivative suit is two suits in one: An action against those who breached their duty to the corporation, and an action against the corporation to compel the company to pursue this claim.

As a so-called defendant in the derivative suit, can the corporation assert any defenses? Since the suit seeks recovery for the corporation, one might well ask why it would ever be in the corporation's interest to assert a defense. Indeed, the suspicion is strong that any defense asserted by the corporation is really an attempt by the real defendants, who are in control of the corporation, to have the company subsidize their defense. Accordingly, courts generally do not allow the corporation to assert a defense on the merits, nor to raise procedural defenses (such as the statute of limitations) designed to protect the real defendants in a suit.[22] On the other hand, the corporation can assert various procedural defenses when the procedure involved is for the protection of the corporation. Hence, the corporation may raise the court's lack of jurisdiction over the corporation or improper service of process upon the corporation.[23] Of far more significance, the corporation can raise a variety of defenses based upon procedures designed to protect the corporation's interest specifically in derivative suits. These include challenges to the plaintiff shareholder's standing, motions to dismiss for failure to make a demand upon the directors or shareholders or based upon a determination by the directors that the suit is not in corporation's best interest, and a demand that the plaintiff post security for the corporation's litigation expenses. We shall discuss these various procedures shortly.

Related questions involve the role of the corporation's attorney. Since the corporation is a party, presumably it will need an attorney. Can the attorney who represents the corporation in the derivative suit also represent the real defendants in the action? Given that the action seeks a recovery for the corporation from the real defendants, such dual representation would seem to represent the sort of elementary conflict-of-interest which violates the ethical rules for an attorney. A number of courts have so held.[24] Other courts, however, have allowed the dual representation, at least in some cases.[25] Perhaps to the extent that the corporation takes a completely passive role in the litigation, there might be little harm in saving the expense of employing separate attorneys for the corporation and the real defendants. Yet, suppose the corporation is

22. *E.g.,* Kartub v. Optical Fashions, Inc., 158 F.Supp. 757 (S.D.N.Y.1958). Occasionally, courts might allow the corporation to assert a defense on the merits when the suit challenges a business practice of the corporation, and, as a result, the adjudication will impact the corporation's future ability to employ a business practice which might be in the company's best interest. Otis & Co. v. Pennsylvania R.R., 57 F.Supp. 680 (E.D.Pa.1944), *aff'd,* 155 F.2d 522 (3d Cir.1946).

23. *E.g.,* Swenson v. Thibaut, 39 N.C.App. 77, 250 S.E.2d 279 (1978).

24. *E.g.,* Cannon v. United States Acoustics Corp., 398 F.Supp. 209 (N.D.Ill. 1975), *aff'd in part,* 532 F.2d 1118 (7th Cir.1976).

25. *E.g.,* Bell Atlantic Corp. v. Bolger, 2 F.3d 1304 (3d Cir.1993).

considering whether to assert the various procedural defenses open to it. An attorney will have a difficult time giving the corporation objective advice on whether to assert the defense if the attorney also represents the real defendants. Still, as a realistic matter, the attorney's lack of objectivity is probably not going to matter. After all, given that the defendants typically control the corporation—or else there would be no need to allow a derivative suit—the corporation generally will assert a defense if it is in the defendants' interest to do so. This is an underlying problem with derivative suits, which we will return to later.

A more significant problem with corporate legal representation in the derivative suit context concerns attorney-client privilege. Corporate counsel may have had communications with directors and officers, the content of which the plaintiff shareholder wishes to discover. If the corporation is the attorney's client, who has control over asserting the privilege? Specifically, since the shareholder plaintiff is suing on behalf of the corporation, does the plaintiff pick up the corporate client's right to obtain information covered by the privilege? In *Garner v. Wolfinbarger*,[26] the court adopted a multi-factor test to answer this question. Among the relevant factors are: Whether the plaintiff is just one shareholder with only a few shares, or whether the demand for the information comes from a number of shareholders with a greater percentage of the outstanding stock; Whether there is reason to doubt that the plaintiff is asserting a colorable claim in the lawsuit, or there are other grounds to question the plaintiff's bona fides; How important is it for the plaintiff to get this information from this source; What is the nature of the plaintiff's action and of the alleged wrongful conduct; Whether the communication between the corporate officials and the corporation's attorney related to past or prospective acts, or whether it involves legal advice concerning the present litigation (which would make the court especially reluctant to give the plaintiff access to the communication); and any interest of the corporation in keeping the communication confidential (for instance because it involves trade secrets).[27]

The final question is whether corporate recovery is the appropriate remedy. For example, to the extent that the defendants in the suit are still in control of the corporation, recovery for the corporation leaves whatever funds the company obtains at the mercy of the defendants. A few courts have ordered the defendants to pay damages directly to the innocent shareholders, instead of to the corporation, based upon this concern.[28] By and large, however, this view does not prevail. After all, if the defendants were not in control over the corporation, there would be no need for a derivative action. Hence, if the defendants' continued control justified personal recovery by the shareholders, this would apply to the vast bulk of derivative suits. As discussed above, however, the

26.   430 F.2d 1093 (5th Cir.1970).

27.   There is some disagreement among the courts as to whether *Garner* applies only to derivative suits. *Compare* Fausek v. White, 965 F.2d 126 (6th Cir.1992), *with* Weil v. Investment/Indicators, Research & Management, 647 F.2d 18 (9th Cir.1981).

28.   *E.g.,* Backus v. Finkelstein, 23 F.2d 357 (D.C.Minn.1927).

interests of other parties impacted by harm to the corporation weighs against shareholder recovery, and, presumably, trumps the concern that the defendants will simply turn around and misbehave with the recovery. Besides, the suit should provide some deterrence to future misconduct.

The more common circumstance in which a court might deny corporate recovery in favor of individual recovery by innocent shareholders occurs when the owner(s) of a large percentage of the outstanding stock should not benefit from the recovery. At first glance, this seems to encompass the situation in which the defendant in the derivative action is a substantial (and especially a majority) shareholder. Some courts have reached this conclusion.[29] In this situation, however, any indirect benefit to the defendant by virtue of corporate recovery turns out to be a wash. To understand why, let us assume that a shareholder owning 51 percent of the corporation's outstanding stock damaged the corporation to the tune of $1 million. The loss suffered by the other shareholders due to this damage will equal $490,000 (49 percent of the million dollar loss in value of the corporation). Under this circumstance, it would hardly reward the wrongdoing shareholder to pay $1 million to the corporation—even though this indirectly benefits the wrongdoing shareholder by $510,000—when the alternative is for the wrongdoing shareholder to pay only $490,000 to the minority shareholders. Hence, it is not surprising that few cases have ordered the defendant to pay damages directly to the shareholders, rather than to the corporation, because the defendant is a substantial shareholder.

Suppose, however, there are shareholders, who are not the defendants in the suit, but who still should not benefit from corporate recovery. In this instance, payment by the defendant to the corporation creates a real transfer of wealth from the defendant to shareholders who, by hypothesis, should not be benefiting from recovery. What sort of shareholders could this be? One possibility would be shareholders who participated in the wrongdoing, but, for one reason or another, are not defendants in the lawsuit.[30] A second possibility would be shareholders who acquiesced in, or ratified, the challenged transaction[31]—albeit courts may not wish to penalize shareholders who voted to approve transactions when the shareholders really could not be expected to fully investigate or understand the merits of what they were voting on. A third possibility would be shareholders who bought their stock at fair value after the wrongdoing—particularly if they bought their stock from the defendant and were aware of the challenged conduct.[32] Such shareholders could receive something of a windfall if the corporation were to recover

29. *E.g.,* Atkinson v. Marquart, 112 Ariz. 304, 541 P.2d 556 (1975).

30. *E.g.,* Chounis v. Laing, 125 W.Va. 275, 23 S.E.2d 628 (1942).

31. *E.g.,* Young v. Columbia Oil Co., 110 W.Va. 364, 158 S.E. 678 (1931). *But see* Keenan v. Eshleman, 23 Del.Ch. 234, 2 A.2d 904 (Sup. Ct. 1938) (allowing corporate recovery despite the fact that numerous shareholders had ratified the challenged transaction).

32. *See, e.g.,* Perlman v. Feldmann, 219 F.2d 173 (2d Cir.1955).

damages when the shareholders paid a price discounted to reflect that damage. Hence, courts might deny corporate recovery, and order instead pro-rata recovery by deserving shareholders, when a large percentage of the corporation's stock is in the hands of persons who should not benefit from corporate recovery.

4.3.2   Who Has Standing to Bring a Derivative Suit?

Concern that corporate recovery might produce an unjust benefit for some shareholders leads us into the question of who can bring a derivative suit. The corporation statutes or court rules which govern derivative suits, as well judicial decisions dealing with such suits, have established four common limitations on who can bring the action:

The first limitation is that the plaintiff must be a shareholder at the time of the lawsuit.[33] Presumably, the rationale for this limitation is that a person who is not a shareholder at the time of the suit would simply be a kibitzer with no real interest in corporate recovery. Actually, as we shall discuss later, the typical plaintiff shareholder in a derivative suit tends to have a minimal economic interest in corporate recovery. In any event, not only must the plaintiff be a shareholder at the time the plaintiff files the suit, but the plaintiff generally must remain a shareholder throughout the life of the action.[34]

The requirement that the plaintiff must be a shareholder raises a number of questions. For example, must the plaintiff be a shareholder of record, or is a mere beneficial interest in stock enough to give standing? Corporation statutes provide different answers to this question.[35] In the absence of statute, courts tend to be generous in conferring standing on the holders of beneficial interests in stock.[36] The limitation of standing to shareholders obviously excludes corporate creditors from bringing derivative suits.[37] Some courts, however, have allowed the holders of bonds, which are convertible into stock, to bring derivative suits even without exercising the conversion option.[38] Interestingly, dissenting directors (unless they are also shareholders) generally lack standing under this requirement to bring a derivative suit against the majority of the board[39]—albeit, a few statutes grant individual directors standing to bring a derivative suit.[40] (Needless to say, if a majority of the board decides to have the corporation pursue an action, this is not a derivative suit.)

---

33. *E.g.,* M.B.C.A. § 7.41.

34. *E.g.,* Lewis v. Chiles, 719 F.2d 1044 (9th Cir.1983).

35. *Compare* M.B.C.A. § 7.40 (1985) (encompassing beneficial owners), *with* M.B.C.A. § 49 (1969) (limited to record holders).

36. *E.g.,* Rosenthal v. Burry Biscuit Corp., 30 Del.Ch. 299, 60 A.2d 106 (Ch. 1948).

37. *E.g.,* Dodge v. First Wis. Trust Co., 394 F.Supp. 1124 (E.D.Wis.1975). *But see* Devereux v. Berger, 264 Md. 20, 284 A.2d 605 (1971).

38. *E.g.,* Hoff v. Sprayregan, 52 F.R.D. 243 (S.D.N.Y.1971). *But see* Simons v. Cogan, 549 A.2d 300 (Del.1988); M.B.C.A. § 7.41 Official Comment.

39. *E.g.,* Wright v. Floyd, 43 Ind.App. 546, 86 N.E. 971 (Ind. Ct. App. 1909).

40. *E.g.,* Ga. St. 14–3–741.

The requirement that the plaintiff maintain his or her ownership throughout the suit poses a problem when the corporation engages in a transaction, such as a merger, which forces the plaintiff to give up his or her shares. Courts have reached different results as to whether the plaintiff's standing will survive such a transaction.[41] The result may depend upon whether the purpose of the transaction was simply to force out the plaintiff and get rid of the suit;[42] whether the plaintiff received shares in another company which succeeded to the rights (including the cause of action) of the corporation on whose behalf the plaintiff originally sought to sue;[43] whether the transaction which removed the plaintiff was itself fraudulent or illegal;[44] and whether the plaintiff acquiesced in the loss of his or her shares.[45]

Suppose that the plaintiff is a shareholder in a parent corporation and wishes to complain about the breach of a duty owned to the subsidiary corporation. A number of courts have recognized such a shareholder's ability to assert a so-called double derivative suit.[46] In other words, since the parent corporation is itself a shareholder, the parent could bring a derivative action on behalf of the subsidiary. In a double derivative suit, the parent's shareholder brings, as a derivative action on behalf of the parent, the parent's derivative action on behalf of the subsidiary.[47]

The so-called contemporaneous shareholder rule provides a second limitation on who can bring a derivative suit. Under this rule, it is not sufficient that the plaintiff is a shareholder at the time of the lawsuit; the plaintiff must also have been a shareholder at the time of the complained of wrongdoing.[48] (An exception exists if the plaintiff obtained his or her shares by operation of law—as, for example, by inheriting the shares—from someone who was a shareholder at the time of the wrongdoing.)

There are several rationales for the contemporaneous shareholder rule. Historically, the rule arose in federal courts out of a concern with collusive attempts to gain diversity jurisdiction. In other words, if the corporation could not bring an action in federal court based upon diversity jurisdiction, those in charge of the company might have an out-of-state individual buy shares and bring a derivative suit in federal court. Needless to say, this rationale cannot explain application of the contem-

41. *Compare* Lewis v. Chiles, 719 F.2d 1044 (9th Cir.1983), *with* Gabhart v. Gabhart, 370 N.E.2d 345 (Ind. 1977).

42. *See, e.g.,* Merritt v. Colonial Foods, Inc., 505 A.2d 757 (Del. 1986).

43. *See, e.g.,* Kessler v. Sinclair, 37 Mass.App.Ct. 573, 641 N.E.2d 135 (Mass. App.Ct.1994).

44. *See, e.g.,* Lewis v. Anderson, 477 A.2d 1040 (Del.1984).

45. *See, e.g.,* Issen v. GSC Enter., 538 F.Supp. 745 (D.Ill.1982).

46. *E.g.,* Brown v. Tenney, 125 Ill.2d 348, 126 Ill.Dec. 545, 532 N.E.2d 230 (Ill. 1988).

47. Courts differ as to whether the corporation in which the plaintiff owns shares must own a controlling interest, as opposed to just some stock, in the corporation which suffered the immediate harm. *Compare* Brown v. Tenney, 125 Ill.2d 348, 126 Ill. Dec. 545, 532 N.E.2d 230 (Ill. 1988), *with* Issner v. Aldrich, 254 F.Supp. 696 (D.Del. 1966).

48. *E.g.,* M.B.C.A. § 7.41(a); Fed. R. Civ. P. 23.1.

poraneous shareholder rule in state courts. Moreover, it is questionable how significant the collusive jurisdiction concern remains in federal courts given that Rule 23.1 of the Federal Rules of Civil Procedure attacks the collusive jurisdiction problem more directly.[49]

A current rationale for the contemporaneous shareholder rule lies in a concern with individuals purchasing shares simply for the purpose of bringing the suit. Yet, what is wrong with buying a lawsuit? Collection agencies buy claims all the time. The notion seems to be that individuals purchasing shares for purposes of filing suit are more likely to bring so-called strike suits—in other words, meritless claims filed in order to extort settlement based upon the suit's nuisance value.[50] The question of whether strike suits are a common problem in derivative litigation is a hotly debated issue to which we shall return. Even if strike suits are a significant problem, however, there is little empirical evidence that individuals who buy shares after the purported wrongdoing are more likely to bring strike suits than are individuals who already own their stock. Indeed, as we shall discuss, the primary force behind most derivative litigation may be the plaintiff's attorney. As a result, the practical impact of the contemporaneous shareholder rule simply may be to force such attorneys to maintain a larger "Rolodex" with the names of relatives and acquaintances who own shares of various corporations and who can serve as derivative suit plaintiffs.

An alternate justification for the contemporaneous shareholder rule parallels our earlier discussion as to why courts sometimes deny corporate recovery which will benefit undeserving shareholders. Specifically, individuals who buy stock after wrongdoing damaged the corporation might obtain a windfall if the corporation were then to recover. Actually, whether there will be such a windfall depends upon the price which the non-contemporaneous shareholder pays for the stock. If the price reflects a discount to take into account the damage which the corporation had suffered, then there is something of a windfall. On the other hand, if the price does not reflect such a discount, then there is no windfall. Why might the price of stock not reflect the damages? One reason would be that the buyer, or the market generally, does not yet know about the damage to the corporation. For this reason, some authority—such as the American Law Institute's Principles of Corporate Governance—will not apply the contemporaneous shareholder rule if the facts about the wrongdoing were not public, or otherwise known to the plaintiff, at the time the plaintiff bought his or her shares.[51]

Yet, even if the buyer or the market knows about the damage, this does not mean that the share price will incorporate a discount fully reflecting the damage. If the buyer expects that the corporation can recover compensation from the wrongdoer, then the price of the shares should reflect this potential recovery (discounted, of course, for the cost

49. Under Rule 23.1, the plaintiff must allege that the suit is not a collusive action brought to confer jurisdiction which the federal courts otherwise would lack.

50. *E.g.,* Lawson v. Baltimore Paint & Chem. Corp., 347 F.Supp. 967 (D.Md.1972).

51. Principles of Corporate Governance § 7.02(a)(1).

of suit and the possibility of non-recovery). Seen in this light, the windfall rationale for the contemporaneous shareholder rule becomes circular: If the rule decreases the likelihood of corporate recovery, this results in buyers after the wrongdoing paying less for the stock, which, in turn, means that corporate recovery will produce something of a windfall for the buyer. Yet, if the rule did not exist, buyers might pay more for the stock, which means that the buyer would not obtain a windfall. Since a higher price would go to shareholders who owned shares at the time of the wrongdoing, this analysis suggests that the real persons denied recovery by the contemporaneous shareholder rule may be those who were shareholders when the wrongful conduct occurred—which seems to be the opposite of the rule's intended result.

In any event, the contemporaneous shareholder rule merely prevents the later purchasing shareholder from bringing a derivative suit. Unless, as we discussed earlier, courts deny corporate recovery, non-contemporaneous shareholders still can enjoy the benefits of corporate recovery if any shareholder who owned stock at the time of the wrongdoing brings a derivative suit. Hence, even if one accepts the windfall rationale, it is unclear how much the rule prevents the problem.

Suppose an individual purchases enough shares to replace the directors and obtain control over the corporation. Then such a buyer could have the new directors vote for the corporation to bring suit, thereby avoiding the contemporaneous shareholder limitation on derivative suits. In several cases, courts have been so concerned with windfall recovery for a shareholder who buys control after the wrongdoing that the courts denied the corporation, itself, the right to sue. For example, in *Bangor Punta Operations, Inc. v. Bangor & Aroostook R.R.*,[52] a party, who bought almost all of the corporation's outstanding stock, had the corporation turn around and sue the prior owners of the stock for unfair transactions with the corporation while the prior owners had been in control of the company. The court denied the corporation recovery on the ground that this would constitute a windfall to the new shareholder.

There are a couple of potential problems with this result. To begin with, it is rather harsh on innocent parties—such as the minority shareholders in *Bangor Punta*—who might have a legitimate interest in corporate recovery. Presumably, a court willing the follow the *Bangor Punta* result should be willing to allow a direct cause of action for the minority shareholders.[53] In addition, the *Bangor Punta* result only makes sense if the new buyer payed a price for the stock which the sellers discounted for the damages from the wrongdoing, coupled with the assumption that there would be no corporate recovery. Otherwise, there is no windfall. Perhaps this will be the case when, as in *Bangor Punta*, the new controlling shareholder purchases the stock from the wrongdoer in a situation in which the purported wrongful conduct was fully disclosed. In situations in which the wrongdoing was not fully

---

52. 417 U.S. 703, 94 S.Ct. 2578 (1974).   **53.** *See, e.g.,* Watson v. Button, 235 F.2d 235 (9th Cir.1956).

disclosed, courts should not assume there will be a windfall.[54] Nor should the court assume that there is a windfall when the wrongdoing is disclosed, but the party purchasing control buys his or her shares from stockholders who were not the wrongdoers. After all, in this instance, the buyer presumably paid a price reflecting the possibility of corporate recovery.[55]

This discussion suggests that the contemporaneous shareholder rule is a mistake. Some jurisdictions, such as California, have weakened the rule by allowing courts to create case-by-case exceptions in situations in which the court finds both that no one else will pursue what appears to be a strong case for the corporation and that the rationales for the rule do not seem to apply.[56]

In any event, application of the contemporaneous shareholder rule requires figuring out when the purported wrongdoing occurred. This is often not as simple it sounds. For example, suppose the plaintiff complains that the directors sold overvalued property to the corporation in exchange for a series of installment payments from the corporation: Is the wrongful conduct when the corporation made the deal, or is there a "continuing wrong" while the corporation actually suffers harm by making the payments? The answer to this question will determine whether a party, who bought his or her shares after the corporation made the deal, but before the corporation completes the payments, can bring a derivative suit. Courts have reached differing results in this sort of situation.[57]

A third limitation on the standing of a derivative suit plaintiff occurs in situations in which the plaintiff is subject to some personal defense. For example, the plaintiff shareholder may have participated in the wrongful conduct. Perhaps the plaintiff ratified, or, at least, acquiesced in, the challenged transaction. Alternately, maybe the plaintiff is guilty of laches. Earlier, we saw how courts might deny corporate recovery if such personal defenses exist against the owners of a large proportion of the corporation's outstanding stock. Along similar lines, courts often deny shareholders subject to such personal defenses the right to bring a derivative suit.[58] Other courts, however, noting that recovery is for the corporation rather than the shareholder, have reached a contrary result.[59]

---

54. *E.g.,* Rifkin v. Steele Platt, 824 P.2d 32 (Colo.Ct.App.1991).

55. On the other hand, if the buyer knew of the wrongdoing, but the innocent selling shareholders did not, then there could be some windfall. *See* Courtland Manor, Inc. v. Leeds, 347 A.2d 144 (Del.Ch. 1975). Even then, however, the buyer may have paid the selling shareholders more then the buyer otherwise would have if the buyer did not intend to have the corporation sue.

56. *E.g.* Cal. Corp. Code § 800(b)(1).

57. *Compare* Palmer v. Morris, 316 F.2d 649 (5th Cir.1963), *with* Chaft v. Kass, 19 App. Div. 2d 610, 241 N.Y.S.2d 284 (1963).

58. *E.g.,* Bloodworth v. Bloodworth, 225 Ga. 379, 169 S.E.2d 150 (1969).

59. *E.g.,* Kullgren v. Navy Gas & Supply Co., 112 Colo. 331, 149 P.2d 653 (1944).

The final limitation on standing is that the plaintiff fairly and adequately represent the interests of the corporation.[60] As we shall discuss later, the plaintiff in a derivative suit often, as a realistic matter, does not represent the interests of the corporation. Yet, courts have held that the fact that the plaintiff may have little idea of what the suit is about, but, instead, simply is acting at the urging of an attorney who wants to bring the suit, does not render the plaintiff an inadequate representative.[61] On the other hand, if the plaintiff is pursuing the action to further some personal side agenda—such as gaining leverage in a wrongful discharge suit against the corporation—then the plaintiff is an inadequate representative.[62]

4.3.3 Demand on Directors

Probably the most significant procedural rule involving derivative suits is the requirement that the plaintiff, prior to bringing the suit, must make a demand upon the directors to take action. Dealing with this requirement calls for us to consider two interrelated questions: (1) Under what circumstances can the plaintiff avoid making such a demand? (2) What is the impact of a board's refusal to take the demanded action?

a. The traditional rule

The requirement that a shareholder must make a demand upon the board of directors prior to bringing a derivative suit is found in some states' corporations statutes,[63] while, in other jurisdictions, the requirement is found in rules of court[64] or has been established by judicial decision.[65] Rule 23.1 of the Federal Rules of Civil Procedure contains a typical codification of the requirement. Rule 23.1 states that the complaint in a derivative suit must allege "with particularity the efforts, if any, made by the plaintiff to obtain the action the plaintiff desires from the directors ... and the reasons for the plaintiff's failure to obtain the action or for not making the effort."

Taken literally, a plaintiff could comply with the language of Rule 23.1 by alleging, for instance, that the plaintiff "made no effort to obtain action from the directors, because the plaintiff was in a bad mood and wanted nothing to interfere with filing a lawsuit." Not surprisingly, such literalism does not capture the meaning of the Rule. Instead, the Rule means that the plaintiff must allege that he or she made a demand for action upon the directors, or the plaintiff must allege a good excuse for not making a demand.[66] To rephrase in substantive rather than pleading terms, under the traditional demand rule as encapsulated in sources

60. *E.g.*, M.B.C.A. § 7.41(2).

61. *E.g.*, Lewis v. Curtis, 671 F.2d 779 (3d Cir.1982). *But see* Mills v. Esmark, Inc., 573 F.Supp. 169 (N.D.Ill.1983).

62. *E.g.*, Zarowitz v. BankAmerica Corp., 866 F.2d 1164 (9th Cir.1989).

63. *E.g.*, Cal. Corp. Code § 800(b)(2).

64. *E.g.*, Del. Ch. Ct. R. 23.1.

65. *E.g.*, Bartlett v. New York, New Haven & Hartford R.R., 221 Mass. 530, 109 N.E. 452 (1915).

66. *E.g.*, Lewis v. Graves, 701 F.2d 245 (2d Cir.1983).

such as Rule 23.1, a derivative suit plaintiff must make a demand upon the directors unless the plaintiff has a good excuse for not doing so. This, in turn, means that a central issue under the traditional demand rule is determining what is an acceptable excuse for not making a demand.

The accepted excuse for not making a demand under the traditional demand rule is that a demand would be "futile." At first glance, this seems like a sensible enough approach. After all, why require the plaintiff to engage in a futile exercise? Unfortunately, court opinions have generated considerable confusion as to what exactly makes a demand futile.

To take a simple example, suppose the plaintiff alleges that a demand would be futile because the directors have already indicated that they will not respond affirmatively to the plaintiff's demand—for instance, the directors already voted not to bring the lawsuit which the plaintiff wishes the corporation to bring. Alternately, the plaintiff might allege that it is predictable that the directors will not comply with a demand, because the plaintiff's demand is for the directors to have the corporation sue the directors themselves or to sue a party who controls the directors. Courts have reached different results as to whether the directors' previous or predictable opposition to the demanded action renders demand futile.[67] Perhaps this divergence in authority represents nothing more than different views of the possibility for repentance. In other words, while some courts might figure that it is futile to make a demand if the directors have already indicated, or logic would predict, their opposition,[68] other courts might feel that the directors can always change their minds and do the right thing.[69] Yet, if this is all that is going on in court opinions discussing whether previous or predictable opposition renders demand futile, then courts and litigants need to engage in a serious reality check. After all, in itself, little of practical impact turns on whether a court requires a plaintiff to make a demand. Specifically, sending a written demand to the directors imposes a *de minimis* financial burden on the plaintiff. Moreover, even if the suit proceeds without a prior demand, the directors, upon learning of the suit, still could take the action which the plaintiff wanted and then seek to dismiss the action as moot. Hence, to spend money litigating over whether likely board opposition renders a demand futile seems to be rather silly.

This discussion suggests that determining futility should entail something more than predicting the directors' likely response to a demand. Rather, to evaluate sensibly what circumstances render a demand futile, we should ask what courts hope to accomplish by requiring a demand. Courts and writers often list up to three purposes for this

67. *Compare* Nussbacher v. Continental Ill. Nat'l. Bank & Trust Co., 518 F.2d 873 (7th Cir.1975), *with* Kaplan v. Peat, Marwick, Mitchell & Co., 540 A.2d 726 (Del. 1988).

68. *See, e.g.,* Lewis v. Curtis, 671 F.2d 779 (3d Cir.1982).

69. *See, e.g.,* In re Kauffman Mut. Fund Actions, 479 F.2d 257 (1st Cir.1973).

requirement.[70] First, there is the goal of avoiding litigation by giving the directors a chance to take corrective action or otherwise to resolve the matter without a lawsuit. In addition, there is the argument that the demand requirement will prevent strike suits—in other words, meritless claims brought to extort settlement. Finally, the demand rule is said to reflect the fundamental principle of corporate law that the board of directors ordinarily has the responsibility to manage the corporation, including by deciding whether or not the corporation should bring a lawsuit.

If the purpose for requiring a demand is to avoid litigation by allowing the directors to correct the problem without a lawsuit, then courts should rarely, if ever, excuse a demand as futile. After all, the directors always might change their minds and do what the plaintiff asks. Moreover, litigating over whether to require a demand certainly seems counterproductive to avoiding litigation costs. Hence, this goal mandates use of a bright line standard, rather than a fact-specific futility test. In any event, while the goal of attempting to resolve problems without litigation sounds good, it is difficult to take seriously. Specifically, if encouraging corrective action without lawsuits is such a worthwhile objective, why limit the demand rule to derivative suits? Why not create a general rule of civil procedure that any plaintiff, before bringing suit, must make a demand on the prospective defendants that they voluntarily give relief?

We encountered the goal of avoiding strike suits before in discussing the contemporaneous shareholder rule. Much the same as in our earlier discussion, even if there is a problem with strike suits in derivative litigation, it is not clear how the demand rule addresses the problem.

This analysis suggests that purpose behind the demand rule lies in observing, insofar as possible, the normal rule of corporate law that the board of directors runs the corporation—including by deciding whether or not the corporation should bring a lawsuit. In other words, the law requires a demand in order to give the board of directors an opportunity to decide whether the corporation should bring the suit which the shareholder is urging. Once we focus upon this purpose, it is possible to clarify the general concept of when a demand is futile. A demand is futile when the law will not allow the directors make the decision regarding whether the corporation should bring a suit.[71] Put differently, if the court is going to ignore what the directors decide regarding bringing a proposed lawsuit, it is a futile exercise to ask the board to make a decision. Notice, under this analysis, the inherent interrelationship between the two inquires with which we started our discussion of the demand rule—(1) when can the plaintiff avoid making a demand, and (2)

---

70. *See, e.g.,* Starrels v. First Nat'l. Bank of Chicago, 870 F.2d 1168, 1173 (7th Cir.1989) (Easterbrook, J, concurring); Dennis Block, Stephan Radin & James Rosenzweig, *The Role of the Business Judgment Rule in Shareholder Litigation at the Turn of the Decade*, 45 Bus. Law. 469 (1990).

71. *E.g.,* Marx v. Akers, 88 N.Y.S.2d 189, 644 N.Y.S.2d 121, 666 N.E.2d 1034 (1996). *But see* Galef v. Alexander, 615 F.2d 51 (2d Cir.1980).

what is the impact of the board's refusal to take the demanded action. Under the futility excuse, the plaintiff can avoid making a demand when the board's refusal has no impact. Conversely, if the board's refusal will have an impact—in other words, the court is going to listen to the board's decision—then a demand is not futile, even (under most authorities) if the court already knows that the board will reject the demand.[72]

Having reached this point, the question now becomes when will a court disregard the directors' decision as to whether the corporation should bring a suit urged by a shareholder. The obvious answer is when the suit would be against the directors themselves.[73] Doctrinally, this follows the from rule that deference to the directors' business judgment does not occur when the directors are in a conflict-of-interest.[74] Needless to say, directors are in a conflict-of-interest when deciding whether the corporation should sue themselves. More fundamentally from a policy standpoint, the whole point of allowing shareholders to bring derivative actions is because otherwise directors will block the corporation from pursuing valid claims against themselves. Along similar lines, this analysis suggests that courts should not defer to the directors' decision if the proposed lawsuit would be against a party who controls the directors (as in the cases dealing with controlling shareholders discussed earlier in this chapter).[75]

The upshot of this discussion is that, as a first approximation, a demand is futile if the demand would be for the directors to have the corporation sue themselves or sue a party who controls the directors. The reason is not because we expect the directors will refuse to sue themselves, but, rather, because the court will not defer to the directors' refusal. Notice incidentally that this analysis clarifies what action the plaintiff is supposed to demand. The relevant demand should be to bring a lawsuit—not for voluntary corrective action (such as undoing whatever transaction the plaintiff is complaining about). After all, as we discussed above, it is poor policy to foment litigation over whether a demand for voluntary corrective action is futile.

Suppose, however, the plaintiff does not demand that the corporation sue all of the directors, but rather the plaintiff only seeks to sue some members of the board: Will a demand still be futile? Courts have held that a demand is futile if plaintiff states a claim against a majority of the board of directors.[76] This follows from the basic concept of majority rule when it comes to decisions by a board of directors. Given majority rule, even if the non-defendant directors wish the corporation to bring suit, the prospective defendants, if the prospective defendants comprise a majority of the board, can outvote the non-defendant directors. Conversely, if the plaintiff only sues a minority of the board,

---

72. *E.g.,* Kaplan v. Peat, Marwick, Mitchell & Co., 540 A.2d 726 (Del.1988).

73. *E.g.,* Barr v. Wackman, 36 N.Y.2d 371, 368 N.Y.S.2d 497, 329 N.E.2d 180 (1975).

74. See § 4.2.1 *supra.*

75. *E.g.,* Papilsky v. Berndt, 59 F.R.D. 95 (S.D.N.Y.1973), *appeal dism'd,* 503 F.2d 554 (2d Cir.1974).

76. *E.g.,* Marx v. Akers, 88 N.Y.2d 189, 644 N.Y.S.2d 121, 666 N.E.2d 1034 (1996).

then courts generally hold that demand is not futile.[77] A suit against a minority of the board still leaves a majority of directors not interested in the lawsuit, and hence the non-defendants are able to control the vote on whether the corporation should sue. As mentioned above, an exception exists if the prospective defendants somehow exercise control over the non-defendant majority. What if the plaintiff sues exactly half of the directors on the board? One court confronted with this situation decided that demand would be excused.[78] The court reasoned that since it takes a majority to pass a resolution deciding that the corporation should bring a suit, the defendant directors had the power to block a suit when they constituted half of the board.

So far, we seem to have derived a simple rule: Demand should be excused if the plaintiff seeks to have the corporation sue a majority (or at least half) of the board of directors or sue a party who controls a majority (or at least half) of the board of directors. There is just one problem with this simple rule. Under it, any shareholder whose attorney possesses a modicum of wit should be able, with rare exceptions, to get the court to excuse demand. Recall from the outset of our discussion that the demand rule is actually a rule of pleading; in other words, sources such as Rule 23.1 of the Federal Rules of Civil Procedure couch the rule in terms of what the plaintiff must allege in his or her complaint. If the allegation that the corporation should sue a majority of the directors excuses demand, then all the plaintiff needs to do is to plead a cause of action against a majority of directors and demand is excused. Will it typically be difficult for a shareholder to plead a cause of action against a majority of the directors? Under modern notice pleading standards, not really. Presumably, a shareholder wishing to bring a derivative suit must be upset about an action the directors took, or about the directors' failure to take some action. If the action involves a conflict-of-interest for directors, then pleading a duty of loyalty claim is straightforward.[79] Let us suppose, however, that most of the directors have no conflict-of-interest in whatever it is that the plaintiff is upset about. In this event, the remaining possible cause of action lies in a claim that the directors breached their duty of care. As we discussed when dealing with the business judgment rule, such claims are very difficult to prove.[80] Yet, the demand rule is not about proof, it is about pleading. Assuming that courts apply normal standards of notice pleading, how difficult is it to allege that a majority of the board was negligent, or grossly negligent, in approving a transaction, or not preventing some action? Presumably, some specification of what the directors did versus what the plaintiff claims they should have done, coupled with some appropriate buzz words

77. *See, e.g.,* Aronson v. Lewis, 473 A.2d 805 (Del.1984).

78. Untermeyer v. Fidelity Daily Income Trust, 580 F.2d 22 (1st Cir.1978).

79. *But see* Marx v. Akers, 88 N.Y.2d 189, 644 N.Y.S.2d 121, 666 N.E.2d 1034 (1996) (after holding that a demand was excused because a majority of the board had raised their own fees, the court then held that the plaintiff had failed to state a cause of action on the merits because the complaint did not contain sufficient allegations to show that the raise was excessive).

80. See § 4.1.2 *supra.*

matching the applicable standard for breaching the duty of care, should do the job.

Some courts have taken pleadings at face value, and held that demand is excused if the plaintiff states a cause of action against a majority of the board (or states a cause of action against a party who the plaintiff alleges controls the board).[81] Many courts, however, find it troubling when a plaintiff shareholder seeks to bootstrap his or her way out of making a demand by pleading broad allegations against a majority of the board. Rule 23.1 itself provides a tool for attacking this problem. It requires the plaintiff to allege "with particularity" the reasons for not making a demand.

This, in turn, raises the question as to how much detail the plaintiff's complaint must contain in order to avoid demand. Various courts have attempted to answer to this question. The Delaware Supreme Court's opinion in *Aronson v. Lewis*[82] provides one of the least articulate, but nevertheless most influential (because of its source), efforts by a court to address the issue.

Aronson was a derivative action brought by Harry Lewis (who made something of a career out of being a plaintiff in derivative suits). Lewis sued all ten of the directors of Meyers Parking System, Inc. He alleged that the directors had breached their duty by approving an employment contract between the corporation and one member of the board, Leo Fink, who also happened to own 47 percent of the corporation's outstanding stock. Fink, who was 75 years old, had retired under a preexisting employment contract and was receiving consulting fees. The new contract reinstated Fink's employment, but provided that Fink could retire again at any time, after which he would again become a consultant to the corporation. The new contract also provided that Fink was entitled to receive compensation even if he was unable to perform services for the corporation. In addition, the corporation's board approved the corporation making interest-free loans to Fink totaling $225,-000.[83] The complaint alleged that a demand was futile essentially for two reasons: First, all the directors were personally liable for the actions complained of and hence would be called upon to have the corporation sue themselves. Second, Fink, having selected each member of the board, dominated and controlled all the directors. The chancery court held that these allegations were sufficient to excuse demand, but the Delaware Supreme Court reversed.

In deciding that Lewis' complaint failed to allege an adequate excuse, the Delaware Supreme Court set out a test which has become the standard for determining if a demand is futile in Delaware and in those jurisdictions influenced by Delaware. Under this test, the trial court,

---

81. *See, e.g.,* deHaas v. Empire Petroleum Co., 286 F.Supp. 809 (D.Colo.1968), *modified and aff'd* 435 F.2d 1223 (10th Cir.1970).

82. 473 A.2d 805 (Del.1984).

83. Fink repaid these loans after Lewis filed suit, showing that filing suit without a demand does not cut off the potential for a voluntary corrective action.

using "its discretion," must determine whether the "particularized" facts alleged in the complaint create a "reasonable doubt" that "(1) the directors are disinterested and independent and (2) the challenged transaction was otherwise the product of a valid exercise of business judgment."[84]

This language is a recipe for confusion. To begin with, "reasonable doubt" deals with the standard of proof in a criminal trial. How a trial court should apply this concept to reviewing allegations in a complaint is anyone's guess.[85] More broadly, the two-pronged test of what the trial court is to examine raises as many questions as it answers. For example, in asking whether the directors are disinterested and independent, is the court speaking of disinterest in deciding whether the corporation should sue, or disinterest in the transaction which the plaintiff challenges? The court's opinion in *Aronson* bounces back and forth between these two possible meanings. The court expresses its test in the conjunctive—the complaint must raise a reasonable doubt about disinterest *and* business judgment. Yet, at various points in applying the test, the court seems to indicate that finding a reasonable doubt on either prong would be sufficient.[86]

Perhaps the reason for the *Aronson* court's inconsistency about the two prongs in its formulation is that the two prongs muddle together a number of interdependent ideas. For example, as the court recognizes, if a majority of the board had a conflict-of-interest when approving the transaction attacked by the plaintiff, then the business judgment rule would not apply to the challenged transaction.[87] This fact, in turn, means that at least a majority of the directors will face potential liability for breaching their duty of loyalty and, accordingly, are not disinterested in deciding upon the suit. Alternately, the court recognizes that the plaintiff may be able to plead facts showing that the challenged transaction is so egregious on its face as to flunk the business judgment rule and thereby leave the directors who approved the transaction facing liability for breaching their duty of care. The prospect of such liability, in turn, means that the directors will not be disinterested in deciding if the corporation should sue. Also, if the challenged transaction is between the corporation and a party who dominates and controls the board, then the directors are neither independent in approving the challenged transaction nor in reviewing a possible lawsuit against the controlling party. In

84. 473 A.2d at 814.

85. More recently, the Delaware Supreme Court responded to the criticism of this choice of terminology by explaining what the court meant was that the plaintiff had a "reasonable belief" that the board lacked independence or that the transaction was not protected by the business judgment rule. Put in more practical terms, the idea is that the plaintiff's claim should not be based upon "mere suspicions" or stated solely in conclusory terms. Grimes v. Donald, 673 A.2d 1207 (Del.1996).

86. The Delaware Supreme Court later described the two prongs as alternatives, rather than as a conjunctive test, in *Levine v. Smith,* 591 A.2d 194 (Del.1991).

87. The court's analysis here seems to ignore the fact that Delaware might apply the business judgment rule to a conflict-of-interest transaction which received approval by a majority of the disinterested directors, even though a majority of the whole board had a conflict-of-interest. See § 4.2.3*b,e supra.*

all of these instances, it turns out then that the same basic fact—be this fact that a majority of the directors approving the challenged transaction were in a conflict-of-interest, or that the transaction was so egregiously stupid as to flunk the business judgment rule despite disinterested director approval, or that the transaction involved a party who controlled the directors—establishes both prongs of the *Aronson* test.[88]

Ultimately, the significance of *Aronson* does not lie in the test it announces, but rather in how the court applied the test to the Lewis' complaint. Lewis alleged that the directors had breached their duty by approving an employment contract for Fink that amounted to "waste." Lewis alleged that the contract constituted waste primarily because Fink was entitled to compensation under the contract even if Fink was unable to perform services. The court held that this allegation was insufficient to avoid demand—indeed, the court commented that the allegation may not even have been sufficient to state a cause of action. In fact, whether the employment contract amounted to waste largely would come down to whether the feature continuing Fink's compensation despite non-performance was a legitimate portion of a compensation package which the directors rationally could conclude was necessary to entice Fink out of retirement, or whether this was simply a back-door attempt to give Fink more financial security in his retirement than Fink was entitled to under the former employment contract. Ultimately, it would be Lewis' burden to prove the latter at trial. Yet, other than pleading his evidence or making general allegations, what else is Lewis supposed to put into his complaint? Turning to the alternate argument for futility, Lewis based his allegation that Fink controlled the board upon the facts that Fink owned 47 percent of the outstanding stock, had personally selected each director, and had received favorable treatment from the board (through the transactions Lewis challenged). The court found these allegations insufficient to establish Fink's control and thereby excuse demand. Again, however, it is unclear what else Lewis was supposed to plead. Is Lewis supposed to plead that the directors saluted Fink each time Fink entered the boardroom? Overall then, the significance of *Aronson* is to grant the trial court discretion to nitpick at the pleadings in search of elusive particularity—at least when faced with a complaint filed by a habitual plaintiff.[89]

Suppose the plaintiff goes ahead and demands that the directors

88. The New York Court of Appeals decision in *Marx v. Akers*, 88 N.Y.2d 189, 644 N.Y.S.2d 121, 666 N.E.2d 1034 (1996), contains a more intelligible, even if not fundamentally different, listing of what a plaintiff might plead to avoid demand. To successfully avoid a demand, the plaintiff might plead that (1) a majority of the board was interested in the challenged transaction, (2) the directors did not reasonably inform themselves before approving the challenged transaction, or (3) the challenged transaction was so egregious on its face as to flunk the business judgment rule. The court in *Marx* included allegations that a majority of the directors were under the control of a party interested in the challenged transaction as a means of pleading that the majority of the directors were interested in the transaction.

89. In the end, Lewis amended his complaint, and the trial court held that the new version stated enough allegations of control by Fink to excuse demand.

have the corporation bring a lawsuit, and the directors refuse:[90] What happens then? Courts generally treat such a decision as a business decision, thereby invoking the so-called business judgment rule.[91] In other words, the court will defer to the directors' decision not to sue unless the plaintiff can show a conflict-of-interest, a lack of good faith, or a lack of due care by the directors in deciding not to sue.

As we discussed above, if the lawsuit would be against a majority of the directors, or a party controlling a majority of the directors, then the directors are in a conflict-of-interest in deciding upon the suit and the court should not defer to their decision regarding the suit. This is why it was a waste of time, in other words "futile," for the plaintiff to have demanded a decision from such a board. Suppose, however, the plaintiff figured "what the heck" and went ahead and made a demand that the directors have the corporation sue themselves. In most jurisdictions, presumably the plaintiff could still point out the obvious conflict-of-interest and the court should not defer to the directors' refusal to comply with the demand.[92] After all, nothing really has changed because the plaintiff graciously gave the directors one more chance to make amends. Nevertheless, this simple logic seems to have escaped the Delaware Supreme Court. The Delaware Supreme Court has held that a plaintiff who makes a demand thereby concedes the directors are disinterested in deciding upon whether to bring the suit.[93] The primary effect of this holding is to create a malpractice trap for attorneys unfamiliar with Delaware peculiarities.[94]

If the lawsuit is not against either a majority of the directors, or a party controlling a majority of directors, then the plaintiff must show that the board's rejection of the demand was in bad faith, or else breached the directors' duty of care as measured under the jurisdiction's interpretation of the business judgment rule. This is an extremely difficult road for the plaintiff to take. Since the directors know that an eager plaintiff is watching their actions, they are unlikely to act without at least the appearance of a reasonable inquiry.[95] Moreover, it is a rare claim which is so overwhelming that one can say the directors would be unreasonable, much less irrational, in deciding that the corporation should not pursue it.[96]

---

90. Needless to say, if the directors respond to the demand by having the corporation bring the suit which the shareholder demanded, then there is no need for the shareholder to bring a derivative suit.

91. *E.g.,* Findley v. Garrett, 109 Cal. App.2d 166, 240 P.2d 421 (1952).

92. *See, e.g.* Galef v. Alexander, 615 F.2d 51 (2d Cir.1980).

93. Levine v. Smith, 591 A.2d 194 (Del. 1991).

94. The Delaware Supreme Court somewhat backed off this point in *Grimes v. Donald,* 673 A.2d 1207 (Del.1996). In an obscure reference, the court stated that just

because a plaintiff made demand does not mean that the board "acted independently [or] disinterestedly" in responding to the demand.

95. Still, sometimes directors can be dumb even if they know that an eager plaintiff is watching. *See* Stepak v. Addison, 20 F.3d 398 (11th Cir.1994) (the court held that the directors acted with gross negligence in rejecting a demand, because they relied upon advice from the law firm which represented the prospective defendants in a related criminal proceeding).

96. For an example of a case in which the court held that the directors breached their duty of care by not prosecuting a

One important wrinkle on this discussion, however, is that the question of whether to defer to the directors' refusal to sue, like the question of whether demand is excused, comes up at the pleading stage. Recall that Rule 23.1 of the Federal Rules of Civil Procedure requires the plaintiff to plead with particularity why the demand was unsuccessful. This, in turn, provides the basis for courts to demand that the plaintiff plead with particularity facts which show that the court should not respect the directors' business judgment against bringing suit. This again allows the court to nitpick at the plaintiff's allegations. For example, in *Levine v. Smith*,[97] the Delaware Supreme Court dismissed as too conclusory an allegation that the directors "did nothing" to inform themselves prior to rejecting the plaintiff's demand. Yet, if, in fact, the directors had taken no action at all to inform themselves prior to rejecting the demand, then the rejection would seem to flunk the business judgment rule. Moreover, it is difficult to understand how one is to plead an absence of action, other than to say that the directors "did nothing." Perhaps the court did not believe that the directors really "did nothing," but what the court believes really happened is not supposed to be the standard in reviewing pleadings.

b. The universal demand rule

The American Law Institute's Principles of Corporate Governance, and the Revised Model Business Corporations Act, take a different approach to the demand rule. They abolish the futility excuse and require demand in all cases.[98] There is one minor caveat to this blanket requirement. Suppose the delay resulting from making a demand and waiting for the board to respond would result in irreparable harm to the corporation. For example, perhaps the statute of limitations is about to run. In this event, the American Law Institute still requires demand, but will allow the plaintiff to make the demand after filing the complaint, while the Model Act still requires a pre-filing demand, but will excuse the plaintiff from waiting for a reply.

What is the rationale behind the universal demand rule? As we discussed above, to the extent that a goal for the demand requirement is to allow voluntary corrective action without a lawsuit, then it makes very little sense to have a futility exception which promotes costly additional litigation over whether the directors will change their ways. Indeed, part of the rationale in the official comment to the Model Act section adopting the universal demand rule is to allow for corrective action without a lawsuit.

Yet, as discussed above, it is unlikely that avoiding litigation through voluntary repentance is the goal of the demand rule—otherwise, a similar rule would extend to all lawsuits. The real goal of the traditional demand requirement has been to preserve, insofar as possible, the role

highly promising claim see Epstein v. Schenck, 35 N.Y.S.2d 969 (Sup. Ct. 1939).

97. 591 A.2d 194 (Del.1991).

98. Principles of Corporate Governance § 7.03; M.B.C.A. § 7.42.

of the board in deciding if the corporation should bring a lawsuit. The futility exception identified those situations in which, based upon the pleadings, the board should not make the decision as to whether the corporation should sue. Court opinions like *Aronson*, in turn, illustrate the difficulty of evaluating whether the board should make the litigation decision when all the court has before it is a complaint alleging that most of the directors breached their duty to the corporation or are under the control of a person who breached a duty to the corporation. To what extent has the universal demand rule avoided this difficulty? The answer is not at all. Instead, under either the American Law Institute's Principles or the Model Act, the court still must decide, based on the pleadings, whether to defer to the directors' decision against bringing a lawsuit.

Under the American Law Institute's Principles, the plaintiff must plead "with particularity" facts which "raise a significant prospect" that the challenged transaction entailed a breach of duty by directors or controlling shareholders. In addition, if the board rejects the demand, then the plaintiff must plead "with particularity" either that a majority of the directors were interested in the challenged transaction or were otherwise not capable of objective judgment in rejecting demand, or that the rejection flunked the business judgment rule.[99] In other words, to continue the suit in the face of a rejection of his or her demand, the plaintiff must plead with particularity the same sort of facts required to establish futility under *Aronson* and similar cases: That a majority of directors entered a conflict-of-interest transaction; that a majority of directors breached their duty of care; or that a majority of directors are under the control of a party who breached his or her duty (which presumably would render such directors incapable of objective judgment in deciding whether the corporation should sue either themselves or the party who controls them). Unfortunately, the American Law Institute does not answer the difficult question as to how much detail the complaint must contain in order to meet the standard of pleading with particularity. The American Law Institute throws in a new wild card, however, when it raises the prospect that the court will not defer to the directors because they are incapable of objective judgment under the circumstances. As we shall discuss later, there is substantial reason to

99. To be more precise, the American Law Institute's Principles calls for the board to communicate its rejection of the demand in a written reply. If this reply states that a majority of the board members were not interested in the challenged transaction, were capable of objective judgment, and rejected the demand, then the plaintiff must plead, with particularity, facts which raise a significant prospect either that the statements in the reply were not correct, or that the rejection flunked the business judgment rule. If the underlying claim involved a breach of the duty of loyalty rather than care, however, then it is sufficient to plead with particularity that the board could not reasonably—rather than just rationally, as is the standard under the American Law Institute's version of the business judgment rule—have concluded that rejecting the demand was in the best interest of the corporation. Principles of Corporate Governance § 7.04(a). Even when dealing with a duty of loyalty claim, however, it may be extraordinarily difficult for the plaintiff to plead, with particularity, facts which show that pursuing a lawsuit is so indisputably in the corporation's interest that reasonable minds could not disagree over whether to pursue the action.

question whether directors ever are capable of objectively judging the corporate interest in a suing a fellow director.

Similarly, under the Model Act, the plaintiff, when faced with a rejection of the plaintiff's demand, must allege "with particularity" that a majority of the board was not "independent" or that the board did not make the rejection in good faith after reasonable inquiry.[100] The Model Act does not define independence, except to say that merely because the complaint names a director as a defendant (even if he or she approved the challenged transaction), or alleges that the defendant selected a director, does not preclude this director from being independent.[101] This, however, does little more than codify *Aronson's* rejection of these exact allegations as being insufficiently particularized to implicate a majority of the board. Presumably, however, if the plaintiff pleads in detail that a majority of the directors breached their duty of care or loyalty, or in detail that the directors were under the control of a party who breached his or her duty, then the Model Act would not consider such directors independent in deciding upon whether to sue themselves or the party who controls them.

All told then, neither the American Law Institute's Principles nor the Model Act change the basic nature of what the plaintiff must plead in order to deprive the directors of their normal role in deciding whether the corporation will sue.[102] What the Principles and the Model Act change is to require a demand in situations in which the court will not listen to the directors' response—in other words, in situations in which the traditional rule recognized that it was a waste of time to ask the directors to make a decision. In light of this analysis, it is not surprising that there has been only limited adoption of this new approach. Some jurisdictions have adopted statutes incorporating the Model Act provision.[103] Also, one court attempted to adopt the American Law Institute's universal demand rule. Specifically in *Kamen v. Kemper Financial Services, Inc.*,[104] the Seventh Circuit decided to interpret Rule 23.1 of the Federal Rules of Civil Procedure to call for universal demand in federal courts, at least when dealing with federal causes of action. The Supreme Court, however, reversed and held that federal courts must follow the rule adopted by the state of incorporation of the corporation in question, unless the state's rule frustrates a specific policy contained in the federal statute under which the plaintiff brought the suit.

4.3.4 *Special Litigation Committees*

We just saw that under the traditional demand rule, if the complaint contains sufficiently detailed allegations of wrongdoing against a majority of the board of directors, the court will excuse a demand as futile and

---

100. M.B.C.A. § 7.44(d).

101. M.B.C.A. § 7.44(c).

102. Except, as mentioned above, insofar as the American Law Institute's Principles may allow the plaintiff to raise the board's lack of objectivity as a reason for

the court to deny deference to the board's decision.

103. *E.g.*, Mich. Comp. Laws Ann. §§ 450.1493a–450.1495.

104. 500 U.S. 90, 111 S.Ct. 1711 (1991).

the plaintiff can proceed with his or her derivative suit. The fact that the complaint does not implicate every member of the board is irrelevant. After all, the innocent minority of the board lacks the votes to decide that the corporation should sue the potentially wrongdoing majority of directors. In the 1970s, however, clever corporate attorneys came up with a way for the innocent minority of the directors to make the decision as to whether the corporation should sue the majority of its board members. This is for the board to create a committee consisting of some or all of the directors who are not defendants in the derivative suit.[105] Often, the reason that these directors are not defendants is because they joined the board after the challenged transaction took place or even after the plaintiff filed the derivative suit. The board then delegates to this committee the board's power to decide if the corporation should pursue the lawsuit against the majority. Such committees often are referred to as special litigation committees.

Special litigation committees, almost without exception, have concluded that the derivative suits which the committees looked into were not in the corporation's best interest.[106] So what happens then? The answer is that the corporation moves to dismiss the suit based upon the committee's determination. Procedurally, these motions are quite different from the motions to dismiss we encountered in discussing the demand rule. The demand rule results in motions to dismiss the plaintiff's complaint for failure to contain adequately particularized allegations to establish either that the plaintiff made a demand or that demand was futile. Alternately, if the plaintiff made and the board rejected a demand, the corporation can move to dismiss the complaint for lack of particularized allegations to establish that the rejection did not come within the business judgment rule. Sources such as Rule 23.1 of the Federal Rules of Civil Procedure provide authority for dismissing the complaint for failure to plead with particularity the facts which either excuse a demand or show that the board improperly rejected a demand. By contrast, courts confronted with motions to dismiss based

---

105. Occasionally, some members of a special litigation committee have been defendants in the derivative action (*e.g.,* Lewis v. Anderson, 615 F.2d 778 (9th Cir. 1979)), even though this seems to frustrate the point of delegating the decision to a committee.

106. This, at least, has been the result in reported decisions involving special litigation committees. *E.g.,* James Cox & Harry Munsinger, *Bias in the Boardroom: Psychological Foundations and Legal Implications of Corporate Cohesion,* 48 L. & Contemp. Probs. 83, 85 (1985). There is a bit of a sample bias problem here, however, since these reported decisions result from motions by the corporation to dismiss the suit based upon the committee's findings. If the committee finds the suit to be in the corporation's interest, the corporation would have no reason to ask the court to dismiss the suit and the committee's action might not result in a reported court opinion. Still, there are no anecdotal reports of favorable committee recommendations regarding a derivative suit and no reports of any case in which the corporation took over and prosecuted a suit against the company's directors based upon a committee's decision. The only reported exceptions to the negative evaluations of derivative suits by special litigation committees occurred in a couple of cases in which the committees recommended dismissing the actions against the corporations' directors, but either settling or continuing the actions against several lower level present or former corporate officials. Joy v. North, 692 F.2d 880 (2d Cir. 1982); *In re* Continental Ill. Sec. Litig., 572 F.Supp. 928 (N.D.Ill.1983).

upon the finding of special litigation committees had no established procedural context into which such motions fit. This fact, coupled with both doctrinal and policy problems presented by the special litigation committee technique, resulted in a divergence of judicial approaches to motions to dismiss derivative suits based upon the negative conclusions of a special litigation committee.

Federal courts were the first courts to confront the special litigation committee technique. Indeed, the very first case to involve a motion to dismiss based upon the recommendation of a special litigation committee went all the way to the United States Supreme Court.[107] The Supreme Court held that, in dealing with motions to dismiss based upon the recommendations of a special litigation committee, the federal courts generally should follow the law of the state of incorporation of the company on whose behalf the shareholder brought the derivative suit. The only exception to this choice of law rule occurs if following the state of incorporation's law will frustrate a specific policy underlying the federal statutory scheme upon which the plaintiff based his or her cause of action.[108] The result of this holding was that federal courts had to guess at what state courts would do when confronted with a procedure no state court had yet encountered.

The first federal courts to confront the special litigation committee technique guessed that the state courts would apply the business judgment rule to the committee's decision.[109] In other words, the court will dismiss the derivative suit upon the committee's recommendation unless the plaintiff can prove that the committee members have a conflict-of-interest, acted in bad faith, or violated their duty of care in recommending against the suit. Critically, under this approach, the question of whether the directors have a conflict-of-interest in considering the lawsuit involves only the directors who are on the special litigation committee. The fact that a majority of the directors who appointed the committee have a conflict-of-interest is irrelevant. Hence, with a modicum of discretion, the board can create a committee whose members are at least facially disinterested.[110] This will leave the plaintiff attempting to prove bad faith or a lack of care on the part of the committee in

---

107. Burks v. Lasker, 441 U.S. 471, 99 S.Ct. 1831 (1979).

108. Section 16(b) of the 1934 Securities Exchange Act provides an example of such a policy. This section expressly allows shareholders to sue on behalf of their corporation to recover short swing profits made by certain designated classes of insiders. See § 6.4.1 *infra*. Since the purpose of the section is to deter trading on inside information by forcing insiders to give up their profits on short swing trades, and, since, in order to achieve this deterrence, the statute expressly allows shareholders to sue on behalf of their corporation if the corporation will not sue, it would frustrate the statutory policy to dismiss such suits based upon a committee's recommendations as to the corporation's interests.

109. *E.g.*, Lewis v. Anderson, 615 F.2d 778 (9th Cir.1979).

110. Such discretion to assure the appearance of disinterest was the norm with the early committees, when corporate attorneys were uncertain how receptive courts would be to this new technique. Once it appeared that courts would be very receptive to this technique, some boards got sloppier about making sure that the committee had the appearance of independence. *See, e.g.*, Hasan v. Clevetrust Realty Investors, 729 F.2d 372 (6th Cir.1984).

recommending against the suit. As pointed out earlier in discussing cases involving the rejection of a demand, proving that directors deciding against a lawsuit acted in bad faith or without due care is a difficult task for the plaintiff. Indeed, in order to create at least the appearance of care, the special litigation committee commonly will take several months to "investigate" the lawsuit, and will prepare an inch thick report in support of its recommendations.[111]

Applying this "business judgment rule approach" to the recommendations of a special litigation committee raises several questions. To begin with, through what procedure will the court determine whether the committee members are disinterested, acting in good faith and acting with due care in recommending against the suit? Is the court supposed to conduct an evidentiary hearing (in other words, a trial) to see if the plaintiff can prove a conflict-of-interest, bad faith or a breach of the duty of care on the part of the committee? While some courts have stated that they will conduct such a trial if necessary,[112] the general proposition has been that the plaintiff can only get such a trial if he or she can show a material issue of fact as to the committee members' disinterest, good faith or due care. If the plaintiff cannot establish a material issue of fact on any of these points, the court will grant a summary judgment based upon the committee's recommendations.[113] Actually, however, it is probably not in anyone's interest to conduct a trial over the committee's recommendations. After all, the plaintiff wants to get to a trial on the merits (if the case does not settle), while the whole point of the committee's recommendation is that further litigation is not in the corporation's interest. Hence, as a practical matter, typically either the court will grant the motion to dismiss in a summary judgment procedure, or the derivative suit will continue despite the committee's recommendation.

Related to the question of what procedure the court will employ, is the issue of whether and to what extent the plaintiff is entitled to undertake discovery before the court decides the motion to dismiss. Without such discovery, the plaintiff is at a severe disadvantage in attempting to show that the committee is not entitled to deference under the business judgment rule. On the other hand, the whole point of the committee's recommendation is that continued litigation (such as taking discovery) is harmful to the corporation. Given this tension, it is not surprising that judicial attitudes have varied as far as allowing the plaintiff to undertake discovery before the court decides whether to dismiss.[114]

---

111. Occasionally, however, special litigation committees will be sufficiently sloppy as to expose bad faith or lack of care. *E.g.,* Watts v. Des Moines Register & Tribune, 525 F.Supp. 1311 (S.D.Iowa 1981) (committee disregarded the opinion of its special counsel that the corporation should pursue some of the causes of action asserted in the derivative suit).

112. *E.g.,* Lewis v. Anderson, 615 F.2d 778 (9th Cir.1979).

113. *E.g.,* Auerbach v. Bennett, 47 N.Y.2d 619, 419 N.Y.S.2d 920, 393 N.E.2d 994 (1979).

114. *Compare* Auerbach v. Bennett, 47 N.Y.2d 619, 419 N.Y.S.2d 920, 393 N.E.2d

Finally, courts have varied in the degree of scrutiny which they will apply in evaluating whether the committee's decision meets the duty of care. In large part, this divergence is a manifestation of the varying views of the business judgment rule, which we discussed earlier.[115] For example, in outlining the differing views of the business judgment rule, we looked at the New York Court of Appeals' decision in *Auerbach v. Bennett*.[116] In *Auerbach*, the Court of Appeals applied the business judgment rule to the recommendation of a special litigation committee. As its interpretation of the business judgment rule, the court held that it would only review the process used by the committee in studying whether to recommend dismissal of the suit, but the court would not consider the substantive merits of the committee's recommendation. By contrast, other courts applying the business judgment rule to committee recommendations have held that the rule does not preclude the court's review of the reasonableness of the committee's decision[117]—which would be consistent with the view that the business judgment rule does not change the standard from ordinary negligence.

The prediction of most of the initial federal court opinions that state courts would apply the business judgment rule to the recommendations of special litigation committees turned out to be overstated. While New York opted for this approach in *Auerbach*, other states went in different directions.

In *Miller v. Register & Tribune Syndicate, Inc.*,[118] the Iowa Supreme Court held that the court would ignore any recommendations by a special litigation committee when a majority the board which appointed the committee were defendants in the derivative suit. The court gave two related rationales for this holding. Doctrinally, if a majority of the board members were defendants in the suit, the board lacked the power, as recognized by the futility exception to the demand requirement, to decide whether the corporation should sue. If the board lacked the power to decide whether to sue, the *Miller* court reasoned, the board must also lack the power to appoint a committee to make this decision. From a policy standpoint, the *Miller* court was concerned with the obvious bias introduced when the defendants in the lawsuit can pick the members of a committee charged with deciding whether the corporation will pursue the suit.

The Delaware Supreme Court took a middle approach in *Zapata Corp. v. Maldonado*.[119] Maldonado brought a derivative action in both federal and Delaware state court, complaining about a board decision to accelerate the exercise date of stock options.[120] A special litigation

---

994 (1979), *with* Gall v. Exxon Corp., 418 F.Supp. 508 (S.D.N.Y.1976).

115. See § 4.1.2 *supra*.

116. 47 N.Y.2d 619, 419 N.Y.S.2d 920, 393 N.E.2d 994 (1979).

117. *E.g.*, Cramer v. General Tel. & Elec. Corp., 582 F.2d 259 (3d Cir.1978).

118. 336 N.W.2d 709 (Iowa 1983).

119. 430 A.2d 779 (Del.1981).

120. The result of this action was to reduce taxes for the recipients of the options, but at the same time to reduce the tax deduction which the corporation received for giving the options.

committee, composed of directors appointed to the board some years after the start of lawsuit, recommended dismissal. The federal district court predicted that Delaware would follow the business judgment rule approach. The Delaware chancery court, however, held that if a demand was futile—which was the case here because most of the board members were recipients of the options—then the committee lacked the authority to terminate the suit. The Delaware Supreme Court rejected both approaches. The Delaware Supreme Court held that even if most of the individual board members were disqualified from deciding whether the corporation should sue themselves, the board as a whole retained the statutory power to delegate decision making authority to a committee of disinterested directors. On the other hand, the Delaware Supreme Court was concerned about the bias in a situation in which committee members were judging the wisdom of a suit against the individuals who appointed the committee members both to the board and to the committee.

The solution the court in *Zapata* came up with was to adopt a two-part approach. First, the court switched the burden of proof on the issues of whether the committee members were disinterested, acting in good faith, and exercising due care, from the plaintiff to the committee. Far more significantly, the court held that the trial court could exercise the trial court's own independent business judgment to determine whether the trial court felt that the suit was in the corporation's interest. Curiously, while the *Zapata* opinion labeled this second step as "the essential key" to achieving the balance it sought, the opinion stated that the trial court has the discretion not to undertake this independent judicial determination of the corporation's interest.[121]

Since *Zapata*, a number of courts have latched onto the idea of undertaking an independent judicial evaluation of whether continuing the derivative suit is in the corporation's best interest when faced with the negative recommendation of a special litigation committee. For example, in *Joy v. North*,[122] the Second Circuit, guessing at what Connecticut courts would do, attempted to refine the *Zapata* approach. The Second Circuit suggested that, in exercising its independent judgment, the court should engage in a largely quantitative balancing of expected corporate gains versus tangible losses from pursuing the action.

One significant aspect of the approach in *Miller* and *Zapata* is to place a premium on whether a demand is futile. If the plaintiff must make a demand, and the board rejects the demand, then it is up to the plaintiff to overcome the business judgment rule. If, however, demand is futile, then, under *Miller*, the court will disregard the recommendations of a special litigation committee, or, under *Zapata*, the court can make

---

121. In *Kaplan v. Wyatt*, 499 A.2d 1184 (Del.1985), the Delaware Supreme Court showed that it meant what it said about the second step being discretionary. In *Kaplan*, the court affirmed a trial court's refusal to apply the trial court's own business judgment before dismissing a derivative suit based upon the recommendation of a special litigation committee.

122. 692 F.2d 880 (2d Cir.1982).

the court's own judgment as to the corporation's best interest in pursuing the suit. Some writers have criticized the significance this places on whether demand is excused.[123] In *Alford v. Shaw*,[124] the North Carolina Supreme Court stated that it would apply a *Zapata* type approach both in cases in which a demand is excused as futile and in cases in which a demand is required. Still, this statement is only dicta, since *Alford* involved a special litigation committee, and a majority of the board which appointed the committee were defendants in the suit. Indeed, it is difficult to imagine that the courts of North Carolina are going to employ their own business judgment to determine the corporate interest in every derivative suit even if the complaint names no directors as defendants.

The distinction drawn by *Zapata* and *Miller* between demand-required and demand-excused cases obviously cannot work under the Model Act's and the American Law Institute's universal demand rule. We saw earlier that the universal demand rule does not make a decisive change in what facts the complaint must allege in order for the plaintiff to pursue a derivative suit. Specifically, the plaintiff still must allege, with particularity, facts establishing a cause of action against most of the directors, or facts establishing that the defendant controls most of the directors—otherwise, the court generally will respect the board's rejection of the plaintiff's demand. Suppose the plaintiff pleads such facts, and the board appoints a special litigation committee: What is the result under the Model Act or the American Law Institute's Principles?

The Model Act follows the first part of the *Zapata* approach.[125] If a majority of the board of directors are not independent and a special litigation committee recommends dismissal, then the burden of proof is on the corporation to establish that the committee members are independent, acted in good faith and based their conclusions on a reasonable inquiry. The Model Act does not follow, however, the second part of the *Zapata* approach and allow the court to exercise the court's own judgment as to the corporation's interest. Instead, the Model Act attacks the bias problem resulting from the defendant directors selecting the members of the special litigation committee by requiring that a majority of the independent directors (even if not a quorum of the board) vote to appoint the committee. One question about this appointment requirement is whether the defendant directors can be involved in the formation of the special litigation committee so long as the actual vote to appoint the committee commands the support of a majority of the independent directors. In addition, similar to the Model Act's approach to disinterested director approval of conflict-of-interest transactions,[126] the Model Act requires that the special litigation committee have at least two members.

123. *E.g.*, James Cox, *Searching for the Corporation's Voice in Derivative Suit Litigation: A Critique of* Zapata *and the ALI Project*, 1982 Duke L. J. 959, 1009–1010.

124. 320 N.C. 465, 358 S.E.2d 323 (1987).

125. M.B.C.A. § 7.44

126. See § 4.2.3*b supra*.

The American Law Institute deals with motions to dismiss a derivative suit based upon the recommendation of the board, or the recommendation of a special litigation committee, in a series of complex provisions.[127] The most critical element of these provisions is to divide derivative suits against directors and controlling shareholders into cases based upon a breach of the duty of care (except for knowing illegality), cases based upon either knowing illegality or breach of the duty of loyalty (but not when dismissal would allow the defendants to retain a significant improper benefit), and cases in which dismissal would allow the defendants to retain a significant improper benefit. The American Law Institute then proposes that the courts apply different levels of scrutiny in reviewing recommendations to dismiss derivative suits, depending upon the category of case. Specifically, the American Law Institute proposes that courts review recommendations to dismiss duty of care cases by following the business judgment rule approach. For cases claiming knowing illegality or breach of the duty of loyalty, the American Law Institute proposes that courts examine whether a special litigation committee's recommendation of dismissal is reasonable. This adopts the view of several federal court opinions which, while following the business judgment approach to dealing with recommendations by special litigation committees, interpreted the business judgment rule to allow a review of reasonableness. On the other hand, in cases in which dismissal would permit the defendants to retain a significant improper benefit, the American Law Institute proposes that the court not dismiss the suit unless the court determines that the likely injury to the corporation from continuing the suit "convincingly outweighs" any adverse impact on the "public interest" from dismissing the action. The basic rationale for this sliding scale of scrutiny is that the court should not apply a lower level of scrutiny to a recommendation to dismiss a derivative suit than the court would have applied in reviewing the underlying transaction challenged in the suit.[128] Interestingly enough, the American Law Institute, like the Model Act, does not follow the *Zapata* approach of having the court make the court's own business judgment as to the corporation's interest. This, in fact, marks a retrenchment from the early drafts of the American Law Institute's Principles.

Incidentally, neither the Model Act nor the American Law Institute's Principles limit their provisions dealing with director recommendations to dismiss derivative suits to recommendations by special litigation committees. By their terms, these provisions can apply to a recommendation of dismissal from the entire board. Still, it is unlikely that these provisions often will apply in that context. After all, unless the plaintiff alleged, with particularity, facts which establish that most of the directors breached their duty, or are under the control of a party who breached his or her duty, the court generally will dismiss

---

127. Principles of Corporate Governance §§ 7.07–7.10.

128. *E.g.*, John Coffee, Jr., *New Myths and Old Realities: The American Law Insti-*

tute Faces the Derivative Action, 48 Bus. Law. 1407 (1993).

the plaintiff's complaint based upon the board's rejection of demand. If the plaintiff alleges with particularity that most of the directors breached their duty (or are under the control of a person who breached his or her duty), and the board as whole nevertheless votes to recommend dismissal, the court would need to decide the merits of the lawsuit in order to determine whether a majority of the board were independent or disinterested in voting on whether to dismiss the suit.

4.3.5 *Demand on Shareholders*

Earlier, we discussed how Rule 23.1 of the Federal Rules of Civil Procedure requires the plaintiff in a derivative suit either to make a demand upon the directors or to plead an excuse for not making such a demand. Rule 23.1 also requires the plaintiff to make a demand for action upon the shareholders "if necessary," or else to plead an excuse for not making a demand upon the shareholders. A number of state courts have adopted similar rules.[129]

On its face, the only difference between Rule 23.1's requirement for a demand on the shareholders, versus on the directors, is the addition of the language "if necessary." What is the impact of this language? A number of federal courts have held that the phrase "if necessary" generally requires the federal court to look to the law of the company's state of incorporation to see whether a demand on the shareholders is necessary.[130] As mentioned earlier, however, the United States Supreme Court recently held that federal courts generally should look to law of the state of incorporation to decide when to require a demand on directors—even though the demand-on-directors portion of Rule 23.1 lacks the "if necessary" language. As a result, it appears that the "if necessary" language adds nothing. In any event, if the "if necessary" language in the Federal Rules means that the federal court should look to state law, then it becomes difficult to figure out what the language means when it appears in a state court rule.

Regardless of the specific language of provisions such as Rule 23.1, the demand-on-shareholders and demand-on-directors rules turn out to be vastly different in operation. The reason for this difference is that courts have accepted more excuses for not making a demand upon the shareholders. This acceptance has marginalized the significance of the demand on the shareholders rule in most of the jurisdictions which impose such a requirement.

One commonly accepted excuse for not making a demand upon the shareholders is the futility excuse we saw before when dealing with the requirement of demand on directors. Specifically, the plaintiff might allege that a demand on the shareholders would be futile because the

129. *E.g.,* Mass. R. Civ. P. 23.1

130. *E.g.,* Jacobs v. Adams, 601 F.2d 176 (5th Cir.1979). The court will not apply the law of the state of incorporation, however, if doing so would frustrate the policy of a federal statute under which the plaintiff brought his or her cause of action. Levitt v. Johnson, 334 F.2d 815 (1st Cir.1964).

proposed lawsuit is against the owner(s) of the majority of the outstanding stock. While courts have accepted this excuse,[131] judicial reactions have been more mixed when the plaintiff alleges that the defendant owns a "controlling percentage" of the outstanding stock, despite owning less than a majority of the shares.[132]

A second possible excuse is to assert that it would be too expensive and burdensome to contact the shareholders to demand action. This expense and burden occurs when dealing with a widely held corporation with numerous, scattered shareholders. Courts have differed in their willingness to accept this excuse.[133] Notice that if a court accepts the excuse that it is too burdensome to make a demand of numerous, scattered shareholders, the combined impact of this and the futility excuse will be to eliminate shareholder demand in the vast majority of cases. The excuse that the defendant owns most of the shares will cover almost all of the derivative suits involving closely held corporations, while the burden excuse will cover most of the derivative suits involving publicly held corporations.

Perhaps the most common excuse is the assert that the shareholders cannot ratify the defendants' conduct. For example, earlier we discussed how a majority vote of the shareholders cannot approve a transaction amounting to waste, over the objections of a minority shareholder.[134] In *Mayer v. Adams*,[135] the Delaware Supreme Court held that if the shareholders cannot ratify the challenged conduct, then a demand on the shareholders is not necessary. The court reasoned that the end result of not suing is the same as ratifying the transaction. Accordingly, if the shareholders cannot ratify a transaction, they also cannot vote to prevent a minority shareholder from bringing a suit challenging the transaction. On the other hand, a shareholder vote in favor of bringing the lawsuit will accomplish nothing—after all, the shareholders lack the authority to have the corporation itself bring the suit. Hence, it is pointless to ask the shareholders to vote on the lawsuit and so a demand is futile.[136]

One issue with this non-ratifiable conduct excuse is to figure out what sorts of actions the shareholders cannot ratify. For example, in *Mayer*, the court accepted the argument that the defendants' conduct amounted to fraud and the shareholders cannot ratify fraud.[137] Actually,

131. *E.g.*, G.A. Enter. v. Leisure Living Communities, Inc., 66 F.R.D. 123 (D.Mass. 1974), *aff'd on other grounds*, 517 F.2d 24 (1st Cir.1975).

132. *Compare* Gottesman v. General Motors Corp., 268 F.2d 194 (2d Cir.1959), *with* Carroll v. New York, New Haven & Hartford R.R., 141 F.Supp. 456 (D.Mass. 1956).

133. *Compare* Levitt v. Johnson, 334 F.2d 815 (1st Cir.1964), *with* Quirke v. St. Louis–San Francisco Railway Co., 277 F.2d 705 (8th Cir.1960).

134. See § 4.2.4a *supra*.

135. 37 Del.Ch. 298, 141 A.2d 458 (S.Ct. 1958).

136. Of course, the shareholders could replace the current directors with individuals who would be willing to have the corporation bring the suit, but the court in *Mayer* felt that it would be a bit much to require the plaintiff to first attempt a proxy contest for corporate control before bringing a derivative suit.

137. *But see* Claman v. Robertson, 164 Ohio St. 61, 128 N.E.2d 429 (1955).

the defendants' so-called fraud in *Mayer* amounted to nothing more than an allegedly unfair conflict-of-interest transaction.

Some courts have rejected the non-ratifiable conduct excuse.[138] Specifically, these courts have differentiated between ratifying a transaction and deciding not to sue over the conduct. Their reasoning is that even if the shareholders cannot ratify the conduct, they may decide that it is not worthwhile to sue over the transaction.

Beyond more liberally recognized excuses, one other factor renders the demand-on-shareholders rule much less important than the demand-on-directors rule. While all jurisdictions have some requirement for a demand on the directors, many jurisdictions do not have any requirement for a demand on the shareholders.[139] Indeed, the Model Act[140] and the American Law Institute's Principles of Corporate Governance[141] propose that there be no requirement for a demand on the shareholders.

4.3.6 *Security for Expenses*

We have seen the fear of so-called strike suits repeatedly invoked to justify restrictions on derivative actions. The enactment of security for expenses statutes provides one of the most notable examples of this sort of legal reaction. In 1944, the New York Chamber of Commerce issued a report (known as the Wood Report) which examined a decade's worth of derivative suits filed in New York. The Report found that less than 10 percent of the suits produced recovery for the corporation. The Report concluded that shareholders with minor interests in the corporation were bringing claims with no merit for the purpose of extorting a settlement in which the corporation (rather than the real defendants) would pay the plaintiff to go away. In reaction, the New York legislature enacted the first security for expenses statute.[142] A number of other states followed New York.[143] Many other states, most notably Delaware, did not.

Security for expenses statutes allow the corporation to require that the plaintiff in a derivative suit post security to cover the expenses which the corporation reasonably expects to incur in the litigation.[144] This requirement has two impacts. The first is that the plaintiff shareholder who loses a derivative suit ends up reimbursing the corporation for much or all of the expenses which the company incurs in the action. This includes the corporation's attorneys' fees, as well as the attorneys' fees of the corporation's directors or officers which the company indemnified. This is in marked contrast to the normal American law rule that all

138. *E.g.*, S. Solomont & Sons Trust, Inc. v. New England Theatres Operating Corp., 326 Mass. 99, 93 N.E.2d 241 (1950).

139. *See, e.g.*, Del. Ch. Ct. R. 23.1; Cal. Corp. Code § 800.

140. *See* M.B.C.A. § 7.42.

141. Principles of Corporate Governance § 7.03(c).

142. N.Y. Bus. Corp. Law § 627.

143. Before 1982, the Model Business Corporation Act contained a section requiring security for expenses. M.B.C.A. § 49 (1969).

144. At least one state allows the real defendants in a derivative suit, as well as the corporation, to require the plaintiff to post security for their expenses. Cal. Corp. Code § 800(c).

parties pay their own attorneys' fees. The corporation's right to this reimbursement does not depend upon finding that the action was frivolous or malicious. The second impact of these statutes comes from the requirement of posting security. Because the plaintiff must post security (in other words, put up a bond) early in the lawsuit, the plaintiff faces up-front costs in pursuing the action, even if the plaintiff ultimately prevails.

Since the theory behind New York's legislation was that shareholders with small interests in the corporation were filing abusive derivative suits, New York's security for expenses statute exempts stockholders owning shares either worth over $50,000, or representing over five percent of a class of stock, from posting such security. Most security for expenses statutes have similar exemptions for stockholders holding over a minimum amount of the corporation's outstanding shares.[145] California, however, took a different approach to dividing derivative suits which require security from those which do not. To order the posting of security under California's statute, the court must find that there is no reasonable possibility the action will benefit the corporation, or, if an individual defendant moves for security, the court must find either that there is no reasonable possibility of corporate benefit or that the defendant did not participate in the challenged transaction.[146] To establish these facts, the court might undertake an evidentiary hearing.[147]

While early critics of security for expenses statutes thought the laws would be a "death knell" for derivative suits,[148] the impact of these statutes has turned out to be rather minor. Most states, including important jurisdictions such as Delaware, do not have such statutes. Plaintiffs have avoided such statutes in many instances by suing in federal court based upon violation of a federal statute.[149] One popular technique for deterring the corporation from moving for security in jurisdictions which have security for expenses statutes has been for plaintiffs to respond to such motions by demanding to see the shareholder list.[150] The ostensible purpose for seeing the list is to encourage other shareholders to join as plaintiffs in the lawsuit. If additional shareholders join the suit as plaintiffs, then the plaintiffs as a group might own enough shares to avoid the security requirement under statutes like New

145. *E.g.*, M.B.C.A. § 49 (1969).

146. Cal. Corp. Code § 800(c).

147. *E.g.*, Bailey v. Fosca Oil Co., 180 Cal.App.2d 289, 4 Cal.Rptr. 474 (1960) (hearing involved six days of testimony).

148. Hornstein, *The Death Knell of Stockholders' Derivative Suits in New York*, 32 Calif. L. Rev. 123 (1944).

149. *See, e.g.*, McClure v. Borne Chem. Co., 292 F.2d 824 (3d Cir.1961) (a derivative suit based upon a federal statute does not need to meet the forum state's security for expenses statute). *But see* Haberman v. Tobin, 480 F.Supp. 425 (S.D.N.Y.1979), *aff'd*, 626 F.2d 1101 (2d Cir.1980) (a deriva-

tive suit must meet the forum state's security for expenses statute insofar as it asserts pendent state law claims along with its federal causes of action). Security for expenses requirements are substantive, and so subject to the forum state's choice of law rule, for purposes of derivative suits brought in federal court under diversity jurisdiction. *E.g.*, Cohen v. Beneficial Indus. Loan Co., 337 U.S. 541, 69 S.Ct. 1221 (1949).

150. *See, e.g.*, Baker v. MacFadden Pub., Inc., 300 N.Y. 325, 90 N.E.2d 876 (1950).

York's. It turns out that corporate directors often prefer to forgo requesting security for expenses, rather than have the corporation's shareholders contacted about a pending derivative suit.

4.3.7   *Settlement and Plaintiffs' Attorneys' Fees*

As mentioned above, the Wood Report in New York found that a large number of derivative suits in that state resulted in settlements in which the corporation, rather than the real defendants, paid off the plaintiff. For example, the corporation might agree to buy the plaintiff's stock at a substantial sum and the plaintiff would then drop the lawsuit. New York responded by enacting its security for expenses statute. Critics of this response, however, pointed out that the cure really did not match the disease. Specifically, the problem of collusive settlements is different from the problem of meritless "strike suits." To see why, let us suppose that a corporation's directors breached their duty and damaged the company by $1 million. Let us also suppose that the plaintiff shareholder owns 100 shares out of a total of 10 million outstanding shares in the corporation. In this instance, a corporate recovery will increase the value of the plaintiff's stock by $10 ($1 million corporate recovery, divided by 10 million shares outstanding, multiplied by 100 shares owned by the plaintiff). Under these circumstances, it is obvious that both the plaintiff (ignoring for the present the plaintiff's attorney's fees) and the wrongdoing directors would be financially better off by any deal which pays the plaintiff directly more than $10, and costs the directors less than $1 million. Hence, there will be a strong temptation to agree to a settlement in which the plaintiff receives, say, $50,000 to drop the suit. Moreover, if the corporation pays the settlement, the defendants are out nothing. Notice that the incentive for the directors to make this sort of deal is actually greater in the situation in which the plaintiff has a strong suit, than in the situation in which the plaintiff's suit lacks merits. After all, in the situation in which the plaintiff has a strong claim, the directors face more risk of personal liability and have already shown themselves to be the type of persons who breach their duty to the corporation.

To solve the problem of abusive settlements at the expense of the corporation, court rules and statutes governing derivative suits generally require that the court approve the settlement of a derivative suit.[151] Indeed, the refusal of New York courts to require such approval[152]—until the New York legislature finally imposed such a mandate[153]—probably contributed to the problem of abusive settlements noted in the Wood Report. Rule 23.1 of the Federal Rules of Civil Procedure provides a typical statement of an approval requirement. The Rule states that derivative suits shall not be dismissed or compromised without court

---

151. *E.g.,* M.B.C.A. § 7.45.

152. Manufacturers Mut. Fire Ins. Co. v. Hopson, 288 N.Y. 668, 43 N.E.2d 71 (1942). New York courts would order the plaintiff to turn over any personal recovery to the corporation, however, if another shareholder discovered the settlement and sued the original plaintiff. *E.g.,* Clarke v. Greenberg, 296 N.Y. 146, 71 N.E.2d 443 (1947).

153. N.Y. Bus. Corp. Law § 626(d).

approval. Rule 23.1 also requires giving the shareholders notice of the settlement, in the manner directed by the court.

Typically, the court will hold a hearing prior to approving a settlement. Sometimes, shareholders who oppose the settlement (often called "objectors") will appear at such a hearing and attempt to convince the court to reject the settlement. The court often will hear evidence as to the merits of the settlement, including consideration as to the likely outcome of a trial and the burdens of further litigation.[154] The general standard is whether the settlement is within a range which is fair to the corporation.[155]

As illustrated above, a small shareholder typically obtains only a *de minimis* benefit even from a substantial corporate recovery in a derivative suit. Under these circumstances, it hardly seems sensible to hire an attorney to bring such an action. What makes such suits feasible is the rule that the corporation must pay the plaintiff's attorney if the suit produces a recovery for the corporation.[156] The theory is that if the plaintiff's efforts have produced a benefit for the corporation, then fairness requires the corporation to reimburse the plaintiff for the cost of producing the benefit. Otherwise, not only would there be an unjust enrichment of the corporation, but shareholders would stop bringing meritorious derivative suits and corporations would not get any benefit in the future.

The rule that the corporation must pay the successful plaintiff's attorney's fees raises a couple of questions. To begin with, what sort of recovery by the corporation will invoke this rule? Older cases had required a monetary recovery by the corporation.[157] Put differently, the litigation had to produce a "common fund" out of which to pay the plaintiff's attorney. By and large, courts have moved away from this view. Instead, if the litigation produces a "substantial benefit" for the corporation—even if the benefit is not monetary—the court can order the corporation to pay the plaintiff's attorney's fees.[158] An example of a substantial benefit might consist of obtaining changes in the corporate management structure designed to prevent future misconduct.[159]

The second question is how much to pay the plaintiff's attorney. There are two principal approaches to setting the fee. Some courts apply a "salvage value" approach.[160] Essentially, this awards the attorney a percentage of the recovery. Other courts apply the "lodestar" approach.[161] Essentially, this is an hourly fee. The court sets the hourly

---

154. *E.g.,* Haudek, *The Settlement and Dismissal of Stockholders' Actions—Part II: The Settlement,* 23 Sw. L.J. 765, 793 (1969).

155. *E.g.,* Goldsholl v. Shapiro, 417 F.Supp. 1291 (S.D.N.Y.1976).

156. *E.g.,* Sprague v. Ticonic Nat'l Bank, 307 U.S. 161, 59 S.Ct. 777 (1939).

157. *E.g.,* Giesecke v. Pittsburgh Hotels, Inc., 180 F.2d 65 (3d Cir.1950).

158. *E.g.,* Bosch v. Meeker Coop. Light & Power Ass'n, 257 Minn. 362, 101 N.W.2d 423 (1960).

159. *E.g.,* Fletcher v. A.J. Indus., 266 Cal.App.2d 313, 72 Cal.Rptr. 146 (1968).

160. *E.g.,* Sugarland Indus., Inc. v. Thomas, 420 A.2d 142 (Del.1980).

161. *E.g.,* Shlensky v. Dorsey, 574 F.2d 131 (3d Cir.1978).

rate based upon a variety of factors and then pays the plaintiff's attorney this rate multiplied by the number of hours worked on the case.

4.3.8   The Fundamental Question: Who Should Represent the Corporation?

Having reached this point, the reader might wonder why the rules governing derivative suits are so complex and often difficult to apply. The answer largely is that derivative suits involve a structural problem which law has attempted to deal with through a series of procedural rules. The result has been to burden the suits with increasingly complex procedural rules, which do not solve the problem. The underlying structural problem involved in derivative suits is the lack of an acceptable candidate to determine when it is in the corporation's interest to pursue a lawsuit against persons in control of the corporation.

As we discussed at the outset of this section, courts allow derivative suits in order to avoid leaving directors in charge of whether to have the corporation sue either the directors themselves or a party who controls the directors. The difficulty, however, is that courts really do not trust the shareholder who brings a derivative suit to look out for the corporation. Courts and writers, as we have repeatedly seen, often express this lack of trust as a concern with "strike suits"—meritless claims brought to extort a settlement.

The question of whether many, or even most, derivative suits amount to strike suits is a subject upon which opinions differ. There have been several efforts to study the question. The failure of these empirical studies to put the matter to rest is not because they produced different data. Rather, the indeterminacy lies in different interpretations as to the meaning of the data produced by these studies. For example, not long ago, Professor Roberta Romano gathered statistics on derivative suits, which she interpreted to suggest that a significant portion of the suits are without merit.[162] She based this interpretation upon the facts that the settlements of derivative suits typically produced what she viewed as little recovery for the corporation, and that the plaintiffs typically lost the derivative suits which did not settle. Yet, others have looked at similar data and reached different conclusions.[163] For instance, the average monetary settlement in the derivative suits examined by Professor Romano was $6 million. Such an amount is slight when divided by the number of shares typically outstanding in the publicly-held corporations involved in these suits. Nevertheless, is the per-share value of the recovery the relevant comparison? After all, managers of corporations have their companies pursue debt collection and other breach of contract actions against third parties for far smaller sums every day. The small recovery in such mundane non-derivative litigation, when measured on a per-share basis, does not mean that these simple

---

162. Roberta Romano, *The Shareholder Suit: Litigation without Foundation?*, 7 J.L. Econ. & Org. 55 (1991).

163. *E.g.*, Jones, *An Empirical Examination of the Resolution of Shareholder Derivative and Class Action Lawsuits*, 60 Boston U. L. Rev. 542 (1980).

contract actions are meritless or not worthwhile. Why appraise the utility of derivative suits against a different yardstick? Moreover, even if the settlements of derivative suits often do not produce substantial corporate recovery—for example, because the settlement calls for changes in management instead of dollar recovery—this does not necessarily mean that the underlying claims were weak. Rather, this could be the result of the plaintiffs agreeing to suboptimal settlements—a problem mentioned earlier in discussing settlements, and one which we will discuss in more detail shortly. Finally, the fact that the plaintiffs usually lost those derivative actions which did not settle does not necessarily mean that most derivative actions were meritless. For one thing, most derivative suits, as is true of lawsuits generally, settle. It could be that defendants—perhaps in order to send a message to future litigants—refuse to settle the cases in which the plaintiffs have the weakest claims. Further, Professor Romano does not distinguish between losses on the merits and losses on procedural issues. Specifically, we have seen how the derivative suit plaintiff faces a number of procedural barriers which can cause the plaintiff to lose the action regardless of the merits of the underlying claim. Hence, criticizing derivative suits based upon the frequency with which plaintiffs lose might involve something of a "Catch 22": Procedural barriers to derivative suits can lead to plaintiffs often losing derivative suits, and then the fact that plaintiffs often lose derivative suits becomes the justification for procedural barriers to derivative suits.

In any event, even if some derivative suits are strike suits, it is by no means clear that the problem is any worse in derivative suits than in other types of litigation. Defendants in all sorts of lawsuits—from securities class actions to personal injury suits—constantly claim that they are the victims of strike suits. Is there something different about derivative suits? In fact, the unique problem with leaving the plaintiff shareholder in charge of deciding whether the corporation should pursue a lawsuit is not the possibility of strike suits. The unique problem lies in the incentive structure underlying derivative suits. This incentive structure can cause the plaintiff to bring a derivative suit which is not in the corporation's interest. This incentive structure also can cause the plaintiff to accept a settlement which it would be the corporation's interest to reject, or to reject a settlement which it would be the corporation's interest to accept.

To understand this incentive structure, it is important to start by recognizing that the party really making the decisions about a derivative suit involving a widely-held corporation typically is the plaintiff's attorney. After all, the plaintiff shareholder normally owns only a tiny fraction of the corporation's outstanding shares. Hence, victory or defeat in the lawsuit will cause a *de minimis* impact upon the value of the plaintiff's stock. Indeed, it does not make economic sense for the usual plaintiff shareholder to bring the suit. The individual who gains by bringing the suit is the plaintiff shareholder's attorney. The attorney hopes to collect fees out of any judgment or settlement. The plaintiff shareholder is often a relative or acquaintance who the attorney asked to serve as plaintiff.

At this point, however, the reader might conclude that the incentive structure seems pretty good. Since, under the rules we discussed earlier, the plaintiff's attorney must obtain a recovery or other benefit for the corporation in order to receive fees, the attorney seemingly has an incentive only to pursue worthwhile claims. Indeed, even if the attorney were to pursue a claim in order to settle based upon the suit's nuisance value, the corporation should gain most of the benefit of the settlement.

The difficulty, however, is that this analysis is too simplistic. Deciding whether to bring a lawsuit is not simply a matter of ascertaining whether one has a possible claim. Instead, a prospective plaintiff must balance the likelihood of success, and the amount of possible recovery, against the tangible and intangible burdens of bringing the suit. The fundamental problem is that the balance of costs versus gains from pursuing a lawsuit is different for the corporation and for the plaintiff's attorney.

For example, suppose a corporation's directors might have breached their duty by paying several corporate officers, who are also directors, compensation which is arguably excessive by an amount of $1 million. Further, let us assume that the suit has a fifty-fifty chance of forcing the officers to reimburse the corporation the $1 million. (To keep things simple, we will ignore the more realistic prospect of settling for some partial recovery.) If the corporation recovers, it must pay the plaintiff's attorney, let us say, 25 percent of the recovery or $250,000. A little simple arithmetic and we end up with a discounted value for the possibility of recovery equal to $375,000 (($1,000,000 − $250,000) × 50%). Against this, however, we must weigh the various costs of the suit to the corporation. For example, as we will discuss later in this chapter,[164] the corporation will be obligated to indemnify its directors' legal expenses if the directors prevail. (The corporation might even be obligated to indemnify the directors if the lawsuit settles or the company prevails, but, for simplicity, we will ignore this. Also, for simplicity, we will ignore the prospect that the corporation might have insurance which will cover the costs of indemnity, but then the claim might cause the corporation to incur greater future insurance premiums.) If we assume that the defendants' likely attorneys' fees will be also $250,000, then the expected cost of indemnity, when discounted for the probability of being required to make the payment, equals $125,000 ($250,000 × 50%). So far, the expected gains outweigh the expected costs of the suit. Yet, there are other costs to the corporation. For example, there might be a negative public relations fallout from the suit, possible losses to the business due to distraction of the officers while they are involved with the litigation, and consequences to the future relationship between the corporation and its managers. On the positive side as far as the future relationship between the company and its managers, perhaps the suit

---

164. See § 4.4.1 *infra*.

will deter further attempts to obtain excessive compensation. On the other hand, the response of the directors to the suit might be less constructive. Perhaps individuals will be less willing to serve on the board of directors if they feel they might be wrongfully accused. Perhaps the corporation will incur increased legal and consulting fees as directors attempt to cover themselves against future challenges. In the end, it may be a close question as to whether the costs of the suit outweigh its gains. Moreover, a change in the likelihood of various outcomes, or different assumptions as to the magnitude of costs or recovery, could make the suit into a clear-cut mistake for the corporation. For example, if the likelihood of recovery was 20 percent (and the probability of losing was therefore 80%), then the discounted expected cost of indemnity ($250,-000 × 80% = $200,000) alone outweighs the discounted expected value of recovery (($1 million − $250,000) × 20% = $150,000).[165]

For the plaintiff's attorney, the calculation will be very different. The attorney's expected recovery comes from the fees ($250,000 in the hypothetical above). This must be discounted by the probability of recovery (so, at a 50% chance of recovery, the upside of the suit is worth $125,000 to the attorney, while it is worth $50,000 if the chance of recovery is only 20%). The critical divergence between the attorney's interest and the corporation's comes on the costs side. Generally, the attorney need not worry about indemnifying the directors' attorneys' fees if the directors prevail. The plaintiff's attorney also need not be concerned about bad publicity for the corporation, distraction of corporate personnel, or the future relations between the corporation and its managers. Instead, the plaintiff's attorney's concern is with the opportunity costs of pursuing the action. Depending upon how busy the attorney is, this could make the suit in the example above worthwhile for the attorney even if there was only a 20 percent chance of recovery—in which case, the suit would not be worthwhile from the standpoint of the corporation. Moreover, the small size of the typical plaintiff's holdings in the corporation means that the costs of the suit for the corporation will not significantly impact the value of the plaintiff's stock.

This discussion suggests that the security for expenses statutes we discussed earlier might be a good idea. They force the plaintiff and his or her attorney to take into account the costs of the suit to the corporation. The problem is that these statutes are overkill. They potentially impose all of the corporation's litigation costs on the plaintiff, but the plaintiff (or his or her attorney) does not obtain all the corporation's recovery. Hence, a suit which might be worthwhile for the corporation might not be worthwhile for the plaintiff's attorney faced with a security for expenses statute.

---

165. The fact that a lawsuit might have only a 20 percent chance of victory for the plaintiff does not mean that the suit is meritless under any legal standard. Such a probabilistic assessment is not the criteria for granting a motion to dismiss a com- plaint for failure to state a cause of action, or for granting a motion for summary judgment. Nor would only a 20 percent chance of prevailing render the suit frivolous for purposes of awarding sanctions.

For instance, consider the incentives created by a security for expenses statute in the example above if there is a 50–50 chance of victory or loss. A 50 percent chance of paying the defendant's $250,000 of attorneys' fees renders the suit not worthwhile for the plaintiff's attorney—who only has a 50 percent chance of receiving $250,000 in fees—but this indemnity risk does not, in itself, completely offset the corporation's prospective $750,000 gain from pursuing the suit. Moreover, the up-front cost of posting security might deter suits which are in the corporation's interest.

Perhaps one could align the interests of the corporation and the plaintiff's attorney by requiring the attorney to pay the same percentage of the corporation's expenses as the court would award to the attorney in fees from any recovery. For instance, if the attorney would receive 25 percent of any corporate recovery as fees, then the attorney will be liable for 25 percent of the corporation's costs from pursuing the action. On the other hand, for this sort of scheme to work, courts must award fees based upon a predetermined percentage of recovery, which, as we shall discuss shortly, creates incentive problems when it comes to settlement.

The divergence between the corporate interest and the interest of the plaintiff's attorney when it comes to settlement stems from a couple of factors. To begin with, there are incentive problems with both of the principal methods used by courts to calculate the fee award for the successful plaintiff's attorney. As we discussed earlier, the salvage value approach sets the fees as a percentage of recovery. This creates an incentive for the attorney to settle early, even when holding out for a larger recovery might be in the corporation's interest. At first glance, this seems counterintuitive, since, under the salvage value approach, the higher the recovery, the higher the fee. The problem is that the amount of work which the attorney must do to increase recovery might not be proportionate to the increase in fees. Specifically, a quick settlement might produce a satisfactory fee with minimal work, whereas pursuing the litigation will require very much more work for the attorney to obtain an increase in fees.[166] On the other hand, the lodestar, or hourly, fee creates an incentive to reject an early settlement in order to stall and put in more hours to obtain more fees. The result can be to increase the burden of the litigation on the corporation because the plaintiff's attorney rejects early settlements which were in the corporation's interest.

There is also the ever present temptation to trade away corporate recovery in exchange for increased recovery by the plaintiff or his or her attorney. At its extreme, the creates the problem of under-the-table payoffs to the plaintiff, which we discussed earlier. Even without reaching this extreme, the plaintiff's attorney's greater concern for his or her fees might lead to a partial sacrifice of corporate recovery. The problem arises because the parties often negotiate attorneys' fees as part of the

---

166. Indeed, this is the economics behind a number of high volume personal injury plaintiff's law practices, which rely on obtaining quick settlements and are ill prepared to actually try a case.

settlement. For example, the agreement may call upon the defendants not to oppose the plaintiff's attorney's fee request. Since the essence of negotiation is the exchange of *quid pro quos*, such fee discussions place the plaintiff's attorney in an evident conflict-of-interest when simultaneously negotiating fees and corporate recovery.[167] Moreover, the availability of fee awards based upon nonpecuniary corporate benefit exacerbates this problem. Negotiating for purported reforms in corporate management provides a means to justify compensation under the substantial benefit test for attorneys fees, and yet imposes minimum hardship on the defendants. This allows the negotiations to follow a path of least resistance, thereby potentially precluding a monetary recovery for the corporation. Indeed, this may explain the substantial number of settlements in Professor Romano's study in which there was no monetary recovery for the corporation. The lodestar approach to setting fees increases this problem, since it does not tie fees to the size of recovery.

These concerns with the motives of the plaintiff shareholder explain the extraordinary efforts made by the courts to preserve a role for the board through the demand-on-directors rule and the courts' willingness to listen to the recommendations of special litigation committees. Nevertheless, it is also difficult to trust the directors' motives when the prospective lawsuit is against members of the board, or a party who might be controlling members of the board. After all, directors who are prospective defendants are unlikely to determine the corporation's interest uninfluenced by their own. Moreover, even directors who are not defendants might be unable to provide a truly disinterested determination of the corporation's interest in pursuing a claim against their colleagues on the board. Because of what a number of writers have labeled "structural bias," directors who have no personal stake in the prospective litigation may still place the interest of the defendants ahead of the company's interest in deciding whether to pursue the claim.[168] This structural bias stems from three sources:

A major source of bias lies in the relationship between corporate management and the board of directors. As discussed earlier in this book,[169] management (and particularly the chief executive officer) of a publicly held corporation often have substantial, if not controlling, influence over the board. Indeed, traditionally, directors in a publicly held corporation owe their positions on the board to management. Since claims in a derivative lawsuit are more often against the management than against the outside directors, the influence of management on the outside directors undermines the ability of non-defendant directors to determine the corporate interest in the typical derivative suit.

---

167. Attempting to ban the practice of negotiating fees at the same time as the parties negotiate corporate recovery introduces uncertainties into the value of the settlement, thereby making it more difficult to settle the case, and, in any event, may be impossible to enforce.

168. *See, e.g.,* Cox & Munslinger, *supra* note 106 at 85–108.

169. See § 3.1.5a *supra.*

The dynamics of litigation (or proposed litigation) against one's colleagues creates a second source of structural bias. Because of group psychology, non-defendant directors normally will be sympathetic toward the defendant directors, and suspicious of the outsider plaintiff shareholder. The court in *Zapata* caught this psychology when the court referred to the possible attitude of non-defendant directors as "there but for the grace of God go I."[170]

Finally, we earlier discussed the selection bias which exists in the special litigation committee process. Specifically, the defendants in the lawsuit typically have selected the members of these committees. This puts the defendants in a position to select individuals who, while not possessing any overt interest in the suit, will nevertheless be sympathetic towards the defendants' position. It is as if one side in a trial could pick the jury, while the other side can only challenge for cause.

The third party involved in deciding the corporate interest in a derivative suit is the court. In fact, the court can play two roles: The first occurs both in applying the demand-on-directors rule and in deciding whether to defer either to a rejection of demand or the recommendations of a special litigation committee. This role entails the court deciding whether the directors or the plaintiff shareholder will make the decision for the corporation as to whether to pursue the lawsuit. *Zapata* introduced a second possible role. Instead of deciding whether the directors or the plaintiff shareholder should make the decision for the corporation, the court itself might decide what course of action is in the corporation's best interest. This is also, to a large extent, the role the court takes in approving a settlement.

Some have criticized the *Zapata* approach on the ground that judges are not experts on when it makes business sense to pursue a lawsuit.[171] Actually, judges, who see how the process works every day, often possess a more realistic understanding of the burdens and benefits of prospective litigation than do business-persons. The real problem with judges deciding the corporate interest in pursuing a lawsuit, or even deciding who will decide the corporate interest, lies in the adversarial process by which courts reach decisions. The result of this process is to create extensive litigation over the wisdom of decisions which have as their purpose avoiding the burdens of litigation. Keep in mind that the question is whether the burden of pursuing litigation against the corporation's directors outweighs the likely benefits to the corporation—or, to put the matter crudely, the issue is whether it is worth the costs to have a trial. Seen in this light, it hardly makes sense to have a trial in order to decide whether it is worth the costs to have a trial (or to have a trial to decide who should decide whether it is worth the costs to have a trial).

Much of the difficulty involved in applying the demand-on-directors rule, and in responding to the recommendations of special litigation

---

170.   430 A.2d at 787.

171.   *E.g.,* Joy v. North, 692 F.2d 880, 898 (2d Cir.1982) (Cardamone, J., dissenting).

committees, stems from the efforts of courts to wiggle around the fundamental fact that it makes no sense to have a trial over whether to have a trial. Ultimately, the reason for not letting the directors decide whether the corporation should sue is that the directors are the wrong-doers, or are under the control of the wrongdoer(s). The problem is that determining whether the directors are, in fact, wrongdoers entails decid-ing the merits of the lawsuit. If a court can resolve the merits on the pleadings (in other words, the complaint does not state a cause of action), or on summary judgment (in other words, there is no material issue of fact), then the court can fairly quickly dispose of the lawsuit on the merits and there is no reason to spend time trying to figure out whether the suit is worthwhile for the corporation (or figuring out who should decide if the suit is worthwhile for the corporation). If the court cannot resolve the merits at these early stages, however, it is too late after a trial has exonerated the directors to say "gee, we should have let the directors decide not to sue after all."

This, in turn, explains why the key to the court's evaluation of either the futility excuse under the traditional demand rule, or the directors' rejection of a demand, is the requirement that the plaintiff plead "with particularity." In other words, courts are desperately at-tempting to make an evaluation of the merits of the plaintiff's claim at the pleading stage by forcing the plaintiff to allege details. Yet, if this is such a good idea, why not do this in all litigation? Why allow the plaintiff in any action to put the defendant(s) to the burden of defending a lawsuit based upon broad allegations? Part of the answer is that courts have concluded it is unfair to force the plaintiff to provide detailed allegations before having the opportunity to take discovery and find out what really happened. This rationale seems more apropos to a derivative suit—in which the typical shareholder has little access to what really went on regarding a director decision before taking discovery—than it is to the typical tort or breach of contract action, in which the plaintiff knows much more what happened. In addition, the move to notice pleading under rules of civil procedure reflected a dissatisfaction with the requirements for more detailed pleadings, under which an attorney's inarticulateness in dealing with the rather stylized art form of pleading, rather than the lack available facts, may have led to dismissal. Indeed, the process of dismissal, amendment, and new motion for dismissal, entailed in trying to assess whether the plaintiff can plead adequately detailed facts, itself adds to the costs of litigation. This was certainly true in *Aronson*, where it took a trip to the Delaware Supreme Court before the plaintiff put enough details in his complaint to survive judicial nitpicking.

As we discussed earlier, the court, as a practical matter, must evaluate the recommendations of a special litigation committee on a motion for summary judgment. In other words, the statements in some opinions that the court will, if necessary, conduct an evidentiary hearing (a trial) if there are material issues of fact as to the committee's independence, good faith or due care (or, under *Zapata*, if the court must resolve material issues of fact in order for the court to determine the corporation's interest) are largely bluff. It does not make any sense to conduct such a trial and, hence, it hardly ever has been done. Instead, if the court denies summary judgment, the recommendations of the special litigation committee become moot.[172]

Yet, if the courts are honest about the concept of material issues of fact, it is difficult to image the courts very often granting summary judgment motions based upon the recommendations of special litigation committees. Admittedly, as discussed earlier, there normally will be little basis for the plaintiff to raise material issues of fact as to the good faith or due care of the committee. After all, the decision about whether to pursue a lawsuit is one on which reasonable minds typically can differ. Hence, unless the committee is unusually sloppy, it can come up with reasonable grounds for not pursuing the action. The same ease of resolution, however, is not true as to the question of whether the committee members are disinterested or independent. We have seen that the members of the special litigation committee typically owe their positions both on the board and on the committee to the defendant directors. There are also practical and psychological pressures for the committee members to sympathize with the defendant directors. Under these circumstances, the independence of the committee seems to present the essence of a material issue of fact.[173]

Resolving this issue opens to door to extensive litigation. For example, the plaintiff might attempt to show a lack of independence of the committee members by exploring possible economic interests of the committee members which their action for or against the defendants could impact.[174] The plaintiff might attempt to show a lack of independence by examining prior votes of the directors on the committee in circumstances in which their vote impacted the defendants[175]—which, in turn, could lead into a morass of side issues as to the merits of earlier conflict-of-interest transactions. The plaintiff might look into who suggested the committee members' nomination to the board and the committee,[176] and what knowledge about the committee members motivated this nomination. Evidence of prior resignations—to ascertain if the defendants had the practical power to remove directors—would seem relevant. Also seemingly relevant would be evidence suggesting a pre-existing hostility toward derivative suits—perhaps because of the committee members' experiences with other corporations.[177] Gathering all

---

172. *See, e.g., In re* Continental Ill. Sec. Litig., 732 F.2d 1302 (7th Cir.1984) (the corporation withdrew its motion to dismiss rather than participate in a mini-trial applying the *Zapata* approach). *But see* Grynberg v. Farmer, 1980 Fed. Sec. L. Rep. (CCH) ¶ 97,683 (D. Colo. 1980) (the court held a two day evidentiary hearing on the committee members' independence).

173. *See, e.g.,* Gall v. Exxon Corp., 418 F.Supp. 508 (S.D.N.Y.1976)

174. *See, e.g.,* Hasan v. Clevetrust Realty Investors, 729 F.2d 372 (6th Cir.1984).

175. *See, e.g.,* deHaas v. Empire Petroleum Co., 286 F.Supp. 809 (D.Colo.1968), *modified on other grounds,* 435 F.2d 1223 (10 Cir.1970).

176. *Id. But see* Aronson v. Lewis, 473 A.2d 805 (Del.1984).

177. *But see* Rosengarten v. IT & T, 466 F.Supp. 817 (S.D.N.Y.1979).

these sorts of evidence could entail extensive discovery, while the presentation and rebuttal of such evidence could require a major trial replete with expert testimony on psychology.

Given the potential for extensive adjudication over the independence of the members of special litigation committees, how have courts been able to grant summary judgments based upon the recommendation of such committees? The answer is that courts tend to ignore the problem by confining the meaning of independence to a lack of any blatant self interest.[178] The difficulty with this approach is that it turns over the fate of the suit to persons who cannot be trusted to put the corporation's interest ahead of the defendants'.

A judicial determination of the corporate interest under a *Zapata* approach also normally would seem to raise numerous issues of material fact. The probability and expected size of recovery, the likely extent of both the plaintiff's attorneys' fees and the attorneys' fees of the defendants which the corporation must indemnify,[179] the impact of the suit on the corporation's public image[180] and on employee productivity, and the suit's likely impact on future relations with the corporation's management, all present difficult factual questions. Resolution of these questions would seem to call for extensive discovery and a major trial.

The fact that there have been no reported major trials to apply the *Zapata* approach raises questions as to whether courts or litigants ever will be serious about obtaining an independent judicial evaluation of the corporation's interest. For example, the Delaware Supreme Court has given the trial court discretion not to apply the court's independent judgment. Also, the prospect of a trial no doubt provides an impetus to settlement, even if the trial is not on the merits. The problem is that this is an incentive to settle for all the wrong reasons. If the plaintiff has a strong case, the ability to put the plaintiff through two trials before he or she can obtain victory on the merits gives the defendants leverage to force the plaintiff to settle for less than justified by the strength of the claim. On the other hand, if the plaintiff has a weak claim, the added burden on the corporation of potentially two trials adds to the nuisance value of the suit. Indeed, the *Zapata* litigation, itself, ended by virtue of a ignominious settlement on the eve of a trial court determination as to the corporation's interest. This settlement—which came about in a related action brought in federal court in Texas—essentially consisted of the plaintiff in the Texas action agreeing to a dismissal, in exchange for the corporation agreeing not to oppose the fee request of this plaintiff's attorney.[181]

---

178. *E.g.,* Mills v. Esmark, Inc., 544 F.Supp. 1275 (N.D.Ill.1982).

179. *See, e.g.,* Note, *Judicially Exercised Business Judgments In Shareholder Derivative Suits: Implementing Zapata Corp. v. Maldonado,* 46 Albany L. Rev. 980, 1007 n.122 (1982) (the briefs filed by the parties in *Zapata* disputed the probable expenditures on attorneys' fees).

180. *See, e.g.,* Joy v. North, 692 F.2d 880 (2d Cir.1982) (the special litigation committee obtained the opinions of two experts concerning the impact of the suit on the corporation's reputation).

181. Maher v. Zapata Corp., 714 F.2d 436 (5th Cir.1983).

Speaking of settlements, some idea as to the potential burden entailed by a judicial determination of the corporation's interest in pursuing a derivative suit can come from examining judicial hearings concerning approval of settlements. Some of these hearings have been as long as major trials.[182] Actually, however, lengthy proceedings have not turned out to be the usual problem when dealing with judicial approval of settlements. The reason is simple. The adversary process depends upon conflict between opposing parties before the court. Such a conflict is present when the recommendation of special litigation committee prompts a motion to dismiss the plaintiff's claim. Hence, one could expect—unless the court cuts off the process by taking a cramped view of material issues of fact—extensive adjudication over motions to dismiss based upon the recommendation of a special litigation committee. With a settlement, however, the situation is radically different. Plaintiff and defendant(s) join hands to present their agreement to the court for approval. Commonly, there is no opposition.[183] On the positive side, the lack of opposition means that the settlement hearing usually will not turn into a major trial. On the negative side, however, the lack of opposition seriously undercuts the ability of judicial approval to protect the corporation from poor settlements.[184] Indeed, the large number of settlements found by Professor Romano in which the corporation received no monetary recovery, and possibly little beneficial non-monetary recovery, raises troubling questions as to the adequacy of judicial approval of settlements to protect the corporation.

Judicial review of settlement agreements has another failing as well. The court can only review the settlement agreement presented to the court. The court cannot review the decision of the plaintiff's attorney to reject a settlement agreement which might have been in the corporation's interest to accept.[185] Nor can the court usually test whether tougher negotiations would have produced a better bargain for the corporation.[186]

A fourth party to determine the corporation's interest in a derivative suit would be the shareholders as a whole. In other words, one could put the question of whether the corporation should pursue the action to a vote by the shareholders. This, in fact, is the underlying idea of the

---

182. *E.g.,* Pergament v. Frazer, 93 F.Supp. 13 (E.D.Mich.1950) (settlement hearing included seven weeks of testimony).

183. Haudek, *supra* note 154 at 805.

184. *E.g.,* Alleghany Corp. v. Kirby, 333 F.2d 327, 347 (2d Cir.1964) (Friendly, J., dissenting).

185. Occasionally, the board might enter an agreement on behalf of the corporation purporting to settle the derivative claims. This is rare, largely because the board typically will view such an action as simply trading lawsuits. After all, the settle-ment agreement is itself a conflict-of-interest transaction, and, hence, the plaintiff can challenge the agreement as a breach of a duty of loyalty and demand that the board prove the deal is fair. *See, e.g.,* Denicke v. Anglo Cal. Nat'l Bank, 141 F.2d 285 (9th Cir.1944).

186. *See, e.g.,* Levin v. Miss. River Corp., 59 F.R.D. 353, 361 (S.D.N.Y.1973), *aff'd,* 486 F.2d 1398 (2d Cir. 1973) (it is not the function of the court to "enter in negotiations with the litigants in the hope of improving the terms of the settlement").

demand-on-shareholders requirement we discussed earlier. Also, shareholders might vote on a settlement.[187]

Naturally, if the prospective derivative suit is against a majority shareholder, then a shareholder vote will not provide an objective assessment of the corporation's interest. This tends to rule out a shareholder determination of the corporation's interest when the derivative suit involves a closely held corporation. The problems with a shareholder vote are different in the widely held corporation. To begin with, obtaining such a vote—which means essentially running a proxy contest—can be very expensive. To the extent the corporation foots some or all of this expense, then we are back to the problem of using a costly process to see if it is worth the cost for the corporation to pursue a claim. On the other hand, imposing the cost of the solicitation on the plaintiff will deter the plaintiff from bringing potentially worthwhile derivative suits. More fundamentally, shareholders in a widely held corporation typically would be grossly ill-informed in voting on whether the company should pursue a derivative suit. Determining if a lawsuit is worthwhile requires information as to the likelihood and magnitude of recovery and as to various tangible and intangible costs entailed in pursuing the litigation. Obtaining and understanding such information normally requires consulting with an attorney. Presumably, few shareholders would go out and consult an attorney to advise them on how to vote regarding a derivative suit. Indeed, many shareholders will not even bother to read whatever materials they receive from those soliciting proxies to vote their shares for or against the suit.

Is there any solution to the problem of who should decide the corporation's interest in pursuing a lawsuit against those in control of the corporation? If none of the existing candidates provides an attractive solution, perhaps the answer is to introduce a new party. One idea is to have the court appoint one or more individuals, who will make the decision as to what action is in the best interest of the corporation when it comes to suing a corporate director. The court in *Miller* stated that such an appointment was within the powers of the trial court. The Model Act now contains a provision authorizing such an appointment.[188] One critical limitation under *Miller* and the Model Act is that such an appointment of independent decision makers only will occur at the request of the corporation—in other words, at the request of a board of directors whose members include the defendants in the lawsuit. Given the risks that such independent decision makers might end up seeing things the plaintiff's way, one would be surprised if there will be too many times when a board containing defendant directors will request the court to appoint independent decision makers. Perhaps a better approach is to have the court automatically appoint a panel of "provisional litigation directors" who could monitor the plaintiff's decisions in

187. *See, e.g.,* Glicken v. Bradford, 35 F.R.D. 144 (S.D.N.Y.1964) (a shareholder vote does not preclude the necessity of the court's finding a settlement to be fair).

188. M.B.C.A. § 7.44(f). *See also* Principles of Corporate Governance § 7.12.

a derivative suit.[189] This panel could not only evaluate the initial decision to bring the suit, but could also keep on top of the decisions regarding the prosecution and settlement of the suit in order to ensure that the plaintiff's attorney acts in the corporation's interest, instead of his or her own.

§ 4.4   Indemnity and Insurance

Having looked at the duties of care and loyalty of corporate directors and officers, and the enforcement of those duties through derivative suits, we now examine two mechanisms whereby the corporation might protect its directors and officers from the financial consequences of claims made against the directors and officers. These mechanisms are indemnity and insurance.

4.4.1   Indemnity

Employers, including corporations, commonly indemnify (in other words, reimburse) their employees for various expenses which the employees incur during the course of work. For example, if an employee must attend a business meeting at the other end of town from the employer's office, the employer generally will reimburse the employee for reasonable expenses (such as cab fare) which the employee paid out of his or her own pocket to get to the meeting. The employee's right to such reimbursement is a matter of express or implied contract (including, in the absence of express agreement, judicial notions as to when requiring indemnity is fair).[1]

Sometimes, the expenses which corporate directors, officers and employees incur as a result of their working for the corporation arise out of the directors, officers or employees becoming embroiled in litigation. Perhaps, an outsider claims that the directors, officers or employees engaged in illegal or tortious activity while working for the corporation. Alternately, perhaps the corporation, or a shareholder suing on its behalf, sues the directors, officers or employees for breaching their duty to the corporation. In either event, the resulting expenses can include the costs, such as attorneys fees, of defending against the lawsuit. Expenses resulting from such litigation also can involve the directors, officers or employees paying a liability which results from losing or settling the suit. To what extent can directors, officers and employees obtain indemnity from the corporation for these expenses?

Indemnifying expenses resulting from litigation raises far more complex and important issues than does reimbursing conventional expenditures (such as business transportation). In fact, every state has found it necessary to address this subject through a provision in the

---

189. For the details of such a proposal, see Franklin Gevurtz, *Who Represents the Corporation? In Search of a Better Method of Determining the Corporate Interest in Derivative Suits*, 46 U. Pitt. L. Rev. 265 (1985).

§ 4.4

1. *E.g.*, Restatement (Second) of Agency §§ 438–440(1958).

state's corporation statute. These statutory provisions vary among the states. Nevertheless, the statutes often draw four distinctions, which will provide the focal points for our discussion.

The first common distinction impacting a corporate official's ability to obtain indemnity, not surprisingly, involves the disposition of the suit; in other words, did the official win, lose or settle the action for which he or she seeks indemnity. Indeed, if one were to make up rules from scratch, as a first approximation, one might say that officials who win in the lawsuit should get indemnity and officials who lose in the lawsuit should not. It turns out, however, that things are nowhere near this simple.

Let us start with the situation a which a corporate official prevails upon the merits after becoming a defendant in a suit arising out of his or her employment. Interestingly, some common law cases had denied indemnity in this situation.[2] These courts reasoned that the corporate official had no claim to indemnity (at least in the absence of an express contract) because the corporation does not benefit from the defense of litigation in which the corporation is not a defendant (particularly if a shareholder had brought the litigation against the official in order to obtain a recovery for the corporation). Still, such a result seems unfair to the official who would not have faced the often considerable expense of becoming a defendant in litigation but for his or her role with the corporation. Moreover, lack of indemnity might deter individuals from serving as directors or officers (albeit, if persons were so concerned, perhaps they would have made an express contract covering the point as a condition of taking the position as director or officer). Besides, it is not clear that the corporation obtains no benefit if its officials defeat non-meritorious charges brought against the officials. After all, if corporate officials are afraid of the expense of defending against even non-meritorious lawsuits, the officials might decline to take legitimate actions on behalf of the corporation. In any event, dissatisfaction with these judicial holdings was part of the agenda leading to the enactment of indemnity statutes. Hence, statutes now require the corporation to indemnify litigation expenses incurred by a corporate official who prevails upon the merits in defense of a suit arising out of his or her job.[3]

Suppose, instead of prevailing upon the merits, the corporate official wins the suit on a procedural point. For example, maybe the statute of limitations has run. Should the official still be entitled to indemnity for litigation expenses? The argument against providing indemnity in these cases is that the lawsuit really has not vindicated the corporate official; in fact, he or she may have acted wrongfully and only escaped liability on a technicality. Still, a rule which denied indemnity in this situation could penalize the corporate official for asserting a legitimate procedural defense, which would frustrate whatever policy allowing the particular

---

2. *E.g.,* New York Dock Co. v. McCol-   **3.** *E.g.,* M.B.C.A. § 8.52.
lom, 173 Misc. 106, 16 N.Y.S.2d 844 (Sup.
Ct. 1939).

procedural defense serves. Moreover, to the extent a corporate official decides to forgo a procedural defense so that the official might be eligible for indemnity, the result can be to increase the costs of litigation and thus increase the amount the corporation must pay as indemnity. For these reasons, most indemnity statutes automatically entitle corporate officials to indemnity when they are successful in the lawsuit on the merits "or otherwise."[4] Some statutes, however, do not provide for automatic indemnity in this situation;[5] albeit, as we shall discuss later, they may allow for indemnity at the option of the corporation.

Things become more complicated once we recognize that litigation often produces partial victories and partial defeats. In this event, is a corporate official entitled to indemnity for some of his or her litigation costs if he or she obtains a partial victory? A Delaware court addressed this issue in *Merritt-Chapman & Scott Corp. v. Wolfson.*[6] The government had indicted Wolfson, an official of Merritt–Chapman, for securities law violations. As a result of a plea bargain, Wolfson plead *nolo contendere* to one of the five counts in the indictment, and the prosecution dropped the other four counts. Wolfson sought indemnity based upon his "success" in obtaining dismissal of four of the counts against him. The court agreed and held that Wolfson was entitled to partial indemnity.

The idea that partial success entitles an official to partial indemnity flows from the language used by Delaware's indemnity statute. The statute calls for indemnity "to the extent" that a corporate official is successful in defense of any suit "or in defense of any claim, issue or matter therein."[7] By contrast, the Model Act's indemnity provisions only require indemnity if the official is "wholly successful." The comments to the Model Act state that the use of the "wholly successful" language is intended to preclude the result in *Merritt-Chapman*.[8]

This raises the question of why not require partial indemnity for partial success. Actually, much of the reason to question the *Merritt-Chapman* result does not go to the issue of partial success, but, rather, goes to the question of what the court meant by success. The dismissal of the four counts came about as plea bargain. This brings up the issue of what to do with settlements; a subject we will address shortly. For now, however, let us ask what the rule should be if a defendant obtains dismissal of some claims, despite the plaintiff's opposition. It might seem rather harsh to deny indemnity entirely if such a corporate official were then to lose on a relatively minor claim which remained. On the other hand, it is common for plaintiffs in litigation to start by asserting a variety of claims, which then get whittled down as facts develop through discovery and the like. Should the corporation need to pay for this process of focusing the claim if significant wrongdoing by the corporate official led to the lawsuit to begin with?

4.   *Id.*

5.   *E.g.,* Cal. Corp. Code § 317(d).

6.   321 A.2d 138 (Del.Super.Ct.1974).

7.   Del. Gen. Corp. Law § 145(c).

8.   M.B.C.A. § 8.52 Official Comment.

Now, let us consider the situation in which the corporate official loses the suit. At first glance, the answer should be simple: no indemnity. It turns out, however, that the indemnity statutes refuse to make things simple. To understand when it might make sense to indemnify a corporate official despite his or her having lost the lawsuit, we must turn to two other distinctions drawn by many of the indemnity statutes.

One distinction is whether the lawsuit against the official was on behalf of the corporation, or whether the suit was on behalf of an outsider to the corporation. It would not seem to make any sense, at least on initial impression, for the corporation to indemnify its official who lost an action brought by or on behalf of the corporation. Otherwise, the whole lawsuit would have been worse than pointless. Yet, perhaps one might argue that the result should be different if the official loses a suit brought by an outsider.

As we discussed earlier in this chapter,[9] corporate officials can face sanctions under regulatory and criminal statutes, or officials can face civil liability to third parties, as a result of actions the officials take on behalf of the corporation. In the earlier discussion, we asked whether the *corporation* can obtain reimbursement *from the official* if the corporation also incurs liability or suffers other damages as a result of the official's action. The indemnity statutes force us to consider the flip-side: Can the *official* who violates criminal or regulatory statutes, or commits a tort, obtain indemnity *from the corporation* for the resulting liabilities and legal expenses? A sensible legal regime would coordinate, at least somewhat, the answers to these two questions. After all, it would be rather silly to have a rule which says unlawful conduct constitutes a breach of a corporate official's duty to the corporation, and, at the same time, have a rule which calls for corporations to reimburse their officials for litigation expenses and liabilities resulting from the officials acting unlawfully. Otherwise, the end result would be that, as soon as the corporation indemnified its official, the company would have a cause of action against the official to get the money back, and then the official would have an action against the corporation for indemnity, and on and on.

On the other hand, as we discussed earlier, it is not settled that unlawful actions necessarily breach a corporate official's duty to the corporation. If the conduct did not breach the official's duty to the corporation, perhaps the company should indemnify the official. The argument for indemnity is that the official might have been trying to advance the corporation's interests through the unlawful conduct. Recall, we mentioned in discussing illegal acts, how a cold analysis of probable outcomes might lead a corporate official to conclude it was in the company's interest to engage in unlawful actions. Moreover, if the corporate official's liability was based upon negligence, the official may not even have realized that he or she was exposing, either him- or herself, or the corporation, to possible liability.

9. See § 4.1.6 *supra.*

Still, there is a serious public policy problem with allowing indemnity in this situation. Doing so undercuts the deterrent purpose of having imposed the sanction personally upon the official (as opposed to just upon the corporation) in the first place. Yet, the concern with undercutting deterrence might not apply if the official was only liable for compensatory damages resulting from a civil wrong. In addition, one might argue that the cost of defending against prosecution is not part of the intended sanctions for law violations. If so, shifting the costs of defense, but not the burden to pay any fines or judgments, to the corporation does not undermine the intended sanction.

Notice, we have now arrived at the third distinction which might impact rights to indemnity. This is a distinction among the type of costs for which the corporate official seeks indemnity. Indemnity statutes sensibly might take different approaches to fines and other damages imposed to deter unlawful conduct, damage awards intended solely to compensate, and the costs of litigating over the official's liability.

This distinction also might cause us to take a second look at the situation in which the official loses an action brought on behalf of the corporation. The idea of the corporation indemnifying one of its officials for the very judgment which the official just paid to the corporation is obviously silly. Maybe, however, the idea of the corporation covering the official's litigation expenses is not always so absurd. Perhaps the issue on which the official lost was a close one and we should not be too critical of the official for litigating the matter. Perhaps obtaining a judicial decision after a full adversary proceeding will provide some guidance which is more worthwhile for the corporation than if the official had simply conceded at the outset. Hence, statutes might want to leave the door open a crack for indemnity of litigation costs even when an official loses an action brought on behalf of the corporation.

Now let us see how our policy analysis compares with what the statutes actually do in situations in which the corporate official lost the action for which he or she seeks indemnity. To understand how the statutes operate in this regard, we need to introduce a yet a fourth distinction commonly employed in the statutes. This distinction is between automatic (or mandatory) indemnity, and permissive indemnity.

As we discussed above, indemnity statutes universally require the corporation to indemnify officials who prevail upon the merits. In other words, the statute gives the official the right to obtain indemnity regardless of whether those in charge of the corporation voluntarily agree to pay. Not surprisingly, no statute provides for such automatic indemnity in favor of a corporate official who loses a lawsuit. Many statutes, however, permit the corporation to indemnify such an official despite the loss. Such statutes raise two questions: Under what circumstances may the corporation indemnify the losing official? And, who decides if the corporation will pay indemnity?

Indemnity statutes set out various criteria for when a corporation may pay indemnity to a corporate official who did not prevail in the lawsuit. Typical criteria include: (1) the official acted in good faith in undertaking the challenged conduct; (2) the official reasonably believed that the challenged conduct was in the best interest of the corporation, or, at least, not opposed to the best interest of the corporation; and (3) if the indemnity claim involves a criminal action, the official had no reasonable cause to believe that the challenged conduct was illegal.[10]

The policy behind these criteria reflects a curious legislative compromise. For example, we might think it overly harsh to punish a person who had no reasonable cause to believe his or her conduct was illegal (the third criteria above). If so, then the solution is to require such belief as part of the mens rea necessary to establish a criminal violation. If the legislature, however, decides that requiring such mens rea would be inconsistent with the purposes of the criminal statute, it seems strange to pass another statute allowing some individuals to obtain relief simply because they violated the law while working for a corporation. As mentioned above, one might draw a distinction in this regard between reimbursement of defense costs and reimbursement of fines. Yet, the indemnity statutes generally do not draw this distinction, but, instead, allow the corporation to reimburse the official for fines as well as defense costs.[11]

Also, as we discussed earlier in the chapter when dealing with the issue of whether officers and directors breach their duty of care to the corporation by engaging in unlawful conduct, it is questionable whether officials ever reasonably can believe that unlawful conduct is in (or at least not opposed to) the corporation's interest. After all, perhaps courts should presume that sanctions are sensible so that reasonable people would not think it worthwhile to engage in unlawful actions. Moreover, most tortious conduct for which a corporate official might be personally liable would involve either intentional or at least negligent misconduct. If so, this would seem to rule out the possibility that the official acted in good faith and could be reasonable in believing that the tortious action was in the corporation's interest.[12] The indemnity statutes, however, expressly reflect a different view. They commonly state that an adverse judgment does not, itself, establish that the official lacked a good faith, reasonable belief that the action was in the corporation's interest.[13]

If losing the suit does not, itself, establish that the corporate official lacked a good faith and reasonable belief that he or she was serving the corporate interest, then the critical question becomes who will decide whether the corporate official meets the criteria for indemnity. Various

---

10. *E.g.*, M.B.C.A. § 8.51(a)(1).

11. *E.g.*, Del. Gen. Corp. Law § 145(a)

12. For example, under the traditional calculus of risk made famous by Judge Learned Hand, a corporate official's decision not to take accident avoidance steps would be negligent only if it would have been cheaper for the corporation to have taken the safety step than it would have been to pay for any accidents, when discounted for the probability that the accident will occur. In other words, a finding of negligence establishes that the official did not act reasonably, even if one views the situation from the interest of the corporation, rather than just from the interest of the injured third party.

13. *E.g.*, M.B.C.A. § 8.51(c).

statutes specify four possibilities. The most common decision makers specified in the indemnity statutes are (1) directors who were not parties to the lawsuit for which the official seeks indemnity; (2) the stockholders; or (3) an independent attorney.[14] Some states allow for a judicial determination as well.[15] Critics might question how well informed or unbiased any of these decision makers are likely to be.

Many statutes even allow indemnity for corporate officials who lose an action by or on behalf of the corporation itself. Often, these statutes impose two additional constraints on indemnity when the official loses an action on behalf of the corporation rather than on behalf of an outsider. The first constraint is the requirement that a court determine that, despite the adjudication of liability, the corporate official is still "fairly and reasonably" entitled to indemnity.[16] In addition, statutes may limit indemnity in this instance to litigation expenses, and exclude amounts the official must pay under a judgment in favor of the corporation.[17] These two limits are consistent with the notion we discussed earlier that occasionally it might make sense for the corporation to pay litigation expenses even for its officials who lost an action brought on the corporation's behalf. Presumably, this should not be the typical case the official lost, but, rather, one which involved a close legal issue which the corporation gained by having resolved either way.

A few states have gone beyond this limited approach to indemnifying officials who lose an action brought on behalf of the corporation. These states have eliminated or greatly reduced the distinction between suits by outsiders and suits on behalf of the corporation, when it comes to permissive indemnification of a losing official.[18] In other words, if an appropriate decision maker (disinterested directors, independent counsel or the shareholders) finds that the official meets the requirements for permissive indemnification (a good faith and reasonable belief that he or she served the corporate interest), then the official can receive indemnity, even for amounts paid to the corporation under a judgment in the corporation's favor. Given our discussion above, this approach does not seem to make much sense. Why then did these states adopt it? The answer is that these states acted in the midst of the legislative panic which followed the *Van Gorkom* decision and the decreased availability of directors' and officers' liability insurance.

There is one other possibility by which some statutes might allow indemnity of a corporate official who loses an action (whether the action is either on behalf of the corporation or by an outsider). A number of statutes, most notably Delaware's, state that the rights to indemnity under the statute are not exclusive of any rights which an official might have to indemnity under a bylaw, agreement or the like.[19] Hence, it

---

14. *Id* at § 8.55

15. *E.g.,* Cal. Corp. Code § 317(e)(4).

16. *E.g.,* Del. Gen. Corp. Law § 145(b).

17. *E.g.,* M.B.C.A. § 8.51(d)(1).

18. *See, e.g.,* James J. Hanks, Jr., *Evaluating Recent State Legislation on Director and Officer Liability Limitation and Indemnification,* 43 Bus. Law. 1207 (1988).

19. Del. Gen. Corp. Law § 145(f). *But see* M.B.C.A. § 8.59.

might seem possible for a corporation to contract with its officials, or provide in its bylaws, for indemnity, even when the officials would not qualify for permissive indemnity under the statute.

It is unclear how far a bylaw or agreement can go in providing indemnity under an indemnity statute such as Delaware's. Can a bylaw or agreement provide indemnity for an official who did not act in good faith? What if the official acted in good faith, but was not reasonable? Can a bylaw or agreement call for the corporation to repay to its official anything which the official had to pay to the corporation under a judgment the corporation received against the official? A number of courts and writers have stated that agreements and bylaws which provide for indemnity are subject to a public policy limit.[20] Yet, what is this limit? Presumably, a bylaw or an agreement must be able to go beyond the precise parameters of indemnity called for under the mandatory and permissive provisions of the indemnity statute, or else the statement that the provisions are not exclusive becomes meaningless. On the other hand, what is the point of the statute delineating limits on permissive indemnification if a bylaw or agreement can provide for indemnity despite any limits?

In *Waltuch v. ContiCommodity Services, Inc.,*[21] the Second Circuit attempted to answer these questions under Delaware law. Waltuch was vice-president and the chief metals trader of ContiCommodity. After silver trades undertaken by Waltuch went awry, the government and private traders brought legal actions against Waltuch and ContiCommodity. ContiCommodity settled the private claims by agreeing to pay over $35 million, in exchange for the dismissal of the claims against both it and Waltuch. Waltuch plea-bargained the government action brought against him by agreeing to a fine and suspension of his trading privileges. Waltuch then sought indemnity from ContiCommodity for over $2 million in legal expenses. ContiCommodity (who evidently had fired Waltuch) refused to pay indemnity, and Waltuch sued. Waltuch argued that he was entitled to indemnity because he was successful in the lawsuit, and, even if not, because a provision in ContiCommodity's articles called for indemnity unless the corporate official was adjudged liable.

The Second Circuit decided that the provision in ContiCommodity's articles calling for indemnity was invalid insofar as it went beyond the limits of permissible indemnity under Delaware's statute (in other words, if it allowed indemnity to those who acted in bad faith or without a reasonable belief that their actions were consistent with the corporation's interest). The court did not resolve exactly what the "nonexclusive" provision of the Delaware statute allowed. Instead, the court simply quoted from several writers, who suggested that the non-exclu-

20. *E.g.,* S. Samuel Arsht, *Indemnification Under Section 145 of Delaware General Corporation Law,* 3 Del. J. Corp. L. 176, 176–177 (1978).

21. 88 F.3d 87 (2d Cir.1996).

sive provision was intended to open up various procedural alternatives for approving permissible indemnity.

Now that we have considered the situation in which the corporate official wins the legal action for which he or she seeks indemnity, and the situation in which the official loses the legal action, we must address the situation in which the parties settle the suit. Since most legal actions settle, the rules regarding indemnity in this situation have the most practical significance. Settlement also creates the most difficult policy questions regarding indemnity. The problem is that a rule which limits indemnity in the case of settlement can discourage settlements. Many times, a settlement might be in the best interest of the corporation. This can be especially true when the corporation might end up indemnifying the increased litigation costs which result if the official refuses to settle. On the other hand, indemnity can provide the means for collusive settlements which largely serve to shift costs to the corporation. As we discussed earlier in this chapter,[22] parties in a derivative suit all too often agree to a settlement whose main feature is that the corporation ends up paying both sides' attorneys' fees.

By and large, statutes have treated settlement as a subject for permissive rather than mandatory indemnity. Occasionally, however, some courts have mistaken settlements for at least partial victory. As mentioned earlier, this occurred in *Merritt-Chapman*. It also occurred in *Waltuch*. The court in *Waltuch* concluded that Waltuch had been successful when, as part of a settlement in which the ContiCommodity paid a substantial sum, the plaintiffs agreed to dismiss the claims against Waltuch as well as ContiCommodity. Perhaps one might defend the result in *Waltuch* on the grounds that Waltuch did not agree to the settlement of the private claims and might have preferred to seek vindication by litigating—albeit Waltuch's agreeing to a plea bargain of the government prosecution renders this improbable.

Now let us look at permissive indemnity following a settlement. One proposition seems easy enough. There is no reason to treat the situation any worse than if the official lost the action. Hence, to the extent the statute allows indemnity for losing officials, the statute also should allow indemnity in the case of settlement. Indemnity statutes follow this principle. Indemnity will be at least as permissible in the case of settlement as it will be when the official loses.

The difficult question is whether we should treat settlements more favorably than losing as far as indemnity. Indemnity statutes might do this in either of two ways.

To begin with, the statute might differentiate between a settlement and an adjudication of liability when it comes to asking whether the official's conduct met the requirements for permissive indemnity—in other words, did the official act in good faith, etc. As we discussed above, indemnity statutes, at least in the context of actions by third parties,

---

22. See § 4.3.7 *supra.*

generally do not treat an adjudication of liability, in itself, as showing that the official's action disqualifies the official from receiving indemnity. Still, even if the judgment itself does not preclude indemnity, specific findings which underlie the judgment might make it very difficult for anyone to conclude that the official's conduct met the requirements for permissive indemnity. In contrast, a settlement presumably leaves the appropriateness of the official's conduct unresolved. Moreover, as discussed above, an adjudication of liability *in favor of the corporation* makes it far more difficult under many statutes for the official to obtain permissive indemnity. For instance, the official may need a court determination that, despite his or her loss, indemnity is still fair and reasonable under the circumstances. The indemnity statutes, by and large, do not impose the same constraints in the case of a settlement of an action on behalf of the corporation.

The second way in which statutes might differentiate between settling and losing a suit is with respect to what expenses the corporation may indemnify. For example, Delaware does not allow the corporation to indemnify amounts which a corporate official paid to the corporation by virtue of a judgment in the corporation's favor. Delaware's statute, however, allows indemnity of amounts paid to the corporation under a settlement.[23]

Do either of these two potential differences in the availability of indemnity for officials who settle rather than lose make sense? Allowing the corporation to indemnify an official for the very sum which the corporation just recovered under a settlement clearly does not make sense. Hence, the Model Act is an improvement over Delaware in refusing to allow such indemnity.[24] Allowing officials to avoid adverse findings for purposes of indemnity by settling is more problematic. Here is where the tension between the worry about collusive settlements versus the desire not to deter settlements comes into play. Perhaps we can best mitigate this tension by returning to the distinction between actions by outsiders and actions on behalf of the corporation. Given the potential for collusion in actions on behalf of the corporation, as well as the fact that it seems strange for the corporation to pay expenses incurred in a less than successful defense against its own legal claim, perhaps there should be adverse inferences drawn from a settlement of an action on behalf of the corporation.

Several additional points are worth noting about indemnity statutes. Some statutes limit their reach to directors and officers,[25] while other statutes reach directors, officers, as well as employees and agents.[26] If the statute addresses only directors and officers, then court decisions under agency law presumably govern the rights of employees and agents to indemnity.[27]

23. Del. Gen. Corp. Law § 145(b).
24. M.B.C.A. § 8.51(d)(1).
25. *E.g.*, M.B.C.A. §§ 8.51–8.56.
26. *E.g.*, Del. Gen. Corp. Law § 145.
27. *E.g.*, M.B.C.A. § 8.58(e).

Naturally, a corporate official cannot seek indemnity for expenses from just any litigation in which the official might become a defendant. The official must become a defendant "by reason of the fact that" he or she was a corporate official.[28] Occasionally, courts must resolve whether an official seeking indemnity became a defendant by virtue of his or her job. For example, in *Heffernan v. Pacific Dunlop GNB Corp,*[29] the court faced the question of whether Heffernan, who had been a director as well as the owner of 6.7 percent of the corporation's stock, was eligible for indemnity when a party, who purchased a controlling amount of stock in the corporation (including Heffernan's 6.7 percent), sued Heffernan for securities fraud. The court held that there was at least a factual issue as to whether the suit arose out of Heffernan's position, rather than just his personal dealings in stock. Specifically, the purchaser claimed that it was Heffernan's status as a director which put Heffernan in a position to know of the facts which the purchaser alleged Heffernan failed to disclose to the purchaser. Moreover, Heffernan's sale of his stock was part of a broader deal—which involved the corporation—whereby the party who later claimed fraud bought a controlling interest in the corporation.

Finally, indemnity statutes commonly allow the corporation to advance to the company's officials the sums necessary to pay the official's legal expenses.[30] True, before resolution of the litigation, we cannot know if the officials will be entitled to indemnity for their legal costs. Yet, if the corporation does not advance the sums, an official may have a difficult time affording a defense. The official must repay these advances if he or she later turns out not to be entitled to indemnity.

4.4.2 *Insurance*

Corporations commonly purchase insurance covering directors' and officers' liabilities (often called "D & O" insurance). Such a policy typically covers two types of claims. First, the policy commonly reimburses the corporation for the corporation's costs of indemnifying the corporation's officers and directors. In addition, the policy typically reimburses directors and officers for expenses and liabilities for which the directors and officers do not obtain indemnity from the corporation. Indeed, corporation statutes often expressly empower a corporation to purchase insurance to cover directors' and officers' liabilities, whether or not the corporation legally could indemnify the directors or officers for those liabilities.[31]

In an era when liability insurance is not only widespread, but sometimes legally required (for driving and in some professions), the notion of corporations purchasing D & O policies seems inoffensive. Admittedly, as discussed earlier in dealing with the duty of care, there is a certain circularity to a corporation purchasing an insurance policy

28. *E.g.,* Del. Gen. Corp. Law § 145(a), (b).

29. 965 F.2d 369 (7th Cir.1992).

30. *E.g.,* M.B.C.A. § 8.53.

31. *E.g.,* M.B.C.A. § 8.57.

which will fund a director's or officer's liability to the corporation itself. Yet, the same is true of malpractice insurance for professionals. Ultimately, it is the patients or clients who pay for a professional's malpractice insurance through the fees the professional charges.

One common problem with insurance is that of "moral hazard"—in other words, the presence of insurance leading to the creation of the loss insured against. If policies could reimburse corporations for fines imposed to deter wrongful conduct, or could reimburse directors or officers either for such fines or for sums wrongfully acquired from the corporation (for instance, in unfair conflict-of-interest transactions), there would be a serious moral hazard problem. For this reason, both insurance law and insurance policies exclude coverage for items such as fines or the obligation to repay sums wrongfully obtained.

Chapter V

SPECIAL PROBLEMS OF CLOSELY HELD CORPORATIONS

[Research References]

> AmJur 2d, Corporations §§ 2243–2502, 2566–2586
> CJS, Corporations §§ 14, 328, 344, 760
> ALR Index: Deadlock; Majority and Minority Stockholders; Voting Trusts
> ALR Digest: Corporations §§ 228, 240, 241
> Am Jur Legal Forms 2d, Corporations §§ 74:1431–74:1464
> Am Jur Pleading and Practice Forms (Rev), Corporations §§ 265, 283, 307.1, 315, 316, 340, 369
> 45 POF3d 1, Grounds for Disregarding the Corporate Entity and Piercing the Corporate Veil
> 2 POF2d 1, Valuation of Stock of Closely Held Corporations
> 28 POF 65

In discussing choice of business form in Chapter I, we noted that corporate law governance and exit rules work well for corporations with numerous, widely scattered shareholders. In the widely held corporation, it makes sense to limit the shareholders' role in governance largely to the election of directors who will manage the corporation, to provide for majority rule, and to follow a free-transfer approach to deal with the departure of existing shareholders. These rules, however, can lead to problems when the corporation has only small number of shareholders—in other words, when the corporation is closely held.[1] These problems, and their possible solutions, are the subject matter of this chapter.

§ 5.1 Judicial and Statutory Remedies for Shareholder Dissension

In a widely held corporation, it is generally not necessary for the shareholders to get along with each other; indeed, shareholders in a widely held corporation typically do not even know who most of their

---

1. This book uses the term "closely held corporation" to refer to corporations with few shareholders. Many courts and writers also refer to such corporations as "close corporations." A number of state corporation statutes, including in such important jurisdictions as Delaware and California, however, use the term "close corporation" to refer to closely held corporations which elect special treatment under the statute. To avoid confusion, this book sticks to the term closely held corporation to describe the generic corporation with few shareholders, and only uses the term close corporation to describe corporations which elect special treatment under these statutes.

fellow shareholders are. This works because the shareholders' role in governing the widely held corporation normally consists only of voting for individuals to serve as directors and voting to approve occasional transactions. Moreover, if a shareholder in a widely held corporation does not like what is going on with the company, he or she generally has the remedy of selling his or her shares in public trading markets.

Things change in the corporation with few shareholders. To use the simplest example, suppose a corporation has only two shareholders.[1] It would be extraordinarily rare for the only two shareholders of a corporation to elect a bunch of strangers to the board of directors, while the two shareholders content themselves with a management role limited to the approval of occasional transactions. Instead, the two shareholders normally will elect themselves (and possibly some cronies) to the board, so that the two shareholders manage the company. Under these circumstances, what happens if the two shareholders do not get along with each other? Generally speaking, this depends upon the division of voting stock between the two shareholders. One possibility is that each shareholder has 50 percent of the stock. In this case, if the two shareholders cannot get along, there is the potential for deadlock. The alternate possibility is for one shareholder to own more voting stock than the other—in other words, we have a majority and a minority shareholder. Under traditional norms of corporate governance, the majority shareholder generally will have his or her way in running the company. As a result, if the minority shareholder does not get along with the majority shareholder, the minority shareholder may become the victim of what is often referred to as a squeeze-out. In a squeeze-out, the majority owner(s) uses the majority's control over the corporation to deprive the minority shareholder of any say in management, and, of more practical importance, to deprive the minority shareholder of any distribution of the business' earnings. Nor will a disenchanted minority shareholder have the same escape available to those who own shares in a widely traded company, as there typically is no outside buyer for this shareholder's stock. After all, who would want to be a minority shareholder at the mercy of a majority owner who already has stomped on one minority shareholder? The situation is little different in the corporation with three, four or any small number of shareholders—except that there is less potential for a deadlock between two equal shareholders (unless there are two equal shareholder factions)—and there is more potential for minority shareholders to face a squeeze-out either by a majority shareholder or a majority faction.

Trapped in such a dysfunctional corporate marriage, equal and minority shareholders often turn to the courts for relief. This section will consider the two principal avenues for such relief.

§ 5.1

1. We do not need to worry about shareholder dissension if a corporation has only one shareholder—at least barring a psychiatric problem involving multiple personalities.

5.1.1 *Fiduciary Duty Claims*

As just stated, one of the primary dangers facing the minority shareholder in a closely held corporation is that he or she will end up as the victim of a squeeze-out. The facts in *Wilkes v. Springside Nursing Home, Inc.*[2] provide a good illustration of a classic squeeze-out. In *Wilkes*, four individuals set up a corporation to operate a nursing home. The four individuals became equal shareholders (each owning 10 shares of stock), elected themselves directors, and divided responsibilities for running the business among themselves. The corporation declared no dividends, but paid equal amounts to the owners as compensation for work performed. Years after the corporation's founding, a falling out occurred between its owners. As a result, three of the owners, acting as directors, cut off the compensation which the fourth, Wilkes, received for working in the business. Soon thereafter, the three other owners, acting as shareholders, did not reelect Wilkes either to the board of directors or as an officer of the corporation. Instead, the three informed Wilkes that they no longer desired either his services or his presence. The end result was to prevent Wilkes from having any say in running the company, and, given that the directors never declared a dividend, to render Wilkes' investment virtually worthless.

This pattern, with variations, has repeated itself countless times among the owners of closely held corporations: The majority shareholder(s) vote a minority shareholder off the board of directors, thereby preventing the minority shareholder from having a voice in making management decisions. Of generally more practical significance, the majority shareholder(s), acting as directors—or occasionally, as in *Wilkes*, as shareholders—fire the minority shareholder from his or her employment with the corporation. Many times, however, other events account for the minority shareholder not working for the company. For example, a minority shareholder might voluntarily retire from employment with the corporation. Or, in many cases, the minority shareholder facing a squeeze-out never worked for the corporation, but, instead, received his or her shares as a result of the death or divorce of a shareholder who worked for the company. In any event, the failure to work for the company frequently deprives the minority shareholder of most or all income from the business. This is because of the extraordinarily common practice of closely held corporations distributing the bulk, if not all, of their income to their owners through salaries rather than dividends. Two factors explain this practice. First, there is a significant tax advantage to payments made as a salary rather than as a dividend— specifically, salaries provide the corporation with a income tax deduction,[3] whereas dividends do not. The second factor is psychological: Individuals running a closely held business often are likely to attribute the earnings of the business to their work. Hence, the result we see in

---

2. 370 Mass. 842, 353 N.E.2d 657 (1976).

3. This assumes that the salary constitutes reasonable compensation for work performed and is not simply a disguised dividend. *See, e.g.,* I.R.C. § 162(a)(1).

Wilkes: The board votes to declare little or no dividends, while the majority continues to receive money from the corporation through salaries and perquisites. Ultimately, the minority shareholder may sell out at a bargain price to the majority.

Wilkes asserted two possible causes of action against the defendant shareholders: breach of an alleged partnership agreement, and breach of fiduciary duty—which illustrates that fiduciary duty claims are often the last refuge of aggrieved parties who cannot think of any more specific causes of action to assert. The chapter of this book dealing with the duties of directors and officers explored fiduciary duties of directors, officers, and even controlling shareholders at some length. Under the traditional analysis of the duties of care and loyalty detailed in that chapter, Wilkes' fiduciary duty claim faced an uphill battle.

To begin with, under a traditional approach, it is necessary to divide the majority's actions into those undertaken in their role as shareholders, and those undertaken as directors (or by controlling the actions of directors). With respect to the actions undertaken solely as shareholders—specifically, voting for directors, and, in *Wilkes*, voting for corporate officers—the majority traditionally has little duty at all.[4] In other words, under a traditional view of fiduciary duties in the corporate context, shareholders can vote for whomever they want, no matter how irrational or disloyal the vote,[5] and there is no relief for a minority shareholder squeezed out of any say in corporate affairs.

By contrast, the actions the majority took in their role as directors are subject to duties of care and loyalty. These actions include the refusal to declare dividends, terminating Wilkes' compensation—or, in the normal case in which directors appoint officers, terminating a minority shareholder's employment—and authorizing continued, or even increased, compensation for the majority shareholders. Yet, even here, Wilkes, or any other minority shareholder facing similar actions, has a difficult row to hoe. The actions which most directly impact Wilkes—cutting off his compensation (or, in the case in which directors terminate the minority shareholder's employment, this termination) and the failure to declare dividends—do not, on their face, involve a conflict-of-interest transaction between the majority owners and the corporation. Hence, under the business judgment rule, courts would apply a highly deferential level of review; for example, they might require that the complaining shareholder prove the board's decision was in bad faith or irrational.[6] Indeed, as discussed when addressing the subject of dividends in an earlier chapter of this book, it will take fairly extraordinary facts before a court would find that directors breached their duty by not declaring a dividend.[7] Moreover, since the directors' duty runs to the

---

4. *E.g.*, Hall v. Hall, 506 S.W.2d 42 (1974).

5. One arguable caveat involves the election of persons who the shareholders know will loot the corporation—a subject

addressed when discussing the sale of corporate control later in this book.

6. *E.g.*, Gottfried v. Gottfried, 73 N.Y.S.2d 692 (Sup. Ct. 1947).

7. See § 2.3.1 *supra*.

corporation and to the shareholders as a group, the minority shareholder who tries to argue that directors breached their duty of care by firing him or her, would need to show more than that there was no legitimate cause for the termination. Instead, the minority shareholder would need to show the decision was irrational from the perspective of the corporation's (or the overall group of shareholders') interest—in other words, that he or she was irreplaceable. This would be pretty well impossible if the corporation flourishes before the matter can reach trial.

Of course, the majority owners' receipt of salaries and perquisites from the corporation involves conflict-of-interest transactions, and, without disinterested approval, the majority bears the burden of proving what they received was fair. Hence, the strongest claim under a traditional fiduciary duty analysis for a squeezed-out shareholder such as Wilkes lies in challenging compensation or other benefits received by the majority from the corporation. Still, courts find a substantial range of compensation to be fair.[8] Moreover, such a challenge does not put any dollars in the minority shareholder's pocket, but, instead, at best operates to give the squeezed-out shareholder leverage in negotiating with the majority.

Fortunately for Wilkes, the Massachusetts Supreme Court did not follow this traditional analysis of fiduciary duty in the corporate context. Instead, the court applied an expanded concept of fiduciary duty ostensibly based upon the notion that shareholders in a closely held corporation owe to each other a fiduciary duty akin to that owed between partners. In the context of a squeeze-out, the court held that this duty requires the majority to show a corporate purpose for actions detrimental to the minority. If there is such a legitimate purpose, then the minority can attempt to prove that the majority could achieve this purpose in a less harmful manner.

The difference between the traditional approach and the court's holding in *Wilkes* is dramatic. The court was willing to review the failure to reelect Wilkes as a corporate officer, and even as a director, despite the fact that these were actions taken solely in the role of shareholders. Moreover, the court placed the burden on the defendants to show a legitimate business purpose for their failure to vote for Wilkes—for example, that Wilkes had engaged in misconduct or was a disruptive individual bent on injuring the corporation. The end result appears to be that majority shareholders in a closely held corporation cannot, without good cause, vote against reelecting a minority shareholder to the board. Similarly, if majority shareholders in a closely held corporation act in their roles as directors to terminate the corporation's employment of a minority shareholder, under *Wilkes*, their action is not entitled to deference under the business judgment rule. Moreover, it will not be necessary for the minority shareholder to show any harm to the corpora-

---

8. *E.g.*, Cookies Food Products, Inc. v.   447 (Iowa 1988).
Lakes Warehouse Distrib., Inc., 430 N.W.2d

tion (or the shareholders generally) from the board's decision to fire him or her as an employee. Taking *Wilkes* at face value, it would appear that directors might not be able to fire a minority shareholder from corporate employment without good cause—albeit, we shall develop a significant qualifier on this conclusion shortly. Finally, apparently under *Wilkes,* it might be up to the directors to justify their refusal to declare dividends, rather than up to the complaining shareholder to show that things had reached such an extreme state that the failure to declare dividends amounted to an abuse of discretion.

Where did the court in *Wilkes* get the notion of an expanded fiduciary duty for shareholders in a closely held corporation? In fact, the Massachusetts Supreme Court had announced this rule two years earlier in its ground-breaking decision in *Donahue v. Rodd Electrotype Co.*[9] *Donahue* did not involve the sort of dramatic squeeze-out found in *Wilkes*. The problem was more subtle. There had been two shareholders of the corporation—an 80 percent shareholder (Rodd) and a 20 percent shareholder (Donahue)—both of whom had worked for the company. Donahue died, leaving his stock to his wife and son. As Rodd grew old, he gave most of his stock to his three children, bringing in his two sons to run the company. The transaction which led to the lawsuit involved the corporation's purchase of most of Rodd's remaining shares so that he could retire.[10] Donahue's widow and son complained when the corporation refused to purchase their shares on the same terms as it purchased the shares owned by Rodd. The trial court dismissed the widow and son's case. Because this was a conflict-of-interest transaction, implicit in the trial court's action was a finding that the transaction was fair to the corporation. Indeed, the price reflected book and liquidating value and did not appear to be excessive. Nevertheless, the Massachusetts Supreme Court reversed. The Supreme Court held that the Rodd family breached their duty by obtaining corporate benefits—the money obtained by selling Rodd's stock to the corporation—not shared with the minority. This duty of equal opportunity, in turn, according to the court, flowed from the court's broader holding that shareholders in a closely held corporation owe to each other substantially the same fiduciary duty as partners owe to each other.[11]

9. 367 Mass. 578, 328 N.E.2d 505 (1975).

10. The Rodd family structured the transaction so that any two of Rodd's three children together owned a majority of the outstanding stock. In this manner, the family avoided the possibility of Donahue's widow and son later allying with a disaffected sibling to take control away from most of the family.

11. As part of this holding, the court in *Donahue* set out a three-part definition of a "close" corporation: (1) a small number of shareholders; (2) no ready market for the

stock; and (3) substantial majority shareholder participation in management. In fact, however, this exercise in defining a close corporation is largely a waste of time. The small number of shareholders is the factor which we have referred to as rendering the corporation closely held. The lack of a ready market for the stock, and the majority shareholder(s)' substantial participation in management, are simply corollaries which normally follow as a practical matter from the small number of shareholders.

Why should shareholders in a closely held corporation owe to each other the same fiduciary duties as partners owe to each other, or have any other fiduciary obligations greater than imposed in a widely held corporation? The facts in *Wilkes* illustrate one possible reason. The parties there originally intended to form a partnership, but were talked out of this by their attorney, who recommended incorporation in order to limit liability to creditors. There is no indication that the parties intended to change the rules of fiduciary duty between themselves based upon this decision. Indeed, it is questionable whether most individuals who form closely held corporations intend by choosing the corporate form to change the rules of fiduciary duty from what they would have been in a partnership—or even realize that this is the impact of their decision.[12] Of course, this does not say that most parties forming a closely held business would choose partnership fiduciary duty rules—even if they chose to form a partnership. Moreover, a number of rules, beyond simply limited liability for the owners, change when forming a corporation rather than a partnership. Still, one must ask why fiduciary duty rules for closely held firms should be different based upon a choice of entity which never took this difference into account (often because this difference is not as transparent as most of the other differences between corporations and partnerships).

In addition, the *Donahue* opinion emphasized the inadequacy of traditional corporate fiduciary duty rules to protect the minority shareholder in a closely held corporation from a squeeze-out. One might say this is the minority shareholder's tough luck, if there is a sound reason the traditional rule's failure to protect such a shareholder. In fact, however, the justifications for the traditional corporate fiduciary duty principles seem geared to a model of a firm with larger numbers of passive owners who delegate management. In the widely held corporation, attempting to impose a duty upon how the shareholders vote their stock is unworkable. Also, in the widely held corporation, board decisions on dividends and termination of employment typically do not present a danger of significantly shifting the financial benefits of the corporation from one set of shareholders to another. Hence, in the widely held corporation context, rules which refuse to impose on shareholders any duties in voting their stock, and which generally give deference to board decisions on dividends and termination of employment, make sense. Looking at the situation in *Wilkes*, however, shows that the assumptions justifying the traditional approach do not apply in a closely held corporation. It was not difficult for the court to inquire into the justifications for three shareholders refusing to reelect Wilkes as a director and officer. Moreover, the effect of terminating Wilkes and not declaring dividends was to shift more of the benefits of corporate ownership to the three defendant shareholders. This benefit to the majority, combined with the personal animosities which precipitated the squeeze-out in *Wilkes*, sug-

---

12. Recall that fiduciary duty was not a factor discussed in Chapter I of this book when outlining the considerations most per- sons look to in choosing between business entities.

gest that the underlying assumptions for deference under the business judgment rule did not apply to the board decisions in *Wilkes*.

Not all jurisdictions subscribe to the notion of an expanded duty between shareholders in a closely held corporation. Indeed, the Delaware Supreme Court rejected such a duty in a case fairly similar to *Donahue*. In *Nixon v. Blackwell*,[13] the Delaware Supreme Court faced a challenge brought by a number of non-employee shareholders of a closely held corporation to actions which provided liquidity for the employee shareholders of the company. Essentially, through the corporation's operation of an employee stock ownership plan and maintenance of key man life insurance policies, the employee shareholders were able to cash out their interests in the corporation upon death or retirement. By contrast, the non-employee shareholders lacked any market to sell their stock (except for occasional offers by the corporation). The trial court held that providing liquidity for the employee shareholders, while not providing similar liquidity for the non-employee shareholders, constituted a breach of fiduciary duty. The Delaware Supreme Court, however, reversed. In so doing, the Delaware Supreme Court specifically rejected the idea that there should be special judicially created rules to protect minority shareholders in a closely held corporation.

In fact, however, in its analysis of the factual situation before the court, *Nixon* may not be as far removed from *Wilkes* as it might appear from the court's broad statements about special rules for closely held corporations. Because the challenged actions constituted conflict-of-interest transactions, the court recognized that the defendants had to prove the actions were fair. The court found that the actions were fair, not only to the corporation, but also to the non-employee shareholders. In so finding, the court pointed to corporate purposes for repurchasing the employee shareholders' stock upon death or retirement—these being to encourage valuable employees to stay with the corporation and to avoid shares falling into the hands of strangers. Hence, the defendants in *Nixon* did prove a legitimate business purpose for their actions, as would have been called for under *Wilkes*. Moreover, to the extent that the Delaware Supreme Court did not examine whether there were less harmful alternatives—for example, how much burden would it be on the company also to repurchase the non-employee shareholders' stock upon death?—there were special facts in the case. Specifically, the court attached great significance to the fact that the corporation was following the practice set up by the founder of the company—who desired to preserve control in the company's employees following his death—while the plaintiffs only had obtained their shares by a succession of inheritance and gifts of stock originally owned by the founder. Nevertheless, one should not underestimate the significance of *Nixon's* rejection of special fiduciary duty rules for closely held corporations. As discussed above, in the classic squeeze-out situation, the traditional approach will

13. 626 A.2d 1366 (Del.1993).

not apply a fairness test to the conduct most prejudicial to the minority shareholder.

The court in *Nixon* based its rejection of special fiduciary duty rules in closely held corporations upon two arguments: the fact that minority shareholders can protect themselves through contract or various other corporate control devises, and the court's view that special close corporation legislation in Delaware preempts the field of special rules for closely held corporations. How persuasive are these arguments? We shall discuss Delaware's special close corporation legislation later in this chapter. Suffice it for now to say that little in the statute addresses the subject of fiduciary duty between shareholders in a closely held corporation, and nothing in the statute expressly preempts the courts from recognizing the special problems in closely held corporations when determining the fiduciary duties of the participants in such companies.[14] Of more general relevance is the court's argument that minority shareholders ought to protect themselves by contracting or the use of various other corporate control techniques (which we will describe later in this chapter). Essentially, the argument is that if minority shareholders do not protect themselves, why should courts bail them out. On the other hand, once we start down this road, we might end up asking why have fiduciary duty rules at all; why not require corporations and their shareholders to contract for duties of care and loyalty if they wish protection?

Still, it is useful to ask why the plaintiffs in *Nixon* did not contract for protections. The answer, as the court itself recognized, is because the plaintiffs received their shares through a process of inheritance and gift, and, hence, never were in a position in which they could bargain for the terms under which they would invest. Indeed, shareholder dissension and squeeze-outs often arise in situations in which shares have passed on to new shareholders by virtue of death, gift or even divorce.[15] Such events introduce into the closely held corporation the sort of shareholders who will not obtain income from salaries and, accordingly, are upset with the common no-dividend policies of a closely held corporation. This, in part, is probably why the founder in *Nixon* established the policies of seeking to repurchase the employee shareholders' stock upon death or retirement. In recognizing, but disregarding, the impossibility of self-protection through contract for those who obtain shares by gift or inheritance, the Delaware Supreme Court seems almost to take a "you get what you pay for" attitude. A more subtle view is that the party who obtains stock by inheritance or gift takes what the donor chose to give— after all, the person who originally bought the shares could have negotiated for protection which would run to donees. Of course, this requires a fair amount of prescience on the part of the original shareholder, while a major justification for fiduciary duty rules is that the law cannot expect

14. About all the statute does in regard to fiduciary duty is to state that shareholders who control the actions of directors pick up the potential liabilities of directors. See § 5.2.2*b infra.*

15. O'Neal & Thompson, O'Neal's Oppression of Minority Shareholders § 2.01 et. seq. (2d ed. 1985) (providing a comprehensive list of the causes of squeeze-outs).

458 SPECIAL PROBLEMS OF CORPORATIONS Ch. 5

individuals to anticipate all of the circumstances in which they should have contracted for protection from abuse.

In any event, it is one thing to decide to apply more expansive concepts of fiduciary duty to shareholders in closely held corporations, it is another to answer the question of what the duty should entail. *Donahue* called for substantially the same duty as partners owe to each other, which is a duty of "utmost good faith and loyalty." Yet, what does a duty of utmost good faith and loyalty mean? In fact, the parameters of the fiduciary duties owed by partners to each other have been a subject of considerable controversy and uncertainty.[16] Moreover, it turns out that fiduciary duty rules are not the significant rules which curb squeeze-outs in partnerships. Rather, the default rules under the Uniform Partnership Act go far to prevent the problem. Specifically, barring contrary agreement, all partners are entitled to participate in management, and no partner is entitled to compensation for services to the partnership (other than through his or her share of the profits).[17] Hence, if the *Wilkes* case involved a partnership, unless Wilkes had agreed in the partnership contract, a majority of partners legally could not have deprived Wilkes of a say in running the business or paid themselves salaries while depriving Wilkes of any compensation. Similarly, had the buy-out of one owner's interest in *Donahue* occurred in a partnership, the transaction arguably would have tripped the Uniform Partnership Act default rule allowing a majority of partners to decide only matters of ordinary business, while requiring unanimous approval for any act which would contravene the partnership agreement.[18] This would have allowed the Donahues to withhold consent to the buy-out of the elder Rodd's interest unless the firm also met their demand for a buy-out. All told, in coming up with an equal opportunity rule, or the requirement of a legitimate business purpose, the court in *Donahue* and *Wilkes* was not really applying partnership fiduciary duty rules (nor, for that matter, was the court applying partnership law default rules). The court was simply making up rules as it went along.

Looking at these two rules, *Donahue's* equal opportunity rule is more difficult to defend than *Wilkes'* business purpose requirement. After all, a rigorous demand that shareholders receive an equal opportunity to obtain all of the benefits of corporate ownership might lead to questionable results. For example, termination of one shareholder from employment, when all of the other shareholders are employed, would be a denial of an equal opportunity to receive earnings from the corporation in the form of a salary. Yet, if a shareholder gives cause for the termination of his or her employment by the company, it seems unreasonable to deny the majority the ability to fire the nonperforming shareholder-employee.[19] It is not surprising then that the Massachusetts

---

16. An effort to codify the fiduciary duties of partners toward each other in the recently promulgated Revised Uniform Partnership Act has created so much resistance that few states so far have adopted the Act.

17. U.P.A. § 18(e), (f).

18. *Id* at § 18(h).

19. Of course, one might argue that retaining all shareholders in employment unless a shareholder gives cause for his or her

Supreme Court expressly backed off of a broader reading of *Donahue* in the *Wilkes* decision. Indeed, perhaps if the court had decided *Donahue* after *Wilkes*, the court might have inquired into the financial burden on the corporation to purchase shares from the Donahue's widow and son on the same terms offered to Rodd. Had the purchase of Rodd's shares served an important corporate purpose—which presumably was the case given the trial court's finding that this transaction was fair to the corporation—and the corporation been unable to afford to extend the same opportunity to all shareholders, then, if *Donahue* came after *Wilkes*, the court might not have found a breach of duty. Given the utility of buy-outs—for example to avoid dissension—and the possible limited liquidity of many small businesses, this more flexible standard seems appropriate.[20]

In contrast to the equal opportunity rule, the rule adopted by the court in *Wilkes*—requiring the majority to show a business purpose for actions harmful to the minority and allowing the minority to attempt to show less harmful alternatives—is not difficult to justify. In fact, in many instances, one almost could arrive at this point under traditional doctrine by expanding the concept of a conflict-of-interest to fit the realities of a closely held corporation. Specifically, as pointed out above, the combination of termination of employment and skimpy dividend policies serves to shift income between the minority and majority shareholders in the closely held corporation. Hence, the business judgment rule is not the appropriate standard. Once one decides to apply a fairness test to these decisions, it is but a short jump to the *Wilkes* rule.[21]

In addition, there was something of a breach of contract involved in *Wilkes*. While the court never needed to resolve Wilkes' partnership contract claim, it appears from the facts that the parties had an understanding that they would all have positions on the board, and all receive compensation from the corporation. Hence, while it might seem extreme to require a showing of cause in order to dismiss a shareholder from employment, and especially to suggest that the majority shareholder(s) must vote to keep the minority shareholder(s) on the board unless

termination is equal opportunity, but this suggests that an equal opportunity rule can become bogged down in attempting to define equal opportunity.

20. *E.g.*, Toner v. Baltimore Envelope Co., 304 Md. 256, 498 A.2d 642 (1985). On the other hand, if the typical corporate purpose for the repurchase is to avoid dissension, then one must ask why not also purchase shares from the complaining minority. Hence, the court might use a little healthy skepticism when applying *Wilkes* to corporate share repurchases. In any event, whether or not *Donahue* survives *Wilkes*, minority shareholders cannot complain about the corporation's failure to repurchase their shares in the absence of corporate purchases from the majority. Goode v.

Ryan, 397 Mass. 85, 489 N.E.2d 1001 (1986). Also, as the court noted in *Donahue*, the equal opportunity rule should not preclude purchases of only some shareholders' stock pursuant to an advance agreement among all of the shareholders for such a buy-out.

21. In fact, in many of the cases purporting to apply an expanded concept of fiduciary duty between shareholders in a closely held corporation, the court was doing little more than dealing with conventional conflict-of-interests in a conventional way. *See, e.g.*, Puritan Medical Ctr., Inc. v. Cashman, 413 Mass. 167, 596 N.E.2d 1004 (1992).

there is legitimate cause to vote differently,[22] enforcing an implied agreement between the parties goes far to justify this result. Understandings along the lines present in *Wilkes* are quite common between the shareholders of closely held corporations.

This analysis of the justification for the result in *Wilkes* suggests that one should not expect courts mechanically to apply the *Wilkes* test without sensitivity to the context which produced it. A recent Massachusetts Supreme Court decision illustrates the point. In *Merola v. Exergen Corp.*,[23] an employee, who also became a shareholder of a closely held corporation, sued after he was fired. The court held that even though the majority shareholder evidently had the corporation fire the plaintiff without cause, *Wilkes* did not apply. Essentially, this was not a situation, like *Wilkes,* in which employment with the corporation was the understood mechanism for providing income from the corporation to its shareholders. Quite the reverse: in *Merola*, the opportunity to buy stock—which the plaintiff sold back to the corporation at a very large profit—was part of the compensation the plaintiff received for being an employee.

Merola points up a broader problem in trying to reconcile *Wilkes* with employment law rules regarding the right to fire at-will employees. Traditionally, courts have held that employers can fire at any time, with or without cause, employees who have no express or implied agreement for employment to continue for a specified term. Various jurisdictions have qualified this rule in differing degrees. For example, most courts will hold that firing an employee for refusing to break the law gives even an at-will employee a claim for wrongful discharge.[24] More broadly, courts in some jurisdictions have held that the implied covenant of good faith and fair dealing tempers the right to fire an at-will employee at any time, with or without cause.[25] Other courts, however, have refused to recognize such a good-faith limit on the right to terminate an at-will employee.[26] To the extent that courts in a state impose a broadly conceived obligation of good faith and fair dealing as a qualifier on the right of an employer to fire at-will employees, then there may not be too great a conflict if the court applies the *Wilkes* test to the termination of a shareholder from an at-will employment with the corporation. After all, the termination, without cause, of a shareholder from corporate employment might both establish a breach of fiduciary duty toward the individual in his or her role as shareholder, and establish a breach of the requirement of good faith toward the individual as an employee. On the other hand, in a jurisdiction which rejects (or narrowly defines) a good-

22. After all, the mere fact that the small number of shareholders in a closely held corporation makes a review of the reasons behind shareholder votes practical, does not state why the court should review such reasons.

23. 423 Mass. 461, 668 N.E.2d 351 (1996).

24. *E.g.*, Tameny v. Atlantic Richfield Co., 27 Cal.3d 167, 610 P.2d 1330, 164 Cal.Rptr. 839 (1980).

25. *E.g.*, Gates v. Life of Mont. Ins. Co., 196 Mont. 178, 638 P.2d 1063 (1982).

26. *E.g.*, Murphy v. American Home Prods. Corp., 58 N.Y.2d 293, 448 N.E.2d 86, 461 N.Y.S.2d 232 (1983).

faith limit on the right to terminate at-will employees, allowing terminated employees, who are also shareholders, to sue claiming breach of
fiduciary duty, risks enabling some terminated employees to make an
end run around the at-will nature of their employment agreement.

Courts have reached different results in attempting to reconcile a
recognition of expanded fiduciary duties between shareholders in closely
held corporations, with the right of employers to terminate at-will
employees. The problem has come up particularly when a shareholder-
employee is a party to a contract which gives the corporation (or other
shareholders) the option to buy his or her shares at a set price following
termination of employment. If the price set by this agreement is significantly less than the value of the shares, there may be a temptation to
fire the shareholder-employee for the purpose of forcing the sale. The
New York Court of Appeals has taken a hard line in favor of an
unrestrained right to fire the shareholder-employee even under these
circumstances. In *Ingle v. Glamore Motor Sales*,[27] and *Gallagher v.
Lambert*,[28] the court held that the unqualified right to fire an at-will
employee trumps the claim of the employee as a shareholder for breach
of fiduciary duty. Actually, one might argue that if the purpose of the
firing was to force the sale of stock at a below market price, then the
firing would violate contractual notions of good faith and fair dealing,
even if courts understandably do not wish to equate good faith with a
requirement of good cause for the firing. Indeed, some courts have held
that deliberately firing an employee just before sales commissions become due, or pension rights vest, constitutes the sort of effort to prevent
a party from enjoying the benefits of a contract which is the most
elementary breach of the obligation of good faith.[29] Hence, in this
situation, there really is not a conflict between contract law principles
which ought to be applicable to employees generally, and corporate law
fiduciary rules governing shareholders in a closely held corporation.[30]
Nevertheless, the New York court rejected both fiduciary duty and good
faith claims in this context. Courts in other jurisdictions, by contrast,
have gone so far as to be willing to recognize the claim made in the role
as a shareholder, even when they would not recognize the claim made in
the role as employee.[31]

27. 73 N.Y.2d 183, 538 N.Y.S.2d 771, 535 N.E.2d 1311 (1989).

28. 74 N.Y.2d 562, 549 N.Y.S.2d 945, 549 N.E.2d 136 (1989).

29. *E.g.*, Fortune v. National Cash Register Co., 373 Mass. 96, 364 N.E.2d 1251 (1977).

30. *See, e.g.*, King v. Driscoll, 418 Mass. 576, 638 N.E.2d 488 (1994). In a strange decision, however, the Massachusetts Supreme Court held that there could be no *Wilkes* claim when the shareholder-employee was fired pursuant to an employment agreement which provided for termination on six months notice (which then triggered an obligation of the shareholder-employee to sell his stock back to the corporation). Blank v. Chelmsford Ob/Gyn, P.C., 420 Mass. 404, 649 N.E.2d 1102 (1995). The rationale was that the contract provision allowing termination preempted any fiduciary duty claim—which is bizarre given that this rationale could cover the typical agreement to at-will employment.

31. *E.g.*, Jensen v. Christensen & Lee Ins., Inc., 157 Wis.2d 758, 460 N.W.2d 441 (App. 1990).

One final question about the expanded fiduciary duty of shareholders in closely held corporations is whether the duty applies to the actions of minority shareholders. At first glance, one might assume this question is moot, for how can minority shareholders have the power to abuse other shareholders? One easy answer is if several minority shareholders group together into a majority faction, as happened in *Wilkes* and *Donahue*. Not surprisingly, the court in *Donahue* expressly decided to treat the Rodds as a group for purposes of holding them to the duty of majority shareholders.

A less obvious potential for abuse by a minority shareholder existed in *Smith v. Atlantic Properties, Inc.*[32] There, provisions in the corporation's articles and bylaws effectively gave a minority shareholder a veto on all corporate actions. The minority shareholder used this veto to prevent the corporation from paying any dividends, with the result that the corporation ended up paying federal penalty income taxes for improperly accumulating income. The court held that the minority shareholder breached his fiduciary duty. This result may be justified by a simple notion of "what is sauce for the goose is sauce for the gander"— or how can a minority shareholder claim that the majority shareholder owes to him or her a fiduciary duty while disclaiming any duty for him- or herself? Besides, if the court is pursuing the partnership analogy, the fiduciary duty exists for all partners.[33]

One danger, however, in the *Smith* approach occurs if the court examines the minority shareholder's veto in isolation. The parties may have agreed to give minority shareholders a veto on corporate actions, not only to protect the minority shareholder from undesirable actions, but also to provide the minority shareholder ammunition to horse-trade with the majority in order to obtain desired actions. Hence, in evaluating whether the minority shareholder breached his or her duty in exercising a veto, the court should consider not only the consequences of the veto, but also the legitimacy of what the minority shareholder sought to achieve.

An additional prospect for possible abuse by minority shareholders, which has come up in a number of cases, involves the purchase of stock that makes the minority shareholder into a majority shareholder. *Zidell v. Zidell, Inc.*,[34] provides an illustration. Two half-brothers, Arnold and Emery Zidell, each owned 37½ percent of the outstanding stock in several related corporations. Jack Rosenfeld (a distant cousin on my mother's side) owned the remaining 25 percent. The plaintiff, Arnold, found out that cousin Jack was interested in selling out, and naively

32. 12 Mass.App.Ct. 201, 422 N.E.2d 798 (1981).

33. Veto powers, whose use might trigger a fiduciary duty for minority shareholders, can exist not only by virtue of shareholder agreements, but also through the operation of laws which require the cooperation of all shareholders in order to obtain desired treatment. *See, e.g.,* A.W. Chesterton Co., Inc. v. Chesterton, 128 F.3d 1 (1st Cir.1997) (minority shareholder breached his fiduciary duty by attempting to transfer his shares in a manner which would have resulted in the loss of the company's S corporation status under federal income tax law).

34. 277 Or. 423, 560 P.2d 1091 (1977).

relayed that information to Emery—who then, in effect, bought Jack's shares for himself. This gave Emery control over the corporations, which he later used to engage in a squeeze-out of Arnold. Arnold sued, asserting a number of theories, including that Emery's purchase breached Emery's duty under *Donahue*. While not rejecting *Donahue*, the Oregon court held that the fiduciary duty laid out in *Donahue* did not require Emery to have the corporation purchase Jack's shares in order to maintain the balance of power between Emery and Arnold. Other courts, however, have held that a stockholder's secretive purchase of shares upsetting the balance of power does violate the shareholder's fiduciary duty.[35] The merits of applying a fiduciary duty to prevent such purchases are that maintaining equality probably corresponds to the original expectations of the parties, and seems likely to produce less strife in the future than would allowing the balance to be upset.

5.1.2 *Dissolution and Other Statutory Remedies for Deadlock and Oppression*

Ultimately, if shareholders in a closely held corporation cannot get along, perhaps the solution is same as in any hopelessly dysfunctional marriage: the parties should get a divorce. Many times, shareholders who cannot get along reach a more or less amicable parting of the ways, as one shareholder (or group of shareholders) buys out the interest of the other shareholder(s). If the shareholders cannot reach a voluntary solution, one or more shareholders may go to court and ask for a judicially ordered corporate divorce. To drop the metaphor, the shareholder(s) will petition the court to dissolve the corporation under statutes which empower the court to undertake this action. Corporation statutes typically authorize the court to dissolve a corporation in case of deadlock, and, in most states, corporation statutes also authorize dissolution when those in control of the corporation have acted oppressively or otherwise wrongfully toward the minority shareholders. Many corporation statutes also authorize the court to order alternate remedies instead of dissolution. Before, however, exploring both the statutory grounds for dissolution, and the alternate remedies a court might order, it is useful to consider the rather vigorous policy debate which has surrounded the topic of dissolving corporations racked with dissension.

a. *Why be afraid of dissolution?*

Historically, many courts have been reluctant to dissolve corporations operating viable businesses despite hopeless dissension among the shareholders. The assumption seems to be that dissolving the corporation means destroying the business, with the result that employees will lose their jobs and the economy will be harmed. Such an assumption misunderstands the practical consequences of ordering dissolution.

In 1977, Professors Hetherington and Dooley published an important study of the consequences of corporate dissolution litigation.[36] They

35. *E.g.*, Hallahan v. Haltom Corp., 7 Mass.App.Ct. 68, 385 N.E.2d 1033 (1979).

36. J.A.C. Hetherington & Michael Dooley, *Illiquidity and Exploitation: A Proposed*

looked at all of the reported cases dealing directly or primarily with suits for involuntary dissolution between 1960 and 1977, and contacted the lawyers for the parties to find out what had happened with the corporation following the lawsuit. It turned out that in a large majority of the cases in which the court ordered dissolution, the end result simply was that defendant shareholder bought out the plaintiff shareholder (albeit, in a few cases, the plaintiff shareholder bought out the defendant). Sometimes, the business was sold to an outsider, or, in the case of service businesses, the former shareholders went into competition. The only businesses which actually were terminated following an order of dissolution were those in a barely marginal or deteriorating financial condition—in other words, businesses which were likely to fail anyway. Interestingly enough, it turned out that the most common outcome following a judicial denial of dissolution was also a buy-out of the plaintiff shareholder by the defendant shareholder. In other words, most of the time, the defendant bought out the plaintiff regardless of whether the court ordered dissolution or not. What then was the point of the litigation? Presumably, the plaintiff who was armed with a dissolution order would be in a better position when negotiating over the price.

Actually, this result should not have surprised anyone, since it corresponds with long experience in dealing with partnerships. As described in discussing choice of business entity at the beginning of this book,[37] partnerships dissolve upon the departure of any member. Nevertheless, the businesses conducted by partnerships do not come to a grinding halt every time a partner dies or demands out. Instead, typically, if the business is viable, the remaining partners will buy out the interest of the departing partner and continue the enterprise.

Given that suits for dissolution mostly end up with a buy-out anyway, Professors Hetherington and Dooley proposed that shareholders in closely held corporations have the right to force the corporation or the other shareholders to buy them out, without having to establish deadlock, oppression, or other such grounds.[38] This sort of no-fault divorce may make a good default rule in the closely held corporation context—as it is most other business forms.[39] It certainly can avoid the sort of

Statutory Solution to the Remaining Close Corporation Problem, 63 Va. L. Rev. 1 (1977).

37. See § 1.1.2*b supra.*

38. Or, under the Hetherington and Dooley proposal, if the corporation or other shareholders refuse to buy out the complaining shareholder, then the complaining shareholder would have the right to force the dissolution of the corporation.

39. See § 1.1.2*b supra.* One disadvantage of this default rule is that it can increase estate taxes for those family controlled businesses in which the owners agreed to more limited rights upon the death of an owner. This is because estate tax rules value an interest in a family controlled business for purposes of setting the estate tax at the greater of the value which the interest actually has under the governing contract, or the value which the interest would have had under state law default rules (such as a rule which gives the estate the right to cash out at fair value). Based upon this concern, there has been some move to repeal the rights of owners in limited liability companies and limited partnerships to cash out their interests. *See, e.g.,* Franklin Gevurtz, *California's New Limited Liability Company Act: A Look at the Good, the Bad, and the Ambiguous*, 27 Pac. L.J. 261, 285–286 (1996). This is an example of letting the tax tail wag the economic dog.

indeterminate "who did what to whom first" litigation which often results from requiring a showing of cause in order to obtain dissolution. Still, it seems extreme to limit, as proposed by Hetherington and Dooley, the ability of shareholders to waive the right to demand a buy-out. After all, partners can, and often do, contract around the default rule which allows partners, at will, to force either a dissolution or a buy-out.

Critics of the Hetherington and Dooley proposal have expressed concern that small businesses might not always be in a liquid position to buy out an owner whenever he or she wants.[40] Yet, the concern that shareholders might imperil illiquid businesses by inopportune demands to cash out seems overblown. If the business is truly unable to afford the demanded cash out, it would be self defeating for the departing shareholder not to try to reach an accommodation. In this regard, we should note that a helpful symmetry exists in dealing with demands by minority shareholders to cash out. The smaller the minority shareholder's interest in the corporation, the easier it is for the corporation to come up with the funds to buy the shareholder's interest. The larger the shareholder's interest, the more the shareholder has to lose by imperiling the business through unreasonable demands to cash out. Nor has experience with partnerships, or other businesses in which owners effectively can demand to cash out, established that inopportune demands to cash out are a frequent problem.

A more realistic concern is that one or more shareholders might seek dissolution of the corporation as a technique to force the other shareholder(s) to give up ownership in the company. (Forcing a shareholder to give up his or her ownership in the company is often referred to as a freeze-out.) For example, suppose a corporation has two shareholders, one of which is financially well healed, while the other is financially strapped. Following dissolution, the well healed shareholder would be a position to outbid the financially strapped shareholder to buy the company's assets and thereafter continue the business without the other shareholder. Moreover, if the bidding produces little competition, the well healed shareholder can acquire the business at much less than it is worth.[41] This prospect has led some courts to refuse to order corporate dissolution,[42] and has been a source of concern in a number of cases involving partnership dissolutions.[43]

---

40. Frank Easterbrook & Daniel Fischel, *Close Corporations and Agency Costs*, 38 Stan. L. Rev. 271 (1986).

41. This scenario assumes that market inefficiencies prevent both the strapped shareholder from obtaining outside financing, and outsiders from entering the bidding on their own. Because outsiders typically lack easily verifiable information about the financial prospects of most closely held businesses, this assumption is not unrealistic.

42. *E.g.,* Wollman v. Littman, 35 App. Div. 2d 935, 316 N.Y.S.2d 526 (1970).

43. *E.g.,* Page v. Page, 55 Cal.2d 192, 10 Cal.Rptr. 643, 359 P.2d 41 (1961). A similar problem can exist if one or more of the shareholders have an advantage which allows them to appropriate the goodwill of the company without paying for it—for example, in a personal service business, some shareholders might have advantage over other shareholders in acquiring the clients.

Still, it is difficult to say how much courts should be reluctant to order dissolution based upon a concern over freeze-outs. After all, majority shareholders have the power to dissolve the corporation, under most statutes, simply by voting for such.[44] Moreover, we shall see in the final chapter of this book that majority shareholders typically possess the ability to freeze out minority shareholders through other techniques, such as mergers. If the law allows majority shareholders to freeze out minority shareholders, what is wrong with allowing minority shareholders, if they have the financial means, from doing the same to the majority? In either event, rather than making it generally difficult to dissolve the corporation, perhaps the answer is for courts to apply the sort of fiduciary duty analysis we found in *Wilkes* to cases in which a shareholder alleges that another shareholder is using dissolution as a freeze-out tool.

A less extreme prospect is that a minority shareholder might use a demand for dissolution or a cash-out as leverage to renegotiate the way the corporation operates. This is often referred to as a hold-up problem. Of course, the difference between a "hold-up" and a reasonable demand often lies in the eye of the beholder.

b. Deadlock

As mentioned at the outset of our discussion of shareholder dissension, in the event of dissension between two 50 percent shareholders (or two 50 percent shareholder factions) there is the potential for deadlock. Such a deadlock can manifest itself on two levels: on the shareholder level with respect to the election of directors, and on the board of directors level with respect to management decisions.

With respect to the election of directors, if two 50 percent shareholders vote for entirely different candidates for the board of directors, no candidates normally will receive sufficient votes to be elected.[45] The result might be disastrous for the corporation if this meant that the corporation then had no directors. Corporation statutes, however, typically allow the old directors to remain in office until the election of new directors[46]—meaning that in case of such an election deadlock, the old

---

44. See § 7.2.2.b *infra*. While voluntary dissolution typically requires the vote of the directors, as well as the shareholders, the owner(s) of a majority of the voting stock should have little trouble convincing the directors to vote to dissolve, or else the owner(s) of a majority of the voting shares can replace recalcitrant directors with more pliable individuals.

45. Under the normal voting scheme for director elections, if the two shareholders (or shareholder factions) vote for entirely different candidates, then each candidate will receive a vote equal to 50 percent of the outstanding stock, which means that not only will no candidate receive a majority, but no candidates will receive a plurality (in

other words, there will not be a group of candidates equal to the number of positions on the board to be filled who receive more votes than any other candidates). This will preclude any individual from being elected. Later in this chapter, we will explore an alternate voting scheme—cumulative voting—which, if effectively used, would allow the each of the two shareholders (or factions) to elect half of the directors despite complete non-cooperation between the two shareholders. If the board has an odd number of directors, however, there can be a deadlock in filling the last position despite cumulative voting.

46. *E.g.*, M.B.C.A. § 8.05(e).

board will remain in power. Moreover, corporation statutes normally authorize the directors to fill vacancies on the board between elections.[47] Hence, unless all the directors die simultaneously in an airplane crash or some such event, a self-perpetuating board can continue along year after year despite a deadlock among the shareholders which prevents the election of new directors.

A board with an even number of directors sets up the potential for a deadlock on the director level. Of course, numerous corporations function perfectly well with a board containing an even number of directors. Occasionally, there may be tie votes on such a board.[48] This is not a deadlock; rather this simply means that the action proposed before the board fails for want of a majority. On the other hand, if the board with an even number of directors has crystallized into two implacably hostile factions so that virtually every motion results in a tie vote (except the always popular motion to adjourn) then we have a deadlock. At first glance, one might assume that if the board is deadlocked and cannot run the corporation, then the company soon will stop functioning. In fact, however, this generally is not what will happen. Instead, as one might recall from the discussion of corporate officers in an earlier chapter, the corporation's chief executive officer—commonly, in small corporations, the corporation's president—has the authority to make at least ordinary business decisions (which have become increasingly broadly defined) for the corporation.[49] Hence, as a practical matter, a deadlock on the board typically results in the faction which occupies the presidency controlling the corporation. For example, in *Gidwitz v. Lanzit Corrugated Box Co.*,[50] two branches of the Gidwitz family each owned 50 percent of the stock in the box company and each occupied two of the four seats on the corporation's board of directors. The family whose member held the corporation's presidency was able to run the corporation for 10 years in the face of a deadlock, until the court ordered a dissolution in response to a suit brought by the other family.

As just suggested, a deadlock can lead to a court order dissolving the corporation.[51] Most jurisdictions have provisions in their corporation statutes which allow a court to dissolve a corporation based upon the existence of a deadlock. The Model Act is fairly typical. Section 14.30(2)(iii) of the Model Act states that a court may dissolve a corporation if the shareholders are deadlocked in voting power and have failed for a period of at least two consecutive annual meeting dates to elect successors to directors whose terms have expired—in other words, if there is a shareholder deadlock which is not just a one annual election occurrence.[52] Section 14.30(2)(I) states that a court may dissolve a

---

47. *E.g.*, M.B.C.A. § 8.10(a).

48. There also can be tie votes on a board with an odd number of directors if some directors abstain or do not show up at the meeting.

49. See § 3.1.1*b supra*.

50. 20 Ill.2d 208, 170 N.E.2d 131 (1960).

51. Albeit, in *Gidwitz*, the court actually ordered dissolution because of oppression rather than deadlock.

52. The notion presumably is that an evenly divided election is not that abnormal an occurrence and often will be corrected at

corporation if the directors are deadlocked in the management of the corporation, the shareholders are unable to break the deadlock, and this deadlock either threatens irreparable injury to the corporation, or means that the business and affairs of the corporation can no longer be conducted to the advantage of the shareholders generally.

From both a policy standpoint, and in terms of applying the dissolution for deadlock statutes, the primary question is what type of harm must the deadlock cause in order to justify dissolution. As we just saw in describing the nature of a corporate deadlock, the company's business commonly can continue merrily along for years despite a deadlock. Indeed, as the court in *Gidwitz* perhaps recognized intuitively when dissolving for oppression rather than deadlock, the real interest protected in dissolving for deadlock may be that of the shareholder or faction who ends up in the de facto status of minority shareholder(s) despite owning 50 percent of the stock.

The place to begin answering the question of what harm deadlock must cause in order to justify dissolution is with the language of the statute. The language in the Model Act and similar statutes, which refers to irreparable injury to the corporation, is obviously highly demanding, and, as we have seen, commonly not met. Accordingly, it is significant that the Model Act and similar statutes specify an alternate harm, besides irreparable injury to the corporation, which can justify dissolution in case of deadlock among the directors. This is when the deadlock prevents the conduct of the corporation to the advantage of the shareholders generally (as opposed to the advantage of some shareholders). At least one court has held that this alternate harm includes a situation, such as in *Gidwitz*, in which one 50 percent faction takes over de facto control and acts in a high handed manner toward the other 50 percent faction.[53]

An even broader reach exists if the statute makes the deadlock itself grounds for dissolution, without requiring any consequential harm. In this regard, notice that the language in the Model Act requiring consequential harm is in the provision dealing with deadlock among the directors. In contrast, the Model Act provision which calls for dissolution when deadlock among the shareholders results in the failure to elect directors does not specify any consequences which the failure to elect directors must cause before the court can order a dissolution. There are a couple of possible reasons for this difference. One reason is a practical drafting concern. Failure to elect directors is a self-defining event. By comparison, if a statute makes deadlock among the board grounds for dissolution without regard to the consequences of the deadlock, then the statute (or the court) will need to define when there is a deadlock and when there are just a lot of tie votes. The other reason lies in policy. Implicit in the provision dealing with deadlock in shareholder election of directors is the notion that shareholders have a right to directors who

the next annual election, but if it repeats itself then we know we have a problem.

53. In re Hedberg–Freidheim & Co., 233 Minn. 534, 47 N.W.2d 424 (1951).

are elected for the term at hand, rather than a self-perpetuating board of holdovers. By contrast, the provision dealing with deadlock on the director level reflects the notion that there is no right to be free of a strife on the board of directors, even to the extent this means inertia sets corporate policy, unless the strife produces some harm to the corporation or the shareholders. Picking up on the distinction between the two provisions, several court opinions have ordered dissolution (or other statutory remedies) based upon the failure to elect directors, without requiring a showing that this failure produced any other harm to the corporation or the shareholders.[54]

There is an additional piece of language in the dissolution statutes which can impact what consequences it takes before a court will order dissolution because of deadlock. The Model Act, and statutes generally, state that a court "may" dissolve a corporation upon finding a shareholder or director deadlock which has the impact specified in the statute—the statutes do not say that the court must order dissolution if the specified deadlock exists. A number of courts have seized upon such discretionary language to deny dissolution. For example, in a much discussed decision, the New York Court of Appeals in *In re Radom & Neidorff, Inc.*[55] denied dissolution despite a deadlock between two 50 percent shareholders which admittedly met the criteria for ordering dissolution set forth in the New York statute (including the failure to elect new directors). The court in *Radom & Neidorff* pointed to the fact that despite the dissension, the corporation was proceeding profitably— and so what if the plaintiff (a 50 percent shareholder) was working as president of the company while the defendant (the other 50 percent shareholder, and the plaintiff's sister) blocked the corporation from paying the plaintiff any salary.[56] *Radom & Neidorff* and similar opinions have provoked critical commentary,[57] and the New York legislature

---

54. *E.g.,* Giuricich v. Emtrol Corp., 449 A.2d 232 (Del.1982) (involving appointment of custodian due to deadlock). One might ask whether the difference between these two levels of deadlock really matters: in other words, is it possible to have a director deadlock without also having a shareholder deadlock, and visa versa? In fact, it is not uncommon to have a shareholder deadlock which does not produce a deadlock on the board of directors. For example, one of two 50 percent shareholder factions may be able to seize control of what was an equally divided board by using their power as directors to fill a vacancy created by the death or resignation of a director who was part of the other faction. *E.g.,* Schwartz v. Marien, 37 N.Y.2d 487, 373 N.Y.S.2d 122, 335 N.E.2d 334 (1975). *Giuricich* involved a similar situation, in that one shareholder had filled the board with its representatives by virtue of having owned a majority of the stock, and refused to give up this control after two minority shareholders exercised options creating a 50–50 division of shares

between them and the former majority shareholder. By contrast, it is more difficult at first glance to see how there can be a director deadlock without a shareholder deadlock which prevents the election of new directors. Otherwise, one would assume that the shareholders would break the deadlock by replacing the directors. Indeed, the Model Acts only calls for dissolution in the event of director deadlock if the shareholders are unable to cure the problem. One explanation here is that cumulative voting could allow two 50 percent shareholders each to fill half the seats on an even numbered board despite complete non-cooperation between the two.

55. 307 N.Y. 1, 119 N.E.2d 563 (1954).

56. For reasons which are unclear, both shareholders had to sign corporate checks. The sister refused to sign checks to pay her brother's salary.

57. *E.g.,* Israels, *The Sacred Cow of Corporate Existence: Problems of Deadlock and Dissolution,* 19 U. Chi. L. Rev. 778

changed the statute to add a provision stating that profitable operation of the corporation is not, in itself, a ground for denying dissolution.[58] Still, in *Wollman v. Littman*,[59] a New York appellate court denied dissolution despite dissension which met the terms of the statute. In *Wollman*, however, it was not simply the lack of harm from the deadlock which provoked the court's reluctance to act. Instead, the court was concerned that the shareholder seeking dissolution was attempting to use dissolution to freeze out the other shareholder.[60]

There is one other type of statute which may allow for dissolution in case of deadlock between two 50 percent shareholders (or 50 percent shareholder factions). California's corporation statute empowers the holder(s) of at least 50 percent of the outstanding shares to dissolve the corporation simply by voting for such.[61] Under such a provision, it is not necessary for the shareholder(s) owning 50 percent to go to court and show that there is a deadlock in order to dissolve the corporation. Indeed, the owner(s) of half of the voting stock can dissolve the company under California's statute even if there is no deadlock. This creates a result very close to the Hetherington and Dooley proposal, at least for 50 percent shareholders. While no one has conducted a study of the impact of this California provision, there have been no reports of California corporations falling victim to inopportune votes for dissolution by 50 percent shareholders. Perhaps this is, in part, because California courts have qualified the right of the owners of 50 percent of the shares to dissolve the corporation. Specifically, California courts require that the shareholder(s) act in good faith for a legitimate business purpose when voting to dissolve.[62]

In our discussion of deadlock so far, we have focused on the normal deadlock between two equal shareholders (or two equal factions of shareholders). Occasionally, however, a deadlock can occur despite unequal share holdings. This can happen when agreements or supermajority vote requirements give a veto power to minority shareholders. Under most statutes, such as the Model Act, the fact that the deadlock results from a veto, rather than from an equal division of stock, is irrelevant to the court's power to order dissolution. Some statutes, however, only expressly authorize the court to order dissolution in the case of a deadlock from an equal division of stock,[63] and, hence, presumably do not cover the situation in which a veto power produces the deadlock.

(1952). *But see* Abram Chayes, *Madame Wagner and the Close Corporation*, 73 Harv. L. Rev. 1532 (1960).

58. N.Y. Bus. Corp. Law § 1111(a)(3).

59. 35 App. Div. 2d 935, 316 N.Y.S.2d 526 (1970).

60. Other courts have been less worried about one shareholder's possible use of dissolution to freeze out another shareholder. *E.g.*, Weiss v. Gordon, 32 App. Div. 2d 279, 301 N.Y.S.2d 839 (1969).

61. Cal. Corp. Code § 1900(a). By contrast, most states require a vote by both the directors and a majority of the outstanding shares in order to voluntarily dissolve a corporation. See § 7.2.2*b infra*.

62. In re Security Finance Co., 49 Cal.2d 370, 317 P.2d 1 (1957).

63. *E.g.*, Kans. Stat. Ann. § 17–6804(d).

c. *Oppression and the like*

The minority shareholder who lacks a veto and faces a squeeze-out obviously cannot seek dissolution based upon deadlock. Fortunately for such a shareholder, the corporation statutes in most jurisdictions also allow the courts to dissolve a corporation for misconduct or abuse of minority shareholders by those in control of the corporation. It is worth noting, however, that the corporation statutes of some important states, such as Delaware, do not have provisions which authorize courts to order dissolution based upon any sort of majority misconduct or abuse of the minority.[64]

The most traditional, and least useful, grounds for dissolution under these statutes speak of fraud, illegality, or misapplication or waste of assets.[65] Far more significantly, the Model Act and most states' corporation statutes also authorize dissolution in case of "oppression."[66] This, however, creates the question as to what the statutes mean by oppression.

The earlier interpretations of oppression speak in terms of wrongful conduct, violations of the duty of good faith and fair dealing, breaches of fiduciary duty, and the like.[67] In other words, under this view, the term conveys a subjective, fault oriented, standard. This is not to say, under this view, that oppression refers only to conduct which breaches the traditional duties of care and loyalty. On the contrary, in *Gidwitz*, the court concluded that abusing the power of the corporation's presidency to deprive the other 50 percent shareholder faction of any role in governing the corporation, either as shareholders or as directors, constituted oppression. Still, while the reach of oppression under this view is broader than breaches of traditional fiduciary duties, the focus remains on bad actions by the defendant(s). Moreover, the standard for measuring oppressive conduct under this approach seems to be little more than the court's gut instinct.

Courts in New York and a number of other states have developed a different test for oppression. This test looks at whether the majority's

---

64. Historically, courts in a few states have held that they can order dissolution, even without statutory authority, for gross misdeeds by those in control of the corporation. *E.g.*, Ross v. American Banana Co., 150 Ala. 268, 43 So. 817 (Ala. 1907). Most courts, however, have held that they cannot dissolve a solvent corporation in the absence of statutory authority. *E.g.*, People ex rel. Barrett v. Shurtleff, 353 Ill. 248, 187 N.E. 271 (Ill. 1933).

65. M.B.C.A. § 14.30(2)(ii), (iv). This is not to say that fraud, illegality or misapplication of assets does not occur. Moreover, as the court recognized in *Brenner v. Berkowitz*, 134 N.J. 488, 634 A.2d 1019 (1993), such misdeeds can constitute grounds for dissolution, even in the absence of oppression, and even when such actions are not

ongoing at the time of the suit. Yet, as the court in *Brenner* makes clear, the presence of such misdeeds does not per se require dissolution. Rather, the court will consider how serious the misdeeds were, how much they prejudiced the shareholder requesting dissolution, and the availability of a less drastic remedy. Given the fact that a derivative suit typically can address this sort of conduct, the presence of a less drastic remedy should preclude dissolution unless the fraud, illegality, or misapplication of assets is egregious and pervasive.

66. *E.g.*, M.B.C.A. § 14.30(2)(ii).

67. *E.g.*, Baker v. Commercial Body Builders, Inc., 264 Or. 614, 507 P.2d 387 (Or. 1973).

conduct frustrated the reasonable expectations of the minority share-holder(s) seeking dissolution.[68] This reasonable expectations test shifts the focus from a subjective, fault oriented, approach, to an approach rooted in notions of implied contract.

New York's highest court adopted this reasonable expectations test in *Matter of Kemp & Beatley, Inc.*[69] Kemp & Beatley, Inc. had eight shareholders, two of which petitioned for dissolution after they lost their employment with the corporation. (One resigned, the other was fired.) The two shareholders argued that prior to the termination of their employment, the corporation had followed a practice of awarding de facto dividends in the form of so-called extra compensation bonuses. Coinciding with the time the two shareholders ceased working for the corporation, the corporation changed its policy and began to pay the extra compensation bonuses based upon working for the company rather than owning stock. (The reader may notice the similarities to the facts in *Wilkes*.) The court held that this constituted oppression. In doing so, the court held that conduct is oppressive when the conduct defeats the reasonable expectations under which a shareholder invested. In this case, when the two petitioning shareholders bought their stock, it was understood by all the shareholders that the so-called extra compensation bonuses really amounted to payments for being shareholders, and that all of the shareholders would be entitled to these bonuses. Changing this policy, in effect, breached the implied agreement under which the petitioners bought their stock.

The court in *Kemp & Beatley* added a significant gloss to the reasonable expectations test when the court explained what it meant by a reasonable expectation. This is not simply a subjective hope which a shareholder had when deciding to invest. Rather, the expectation must be one which the majority knew or should have known that the petition-ing shareholder had at the time the petitioning shareholder bought his or her stock. Moreover, the expectation, viewed objectively, must be both reasonable and central to the petitioning shareholder's decision to in-vest. Notice the parallel between these requirements and contract law doctrines which derive from the so-called objective theory of contracts. The plaintiffs' expectation of receiving the extra compensation bonuses in *Kemp & Beatley* met these criteria, for not only was it known by all the shareholders, but it went to the very heart of how the shareholders intended to receive any return on their investment.

One problem with the reasonable expectations test as developed in *Kemp & Beatley* is that the court referred to the expectations which the complaining shareholder had at the time he or she chose to invest (in other words, bought the stock). Suppose, however, that the complaining shareholder did not purchase his or her shares, but, instead, received the

---

68. In addition to court opinions defin-ing oppression in terms of reasonable expec-tations, a couple of states expressly have included defeat of reasonable expectations as a grounds for dissolution in the states' corporation statutes. *E.g.,* Minn. Stat. § 302A.751 subd. 3a.

69. 64 N.Y.2d 63, 484 N.Y.S.2d 799, 473 N.E.2d 1173 (1984).

stock as a gift or inheritance. In fact, as we have already seen, it is quite common for dissension to arise after widows and children, who do not go to work for the corporation, receive shares from the original shareholders, and then complain when they do not receive any income from the company.

In *Meiselman v. Meiselman*,[70] the court faced the of problem of defining the reasonable expectations of a shareholder who essentially inherited his shares. The plaintiff and defendant in *Meiselman* were brothers. Their deceased father had given the defendant 70 percent of the stock in several corporations, while giving the plaintiff 30 percent. Both brothers worked for the companies until the defendant had the corporations fire the plaintiff (after the plaintiff sued his brother over excluding the plaintiff from a meaningful role in managing the companies). The plaintiff then sued for dissolution. In response, the court applied the reasonable expectations test.[71] Significantly, the court held that reasonable expectations were not limited to expectations which existed at the time the complaining shareholders purchased their stock. Instead, the court held that the trial judge should examine the entire history of the parties' relationship to see how expectations have developed over a course of dealing. This would allow a party, such as the plaintiff in *Meiselman*, to establish that his or her receipt of a significant ownership in the corporations (even through gift or inheritance), as well as his or her working for the corporations and having had a voice in running the corporations, created reasonable expectations which the majority shareholder's action frustrated.

The notion of determining expectations from a course of dealing is consistent with an implied contract sort of approach. One might ask, however, why protect the expectations of one who never gave consideration for the stock? Of course, in *Meiselman*, the defendant brother never paid for his stock either. In any event, since the brothers received their shares by gift from their father, perhaps the justification for protecting reasonable expectations in this case lies, not in an implied contract, but rather in carrying out the intent of the donor. Yet, if this is the rationale for applying a reasonable expectations test on behalf of shareholders who receive their stock through gift or inheritance, then, in assessing reasonable expectations for such shareholders, courts should consider what corporate practices the donor had in mind. While the Delaware Supreme Court in *Nixon* did not deal with a suit for dissolution, or purport to be applying a reasonable expectations test, notice how this analysis of reasonable expectations in the case of shares received by gift or inheritance corresponds with the significance which the *Nixon* court attached to the fact that the corporation's founder had established the practices challenged by the plaintiff shareholders (who had received

70. 309 N.C. 279, 307 S.E.2d 551 (1983).

71. Interestingly, the statute involved in *Meiselman* did not list "oppression" as grounds for dissolution. Instead, it authorized dissolution when "reasonably necessary for the protection of the rights or interests of the complaining shareholder."

their shares through gift and inheritance of shares owned by the founder).

The courts in both *Kemp & Beatley* and *Meiselman* cautioned that the frustration of the plaintiff's reasonable expectations must not be the fault of the plaintiff. For example, we have seen that a common expectation for shareholders in a closely held corporation is to receive income by working for the corporation. Yet, courts might not be inclined to dissolve a corporation at the urging of a shareholder who complains about the frustration of his or her expectation of employment, when the shareholder gave the corporation good cause fire the shareholder.[72] Notice, in this regard, how the reasonable expectations test comes to resemble the holding in *Wilkes*—only the remedy changes.

Still, even if a shareholder gives good cause for the corporation to terminate his or her employment, or voluntarily quits, this does not mean that the majority's conduct might not unjustifiably frustrate the shareholder's reasonable expectations. After all, stockholders should be entitled to a share of a corporation's profits as a return on their ownership interest. In other words, the notion among some closely held business owners that profits belong to those who work for them, fails to give appropriate recognition to the role of capital—both that originally invested for stock, as well as earnings retained in the corporation over the years to grow the business—in producing profits. Hence, a failure ever to declare dividends, so that the non-employees' stock becomes worthless, can justify dissolution, regardless of why it is that the complaining stockholders do not work for the company.[73]

So far, we have focused on expectations which involve the shareholders obtaining a return on their investment, either through employment with the corporation or otherwise. This does not exhaust the list of reasonable expectations. A shareholder might reasonably expect that he or she would have a position on the board of directors—albeit, there is an easier remedy than dissolving the corporation for a shareholder booted off the board.[74] It is not at all uncommon in a family business for shareholders to expect that their children would have jobs with the corporation when the children reach working age. Nevertheless, while not ruling out such a claim for all cases, the court in *Brenner v. Berkowitz*[75] held that the complaining shareholder would have a heavy burden to sustain such nepotistic ambitions as constituting a reasonable expectation in the face of the need for the corporation's management to have some flexibility in deciding who to employ.

---

72. *E.g.*, Exadaktilos v. Cinnaminson Realty Co., 167 N.J.Super. 141, 400 A.2d 554 (N.J. Super. Ct. 1979), *aff'd*, 173 N.J.Super. 559, 414 A.2d 994 (N.J.1980).

73. *E.g.*, Gimpel v. Bolstein, 125 Misc.2d 45, 477 N.Y.S.2d 1014 (1984). *See also* Stumpf v. C.E. Stumpf & Sons, Inc., 47 Cal.App.3d 230, 120 Cal.Rptr. 671 (1975) (applying California's statute, which authorizes dissolution of corporations with less

than 35 shareholders whenever reasonably necessary for the protection of the rights and interests of the complaining shareholder(s)).

74. *E.g.*, Brenner v. Berkowitz, 134 N.J. 488, 634 A.2d 1019 (1993) (the court ordered the reinstatement of the plaintiff on the board, rather than dissolution).

75. 134 N.J. 488, 634 A.2d 1019 (1993).

Statutes authorizing judicially ordered dissolution sometimes impose a standing requirement limiting which shareholders can seek dissolution. This is typically not an issue in a deadlock situation, since normally a deadlock involves 50 percent shareholders. When dealing with oppression or other wrongful conduct, however, a petition for dissolution might come from a shareholder with only a small interest in the corporation. It is possible to be suspicious of the motives of a shareholder, who seeks to dissolve the company, when this shareholder has only a small interest in the corporation. Some legislatures have responded to this concern by setting a minimum percentage of the outstanding stock which a shareholder must own in order to have standing to petition for dissolution.[76] Nevertheless, given that courts normally have discretion in deciding whether to order dissolution, even if the statutory criteria are met, it would seem that courts are capable of rejecting opportunistic claims made by shareholders with little interest in the corporation. Hence, most states, including the Model Act, impose no minimum share holding requirement for standing to seek dissolution.

d.　Alternate remedies

Recent court opinions and literature dealing with statutory remedies for deadlock and oppression have given considerable attention to remedies short of dissolving the corporation. This is understandable if one starts with the premise that corporate dissolution is a drastic remedy, and so should be a last resort. If, on the other hand, one concludes that the fears of dissolution are overstated, then perhaps the emphasis on seeking alternate remedies is not entirely warranted.

In any event, many corporation statutes expressly authorize the courts to order remedies short of dissolution to deal with deadlock or oppression. For example, Section 14.32 of the Model Act authorizes the court to appoint a custodian to run the corporation in lieu of dissolving the company. In addition, Section 14.34 of the Model Act gives the corporation or the non-petitioning shareholders an option to avoid dissolution by purchasing at fair value the stock owned by the shareholder who petitioned the court for dissolution. Even without statutory authorization, many courts have held that the court, under the court's general equity powers, has the ability to order remedies short of dissolution.[77] For example, a court, under its general equity power, might order an end to conduct found to constitute oppression, or might order a buy-out instead of dissolution.

In some instances, it is easy to see that there is a more appropriate remedy than dissolution to deal with the plaintiff's complaint. For example, failure to reelect a minority shareholder to the board of

---

76. *E.g.*, Cal. Corp. Code § 1800(a)(2).

77. *E.g.*, Davis v. Sheerin, 754 S.W.2d 375 (Tex. Ct. App. 1988). *See also* Brenner v. Berkowitz, 134 N.J. 488, 634 A.2d 1019 (1993) (under its equity powers, a court can add to the remedies available under a stat-ute which provided for dissolution or a court ordered buy-out). *But see* Giannotti v. Hamway, 239 Va. 14, 387 S.E.2d 725 (1990) (holding that the court is unauthorized to go beyond the relief specified in the dissolution statute).

directors might frustrate, in many instances, the shareholder's reasonable expectation. Yet, if this is all there is to the plaintiff's complaint, reinstatement to the board seems to be an adequate solution.[78] In other situations, however, attempting to rectify specific misconduct becomes impractical. For instance, a common claim of oppression arises if the majority has the corporation terminate, without cause, a minority shareholder's employment. Yet, ordering reinstatement of employment can create the sort of ongoing judicial supervision difficulties which make courts reluctant to grant specific performance of personal service contracts. A borderline situation as far as the practicality of a corrective order occurs when the failure to declare dividends constitutes the oppressive conduct. A court might order the payment of dividends.[79] While such an order can embroil the court in an annual (or perhaps quarterly) task of assessing how much of its earnings a corporation needs to retain, it is unclear whether this will be as difficult as mediating constant disputes about whether a shareholder-employee, who the majority wants to fire, continues to perform satisfactory work.

A number of statutes contain remedies short of dissolution to break deadlocks. For example, Section 226 of the Delaware General Corporation Law authorizes a court to place a custodian in charge of a deadlocked corporation. Unless the court orders liquidation, the custodian's task is to continue the business. Section 353 of Delaware's corporation statute expands the options available to a court when dealing with a deadlock in a corporation which has elected special close corporation treatment under Delaware's law. Under Section 353, a court can appoint a provisional director, who can break a tie on an evenly divided board.

It is not entirely clear why statutes like the Model Act and Delaware's law seem to favor appointment of custodians over provisional directors. Appointment of a custodian places the corporation entirely under the control of a person with no financial stake in its welfare, and who may or may not have any expertise in the business. Actually, it is unlikely that the type of individual who the court will select will run amok with control of the company. On the contrary, the custodian is likely to view his or her role as a holding action, allowing the business to muddle along. This is probably alright for the short term, but may not be conducive to the long run health of the company. By contrast, a provisional director only has power insofar as he or she votes with one faction or the other.[80] Hence, persons with a financial stake still essentially make decisions for the corporation—the provisional director simply picks which side's decision prevails. Under these circumstances, there is no reason that the provisional director cannot support even dramatic business initiatives which one faction might propose. In any event, one would think that the court should be careful to select an impartial custodian or

78. Brenner v. Berkowitz, 134 N.J. 488, 634 A.2d 1019 (1993).

79. *See, e.g.,* Patton v. Nicholas, 154 Tex. 385, 279 S.W.2d 848 (1955).

80. *See, e.g.,* Abreu v. Unica Indus. Sales, Inc., 224 Ill.App.3d 439, 166 Ill.Dec. 703, 586 N.E.2d 661 (1991) (provisional director exceeded his authority in unilaterally appointing an auditor).

provisional director.[81] Additionally, one would think that a custodian or provisional director should be subject to the same fiduciary duties as a director—albeit, the issue is not settled.[82]

The remedies short of dissolution which we have been looking at so far consist essentially of efforts to correct the plaintiff's specific complaints—in other words, court orders designed to stop or undo oppressive conduct or to break the deadlock. It turns out, however, that much of the attention involving remedies short of dissolution does not involve such complaint-specific corrective efforts. Rather, a great deal of the focus of courts and writers has turned to the use of court ordered buy-outs as an alternative to dissolution.[83] Specifically, instead of dissolving the corporation, the court will order the corporation or the defendant shareholders to buy all of the stock owned by the plaintiff shareholder (or, sometimes, the court will order the defendant shareholders to sell all of their stock to the plaintiff shareholder). In either event, if the parties cannot agree, the court will set the price for this buy-out.

At first glance, having the court order a buy-out instead of dissolution seems like a brilliant idea. For one thing, it apparently avoids the potential that dissolution could destroy a viable business—albeit, we saw earlier that dissolution orders do not destroy viable businesses. More realistically, since a court-ordered dissolution typically leads to a buy-out instead of a dissolution anyway, why not have the court short circuit the process by ordering a buy-out instead of a dissolution in the first place? To answer this question, one must pose another: What practical differences can there be in the outcome between the situation in which the court orders a dissolution and the parties then work out a buy-out, and the situation in which the court just goes ahead and orders a buy-out? The answer is that in ordering a buy-out, the court can face the need to make two critical decisions, which the court would not need to make if the court ordered dissolution.

The first decision which a court might need to make after it decides to order a buy-out is who will buy out whom. One might assume that the answer to this question is obvious—the shareholder(s) opposing dissolution (or perhaps the corporation) will buy out the shareholder(s) suing for dissolution. In fact, this is the way most of the lawsuits have ended up out when the court orders dissolution and the parties then negotiate a buy-out instead of letting dissolution take place. This shows that shareholders who sue for dissolution usually want out of the business. Consistent with this view, court ordered buy-outs normally call for the defendant shareholders or the corporation to buy out the plaintiff's

81. *But see id.*

82. *See, e.g.,* Valley View State Bank v. Owen, 241 Kan. 343, 737 P.2d 35 (Kan. 1987) (refusing to find a custodian liable to creditors for the negligent loss of corporate assets).

83. *See, e.g.,* Haynsworth, *The Effectiveness of Involuntary Dissolution Suits as a*

Remedy for Close Corporation Dissension, 35 Clev. St. L. Rev. 25 (1987) (in lawsuits brought seeking corporate dissolution in which an opinion was reported in 1984 through 1985, a court ordered buy-out was the most frequent result).

interest in the company.[84] Indeed, the Model Act and a number of other statutes[85] give the corporation and the other stockholders the option to buy out the plaintiff's shares in lieu of dissolution, but do not give the plaintiff an option to buy out the other stockholders' shares. Nevertheless, occasionally, the shareholder who sues for dissolution when faced with deadlock or oppression wants to continue the business and feels that the other shareholder(s) should be the one(s) to sell their stock. Some courts have been willing to order the defendant shareholders to sell out to the plaintiff shareholder. For example, in *Muellenberg v. Bikon Corp.*[86] the court ordered the majority shareholders to sell their stock to the plaintiff minority shareholder. Significantly, however, the New Jersey statute involved in *Muellenberg* stated that any shareholder who was a party to the dissolution action could request a court order allowing a buy-out of any other shareholder. Hence, it is not clear that courts operating under the Model Act, or other statutes which give a buy-out option to the corporation or shareholders other than the plaintiff, could authorize a buy-out by the plaintiff.

If both the plaintiff and the defendant want to buy out the other, then the court which orders a buy-out must choose which party gets to buy. An economically efficient way to make this choice would appear to be to conduct an auction. In this manner, the shareholder who thinks that he or she can make the most money running the company should be willing to pay the most, and will outbid the other shareholder(s). Admittedly, this might not work out if shareholders have unequal access to capital. A financially strapped shareholder, however, typically is not going to ask the court to allow him or her to buy the other shareholders' stock, and so it is unlikely that the court would face a situation in which unequal access to capital would prejudice an auction between two shareholders who both seek to buy the business. In any event, dissolving a corporation should produce an auction if the shareholders are unable to come to an agreement for a buy-out. This is because, following dissolution, the assets of the corporation are liquidated, in other words, sold.[87] There is no legal reason that such a sale cannot include the business as a whole, and presumably such a sale should be made to the highest bidder. Hence, dissolution and liquidation appears to constitute an efficient means of choosing between shareholders who wish to continue the business, albeit not together.

By contrast, courts choosing between shareholders in ordering a buy-out have looked at a variety of a factors. Some courts have looked at the relative ability of the shareholders to afford the buy-out;[88] in other words, they have favored the wealthier shareholder(s). In *Muellenberg*, the court noted that the plaintiff minority shareholder was not only financially able to buy out the majority shareholders, but, also, the

84. *E.g.*, Davis v. Sheerin, 754 S.W.2d 375 (Tex. Ct. App. 1988).

85. *E.g.*, New York Bus. Corp. Law § 1118.

86. 143 N.J. 168, 669 A.2d 1382 (1996).

87. See § 7.4.1*b infra*.

88. *E.g.*, Hendley v. Lee, 676 F.Supp. 1317 (D.S.C.1987).

plaintiff was the most active shareholder, and had been responsible for developing most of the company's contacts and for generating all the company's income the last ten years. Yet, if the plaintiff in *Muellenberg* had sufficient financial resources and been in the best position to continue the business, he should have been able to outbid the majority shareholders if the court ordered a dissolution. By ordering a buy-out rather than dissolution, the court precluded the *Muellenberg* defendants' ability to prove through competitive bidding that they, and not the plaintiff, could make the most efficient use of the corporation.

An even worse approach exists under the Model Act and similar statutes, which give the buy-out option exclusively to the corporation and the stockholders other than the shareholder seeking dissolution. In a situation in which two shareholders (or factions) wish to oust each other from the corporation, the Model Act penalizes the one who goes to court seeking dissolution. The incentive this creates is to be as obnoxious as one can be toward the other shareholder(s) in order to force the other shareholder(s) to blink first. Put differently, this approach can reward oppressive behavior.

The second question which a court must resolve if it orders a buy-out is the price. If the court orders a dissolution, the shareholders will be left to negotiate their own price for a buy-out, or, if they cannot agree and want to push things to the limit, a liquidation sale of the business will set the price. Statutes calling for a buy-out alternative to dissolution commonly let the shareholders in the first instance attempt to negotiate a price. If the shareholders cannot reach agreement, in the case of a court-ordered buy-out, the court will set the price at the so-called fair value of the stock.

This judicial valuation has strengths and weaknesses relative to the alternative of ordering dissolution and a liquidation. On the positive side, judicial valuation can avoid the prospect of an unfairly low price which would result from a liquidation sale in which only one shareholder (or group of shareholders) is in a position to bid. This might occur either because only one shareholder (or group) has the financial resources to buy the business, or because one shareholder (or group) already holds the key—such as having the business contacts, personally owning property critical to the business, or the like—to continuing the business.[89] The downside of judicial valuation is that it substitutes a battle of hired expert witnesses for the market as a price setting mechanism. This

---

89. Given the low price possible in a liquidation sale in which only one shareholder (or group of shareholders) desires to continue the business, one might ask why do shareholders who want out of the business seek dissolution, and why do shareholders who want to continue the business commonly negotiate for a buy-out when faced with an order dissolving the corporation. Part of the answer is that liquidation of the corporation creates the need to pay off the company's debts and can result in the loss of franchises and other rights which may not be assignable following a corporate dissolution. Hence, a negotiated buy-out may be preferable to dissolution for both sides. Besides, even receiving his or her share of the proceeds from a low price in a liquidation sale may look good to a shareholder cut off from all corporate earnings.

analysis suggests that a judicially set price is probably better when only one party is interested in continuing the venture, but that a liquidation auction works better to set the price when both sides want to buy out the other.

One issue which has come up when courts set a price at which the corporation or the other shareholders will buy out a minority shareholder who sued for dissolution is whether to apply a so-called minority discount. The argument for such a discount is that an arms-length buyer would reduce the price which he or she is willing to pay to acquire a minority interest in a closely-held corporation to take into account the precarious position of a minority shareholder in a closely held corporation (who faces the danger of a squeeze-out by the majority). Hence, if fair value equals what an arms-length buyer would pay, there should be a minority discount. The problem with this argument is that it is circular: The purpose for ordering dissolution or a buy-out is to protect a minority shareholder faced with oppression. Hence, to the extent that courts protect minority shareholders—including by refusing to apply a minority discount in setting the price for a buy-out—then arms-length buyers of minority interests face less risk of disastrous squeeze-outs and have less reason to demand minority discounts in negotiating a price. Viewed another way, applying a minority discount rewards the majority for oppressive conduct, since the more oppressively the majority acts, the more an arms-length buyer would have demanded a discount to purchase the minority's interest. Given this analysis, it is not surprising that most courts refuse to apply a minority discount in setting a price at which a majority will buy out a minority in lieu of dissolution.[90]

Courts have had somewhat more difficulty deciding whether to discount the value of the minority's shares because of a lack of easy marketability.[91] An appropriate analysis here would ask why the shares are not easily marketable. To the extent that the lack of market reflects the hazards of being a minority shareholder in a closely held corporation, then the so-called marketability discount is really a disguised minority discount. To the extent, however, that the lack of marketability reflects the lack of a developed trading market for any interest in a closely held business, majority or minority, or, indeed, the limited market of persons to buy the whole business, then marketability is an appropriate criteria in setting value. In this instance, a marketability discount simply takes into account that outsiders, who face greater information gathering costs and risks of misinformation when purchasing a closely held business, demand a greater return on their investment than they would when investing in public companies subject to reporting requirements and the scrutiny of numerous independent investment analysts.

90. *E.g.,* Charland v. Country View Golf Club, Inc., 588 A.2d 609 (1991).

91. *Compare* Charland, *supra, with* Matter of Dissolution of Gift Pax, Inc., 123 Misc.2d 830, 475 N.Y.S.2d 324 (1984), *aff'd,* 107 App. Div. 2d 97, 486 N.Y.S.2d 272 (1985).

§ 5.2   Special Governance Arrangements for Closely Held Corporations

In the previous section, we looked at after-the-fact resolution of shareholder dissension in closely held corporations—specifically, we explored judicial and statutory remedies available to the minority shareholder who finds him- or herself at the mercy of the owner(s) of a majority of the corporation's stock, as well as statutory remedies available to equal shareholders faced with a deadlock. In this section, we switch to a before-the-fact perspective and examine the methods sometimes employed by shareholders to avoid the situations encountered in the previous section. Predominately, we will focus upon techniques to protect the minority shareholder from the majority. (Naturally, ownership of a majority of the stock provides its own protection without special planning.) As far as planning to deal with deadlocks between equal owners, we shall explore arbitration in this section, while the next section of this chapter, dealing with share transfer restrictions, will look at advance agreements allowing one shareholder to buy out another in cases such as dissension between the owners.

5.2.1   *Ensuring Positions on the Board of Directors for Minority Shareholders*

We noted in discussing choice of entity at the beginning of this book that individuals, who own a substantial percentage of a business, commonly wish to have a say in managing the business. The default rule for partnerships, and, in most states, for limited liability companies, accommodates this desire by calling for direct governance by all of the owners.[1] Corporate law is different, since it places ultimate managerial authority in a board of directors. Hence, having a say in managing a corporation typically means having a position on the board of directors. Normally, those who hold a majority of the stock have the power to decide who will serve on the board. As a result, minority shareholders, who wish to ensure themselves a position on the board, must employ various techniques to achieve this goal.

a.   *Cumulative voting*

Cumulative voting is a technique created to give minority shareholders sufficient voting power to elect themselves to the board of directors. Widely held corporations sometimes allow cumulative voting, but its primary significance lies in closely held corporations, since it takes control of a fairly large percentage of the company's outstanding stock in order for cumulative voting to have an effect.[2]

To understand cumulative voting, one must start by understanding the mechanics of so-called straight voting (the voting scheme normally followed) in an at-large election for several positions on a board. In an

§ 5.2

1. See § 1.1.2c *supra.*

2. For an argument that cumulative voting may be useful in public corporations as a mechanism to allow institutional inves- tors to obtain representation on the board, see Jeffrey Gordon, *Institutions As Relational Investors: A New Look at Cumulative Voting*, 94 Colum. L. Rev. 124 (1994).

at-large election to fill more than one seat on a board—be it a county board of supervisors, a school board, or a corporation's board of directors—instead of dividing up the electorate into districts (as in legislative races), each voter votes to fill as many positions as are available for election to the board. For example, if there are five open seats on a board, each voter in an at-large election will vote for five candidates. Crucially, the candidates are not running for a particular seat on the board, but, rather, all of the candidates are running against all of the other candidates to be one of the top vote getters and so elected to the board. In other words, the victors in an election to fill five open slots on a board are the first, second, third, fourth and fifth top vote getters. In a public election, say for school board, each voter will place one vote (since, in a public election, the rule is one-person-one-vote) on as many candidates as there are open positions. In a corporate election, where the normal rule is one-share-one-vote, each shareholder will place as many votes as he or she owns voting shares on as many candidates as there are open seats. So, if five directors are to be elected, an individual owning 100 voting shares would cast 100 votes each for five candidates. Notice that total votes cast by each shareholder will equal the number of voting shares he or she owns, multiplied by the number of directors to be elected. So, in the example of an election to fill five director positions, a shareholder owning 100 shares will cast a total of 500 votes. Under straight voting, however, the shareholder cannot give any one candidate more votes than the number of voting shares which the shareholder owns.

Cumulative voting allows a minority shareholder to avoid the dilution of his or her voting power which occurs when the shareholder must spread out his or her votes among a number of candidates equal to the number of positions to be filled. Instead, under cumulative voting, a shareholder can concentrate all of his or her votes—which, we just saw, equals the number of his or her voting shares multiplied by the number of director positions to be filled in the election at hand—on less candidates than there are positions to fill. For example, a minority shareholder might put all of his or her votes on just one candidate (such as the shareholder him- or herself). Ultimately, under cumulative voting, the shareholder can divide up his or her votes however he or she sees fit.

To see the effectiveness of cumulative voting, consider how it would have worked in a situation based upon the *Wilkes* case discussed earlier in this chapter. Assume the corporation has four shareholders, each owning 10 shares of stock, and that the corporation's bylaws call for a four-person board of directors. Under straight voting, if three shareholders gang up on the fourth—which is what happened in *Wilkes*—the fourth will be powerless to get himself reelected to the board. After all, the three shareholders will vote 30 shares for their four candidates, while the fourth shareholder will vote only 10 shares for four candidates, meaning that the four individuals supported by the majority block will be the four top vote getters and so elected to the four positions on the board. Cumulative voting, however, would allow our estranged shareholder to take his 40 total votes (10 shares multiplied by the four positions on the board to be filled) and place them on fewer than four candidates. For instance, our estranged shareholder in this example could vote all 40 votes for himself as a director. The three shareholders ganging up on this individual have a total of 120 votes to play with (30 shares owned between the three individuals, multiplied by the four positions on the board to be filled). There is no way for these three individuals to spread their 120 votes among four candidates so that all four of their candidates would receive more than 40 votes and thereby preclude the estranged shareholder from being among the top four vote getters and so elected to the board. Specifically, if the "gang of three" in this example put 41 votes on two candidates, they would only have 38 votes left to cover both of the last two candidates. The estranged shareholder would then receive the third highest vote total, and so be among the four individuals elected.

What must occur in order for a corporation's shareholders to have the right to use cumulative voting? In most jurisdictions, to allow cumulative voting, the corporation's articles must contain a provision stating that shareholders may vote in this manner.[3] Some jurisdictions allow shareholders to employ cumulative voting unless the articles contain a provision denying shareholders this right.[4] A few jurisdictions go beyond this to require that corporations give their shareholders the right to vote cumulatively regardless of what the articles provide.[5] Indeed, some states have felt this is such an important right, that the state's constitution, rather than just the state's corporation statute, requires corporations to allow cumulative voting.[6] At one time, state laws which require corporations to allow cumulative voting were fairly common. However, laws requiring corporations to allow cumulative voting have waned considerably in recent years.

State laws which empower corporations to permit cumulative voting have raised little controversy—albeit one could always debate whether the default rule should call for cumulative voting or straight voting barring a specific provision in the articles.[7] By contrast, state laws which mandate corporations to allow cumulative voting have generated considerable disagreement.[8] Historically, the notion behind mandatory cumulative voting rights is that large minority shareholders should be entitled to representation on the board as a natural part of a representative democracy, and, also, that allowing the minority to keep an eye on what was going on through representation on the board—even if the minority

---

3. *E.g.*, Del. Gen. Corp. Law § 214; M.B.C.A. § 7.28(b).

4. *E.g.*, 15 Pa. Cons. Stat. Ann. § 1758(c).

5. *E.g.*, Cal. Corp. Code § 708(a). *But see* Cal. Corp. Code § 301.5 (corporations with shares listed on national stock exchanges may adopt an article provision eliminating cumulative voting).

6. *E.g.*, Az. Const. Art. 14 § 10.

7. The common expectation that substantial shareholders will have some say in management suggests that cumulative voting should be the default rule, especially in closely held corporations.

8. *E.g.*, John Sobeski, *In Support of Cumulative Voting*, 15 Bus. Law. 316 (1960); Ralph Axley, *The Case Against Cumulative Voting*, 1950 Wis. L. Rev. 278.

could not actually dictate decisions—would help avoid misconduct by the majority. Opponents of cumulative voting have argued that it can lead to dissension among board members and to the election of some members who view their role as looking out for the interests of one shareholder rather than the overall good of the corporation. Of course, the fundamental question in all this is why the pros and cons of cumulative voting are not a subject which the shareholders in a given corporation can decide for themselves, rather than being mandated by state law. Presumably, the rationale for a mandatory rule is that, since the whole goal of cumulative voting is to protect minority shareholders, under an optional approach the majority will deprive the minority of the right to vote cumulatively, especially when it may be most useful.

Several factors undermine the effectiveness of cumulative voting as a tool to guarantee directorships for minority shareholders. To begin with, the minority shareholder must control a substantial percentage of the outstanding voting stock before even cumulative voting will enable the shareholder to elect a director. The number of positions on the board up for election dictates the percent of stock which a shareholder needs in order to elect a director by cumulating all of his or her votes on one candidate. Specifically, to have assurance that he or she can elect one board member through cumulative voting, a shareholder must control one more share than the total number of voting shares divided by one plus the number of directors to be elected—or $1 + V/(1+D)$, where V is the number of voting shares and D is the number of directors to be elected.[9] Hence, if there are three directorships to fill, it takes one more share than one-quarter of the voting shares $(1 + V/(1+3))$ to assure the ability to elect a single director.

Notice from this formula that there is an inverse relationship between the number of board positions subject to the election and the percent of stock which it takes to elect a director through cumulative voting—in other words, the less the number of positions to be filled, the greater the percentage of the outstanding stock required in order to elect

9. To determine how many shares it takes to elect two directors, one simply multiplies this formula by two; to determine how many for three directors, one multiplies by three, and so on. This formula ignores fractions of shares, and assumes that the stockholders vote all of the outstanding shares to the maximum possible effect under cumulative voting. In fact, stockholders often do not make optimum use of cumulative voting. *See, e.g.,* Stancil v. Bruce Stancil Refrigeration, Inc., 81 N.C.App. 567, 344 S.E.2d 789 (1986). Indeed, in many situations, maximizing the effectiveness of cumulative voting calls for some strategy. *E.g.,* Glazer, Glazer & Grofman, *Cumulative Voting in Corporate Elections: Introducing Strategy Into the Equation,* 35 S.C. L. Rev. 295 (1984). For example, if a majority stockholder expect-

ed that the minority would not take advantage of cumulative voting, the majority stockholder would be best to spread his or her votes evenly across as many candidates as there are openings on the board. In this way, the majority stockholder would elect all of the directors. Following this strategy would be very dangerous, however, if a large minority votes cumulatively, since the majority stockholder can end up electing only a minority of the board if the majority spreads its votes too thinly and the minority counters with an optimum use of the minority's votes. To avoid unfair surprises becoming part of cumulative voting strategy, statutes sometimes require that shareholders give advance notice of their intent to vote cumulatively. *E.g.,* M.B.C.A. § 7.28(d); Cal. Corp. Code § 708(b).

a director by cumulative voting. This means that the majority can decrease the effectiveness of cumulative voting by reducing the number of positions up for election to the board. To go back to the example based upon *Wilkes*, if the board had only two members, the gang of three would be able to prevent the estranged fourth shareholder from gaining election by cumulative voting.[10]

Two methods exist to reduce the number of positions on the board up for election. The obvious one is to reduce the size of the board.[11] Alternately, one might use staggered terms to reduce the number of directors elected at one time without reducing the size of the board.[12] Staggered terms mean that not all of the board stand for election at one time. For example, directors might have three-year terms in office, with one-third of the positions on the board up for election at each annual shareholders meeting. The reader might recognize staggered terms as the model followed by the United States Senate.

A number of lawsuits have challenged the use of staggered terms to reduce the effectiveness of cumulative voting in states whose laws required corporations to allow cumulative voting. In a situation in which the state's corporation statute both requires corporations to allow cumulative voting and yet expressly allows corporate boards to have staggered terms, it is a difficult to argue persuasively that staggered terms are illegal because they undercut the effectiveness of cumulative voting.[13] After all, what the legislature gives, the legislature can take away. The more difficult issue arises when the state constitution contains the requirement that corporations allow cumulative voting. In this instance, it is possible to argue that the state statute allowing staggered terms is unconstitutional by virtue of the state's constitutional right of cumulative voting. At least one court reached this conclusion.[14] Other courts, however, have rejected the constitutional challenge by reasoning that so long as the shareholders have the right to cumulate their votes, the constitution does not require that there be any particular level of effectiveness to cumulative voting.[15] After all, even without staggered terms, the effectiveness of cumulative voting depends upon the size of board. Still another approach has been to uphold staggered terms against a constitutional challenge unless the staggered terms completely destroy the effectiveness of cumulative voting by having only one director elected at a time.[16]

10. The gang of three would have 60 votes to use (30 shares multiplied by two positions to fill). If they place 30 votes each on two candidates, both of their two candidates would outpoll the fourth shareholder—who only has 20 votes (10 shares multiplied by two positions) to work with.

11. For a discussion of the rules governing the size of the board, see § 3.1.2a *supra*.

12. See § 3.1.2a *supra*.

13. *See, e.g.*, Humphrys v. Winous Co., 165 Ohio St. 45, 133 N.E.2d 780 (1956).

14. Wolfson v. Avery, 6 Ill.2d 78, 126 N.E.2d 701 (1955). Illinois subsequently repealed its constitutional provision requiring corporations to allow cumulative voting.

15. *E.g.*, Janney v. Philadelphia Transp. Co., 387 Pa. 282, 128 A.2d 76 (Pa. 1956).

16. Bohannan v. Corporation Commission, 82 Ariz. 299, 313 P.2d 379 (1957).

In states in which cumulative voting depends upon a provision in the articles, a simple way for the majority to prevent cumulative voting is to change the articles so that cumulative voting is not allowed.[17] One other approach would be for the majority to attempt to remove directors which the minority elected through cumulative voting. Often, however, statutes prevent removal of directors elected under cumulative voting unless the shares voted against removal would not have been sufficient, even if voted cumulatively, to elect the director in the first place.[18]

b. *Shareholder voting agreements*

Contracts between shareholders to vote their stock in a prescribed manner—variously referred to as shareholder voting or pooling agreements—constitute another way in which minority shareholders may attempt to ensure election to the board. Such agreements might accomplish this goal either by combining minority interests together into a majority, or by obtaining a majority shareholder's commitment to vote for the minority.

In the late 19th and early 20th centuries, a number of court opinions held that shareholder voting agreements were contrary to public policy and unenforceable.[19] The notion was that agreeing upon how to vote one's shares interfered with a shareholder's duty to vote according to his or her independent judgment and in the best interest of the corporation. Courts also expressed concern that such agreements separated the control over how stock was voted from the ownership of the stock. This hostility to voting agreements has faded away. For example, in *Ringling Brothers–Barnum & Bailey Combined Shows, Inc. v. Ringling*,[20] the Delaware Supreme Court upheld a shareholder voting agreement against challenges to its validity.

Ringling involved a voting agreement entered into between two individuals owning shares in the corporation which operated the famous circus. The original Ringling brothers had all died, leaving ownership of the corporation essentially divided between three successors-in-interest.[21] Two of three shareholders entered a voting agreement in order to maximize the number of directors they could elect by virtue of cumulative voting.[22] After a falling out, one of the two shareholders refused to

---

17. *See, e.g.,* Maddock v. Vorclone Corp., 17 Del.Ch. 39, 147 A. 255 (1929).

18. *E.g.,* M.B.C.A. § 8.08(c).

19. *E.g.,* Haldeman v. Haldeman, 176 Ky. 635, 197 S.W. 376 (1917).

20. 29 Del.Ch. 610, 53 A.2d 441 (1947).

21. One of the three blocks was held in the estate of John Ringling (who had been the leading brother). A sister and nephew of the original Ringling brothers controlled these shares by virtue of being executors of the estate.

22. Earlier, financial difficulties had forced the shareholders to relinquish con-

trol over the corporation to creditors pending repayment of loans. The creditors placed the nephew who controlled John Ringling's estate in charge of the circus, leading to resentment by the other two shareholders. The two other shareholders, in turn, entered a voting agreement which took effect upon the repayment of the loans. By virtue of the agreement, these two shareholders could elect five of the corporation's seven directors through cumulative voting, whereas if the two shareholders did not coordinate their votes, they each only could elect two directors, and the nephew—who controlled a somewhat larger number

vote in accordance with the agreement,[23] resulting in a lawsuit. The trial court upheld the agreement against challenges from the defendant, and the Delaware Supreme Court affirmed. The court rejected the argument that the agreement impermissibly separated control from ownership, noting that, even though the agreement provided for binding arbitration, the agreement could not be enforced unless one of the two shareholders who were a party to the agreement sued to force compliance with the arbitrator's decision. Hence, control over the election of directors ultimately remained in the hands of shareholders, rather than being in the hands of an individual with no stake in the company. The court also backhandedly dismissed the notion of a duty of shareholders to exercise independent judgment in voting. The court pointed out that shareholders have no duty to vote at all, and, therefore, the court reasoned, shareholders can vote however they please.

Actually, the *Ringling* opinion never really grapples with the difficult issue regarding shareholder voting agreements. This issue concerns the interest of the stockholders who are not a party to the agreement. After all, if every shareholder in the corporation is a party to the voting contract, it is difficult to see why such a contract should be any more subject to challenge than the typical partnership agreement which specifies the management roles of the various partners. The problem with the agreement in *Ringling* lay in the possible prejudice to the third shareholder of the circus company, who never agreed to the voting contract. True, any minority shareholder is always subject to the risk that voting coalitions will form against him or her. The difference with a legally enforceable voting agreement is that outside shareholder loses the ability to attempt to break up the coalition by persuading one of the allied shareholders to vote with the outside shareholder.

These concerns, however, appear to be water under the dam as legislatures have reinforced decisions like *Ringling* by enacting statutes which state that shareholder voting agreements are valid.[24] Significantly, the statutes validating shareholder voting agreements generally do not contain the limitations commonly found in statutes, which we will discuss later, that allow shareholder agreements to control particular board decisions. Specifically, statutes validating shareholder voting agreements typically do not limit their reach to close corporations,[25] nor do they generally require that all of the shareholders be party to, or at least have notice of, the agreement in order for it to be valid.[26]

of shares—could elect three persons to the board.

23. The agreement called for the two shareholders to meet before each election and agree upon how to vote, and, if they could not agree, the contract required them to vote as instructed by an arbitrator.

24. *E.g.*, Del. Gen. Corp. Law § 218(c); M.B.C.A. § 7.31(a).

25. California had been an exception to this proposition until the legislature amend-

ed the state's statute validating shareholder voting agreements to reach beyond statutory close corporations. Cal. Corp. Code § 706(a).

26. *Compare* N.Y. Bus. Corp. Law § 620(a) (validating shareholder voting agreements as long as in writing and signed), *with* N.Y. Bus. Corp. Law § 620(b) (validating shareholder agreements restricting the board in the management of the corporation only if the agreement is placed

Does this mean that no challenge remains to the validity of shareholder voting agreements? The answer is no. To begin with, the consideration for such agreements can sometimes present a problem. In the typical pooling agreement, the parties all promise to vote in accordance with the agreement. Promising to vote in accordance with the contract, in exchange for the other party's promise to do the same, should constitute, under ordinary contract law, adequate consideration to create an enforceable contract. The court in *Ringling* had no trouble seeing this (albeit, the agreement in *Ringling* also contained a mutual right of first refusal to buy the other stockholder's shares, thereby arguably providing some added consideration for the voting promises). Curiously, however, some court opinions have refused to find that exchanging mutual voting promises alone constitutes adequate consideration to create an enforceable contract.[27]

At the other extreme from trading votes, suppose a party offers to pay cash in exchange for a shareholder's promise to vote in accordance with the contract. Here, one confronts the well-established doctrine that buying votes for cash[28] is contrary to public policy.[29] At first glance, the prohibition on vote buying seems sensible enough. After all, courts would hardly enforce a vote buying agreement involving an election for public officials. Yet, maybe there is a difference between corporate elections and the elections of public officials. Specifically, persons legally buy corporate votes all the time; all one has to do is buy stock. This is where we get into the concern about separating control from ownership. A person, who buys stock, gains the advantage and suffers the detriment from however the person chooses to vote the shares. A person who buys the votes, but not the stock–in other words, who separates control from ownership— does not feel the economic impact of his or her voting decisions. This makes us suspicious of the motives of one who only buys the votes and not the stock. On the other hand, if the person giving pecuniary consideration for votes already is a substantial shareholder, or there is some other reason to allay any suspicion as to the motives for the contract, then maybe courts should not automatically condemn the contract.[30]

The specific provisions of a shareholder voting agreement also might create questions as to the agreement's validity. A simple promise by the parties to vote for each other (or for each other's nominees) raises little problem. In *Ringling*, such a promise would not have accomplished the parties' objective, since the purpose of the agreement was to gain the

in the certificate of incorporation, all of the shareholders agreed to the restriction at the time it was made, later shareholders receive notice of the restriction, and the corporation's stock is not publicly traded). *But see* Tex. Bus. Corp. Act § 2.30(B).

27. *E.g.*, Johnson v. Spartanburg County Fair Ass'n, 210 S.C. 56, 41 S.E.2d 599 (1947).

28. Or for some other pecuniary benefit personal to the shareholder who gives up his or her vote, such as cancellation of a personal debt.

29. *E.g.*, N.Y. Bus. Corp. Law § 609(e); Macht v. Merchants Mortgage & Credit Co., 22 Del.Ch. 74, 194 A. 19 (1937).

30. *E.g.*, Schreiber v. Carney, 447 A.2d 17 (Del.Ch.1982).

power to elect a fifth director. Had the parties in *Ringling* simply agreed to agree in the future on how to vote, presumably there would not have been a contract. Agreeing to arbitration avoided this problem, but potentially created another. The defendant in *Ringling* argued that the arbitration provision violated public policy by separating control from ownership. As discussed above, the court in *Ringling* did not find this argument persuasive. Some courts, however, have.[31]

Another approach sometimes used in drafting shareholder voting agreements is to focus less on specifying who the parties will vote for, and more on equalizing their voting power. For example, the owner of a majority of the voting shares could agree not to vote the number of shares he or she owns which are in excess of the number of shares owned by another stockholder. So long as the agreement speaks in terms of a promise not to vote some shares, there should be little problem. Sometimes, however, the agreement speaks in terms of altering the voting power of shares. In this event, a court might hold the agreement is invalid for attempting by side contract to do something—changing the voting power of stock—which, by statute, can only be done through a provision in the corporation's articles.[32]

Finally, statutes seeking to validate shareholder voting agreements may have the effect of invalidating some voting agreements for failure to comply with the statute. For example, such statutes commonly state that a voting agreement is valid if in writing and signed. The negative implication of such statutes is that oral voting agreements may not be valid—in other words, the statute might turn into something of a statute of frauds.[33]

Even if a shareholder voting agreement is enforceable, there may be problems concerning the remedy. *Ringling* provides a good illustration. Money damages would not have been a useful remedy; it is unlikely that the plaintiff sustained any monetary damages. Yet, the court did not award specific performance. Rather, it only invalidated the defendant's votes.[34] It is difficult to understand a reluctance to award specific performance in this sort of case. Money damages generally are inadequate, and ordering a party to vote in accordance with the contract is hardly likely to create the supervision difficulties which deter courts from ordering specific performance of personal service contracts. Recog-

---

31. *E.g.*, Roberts v. Whitson, 188 S.W.2d 875 (Tex.Civ.App.1945). We shall return to the subject of arbitration as part of shareholder agreements later in this chapter.

32. *Compare* Nickolopoulos v. Sarantis, 102 N.J.Eq. 585, 141 A. 792 (1928), *with* Sankin v. 5410 Conn. Ave. Corp., 281 F.Supp. 524 (D.D.C.1968), *aff'd*, 410 F.2d 1060 (D.C.Cir.1969). *But see* M.B.C.A. § 7.32(a)(4).

33. *But see* Del. Gen. Corp. Law § 218(d) (indicating that the section is not intended to invalidate any voting agreement which is not otherwise illegal).

34. Actually, it unclear whether the plaintiff would have been better off with more complete relief in this particular case. Invalidating the defendant's votes left the board equally divided between three directors elected by virtue of the plaintiff's votes and three directors elected by virtue of the nephew's votes. Had the court ordered to defendant to vote as commanded by the arbitrator, a new alliance between the defendant and the nephew would have comprised a majority of the board.

nizing this, a number of modern statutes expressly authorize courts to order specific performance of shareholder voting contracts.[35]

Sometimes, parties attempt to create self-help specific performance by having the agreement contain a grant of proxies to carry out the promised votes. In other words, as part of their contract, each party to the contract grants to the other parties, or to some neutral individual, a proxy authorizing the recipient of the proxy to vote the stock in accordance with the contract's terms. Naturally, for this scheme to work, the parties must not have the power to revoke the proxies they granted under the agreement, or else a party refusing to comply with the contract can simply revoke his or her proxy and we are back to where we started. Unfortunately, simply having each party promise, as part of the contract, not to revoke the proxy may not serve to make the proxy, in fact, irrevocable. True, assuming there is consideration for the promise not to revoke the proxy, the party giving the proxy lacks the right to revoke it, and may be liable for damages. Traditionally, however, courts have held that, since a proxy is a species of agency, the party giving the proxy retains the power, even if not the right, to revoke the proxy despite a promise not to do so.[36] Accordingly, we are back to a situation in which the only remedy may be money damages in a circumstance in which there typically is no monetary damage.

Historically, common law courts recognized an exception to the rule that persons retain the power (even if not the right) to terminate authority despite a binding contract not to do so. This exception covered authority which was "coupled with an interest." Typically, this referred to some sort of property interest in the subject matter of the authority. For example, a borrower might grant the lender a lien on the borrower's property coupled with the authority to sell the collateral in the event of non-payment of the loan. Here, the authority is coupled with a property interest (the lien) in the subject matter of the agency (the collateral). Hence, the borrow lacks the power, as well as the right, to terminate the authority to sell the collateral in the event of non-payment of the loan. Applying this "coupled with an interest" concept to proxies, a proxy granted to vote shares pledged as collateral for a loan, or a proxy given to one who has contracted to buy the shares (but perhaps will not be able to vote the shares because the transfer will take place after the record date establishing who can vote the shares in the next election) would be irrevocable if so provided by the proxy.[37] This, however, would not have helped in the situation in *Ringling*—even if the parties had exchanged proxies to vote each others' shares in that case—unless, perhaps, the right of first refusal in the agreement would have constituted a sufficient interest in the other party's shares.

35. *E.g.*, M.B.C.A. § 7.31(b). Even without a statutory command, some courts have been willing to order specific performance of a voting contract. *E.g.*, Weil v. Beresth, 154 Conn. 12, 220 A.2d 456 (1966).

36. *E.g.*, In re Chilson, 19 Del.Ch. 398, 168 A. 82 (1933).

37. *E.g.*, Calumet Indus., Inc. v. Mac-Clure, 464 F.Supp. 19 (N.D.Ill.1978).

Some states, by statute or court opinion, have expanded the concept of "coupled with an interest" in the case of a proxy to include a property interest in the corporation, rather than just a property interest in the specific shares to which the proxy pertains.[38] This will pick up a proxy granted to the other shareholders who are parties to a shareholder voting agreement.[39] It presumably will not, however, save the proxy granted to an outside neutral party who owns no shares in the corporation (such as the arbitrator in *Ringling*). A number of statutes recognize that this whole "coupled with an interest" approach may be rather pointless.[40] These statutes make proxies irrevocable if so agreed as part of a valid shareholder voting contract.[41]

If parties to a shareholder voting contract use irrevocable proxies in order to achieve a self-help remedy, there is a practical reason to give the proxies to a neutral third party instead of to the parties to the contract. Otherwise, a party to the contract could vote the proxies in breach of the agreement, and the parties are back in court to enforce the contract. Granting irrevocable proxies to a neutral third party, however, may create another problem as to the legality of the agreement. This arrangement starts to look like a voting trust because the neutral third party can vote shares much like the trustee of a voting trust. This fact might lead a court to conclude that the contract is indeed a voting trust, and to rule that the agreement is illegal because the agreement does not comply with the specific statutory requirements governing voting trusts (which we shall discuss shortly). In *Abercrombie v. Davies*,[42] the Delaware Supreme Court held that an elaborate voting agreement, which included granting irrevocable proxies to so-called agents, was in fact a voting trust, and was therefore illegal for failing to comply with the voting trust statute. Few cases have gone this far, however, and corporation statutes in Delaware and elsewhere now often contain provisions which state that

---

38. *E.g.*, Del. Gen. Corp. Law § 212(e); State ex rel. Everett Trust & Savings Bank v. Pacific Waxed Paper Co., 22 Wash. 2d 844, 157 P.2d 707 (1945).

39. The Model Act states that "coupled with an interest" includes being a party to a shareholder voting agreement. M.B.C.A. § 7.22(d)(5).

40. Some courts have attempted to rationalize the "coupled with an interest" limitation as a way to prevent the incentive problem which could occur when an individual holds a proxy to vote another person's stock, but has no interest in the stock, or in the corporation's welfare generally. *E.g.*, Haft v. Haft, 671 A.2d 413 (Del.Ch.1995). Of course, if a person, who has no interest in the corporation's welfare, gives consideration to gain control over the voting of stock, we apparently have a vote buying problem and a reason to void the entire agreement regardless of the coupled with an interest rubric. On the other hand, the coupled with an interest approach seems to rule out granting irrevocable proxies to an

arbitrator, despite the fact that in *Ringling* the court found that it was perfectly appropriate to let such a stranger decide how the shareholders should vote their stock. One might respond that the *Ringling* court only disposed of the concern about placing control over voting in the hands of a nonshareholder by pointing out that the contract there could not be enforced unless a shareholder acted to enforce it. Nevertheless, even if the arbitrator has the proxies to carry out his or her order without any shareholder suing to enforce the arbitrator's decision, the arbitrator still cannot act if all of the shareholders who are parties to the voting agreement oppose the arbitrator and agree among themselves to revoke the proxies given to the arbitrator. After all, it is within the power of all of the parties to a contract to revoke or modify the contract.

41. *E.g.*, Cal. Corp. Code § 705(e)(5).

42. 36 Del.Ch. 371, 130 A.2d 338 (1957).

the voting trust provisions are not to render shareholder voting agreements and proxies illegal so long as the agreements and proxies are otherwise legal.[43]

c. Voting trusts

Having introduced voting trusts during our discussion of shareholder voting agreements, now is a good time to take a closer look at such trusts. In a voting trust, shareholders transfer their stock to one or more persons who take title as trustees. The trustees have a fiduciary, as well as a contractual, obligation to carry out the terms of the agreement under which they received the shares.[44] Because the trustees become the legal owners of the stock, their right to vote the stock does not depend upon a court's ordering specific performance of a voting agreement or finding a proxy coupled with an interest. Hence, a voting trust can provide a self-executing mechanism for ensuring the voting of shares in accordance with an agreed plan. Since the trustees receive their title in trust to act for the benefit, typically, of the former shareholders, the former shareholders give up legal title but retain beneficial ownership. This means that the trustees normally forward to the former shareholders any dividends received from the corporation, and transfer the stock back to the former owners upon termination of the trust. To evidence their beneficial ownership, the former owners often receive certificates from the trustee.

Voting trusts can be useful for a variety of purposes beyond securing positions on the board for minority shareholders in a closely held corporation. For example, before the shareholder voting agreement in *Ringling* went into effect, a voting trust held the stock in the circus corporation. Creditors of the circus had insisted upon this arrangement in order to make sure that the company had management acceptable to the creditors until the company repaid their loans. The use of voting trusts to ensure management acceptable to creditors might occur in public as well as closely held corporations. Along similar lines, an elderly shareholder owning a controlling interest in a corporation may wish to pass the beneficial interest in his or her stock to junior members of the family, but lack confidence in the junior members' ability to run the company. Placing the stock in a voting trust with trustees in whom the elderly shareholder has confidence may be an answer. Individuals might also transfer their shares to a voting trust and then sell off part of their beneficial interest. In this way, a voting trust can facilitate retention of control despite cashing out some of one's interest. To the extent that the purpose of the trust is detrimental to the corporation, however, some courts might hold that the trust is illegal.[45]

Similarly to the early judicial attitude toward shareholder voting agreements, some older court opinions condemned voting trusts for

---

43. *E.g.*, Del. Gen. Corp. Law § 218(d). *See also* M.B.C.A. § 7.31(a).

44. *See, e.g.*, Bryson v. Bryson, 62 Cal. App. 170, 216 P. 391 (1923).

45. *E.g.*, Grogan v. Grogan, 315 S.W.2d 34 (Tex.Civ.App.1958).

separating control from ownership.[46] Technically, however, a voting trust does not separate control at least from the legal title to the stock. Moreover, the incentive problem created when individuals do not feel the economic impact of their vote is ameliorated to some extent in the voting trust context by the fiduciary obligation of a trustee to the beneficiary of the trust. Hence, many older opinions do not condemn voting trusts.[47] In any event, most states now have statutes which expressly validate voting trusts.[48]

Generally, the statutes which validate voting trusts also set out specific requirements for the creation of such trusts.[49] Typically, to establish a voting trust, the statutes require the transfer of shares to the trustee pursuant to a written agreement between the trustee and the transferring shareholder(s). Significantly, the voting trust statutes commonly require that the parties file the trust agreement with the corporation, thereby providing shareholders who are not participants in the trust with potential notice of the trust's existence. This filing requirement stands in marked contrast to the normal lack of such a notice requirement for shareholder voting contracts. The resulting divergence in statutory treatment accounts for the problem we discussed earlier in which courts sometimes condemn shareholder voting agreements with irrevocable proxies as being, in effect, an illegal secret voting trust—in other words, a voting trust which did not comply with the statutory filing requirements.

This, in turn, leads to the question: When is an agreement which does not explicitly transfer legal title in stock to a trustee nevertheless a voting trust? Delaware courts have devised a three-part test: (1) The separation of voting rights from beneficial ownership; (2) This separation is irrevocable for a definite period of time; and (3) The object of the agreement is voting control over the corporation.[50] One problem, however, with this test is that it has the potential to turn practically every voting agreement with irrevocable proxies into a voting trust. More fundamentally, from a policy standpoint, why should the law require voting agreements with irrevocable proxies to be on file with the corporation when the law does not require the same of voting agreements without irrevocable proxies? After all, there appears to be little difference as far as the impact on non-party shareholders between voting agreements with irrevocable proxies and voting agreements without

---

46. *E.g.*, Shepaug Voting Trust Cases, 60 Conn. 553, 24 A. 32 (1890).

47. *E.g.*, Carnegie Trust Co. v. Security Life Ins. Co., 111 Va. 1, 68 S.E. 412 (1910).

48. *E.g.*, Del. Gen. Corp. Law § 218(a); M.B.C.A. § 7.30.

49. Failure to comply with all of the statutory requirements for forming a voting trust may, or may not, render the trust invalid, depending upon the severity of the mistake and the general attitude of the court toward voting trusts and voting trust statutes. *Compare* Smith v. Biggs Boiler

Works Co., 32 Del.Ch. 147, 82 A.2d 372 (1951), *with* Reserve Life Ins. Co. v. Provident Life Ins. Co., 499 F.2d 715 (8th Cir. 1974).

50. *E.g.*, Lehrman v. Cohen, 43 Del.Ch. 222, 222 A.2d 800 (Sup. Ct. 1966). Interestingly, Delaware courts also have been willing to hold that an agreement labeled a voting trust may not, in fact, be a voting trust for purposes of the statutory requirements. Oceanic Exploration Co. v. Grynberg, 428 A.2d 1 (Del.1981).

proxies, at least if the court is willing to specifically enforce shareholder voting agreements. Given these practical and policy problems with attempting to characterize some voting agreements as voting trusts, it may be just as well that, as mentioned earlier, the voting trust statutes now often contain provisions disclaiming an intent to invalidate otherwise legal shareholder voting agreements and proxies. Of course, this forces one to ask: Why have requirements in voting trust statutes that do not apply to voting agreements, when voting agreements generally have the same effect on non-party shareholders as does a voting trust?[51]

One other common feature of statutes validating voting trusts is that these statutes typically provide that the trust terminates 10 years after creation of the trust[52] (albeit, the statutes typically contain provisions allowing parties to extend the trust for additional 10 year periods by written agreement entered into prior to the trust's expiration[53]). Since voting agreements generally are not subject to similar time limits, this creates a second questionable difference in the treatment of voting agreements versus voting trusts, and again can lead to arguments over whether a voting agreement is in fact a voting trust.

Presumably, the reason for limiting the length of a voting trust lies in concerns about changing circumstances over time rendering obsolete the original intent behind the trust and the instructions in the trust agreement—albeit, one might wonder why this is not a danger which the founders of the trust can assess for themselves. Even before expiration of 10 years, however, circumstances can arise which were not anticipated in drafting the trust agreement. For example, the trust agreement normally contains instructions concerning the election of directors—either telling the trustees who to vote for, or granting discretion to the trustees—since selection of directors typically is the whole point of the voting trust. The parties creating the trust may forget, however, that shareholders occasionally vote on matters other than the election of directors, such as amendment of the articles, sales of substantially all assets, mergers, and the like. This creates problems when the trust agreement contains no instructions as to how, or even whether, the trustees are to vote

---

51. The problem is not confined to shareholder voting agreements. Once we start condemning arrangements which have an effect equivalent to a voting trust on the ground that the arrangement does not comply with the voting trust statute, all sorts of arrangements may be swept away. *See, e.g.,* Hall v. Staha, 303 Ark. 673, 800 S.W.2d 396 (1990) (the court held that a limited partnership, which existed to hold stock in a corporation, was an illegal voting trust).

52. *But see* Del. Gen. Corp. Law § 218(a).

53. If not all of the beneficial owners agree to the extension, the statutes generally allow an extension covering the shares of the beneficial owners who agree. *E.g.,* M.B.C.A. § 7.30(c). The ability of a majority shareholder to decline participation in an extension of the trust is a weakness of the voting trust as a tool to ensure minority shareholders retain membership on the board of directors. Nor is this a problem that the parties can circumvent through advance planning, since the statutes typically limit the ability of the beneficial owners to agree to an extension far in advance of the trust's termination. *See, e.g.,* Cal. Corp. Code § 706(b) (allowing extensions within two years of the trust's expiration); N.Y. Bus. Corp. Law § 621(d) (allowing extensions within six months of the trust's expiration); M.B.C.A. § 7.30(c) (extension may be entered at any time, but only lasts 10 years from the date the first shareholder signs the extension).

concerning such matters.[54] Other questions the trust agreement may neglect to answer include whether the trustees can vote for themselves to be directors,[55] what happens when multiple trustees disagree on how to vote,[56] and whether the beneficial owners, if they all agree, can terminate the trust prior to the stated expiration of its term.[57]

In addition to the normal rules of contract interpretation, courts confronted with such gaps in voting trust agreements can bring to bear the fiduciary obligation of the trustees to the beneficiaries of the trust. Indeed, even in cases in which the trust agreement seems clearly to grant powers to the trustees, courts might limit the actions of trustees when those actions are contrary to the interests of the beneficiaries. For example, in *Brown v. McLanahan*,[58] trustees voted to amend the corporation's certificate of incorporation to shift voting rights from preferred stock—which was in the voting trust—to debentures. The trust was about to expire (because of the 10 year limit) and the trustees acted to prevent the preferred shareholders taking control of the corporation away from the trustees, who were debenture holders. Despite the trust agreement empowering the trustees to vote on certificate amendments, the court held that the action breached the trustee's fiduciary duty to the preferred shareholders. Interestingly, in reaching this conclusion, the court rejected the argument that the trustees' fiduciary duty in this case should run to the debenture holders because the trust agreement essentially had been imposed to protect the interests of the debenture holders as part of a bankruptcy reorganization plan for the corporation. The court pointed out that the debenture holders originally also had received the beneficial interest in the preferred stock in the reorganization plan, but the debenture holders had sold their interest in the preferred stock. Having sold their beneficial interest in the trust property, the debenture holders could no longer assert that they were the real beneficiaries of the trust. Accordingly, the court's opinion does not address the difficult question as to where the trustee's obligation will run in a case in which a creditor forces shareholders to put their stock in trust pending repayment of corporate debt.

One other question sometimes created by voting trusts involves the rights of the beneficial owners. Specifically, to what extent do the beneficial owners retain the rights of shareholders to inspect corporate records, bring derivative suits, and the like? Earlier sections of this book dealing with inspection rights and derivative suits considered the stand-

---

54. *E.g.*, Clarke Memorial College v. Monaghan Land Co., 257 A.2d 234 (Del.Ch. 1969) (holding that the trustees could vote to authorize the sale of land which was the corporation's sole asset, even though the trustees could not vote to dissolve the corporation).

55. *See* Taft Realty Corp. v. Yorkhaven Enterprises, Inc., 146 Conn. 338, 150 A.2d 597 (1959) (holding that the trustees can vote for themselves as directors, barring other provision in the trust agreement).

56. *See* Del. Gen. Corp. Law § 218(a) (majority rule, barring other provision in the trust agreement, but if an even number of trustees disagree, then split up how the shares are voted).

57. *See* H.M. Byllesby & Co. v. Doriot, 25 Del.Ch. 46, 12 A.2d 603 (1940) (holding that the beneficiaries, if they all agree, can terminate the trust early if no third party has relied upon the existence of the trust).

58. 148 F.2d 703 (4th Cir.1945).

ing of persons who have beneficial ownership, but not legal title, to stock, to assert the rights of a shareholder in these contexts.[59]

d. Classified shares

Yet another way to ensure that a minority shareholder can elect him- or herself to the board of directors is by having the corporation issue two or more classes of stock with differing voting rights. For example, suppose two individuals form a corporation and agree to have equal representation on the board of directors, but (presumably because one party contributes more capital) the two parties agree to an unequal division of the rights to receive dividends and liquidating distributions from the corporation. Having the articles authorize the corporation to issue two classes of stock, equivalent in all respects except that one class has the right to vote and one class does not, could accomplish the parties' objective. The parties could each purchase 50 percent of the voting stock—thereby ensuring that neither party had the power to vote the other off of the board—while the individual who is to receive the greater share of the dividends would purchase additional nonvoting stock. A variation of this idea is to have the articles authorize the corporation to issue different classes of stock that are entitled to an unequal number of votes per share—say one class could have two or three votes per share, while the other class is only entitled to the traditional one vote per share. Issuing the stock with more votes per share to a party who will receive a smaller economic interest in the corporation can give this party an equal vote to a person receiving a greater interest in the company, but who will receive the shares with only one vote per share.

Use of nonvoting or super-voting shares can work to ensure that each shareholder retains his or her position on the board in the two-person corporation. This solution, however, breaks down in the corporation with more than two shareholders (or two cohesive shareholder groups). The problem is that shifting alliances among multiple shareholders make it impossible to prevent any shareholder from ending up in the minority (as happened the *Wilkes* case). A possible solution here is to get away from the at-large election format in which all shareholders vote to fill all of the positions on the board. Instead, the articles could authorize several classes of shares, each class being entitled to elect some fraction of the board members. The facts which faced the Delaware Supreme Court in *Lehrman v. Cohen*[60] provide a good illustration of this technique.

Two families, the Lehrmans and Cohens, essentially owned the supermarket corporation involved in *Lehrman*. The company issued three classes of stock. The Lehrmans received all of the shares of one class (cutely named class AL), which was entitled to elect two members of the board. The Cohens received all of the shares of a second class (class AC, naturally), which was also entitled to elect two directors.

59. See §§ 3.1.3c, 4.3.2 *supra*.   **60.** 43 Del.Ch. 222, 222 A.2d 800 (1966).

Notice how this arrangement guaranteed each family could fill two positions on the board. The corporation also issued a third class of shares to the corporation's attorney—who was named Danzansky (and so this class imaginatively was named class AD). The AD shares had the right to elect one director to the corporation's five-person board and the right to receive repayment of the rather nominal purchase price of the shares back from the corporation upon the company's liquidation; but the AD shares otherwise lacked any of the rights normally associated with stock (such as the right to receive dividends). Essentially, the AD shares were designed simply to ensure that Danzansky would be on the board to act as a tie-breaker. Lehrman (perhaps understandably) got upset when Danzansky and Cohen voted to make Danzansky president of the company under a 15–year employment contract. Lehrman then sued claiming that the AD shares constituted an illegal voting trust. This argument seems to be clutching at straws, and, not surprisingly, the Delaware Supreme Court rejected it. After all, Danzansky did not receive the power to vote anyone else's stock by trust or proxy. Moreover, there was no problem of the arrangement being a secret from Lehrman. Still, Danzansky did not have much of an economic stake in the corporation to correspond to his voting power. Yet, to condemn the agreement on those grounds would doom all efforts at outside arbitration of corporate management disputes. Indeed, the court rejected Lehrman's alternate argument that the AD shares had an improper purpose (this being to create a mechanism for arbitrating disputes among directors).

As discussed earlier when dealing both with forming and financing a corporation,[61] corporation statutes typically provide that a company's articles may authorize classes of stock with different voting and other rights. As a result, courts generally uphold the sort of classified stock schemes outlined above.[62] In addition to rejecting the notion that such schemes somehow equal an illegal voting trust (in *Lehrman*), courts have also rejected arguments that such schemes violate state laws requiring corporations to allow cumulative voting.[63]

Much as in the case of voting trusts, parties creating a classified stock arrangement may ignore the fact that shareholders occasionally vote on matters other than electing directors, including amending the articles, mergers and the like. Issuing multiple classes of stock with different voting rights can raise a number of questions when such votes occur. For example, can shares lacking the right to vote for directors, nevertheless vote on these other matters? Also, if some shares possess greater voting power in electing directors, does such weighted voting apply in voting on other issues? In the absence of guidance in the articles, the court is left essentially to choose between assuming consistency in voting rights across all matters (in other words, nonvoting or

61. See §§ 1.4.1, 2.1.1*b supra*.

62. *E.g.,* Hampton v. Tri–State Finance Corp., 30 Colo.App. 420, 495 P.2d 566 (1972) (upheld issuing nonvoting common stock).

63. *E.g.,* Diamond v. Parkersburg–Aetna Corp., 146 W.Va. 543, 122 S.E.2d 436 (1961).

super-voting shares are always nonvoting or super-voting no matter what the election), and applying the rule that any deviation from treating all shares equally must be spelled out in the articles.

5.2.2   Controlling Specific Management Decisions

Merely obtaining a position on the board does not, of course, give a minority shareholder protection against a majority of directors making decisions for the company (on matters such as jobs, salaries, dividends and business policy) which are contrary to the minority shareholder's interest and expectations. Hence, shareholders in closely held corporations often use various techniques to control specific management decisions which ordinarily would be within the board's discretion.

a.   Shareholder agreements controlling board decisions

In a partnership (or limited liability company), making an advance arrangement to govern specific management decisions is, at least from a legal standpoint, a straightforward matter: All that the parties need to do is to set out the decisions upon which they have advance agreement in their partnership (or limited liability company operating) contract. If the parties so desire, the contract can specify what owners will have what jobs and at what salaries, what profits the company will distribute or reinvest, and what business policies the company will follow. There may be practical difficulties in seeking to anticipate and draft for all these future decisions in a contract made as early as the start of the venture, but, in the partnership or limited liability company, there is no legal rule which states that the parties cannot try.

Shareholders in closely held corporations often attempt to follow this same approach to govern decisions ordinarily made by the board of directors. For example, in *McQuade v. Stoneham*,[64] three shareholders of the corporation which operated the then New York Giants baseball team entered an agreement regarding the management of the company. McQuade (who was a New York City magistrate) and John McGraw (the well-know manager of the Giants) had each purchased a small number of shares in the corporation from Stoneham (who owned a majority of the corporation's shares). In part, the agreement operated as a shareholder voting contract, calling upon Stoneham, McGraw and McQuade to vote for each other as directors. The agreement, however, went significantly beyond this. Stoneham, McGraw and McQuade agreed to "use their best efforts" to have Stoneham be president, McGraw be vice president, and McQuade be treasurer, of the corporation, and the contract specified the salaries each was to receive in those positions. The contract also required unanimous agreement of the three shareholders to change salaries, capitalization, bylaws or business policy of the company in a way which would "interfere with the rights of minority shareholders." After the board (apparently acting under Stoneham's influence) fired McQuade from his position as treasurer, and the shareholders (essentially Stone-

---

64.   263 N.Y. 323, 189 N.E. 234 (1934).

ham) did not reelect McQuade as a director, McQuade sued. The New York Court of Appeals, however, held that the contract was contrary to public policy and void.

One problem with the contract in this particular case was that McQuade's participation violated a New York statute which prohibited a magistrate from engaging in any outside business. The majority of the court was not content to rule against McQuade only on this ground, however. Rather, the majority of the court held that the contract also violated public policy because of its attempt to control decisions made by the board of directors—specifically, in this case, the decision as to who the company should employ as officers and at what salaries. In other words, a contract which seemingly would be perfectly appropriate if made among partners in a partnership, violated public policy because it was among shareholders in a corporation.

To understand the broader holding in *McQuade*, it helps to ask just how the parties were going to carry out the contract to maintain the three individuals in the specified positions and at the specified salaries. The contract stated that the parties would use "their best efforts," but in what capacity would they use those efforts? This is not as simple as with a shareholder voting contract, which is a promise by shareholders as to how they will vote as shareholders. The problem is that appointing officers and setting salaries are decisions ordinarily within the power of the board of directors.

Perhaps this was an agreement between the parties as to how they would vote as directors. After all, the contract contained a shareholder voting agreement which would ensure that the parties were directors. The problem with this construction, according to the court in *McQuade*, is that directors may not contract away their obligation to exercise independent judgment in deciding what is best for the corporation. Recall, we noted earlier how a few courts had ruled that shareholder voting agreements were contrary to public policy because shareholders had a duty to exercise independent judgment in voting. This argument has far greater resonance for director action than for shareholder voting. After all, as discussed previously, shareholders, by and large, traditionally lack any duty when voting. As the *Ringling* court pointed out, shareholders would not breach any duty by ignoring corporate affairs and not voting at all. By contrast, directors assume a duty of care and loyalty to the corporation. Hence, it certainly plausible to say that directors breach their duty by contracting away their votes, and that any voting contract by directors is contrary to public policy.

Okay, if the parties could not couch the contract as an agreement governing how they would vote as directors, perhaps the parties intended to carry out the agreement as shareholders. The problem with this interpretation, according to the court in *McQuade*, is that it illegally impinges upon the board of directors' power to manage the corporation. Specifically, the corporation statute grants the board of directors the power to manage the company, which normally includes deciding who to employ and at what salaries. To uphold a contract in which shareholders, acting as shareholders, decide who the corporation will employ and at what salaries, would contravene the statute giving this power to the board. In sum then, shareholder contracts attempting to dictate actions within the board's authority become impaled upon the horns of a dilemma: If the parties cast the contract as an agreement concerning how they will vote as directors, then the contract calls for the directors to breach their duty to exercise independent judgment; if the parties cast the agreement as an attempt by shareholders to make specific management decisions, then the agreement contravenes the statute empowering the board to manage the corporation. Some shareholders have argued that they are binding each other as partners who are conducting their partnership through a corporation. This rationalization, too, has received a hostile response from the courts.[65]

While the *McQuade* opinion and similar holdings have a certain logic, the objections they make are rather abstract. After all, who exactly is hurt by a shareholder agreement seeking to control decisions ordinarily made by the board of directors? Also, why should parties be condemned for attempting to make an agreement controlling business decisions, which if done in a partnership, would not only be permissible, but would be applauded as good planning that avoids the need for courts to apply the Uniform Partnership Act's default rules? Indeed, it would seem that courts should encourage efforts by minority shareholders to protect themselves by contract, since such contracts might avoid the need for minority shareholders to run to court complaining about breaches of fiduciary duty by the majority or seeking to invoke statutory remedies against oppressive actions.

Shortly after *McQuade*, it appeared that the New York Court of Appeals had a change of heart. In *Clark v. Dodge*,[66] the Court of Appeals dealt with an agreement between two shareholders of two corporations which produced certain medicines. Clark owned 25 percent of the stock in each company, while Dodge owned 75 percent. Only Clark, however, knew the formulas for the medicines. Under the contract, Clark promised to disclose to Dodge's son the formulas. In exchange, the agreement pledged Dodge to vote his stock for Clark to remain as a director. More significantly, Dodge promised to make sure that Clark would continue as general manager of one of the corporations so long as Clark was "faithful, efficient and competent," and that Clark would receive one-quarter of the net income of both corporations either by way of salary or dividends. Moreover, the agreement prohibited the payment of excessive salaries to other employees which would reduce the share of the net income owed to Clark. After Dodge breached the contract, Dodge defend-

65. *E.g.*, Jackson v. Hooper, 76 N.J.Eq. 592, 75 A. 568 (1910). The concurring opinion in *McQuade* attempted to avoid the dilemma underlying the majority's argument by suggesting that the parties could vote as shareholders to elect directors who would be inclined to carry out the provisions regarding positions and salaries. *See also* Hart v. Bell, 222 Minn. 69, 23 N.W.2d 375 (1946).

66. 269 N.Y. 410, 199 N.E. 641 (1936)

ed on the basis of the *McQuade* decision. The Court of Appeals, however, refused to void the agreement.

Given the similarity of the agreements involved, can one reconcile *McQuade* and *Clark*? One distinction is that all of the shareholders were party to the agreement in *Clark*, whereas there were other minority shareholders who were not a party to the contract in *McQuade*. Indeed, at one point in its opinion, the court in *Clark* focused upon the fact that the agreeing parties were the sole shareholders. Courts in other jurisdictions also have drawn a distinction between agreements controlling board actions when all shareholders are a party to the contract, and agreements only among some shareholders who attempt to control board policy—holding that the former, but not the latter, are valid.[67] This distinction makes sense. The presence of non-assenting shareholders answers the question as to who might be hurt if directors fail to exercise the directors' best judgment as to the corporation's interest on a case-by-case basis. The potential prejudice to non-party shareholders is especially apparent when one notices that the typical subject matter of the agreements in cases such as *McQuade*, *Clark* and the like involves payment of salaries to the parties to the agreements. Also, a rule which validates shareholder agreements controlling matters such as salaries and the like, only if all of the shareholders assent, places shareholder agreements on the same plane as agreements among partners. Specifically, when we spoke earlier as to how the law not only allows, but encourages, partners to make an agreement controlling the management of their firm (including by setting compensation), this is through an agreement among all of the partners, not simply a majority.[68]

The distinction based upon the presence of non-assenting shareholders raises one question, however: Should it be up to the non-assenting shareholders to object to the contract, or can one of the shareholders who entered the deal use the existence of such shareholders as an excuse to avoid his or her promise? For example, in *McQuade*, none of the non-party shareholders objected to the contract—indeed, McQuade claimed that Stoneham dismissed him because McQuade tried to look out for the interest of the other shareholders. Hence, one could make the rule be that shareholder agreements controlling board action are valid as between the parties to the agreement, but invalid if challenged by any non-assenting shareholder. On the other hand, if one wishes to deter agreements made by less than all of the shareholders, then courts should let a party use the presence of non-assenting shareholders as an out. Such deterrence might be desirable if one fears that non-assenting shareholders in many cases will not be aware of agreements controlling board action to the possible prejudice of the non-party shareholders.

Unfortunately, the hope that the New York Court of Appeals, through the combination of *McQuade* and *Clark*, had created a sensible rule keyed to the presence or absence of non-assenting shareholders,

67. *E.g.*, Glazer v. Glazer, 374 F.2d 390 (5th Cir.1967).

68. *See, e.g.*, Uniform Partnership Act § 18.

took a blow some years later. In *Long Park, Inc. v. Trenton–New Brunswick Theatres Co.*,[69] the Court of Appeals dealt with an agreement made by the only three shareholders of a corporation. The agreement provided that one of the shareholders would manage the company for 19 years (subject to the right of the other shareholders to arbitrate the question of changing management if they were dissatisfied). The court struck down the agreement because the agreement took away the board's authority to manage the company. In reaching this result, the court distinguished *Clark* as involving only a "slight impingement or innocuous variance from the statutory norm" of board management.

The problems with the *Long Park* decision are not only that it struck down an agreement without identifying anyone hurt by the parties' action, but also that the court's opinion fails to provide much of a workable standard to guide shareholders making contracts. For example, the court seems to say that the contract in *Clark* was okay because it did not take away all power from the board to manage the business, as did the agreement in *Long Park*. Yet, the agreement in *Clark* required the board to continue Clark as general manager so long as he was competent. In that position, Clark was the corporation's chief executive officer, a post which traditionally places its holder largely in charge of business operations. True, unlike the shareholder in *Long Park*, Clark's power as general manager was subject to the ultimate authority of the board, which could always countermand his decisions. Suppose, however, the parties had coupled the provision maintaining Clark as general manager, with a shareholder voting agreement calling for only two directors—Clark and Dodge. Under those circumstances, the power of the board to countermand any action by Clark would exist in theory, but not in practice, since Clark would have an effective veto on board resolutions. Would this render the agreement invalid under *Long Park*?

Judicial reactions outside of New York exhibit much the same ambivalence toward shareholder contracts controlling board actions as found in *McQuade*, *Clark* and *Long Park*. Many courts outside of New York have been sympathetic to such agreements. For example, in *Galler v. Galler*,[70] the Supreme Court of Illinois upheld a shareholder agreement which, among other things, set the dividends the corporation would pay and required the corporation to pay a pension to the widow of either of the two contracting shareholders in the event either of the contracting shareholders died. Interestingly, the two contracting shareholders in *Galler* did not own all of the stock—each owned 47½ percent—albeit, the non-party shareholder did not come forward to raise objections to the agreement. The opinion in *Galler* has been influential, particularly in its rationale that closely held corporations deserve special treatment. On the other hand, there continue to be court opinions in states beyond New York—albeit, less so in recent years—that raise

69.   297 N.Y. 174, 77 N.E.2d 633 (1948).   **70.**   32 Ill.2d 16, 203 N.E.2d 577 (1964).

questions as to the validity of shareholder agreements governing decisions ordinarily made by the board.[71]

b. Statutes which validate shareholder agreements controlling board decisions and which establish special treatment for electing close corporations

Earlier, we discussed how state legislatures responded to the uncertain judicial treatment of shareholder voting agreements and voting trusts by enacting validating statutes. Many state legislatures likewise have responded to hostile or uncertain judicial treatment of shareholder contracts controlling board actions. The statutes validating shareholder contracts controlling board actions, however, exhibit greater variation and complexity than statutes dealing with voting contracts and voting trusts—and, as a result, practitioners and students often are confused as to the impact of such statutes. Accordingly, it useful to explore these statutes in some depth.

Statutes expressly validating shareholder agreements which control board actions fall into two broad camps. In the first camp, there are what one might label "general applicability validating statutes"—general applicability because the corporation does not need to elect special status in order for the statute to validate shareholder agreements controlling management decisions. New York's law provides an illustration of a general applicability validating statute. In reaction to the *Long Park* decision, the New York legislature added Section 620(b) to the New York Business Corporation Law. Section 620(b) validates shareholder agreements which otherwise could be invalid because the agreement restricts the board in managing the corporation—either in that the agreement commands certain board decisions or in that the agreement transfers management authority to someone other than the board.

Several requirements exist for an agreement to come within Section 620(b)'s protection. These requirements, as noted earlier, go well beyond the simple writing requirement for a valid shareholder voting contract under Section 620(a). In large part, these requirements appear directed at codifying the distinction we suggested earlier between *Clark* and *McQuade*—this being that agreements controlling board action should be legal if all of the shareholders assent, but not legal if some of the shareholders do not assent. Much of the complexity in Section 620(b) results from dividing non-consenting shareholders into two groups. There can be individuals who owned stock at the time that other shareholders made a contract controlling board actions, but who did not agree to the contract (either because no one asked them or because they declined when asked). Here, Section 620(b) takes a simple approach: Section 620(b) does not validate the contract. The complexity comes from dealing with a second type of non-consenting shareholder—this being the shareholder who only acquired his or her stock after earlier shareholders

71. *E.g.*, Capital Investments v. Whitehall Packing Co., 91 Wis.2d 178, 280 N.W.2d 254 (1979) (dicta); Kennerson v. Burbank Amusement Co., 120 Cal.App.2d 157, 260 P.2d 823 (1953) (involving similar facts and holding to *Long Park*).

entered the agreement. In this situation, there is a need to balance the interest of the non-assenting new shareholder against the interest of the individuals who made the contract and still remain shareholders. (After all, the minority shareholders who might be relying upon the contract for protection often will not have been the persons who transferred stock to the new shareholder.) New York's statute largely takes a notice approach to deal with this problem: The agreement is valid if the new shareholders have notice of it. (To facilitate this notice, Section 620(g) requires the stock certificates to note conspicuously the existence of the agreement.) In the case of shares traded in public markets, however, buyers technically may have notice of special agreements governing the corporation, but might not pay much attention. Accordingly, while New York does not require that the corporation limit the number of its shareholders, or elect special close corporation treatment—as done by states in the second camp—Section 620(c) disqualifies corporations with shares listed on national stock exchanges or regularly quoted by over-the-counter market makers from taking advantage of Section 620(b).[72]

Section 620(f) of New York's statute provides that the effect of the agreement validated by Section 620(b) is to relieve the directors, and impose upon the shareholders making the agreement, any liability for breaching a duty by carrying out the decisions dictated by the agreement. The rationale for this provision is not difficult to understand. If shareholders, rather than directors, are making management decisions, then shareholders, rather than directors, should assume a duty of care and loyalty. Indeed, it is likely that courts would have figured this out even if the statute had been silent on the point. It is important not to misunderstand the impact of this liability provision. Shareholders do not become liable simply by virtue of making business decisions, any more than directors are liable for making business decisions. Rather, only if a decision made by the shareholders flunks the business judgment rule should the shareholders who made the decision be liable, just as directors only would be liable if the directors' decision flunks the business judgment rule. The statute makes this point by placing on the contracting shareholders the liabilities "imposed on directors by this chapter" (in other words, the liability which the directors can face under the corporation statute).

One requirement of Section 620(b) is more problematic. Section 620(b) requires the parties to place the agreement controlling board action in the certificate of incorporation. Placing the contract in a side document (or even the bylaws) does not meet the statute. The requirement that the parties must place the agreement in the corporation's certificate of incorporation creates the potential for shareholders, who do not hire an attorney, or whose attorney does not bother to read the statute, to muck things up.[73] One might say to such shareholders "tough

72. One might also argue that if the corporation's stock is traded on public markets, minority shareholders can sell their stock in case of dissatisfaction, and, therefore, have less need for contractual protections.

73. *E.g.*, Adler v. Svingos, 80 App. Div. 2d 764, 436 N.Y.S.2d 719 (1981).

luck" if there was some purpose to the certificate placement requirement. Given the general notice rule, however, it is difficult to understand what purpose the legislature had in mind for the requirement that the agreement appear in the certificate.

In light of this discussion concerning the certificate placement requirement, Section 7.32 of the Model Act marks an improvement over the New York statute. Section 7.32 largely copies the approach of New York's Section 620(b). Section 7.32, however, allows the agreement to be in the articles, bylaws, or a separate written document signed by all of the shareholders and "made known to the corporation." (Of course, if all of the shareholders sign an agreement, it is difficult to see how the "corporation" would not know about it.) Section 7.32 of the Model Act also is broader in the scope of its protection than New York's Section 620(b). For example, under Section 7.32, a shareholder agreement can eliminate the board of directors altogether in favor of direct governance by the shareholders—something which Section 620(b) might not cover. Section 7.32 also states that agreements falling within the section's protection are not subject to challenge under any other provision of the statute, whereas Section 620(b) only speaks about challenges based upon the contention that the agreement improperly controls the board or transfers the board's authority. Incidentally, while Section 7.32, like Section 620(b), uses notice—specifically, by requiring that the stock certificates note the existence of the agreement—to deal with the problem of shareholders who acquire their stock after the agreement, failure to provide such notice does not void the contract under Section 7.32. Rather, such a failure entitles purchasers of stock without knowledge of the agreement to rescind their purchase. Another difference between Sections 7.32 and 620(b) is that Section 7.32 creates a default rule limiting the term of the agreement to 10 years unless the agreement provides otherwise.

The second camp of statutes are those which require corporations to make an election to be a "close corporation" in order to take advantage of the statutes' provisions validating shareholder agreements impinging upon the board's control. Delaware was one of the states which pioneered this type of statute. There are three essential differences between these elective close corporation statutes and the general applicability validating statutes discussed above.

The first difference is that the elective close corporation statutes normally are more restrictive as to which corporations even can elect to come under the statutes' special provisions than are the general applicability validating statutes like New York's and the Model Act. In contrast to New York and the Model Act's coverage of all corporations without publicly traded stock, the elective close corporation statutes typically limit the number of shareholders a corporation can have if it wishes to elect to be a close corporation under the statute. For example, under Delaware's statute, an electing corporation can have no more than 30 shareholders.[74] This limit reflects the notion that it is the number of shareholders which dictates appropriate rules for corporate governance— for example, corporations with few shareholders do not gain the same efficiencies from central management by a board of directors as do corporations with numerous shareholders. Delaware's statute also requires that corporations, wishing to elect close corporation status, must restrict the transfer of their stock (presumably because of concern with prejudice to new shareholders), and must not make a public offering of stock (presumably for similar reasons).[75]

The second difference in these elective close corporation statutes is the one already mentioned: To trigger the statute, the shareholders must elect close corporation status. Typically, the mechanics of such an election simply entails placing a provision in the corporation's articles, which states that the corporation is a close corporation.[76]

The rationale for the election requirement perhaps stems from the third difference between the elective close corporation statutes and the general applicability validating statutes. Electing close corporation status triggers more provisions in the statute than just those which validate shareholder agreements seeking to control actions ordinarily made by the board of directors. Actually, it is easy to exaggerate the scope of the provisions triggered by a close corporation election under most of these statutes. Delaware provides a useful illustration. Delaware's corporation statute contains a whole subchapter of provisions dealing with electing close corporations.[77] Most of these provisions, however, simply deal with obtaining or maintaining the close corporation election. The actual impact of making the election turns out to be rather limited.

Primarily, as already suggested, the close corporation election triggers provisions validating shareholder agreements despite the challenge that the agreement interferes with the board's discretion to manage the corporation.[78] Also, electing close corporation status under Delaware's statute enables the shareholders to take the broader actions which we saw sanctioned by Section 7.32 of the Model Act—such as dispensing with the board of directors altogether.[79] Much as under New York's Section 620(b), or Section 7.32 of the Model Act, shareholders who

74. Del. Gen. Corp. Law § 342(a)(1).

75. *Id* at § 342(a)(2) and (3).

76. *E.g.*, Del. Gen. Corp. Law § 343(a). Statutes vary as to whether it takes a unanimous vote of the shareholders to amend the articles in order to make a close corporation election when the incorporators did not originally make this election. *Compare* Del. Gen. Corp. Law § 344 (two-thirds vote sufficient), *with* Cal. Corp. Code § 158(b) (requiring unanimous vote of shares of all classes).

77. Del. Gen. Corp. Law §§ 341–356. California's corporation code provisions dealing with electing close corporations illustrates a different stylistic approach. Per-

haps to make things challenging for persons reading the code, California scatters the provisions dealing with companies electing close corporation status throughout the state's corporations statute.

78. Del. Gen. Corp. Law § 350. Section 354 of Delaware's statute supplements Section 350 by protecting a shareholder agreement against the challenge that the agreement is invalid as constituting an attempt to manage the corporation as if the company was a partnership—which is a response to the *Jackson v. Hooper* opinion cited earlier in discussing the *McQuade* rationale.

79. Del. Gen. Corp. Law § 351.

control the actions of directors will pick up, under Delaware's statute, the potential liabilities of directors.[80] One interesting feature of Delaware's statute is that not all of the shareholders need to agree in order for a contract controlling board action to be valid. Specifically, Delaware's statute makes such a contract among shareholders holding a majority of the outstanding stock valid "as between the parties to the agreement." In other words, Delaware follows the approach we discussed earlier, which requires non-assenting shareholders to challenge the agreement themselves, rather than allowing a party to the contract to point to the existence of non-assenting shareholders as grounds to let the party out of his or her agreement.[81]

So, what else does the close corporation election under Delaware's statute accomplish besides validating shareholder contracts controlling decisions ordinarily made by the board? About the only other thing is to empower the court to appoint a provisional director to break deadlocks on the board of an electing close corporation[82]—which, as we discussed earlier, goes somewhat beyond the scope of judicial action available to deal with deadlocks in Delaware corporations generally. This approach of authorizing somewhat greater judicial intervention in case of shareholder dissension—either by granting more shareholders standing to ask for intervention, relaxing the standards for the court to award relief, or expanding the range of remedies—is found in a number states' elective close corporation provisions.[83]

Experience with statutes creating special treatment for corporations electing close corporation status probably has disappointed the advocates of such legislation. A number of studies of corporate filings have found that only a small fraction of eligible corporations elect to be close corporations.[84] This fact, in turn, raises the question as to why few persons take advantage of the election.

Perhaps shareholders, or their attorneys, are unaware of these statutes—albeit, by and large, books on corporate law do not ignore these statutes. Alternately, perhaps shareholders, or their attorneys, do not find the statutes useful. As we just discussed, the predominant impact of a close corporation election under these statutes is to validate

---

80. *Id* at § 350.

81. Placing the close corporation election in the certificate of incorporation presumably gives non-party shareholders notice at least of the possibly that there might be a shareholder agreement controlling director actions.

82. Del. Gen. Corp. Law § 353.

83. *E.g.*, Cal. Corp. Code § 1800(a)(2). Special treatment of closely held corporations under entirely different laws sometimes leads individuals into confusion as to the scope of elective close corporation statutes such as Delaware's. For example, as discussed earlier in this chapter, some courts have adopted a special rule of fiduciary duty for shareholders in closely held corporations. Elective close corporation statutes following Delaware's approach generally do not address fiduciary duty (beyond imposing the duties of directors on shareholders who control the board's actions). Nor do elective close corporation statutes such as Delaware's provide special income tax treatment (under Subchapter S) or exemptions from securities law requirements; those are subjects of entirely different legislation.

84. *E.g.*, Comment, *Assessing the Utility of Wisconsin's Close Corporation Statute: An Empirical Study*, 1986 Wis. L. Rev. 811.

shareholder agreements controlling decisions ordinarily made by the board of directors. Maybe, shareholders, or their attorneys, do not think this statutory validation is necessary. As discussed earlier, recent court opinions are more likely to uphold, than to strike down, these sort of agreements—even in the absence of a statute. Still, in many, if not most, jurisdictions, an attorney is unlikely to find a court opinion clearly holding that such agreements are beyond challenge for treading on the board's discretion. Another reason that an election may be unnecessary is because the shareholders in the particular corporation did not make an agreement controlling what are ordinarily board decisions. Needless to say, shareholders do not need to ensure the validity of an agreement they do not make. In fact, one study, which found low usage of statutory close corporation elections, also found shareholder agreements controlling board action were not that common.[85] This, however, raises the question of whether the failure to make such agreements reflects the lack of need for this sort of protection of minority shareholders, or a failure of minority shareholders, or their attorneys, to recognize the need for such contracts. Finally, perhaps shareholders, or their attorneys, perceive some disadvantage to the close corporation election which outweighs its utility. So far, our discussion has not demonstrated much burden or additional impact to a close corporation election. So, where is the problem?

One concern some attorneys seem to have with close corporation elections—and, indeed, with shareholder agreements controlling board actions generally—is possible liability of the shareholders to creditors based upon piercing the corporate veil. This concern stems from the idea that the observance of so-called corporate formalities is a factor which courts consider in deciding whether to pierce the corporation. As discussed earlier in this book when exploring piercing, this idea may be something of a myth.[86] In any event, to the extent that statutes expressly empower shareholders to control board actions, or even to do away with the board, it would be rather perverse for courts to turn around and use such control as grounds to pierce. One suspects that even a court which took seriously the notion that disregarding corporate formalities is a factor in piercing would ignore informality sanctioned by statute.[87] Just to provide added assurance, some states (such as California) have included, as part of their elective close corporation statutes, provisions which state that the failure to observe certain corporate formalities pursuant to an agreement validated by the close corporation statute is not a factor to be used in favor of piercing.[88]

The provisions addressing piercing in some elective close corporation statutes, in turn, have caused a number of writers and practitioners to

---

85. *Id.*

86. See § 1.5.4 *supra.*

87. *See, e.g.,* Abraham v. Lake Forest, Inc., 377 So.2d 465 (La.Ct.App.1979) (noting that the failure to hold shareholders and directors meetings is not a factor supporting piercing the corporate veil when the

lack of meetings was sanctioned by a provision in the state's corporation statute allowing use of unanimous consent in lieu of meetings.)

88. *E.g.,* Cal. Corp. Code § 300(e).

view close corporation statutes as, in fact, serving an independent function of allowing informal operation of corporations by their shareholders without fear of piercing based upon the non-observance of corporate formalities.[89] The history of these statutes suggests this was not their intended effect. Some writers have criticized this potential impact of close corporation statutes.[90] Such criticism seems overblown. Recall that the target of a piercing case is a dominant shareholder—typically a sole or majority shareholder—who abuses his or her control over the corporation to the prejudice of creditors. A sole or majority shareholder does not need close corporation statutes to run the corporation as he or she wishes. Rather, these statutes serve to protect minority shareholders, by ensuring that majority shareholders, like Stoneham and Dodge, cannot get out of contracts made with the minority. Hence, the statutes do not sanction the sort of conduct which ought to be relevant to piercing the corporate veil.[91]

Given the infrequency with which shareholders of closely held corporations elect close corporation status, the main significance of elective close corporation statutes may, in fact, lie in their influence on judicial treatment of *non*-electing corporations. Indeed, the two leading cases invoking Delaware's close corporation provisions involved corporations which did not make the election. These two cases suggest two opposite ways such statutes can influence judicial thinking.

In *Nixon v. Blackwell*,[92] the Delaware Supreme Court drew a negative implication from the statute in resolving a case dealing with a corporation which did not make a close corporation election. Actually, the court's invocation of Delaware's close corporation statute in *Nixon* is curious, since nothing in the statute would have been relevant to the issue in the case even had the shareholders elected close corporation treatment under Delaware's law. The case involved a challenge made by minority shareholders who were left out of share repurchases funded by the corporation. The minority shareholders urged the Delaware court to hold that shareholders in closely held corporations owe a special fiduciary duty to each other. We explored this issue earlier in this chapter. For now, what is interesting about *Nixon* is the fact that a portion of the court's rationale for rejecting a special fiduciary duty is the notion that Delaware's close corporation statute preempts the field of special rules for closely held corporations. The minor details that nothing in Delaware's close corporation statutory provisions either expressed such a preemptive intent, or addressed the subject of fiduciary duty (except

89. *E.g.*, Consumer's Co-op. v. Olsen, 142 Wis.2d 465, 419 N.W.2d 211 (1988).

90. *E.g.*, Dennis Karjala, *An Analysis of Close Corporation Legislation in the United States*, 21 Ariz. St. L.J. 663 (1989).

91. One qualifier on this discussion, however, stems from the typical subject matter of shareholder contracts controlling board decisions. These contracts commonly seek to ensure salaries or other distributions to minority shareholders. If the salary provided by the contract is unfair to the corporation, or the distribution violates dividend rules, then the minority shareholder may face liability to creditors, just as would a dominant shareholder who engaged in abusive self-dealing with the corporation.

92. 626 A.2d 1366 (Del.1993).

when shareholders enter contracts dictating actions of the board), did not seem bother the court.

A majority of the New York Court of Appeals had different reaction to Delaware's statute in *Zion v. Kurtz*.[93] *Zion* involved an agreement between the only two shareholders in a Delaware corporation. This agreement gave the minority shareholder a veto on all corporate activities. The shareholders had not made a statutory close corporation election, but the court nevertheless held that the agreement was valid. The majority of the court's precise holding relied upon a clause in the shareholder agreement, which stated that the defendant would execute whatever documents were necessary to carry out the contract. This clause, the majority of the court reasoned, required the defendant belatedly to amend the certificate of incorporation in order to make a close corporation election. In being willing to allow such an after-the-fact remedy, the majority of the court viewed Delaware's close corporation statute as expressing a general public policy that there is nothing wrong with shareholder agreements controlling board actions.

Technically, *Nixon* and *Zion* are not inconsistent, as their holdings involve entirely different issues. The two courts' use of the statute, however, reflects very different philosophies: One court drawing the sort of negative implication which, if applied to shareholder contracts controlling board decisions, could lead a court to invalidate such contracts in corporations which do not take advantage of a close corporation election; the other court finding that the statute shows there really is nothing wrong with such contracts, even in corporations which do not make a close corporation election. In either event, the need for courts to engage in this sort of analysis may suggest the superiority of the general applicability validating statutes as a mechanism to deal with shareholder agreements controlling board actions. Put differently, the elective close corporation statutes may have pretended to accomplish too much, and ended up accomplishing very little.

In addition to the two types of statutes explicitly intended to validate shareholder agreements controlling board actions, there is another type of statutory provision which can bear upon the validity of such agreements. Recall, under the rationale in *McQuade*, the reason that shareholders cannot carry out an agreement making business decisions in their capacity as shareholders is because this would contravene the provision in the corporation statute which states that the board shall manage the corporation. In this light, it is potentially significant that modern acts typically add a caveat to this portion of the corporation statute. For example, Section 141(a) of Delaware's statute states that the business of the corporation shall be managed by or under the direction of the board "except as may be otherwise provided ... in [the company's] certificate of incorporation." Such provisions raise the possibility that shareholders could ensure the validity of agreements controlling actions

---

93. 50 N.Y.2d 92, 428 N.Y.S.2d 199, 405 N.E.2d 681 (1980).

of the board merely by including such agreements in the corporation's articles.

The *Lehrman* opinion discussed earlier in dealing with classified shares, in fact, supports this possibility. The challenged class of stock in *Lehrman* existed in order to create a mechanism for arbitrating disputes between the directors. If the shareholders simply had made an agreement to submit such disputes to arbitration, then there certainly would be an issue of the agreement improperly impinging upon the board's discretion to manage the corporation. Nevertheless, the court rejected the plaintiff's alternate challenge to the classified stock scheme—that the scheme constituted an impermissible delegation of the board's authority to an arbitrator. In doing so, the court relied upon the caveat in Section 141(a), and the fact that the classified stock scheme was in the company's certificate of incorporation.

Still, all the certificate of incorporation actually did in *Lehrman* was to authorize the issuance of a class of stock with certain voting and limited economic rights. Corporation statutes expressly allow articles to designate rights for different classes of stock. Hence, it is unclear whether *Lehrman* stands for the proposition that shareholders can place any agreement controlling board action in the articles and have the agreement be valid merely because it is in the articles. Indeed, such a rule would create some rather strange results. For example, typically it only takes a vote of a majority of the shares, not unanimity, to amend the articles.[94] If shareholder agreements controlling board action are valid simply by virtue of being in the articles, what is to stop a majority of shareholders from making such an agreement by amending the articles? Allowing the majority to do this, however, would circumvent the rule in many jurisdictions' statutes or court decisions that shareholder agreements controlling board actions are valid only if all shareholders agree.

c. *Arbitration agreements*

We already have encountered a couple of cases in which shareholders in closely held corporations agreed to arbitration in the event of disputes between themselves. As just mentioned, *Lehrman* involved a scheme to place on the board a person who would serve as a tie-breaker—essentially an arbitrator—in the event of deadlock between the other directors. In *Ringling*, the agreement called for arbitration in the event the parties could not agree upon how to vote their shares. Arbitration agreements raise a number of legal issues.

At one time, courts were unwilling to enforce arbitration agreements generally, and so commonly held that parties could revoke, at any point prior to the award, an agreement to arbitrate. Most states, however, now have statutes which make agreements to arbitrate future disputes enforceable.[95] These statutes also often overrule court decisions which

---

94.   See § 7.4.2 *infra.*   **95.**   *E.g.*, N.Y.Civ. Prac. Law § 7501.

refused to enforce agreements to arbitrate a dispute unless the dispute was justiciable—in other words, presented the sort of issue that would be an appropriate subject for a court to resolve in a lawsuit—which otherwise would be a problem with a dispute over what would be a better business decision or who parties should vote for as a director.[96]

Nevertheless, we already have seen how arbitration provisions in shareholder agreements face possible challenges even if arbitration agreements generally now are enforceable. An arbitration provision in a shareholder voting agreement, as in *Ringling*, faces the challenge that the parties have separated control over the voting of stock from the ownership of the shares. Arbitrating board decisions, as in *Lehrman*, faces the challenge that the arbitration agreement impermissibly usurps the board's discretion. We already saw how the *Ringling* court rejected the challenge that the arbitration agreement improperly separated control from ownership—albeit some other courts have agreed with this challenge. In *Application of Vogel*,[97] New York courts considered the argument that an arbitration agreement impermissibly usurped the board's discretion.

Vogel involved an arbitration clause contained in a shareholder agreement made between the two 50 percent shareholders of a corporation. The corporation conducted a moving and storage business, and had the option to purchase the warehouse out of which the company operated. The two shareholders, who were also the only two directors, disagreed on whether to exercise the option, and the plaintiff shareholder demanded arbitration of the question. In ordering arbitration, the appellate court stated that if the dispute had involved simply a matter of business judgment or everyday management, then an agreement to arbitrate might well run afoul of the statutory provision empowering the board to manage the corporation. In this particular case, however, the dispute over exercising the option involved a one-time matter which went to the very existence of the company—since, without the warehouse, the company would go out of business. The idea that one-time, critical questions might be better subjects for arbitration than continuing disagreements over day-to-day management certainly has a practical appeal—after all, constant arbitration would be an awkward way to run a business. Yet, it is difficult to see the basis for the court making this a rule as to what the law will allow parties to arbitrate, rather than leaving the practicalities for the parties to decide. In any event, the New York Court of Appeals affirmed the appellate court's result without much discussion.

One added wrinkle in this area stems from the Federal Arbitration Act. This federal statute makes agreements to arbitrate disputes arising out of transactions in interstate commerce as valid and enforceable as

96. *E.g.*, Application of Burkin, 1 N.Y.2d 570, 136 N.E.2d 862, 154 N.Y.S.2d 898 (1956).

97. 25 App. Div. 2d 212, 268 N.Y.S.2d 237 (1966), *aff'd* 19 N.Y.2d 589, 278 N.Y.S.2d 236, 224 N.E.2d 738 (1967).

any other contract.[98] In other words, the act preempts state laws singling out arbitration agreements for unfavorable treatment. To the extent that the management of a particular corporation constitutes an activity in interstate commerce, then the act could preempt a state from preventing the arbitration of management disputes[99]—at least if the state does not show similar hostility toward any contract involving control over voting or director decisions.

From a policy standpoint, the objection to arbitration agreements in the corporation context is that it allows a stranger with no economic interest in the corporation either to tell shareholders how to vote their stock (if the arbitration clause is in a shareholder voting contract), or to make management decisions for the corporation (if the arbitration provision is part of a shareholder agreement seeking to control actions of the board). Yet, this objection to arbitration applies to any commercial contract containing an arbitration clause, and, hence, does not seem to justify treating arbitration clauses in shareholder agreements any worse than arbitration provisions in commercial contracts generally. Of course, the 15 year employment contract for the "neutral" director in *Lehrman* may lead one to pause before assuming there is no potential for arbitrators to abuse their position. Perhaps an answer here, however, is for courts to void transactions in which one party, in effect, has bribed the arbitrator.

d. *Supermajority requirements*

We have already encountered a couple of cases—*McQuade* and *Zion*—in which minority shareholders sought to protect themselves from undesired board actions by obtaining a veto. In these two cases, the parties made the veto part of a shareholder agreement under which the board could not take certain actions without the consent of the minority shareholders. This raised the problem we have discussed about shareholders attempting to control actions by the board. Suppose, however, the parties had placed a provision in a governing document for the corporation—the articles or bylaws—which required a unanimous vote by the directors in order to approve certain actions by the board. If the parties then combined the unanimous vote requirement with one of the techniques we discussed earlier for ensuring that minority shareholders retain a position on the board of directors, the end result would be to give minority shareholders the same veto that the agreements sought in *McQuade* and *Zion*. This illustrates that supermajority voting requirements can be a handy tool to protect minority shareholders.

As with so many of the other techniques we have discussed to protect minority shareholders, supermajority voting requirements encountered at least some hostility from the courts.[100] Perhaps the most notorious example came in the New York Court of Appeals' decision in

---

98. 9 U.S.C. § 2.

99. *See* Goodwin v. Elkins & Co., 730 F.2d 99 (3d Cir.1984) (involving an arbitration provision in a partnership agreement).

100. *But see* Katcher v. Ohsman, 26 N.J.Super. 28, 97 A.2d 180 (1953).

Benintendi v. Kenton Hotel.[101] The shareholders in *Benintendi* adopted a set of corporate bylaws which required a unanimous vote for pretty much everything the shareholders could think of. Specifically, the bylaws required a unanimous vote by the shareholders to elect any directors, or to approve any other action requiring a shareholder vote. The bylaws also required a unanimous vote by the directors to pass any resolution of the board. Finally, the bylaws required a unanimous vote by the shareholders to amend the bylaws. The court held that all of these unanimity requirements were invalid, except for the requirement of a unanimous vote to amend the bylaws.[102] The bylaws requiring unanimous shareholder votes to elect directors or to take any other action requiring shareholder approval (except amend the bylaws) entailed the simplest problem. The court held that these bylaws conflicted with various sections of the corporation statute which set out the vote of the shareholders required to take certain actions. For example, the corporation statute stated that directors shall be chosen by a plurality of votes cast at an election. The court found that the provisions in the corporation statute addressing the vote required for action by the board of directors were less clear cut. Nevertheless, the majority of the court, largely looking to common law cases and the majority of the court's own sense that a unanimity requirement for director action would be unworkable, held that the bylaw requiring unanimous director votes was also contrary to public policy.

The court's analysis in *Benintendi* points up an ambiguity which may occur in statutes addressing shareholder and director votes: When the statute simply specifies a vote required for shareholder or director approval, did the legislature really intend a mandatory rule required of all corporations, or did the legislature intend awkwardly only to supply a default rule subject to the governing documents of the corporation? Corporation statutes in most states now remove the ambiguity and explicitly allow for supermajority voting requirements.[103]

Statutes explicitly allowing supermajority voting requirements also should eliminate the prospects for a court invalidating such a requirement because the court feels the requirement is unworkable. Indeed, the court's argument on this point in *Benintendi* is rather silly. There were only two shareholders of the corporation in *Benintendi*. If each had owned half the stock, the result would have been to create, for all practical purposes, much the same requirement of unanimity as the parties sought through the bylaw provisions. The only reason the parties needed the bylaws to require unanimity is because the division of stock was unequal. Moreover, had the two formed a partnership, then, under the Uniform Partnership Act's default rule, every decision would have required unanimity of the two partners.[104] The fact is two-person part-

---

101. 294 N.Y. 112, 60 N.E.2d 829 (1945).

102. A lot of good upholding the amendment provision did for the minority share-

holder after the court gutted the key provisions of the bylaws.

103. *E.g.*, Del. Gen. Corp. Law §§ 141(b), 216; M.B.C.A. §§ 7.27, 8.24(c).

104. *E.g.*, Summers v. Dooley, 94 Idaho

nerships somehow manage to exist all of the time with the very arrangement which the court condemned as unworkable. Of course, as the number of shareholders grows, the greater becomes the prospect for deadlock from unanimity requirements. Still, this seems to be a consideration which owners (at least of a closely held business) can weigh for themselves.[105]

As we have seen repeatedly, statutes allowing various corporate control mechanisms often contain requirements which can create problems for parties who do not pay attention. This is true of the statutes allowing supermajority voting requirements. For example, some statutes validate supermajority voting requirements if placed in the corporation's articles.[106] In this event, placing the voting requirements in the bylaws renders the voting requirement invalid.[107] Similarly, if the statute validates supermajority voting requirements when placed in the corporation's articles or bylaws, veto provisions in shareholder agreements, such as in *McQuade* and *Zion*, face a new objection. Even if the agreement gets past the problem of impinging upon the board's discretion—either because the agreement calls for a veto on issues (such as a merger or election of directors) appropriately the subject for a shareholder vote, or because the jurisdiction allows agreements by shareholders to control board actions—a court might find that the veto is invalid as constituting a supermajority voting requirement which is not in the articles or bylaws as required by the statute. Whether the court reaches such a result might depend upon how the court interprets the agreement—in other words, have the parties agreed to require a supermajority vote for corporate action, or is this an agreement by the parties to vote against any action opposed by any shareholder.[108]

Placement of supermajority requirements in the articles or bylaws raises an issue of tremendous practical importance: Given the fact that corporation statutes typically allow the amendment of articles or bylaws by majority vote, what is to prevent a majority shareholder from amending the articles or bylaws to remove a supermajority voting requirement which gives minority shareholders a veto of various decisions? The best answer is for the bylaws or articles to contain a provision requiring a supermajority (say unanimous) vote to amend the articles or bylaws. Notice this is what the bylaws did in *Benintendi*. In the absence of such self-protection, statutes and courts may or may not help the minority.[109]

87, 481 P.2d 318 (1971).

105. One technique shareholders can use to limit the potential for deadlock is to set the supermajority voting requirement at some point less than unanimity (say 90 percent). This avoids giving a veto to shareholders with only a minor interest in the corporation.

106. *E.g.*, N.Y. Bus. Corp. Law §§ 616, 709. New York's statute also requires notice of the supermajority requirement to be on the stock certificates.

107. *E.g.*, Model, Roland & Co. v. Industrial Acoustics Co., 16 N.Y.S.2d 703, 261 N.Y.S.2d 896, 209 N.E.2d 553 (1965).

108. *Compare* Gazda v. Kolinski, 91 App. Div. 2d 860, 458 N.Y.S.2d 387 (1982), *aff'd*, 64 N.Y.2d 1100, 489 N.Y.S.2d 907, 479 N.E.2d 252 (1985), *with* Adler v. Svingos, 80 App. Div. 2d 764, 436 N.Y.S.2d 719 (1981).

109. *Compare* M.B.C.A. §§ 7.27, 10.21, 10.22 (amendment to articles or bylaws to delete, change or add a supermajority voting requirement requires the same super-

Blount v. Taft,[110] illustrates what can happen when shareholders place supermajority requirements in documents subject to amendment by majority vote. The shareholders in *Blount* placed into the bylaws of their corporation a provision establishing an executive committee of the board of directors. The bylaws stated that the executive committee would be comprised of representatives of the three families who held shares in the corporation, and that any hiring of employees by the corporation would require a unanimous vote of the executive committee. Unfortunately for the members of the family who had desired this unanimity provision—in order, evidently, to combat nepotistic hiring practices by one of the other families—the bylaws contained a provision allowing amendment of the bylaws by majority vote of the directors. The two other families later used this power of amendment to get rid of the special provisions concerning the executive committee. The court took the understandable position that the bylaw allowing amendment by a majority of the directors authorized this action. Interestingly, the family member, who had overlooked the danger of agreeing to place a unanimity requirement in bylaws subject to amendment by majority vote, was an attorney.

The plaintiffs in *Blount* expended much energy attempting to convince the court that the bylaw provision concerning hiring constituted a shareholder agreement within the meaning of the state's statute validating shareholder agreements controlling board actions—an inquiry which the court quite reasonably found irrelevant to the issue before it. As the court noted, had the parties placed the provisions about the executive committee in a side contract between the shareholders, then, under normal contract rules, a majority could not have amended the contract over the minority's objection (unless the contract allowed such an amendment). This illustrates the danger minority shareholders create for themselves when they place protective agreements in documents—the bylaws or articles—which the statutory default rule typically allows the majority to amend, instead of placing such agreements in a separate contract. Sometimes, however, there may be good reasons for placing the agreement in articles or bylaws—as, for example, when the state statute provides that the agreement is valid if placed in the articles. A worthwhile solution in this case might be for the articles or bylaws to require a

---

majority vote as the amendment would delete, change or add), *with* Del. Gen. Corp. Law §§ 109, 141(b), 216 (containing no supermajority voting requirement to amend the bylaws in order to delete or change a supermajority voting requirement in the bylaws). Interestingly, Delaware's statute demands that the vote in favor of amending the articles in order to delete or change a supermajority voting requirement contained in the articles, as opposed to the bylaws, equal at least the supermajority vote which the amendment would delete or change. Del. Gen. Corp. Law § 242(b)(4). Notice also that the Model Act requires a supermajority vote of equal magnitude not only to delete or change an existing supermajority voting requirement, but also to establish a supermajority voting requirement by amendment in the first place. The rationale for requiring an equal magnitude supermajority vote to lower or remove an existing supermajority requirement is easy to see. On the other hand, the rationale for imposing an equal magnitude supermajority vote requirement to adopt an amendment establishing a supermajority requirement is less clear.

110. 295 N.C. 472, 246 S.E.2d 763 (1978).

supermajority vote for any amendment changing or removing the provision protecting the minority. Indeed, this discussion points up an important use of supermajority voting requirements. In addition to giving minority shareholders a veto over corporate decisions, supermajority voting requirements can provide a handy backstop to prevent the majority from amending corporate articles or bylaws to remove other minority protections, such as cumulative voting.

Sometimes shareholders may attempt to use high quorum requirements to accomplish the same goals as a supermajority voting requirement. Corporation statutes commonly set the quorum for a shareholder or director meeting—in other words, the percent of the shareholders or directors who must be present at the meeting in order to take action—at a majority, but the statutes often allow bylaws or articles to require a greater or lesser percentage for a quorum.[111] Setting a high quorum (such as 100 percent) can allow a shareholder or director to block action by staying away from a meeting—so long as the shareholder or director discovers that undesired action will come to a vote at the meeting in time to stay away. One problem with this approach, however, is that a court might hold a director, who deliberately stays away from a meeting to block action, thereby breached his or her duty, and cannot challenge action taken at the meeting as invalid for lack of quorum.[112] Given the lack of any duty of shareholders to attend shareholder meetings, a shareholder's deliberate absence to break a quorum presumably should not preclude the shareholder's ability to raise the lack of a quorum in a challenge to the action taken at a meeting of the shareholders.[113]

e.   Employment contracts and shareholder election of officers

As evident from the earlier discussion of *McQuade* and *Clark*, one of the most critical board decisions a minority shareholder often wishes to guarantee is his or her continued employment by the company. The typical pattern of closely held corporations distributing much of their earnings to their owners through salaries renders continued employment important to provide a source of income from the company. Being an officer in the corporation also can provide authority over specific aspects of the company's operations about which the shareholder may have a particular concern. A couple of methods beyond the techniques described above exist for ensuring continued employment.

One approach is to make a contract between the corporation and the shareholder, in which the company agrees to employ the shareholder for a specified period of time in a particular position and at a given salary, and the shareholder agrees to work for the company under these terms.

111. *E.g.*, Del. Gen. Corp. Law §§ 141(b), 216; M.B.C.A. §§ 7.25(a), 8.24(b).

112. *See* Gearing v. Kelly, 11 N.Y.2d 201, 227 N.Y.S.2d 897, 182 N.E.2d 391 (1962) (holding that a shareholder, who encouraged the director's absence, also could

not challenge the validity of the board's action based upon the lack of a quorum).

113. *See* Hall v. Hall, 506 S.W.2d 42 (Mo.App.1974) (holding that a shareholder is legally entitled to stay away from a shareholder meeting in order to prevent any action).

Notice that since this contract is between the corporation and the shareholder-employee, and is approved by the board of directors, this contract avoids the charge that shareholders are usurping the discretion of the board. Some older court opinions questioned the authority of a board of directors to approve an employment contract extending beyond its term in office.[114] Most courts, however, recognize that the board, under its power to manage the company, can bind the corporation to a long-term employment contract, just as the board can bind the firm to all kind of contracts.[115] A number of corporation statutes reinforce this view.[116] Still, such contracts may occasionally run into a problem if a court interprets a particular corporation's articles or bylaws to limit the term of the office which is the subject of the contract, and to override any contractual right to continue in office past that term.[117]

Long term employment contracts are more useful in securing sustained income, than they are as a tool to obtain continued power over the running of the business. Their inability to realize the latter goals stems from two problems. To begin with, as discussed earlier in this book, an officer's authority is subject to commands from higher corporate officers, and, ultimately, to the overriding power of the board of directors.[118] In addition, should the board terminate an officer in breach of an employment contract, most courts limit relief to money damages, and will not require the board to reinstate the officer.[119]

A second approach shareholders can take to ensure that they retain certain offices is to have the shareholders elect officers. Many statutes enable a corporation's articles (or sometimes bylaws) to call for shareholder election, instead of the directors' appointment, of the corporation's officers.[120] If shareholders elect officers, they could agree who to elect as part of a shareholder voting contract, rather than as part of a contract seeking to control actions of the board.

§ 5.3 Share Transfer Restrictions

Shareholders in closely held corporations commonly make contracts restricting each others' ability to sell or otherwise transfer stock. There are several motivations for such restrictions. Primarily, there is the concern about the impact of share transfers upon the harmonious management of the corporation. The reporters are littered with cases in

---

114. *E.g.*, Borland v. John F. Sass Printing Co., 95 Colo. 53, 32 P.2d 827 (1934).

115. *E.g.*, In re Paramount Publix Corp., 90 F.2d 441 (2d Cir. 1937).

116. *E.g.*, M.B.C.A. § 8.44(b).

117. *E.g.*, Pioneer Specialties, Inc. v. Nelson, 161 Tex. 244, 339 S.W.2d 199 (1960).

118. See § 3.1.1*b supra*. Indeed, an employment contract which stated that the officer's authority would not be subject to countermand by the board raises an issue of unlawful delegation by the board of its statutory authority. *See, e.g.*, Kennerson v. Burbank Amusement Co., 120 Cal.App.2d 157, 260 P.2d 823 (1953).

119. *E.g.*, Zannis v. Lake Shore Radiologists, Ltd., 73 Ill.App.3d 901, 29 Ill.Dec. 569, 392 N.E.2d 126 (1979) (despite the contract containing an advance agreement to specific performance).

120. *E.g.*, N.Y. Bus. Corp. Law § 715(b); Del. Gen. Corp. Law § 142(b).

which the original participants in a closely held corporation got along for years, only to have relationships deteriorate into litigation following the entry of new shareholders when some of the original participants sold out, died or otherwise disposed of their interest. In addition, there are various technical reasons to restrict share transfers. For example, such transfers might undermine the enforceability of contracts among the shareholders either governing the voting of shares[1] or dictating decisions by the board.[2] Stock transfers also can endanger compliance with securities laws.[3]

The flip-side of the non-transferring shareholders' concerns about new owners is the liquidity concern of the shareholder who wants out of his or her investment. This liquidity concern presents an obvious tension in contracting to restrict the transfer of shares. Yet, even without a contractual restriction on transfer, shareholders in a closely held corporation typically face a liquidity problem. This is because often there is no one interested in purchasing their stock. Hence, agreements dealing with share transfers often serve another function which can be of equal, if not greater, importance than keeping out new shareholders. This function is to provide a buyer for the stockholder who will depart the scene.

In this section we shall explore two broad types of share transfer restrictions. To begin with, there are consent restraints. These prevent a shareholder from transferring his or her stock without the permission of other shareholders (or perhaps the corporation). Notice that some restrictions, which at first glance do not appear to be consent restraints, really are such restraints. Specifically, a restriction which reads as an absolute prohibition on transfer—either under all, or just certain, circumstances—effectively functions as a consent restraint, since the other parties to the contract always can waive the restriction. The second broad category of share transfer restrictions encompasses advance buy-out agreements, which include rights of first refusal, first options and buy-sell agreements. Unlike consent restraints, these buy-out agreements do not prevent the transfer of stock. Rather, they control who will be the purchaser, and perhaps the terms of the sale. Specifically, a right of first refusal gives the other shareholders or the corporation the right to purchase the stock at the price offered by an outside buyer, before a shareholder can sell to the outsider. A first option also gives the other shareholders or the corporation the right to purchase the stock before a shareholder can transfer his or her shares to an outsider—but, in this case, at a price specified in the first option rather than matching what the outsider would pay. A buy-sell agreement either requires the shareholder to sell, and the other shareholders or the corporation to buy, the shares upon a triggering event, or else gives one or the other party the

---

§ 5.3

1. *See, e.g.*, Bond v. Atlantic Terra Cotta Co., 137 App.Div. 671, 122 N.Y.S. 425 (1910) (shareholder voting agreement did not bind successor-in-interest without notice of the agreement).

2. *See, e.g.*, Del. Gen. Corp. Law § 342(a)(2) (requiring share transfer restrictions in order to elect close corporation status).

3. See § 6.2.2a *infra*.

option to force such a sale upon the triggering event. Buy-sell agreements can serve to control transfers in situations, such as death, in which consent restraints will not work. (Decedents cannot very well keep their stock until they receive consent for a transfer.) Buy-sell agreements can serve other functions as well. Such agreements often ensure liquidity for shareholders even when there is no outside buyer for their stock. They also can provide a tool to deal with deadlock in a closely held corporation—in essence providing something of a prenuptial agreement setting out the terms of a divorce should shareholders simply be unable to get along.

5.3.1 Validity

The common law generally has been hostile toward contracts which restrict the right of owners to transfer their property. Accordingly, a basic doctrine of property law has evolved that courts will enforce restraints on alienation only if the restraint is reasonable. Courts have applied this doctrine to restrictions on the ability of a shareholder to sell his or her stock.

This, in turn, raises the question as to when a share transfer restriction is reasonable and when such a restriction is unreasonable. One obvious factor is the purpose for the restraint.[4] Indeed, the Model Business Corporation Act only authorizes restrictions on the shareholders' right to transfer their stock if the restriction is for a "reasonable purpose"—which includes maintaining the corporation's status (for example as an S corporation for income tax purposes), preserving securities law exemptions, or some other reasonable purpose.[5]

Balanced against the purpose for the restraint is the degree to which the restriction blocks any transfer. Here, there is a need to draw a distinction between consent restraints and advance buy-out agreements. Consent restraints generally burden a shareholder's ability to transfer his or her stock to a greater extent than do advance buy-out agreements. Accordingly, courts often have struck down consent restraints. For example, in *Rafe v. Hindin*,[6] a New York appellate court held that a contract between two 50 percent shareholders of a corporation, under which each agreed not to transfer his stock without the consent of the other shareholder, was an illegal restraint on alienation. Other courts,

4. *See, e.g.*, Fayard v. Fayard, 293 So.2d 421 (Miss.1974) (maintenance of harmony among the owners justified restricting the transfer of shares to members of the family, but not restricting transfers within the family).

5. M.B.C.A. § 6.27(c). Section 202 of Delaware's corporation statute, by contrast, contains an ambiguity as to whether the validity of a share transfer restriction depends upon finding a reasonable purpose. The section states that restrictions to maintain tax status are conclusively presumed to be for a reasonable purpose, but the section never comes out and says that share transfer restrictions actually must be for a reasonable purpose. In the absence of a definitive interpretation from the Delaware Supreme Court, several courts have reached conflicting conclusions as to the need for a reasonable purpose under Delaware's Section 202. *Compare* Grynberg v. Burke, 378 A.2d 139 (Del.Ch.1977), *with* St. Louis Union Trust Co. v. Merrill Lynch, Pierce, Fenner & Smith, Inc., 562 F.2d 1040 (8th Cir.1977).

6. 29 App. Div. 2d 481, 288 N.Y.S.2d 662 (1968).

however, have upheld similar consent restraints.[7] Several factors may impact the willingness of a court to uphold a consent restraint. The court's opinion in *Rafe* suggests that one factor might be whether the agreement imposes any conditions upon the power of the non-transferring shareholder(s) to withhold consent. Specifically, the court there seemed to have been willing to allow the restraint if the agreement had stated that the non-selling shareholder could not withhold consent "unreasonably."[8] Another factor might be whether the restriction lasts perpetually, or whether, instead, the shareholder at some future point will have the right to sell his or her shares without consent.[9] Also, what the court thinks of the purpose for the restraint will impact the court's decision. Indeed, the differing willingness of courts to uphold consent restraints appears in large part to reflect differing assessments as to how important it is for shareholders in closely held corporations to maintain harmonious relationships through the right to veto new entrants.[10]

This, in turn, raises the question as to whether courts should be liberal in allowing consent restraints in order to maintain harmony in closely held corporations. Justice Holmes presented the case for such liberality when he wrote in dicta that he saw no more objection to shareholders retaining the right to choose their associates than there is to partners having this right.[11] Holmes was referring to the fact that not only does the law allow partners to agree to give each other a veto on new entrants into the firm, but this is the default rule under partnership law.[12] Why should there be any difference in a closely held corporation? One difference between corporations and partnerships is that, at least under partnership law default rules, a partner who wants to cash out can assign his or her economic interest in the firm—even if the assignee does not become a new partner—or even dissolve the firm and force liquidation.[13]

Actually, from a practical standpoint, a consent restraint may be an ill-designed method of maintaining harmony among owners in a closely held corporation. After all, if a shareholder wants out and the other shareholders block a sale, one imagines that relations among the share-

---

7. *E.g.*, Colbert v. Hennessey, 351 Mass. 131, 217 N.E.2d 914 (1966).

8. The shareholder seeking to uphold the restriction argued that there was an oral agreement not to withhold consent unreasonably, but, because of the parol evidence rule, the court refused to consider whether there was, in fact, such an oral agreement.

9. *E.g.*, Gray v. Harris Land & Cattle Co., 227 Mont. 51, 737 P.2d 475 (1987) (upheld a consent restraint after noting that it was not perpetual).

10. *Compare* Tracey v. Franklin, 31 Del. Ch. 477, 67 A.2d 56 (1949) (desire to solidify ownership in the existing two owners is not a legally sufficient purpose to justify a consent restraint on alienation), *with* Lon-

gyear v. Hardman, 219 Mass. 405, 106 N.E. 1012 (1914) (right to choose one's associates in order to maintain harmony among the owners justifies a consent restraint in a closely held corporation).

11. Barrett v. King, 181 Mass. 476, 479, 63 N.E. 934, 935 (1902).

12. U.P.A. § 18(g).

13. *Id* at §§ 27, 31(1)(b), 38(1). Also, in an ordinary partnership, a new partner's actions can create unlimited personal liability for the other partners—albeit, this is not the case in limited partnerships, limited liability companies and limited liability partnerships, and yet the default rule often remains that existing members can veto new entrants.

holders will not remain good. Ultimately, one suspects that a consent restraint will turn into a buy-out by the non-transferring shareholders of the shareholder who sought consent to sell. To the extent, therefore, that judicial hostility toward consent restraints forces shareholders instead to make advance buy-out agreements, the result may be to push shareholders into negotiating early on the agreement they will ultimately need anyway. This can give shareholders a clearer understanding of the ultimate impact of their actions.

In any event, statutes in a number of jurisdictions have sought to reduce the hostility toward consent restraints. The Model Act expressly allows consent restraints so long as "the requirement is not manifestly unreasonable."[14] While this language still leaves the court with room to invalidate a consent restraint for being unreasonable, the evident intent is to tell the court that finding consent restraints to be unreasonable should be the exception rather than the rule. Delaware's statute appears to go even further. It states that consent restraints are permitted, without expressing any qualifier as to reasonableness.[15]

In contrast to the uncertain authority confronting consent restraints, courts are likely to uphold advance buy-out agreements. After all, such agreements do not prevent a shareholder from selling out whenever he or she wishes—they just alter who might be the buyer and what might be the terms. In the case of a right of first refusal, the agreement does not even alter the essential terms. Hence, there is generally little question that a right of first refusal constitutes a reasonable restraint.[16]

Unlike rights of first refusal, first options alter the price which the selling shareholder will receive. In fact, it is possible to set the price which the corporation or non-selling shareholders must pay in order to exercise the first option so low that the effect of a first option becomes much the same as a consent restraint. For example, suppose a contract gave the corporation an option to purchase a shareholder's stock for one-tenth of one penny per share before a shareholder could sell his or her stock to an outsider. With such a price, there is little point to a shareholder even considering selling his or her shares without some assurance that the corporation will not exercise its option. Hence, there is very little practical difference between this first option and a contract simply stating that a shareholder cannot sell his or her stock without the consent of the corporation.

---

14. M.B.C.A. § 6.27(d)(3).

15. Del. Gen. Corp. Law § 202(c)(3). As noted above, Delaware's statute is ambiguous as to whether the validity of share transfer restrictions depends generally upon finding a reasonable purpose.

16. *E.g.,* Groves v. Prickett, 420 F.2d 1119 (9th Cir.1970). It is possible, however, that the parties having the right of first refusal (or a first option) will have such a long time to exercise the right, or that so many shareholders will have a right of first refusal, that the mechanics and delay of giving the shareholders the opportunity to exercise their right will unreasonably deter sales. It would be a pretty rare agreement that is so extreme as to create this problem *See, e.g.,* Ling, Inc. v. Trinity Sav. & Loan Ass'n, 482 S.W.2d 841 (1972) (not finding a problem under the facts present).

Nevertheless, courts usually have upheld first options despite arguments that the price was so much less than the value of the shares as to render the restriction unreasonable.[17] The New York Court of Appeals gave the rationale for this proclivity in *Allen v. Biltmore Tissue Corp.*[18] The court explained that it is very difficult to value the shares of a closely held corporation, and, therefore, parties creating a first option need leeway to establish a price formula without fear of later litigation quibbling over whether the price was, in fact, fair. In *Allen*, a bylaw required the corporation's shareholders, before they could sell to an outsider, to give the corporation the opportunity to buy their stock back at the price the shareholders originally paid the corporation to purchase the stock. It is very likely that, as time passes, this initial price for the stock will diverge considerably from the actual value of the shares. Yet, this formula has a significant advantage in terms of simplicity, which shareholders ought to be allowed to weigh against the desire to achieve greater accuracy in hitting the present value of the stock. All told, *Allen* quite appropriately seems to hold that so long as there is some rationale for the price formula—rather than representing purely a punitive attempt to deter transfers—courts should not set aside first options as an unreasonable restraint on transfer.[19]

The enforceability of share transfer restrictions sometimes raises issues beyond the broad concern about unreasonably restraining alienation. For example, can a party enforce a share transfer restriction against persons who never consented to the restriction? This question arises in a couple of circumstances. To begin with, share transfer restrictions often appear in corporate articles or bylaws—both of which normally are subject to amendment by a less than unanimous vote. Can a majority of shareholders amend the articles or bylaws to add a share transfer restriction and have the amendment bind shareholders who voted against it? Many statutes, quite understandably, provide that such amendments are not binding on dissenting shareholders.[20] A more fre-

---

17. *E.g.*, In re Estate of Mather, 410 Pa. 361, 189 A.2d 586 (1963). *But see* Hicks v. Rucker Pharmacal Co., 367 So.2d 399 (La. Ct.App.1978). Courts have also rejected the argument that enforcing agreed upon low price terms violates the fiduciary duty owed between shareholders in a closely held corporation. *E.g.*, Evangelista v. Holland, 27 Mass.App.Ct. 244, 537 N.E.2d 589 (1989).

18. 2 N.Y.2d 534, 141 N.E.2d 812, 161 N.Y.S.2d 418 (1957).

19. Logically, a court should treat a first option with a deliberately punitive price term as the equivalent of a consent restraint—which means the restriction may, or may not, be valid, depending upon the circumstances.

20. *E.g.*, Del. Gen. Corp. Law § 202(b); M.B.C.A. § 6.27(a). Even without a statute, some courts might prevent such an amendment from applying to dissenting shares.

E.g., B & H Warehouse, Inc. v. Atlas Van Lines, Inc., 490 F.2d 818 (5th Cir.1974). *See also* Lambert v. Fishermen's Dock Co-op., Inc. 61 N.J. 596, 297 A.2d 566 (1972) (amendment changing the price in a buy-sell agreement cannot affect the "vested rights" of dissenting shares). California had provided a significant counterpoint by allowing amendments to bind dissenting shares. Tu-Vu Drive-In Corp. v. Ashkins, 61 Cal.2d 283, 391 P.2d 828, 38 Cal.Rptr. 348 (1964). The California legislature, however, overruled *Tu-Vu Drive-In* and no longer allows an amendment of the articles to restrict the transfer of dissenting shares. Cal. Corp. Code § 204(b). One question raised by statutes and court opinions which prevent transfer restrictions in the articles or bylaws from applying to dissenting shares is why this sort of amendment to articles or bylaws should be subject to different rules than any other amendment to

quent problem with non-consenting parties involves the enforceability of the restriction against a transferee of the shares. Statutes commonly handle this problem by requiring that stock certificates contain conspicuous notice of the restriction—otherwise, the restriction will not impact the rights of a transferee without knowledge of the restriction.[21]

5.3.2 Drafting

Poor drafting of share transfer restrictions has resulted in considerable litigation over the years. There are a number of terms in a share transfer restriction which can provoke litigation.

This starts with the term setting out what transfers the agreement restricts, or what events trigger a buy-out under an advance buy-out agreement. For example, transfer restrictions often require consent, or else give the other shareholders or the corporation an option to buy, before a shareholder can "sell" or "dispose of" his or her shares. This can create litigation over whether a sale or disposition includes an involuntary transfer upon bankruptcy,[22] death[23] or divorce,[24] and whether this includes gifts.[25] Ambiguity also can arise over whether the restriction will apply to offers to sell the entire company,[26] and whether it covers sales between existing shareholders rather than to outsiders.[27] Often, courts, reciting the rationale that restraints on alienation are disfavored and therefore narrowly construed, resolve these questions against applying the restriction.[28] In some instances, a more honest approach might simply be to say that share transfer restrictions should not curb the rights of parties—such as divorcing spouses who assert a claim to the stock under community property laws, or creditors of bankrupt shareholders—who have significant equities in their favor, and whose interests were not represented by those agreeing to the restrictions.[29] (Indeed, the bankruptcy code overrides most transfer restrictions

the articles which might impact the economic rights of stock.

21. *E.g.*, Del. Gen. Corp. Law § 202(a); M.B.C.A. § 6.27(b). *See also* U.C.C. § 8–204(a) (requiring conspicuous notice of transfer restrictions imposed by the issuer of a security); Ling & Co. v. Trinity Sav. & Loan Ass'n, 482 S.W.2d 841 (Tex.1972) (addressing the issue of what constitutes conspicuous notice). While the share certificates must provide notice to transferees, by and large there is no requirement that the parties place the restriction itself in the corporation's articles (or bylaws) as opposed to a side contract. *E.g.*, Rafe v. Hinden, *supra*. *But see* Carlson v. Ringgold County Mut. Tel. Co., 252 Iowa 748, 108 N.W.2d 478 (1961).

22. *E.g.*, Matter of Trilling & Montague, 140 F.Supp. 260 (E.D.Pa.1956).

23. *E.g.*, Globe Slicing Machine Co. v. Hasner, 333 F.2d 413 (2d Cir.1964).

24. *E.g.*, Earthman's, Inc. v. Earthman, 526 S.W.2d 192 (Tex.Civ.App.1975).

25. *E.g.*, Louisiana Weekly Publ. Co. v. First Nat. Bank of Commerce, 483 So.2d 929 (La.1986).

26. *E.g.*, Frandsen v. Jensen–Sundquist Agency, Inc. 802 F.2d 941 (7th cir.1986).

27. *E.g.*, Remillong v. Schneider, 185 N.W.2d 493 (N.D.1971).

28. *E.g.*, Earthman's, Inc. v. Earthman, 526 S.W.2d 192 (Tex.Civ.App.1975).

29. Shareholders are likely to balance the interests of some prospective transferees, such as heirs and purchasers, against the concerns about new entrants into the corporation. Other prospective transferees, such as a shareholder's divorcing spouse or personal creditors, can expect no such effort to weigh their interests in agreeing to a share transfer restriction—quite the contrary.

triggered by bankruptcy.[30]) In the absence of such third party interests, courts might do well to consider the purpose for the restriction when interpreting its scope. For example, in deciding if the restriction reaches transfers among the existing shareholders, as well as to outsiders, a court might wish to note that such intra-shareholder transfers often produce significant strife by upsetting the balance of power within a corporation.[31] If the purpose for the restraint is to avoid disharmony within the corporation, this suggests that courts should interpret ambiguous restrictions to cover intra-shareholder transfers.

In addition to specifying what events trigger the contract, an advance agreement for a buy-out must state who has the option to demand the buy-out—the would-be buyer, the would-be seller, or both. Presumably, this reflects who the contract protects: the non-transferring shareholders from problems with new entrants, the shareholder who wants out from the problem of finding a buyer, or both sides. Litigation can arise when the contract gives the choice about forcing the buy-out (or granting consent to a sale) to the corporation. Typically, the intent of giving the choice to the corporation is to protect the non-transferring shareholders. Sometimes, however, the person who would be subject to the restriction—either because this is the person who wishes to dispose of his or her stock, or because this is the person who would purchase the stock if the corporation does not enforce the restriction—is in control of the corporation. If the agreement itself does not disqualify the interested party from making the decision for the corporation, then the court must determine whether the interested party breached his or her fiduciary duty in having the corporation grant consent to a transfer or decline to exercise its option to purchase.[32]

Another circumstance in which courts might need to consider the applicability of fiduciary duty (or else obligations of good faith and fair dealing) regarding the exercise of an advance buy-out agreement occurs when those in charge of the corporation can take action which will trigger the corporation's right to purchase stock under terms which will advantage the non-selling shareholders. Many times, buy-sell agreements obligate shareholders, who are also employees, to sell their shares back to the corporation at the termination of employment. If the stock has risen significantly in value, while the price which the corporation must pay to purchase the shares has not, this can create a temptation to terminate the shareholder's employment in order to trigger the buy-out. The result is to force the court to consider whether such a tactic breaches any fiduciary duty owed between the shareholders, or whether there are any contractual protections against the firing—either based employment for a term, or implied obligations of good faith. Earlier in this chapter, we looked at the resulting interface between the doctrines

30. Bkrcy. Code § 541(c).

31. *See, e.g.,* Zidell v. Zidell, Inc., 277 Or. 423, 560 P.2d 1091 (1977).

32. *Compare* Lash v. Lash Furniture Co. of Barre, Inc., 130 Vt. 517, 296 A.2d 207 (1972), *with* Boss v. Boss, 98 R.I. 146, 200 A.2d 231 (1964).

regarding at-will employment and fiduciary duty among shareholders in a closely held corporation.[33]

There is also a potential interrelationship between advance buy-out agreements, and shareholder suits seeking dissolution under statutes providing for dissolution upon deadlock or oppression. One potential purpose for an advance buy-out agreement is to serve as a sort of prenuptial agreement setting out the terms of a divorce if shareholders cannot get along. If this is the purpose of the agreement, then courts should not allow a shareholder to circumvent his or her agreement by seeking a judicial order either dissolving the corporation or commanding a buy-out at a price set by the court. On other hand, advance buy-out agreements often are not intended to serve the function of dealing with deadlock or oppression. If the agreement did not contemplate such events, then there is no reason for the court to deny dissolution based upon the presence of the agreement, nor, if the court orders a buy-out in lieu of dissolution, does the price set by the advance buy-out agreement necessarily dictate the fair value of the stock.[34] In other words, as some courts have recognized,[35] the court must determine whether the parties intended the advance buy-out agreement to apply to dissension between the shareholders which has degenerated into arguable deadlock or oppression. Unfortunately, drafters of advance buy-out agreements often are not clear as to whether events which precipitate a dissolution suit, trigger the buy-out agreement.

There is a practical connection between the problems we have just discussed concerning the triggering events in an advance buy-out agreement and the price term in the agreement. Specifically, the more the price term favors one side or the other, the more likely there is to be a dispute over whether the triggering event occurred. Unfortunately, there is trade-off involved in drafting a price term for an advance buy-out agreement, which we mentioned in discussing the New York Court of Appeal's opinion in *Allen*. This trade-off is between ease of application versus seeking to have the price term accurately reflect the "fair" value of the stock.

In *Allen*, the price was what the shareholders originally paid the corporation for their stock. This is an example of a fixed price. *Allen* illustrates the problem with a fixed price. While the price presumably was fair at the time the shareholders bought their stock—unless there was some sort of bargain purchase involved—inevitable changes in the worth of the company over time create a divergence between the fixed

33. See § 5.1.1 *supra*.

34. For a variety of reasons, the parties to an advance buy-out contract may agree to a bargain price when the buy-out will occur through no fault of the buyer, as, for instance, in the event of a buy-out triggered by a shareholder's death. For a court to treat such a bargain price as the fair value for purposes of a buy-out which the court orders in response to oppression would not only use the advance buy-out agreement in a way the parties never intended, but would also create perverse incentives. Specifically, it would create an incentive to act oppressively in order to trigger a favorably priced buy-out.

35. *E.g.*, Matter of Pace Photographers, Ltd., 71 N.Y.2d 737, 530 N.Y.S.2d 67, 525 N.E.2d 713 (1988).

price and the shares' actual value. Sometimes, agreements call for the shareholders periodically to meet and revise the fixed price—although owners of a closely held corporation may well forget to perform this task.[36]

Another relatively simple approach to setting the price is to use book value. Book value is the value of the shares as shown on the corporation's balance sheet. (If only one class of stock is outstanding, the per share book value will equal assets minus liabilities divided by the number of shares.) While simple, book value also typically diverges from the shares' real value. This is not only because the values of a corporation's assets often are different than the assets' book values—which, by accounting custom, are based upon the assets' costs, less, in appropriate cases, an allowance for depreciation—but, often more significantly, also because book value does not reflect the added worth of a going business (generally referred to as goodwill). Moreover, since choices between various acceptable accounting procedures (such as the method for setting depreciation) can significantly impact book value in many cases, using book value as a basis for pricing may not always avoid litigation over the price.[37]

A common approach is to call for appraisers to set the price of the shares. Of course, this raises the question as to what valuation method the appraisers are supposed to use under the agreement. In addition to, or in lieu of, looking at book value, appraisers may attempt to value the shares based upon the future earnings of the business.

Indeed, an agreement may set the price based upon a formula keyed to future earnings without calling for the use of appraisers. Such future earnings based valuation is economically sound. After all, the purpose of owning a business (or a piece of the business in the case of stock in a corporation) normally is to obtain the future earnings from that business. The problem is that both the prediction of future earnings and the determination of the present value of those future earnings are matters upon which there is likely to be room for considerable disagreement.

Still other methods of setting the price may work in specialized circumstances. For example, a right of first refusal sets the price by what the prospective outside purchaser will pay. Another method to set the price exists when two owners cannot get along. One owner may set the price, while giving the other owner the choice of whether to buy or to sell at that price. (Notice how this gives the first owner an incentive to set the price neither too high nor too low. This only works, however, if both owners have adequate funds to buy out the other.)

Drafting share transfer restrictions can raise a number of other issues. For example, litigation can arise over whether an advance buy-

---

36. *E.g.*, Helms v. Duckworth, 249 F.2d 482 (D.C.Cir.1957). In *Helms*, the court held that a shareholder would breach his or her fiduciary duty by deliberately refusing to negotiate, in good faith, the periodic revisions called for in such an agreement.

37. *E.g.*, Aron v. Gillman, 309 N.Y. 157, 128 N.E.2d 284 (1955).

out agreement can apply to less than all of a stockholder's shares[38]—so-called block busting. This could be highly significant in a situation in which a corporation has two 50 percent shareholders, so that the purchase of even one share under the advance buy-out agreement would give the purchasing shareholder a majority and dramatically reduce the value of the selling shareholder's remaining stock. With a buy-sell agreement, a question can arise over when the selling shareholder's status as a shareholder terminates—upon the occurrence of the triggering event for the buy-sell agreement, or when the shareholder actually gives up the shares. This can be important, for example, if the selling shareholder wishes to claim that breaches of fiduciary duty toward the corporation lowered the value of his or her shares, and hence the price he or she will receive under the agreement. If the selling shareholder's status terminated upon the triggering event, he or she may lack standing to bring such a claim.[39] Parties drafting an advance buy-out agreement also must give careful thought to whether the purchaser should be the other shareholders or the corporation. This decision can have significant tax consequences, which are beyond the scope of this book. Purchases by a corporation of its outstanding stock are subject to statutory financial limitations for the protection of creditors—which are discussed elsewhere in this book.[40]

---

38. *E.g.*, Rainwater v. Milfeld, 485 S.W.2d 831 (Tex.Civ.App.1972).

39. *E.g.*, Stephenson v. Drever, 16 Cal.4th 1167, 69 Cal.Rptr.2d 764, 947 P.2d 1301 (1997).

40. See § 2.3.3*b supra*.

Chapter VI

SECURITIES FRAUD AND REGULATION

[Research References]

AmJur 2d, Securities Regulation–Federal §§ 1 et seq.; Securities Regulation–State §§ 1 et seq.

CJS, Securities Regulation and Commodity Futures Trading Regulation §§ 4–490

ALR Index: Bonds and Securities; Federal Securities Exchange Act; Fraud and Deceit; Investment Securities; Securities Exchange Act; Uniform Securities Act

ALR Digest: Corporations §§ 221–223; Securities Regulations §§ 1 et seq.; Trial § 364.5

Am Jur Legal Forms 2d, Corporations §§ 74:2614–74:2638; Securities Regulations §§ 231:11 et seq.

Am Jur Pleading and Practice Forms (Rev), Corporations §§ 126–142; Securities Regulation, Forms 1–60.5

45 Am Jur Trials 113, Third–Party Accountant Liability–Prospective Financial Statements Used in Securities Offerings

22 POF3d 559, Legal Malpractice in a Securities Offering

11 POF2d 271, Failure to Disclose Material Facts to Stock Purchaser; 9 POF2d 577, Participation by Corporate Officer in Illegal Issuance of Securities

---

Thus far in this book, our focus has been almost entirely on state corporate law. One of the primary problem areas we have discussed is how state corporate law seeks to protect shareholders from the danger posed by incompetent or disloyal directors and officers. We saw that the basic approach of state corporate law is to focus on the conception of the shareholders as the owners of the corporation, and to impose duties of care and loyalty upon the directors and officers both toward the corporation and toward the shareholders as the corporation's owners.

In this chapter, we shift our focus in a couple of ways. To begin with, in large part, we will be dealing with federal rather than state law. More fundamentally, this chapter involves a conceptual shift in the law's approach to protecting shareholders from incompetent or disloyal directors and officers. Instead of looking at the shareholders as owners entitled to ongoing obligations from their agents, we now look at the shareholders as investors, who make decisions to purchase or sell stock. Seen in this light, one danger posed by incompetent or disloyal directors and officers is that such individuals might induce investors to become shareholders by false or incomplete statements about the company and its prospects. A second danger is that disloyal directors and officers might take advantage of their knowledge of what is going on inside the corporation to buy out some shareholders before these shareholders learn of favorable developments at the corporation. Given such dangers, what protections does the law accord to persons in their role as investors deciding whether to buy or sell stock in the corporation?

§ 6.1   Common Law

Before the enactment of state and federal statutes known as securities laws, an action under the common law of fraud and deceit was the principal weapon available to persons claiming that false or misleading statements led them to lose money in the purchase or sale of stock, or complaining that corporate officials took unfair advantage of inside information in buying or selling stock. While the securities laws now dwarf the common law as a source of remedies for securities fraud and trading on inside information, it is nevertheless useful to begin with an exploration of the common law doctrines relevant to such conduct. For one thing, from time to time, including quite recently, a resurgence occurs in efforts to use common law theories against such conduct. More fundamentally, an awareness of the limitations found in the common law of fraud and deceit enables one to understand a division which exists between two judicial approaches to the securities laws. One approach is to view the enactment of the securities laws as a legislative reaction to the failure of the common law to provide adequate investor protection— which means interpreting the securities laws to avoid the limits of common law actions. The conflicting approach, which, in the 1970s, became the dominant view on the United States Supreme Court, is to assume that the use of common law terms (like "fraud") by the securities laws imports common law limitations which went with those terms. In either event, it helps to know the limitations found in the common law of fraud and deceit.

6.1.1   False or Misleading Statements

False or misleading statements can produce a variety of consequences under the common law. Two of the most important consequences are to allow parties to void contracts induced by fraud, and to create the basis for recovery from those who commit the tort of fraud or deceit. A comprehensive exploration of the elements of fraud and deceit is well beyond the scope of this book. For our purposes, it is adequate to outline the basic elements with a focus on false or misleading statements impacting the purchase or sale of stock.

The first element of a claim for fraud or deceit is that the defendant made a false or misleading statement of material fact. A "material" fact is a fact that a reasonable person would attach importance to in deciding what to do about the transaction in question.[1] The reason for saying

---

§ 6.1

1.   The Restatement of Torts also views   a fact as material if the defendant knows, or has reason to know, that the plaintiff

false "or misleading" is because literal truth is not sufficient to avoid fraud if the defendant designs the statement to mislead the listener. For example, suppose a party selling a racehorse states that the horse has "beaten national champion racers." If the national champion racers the horse has beaten were humans (rather than horses), this statement would be literally true, but is misleading, and is, therefore, fraudulent. Such misleading statements are often referred to as "half-truths."

Courts have struggled with the question of when statements of promise, opinion or prediction constitute statements of material "fact" sufficient to support a claim of fraud. Promises constitute false statements of fact if, at the time the defendant made the promise, the defendant had no intent to perform.[2] Here, the rule is straight-forward, even if proof of the defendant's secret intent is often anything but straight-forward. By contrast, judicial views on when an opinion constitutes a statement of fact sufficient to support an action for fraud are less clear-cut. Numerous cases have characterized broad qualitative statements, such as "this is the best product on the market," as simply "puffing" upon which the plaintiff should not have relied.[3] On the other hand, when there are particular reasons for the plaintiff to rely on the defendant's representation—as, for instance, the defendant was a expert upon the subject matter of the opinion, while the plaintiff was not—then courts will find that the defendant's expressing an opinion which the defendant does not honestly hold can be actionable.[4] Notice that since opinions or predictions as to the prospects for a business are often precisely the sort of statements which induce persons to buy or sell stock, the traditional hesitancy of common law courts to recognize fraud claims based upon statements of opinion or prediction can limit significantly the utility of the common law of fraud to deal with false statements in stock transactions.

The second element of an action for fraud or deceit has come to be known as scienter. This generally means either that the defendant knew the statement was false, or, at least, did not believe the statement was true.[5] Under the leading case of *Derry v. Peek*,[6] scienter also exists if the defendant was reckless as to whether the statement was true or false. The *Derry* case—in which the plaintiff failed to prove that an English company's directors knew of, or were reckless toward, the falsity of statements made in a prospectus used to sell shares in the company— illustrates that proof of scienter often presents a stumbling block for individuals induced to purchase or sell stock by false statements.

regards the fact as important (even though a reasonable person would not regard the fact as important). Restatement (Second) of Torts § 538(2).

2. *E.g.*, Burgdorfer v. Thielemann, 153 Or. 354, 55 P.2d 1122 (1936).

3. *See, e.g.*, Bertram v. Reed Automobile Co., 49 S.W.2d 517 (Tex.Civ.App.1932).

4. *See, e.g.*, Vulcan Metals Co. v. Simmons Mfg. Co., 248 F. 853 (2d Cir.1918).

5. In other words, the defendant realized that he or she did not know if the statement was true or false.

6. 14 App. Cas. 337 (H.L. 1889).

While fraud requires proof of scienter, most jurisdictions also recognize a tort of negligent misrepresentation. Such recognition, however, comes most readily when the negligent misrepresentation leads to personal injury or property damage. Courts are more divided about whether to recognize a claim in situations in which a negligent misrepresentation produced only economic loss. Even among the courts prepared to recognize a claim for economic loss resulting from negligent misrepresentation, such recognition may depend the existence of a special relationship between the plaintiff and the defendant.[7] While there is little authority for imposing strict liability for damages from innocent misrepresentations, a court can order rescission of a contract entered on the basis of a false statement of material fact made by one party to the contract, even if the defendant neither knew, nor should have known, of the error.[8] In terms of false statements impacting the purchase or sale of stock, what is important to notice about both the tort of negligent misrepresentation, and the availability of rescission, is how these actions can require privity between the defendant and the plaintiff—which leaves out, for example, unintended false statements by a corporation that impact the trading price of its stock in resale markets.

The third element of an action for fraud or deceit also involves the defendant's state of mind. The defendant must intend to induce the plaintiff's reliance on the statement. Accordingly, a defendant will not be liable to a person whom the defendant neither intended to hear the misstatement, nor realized would hear the statement. This element also historically created a particular problem in the case of misrepresentations impacting the purchase or sale of stock. For example, in *Peek v. Gurney*,[9] the English House of Lords held that directors, who prepared a prospectus containing false statements for the purpose of inducing individuals to buy stock from the corporation, could not be liable to a person who thereafter bought stock resold by an existing shareholder. Hence, the circle of persons who might have a claim under the common law based upon intentional misrepresentations concerning stock traditionally has not been that much broader than those who could successfully make a claim based upon negligent misrepresentations or for rescission.

The fourth element is the plaintiff's justifiable reliance on the false or misleading statement. Reliance is the normal mechanism by which a false statement causes harm to the plaintiff. In other words, if the plaintiff never heard the false statement, did not believe the false statement, or would have taken the same action even if the plaintiff knew the statement was false, then it is difficult, as a general proposition, to see how the false statement caused damages to the plaintiff.

The qualifier that the reliance must be "justifiable" encapsulates the idea that the plaintiff cannot blindly ignore obvious warning signs of

7. *See, e.g.*, International Products Co. v. Erie R. Co., 244 N.Y. 331, 155 N.E. 662 (1927).

8. *E.g.*, Ross v. Harding, 64 Wash.2d 231, 391 P.2d 526 (1964).

9. [1893] 6 H.L. 377.

falsity and claim to be deceived.[10] Occasionally, courts might refer to reasonable reliance.[11] When dealing with fraud (as opposed to negligent misrepresentation), this is a misnomer, since it suggests that a plaintiff who is unreasonable (in other words, negligent) in believing the false statement cannot recover. Yet, just as contributory negligence is not a defense to an intentional tort, courts will not let off a defendant committing intentional deceit, just because the plaintiff is gullible.[12]

The element of reliance can pose a particular problem when false representations impact the prices at which stocks are bought and sold in active trading markets. As we will discuss later in this chapter,[13] it is possible in this event for a party to over- or under-pay for stock due to a false representation which the party never heard. Nevertheless, under a traditional view of common law fraud and deceit, the lack of individual reliance would preclude recovery.[14]

Finally, there is the element of damages. Two different measures of damage have support in the cases.[15] The traditional tort measure is known as the out-of-pocket measure. This is the difference between what the plaintiff paid, and the real value of what the plaintiff received in the transaction (or, if the fraud induced the plaintiff to sell, rather than buy, the difference between what the plaintiff received, and the actual value of what the plaintiff gave up in the transaction). An alternate measure is to compare the real value of what the plaintiff received, with the value the purchased item would have had if the false statements had been true. This is known as the benefit of the bargain measure.

6.1.2 Trading on Inside Information

As stated above, the first element of a claim for fraud or deceit is a false or misleading statement of material fact. Suppose, however, the plaintiff complains, not about what the defendant told him or her, but rather about what the defendant did not say. For example, a seller of property might neglect to inform the buyer of a possible flaw in the property. Many times, such omissions might turn statements made by the defendant into half-truths. Yet, many other times, the plaintiff will have difficulty creating a credible argument that the defendant's silence rendered something the defendant said misleading. In this event, the plaintiff will be reduced to arguing that the silence, itself, constitutes fraud.

Historically, courts had not been receptive to the argument that silence equals fraud; preferring instead the notion of caveat emptor. A long-standing exception exists when the defendant has a fiduciary relationship with the plaintiff. More recently, many courts have become

---

10. *E.g.*, Williams v. Rank & Son Buick, Inc., 44 Wis.2d 239, 170 N.W.2d 807 (1969).

11. *E.g.*, Nielsen v. Adams, 223 Neb. 262, 388 N.W.2d 840 (1986).

12. *E.g.*, Chamberlin v. Fuller, 59 Vt. 247, 9 A. 832 (1887).

13. See § 6.3.1e *infra*.

14. *E.g.*, Mirkin v. Wasserman, 5 Cal.4th 1082, 858 P.2d 568, 23 Cal.Rptr.2d 101 (1993).

15. *E.g.*, Hinkle v. Rockville Motor Co., 262 Md. 502, 278 A.2d 42 (1971).

willing to turn silence into fraud under a number of circumstances, including when the defendant has access to the facts and the plaintiff does not, and under circumstances in which business custom creates an expectation of disclosure.[16]

Turning from the general subject of non-disclosure as fraud, to the specific subject of how the common law has treated corporate officials trading on inside information, we must divide our discussion into two parts: (1) claims that such trading defrauded the other party to the purchase or sale, and (2) claims that such trading breached a fiduciary duty to the corporation.

a. Trading on inside information as fraud

In the years before the federal securities laws became the focal point for lawsuits dealing with trading on undisclosed inside information, a number of courts confronted the question of whether such trading constituted common law fraud. The typical scenario entailed a director or officer of a corporation purchasing stock from a shareholder of the corporation, without disclosing to the shareholder highly favorable developments regarding the corporation. When the former shareholder later learned of the favorable developments and regretted his or her sale, the former shareholder would sue the director or officer who bought the shares, claiming fraud. Such suits provoked a mixed reaction from the courts.

Courts following the so-called majority rule rejected the selling shareholder's claim.[17] These courts operated under the general principle that silence is not fraud unless the parties to the transaction stand in a fiduciary relationship. While directors and officers are fiduciaries, courts following the so-called majority rule viewed the directors' and officers' fiduciary relationship to be with the corporation, rather than with individual shareholders (at least when the director or officer was transacting business with a shareholder in the director's or officer's personal, rather than official, capacity). Hence, since there was no fiduciary relationship between the director or officer and the selling shareholder, there was no duty to disclose inside information and no fraud.

By contrast, courts following the so-called minority or Kansas rule viewed the fiduciary relationship of directors and officers to be with the individual shareholders, as well as with the corporation. Accordingly, directors and officers, under this view, had a duty to disclose material facts to any shareholder from whom a director or officer purchased stock.[18]

The United States Supreme Court, in *Strong v. Repide*,[19] came up with an intermediate approach. This approach is known as the "special

---

16. *E.g.*, Ollerman v. O'Rourke Co., 94 Wis.2d 17, 288 N.W.2d 95 (1980).

17. *E.g.*, Hooker v. Midland Steel Co., 215 Ill. 444, 74 N.E. 445 (1905).

18. *E.g.*, Hotchkiss v. Fischer, 136 Kan. 530, 16 P.2d 531 (1932).

19. 213 U.S. 419, 29 S.Ct. 521 (1909).

facts" doctrine. Strong owned stock in the Philippine Sugar Estates Development Company. Repide was a director, the principal officer, and the owner of three-fourths of the shares of the company. The company's only asset was some land in the Philippines which the government wanted to acquire. The company's shareholders authorized Repide to negotiate the sale of the land to the government. The negotiations dragged on for months, but finally reached a point at which it appeared an agreement was probable. Shortly before Repide reached a deal with the government, Repide, acting through intermediary, purchased Strong's shares. When Strong later learned of the sale of the land to the government at a price which made her shares worth ten times what Repide had paid, she sued.[20]

In holding that the trial court properly found fraud, the Supreme Court assumed, for the purposes of argument, that directors generally do not have a duty to disclose knowledge affecting the value of the stock when the directors purchase stock from a shareholder. The Supreme Court stated, however, that special facts took the case before the Court out of this general rule—hence, the notion of a special facts doctrine. The problem, however, with the special facts doctrine is determining what are special facts. Indeed, the *Strong* opinion, itself, provides something of a Rorschach test in which every reader sees whatever he or she is inclined to see. For example, the opinion refers to the prospect of a favorable sale of the corporation's sole asset as a "most material fact." Some courts have interpreted this reference to mean that special facts simply involves the materiality of the facts which the defendant did not disclose.[21] Such an interpretation, however, would make the special facts doctrine swallow the general no duty rule, since, unless the undisclosed fact is material, even a fiduciary would not have a duty to disclose the fact. By contrast, the Supreme Court in *Strong* spent considerable time discussing how Repide took steps to hide his identity as the purchaser from Strong's agent—presumably based on the fact that had Repide's identity as the prospective purchaser been known, Strong's agent would have figured that something was up with the land negotiation. If this is the special fact, then *Strong* does little more than apply the well recognized notion that an agent's misrepresenting the existence or identity of his or her principal constitutes fraud when the agent knows that the principal's identity is material to the party the agent is dealing with.[22]

In any event, there might be far less significance to the split between the majority rule, the minority rule and the special facts doctrine than the literature often suggests. This is because, in a couple of contexts (which occupy much of the field), courts applying the common law generally agreed that corporate officials have no duty to disclose

---

20. Strong sued in the Philippine Courts at a time in which the United States controlled the Philippines, which accounts for the case ending up in the United States Supreme Court.

21. *E.g.*, Bailey v. Vaughan, 178 W. Va. 371, 359 S.E.2d 599 (W. Va. 1987).

22. *E.g.*, Barnes v. Eastern & Western Lumber Co., 205 Or. 553, 287 P.2d 929 (1955).

inside information, regardless of which of the three approaches above the court otherwise was inclined to take. One context is when directors and officers sell stock to non-shareholders, rather than purchase stock from shareholders.[23] After all, even if the directors and officers have a fiduciary relationship with shareholders, they do not have such a relationship with non-shareholders. More significantly, courts would not find a disclosure duty when the directors or officers purchased shares through transactions in impersonal stock markets. Indeed, in a case often cited for the so-called majority rule—*Goodwin v. Agassiz*[24]—one of the court's rationales for not finding fraud was that the directors purchased the plaintiff's share through a stock exchange in which the identities of the parties were unknown to each other.

>   *b. Trading on inside information as a breach of duty to the corporation*

In 1969, the New York Court of Appeals handed down a decision which, for a brief period, appeared as if it would revitalize state law as a source of remedies for trading on inside information. The case is *Diamond v. Oreamuno.*[25] Oreamuno was the chairman of the board, and Gonzalez was the president, of Management Assistance, Inc. (MAI). MAI suffered a sharp decline in its earnings. Prior to MAI publicly reporting this decline, Oreamuno and Gonzalez sold off a large quantity of the MAI stock they owned at $28 per share. After disclosure of the earnings decline, the price of the stock fell to $11 per share. Diamond, a shareholder of MAI, brought a derivative suit on behalf of the corporation, seeking to force Oreamuno and Gonzalez to pay to the company the $800,000 more they had received for their stock by selling at $28 rather than $11 per share.[26] The trial court dismissed the complaint for failure to state a cause of action, and, after the intermediate appellate court reversed, the matter ended up in the Court of Appeals.

Oremumo and Gonzalez did not dispute that they had a fiduciary duty to MAI. Their argument was that their stock sales did nothing to harm MAI, and, therefore, there were no damages for MAI to collect through a derivative suit. The Court of Appeals rejected this argument based upon two alternative rationales.

The broader rationale was that the corporation could recover even if it sustained no damages. The notion is that a fiduciary should not profit from his or her position—at least without the beneficiary's consent— even if the beneficiary suffers no loss. Accordingly, the fiduciary must turn over to his or her beneficiary any profit made without the beneficiary's consent from the fiduciary's position. Put differently, this rationale

---

23. *See, e.g.,* Joseph v. Farnsworth Radio & Television Corp., 99 F.Supp. 701 (S.D.N.Y.1951).

24. 283 Mass. 358, 186 N.E. 659 (1933).

25. 24 N.Y.2d 494, 301 N.Y.S.2d 78, 248 N.E.2d 910 (1969).

26. As we shall see later in this chapter, Section 16(b) of the 1934 Securities Exchange Act provides for this is the type of remedy. Oreamuno and Gonzalez evidently avoided liability under Section 16(b) by not repurchasing stock in MAI after the price had fallen.

treats inside information as a species of corporate property. Just as the corporation is entitled to recover whatever profits an agent makes through unauthorized use of the corporation's tangible property, so the corporation is entitled, under this reasoning, to whatever profits the director or officer makes through trading on inside information from the corporation.

The alternative rationale in *Diamond* is factual rather than doctrinal. Specifically, the court suggested that the corporation suffered reputational harm from its officials trading on inside information. While, at first glance, this suggestion might seem to be a make-weight, in fact, it captures one of the principal policy reasons often asserted for laws to prohibit trading on inside information. As we shall discuss in some detail later, such trading presumably causes investors to discount the amount they are willing to pay for a corporation's stock, and thereby raises the corporation's cost of capital.[27]

In any event, subsequent cases in other jurisdictions have been reluctant to follow *Diamond*,[28] and, perhaps because the federal remedies turned out to be more effective than the court in *Diamond* predicted, there has not been any great rush of shareholder plaintiffs pursuing claims under the *Diamond* rationale.

§ 6.2 Securities Laws

In the prior section, we saw that the common law action for fraud and deceit provided only limited protection for investors who had been led to purchase stock by false or misleading statements. More broadly, the common law generally did nothing to protect against investment decisions made in ignorance, rather than based on false information. This state of affairs—particularly when coupled with well publicized frauds and economic downturns—led legislatures to decide that the law needed a more robust response to protect persons urged to invest in corporations and other business ventures. As a result, first state legislatures, and then Congress, enacted statutes known as securities laws.

6.2.1 *State Securities (or "Blue Sky") Laws*

Worried that the state's farmers were falling victim to shady operators selling investments which possessed little more substance than buying so many square feet of blue sky, Kansas passed the first state securities (or so-called blue sky) law in 1911. Since then, all states have enacted such statutes. These statutes vary widely. Nevertheless, they

27. The defendants also argued that corporate recovery would tread upon an area regulated by the federal securities laws, and created the prospect for overlapping damage claims by the corporation and by other traders in the market. The Court of Appeals' response was anything but prescient, as the court expressed skepticism that federal laws would provide much relief against those trading on inside information—which, as we shall see later, turned out not to be the case. The court was on more solid ground in pointing out that the federal securities laws did not preempt state corporate law, and in stating that the court could deal with problems of overlapping recovery when and if the problem actually arose.

28. *E.g.*, Schein v. Chasen, 313 So.2d 739 (Fla.1975).

typically contain one or more of three types of provisions. The simplest type of provision imposes sanctions, such as criminal prosecution, for fraud in selling securities. A much more elaborate type of provision requires registration and regulation of persons, such as brokers, who trade securities in the state. The type of provision which has the most impact on corporate law, however, imposes a requirement that persons must "register" any securities sold in the state. Since the definition of securities under state blue sky laws invariably includes corporate stock,[1] this third type of provision prevents a corporation from selling stock within a state unless the corporation registers the stock (or the statute provides an exemption for the type of transaction in question).[2]

What exactly does registration of securities under state blue sky laws entail? Because state securities laws vary widely, it would take an entire treatise just on state blue sky laws to give a definitive answer to this question. Still, the enactment of the Uniform Securities Act by most states allows us to discern a predominant pattern.[3] The 1956 version of the Uniform Securities Act established three methods of registering the sale of securities in a state: notification, coordination and qualification.[4] Notification allows seasoned companies meeting certain financial tests to file a shortened registration statement. Issuers have made little use of the notification procedure, however, and the 1985 revision of the Uniform Securities Act replaced it with a new registration procedure called filing. Filing allows blue chip companies to avoid merit review (which we will describe shortly) of their offerings. More broadly useful is the coordination procedure. This allows a company registering under the 1933 Securities Act (which we shall discuss shortly in dealing with federal securities laws) to file copies of its federal materials with the appropriate state agency, instead of preparing entirely new disclosure documents for the state. Otherwise, the issuer must register by qualification. This requires preparation and filing of an extensive disclosure document.

Disclosure, however, is not the worst burden imposed by blue sky laws—especially for a company going public and therefore preparing federal disclosure materials anyway. Rather, a significant requirement contained in a number of state securities laws is merit review. Specifical-

---

§ 6.2

1. *E.g.,* Cal. Corp. Code § 25019.

2. The question of when a sale of stock takes place within a state can present a difficult issue, and, indeed, it is possible, when the selling company is in one state, and the purchasing investors are in another state, for courts to consider the sale to take place in both states. *See, e.g.,* Benjamin v. Cablevision Programming Investments, 114 Ill.2d 150, 102 Ill.Dec. 296, 499 N.E.2d 1309 (1986).

3. The Uniform Securities Act was originally promulgated in 1956. A revised version came out in 1985. The Uniform Securities Act, however, has been far less successful in achieving uniformity among the states than have many other uniform statutes, such as the Uniform Partnership Act. For one thing, many of the most important commercial states, such as New York, have been among the states not adopting the Uniform Securities Act. In addition, many of the states which base their blue sky law on the Uniform Securities Act have made substantial modifications. Moreover, much of state blue sky "law" consists of the rules and determinations of the state agencies which enforce the statutes.

4. Uniform Securities Act §§ 302–304.

ly, a number of state securities laws either require the seller to receive a state official's approval of the merits of the proposed offering before the issuer can sell the securities, or else allow the state official to stop an offering which the official finds to be unsatisfactory on its merits.[5]

Generally, the statutory standards for merit review are quite vague. For example, a common formulation is whether the offering is "fair, just and equitable."[6] Hence, these statutes essentially vest the state agency administering the statute with broad discretion to decide what offerings are worthy of sale in the state. The specific criteria applied in the exercise of this discretion vary from state to state (and even over time within the same state as personnel in government change).[7] Nevertheless, the two common themes are (1) whether the investment is too risky to be sold to anyone but perhaps sophisticated and well-healed investors, and (2) whether the insiders are too greedy in terms of how little of the company they are willing to give up to obtain the new investors' money.

The idea that state officials should protect investors from making their own choices might strike many as rather paternalistic—albeit, government agencies keep all sorts of products off the market for the good of prospective consumers of those products, and most states do not have unlimited legalized gambling. Even if merit review is an appropriate protection, however, the patchwork of varying state regulations creates a burden on nationwide plans to sell securities. For decades, companies seeking to sell stock lived with this burden. (Indeed, numerous young associates in law offices over the years cut their legal research teeth in the corporate arena by undertaking what was known as a blue sky survey; which meant checking out all of the state laws and regulations that might be applicable to a proposed offering.) Recently, Congress decided that the burden of compliance with state registration requirements was too much for companies with stock listed for trading on the national exchanges. Accordingly, Congress amended the 1933 Securities Act to preempt state securities laws from requiring the registration of so-called covered securities—which are securities listed (or that will be listed after their distribution) for trading on the New York or American Stock Exchanges or on the National Market System of the NASDAQ Stock Market.[8]

6.2.2   The 1933 Securities Act

The 1933 Securities Act constituted the first foray by the federal government into what had theretofore been the state domain of regulating the sale of stocks and other securities. The Act was part of the "New

5. *E.g.*, Cal. Corp. Code § 25140.

6. *Id.* The Uniform Securities Act contains an alternate formulation, which asks whether the offering would "work a fraud upon purchasers" or "would be made with unreasonable amounts of underwriters' and sellers' discounts, commissions, or other compensation, or promoters' profits or participation, or unreasonable amounts or

kinds of options." Uniform Securities Act § 306.

7. *See, e.g.,* Brandi, *Securities Practitioners and Blue Sky Laws: A Survey of Comments and a Ranking of States by Stringency of Regulation,* 10 J. Corp. L. 689 (1985).

8. Sec. Act. § 18.

Deal" legislation enacted by Congress at the start of the Roosevelt administration to cope with the Great Depression. The Act reflects two basic assumptions.

One assumption underlying the Securities Act was Congress' view that sales of stock and other investments through the dissemination of false or even incomplete information was not simply a matter of private concern, but had an impact on the national economy. It is easy to see how Congress came to this view while legislating in the midst of the Great Depression. The conventional wisdom at the time held that the stock market crash of 1929 had precipitated the depression. Moreover, the conventional wisdom at the time (as reflected in the hearings leading up to the enactment of the 1933 Act) believed that the stock market crash represented the collapse of a market bubble created in large part by fraud.[9]

Even if one no longer subscribes to this historical view, there is a strong argument that fully and accurately informed stock and other securities markets are important to a healthy economy. To begin with, the stock and other securities markets allocate capital to various businesses. Presumably, accurately and fully informed stock and other securities markets will allocate capital to the most productive firms where the capital can do the most good for the economy.[10] Misinformed, or not fully informed, stock and other securities markets may allocate capital in less useful directions. The availability of complete and accurate information also impacts how much total capital society will invest in productive ventures, and what rate of return investors will demand for putting up their funds. Frauds and lack of information create risks for investors—who, after all, might be fooled into putting their money into unsound investments. Such risks make some prospective investors unwilling to invest (better to keep the money safely hidden in a mattress), and make other prospective investors demand a higher rate of return to compensate for the added risk. The end result is to decrease the supply of capital available to promote economic growth, and to increase the cost of that capital—thereby slowing economic expansion.[11]

9. Revisionist historians have challenged the traditional narrative of the relationship of the stock market crash to the Great Depression, arguing, for example, that Congress, itself, may have caused the depression through the Smoot–Hartley tariff, or that the cause lay in the Federal Reserve's contraction of the money supply.

10. The performance of companies reflects both the demand for their products and the efficiency of the companies' managements in producing goods and services to meet that demand. Accordingly, accurate information about company performance (and the prospects for future performance) informs potential investors of where there is the greatest demand for goods and services and what managements are best able

to meet this demand. The rational desire of investors to purchase securities which have prospects for solid performance should, as a result, move capital to where it can do the most to produce the goods and services desired by society in the most efficient manner.

11. Given that a lack of complete and accurate information raises the cost of capital to businesses, one might argue that individual businesses have an incentive to provide complete and accurate information without the need for a regulatory requirement. The problem with such a voluntary approach is that some individual businesses and managers always spoil things for everyone by succumbing to the temptation to make a short-term gain through false or

The second assumption behind the 1933 Securities Act was Congress' view that the appropriate mechanism to protect investors is simply to ensure complete and accurate disclosure. In other words, Congress rejected the approach of many state blue sky laws, which sought to protect investors by prohibiting the sale of securities unless a state agency decided that the investment was a sound one. Instead, Congress decided that, once investors had full and accurate information, it was up to the investors to protect themselves.[12]

The basic approach of the 1933 Securities Act borrowed partially from state securities laws, as well from a statute passed by the English Parliament in response to some noted failures of common law fraud actions to protect investors in England. This approach is to require the registration of securities before their issuance, with registration involving the preparation, filing and dissemination to investors of an extensive disclosure document. Exploring this requirement calls for us to address two questions: (1) When must one register? and (2) What does registration entail?

a.   The scope of the registration requirement

The basic thrust of the 1933 Securities Act is to require registration of public offerings of newly issued securities. The Act, however, does not come out and directly state this. Instead, the structure of the Act is to start with a blanket requirement of registration for all securities sales and then work the Act's way backwards by creating exemptions.

The 1933 Securities Act revolves around Section 5 of the statute. This section contains three prohibitions. Section 5(a) prohibits use of the mail or means of transportation or communication in interstate commerce to sell (or deliver for or after a sale) a security, unless a registration statement is in effect. In other words, one cannot sell a security unless one has registered under the Act.[13] Section 5(c) prohibits use of the mail or means of transportation or communication in interstate commerce to make offers to sell or buy any security, unless a registration statement is filed.[14] Finally, Section 5(b) prohibits the use of any "prospectus" (essentially any written document, or radio or televi-

incomplete disclosure. Since it is difficult for investors to know which businesses are the rotten apples, the cost of capital goes up for everyone.

12. Up until recently, however, Congress respected the right of the states to approach the matter differently, and did not seek to preempt state merit regulation.

13. The language about use of mails or interstate commerce is to make the statute constitutional. It seems that the drafters of the United States Constitution inconveniently had overlooked the need to empower Congress specifically to regulate securities transactions, and so Congress had to rely on its power over the mails and interstate commerce. Since it is pretty dif-

ficult to sell securities without using the mail or a telephone or some other means of transportation or communication in interstate commerce, this jurisdictional limitation has little practical impact.

14. At first glance, Section 5(c) seems repetitive of Section 5(a). A careful reading, however, illustrates that Section 5(c) has the impact of dividing the time prior to registration of securities into two periods— before filing the registration materials, at which time there can be no offers to sell or buy the securities in question, and after filing the registration materials, but before the registration becomes effective, during which time there can be offers, but no sales.

sion communication, seeking to sell a security) unless the prospectus meets the requirements of the statute. Section 5(b) also requires delivery of a prospectus meeting the requirements of the statute to purchasers of securities when the security is delivered following its sale.

Since the prohibitions of Section 5 hinge upon whether one is selling a "security," the definition of a security is critical to the reach of the statute. The very first substantive term in the statute (Section 2(a)(1)) defines the word "security" for purposes of the Act. The definition is quite broad. Among the laundry list of items considered to be securities is an "investment contract." Court decisions have held that an investment contract includes any contract by which a person invests money in a common enterprise with profits to come solely from the efforts of others.[15] Hence, all sorts of investments—such as purchasing a row of orange trees in a grove under central management—can be securities. For purposes of this book, which is concerned about corporate law, what is important about the definition of a security is that the definition, not surprisingly, includes "stock."[16]

If the drafters of the 1933 Securities Act had left things with Section 5, then anyone who sold stock would need to register. This would include the one-person corporation, which issues all of its shares to the person who founded the company and will be the company's sole owner, and a person who calls his or her broker to sell the 100 shares of General Motors stock which he or she owns. Requiring the seller to prepare an extensive disclosure document obviously would be silly in such cases. After all, in the first instance, the sole owner of the corporation would end up preparing a document for him- or herself to read, while, in the second instance, the selling shareholder typically does not know anything more about the company to put into such a document than does anyone else in the market. Accordingly, the 1933 Act contains various exemptions to narrow the reach of its registration requirement. Section 3 of the Act exempts various securities, and Section 4 of the Act exempts various transactions, from registration. While there are numerous exemptions, a few are the most important as far as corporate law.

Section 4(2) of the Securities Act will cover the situation in which a corporation issues shares to the individual or individuals who founded the corporation and will be in charge of the company. This provision exempts transactions by the issuer which do not involve any public offering. (For obvious reasons, Section 4(2) is often referred to as the

---

15. *E.g.*, SEC v. W.J. Howey Co., 328 U.S. 293, 66 S.Ct. 1100 (1946). *See also* SEC v. Glenn W. Turner Enterprises, Inc., 474 F.2d 476 (9th Cir.1973) (holding that an investment contract still exists even if the investors provide some services to the venture, so long as the essential managerial efforts come from someone other than the investors).

16. While the mere label of something as "stock" does not mean it is stock for

purposes of the securities laws (*e.g.*, United Housing Foundation, Inc. v. Forman, 421 U.S. 837, 95 S.Ct. 2051 (1975)(units entitling one to live in a cooperative apartment house were not stock for purposes of the securities laws)), ownership interests in a for-profit corporation, which entitle one to dividends and the like, clearly are stock. *E.g.*, Landreth Timber Co. v. Landreth, 471 U.S. 681, 105 S.Ct. 2297 (1985).

private offering exemption.) Unfortunately, once one goes beyond the situation in which the corporation is issuing shares to the persons in charge of the company, it is often not clear when one has gone beyond the bounds of a private offering. Indeed, court holdings do not limit the meaning of a "public offering" for purposes of Section 4(2) to situations in which the corporation sells stock to the public at large.[17]

What exactly are the criteria for the private offering exemption? Court opinions have pointed to two seemingly disparate tests. One test is a list of four factors (which stem from a 1935 Securities Exchange Commission General Counsel Opinion). These factors include: how many units in total are offered; how much money the offering raises; the manner in which the issuer makes the offering; and the number of offerees and their relationship to the issuer.[18] Actually, however, this list provides a largely useless test. The number of units (such as shares of stock) offered is a function of the price per unit. Even a one-person corporation could issue its sole owner thousands of shares if the price per share is low enough. Yet, this would certainly not be a public offering. On the other hand, a limited partnership might issue only several hundred units (limited partnership interests); yet this would probably entail a public offering. Similarly, the size of the offering (in terms of dollars raised) generally does not lead to different results in decided cases. In fact, private placements to institutional investors can run into the tens or hundreds of millions of dollars. The manner of offering— more specifically the lack of general solicitations or advertising—is a relevant factor; although one which is probably a necessary, but hardly a sufficient, condition for a private offering. This brings one to the number of offerees and their relationship with issuer. The relationship part of this factor is more important than the number. Indeed, some courts have held that even an offer to one person could be a public offering,[19] while, at the other end, there is no maximum number which, in itself, constitutes an offering public versus private.[20]

Far more useful is the Supreme Court's test in *SEC v. Ralston Purina Co.*[21] This approach examines whether the offerees could fend for themselves, rather than needing the protection of registration. Clearly the promoters or top managers of a company hardly need the protection of reading a registration statement for which they would have provided the information.[22] Moving beyond insiders, sophisticated investing institutions, like banks or venture capital funds, know what information to demand without reading a registration statement.[23]

---

17. *See, e.g.,* Doran v. Petroleum Management Corp., 545 F.2d 893 (5th Cir.1977).

18. *Id.*

19. *E.g.,* G. Eugene England Foundation v. First Federal Corp., 663 F.2d 988 (10th Cir.1973).

20. *E.g.,* SEC v. Ralston Purina Co., 346 U.S. 119, 73 S.Ct. 981 (1953).

21. 346 U.S. 119, 73 S.Ct. 981 (1953).

22. On the other hand, more junior corporate employees, as were involved in *Ralston Purina,* might not know enough about what is going on in the corporation to protect themselves without a registration statement.

23. Notice that the test for a private offering focuses on the persons who receive an "offer"—which the 1933 Act defines to reach well beyond what is an offer under

The problem with the private offering exemption is that once one gets beyond offers to top management and sophisticated investing institutions, it is never entirely clear whether the exemption will apply. Yet, many small businesses need to raise money from a few investors, and it might stifle small business development if any effort to raise money from a few investors required the expense of preparing for a registration under the 1933 Act. This concern led the Securities Exchange Commission—the federal agency which administers the Securities Act—to develop exemptions which would alleviate unnecessary burdens on small businesses seeking to raise money. In 1982, the Securities Exchange Commission adopted an integrated set of exemptions grouped together under the title Regulation D. While the Commission several times has amended Regulation D, the consensus seems to be that these exemptions have proven largely successful in reconciling the protection of investors with the fundraising needs of smaller businesses.

Regulation D contains three specific exemptions. Rule 504 provides an exemption for offerings of no more than $1 million. The principal limitation of Rule 504 is that, unless there is disclosure under state securities laws, offerings under Rule 504 normally cannot include a "general solicitation"—which might encompass any efforts to sell securities to persons who do not have some preexisting relationship with either the business or persons associated with the business.[24]

Rule 505 allows an exemption for selling up to $5 million worth of securities. Unlike Rule 504, however, Rule 505 limits the number of purchasers (up to 35 plus any number of so-called accredited investors[25]) and requires the purchasers' receipt (unless they are accredited investors) of specified information. Also, Rule 505 limits general solicitations regardless of compliance with state securities laws.

Both Rules 504 and 505 contain dollar limits because both exemptions stem from the Securities Exchange Commission's authority under Section 3(b) of the Securities Act. Section 3(b) empowers the SEC to create exemptions when the Commission concludes registration is not needed "by reason of the small amount involved or the limited character of the public offering." By contrast, Rule 506 provides an exemption without any dollar limit. Essentially, Rule 506 differs from Rule 505 in two ways. Conceptually, Rule 506 differs from Rule 505 (and 504) because the authority for Rule 506 does not come from Section 3(b) (which extends only to offerings up to $5 million). Instead, Rule 506 is

contract law—rather than just the persons who actually end up purchasing the securities. Keep in mind also that even if the initial buyer of securities does not need the protection of reading a registration statement, the initial buyer might turn around and resell the securities to persons who do need such protection. Indeed, this is what an underwriter does in a public offering. Hence, avoiding a public offering typically requires limitations on resales of securities by the initial purchasers.

24. An exception exists if the offering is made to certain limited classes of wealthier or more knowledgeable investors pursuant to a state law exemption which allows general solicitations.

25. Regulation D contains a laundry list of persons who fit the definition of accredited investors, including certain insiders, institutions and wealthy individuals.

an "interpretation" of the private offering exemption found in Section 4(2). Moreover, it is not an interpretation of what Section 4(2) requires for every private placement. Rather, it is a "safe harbor," within which the Securities Exchange Commission deems a private offering to occur, but outside of which issuers take their chances with the standards developed under the case law. Practically speaking, Rule 506 differs from Rule 505 by imposing a trade-off: no dollar limit, but now the up to 35 unaccredited purchasers must all be sophisticated (or, more precisely, the purchaser, or his or her "purchaser representative," must have knowledge and experience in financial and business matters making him or her capable of evaluating the merits and risks of the prospective investment). Besides lacking any dollar limit, Rule 506 has one other significant advantage over the other exemptions in Regulation D. Section 18 of the 1933 Securities Act preempts the states from requiring registration of any security the sale of which is exempt from federal registration by virtue of Rule 506. (Without such preemption, sellers of securities seeking to avoid state registration must look for exemptions in the blue sky laws of the state(s) in which they are selling the securities.)

What about the average investor's sale of his or her shares? Section 4(2) and Regulation D do not apply, since these exemptions only cover sales by the issuer (in other words, in the case of stock, sales by the corporation). Section 4(1) of the 1933 Act, however, exempts transactions by one who is not an "issuer, underwriter, or dealer." Hence, Section 4(1) is the provision which exempts the existing stockholder's sale of his or her shares in the corporation, so long as the stockholder is not a dealer in securities, and so long as the transaction does not involve an underwriter.

Unfortunately, the question of whether a given sale involves an underwriter is not as simple as one might suppose. This is because the definition of an underwriter in the Securities Act is not limited to the investment banking firms one normally thinks of as underwriters. Rather, Section 2(11) of the Act defines an underwriter to include "*any person* who has purchased from an issuer with a view to . . . *the distribution* of any security, *or participates* . . . in any *such undertaking*." (Emphasis Added.) Thus, whether a seller of securities is an underwriter generally depends on whether his or her sale is part of a "distribution." Moreover, when a party who is in control of the issuer sells some of his or her securities, an additional complication arises by virtue of the last sentence in Section 2(11). If this controlling person sells through a broker, the broker can be an underwriter, as one who "offers or sells for an issuer [defined under the last sentence of Section 2(11) to include, for this purpose, a person controlling the issuer] in connection with the distribution." Notice this again means that underwriter status depends on whether the sale constitutes part of a "distribution."

As one might have guessed, it is often not clear when an existing shareholder's sale of his or her stock is part of a distribution. To provide guidelines on when a sale is part of a "distribution," the SEC promulgated Rule 144. This rule contains a fairly complex set of requirements looking to how long the seller owned the securities, the quantity of securities sold, and the availability of public information about the issuer, which, if met, place the seller in a safe harbor under which the SEC will not consider the sale to involve an underwriter. If the sale does not fall within the Rule 144 safe harbor, the sale still might not be part of a distribution. There are two important contexts in which this is commonly the case. The first is a sale of registered shares by a non-affiliate of the issuer.[26] Hence, it is Section 4(1), unqualified by Rule 144, which allows the ordinary stockholder to sell his or her General Motors shares without registering. At the other extreme, suppose a shareholder sells his or her shares to an insider or to a sophisticated and fully informed purchaser. While this might seem to fit the private offering exemption, as stated above, Section 4(2) applies only to transactions "by the issuer." On the other hand, such a private transaction would not seem to be part of a "distribution," and so Section 4(1) should apply even without Rule 144. This is sometimes referred to as the "Section 4(1½) exemption," since it represents something of a cross between Sections 4(1) and 4(2), although it falls under the former Section.

Before leaving the subject of who is required to register, it might be useful to ask what happens if a person sells securities without a required registration. In addition to exposing the seller to criminal penalties, Section 12(1) of the 1933 Act gives each buyer of such securities the right to demand his or her money back.

b. What registration entails

As evident from the discussion thus far, registration under the 1933 Securities Act requires the preparation and filing with the Securities Exchange Commission of a disclosure document known as a registration statement. This registration statement contains two parts. Part I is the prospectus. The issuer not only files this part with the SEC, but, as stated in our discussion of Section 5, the issuer must deliver a copy of the prospectus to each purchaser of the securities.[27] Part II of the registration statement contains additional information. The issuer files Part II with the SEC, where it is available for public inspection; but the issuer need not deliver copies of Part II to each purchaser.[28] The preparation of a registration statement is a job for specialists in securi-

---

26. Rule 144 only covers sales of "restricted securities"—that is securities never sold through a public offering—and sales involving an "affiliate" of the issuer. An affiliate of the issuer includes persons, for example, who control the issuer.

27. Since this delivery must accompany the delivery of the purchased securities, it would seem a little late to do any good. To deal with this problem, the SEC requires delivery of a preliminary prospectus to the prospective buyers before the sale takes place.

28. Needless to say, most buyers are not going to review materials at the SEC's offices. The notion, however, is that professional securities analysts will review such materials, and that the analysts' distillation of the information, and the action of the analysts' clients based upon recommendations from the securities analysts, will lead to the price of the securities reflecting the information contained in Part II of the registration statement. More recently, SEC filings have become available over the Internet.

ties law.[29] For our purposes, it is sufficient to explore how the provisions of the Securities Act seek to ensure complete and accurate information goes into the registration statement.

The obvious mechanism for ensuring complete information goes into the registration statement is through the Securities Exchange Commission's specification of the contents of these documents. Over the years, the Commission has refined its registration forms, with the goals of ensuring meaningful disclosure, and, at the same time, avoiding unnecessary burdens upon issuers. Among the Commission's initiatives have been efforts to coordinate registration filings under the 1933 Act, with required filings (which we shall discuss shortly) under the 1934 Securities Exchange Act. Other initiatives have included the development of special, less burdensome, forms for small businesses, and for offerings by more seasoned issuers.

As our earlier discussion of Section 5 noted, there is a gap between the time the issuer files the registration statement with the SEC, and the time the statement becomes effective (during which interval those selling the securities can make oral offers, but there cannot be sales of the securities). This gap allows the Commission's staff to review the registration statement.[30] While the staff cannot confirm the accuracy of the statements made in the document, the staff can, and does, point out to the issuer areas in which the document is incomplete or does not give sufficient emphasis to certain facts (such as the risks entailed in purchasing the securities). Indeed, while the Commission cannot prevent the sale of securities whose merits are not evident to the Commission, the staff can make sure that the prospectus makes the investment look unappetizing.

The Securities Act's mechanism for ensuring the accuracy of registration statements (as well as the accuracy of other communications made in selling securities) is to contain some rather sobering liability provisions. In particular, Section 11 of the Securities Act creates liability for any untrue statements of material fact contained in the registration statement (or for any omissions of material facts either required to be in the registration statement or which render statements made in the registration statement misleading). What makes Section 11 scary for

29. Indeed, the standard legal malpractice insurance policy excludes coverage of liabilities arising out of securities work. To obtain such coverage, the attorney must purchase a supplement to the policy. Insurance companies will not sell such a supplement without being satisfied as to the competence of the attorney to handle securities work.

30. Section 8 of the Securities Act provides that a registration statement automatically will become effective 20 days after its filing (or 20 days after the filing of the last amendment to the statement), unless the SEC seeks to prevent the statement from becoming effective, or the SEC agrees to shorten the time. This, however, is not the way things work in the real world. Instead, the SEC essentially bribes issuers into giving the agency longer to conduct its review. The agency's leverage is to allow issuers whose registration statements meet with the staff's acceptance to insert the price term in the document shortly before the statement becomes effective. Otherwise, the issuer would be stuck selling the securities at a price set 20 days before the sale (which could not take into account the constantly changing market conditions).

those involved in preparing a registration statement are several critical differences between the requirements for imposing liability under Section 11, and the requirements for imposing liability under the common law action for fraud or deceit.

To begin with, Section 11 imposes liability upon a number of parties who may not actually have made the false statement. Specifically, the Section imposes liability upon the issuer, every person who signed the registration statement, every director of the issuer, every person who provides an expert certification of any portion of the registration statement,[31] and the underwriter(s) of the offering.

More dramatically, Section 11 does away with the common law fraud requirement of scienter. Instead, the issuer is strictly liable for any misrepresentations in the registration statement. The other defendants can be liable unless they can establish what is often referred to as their due diligence. Broadly speaking, this creates liability for negligent misrepresentations, with the burden of proof on the defendants to show they were not negligent. This part of Section 11 has tremendous practical implications. It encourages all of the prospective defendants to undertake and document their efforts to investigate the accuracy of the registration statement. On the positive side, this has meant that there have been relatively few cases in which prospectuses contained false statements. On the negative side, this fear and double checking has made the process of preparing a registration statement amazingly expensive.

Finally, with one exception, Section 11 creates liability without the plaintiff needing to prove reliance. Instead, it would be up to the defendants to show that the plaintiff knew the challenged portion in the registration statement was false.

Two other liability provisions reinforce Section 11. Section 12(a)(2) allows a suit for false or misleading statements contained in any prospectus or oral communication used to sell securities. Hence, Section 12(a)(2) will cover misrepresentations made outside of the registration statement.[32] Like Section 11, there is no requirement of scienter under Section 12(a)(2). Rather, it is up to the defendant prove his or her lack of negligence in failing to discover the truth. Nor is there any need for the plaintiff to prove reliance under Section 12(a)(2), so long as the plaintiff did not know the statements were false. The principal restriction of Section 12(a)(2) vis-a-vis Section 11 is that the misrepresentation must be made by the person who sold the plaintiff the securities in question. Section 17(a) prohibits fraud, or making false or misleading statements,

---

31. For example, the accountants who provide audited financial statements.

32. Curiously, the Supreme Court has held that the term "prospectus" for purposes of Section 12(a)(2) refers only to the prospectus prepared in accordance with the requirements which the Securities Act imposes on the document used in public offerings. Gustafson v. Alloyd Company, 513 U.S. 561, 115 S.Ct. 1061 (1995). Not only does this opinion give short shrift to the Securities Act's definition of a "prospectus" as any writing or television or radio advertisement used to sell a security, but it also creates an odd divergence in liability for false statements, depending upon whether they are oral or in writing.

in the offer or sale of any securities. Violation of Section 17(a) can lead to an action by the Securities Exchange Commission for injunctive relief or to a criminal prosecution.

6.2.3   *The 1934 Securities Exchange Act*

The 1933 Securities Act has a fairly narrow focus, this being, for the most part, ensuring full and accurate disclosure during the initial public issuance of stock or other securities. To use a common metaphor, the 1933 Act seeks to ensure adequate information while new securities flow through the spigot into the public marketplace. The 1934 Securities Exchange Act, by contrast, is concerned with what happens with the securities and their owners as they trade in marketplace—to continue the metaphor, with what happens to the securities as they are in the tub. Such a concern, in turn, means that the Securities Exchange Act must deal with a variety of different problems, and, as a result, the 1934 Act contains a hodgepodge of provisions.

Earlier in this book, we explored the impact of one provision in the 1934 Act, that being the regulation of proxy solicitations pursuant to Section 14(a) of the Act. Later in this chapter, we will explore provisions of the 1934 Act addressing fraud and insider trading. Later in this book, we shall examine provisions added by amendment to the 1934 Act, which regulate tender offers. For now, it is useful simply to take notice of provisions in the Securities Exchange Act that complement the Securities Act by ensuring a continuous flow of fresh information reaches the market concerning the issuers of publicly traded securities.

Section 12(a) of the 1934 Securities Exchange Act requires companies with securities traded on a national exchange (such as the New York Stock Exchange) to register the securities.[33] Section 12(g)—which Congress added to the Securities Exchange Act in 1964—significantly expands the scope of companies required to register under Section 12. It calls for every company with over $1 million in assets, and a class of equity securities (stock, for a corporation) held by 500 or more persons, to register the securities. (Of course, $1 million today does not buy as much as $1 million did in 1964. Hence, the Securities Exchange Commission has adopted a rule[34] which limits the requirement of registration under Section 12(g) to companies with over $10 million in assets.) Unlike, registration under the 1933 Act, what is most significant about registration under Section 12 of the 1934 Act is not the initial filing. Rather, the main significance as far as providing disclosure is the requirement in Section 13(a) that companies with securities registered under Section 12 file periodic reports as dictated by the Securities Exchange Commission. The Commission requires such companies to file annual reports (on From 10–K), quarterly reports (on Form 10–Q) and reports for certain significant events (on Form 8–K). Hence, the 1934 Act

33. To be more precise, Section 12(a) prevents trading of unregistered securities on a national securities exchange; which effectively means the issuer must register the securities. Section 12(b) sets out the procedure for registration.

34. Exch. Act Rule 12g–1.

works to ensure that a regular stream of information concerning corporations with widely held stock reaches the market.

As might be expected, the 1934 Securities Exchange Act contains provisions seeking to ensure accuracy in disclosure by imposing liability for false or misleading statements. Section 18(a) gives parties who read and relied upon false or misleading statements contained in documents filed under the Securities Exchange Act a cause of action against the person(s) who made the false or misleading statements. Section 18(a) imposes the burden of proof on the defendant to show that he or she acted in good faith and did not know of the falsity. It turns out, however, that the express remedy in Section 18(a) has not been all that important. This is because of the dramatic growth of what started out as an almost accidental remedy—this being the implied right of action under Rule 10b–5.

§ 6.3 Rule 10b–5

The previous section of this chapter provided an overview of how state and federal securities laws seek to ensure that investors have access to accurate information regarding securities including corporate stock. It turns out that one administrative rule promulgated pursuant to the 1934 Securities Exchange Act has developed a significance dwarfing much of the rest of the securities laws. This rule has the unassuming title, "Rule 10b–5."

Rule 10b–5's current significance stands in contrast to its humble origins. The Securities Exchange Commission promulgated Rule 10b–5 pursuant to the Commission's authority under Section 10(b) of the 1934 Securities Exchange Act. Section 10(b) makes it unlawful to use the mails, or any means of interstate commerce, to employ, in connection with the purchase or sale of any security, any manipulative or deceptive device or contrivance in contravention of rules promulgated by the Securities Exchange Commission. To put it more simply, the idea behind Section 10(b) is to complement the specific requirements and prohibitions in the federal securities laws with a catch-all provision empowering the SEC to define and prohibit manipulative or deceptive conduct which otherwise might fall between the cracks in the statutory scheme.[1]

§ 6.3

1. In authorizing the SEC to make up rules, rather than Congress itself specifying the prohibited conduct, Section 10(b) is similar to Section 14(a) of the 1934 Securities Exchange Act, which was discussed in an earlier chapter of this book. There are a couple of differences, however, between the two sections. Section 14(a) authorizes rules to regulate proxy solicitations—conduct which is not intrinsically bad, but which Congress found in need of regulation—whereas Section 10(b) addresses manipulative and deceptive actions (which, of course, is intrinsically bad conduct). This difference, in turn, has led to rules under Section 14(a) which create an overall regulatory scheme governing proxy solicitations, whereas the rules under Section 10(b) constitute an ad hoc effort to define and prohibit types of conduct which the SEC has found to be manipulative or deceptive. A second difference between the two sections is that Section 14(a) limits its reach to securities registered under Section 12 of the 1934 Securities Exchange Act. Section 10(b) expressly reaches any security.

As one might glean from Rule 10b–5's designation, Rule 10b–5 was not the first rule the Securities Exchange Commission thought up in carrying out the Commission's authority under Section 10(b). Rather, Rule 10b–5 came about as a casual (almost thoughtless) response to a particular problem facing the Commission. In 1942, the Commission's staff learned of an incident in which a corporation's president was going around lying to the corporation's shareholders in order to buy up stock on the cheap. The staff's problem was that the specific anti-fraud provisions of the federal securities laws were concerned with misrepresentations to sell securities, and did not prohibit lying in the course of purchasing securities. For example, Section 17(a) of the 1933 Securities Act prohibited fraud or misrepresentations in the "offer or sale" of a security. To close this gap, the staff proposed a new rule under Section 10(b). This new rule, in large part, borrowed the language of Section 17 of the 1933 Securities Act and substituted the word "purchase" for the word "offer." The Commission, with little deliberation, adopted the staff's proposed new rule as Rule 10b–5.[2]

In a nutshell, Rule 10b–5 makes it unlawful to commit fraud in connection with the purchase or sale of a security. To fall within the prohibition, the fraud must involve the use of either the mail, means or instrumentalities of interstate commerce, or a facility of a national securities exchange. This limitation mirrors the jurisdictional language in Section 10(b), which, in turn, was Congress' way of ensuring that the statute fell within Congress' constitutional authority. Courts have liberally interpreted the jurisdictional requirement: For example, it is not necessary that the defendant actually make false statements through the mail or by instrumentalities of interstate commerce, as long as there occurs some use of the mail or instrumentalities of interstate commerce (such as the telephone[3]) in connection with the fraud (say to mail the securities involved).[4] Hence, it would be a rare case in which someone committing a fraud involving the purchase or sale of a security will manage to avoid any use of either the mail or any instrumentalities of interstate commerce.

Rule 10b–5's specification of prohibited fraud is rather verbose, being set out in three parts. The first part makes it unlawful "[t]o employ any device, scheme or artifice to defraud," while the third part prohibits engaging "in any act, practice, or course of business which operates or would operate as a fraud or deceit upon any person." The reader may be forgiven for thinking these two parts are largely redundant, and, indeed, for as much as the courts seem to have focused on this language, the Commission simply could have said that it is unlawful to commit fraud. The middle part of the rule makes it unlawful "[t]o make

---

2. For a participant's recollection of how Rule 10b–5 came into being, see Milton Freeman, *Comments at the Conference on Codification of the Federal Securities Laws*, 22 Bus. Law. 793, 922 (1967).

3. *E.g.*, Loveridge v. Dreagoux, 678 F.2d 870 (10th Cir.1982) (intrastate telephone call is a use of an instrumentality of interstate commerce).

4. *E.g.*, Kline v. Henrie, 679 F.Supp. 464 (M.D.Pa.1988).

any untrue statement of a material fact or to omit to state a material fact necessary in order to make the statements made ... not misleading." Since false or misleading statements of material fact seemingly fit within the definition of fraud, it is unclear how much the middle part of the rule added to the first and third prohibitions.[5]

Rule 10b–5 only prohibits fraud in connection with the purchase or sale of a security, as opposed to fraud in connection with the purchase or sale of used cars or any of the myriad of other sorts of property whose purchase or sale might be accompanied by fraud. This, in turn, raises the policy question of why make a special federal case out of fraud in connection with the purchase or sale of securities (as opposed to used cars or whatever). The rationale presumably goes back to the apparent impact of securities transactions on the national economy which, in Congress' mind, justified the overall federal securities laws. Put simply, fraud in connection with enough securities transactions might trigger a national economic depression, whereas fraud in connection with the sale of used cars would not have such an impact. Significantly, however, the SEC, taking its lead from the language of Section 10(b), did not confine the reach of Rule 10b–5 to publicly traded securities. As a result, fraud in connection with the purchase or sale of stock in a closely held corporation comes within the prohibition of Rule 10b–5[6]—even though the potential impact of fraud in connection with the purchase or sale of stock in closely held corporations (even if a common occurrence) on the national economy seems remote at best.

In applying Rule 10b–5, it avoids confusion if we separate the analysis by the context in which Rule 10b–5 cases arise. There are three principal contexts to address: (1) misrepresentations; (2) trading on inside information and non-disclosure; and (3) breaches of fiduciary duty involving the purchase or sale of securities.

6.3.1 *Liability for Misrepresentations*

As stated above, Rule 10b–5 explicitly prohibits making false or misleading statements of material fact in connection with the purchase or sale of a security. This prohibition raises many of the same issues confronted when dealing with the common law of fraud or deceit, and when dealing with the prohibition under Securities Exchange Commission's Rule 14a–9 on making false or misleading statements in soliciting proxies (which was discussed in an earlier chapter).

a. *False or misleading statement of fact*

The first element of a Rule 10b–5 claim based upon a false or misleading statement of material fact is, not surprisingly, to find a

---

5. One possible difference is that fraud traditionally imports the notion of an intent to deceive, while the middle part of Rule 10b–5 avoids any language regarding intent. We shall see, however, that the Supreme Court has held that Section 10(b) precludes applying Rule 10b–5 to unintended falsehoods.

6. *See, e.g.,* Rochez Bros., Inc. v. Rhoades, 491 F.2d 402 (3d Cir.1973). Moreover, as discussed earlier in this chapter, the definition of "securities" goes far beyond stock. See § 6.2.2a *supra.*

statement of fact which is false or misleading. This element sometimes requires resolution of subtle issues. For example, suppose corporate management denies that they are engaged in "negotiations" for a merger of the company.[7] If the management had some preliminary discussions with a possible merger partner, is this statement false? The answer presumably depends upon the meaning of "negotiation." In dealing with such interpretation questions, a court might well adopt an empirical approach: Bring in some investors as witnesses and ask them what they took the statement to mean.[8] Moreover, it is important to keep in mind that even if a statement is literally true, the statement may be misleading—commonly because of the statement's failure to disclose other facts. For example, even if literally true, a denial that a company's management is engaged in merger negotiations might be misleading if the statement fails to disclose that the corporation's management has been contacted about a merger and is planning to enter into merger negotiations. Indeed, in some circumstances, the failure to disclose all of the facts, combined with an overly pessimistic, or an overly optimistic, tone to the statement of literally true facts, can produce a misleading result.[9]

A different sort of problem with finding that a statement constitutes a false or misleading statement of fact arises when the statement in question is an opinion or a prediction. For example, corporate managers may provide investors with a projection of the firm's expected earnings for the next year, or those in charge of the company might express their view as to the value of the company's stock or assets. As discussed earlier in this chapter,[10] common law courts have long struggled with the question of whether and when opinions or predictions constitute false statements of fact upon which a plaintiff can ground an action for fraud or deceit. In the context of false or misleading proxy solicitations within the meaning of Securities Exchange Commission's Rule 14a–9, the Supreme Court, in *Virginia Bankshares, Inc. v. Sandberg*,[11] suggested that a statement to the effect that a price was "fair" or "high" could constitute a false statement of fact—as opposed to an unactionable opinion—when the speaker did not believe the statement about price, and the objective evidence as to value did not support the statement.[12]

Of course, if the mere fact that some persons disagree with an opinion, or, especially, if the mere fact that a prediction does not come to pass, turns an opinion or prediction into a false statement of fact, then the result could be that the sort of opinions and predictions which are common in investment discussions would become, in effect, insurance policies for anyone buying a security that turns into a bad investment.

---

7. *See* Basic, Inc. v. Levinson, 485 U.S. 224, 108 S.Ct. 978 (1988).

8. *See, e.g.*, SEC v. Texas Gulf Sulfur Co., 401 F.2d 833 (2d Cir.1968) (trial court heard testimony from investors concerning how they understood and reacted to a press release).

9. *Id.*

10. See § 6.1.1 *supra*.

11. 501 U.S. 1083, 111 S.Ct. 2749 (1991).

12. For a full discussion of the court's opinion on this issue, see § 3.2.2a *supra*.

Perhaps one might argue that this would not be a bad result. Indeed, for a long time, the Securities Exchange Commission took the position that companies should not provide investors with earnings projections, valuation estimates and other so-called soft information. The Commission worried that such information might mislead investors. Accordingly, the Commission refused to allow companies to include such information in documents (such as registration statements) filed with the Commission. The problem, however, with this view is that projections and the like are precisely the sort of information which sophisticated investors find the most useful. After all, any investment essentially constitutes a purchase of a future stream of earnings. Hence, one cannot rationally value an investment without an estimate of future earnings. Ultimately, the SEC changed its view of so-called soft information, both to allow such information in documents filed with the Commission, and to create a safe-harbor for when the Commission will not consider such information in filed documents to be false or misleading.[13]

Under the SEC's safe harbor provisions, the key for deciding whether an opinion or prediction constitutes a false statement is whether the person making the statement provided the information in good faith (which presumably depends upon whether the speaker, him- or herself, believed the opinion or prediction), and whether the speaker had a reasonable basis for the opinion or prediction. Court decisions applying various provisions of the securities laws, including Rule 10b–5, have adopted basically the same test.[14] Interestingly, the Commission's rules and these lower court decisions seem to indicate that the test is a disjunctive one: lack of good faith or lack of a reasonable basis will make a statement of opinion or prediction false. By contrast, the Supreme Court's holding in *Virginia Bankshares* seems to require a conjunctive test: there must both be a lack of a subjective belief and a lack of an objective basis for the opinion in order for the opinion to constitute a false statement of fact.[15] In any event it may be impossible to answer the question of whether the test for actionable opinions and predictions is conjunctive or disjunctive, without going into other elements of the Rule 10b–5 claim. This is because statements of opinion or prediction made in good faith, but without a reasonable basis, might be false, but still not violate Rule 10b–5 due to lack of scienter, while statements of opinion or prediction with a reasonable basis, but which do not truly reflect the speaker's state of mind, might be false, yet not material.

13. Sec. Act Rule 175; Sec. Exch. Act Rule 3b–6.

14. *E.g.*, In re Donald J. Trump Casino Securities Litigation—Taj Mahal Litigation, 7 F.3d 357 (3d Cir.1993).

15. One reconciliation of *Virginia Bankshares* with the SEC safe harbor rules for soft information lies in the fact that *Virginia Bankshares* concerned private claims under Rule 14a–9, and the court's refusal to recognize a claim based solely on a misrepresentation of the speaker's state of mind, without regard to the objective reasonableness of the opinion, stemmed from the court's concerns over the abuse of private litigation. By contrast, the SEC rules address what constitutes a false statement for the purpose, in the first instance, of SEC enforcement actions.

b. *Materiality*

As with common law fraud, as well as under various other anti-fraud provisions in the securities laws, false or misleading statements will not violate Rule 10b–5 unless the statements are false or misleading as to material facts. After all, why get upset about misstatements concerning facts which are trivial in any event? The Supreme Court has held that the standard for materiality in the context of Rule 10b–5 is essentially the same as the standard which the Supreme Court adopted for claims under Rule 14a–9: A fact is material if there is a substantial likelihood that a reasonable investor would find the fact important (in the context of Rule 10b–5, in deciding whether to buy or sell a security).[16] While there can be as many different issues concerning materiality as there are different false or misleading statements, there are a couple of recurring types of materiality issues found in many Rule 10b–5 cases.

One recurring type of materiality issue found in a number of Rule 10b–5 cases involves the significance of facts showing the possibility of a future event, when the importance of the event is clear if the event actually occurs, but, at the time the statement is made, it is not clear whether the event will occur. For example, in *Basic, Inc. v. Levinson*,[17] the Supreme Court confronted a situation in which a corporation denied three times that it either was in merger negotiations or was aware of facts which would account for unusually heavy trading in the corporation's stock. In fact, the corporation was in discussions which ultimately resulted in a merger, the terms for which gave the corporation's shareholders a price for their stock well above the stock's pre-merger market price. Needless to say, reasonable investors would find such a premium price merger, if it actually occurs, to be an important fact in deciding whether to buy or sell the corporation's stock. The problem is that the corporation made the statements at a time in which the merger discussions could have fallen through and there would have been no merger. Does this mean that a reasonable investor would not have cared about the existence of the merger discussions in deciding whether to buy or sell?

The Supreme Court in *Basic* decided that the materiality of facts relating to contingent events, such as a merger under discussion, depends upon the magnitude of the event and its probability of occurring. In other words, the more impact the event will have, the less certain its

---

16. Basic, Inc. v. Levinson, 485 U.S. 224, 108 S.Ct. 978 (1988). In *TSC Indus., Inc. v. Northway, Inc.*, 426 U.S. 438, 96 S.Ct. 2126 (1976), the Supreme Court held that a fact was material for purposes of Rule 14a–9 if there was a substantial likelihood that a reasonable shareholder would consider the fact important in deciding how to vote—the focus on shareholder voting reflecting the fact that Rule 14a–9 deals with false or misleading proxy solicitations. For a discussion of the Supreme Court's analysis of materiality in *TSC Industries*,

see § 3.2.2b *supra*. As discussed when dealing with materiality under Rule 14a–9, the standard for materiality is that a reasonable shareholder or investor would take the fact into account in deciding what to do, but this does not mean that a reasonable shareholder or investor necessarily would have acted differently based upon the true fact. *E.g.,* Folger Adam Co. v. PMI Indus., Inc., 938 F.2d 1529 (2d Cir.1991).

17. 485 U.S. 224, 108 S.Ct. 978 (1988).

occurrence need be in order for investors to find the possibility of its happening to be significant; the more likely the occurrence, the less impact the event need produce in order for investors to take it into account. This sort of weighing of the magnitude and the likelihood of an event might remind the reader of half of the famous Learned Hand equation for measuring whether the failure to take steps to avoid accidents constitutes negligence.[18]

One potential problem with the Supreme Court's approach to materiality in *Basic* is that it is highly fact specific, and, as a result, it is difficult to predict in advance when merger discussions (or facts showing other potential events) have reached a state in which the likelihood of the event occurring is sufficient to render the possibility material. Nevertheless, the Supreme Court rejected the defendants' pleas for a bright line test of materiality. To the extent that one is dealing with a false or misleading statement, the Supreme Court's lack of sympathy is understandable. After all, if the defendants are worried about whether a false or misleading statement will be material, the answer is not to make the false or misleading statement. If there are business reasons to avoid premature disclosure of merger negotiations or the like, the Supreme Court suggested that the appropriate course is to keep one's mouth shut, rather than to dissemble.

The Supreme Court's rejection of a bright line test is consistent with a broader, and important, message in the Court's opinion. This message is that materiality simply involves the question of whether a reasonable investor would, in fact, find a statement important in deciding upon the purchase or sale of a security. Hence, the Supreme Court rejected the approaches of various Court of Appeals opinions which had used the materiality element as a convenient dumping ground under which to take into account all sorts of factors that have nothing to do with the importance investors attach to various statements.[19] In the *Basic* situation itself, this meant that business reasons for keeping merger negotiations secret were irrelevant to whether the existence of such negotiations was material.[20]

---

18. In applying this magnitude and probability test to merger discussions, the court in *Basic* recognized that the magnitude of a merger's importance to a corporation's shareholders could depend upon the size of the two companies involved (a large corporation's shareholders might not care much about a merger with a very small other company), and whether shareholders would receive a premium price for their shares over the current market price; while the probability of the merger actually occurring could be indicated by how much interest there was in the merger at the highest corporate levels (as opposed to a pair of middle managers chatting about a possible merger over drinks in a bar).

19. *See, e.g.,* Flynn v. Bass Bros. Enterprises, Inc., 744 F.2d 978 (3d Cir.1984) (creating a multi-factor test for when so-called soft information—an earnings projection or the like—is sufficiently material to require disclosure).

20. The Supreme Court in *Basic* also rejected an approach (which the Court of Appeal had followed in the case) under which the existence of the false statement could render the misstated facts material, even if the facts might not otherwise have been material. The Supreme Court reasoned that this approach seemed to be mixing up different elements of a Rule 10b–5 claim. While this result is logical, it may ignore psychology. Specifically, it may be

A second common materiality issue involves the impact of context. Specifically, defendants often argue that false or misleading statements are not material because surrounding disclosures undercut the significance which a reasonable person would attach to the false or misleading statements.[21] To use an unrealistic example, a statement misrepresenting a corporation's earnings might not be important to a reasonable investor if the misrepresentation was followed immediately by the disclaimer "We made up these earnings figures as an illustration of what we would like the company to achieve; This is not actually the earnings of the company." The notion that warnings and caveats might render misstatements not material has come to be known as the "bespeaks caution" doctrine.[22] Of course, persons do not commonly make blatantly false statements followed by disclaimers which point out that the speaker lied. Rather, the typical situation in which the bespeaks caution doctrine comes up involves projections or opinions, followed by warnings that the projection might not pan out or the opinion might be wrong. Indeed, Congress, as part of 1995 amendments to the Securities Exchange Act, added a safe harbor provision which essentially codifies the bespeaks caution doctrine for so-called forward looking statements when accompanied by meaningful cautionary language.[23]

One danger with the bespeaks caution doctrine is that its thoughtless application could allow persons to give projections or opinions which the speaker does not, in fact, believe in, and which lack any sort of reasonable basis, but avoid liability by accompanying the projections or opinions with boilerplate warnings which investors often ignore. To avoid this danger, most courts applying the bespeaks caution doctrine have required that the cautionary language be detailed and specific in laying out just why the projections might not pan out or why the opinions might be wrong.[24] In this regard, notice that a requirement that the caveats or warnings must be specific to the reasons why the projections may not pan out or the opinion might be wrong builds in a degree of proportionality between the required warnings and the degree to which the defendant's statement is false or misleading. In other words, the more the defendant's statement lacks a reasonable basis or was not made in good faith, the stronger the warning should be. In an extreme case in which a defendant simply made up a projection out of

human nature to attach greater significance to a fact which a speaker lied about than the listener might have attached to the fact had it been truthfully disclosed to begin with—perhaps based upon the supposition that the speaker would not have bothered to lie if the fact was not important.

21. While typically couched as an issue of materiality, it is also possible that surrounding disclosures will render a statement not even false or misleading. In other words, a statement should not be considered false or misleading if the only way it receives a false or misleading interpretation is when taken out of context (unless there

is some reason to suspect that investors will read the statement out of context). Yet another impact of surrounding disclosures is to raise an issue as to whether the plaintiff was justified in relying on the misstatement. *E.g.*, Schlesinger v. Herzog, 2 F.3d 135 (5th Cir.1993).

22. *E.g.*, In re Donald J. Trump Casino Securities Litigation—Taj Mahal Litigation, 7 F.3d 357 (3d Cir.1993).

23. Sec. Exch. Act § 21E.

24. *E.g.*, In re Donald J. Trump Casino Securities Litigation—Taj Mahal Litigation, 7 F.3d 357 (3d Cir.1993).

thin air and did not really believe the projection him- or herself, a warning giving specific reasons why the projection might not pan out should start with the fact that the defendant made up the projection out of thin air and does not really believe it him- or herself.[25]

c. Fault

The second part of Rule 10b–5's three-part specification of wrongful conduct simply says that it is unlawful to make a false or misleading statement of material fact. It does not say that to violate the rule the speaker must intend to make a false or misleading statement, or, at least, be reckless or negligent in making such a statement. Hence, looking at the language of Rule 10b–5 alone, it is possible to argue that there can be strict liability under Rule 10b–5 for making false or misleading statements in connection with the purchase or sale of a security.[26] It turns out, however, that not only is there no strict liability for false statements under Rule 10b–5, even negligence is not enough to produce liability. The reason we can assert this unqualified conclusion is because the Supreme Court has addressed the issue of culpability under Rule 10b–5.[27]

In *Ernst & Ernst v. Hochfelder*,[28] the Supreme Court dealt with an action brought by the defrauded customers of a securities brokerage firm against the accounting firm (Ernst & Ernst) who audited the brokerage firm. The customers claimed that Ernst & Ernst was liable under Rule 10b–5 for having aided and abetted the fraud which a broker in the firm perpetrated on the customers, because Ernst & Ernst negligently failed to discover the fraud in performing its audits. The Supreme Court held

---

25. One other question as to the materiality of statements of opinion or prediction is whether the reasonable investor really cares about the speaker's state of mind. In other words, if an opinion or prediction has an objectively reasonable basis, would a reasonable investor find it important that the speaker, in fact, neither holds the opinion or believes in the prediction (or, conversely, if an opinion or prediction lacks an objectively reasonable basis, would a reasonable investor care whether a speaker holds such a view). The answer might depend upon the situation. For example, if the speaker is a person in whose judgment the investor places particular confidence (such as the board of directors of a shareholder's corporation), then the lack of an honest belief in an expressed opinion could well be material, even if the opinion has an objectively reasonable basis. After all, opinions might have an objectively reasonable basis on both sides of an issue such as whether a price offered for one's shares represents a good deal. In such an event, a reasonable investor might defer to the opinion of a person in whose judgment the investor has confi-

dence, and so what is important is that the opinion expressed by such a person reflect the person's honest belief. Alternately, opinions by persons on the opposite side of a proposed transaction might be important to a reasonable investor regardless of whether the opinion has a reasonable basis. For example, an opinion on the value of shares by a person offering to purchase stock could be material, even if the opinion is based upon an astrological forecast, since such an opinion gives the potentially selling shareholder an idea of how high a price this particular buyer is willing to pay.

26. In lacking language requiring fault, this part of Rule 10b–5 is much the same as Rule 14a–9, which prohibits false or misleading statements in soliciting proxies.

27. This is something the Supreme Court has not done for Rule 14a–9—where most lower courts have held that negligence is sufficient to produce liability for a false or misleading proxy solicitation. See § 3.2.2c *supra*.

28. 425 U.S. 185, 96 S.Ct. 1375 (1976).

that negligence was not sufficient to violate Rule 10b–5. Rather, the Court held, in order to violate Rule 10b–5, there must be "scienter."[29]

The basis for the Supreme Court's holding in *Ernst & Ernst* lies, not in the language of Rule 10b–5, but in the language of Section 10(b). As discussed earlier, Section 10(b) of the 1934 Securities Exchange Act empowers the SEC to make up rules banning manipulative or deceptive devices or contrivances. Since the SEC's authority to adopt Rule 10b–5 comes from Section 10(b), Rule 10b–5 cannot impose strict liability for making false or misleading statements, or even impose liability for negligently making false or misleading statements, unless unintended or negligently made false or misleading statements equal a manipulative or deceptive device or contrivance.[30] Looking at the terms "manipulative," "device," and "contrivance," the Supreme Court in *Ernst & Ernst* held they did not encompass unintended or negligent misstatements. After all, terms like manipulating, devising or contriving normally speak of intentional misconduct. In everyday parlance, or in traditional legal usage, one simply would not say that an individual accidentally manipulated the market, or negligently devised or contrived to spread false information. Moreover, the legislative history of Section 10(b), according to the Court, while slight, did not seem to contemplate that the Section would address negligent or unintended conduct. Finally, the Court noted that interpreting Section 10(b) and Rule 10b–5 to create liability for negligence could render the express private remedy provisions of the 1933 and 1934 securities acts largely surplusage (which is contrary to the rule that courts should interpret statutes to give every section impact). After all, as mentioned earlier in this chapter,[31] a principal advantage of these express private remedy provisions lies in their standards as to fault. Interpreting Rule 10b–5 to create the same liberal standard of fault—when Rule 10b–5 actions might not have the same procedural limitations as imposed by these express private remedy provisions[32]—could make the express private remedy provisions useless.[33]

29. Because the Supreme Court disposed of the case based upon the issue of scienter, it was years later before the Supreme Court resolved the question of whether there can be aiding and abetting liability under Rule 10b–5.

30. By contrast, the Securities Exchange Commission adopted Rule 14a–9 pursuant to the agency's authority under Section 14(a) of the 1934 Securities Exchange Act. The language of Section 14(a) gives the SEC pretty much carte blanch to adopt whatever regulations the Commission thinks are appropriate to regulate proxy solicitations. Hence, if the SEC wants to impose strict liability upon those who make false or misleading proxy solicitations, there is nothing to stop the Commission from adopting a rule to do so.

31. See § 6.2.2*b supra*.

32. For example, at the time the court decided *Ernst & Ernst*, lower courts held that Rule 10b–5 actions were subject to a longer statute of limitations than the statute of limitations applicable to the express private remedy provisions of the securities laws—something, however, the Supreme Court later changed.

33. The concern about rendering the express private remedy provisions in the 1933 and 1934 securities acts redundant might suggest that the requirement of scienter only applies to private actions brought under Rule 10b–5, but not to actions brought by the SEC. On the other hand, the basic rationale in *Ernst & Ernst* hinges on the meaning of the language in Section 10(b). Since the basic rationale goes to the scope of the statutory prohibition, rather than judicially made up ground rules for an im-

While the Supreme Court's opinion in *Ernst & Ernst* makes it indisputable that violations of Rule 10b–5 only exist if there is scienter, this does not remove all questions as to the element of culpability under Rule 10b–5. Most critically, this holding forces one to ask what is scienter. The Supreme Court's opinion in *Ernst & Ernst* defined scienter as "a mental state embracing intent to deceive, manipulate, or defraud."[34] This definition, however, raises almost as many questions as it answers. These questions start with what do we mean by "intent?"

Conventionally, as every student of tort law soon learns, intent refers either to a purpose to achieve an outcome, or to knowledge that an outcome is substantially certain to occur as a result of one's contemplated action (even if this outcome is not desired). Suppose, however, an individual recklessly takes an action which produces an undesirable outcome. The Supreme Court in *Ernst & Ernst* expressly left open the issue of whether recklessness could be sufficient for a violation of Rule 10b–5.

Lower court opinions subsequent to *Ernst & Ernst* have fairly unanimously held that recklessness is sufficient for a violation of Rule 10b–5.[35] There are several reasons for these holdings. One is the fact that recklessness, according to courts applying common law, constitutes scienter sufficient to support an action for fraud or deceit.[36] Closely related to this factor may be the feeling among lower courts that, since the holding in *Ernst & Ernst* seems based mostly upon a rather dry statutory reading of terms known to the common law (rather than any overarching policy), the courts may as well extend liability as far would common law decisions using the same terms. Finally, it may be pointless not to recognize an action based upon recklessness. This is because a finder of fact, faced with evidence that a defendant made a false or misleading statement with a reckless disregard for facts in front of the defendant, often will find that the defendant, in all likelihood, actually knew the statement was false, and hence there is scienter even under a narrow definition. Allowing an action based explicitly upon recklessness reaches the same result, without the need for the finder of fact to speculate on whether the defendant's purported ignorance in the face of patent warnings was real or just feigned.

While lower courts are unanimous that recklessness is sufficient for liability under Rule 10b–5, they are badly divided upon what recklessness entails. Some courts have found recklessness under formulations

plied private cause of action, it was not surprising that, a few years after *Ernst & Ernst,* the Supreme Court held the SEC must establish scienter in order to show a violation of Rule 10b–5. Aaron v. SEC, 446 U.S. 680, 100 S.Ct. 1945 (1980). Interestingly, in *Aaron,* the court held that SEC actions to enjoin violations of Section 17(a) of the Securities Act do not require a showing of scienter. In reaching this conclusion, the court noted how the language of parts two and three of Section 17(a)—which had

served as the model for parts two and three of Rule 10b–5—do not contain language requiring scienter. The result is to emphasize that *Ernst & Ernst* keys off an interpretation of Section 10(b), not Rule 10b–5.

34. 425 U.S. at 194 note 12.

35. *E.g.,* Sundstrand Corp. v. Sun Chem. Corp., 553 F.2d 1033 (7th Cir.1977).

36. See § 6.1.1 *supra.*

which make recklessness sound like a worse case of negligence.[37] Probably more courts have emphasized, however, that, in light of *Ernst & Ernst*, recklessness must entail something more than a greater degree of negligence.[38] Rather, recklessness under these formulations entails an awareness by the defendant of facts warning the defendant of the falsity.[39] Yet, other courts have chosen to define recklessness based upon multiple factors, including the relationship of the defendant to the plaintiff, and how much effort it would have taken for the defendant to check out the information which turned out to be false or misleading.[40]

If one's goal is to find a workable definition that will differentiate recklessness from negligence—as opposed to seeking to circumvent the Supreme Court's opinion in *Ernst & Ernst*—then the approach of those courts focusing on the defendant's awareness of facts warning of the falsity seems about right. Under this approach, negligence can be understood as focusing upon the failure of a defendant to investigate facts before speaking in circumstances where a reasonable person would have investigated. The defendant's relationship to the plaintiff, or the ease of investigation, suggest reasons why a reasonable person might have investigated, but really do not go beyond negligence. If recklessness equates to scienter (a term which connotes knowledge) rather than negligence, it is because the circumstance is one in which the defendant is aware of facts which warn the defendant that the defendant might be making a false or misleading statement, and the defendant consciously chose to ignore those facts. Indeed, it is this situation in which, if recklessness is not sufficient for a Rule 10b–5 violation, the finder of fact might well conclude that the defendant actually knew of the falsity anyway. Put simply then, if the thrust of the plaintiff's complaint is that the defendant should have checked the facts before speaking, this is negligence; if the plaintiff's claim is that the defendant consciously ignored the implication of facts of which the defendant was aware, then there may be recklessness.[41]

Beyond the question of what is entailed by intent, there is the question of what exact result the defendant must intend when one says that there was an intent to "deceive." There are a host of steps which must occur in order for a false or misleading statement to deceive a

37. *See, e.g.,* Rolf v. Blyth, Eastman Dillon & Co., 570 F.2d 38 (2d Cir.1978).

38. *E.g.,* Sanders v. John Nuveen & Co., 554 F.2d 790 (7th Cir.1977).

39. *E.g.,* Sundstrand Corp. v. Sun Chem. Corp., 553 F.2d 1033 (7th Cir.1977).

40. *E.g.,* Vucinich v. Paine, Webber, Jackson & Curtis, Inc., 739 F.2d 1434 (9th Cir.1984). *But see* In re Silicon Graphics Inc. Securities Litigation, 183 F.3d 970 (9th Cir.1999).

41. This view of recklessness finds support in the standards developed to deal with the First Amendment privilege in defamation cases. Under the Supreme Court's fa-

mous decision in *New York Times v. Sullivan*, 376 U.S. 254, 84 S.Ct. 710 (1964), public officials, in order to recover for defamation, must show the defendant knew the defamatory statement was false, or acted in reckless disregard of its truth or falsity. Courts, applying this test, often differentiate between claims that the defendant simply failed to investigate when a reasonable person would have, and claims that the defendant consciously ignored facts which should have alerted the defendant to the falsity. *See, e.g.,* St. Amant v. Thompson, 390 U.S. 727, 88 S.Ct. 1323 (1968).

person in connection with the purchase or sale of a security. A speaker may or may not have intended various of these steps. Specifically, the speaker may not have intended even to make the statement—as might occur when some internal notes inadvertently become public. The speaker may have intended publication of the statement, but not have intended the interpretation which renders the statement false or misleading. The speaker might have intended the interpretation which renders the statement false or misleading, but thought the statement was true. The speaker might have made the statement knowing that it was false or misleading, but did not intend any persons to rely on the statement in buying or selling securities. When the Court in *Ernst & Ernst* says that there must be an intent to deceive in order to find a violation of Rule 10b–5, which of these steps must the defendant intend?

In the vast majority of cases involving Rule 10b–5 claims for false or misleading statements, if there is an issue about intent, it goes to the defendant's contention that he or she believed that the statement was true, and, in this sense, lacked an intent to deceive. Hence, the issue of scienter often can be labeled more precisely as the issue of the defendant's knowledge of falsity. In this light, it becomes easy to understand why the discussion of recklessness above focused on the defendant's disregard of facts which warned the defendant that the defendant's statement was not true.[42]

Suppose the defendant's statement involves an opinion or prediction: What does knowledge of falsity mean is this context? If the defendant did not, in fact, hold the opinion he or she expressed, or did not believe his or her own prediction, this should certainly suffice for scienter. Such a state of mind might also, in itself, render the opinion or prediction false or misleading—albeit, the reader may recall the Supreme Court's requirement in *Virginia Bankshares* that such a misrepresentation of the speaker's state of mind be accompanied by an objective lack of basis, in order to state a claim under Rule 14a–9. Suppose, however, the defendant believes in his or her prediction or opinion, even though the opinion or prediction lacks any reasonable basis. As discussed above, under SEC rules and lower court opinions, the lack of a reasonable basis can make an opinion or prediction into a false statement of material fact. Does a speaker's foolish belief prevent such a baseless opinion from violating Rule 10b–5 due to a lack of scienter? Reinforcing this prospect, Congress amended the Securities Exchange Act in 1995 to add a safe harbor provision protecting so-called forward looking statements (earnings projections and the like made by corporations). In addition to codifying the bespeaks caution doctrine, as discussed earlier, this provi-

42. In between the situation in which the defendant knows that his or her statement is false, and the situation in which the defendant recklessly disregards facts which warn the defendant that the statement is false, is the situation in which the defendant knows that he or she has no idea of whether the statement is true or false. Tra- ditionally, common law courts have treated such knowledge of one's ignorance as sufficient knowledge of falsity. Hence, knowledge of one's ignorance should meet the scienter requirement, even if courts were to hold that recklessness is not enough for a Rule 10b–5 violation.

sion requires the plaintiff to prove actual knowledge by a corporate officer that the forward looking statement was false or misleading.[43] Still, it may be possible for a speaker to have scienter (or actual knowledge that an opinion or prediction is false or misleading), even though the speaker personally believes the opinion or prediction. This could be the case when the speaker is aware of those facts (including the lack of facts) which establish that there is no reasonable basis for the opinion or prediction, and is also aware of the implication of those facts on the opinion or prediction expressed.[44] In other words, scienter might hinge on what the speaker knew, not whether the speaker maintained a religious-like faith in the face of such knowledge.

Occasionally, the question about intent goes, not to the defendant's knowledge of falsity, but rather to why the defendant made the statement. For example, in *Basic*, there is no indication that the corporate officials issued their denials because the corporation, or its officials, had any desire for Basic's shareholders to sell their stock. Rather, those in charge of the corporation wanted to keep the merger discussions secret probably because the other party to the discussions demanded this as a condition to the discussions taking place. Does it matter under Rule 10b–5 that the defendant did not desire to induce the action which the plaintiffs took? The answer apparently is no.

In *Basic* itself, no one seems to have cared why the corporation made the false statements. About the closest anyone came to raising the issue is an aside in Justice White's dissent in which he questioned whether Rule 10b–5 should apply to statements made by those, like Basic, who were neither buying nor selling stock themselves. Several lower court opinions contain potentially more helpful discussions.

In *SEC v. Texas Gulf Sulfur Co.*,[45] the Second Circuit dealt, much like in *Basic*, with a misleading press release by a corporation (Texas Gulf Sulfur) who was not trading stock. Rather than couch its argument in terms of intent to deceive, Texas Gulf Sulfur focused on the language of Rule 10b–5 which requires that the fraud be "in connection with the purchase or sale or any security." The company argued that, if it was not buying or selling stock nor otherwise acting with bad motives, there was not the requisite connection between its false or misleading statement and the purchase or sale of a security. The Second Circuit rejected this argument, finding that the requisite connection between the false statement and the purchase or sale of a security came from the actions of those in the market who sold stock in reliance on the press release. What is interesting about the opinion in terms of our discussion of intent to deceive lies in a couple of not entirely consistent formulations with which the Second Circuit expressed this result. At one point, the court states that the requisite connection between a false statement and the

43. Sec. Exch. Act § 21E(c)(1)(B).

44. If the speaker knows the facts which show his or her opinion or prediction lacks a reasonable basis, but is not subjectively aware that these facts would lead most folks to reject the speaker's opinion or prediction, then all that may exist is negligence or perhaps recklessness.

45. 401 F.2d 833 (2d Cir.1968).

purchase or sale of a security is present if the statement is "reasonably calculated" to affect traders in the market. The phrase "reasonably calculated" might suggest that, even if the defendant is not trading, the defendant must have some intent that its false or misleading statement impact traders in the market. Yet, at another point in its discussion, the Second Circuit states that the "in connection" with requirement is met simply if the false statement is of a sort which would cause reasonable investors to rely upon it (which is little more than materiality).

Perhaps we might reconcile the two formulations in *Texas Gulf Sulfur*, as well as the requirement of an intent to deceive, by going back to the concept that intent includes knowledge that a consequence will follow from one's action, even if this consequence is not desired. If a person makes a false statement of material fact which the speaker knows will reach traders in an active securities market, by the very definition of material fact, the speaker knows that someone is almost sure to rely on the statement in purchasing or selling a security. Hence, the requisite intent to deceive, or to induce reliance, in connection with the purchase or sale of a security exists, even though the speaker is not trading stock, and even though the speaker might not desire that anyone rely on the false statement in trading stock.[46]

The requirement that the defendant must have an intent to deceive in order to violate Rule 10b–5 obviously increases the burden on the plaintiff to prove his or her case. Barring a confession by the defendant, the plaintiff often will seek to prove knowledge of falsity indirectly by showing that facts came to the defendant's attention which presumably tipped the defendant off to the falsity (which is why proof of knowledge often overlaps with proof of recklessness[47]). Alternately, a plaintiff might hope to prove knowledge of falsity by showing that the defendant had a strong motive to lie.[48] In either case, plaintiffs traditionally often hoped

---

46. In a recent decision—*In re Carter–Wallace, Inc. Securities Litigation*, 150 F.3d 153 (2d Cir.1998)—the Second Circuit returned to the subject of false statements by a corporation who did not trade stock. Carter–Wallace, a drug company, ran advertisements in medical journals extolling the virtues of its new anti-epileptic drug. Broadly speaking, these ads stated that no life-threatening side effects had been attributed to the drug, whereas Carter–Wallace had already received reports of some fatal complications (and ultimately had to send letters to doctors recommending that most patients stop using the drug). The District Court found the ads were false, but, since they appeared in medical journals directed toward doctors, the District Court held that the ads were not in connection with the purchase or sale of a security. The Court of Appeals reversed, holding that if, in fact, market participants (such as stock analysts) used the ads in evaluating Carter–Wallace's stock, then the requisite connection be-

tween the fraud and securities transactions existed. The possibility that Carter–Wallace was attempting to deceive doctors into prescribing its drug, rather than stock traders into buying its stock, was irrelevant. *See also* Heit v. Weitzen, 402 F.2d 909 (2d Cir.1968).

47. In other words, if facts came to the defendant's attention which warned of the falsity, then the defendant either knew the statement was false or else recklessly ignored the warnings.

48. We are likely to be suspicious that the salesperson, who makes false claims extolling the product he or she is selling, knew that the claims were false, whereas we can readily accept that a neutral observer, who makes false statements about a product, made an innocent mistake. Similarly, we are likely to be suspicious that corporate officials, who were responsible for issuing untrue statements about the corporation, knew that the statements were

to uncover evidence to prove the defendant's scienter by taking discovery after filing the lawsuit. However, in amendments made in 1995 to the Securities Exchange Act, Congress added provisions directed at perceived abuses of private securities lawsuits. One of the perceived abuses was the filing of lawsuits every time a corporate pronouncement turned out wrong, with the goal of fishing around during discovery for evidence that corporate officials knew of, or were reckless toward, facts suggesting the pronouncement was wrong.[49] To make sure that the plaintiff has the goods on the defendant before launching the lawsuit, one provision in the 1995 amendments requires that a plaintiff in a private action under Rule 10b–5 plead "with particularity facts giving rise to a strong inference that the defendant acted with the required state of mind."[50] This provision has a couple of potential impacts, both of which have led to disagreement among the courts.

One impact of the pleading provision in the 1995 amendments is to raise questions as to whether a motive to lie constitutes sufficient evidence of knowledge of falsity.[51] The argument here stems from the fact that the provision calls for pleading facts creating a "strong inference" of scienter. The defendant's incentive to make a statement, which turned out to be false, might establish only a relatively weak inference that the defendant knew the statement was false. Hence, one might argue that a motive to lie is no longer a sufficient pleading of scienter, and, if motive is not a sufficient pleading of scienter, presumably motive is no longer sufficient proof of scienter.

Moreover, in requiring the plaintiff to plead with particularity facts giving rise to a strong inference, some courts have felt Congress is demanding that the plaintiff virtually plead his or her evidence regarding state of mind. For example, in a recent decision,[52] the Ninth Circuit found a complaint inadequate in pleading scienter, even though the complaint alleged that corporate officials had made optimistic statements about corporate performance despite the officials being privy to internal corporate reports which indicated that there were problems with a key product. The Ninth Circuit demanded more detail about these internal reports, including how the plaintiff knew about them. Under this sort of approach, it seems almost as if the plaintiff is supposed to plead his or

---

false, when those officials had some personal interest in hiding the truth; for example, the officials were selling their own stock (and hence wanted to keep the market price up) at the time the officials issued the statements.

49. Much of the problem with such "sue first and investigate later" litigation lies in the burden which discovery imposes on the defendant. Indeed, some plaintiffs' attorneys might figure that the burden of discovery gives the plaintiff leverage for a settlement, even if the discovery ultimately turns

up nothing. Whether this fact suggests the need to rethink the discovery process in lawsuits generally, rather than just attacking securities fraud lawsuits, is a interesting question.

50. Sec. Exch. Act § 21D(b)(2).

51. *Compare* Press v. Chemical Inv. Serv. Corp., 166 F.3d 529 (2d Cir.1999), *with* In re Silicon Graphics Inc. Securities Litigation, 183 F.3d 970 (9th Cir.1999).

52. In re Silicon Graphics Inc. Securities Litigation, 183 F.3d 970 (9th Cir.1999).

her witness list on the issue on scienter. Other courts, particularly the Second Circuit, have refused to be this demanding.[53]

d. *Private cause of action*

Rule 10b–5 simply says that "it shall be unlawful" to commit fraud, etc., in connection with the purchase or sale of a security. Similarly, Section 10(b) of the 1934 Securities Exchange Act simply says that "it shall be unlawful" to use a manipulative or deceptive device, etc., in violation of Securities Exchange Commission rules. Neither Rule 10b–5 nor Section 10(b) state what happens if a person breaks the Rule. The reader may recall we confronted the same situation when dealing with Rule 14a–9 and Section 14(a) of the 1934 Securities Exchange Act. As discussed when dealing with Rule 14a–9 and Section 14(a), other sections in the Securities Exchange Act allow the Securities Exchange Commission to bring an administrative proceeding or a civil action to stop violations of the statute, and subject persons who wilfully violate provisions of the statute to criminal penalties.[54] However, the 1934 Act (with a minor exception resulting from an amendment we shall discuss later) does not expressly provide any remedy for persons injured by a violation of Rule 10b–5 (just as the Act does not expressly provide any remedy for persons injured by virtue of a violation of Rule 14a–9).

We saw earlier how the Supreme Court held that persons injured by false or misleading proxy solicitations have an implied right of action against those who violated Rule 14a–9. Courts also have recognized such an implied private right of action for those injured by a violation of Rule 10b–5. The recognition of the implied private right of action under Rule 10b–5, however, has a different history from what happened with Rule 14a–9.

A few years after the SEC promulgated Rule 10b–5, a Federal District Court held that private parties injured by a violation of Rule 10b–5 have an implied private cause of action against the person violating the Rule.[55] To the District Court in this early case, the existence of an implied private cause of action seemed to follow as a straight-forward application of traditional tort law principles. Specifically, courts applying the common law generally hold that a party, injured by a violation of a statute enacted for the protection of a class of persons which includes the injured party, has a tort claim against the person violating the statute.[56] Over the decades since this District Court decision, the overwhelming majority of lower courts faced with private claims for violation of Rule 10b–5 have seen little problem in recognizing the existence of such an implied private cause of action. It was not until the early 1970s that the first private Rule 10b–5 claim reached the Supreme Court. In

---

53. *E.g.*, Press v. Chemical Inv. Serv. Corp., 166 F.3d 529 (2d Cir.1999).

54. See § 3.2.2d *supra.*

55. Kardon v. National Gypsum Co., 73 F.Supp. 798 (E.D.Pa.1947).

56. When dealing with unintended personal injury, this claim generally carries the label "negligence per se." This general tort rationale was one of the three rationales used by the Supreme Court in implying a private cause of action for violations of Rule 14a–9. See § 3.2.2d *supra.*

this case, the Supreme Court upheld the plaintiff's claim without even discussing the question of whether an implied private right of action exists under the Rule.[57] Given the Supreme Court's recognition of an implied private right of action under Rule 14a–9 a few years earlier, the court's unspoken assumption that an implied private cause action exists under Rule 10b–5 was not surprising. By the late 1970s, however, the Supreme Court's attitude toward implied private causes of action for violation of federal statutes had changed. Since there was not yet a Supreme Court opinion expressly holding (as opposed to assuming) that such a cause of action exists under Rule 10b–5, one might have wondered whether the Supreme Court would decide that no such implied private cause of action existed under Rule 10b–5 after all. Any fear (or hope) of a retrenchment evaporated in 1983, when the Supreme Court held that defrauded purchasers of securities could bring an action for violation of Rule 10b–5, even if such purchasers also could bring an action under the express civil remedy provisions of the 1933 Securities Act.[58]

Interestingly, the Supreme Court's rationale for an implied private right of action under Rule 10b–5, as expressed in more recent Rule 10b–5 cases before the Court,[59] is quite different from the Supreme Court's rationale for an implied private right of action under Rule 14a–9. The contemporary rationale for an implied private right of action under Rule 10b–5 focuses on the passage of time, coupled with Congressional acquiescence, since the lower courts first recognized an implied private cause of action under Rule 10b–5. The notion is that, while the Supreme Court might have decided the question differently had the issue just arisen for the first time, decades of judicial recognition of an implied private claim under Rule 10b–5 without objection from Congress (who has fiddled with the 1934 Act in other particulars), suggests that the implied private cause of action is consistent with Congress' intent. Indeed, Congress' adoption, in 1995 amendments to the 1934 Securities Exchange Act, of extensive provisions regulating private securities law claims largely involving Rule 10b–5 would seem to remove any doubt that Congress considered the implied private claim under Rule 10b–5, at least in general, to be consistent with Congress' intent.

Allowing persons injured by a violation of Rule 10b–5 to bring a claim against the party committing the violation raises additional issues not confronted in a case brought by the SEC or a federal prosecutor. These issues include: How does a private plaintiff establish that the

57. Superintendent of Insurance of New York v. Bankers Life & Casualty Co., 404 U.S. 6, 92 S.Ct. 165 (1971).

58. Herman & MacLean v. Huddleston, 459 U.S. 375, 103 S.Ct. 683 (1983). Finding an overlap between implied private claims under Rule 10b–5, and express private claims under provisions the 1933 Securities Act, might have offended statutory interpretation principles if the result rendered the 1933 Act provisions entirely redundant of the Rule 10b–5 claim. The Supreme Court, however, had already avoided this problem by requiring scienter for a Rule 10b–5 claim—something not required under the 1933 Act express private remedy provisions.

59. *See, e.g.,* Basic, Inc. v. Levinson, 485 U.S. 224, 108 S.Ct. 978 (1988).

defendant's misrepresentation caused harm to the plaintiff? What remedy can the plaintiff obtain? And, are there any private parties who cannot bring an action under Rule 10b–5 despite having suffered injury by virtue of a violation of the Rule? (By contrast, the SEC or a federal prosecutor essentially need only show that the defendant violated Rule 10b–5 by making a false or misleading statement of material fact with scienter.[60])

e. Reliance and causation

As discussed earlier in this chapter, in a traditional common law fraud case, the plaintiff establishes that the defendant's misrepresentation caused the plaintiff's injury by asserting that the plaintiff relied on the defendant's misrepresentation to take some action which the plaintiff, now knowing the true facts, regrets. Reliance is also the manner in which a private plaintiff in a Rule 10b–5 case establishes a link between a defendant's misrepresentation and the plaintiff's injury.[61] The traditional manner for a plaintiff in a common law fraud case to prove reliance is to testify that he or she heard (or read) the defendant's misrepresentation; that he or she believed it; and that this belief influenced him or her to enter into a transaction (typically with the defendant) which he or she would not have entered (at least under the same terms) had he or she known the truth. This sort of proof of reliance also is the norm in a Rule 10b–5 case involving direct dealings between the plaintiff and defendant.[62] Many Rule 10b–5 cases, however, do not involve direct dealings between the plaintiff and defendant. Instead, they involve misleading corporate pronouncements, and persons trading in active stock markets. The *Basic* case (discussed when dealing with materiality) provides an illustration.

As mentioned earlier, Basic Inc.'s management issued press releases and statements which falsely denied that the corporation was in merger negotiations or that the management knew of any facts which could account for the unusually heavy trading in the corporation's stock. After Basic announced a merger which would give the shareholders a price for their stock in excess of the current market price, the plaintiffs filed a complaint on behalf of a class consisting of all persons who had sold their stock in Basic between the time of the false statements and the announcement of the merger. The element of reliance, however, created two potential problems for the plaintiffs: one substantive and the other procedural. The substantive problem is that it is questionable how many class members actually had read or heard Basic's denials before selling their Basic shares. After all, a denial of merger negotiations is not necessarily (depending upon how prevalent the rumors of merger negoti-

---

60. *See, e.g.,* SEC v. Rana Research, Inc., 8 F.3d 1358 (9th Cir.1993) (the SEC need not prove any investor actually relied on a false statement).

61. *E.g.,* Basic, Inc. v. Levinson, 485 U.S. 224, 108 S.Ct. 978 (1988).

62. *See, e.g.,* Simon v. Merrill Lynch, Pierce, Fenner & Smith, Inc., 482 F.2d 880 (5th Cir.1973).

ations are) the sort of dramatic announcement which will catch pretty much every trader's attention. If a class member had not heard or read the false press releases, the member could not get past even the first step in the traditional proof of reliance. It was the procedural problem, however, which brought the question of reliance before the Supreme Court. The procedural problem involved the requirements for certifying a class action. If each person who sold Basic stock during the relevant period needed to prove reliance on the false statements, then the burden of attempting in one trial to adjudicate whether each class member relied on the misrepresentation would predominate over the efficiency gained from having just one trial of the common issue of whether there was a misrepresentation of material fact. In this case, it would be inappropriate to have a class action. Nevertheless, the District Court certified the class. To do so, the District Court—in a portion of its decision affirmed by a plurality of the Supreme Court[63]—employed the so-called "fraud on the market theory."

The label "the fraud on the market theory" has a magical ring to it which sometimes tempts students of the law to attribute to the theory all sorts of significance beyond what the theory really possesses. The theory does not change the nature of what is a false or misleading statement of material fact, or obviate the need to prove the defendant acted with scienter. All the theory provides is a means for traders in an active securities market to prove their reliance on a false or misleading statement of material fact, without each trader testifying that he or she heard, believed and was influenced by the false statement.

The fraud on the market theory reflects the notion that false or misleading statements of material fact will impact the price of stock traded in a well developed market. For instance, if a corporation falsely claims to have discovered gold, the price of the corporation's stock will be higher in a well developed market than if the corporation had not made the false claim. Conversely, if a corporation falsely denies having struck copper, the price for the corporation's outstanding stock in a well developed market will be lower than if the corporation had told the truth. This impact of false information on stock prices in a well developed market is often said to be a corollary of something called the "Efficient Capital Market Hypothesis." The Efficient Capital Market Hypothesis is a fancy way of saying that stock prices in active trading markets move very rapidly in response to information relevant to a stock, and, thus, the stock's price will incorporate in very short order the information.[64] One key question about the Efficient Capital Market Hypothesis is what types of information it covers. Here, the hypothesis

---

63. Only four justices joined in this portion of the Supreme Court's opinion in *Basic*; two justices dissented as to this portion, and three judges disqualified themselves from ruling on this case.

64. It is useful not to overstate what is meant when one says that a market is

efficient. For our purposes, all one needs to say is that the price of stock incorporates information, not necessarily that the price represents the "true" worth of the stock. After all, stock prices often reflect a lot of silly investor psychology, as well as relevant information.

breaks down into three flavors. The weak form, which is not relevant to the fraud on the market theory, states that the price incorporates all information one can glean from looking at past price movements.[65] The semi-strong form is relevant to the fraud on the market theory. This form holds that the price incorporates all publicly available information—which will include misleading corporate press releases. The strong form of the hypothesis holds that the market price incorporates all information, including information not supposed to be known outside the corporation. Interestingly, the strong form would undercut the fraud on the market theory, since it says that the price of stock will reflect the fact that the false public statements are a lie. Fortunately for the fraud on the market theory, the empirical evidence supports the semi-strong, rather than the strong form, of the Efficient Capital Market Hypothesis.[66] Incidentally, one amusing aspect of the Efficient Capital Market Hypothesis is that it will work only if, at least to some extent, stock traders do not believe it, since it is through the actions of traders gathering and acting on information that the price of stock impounds the data. If all traders assumed that the price of stocks already takes into account all information, they would not bother to collect information about companies, or to buy and sell stock based upon the information they collect, and the market would not be efficient.

So far we have seen that false statements of material fact presumably impact the price of a corporation's stock in active trading markets. This still leaves the question of how this impact on price establishes the plaintiff's reliance. The Supreme Court's opinion refers to the plaintiffs' reliance on the integrity of the market price. In fact, however, the Court's insistence on couching the issue as one of reliance tends to confuse the matter. It is simpler to understand the impact of the fraud on the market theory if one thinks in terms of causation. After all, as stated above, the reason one discusses reliance in a fraud case is because a plaintiff's action in reliance on a false statement is the normal mechanism by which a false statement causes harm to a plaintiff. What the fraud on the market theory shows is a mechanism by which a false statement can cause harm to a party who trades in an active securities market, despite the party's never even being personally aware of the false statement. A false positive statement about a corporation will cause the buyer of stock to pay more than he or she would have if the truth were known, while a false negative statement about a corporation (as in *Basic*) will cause the seller of stock to receive less for his or her shares than he or she would have if the truth were known.

Of course, one might dismiss the *Basic* opinion's insistence on framing the issue as one of reliance, rather than causation, as only of academic concern. It turns out, however, that this characterization leads

---

65. This, of course, is heresy to the many stock traders who spend countless hours poring over stock price charts, looking for trend lines, resistance points and other such clues upon which to buy or sell stock.

66. *E.g.*, R. Brealey & S. Myers, Principles of Corporate Finance, 290–310 (4th ed. 1993).

to one practical consequence. The Court held that the fraud on the market theory operates as a rebuttable presumption of reliance. Defendants might rebut the presumption by showing that market makers were privy to the truth and disregarded the false statement, or by showing that the truth otherwise had leaked out and dissipated the impact of the false statement on the stock price before a plaintiff traded. This is logical. After all, if the traders in the market do not believe the "Boy Corporation" when they hear the company falsely cry "wolf," then the market price will not reflect the false information and the fraud will not cause harm to the traders who did not hear the statement. The Supreme Court also stated, however, that defendants could rebut the presumption of reliance by showing that a particular plaintiff would have traded even if he or she was aware the corporation's statement was false (perhaps because the particular plaintiff was under some legal compulsion to sell). It is here that the Court's insistence on viewing the issue as one of reliance produces a silly result. A person who had no choice about selling may not be relying on a false statement, but certainly is damaged by its impact of depressing the market price. There seems little policy reason why such a person should not be able to recover for these damages.[67]

In any event, in order to trigger the fraud on the market presumption, the stock must be traded in a well developed securities market. After all, it takes the action of numerous persons who pay attention to developments at a corporation, and who buy or sell the corporation's stock in accordance with those developments, in order for false statements about a corporation to impact the price of a corporation's stock paid or received by traders who themselves may be unaware of the false statements. In evaluating whether a stock is traded in a well developed market, courts might look at the trading volume, how many stock analysts follow the stock and how many professionals make a market in the stock, how rapidly the stock price has moved in response to corporate news in the past, and the corporation's eligibility to use federal securities law registration statements adapted to more widely traded securities.[68] Notice that these factors go to the particular market for the corporation's stock, not the general stock market in which the stock trades. In other words, it is possible that a corporation's stock might be listed for trading on an exchange, but nevertheless have attracted so little trading and interest by professionals that the market for this corporation's stock

67. Indeed, the court has shown much more sophistication in dealing with the impact of misleading proxy solicitations. In the proxy context, the court has allowed parties who voted against actions sought through misleading proxy solicitations to bring a lawsuit, even though such parties obviously did not believe or rely upon the misleading solicitation. This is because, in the proxy context, the court recognized that harm may come from the actions of others who rely on misleading communications. See § 3.2.2e *supra*. The fraud on the market theory involves, in many ways, the same sort of collective action phenomenon as proxy voting. Of course, if the plaintiff had a choice about buying or selling in a market the plaintiff knows is impacted by a false statement, then one might not be very sympathetic to a plaintiff who could have avoided the harm. Yet, whether the plaintiff's conduct justifies denying recovery should depend upon why the plaintiff did not wait before buying or selling.

68. *E.g.*, Freeman v. Laventhol & Horwath, 915 F.2d 193 (6th Cir.1990).

is not well developed or efficient. Incidentally, when a corporation makes its first public offering of stock, it is pretty clear that the stock, at this point, is not traded in a well developed market. Nevertheless, some courts have applied a variant of the fraud on the market theory to misrepresentations used in making the initial public offering.[69] This variant (sometimes called the fraud created the market theory) is based upon the notion that if the misrepresentation allowed the offering to gain the necessary backing of underwriters and government officials, then, without the misrepresentation, the plaintiff would never have been able to buy the stock, and, hence, there is reliance.

A different sort of problem with reliance sometimes comes up in cases in which the plaintiff actually did hear, believe and act upon the defendant's false statement. Many times, a defendant will argue that the plaintiff was not reasonable in relying upon the defendant's false statement. As discussed when dealing with common law fraud earlier in this chapter,[70] while courts sometimes state that the plaintiff must prove he or she "reasonably" relied on the defendant's false statement, it is better to speak of "justifiable" reliance. Otherwise, one might become confused into thinking that the plaintiff's failure to meet the standard of the reasonable prudent person in response to a lie should exonerate an individual who intentionally deceived the plaintiff. This result would provide a legal, as well as a practical, reward for flim-flam artists who target the naive, and would be contrary to the normal tort law approach that contributory negligence is not a defense to an intentional tort. Hence, a defendant in a Rule 10b–5 case (which requires scienter for liability) should not avoid liability by asserting that the plaintiff negligently failed to check out the statement (in other words, did not perform a "due diligence" investigation).[71] Nevertheless, when a plaintiff completely closed his or her eyes to patent warnings of the fraud, then considerations of judicial economy suggest that the court in a Rule 10b–5 case, just as in a common law fraud case, will not necessarily rescue the plaintiff from his or her own folly.[72]

The question of when the plaintiff has sufficiently ignored patent warnings so as to preclude a finding of justifiable reliance is often not an easy one. A common problem in this regard occurs when the plaintiff did not read documents in his or her possession which contradicted the false statements.[73] In resolving questions of justifiable reliance, courts might

---

69. *E.g.*, Shores v. Sklar, 647 F.2d 462 (5th Cir.1981).

70. See § 6.1.1, *supra.*

71. *E.g.*, Dupuy v. Dupuy 551 F.2d 1005 (5th Cir.1977). The date of *Dupuy* is worth noting. It is after the Supreme Court, in *Ernst & Ernst*, held that negligence is insufficient for liability under Rule 10b–5. Before *Ernst & Ernst*, a number of lower courts assumed that negligence of the defendant was sufficient for liability under Rule 10b–5. If the defendant was only negligent in making the false statement, it may

make sense to bar recovery by a plaintiff who was negligent in not investigating the defendant's representations. This may explain some pre-*Ernst & Ernst* lower court opinions which held that the plaintiff must establish his or her due diligence in order to recover under Rule 10b–5.

72. *See, e.g.,* Kennedy v. Josephthal & Co., 814 F.2d 798 (1st Cir.1987).

73. *Compare* Zobrist v. Coal–X, Inc., 708 F.2d 1511 (10th Cir.1983), *with* Gower v. Cohn, 643 F.2d 1146 (5th Cir.1981).

distinguish between defendants who knew their statements were false, and defendants who were only reckless themselves in making the false statement—the notion being that the plaintiff's conduct should not serve to exonerate the defendant unless the plaintiff's conduct was equally as culpable as the defendant's.

As we have emphasized at several points in this discussion, proving reliance is a means of proving causation, or, put differently, the plaintiff's reliance on a false statement is the normal mechanism by which a false statement causes harm to the plaintiff. Since reliance on the false statement caused the plaintiff to enter a transaction which the plaintiff now regrets, courts often refer to reliance as establishing "transaction causation."[74] The reason for courts to introduce this new term lies in the fact that courts have held that the plaintiff must not only prove transaction causation, the plaintiff must also prove something called "loss causation."[75] Loss causation does not mean simply that the plaintiff suffered a loss in the transaction which the plaintiff entered in reliance on the fraud. Rather, loss causation embodies the idea that the reason the transaction turned out to be a loser must have something to do with the substance of the misrepresentation. A simple example illustrates the point. Suppose a corporation, which operates a cargo ship, induces an investor to purchase the corporation's stock by misrepresenting the cargo carrying capacity of the ship. If, shortly after the purchase, the ship sinks in a storm (for reasons having nothing to do with the ship's cargo carrying capacity), the investor might argue that, but for his reliance on the misrepresentation, he would not have purchased the stock (or would have paid less for the stock) and would not have suffered the loss (or as much loss) in the value of the stock resulting from the ship's sinking. Notice, as this example illustrates, that transaction causation serves to establish "but for" causation. By contrast, the requirement of loss causation follows from notions of proximate cause. Since the sinking of the ship in the storm had nothing to do with the substance of the misrepresentation, it would seem unfair for the plaintiff to be able to recover the plaintiff's loss in this instance. Of course, real world examples of situations in which loss causation issues arise rarely are as cut and dry as this example. Instead of storms at sea, the question might be the far more difficult one of whether general economic forces or events would have produced the same loss for the plaintiff's investment even had the defendant's representations been true.[76] In a potentially significant provision, the 1995 amendments to the 1934 Securities Exchange Act state that the burden of proving loss causation shall be on the plaintiff[77]—which means it will be up to the plaintiff in these difficult cases to show that general economic forces or events would not have produced the same loss.

74. *E.g.*, Harris v. Union Elec. Co., 787 F.2d 355 (8th Cir. 1986).

75. *E.g.*, Huddleston v. Herman & MacLean, 640 F.2d 534 (5th Cir.1981), *aff'd in part and rev'd in part on other grounds*, 459 U.S. 375, 103 S.Ct. 683 (1983).

76. *See, e.g.*, Bastian v. Petren Resources Corp., 892 F.2d 680 (7th Cir.1990).

77. Sec. Exch. Act § 21D(b)(4).

f. Remedies

As discussed earlier in this chapter,[78] courts recognize a number of remedies and measures of damage in cases of common law fraud and deceit. Similar remedies and measures of damage generally are available in cases of false or misleading statements in violation of Rule 10b–5.

The most common remedy in Rule 10b–5 cases is a damage award measured by the out-of-pocket loss—in other words, the difference between the stock's (or other security's) actual value at the time of the fraud, and, either, what the plaintiff paid for stock (in the case of a plaintiff who purchased based upon a misrepresentation), or what the plaintiff received for the stock (in the case of a plaintiff who sold based upon a misrepresentation).[79]

Suppose, however, the plaintiff bought stock based upon false representations, which, if true, would make the stock worth more than the plaintiff paid for the stock. In this event, the plaintiff would much rather obtain a damage award measured by the difference between the stock's actual value at the time of the fraud, and the value the stock would have had if the representations had been true. This is referred to as the benefit-of-the-bargain measure of damages. By and large, courts have refused to grant benefit-of-the-bargain damage awards in Rule 10b–5 cases.[80] In part, this refusal reflects a concern that such a measure might be too speculative (since it requires the court to compare two values for the stock on which there may be evidentiary dispute, instead of comparing one disputable value and a simple dollar sum under the out-of-pocket-loss approach). In addition, some courts in Rule 10b–5 cases have felt that such a measure of damage conflicts with Section 28 of the 1934 Securities Exchange Act, which prohibits, in any action brought under the 1934 Act, recovery "in excess of ... actual damages."

As just mentioned, the actual value of stock, and the value the stock would have had if a misrepresentation had been true, are subjects upon which the plaintiff and defendant might well present conflicting evidence. Since valuation of stock is more of an art than a science, judicial resolution of this evidentiary conflict often will not be easy. Suppose, however, the stock involved is traded in an active market. In this event, a court might use the market price of the stock as the measure of the stock's value. Of course, if the market price reflects the false statement (as under the fraud on the market theory), then the market price does not show what the stock is actually worth at the time of the fraud. Rather, this market price shows what the stock is worth (at least in the market's estimation) if the false statement had been true. Notice this means that in the case in which a plaintiff buys or sells in a well developed market impacted by a false statement, the benefit-of-the-bargain and out-of-pocket measures of damages are the same. On the other hand, is there any way to use the market price to figure out what

78. See § 6.1.1 *supra.*

79. *E.g.,* Harris v. Union Elec. Co., 787 F.2d 355 (8th Cir.1986).

80. *E.g.,* Madigan, Inc. v. Goodman, 498 F.2d 233 (7th Cir.1974).

the stock really was worth at the time of the fraud? The answer courts have used is to look at the market price of the stock after the true facts became public.[81]

· There are a couple of objections one might make to using the difference between the market price paid or received by the plaintiff during the fraud, and the market price after disclosure of the true facts, as the measure of damages. First, the plaintiff might argue that market price does not always reflect "true" value, because stock markets often are influenced by investor psychology and such factors. The simple answer is that this should not matter because, even if the market price varies from "true" value, it is a price available to the plaintiff, and, accordingly, the plaintiff can always take advantage of, or protect him- or herself against, any variation between market price and "true" value by the simple act of buying or selling stock.[82]

Alternately, the defendant might argue that the market price after disclosure could reflect other factors besides just the disclosure. For example, only part of the decline in the price of stock following disclosure that optimistic pronouncements were misleading might reflect the adjustment for the accurate information; part of the decline might reflect independent developments at the corporation or general market factors. To the extent the court can figure out how much the stock price changed as a result of factors independent of the disclosure, then, for the reason explained when dealing with loss causation above, the measure of damages should subtract this amount. On the other hand, if it is not clear how much of the change came from independent factors, then courts presumably will follow the traditional approach of resolving uncertainties in amount of damages (as opposed to uncertainties as to the existence and causation of any damages) against the wrongdoer.[83]

---

81. *E.g.,* Mitchell v. Texas Gulf Sulfur Co., 446 F.2d 90 (10th Cir.1971).

82. To illustrate, suppose a person is fooled into buying stock by misleading optimistic pronouncements. Assume also that, after disclosure of the fraud, the price of the stock goes down, but, because of irrational exuberance in the stock market, not all the way down to the stock's "true" value. The plaintiff should not be able to argue that a measure of damages based upon the difference in market prices understates his loss. After all, if the plaintiff thought that the stock was overvalued after the disclosure, the plaintiff could always sell at this point. Hence, any further losses the plaintiff incurs as a result of a later decline in the price of the stock are the result of the plaintiff's independent investment decision to hold the stock after learning of the fraud, and not the result of the fraud. Because part of the rationale for measuring damages based upon the market price after disclosure of the fraud is that the plaintiff can then purchase or sell shares, this mea-

sure of recovery is sometimes referred to as a "cover" measure.

83. *See, e.g.,* Mitchell v. Texas Gulfur Co., 446 F.2d 90 (10th Cir.1971). One might ask whether the 1995 amendments to the 1934 Securities Exchange Act alter this result. Specifically, as discussed above, one provision in the amendments states that the plaintiff has the burden to prove loss causation. Does this provision mean that the plaintiff will lose completely in case of uncertainty as to precisely how much of a change in stock price after disclosure of fraud reflects factors independent of disclosure? Probably not, since courts presumably will interpret this provision consistently with the traditional distinction between uncertainties in whether the defendant's action caused damage, and uncertainties in the precise amount of damage caused.

Actually, the post-disclosure market price often will overstate the plaintiff's out-of-pocket damages, even if the change in price reflects only the impact of the disclosure.

The fact that stock prices are constantly moving in response to factors independent of disclosure of fraud makes the timing of the market price used to measure damages potentially critical. The moment of disclosure is presumably too soon, since even efficient markets need a little time for the price to reflect new data. Moreover, the court might wish to ensure the plaintiff had a reasonable amount of time to learn of, and react to, the disclosure, since part of the rationale for looking to the market price after disclosure of the fraud is that the plaintiff could have protected him- or herself from further price changes by purchasing or selling shares.[84] The 1995 amendments to the 1934 Securities Exchange Act contain a provision which speaks to this issue. This provision limits damage awards measured by the market price of stock after disclosure of fraud to an amount no greater than the difference between what the plaintiff paid or received for the stock and the mean average market price of the stock during the period 90 days after disclosure of the fraud.[85]

An alternate remedy traditional in fraud cases is to rescind the transaction—in other words, give the plaintiff who purchased, based upon fraud, his or her money back, and give the plaintiff who sold, based upon fraud, his or her property (such as stock) back, while the plaintiff returns any consideration the plaintiff received to the defendant. In light of the traditional common law recognition of this remedy, as well as the fact that Section 29 of the 1934 Securities Exchange Act states that any contract made in violation of the Act shall be void, it is not surprising that courts have awarded rescission as a remedy in Rule 10b–5 cases.[86]

For one thing, the true facts at the time of the fraud's disclosure frequently will not have the same degree of uncertainty as to their ultimate impact as would the true facts at the time of the misrepresentation. For example, in *Basic*, the misrepresentation consisted of denying that the corporation was negotiating a merger. Accurate disclosure of this fact would have led to a price higher than the price resulting from the false denials, but this price increase would have a discount to reflect the risk that the parties would not reach agreement on a merger. By comparison, the disclosure occurred when Basic, Inc. announced that the corporation had reached agreement upon a merger. The price increase resulting from this disclosure did not have a discount to reflect the risk that the two sides would fail to reach an agreement. Moreover, this discussion operates on the assumption that the appropriate comparison in a situation such as in *Basic* is between the stock price resulting from the false denials the corporation issued and the stock price which would have resulted from accurate disclosure regarding the merger negotiations. The corporation in *Basic*, however, could have avoided violating Rule 10b–5 by keeping its mouth shut. Hence, one might argue that the appropriate comparison is between the price resulting from the false denials and the price the stock would have had if Basic, Inc. had refused to comment on the cause of unusual trading in its stock. The price resulting from such silence presumably would have been somewhat less than the price the stock would have had if Basic, Inc. confirmed the company was in merger negotiations.

84. *E.g.*, Mitchell v. Texas Gulf Sulfur Co., 446 F.2d 90 (10th Cir.1971).

85. Sec. Exch. Act § 21D(e). The evident purpose for averaging post-disclosure prices is to limit the potential for factors independent of the fraud to impact the damage award. The existence of this provision reinforces the conclusion reached earlier that placing the burden of proving loss causation on the plaintiff does not mean that the plaintiff loses unless the plaintiff can show precisely how much of post disclosure price changes resulted from the disclosure—since, if the plaintiff loses in the case of such uncertainty, there would no point to averaging to limit the effect of uncertainty.

86. *E.g.*, Randall v. Loftsgaarden, 478 U.S. 647, 106 S.Ct. 3143 (1986) (holding

Notice that the rescission remedy can allow a plaintiff defrauded into selling his or her shares to obtain the shares back—or, if the defendant no longer has the shares, to obtain the profit the defendant made on selling the shares—even though the shares increased in the value after the fraudulent purchase for reasons independent of the fraud.[87] The idea is to deprive the defendant of any profit from the defendant's wrongdoing, even if this means that the plaintiff ends up enriched. As this discussion illustrates, the rescission remedy allows the plaintiff to hedge his or her bets—rescinding or seeking out-of-pocket damages depending upon which way the stock goes. To limit the potential unfairness of such hedging, courts may deny the remedy of rescission to the plaintiff who dawdles too much.[88] It is also worth noting that a recessionary remedy presumably would be inappropriate when the defendant is not the other party to the trade (as, for example, with the misleading corporate press releases in *Basic*); nor would such a remedy seem called for when the stock is actively traded, and so the plaintiff could always purchase or sell shares on the market to return to his or her pre-fraud portfolio.

Incidentally, one disadvantage of Rule 10b–5 actions relative to state law actions for fraud is that punitive damages are unavailable under the 1934 Act.[89]

g. Standing

In *Basic*, the plaintiff class consisted of persons who sold their stock after the misleading press releases. Yet, there was another class of persons who, arguably, might have suffered injury due to Basic, Inc.'s misleading statements. This would be persons who would have purchased Basic stock, but, after reading or hearing of the denials of merger negotiations, decided not to do so. Why was there no class action on behalf of such non-purchasers? One answer is that the Supreme Court, in *Blue Chip Stamps v. Manor Drug Stores*,[90] held, in order to bring a private action under Rule 10b–5, the plaintiff must have been a purchaser or seller of stock or other securities.

Blue Chips Stamps arose out of an antitrust consent decree which required Blue Chips Stamps Company to offer stock in itself to retailers who gave Blue Chips trading stamps to their customers.[91] The plaintiff retailer did not accept this offer, and later regretted its decision. Accord-

---

that persons induced to invest in tax shelters by fraud were entitled to rescind and obtain return of the money they paid, without any reduction in recovery to reflect the plaintiffs' tax savings).

87. *E.g.*, Janigan v. Taylor, 344 F.2d 781 (1st Cir.1965). *But see* Thomas v. Duralite Co., 524 F.2d 577 (3d Cir.1975) (not allowing recovery of subsequent appreciation resulting from the defendant's special skill and effort after the fraudulently induced purchase).

88. *E.g.*, Baumel v. Rosen, 412 F.2d 571 (4th Cir.1969).

89. *E.g.*, Manufacturers Hanover Trust Co. v. Drysdale Sec. Corp., 801 F.2d 13 (2d Cir.1986).

90. 421 U.S. 723, 95 S.Ct. 1917 (1975).

91. Older readers will recall with nostalgia those days of receiving stamps with every purchase of groceries and such, and gluing the stamps into books to be exchanged for various goods at the Blue Chip Stamps (or Green Stamps) redemption center.

ing to the plaintiff's complaint, Blue Chip Stamps Company recognized that it could sell to the public at a higher price any stock which the retailers did not purchase—evidently, the price fixed by consent degree having been a bargain. Because of this, Blue Chip Stamps Company allegedly set out to discourage the retailers from purchasing the stock by making misleading statements in the prospectus which accompanied the offer to the retailers. The Supreme Court held that, because the plaintiff was not a buyer or seller of a security (rather, the plaintiff was complaining about its decision not to buy), the retailer's complaint did not state a cause of action.

The Supreme Court put forth several rationales for giving only purchasers or sellers of securities standing to bring a private suit under Rule 10b–5. The first rationale looked to the language of Section 10(b) and Rule 10b–5, both of which require the deceptive or manipulative conduct, or the fraud, to be "in connection with the purchase or sale of [a] security." Accordingly, without some purchase or sale of a security (and without this purchase or sale having some relationship to the fraud), there is no violation of Rule 10b–5. A problem, however, with this rationale in the situation facing the Court in *Blue Chip Stamp*s is that the fraud did have some relationship to a sale of securities: By deceiving the plaintiff into not buying the stock, the defendant had more stock to sell in the later public offering. Another rationale for this rule regarding standing was that some years earlier the Second Circuit had held that only purchasers or sellers have standing to bring a private cause of action under Rule 10b–5.[92] Thereafter, other lower courts followed this holding, and Congress had not seen fit to adopt an amendment to change the result despite urging from the Securities Exchange Commission. The Supreme Court, however, was not content with these and several other technical statutory construction arguments. Indeed, the Supreme Court admitted it was hard to divine the intent of Congress when dealing with a judicially created cause of action that had grown (like a "judicial oak" from a "legislative acorn") out of a statutory section and an administrative rule, both of whose drafters probably never anticipated private lawsuits. Hence, the Court looked to policy concerns.

Turning to policy, the majority opinion by Justice Rehnquist indulged in a diatribe about the danger of meritless securities lawsuits brought to extort settlement by using the leverage of burdensome discovery. One problem with this rationale is that it does not explain why suits by non-purchasers or non-sellers are more likely to be meritless strike suits than are suits by purchasers or sellers. In any event, the hostility toward securities lawsuits reflected in this portion of Justice Rehnquist's opinion presaged a shift in the attitude by the Supreme Court toward Rule 10b–5. After *Blue Chip Stamps*, a number of Supreme

---

92. Birnbaum v. Newport Steel Corp., 193 F.2d 461 (2d Cir.1952). Because *Birnbaum* was the first case to adopt the requirement that a plaintiff in a private Rule 10b–5 lawsuit must be purchaser or a seller of securities, this standing requirement was generally known, before *Blue Chip Stamps*, as the "*Birnbaum* Rule."

Court decisions, such as the *Ernst & Ernst* decision discussed earlier, seemed to retrench on the reach of the Rule.

More focused discussions, in Justice Rehnquist's opinion and in a concurring opinion by Justice Powell, raised a concern about the difficulty of proving or disproving that a plaintiff, who did not buy, or did not sell, would have acted differently absent the fraud, coupled with the danger that an unlimited class of individuals could always claim that, if only they had known the truth, they would have bought or would have sold (and this would have made them rich). Actually, the situation in *Blue Chip Stamps* was not one in which this concern was particularly apropos, since the plaintiff alleged that the government was forcing Blue Chips Stamps Company to make an offer at bargain prices to a distinct class of persons. This is why the Court of Appeals in *Blue Chip Stamps* had held this particular case fell outside of the *Birnbaum* Rule—an approach rejected by the Supreme Court, who worried about destroying the standing rule by making case-by-case exceptions. By contrast, the situation in *Basic* seems to present precisely the potential the court in *Blue Chip Stamps* feared. An unlimited class of persons might have claimed that, if Basic did not lie about the merger, they would have bought Basic stock and made lots of money. On the other hand, even if non-purchasers in the *Basic* situation had standing, they would have faced a problem—which makes one question whether this rationale in *Blue Chip Stamps* is not exaggerated. The problem is that, if Basic did not lie, the price paid by any purchasers for Basic stock would have been higher, and so it is not clear how much those who did not buy Basic stock were injured by the fraud.

In any event, several questions remain about the limitation of standing to purchasers or sellers. To begin with, does this limitation apply to private suits brought for injunctive relief rather than for monetary damages? Lower courts are divided on this question.[93] One rationale for excepting injunction actions from the purchaser-seller rule is to draw a parallel to SEC enforcement actions. Obviously, the limitation of standing to those who purchased or sold securities does not apply to the Securities Exchange Commission bringing an enforcement action (nor to the Justice Department bringing a criminal prosecution). On the other hand, as mentioned above, without a purchase or sale of a security in connection with the fraud, there is no violation of Rule 10b–5 or Section 10(b). Does this mean that if the SEC learns of a person going around lying in an effort to purchase securities, the Commission must wait until someone falls victim before the Commission can do anything to stop the fraud? The answer is no. Rather, the 1934 Act expressly authorizes the Commission to seek an injunction against a person who is

---

93. *Compare* Mutual Shares Corp. v. Genesco, Inc., 384 F.2d 540 (2d Cir.1967), *with* Cowin v. Bresler, 741 F.2d 410 (D.C.Cir.1984). While *Mutual Shares* precedes *Blue Chip Stamps*, one of the rationales in *Blue Chips Stamps* is the long-standing adherence of the lower courts to the *Birnbaum* rule, and nothing in *Blue Chip Stamps* indicates that the Supreme Court meant to alter the *Birnbaum* rule as applied by the lower courts.

about to engage in acts violating the statute.[94] Similarly, courts could decide that they do not need to wait until a violation of Rule 10b–5 when a private party brings an action seeking to enjoin those who are about to violate the Rule. From a policy standpoint, an injunction action might not present the same danger of plaintiffs making up claims about what they would have done if only they had known the truth. Rather, the fact that the plaintiff seeks an injunction suggests the plaintiff might not be claiming to have been fooled at all, but is worried about the effect of the fraud on someone else (which presumably will affect the plaintiff negatively).

The possibility that a false statement might injure a person who does not believe the statement is one we encountered before in dealing with misleading proxy solicitations. For example, a misleading proxy solicitation might lead a majority of shareholders to vote for a poor merger to the detriment of a shareholder who unsuccessfully opposed the merger. We saw earlier that, if it is too late for an injunction, such a shareholder might bring an action for damages under Rule 14a–9. Does such a shareholder also have standing to bring an action for damages under Rule 10b–5? The answer is yes, because courts consider mergers and the like to be "sales" for securities law purposes, and a person forced to exchange his or her shares in a merger or the like is a seller, even though this person had no choice in the matter.[95] This is sometimes referred to as the "forced seller" doctrine. Not surprisingly, in a number of cases, it is not clear whether a transaction constitutes a forced sale.[96] As the forced seller doctrine illustrates, the definition of a "sale" for securities law purposes, including with respect to Rule 10b–5, is broader than what one normally thinks of as a sale, or what constitutes a sale for purposes of other areas of law.[97]

Defendants sometimes argue that grounds, other than the purchaser-seller requirement, exist in the case at hand to deny a plaintiff the right to bring a private Rule 10b–5 action. For example, the defendant may assert that the plaintiff was "in pari delicto" with the defendant— in other words, the plaintiff should not be able to prevail because the plaintiff engaged in misconduct too. This is most likely to come up when a person, who illegally bought or sold stock based upon a tip, sues the person who give him or her the tip because the tip turned out to be wrong.[98] In *Bateman Eichler, Hill Richards, Inc. v. Berner*,[99] the Su-

94. Sec. Exch. Act § 21(d)(1). Indeed, if the SEC learns of an abortive effort to disseminate false information about securities, the Commission may request, as a sort of prophylactic remedy, a permanent blanket injunction against violating Rule 10b–5. *See, e.g.,* SEC v. Rana Research, Inc., 8 F.3d 1358 (9th Cir.1993).

95. *E.g.,* Alley v. Miramon, 614 F.2d 1372 (5th Cir.1980). Presumably, the fact that the plaintiff voted against the transaction should not cause the plaintiff to lose for lack of reliance.

96. *Compare* Dudley v. Southeastern Factor & Finance Corp., 446 F.2d 303 (5th Cir.1971), *with* Arnesen v. Shawmut County Bank N.A., 504 F.Supp. 1077 (D.Mass. 1980).

97. *See, e.g.,* Chemical Bank v. Arthur Andersen & Co., 726 F.2d 930 (2d Cir.1984) (pledge of securities equals a sale).

98. We shall explore a little later the question of when buying or selling stock based upon a tip of information regarding the stock is a violation of Rule 10b–5.

99. 472 U.S. 299, 105 S.Ct. 2622 (1985).

preme Court decided that the in pari delicto defense normally would not apply to the illegal, but false, tip situation. The Court felt that trading on a tip was typically not as bad a conduct as providing the tip, and that it would facilitate enforcement of Rule 10b–5 if persons who received false tips could sue the tipper.

h. Aiding and abetting and multiple defendants

The *Ernst & Ernst* case discussed earlier came from the effort of defrauded parties to sue persons beyond the individual who committed the fraud—in *Ernst & Ernst*, the target being the accounting firm who failed to discover the fraud. The motive for suing the accountants (or, God forbid, even the lawyers) of persons committing fraud is practical; the accountants and lawyers have money, whereas the party committing the fraud is often (as in *Ernst & Ernst*) broke. The theory the plaintiffs used in *Ernst & Ernst* is that the accountants aided and abetted the fraud by their failure to discover it. The Supreme Court in *Ernst & Ernst* avoided the need to address the aiding and abetting theory by holding that negligent conduct (which is all that the plaintiffs in *Ernst & Ernst* claimed) was not enough for liability under Rule 10b–5. It was not until almost two decades later that the Supreme Court decided whether attorneys, accountants, or anyone else, who knowingly or recklessly facilitated in some manner another person's misrepresentations, could be liable under Rule 10b–5.

In *Central Bank of Denver, N.A. v. First Interstate Bank of Denver, N.A.*,[100] the Supreme Court held that there could not be aiding and abetting liability in a private suit under Rule 10b–5. Like *Ernst & Ernst*, the aiding and abetting claim in *Central Bank* involved a failure to discover fraud by a party whose job it was to do so. Specifically, Central Bank, as the indenture trustee for some development bonds, received, from the bonds' issuer, an appraisal of the value of the collateral for the bonds. Despite warnings that the appraisal was inflated, Central Bank delayed undertaking an independent appraisal of the property. This allowed the borrower to issue additional bonds—which the plaintiffs purchased—based upon an inflated appraisal.

In rejecting the aiding and abetting claim against Central Bank, the Supreme Court's reasoning was reminiscent of its reasoning in *Ernst & Ernst*. Looking to the language of Section 10(b), the Court saw nothing which said that SEC rules could make it unlawful to aid another person in engaging in manipulative or deceptive conduct. The Court also noted that the express private remedy provisions in the securities acts did not include aiding and abetting liability, and the Court worried that aiding and abetting liability might make it difficult for small firms to get professional services from accountants and lawyers.

The result in *Central Bank* does not mean that accountants, attorneys, and the like, whose clients commit fraud, are off the hook as far as

100. 511 U.S. 164, 114 S.Ct. 1439 (1994).

possible liability under Rule 10b–5. To begin with, as the Court in *Central Bank* pointed out, accountants, attorneys and others might sufficiently participate in the fraud so that their own conduct constitutes the making of a misrepresentation, or is otherwise fraudulent or deceptive. For example, accountants who knowingly make false representations in reporting the results of audits,[101] or attorneys who knowingly make false representations in opinion letters they prepare for clients,[102] can be liable under Rule 10b–5 for their own fraud when they know the client will use the false representations to defraud a person in connection with the purchase or sale of a security.[103] In addition to the prospect of liability for their own fraud, aiding and abetting liability for attorneys, accountants and the like is not completely dead. Specifically, in the 1995 amendments to the Securities Exchange Act, Congress added a provision to the statute allowing the Securities Exchange Commission to bring actions against persons who aid and abet violations of the Act or SEC rules under the Act.[104]

The possibility that multiple parties might participate in fraud in violation of Rule 10b–5 raises the question of how much of the plaintiff's damages each wrongdoer must pay. In *Musick, Peeler & Garrett v. Employers, Insurance of Wausau*,[105] the Supreme Court held that defendants in Rule 10b–5 cases had an implied right to contribution from other persons violating the Rule. In the 1995 amendments to the Securities Exchange Act, Congress altered the previous rules regarding the liabilities of multiple defendants in Rule 10b–5 cases (which had followed the traditional tort law approach of joint and several liability, coupled with the right to contribution). A provision in the 1995 amendments creates a new regime of proportionate liability for defendants whose scienter is based upon recklessness rather than knowledge of falsity.[106]

i. Procedural issues

Securities fraud actions under Rule 10b–5 can raise a number of procedural issues. While a detailed exploration of these issues is beyond the scope of this book, a brief look might be handy.

Since neither Rule 10b–5, nor the 1934 Securities Exchange Act, expressly create a private right of action under Rule 10b–5, it is not surprising that neither the Rule nor the statute specify the statute of limitations for implied actions under Rule 10b–5. In *Lampf, Pleva,*

---

101. *E.g.*, Anixter v. Home–Stake Prod. Co., 77 F.3d 1215 (10th Cir.1996).

102. *E.g.*, Kline v. First Western Gov't Sec., Inc., 24 F.3d 480 (3d Cir.1994).

103. Distinguishing conduct which makes an attorney, accountant or other individual liable for his or her own misrepresentation or fraud, from conduct which only constitutes aiding and abetting another person's fraud, sometimes can be tricky. *Com-*

pare In re Software Toolworks, Inc. Sec. Lit., 50 F.3d 615 (9th Cir.1994), *with* Vosgerichian v. Commodore Int'l, 862 F.Supp. 1371 (E.D.Pa.1994).

104. Sec. Exch. Act § 20(f).

105. 508 U.S. 286, 113 S.Ct. 2085 (1993).

106. Sec. Exch. Act § 21D(g).

Lipkind, Prupis & Petigrow v. Gilbertson,[107] the Supreme Court decided to borrow, for implied actions under Rule 10b–5, the statute of limitations specified in a couple of sections of the 1934 Securities Exchange Act (Sections 9(e) and 18(e)), which cover a pair of express private causes of action created by the 1934 Act. As a result, the statute of limitations for private actions under Rule 10b–5 is the earlier of one year after discovery of the fraud, or three years after the fraud took place.

Federal courts have exclusive jurisdiction to hear actions brought under the federal securities laws, including for violation of Rule 10b–5.[108] Traditionally, plaintiffs often viewed bringing an action in federal, rather than state, court to be advantageous for reasons including obtaining personal jurisdiction over the defendant, and avoiding certain state procedural rules regarding derivative suits. The 1995 amendments to the 1934 Securities Exchange Act, however, altered the balance of advantage favoring federal filings, and led to the filing of more securities fraud suits in state courts. This development, in turn, prompted Congress to pass legislation which preempted state law securities fraud class actions.[109]

As suggested by the title of the legislation containing the 1995 amendments to the 1934 Securities Exchange Act—"The Private Securities Litigation Reform Act"—these amendments include a number of provisions addressing procedural aspects of private lawsuits brought under Rule 10b–5. Among the most important provisions are various reforms directed at class actions involving securities fraud. For example, the amendments contain provisions altering the selection and role of the lead attorney in securities fraud class actions.[110]

6.3.2 *Trading on Inside Information and Non–Disclosure*

We now turn from the situation in which the defendant makes a false or misleading statement, to the situation in which the defendant makes no statement at all (except perhaps to say "buy" or "sell"). Specifically, our concern is when does the failure to speak violate Rule 10b–5. Of course, if a person has nothing interesting to say, then presumably no one will bring a lawsuit complaining of this individual's silence. The problem arises when an individual knows facts (often referred to as inside information) which other traders do not know, and

107. 501 U.S. 350, 111 S.Ct. 2773 (1991).

108. Sec. Exch. Act § 27. If a plaintiff has state law claims, as well as a claim under Rule 10b–5, then the plaintiff might be able also to bring the state law claims in federal court under pendent jurisdiction.

109. Sec. Act § 16, as added by the Securities Litigation Uniform Standards Act of 1998. Securities fraud class actions are class actions based upon allegedly false statements or omissions of material fact, or any other sort of manipulative or deceptive devices or contrivances, in connection with the purchase or sale of a so-called covered security. Covered securities, for the most part, are securities listed for trading on the New York or American Stock Exchange or on the National Market System of the NASDAQ Stock Market. Actions on behalf of over 50 persons, in which the common issues predominate, constitute class actions for this purpose, even if the actions were not brought as a class action. State law derivative suits on behalf of the corporation are not preempted; nor are class actions based upon shareholders' voting decisions, decisions in response to a tender offer, or decisions to exercise appraisal rights

110. Sec. Exch. Act § 21D(a).

this individual does not disclose those facts. Such non-disclosure can occur in two contexts: (1) non-disclosure by a person who buys or sells securities while knowing facts which the other party to the purchase or sale does not know; and (2) non-disclosure by a person who does not buy or sell securities (nor pass the information off for another person to buy or sell securities). The first context often is referred to as trading on inside information, and will be the focus of most of our attention.

a.   *When does trading on undisclosed information violate Rule 10b–5?*

There is no dispute that making false or misleading statements of material fact in connection with the purchase or sale of securities is unlawful—the middle part of Rule 10b–5's three-part prohibition says as much.[111] At first glance, some readers might be tempted to conclude that the middle part of Rule 10b–5's three-part prohibition also renders silence unlawful, since the part speaks of omissions of material facts. A more careful reading, however, establishes that the middle part renders omissions unlawful only if the omission makes a statement misleading, and, with pure silence, there is no statement for the omission to make misleading. Hence, the one portion of Rule 10b–5 which clearly does not prohibit pure silence is the middle part of Rule 10b–5's three-part prohibition.

If any language in Rule 10b–5 renders pure silence unlawful it must be the first and third parts of the rule's three-part prohibition. Since these portions of the rule prohibit actions "to defraud" or which "operate as a fraud or deceit," the question becomes when does silence—or, more precisely for purposes of our present discussion, trading on undisclosed inside information—equal fraud for purposes of Rule 10b–5?[112] Logically, a court could take one of two basic approaches to answer the question of when trading on undisclosed inside information equals fraud for purposes of Rule 10b–5.

One approach to deciding when trading on undisclosed inside information equals fraud for purposes of Rule 10b–5 is to look to the common law. After all, the terms fraud and deceit are terms used in the common law. Hence, it would not be illogical to assume that the drafters of Rule 10b–5, in choosing terms from the common law, meant to incorporate

---

111. Of course, after *Ernst & Ernst*, the defendant must have scienter.

112. As *Ernst & Ernst* makes clear, Rule 10b–5 cannot go beyond what Section 10(b) means when the section speaks of manipulative or deceptive devices and contrivances. Hence, if Congress, in enacting Section 10(b), only meant to allow the SEC to prohibit trading on undisclosed inside information under certain circumstances (such as when the common law treated such trading as fraud), then the court could not give a broader reach to Rule 10b–5. On the other hand, it is one thing to conclude broadly that the terms of Section 10(b) bespeak intentional wrongdoing; it is quite a different matter to read into Section 10(b) a specific interpretation of when silence equals a manipulative or deceptive device or contrivance. After all, if Congress meant to codify specific theories as to when trading on inside information equals fraud, then what was the point of drafting Section 10(b) as a grant of authority to the SEC to make rules, rather than Congress itself specifying the precise conduct Congress intended to prohibit?

the interpretation which courts in common law cases had given those terms. One problem with this approach, however, when it comes to trading on undisclosed inside information is that, if courts decide to apply the common law, they immediately must ask, "the common law according to whom?" In other words, did the SEC, in adopting Rule 10b–5, mean to incorporate the so-called majority rule for trading on inside information, the so-called minority or Kansas rule, or the so-called special facts rule? Moreover, if the SEC, in adopting Rule 10b–5, meant to incorporate common law definitions of the terms fraud and deceit, did the Commission mean to freeze those definitions as the common law stood in 1942, or are the federal courts, when interpreting Rule 10b–5, to change the meaning of the terms fraud and deceit under Rule 10b–5 whenever courts applying the common law change their view on questions such as when trading on undisclosed inside information constitutes fraud?

An alternate approach to answer when trading on undisclosed inside information equals fraud for purposes of Rule 10b–5 is to look to the policies behind the rule, as well as the policies behind Section 10(b) and the Securities Exchange Act in general. After all, if Rule 10b–5 meant solely to prohibit conduct already prohibited under the common law of fraud or deceit, then what was the purpose of even having the rule?[113] Unfortunately, as we shall see, there is considerable debate as to when, or even whether, the law should, as a policy matter, prohibit trading on undisclosed inside information.

It turns out that the Supreme Court, in a series of decisions which delineate when trading on undisclosed inside information violates Rule 10b–5, has followed neither of these two approaches. Instead, the Court has adopted tests which draw upon common law concepts, but do not reach results consistent with decisions applying the common law. At the same time, the Supreme Court's tests for illegal trading on inside information reflect no overarching policy (save to appeal to the instincts of a majority of the justices of the Court).

The Supreme Court's efforts to delineate when trading on undisclosed inside information violates Rule 10b–5 began in *Chiarella v. United States*.[114] Chiarella worked for a financial printing company. The printing company's customers included firms who were going to make tender offers to buy, at a premium price, outstanding stock of other corporations.[115] Despite the customers having blanked out the names of the target corporations in the documents given to the printing company,

113. Perhaps one might argue that Rule 10b–5 serves a useful purpose even if the rule does not go beyond existing state law prohibitions, since the rule and the statute bring to bear the resources of federal enforcement authorities (the SEC and the Department of Justice) to aid state efforts to police securities fraud.

114. 445 U.S. 222, 100 S.Ct. 1108 (1980).

115. The customers were what are often referred to as "acquiring firms," since they were attempting to acquire control of other corporations. The corporations whose stock the customers planned to buy are known as "target corporations," since these corporations are the target of a takeover attempt.

Chiarella was able to figure out the identities of the target corporations from the surrounding material in the documents. He made around $30,000 by purchasing stock in the target corporations prior to the announcements of the tender offers. Ultimately, the SEC uncovered Chiarella's trading, whereupon he lost his job, he entered a consent decree with the SEC giving up his trading profits, and the U.S. Attorney prosecuted and convicted Chiarella of criminally violating Section 10(b) and Rule 10b–5. Chiarella appealed his conviction all the way to the Supreme Court, who overturned the conviction.

Looking back on *Chiarella* two decades after the decision, it is now clear that Chiarella did violate Rule 10b–5. In order to understand how the Supreme Court nevertheless could overturn Chiarella's conviction, it is important to separate the actual holding in the case, from the court's rationale, and from a critical issue which the court expressly left open. The holding in the case involves a jury instruction. The District Court judge instructed the jury that all they needed to find in order to convict Chiarella was, in purchasing the stock, Chiarella used material non-public information at a time he knew other people trading in the securities market "did not have access to the same information."[116] The actual holding in *Chiarella* was that this instruction was wrong—in other words, the simple fact that one person possesses material non-public information which is inaccessible to other traders in the market does not, in itself, create a duty to disclose the information before trading. Hence, the starting point of Supreme Court doctrine regarding trading on inside information and Rule 10b–5 is a negative: There is no equal access rule.[117]

If mere possession of material information not accessible to other traders is insufficient to create a duty to disclose before buying or selling stock, then the inevitable question becomes what, if anything, can create such a duty? The Supreme Court in *Chiarella* could have responded to this question in several ways: The Court could have refused to answer the question, as unnecessary to the resolution of the case before it—but

116. 445 U.S. at 231. The Supreme Court characterized this instruction has adopting a "parity-of-information" rule. It would be more precise, however, to refer to the instruction as adopting an "equal access" rule, thereby avoiding confusing the instruction with an "equal information" rule. The difference is that an equal information rule would say that any time one trader knows material facts which the other party to the trade does not know, there would be a duty to disclose before trading; whereas an equal access rule says that the duty to disclose only arises when one party knows material facts which the other party to the trade, not only does not know, but could not legally have found out. The significance of this distinction lies in the fact that, as we shall discuss later, the policy justification for an equal access rule is different (and stronger) than the policy justification for an equal information rule (which virtually no one advocates).

117. The Supreme Court's opinion is not entirely clear as to whether the court is interpreting Rule 10b–5, or Section 10(b). The court's opinion actually refers to the scope of Section 10(b) and Congress' intent, more than the opinion refers Rule 10b–5 and the SEC's intent, which suggests the court is holding that an equal access rule would go beyond what Congress meant in Section 10(b) by a manipulative or deceptive device or contrivance. If so, the SEC could not adopt an explicit equal access rule under Section 10(b). Unlike the *Ernst & Ernst* opinion, however, the court in *Chiarella* never explains how an equal access rule contradicts the actual language used by Section 10(b).

this would have led to chaos. The Court could have said that almost nothing can produce such a duty—which, as discussed earlier in this chapter, reflects the apparent approach of many, if not most, common law opinions. The Supreme Court in *Chiarella*, however, chose neither path. Instead, the Court came up with a rationale which a later Supreme Court opinion would refer to as the "traditional" or "classical" theory.

In the traditional or classical theory, the Supreme Court in *Chiarella* sought to reconcile the Court's holding with the results of a Securities Exchange Commission administrative proceeding, and a number of lower court decisions, which had found individuals violated Rule 10b–5 by trading while in possession of undisclosed inside information. The Securities Exchange Commission administrative proceeding[118] was a disciplinary action (pursuant to the SEC's authority to regulate stock brokers) against the Cady, Roberts brokerage firm. A broker in the Cady, Roberts firm received a tip from a corporate director (who was also associated with Cady, Roberts) that the corporation's board had just voted to cut the dividend, whereupon the brokerage firm was able to sell the firm's and the firm's clients' stock in the corporation before the corporation announced to the public the board's decision. The Commission held that the brokerage firm violated Rule 10b–5 (as well as Section 17 of the 1933 Securities Act). A few years after *Cady, Roberts*, the Securities Exchange Commission brought an action against various officials of Texas Gulf Sulfur Company.[119] These officials purchased stock in the corporation after the corporation made a major copper discovery, but before public disclosure of this discovery. The Second Circuit held that this conduct violated Rule 10b–5.

In order to reconcile both *Cady, Roberts* and *Texas Gulf Sulfur* with its holding in the case at hand, the Supreme Court in *Chiarella* focused on the fact that the defendants in *Texas Gulf Sulfur* were directors, officers, and other employees (in popular parlance, "insiders") of the corporation whose stock the defendants purchased or sold, while, in *Cady, Roberts*, the broker had received a tip from such an insider. The significance of this fact, according to the Court in *Chiarella*, is that insiders have a fiduciary relationship, or a relationship of trust and confidence, with the shareholders of the corporation in which the insiders are directors, officers or employees. This relationship between the insider, and the party with whom the insider trades, creates, according to the Court in *Chiarella*, a duty on the insider either to disclose material information before trading or else to abstain from the trade. Since Chiarella was not an insider in the corporations whose stock he purchased (he was an employee of a printing company), nor had he received information from insiders of the corporations whose stock he

118. In re Cady, Roberts & Co., 40 S.E.C. 907 (1961).

119. SEC v. Texas Gulf Sulfur Co., 401 F.2d 833 (2d Cir.1968). As evident from the title of the case, the SEC also named the corporation as a defendant. The charge against the corporation was that it issued a misleading press release. The reader may recall the earlier discussion of issues raised by the press release aspect of the *Texas Gulf Sulfur* opinion.

purchased (since the printing company's customers were the acquiring firms and Chiarella bought stock in the target corporations), Chiarella had no duty under the traditional or classical theory.

Unfortunately, the traditional or classical theory suffers from a number of flaws. To begin with, this theory was not the rationale used by the SEC in *Cady, Roberts* or by the court in *Texas Gulf Sulfur*. Indeed, the thrust of the *Cady, Roberts* opinion was to respond to the brokerage firm's contention that, since they were not insiders, Rule 10b–5 did not prohibit the brokerage firm's trading without disclosure. The Commission rejected this argument by reasoning that the obligation to disclose arose from a relationship giving access to information intended only to be available for a corporate purpose rather than personal benefit, coupled with the unfairness of one party taking advantage of information which he or she knows is unavailable to those with whom he or she is dealing. This reasoning seemingly applies to Chiarella, who had a relationship with the printing company and its customers which gave Chiarella access to information for the purpose of printing the customers' documents (and not for his personal benefit), and Chiarella took advantage of the information to trade with persons who lacked the same access to information about the forthcoming tender offers. Similarly, the Second Circuit in *Texas Gulf Sulfur* did not focus on the officials' status as insiders in finding that they had a duty to disclose before trading. Rather, after expressing the view that the policy of Rule 10b–5 is to ensure all investors have relatively equal access to material information, the Second Circuit stated that "anyone in possession of material inside information" must disclose or abstain.[120]

If the traditional or classical theory did not come from *Cady, Roberts* or *Texas Gulf Sulfur*, where did theory come from? The Supreme Court in *Chiarella* suggests that the theory comes from the common law concerning fraud. It is true, as discussed earlier in this chapter, that one of the exceptions recognized by the common law to the normal rule that silence is not fraud occurs when there is a fiduciary relationship between the two parties to a transaction. The problem, however, is that courts applying the common law were virtually unanimous in holding that this exception did not apply to the sort of impersonal market trading involved in *Cady, Roberts* and *Texas Gulf Sulfur* (and most courts applying the common law would not even apply the exception to face-to-face trading between corporate insiders and shareholders).[121] Hence, in the traditional or classical theory, the Supreme Court in *Chiarella* adopted the results of *Cady, Roberts* and *Texas Gulf Sulfur* while ignoring the rationale of these decisions, and adopted the broad rationale of common law fraud cases while ignoring the actual results of common law decisions.

120. 401 F.2d at 848. This language in *Texas Gulf Sulfur* explains how the District Court in *Chiarella* came up with the challenged jury instruction.

121. See § 6.1.2a *supra*.

To top it off, the *Chiarella* opinion's traditional or classical theory will not even follow its own logic. The Supreme Court in *Chiarella* explained that the duty to disclose arose out of the fiduciary relationship between the corporation's officials and the corporation's shareholders, coupled with the notion that when two parties to a transaction stand in a fiduciary relationship, there is a duty of full disclosure between them. This explains the duty in a situation like *Texas Gulf Sulfur* in which insiders purchase stock from the existing shareholders without disclosing good news regarding the company. Suppose, however, as in *Cady, Roberts*, an insider (or the tippee of an insider), knowing undisclosed bad news about the corporation, sells stock to someone who is not yet a shareholder. This would seem to be an instance of an arms-length transaction, since there is not yet a fiduciary relationship at the time of the sale. Yet, the Court in *Chiarella* stated that it would not follow its own logic to such a result. Perhaps one might respond by pointing out that, as a result of the sale, there will become a fiduciary relationship between the insider and the buyer, and so it is not unprecedented to move the disclosure obligation forward to the transaction which creates the relationship.[122] Yet, even this rationalization may not apply if, as in *Texas Gulf Sulfur*, insiders purchase options either to buy or sell the corporation's stock (so-called "calls" or "puts"). In the case of such options trading, it is quite common that parties to the transaction may not, at the time the option is entered, or ever, have more than transitory ownership (if that) of stock in the corporation.

One evident gap in our discussion of the traditional or classical theory so far is to explain the result in *Cady, Roberts*. After all, the party trading on undisclosed information in *Cady, Roberts* was not an official of the corporation. In *Dirks v. SEC*,[123] the Supreme Court filled in this gap.

Dirks arose out of a massive fraud at the Equity Funding company.[124] Dirks was an investment analyst. A disgruntled ex-Equity Funding official, named Secrist, tipped Dirks off to the fraud in the hope that Dirks would expose the scheme. Dirks investigated, and, after Dirks received confirmation of Secrist's charges from several Equity Funding employees, Dirks alerted his brokerage firm's clients to the fraud at Equity Funding.[125] The clients were then able to unload their Equity Funding stock prior to the fraud becoming public knowledge. The Securities Exchange Commission—who, some suspect, may have been

---

122. *See, e.g.*, Herring v. Offutt, 266 Md. 593, 295 A.2d 876 (1972) (holding that prospective partners have a duty of disclosure in forming their partnership).

123. 463 U.S. 646, 103 S.Ct. 3255 (1983).

124. Equity Funding was, for the most part, an insurance company, whose stock kept increasing in price as the company reported to the public ever increasing income. In fact, however, the company never

made a profit. Instead, the company's officials simply made up much of the income the company reported. The officials accomplished this by techniques such as programing the company's computers to record that the company received premiums from what were actually fictitious insurance policies.

125. Dirks also contacted the Securities Exchange Commission and a reporter for the Wall Street Journal to report the fraud.

miffed that Dirks discovered a fraud which the agency should have—censured Dirks for violating Rule 10b–5 by tipping his firm's clients to the fraud so that the clients could sell prior to the information becoming public. Dirks appealed his censure ultimately to the Supreme Court, which overturned the SEC's action.

The challenge for the Supreme Court in *Dirks* was to set out an approach which would reconcile finding a violation by the tippee in *Cady, Roberts*, with the notion that, under the traditional or classical theory, only insiders have a duty to disclose before trading. One possible approach would be to say that anyone who obtains information from an insider picks up the insider's duty. This was the approach used by the SEC in censuring Dirks. The Supreme Court, however, rejected this sort of "tainted fruit" approach. Instead, the Supreme Court's opinion in *Dirks* essentially divides persons who receive information from corporate officials into three categories. In two of these categories, recipients of information from insiders have a duty to disclose before trading (or else to abstain from trading if the recipient cannot disclose the information), and in the third, residual, category there is no duty.

The first category of persons receiving information from corporate officials consists of persons commonly referred to as "temporary" or "constructive" insiders (or even "Footnote 14" insiders, since the Supreme Court discussed such folks in Footnote 14 of its opinion). These temporary insiders consist of persons like underwriters, accountants, lawyers and consultants, who enter into a confidential relationship with the corporation and are given access to corporate information solely for corporate purposes. These temporary insiders have the same obligations with respect to trading on information they receive from the corporation as do corporate officials. For temporary insider status to exist, the corporation must expect, and the relationship must imply, a duty to keep information from the corporation confidential.[126] Finding a duty of confidentiality is easy in the case of an attorney, where the rules of the profession require confidentiality. It is more problematic in the case of underwriters, where, in some circumstances, there may be an implied understanding of confidentiality, but, in other circumstances, there might be no such understanding.[127]

126. The court does not explain why the expectation of confidentiality serves to create a fiduciary relationship between the temporary insider and the corporation's shareholders.

127. *See, e.g.*, Walton v. Morgan Stanley & Co., 623 F.2d 796 (2d Cir.1980). In many cases, corporations provide information in confidence to members of a firm—a law firm, an accounting firm, an underwriting firm, a consulting firm, and so on. In this event, various employees of the firm will have access to the information. For example, information provided to lawyers also might be seen by secretaries and paralegals who work for the law firm. Such employees should also be considered temporary insiders of the corporation. *See, e.g.*, SEC v. Musella, 578 F.Supp. 425 (S.D.N.Y.1984). This, in turn, might lead the reader to ask why Chiarella was not a temporary insider, since the printing company received information with an expectation that the information be confidential. The answer is that the printing company's customers were the acquiring firms, whereas Chiarella bought stock in the target corporations. Hence, Chiarella was not a temporary insider of the corporations whose shares he purchased.

The second category of persons receiving information from corporate officials—and the category with which the *Dirks* opinion primarily is concerned—are "tippees" who receive information in breach of the insider's duty to refrain from profiting on undisclosed inside information. A tippee is an individual who receives information (a tip) from a person (a tipper) who provides the information to the tippee with the expectation that the tippee will buy or sell based upon the information. The brokerage firm in *Cady, Roberts* was a tippee; so was Dirks and Dirks' firm's clients (since Secrist apparently intended Dirks to pass on the information for trading, which Secrist hoped would precipitate the exposure of the fraud). The court in *Dirks* held that not all tippees have a duty to refrain from trading on undisclosed inside information. Instead, to explain both why and when tippees were under such a duty, the court went back to a concept it had suggested in a footnote in *Chiarella*. This concept is that the tippee's liability flows from having acted as a "participant after the fact" in the insider's breach of the insider's duty not to trade on inside information without disclosure.[128] Specifically, the court reasoned that an insider should not be able to accomplish indirectly what the insider could not legally do directly. Hence, since it would be illegal for an insider to profit by trading on undisclosed inside information, it also should be illegal for the insider to profit by passing on information for another person's use in trading.[129]

This rationale for why trading by tippees on undisclosed inside information can violate Rule 10b–5 led the court in *Dirks* to adopt a two-pronged test for when trading by tippees will violate Rule 10b–5. Under this test, there is a violation when (1) an insider breaches his or her duty by passing on a tip in order for the insider to obtain some personal benefit, and (2) the tippee "knows or should have known" that passing on the tip was a breach of the insider's duty.

The *Dirks* test for illegal tipping raises a number of questions. To begin with, consider the personal benefit portion of the test. Normally, when one thinks of who benefits by tipping, one thinks of the benefit flowing to the tippee, who, after all, makes the money by trading on the tip. The *Dirks* test, however, somewhat counter-intuitively looks at the benefit to the tipper. What sort of benefit can the tipper get from tipping? Perhaps the tippee will pay cash for the tip (as the notorious Ivan Boesky did). Alternately, perhaps two insiders at different firms will trade tips. Suppose, however, the tipper simply makes a gift of the information (as, one suspects, often happens with tipping among family and friends). The court in *Dirks* states that gifts produce a personal

---

128. It is not entirely clear where the Supreme Court obtained the concept of a "participant after the fact." Historically, criminal law penalized individuals who were accomplices after the fact. Being an accomplice after the fact, however, probably is a species of aiding and abetting liability, which the Supreme Court held in *Central Bank* could not produce civil liability under Section 10(b).

129. Implicit in this reasoning is the notion that the insider's breach of duty results from making a profit through corporate information, rather than from simply transacting business with a person with whom the insider has a fiduciary relationship without having made disclosure of all material facts.

benefit for the giver. This notion in *Dirks* owes less to the old saying "that it is better to give than to receive," than it does to the step transaction doctrine found in tax cases. In the tax field, courts sometimes disregard tax differences which depend upon the formal order in which a taxpayer carries out a multi-step transaction when the end substantive result of the transaction will be the same no matter which order the taxpayer carries it out. Along the same line, since giving information for a tippee to turn into cash through trading produces the same result as the insider, him- or herself, trading on the information and then giving the tippee cash, the court in *Dirks* stated that a gift of information is equivalent to the insider, him- or herself, trading. In any event, beyond the gift context, warm and fuzzy feelings apparently do not count as a personal benefit. Otherwise Secrist's satisfaction from the good deed of exposing the fraud (and the even greater satisfaction of revenge upon one's former employer) should have been a sufficient personal benefit to create liability for Dirks.[130]

Other questions arise from the Supreme Court's statement in *Dirks* that, for the tippee to be liable, the tippee must know or "should have known" of the insider's breach. "Should have known" sounds like the language of negligence; yet, as discussed earlier, in *Ernst & Ernst*, the Supreme Court held that negligence was not enough for liability under Rule 10b–5. Presumably this was just a slip of the pen in writing the opinion. In any event, what exactly must the tippee know in order to know of the insider's breach? For example, suppose the tippee is aware that the information comes from an insider and that the insider received a personal benefit from giving the tip (say, the tip was a gift). Is this

---

130. A practical explanation for the Supreme Court's refusal to find that Secrist personally benefited from the psychological satisfaction Secrist obtained is that the court did not want to create a test which deters the exposure of fraud. One broader rationalization for this result, however, is to suggest that there is no illegal tipping if the insider's personal benefit coincides with a benefit to the corporation or its shareholders from passing on the information. After all, the key to liability under the court's approach in *Dirks* is that the insider breached his or her duty in passing on the tip. If passing on the tip somehow furthered a legitimate corporate purpose, then arguably there would be no breach of duty. (In *Dirks*, one might say that the corporation benefited by exposing and stopping the fraud, even though, in the short run, the result of the exposure was to force Equity Funding into bankruptcy.)

It is also worth noting that the personal benefit ordinarily must come from passing on the information for the purpose of the tippee trading on the information. For example, suppose an insider, faced with po-

tential personal liability due to some calamity at the corporation, retains, on his or her own behalf, an attorney. The insider obtains a personal benefit from providing the attorney with sufficient information concerning the calamity so that the attorney can give informed advice to the insider. Nevertheless, if the attorney were to trade on the information, this would not fit within the *Dirks* test for tippee liability. This is because the insider did not provide the information to the attorney for the attorney to trade upon, and, hence, the insider did not attempt to achieve indirectly something (trading on inside information) which the insider could not do directly. Lower court authority exists, however, for an arguable exception to the notion that there is no violation of Rule 10b–5 under the personal benefit test unless the insider passes on the information for trading. This exception arises if the insider sells confidential corporate information under circumstances where the insider knows the information will be misused, but is not necessarily aware that the misuse will involve stock trading. *See* United States v. Libera, 989 F.2d 596 (2d Cir.1993).

enough to show the tippee knew of the breach, or is it also necessary to show that the tippee was aware of the law of trading on inside information which renders tipping for personal benefit illegal? Most likely, courts will apply the old saw about "ignorance of the law is no excuse," but the matter is by no means free from doubt.[131] Also, suppose the tippee is unaware of the insider's breach. This precludes liability for the tippee; but what about the liability of the tipper? Since the tipper still tipped for personal benefit, the tippee's ignorance presumably should not preclude the tipper's liability; but there is no definitive authority on the question.

As *Dirks* illustrates, often there can be chains of tipping, as one tippee turns around and becomes a tipper by passing the information off to others. When dealing with chains of tipping, questions might arise both as to personal benefit and as to knowledge of the breach. For example, Dirks received a benefit by passing on the information to his firm's clients—since this is what induces clients to trade with a brokerage firm which employs investment analysts like Dirks. The personal benefit to Dirks is irrelevant, however, because Secrist, the insider, did not breach a duty by gaining a personal benefit, and, accordingly, Dirks did not participate in a breach no matter what Dirks did with the information. On the other hand, if the insider benefits from providing the information to the initial tippee, how does the personal benefit test apply if the initial tippee then tips someone else, who tips someone else, and so on? Specifically, must the benefit of the subsequent tipping flow all the way back to the insider; or is it sufficient that each tippee gains a personal benefit when he or she turns around and becomes a tipper; or, so long as there was a personal benefit to the insider from the initial tip, does it matter whether there is any benefit flowing up the chain from further tipping? So far, there is little authority on these questions.[132] Turning to knowledge of the breach, how much must a remote tippee know of the original insider's breach in order to be liable? After all, a remote tippee is unlikely to know the original source of a tip which has gone through several hands, much less the circumstances under which the insider gave the original tip. Still, the circumstances might be such to suggest to the remote tippee that in all likelihood the information

---

131. Section 32 of the 1934 Securities Exchange Act precludes imposing a jail sentence upon an individual for violating a rule promulgated under the Act, however, if the individual proves he or she was ignorant of the rule he or she violated.

132. The lack of authority may in part be a function of the fact that, in many instances, benefit to the tippee who turns around and tips also could be conceived of as a benefit to the insider who originally tipped. For example, if an insider sold the information for money to a tippee, who then resells the information to an other tippee, one might argue that the second tipping indirectly benefited the insider, be-cause the first tippee's motivation for paying the insider for the information may have come, at least in part, from the intent of reselling the information. Similarly, if an insider tips as a gift, part of the value of such a gift is the ability to make a gift of the information to others. Hence, one might argue that subsequent gifts of information, not only benefit the tippees who make the gifts, but also benefit the original insider. On the other hand, suppose an insider tips her husband as a gift, who then tips his mistress as a gift. The insider no doubt would be shocked to hear that the gift to the mistress was a benefit to the insider.

originated with an illegal tip. Are such general grounds for suspicion enough for the tippee to be liable? There is limited authority on this question.[133]

The third category of persons who receive information from insiders includes everyone who does not fall either into the category of temporary insiders or into the category of tippees who receive information in breach of the insider's duty not to profit from trading on undisclosed inside information. Under *Dirks*, persons in this residual category can trade on undisclosed inside information without violating Rule 10b–5—at least so long as liability rests only on the traditional or classical theory.

Incidentally, we have been treating Secrist as an insider even though, at the time Secrist talked with Dirks, Secrist was no longer employed by Equity Funding. An implicit assumption in the *Dirks* opinion is that former insiders remain subject to the duty not to trade on undisclosed inside information which the former insider obtained while he or she was an insider. This is because any other rule would leave a huge loophole for insiders to tender a timely resignation whenever they become privy to some juicy tidbit of inside information.

Our discussion so far does not explain why it is *now* clear that Chiarella violated Rule 10b–5. The answer lies in an issue the Supreme Court expressly left open in *Chiarella*. Suspecting that a majority of the Supreme Court justices might not be sympathetic to the equal access rule, the government presented the Supreme Court with an alternate theory to support Chiarella's conviction. This theory is that Chiarella breached his duty to his employer's customers (the acquiring firms). In essence, Chiarella, to use Chief Justice Burger's colorful language, "misappropriated—stole to put it bluntly—valuable nonpublic information entrusted to him in the utmost confidence."[134] Unwilling to send a person to jail based upon a theory which was never before the jury, the Supreme Court refused to resolve the viability of this alternate theory.[135]

It took almost two decades before the Supreme Court resolved the viability of this alternate theory—which has since come to be known as the "misappropriation theory."[136] The resolution came at the expense of a wayward attorney in *United States v. O'Hagan*.[137]

133. *See, e.g.,* SEC v. Musella, 678 F.Supp. 1060 (S.D.N.Y.1988) (holding remote tippees liable when they consciously chose not to ask their tipper about the source of the information, which they suspected).

134. 445 U.S. at 245.

135. Chief Justice Burger (who had something of a law and order reputation) filed a sole dissent on the issue of whether the jury instruction was adequate to convict based upon the alternate theory.

136. It looked like the Supreme Court was going to resolve the viability of the misappropriation theory when the court handed down its decision in *Carpenter v. United States*, 484 U.S. 19, 108 S.Ct. 316

(1987). *Carpenter* arose out of a scheme by a Wall Street Journal reporter and several of his friends to trade on their advance knowledge of the contents of the Journal's "Heard on the Street" column. (The publication of this column often impacted the stocks of the corporations discussed in the column.) The Supreme Court unanimously held that the defendants violated the federal mail and wire fraud statutes by misappropriating the Wall Street Journal's proprietary information through the defendants' trading. (In reaching this conclusion, the court noted that the Journal's policy prohibited its employees from using information gained through their work at the Journal in this manner.) The Supreme Court (on which there was one vacancy at

The facts out of which the *O'Hagan* case arose provide an object lesson for all attorneys and prospective attorneys—even putting aside the issue of trading on inside information. O'Hagan was a partner at a prominent Minneapolis law firm. According to news accounts, O'Hagan got into financial trouble (despite his substantial income as a partner) by playing the market. He then embezzled from client trust accounts in order to cover his trading losses. Then, in order to replenish the trust accounts and thereby cover up the embezzlement, O'Hagan engaged in the conduct which led to the Supreme Court's decision. Specifically, an English company (Grand Metropolitan) had retained O'Hagan's law firm to act as local counsel in connection with Grand Metropolitan's planned tender offer for the stock of a corporation (Pillsbury) headquartered in Minneapolis. While O'Hagan did no work on this matter, he learned of the tender offer (according to news accounts by finagling the information out of a partner who knew about the representation). O'Hagan then purchased Pillsbury shares and options to buy Pillsbury shares, and, as a result, made over $4 million profit after announcement of the tender offer.[138] Upon (the not surprising) discovery of his trading by the SEC,[139] O'Hagan was indicted and convicted of violating Section 10(b) and Rule 10b–5—as well as violating the federal mail fraud statute, Rule 14e–3(a),[140] and even federal money laundering statutes. He was sentenced to 41 months in prison.[141] It looked like O'Hagan's luck might turn when the Eighth Circuit Court of Appeals reversed O'Hagan's federal law convictions on all counts. Then the matter reached the Supreme Court.

The Supreme Court held that O'Hagan violated Rule 10b–5—despite the fact that he was neither an insider nor had he received information from an insider of the corporation in whose stock he traded (Pillsbury), and, hence, O'Hagan's trading did not come within what the court labeled as the traditional or classical theory for finding a violation of Rule 10b–5. Instead, the court based the violation on O'Hagan's having misappropriated confidential information (the plans for a tender offer) from both his law firm and from the firm's client (Grand Metropolitan).

the time) split 4–4, however, on the question of whether this conduct violated Rule 10b–5. Since the principal difference between Rule 10b–5 and the mail and wire fraud statutes is that Rule 10b–5 only prohibits fraud "in connection with the purchase or sale of [a] security," the result in *Carpenter* indicated that all the justices viewed trading on information given in confidence to be fraud, but the justices were sharply divided upon whether such trading was a fraud in connection with the purchase or sale of a security.

137. 521 U.S. 642, 117 S.Ct. 2199 (1997).

138. The brazenness of O'Hagan's conduct is especially surprising since part of his area of practice was securities litigation.

139. O'Hagan's position in Pillsbury call options (he owned the largest position in call options to Pillsbury stock at one point) would seem bound to attract attention.

140. The Securities Exchange Commission promulgated Rule 14e–3(a) in the wake of *Chiarella.* Using the Commission's authority under Section 14(e) of the Securities Exchange Act, Rule 14e–3(a) attacks trading on inside information dealing with tender offers. We shall explore this rule later.

141. A state court conviction for embezzling the client trust accounts already had landed O'Hagan in state prison. Needless to say, O'Hagan also was disbarred.

Reaching this result required the court to take two steps: The first step was to reaffirm the result the court already had reached in *Carpenter*—this being to find that misappropriating information can equal a fraud. The second step was to resolve the question which evidently split the justices in *Carpenter* (and provoked dissents in *O'Hagan*)—the question being whether such a fraud was "in connection with the purchase or sale of [a] security." Taking a literalist approach, the majority of justices in *O'Hagan* reasoned that, since the very act by which O'Hagan misappropriated information was purchasing stock, the fraud (misappropriating the information by trading on it) was in connection with the purchase of a security.[142]

Actually, while the dispute among the justices in *O'Hagan* involved the "in connection with" question, when it comes to defining the scope of the misappropriation doctrine, it is more important to focus on the first step taken by the court in *O'Hagan*—this being to equate misappropriating confidential information with fraud. There are two theories under which misappropriating confidential information by trading on it can equal fraud.

The broader theory formed the basis for Chief Justice Burger's dissent in *Chiarella*. This theory, which traces its roots back to an early article on common law fraud,[143] takes a utilitarian approach to deciding when silence between two parties to a transaction equals fraud. Under the utilitarian theory, the reason that silence normally is not fraud, despite one party's knowing material facts unknown to the other party to the transaction, is to encourage hard work in gathering and analyzing information. On the other hand, if the hard work essentially consists of stealing information, this effort obviously is not something society wishes to reward or encourage. Hence, under this logic, the law should create a duty to disclose misappropriated information to the other party to the transaction—which would remove the reward from using ill-gotten information, and would place the parties to the transaction on equal footing.[144]

Chief Justice Burger's utilitarian theory was not the theory adopted by the court in *O'Hagan*. Instead, the court adopted what might be labeled the "sneaky theft" theory. The notion here is that an individual, such as O'Hagan, who stands in a fiduciary relationship, expressly or implicitly represents to his or her employer or client that he or she will act loyally—in other words, that he or she will not embezzle money entrusted to his or her care, nor misuse information which his or her employer or client made available and does not wish disclosed or traded

---

142. The dissent felt the connection was absent because the defrauded parties were O'Hagan's firm and its client rather than the other parties to O'Hagan's purchases of stock and options. In essence, the dissent operated on the assumption that a fraud is not in connection with the purchase or sale of securities unless the defendant's action defrauds a person when that person purchases or sells securities.

143. W. Page Keeton, *Fraud—Concealment and Non–Disclosure*, 15 Tex. L. Rev. 1 (1936).

144. Which is desirable in the absence of any reason to reward obtaining information.

upon. If, without disclosing to the employer or client the fiduciary's subversive intention, the fiduciary then embezzles the money or misuses the information entrusted to the fiduciary, the fiduciary has lied in making this express or implicit representation of loyalty, and thereby has defrauded the employer or client.

The difference between these two misappropriation theories has a couple of potentially significant impacts. To begin with, it might impact private suits under Rule 10b–5. The utilitarian theory creates a duty to disclose the ill-gotten information to the other party to the transaction (or else abstain from trading). Since the disclosure duty runs to the other party to the transaction, the non-disclosure constitutes a fraud on the other party to misappropriater's purchase or sale of stock. Not only would this logic have avoided the "in connection with" issue, but it also suggests that the other party to the purchase or sale can sue the misappropriater for violating Rule 10b–5. By contrast, under the sneaky theft theory, the fraud is on the person from whom the defendant misappropriated the information. This means that the persons trading with the misappropriater were not defrauded and, therefore, could not bring a suit under Rule 10b–5.[145] Moreover, since the party from whom the information was misappropriated is not buying or selling stock (at least with the misappropriater), this party lacks standing under *Blue Chip Stamps* to bring a private Rule 10b–5 action.[146]

The two theories also produce potentially different results as to what constitutes a misappropriation. To take an extreme example, suppose a person steals information at gunpoint. The utilitarian theory would impose a duty to disclose such ill-gotten information before trading, and, accordingly, non-disclosure would constitute fraud. Such armed robbery would not constitute fraud under the sneaky theft theory, however, since there is no pretense of loyalty. Of course, there is not likely to be too much armed robbery of confidential corporate information useful for stock trading. Obtaining such information through burglary, however, is a realistic prospect.[147] A burglary involving forced entry presumably would not constitute fraud under the sneaky theft theory, but would create a duty to disclose under the utilitarian theory. Some burglaries, however, might lead to a fairly subtle inquiry under the sneaky theft theory as to whether the defendant used a misrepresentation to gain access. For instance, would a computer hacker's efforts to gain entry to a secured database constitute a misrepresentation to the computer containing the data?[148]

---

145. *E.g.*, Moss v. Morgan Stanley Inc., 719 F.2d 5 (2d Cir.1983). We shall see later a statutory caveat to this result.

146. *E.g.*, In re Ivan F. Boesky Securities Litigation, 36 F.3d 255 (2d Cir.1994).

147. *See* United States v. Cherif, 943 F.2d 692 (7th Cir.1991).

148. One potential problem under the sneaky theft theory arises from the Court's observation in *O'Hagan* that disclosure to the source of the information of the fiduciary's intent to trade on the information precludes the fraud. While this observation follows logically from the basic rationale behind the sneaky theft theory, a question might arise as to the timing of the disclosure. Specifically, the Court seems to suggest that disclosure at the time of the trade would be sufficient. Yet, under this timing, a fiduciary could gain information while

In some cases, whether there is a misappropriation might be at issue under either theory. Specifically, it might not be clear whether the defendant had a fiduciary relationship with the person providing information to the defendant such that the information provider legitimately could expect (barring the defendant's disclosure of his or her intention to act to the contrary) that the defendant would not use the information for trading. For example, in *United States v. Chestman*,[149] the Second Circuit, in a closely divided decision, refused to find such a relationship when a husband received information from his wife, who told him not to tell the information to anyone else. By contrast, in *United States v. Reed*,[150] the District Court found such a relationship when a father disclosed confidential information to his son.[151]

Two other points are worth noting about the misappropriation theory. To begin with, if the person who provides information approves of, or does not care about, use of the information to trade, then there is no misappropriation. This notion of sanctioned trading on non-public information might strike some people as strange, but follows logically from the nature of the misappropriation theory.[152] In addition, while *O'Hagan* did not involve tipping, and *Dirks* only discussed tipping by insiders, presumably tipping by a misappropriater of information would invoke the same personal benefit test as *Dirks* applied to insiders.[153]

As suggested by the discussion thus far, whether trading on undisclosed inside information violates Rule 10b–5 typically hinges on whether there is a breach of duty as recognized in either the classical or the misappropriation theories. There are, however, some other potential issues. To begin with, the undisclosed information must be material. After all, there seems even less point to complain about the non-disclosure of immaterial facts, than there would be to complain about the misrepresentation of such facts. The standard for materiality is the same for trading on inside information as it is for a misrepresentation.[154] As with misrepresentations, a recurrent materiality problem in non-disclosure cases involves facts which show the possibility, but not the certainty, of a future event. For example, much of the focus in the *Texas Gulf*

---

deceptively feigning an intent not to misuse the information, and then avoid liability under Rule 10b–5 by telling the employer or client "so long sucker, I am off to trade."

149. 947 F.2d 551 (2d Cir.1991).

150. 601 F.Supp. 685 (S.D.N.Y.), *rev'd on other grounds*, 773 F.2d 477 (2d Cir. 1985).

151. A wag might seek to reconcile *Reed* with *Chestman* through the old saying that "blood is thicker than water." The main opinion in *Chestman* asserted that the difference lay in the father and son's repeated practice of discussing confidential business information, unlike the husband and wife in *Chestman*. In any event, when courts effectively hold that husbands and wives should

not trust their spouses with confidential information, one should not be surprised at the sorry state of marriage these days.

152. Because the classical theory keys off of the duty of disclosure owed by an insider to his or her corporation's shareholders, presumably superiors at a corporation could not sanction insider trading in the corporation's own stock—at least unless one could say the corporation's shareholders (and prospective shareholders) approved.

153. *See, e.g.,* United States v. Carpenter, 791 F.2d 1024 (2d Cir.1986), *aff'd*, 484 U.S. 19, 108 S.Ct. 316 (1987)

154. *E.g.,* Basic, Inc. v. Levinson, 485 U.S. 224, 108 S.Ct. 978 (1988).

Sulfur decision discussed earlier was not on the question of duty—since the Second Circuit followed an equal access approach—but rather on the question of whether preliminary indications of a potentially major copper discovery were material.

Moreover, there is no point requiring disclosure of facts already known to traders in the market. Accordingly, in addition to being material, the non-disclosed information must be non-public. This element also became an issue in the *Texas Gulf Sulfur* case. Some of the insider trading occurred immediately after the corporation announced the copper discovery. As the court recognized, simply because the corporation has made a public announcement does not mean that the information is immediately public. Otherwise, insiders could always beat the market, since they are prepared to react based upon their preexisting knowledge of the facts, while it takes other traders in the market a little time to hear and digest the news.

We have not mentioned scienter, or intent, in the context of trading on undisclosed inside information—except with respect to the requirement that a tippee know of the tipper's breach, and with respect to the tipper's motive for tipping. This is because scienter does not come up as an issue in an insider trading case with anywhere near the frequency scienter arises as a concern with misrepresentations. For example, it does not make any sense to talk about knowledge of falsity by a person trading on undisclosed information. The insider does not accidentally or negligently trade. Perhaps the only issue of mistaken belief might arise if the insider thought that the information in question was already known to the public.

One sort of intent issue has arisen in a number of recent court decisions. The issue is whether it is necessary to show that the insider "used," rather than simply possessed, inside information at the time of the trade. By used, we mean that the information, at least in some part, motivated the insider to make the purchase or sale in question. Normally, as in *Chiarella*, *Dirks* and *O'Hagan*, it fairly obvious that the inside information motivated the defendant's trade. Occasionally, however, insiders might claim that they would have bought or sold the same amount of stock at the same time even if they did not know of the undisclosed inside information. A credible example of this occurs when the insider's transactions follow a predictable pattern which did not change upon the receipt of the information. The circuits have split upon the use versus possession issue.[155]

Resolution of the use versus possession issue depends on two arguments—one doctrinal, the other practical. The doctrinal argument is whether the breach of duty under either the classical or the misappropriation theories stems from merely possessing undisclosed inside information when one trades. The answer to this question is easy under the misappropriation theory. It is the use of the information that constitutes

155. *Compare* United States v. Smith, 155 F.3d 1051 (9th Cir.1998), *with* United States v. Teicher, 987 F.2d 112 (2d Cir. 1993).

a misappropriation. In other words, if O'Hagan would have bought the Pillsbury stock even without knowledge of the takeover, then no one can complain that he stole the inside information by trading on it. The doctrinal answer is more difficult in the case of the classical theory. We must ask why exactly a fiduciary relationship between insider and shareholder creates a duty to disclose. One possible answer is that it is unfair for the insider to use his or her superior access to information to profit at the expense of his or her beneficiary. If this is the rationale, then, as with misappropriation, logically if there is no use of the information, then there is no breach of duty. On the other hand, a rationale behind the common law requirement of full disclosure whenever parties in a fiduciary relationship transact business with each other is that parties in such a relationship of trust expect full disclosure of any material facts without having to ask. If this is the rationale for the classical theory in *Chiarella*, then the lack of use of the information is irrelevant.

The practical argument concerning the use versus possession issue involves the concern that it will be difficult to prove or disprove that inside information motivated a purchase or sale. Actually, looking at the reported cases of insider trading, in few of them does there appear to be much doubt on this score. Moreover, one Court of Appeals has adopted a sensible solution: This is to presume that the defendant used the inside information he or she possessed unless the defendant can prove to the contrary.[156] The mere fact that a defendant might already have been considering a transaction, or had independent reasons to undertake a transaction, hardly constitutes a showing of non-use; since, by definition, the possession of material information will impact a decision, if only to confirm a decision one was leaning toward but still might not have undertaken. About the only showing which could work would be the insider's adherence to some sort of long-standing autopilot approach to stock transactions.

b. Why is there anything wrong with trading on inside information?

Having explored what the law is regarding trading on inside information, let us turn to the question of what the law should be. In Heaven, the rule would be that one party to a proposed transaction always discloses material information unknown to the other side—in other words, there would be an equal information rule. This rule reflects the ideal that it is unfair to enter a transaction when a person knows that the other side might not make the same agreement if the other side knew all the facts. After all, the basis for what is fair or moral is avoiding conduct toward others to which one would object if done toward oneself, and most folks feel cheated by non-disclosure of material facts. Moreover, from the standpoint of economic efficiency (assuming this is a legitimate consideration in Heaven), the object is to promote transactions in which both sides feel better off for having made the deal based

---

156. SEC v. Adler, 137 F.3d 1325 (11th Cir.1998).

upon complete information. By contrast, transactions which simply shift wealth from one party (without information) to another party (who possesses information) seemingly represent a zero-sum game which produces nothing for the gross domestic product of Heaven. Accordingly, the twin considerations of fairness (or morality) and efficiency suggest an equal information rule for Heaven.

Earth, however, is not Heaven, and few here advocate an equal information rule. The problem is that information is both something of value to society and something which often takes work to produce. In order to encourage the production of information, presumably there must be some reward. This is why governments grant patents to inventors. An equal information rule, at least to some extent, undermines the incentives to search for undiscovered values obtainable from entering a transaction. After all, why bother to spend time searching for unappreciated reasons, say, to invest in a company, when one must disclose the information to the existing stockholders, who will charge more for the stock as a result? The facts in *Dirks* provide an extreme illustration of this point. Dirks worked as an investment analyst, which means that someone must pay Dirks to provide information about what stocks to buy or sell. If Dirks or his clients must immediately provide any material information to everyone in the market, what incentive does anyone have to pay Dirks, and what incentive does Dirks have to spend time investigating companies (including by helping uncover fraud)? Moreover, given the morality of the traditional work ethic, perhaps it is consistent with notions of fairness for individuals, who work to produce information, not to share this information with others who could have worked to obtain the information for themselves.

Suppose, however, a person does not gain knowledge by working hard to gather information available to anyone who puts in the effort, but rather obtains the knowledge because of some superior access. For example, in order to carry out their jobs, corporate officers, directors, and even employees have access to information concerning the corporation, which is not available to outsiders. Alternately, the superior access might consist simply of being in the right place at the right time to overhear a conversation.[157] In this event, there seems no reason—either in terms of creating incentives for gathering information, or in terms of fairness towards those who work to obtain something others could have—to allow individuals to trade on the information without disclosing the information to those who lack access. This notion leads one toward the equal access rule rejected by the Supreme Court in *Chiarella*.[158] The utilitarian version of the misappropriation theory set forth in Chief Justice Burger's dissent in *Chiarella* provides a variation on this rationale for an equal access rule: If the work employed to gather information consists of socially undesirable activities (say, burglary), then the law

157. *See* SEC v. Switzer, 590 F.Supp. 756 (W.D.Okla.1984).

158. For a noted article advocating an equal access rule, see Victor Brudney, *Insiders, Outsiders, and Informational Advantages under the Federal Securities Laws,* 93 Harv. L. Rev. 322 (1979).

need not reward the misappropriater by allowing him or her to profit from trading without disclosure. A major problem, however, with an equal access rule is defining when access is unequal (or when information was gathered in socially undesirable ways). For example, the investment insights of one with superior analytical abilities might not be available to those less gifted no matter how hard they try; yet few would argue for a duty to disclose in this situation. Similarly, the acquiring company's knowledge of its intent to make a premium price tender offer for stock in the target corporation reflects both facts open for discovery by anyone (whatever synergies or opportunities justify paying a premium price for control of the target), as well as a fact (the acquirer's subjective decision to make the offer) which is inaccessible to anyone outside of the acquiring company.

If one rejects (as the Supreme Court did) the idea that unequal access to information, in itself, justifies a duty to disclose, then the question becomes what, if any, policies are served, or undermined, by the Supreme Court requiring corporate insiders to disclose non-public information before trading. To say that there is a fiduciary relationship between the insider and the corporation's shareholders begs the question: Why should a fiduciary relationship lead to a duty to disclose?

One rationale for imposing on fiduciaries a duty to disclose flows from the concept that a fiduciary relationship involves trust between two parties. When parties in a relationship which involves such trust transact business with each other, they may expect that the other party will disclose any facts material to the transaction without needing to be asked. It is as if each party implicitly represents to the other party that "if there is anything you should know about this deal, I will tell you." When the fiduciary fails to disclose, this implicit representation becomes false.[159] Still, while this rationale might explain why there should be a duty to disclose when a corporate insider purchases shares from a current stockholder in a face-to-face transaction, it does not seem apropos to the impersonal market transactions involved in the vast majority of insider trading cases. A party who places an order with a broker for execution through a stock exchange or the like would be unaware that he or she is dealing with an insider. How can a party assert that he or she was trusting in the insider to disclose any material facts without being asked, when the party was unaware that he or she was trading with an insider?

An alternate rationale for forbidding insiders from trading on undisclosed inside information involves the unfairness of using information to the detriment of a person on whose behalf the fiduciary is supposed to act; especially if the reason the fiduciary received the information in the first place was to act for the benefit of the person against whom the fiduciary uses the information. Since corporate insiders receive informa-

---

159. There is, however, a certain degree of circularity to this sort of reasoning, since part of the reason for this trust is that the law traditionally has imposed an obligation on fiduciaries to disclose material facts.

tion from the corporation in order to act for the ultimate benefit of the corporation's shareholders and prospective shareholders, it seems unfair to allow corporate insiders to profit at the expense of the corporation's shareholders or prospective shareholders by exploiting the insider's informational advantage over the shareholders or prospective shareholders. Again, however, this rationale seems more persuasive in face-to-face dealings than in impersonal market transactions. The reason in this instance is not, however, because the participant in an impersonal market transaction is unaware that he or she is dealing with an insider. Rather, the problem is that in an impersonal market transaction, unlike face-to-face transactions, the party with whom the insider deals presumably would have dealt with someone else on no better terms if the insider had stayed out of the market.[160]

The analysis so far suggests that once the Supreme Court rejected the equal access approach, then the common law cases had it right, and the Supreme Court had it wrong, with respect to whether impersonal market trading by corporate officials with inside information should constitute fraud. Still, just as the fraud on the market theory recognized that the effect of a misrepresentation on traders in an active stock market as a whole could substitute for individualized reliance, so it is possible to argue that trading on inside information by corporate officials creates an unfair or fraudulent impact on the group of shareholders and prospective shareholders of the corporation when viewed as a whole.

To understand why the overall impact of trading on inside information by corporate officials might be considered unfair, let us return to the question of who is hurt when a corporate official trades on inside information. Needless to say, the profit the insider makes by purchasing stock before the market learns of good news must come from someplace (or the loss the insider avoids by selling stock before the market learns of bad news must go someplace else). As we just saw, the insider's profit (or avoided loss) does not necessarily come at the expense of the person(s) who traded with the insider. True, if the insider disclosed before trading, the person(s) who traded with the insider would not have made the same deal. If, however, the insider abstained from trading, then the person(s) who dealt with the insider simply would have traded with someone else. Notice this means that the effect of the insider's trading can be to displace another trader who otherwise would have made the purchase or sale the insider did. This displaced trader, in turn, displaces another trader, and so on, like a line of dominoes. One writer has labeled this phenomenon "The Law of Conservation of Securities."[161] The result is to push the displaced traders into slightly higher priced trades by the demand created through the insider's purchases, or into slightly lower priced trades by the supply created through the insider's sales, until the

160. Keep in mind that, while the party dealing with the insider may avoid poor trades if the insider discloses, the law does not require the insider to disclose if the insider refrains from trading in shares.

161. William Wang, *Trading on Material Nonpublic Information on Impersonal Stock Markets: Who Is Harmed, and Who Can Sue Whom Under SEC Rule 10b–5?*, 54 S. Calif. L. Rev. 1217 (1981).

last person who would have bought or would have sold the number of shares traded by the insider decides not to trade. Since all of these displaced traders—who, as a group, lost the profit the insider made, or incurred the loss the insider avoided—constitute shareholders or prospective shareholders, the effect of insider trading is to enrich the insider at the expense of those for whose benefit the insider received the inside information in the first place.

We also can argue that there is a an implicit misrepresentation involved when insiders trade without disclosure of material facts, even in impersonal market transactions. This argument is a variant on the fraud on the market theory: Insiders are fiduciaries of, and trusted by, the shareholders and prospective shareholders of the corporation as a group, and have implicitly represented to the shareholders and prospective shareholders as a group that the insiders will disclose any material inside information before trading. The market price of the corporation's stock presumably has impounded this representation, and shareholders and prospective shareholders purchase and sell stock in reliance on the assumption that either (1) the market price will reflect disclosure of all material facts known to insiders, or, (2) at least insiders, who cannot disclose inside information, will not use their information advantage to displace other traders from obtaining profits or avoiding losses.

There are a number of corollaries and counter arguments to both the fairness and the implicit misrepresentation arguments for prohibiting corporate officials from trading on undisclosed inside information. To begin with, the fairness argument ultimately comes down to the insiders obtaining more wealth, and the shareholders and prospective shareholders obtaining less wealth, by virtue of the insider's access to corporate information. Some writers have argued that there is nothing wrong with this.[162] After all, any compensation paid by the corporation to its officials has the ultimate effect of shifting wealth from shareholders to officials. Hence, one might argue that the ability to use corporate information is simply another form of compensation. Indeed, it might be an efficient form of compensation. It does not cost the corporation any dollars out-of-pocket, and rewards the insiders for developments (like striking copper) which cause the value of the corporation's stock to rise—which enriches the enterprise and all those who hold the stock. There are, however, a couple of problems with allowing use of inside information as a form of compensation to corporate officials. To begin with, allowing officials to sell their stock before disclosure of bad news enables officials to avoid the consequences of bad developments at the corporation—which does not seem to provide the best incentives. (Indeed, if insiders purchase "put" options, they could actually profit on bad corporate developments, which seems to be a perverse incentive.) Moreover, unlike a negotiated compensation package, allowing insiders to trade on corporate information means that each insider, within broad limits, essentially sets his or her own level of compensation by deciding how much he or she chooses

162. *E.g.*, Henry Manne, Insider Trading and the Stock Markets (1966).

to trade. Few business owners would agree to a compensation scheme which says to their employees "here is the cash drawer; help yourself to whatever you think you deserve."

Notice also that the implicit misrepresentation argument when dealing with impersonal market trading depends upon the market price for a corporation's stock reflecting the assumption that corporate officials either will disclose material inside information or else abstain from trading. Yet, just as one can rebut the fraud on the market presumption in the case of an affirmative misrepresentation by showing that participants in the market did not believe the misrepresentation, so one could point out that if participants in the market expect corporate officials to trade on undisclosed inside information, the price of corporate stock will reflect this expectation. In other words, if traders in the market expect that insiders regularly will exploit the insiders' information advantage to shift profits toward, and losses away from, the insiders, other traders will discount the price they are willing to pay for corporate stock to reflect this expectation. Accordingly, if the law explicitly allowed corporate officials to trade on undisclosed insider information, there would be no implicit misrepresentation reflected in the price of corporate stock. Perhaps this means that the appropriate rule is not one which prohibits corporate officials from trading on undisclosed inside information, but rather one which makes it clear that such officials are free to do so.

In fact, however, many writers have argued that the reaction of other traders in the market to corporate officials trading on undisclosed inside information provides the most persuasive justification for the federal securities laws to prohibit such insider trading.[163] The notion is that if investors discount the amount they are willing to pay for corporate stock to take into account the impact of corporate officials trading on inside information, then corporations face a higher cost to obtain capital. Notice how this rationale corresponds to an underlying concern behind the federal securities laws discussed earlier in this chapter: The decreased willingness of persons to invest in corporate stock because of fraud and lack of accurate information—or because of rampant trading on undisclosed inside information—might make it more difficult for enterprises to raise needed capital, and thereby undermine the general health of the economy.

While possessing a theoretical logic, there are a couple problems with this "market confidence" rationale. To begin with, if corporations desire to lower their cost of capital, perhaps the corporations simply can contract with their officials not to trade on undisclosed inside information, and advertise this restriction to the public. If corporations do not do this for themselves, why should the government worry about the companies' cost of capital? Yet, for such a self-help approach to work, the trading public must be convinced that the corporations will enforce the restriction—which is something that individual corporations may lack

---

163. *E.g.*, Joel Seligman, *The Reformulation of Federal Securities Law Concerning*   *Nonpublic Information*, 73 Geo. L.J. 1083 (1985).

both the willingness[164] and the ability[165] to do. A second problem with the market confidence rationale is empirical: Both the conventional wisdom, and considerable evidence, suggest that there is quite a bit of trading on undisclosed inside information going on.[166] Nevertheless, ample capital still seems to flow into the stock market.[167]

Reconciliation of the impact of trading on inside information and the broader goals of the federal securities laws raises other issues. Recall from the discussion earlier in this chapter that the basic philosophy of the federal securities laws is to bring information about corporations and securities to the market, thereby lowering the potential for fraud, increasing investor confidence, and allocating capital in an efficient manner. Trading by corporate officials on undisclosed inside information, and the prohibition of such trading, have an ambivalent impact on the flow of information to the market. At first glance, prohibiting trading on undisclosed inside information would seem to increase the flow of information to the market, because, if corporate officials wish to purchase or sell stock, they must disclose material facts to the public. Yet, the matter is not this simple. This is because corporate officials do not need to disclose material facts if they abstain from trading. Moreover, in many cases, corporate officials will not be able to disclose the information, because the interest of the corporation requires keeping the development secret.[168] This has led some writers to argue that trading on undisclosed inside information is actually a good thing.[169] Such trading, the argument runs, moves the price of a corporation's stock in a manner reflective of non-public information—higher upon undisclosed good news, and lower upon undisclosed bad news. In this way, non-public information ends up impounded in the price of stock, and so investors can have confidence that the price of stock reflects accurate information, and capital is allocated efficiently. Put differently, if one cannot have immediate disclosure, trading on inside information provides a second best solution. Yet, this effect of trading on inside information is clearly a second best solution to more prompt disclosure, since the impact of such trading on the market price will not be the same as full disclosure, and the lack of transparency to the process hardly seems likely to inspire investor confidence. Moreover, allowing insiders to profit from non-public information might create an incentive to delay disclosure (in order to allow the insiders time to trade). If so, the disadvantage of encouraging delay in disclosure could swamp any gains from impounding non-public information in the price of stock through insider trading.

---

164. Since those engaged in insider trading often are the persons in charge of the corporation.

165. Since corporations might not be as well placed to discover trading on undisclosed inside information as are the stock exchanges (who can monitor for suspicious trades).

166. *See, e.g.,* H. Nejat Seyhun, *The Effectiveness of the Insider–Trading Sanctions,* 35 J.L. & Econ. 149 (1992).

167. *But see* Demsetz, *Corporate Control, Insider Trading and Rates of Return,* 76 Amer. Econ. Rev. 313 (1986) (the stock market tends to discount the stocks of corporations whose insiders trade heavily).

168. For example, in *Basic,* the other party to the merger negotiation might have insisted that the negotiations be kept secret.

169. *E.g.,* Manne, *supra* note 162.

Having explored the policy arguments for limiting the ability of insiders to trade on non-public information concerning the corporations for which they work, what are the policy arguments for prohibiting the misappropriation of information regarding other companies? As explained earlier, the utilitarian theory used by Chief Justice Burger is a variation of the equal access rule, and follows from the policies for that rule discussed above. The sneaky theft theory adopted by the Supreme Court in *O'Hagan* reflects a different policy—this being to protect property rights in information. In fact, this approach treats information useful for stock trading as a sort of trade secret subject to federal protection. Why there should be a special federal protection against the sneaky misappropriation of information useful for stock trading is not entirely clear.

    c. *Sanctions for trading on inside information in violation of Rule 10b–5*

The observant reader may have noticed one interesting contrast between the cases we discussed dealing with Rule 10b–5 claims arising out of misrepresentations and the cases we discussed dealing with Rule 10b–5 claims based upon trading on inside information. While the misrepresentation cases were, for the most part, actions brought by private parties, the bulk of the trading on inside information cases were SEC enforcement actions or criminal prosecutions. The prevalence of SEC enforcement actions and criminal prosecutions against persons illegally trading on inside information serves to remind us that the primary enforcement mechanisms expressly provided for by the Securities Exchange Act are actions by the SEC, or, in the case of a wilful violations, criminal prosecutions.

Interestingly, the express penalties provided for by the Securities Exchange Act for violating Rule 10b–5 through trading on inside information are now greater than the penalties for violating Rule 10b–5 through misrepresentations. This disparity is the result of amendments to the statute in 1984 and 1988. These amendments resulted from a perception that the general enforcement provisions of the 1934 Act did not provide incentives sufficient to deter persons from illegally trading on inside information. Specifically, before 1984, the SEC could seek an injunction against future violations by a person caught engaging in illegal trading on inside information. Courts, under their general equitable powers, might even order those engaged in such illegal trading to disgorge any profits made—as the court did in *SEC v. Texas Gulf Sulfur Co.* Yet, neither of these consequences from an SEC action cause the illegal trader to be significantly worse off for having traded. As a result, a person faced with the opportunity to trade illegally on inside information might figure that he or she should give it a try, since he or she might not get caught, and, if he or she did get caught, the consequence simply would be to give up the profits made and be told not to do it again. Of course, this ignores the prospect of a criminal prosecution. Yet, the maximum fine provided before 1984 for violating Rule 10b–5, including by trading on inside information, was significantly smaller than the profits potentially available from such trading. This left only the prospect of a jail sentence as a real deterrence; yet imprisonment might seem a rather excessive penalty given the uncertain degree of moral culpability attached to trading on inside information.

In 1984, Congress added Section 21A to the Securities Exchange Act. This section empowers the SEC to seek a civil penalty for illegal trading on inside information of up to three times what the defendant made on the illegal trades.[170] In 1988, Congress amended Section 21A to extend potential liability to so-called controlling persons (such as employers) of parties who engage in illegal trading on inside information. Such a controlling person can be liable for a civil penalty up to the greater of $1 million or three times the illegal trader's profits, if either the controlling person knew or recklessly disregarded the fact that the illegal trader was likely to illegally trade or the controlling person failed to meet requirements which the 1988 amendments imposed on brokers to establish internal controls to protect against securities law violations.

The provisions in the Securities Exchange Act authorizing SEC enforcement actions and criminal prosecutions do not explain the relative scarcity of private actions for trading on inside information; indeed, Congress' decision to enhance the penalties specifically for unlawful trading on inside information may have been, in part, a reaction to, rather than the cause of, the lack of effective private actions. What then accounts for the lack of effective private actions against those trading on inside information—at least as compared with the numerous private Rule 10b–5 actions against those charged with misrepresentations? One critical difference lies in the problem of proving that the defendants' trading caused harm to private plaintiffs.

With misrepresentations, the plaintiff's action in reliance on the false statement normally provides the link between the false statement and the harm suffered by the plaintiff. It becomes conceptually more difficult to speak of reliance establishing the link between illegal act and harm to a private plaintiff when the violation of Rule 10b–5 involves non-disclosure, rather than a false or misleading statement. After all, how can a plaintiff rely on what is not disclosed to him or her?[171] An evident answer is for the plaintiff to assert that he or she would not have made the same trade had he or she known the fact(s) which the defendant did not disclose. Indeed, since the non-disclosed fact(s) must be material—or else there would be no violation of Rule 10b–5—it might make sense to presume that the plaintiff, more likely than not, would have acted differently had disclosure occurred. The Supreme Court

170. Since this penalty is in addition to disgorgement of profits, the illegal trader can end up paying four times his or her illegal profits. The 1984 amendments also increased the maximum criminal fine for violating the Securities Exchange Act from $10,000 to $100,000, while 1988 amendments increased the fine again from $100,- 000 to $1 million (and the possible jail time from 5 years to 10 years).

171. Along the same line, the market price of stock cannot reflect a false statement in the case in which the complaint is non-disclosure rather than misrepresentation.

seemingly adopted this sort of reasoning in *Affiliated Ute Citizens of Utah v. United States.*[172]

In *Affiliated Ute*, the defendants were employees of a bank which acted as the transfer agent for shares in the Ute Distribution Corporation. The Ute Distribution Corporation managed assets on behalf of the Ute tribe. So-called mixed-blood descendants of tribe members had received shares in the corporation. The defendants, either personally purchased, or arranged to have other non-tribe members purchase, shares from some descendants. The defendants did not tell the descendants that the defendants had developed a market in which non-Native–Americans were trading the shares at a higher price than received by the descendants. In reversing the Court of Appeals' decision that the plaintiffs had not proven reliance, the Supreme Court held that, in the case before it—"involving primarily a failure to disclose"—positive proof of reliance was not necessary.

It is easy to understand why a court essentially would presume reliance or causation in a case, such as *Affiliated Ute*, involving non-disclosure during face-to-face trading. Since the non-disclosed fact must be material, most plaintiffs can credibly claim they would have acted differently had the defendant disclosed the fact.[173] Had the defendants not traded (nor, as in *Affiliated Ute*, arranged the trading by others), then the plaintiffs probably also would not have purchased or sold—or, at least, the plaintiffs would have had an opportunity to make a fully informed trade with someone else.

Things become considerably more complicated, however, in the typical case involving non-disclosure during impersonal market trading. If a court focuses on the non-disclosure, then it is logical to presume, like *Affiliated Ute*, that reliance or causation exists, because disclosure of a material fact likely would have altered other traders' willingness to enter the transaction.[174] On the other hand, a person prohibited from trading on inside information would not violate Rule 10b–5, even without disclosure, if this person refrains from purchasing or selling the stock. Yet, if the person illegally trading on inside information had abstained from trading, the parties with whom this person dealt would have been no better off. This is because, as discussed earlier, ordinarily the parties who sold to or bought from the illegal trader through impersonal market transactions would have sold or bought anyway on no better terms had the illegal trader refrained from buying or selling.[175] Accordingly, if one

172. 406 U.S. 128, 92 S.Ct. 1456 (1972).

173. If, however, the defendant establishes that the plaintiff would have bought or sold even had there been disclosure—perhaps by showing that the plaintiff already knew the non-disclosed fact—then the defendant can defeat a finding of reliance or causation. *E.g., Shores v. Sklar,* 647 F.2d 462 (5th Cir.1981).

174. Alternately, using the fraud-on-the-market concept, one can presume that the market price would have reflected the disclosure, and, hence, even traders who never would have heard the disclosure still would not have traded on the same terms had the defendants disclosed.

175. We know this because, in an impersonal market trade, typically each party either has contacted a broker on his or her own initiative, or has traded at the suggestion of a broker who was not reacting to the defendant's order, and so the person who

focuses on the defendant's trading (as opposed to staying out of the market), then it becomes difficult to say that the defendant's illegal conduct caused any loss to the party who dealt with the defendant.

Further complicating the situation is the fact that it makes little practical or policy sense to limit private recovery, in the case of illegal trading on inside information through impersonal markets, only to the person(s) who actually traded with the defendant. From a practical standpoint, the person(s) who traded with the defendant through an impersonal market rarely will bring a lawsuit, for the reason that any individual who traded with the defendant is unlikely to learn that he or she traded with a party abusing inside information.[176] From a policy perspective, it seems unfair to award recovery among traders making almost identical trades on the basis of the random chance of whose buy or sell order happened to match up with the defendant's sell or buy order. Besides, if the theory of reliance or causation is that the plaintiff would not have made the same trade had there been disclosure, this will apply to all traders in the market who traded after the defendant would have made disclosure, and not just the person dealing with the defendant.[177] Following this logic, the class of plaintiffs who might claim that the defendant's non-disclosure caused them injury includes everyone who traded between the time of the defendant's transaction (when the defendant should have disclosed) and the ultimate disclosure of the facts in question.

These various considerations produced disagreement among the lower courts on the question of who could recover in a private action against defendants illegally trading on inside information through impersonal market transactions. In *Fridrich v. Bradford*,[178] the court refused to allow recovery by plaintiffs who had sold their shares during the time period between illegal purchases by a tippee (who had inside information about an impending merger), and the corporation's announcement of the merger. Not only did the court point out that the plaintiffs would have

dealt with the defendant still would have issued his or her order even if the defendant did not trade. Moreover, there are typically plenty of other traders in the market to take the defendant's place if the defendant did not issue a purchase or sell order. An exception to the conclusion that the party dealing with the defendant still would have traded even if the defendant stayed out of the market might exist, however, if trading by the defendant(s) is so extensive as to move the price, and this price move induced the party dealing with the defendant to enter the market.

176. This is a function of search costs and incentives. Specifically, one would need to search trading records to determine who traded with the person abusing inside information. From the standpoint of any individual trader who happens to hear of the illegal trading, the odds of being the person

who traded with the insider might be sufficiently small so as to discourage making the effort to investigate whether one happens to be the lucky potential plaintiff. From the standpoint of attorneys who might wish to inform prospective clients of the potential for a suit (despite obvious ethics concerns), a recovery measured only by the losses of those who traded with the insider might not be large enough to justify searching for these traders.

177. After all, as a practical matter, the defendant only could have disclosed through a public announcement, because there is little way for the defendant to have made a targeted disclosure just to the person at the other end of an impersonal market trade.

178. 542 F.2d 307 (6th Cir.1976).

traded on no better terms had the tippee abstained from trading, but the court worried about the draconian amount of liability which the tippee would have faced if the court allowed recovery.[179] Other courts have allowed recovery by persons who would have avoided poor trades if the defendant had disclosed inside information before buying or selling. These courts, however, have sought to prevent the potential for draconian damage awards by limiting recovery to those who traded around the same time as the defendants,[180] and by limiting the total damages to the amount of the defendants' profits.[181]

Congress liked the compromise idea of those courts which had allowed recovery, but had limited recovery to prevent draconian damage awards. As a result, Congress amended the Securities Exchange Act in 1988 by adding Section 20A. Section 20A creates an express private cause of action against persons who violate the 1934 Act by trading on inside information. To take advantage of this cause of action, the plaintiff must have purchased "contemporaneously" with a defendant who illegally sold using inside information, or else the plaintiff must have sold "contemporaneously" with a defendant who illegally bought using inside information.[182] Section 20A limits the total recovery in favor of all plaintiffs bringing an action pursuant to the section to the total of the profits the defendant made (or the loss the defendant avoided) by virtue of the illegal trades (less any payment already made by the defendant pursuant to Section 21A).

Congress had a second motivation in enacting Section 20A. As discussed earlier, the sneaky theft misappropriation theory conceives of trading on misappropriated information as a fraud upon the party from whom the defendant obtained the information, not upon the party with whom the defendant trades. Moreover, the defendant's fraud consists of misappropriating the information by trading, not in the failure to disclose the information before trading.[183] Under this logic, as mentioned earlier, neither the party with whom the misappropriater trades, nor other traders in the market who would have acted differently had there been disclosure, have a claim under Rule 10b–5 against the party trading on misappropriated information. The legislative history of Section 20A indicates, however, that Congress saw things differently. Hence, Section 20A allows contemporaneous traders to sue those who violate Rule 10b–5 by trading on inside information, apparently even if the violation is based upon the misappropriation theory.

179. Since the trading occurred in April, and the disclosure took place in June, the defendants could have faced potential liability—if all the sellers during the period sued—of around $3.7 million, whereas the tippee had made a profit of only $13,000 on his purchase.

180. See, e.g., Shapiro v. Merrill Lynch, Pierce, Fenner & Smith, Inc., 495 F.2d 228 (2d Cir.1974).

181. E.g., Elkind v. Liggett & Myers, Inc., 635 F.2d 156 (2d Cir.1980).

182. Contemporaneously probably means not more than a few days apart from the defendant's purchases. See, e.g., Neubronner v. Milken, 6 F.3d 666 (9th Cir. 1993).

183. Indeed, such a disclosure of information intended to be kept confidential would itself constitute a misappropriation.

Incidentally, the 1984 and 1988 amendments to the Securities Exchange Act make it clear that Congress believed that, at least under some circumstances, trading on inside information violates Rule 10b–5 and Section 10(b)—otherwise enacting these penalty provisions makes no sense. Congress, however, refused to define when trading on inside information violates Rule 10b–5 or Section 10(b). Instead, Sections 20A and 21A simply create penalties and private causes of action when there is trading in violation of any provision in the Securities Exchange Act.

d.   Disclosure duties of those who do not trade

So far, we have asked when does trading on undisclosed inside information violate Rule 10b–5. Suppose, however, the party who possesses material information unknown to others does not purchase or sell stock (nor pass the information on for anyone else to purchase or sell stock). In this event, can non-disclosure constitute fraud in violation of Rule 10b–5?

While the Supreme Court has never directly addressed this question, the implication of Supreme Court opinions is that non-disclosure by a party not trading in stock (or tipping others to trade) will not, as a general proposition, constitute fraud in violation of Rule 10b–5. To begin with, it would see rather silly for the Supreme Court, in decisions such as *Chiarella* and *Dirks*, to speak of an insider's duty either to disclose material non-public information or else abstain from trading, if there is a duty to disclose material non-public information even if one does not trade. Moreover, since the classical theory in *Chiarella* and *Dirks* bases the disclose *or abstain* obligation upon the insider's fiduciary relationship to the corporation's shareholders, the existence of a fiduciary relationship would not appear to create a disclosure obligation in the absence of trading. If a fiduciary relationship does not create a general disclosure obligation for those who do not trade, it is not clear what else could.

The Supreme Court's opinion in the *Basic* case discussed earlier reinforces the view that non-disclosure in the absence of trading generally is not a violation of Rule 10b–5. In *Basic*, the defendants argued that the test for determining whether the corporation's false denials of merger discussions were material should take into account business reasons for keeping merger discussions confidential. The court rejected this need for secrecy argument as going to the corporation's duty to disclose, but inapposite to the question of materiality. The court also noted that silence, absent a duty to disclose, is not misleading under Rule 10b–5. These comments by the court would not make much sense if corporations had a general duty to disclose any material facts to their shareholders.

There are sound policy reasons to reject an interpretation of Rule 10b–5 under which mere possession of material information would trigger a disclosure obligation for those who do not trade stock—even if the person in possession of material information is the corporation or another party with a fiduciary relationship to the corporation's share-holders. To begin with, if possession of material information triggers such a general disclosure obligation, then the Supreme Court's refusal in *Basic* to consider a bright line test for materiality becomes much more questionable. After all, it is one thing to tell corporate managers, who are uncertain as to whether an event is material, that they can always keep silent and abstain from trading; it is quite a different matter to refuse to provide workable guidance if the corporation is supposed to announce developments as soon as they become material.[184] Moreover, a rule which required corporations to disclose events when the events became material would need exceptions for situations in which there are legitimate business reasons not to disclose. Such reasons might include the need for secrecy (as in *Basic*) or the need to double check on the accuracy of information before disclosure.[185] A court which created a general disclosure obligation subject to a legitimate business reasons exception, in turn, would need to address the question of how much deference to give to the corporation's directors' assessment as to the business reason for non-disclosure. Application of a highly deferential business judgment rule could produce results little different from not having a general disclosure obligation at all. Greater scrutiny of deci-sions by directors not to disclose could produce excessive paranoia in board rooms every time some material event occurs in the corporation. Finally, and most significantly, interpreting Rule 10b–5 to create a general disclosure obligation would be inconsistent with the overall scheme of the securities laws. After all, why have specific affirmative disclosure obligations under other sections of the securities laws, if Rule 10b–5 obligates corporations automatically to disclose any material fact?

If non-disclosure in the absence of trading generally does not violate Rule 10b–5, are there any circumstances in which non-disclosure without trading can violate the rule? As discussed in dealing with misrepresenta-tions and Rule 10b–5, omissions to state material facts violate Rule 10b–5 when the omitted facts render statements made misleading. In a couple of circumstances, courts have been quite expansive in the courts' willingness to tie together omissions with statements in order to find violations of Rule 10b–5.

One circumstance in which courts have stretched the notion that an omission violates Rule 10b–5 if the omission makes a statement mislead-ing involves the duty to correct prior statements made by the corpora-tion. There are two variations on this theme. The first occurs when the corporation made a statement which was false at the time the corpora-tion made the statement, but the corporation (or, more realistically, the corporate officials responsible for making the statement) did not know

---

184. While boards of corporations with stock listed for trading on the national stock exchanges live with exchange require-ments for prompt disclosure of material events, the consequences of misjudging when an event becomes material is much less severe when the question is one of compliance with listing requirements than it is when the outcome could be corporate liability in a class action under Rule 10b–5.

185. *E.g.*, Financial Industrial Fund, Inc. v. McDonnell Douglas Corp., 474 F.2d 514 (10th Cir.1973).

the statement was false—which means the statement did not violate Rule 10b–5 due to lack of scienter. If the corporation (through its officials) later learns of the mistake, courts have held that the failure to issue a corrective disclosure violates Rule 10b–5—at least if the statement is still material to investors.[186]

A more difficult problem occurs if the corporation's statement was correct at the time the corporation made the statement, but later events render the statement no longer accurate. Here, some courts have held that the corporation has a duty to update the statement.[187] On the other hand, a general duty to update statements when subsequent facts render the statements no longer accurate could turn into a general disclosure obligation every time material events occur in the life of the corporation. After all, business circumstances are constantly changing such that an accurate snapshot of the corporation's business one day is obsolete the next. Hence, prospective plaintiffs seemingly might always be able to find some statement by the corporation which later events have rendered obsolete. Moreover, corporate statements typically do not become misleading by virtue of later events, because reasonable investors understand statements to speak to the situation at the time the statement is made. There is, however, one exception to such an understanding. This is when a statement offers a prediction of future events. Following this logic, the Court of Appeals in *Backman v. Polaroid Corp.*,[188] held that corporations only have a duty to update so-called forward looking statements (in other words, predictions of future earnings and the like) which subsequently turn out to be mistaken. In any case, determining whether subsequent events have rendered earlier statements no longer accurate often can present a difficult issue.[189]

Another circumstance in which some courts seem willing to take an expansive view of when non-disclosure renders statements false involves the need to correct rumors or other market chit-chat. In this circumstance, the underlying issue is whether statements nominally made by other persons somehow become statements by the corporation, thereby creating a duty for the corporation to correct, or otherwise to disclose, in order to prevent such statements from being misleading. There are several possibilities for attributing rumors or market chit-chat to the corporation. One is if the rumors come from corporate personnel.[190] Another possibility is if corporate officials have involved themselves in

---

186. *E.g.*, Backman v. Polaroid Corp., 910 F.2d 10 (1st Cir.1990). It hardly seems too much to ask that a corporation, which learns of its mistake, should correct false statements still being relied upon by investors. Of course, if, by the time corporate officials learn of the mistake, reasonable investors no longer care about the statement, then there is not much point to issuing a correction.

187. *E.g.*, Greenfield v. Heublein, Inc., 742 F.2d 751 (3d Cir.1984).

188. 910 F.2d 10 (1st Cir.1990).

189. *See, e.g.,* In re Time Warner, Inc. Securities Litig., 9 F.3d 259 (2d Cir.1993).

190. *See* State Teachers Retirement Board v. Fluor Corp., 654 F.2d 843 (2d Cir.1981). On the other hand, basic notions of agency suggest that corporations should not be responsible for rumors, even if the rumors come from corporate personnel, unless one can say that the personnel spread the rumors in the scope of their employment.

discussions with stock analysts to such an extent that mistakes in an analyst's report concerning the corporation can be attributed to the corporation.[191] An extreme possibility would lie in a notion that investors might interpret silence from the corporation in the face of rumors or stock analysts' reports as confirmation of the rumors or the reports. Unless the corporation did something to encourage such an interpretation, however, it is difficult to blame the corporation for, or require the corporation to respond to, investors' interpretations.

6.3.3 Breaches of Fiduciary Duty as Fraud: The Attempt to Use Rule 10b–5 to Federalize Corporate Law

Before 1977, it appeared that the greatest impact of Rule 10b–5 might not lie in pursuing misrepresentations inducing investors to purchase or sell stock, or in attacking trading on inside information—not that these two areas were not highly important before 1977. Rather, there appeared to be an even more dramatic use of the rule, this being to federalize a significant portion of corporate law. Specifically, for few years, it appeared that Rule 10b–5 provided the basis to bring a federal cause of action against corporate directors and controlling shareholders who breached their duty of loyalty, so long as one could connect this breach in some loose manner to a purchase or sale of a security.

The Court of Appeals decision in *Schoenbaum v. Firstbrook*,[192] illustrates this possibility. This was a derivative suit by a minority shareholder of an oil company against the controlling shareholder and the directors of the company. The complaint alleged that the directors had the oil company issue additional stock to the controlling shareholder at an unfairly low price. The court held that this conduct could constitute fraud in connection with the sale of a security.

Interestingly, it was the Supreme Court, itself, which added significant fuel to this potential use of Rule 10b–5. In *Superintendent of Insurance v. Bankers Life & Casualty Co.*,[193] the Supreme Court confronted your basic corporate looting. An insurance company owned some treasury bonds. A certain Mr. Begole bought all of the insurance company's stock from Bankers Life. Begole then had the insurance company sell the bonds so that Begole could use the proceeds essentially to pay Bankers Life for the stock. The Supreme Court held that this constituted fraud in connection with the purchase or sale of a security (the treasury bonds). Where was the fraud? Well, not surprisingly, Begole did not tell the directors of the insurance company, who approved the insurance company's sale of the treasury bonds, that he intended to steal the proceeds; instead Begole told the directors that he intended to have the company reinvest the money in a certificate of deposit. Moreover, the Supreme Court treated this fraud as being in connection with the sale of a security, even though the fraud had nothing to do with the treasury bonds, but rather involved what Begole intended to do with the proceeds

191. Elkind v. Liggett & Myers, Inc., 635 F.2d 156 (2d Cir.1980).

192. 405 F.2d 215 (2d Cir.1968).

193. 404 U.S. 6, 92 S.Ct. 165 (1971).

of their sale. While the Court's opinion stated that Congress in Section 10(b) did not seek to regulate transactions which "constitute nothing more than internal corporate mismanagement," the Court's opinion is also full of language as to how the disregard of trust relationships by fiduciaries is all part of a seamless web with manipulation and the like.

A few years later, the Supreme Court took much of the wind out of the sails of this use of Rule 10b–5. This occurred in *Santa Fe Industries, Inc. v. Green.*[194] Santa Fe Industries owned 95 percent of the stock in Kirby Lumber Corp. Pursuant to Delaware's corporation statute, Santa Fe undertook a "short-form" merger which cashed out the minority shareholders of Kirby Lumber, including Green. As we shall discuss in a later chapter, in a short-form merger under Delaware law, there is no stockholder vote, and the only recourse for a removed minority stockholder is to seek payment of the fair value of the minority stockholder's shares as set by a court supervised appraisal. Green, however, brought an action in federal court seeking to set aside the merger as a violation of Rule 10b–5. Specifically, Green claimed that Santa Fe had obtained a "fraudulent" valuation of Kirby Lumber's stock in order to justify paying an inadequate price for the stock in the merger, and that this conduct constituted a device or scheme to defraud the minority shareholders. In an opinion which would have had tremendous implications, the Second Circuit thought that this complaint stated a claim under Rule 10b–5. Critically, the Second Circuit did not base its acceptance of the complaint upon any deception of the minority shareholders—since the corporation fully disclosed to the minority shareholders the facts upon which Green based his attack on the so-called fraudulent valuation. Instead, the Second Circuit equated a controlling shareholder's breach of fiduciary duty (by treating the minority unfairly) to fraud. The Supreme Court, however, would have none of this and reversed the Second Circuit. Rather, according to the Supreme Court, to constitute fraud in violation of Rule 10b–5 and Section 10(b), there must be some misrepresentation, non-disclosure, or conduct which in some other manner is deceptive.

Actually, the Second Circuit's decision in *Santa Fe* was not as far out as it sounds. As we have seen elsewhere, it is not that unusual for state courts to refer to unfair conflict-of-interest transactions as "fraud."[195] Moreover, the Second Circuit's decision coincided with renewed criticism of Delaware's role in leading a "race to the bottom" in the protections accorded to minority shareholders from unfair actions by those in control of the corporation.[196] One way to impede such a race is to use Rule 10b–5 as the springboard to develop federal standards for the protection of minority shareholders. Still, one must ask how far courts should go in expanding the reach of a rule whose original purpose was to stop a corporation's president from lying in order to buy securities on the cheap. It is unlikely that Congress in enacting Section 10(b), or the

194. 430 U.S. 462, 97 S.Ct. 1292 (1977).   **196.** See § 1.2.3 *supra.*
195. See § 4.3.5 *supra.*

SEC in adopting Rule 10b–5, meant to create the basis for a federal law of corporate fiduciary duty.

In any event, the Supreme Court's decision in *Santa Fe*, itself, introduced considerable uncertainty into this area. This is because the scope of the decision is open to dispute. A final portion of the Court's opinion—from which a couple of justices, in concurring opinions, pointedly distanced themselves—suggests that Rule 10b–5 should not intrude on areas of corporate governance traditionally regulated by state law. Under this language, Rule 10b–5 should not reach transactions involving breaches of fiduciary duty by majority shareholders and corporate directors, where state corporate law traditionally provides a remedy. By contrast, in its actual holding, the Supreme Court only addressed the question of whether unfair transactions could equal fraud when the plaintiff is unable to claim any harm based upon false statements or non-disclosure. If one confines *Santa Fe* to this actual holding, then Rule 10b–5 actions are still available in situations in which majority shareholders or corporate directors have breached their fiduciary duties in transactions involving stock, so long as one can find some misrepresentation or non-disclosure.

In fact, a number of lower court decisions have followed the narrow interpretation of *Santa Fe* in order to allow Rule 10b–5 claims based upon conflict-of-interest transactions involving the purchase or sale of stock. For example, in *Goldberg v. Meridor*,[197] the Court of Appeals for the Second Circuit confronted a situation much like it had earlier faced in *Schoenbaum*. The court held that the parent corporation had violated Rule 10b–5 in a transaction in which the subsidiary issued shares to the parent for inadequate consideration. The key, according to the court, was that Goldberg's complaint alleged the parent had failed to disclose, or had made a misleading disclosure of, material facts about the transaction to the minority shareholders.

Decisions such as *Goldberg* raise a number of issues. To begin with, who exactly is the victim of the misrepresentation or non-disclosure by the controlling shareholder or defendant directors? In *Superintendent of Insurance*, Begole lied to the corporation's directors, and thereby defrauded the corporation. In *Santa Fe*, the plaintiff unsuccessfully tried to argue that defendants directed a misrepresentation or non-disclosure at the minority shareholders in order to lull the minority shareholders into forgoing their rights; hence, had there been a misrepresentation or material non-disclosure, the minority shareholders would have been the victims of the fraud. *Goldberg* straddles these two concepts. As in *Superintendent of Insurance*, the fraud was upon the subsidiary corporation, since it was the subsidiary corporation which received inadequate consideration for stock issued to the parent. Yet, there was no misrepresentation to any members of the subsidiary's board, since they were all fully aware of the facts, and, indeed, were all part of the conspiracy to victimize the subsidiary. Instead, the court found that the corporation

---

197.　567 F.2d 209 (2d Cir.1977).

was defrauded by the non- or misleading disclosure to the minority shareholders.[198] Incidentally, since the defendants in *Goldberg* defrauded the corporation when the corporation sold shares in itself, the plaintiff shareholder could bring a derivative suit on behalf of the corporation despite the fact that the plaintiff shareholder did not purchase or sell stock, and, hence, the plaintiff shareholder would have no standing to bring a Rule 10b–5 lawsuit on his own behalf.

The prospect that a minority shareholder, like Goldberg, might bring a lawsuit claiming that misrepresentations or non-disclosure aimed at the minority shareholders served to defraud the corporation, raises the question of how does the plaintiff show a causal link between the false statement (or non-disclosure) and the harm of which he or she complains? In a situation in which the minority shareholder claims that the shareholders were duped in voting for essential approval of the transaction, then causation is straightforward. Indeed, in this situation, the plaintiff might also have a claim under Rule 14a–9 for a misleading proxy solicitation. A problem, however, arises when, as in *Goldberg*, and as in *Santa Fe*, the defendant is a controlling shareholder who does not need the minority shareholders' votes (or else the matter requires only board action and not a vote of the shareholders). Recall that this same sort of causation question arose in dealing with misleading proxy solicitations by a majority shareholder in *Virginia Bankshares*.[199] In *Goldberg*, the court found causation based upon the notion that, with full disclosure, the minority shareholders could have sued to enjoin the transaction.[200] Many times, however, the situation is such that the misrepresentation or non-disclosure rendered the minority shareholders no worse off in terms of bringing a state court action. Perhaps, as in *Virginia Bankshares*, the minority shareholders still would have had a viable state claim despite whatever action the shareholders took in reliance on the misleading statement. Alternately, the minority shareholders might not have been able to enjoin the merger even if they knew the truth. This might be the case because the statute, like the short-form merger statute in *Santa Fe*, limits the remedies of the minority shareholder; or because the minority shareholders would have lost on the merits in arguing that the transaction in question was unfair. This latter prospect, in turn, raises the question of whether the plaintiff must show that he or she actually would have prevailed had the misleading disclosure not caused the plaintiff to delay instituting a state action—a question upon

---

198. Curiously, the court stated that the test for determining the materiality of the facts misstated or not disclosed to the shareholders is whether the facts would have been important to a reasonable and disinterested *director* in voting upon the transaction. In a later opinion, the Second Circuit clarified that non-disclosure to the shareholders does not constitute a fraud on the corporation if the transaction in question does not require shareholder approval, and if the transaction receives approval from fully informed disinterested directors who constitute a majority of the board. Maldonado v. Flynn, 597 F.2d 789 (2d Cir. 1979).

199. See § 3.2.2e *supra*.

200. Some other lower Federal courts have rejected this sort of causation as addressing issues beyond the purposes of the securities law. *E.g.*, Isquith v. Caremark International, 136 F.3d 531 (7th Cir.1998).

which lower courts are in disagreement.[201] Regardless of this disagreement, notice that a critical aspect of the *Goldberg* approach to causation is to make the plaintiff's case depend upon state law standards for fiduciary duty, since such standards dictate whether the shareholders would have been able to stop the defendant's action had the shareholders received accurate disclosure. Hence, the highly significant result of *Santa Fe*, even as interpreted by cases such as *Goldberg*, is, for better or worse, to eliminate the prospect that Rule 10b–5 could serve as a source of federal standards of substantive fiduciary duty which would trump lax laws in some states.[202]

§ 6.4 Other Federal Laws Dealing with Trading on Inside Information

In the prior section, we spent considerable time addressing the question of when trading on undisclosed inside information violates Section 10(b) of the 1934 Securities Exchange Act and Rule 10b–5 promulgated by the Securities Exchange Commission pursuant to Section 10(b). This is because Rule 10b–5 provides the primary law currently used to address trading on undisclosed inside information. Nevertheless, a number of other federal laws deal with trading on inside information—as witnessed by the fact that in several of the cases we discussed in the prior section, the government charged the defendant with violating federal laws in addition to Rule 10b–5 and Section 10(b). Indeed, when Congress enacted the 1934 Securities Exchange Act, Congress meant the Act to attack trading on inside information; yet, Section 10(b) was not the tool Congress had in mind for this task. Rather, this role was supposed to fall to Section 16 of the Act.

201. *Compare* Kidwell ex rel. Penfold v. Meikle, 597 F.2d 1273 (9th Cir.1979) (must show would have succeeded in the suit), *with* Healey v. Catalyst Recovery, 616 F.2d 641 (3d Cir.1980) (must show reasonable probability of success), *and with* Alabama Farm Bureau Mutual Cas. Co. v. American Fidelity Life Ins. Co., 606 F.2d 602 (5th Cir.1979) (only must show a reasonable basis for relief under state law).

202. The reader may be struck by an apparent inconsistency between this discussion of breach of fiduciary duty as a violation of Rule 10b–5, and the earlier discussion of the impact of fiduciary relationships on the legality of trading on inside information. The simple answer is that the Supreme Court has held that a breach of fiduciary duty, in itself, does not constitute fraud, but the existence of a fiduciary relationship can turn non-disclosure of material information, or trading on information received in confidence, into fraud. Moreover, there is nothing logically, or from a policy matter, inconsistent with stating that the existence of relationships of trust (in other words, fiduciary relationships), as defined under federal standards, can create a duty to disclose which will turn silence into fraud, and, at the same time, holding that Rule 10b–5 cannot reach arguable breaches of fiduciary duty based solely upon substantive unfairness in fully disclosed transactions. In the former case, the concern lies in asymmetries in information—the central concern of the securities laws—whereas, in the latter case, the concern lies only in the abuse of power, which, in itself, is not the general concern of the securities laws. Still, it is a little more difficult to say where the abuse of a fiduciary relationship entailed by misappropriating information logically fits in this analysis. If one focuses solely on the theft of information, then the misappropriation theory appears to be an attempt to use Rule 10b–5 as a device to police substantive fiduciary duty, contrary to the rationale of *Santa Fe*. On the other hand, the *O'Hagan* rationale is that a fraudulent silence exists in the fiduciary's failure to disclose his or her intent to misuse information given in confidence—which is not dissimilar from the rationale in *Superintendent of Insurance*.

6.4.1 Section 16

In Section 16 of the 1934 Securities Exchange Act, Congress used a moderately blunt instrument to attack trading on inside information. To understand Congress' thinking, it is helpful to consider several approaches the law might use to deter unfair trading on undisclosed inside information.[1]

Rule 10b–5 follows what one might label a scalpel approach to the problem. Prosecution under Rule 10b–5 requires proof that an individual, who had a duty not to do so, made specific trades while in possession of material non-public information. In 1934, Congress believed that proving abuse of information in specific trades would be so difficult as to render the scalpel approach infeasible. The subsequent use of Rule 10b–5 to prosecute numerous trading on inside information cases suggests that Congress was unduly pessimistic about the scalpel approach. Still, the fact that studies have shown corporate insiders generally out perform the market in the insiders' dealing with their own corporations' stocks[2] indicates that Congress was not totally wrong. The very fact that corporate insiders generally buy low and sell high in dealing with their own corporations' stocks suggests that insiders commonly must possess material (at least in an economic sense) information about their companies not shared by other participants in the market. Nevertheless, for practical reasons, Rule 10b–5 prosecutions typically only involve trading on inside information concerning dramatic developments—for the most part, takeovers and highly significant earnings announcements—rather than the more subtle sorts of inside information which often may allow insiders to optimally time their trades.

At the other extreme, the law could take a sledgehammer approach to the problem. This would be to prohibit insiders, such as officers and directors, from trading in their own corporations' stocks. Many law firms adopt this sort of approach as a matter of internal ethics by adopting firm policies prohibiting lawyers in the firm from owning stock in corporate clients. The problem, however, with the law prohibiting officers and directors of corporations from buying and selling stock in their corporations is that this could create strong disincentives for officers and directors to own stock in their companies. After all, even if the law made an exception to such a no purchase or sale rule to allow officers and directors to buy stock from the corporation under certain controlled conditions, how much stock will officers and directors want to own they cannot resell it? Yet, the general view is that the law should encourage, not discourage, officers and directors owning stock in their corporations. Such stock ownership gives officers and directors an incentive to manage their corporations in the interests of the stockholders.

Section 16 takes a middle approach between these two extremes—a sort of moderately blunt instrument. The idea is to identify a category of

---

§ 6.4

1. This assumes that at least some such trading is unfair and should be deterred.

2. *E.g.*, H. Nejat Seyhun, *The Effectiveness of the Insider–Trading Sanctions*, 35 J.L. & Econ. 149 (1992).

transactions in which the abuse of inside information seems likely. Moreover, since some of the transactions in this category might be innocent, one would not wish to prohibit such transactions. Instead, by forcing insiders to give up any profits the insiders make in this category of transactions, the law could deter abuse of inside information, without either the proof problem entailed in the scalpel approach, or the problem of substantially deterring insiders from owning stock in their corporations as under the sledgehammer approach.

The category of transactions identified by Section 16 in which the abuse of inside information seems likely is when corporate insiders (as defined by the statute) purchase and, within six months, sell, or sell and, within six months, purchase, stock in a corporation. The supposition is that individuals trading on inside information would not wish to hold stock for over six months after a purchase motivated by inside information (or refrain from repurchasing stock for over six months after a sale motivated by inside information), since, during the six month period, the insider risks changes in the market or with the corporation eliminating the profit achieved by the initial trade. Such purchases and sales, or sales and purchases, within a six month period commonly are referred to as short-swing trades. Section 16(b) provides that officers, directors, and owners of over 10 percent of the stock of a corporation which is required to register under the 1934 Act must give to their corporation any profits they make on short-swing trades of stock of their corporation. Section 16(a) aids in the enforcement of Section 16(b) by requiring the designated insiders to file public reports of their purchases and sales of stock in their corporations.[3]

Actually, the supposition that removing profits from short-swing trades is likely to deter abuse of inside information seems questionable. All an insider must do to avoid the impact of Section 16(b) is to hold stock over six months after the purchase (or not repurchase stock in the corporation less than six months after one has sold). True, the insider is at risk that subsequent market changes could wipe out some of the insider's gains—or, if the market changes too much, the insider may need to make an offsetting trade within six months and forgo all of his or her profits from the initial trade. Yet, how often is such a dramatic change in the market going to occur? Hence, the principal impact of Section 16(b) may be simply to create something of a trap for insiders who engage in short-swing trades (perhaps because of the insiders' ignorance of the section, or because of some independent compelling factor behind the trades). Of course, since the only consequence of

---

3. The reporting requirements of Section 16(a) reach transactions which would not produce liability under Section 16(b), which suggests that Section 16(a) serves a disclosure function—giving the market an idea of what insiders are up to—beyond simply easing the enforcement of Section 16(b). Section 16(c) reaches a second type of transaction in which one might suspect the use of inside information. Section 16(c) pro-

hibits short-selling (in other words, entering a contract to sell stock ones does not yet own) by designated insiders. Short selling provides a mechanism whereby a person who anticipates a stock's price to decline can make a profit. Section 16(d) and Section 16(e) exempt from liability under Section 16(b) certain market maker and arbitrage transactions.

Section 16(b) is to give up the insiders' profits, the result is hardly the end of the world for those ensnared in the trap. Nevertheless, Section 16(b) has generated considerable litigation to clarify ambiguities as to the scope of the statute—which makes one wonder whether Section 16(b) was really worth the candle.[4]

One area in which there has been considerable litigation under Section 16(b) involves questions about who the section reaches. Section 16(b), read in conjunction with Section 16(a), states that it reaches officers and directors of corporations which have a class of equity securities (stock) registered pursuant to Section 12 of the 1934 Act, and owners of more than 10 percent of the outstanding shares of any class of stock which is so registered. As discussed earlier in this chapter, Section 12 of the 1934 Act requires corporations to register classes of stock which are listed for trading on a national exchange, or held by over 500 persons (so long as the corporation has at least $10 million in assets). Hence, Section 16(b), like the proxy rules under Section 14(a), and very much *un*like Section 10(b) and Rule 10b–5, only reaches a limited universe of publicly traded corporations.

While the specification of which corporations Section 16 reaches is straightforward, the determination of who is an officer, director, or owner of over 10 percent of the stock of such corporations sometimes leads to questions. Take the subject of who is an officer for purposes of Section 16. As discussed earlier in this book, there is no generally accepted demarcation under state corporation law separating when an individual is a corporate "officer" versus just an executive employee. For example, while one might normally assume that a vice president is a corporate officer, some corporations (like banks and brokerage firms) hand out the title willy nilly. This fact led the court in *Merrill Lynch, Pierce, Fenner & Smith, Inc. v. Livingston*,[5] to adopt a test for determining whether an individual is an officer for purposes of Section 16, which the court geared to the purposes of the section. Specifically, the test is whether the individual has the sort of executive responsibilities or decision-making authority likely to give the individual access to inside information of corporate-wide significance (as opposed to the narrower sort of inside information accessible to corporate employees in general). An interpretive rule adopted by the Securities Exchange Commission in 1991 similarly tests officer status by whether an individual has a policy-making function.[6]

By contrast, the position of director has a well defined meaning. Even here, however, questions can arise under Section 16. Specifically, a court occasionally may decide that persons, who are themselves not officially on the board of directors, might nevertheless be directors

---

4. Because Section 16(b) only questionably serves the policy of preventing trading on inside information, some writers have suggested that the section serves other purposes, such as discouraging corporate insiders from manipulating corporate events in order produce sharp swings in stock prices.

E.g., Report of the Task Force on Regulation of Insider Trading, Part II: Reform of Section 16, 42 Bus. Law. 1087, 1089–92 (1987).

5. 566 F.2d 1119 (9th Cir.1978).

6. Sec. Exch. Act. Rule 16a–1(f).

within the meaning of Section 16. This might occur when a person (including a firm) delegates an individual to sit on the board as the person's representative.[7]

Questions also can arise about who is an owner of more than 10 percent of the outstanding shares of any class of a corporation's registered stock. For example, suppose a party owns corporate bonds which are convertible into a corporation's stock, or owns options to purchase a corporation's stock. Are the bonds or options "equity securities?" If so, does the owner of more then 10 percent of the number of outstanding such convertible bonds or options count as an insider for purposes of Section 16? Since the over–10 percent ownership test is based upon the notion that major shareholders have the clout to gain inside information, a sensible approach to these questions is to ask what sort of clout does an owner of convertible bonds, or options to purchase stock, have by virtue of this ownership. Presumably, the owner has some clout by virtue of the threat of either conversion or exercise of the options. Following this sort of logic, both a court opinion[8] and an SEC regulation[9] deem the convertible bond or option owner to own the underlying stock which the bond or option owner would have the right to obtain upon conversion or exercise of the option (which means that the 10 percent ownership test is measured against the total outstanding stock, rather than against just the outstanding bonds or options).

One question which took two Supreme Court opinions to resolve—despite language in Section 16(b) addressing the point—is when must a person own over 10 percent of the outstanding stock in order to count as an insider. The last sentence in Section 16(b) states that an individual must own over 10 percent of the outstanding stock at both the time of the purchase and the time of the sale in order to count as an insider based upon ownership of stock. In *Reliance Electric Co. v. Emerson Electric Co.*,[10] the Supreme Court dealt with a situation in which the owner of over 10 percent of the corporation's outstanding shares sold off enough stock to bring the owner's holdings to 9.96 percent of the outstanding stock, whereupon the owner sold off the rest. The court held that the second sale did not come within Section 16(b), regardless of the fact that the two-stage sell-off was all part of a pre-existing plan. In *Foremost-McKesson, Inc. v. Provident Securities Co.*,[11] the Supreme Court held that a person is not an owner of over 10 percent of the outstanding stock in making the very purchase which puts the person over the 10 percent threshold. After all, if the notion is that ownership of over 10 percent of a corporation's outstanding stock gives a person clout to gain inside information, the law cannot presume the person to have this clout at the moment the person decides to purchase the very shares which will give the clout.[12]

7. *E.g.*, Feder v. Martin Marietta Corp., 406 F.2d 260 (2d Cir.1969).

8. Chemical Fund, Inc. v. Xerox Corp., 377 F.2d 107 (2d Cir.1967).

9. Sec. Exch. Act Rule 16a–4(a).

10. 404 U.S. 418, 92 S.Ct. 596 (1972).

11. 423 U.S. 232, 96 S.Ct. 508 (1976).

12. This made sense in the context involved in *Foremost* in which the purchase placing the defendant over the 10 percent

Since Section 16(b) states that an over–10 percent shareholder must be such both at the time of the purchase and at the time of the sale, but does not state anything similar as to officers and directors, the negative implication is that officers and directors need not have been officers and directors at both points.[13] Hence, under the SEC's interpretive rules, a purchase or sale taking place after a director or officer resigns (but not before a person becomes an officer or director) can be matched with a sale or purchase which took place while the person was an officer or director, in order to create liability under Section 16(b).[14]

Beyond the issue of who Section 16(b) reaches, determining whether an insider has made any profit from short-swing trades (and, if so, how much) can lead to questions. For example, suppose an insider buys 100 shares of his or her corporation's stock at $50 per share; a month later sells the 100 shares at $30 per share; a month later buys 100 shares at $20 per share; and one month later sells the 100 shares at $25 per share. Has the insider made a profit from his or her trades? If one looks at the total results, the insider has lost $1500 (a $2000 loss on the 100 shares bought at $50 per share and sold at $30 per share, offset by only $500 made on the 100 shares purchased at $20 per share and sold at $25 per share). Alternately, if one disregards the loss on the first purchase and sale as irrelevant, one might say that the insider made $500 on the purchase at $20 per share and sale at $25 per share. It turns out, however, that neither of these answers is correct. Instead, the approach followed by the courts[15] is simply to match the highest sale(s) and with the lowest purchase(s) within six months (disregarding any left over losing combinations) to achieve the largest mathematical "profit"—in this example, matching the $30 sale with the subsequent $20 purchase gives a profit of $1000. Presumably, the notion is that any good combination might have been the result of inside information; whereas even one with access to inside information still occasionally might make poor trades.

Sometimes the problem lies not in calculating the amount of profit resulting from short-swing trades, but rather in the need to ask whether it was the insider who really made the profit. This occurs when someone other than the insider made the short-swing trades.[16] For example,

mark took place before the sale within six months. The lack of inside information rationale does not logically apply, however, if a person owning over 10 percent sells enough stock to go below 10 percent, and then, within six months, purchases stock bringing him or her back over the 10 percent line. This is because in the sale-repurchase scenario, the decision to begin the short-swing trade (potentially based upon knowledge that the stock will decline in value) was made at the time the person presumably had access to inside information by virtue of his or her stockholding. The Court in *Foremost* left open the issue of when to measure share holdings in the sale-repurchase scenario.

13. *E.g.*, Adler v. Klawans, 267 F.2d 840 (2d Cir.1959).

14. Sec. Exch. Act Rule 16a–2(b).

15. *E.g.*, Smolowe v. Delendo Corp., 136 F.2d 231 (2d Cir.1943).

16. A person other than the insider might have made both the purchase and the sale in question, or such a person might have made a purchase, while the insider made a sale, or such a person might have made a sale, while the insider made a purchase.

suppose a partnership in which the insider is a partner made short-swing trades. In this event, courts will deem the insider to make a profit equal to his or her proportionate interest in the profits the partnership made on the trades.[17] Deciding if trades by relatives of insiders create a profit for the insider can present a very difficult question, the resolution of which may depend upon the facts of each case.[18]

Finally, questions can occur about when there is a "purchase" or a "sale" for purposes of Section 16(b). The Supreme Court's opinion in *Kern County Land Co. v. Occidental Petroleum Corp.*,[19] set out the standard on this issue.

In *Kern*, the Supreme Court faced the question of whether two transactions by a party who unsuccessfully attempted to make a hostile takeover constituted sales within the meaning of Section 16(b). Specifically, Occidental Petroleum Corporation launched a tender offer for the stock of Kern County Land Company, and ultimately acquired around 20 percent of Kern's outstanding shares. Because Occidental acquired its stock in stages, some of the purchases took place after Occidental owned more than 10 percent of the outstanding Kern shares. Unfortunately for Occidental, Kern's board agreed to a defensive merger with another oil company (Tenneco, Inc.). Upon recognizing it had lost the battle for Kern, Occidental sold Tenneco an option to purchase the Tenneco stock which Occidental would receive in exchange for Occidental's Kern stock in the Kern–Tenneco merger. Seeking to avoid the impact of Section 16(b), the option agreement did not allow Tenneco actually to purchase the stock until more than six months after Occidental's purchases. Before this six month milestone was reached, however, the Kern shareholders (with Occidental abstaining) approved the Tenneco merger, and the Kern shareholders (including Occidental) became both entitled and obligated to exchange their Kern shares for Tenneco shares. Following the merger, Kern sued Occidental under Section 16(b). Kern argued that both the sale of the option to Tenneco, and the exchange of shares mandated by the merger, constituted "sales" of stock within the meaning of Section 16(b) (and these sales produced a profit when matched with Occidental's purchases).

To determine whether these so-called unorthodox transactions constituted sales, the Supreme Court decided to apply a pragmatic test. The Court asked whether the transactions carried the potential for the abuse of inside information. Holding that the potential for abuse was not present given the facts before it, the Supreme Court decided that the two transactions were not sales within the meaning of Section 16(b).

17. *E.g.*, Blau v. Lehman, 368 U.S. 403, 82 S.Ct. 451 (1962).

18. *See, e.g.*, Whiting v. Dow Chem. Corp., 523 F.2d 680 (2d Cir.1975) (The court considered a wife's trades to create a profit for her husband—who was a director—when the couple used the wife's income to pay many of their living expenses and the transactions by the wife were part of a common plan jointly managed by the husband and wife); Sec. Exch. Act Rule 16a–1(a)(2)(ii)(A) (creating a rebuttable presumption that an insider has an indirect beneficial interest in stock held by his or her immediate family).

19. 411 U.S. 582, 93 S.Ct. 1736 (1973).

There are a couple of troubling aspects to the Supreme Court's opinion in *Kern*. To begin with, the Court's approach in *Kern* seems inconsistent with the Court's rationale in *Reliance Electric*. In *Reliance Electric*, the Court held that it would not integrate both parts of a planned two-stage sell-off together (in order to bring the second part within the reach of Section 16(b)), since this would be inconsistent with the sort of objective, mechanical way in which Congress intended Section 16(b) to operate. Yet, in *Kern*, the Court seems to have replaced an objective, mechanical approach with an examination of the potential for abuse of inside information. Perhaps one might reconcile *Kern* with *Reliance Electric*—other than by suggesting cynically the Supreme Court does not like Section 16(b)—by pointing out that it is not self-evident whether selling a call option, or being forced to exchange shares in a merger, constitute sales of stock. Hence, there was no simple mechanical approach available to the Court in *Kern*.

Even so, the Court in *Kern* could have applied its pragmatic test in a more objective fashion. Specifically, in deciding that there was no potential for abuse of inside information, the Court focused in large part upon how Occidental was attempting a hostile takeover. Indeed, so bad was the blood between Occidental and Kern's board that Kern's board attempted to deny Occidental the information to which Occidental was entitled as an ordinary shareholder. Hence, Occidental hardly had access to the sort of inside information one normally assumes is accessible to a major shareholder. Yet, this sort of evaluation of whether a statutory insider actually had inside information is precisely the sort of inquiry Section 16(b) seeks to preclude. Indeed, if Occidental had sold the shares outright, the fact that Occidental lacked access to inside information would not have precluded liability under Section 16(b). Why then should the fact that the transactions were unorthodox allow such an inquiry?

In fact, the *Kern* court's initial instinct to evaluate whether the transactions carried the potential for abuse was sensible. The problem was that the Court got sidetracked by the question of whether Occidental had inside information. Instead, the Court should have stayed focused on the nature of the two questioned transactions themselves—which, after all, created the issue. Specifically, the Court should have asked: "Assuming Occidental had inside information, did the merger or the option contract constitute mechanisms to profit on the information along the lines of a sale following a purchase?"

Had the Court asked these questions, then the outcome might have been different. After all, if we assume that Occidental's status as an owner of over 10 percent of the stock gave it access to inside information, then one piece of information accessible to it would be the prospects for a merger. Following this line, buying additional shares based upon the knowledge that the shares will be exchanged in a forthcoming merger is a typical way to exploit inside information. True, as the Court emphasizes, Occidental could not prevent the merger or resulting exchange of shares.[20] Occidental did have a choice, however, about the additional share purchases.

The Court's analysis of the option at least got around to asking the right question—if Occidental had inside information, was the option a way to exploit it? The problem, however, is that the economics of stock options is more complex than the Court seemed to realize. One point is easy: If Occidental had purchased an option entitling Occidental to sell the shares (a put), then there would be a sale. Otherwise Section 16(b) would be a dead letter, since an insider could always purchase a put to protect against market risk while the insider waited out the six months. Because the call gave the option to Tenneco, the Court felt that the situation was different. Yet, by selling the call, Occidental may have locked in at least some profit despite whatever the Kern–Tenneco stock subsequently did.[21]

More recently, the Securities Exchange Commission adopted a rule dealing with the question of when the acquisition, disposition, or exercise of puts and calls constitute a purchase or sale for purposes of Section 16(b).[22] The basic approach of this rule is to treat the increase or decrease in a put or call position, rather than the exercise of the put or call, as the purchase or sale.[23]

In any event, if a designated insider makes a profit from short-swing trades in his or her corporation's stock, Section 16(b) requires the insider to pay the profit to the corporation in question. One obvious problem is that directors often will be disinclined to vote to have the corporation sue themselves, major shareholders, or perhaps even corporate officers. The solution is one we have encountered before: Allow shareholders to bring a derivative suit on behalf of the corporation. Significantly, however, derivative suits under Section 16(b) are not subject to many of the procedural hurdles which plague derivative suits in general.[24] For example, since Congress expressly empowered shareholders to bring derivative suits to enforce Section 16(b) if the corporation's directors do not pursue the action, and since the purpose of

20. Indeed, some subsequent lower court opinions have interpreted *Kern* to stand for the proposition that only involuntary transactions constitute unorthodox transactions subject to the pragmatic test. *E.g.*, Colan v. Mesa Petroleum Co., 951 F.2d 1512 (9th Cir.1991).

21. Specifically, if the Kern–Tenneco stock increased in value before expiration of the six months, then Tenneco would exercise the option, thereby limiting Occidental's profit to the option price and the premium. Yet, limiting Occidental's upside would also have been the result of an outright sale of the shares at the time Occidental sold the option. Suppose the shares declined in value. Once the market price for the shares reached the price at which Occidental purchased them, Occidental could

have protected itself against further loss by selling the shares at the same price Occidental bought them (or by purchasing a put). This sale seemingly would not have produced any profit for purposes of Section 16(b), yet Occidental still would have pocketed the premium Tenneco paid for the call.

22. Sec. Exch. Act. Rule 16b–6.

23. To avoid Section 16(b) interfering with the use of stock options as executive compensation, Rule 16b–3 generally excludes stock option compensation schemes from Section 16(b).

24. *See, e.g.,* Gollust v. Mendell, 501 U.S. 115, 111 S.Ct. 2173 (1991) (no continuous ownership requirement for a shareholder who brings an action pursuant to Section 16(b)).

Section 16(b) is not necessarily to further the interests of the corporation involved, there is no room in dealing with Section 16(b) for the board or a special litigation committee to recommend dismissal of the suit as not in the best interest of the corporation.

6.4.2 Rule 14e–3(a) and the Mail and Wire Fraud Statutes

In our earlier discussion of the application of Rule 10b–5 to trading on inside information, we saw that it is not self-evident when such trading equals a "fraud," which is what Rule 10b–5 prohibits. Given this ambiguity, one might have been tempted to ask why the Securities Exchange Commission did not simply adopt a rule explicitly addressing such trading. Prior to the Supreme Court's decision in *Chiarella*, the Commission may have felt this was unnecessary, because lower court opinions (taking their lead from the Commission's decision in *Cady, Roberts*) applied an equal access rule to decide when trading on inside information violated Rule 10b–5. After *Chiarella*, the Commission's rule-making options under Section 10(b) may be severely limited with respect to trading on inside information, since the Supreme Court, in *Chiarella*, seems to have been interpreting the scope of Section 10(b), rather than just Rule 10b–5. As a result, the Commission turned to its rulemaking authority under Section 14(e) of the Securities Exchange Act in order finally to adopt a rule specifically prohibiting trading on inside information—albeit, only when dealing with tender offers.

We shall discuss Section 14(e)—which was added to the Securities Exchange Act as part of the Williams Act—when we address tender offers in the final chapter of this book. For now, it is sufficient to note that Section 14(e) makes it unlawful to engage in fraudulent conduct in connection with tender offers, and, highly significantly, the section also grants the Securities Exchange Commission authority to promulgate rules reasonably designed to prevent such fraudulent conduct. It was this authority which the Commission used following the *Chiarella* decision to adopt Rule 14e–3(a). Rule 14e–3(a) makes it unlawful to trade on material information concerning a tender offer, when one knows, or has reason to know, that the information is non-public and comes from the acquiring company, the target company, insiders of such companies, or persons working on behalf of either company in connection with the tender offer.

For many years, it was uncertain whether the SEC had exceeded its rulemaking authority in adopting Rule 14e–3(a). After all, if *Chiarella* stands for the proposition that an equal access rule would go beyond proscribing deceptive or manipulative conduct within the meaning of Section 10(b), then such a rule might seem go beyond prohibiting fraud or the like for purposes of Section 14(e). Nevertheless, in *United States v. O'Hagan*,[25] the Supreme Court upheld Rule 14e–3(a).[26]

---

25. 521 U.S. 642, 117 S.Ct. 2199 (1997).

26. The Supreme Court left open, however, possible challenges to the scope of Rule 14e–3(b) which the Court of Appeals had not considered.

The Court's rationale in *O'Hagan* is that Section 14(e) empowers the SEC, not only to make rules prohibiting fraudulent conduct, but also to make rules reasonably designed to prevent fraudulent conduct. Rule 14e–3(a) can be seen as preventing fraudulent conduct—specifically, tips in breach of an insider's duty, and the misappropriation of information—even though the prohibition under Rule 14e–3(a) reaches beyond such fraudulent conduct. The argument for this utility of Rule 14e–3(a) is similar to the rationale behind Section 16(b). We suspect that much, if not most, of the time a person trades based upon knowledge of non-public information concerning a tender offer, the knowledge came through a tip in breach of duty or through misappropriation; but it might be difficult to prove this occurred. By eliminating the problem of proving that trades concerning tender offers stemmed from illegal tips or misappropriation of information, Rule 14e–3(a) can be seen as preventing fraudulent conduct.

Using the mail and wire fraud statutes against trading on inside information embodies a very different approach from Rule 14e–3(a). Instead of adopting a rule specifically addressing such trading, instituting prosecutions under the mail and wire fraud statutes brought into play laws whose original purpose had less to do with trading on inside information than did Section 10(b) and Rule 10b–5. In terms of the development of the law of trading on inside information, a prosecution under the mail and wire fraud statutes gave the Supreme Court an opportunity to decide that misappropriating information by trading constitutes fraud.[27] Following the Supreme Court's acceptance of the misappropriation theory under Rule 10b–5, however, the only remaining significance of mail and wire fraud prosecutions for trading on inside information is to allow the government to pile on more criminal penalties for those engaged in such trading.

27. Carpenter v. United States, 484 U.S. 19, 108 S.Ct. 316 (1987).

Chapter VII

MERGERS AND ACQUISITIONS

[Research References]

AmJur 2d, Corporations §§ 2503–2732

CJS, Corporations §§ 792–810

ALR Index: Acquisition of Company; Liquidation or Dissolution; Merger; Takeovers

ALR Digest: Corporations §§ 30–40

Am Jur Legal Forms 2d, Corporations §§ 74:2651–74:2848

Am Jur Pleading and Practice Forms (Rev), Corporations §§ 335–358

59 Am Jur Trials 231, Contractual Indemnifications and Releases From Environmental Liability

34 POF3d 387, CERCLA Liability of Parent, Subsidiary and Successor Corporations

46 POF2d 313, Products Liability: Continuation of Business Enterprise or Product Line by Successor Corporation; 20 POF2d 609, De Facto Merger of Two Corporations

---

If one thinks as corporate law as a chess game, Chapter I on corporate formation could be considered a discussion of the opening moves, while Chapters II through VI could be viewed as a discussion of the struggle for control of the center during the middle game. Now, we turn to what one might visualize as the end-game in corporate law—the subject of mergers and acquisitions.[1]

§ 7.1 Sale of Control

A party seeking to acquire a corporation typically will attempt to secure the cooperation of the individuals currently in control of the corporation. In a corporation with widely dispersed shareholdings, the directors (and particularly those directors who are also full-time managers) are the individuals in control. In the corporation in which an individual or cohesive group (such as a family) owns a majority of the outstanding voting stock, the individual or group holding the majority interest will have the ultimate control by virtue of the majority's ability to dictate who serves on the board. Even without holding a majority of shares, an individual or cohesive group may own enough stock to determine, as a practical matter, who gets elected to the board, and thereby have working control of a corporation whose other shares are widely dispersed.

---

1. For many companies, bankruptcy might be a more likely end-game—but the subject of corporate bankruptcy is beyond the scope of this book.

Securing the cooperation of the individuals in control of the corporation can smooth the path (and, indeed, is often a necessary prerequisite) for the complete acquisition of the company. Alternately, if the cooperation of those in control of the corporation can pass working control over the company to the acquirer, this sometimes might be all the acquirer desires. Under these circumstances, it might make economic sense from the prospective acquirer's standpoint to offer the individuals in control of the corporation something more than simply the opportunity to sell their stock at the same price the prospective acquirer, or anyone else, is willing pay minority shareholders for the minority's stock. At the same time, one might expect persons with control to seek to exploit their position by demanding such a payment. This section takes a look at the legal rules governing the permissibility of payments to those currently in control of a corporation by persons seeking control, and the controversial question of whether controlling shareholders should be able to receive a premium for selling their stock, which is not available to minority stockholders.

7.1.1 The Traditional Rules

The legal rules governing dealings between a person seeking to acquire control of a corporation, and the individual(s) currently in control, reflect the interplay of two broad principles. One principle is that a stockholder traditionally has little fiduciary duty when acting solely as a stockholder. After all, one is not elected or appointed to be a stockholder by persons who expect, in return, care and loyalty in looking out for their interest; rather, one purchases stock in order to enjoy selfishly the benefits of ownership. Following this broad principle, courts hold, as a general rule, that stockholders can sell their shares at whatever price a buyer will pay, and, if (as is normally the case) a buyer will pay more for a controlling block than the buyer will pay for minority holdings, the selling stockholder is not obligated to share the premium with the other stockholders.[1]

The competing principle impacting dealings in control is that corporate directors do have a fiduciary obligation to the corporation and all of the shareholders. This principle is supplemented by two other notions: a controlling shareholder who tells directors what to do will pick up the duties of a director, and a person who aids in the breach of duty by corporate fiduciaries can become liable for the results of this aid. This competing principle (and supplementary notions) lead to four limitations on the ability of those currently in control of a corporation to extract compensation for their cooperation with a person who seeks to acquire control.

§ 7.1
1. *E.g.*, Zetlin v. Hanson Holdings, Inc., 48 N.Y.2d 684, 397 N.E.2d 387, 421 N.Y.S.2d 877 (1979).

a. Sale to looters

One limitation on the right to transfer control arises if the person who acquires control loots the corporation (in other words, misappropriates the corporation's assets). In this event, the person who sold a controlling block of stock to the looter, or otherwise helped the looter gain control of the corporation, can be liable for damages the corporation sustains as a result of the looting.[2] There are a pair of rationales for this liability. If any steps to transfer control of the corporation to the looter involve actions taken as a director (or by controlling the directors)—as, for example, resignation from the board and the appointment of the looter and his or her cronies to the board—then the duties of care and loyalty of corporate directors come into play. In addition, the transfer of a controlling block of stock to the looter serves to aid in the forthcoming breach of the duties which the looter will assume to the corporation as a result of the looter's taking control of the board. This concept of liability based upon supplying the means for another person's wrongful conduct is not unusual in the law. Indeed, the sale of a controlling block of stock to a looter is not that much different than renting an automobile to a person who is drunk. While the sale to looters limitation is not controversial, a couple problems can arise in its application.

The first problem in applying the sale to looters limitation arises from the fact that a prospective looter typically lacks the curtesy to inform the person from whom the looter buys stock of the looter's plans to loot the corporation. After the looting occurs, and the victimized minority shareholders or creditors sue the person who sold control to the looter,[3] the typical response of the seller is to say "Sorry, I did not know I was selling to a looter." The question then becomes what obligation did the seller of a controlling block of shares have to check out the buyer.

There are several approaches one could take to answer this question. At one extreme, the rule could be that sellers will not be liable unless they know the buyer plans to loot.[4] At the other extreme, a few courts suggest that the seller has a duty to investigate a buyer even in the absence of any reason for suspicion.[5] Most courts, however, take an intermediate approach under which the liability of the seller will depend upon whether facts came to the seller's attention which should have alerted the seller of the need for further investigation. In fact, this middle approach is the most consistent with general tort law principles applied to persons who sell alcoholic drinks, guns, cars and other items to persons who injure third parties.

This intermediate approach, in turn, raises the question as to what sort of facts should make a seller suspicious. One such fact would be the

---

2. *E.g.*, DeBaun v. First Western Bank & Trust Co., 46 Cal.App.3d 686, 120 Cal. Rptr. 354 (1975).

3. Since the looter, or his or her loot, may have disappeared.

4. *See, e.g.*, Levy v. American Beverage Corp., 265 App.Div. 208, 38 N.Y.S.2d 517 (1942).

5. *See, e.g.*, Northway, Inc. v. TSC Indus., Inc., 512 F.2d 324 (7th Cir.1975), *rev'd on other grounds*, 426 U.S. 438, 96 S.Ct. 2126 (1976).

prior history of the buyer—in other words, has the buyer looted before. For example, the court in *DeBaun v. First Western Bank & Trust Co.*, [6] pointed to the financial history of the buyer, which was notable for the failure of firms he controlled, as one fact which should have alerted the seller to potential problems. Of course, a history of failure might only show that the buyer is a person with bad luck (or, more likely, a bad judge of what companies to purchase), rather than a thief.

The nature of the corporation's assets is another factor which can raise suspicions. For instance, in holding the seller should have suspected possible looting in *Gerdes v. Reynolds*,[7] the court attached great importance to the fact that the corporation's assets consisted almost entirely of readily saleable securities. This fact actually had dual significance. To begin with, a prospective looter can much more readily make off with liquid assets than can a looter convert a corporation's manufacturing plant. Hence, a corporation with mostly liquid assets (like an investment fund) is much more likely to be the target of a looter than is a manufacturing company. The court also noted that it was difficult to give a legitimate explanation for the hefty premium paid by the buyer for the selling shareholder's stock, in a situation in which the corporation's assets consisted largely of securities anyone could have purchased on the market.

The suggestion of the court in *Gerdes* that the size of the premium was grounds for suspicion should be taken with some care.[8] Otherwise, if one simply views a premium as grounds for suspicion, the common practice of paying a premium for control effectively mandates an automatic investigation of every buyer. *Gerdes* is not to the contrary. Rather, the court seemed to be applying a fairly sophisticated view of the overall economics of the situation. Since the corporation simply had a portfolio of securities, the company only possessed very limited goodwill or going concern value to justify paying significantly greater than the asset value for the company's stock. For the same reason, there was not any evident prospect to improve the corporation's earnings through better management—or to gain any synergistic advantages by combining with another company—which legitimately might justify paying a premium for control. Hence, all that made economic sense was to suspect looting.

Finally, the nature of the sale itself could raises suspicions. The failure of the buyer to conduct a normal investigation into the corporation's business operations makes one wonder about the buyer's motives for the transaction.[9] Sometimes, courts have pointed to the fact that the buyer lacked the funds to make the purchase, and expected to use the corporation's assets.[10] One must exercise a certain degree of caution

6. 46 Cal.App.3d 686, 120 Cal.Rptr. 354 (1975).

7. 28 N.Y.S.2d 622 (Sup. Ct. 1941).

8. *See, e.g.,* Clagett v. Hutchison, 583 F.2d 1259 (4th Cir.1978).

9. *See, e.g.,* Swinney v. Keebler Co., 480 F.2d 573 (4th Cir.1973) (but not finding the buyer's failure to conduct a normal investigation of the business to be so suspicious as to require the seller to investigate the buyer).

10. *E.g.,* Insuranshares Corp. v. Northern Fiscal Corp., 35 F.Supp. 22 (E.D.Pa. 1940).

here, however, to distinguish prospective looters from persons planning a permissible leveraged buy-out.

In addition to the question of when the seller should have known he or she was selling to a looter, there is also can be a question of what conduct by the purchaser constitutes looting.[11] The classic case of *Perlman v. Feldmann*,[12] illustrates the reach of the sale to a looter concept.

Feldmann, members of his family, and some friends and associates, together owned 37 percent of the outstanding stock in Newport Steel Corporation. Due to the wide dispersal of the remaining outstanding stock, this was sufficient to give Feldmann working control over Newport. Newport was a fairly marginal steel producer with old mills, and normally could not compete in selling steel to customers outside of its local area. The Korean War, however, had created a shortage of steel. Normally, one would have expected the price of steel to rise due to the shortage, but government pressure during the war led steel producers not to raise prices. Feldmann, however, had come up with a clever alternative. Instead of raising prices, he obtained interest-free loans for Newport from prospective customers (in exchange for commitments to sell the prospective customers future steel production). Newport used the interest-free loans to finance improvements in its plants. A group of steel users had another idea. They formed a syndicate to purchase the stock owned by Feldmann and his family and associates, for a price which represented a significant premium over the market price for Newport stock ($20 per share, as opposed to a market price which had never exceeded $12 per share). This, in turn, generated a lawsuit by minority shareholders in Newport, who argued that Feldmann must turn over the premium to the corporation.

The Court of Appeals held that Feldmann and his family and associates breached a fiduciary duty, and had to give up whatever portion of the price they received for their Newport stock which represented payment for selling the power to control to whom Newport would sell steel.[13] While, as we shall discuss shortly, it is possible to read more into the court's opinion, the simplest way to understand the outcome is as a variation of the sale to looters limitation. The members of the buyer syndicate planned to have Newport sell steel to themselves—in other words, they were going to use their control over Newport to enter into conflict-of-interest contracts with the corporation. Of course, as discussed in an earlier chapter,[14] there is nothing wrong per se with entering into a conflict-of-interest transaction with one's corporation. The problem arises when the conflict-of-interest transaction is unfair to

11. For example, one might ask what is the difference between the looter's use of the corporation's assets to pay for his or her purchase of the corporation's stock, and a permissible leveraged buy-out. We shall address leveraged buy-outs later in this chapter.

12. 219 F.2d 173 (2d Cir.1955).

13. The court did not have the defendants pay this amount to Newport, since this, in effect, would return a portion of the payment to the buyer syndicate (who now owned a considerable fraction of Newport's outstanding stock). Instead, the court ordered pro-rata recovery by the minority shareholders of Newport.

14. See § 4.2.1 *supra*.

the corporation. Indeed, the misappropriation of assets involved in looting is simply the most extreme case of an unfair conflict-of-interest transaction—the looter takes corporate assets and gives nothing in return.[15] While not reaching anywhere near the extreme of outright theft, the conflict-of-interest transactions planned by the buyer syndicate in *Perlman* were arguably unfair to Newport. Specifically, arms-length sales by Newport—which is the definition of fairness—were extracting interest-free loans under the Feldmann plan. There is no indication that the members of the buyer syndicate planned to give the same added consideration to Newport for their steel purchases.

There are a couple of problems with the sort of sale to "quasi" looters limitation suggested by *Perlman*. One pesky fact, pointed to by critics of the court's opinion,[16] is that the price of Newport stock on the market actually increased after the sale by Feldmann, which arguably is inconsistent with the notion that the buyer syndicate planned transactions which would not be at least as good for Newport as the Feldmann plan. This fact, in turn, illustrates that it often will be highly debatable whether a buyer's post-sale transactions are fair to the corporation. Moreover, uncertainty as to the fairness of the buyer's post-sale dealings with the corporation compounds the difficulty of resolving whether the selling shareholder should have known of the buyer's arguably bad intentions. After all, short of blatant looting, how is the seller supposed to know whether, at some future time, a court will find the buyer's conflict-of-interest transactions to be unfair? Seen in this light, *Perlman* may reflect a unique set of facts which produced a holding of little general applicability.

b. *Sale of directorships*

A second limitation on the ability to cooperate with a party seeking control over a corporation involves the "sale of directorships." It is quite common, following the sale of a controlling block of stock, for the corporation's current directors to resign serially from the board, and appoint the buyer's nominees, one at a time, to fill the vacancies.[17] Indeed, many times, the contract purchasing the shares expressly requires this to occur. The difficulty is this looks like the sale of a corporate office by its current holder.[18] Since positions on the board are

---

15. Of course, if all the buyer obtains is a pro rata share of a distribution of corporate surplus to all stockholders (as in a dividend), this is not looting, even though the corporation receives nothing in return for such a distribution.

16. *E.g.*, Frank H. Easterbrook & Daniel R. Fischel, *Corporate Control Transactions*, 91 Yale L.J. 717 (1982).

17. In other words, one of the current board members will resign, and then the remaining board members—using their power to fill vacancies between annual elections—will appoint one of the buyer's nomi-

nees to be a director. Then, a second one of the current board members will resign, and the rest of the directors will appoint a second one of the buyer's nominees to the board, and so on, until the buyer's nominees have replaced all of the existing board members.

18. This would be clear if the board members received compensation explicitly in exchange for their agreements to resign and appoint specified parties to the board. Such an explicit characterization, however, would be rare. Commonly, the express or implied agreement to replace the directors

not the property of the current directors, and since directors (and persons who act to control directors) have a fiduciary duty to act in the best interest of the corporation (rather than in their personal interest) when performing actions such as filling vacancies on the board, it would seem obvious that directors have no right to sell their positions.[19]

On the other hand, it might appear to be an empty formality to require the buyer of a controlling block of stock to call a shareholders' meeting to replace the directors, when the replacement of the current directors at such a meeting would be a forgone conclusion (as it normally would be if the buyer acquired a majority of the voting stock). Moreover, in a corporation in which the shareholders lack the power to remove directors without cause (say, because the directors have staggered terms), it would seem poor policy to tell directors, who have sold their stock to a party acquiring a controlling interest, that they cannot resign and thereby clear the way for a new controlling stockholder to put his or her ideas into play. After all, normally one would assume that the purchaser of a large percentage of the corporation's stock has better incentives for efficient corporate decisions than would directors simply hanging on until an annual election. For these reasons, many courts have allowed the seriatim replacement of directors at the behest of a person purchasing a controlling block of stock.[20]

This sort of pragmatic approach to the sale of directorships issue, however, raises a question: What proportion of the outstanding voting stock must change hands in order for the court to allow the seriatim replacement of directors? Purchase of a majority of the voting stock should be enough, since then we know the buyer normally has the votes to replace the directors at a special shareholders meeting. Many courts have been willing to go below the fifty percent threshold if the court is convinced that the buyer purchased sufficient stock to give working control in view of the high dispersion of the remaining shareholdings.[21] At least one well respected jurist, however, has questioned whether courts should allow replacement of directors at less than a majority purchase.[22] After all, without an election, one never can be sure that a less than 50 percent block of stock gives its owner working control—at least if the owner did not start with the additional advantage of already holding positions on the board.[23]

is part of a transaction in which there is a sale of stock. In this event, the argument is that part or all of any premium over the current market price for the stock, which the buyer is paying to the seller, is consideration, not for the stock, but for the seller's promise to act as a director him- or herself, and to use the seller's influence over the other directors, to replace the board members with the buyer's nominees. *See, e.g.,* Gerdes v. Reynolds, 28 N.Y.S.2d 622 (Sup. Ct. 1941).

19. *E.g.,* Petition of Caplan, 20 App. Div. 2d 301, 246 N.Y.S.2d 913, *aff'd.,* 14

N.Y.2d 679, 198 N.E.2d 908, 249 N.Y.S.2d 877 (1964).

20. *E.g.,* Carter v. Muscat, 21 App. Div. 2d 543, 251 N.Y.S.2d 378 (1964).

21. *E.g.,* Essex Universal Corp. v. Yates, 305 F.2d 572 (2d Cir.1962).

22. *Id.* at 581 (Friendly, J concurring).

23. The fact that a selling shareholder was able to convince the other directors to resign and appoint the buyer's nominees to the board might suggest working control which flows from the transferred block of stock; but this assumes that the other di-

c. *Side contracts with the buyer*

At the other end from selling offices, lies the fact that many times a party seeking to acquire a corporation wishes to retain the services of the corporation's key personnel—or, at the very least, to ensure that key personnel remain available for consulting and do not go into competition with the corporation. Accordingly, a party acquiring a corporation often will enter into employment, consulting or non-competition agreements with some or all of the corporation's current officers and directors. To the extent that the employment, consulting or non-competition agreement is a bona fide effort to obtain continued services or prevent competition from the corporation's former managers, then the agreement, itself, raises little problem under corporate law.[24] On the other hand, sometimes, what parties denominate as an employment or consulting agreement, is really a bribe to directors for selling out the shareholders' interests while negotiating the sale of the corporation. In this event, the agreement obviously constitutes a breach of the directors' fiduciary duty.[25]

A more subtle and pervasive problem lies, not in the validity of such side agreements themselves, but rather stems from the common practice of negotiating such agreements at the same time the directors are negotiating the sale of the overall company. The concern is that the parallel negotiation of both the individual employment contracts and the sale of the business puts the board in something of a conflict-of-interest. After all, the more vigorously the board negotiates the sale, the more it may upset the party with whom the board's members are negotiating for future employment. A possible prophylactic rule would be to prohibit simultaneous negotiation of the sale of the company and individual employment or other such contracts; but such a rule may be impractical and difficult to enforce. At the very least, it would seem to be a good idea for a court, when presented with a challenge to a board decision regarding the sale of the corporation, to subject the board's action to a greater degree of scrutiny for fairness than normally applied to an arms length deal, when there has been the simultaneous negotiation of the sale of the company and individual employment and other such contracts by members of the board.[26]

d. *Usurping an opportunity*

The last of the four traditional limitations on transfers of control has less acceptance among the courts than the limitations discussed so

---

rectors resigned because they knew the sale of stock would result in their replacement anyway at the next shareholders' meeting. It is possible, however, that the current board members resigned simply out of a sense of personal loyalty to the selling shareholder, or, worse, they resigned because they were selling some of their own shares and received a better price, in effect, for their agreement to resign and appoint the buyer's nominees to the board.

24. *E.g.*, Smith v. Good Music Station, Inc., 36 Del.Ch. 262, 129 A.2d 242 (1957).

25. *See, e.g.*, Barr v. Wackman, 36 N.Y.2d 371, 329 N.E.2d 180, 368 N.Y.S.2d 497 (1975).

26. *See, e.g.*, Smith v. Good Music Station, Inc., 36 Del.Ch. 262, 129 A.2d 242 (1957).

far. This limitation arises in situations in which a court might view the sale of a controlling block of stock at a premium price, which is not also available to minority shareholders, to constitute the usurpation of an opportunity which otherwise would have been available, directly or indirectly, to all of the shareholders. The situation facing the court in *Brown v. Halbert*[27] provides a good illustration.

Brown arose out of the purchase of a savings and loan. Halbert owned a majority of the outstanding stock in the savings and loan, and was also the savings and loan's president and chairman of its board. The purchaser (another savings and loan) initially contacted Halbert to ask if his savings and loan was for sale. Halbert, evidently without consulting the other directors or shareholders, replied that the savings and loan was not for sale, but that he would sell his shares, and named a price which represented a substantial premium over book value. After selling his stock in this manner, Halbert then aided the buyer to purchase included the minority shares for much less than he received. This aid included advising minority shareholders to sell because the new buyer did not intend to have the corporation pay much dividends.

The court in *Brown* condemned Halbert's conduct as a breach of his fiduciary duty. At first glance, this result seems easy to justify. It is one thing to sell one's stock at the best price obtainable; it is quite a different matter to block a transaction which would have been equally beneficial to all stockholders in order to restructure the deal to obtain a premium just for oneself.

Not all courts, however, accept the *Brown* court's condemnation of such a transaction.[28] One concern might be that *Brown* places too much emphasis on the manner in which the purchaser couches the initial expression of interest, and that this will lead purchasers not to make initial statements which suggest an interest in buying the whole corporation in a deal which will not include a premium for controlling shares. It is not clear, however, how much incentive a purchaser will have to censor communication in this manner—after all, it is not the purchaser who obtains the extra consideration. Indeed, deals to purchase the whole company with the same per share consideration ultimately going to every stockholder take place all the time.

One other question might concern the role in which Halbert breached his duty. Since the purchaser appears originally to have contacted Halbert in Halbert's roles as president and chairman of the savings and loan, one might say that Halbert breached his duty as president and chairman by not, at the least, communicating the expression of interest to the rest of the board members. Suppose, however, Halbert passed on the buyer's expression of interest, but then, as the majority shareholder, voted against any deal which did not give himself a premium price for his shares. In this event, would the traditional right of shareholders to

---

27. 271 Cal.App.2d 252, 76 Cal.Rptr. 781 (1969).

28. *E.g.,* Tryon v. Smith, 191 Or. 172, 229 P.2d 251 (1951).

vote their selfish interest when acting solely as a shareholder mean that there was no breach of duty?

Not long ago, the Delaware Supreme Court, in *Thorpe v. CERBCO, Inc.*,[29] considered whether a controlling stockholder legally can use his or her voting power to block a transaction beneficial to all of the stockholders in order to obtain a premium just for him- or herself. The Erikson brothers owned stock giving them a majority of the voting power over CERBCO, and were two of the company's four directors. Another company (INA) approached the Eriksons about purchasing CERBCO's only profitable subsidiary. Like Halbert, the Eriksons did not inform CERBCO's other board members of this offer, but instead made a counterproposal to sell the Eriksons' stock in CERBCO to INA.[30] Consistent with *Brown*, the Delaware Supreme Court held that this conduct breached the Eriksons' fiduciary duty as directors of CERBCO. Nevertheless, the Delaware Supreme Court, for the most part, affirmed the Chancery Court's refusal to award damages. The court's rationale was that the Eriksons had the votes as shareholders to block the sale of CERBCO's subsidiary to INA.[31] Hence, even if the Eriksons had performed their duty as directors in passing on INA's offer, CERBCO still would have been unable to sell the subsidiary. Explicit in this rationale was the view that the Eriksons had the right to vote their shares selfishly to block the sale of the subsidiary.

Still, even if cases like *Brown* and *Thorpe* allow a majority shareholder to vote, as a shareholder, to block sales which do not give the majority shareholder a premium above what the other shareholders receive, these cases occasionally might provide a useful rule in preventing a shareholder with a controlling, albeit not a majority, interest from attempting a veto the shareholder does not necessarily have the votes to back up.

The *Perlman* case discussed above also might fit within the usurping an opportunity category. Portions of the court's opinion express the notion that Feldmann took an opportunity available to the corporation as a whole—this being to extract greater compensation for allocating steel in a time of shortage—and converted it to his own profit in the form of an increased premium for selling his stock.

7.1.2 *Proposals to Require Equal Treatment*

Over the years, a number of court decisions have been hailed (or castigated, depending upon one's viewpoint) as providing the "camel's nose under the tent" for a rule which generally would require controlling stockholders to share with all of the other stockholders any premium the controlling stockholders receive for selling a controlling block of

29. 676 A.2d 436 (Del.1996).

30. In the end, negotiations to purchase the Eriksons' stock broke down, with the result that neither the subsidiary nor the stock was sold.

31. The subsidiary constituted a sufficiently large amount of CERBCO's assets as to require shareholder approval under the statutory provision governing a sale by a corporation of substantially all of its assets.

stock. Indeed, while both opinions dutifully recite the traditional rule that controlling stockholders can sell their shares for a premium, both the *Brown* and *Perlman* decisions discussed above contain some intimations in the direction of an equal treatment obligation.

For example, as we just saw, the *Brown* decision might become something of a dead letter when dealing with majority shareholders, if such shareholders can use their power as shareholders to vote down any deal which does not give themselves a premium price over what the other stockholders will receive. Hence, it would not seem out of the question for a subsequent court to disagree with the Delaware Supreme Court's view in *Thorpe*, and hold that majority shareholders would breach their fiduciary duty by voting in such a selfish manner. Indeed, shortly after *Brown*, the California Supreme Court handed down a notable decision which might go even further with the idea that majority stockholders have a duty to let minority stockholders participate equally in the benefits of transactions involving the transfer of control. This decision came in the case of *Jones v. H.F. Ahmanson*.[32]

Ahmanson, like *Brown*, involved a savings and loan; in this case, however, the transaction did not involve the sale of control to an outside buyer. Rather, the transaction involved the establishment of a holding corporation by the group owning a majority of the stock in the savings and loan. The reason for creating the holding company lay in the marketability of the savings and loan stock. Specifically, the stock in the savings and loan had limited marketability due to the stock's high per share price. By transferring their savings and loan stock to the holding company in exchange for holding company stock with a much lower per share price—because the holding company issued a larger number of shares—the majority group achieved for themselves the ability to make money by selling some of their holding company stock (albeit, they retained enough stock in the holding company to continue to control the holding company, and thereby to continue to control the savings and loan). The minority shareholders left out of this deal sued, and the California Supreme Court held that the plaintiffs had stated a cause of action against the majority group for violating the majority group's fiduciary duty.

In broad strokes, the California Supreme Court held that majority shareholders have a duty "of good faith and inherent fairness to the minority in any transaction where control of the corporation is material."[33] When it comes to greater specificity, however, both the language and the relevant facts in the *Ahmanson* opinion make determining the scope of this duty a study in measured ambiguity. For example, does the reference to any transaction where control is material mean that controlling shareholders, acting solely as shareholders either in selling or in voting their controlling block of stock, have a duty to the minority; or does control refer only to controlling shareholders exercising their power

---

32. 1 Cal.3d 93, 81 Cal.Rptr. 592, 460 P.2d 464 (1969).

33. *Id* at 112, 81 Cal. Rptr. at 602, 460 P.2d at 474.

of control by dictating actions of the board? Focusing on the defendants' formation of the holding company, it appears that the court meant to create a duty which could encompass simply the transfer of controlling shares; yet, it is possible to argue for a narrower interpretation. Specifically, the defendants had used their control over the board of the savings and loan to have the corporation give certain guarantees which allowed the marketing of the holding company's stock. Also, the defendants had used their control over the savings and loan to have the savings and loan not carry out a stock split, which would have increased the marketability of the minority's, as well as the defendants', shares.[34]

Moreover, even if controlling stockholders have a duty under *Ahmanson* when taking actions solely in their role as stockholders, does this duty require a sharing of benefits with the minority, or is it sufficient simply that controlling stockholders not take actions which make the minority worse off than the minority was before? The court cites *Brown*, among other cases, as standing for the proposition that any use by the majority of the power to control the corporation must benefit all shareholders proportionately, and the thrust of the complaint is that the majority left out the minority from the opportunity to market their stock. Yet, the opinion also speaks of a duty not to act to the detriment of the minority, and it is possible to argue that the formation of the holding company put the minority into a worse position than the minority was before (because of the perception of prospective future buyers of the minority's stock that the savings and loan will operate in the future for the benefit of the holding company). Notice, critically, to the extent *Ahmanson* stands for the proposition that controlling stockholders have a duty to share benefits with the minority from any transaction in which the power of control played a role, then the upshot would seem to be that controlling shareholders must share with the minority any premium the controlling shareholders receive for selling the power of control over the corporation.

Perlman also is subject to a broader reading suggesting a general duty to share any premium paid for control. As stated above, the simplest reading is that Feldmann sold control to a party he knew was going to going to engage in "quasi" looting by entering unfair conflict-of-interest transactions with Newport. A somewhat broader interpretation is that Feldmann converted for his own profit the opportunity the corporation had to take advantage of the steel shortage. Yet, suppose the buyer sought control from Feldmann simply to increase corporate profits by more efficient management. Perhaps one could argue that the opportunity to increase profits belongs to all the shareholders, and Feldmann should not be entitled to obtain a disproportionate share of the value of this opportunity by obtaining a premium for selling control.[35]

34. Note, however, that a stock split could have required approval by the defendants in their role as shareholders, thereby returning us to the question of whether a stockholder can vote his or her stock to gain advantages for him- or herself not shared with the other stockholders.

35. This so-called opportunity analysis, however, is a bit too facile. After all, unlike the situation in *Perlman*, the minority

The broader implications of cases like *Perlman*, *Brown*, and *Ahmanson* bring us to the question of whether controlling shareholders should be able to keep for themselves a premium for selling a controlling block of stock, when this premium is not also available to the minority shareholders. The long-running debate about this question revolves around two sets of considerations: concerns of fairness or equity, and more practical considerations of economic efficiency.

One can always say that it seems unfair for some stockholders to receive a greater price for their shares than other stockholders receive; yet, in this sense, life is unfair. A more focused fairness argument keys off the notion that controlling shareholders, who receive a greater per share price for control, are, in effect, selling something which does not belong to them. One common argument along this line is that the power to control the corporation belongs to the corporation.[36] Yet, it is not entirely clear why the power to control, through voting as a shareholder, belongs to the corporation, rather than the shareholder. Perhaps the argument is similar to the prohibition upon the sale of offices. This might make sense to the extent that one views shareholder voting, like acting as a director or officer, as the exercise of a fiduciary obligation to act for the benefit of the corporation. This, however, makes the argument somewhat circular: Control becomes an asset of the corporation because a shareholder has an obligation to use control for the benefit of the corporation; and the reason the shareholder has an obligation to use control for the benefit of the corporation seems to be because control is an asset of the corporation. Another sort of fairness rationale is to argue that control over the corporation only has value insofar as there is an entire corporation to control. Hence, no stockholder should be entitled to more than his or her pro-rata share of the value of the right to control the corporation.

The alternate arguments concern issues of corporate efficiency. Here, one must begin by asking why buyers pay more for the power to control the corporation. Perhaps some folks just plain like power.[37] Assuming, however, as all good economists like to say, that individuals are rational wealth maximizers, the buyer must be paying a premium for control because the buyer expects to profit from the exercise of control over the corporation. Broadly speaking, there are two ways in which the

stockholders will obtain their pro-rata share of the so-called corporate opportunity involved in selling to a party who increases corporate profits. In this instance, the premium charged by the selling controlling stockholder simply impacts the allocation of the corporation's gain between the seller and the buyer. Yet, the common demand for a control premium increases the costs of purchasing control, and thus deters buyers in situations in which the buyer cannot increase profits enough to justify paying off the current controlling shareholder. In effect then, the controlling stockholder's diversion of the corporation's opportunity to increase profits through better management occurs when the controlling shareholder does *not* sell without a premium, rather than when the controlling shareholder sells at a premium.

36. *E.g.*, Adolph A. Berle, Jr., *"Control" in Corporate Law*, 58 Colum. L. Rev. 1212 (1958).

37. Which might explain why some wealthy individuals spend millions of dollars of their own money on seeking election to public office.

buyer could hope to profit from control: The buyer might figure, with his or her superior management, or through some synergistic business combination, the corporation can make more money after he or she takes control. Alternately, the buyer might figure, with control, he or she can obtain a disproportionate share of the corporation's wealth (either through outright looting or by entering into more subtly unfair conflict-of-interest transactions). From the standpoint of economic efficiency, the object of the law should be to place the least barriers in the way of the first type of buyer, and to try and block sales to the second type of buyer.

While there is general agreement about this objective, writers disagree about the best way to reach the goal. A much noted article[38] argued that the best way to achieve the goal is to adopt a rule under which any offers to purchase a controlling interest in the corporation must be open on a pro-rata basis to all shareholders. In other words, if a purchaser wishes to buy 51 percent of the corporation's voting stock, the purchaser could not simply go to a shareholder who currently owns the 51 percent and offer this shareholder a premium to sell the stock. Instead, the purchaser would need to offer to buy 51 percent of the voting stock held by each shareholder. The rationale for such an equal sharing rule is not fairness, but rather incentives. To see how, let us first suppose that the buyer plans to exploit control by gaining a disproportionate share of corporate wealth (say by looting). In this event, the current controlling shareholder would not wish to sell unless the buyer purchases all of the current controlling shareholder's stock.[39] Yet, under the equal sharing rule, if the current controlling shareholder demands the buyer purchase all of the current controlling shareholder's stock, then the buyer must also offer to purchase all of every shareholder's stock. This, however, removes the ability to profit by obtaining a disproportionate share of the corporation's wealth at the expense of the other stockholders—since there now are no other stockholders after the purchase by the looter.[40] By contrast, a buyer who plans on profiting by increasing corporate earnings should be willing to purchase all of the outstanding stock (and thereby avoid sharing the profits resulting from the buyer's superior management with anyone else). If the buyer lacks the funds to purchase all of the corporation's outstanding stock, then a buyer who has plans to increase corporate profits should be able either to convince the current controlling shareholder not to insist on selling all of the current controlling shareholder's stock, or else convince the minority shareholders to retain their stock.

Critics of the equal sharing idea have argued that this incentive analysis is not realistic. The problem is that a party seeking a controlling interest in order to increase corporate profits might lack funds to buy

38. William D. Andrews, *The Stockholder's Right to Equal Opportunity in the Sale of Shares*, 78 Harv. L. Rev. 505 (1965).

39. This assumes the current controlling shareholder suspects that the buyer plans to loot.

40. Of course, to the extent that looting can come at the expense of the corporation's creditors, as in a bank where one can loot at the expense of the depositors, then the looter still could afford to buy out all the shareholders at a premium.

out 100 percent of the current shareholders. At the same time, current shareholders cannot be sure that a party proposing to purchase a controlling interest will succeed in increasing profits.[41] Hence, the current shareholders, and especially the current controlling shareholder, might insist on an all or nothing deal. Without the ability just to buy out the current controlling shareholder—which the equal sharing rule prevents—the strapped-for-funds purchaser cannot make the deal, and a potentially beneficial transfer of control will not take place.

Moreover, there is an additional reason why a current controlling shareholder might not agree to a partial sale of his or her interest. Perhaps the current controlling shareholder is profiting from control through favorable conflict-of-interest transactions. In this instance, the current controlling shareholder might need something of bribe to sell out. Admittedly, a payoff to the current controlling shareholder to stop doing something he or she should not be doing anyway seems like a premium the current controlling shareholder should not be allowed to keep. Yet, from a practical standpoint, the minority shareholders might be better off if a buyer promising honest and efficient management is allowed to make the payment, than the minority shareholders will be if a moralistic condemnation of this transaction keeps the minority exploited by the current controlling shareholder.

In any event, as we have seen, courts have not adopted an equal sharing rule. We shall see later in this chapter, however, that provisions in both federal securities laws and some state takeover statutes can limit the ability to pay a control premium just to some shareholders.

§ 7.2 Mechanics of Corporate Mergers and Acquisitions

Perhaps few other corporate transactions provide the participants with such different options to achieve the same basic result, and, accordingly, place such a premium upon form, as does the acquisition of one business conducted through a corporation by another corporation. Specifically, there are three basic approaches the participants can take to structure such a transaction: The participants can undertake a statutory merger or consolidation in which the two corporations involved become one. Alternately, the participants can have one corporation sell all or substantially all of its assets to the other corporation. Finally, one corporation can purchase most or all of the outstanding stock in the other corporation from the other corporation's shareholders. Moreover, there are numerous variations on each of these three basic approaches.

The existence of these different avenues to reach more or less the same end result would be only of technical interest were it not for one other fact: The route chosen can lead to significantly different results under a variety of laws. For example, the Internal Revenue Code

41. Given human nature, one expects the current controlling shareholder typically will be skeptical of the buyer's claims that the buyer will increase corporate profits, since such a claim commonly presupposes the ability to do a better job than the management provided by the current controlling shareholder.

contains provisions[1] allowing tax-free treatment for some mergers (referred to in tax lingo as an "A reorganization"), some purchases of the outstanding stock in another corporation (referred to as a "B reorganization") and some sales of substantially all of a corporation's assets (referred to as a "C reorganization"). The principal requirement for such tax-free treatment involves the consideration received by the shareholders who give up their stock in the transaction. The notion is that if the shareholders receive stock in the corporation continuing the business, then they simply have changed the form of their investment, but have not cashed out, and so should not need to recognize gain. The precise requirements for this tax-free treatment are well beyond the scope of this book.[2] What is interesting for present purposes is to note that these requirements for tax-free treatment differ substantially in the degree to which they restrict what consideration the shareholders must receive— as well as with respect to a number of other aspects of the transaction— depending upon whether the transaction is a merger, purchase of stock, or sale of assets.[3]

In this section, we shall focus on the corporate law differences which depend upon how parties structure the acquisition or combination of corporate businesses.

7.2.1 Statutory Merger

Every state's corporations statute contains a provision allowing two or more corporations to merge into one corporate entity.[4] This entity could be one of the corporations which existed before the combination. In this event, the corporation which continues to exist after the merger is known as the surviving corporation; the corporation which ceases to exist as a legal entity as a result of the merger is variously referred to as the disappearing or merged corporation; and we often say that the disappearing corporation merged into the surviving corporation. Alternately, the corporate entity emerging from the merger could be a new corporation created by the transaction—in which case, some statutes refer to the transaction as a consolidation rather than a merger.[5] As we shall discuss a little later, the surviving corporation (or new corporation in a consolidation), by operation of law, generally obtains all of the assets, and becomes liable for all of the debts, of the disappearing corporation(s)

Procedurally, the statutory merger provisions call upon the boards of the merging companies to agree upon a plan of merger.[6] This "marriage" contract sets forth the various terms and conditions of the transaction. This includes items such as: which corporation will survive

---

§ 7.2

1. I.R.C. §§ 354, 361, 368.

2. For a detailed examination of this subject, see Franklin Gevurtz, Business Planning 959–999 (2d ed. 1995).

3. Broadly speaking, the statutory merger is the easiest form to qualify for tax-

free treatment, while the purchase of stock is the most difficult.

4. *E.g.*, M.B.C.A. § 11.02(a).

5. *E.g.*, Del. Gen. Corp. Law § 251(a). In a consolidation, both of the preexisting corporations disappear.

6. *E.g.*, M.B.C.A. §§ 11.02, 11.04(a).

the merger; any changes in the articles of the surviving corporation (for instance, changing the name or authorized stock) or else providing new articles in the case of a consolidation; provisions for the management of the surviving company (such as roles for the former officials of the merging firms); and various representations, warranties, and contingencies terminating the transaction (for example, in case too many shareholders seek to exercise appraisal rights). Most important, the plan of merger specifies what the shareholders of each of the merging companies get. After all, the shareholders of the disappearing corporation must exchange their stock in that company for something else; while the stockholders of the surviving firm may, or may not, simply keep their shares. In this regard, it is useful to note that most state corporation statutes do not restrict the consideration stockholders can receive as part of a plan of merger to shares in the surviving company. Rather, the plan might call for the shareholders to receive debt securities, cash or other property in whole or in part payment for their stock (or the plan might even cancel some shares without consideration).[7]

a. Shareholder protections

Inevitably, not all of the stockholders may be pleased with the terms of the merger agreement. The shareholders possess three legal protections against a merger contrary to their wishes; or, viewed from the other perspective, the proponents of the merger face three potential hurdles from the stockholders of the merging companies:

(1) Voting rights

The first protection of the shareholders in a merger is the requirement that they receive the opportunity to vote on approving the transaction. Corporation statutes vary in how they handle several particulars of this requirement. For example, statutes differ in the level of approval needed (at least in the absence of a valid supermajority provision in the articles). Most modern statutes require a simple majority vote in favor of the merger,[8] but some statutes contain a more traditional supermajority requirement.[9] In either event, statutes often measure the applicable percentage against the number of outstanding shares, rather than against the number of shares represented at the meeting (as would be the rule applied to more ordinary matters put to a shareholder vote). A second area of difference among corporation statutes exists with respect the overlapping questions of whether otherwise non-voting stock can vote on the merger, and the necessity of approval by separate classes of shares (at least in the absence of governing provisions in the articles).[10]

---

7. *E.g.*, M.B.C.A. § 11.02(c)(3).

8. *E.g.*, M.B.C.A. § 11.04(e).

9. *E.g.*, N.Y. Bus. Corp. Law § 903(a)(2) (requiring a two-thirds vote for corporations in existence prior to 1998, unless the corporation's articles expressly calls for only a simple majority vote). As we shall discuss when dealing with tender offers later in this chapter, however, a number of states have adopted takeover statutes which raise the vote needed for a merger with a company which recently obtained a substantial percentage of the other merging corporation's outstanding stock. *E.g.*, Del. Gen. Corp. Law § 203.

10. *Compare* Del. Gen. Corp. Law § 251(c) (only requiring approval by the shares entitled to vote, and not requiring

Notice that statutes (like Delaware's) which do not allow all shares to vote, and do not require separate approval by each class of shares, create conflict-of-interest problems and the potential for opportunistic abuse when it comes to deciding what the holders of the different classes of stock will receive in a merger. After all, the more consideration which goes to the holders of one class of stock, the less there is to give to the holders of other classes of stock. If one class of stock has the votes the approve the merger despite opposition of holders of other classes, one suspects the class with the votes will get a better deal.

The requirement of a shareholder vote not only might impede the merger because of the prospect of disapproval, but also because of the administrative burden and cost of obtaining the vote (including compliance with the federal proxy regulations for 1934 Securities Exchange Act reporting companies). Hence, before imposing this burden, it is useful to ask whether a shareholder vote would serve any purpose, and whether the merger at hand really impacts the shareholders sufficiently to justify a vote. These thoughts explain the varying exceptions to the requirement of stockholder approval found in some of the state corporation statutes.

For example, the desire to avoid imposing an added burden only to get to a pre-ordained outcome explains, in part, the short-form merger provisions found in many state corporation statutes. Under these provisions, when the parent company owns an overwhelming percentage (typically 90 percent) of the shares in its subsidiary, a vote of the parent's board can merge the subsidiary corporation into the parent without the approval of either company's stockholders (and often without the approval of the subsidiary's board of directors).[11] Yet, the fact that the outcome is obvious before the vote with a 90 percent owned subsidiary only explains why the subsidiary's shareholders (and even the subsidiary's directors) do not get the opportunity to vote. What explains denying the vote to the parent corporation's shareholders? The answer lies in the impact of such a merger on the parent corporation and its shareholders. Given that the parent already owns at least 90 percent of the subsidiary involved in a short-form merger, how much impact can such a merger have on the parent's shareholders? After all, under these circumstances, the subsidiary's minority shareholders are hardly likely to receive so much cash, or stock in the parent, as to affect significantly the interest of the parent's present stockholders. Nor does such a merger significantly change the nature of the business conducted by the parent.

Some statutes have expanded upon the logic that if the merger does not significantly impact a corporation's shareholders, then the law should not require a shareholder vote on the merger. Specifically, a

separate approval by each class), *with* Cal. Corp. Code § 1201(a) (requiring separate approval by each class of shares, except for preferred shares whose rights remain unchanged in the merger); M.B.C.A. § 11.04(e), (f)(1) (requiring approval by the shares entitled to vote, but also separate approval by a majority of each class of shares if the merger converts the shares into other securities or cash or property, or if the plan of merger contains any provision which would require approval by that class if undertaken as an amendment to the articles of incorporation).

11. *E.g.*, M.B.C.A. § 11.05.

number of modern statutes allow the surviving company in a merger to forego a vote of its shareholders if its articles will not change, its shareholders will not exchange their stock for different shares, and the company will issue a relatively small amount of its common stock (typically no more than 20 percent of the number already outstanding) as part of the plan of merger (thus meaning little dilution of its shareholders' interests).[12]

(2) Appraisal rights

A second protection accorded to shareholders opposing a plan of merger is the right to demand the corporation cash them out at a fair price set by appraisal.[13] As explained when describing the history of American corporate law in the first chapter of this book, this appraisal right originated as something a compromise. The compromise occurred when corporations statutes abandoned the traditional rule that fundamental changes, such a mergers, required unanimous approval of the stockholders. In abandoning the unanimity requirement, state legislatures worried, both on constitutional law and fairness grounds, about allowing alteration, over minority shareholders' objections, of what one might view as a contract among the shareholders. To ameliorate these concerns, the idea arose to give the shareholders, who dissented from the merger, the right to demand the corporation buy back their stock. In this way, dissenting shareholders would not be bound to remain owners in a venture when the majority had made a fundamental change in the nature of the enterprise from what the shareholders originally bought into.

As with many compromises, appraisal statutes have satisfied neither side. From the standpoint of those favoring greater majority prerogatives, appraisal rights introduce unjustified uncertainty into mergers. Specifically, the existence of appraisal rights creates a risk for the proponents of the merger that so many stockholders might exercise the right that the surviving corporation will have difficulty funding the repurchases. To critics, this uncertainty has no modern justification.[14] Whatever the understanding was among Nineteenth Century investors, contemporary corporate shareholders recognize they bought an investment in an evolving venture which can change its nature dramatically without the concurrence of all shareholders. Indeed, the fact of the matter is that corporations radically change the nature of their business, risks and financial structure all the time through transactions which, because they do not involve a merger, do not even require a shareholder vote, let alone trigger appraisal rights.

12. *E.g.*, M.B.C.A. § 11.04(g). *See also* Cal. Corp. Code § 1201(b),(c),(d) (not requiring approval by shareholders of a merging corporation, whether or not the survivor, if those shareholders will end up owning five-sixths of the voting stock of the company surviving the merger (or its parent), unless their company amends its articles, or else these shareholders exchange their stock in the merger for shares with different rights).

13. *E.g.*, M.B.C.A. §§ 13.01 *et. seq.*

14. *E.g.*, Ernest Folk, *De Facto Mergers in Delaware:* Hariton v. Arco Electronics, Inc., 49 Va. L. Rev. 1261 (1963).

On the other hand, the same uncertainty complained of by critics of appraisal rights might, in fact, provide a continuing justification for such rights. The risk that so many shareholders will exercise their appraisal rights that the corporation will have trouble funding the payout, creates an incentive for the boards involved to be sure they have made an attractive deal for their shareholders. This serves as a discipline against directors sacrificing the shareholders' interests for the directors' own interests in negotiating a merger, or else just plain making foolish mistakes in entering the merger agreement.[15]

Still, appraisal rights have not constituted an ideal protection from the standpoint of objecting shareholders. One problem is that the statutory provisions creating appraisal rights commonly require shareholders wishing to assert the rights to comply with exacting requirements which can trip up many persons. For example, statutory appraisal provisions often require the shareholder to give written notice of his or her intent to demand appraisal *before* the vote on the merger, meaning tough luck for the shareholder who takes a long vacation, or is just not paying close enough attention.[16]

A more fundamental complaint with appraisal rights involves the price which the dissenting shareholder will receive for his or her shares. Perhaps the corporation and the dissenting shareholder(s) can reach an agreement on the price.[17] Otherwise, to set the price, the statutes call for a judicially supervised appraisal to establish the "fair value" of the shares.[18] This is why we have been referring to the right of dissenting shareholders to cash out as an "appraisal right." The statutes themselves normally provide little guidance as to the definition of fair value—except some statutes state that this value excludes any element arising from the merger itself.[19] Judicially developed standards for setting the

15. This rationale, however, still leaves the question of why the added discipline of appraisal rights is needed for mergers, but not for other board decisions. Indeed, in an earlier chapter, we considered the related difficulty of trying to figure out any principled basis for distinguishing those transactions which require shareholder approval, from those transactions which the board can undertake on its own. See § 3.1.3a *supra*.

16. M.B.C.A. § 13.21. *See also* M.B.C.A. §§ 13.22–13.23 (requiring further timely action by the shareholder to perfect appraisal rights after the vote). One idea behind short time limits is to prevent shareholders from hedging their bets by stalling while they see how the merger turns out. Moreover, needless to say, a shareholder who votes in favor of the merger cannot exercise appraisal rights.

17. The Model Act contains provisions designed to encourage the shareholder and corporation to agree on a price, including empowering the court to assess the costs of appraisal and attorneys fees against either side if the court finds the party acted arbitrarily, vexatiously or not in good faith in pushing the matter to a judicial appraisal. M.B.C.A. § 13.31.

18. *E.g.*, M.B.C.A. § 13.30.

19. *E.g.*, Del. Gen. Corp. Law § 262(h). The evident notion behind excluding any element of value arising from the merger is that a person who dissents from a merger should not be able to gain any benefit from the transaction. While this seems logical, in fact, it might undercut some of the utility of appraisal rights. Specifically, it is not inconsistent for a shareholder to claim that a merger increased the value of the combined entity, and hence the worth of his or her shares, but, nevertheless, to complain that the merger was unfair because too much of this gain went to other participants in the merger (most likely those in control of the corporation). If appraisal rights are to serve as a discipline on potentially unfair division

fair value of dissenting shares traditionally have tended to be conservative, with the result that appraisals often have not been very good deals for dissenting shareholders.

For many years, most courts have used what is known as the "Delaware block method" to value shares in an appraisal proceeding. Under the Delaware block method, the appraisers value the dissenter's stock using three different approaches: the value of the stock based upon the value of the corporation's assets less its liabilities and divided by the number of shares outstanding ("net asset value"), the value based upon the corporation's earnings per share multiplied by the price/earnings ratio of the stock of similar corporations ("earnings value"), and the value as reflected in the price at which the shares have traded recently in the stock market ("market value"). The court then values the shares by taking a weighted average of these three measures. So, for example, if the market value of the stock was $25 per share, the earnings value was $50 per share, and the net asset value was $100 per share, and the court assigned a weight of 10 percent to market value, 40 percent to earnings value, and 50 percent to net asset value, the appraised value of the shares would be: ($25 x 10%) + ($50 x 40%) + ($100 x 50%) = $72.50.[20]

While the Delaware block method looks like a neat mathematical way of valuing stock, in fact, it produces highly questionable results. To begin with, let us consider the notion of using a weighted average of three very different approaches to stock valuation. At first glance, this seems sensible. After all, valuation is far from an exact science, and by averaging together different approaches one might limit the impact of the inevitable flaws in any one approach.[21] The problem is that this averaging process contains an inherent prejudice toward undervaluing shares.[22] To see why, let us start by the considering the situation in which earnings value is greater than asset value—in other words, the value of the shares based upon the expected future earnings of the corporation is greater than the value computed by figuring out the worth of each separate corporate asset, totaled this up, and subtracted the company's debts. In fact, this is the result we should expect: Unless the

of the merger gains—rather than leaving a lawsuit for breach of fiduciary duty as the only potential remedy—than the valuation should include the impact of the merger. Interestingly enough in light of this discussion, the Delaware courts have suggested a different rationale for excluding elements of value arising from the merger. This new rationale is to exclude overly speculative valuations which represent a mere guess at the effect of the merger. *E.g.*, Weinberger v. UOP, Inc., 457 A.2d 701 (Del.1983). Under this rationale, less speculative values created by the merger might be considered—particularly insofar as one might argue that the value of the pre-merger corporation includes the company's attractiveness as a merger partner. In any event, if the impact of the merger is to *decrease* the value of the objecting shareholder's stock—which is what the shareholder asserting appraisal rights commonly must believe—than it would undermine the purpose of the appraisal right to take such a decrease into account.

20. *E.g.*, Piemonte v. New Boston Garden Corp., 377 Mass. 719, 387 N.E.2d 1145 (1979).

21. Moreover, in assigning how much weight to give each measure, the court will assess how apropos each measure is to the valuation at hand.

22. Schaefer, *The Fallacy of Weighing Asset Value and Earnings Value in the Appraisal of Corporate Stock*, 55 S. Cal. L. Rev. 1031 (1982).

managers of the corporation have structured the venture inefficiently, the whole should be worth more than the sum of the parts.[23] In this event, earnings value reflects the real worth of the stock, since the purpose of the corporation is to earn profits, and there is no reason to care about the separate worth of assets if one does not plan to sell off the assets. Hence, averaging earnings value with asset value simply lowers the price paid to the shareholders based upon a figure (asset value) which is largely irrelevant. Suppose, however, the asset value is greater than the value based upon expected earnings. This tells us that the efficient thing to do is break up the corporation and sell off the pieces. Indeed, one suspects this is often what will happen after the merger. Again, averaging earnings value with asset value undervalues the dissenter's shares, since future earnings potential is irrelevant if the efficient thing to do is sell off the assets rather than continue the venture.

In addition to the problem introduced by averaging the results of different approaches to stock valuation, there are also problems with the way in which courts applying the Delaware block method have insisted that the appraisers perform the specific valuations. This is particularly the case with respect to earnings valuation. The basic concept behind earnings valuation is that in purchasing any investment, such as a share of stock, one essentially is buying a future stream of income. Hence, the value of the investment depends upon two variables: (1) What one expects the future stream of income to be; and (2) What the present value of the expected future income is, given both the time value of money, and the risk that the expected future income might not materialize.

Courts applying the Delaware block method compute the expected future income under an approach which is contrary to modern financial theory. To start with, courts have looked at earnings computed in accordance with accepted accounting principles. In fact, however, cash flow typically provides an economically more realistic measure of future income.[24] More importantly, courts applying the Delaware block method base their expectation of future income upon an average of past income. Specifically, the norm is to compute the average of the last five years' of corporate earnings per share (disregarding any one-time extraordinary items which may have distorted a particular year's earnings).[25] The court then assumes this five year average predicts the corporation's future earnings. This approach, however, seriously understates the value of any company with growing earnings (which is what most efficiently run

---

23. This is the point of purchasing a bunch of assets and putting them together into a profit making venture.

24. To see why, assume a corporation purchased for $1 million a manufacturing plant with an expected life of 20 years. Straight line depreciation would lower the corporation's earnings for accounting purposes by $50,000 each year (1/20 of $1 million). Yet, to treat the corporation's annual earnings as $50,000 less because in 20 years

the company will no longer have the plant ignores the fact that until that time the corporation (or its owners) have the extra money to invest. Keep in mind that because of the time value of money, $50,000 per year for 20 years is worth more than $1 million 20 years in the future.

25. *See, e.g.,* Francis I. duPont & Co. v. Universal City Studios, Inc., 312 A.2d 344 (Del.Ch.1973), *aff'd.,* 334 A.2d 216 (1975).

companies should be). To illustrate, assume a company made steadily growing earnings per share over the last five years of $2.00, $2.50, $3.00, $3.50, and $4.00. All other factors being equal, one would expect future earnings of this company to be at least $4.00 per share, and presumably more. Yet, taking the five year average predicts earnings per share of only $3.00.

There are also flaws in the manner in which courts applying the Delaware block method compute the present value of the predicted future earnings. Courts applying the Delaware block method compute the present value of the predicted future earnings by multiplying the earnings by the price/earnings ratio of similar companies. This is justified if the comparison firms have *both* similar risks and similar expectations for future earnings growth. If, however, the comparison firms have similar risks, but not similar expectations for future earnings growth, then one should not expect that investors would value the stock at the same price/earnings ratio.[26] To obtain a more accurate computation of the present value of expected future earnings, modern financial economists have developed an approach which is more sophisticated than simply a price/earnings comparison. This approach employs a rather complex theory referred to as the capital asset pricing model. While a discussion of this approach is well beyond the scope of this book, the essential idea is that the expected rate of return for stock should be a linear function of the stock's expected volatility relative to the overall stock market.[27]

Within the last couple of decades, the Delaware courts have come to recognize the weakness of the Delaware block method—creating the irony that the method now is least likely to find application in the jurisdiction for which the method is named.[28] Specifically, in *Weinberger v. UOP, Inc.*,[29] the Delaware Supreme Court instructed the Chancery Court to use, in future appraisals, any valuation techniques generally considered acceptable in the financial community, including valuation based upon discounted cash flow.[30] The New York legislature similarly

---

26. For example, if investors in the stock market pay a price for a particular corporation's stock equal to 15 times the company's most recently reported earnings per share, this reflects both investors' expectations for future growth in the company's earnings (the more the investors expect the earnings to grow in the future, the greater a multiple over the present earnings investors are willing to pay), and the riskiness of the stock (the riskier the stock, the greater a return on investment demanded by investors, and, hence, the lower a multiple over current earnings investors are willing to pay). Hence, the fact that stock in a corporation with similar riskiness currently sells at 15 times earnings per share does not mean that the corporation whose stock is being appraised is worth only 15 times earnings per share, if the appraised corpo-

ration expects greater growth in future income than the comparison company.

27. For a judicial explanation and application of the capital asset pricing model to obtain the present value of expected future earnings (for purposes of a valuation in a bankruptcy proceeding), see In re Pullman Construction Indus., Inc., 107 B.R. 909 (Bkrtcy.N.D.Ill.1989).

28. *See, e.g.,* Leader v. Hycor, Inc., 395 Mass. 215, 479 N.E.2d 173 (1985) (Massachusetts court rejected the argument that the Delaware block method is outmoded).

29. 457 A.2d 701 (Del.1983).

30. The Delaware Chancery court's decision in *Gilbert v. MPM Enterprises, Inc.*, 709 A.2d 663 (Del.Ch.1997), provides an illustration of the discounted cash flow ap-

has acted to liberalize valuation methods used in appraisal proceedings.[31]

One part of the Delaware block method we have not spent much time discussing is market valuation—in other words, the price the stock recently has traded at on the market. At first glance, this might seem strange, since presumably the best measure of a stock's value would be what investors are willing to pay for the stock and other investors are willing to sell the stock for. When dealing with a closely held corporation, the simple explanation for giving little or no credence to market value is that there is little or no market. At best, there might be an occasional sale, typically between the existing owners. Yet, the circumstances of such a sale (such as the motivations for the transaction and the bargaining positions of the parties involved), are likely to be sufficiently unique so that the sale price will provide little guidance as to the value of the stock (even if the transaction was relatively recent).[32] Even if the corporation is not closely held, the stock might be so thinly traded as to raise skepticism as to the utility of the market price as a measure of value.[33]

Suppose, however, the stock subject to appraisal is widely traded. In this event, one might assume that the market provides the best measure of the stock's worth. Indeed, if shareholders who want out could sell their shares easily in an active market, one might question whether an appraisal remedy is even necessary. This thinking has led a number of states to deny appraisal rights to shares listed for trading on a national stock exchange or the NASDAQ, or held by a very large number of shareholders (such as 2000).[34] This exclusion, however, has not been without controversy. One bone of contention is the fundamental question of whether markets provide the best measure of a stock's worth. More specifically with respect to appraisal rights, the market exception suffers from a potential circularity problem. To see why, consider what will happen to the market price of stock following the announcement

---

proach. Instead of basing its estimate of future earnings on an average of past years' earnings, the court looked to a three year financial forecast prepared by the corporation's management before the merger, extrapolated to assume continued growth for the next two years at the same pace as forecasted for the prior three years. The court then used a discount rate derived from the capital asset pricing model to compute the present value of the projected future earnings combined with the value of the corporation at the end of the five year period for which there were specific earnings projections.

31. N.Y. Bus. Corp. Law § 623(h)(4).

32. As a realistic matter, the lack of a market lowers the value of stock. Nevertheless, most courts have not been sympathetic to the argument that appraisals of shares for which there is no ready market should reflect a discount for lack of marketability. *E.g.*, In re Valuation of Common Stock of McLoon Oil Co., 565 A.2d 997 (Me.1989). *But see* In re Friedman v. Beway Realty Corp., 87 N.Y.2d 161, 638 N.Y.S.2d 399, 661 N.E.2d 972 (1995). The notion is that appraisals are designed to give every shareholder his or her proportionate interest in the value of the overall company, rather than just the value of his or her individual shares. For the same reason, most courts reject so-called minority discounts in appraisal proceedings. *Id. But see* Hernando Bank v. Huff, 609 F.Supp. 1124 (N.D.Miss. 1985), *aff'd.*, 796 F.2d 803 (5th Cir.1986).

33. *E.g.*, Piemonte v. New Boston Garden Corp., 377 Mass. 719, 387 N.E.2d 1145 (1979) (assigning only 10 percent weight to market valuation when the stock was thinly traded).

34. *E.g.*, Del. Gen. Corp. Law § 262(b).

that the corporation's board has proposed a merger on terms which give public shareholders a poor deal (particularly if the public holds only a minority of the outstanding shares, and so lacks the votes to block the deal). Presumably, the price of the stock on the market will go down to reflect the impact of the merger. Hence, denying appraisal rights on the ground that shareholders always can dump their stock on the market seems to remove the rights in one of the situations in which such rights otherwise might serve the most utility of disciplining board merger decisions.

State corporation statutes often contain a number of other exclusions from appraisal rights. For example, many states limit the rights to holders of shares entitled to vote on the merger, plus minority shareholders of the subsidiary in a short-form merger.[35]

(3) Fiduciary Duty

A third protection for dissident shareholders is to initiate a court action challenging the merger as a breach of the directors' or controlling stockholders' fiduciary duty. Such a challenge might involve either duty of care or duty of loyalty claims. By and large, duty of loyalty claims arise in the context of parent-subsidiary and freeze-out mergers. We will defer consideration of such mergers until later point in this chapter. By contrast, a challenge to a merger between two companies in an arms-length relationship involves a duty of care claim. Such a duty of care claim faces an uphill battle to surmount the business judgment rule. For instance, complaints about the substantive merits of the deal probably will go nowhere unless the inadequacy in the value of what the stockholders received in the merger is "so gross as to lead the court to conclude that it was due not to an honest error in judgment but rather to bad faith, or to a reckless indifference".[36] Still, in a much noted case,[37] a court found directors liable for approving a merger in a grossly ill-informed manner.

One important wrinkle, however, differentiates possible fiduciary duty challenges in the merger context from fiduciary duty challenges in general. This involves the impact of appraisal rights. If shareholders have the right to cash out at a fair price set by appraisal, one might ask why the shareholders also need the ability to bring a suit complaining that the merger breached the directors' or controlling shareholder's fiduciary duties. This sort of thinking has affected a number of legislatures in enacting statutory provisions creating appraisal rights, as well as some courts in interpreting such statutes. Specifically some statutes expressly state, and courts have interpreted some other statutes to imply, that, with various exceptions, appraisal constitutes the exclusive remedy for shareholders dissatisfied with a merger. The result can be to preclude shareholders from challenging the merger based upon breach of

---

35. *E.g.*, M.B.C.A. § 13.02(a)(1).

36. Cole v. National Cash Credit Ass'n, 18 Del.Ch. 47, 156 A. 183 (1931).

37. Smith v. Van Gorkom, 488 A.2d 858 (Del.1985).

fiduciary duty.[38] We shall discuss this subject in greater detail later in this chapter when we explore freeze-out mergers (which constitute the principal context in which the issue arises).

The presence of multiple classes of stock can lead to additional fiduciary duty challenges in the event of a merger. Specifically, the owners of one class of stock (say the preferred) might complain that the holders of another class of stock (say the common) received an unfair amount of the consideration in the merger at the expense of the complaining shareholders.[39] Alternately, holders of one class of shares might complain about a merger agreement which left them still holding their stock, while other shareholders received the opportunity to make an apparently favorable exchange.[40] Presumably, the degree of scrutiny applied by the court to such decisions should depend upon the degree to which the directors either had a personal interest in making the decision which arguably favored one class over another, or were under the control of the owners of the allegedly favored class.

Incidentally, given the differences in state laws concerning the rights of shareholders in a merger, what happens when the proposed merger is between companies incorporated in different states? State statutes generally contain separate provisions dealing with mergers between domestic and foreign corporations in an effort to answer such questions (typically providing each corporation follows its own state's procedures governing shareholder rights).[41]

b.   Succession to assets and liabilities

Thus far, our focus has been on the impact of the merger on the shareholders of the merging corporations. Now let us take a closer look at the impact of the merger on the corporation which emerges from the transaction. As stated above, the central concept is that this corporation (be it the surviving corporation in a merger or the new corporation in a consolidation) succeeds by operation of law to all of the assets and liabilities of the disappearing corporations[42]—much like an ameba absorbs its prey. While the basic concept is straightforward, occasionally questions or problems arise in its application.

Let us start with the assets. Suppose that the disappearing corporation possessed certain contract rights (say, rights under a patent licensing agreement), which the contract states are non-assignable. In this event, does the surviving corporation succeed to the rights or does the non-assignability clause trump? In a rather surprising result, one court has held that the transfer of assets to the surviving corporation in a

38. *E.g.*, Steinberg v. Amplica, Inc., 42 Cal.3d 1198, 233 Cal.Rptr. 249, 729 P.2d 683 (1986).

39. *See, e.g.*, Jedwab v. MGM Grand Hotels, Inc., 509 A.2d 584 (Del.Ch.1986) (finding the division to be fair).

40. *See, e.g.*, Dalton v. American Investment Co., 490 A.2d 574 (Del.Ch.), *aff'd*, 501

A.2d 1238 (Del.1985) (finding that the board did not breach its duty in accepting a deal to exchange the just the common, but not the preferred, stock, when the impetus for this structure came from the buyer).

41. *E.g.*, M.B.C.A. § 11.02(b).

42. *E.g.*, M.B.C.A. § 11.07(a).

merger is just the same as a sale, and so is subject to a contractual prohibition on the assignment of patent rights.[43] Actually, the practical result of this holding might simply be to create a trap for the unwary, since, as we shall see, it is often fairly easy to structure a merger to avoid any argument that the transaction even attempted an assignment otherwise subject to the non-assignment clause.

At first glance, the surviving corporation's automatic assumption of the disappearing corporation's liabilities would seem to be an undesirable feature of a merger from the standpoint of those organizing the transaction. In fact, however, the practical impact of this feature of a merger is more complicated. To begin with, normally the merger agreement will lower the consideration received by the shareholders of the disappearing corporation to reflect the assumed debts. This protects the interests of the shareholders of the surviving corporation, and generally should be acceptable to the former shareholders of the disappearing corporation.[44] This works well, however, only with known debts. The real problem lies with latent liabilities. For example, a product manufactured by the disappearing corporation years before the merger might cause an injury years after the transaction.[45] The prospect of such future claims makes it much more difficult to reach agreement on an adjustment in the consideration received by the disappearing corporation's shareholders.

In one type of transaction, the surviving corporation's automatic assumption of liabilities as a result of a merger is, in fact, the sole reason for the merger. This is in a leveraged buy-out. Broadly speaking, a leveraged buy-out is a fancy way of saying that the purchaser of a business borrowed the money to pay for the purchase. Moreover, the buyer's expectation is to use the earnings of the business to pay off the loan. (Otherwise, why purchase the business?) In this broad sense, when my father borrowed money to buy out his brother's share of a family owned furniture store, it was a species of leveraged buy-out. The obvious danger with a leveraged buy-out is that the earnings of the business might not be sufficient to pay off the loan—which ultimately was the fate of the family furniture store.[46] To protect themselves from this

---

43. PPG Indus., Inc. v. Guardian Indus. Corp., 597 F.2d 1090 (6th Cir.1979). *But see* Dodier Realty & Inv. Co. v. St. Louis Nat'l. Baseball Club, Inc., 361 Mo. 981, 238 S.W.2d 321 (Mo. 1951); M.B.C.A. § 11.07(a)(3). Interestingly enough, the court in *PPG* chose not to follow statements in both a leading corporate law multi-volume treatise and a leading patent law treatise that the surviving corporation in a merger obtained patent rights owned by the disappearing corporation despite non-assignment clauses. This just goes to show that one must take whatever is written in a treatise with a grain of salt.

44. This is because the alternative transaction, in which a corporation simply

buys another corporation's assets without assuming the selling corporation's debts, normally would require payment of the selling corporation's debts prior to distribution of the remaining proceeds to the selling corporation's shareholders—thereby leaving the disappearing or selling corporation's shareholders the same net return in either case.

45. *See, e.g.,* Ramirez v. Amsted Indus., Inc., 86 N.J. 332, 431 A.2d 811 (1981).

46. Fortunately, my father became an attorney and probably a lot happier than he would have been had he stayed in the furniture business.

danger, parties lending money for leveraged buy-outs typically want collateral.

The lender's desire for collateral poses a particular problem when the leveraged buy-out involves a corporation. The borrower who uses the loan to purchase the outstanding stock in the corporation could offer the purchased stock as collateral. Stock, however, is not a particularly good collateral from the standpoint of the lender. The reason is that if the corporation fails to generate sufficient earnings to service the loan (or, worse, goes bankrupt trying), obtaining ownership of the stock will place the creditor last in line for whatever is left over after the corporation pays its other creditors. Hence, parties making loans for leveraged buy-outs commonly wish to "loan to the assets"—in other words, have the corporation's assets secure the loan.[47] This desire, however, forces us to ask how a corporation can become liable for a loan used to purchase the corporation's outstanding stock. A simple-minded approach might be to have the corporation guarantee the purchaser's loans. Notice, however, that such a contract does nothing for the corporation, and, accordingly, might be subject to attack as ultra vires.[48]

Now consider the utility, for parties planning a leveraged buy-out, of the rule that the surviving corporation in a merger becomes liable for the disappearing corporation's debts. Suppose the purchaser sets up a new corporation to borrow money and purchase the outstanding stock in an existing corporation. The new corporation then could merge into the corporation whose outstanding stock it purchased, with the result that the surviving corporation would become liable for the loans used to purchase the outstanding stock in itself. Neat trick.[49]

From a policy perspective, this transaction illustrates the problems created by the use of merger statutes to accomplish something which the legislature probably never contemplated. Presumably, the notion behind the surviving corporation's automatic assumption of the disappearing corporation's debts in a merger is that this constitutes a quid pro quo for the surviving corporation's obtaining the disappearing corporation's assets—which the disappearing corporation otherwise would have used to pay its debts. The problem in a merger to carry out a leveraged buy-out is that the assets of the disappearing corporation consist of stock in the surviving corporation—which is worthless to the surviving corporation. Hence, all the surviving corporation gets in the deal is more debt. This fact, in turn, leads to complaints from the surviving firm's pre-merger creditors—particularly if the surviving firm goes bankrupt after the leveraged buy-out.

---

47. Tax laws and margin rules also can favor placing the corporation on the hook for the loans. *See* Gevurtz, *supra* note 2 at 845–850.

48. *See, e.g.,* Real Estate Capital Corp. v. Thunder Corp., 31 Ohio Misc. 169, 287 N.E.2d 838 (1972).

49. The typical leveraged buy-out is a bit more complex than this description because of the common use of short-term (or bridge) loans to obtain the stock. After the merger, the surviving corporation replaces the bridge loans with longer term loans secured by its assets.

Doctrinally, creditors have attacked leveraged buy-outs using several theories. Two of these theories rely on putting together the various individual pieces of a leveraged buy-out to identify its ultimate economic impact. Notice that the shareholders of the original corporation who sold in the leveraged buy-out ended up with cash. The corporation ended up in debt to repay loans which directly or indirectly supplied this cash. Hence, the end result of the leveraged buy-out is equivalent to the corporation, itself, borrowing to repurchase its stock, and ought to be subject to the limits for the benefit of creditors which corporation statutes create on corporate share repurchases.[50] Some courts have had no problem is seeing this logic;[51] albeit the multiple steps of a leveraged buy-out have snowed less astute courts.[52]

Other courts have put the steps of a leveraged buy-out together to declare that the transaction can constitute a fraudulent conveyance—as a transfer without fair consideration which rendered the corporation insolvent. One question under the fraudulent conveyance theory, however, is who exactly is the recipient of the transfer without consideration.[53] Some courts have held that the parties who made the loans for the leveraged buy-out are the recipients of a transfer without consideration.[54] Yet, these lenders have given consideration—this being the loans. The argument is that, since the consideration ultimately ended up in the hands of the shareholders, rather than the corporation, there was no consideration *to the corporation* in exchange for the corporation's IOU and the pledge of the corporation's assets as collateral. On the other hand, what about the shareholders who sold their stock in the leveraged buy-out? They were the ones who ultimately received the proceeds of the loans. The shareholders' argument, much like the leveraged buy-out lenders', is that the shareholders gave consideration—in this case the stock sold in the leveraged buy-out. One court has suggested that the validity of this argument depends upon whether the shareholders were unaware that the proceeds of the sale ultimately came from debt incurred by the corporation.[55]

Finally, creditors might argue that the directors breached their fiduciary duty in going along the leveraged buy-out. This argument brings us back to the issue addressed in an earlier chapter as to whether directors have a duty to the corporation's creditors.[56] For reasons outlined in this earlier discussion, if the leveraged buy-out renders the corporation insolvent (or even near insolvent), then such a duty should exist.

50. See § 2.3.3b *supra*.

51. *E.g.*, Munford v. Valuation Research Corp., 97 F.3d 456 (11th Cir.1996).

52. *E.g.*, In re C–T of Virginia, Inc., 958 F.2d 606 (4th Cir.1992).

53. Another question under the fraudulent conveyance theory is whether the transaction left the corporation insolvent.

54. *E.g.*, United States v. Tabor Court Realty, 803 F.2d 1288 (3d Cir.1986).

55. Wieboldt Stores, Inc. v. Schottenstein, 94 B.R. 488 (N.D.Ill.1988).

56. See § 4.1.5a *supra*.

c. *Triangular and upside-down mergers*

The discussion of mergers thus far has suggested a number of potential disadvantages of mergers as a mode to structure a corporate acquisition. These include the automatic assumption by the surviving corporation of potential latent liabilities of the disappearing corporation, the potential loss of non-transferable contract rights, and the burdens of shareholder voting and appraisal rights. The desire to avoid these sorts of disadvantages (from the prospective of corporate planners), while, at the same time, obtaining the advantages (under tax and other laws) of the merger over the sale of assets and the purchase of stock modes of structuring an acquisition, have led corporate planners to develop the triangular and upside-down mergers.

A triangular merger simply means that the merger takes place between one corporation (commonly called the "target corporation") and a subsidiary of another corporation (this other corporation commonly being called the "acquiring corporation"), rather than between the target corporation and the acquiring corporation itself. This subsidiary might be either an existing corporation which is actually conducting some business before the merger, or, commonly, a new corporation set up just for purposes of the merger. The corporation surviving the merger might be either the subsidiary, in which case the transaction is referred to as a "forward triangular merger," or the target corporation, a so-called "reverse triangular merger."

One obvious utility of the triangular merger is to avoid the acquiring corporation automatically becoming liable for the target's debts. Instead, since the merger is between the target corporation and a subsidiary of the acquiring corporation, only the subsidiary will become liable for the target corporation's debts (barring grounds for piercing the corporate veil).

As with any merger, the shareholders of the merging companies in a triangular merger receive in exchange for their shares the type of consideration provided by the plan of merger. Invariably, the plan of merger will provide the acquiring corporation with stock in the corporation surviving the merger, since this is the point of the whole transaction.[57] In principle, the target corporation's pre-merger shareholders also could receive shares in the surviving company; in other words, keep their shares in the target corporation in a reverse triangular merger, or exchange for stock in the surviving subsidiary in a forward triangular merger. Ordinarily, however, this is unsatisfactory from the standpoint of both parties to the merger. Ownership of less than 100 percent of the stock of the subsidiary following the merger will leave the acquiring corporation subject to minority shareholder lawsuits regarding any parent-subsidiary dealings. At the same time, the target corporation's pre-

---

57. In a forward triangular merger, the acquiring corporation simply can keep the shares it already owned in its subsidiary; in a reverse triangular merger, the acquiring corporation exchanges the shares it owned in its subsidiary for shares in the target corporation.

merger shareholders typically would rather not end up with shares in a controlled subsidiary, since such shares are often not easily marketable. An alternative is to provide the target corporation's pre-merger shareholders with cash or other property in exchange for their stock. Another alternative is for the target corporation's pre-merger shareholders to receive stock in the acquiring corporation. These two alternatives, however, posed a problem under merger provisions in older corporation statutes, since such provisions commonly limited the consideration which shareholders could receive in the merger to stock in the surviving corporation.[58] Presumably, stock in the acquiring corporation fits within the ambit of property, and so is permissible consideration under those statutes allowing the plan of merger to call for the exchange of shares for cash or other property. Just to be totally clear, many statutes explicitly list shares in any other corporation as acceptable consideration for the shareholders to receive in a merger.[59]

Mechanically, undertaking a triangular merger means going through the same procedures as for any merger (since most state statutes do not provide any special provisions for such transactions.) Notice, however, a critical distinction as far as obtaining shareholder approval (or granting appraisal rights) on the acquiring corporation's side. The merging corporation is not the acquiring corporation, but rather is the subsidiary of the acquiring corporation. This means it is the acquiring corporation (acting through the acquiring corporation's board of directors) who must vote, as the one and only shareholder of the merging subsidiary, to approve the merger, and it is the acquiring corporation, as the one and only shareholder of the merging subsidiary, who possesses appraisal rights (which, needless to say, it will not exercise). The shareholders of the acquiring corporation, themselves, have neither a vote nor appraisal rights—after all, their corporation is not merging—despite the fact that they may suffer dilution of their interests by virtue of the acquiring corporation's issuing stock to the pre-merger shareholders of the target corporation, just like in a non-triangular merger.[60]

There are several possible limitations on the use triangular mergers to deprive the acquiring corporation's shareholders of the voting and appraisal rights which these shareholders would have if the acquiring corporation itself was one of the merging companies. If the acquiring

---

58. Stock in the acquiring corporation would not meet this limitation, since the acquiring corporation is not one of the merging corporations; rather, the acquiring corporation is a shareholder of one of the merging corporations.

59. *E.g.*, M.B.C.A. § 11.02(c)(3). Technically, there are a couple of exchanges of stock involved in a triangular merger. Prior to the merger, the acquiring corporation transfers either cash, property, or stock in itself, to the subsidiary in return for stock in the subsidiary. Then, as part of the merger, the surviving corporation ex-

changes the cash, property, or stock in the acquiring corporation, which the subsidiary previously received, for all of the stock in the target corporation owned by the target corporation's pre-merger stockholders.

60. As noted above, technically, the acquiring corporation issued its stock to its subsidiary in exchange for newly issued stock in the subsidiary—a transaction which does not require shareholder approval unless the acquiring corporation needed to amend its articles to increase the amount of authorized shares.

corporation has shares listed on a major stock exchange, the exchange rules might require the corporation to put the acquisition to a vote of its stockholders (depending upon how many shares the acquiring corporation will issue in the transaction).[61] Perhaps a court might find the defacto merger doctrine—which we shall discuss shortly—applicable to a triangular merger under some circumstances.[62] A few states' (such as California's) corporation statutes grant voting and appraisal rights to the shareholders of an acquiring corporation in a triangular merger if they incur significant dilution of their interest as a result of the transaction.[63]

Notice, in a reverse triangular merger, the shareholder of the *disappearing* corporation (this being the acquiring corporation) ends up owning most or all of the *surviving* corporation's stock. This idea has uses beyond triangular mergers. There is no reason that the corporation, whose shareholders will end up owning most of the combined enterprise, must be the surviving corporation in a non-triangular merger. Instead, the corporation, whose shareholders will end up with only a minority interest in the combined enterprise after the merger (or even cashed out altogether), could be the surviving firm. This is often referred to as an upside-down merger. The earlier discussion of the problem of non-assignable contract rights points up one major utility of reverse triangular and up-side down mergers. By having the corporation with such rights be the company surviving the merger—even if this company's shareholders will end up as the minority owners or cashed out—the parties can argue that there was no attempted transfer of non-assignable contract rights from the disappearing corporation to the surviving corporation.

7.2.2 *Sale of Assets and Dissolution*

The second basic mode for structuring the acquisition or combination of corporate businesses is for one corporation to sell its assets to another corporation. Very often, the purchasing corporation will assume some or all of the selling corporation's liabilities, and the selling corporation will dissolve following the sale. If the parties undertake these two additional steps, the result of a sale of assets transaction largely parallels a statutory merger; yet the rights of the shareholders, and the impact of the transaction on certain creditors, can be radically different.

a. *Corporate mechanics for a sale of substantially all assets*

As with a statutory merger, a sale of substantially all assets from one corporation to another generally requires the boards of the two

61. *E.g.*, N.Y.S.E. Listed Company Manual § 312.03(c) (requiring shareholder approval to issue common shares in any transaction, other than to raise money, in which the newly issued common stock will equal at least 20 percent of the formerly outstanding common shares); *see also* M.B.C.A. § 6.21(f).

62. In re Penn Central Securities Litigation, 367 F.Supp. 1158 (E.D.Pa.1973). *But see* Terry v. Penn Central Corp. 668 F.2d 188 (3d Cir.1981).

63. *E.g.*, Cal. Corp. Code §§ 1200(e), 1201(a),(b).

companies to reach an agreement.[64] This contract of sale covers much the same ground as a merger plan—for instance, specifying the price (albeit not necessarily the ultimate distribution of the consideration to the selling corporation's stockholders), and any representations, warranties and contingencies. Because the sale of substantially all of a corporation's assets typically entails the conveyance of a considerable number of individual properties, the drafting of the contract of sale and related documentation can be significantly more complex than drafting a merger agreement.

Several potentially critical differences between a sale of assets and a statutory merger involve the rights of the shareholders of the two corporations involved. Let us start with the shareholders of the selling corporation. At first glance, the rights of the stockholders of the selling company seem the same as the rights of stockholders in a merging corporation. Specifically, state corporation statutes require a corporation to obtain the approval of its shareholders in order to sell substantially all of its assets outside the ordinary course of business.[65]

Notice, however, that the question of what transactions trigger the requirement of shareholder approval is not as straightforward for sales of assets as it normally is for mergers. This is because often it is not clear whether the transaction constitutes a sale of "substantially all" of a corporation's assets. For example, in *Katz v. Bregman*,[66] a shareholder sued to enjoin the sale of the corporation's Canadian subsidiary. The Canadian subsidiary constituted over 51 percent of the corporation's total assets, and produced around 45 percent of the corporation's sales (and the corporation's only profits during the last four years). Sale of the subsidiary also would mark the abandonment of the corporation's historic business, which was being a producer of steel drums. While, under these facts, the sale was undoubtedly highly significant, it would not appear to fit what most folks would think of as a sale of substantially all assets. Nevertheless, the court held that the transaction constituted a sale of substantially all assets and required a shareholder vote.

The court's approach in *Katz* seems less geared toward a quantitative assessment of the assets sold, than it seems to represent a qualitative assessment of when a transaction so fundamentally redirects a corporation's business as to call for approval from the shareholders. While this makes a certain amount of policy sense, unfortunately it

64. Actually, corporation statutes only specifically address the role of the selling corporation's board. *See, e.g.,* M.B.C.A. § 12.02(a) (corporation may sell substantially all assets on terms and conditions determined by the board and approved by the shareholders). Whether the purchasing corporation's board must approve the deal depends upon the general principles of corporate authority discussed earlier in this book. See § 3.1.1*b supra.* It is possible that the transaction might be sufficiently ordinary that a corporation's president, or even lower level officers, would have authority to

enter the contract on their own—as, for example, if a "Fortune 500" corporation were to buy all of the assets of a corporation whose sole business is to operate one local hardware store. Commonly, however, the purchase of substantially all of the assets of a corporation would be a significant enough transaction to go before the buyer's board for approval.

65. *E.g.,* Del. Gen. Corp. Law § 271(a).

66. 431 A.2d 1274 (Del.Ch.1981).

ultimately might turn into a quixotic exercise. For instance, in *Katz*, the corporation's board might have avoided the court's result simply by reordering the transactions the corporation undertook. Specifically, the company earlier had sold off a number of diverse and unprofitable operations, and the board planned to use the proceeds of the sale of the Canadian subsidiary to embark upon new lines of business. Had the board borrowed to embark upon the proposed new endeavors, and retained the unprofitable other business lines until after the sale of the Canadian subsidiary, then it might have been much more difficult for the court to characterize the sale of the subsidiary, itself, as a dramatic change in corporate direction. In any event, this sort of expansive approach to defining a sale of substantially all assets is not universally accepted. For example, the Model Act's new sale of assets provision limits the requirement of a shareholder vote to dispositions which "would leave the corporation without significant continuing business activity."[67]

Even when there is a sale of substantially all assets, there still may be differences in the rights of the shareholders of the selling corporation, as compared with the rights of shareholders of a merging corporation. For example, some states differentiate between the precise vote required for a merger, and that required to sell a company's assets.[68] More significantly, some states do not provide appraisal rights for the selling corporation's shareholders in a sale of assets transaction.[69] Of course, if a corporation sells its assets for cash, and soon liquidates, there is little point to an appraisal and cash-out—a fact reflected in many statutes which otherwise provide appraisal rights upon a sale of substantially all assets.[70] Note, however, that a statute's failure to provide appraisal rights is a two-edged sword: No longer can the proponents of the transaction argue the statutory appraisal provision preempts any claim for breach of fiduciary duty.

The more significant distinction between a merger and a sale of assets transaction lies, not in the rights of the selling company's shareholders, but in the rights of the stockholders of the buyer. Under most statutes, the buying corporation's shareholders possess neither the right to vote, nor appraisal rights. Several developments, however, have eroded this distinction.

To begin with, as noted earlier, a number of corporation statutes do not require approval of a merger by (or grant appraisal rights to) the shareholders of the corporation surviving the merger, so long as the

67. M.B.C.A. § 12.02(a).

68. *E.g.*, Cal. Corp. Code §§ 1001(a)(2), 1201(a) (requiring a class vote to approve a merger in certain circumstances in which approval by voting shares without a class vote would be sufficient for a sale of assets transaction producing the same economic result). Such distinctions in voting rights make sense when the inherent nature of a sale of assets transaction provides other protections. For example, owners of non-voting preferred stock have the protection of their liquidation preferences in a sale of assets for cash followed by a corporate dissolution.

69. *See, e.g.*, Del. Gen. Corp. Law § 262(b).

70. *E.g.*, N.Y. Bus. Corp. Law § 910(a)(1)(B).

shareholders' rights do not change, and if the shareholders do not suffer significant dilution through the issuance of new stock in the merger. This corresponds to the impact of the transaction on the buyer's shareholders in many, if not most, sale of assets transactions. Hence, in many, if not most, sale of assets transactions, the buyer's shareholders would not have been entitled to a vote or to appraisal rights under a number of corporation statutes, even if the parties had cast the acquisition as a merger rather than a sale of assets.

Often, however, the purchaser's stockholders in a sale of assets transaction will suffer significant dilution through the issuance of additional common shares in exchange for the selling corporation's properties. In this case, the rules of the major stock exchanges may require the corporation, if it has shares listed on the exchange, to put the transaction (regardless of how structured) to a shareholder vote.[71] Moreover, if the purchasing corporation agrees to pay with its stock, but has insufficient authorized and unissued shares, the board will need to go to the stockholders to approve an amendment of the articles increasing the number of authorized shares. Hence, in many cases of substantial dilution, the buying corporation's shareholders will get to vote on a sale of assets transaction, as they would on a merger.

b. Corporate mechanics for dissolution and liquidation

After selling all or substantially all of its assets, the selling corporation could keep or reinvest the proceeds (depending upon whether it received stock in the purchasing corporation, or cash) and continue to exist indefinitely. Commonly, however, the selling corporation will dissolve after the sale, and distribute the proceeds of the sale to the selling corporation's shareholders—who would like to get their hands on the proceeds.

Terminating a corporation after selling its assets involves three basic activities. One is to carry out the formalities specified by statute to dissolve the company. In this regard, it is useful to differentiate two terms: "dissolution," which refers to the legal process of ending the corporation's existence as an entity, and "liquidation," which refers to the practical process of disposing of the assets of the company. Typically, to voluntarily dissolve a corporation, state statutes call for a vote by the company's directors and shareholders (or, under some statutes, just the shareholders[72]), and the filing of an appropriate document (often called a certificate or articles of dissolution; sometimes preceded by a "statement of intent to dissolve") with the Secretary of State (or similar state official).[73]

The second basic activity involved in terminating a company after the sale of its assets is to pay off its creditors. Failure to do so prior to distributing money or property to the stockholders can lead to liability

---

71. See note 61 *supra*.

72. *E.g.*, Cal. Corp. Code § 1900(a).

73. *E.g.*, M.B.C.A. §§ 14.02, 14.03.

for the recipient shareholders under either equitable or statutory theories, as well as liability for the directors approving the distribution.[74]

Finally, the corporation will distribute to its stockholders whatever is left of its cash or properties after paying its creditors. Needless to say, the corporation must make this distribution in accordance with any liquidation preferences between classes of shares.

c. Creditors' rights

As we just saw, the basic scheme for protecting the corporation's creditors in the event a corporation sells all of its assets and dissolves, is to require that the creditors receive payment prior to distribution of the proceeds of the sale to the corporation's shareholders. This scheme, however, raises a couple of issues.

The first issue involves the impact of any agreement by the buyer to assume liabilities of the selling corporation.[75] Presumably, creditors are not going to complain about actually receiving payment from the purchasing company. Prior to complete payment, however, the question can arise as to whether the buyer's assumption of debts allows the selling corporation to distribute its assets to its shareholders, without the shareholders being at risk in the event of the buyer's non-payment of the debts. Authorities are divided on this question.[76]

A far more pervasive issue concerns claims whose existence was unknown at the time of the sale or dissolution, or which arose after the sale or dissolution. The two most common types of such claims involve defective products, which were manufactured prior to the sale of assets and dissolution of the manufacturing corporation, but which injure a person some time after the asset sale and dissolution, and claims for environmental damage based upon dumping which occurred prior to the asset sale and dissolution, but which only become known after the sale and dissolution. In these sorts of cases, the question becomes who is liable for such claims.

One possibility is for the shareholders of the selling corporation to be liable for claims which mature after dissolution. After all, the basic rule is that the shareholders are not supposed to receive the assets of their corporation unless the debts are satisfied. Following this logic, courts applying the common law have held that the former shareholders can be liable for debts which only come home to roost after corporate

---

74. *See, e.g.,* Del. Gen. Corp. Law §§ 281, 282.

75. One might ask why a buyer would agree to assume any liabilities. One factor is simply a comparison of the cost of capital. If the buyer assumes the selling company's debts, and lowers the purchase price accordingly, it may avoid the need to raise added funds at a higher cost than the interest rate charged by the selling corporation's creditors. The buyer's assumption of the selling corporation's debts also, in some situations,

might aid in qualifying the transaction as a tax-free C reorganization.

76. *Compare* Darcy v. Brooklyn & N.Y. Ferry Co., 196 N.Y. 99, 89 N.E. 461 (1909) (creditors must agree to the buyer's assumption of liability), *with* Cal. Corp. Code § 2005(a) (assumption of liability by a person or corporation, reasonably and in good faith determined by the dissolving company's board to be financially responsible, is adequate).

dissolution[77]—at least to the extent of the distribution the shareholders received from the corporation. Now, however, special provisions in corporation statutes usually regulate this subject. These provisions typically attempt to reach a compromise of the two competing interests at stake in this situation. One interest is that of the creditors, who could not assert claims which the creditors did not yet have, or know they had, at the time of the corporation's dissolution. Against this is the interest of the shareholders, who reasonably might ask for some finality in their right to keep distributions made by the corporation after the corporation paid off all of the debts the corporation knew about. A common statutory compromise is to allow post-dissolution claims against the shareholders, but to bar such claims after a certain number of years (such as five).[78]

For reasons of practicality, the far more frequent target for post dissolution creditors is the purchasing corporation. In contrast to the statutory merger, the traditional rule with a sale of assets is that the purchaser only bears those liabilities of the selling company which the purchaser agrees to assume.[79] The incentive, however, of both purchaser and seller is for the purchaser not to agree to assume unknown or later arising claims in a sale of assets transaction. For one thing, it is difficult to figure out how much to adjust the price to take into account the buyer's assumption of uncertain future claims. Moreover, there is less willingness on the part of the seller to accept downward adjustments in the price to offset the assumption of future or unknown claims. After all, given the impracticality of suing scattered shareholders, as well as the statutory time limits on liability just discussed, it is likely in many cases that the selling corporation's shareholders will be able to keep any liquidating distributions they receive despite later arising claims. Hence, the buyer's agreement to assume such debts may have limited value to the selling corporation's shareholders.

Courts have recognized four traditional exceptions under which the purchaser will become liable for the selling corporation's debts, despite the lack of an express agreement to assume such debts.[80] To begin with, the court might find an implied agreement to assume the liability— albeit, sale of asset contracts typically contain language designed to avoid any such implication. Alternately, the court might view the transaction as constituting a fraudulent conveyance—for instance because the purchaser paid the selling corporation's shareholders, rather than the selling corporation.[81]

77. *See, e.g.,* Pacific Scene, Inc. v. Penasquitos, Inc., 46 Cal.3d 407, 250 Cal.Rptr. 651, 758 P.2d 1182 (1988) (holding that provisions of the California corporation statute had preempted the common law theory).

78. *E.g.,* M.B.C.A. § 14.07. These statutory provisions typically require published notice of the dissolution to start the clock running. Another compromise might be to have the corporation set aside some funds, or make some other provision, for claims likely to arise after dissolution. *See, e.g.,* Del. Gen. Corp. Law §§ 280, 281.

79. *See, e.g.,* McKee v. Harris–Seybold Co., 109 N.J.Super. 555, 264 A.2d 98 (Law Div.1970), *aff'd,* 118 N.J.Super. 480, 288 A.2d 585 (App.Div.1972).

80. *Id* (setting out the traditional exceptions to non-liability of the purchasing corporation).

81. *E.g.,* Luedecke v. Des Moines Cabinet Co., 140 Iowa 223, 118 N.W. 456 (1908).

Closely related to the fraudulent conveyance exception is the situation in which the court concludes that the purchasing corporation is merely a continuation of the selling corporation. The mere continuation exception arises when the owners of an existing corporation set up a new corporation to purchase the existing corporation's assets and continue the business. Under these circumstances, the whole purpose of the sale is to allow the owners to continue the business without the debts of the former corporation. In evaluating this situation, some courts tend to talk about whether the new corporation picked up the old company's employees, management and business to such an extent that the new corporation is a mere continuation of the old,[82] while other courts see the more pertinent inquiry as whether the price paid in the asset sale was sufficiently suspect that the transaction smacks of a fraudulent conveyance.[83] In fact, however, these two approaches are not irreconcilable. One danger in this sort of transaction is that even paying a fair price for the tangible assets still allows the new corporation to pick up various intangible values of the existing business (goodwill and going concern value) without paying for such intangibles.[84] Hence, whether they realize it or not, courts have been on the right track when, in applying the mere continuation exception, they inquire as to whether the purchasing corporation picked up the same employees and organization of the selling corporation (thereby appropriating the going concern value of the selling corporation), and whether the new corporation held itself out to old corporation's customers as the successor of the selling corporation (thereby picking up the goodwill of the selling corporation).

The most expansive of the four traditional exceptions to the rule of no liability for the purchasing corporation in a sale of assets transaction occurs if the court characterizes the transaction as a "de facto merger." The rationale behind the de facto merger exception is that when the end result of a transaction is the substantially same as a merger between two corporations—except to leave out a few unfortunate creditors of the selling corporation—then the courts should treat the transaction as if it was a merger for all purposes, including the automatic assumption by the purchasing corporation of all of the debts of the selling corporation. An obvious problem with the de facto merger exception is figuring out when the sale of assets transaction looks enough like a merger to demand that the buyer assume all of the debts of the seller. Some of the factors which make the transaction look like a merger are the degree to which the buyer picks up the seller's organization, management and personnel, whether the selling corporation promptly dissolves or at least becomes inactive after the sale, and, most critically, whether the purchasing corporation pays for the selling corporation's assets with stock in the purchasing corporation, rather than with cash (cash being the kiss of

82. *See, e.g.,* United States v. Carolina Transformer Co., 978 F.2d 832 (4th Cir. 1992).

83. *See, e.g.,* Ortiz v. South Bend Lathe, 46 Cal.App.3d 842, 120 Cal.Rptr. 556 (1975).

84. *See, e.g.,* J.F. Anderson Lumber Co. v. Myers, 296 Minn. 33, 206 N.W.2d 365 (1973) (where the court seemed to have missed the point).

death for any attempt to characterize the transaction as a de facto merger).[85]

A number of courts have gone beyond the four traditional exceptions under which the purchasing corporation may become liable for the selling corporation's debts. California pioneered a so-called "product line" exception to deal with defective product cases.[86] This exception makes the purchaser, who continues to manufacture essentially the same product as the defective item made by the selling corporation, liable for any post-sale-of-assets injury caused by a defective product previously made by the selling corporation. The product line exception has the merit of attempting to carry out the purposes of products liability by internalizing the costs of defective products in the price of the product. By contrast, the traditional approach often allows the buyer and seller in a sale of assets transaction to deliberately externalize costs, based upon both parties' calculation that the selling shareholders will never have to return liquidating distributions to cover later arising products liability claims, and, hence, it is in neither party's interest for the buyer to assume such liabilities. Nevertheless, many courts have refused to follow the product line approach.[87]

Environmental statutes create added prospects for the purchaser of assets to become liable for claims based upon the selling company's pre-sale conduct. For instance, the Comprehensive Environmental Response, Compensation, and Liability Act (CERCLA) may impose liability upon the purchaser of property containing hazardous waste, even if an earlier owner—for instance, the selling company in a corporate acquisition—disposed of the waste upon the property.[88]

d. The de facto merger doctrine and related efforts at equivalence

The de facto merger idea just discussed in the context of creditor claims also can impact the rights of shareholders in sale of assets transactions. Specifically, some courts have characterized sale of assets transactions, which produce the same basic result as a merger, to be de facto mergers, and, accordingly, have demanded that the corporations involved grant their shareholders the same rights the shareholders

---

85. *See, e.g.,* Shannon v. Samuel Langston Co., 379 F.Supp. 797 (W.D.Mich.1974).

86. Ray v. Alad Corp., 19 Cal.3d 22, 560 P.2d 3, 136 Cal.Rptr. 574 (1977).

87. *E.g.,* Stratton v. Garvey Int'l, Inc., 9 Kan.App.2d 254, 676 P.2d 1290 (1984). Courts also are divided upon whether the governing law on this issue is the law of the buyer's (or seller's) state of incorporation, or the plaintiff's home state. *Compare* Litarowich v. Wiederkehr, 170 N.J. Super. 144, 405 A.2d 874 (1979), *with,* Brown v. Kleen Kut Mfg. Co., 238 Kan. 642, 714 P.2d 942 (Kan. 1986).

88. *E.g.,* New York v. Shore Realty Corp., 759 F.2d 1032 (2d Cir.1985). *But see*

42 U.S.C. §§ 9601(f)(35), 9607(b) (creating a possible defense for innocent purchasers who prove they conducted all appropriate inquiry into the previous ownership and uses of the property consistent with good commercial and customary practice and did not discover the waste). When the purchasing corporation did not buy the polluted property, but bought substantially all of the polluting company's other assets, courts still might impose liability upon the purchasing corporation based upon the other purchaser liability theories outlined above. *E.g.,* United States v. Carolina Transformer Co., 978 F.2d 832 (4th Cir.1992).

would have had in a statutory merger. The leading case applying this approach is *Farris v. Glen Alden Corp.*[89]

Farris arose out of a transaction in which Glen Alden, a Pennsylvania corporation, agreed to buy all of the assets of List Industries. The agreement provided that Glen Alden would pay for List's assets with Glen Alden stock, and assume List's liabilities. List was to dissolve and distribute the Glen Alden stock to List's shareholders. Glen Alden was to change its name to List Alden, and the directors of both corporations would become directors of List Alden. Farris, a shareholder in Glen Alden, sued to enjoin the transaction. Farris argued that, in reality, the transaction constituted a merger recharacterized in an attempt to deny him the appraisal rights he was entitled to under the merger provisions of Pennsylvania's corporation statute.

In agreeing with Farris' claim, the Pennsylvania Supreme Court framed the question as whether the transaction fundamentally changed the corporate character of Glen Alden and the interest of Farris as a shareholder in the corporation. In giving an affirmative answer to this query, the court focused upon the facts that (1) the transaction would change the nature of Glen Alden's business from primarily a coal mining company into a diversified holding company; (2) control would pass to the former directors of List (who would hold 11 of the 17 directorships in List Alden's new board); (3) after the transaction, the former List shareholders would hold most of the outstanding stock in List Alden; and (4) the price Glen Alden agreed to pay resulted in a dilution of the book value of Farris' shares.

One evident problem with the de facto merger doctrine as applied in *Farris* is that is uncertain when a court will characterize a transaction as a de facto merger. For example, a significant fact which made *Farris* a sympathetic case for such a characterization was that the transaction constituted an upside-down sale of assets. Specifically, the shareholders and directors of the so-called selling corporation (List) ended up with most of the stock and most of the board positions in the so-called purchasing corporation (Glen Alden); in other words, for practical purposes, the company in which the plaintiff held stock was the one being acquired, rather than the one doing the acquiring. Would a court still be willing to characterize a transaction as a de facto merger if the shareholders and directors of the purchasing corporation remained the majority after the transaction, and so the nominal purchasing corporation really was the acquirer?[90]

This workability concern about the de facto merger doctrine, however, was not the reason that the Delaware Supreme Court rejected the

---

89. 393 Pa. 427, 143 A.2d 25 (1958).

90. Moreover, another fact which made the court sympathetic to Farris' claim is that, at least as measured by book value (for whatever this is worth), the purchasing corporation's shareholders got a bad deal. The fact that the purchasing corporation might have overpaid, however, has nothing to do with whether the transaction is equivalent in any sense to a merger.

doctrine in *Hariton v. Arco Electronics, Inc.*[91] *Hariton*, like *Farris*, involved one corporation's (Arco Electronics) proposed sale of all its assets for in exchange stock in the purchasing corporation, followed by the dissolution of the selling corporation. Unlike Farris, Hariton was a shareholder in the selling corporation, rather than the purchasing corporation. Nevertheless, Hariton sought to invoke the de facto merger doctrine, because Delaware's corporation statute did not provide appraisal rights to the shareholders of a corporation selling all of its assets, as the statute did for shareholders of a merging corporation. The court held that there was no place for the de facto merger doctrine—at least vis-a-vis the rights of the shareholders as opposed to creditors—in Delaware. The court based this holding upon the notion that the sale of assets and the merger provisions in Delaware's corporation's statute were of "equal dignity." Hence, if the sale of assets provision on its face applied to the transaction, then there was nothing wrong with following the sale of assets provision—even though the outcome was to produce the same end result of a statutory merger, but without meeting the requirements of the statutory merger provision.

To a cynic, *Hariton* provides "Exhibit A" for an interest group based theory of Delaware corporate law. The court allowed management to structure a transaction to avoid shareholder protections, thereby reinforcing Delaware's management friendly reputation. Moreover, the court's equal dignities rationale seems to suggest that one of the purposes of the Delaware corporation statute is to provide an incentive to hire creative attorneys familiar with the statute. What other rationale could it serve to draft a statutory provision which mandates certain shareholder protections (voting and appraisal rights) for one type of transaction, and then draft a second statutory provision which allows clever attorneys to avoid the shareholder protections by nominally re-characterizing the deal?

Perhaps a more charitable view of *Hariton's* equal dignities rationale is that the court felt, if the legislature is going to make an inconsistent mess of the law, it is up to the legislature to clean it up. California's legislature has endeavored to do so. Specifically, California (joined to a greater or lesser extent by several other states) has taken the equivalence concept underlying the de facto merger doctrine one step further. California's statute creates a set of requirements for stockholder approval, and rights of shareholder appraisal, which apply for all reorganizations.[92] The California code, in turn, defines the term reorganization to include statutory mergers (other than short-form mergers), acquisitions of stock in exchange for the acquirer's (or its parent's) stock, and, of relevance here, acquisitions of substantially all of a corporation's assets in exchange for the acquirer's (or its parent's) stock or long-term (over 5–years) unsecured debt securities.[93] What this means in a sale of

91. 41 Del.Ch. 74, 188 A.2d 123 (Sup. Ct. 1963).

92. Cal. Corp. Code §§ 1200 *et. seq.*, 1300 *et. seq.*

93. Cal. Corp. Code § 181.

assets in exchange for the purchaser's stock is that both the seller's and the buyer's shareholders possess voting and appraisal rights.[94]

7.2.3   *Purchase of Stock*

A third possible mode for an acquisition is to structure the transaction as the purchase of most or all of one corporation's outstanding stock by another corporation. The purchasing corporation then either can run the corporation whose stock it purchased as a subsidiary, or liquidate the corporation whose stock it purchased, thereby achieving the same end result as a merger. (Indeed, this final step could be a parent-subsidiary merger.) Again, however, despite the similarity of outcome between such a purchase of stock transaction, and a merger, the mechanics are very different.

To begin with, there is a critical difference between a purchase of stock transaction, and both a merger and a sale of assets transaction, with respect to the role of the boards of directors. The purchase of stock transaction does not require any agreement between the board of the purchasing company and the board of the company whose stock is purchased. Rather, the contract is between the purchasing company (requiring approval by its board of directors if the transaction is large enough) and the individual shareholders whose stock the purchasing corporation will buy. This means the acquisition can go forward even if the board of the corporation whose stock is purchased opposes the transaction—making the stock acquisition the vehicle of choice for a "hostile take-over."[95]

There are also significant differences with respect to shareholder voting and appraisal rights between the purchase of stock and other modes of corporate acquisition. As with the sale of assets transaction, most statutes accord neither voting nor appraisal rights to the stockholders of the purchasing corporation. Again, the stock exchange rules may require purchasers with shares listed on the exchange to put the transaction to a vote of their shareholders if the acquisition entails issuing a substantial amount of the corporation's common stock. Moreover, when the purchasing corporation liquidates the purchased corporation following the purchase of stock, a court might deem the whole acquisition to constitute a de facto merger which must follow the state's merger statute.[96] California's statute, as noted above, attempts to create largely equivalent protections in all "reorganizations." In the context of sale of

---

94. Except for shareholders who end up with at least five-sixths of the buyer's outstanding stock (and without any change of their rights).

95. Of course, parties can use a purchase of stock in a "friendly acquisition," and such a transaction can involve agreement between the respective boards of directors—essentially, setting out the terms of the purchasing corporation's offer to the shareholders, and an agreement by the board of the corporation whose shares will be purchased to recommend the shareholders accept this offer.

96. Applestein v. United Bd. & Carton Corp., 60 N.J.Super. 333, 159 A.2d 146 (Ch.), *aff'd*, 33 N.J. 72, 161 A.2d 474 (1960). *But see* Orzeck v. Englehart, 41 Del.Ch. 361, 195 A.2d 375 (1963).

stock transactions, this can mean requiring a vote of the purchasing corporation's stockholders (and granting them appraisal rights).[97]

What about the shareholders of the corporation whose stock is purchased? Traditionally, they vote "with their feet;" individually accepting or rejecting the purchasing corporation's offer. For this reason, even California's statute does not require a formal vote by the shareholders of the corporation whose stock is purchased (as opposed to the shareholders of the purchasing corporation).[98]

Shareholders who do not wish to sell their stock to the purchasing corporation present a very different challenge in the purchase of stock mode of acquisition than in a merger or in a sale of assets transaction. On the one hand, such shareholders traditionally lack appraisal rights.[99] On the other hand, if the buyer does not wish to leave minority interests outstanding, the lack of compulsion in a purchase of stock mode of acquisition poses a problem. Later, this chapter will deal with techniques to remove an objecting minority. For now, it is useful to note that some statutes create a procedure for a mandatory (rather than a voluntary) purchase of shares mode of acquisition (typically referred to in the statutes as a "share exchange").[100] The trade-off these statutes impose in order to gain the compulsion of the minority is to require adherence to procedures—including approval by both boards of directors, an affirmative vote by the exchanging stockholders, and appraisal rights for the exchanging shareholders—which largely parallel the requirements for a sale of assets transaction.

Traditionally, a purchase of stock transaction has represented a middle ground between the statutory merger and the sale of assets transaction as far as the buyer's succession to the purchased corporation's liabilities. Unlike the sale of assets transaction, the buyer cannot pick and choose which liabilities it will assume and thus eschew the assumption of unknown claims. Instead, in purchasing a corporation's outstanding stock, the purchaser now owns a corporation which remains subject to all its former debts. This means, if unknown claims prove overwhelming, the buyer could end up with an insolvent subsidiary and thereby lose its entire investment. In contrast to the statutory merger, however, the buyer itself does not automatically become liable for the purchased corporation's debts. Hence, at worst—assuming no grounds for disregarding the subsidiary's separate corporate status—the buyer stands to lose what it paid for the stock, but no more.

---

97. Cal. Corp. Code §§ 1200(b), 1201(a), (b), 1300. This assumes that the exception for shareholders who suffer little dilution of their interest, or other change in their rights, does not apply.

98. Later, however, we shall discuss some state takeover statutes which require the purchase of a controlling percentage of stock to receive approval by a vote of the other shareholders. *E.g.*, Ohio Gen. Corp. Law § 1701.831.

99. This is true even in California. *See* Cal. Corp. Code §§ 1200(b), 1201(a), 1300(a). One should note, however, that at least one state has enacted a takeover statute which essentially gives appraisal rights in a purchase of stock mode of acquisition. Penn. Bus. Corp. Law §§ 2542–2547. We shall discuss this more in dealing with tender offers later in this chapter.

100. *E.g.*, M.B.C.A. § 11.03.

§ 7.3 Tender Offers

In the prior section of this chapter, we saw that there are three primary ways in which to structure the purchase of the business conducted by a corporation (which is commonly referred to as the target corporation): The individual or company seeking to acquire the target corporation's business (the "acquirer") can have itself (if the acquirer is a corporation), or a corporation controlled by the acquirer, merge with the target corporation; the acquirer can purchase substantially all of the assets of the target corporation; or the acquirer can purchase most or all of the stock owned by the existing shareholders of the target corporation (thereby becoming the majority or sole shareholder of the target corporation).[1] We also saw that there is a critical divergence among these three techniques as far as the role of the target corporation's board of directors. In both the merger and the sale of assets, the target corporation's board of directors plays a gatekeeping role, in that the board must approve the transaction before the shareholders of the target can vote upon it. By contrast, an acquirer can seek to purchase most or all of the outstanding shares in the target corporation directly from the existing stockholders, without any approval from—and, indeed, over the opposition of—the target's board of directors. Broadly speaking, a direct solicitation of a corporation's stockholders to sell their shares to an acquirer is known as a tender offer (because the acquirer is asking the existing stockholders to tender their shares for sale).[2]

Up until a few decades ago, the use of a tender offer to attempt to purchase a corporation over the opposition of the existing board of directors was considered something of a breach of business etiquette, and was not often done. This attitude changed in the 1960s and 1970s, and, by the 1980s, the business papers were full of tales of hostile takeovers and takeover attempts. Paralleling this development, there occurred an explosion in litigation spawned by hostile takeover efforts, and a corresponding growth of judicial doctrines, and legislation, governing both tender offers, and responses to such offers by the corporation's board of directors. Not surprisingly, these events, in turn, have led to a vigorous debate over what legal rules should govern takeover battles. The law governing the hostile tender offer is the subject we will explore in this section.

§ 7.3

1. Actually, it is unlikely that an acquirer will be able to convince all of a publicly held corporation's shareholders to sell out. Accordingly, if the acquirer desires 100 percent ownership, or direct access to the target's assets, the acquirer may push through a merger with the target after the acquirer has obtained a majority or controlling amount of the target's outstanding voting stock, and a corresponding control over the target corporation's board. This is known as a two-step acquisition.

2. The acquirer might seek to buy shares through open market purchases as individual stockholders decide to sell their shares through the stock exchange. Waiting around for stockholders to call their brokers and sell through the stock exchange, however, tends not to be a very efficient way of obtaining a majority of the outstanding shares—albeit, acquirers typically precede a tender offer by purchasing as many shares as they can on the market.

7.3.1 *Takeover Defenses and the Board of Directors' Fiduciary Duties*

a. *The arsenal*

As stated above, corporate law establishes no formal gatekeeping role for the target corporation's board of directors when an acquirer makes a tender offer to the shareholders of the target corporation. Nevertheless, various techniques exist whereby the target corporation's board of directors might seek to exercise an effective veto over the acquisition of the target corporation though a tender offer.

Among the takeover defenses commonly erected prior to a hostile tender offer are a variety of so-called "shark repellent" article and bylaw provisions. For example, the corporation's articles or bylaws might contain a provision giving staggered terms to the corporation's board of directors. We discussed staggered terms for directors in an earlier chapter dealing with corporate governance. If a board of directors has staggered terms (much like the United States Senate), it takes several elections before a purchaser of a majority of the corporation's stock can replace all (or even most) of the corporation's directors. While this will not do much good if the shareholders have the power to remove directors with or without cause, under Delaware's corporations statute (as discussed earlier in this book[3]) shareholders cannot remove directors without cause when directors have staggered terms (unless the certificate of incorporation provides to the contrary). Still, the effectiveness of staggered terms as a takeover defense is limited. The problem is primarily psychological rather than legal. Even if the buyer cannot remove the incumbent directors, the directors may feel pressure to resign, rather than oppose a majority shareholder.

Additional shark repellents include bylaw or article provisions limiting the power of shareholders to call, or make motions at, a shareholders' meeting, or to act by written consent in lieu of a meeting. Such provisions seek to crimp an acquirer's ability to replace the existing directors through an early shareholders' meeting or by the written consent of most of the shareholders, or otherwise to put the acquirer's plans into play without working through the incumbent board.

Still other anti-takeover provisions sometimes found in corporate articles include supermajority requirements for a merger with a "related person" (typically defined as someone holding over a certain percentage of the company's outstanding stock). This is sometimes coupled with a so-called "fair price amendment." The fair price amendment waives the supermajority requirement for a merger with a related person if the shares cashed out in the merger receive a price at least equal to a formula specified in the provision. The price formula tends to be quite generous, often looking to the highest price the acquirer paid to anyone for their shares in the target corporation, or at which the target's stock traded over several prior years, or looking to earnings or premium

---

3. See § 3.1.2a *supra*.

computations which can even go higher. Notice, these supermajority and fair price provisions came into play if the acquirer buys a majority, or at least a potentially controlling percentage, of the voting stock directly from the shareholders, and then seeks to complete the acquisition of the target corporation through a merger—in other words, these article provisions make it potentially more difficult or expensive to undertake a two-step acquisition. A significant variation on the fair price amendment gives shareholders, who do not sell to the party seeking to acquire the corporation, the right to demand that the corporation redeem their stock following any person's acquisition of a certain percentage of shares— even if the buyer does not propose a merger. The price the corporation must pay in this redemption is based upon a generous fair price formula. Notice the incentive such a fair price provision can create for shareholders faced with an offer to buy their stock, if the price formula is very generous toward those who do not tender in response to the offer.

Yet other anti-takeover article provisions work by altering the voting rights of various classes of stock. For example, a corporation might issue a class of stock having a greater number of votes per share to parties unlikely to sell out to a hostile acquirer. Another alternative would be an article provision limiting the right of stockholders to vote more than so many shares, or requiring new stockholders to undertake a waiting period after the purchase before they obtain voting rights. Such caps or waiting periods thwart efforts to gain control of the corporation by purchasing a majority of the outstanding voting stock. One problem with altering the traditional voting rights of common stock in any of these manners is that this can result in delisting the company's shares from the stock exchanges.[4]

Perhaps the most effective and common takeover defense is a so-called "poison pill."[5] What exactly is a poison pill? While there are a number of variations, in its original form a poison pill consists of a series of convertible preferred stock, which the corporation issues to its common shareholders as a stock dividend. These preferred shares may or may not have voting or much dividend rights; this is not the important feature of the stock. What makes the shares a "poison pill" is their conversion rights, and specifically the so-called "flip-over" provision. Under this provision, if an acquiring corporation purchases more than a certain percentage of the target's outstanding common stock, and then merges with the target, the holders of the preferred can convert the

---

4. At one point, it appeared the stock exchanges would relax their listing requirements concerning the voting rights of common stock. In response, the Securities Exchange Commission adopted a rule (Rule 19c–4) which required the stock exchanges to refuse to list the stock of corporations that issued classes of shares with more than one vote per share. The District of Columbia Circuit Court of Appeals, however, held this rule was beyond the Commission's authority under the 1934 Securities Exchange Act. Business Roundtable v. SEC, 905 F.2d 406 (D.C.Cir.1990). Thereafter, the Securities Exchange Commission was able to persuade the stock exchanges voluntarily to retain the restrictions.

5. Corporate directors who issue poison pills do not like to call the defense by this name in public, and so official corporation pronouncements refer to the defense as a "shareholders' rights plan," or the like.

preferred shares into the *acquirer's* common stock at a highly favorable ratio (such as the equivalent of paying half the current market price for the acquirer's common stock). Notice that the impact of the flip-over provision is to deter a two-step acquisition, much like the supermajority voting requirement for mergers with a related party or a fair price amendment. A critical difference with a poison pill from these article provisions, however, is that the board of directors might be able to issue the preferred without going to the shareholders to amend the articles. In addition to the flip-over conversion option, the poison pill preferred is subject to an important redemption provision. This provision empowers the board of the target corporation to redeem the preferred at a modest price for a short period of time following the start of a takeover attempt. The result is that the target's board can remove the poison pill if the directors of the target corporation decide to support the acquisition.

The poison pill defense has mutated over time (like a virus). To begin with, plan designers came up with a couple of additional types of poison, which are often referred to as "flip-in" and "back-end" provisions. A flip-in option is like a flip-over, except that the flip-in becomes effective after an acquirer buys a certain percentage of the target corporation's outstanding common stock, even if the acquirer does not merge with the target corporation. In this event, the holders of poison pill preferred can convert it into stock or other securities of the target corporation at a highly favorable ratio. The back-end provision gives the holder the right to force the target corporation to redeem the poison pill preferred at a very generous price. Notice how the exercise of the flip-in and back-end provisions makes the target common stock purchased by the acquirer much less valuable. The designation of the rights of the poison pill preferred, however, denies the flip-in or back-end rights to any preferred shares purchased by the acquirer. In addition to the development of the flip-in and back-end poison features, corporate boards now attach the poison pill to different types of securities. Specifically, recognizing that there is no necessity for the flip-over, flip-in or back-end rights to attach to preferred shares, many boards have distributed, as a dividend to their shareholders, warrants containing these features, or convertible debt securities with the same options.[6] An important recent mutation has been the development of what is referred to as a "dead hand" poison pill. This limits the ability of newly elected directors to redeem the poison pill securities. The idea is to prevent an acquirer from persuading a majority of the shareholders to replace the existing directors with new board members, who will redeem the poison pill securities and thereby clear the way for a tender offer.

The defenses outlined thus far are typically in place prior to any hostile offer. If the target's board has not adopted such defenses, or if its defenses appear inadequate (which the very failure to deter a hostile bid

---

6. Debt instruments (bonds) also might contain other terms which serve to deter takeovers, such as limitations on the incurring of additional indebtedness by the corporation, or on mergers and other such transactions. While such provisions can deter takeovers, they also protect the legitimate interests of the bond holders.

might indicate), then other defenses exist which the target's board can adopt while under siege. The most straight-forward, and non-controversial, defense is to communicate with the shareholders in an effort to persuade them not to tender their stock. Unfortunately from the standpoint of the incumbent board, shareholders presented with the opportunity to sell their stock at a significant premium over the existing market price typically will scurry to take the offer, much like rats off a sinking ship.[7] Sometimes the target's board will seek to persuade other parties to oppose the bid. For example, the board might launch a public relations campaign in the hope that opposition by employees, customers, members of the business community and the community generally might cause the buyer to reconsider. More dramatically, the target's board might institute a lobbying campaign directed at the state legislature, hoping to convince the legislature to enact anti-takeover legislation. We shall examine some of the resulting legislation later. Alternately, the target corporation might sue the buyer, claiming that the buyer's tender offer solicitation contains misrepresentations or omissions which make the solicitation misleading. We also shall consider such litigation later.

One of the more amusing, if not often used strategies, is known as a "Pac Man" defense. This refers to attempting to buy a majority of the acquiring corporation's shares before the acquirer can purchase a majority of the target corporation's outstanding voting stock. If both corporations end up owning a majority of each others' shares, apparently neither corporation will have the right to vote the shares it owns in the other.[8]

A number of takeover defenses involve purchasing or selling shares in the target corporation. For example, the target might repurchase some of its outstanding shares on the open market or through its own tender offer (called a "self-tender"). Such repurchases, the directors hope, create competition for the hostile acquirer and raise the price of the target's stock. Of course, while the repurchase might raise the price per share paid by the hostile acquirer, there are less shares left for acquirer to buy.[9]

Instead of the target corporation seeking to buy shares in competition with the acquirer, an alternate strategy is to have the target corporation buy the shares in the target owned by the prospective acquirer. Since this essentially means paying off the acquirer to go away,

---

7. Actually, many of the target's shareholders often will not even wait to sell their shares to the party who made a tender offer. Instead, many existing shareholders will react to the increase in the market price of the target's shares, which typically follows the announcement of a tender offer, by selling their shares in the market. This provides a sure profit, whereas the tender offer might fall through. Various professional traders (often called arbitragers) will purchase the shares in order to tender them either to the party who made the tender offer or to any higher bidder. Needless to say, such arbitragers have little patience to hold the shares in response to the board's pronouncements about the long-term prospects for the corporation.

8. *E.g.,* M.B.C.A. § 7.21(b).

9. This would not be a problem, however, if the existing directors or their allies hold a large block of stock which could become the majority after a corporate repurchase.

this strategy is often referred to as "greenmail." On the other hand, paying off one potential acquirer to go away might tempt others to threaten a takeover.

Perhaps better than share repurchases by the target corporation, would be to find a friendly buyer for the target's outstanding stock. The board may encourage another firm to enter the bidding for the corporation. Such a company often is referred to as a "white knight." Better yet (from the standpoint of the target's board) might be to find a purchaser who will buy enough of the outstanding stock in the target corporation to stop the hostile bidder, but not enough to take control (presumably because managers or other non-selling stockholders own the balance). Such a party is often referred to as a "white squire."[10] An attractive choice to make such a partial purchase could be an Employee Stock Ownership Plan (an ESOP) set up by the target for the benefit of its employees, and with friendly individuals acting as trustees.[11] Still another bidder could be a corporation organized by management (often with outside investors and with considerable borrowed money) to buy the shares. This is often referred to as a "management buy-out" or MBO. Also, because of the usually large use of borrowed money, it is one type of leveraged buy-out, or LBO.

The opposite approach from having the target corporation or someone else buy the target's shares is for the target to issue more stock. The notion is to keep supplying more stock which the hostile bidder will need to buy. The result, however, can be to lower the price of the target's shares and make the bidder's offer look all the more attractive.

Having the target corporation issue new shares to a friendly party— a white knight, a white squire, an ESOP, or a firm set up for an MBO— might hold promise. For example, issuing shares to a white knight gives the white knight an advantage over a competitive bidder in seeking to be the first to acquire a majority of the target's outstanding voting stock. For this reason, such a share issuance often is referred to as a "leg-up." Another impact of a leg-up is to act as a consolation prize for the white knight if it loses the bidding war with the hostile acquirer. Specifically, since the leg-up agreement invariably sets the price for the shares sold to the white knight at less than what a hostile acquirer must offer to outbid the white knight, if the white knight loses the war, the white knight

---

10. In order to ensure that the white squire does not turn around and decide to buy control, the board might have the white squire enter what is referred to as a "standstill agreement" promising not to purchase further stock in the target for a certain length of time.

11. Actually, the law governing pensions might preclude the trustees from exercising their discretion to support the incumbent directors in turning away an effort to take control of the corporation. E.g., Donovan v. Bierwirth, 680 F.2d 263 (2d Cir.1982) (the court held that the trustees

of an ESOP breached their fiduciary duty under ERISA by their actions siding with management during a tender offer). One response has been to include in the documents setting up the ESOP a provision calling for "mirrored voting." This requires the trustees to vote the shares not yet allocated to specific employees—which typically are the vast majority of the shares in the trust—in the same percentages as the employees (who presumably will oppose a takeover) vote the shares which have been allocated to specific employees.

typically can turn around and sell the shares it bought in the leg-up to the hostile acquirer at a substantial profit. Notice how this impact means that a leg-up can serve to entice a white knight to enter the bidding.

Another constellation of takeover defenses involve transactions which make target corporation, as a business, less attractive to the acquirer. Such tactics often go under the rubric of "scorched earth;" albeit, in some cases, the transaction might entail a profitable restructuring, the untapped opportunity for which being what tempted the prospective buyer. For example, perhaps the target corporation possesses a large amount of spare cash on hand, which it might use to repurchase its stock. Alternately, the target corporation might borrow heavily in order to repurchase its outstanding stock. Consider the effect of either of these two actions on the desirability of the target as a takeover candidate. After all, the buyer may have planned to use the target's cash to help finance the purchase, and a debt laden company might not seem such a good buy—especially if the acquirer planned to borrow heavily itself to make the purchase.

As another example of this sort of tactic, the target could sell a line of business it suspects the buyer is really after (a "crown jewel"). In some instances, the board might have the target corporation contract to sell a crown jewel or other significant assets to a white knight if the white knight loses out to the hostile bidder in the race to purchase the entire target corporation. This is known as a "lock-up" agreement. Such an agreement has several impacts. In addition to making the target less attractive to the hostile bidder, a lock-up can serve to entice a white knight to enter the bidding for the target by assuring the white knight of a consolation prize—the favorably priced purchase of assets—if the white knight loses in the bidding for the target. A lock-up also can encourage shareholder approval of whatever merger agreement the board might have negotiated with the white knight, since failure to approve the merger will result in the corporation selling, at a low price, some valuable assets.

The opposite approach from divesting lines of business would be acquire additional lines of business which make the target corporation less attractive to particular acquirers (perhaps because the acquisitions create antitrust problems for a particular acquirer, or because the acquisitions preemptively achieve the synergies which the acquirer hoped its acquisition of the target corporation would obtain).

b. The legal standard for reviewing defenses

When the directors of target corporations decide to use these various anti-takeover defenses, the result is often to precipitate a lawsuit asserting that the directors breached their fiduciary duties. After all, if the defense is effective, the result can be to disappoint both the company or individual who sought to acquire the target corporation, as well as numerous shareholders of the target corporation who were salivating at the opportunity to sell their stock at a premium price. A threshold question which the court must resolve when confronted with such a lawsuit is what standard to apply in reviewing the decision by the directors of the target corporation to employ the challenged defense(s).[12]

Some courts apply the business judgment rule to board decisions involving takeover defenses, just as the court would do with any ordinary decision by the board of directors.[13] After all, for the most part, the defenses outlined above do not entail transactions between the target corporation and its directors, or between the target corporation and other firms in which the directors have a stake. As such, these defensive steps do not constitute a traditional conflict-of-interest transaction, which would call for applying the fairness test in the absence of disinterested approval.[14]

The obvious problem with applying the business judgment rule to decisions to engage in takeover defenses is that the directors do have a conflict-of-interest, even if such defenses do not constitute traditional self dealing. After all, a takeover presumably will result in the replacement of the current directors, which is something that most directors have both a financial and a psychological interest to avoid. The psychological interest in opposing a takeover is likely to be especially strong insofar as one of the significant motivations for a hostile takeover is the acquirer's belief that the current management has done a crummy job of running the corporation and the acquirer can do better.

Some courts have responded to the potential interest of the directors in avoiding a takeover by adopting a "primary motive" test: The business judgment rule will apply unless the primary motive of the directors for the defensive step was to preserve their control, rather than advance the interests of the corporation or its shareholders.[15] The problem with this test is its workability. Specifically, unless the directors confess that

12. Another threshold question involves the standing of the plaintiff to bring the action. The standing of the disappointed shareholders who sought to sell out seems obvious—they are the persons on whose ultimate behalf the directors act, and hence the disappointed shareholders can claim that the directors breached the directors' fiduciary duty to the shareholders in taking the defensive step(s). Because the harm typically is suffered directly by the target's shareholders—who lost the opportunity for a profitable sale of their shares—rather than by the target corporation, this generally would seem to be a direct rather than a derivative claim. The standing of a disappointed potential acquirer is less obvious; after all, the board owes a potential acquirer, as such, no fiduciary duty. Once the potential acquirer buys a few shares in the target on the open market, however, the potential acquirer becomes another shareholder to whom the board owes a duty; albeit, only as a shareholder, and not as a

potential acquirer. *See, e.g.,* Paramount Communications, Inc. v. Time Inc., 571 A.2d 1140 (Del.1989).

13. *E.g.,* Treadway Companies, Inc. v. Care Corp., 638 F.2d 357 (2d Cir.1980).

14. There are exceptions. For example, the target corporation's board might have the corporation enter a contract with a firm set up by some or all of the directors to undertake a defensive MBO, which contract gives the management buy-out firm an option to purchase some shares or assets from the corporation (a lock-up or leg-up agreement). This defensive step does involve a traditional conflict-of-interest transaction and so is subject to review under the fairness test in the absence of disinterested director or shareholder approval. *E.g.,* Mills Acquisition Co. v. Macmillan, Inc., 559 A.2d 1261 (Del.1989).

15. *See, e.g.,* Johnson v. Trueblood, 629 F.2d 287 (3d Cir.1980).

their motive was primarily to preserve their power,[16] how is the court going to figure out whether preserving power was the primary motive? Often, the only available evidence of the directors' motive will be the existence or non-existence of a corporate or shareholder interest advanced by the defensive step. Yet, if the court simply accepts on its face any purported corporate or shareholder interest rationale offered by the target's board for the defense, then the primary motive test simply becomes an exercise in conjuring up plausible sounding rationales for fending off a tender offer. On the other hand, if the court scrutinizes the purported corporate or shareholder interest rationale in order to see if it effectively refutes the notion that the directors acted primarily to preserve their control, then the question becomes what degree of deference will the court give the directors in this review. Applying the business judgment rule would create a bootstrap in which a highly deferential standard is used to find facts which, in turn, justified applying the highly deferential standard to start with. Applying less deferential scrutiny, however, would render the primary motive test pointless, since, after the directors' corporate or shareholder interest rationale has passed greater scrutiny, it is a little late for the court to go back and say it should have reviewed the rationale under the business judgment rule after all.

A few courts have viewed the conflict which the directors face in opposing a takeover as sufficient to require application of a fairness review, just as with any other conflict-of-interest transaction.[17] A problem with this approach, however, is that all sorts of decisions, at least indirectly, impact the directors' retention of control over the corporation. If courts apply the rigorous scrutiny of fairness review to any decision which might impact the directors' continued control, then courts can end up second guessing much of what any board decides.

Given that the situation faced by the board in dealing with a threatened takeover is neither as free of conflict-of-interest as the normal business transaction subject to the business judgment rule, and yet might not involve quite as clear-cut a conflict-of-interest as exists when directors are doing business with their corporation, it is not surprising that courts have developed an intermediate standard to review board decisions to employ takeover defenses. In *Unocal Corp. v. Mesa Petroleum Co.,*[18] the Delaware Supreme Court set out a two-part test to review directors' decisions to employ takeover defenses. Under the first part of the *Unocal* test, the directors must prove that they possessed reasonable grounds for believing a threat to corporate policy and effectiveness existed.[19] The second part of the test requires that the defensive measure used be reasonable in relation to the threat posed.

16. Not only would such a confession be unlikely because of its impact on litigation, but, given the historic human capacity to come up with rationalizations for maintaining power, one suspects in many instances the directors will not even admit to themselves that the desire to preserve control for its own sake is their primary motive.

17. *E.g.,* Heckmann v. Ahmanson, 168 Cal.App.3d 119, 214 Cal.Rptr. 177 (1985).

18. 493 A.2d 946 (Del.1985).

19. Actually, the Delaware Supreme Court had developed the first part of the *Unocal* test some years earlier in *Cheff v.*

Notice two potentially critical differences between the *Unocal* test and the ordinary business judgment rule. To begin with, the *Unocal* test shifts the burden of proof to the directors to show a justification for their conduct—much like the fairness test applied to conflict-of-interest transactions. In addition, in requiring that the board have "reasonable" grounds for believing a threat existed, and that the defense be "reasonable" in relation to the threat posed, the *Unocal* test would appear to call for a review of the directors' decision under a sort of objective standard which is much less deferential than the business judgment rule. Just to keep everyone guessing, however, the Delaware Supreme Court in subsequent cases seems to have waffled on the degree of scrutiny which the *Unocal* test entails.

In some cases, the Delaware Supreme Court seemingly shifted the *Unocal* requirement of reasonableness toward greater deference to the board's business judgment. For example, in *Paramount Communications, Inc. v. Time Inc.*,[20] the Delaware Supreme Court expressed disapproval of several Delaware Chancery Court decisions, which, the Supreme Court felt, had impermissibly intruded on the business judgment of the target's directors by holding that the directors did not have reasonable grounds to oppose tender offers at a price which the Chancery Court viewed as fair. Similarly, in *Unitrin, Inc. v. American General Corp.*,[21] the Delaware Supreme Court held that the Chancery Court did not accord proper deference to the business judgment of target's board, when the Chancery Court held that a defensive step was disproportionate to the threat posed because the specific defense was, in the Chancery Court's opinion, unnecessary. In other words, whatever reasonableness entails under the *Unocal* test, it does not mean that the court should second guess board decisions to anywhere near the same extent as the court would under the fairness standard.

Moving in the opposite direction, however, the Delaware Supreme Court in *Revlon, Inc. v. MacAndrews & Forbes Holdings, Inc.*,[22] created a heightened level of scrutiny for situations in which the board decides that the sale of the corporation is inevitable. This heightened scrutiny involves both a narrowing of the range of acceptable goals for the board's action—now the sole acceptable goal is to obtain the best price for the stockholders—and a greater willingness to second guess the directors' actions. Unfortunately, subsequent Delaware cases have illustrated that *Revlon*'s qualifier on the *Unocal* test is anything but clear, both in terms of when the heightened scrutiny will apply, and in terms of what exactly such heightened scrutiny entails. Perhaps this is because Delaware courts never have articulated clearly the rationale behind the *Revlon* qualifier.

To understand the problem, consider the situation which confronted the court in *Revlon*. Two parties bid to acquire the target corporation—a

Mathes, 41 Del.Ch. 494, 199 A.2d 548 (Sup. Ct. 1964).

20. 571 A.2d 1140 (Del.1989).

21. 651 A.2d 1361 (Del.1995).

22. 506 A.2d 173 (Del.1985).

hostile acquirer and a white knight. Both bidders offered to cash out all of the existing shareholders. Under this circumstance, it is understandable how a court could say that the only legitimate objective for a target's board, which has decided to sell to one of the two bidders, is to seek the highest price for the existing shareholders; after all, what other legitimate objective could the board have in this situation?[23] Moreover, in such a situation, it seems logical to suggest, as the court did, that the reasonable way to obtain the best price is to conduct a fair auction between the two bidders, rather than favoring the white knight.

Once we leave this simple scenario, however, neither the ground rules, nor the rationale, for applying *Revlon* are clear. For example, in the *Time* decision mentioned above, Time's board favored a merger with Warner, over a takeover bid from Paramount. Some upset Time shareholders argued that the decision of Time's board to merge with Warner put Time up for sale, and thereby triggered the *Revlon* qualifier. The Delaware Supreme Court rejected this argument. How did the situation in *Time* differ from *Revlon*? The court stated that the difference lay in the fact that the transaction favored by Time's board did not involve the breakup of Time (as did both bids in *Revlon*). Also, the court found it significant that Time's board had not initiated an active bidding process to sell the company.[24] Interestingly, the Delaware Supreme Court attached no significance to an obvious difference between the situation in *Time* and that in *Revlon*: Unlike the two all-cash bids in *Revlon*, the contest in *Time* was between a cash offer (from Paramount), and the favored merger with Warner in which Time's shareholders would retain their ownership in the combined entity. Why might this difference matter? To the Chancery Court in *Time*, this meant that the board's choice contemplated no shift in control over Time, since control over Time would remain in whatever transitory alliance among numerous unaffiliated shareholders created a majority vote in a given election.[25] An even simpler answer might be to say that if the choice comes down to two cash bids, the only issue from the standpoint of the shareholders presumably is which bid gives the best price.[26] Hence, the only reasonable goal for the board is to get the most cash for the shareholders. This is no longer true, however, if one choice leaves the shareholders still as equity owners whose economic fate is tied to the future of the corporate enterprise.

23. As we shall discuss shortly, the only possibility lies in a claim that the board had the right or duty to look out for the interests of persons other than the shareholders.

24. As the board did in *Mills Acquisition Co. v. Macmillan, Inc.*, 559 A.2d 1261 (Del.1989) (holding that *Revlon* applied).

25. The lack of a control shift over Time was certainly true as the deal ended up, since the former Warner shareholders received cash rather than Time stock. Even as the Time–Warner merger was originally structured, however, the Chancery Court viewed control over Time to be unchanged,

despite the receipt by the former Warner shareholders of a majority of the voting stock in Time. Essentially, the Chancery Court conceived of the former Warner shareholders as indistinguishable from the original Time shareholders—in both cases, the shareholders were simply numerous unaffiliated investors in a fluid market.

26. Albeit, perhaps some shareholders might have social policy concerns about the impact of the transaction on employees or other stakeholders in the corporation.

In any event, the grounds for triggering the *Revlon* qualifier were soon to shift in another case involving Paramount. In *Paramount Communications, Inc. v. QVC Network Inc.*,[27] it was Paramount's board which decided to favor one bidder (Viacom Inc.) over another bidder (QVC). Since the board had not initiated an auction, and the Viacom deal did not involve the breakup of Paramount, Paramount's board assumed that *Revlon* did not apply. The Delaware Supreme Court, however, pulled a surprise on Paramount's board. The court focused on the fact that the deal Paramount's board made with Viacom would leave Viacom's controlling shareholder (Sumner Redstone) in control of the combined entity.[28] By contrast, the transaction in *Time* had left control in whatever fluid aggregation of unaffiliated shareholders might come together to cast a majority vote in any given election—in other words, the Delaware Supreme Court belatedly decided to rely on the rationale of the Chancery Court in *Time*. Yet, this result raises the question of why a shift in control should trigger the *Revlon* rule. The court in *QVC* gave a couple of rationales: a concern with the loss of effective voting power for the unaffiliated shareholders once a single person owns a majority of a corporation's outstanding voting stock, and the fact that the transaction, in essence, involved the sale of a valuable asset belonging to the public shareholders (the ability to obtain a premium price for selling control over the corporation). Neither of these rationales is particularly persuasive. The Delaware Supreme Court has often displayed—as we will see it did in *Time*—a lack of solicitude toward actions which undercut shareholder voting power. Similarly, by allowing any takeover defenses, the Delaware Supreme Court has enabled the target's board to undercut the ability of shareholders to extract a premium from selling control over the corporation.

In the end, the outcome in *Time* and *QVC* is to create something of a paradox—the paradox of Paramount's paramours if you will—as far as the application of *Revlon*. The shift in control in *QVC* to a stranger from Paramount[29] triggered intense scrutiny. By contrast, in *Time*, the court applied lesser scrutiny to Time's marriage to Warner—even though this marriage left Time's board and management in charge of the combined entity.[30] As a result, the rule appears to be the greater the conflict-of-interest by the target's board (as far as retaining the current directors' and managers' power), the less the court's scrutiny of the board's action.

Not only is it unclear when the *Revlon* qualifier is triggered, it is also unclear what *Revlon* requires. *Revlon*'s condemnation of the directors' favoritism for the white knight's bid might suggest some sort of duty to the bidders to conduct a fair auction for the target. Subsequent

27. 637 A.2d 34 (Del.1994).

28. This was because Mr. Redstone owned an overwhelming majority of the voting stock in Viacom, and most of the consideration received in the merger by the shareholders of Paramount would consist of cash and non-voting stock in Viacom.

29. Albeit, Paramount's CEO was to be CEO of the combined company.

30. Indeed, a critical component of the Time–Warner deal was the retention of "Time culture" for the company by assuring that senior Time executives would end up in charge.

cases, however, have clarified that *Revlon* does not change the basic fact that the board's duty runs to the shareholders, not to the bidders. Hence, the board can tilt the playing field between two bidders for the corporation, so long as it advances the interests of the shareholders to do so.[31]

A more difficult problem comes from the basic holding of *Revlon*— that the goal of the board in a sale situation is solely to get the best price for the shareholders. This is straightforward when, as in *Revlon*, the comparison is between two all cash offers.[32] Once, however, the Delaware Supreme Court in *QVC* expanded the *Revlon* qualifier to reach non-cash offers, this becomes far less straightforward. After all, the value of the equity interest received in a transaction such as the Paramount–Viacom deal depends both upon how much interest the target's shareholders receive in the combined entity and upon the future success of the combined entity. To say that the board's sole duty is to pick which offer is economically superior for the shareholders—cash now, or a continuing stake in an expanded corporate enterprise—fails to explain how this choice is any different than other decision by directors in response to a cash bid for the company. Certainly, the court could hardly be saying that the board in a non-*Revlon* situation is entitled to block a cash offer if the board did not feel that the shareholders would ultimately be better off economically, at least in the long run, by retaining their interest in the company.

In any event, even though the *Unocal* test (including the special qualifier in *Revlon*) was developed only by the Delaware Supreme Court, given Delaware's prominence as the state of incorporation of most of the companies involved in the major takeover battles, this test has become the dominant approach for reviewing claims that directors breached their fiduciary duties in instituting takeover defenses.

Some voices in academic circles have argued for a different approach. These writers have asserted that courts should find that boards have no power at all to employ takeover defenses—put differently, that courts should insist directors remain passive in the face of tender offers.[33] Doctrinally, there is not much basis for this position. Specifically, even if one views takeover defenses as presenting a full fledged conflict-of-interest for the board, this would call for fairness scrutiny, rather than a ban on all defenses. Perhaps one might argue that takeover defenses constitute an impermissible interference with the rights of stockholders to vote or to alienate their shares. Certainly this would be true if directors simply canceled corporate elections or refused to recognize any share transfers to an acquirer. Yet, the various defenses

---

31. *E.g.*, Mills Acquisition Co. v. Macmillan, Inc., 559 A.2d 1261 (Del.1989).

32. Even with two cash offers, there might be more than just the price to consider. Specifically, there might be issues regarding the timing and assurance of payment.

33. *E.g.*, Easterbrook & Fischel, *The Proper Role of a Target's Management in Responding to a Tender Offer*, 94 Harv. L. Rev. 1161 (1981).

described above do not outright deprive the stockholders of their votes, or the right to sell their shares; instead, the defenses only create greater or lesser potential disincentives toward takeovers. Ultimately, therefore, the argument for a passivity rule is based not on doctrine, but on policy: The proponents of this rule view takeovers as a positive development, and wish to prevent corporate directors from impeding such takeovers.

From a policy standpoint, the argument for a ban on takeover defenses confronts two problems. One problem is a matter of practical definition: Can we figure out what constitutes a takeover defense?[34] Specifically, suppose one defines a takeover defense as any action taken by the board for the purpose of making a takeover less likely. Alternately, one might define a takeover defense as any action which has the effect of making a takeover less likely. The problem with either of these definitions is that board actions to increase corporate profits then become takeover defenses, since one motivation for increasing corporate profits is to avoid the corporation turning into a takeover target, and the impact of increasing profits is to reduce the incentive for the shareholders to sell out to an acquirer. While this might seem like a silly example, in fact, as discussed above, often times the response of the target's board to an uninvited tender offer is to carry out preemptively the sort of profitable corporate restructuring, the previously untapped opportunity for which had tempted to acquirer to make the tender offer in the first place.

The more fundamental problem with banning takeover defenses lies in the possibility that such defenses can serve legitimate interests. This possibility, in turn, brings us to the consideration of what objectives, if any, should lead a court to uphold use of a takeover defense in a particular case.

c. *Permissible goals for takeover defenses*

Ultimately, whether the standard of review is the business judgment rule, the primary motive test, the fairness test, or the *Unocal* test (including as qualified by *Revlon*), the first step in applying the standard must be to ask whether the directors had a legitimate goal for instituting the defense. Sometimes, the justification for the directors' action has nothing to do with its potential impact on tender offers. For example, directors might assert that they voted to sell corporate stock to an ESOP in order to provide compensation to corporate employees in a manner which furthered the corporate interest (because of potential tax and incentive advantages of this form of compensation), and any impact of the transaction on prospective tender offers was incidental.[35] While the effect of the directors' action on a tender offer might call for more

---

34. This problem of definition also exists under *Unocal* or any other test which applies different levels of scrutiny to takeover defenses. The stakes are no where near as high, however, when the question is the level of scrutiny, as they would be under a rule which banned takeover defenses.

35. *See, e.g.,* Shamrock Holdings Inc. v. Polaroid Corp., 559 A.2d 257 (Del.Ch.1989). *But see* NCR Corp. v. AT & T Corp., 761 F.Supp. 475 (S.D.Ohio 1991) (finding an entrenchment motive).

careful scrutiny, the legitimacy of such normal business rationales does not raise any issues beyond those involved with reviewing board actions in general. What is new in the tender offer context is when the board forthrightly defends its action as an appropriate response to the tender offer.

To find appropriate goals for actions specifically directed at tender offers, it might be helpful to focus on a basic jurisdictional question: Why should directors, rather than just shareholders, have a veto on whether to sell the company? Notice that the structure of corporate law displays a certain ambivalence as to this question—giving the directors a gatekeeping role for mergers and sales of substantially all assets, but allowing the acquirer and the shareholders to bypass the board if the acquirer purchases most or all of the corporation's outstanding stock directly from the shareholders. Hence, from a doctrinal standpoint, there may be no obviously correct answer about whether the board should create a self-help gatekeeping role in responding to tender offers. Instead, the issue might be one of practical advantage.

One inherent advantage the board of directors has in responding to an offer to buy the company lies in the board's ability to take coordinated action, in contrast to the atomistic response of individual stockholders. This potential advantage has both a defensive and an offensive aspect. Defensively, the directors might seek to prevent the party making a tender offer from forcing the stockholders to sell, when the stockholders really did not want to sell. Here, one confronts the phenomenon of coercive two-tier or partial tender offers. In fact, this was the justification which led the Delaware Supreme Court to uphold the takeover defense in *Unocal*. Specifically, suppose the acquirer, as in *Unocal*, offers to purchase enough shares to give it a majority, rather than all, of the target's outstanding shares. Further, suppose the acquirer offers a price which is greater than the current trading market, but perhaps not sufficiently high to move the holders of a majority of the stock to wish to sell.[36] Suppose also the acquirer states that the it might seek to force those with shares it does not purchase in the first tier of its offer to sell in a second phase.[37] Moreover, implicit, if not explicit, in this statement might be that those forced to sell in the second phase will not receive as much as those who accept the initial offer (perhaps because, as threatened in *Unocal*, the later sellers will receive a package of debt securities rather than cash). How will shareholders react to this offer? If a majority reject it, then it comes to nothing. But, lacking the practical ability to organize a concerted response, each stockholder must worry about how the other shareholders will react (knowing that the other stockholders are also worrying about his or her response). This could

36. Keep in mind, the current trading level represents the price at which enough shareholders are willing to sell to satisfy the demand at this price. By definition, the stockholders who are not selling in the current market find the price less (perhaps substantially) than they think the stock is worth to retain.

37. The techniques for forcing out minority stockholders will be explored later in this chapter.

lead shareholders, who do not find the price adequate if all other things were equal, to nevertheless tender their shares in order to make sure they are not stuck in the non-tendering minority who will get a worse deal. Can some of the takeover defenses outlined earlier help here? Notice how a number of the defenses—such as supermajority requirements for mergers with a large shareholder, fair price amendments, or flip-over provisions in a poison pill—seek to limit the acquirer's ability to complete a follow-on merger which might force out non-selling stockholders, and thereby curb the coercive aspects of the two-tier tender offer.

A more ambitious goal for a takeover defense is to try to force the acquirer to pay a higher price, even if the acquirer presented a non-coercive offer[38] for the target's shares. The notion here is that while the acquirer may offer a price the stockholders would willingly accept, the shareholders would not object to more. Using the board of directors' advantage in taking coordinated action offensively might obtain a higher price for the shareholders than would an uncoordinated acceptance or rejection of an offer by individual shareholders.[39] One question about this goal is whether it justifies takeover defenses other than communication with the shareholders, since the board might always seek to persuade the shareholders to let the board negotiate for the sale of the company. Yet, the board's ability to negotiate on behalf of the shareholders might be more effective if the board holds a key—other than the possibly limited self-discipline of individual shareholders—which prevents the acquirer from ignoring the board. In this light, notice the utility of the feature in a poison pill plan which allows the board to redeem the poison pill securities if the board agrees to the acquisition. Indeed, in upholding poison pill plans, one justification pointed to by courts is that such plans, in effect, give the target's board "a gavel to run an auction"[40] for the target. Moreover, one way to increase the price paid is to seek out an alternative buyer—be it a white knight, white

---

38. In other words, an offer in which the acquirer indicates its intention to pay the same price to any non-tendering shareholders if the acquirer later forces them to sell out.

39. Some writers have argued that efforts by the board to jack up the price the acquirer ultimately must pay for the target, while possibly raising the return for the shareholders of the individual target company, are counterproductive for the overall body of shareholders of all companies. By raising the price of takeovers, the argument goes, there will be less of them. *E.g.*, Easterbrook & Fischel, *supra* note 33. This contention, however, is part of an overall argument in favor of a legal rule requiring director passivity in the face of a tender offer, since, without a ban on efforts to force bidders to pay more by all prospective

targets, it would appear futile for any one board to remain passive in the hope of increasing takeovers economy wide. More fundamentally from a policy standpoint, acceptance of the notion that a corporation's directors should not seek the best deal for the company's shareholders, because this might be contrary to the interests of the overall body of shareholders of all companies, throws into doubt basic tenets of corporate and antitrust law. After all, attempting to achieve success in the competitive marketplace invariably means taking actions which might be detrimental to the interests of shareholders who hold investments in competing companies.

40. CRTF Corp. v. Federated Dep't Stores, 683 F.Supp. 422, 439 (S.D.N.Y. 1988).

squire, an MBO, or the target itself—who might provide a little price-raising competition.

The prior two rationales flowed from the board's structural advantage of being able to take unified action in dealing with an acquirer. A third rationale for imposing a takeover defense, by contrast, flows from an assumption that the board is more knowledgeable or intelligent than most shareholders. Specifically, this rationale is to assert that the board recognizes, while the shareholders do not, that the shareholders ultimately would better off holding, rather than selling, their shares. This sort of rationale is more problematic than the prior two goals for takeover defenses, and, not surprisingly, judicial reactions to this objective have displayed greater ambivalence than the favorable judicial reactions to the prior two rationales.

Probably the high point for the "board knows best" rationale came in the Delaware Supreme Court's decision in *Time*. As mentioned earlier, this decision arose out of Paramount's battle to take over Time Inc. The prologue to this battle was that Time's board had entered into a merger agreement with Warner Communication. The original merger agreement called for the stockholders in Warner to obtain stock in the combined entity. This stock deal, however, required a vote of the Time shareholders. Before such a vote could take place, Paramount beamed in with a generous tender offer to the Time shareholders. This, in turn, caused Time's board to restructure the transaction with Warner to give cash, instead of stock, to the Warner shareholders—which meant that Time's shareholders did not get to vote on the deal. Completion of the Time–Warner combination would make Time no longer attractive to Paramount.[41] Paramount and some disappointed Time shareholders sued, but the Delaware Supreme Court upheld the action of Time's board. The court viewed the board's action as a takeover defense calling for the *Unocal* test, but concluded that Time's board reasonably viewed Paramount's offer to be a threat to Time and its shareholders. What exactly was the threat? Bluntly, it appears Time's board decided Time (and, hence, its shareholders) would be economically better off through the combination with Warner, than through the acquisition by Paramount, and Time's shareholders would be too ignorant, mistaken or confused to figure this out.

Many observers have interpreted *Time*'s application of the *Unocal* test as watering down the scrutiny suggested by *Unocal*, since the court undertook little objective analysis to see if Time's board was, in fact, correct that the Warner merger was a better combination for the long-run interests of the shareholders.[42] Moreover, the implications of this interpretation of *Time* are staggering, since a board might always take a patronizing (and self-interested) attitude that it knows what is in the company's best interest, that shareholders are often ignorant or con-

41. This largely was because the goal of either combination was to gain synergies from combining a movie studio with cable television networks showing recent movies.

42. The subsequent performance of the combined Time–Warner company did not support the board's conclusion.

fused, and that no uninvited outsider could possibly do a better job than it.[43] In fact, however, *Time* might not constitute the unqualified endorsement of the "board knows best" rationale, which the opinion, at first glance, seems to represent. To understand why, it is useful to look separately at the actions taken by Time's board.

The first action by Time's board was entering the initial merger agreement with Warner. In fact, it is the merger with Warner which ultimately made Time unattractive to Paramount, since it preemptively captured the synergies Paramount sought from merging with Time. Yet, to subject the Time–Warner merger to intense scrutiny as a takeover defense, because it made Time unattractive to other movie studios, would result in characterizing many, if not most, corporate acquisitions and restructuring as takeover defenses. After all, shrewd acquisitions and restructuring often might preempt the incentive for an outside acquirer to take over a corporation in order to push through the same sort of acquisition or restructuring. Hence, one can understand applying a deferential business judgment rule approach here.

Perhaps greater scrutiny could be given to the failure of Time's board to call off the Time–Warner merger in the face of Paramount's tender offer. Indeed, as Paramount's board was later to discover in *QVC*, the Delaware Supreme Court will view a board's refusal to change preexisting merger plans to accommodate a better tender offer to be a takeover defense subject to judicial scrutiny. Yet, what criteria is a court supposed to use in comparing the long-range shareholder interest in choosing between two strategic combinations involving a corporation? Once again, one might understand why a court would be reluctant to substitute its judgment for the directors'.

Finally, there is the decision by Time's directors to restructure the agreement with Warner in order to preclude a vote for Time's shareholders. In fact, this is what the court and parties most focused on as the takeover defense. At first glance, this action by the board seems virtually indefensible, since it is in reference to this action that Time's board most needed to put forth its patronizing and self-serving "shareholders are dumb" rationale. Yet, a judicial condemnation of this action by Time's board would have created some significant inconsistencies with accepted doctrine under Delaware corporate law. Specifically, if the court were to

---

43. Indeed, under this interpretation, *Time* represents a retreat to an earlier approach of the Delaware Supreme Court. As noted previously, the first prong of the *Unocal* test—the requirement that the directors prove that they had reasonable grounds for believing that the takeover presented a threat to the corporation—came from the two-decade earlier decision of the Delaware Supreme Court in *Cheff v. Mathes*, 41 Del. Ch. 494, 199 A.2d 548 (Sup. Ct. 1964). While the test as announced in *Cheff* sounded demanding, its actual application in *Cheff* was rather weak kneed. Specifically, the court approved the target board's payment of greenmail based upon the threat presented by the hostile acquirer's "bad reputation" and apparent plans to change the target corporation's sales practices. The court noted that the directors believed that the corporation's sales practices—which consisted of using high-pressure, deceptive, door-to-door sales tactics—were essential to the company's success. Interestingly, shortly after the *Cheff* decision, the Federal Trade Commission put a stop to the use of these so-called vital sales practices.

condemn structuring a merger agreement to avoid a shareholder vote, the result would be to undercut the Delaware Supreme Court's opinion in the *Hariton* case discussed earlier in this chapter.[44] After all, in *Hariton*, the court concluded there was nothing wrong in picking an available statutory form to combine businesses based upon the fact that the chosen form deprives shareholders of appraisal rights, or, presumably, based upon the fact that the chosen form deprives shareholders of the opportunity to vote on the transaction. Should it make any difference that Time switched the initial structure to remove the need for a shareholder vote after Paramount's tender offer?[45] This sequence of events makes it clear that Time did not want a shareholder vote on the merger with Warner, because Time thought its shareholders might turn down the merger in favor of Paramount's bid. Yet, a common reason for structuring a corporate combination from the outset to avoid a shareholder vote presumably is to avoid the risk of losing the vote, and *Hariton* suggests this is perfectly okay. Hence, it would seem also to undercut *Hariton* for the court to condemn restructuring the merger to remove the need for a shareholder vote.[46]

A significant contrast with the Delaware Supreme Court's acceptance of Time's "board knows best" rationale was the lack of deference accorded by the Delaware Supreme Court in *QVC* to the assessment by Paramount's board of the value of a strategic alliance with Viacom. This takeover battle arose when Paramount, rebuffed in its efforts to marry Time (which owned the HBO cable network), entered into a merger agreement with Viacom (the owner of Showtime). Just as Time's marriage announcement triggered a hostile bid from Paramount, Paramount's announcement triggered a hostile bid from QVC (the Home Shopping Channel). Paramount's board had the same sort of negative reaction to this new suitor, which Time's board had to Paramount. Specifically, Paramount's board refused to consider QVC's offer, or to rescind the leg-up stock option and termination fee agreement Paramount made with Viacom. In this case, however, the Delaware Supreme Court decided that the board did not know best. As discussed earlier, perhaps the difference lies in the fact that the Paramount–Viacom deal triggered the greater scrutiny of *Revlon*. Perhaps the fact that the principal defensive step in *QVC* consisted of a leg-up granted to Viacom—rather than structuring a merger to deprive shareholders of a vote—meant that the court could impose greater scrutiny without under-

---

44. See § 7.2.2d *supra*.

45. Actually, by using a triangular merger in which Warner merged into a newly created subsidiary of Time, Time's initial structure had avoided any requirement under Delaware corporate law for a vote by Time's shareholders. Rather, the requirement for a vote by Time's shareholders was the result of stock exchange rules. Hence, it becomes extraordinarily difficult to condemn Time's board for restructuring the merger agreement to deprive shareholders of a vote which Delaware's law had never seen fit to require in the first place.

46. Moreover, the practical impact of holding that it would have been acceptable to choose a structure initially to deprive the shareholders of a vote, but not to change the structure in response to a tender offer, simply might be to encourage initial choices of structure to deprive shareholders of a vote.

MERGERS AND ACQUISITIONS Ch. 7

cutting *Hariton*.[47] Perhaps the real difference lies in the court's conclusion that Paramount's directors had not carefully considered relative merits of the Viacom and QVC bids—in which case, *QVC* might stand for little more than an application of the *Van Gorkom* decision discussed in an earlier chapter dealing with the duty of care.[48] Put differently, it is hard for sloppy boards to argue that they know better than the shareholders.

Looking at both *Time* and *QVC*, notice that the "board knows best" rationale seems to present the most difficult challenge for the courts when the context involves board choices between competing strategic combinations (as opposed to a decision simply to chase away a hostile bidder in favor of continuance of the corporate status quo). There are a couple of reasons for this. One is practical. The various defensive weapons in the target board's arsenal are often more effective in stalling a takeover while the board seeks a white knight, than they are in completely blocking a determined acquirer in order to allow the target to remain independent. More fundamentally, as suggested in the discussion of *Time*, it is much more difficult for the court to second guess board actions to undertake a strategic combination, than it is for the court to cast aside board actions to prevent a takeover solely in order for the target corporation to remain independent. For one thing, the law clearly contemplates that part of the directors' task is to initiate corporate combinations; whereas, as discussed earlier, there is no similarly explicit power for directors to chase off parties making tender offers. In addition, it is much easier to challenge the directors' judgment in chasing off a premium price tender offer in favor a continuing the status quo upon which there is track record for all to see, than it is to say what the future will hold as the corporation embarks upon a new strategic alliance—particularly an alliance based upon the same sort of synergies which motivated the competing hostile offer. Still, there is a problem with the "board knows best" rationale particularly in the context of choosing between strategic alliances. Such combinations would seem to represent the sort of fundamental transactions upon which the shareholders should vote. Indeed, the specific complaint in *Time* and *OVC* concerns actions by the board which either deprived shareholders of the vote (in *Time*) or so stacked the deck that there was no point presenting the shareholders with the competing bid (in *QVC*). Hence, perhaps the real issue presented by *Time* and *QVC* is not the limits of takeover defenses at all, but rather what are the limits on the board's ability to force through a shotgun corporate marriage over the objections of the shareholders—whether or not there is a competing bidder. In other words, *Time* and *QVC* might cause one to reconsider the issues of shareholder approval of corporate combinations we discussed earlier in this chapter when dealing with cases such as *Hariton*.

47. This is not to suggest that such a distinction makes much policy sense.

48. See § 4.1.2d *supra*.

Moving beyond the board knows best rationale, we arrive at the question of whether the directors can act for objectives other than the shareholders' economic benefit. Specifically, can the target's directors oppose a takeover based upon concerns regarding its impact upon the corporation's creditors, employees, customers or even the community in general? Judicial opinions have not always supplied consistent standards.

For example, in *Unocal*, the Delaware Supreme Court stated that the target's board could consider the interests of creditors, customers, employees and perhaps even the community in general in assessing whether the takeover bid constituted a threat justifying the deployment of a takeover defense. This, however, was dicta in the case, because the threat identified in *Unocal* consisted of coercing the shareholders with a partial tender offer.

When it actually came time to deal with a board's efforts to justify its action based upon the interest of someone other than the shareholders, the Delaware Supreme Court saw things differently. Specifically, in *Revlon*, the court confronted a situation in which the board favored one cash bid for the company over another cash bid. The directors argued that the favored bid better protected certain note holders (creditors) of the target company. The court rejected the argument, holding that the directors' duty in choosing between two cash bids was to get the highest price for the shareholders. It was up the note holders to protect themselves by the contract they made with the corporation. In other words, as interpreted by *Revlon*, *Unocal* only allows the target's board to look out for parties other than the shareholders to the extent that it would be in the shareholders' long-range interest to do so—which cannot be the case when the shareholders are cashing out.

As discussed earlier in this book, the idea that directors should not consider the interests of parties other than the shareholders, unless one can somehow rationalize such consideration as producing a long-range benefit for the shareholders, is not a popular notion with many state legislatures. Accordingly, we noted earlier that a number of states have added provisions to their corporations statutes explicitly allowing directors to consider other constituencies in responding to a takeover bid.[49]

In any event, in at least one instance it would appear directors can oppose an acquisition based upon concerns other than shareholder welfare. This would be if the buyer plans to loot the corporation—in other words, to misappropriate its assets.[50]

d. Issues raised by specific defenses

The second prong of the *Unocal* test shifts our attention from the justification for the target's board taking any action, to an examination

49. See § 4.1.5*b supra*.

50. *See, e.g.,* Gerdes v. Reynolds, 28 N.Y.S.2d 622 (Sup. Ct. 1941). While looting would harm any non-selling shareholders, presumably the directors right, if not duty, to oppose the acquisition would extend even if the looter offered to buy every share and therefore only act to the detriment of the corporation's creditors. *Cf* Francis v. United Jersey Bank, 87 N.J. 15, 432 A.2d 814 (1981).

of the action(s) which the target's board chose to take. Specifically, under *Unocal*, the defensive action(s) must be reasonable in relationship to the threat posed—put differently, there must be proportionality between the justification and the response. In addition to this overarching requirement, some tactics in the defensive arsenal are subject to more specific challenges under corporate law.

Shark repellent article provisions—*e.g.*, staggered terms, supermajority voting requirements for mergers with related parties, fair price amendments, and adjustments to the voting rights of shares—have provoked few, if any, negative judicial reactions.[51] In part, this is because there typically is specific legislative sanction for article provisions to create staggered terms, to establish supermajority voting requirements, and to specify the rights of stock. In addition, the fact that it took a vote of the shareholders to amend the articles to add such shark repellents presumably would make a court more willing to sustain such actions against any complaint that the article provision interferes with the shareholders' rights.[52] Bylaw provisions adopted by the board of directors, which seek to curb shareholder voting rights, are a different story. As we saw in an earlier chapter dealing with corporate governance, courts (as well as legislatures) have imposed limits on unilateral attempts by directors to disenfranchise the shareholders.[53]

Not surprisingly, poison pills have been subject to a number of challenges. In *Moran v. Household International, Inc.*,[54] the Delaware Supreme Court dismissed many of the arguments against poison pills. The poison pill in *Moran* involved warrants with a flip-over provision. Moran (a director in Household International, and the chairman of Household's largest single shareholder) voted against the board's adoption of the poison pill, and then, having been outvoted, sued to invalidate the poison pill. Moran's first challenge involved the board's authority to issue the warrants. While Delaware's corporation statute expressly authorizes a corporation's board to issue options to purchase shares (in other words, warrants), Moran argued that the legislature intended this power only as a device to finance the corporation, not for use as a takeover defense. Not finding any language in the pertinent section of Delaware's statute which limited the purpose for which a corporation could issue warrants, and quoting *Unocal* about need of corporate law to grow and develop, the Delaware Supreme Court rejected this argument. This reaction is hardly surprising: It is entirely consistent with the sort of "bonus points for the creative use of corporation statutes" philosophy which, as discussed earlier in this chapter, the Delaware Supreme Court displayed in rejecting the de facto merger doctrine in *Hariton*. Along the

---

51. *See, e.g.,* Williams v. Geier, 671 A.2d 1368 (Del.1996) (upheld a provision in the certificate of incorporation under which shares lost significant voting power if they were transferred, and regained their voting power after the new owner held the shares three years). *But see* Asarco, Inc. v. Holmes A. Court, 611 F.Supp. 468 (D.C.N.J.1985).

52. *See, e.g.,* Stroud v. Grace, 606 A.2d 75 (Del.1992).

53. See § 3.1.3*b supra.*

54. 500 A.2d 1346 (Del.1985).

same lines, the court rejected Moran's argument that the rights of the warrant holders to purchase Household preferred shares was a sham, because the terms of the rights were not designed to make their exercise for preferred shares attractive.

Incidentally, by attaching the flip-over provision to warrants, the designers of Household's poison pill avoided the question confronted by earlier plans as to whether the corporation's articles authorized the company to issue convertible preferred stock with flip-over features. In the earlier plans using convertible preferred stock, the boards took advantage of so-called blank check provisions in the articles, which give the board the power to set the specific rights of a series of shares at the time the corporation issues the stock. Originally, such blank check provisions were intended to allow flexibility in raising capital for the corporation by enabling the board to adjust the terms of the stock to match the market. Presumably, however, the Delaware Supreme Court would be no more sympathetic to an argument that issuing poison pill preferred stock was contrary to the intent of a blank check article provision, than the court was to Moran's argument regarding the intent of the statute authorizing corporations to issue warrants.

One interesting question raised by a flip-over provision is how can one company create an obligation for another corporation to sell stock at a favorable price. Notice the feature comes into play if there is a merger of the two firms, when, as discussed earlier in this chapter, the surviving entity becomes liable for the obligations of the merging firms. Indeed, as the court in *Moran* pointed out, warrants commonly contain "anti-destruction" clauses, which are designed to ensure that option owner still can purchase securities after a corporate merger—albeit, such clauses are intended to ensure that future mergers do not destroy the value of the option, rather than act as a punishment for engaging in a hostile takeover.[55]

Flip-in and back-end provisions raise a different issue. Such provisions preclude the acquirer from exercising any flip-in or back-end rights for any poison pill securities the acquirer obtains. Courts outside of Delaware have reached conflicting results as to whether a corporation can discriminate between its securities holders in this manner.[56] As we shall soon see, the Delaware Supreme Court has had no problem with such discrimination against the acquirer in another context.

The bulk of Moran's argument, and the bulk of the Delaware Supreme Court's opinion, was directed at the poison pill's impact of blocking takeovers. Given *Unocal*, the fact that the poison pill was a takeover defense was hardly enough to condemn it. Indeed, the court viewed the poison pill as less drastic—both in terms of its impact on the

55. In any event, no hostile acquirer has yet had the nerve to push through a merger and then claim that the acquirer was not bound by the target's poison pill flip-over provision.

56. *Compare* Amalgamated Sugar Co. v. NL Indus., Inc., 644 F.Supp. 1229 (S.D.N.Y. 1986), *with* Harvard Indus. v. Tyson, 1986–87 Fed. Sec. L. Rep. (CCH), ¶ 93,064 (E.D. Mich. 1986).

corporation, and in terms of a hostile acquirer's ability to buy the company despite this defense—than some of the scorched earth tactics used in takeover battles. As discussed earlier, the flip-over provision only comes into play with a two-step acquisition, and, as such, the court in *Moran* viewed the flip-over as an appropriate defense against the coercive effect of two-tier tender offers. More broadly, the court in *Moran* attached considerable significance to the fact that the board could redeem the poison pill when faced with a tender offer, and the court warned that the board could not arbitrarily refuse to redeem the poison pill. In other words, under *Moran*, the time to judge whether a board's use of a poison pill was a proportionate response to a legitimate threat was after the board decided whether or not to withdraw the poison pill.

Moran's focus on redemption, in turn, raises the question of when a board's refusal to redeem a poison pill will violate the *Unocal* test. Following *Moran*, several Delaware Chancery Court decisions held that the board's refusal to redeem the pill, when confronted with a non-coercive tender offer at a price the court found to be fair, violated *Unocal*;[57] but, as discussed earlier, the Delaware Supreme Court in *Time* expressed disapproval of these opinions. On the other hand, does this mean that the target's board can use the pill as bargaining leverage to demand a price from the acquirer, no matter how ridiculously high the price the board demands? Alternately, can the target's board decide that the shareholders would be better off holding their stock no matter what the price, and, accordingly, refuse to withdraw the pill as part of a "just say no" philosophy towards tender offers? The law is unclear on these questions—in substantial part because these questions bring us back to ambivalence surrounding the "board knows best" justification for imposing a takeover defense.

One other rationale expressed by the court in *Moran* for upholding the poison pill was that a prospective acquirer still could launch a proxy contest to elect directors who would redeem the poison pill before a triggering share acquisition terminated the corporation's redemption option—in other words, the poison pill did not completely block the shareholders' ability to sell the company. Nevertheless, some target boards and their legal advisors have been willing to push the envelop by deploying dead hand poison pills. As discussed earlier, a dead hand poison pill limits the ability of newly elected directors to redeem the poison pill securities. Not surprisingly, such efforts have met a frosty reception from Delaware courts. For example, in *Quickturn Design Systems, Inc. v. Shapiro*,[58] the Delaware Supreme Court invalidated a milder variant of the dead hand poison pill—called the "no-hand" poison pill. The no-hand poison pill only delayed for six months the ability of newly elected directors to redeem the poison pill securities—rather than permanently allowing only directors who were on the board at the time the board adopted the poison pill to redeem the poison pill securities.

---

57. *E.g.*, City Capital Associates v. Interco Inc., 551 A.2d 787 (Del.Ch.1988).

58. 721 A.2d 1281 (Del.1998).

The court held that precluding a board from deciding whether to redeem the poison pill securities constituted an infringement on the board's statutory powers to manage the corporation, which could only be done by a provision in the certificate of incorporation.

Several important Delaware Supreme Court decisions involve the use of corporate share repurchases as a takeover defense. For example, the takeover defense employed by the target corporation in *Unocal* was a selective self-tender. Specifically, Unocal's board adopted a resolution which stated that, if Mesa Petroleum[59] purchased a majority of Unocal's voting stock, Unocal would repurchase all of the remaining outstanding stock, except the shares owned by Mesa. Funding this repurchase would have left Unocal heavily in debt and a much less desirable acquisition for Mesa, who sued to challenge the action. The Delaware Supreme Court found that this selective self-tender was a proportionate response to the threat posed by Mesa's coercive two-tier tender offer.

In fact, however, the court's analysis in *Unocal* is remarkably sloppy, and the selective self-tender may have been a disproportionate response to the threat identified. To see why, recall that the threat of a coercive two-tier tender offer comes from the fear that shareholders, who do not tender, will be forced to sell in a lower-priced second stage. The corporation's promise to buy any non-tendering shares can remove this fear, and hence seems to be an appropriate response. The problem lies in the price. If the corporation offers the same price offered by the outside bidder, this removes the coercion, since shareholders know that they will not be any worse off by not tendering their stock, even if a majority of their fellow shareholders accept the offer. By offering a price significantly above Mesa's bid, however, Unocal's board created a reverse incentive (or coercion), since refusing to tender leaves a shareholder eligible to receive a higher price than offered by Mesa.[60] Of course, if all shareholders succumb to this incentive, then no one tenders to Mesa, and no one receives the greater sum from Unocal either. The end result is to blow off the tender offer without, in fact, offering the shareholders a superior alternative.

Does the reverse incentive mean that the court should have stopped Unocal's self tender? Not necessarily. Mesa could have responded by matching or exceeding Unocal's price—which would have restored the incentive for Unocal's shareholders to tender to Mesa. Hence, the self-tender could have been an appropriate tactic to negotiate a better price for the Unocal shareholders. Notice, this means that the coercive partial tender rationale was something of a red herring in the case. Moreover, had the court forthrightly viewed the self-tender as a device to raise the

59. Mesa was a company controlled by T. Boone Pickens, which had made a tender offer to obtain a majority of Unocal's shares.

60. Actually, the incentive impact of Unocal's self-tender is a little more complicated because the corporation intended to offer debt securities rather than cash. Assuming, however, that the debt securities would pay an interest commensurate with their risk, then the cash value of the debt securities should equal roughly their principal amount.

price to the level set by the self-tender, it should have asked whether this was a realistic price for the company. In fact, the directors seem to have set the self-tender price well above the price which Unocal's investment bankers identified as what the shareholders should get from a sale of 100 percent of the company's stock.[61]

Unocal's self-tender raised one other issue. Mesa charged that the self-tender unlawfully discriminated among shareholders by excluding Mesa from eligibility to tender its shares. As the court pointed out, however, this sort of discrimination is simply the flip side of the discrimination practiced by the corporation in paying greenmail—which is an offer to repurchase stock open only to the hostile bidder, and not to the target's other shareholders.[62] Moreover, since the purpose of the self-tender was to protect the other shareholders from Mesa's action, it would make no sense to open the tender to Mesa.[63]

More recently, the Delaware Supreme Court dealt with share repurchases by the target corporation in *Unitrin, Inc. v. American General Corp.*[64] Here, the target company (Unitrin) had launched a major program of repurchasing its stock in response to a hostile tender offer from American General. The impact of the share repurchases was to increase the percentage of the outstanding voting stock owned by the directors (who did not sell their stock) from 23 to 28 percent—which was enough to block a merger with a related party under Unitrin's certificate of incorporation.[65] The Chancery Court held that this was disproportionate to the threat posed, because Unitrin's poison pill already provided sufficient protection against the threat of an inadequately priced hostile tender offer. As stated earlier, the fact that the Chancery Court viewed the defense as an unnecessary bit of piling on was not sufficient in the Delaware Supreme Court's mind to condemn the defense as disproportionate.

To the Supreme Court in *Unitrin*, it was critical to ask whether the defense was coercive or preclusive. The court's concern with defenses which are coercive is curious in light of the impact outlined above of the Unocal self-tender; in any event, the Unitrin repurchase did not have any such coercive impact. Nor was the repurchase preclusive—despite giving the directors the power to block a merger with a shareholder owning at least 15 percent of Unitrin's stock. The court pointed out that,

61. Mesa had offered $54 per share; the investment bankers opined that the minimum price should be $60 per share for 100 percent of the company; Unocal's self-tender was for $72 per share. Admittedly $60 per share represented a minimum price, but there is nothing in the court's opinion which suggests that Unocal's board had any basis for assuming that all of the company's shares should have fetched $72 per share.

62. As noted earlier, the Delaware Supreme Court upheld greenmail in *Cheff.* Some state corporation statutes, however, can require such payments to receive share-

holder approval. N.Y. Bus. Corp. Law § 513(c).

63. As we shall discuss later, however, the Securities Exchange Commission, using the Commission's authority under the Williams Act, has adopted a rule prohibiting discriminatory self-tenders.

64. 651 A.2d 1361 (Del.1995)

65. Unitrin's certificate of incorporation contained a supermajority provision requiring a 75 percent vote to approve a merger with a person owning 15 percent or more of Unitrin's outstanding stock.

before American General acquired 15 percent of Unitrin's stock, American General could launch a proxy contest to replace Unitrin's board with directors who would pull the poison pill and who would approve a merger with American General (which the shareholders could approve by a simple majority if they voted before American General bought 15 percent of the outstanding stock). Hence, the defense did not preclude a takeover.

So long as the defense is not coercive or preclusive, then, according to the *Unitrin* opinion, the defense need only be in the "range of reasonableness." In remanding the matter to the Chancery Court, the Delaware Supreme Court explained that whether a defense was within the range of reasonableness depended, in part, upon whether the defense corresponded to the magnitude of the threat—albeit, if a defense was unnecessary to meet a threat, it is difficult to understand how the defense could nevertheless correspond to the magnitude of the threat. In addition, the defense might be in the range of reasonableness if it is the sort of statutorily authorized decision which the board routinely makes in a non-takeover context. Along this sort of line, the court suggested that the directors might justify the share repurchases as a means of providing liquidity for shareholders who desired it.

Attempting to attract a white knight, in and of itself, is not a controversial defense. Problems arise, however, when the target's directors offer various inducements to the white knight. This returns us to the subject of lock-ups and leg-ups, as found in *Revlon* and *QVC*. While the target's board lost in both cases, in neither case did the Delaware Supreme Court categorically condemn lock-ups or leg-ups. This reflects the fact that lock-ups and leg-ups have a mixed impact, which makes it necessary to evaluate the tactic based upon its specific use in a specific context. On the positive side, a lock-up or leg-up agreement, by giving the bidder a consolation prize should it lose out to another acquirer, can entice a party into making a first bid for the target corporation (as in *QVC*), or can entice a party into bringing to the shareholders a potentially better offer than is already before them (as argued in *Revlon*). On the other hand, as explained earlier, lock-ups and leg-ups can chase away other bidders (as, for instance, if the lock-up conveys the target's crown jewel to one bidder), and can have a coercive impact on the target's shareholders when voting on the favored merger.[66] Presumably then the question becomes one of balancing what the target's shareholders received by virtue of the lock-up or leg-up, versus what they gave up. In *Revlon*, the board obtained a marginally higher priced bid by giving the lock-up to the white knight. The court concluded that the lock-up's effectively precluding any higher further bids from the hostile acquirer outweighed obtaining this marginally higher bid. In *QVC*, the court

---

66. As explained earlier, if the shareholders vote down the merger with a party who obtained a lock-up or leg-up entitling this party to a bargain purchase of major assets or a major quantity of stock, the result could be to devalue significantly the target corporation. To avoid this devaluation, shareholders might vote to approve a merger they otherwise opposed.

viewed the terms of the leg-up option to be so generous as to constitute a draconian defense.[67]

Notice that our discussion of fiduciary duty with respect to tender offers has focused on challenges to the actions of the target corporation's board. Yet, what about challenges to the conduct of the party making a tender offer? In fact, one of the rationales justifying the target's board employing takeover defenses is to combat tactics (such as coercive two-tier tender offers) which state courts view as unfair to the target's shareholders. Still, this does not mean that shareholders successfully can sue a prospective acquirer under state common law for engaging in coercive or unfair tactics in making a tender offer. The reason is simple: At least before the acquirer becomes a controlling shareholder, the acquirer owes no fiduciary duty to the target's stockholders.[68] Congress and state legislatures, however, concluded that, fiduciary duty or not, there should be some constraints on the conduct of the party making a tender offer.

7.3.2 Federal Regulation of Tender Offers Under the Williams Act

The development of the hostile tender offer in the 1960s provoked a fairly quick response from the United States Congress. Congress was concerned that acquirers were structuring tender offers in order to stampede shareholders into selling their stock based upon inadequate information. For example, an acquirer might announce its tender offer after the close of business on a Friday, with shareholders given only until early the next week to accept.[69] Moreover, the offer might seek only a limited number of shares (say, enough to give the acquirer a majority) and might be open on a first-come, first-served basis—meaning that if a shareholder did not hurry to respond, the offer might already be fully taken by stockholders who acted faster. Compounding the shareholders' difficulty in deciding how to respond, the offer might provide little information about the acquirer, the acquirer's source of funds, or the acquirer's future plans for the company. To Congress, the resulting potential for shareholders to make ill-informed decisions in response to a tender offer seemed to parallel two problems already attacked by the securities laws: ill-informed decisions to buy securities, and ill-informed decisions to grant proxies. Accordingly, it seemed a natural enough response to amend the 1934 Securities Exchange Act to add provisions (Sections 13(d), 13(e), 14(d), 14(e) and 14(f)) addressing tender offers

---

67. Specifically, the agreement gave Viacom an option to purchase an amount of shares which would equal almost 20 percent of Paramount's outstanding stock, without putting up any cash; or Viacom could elect simply to have Paramount pay it the difference between the option price and the market price of Paramount's stock. This difference reached almost $500 million.

68. Moreover, as discussed in an earlier chapter, it is not clear that even a control-

ling shareholder would owe a duty to his or her fellow stockholders when taking actions solely in his or her role as a shareholder (such as offering to buy stock from other shareholders). See § 4.2.4*b* supra.

69. A tender offer following such timing was often referred to as a "Saturday night special."

and related matters. This amendment, made by Congress in 1968, is known as the Williams Act.

a. Disclosure requirements

As evident from what we just discussed, a principal thrust of the Williams Act is to require disclosure by persons making tender offers (or otherwise seeking to obtain a controlling amount of a corporation's outstanding stock). The Williams Act imposes formal disclosure requirements in two main situations.

One situation requiring disclosure occurs after a person obtains shares giving him or her beneficial ownership of over five percent of any class of equity securities registered under Section 12 of the Securities Exchange Act.[70] Section 13(d) of the Securities Exchange Act (which the Williams Act added) obligates any person who breaks the five percent threshold, within ten days after acquiring the shares, to send to the issuer of the purchased securities and to any exchange on which the securities are traded, and to file with the Securities Exchange Commission, a statement containing certain specified disclosures (a Schedule 13D).

Disclosure under Section 13(d) entails giving information about the acquirer, the source of the acquirer's funds, the number of shares the acquirer owns or has a right to buy, any arrangements the acquirer has with respect to the issuer's securities, and the acquirer's purpose for purchasing the shares (such as to obtain control, to liquidate or merge the issuer, or to make any other major change in the target's business or structure). Overall, this disclosure is not particularly burdensome to prepare (in comparison, for instance, with preparing a registration statement for a public offering of securities). Nevertheless, acquirers seek to delay making a Section 13(d) disclosure for as long as legally possible. The reason is not difficult to understand. Before filing under Section 13(d), the acquirer might be able to purchase shares on the stock market at previously prevailing prices, whereas, once the acquirer files a Schedule 13D announcing the acquirer's intention to make a premium price tender offer, the market price of the target's stock will shoot up.

This, in turn, raises an interesting policy question—concerning which the Securities Exchange Act displays a fair amount of ambivalence—as to whether persons seeking to purchase control of a corporation ought to be able to purchase stock at prevailing market prices from shareholders who are ignorant of the buyer's plans to pay a greater price in order to obtain control. Certainly such information would be most material to a shareholder in deciding whether to sell his or her stock; yet, as discussed in an earlier chapter, non-disclosure of one's own intent to pay more for shares is not considered to constitute illegal trading on

---

70. Section 12 of the 1934 Securities Exchange Act requires registration of securities listed for trading on a national stock exchange or held by over 500 shareholders (so long as the company has over $10 million in assets). Acquisition of over five percent of certain other specialized types of shares, such as those issued by a registered closed-end investment company, also triggers the disclosure obligation.

inside information.[71] Section 13(d) splits the baby: allowing an acquirer to accumulate at least five percent of the stock with no obligation of disclosure, but ten days after the acquirer goes over the magic five percent threshold, the acquirer effectively is no longer able to purchase from shareholders ignorant of the acquirer's intent.

Generally, Section 13(d)'s trigger for disclosure—acquisition of over five percent of a class of registered shares—is fairly easy to apply. Sometimes, however, application of Section 13(d) is not so straightforward. One source of difficulty lies in Section 13(d)(3). This provision deems two or more parties, who act as a group for the purpose of acquiring, holding or disposing of securities, to be one person under Section 13(d). This is necessary, otherwise parties could avoid Section 13(d) filings by having a number of individuals working together each purchase less than five percent of the target's shares.

While the rationale behind Section 13(d)(3) is simple, application of the group concept raises some questions. To begin with, how much of an agreement must exist between persons before they constitute a group? In fact, there is no requirement that there be a formal written agreement in order to constitute a group; all that is necessary is that the parties have some common understanding.[72] This, in turn, leads to the question of what exactly the group must plan to do. Section 13(d)(3) refers to groups acting not just for the purpose of acquiring, but also groups formed for the purpose of disposing or even holding securities.[73] Hence, if several shareholders gather together to try and sell their stock,[74] or to gain control of a corporation,[75] Section 13(d)(3) could apply, even though the shareholders do not plan to buy any more stock.[76] This broad reach, however, creates a quandary: Even if the purpose of a Section 13(d)(3) group need not be to acquire shares, Section 13(d) only requires filing a Schedule 13D after an acquisition places a person (including a group under Section 13(d)(3)) over the five percent threshold. Where is the acquisition of stock triggering the 13D filing requirement when dealing with groups formed to hold or dispose of, rather than acquire, stock? The answer is that the triggering acquisition takes place upon the formation of the group (assuming the group members' total ownership exceeds five percent), since, at this point, the group (treating it as something of a separate entity) is deemed to obtain the shares theretofore owned individually by its members.[77]

Another problem in applying Section 13(d)'s trigger involves determining when a person has acquired beneficial ownership of shares. Rule

---

71. See § 6.3.2d *supra.*

72. *E.g.,* Wellman v. Dickinson, 475 F.Supp. 783 (S.D.N.Y.1979), *aff'd,* 682 F.2d 355 (2d Cir.1982).

73. Why Congress drafted Section 13(d)(3) with such a scope is unclear.

74. Wellman v. Dickinson, 475 F.Supp. 783 (S.D.N.Y.1979), *aff'd,* 682 F.2d 355 (2d Cir.1982).

75. *E.g.,* GAF Corp. v. Milstein, 453 F.2d 709 (2d Cir.1971).

76. *But see* Bath Indus., Inc. v. Blot, 427 F.2d 97 (7th Cir.1970).

77. *E.g.,* Sec. Exch. Act Rule 13d–5(b).

13d–3, promulgated by the Securities Exchange Commission, specifies a number of criteria for determining who is the beneficial owner of shares for purposes of Section 13(d).

Finally, several exceptions exist to the requirement for a 13D filing. For example, Section 13(d)(6)(B) excludes, from Section 13(d)'s filing requirement, acquisitions of no more than two percent of the class of shares in one year—even if such an acquisition otherwise would trigger Section 13(d) by putting the acquirer over the five percent threshold.[78]

Section 14(d) of the Securities Exchange Act (which the Williams Act added) contains the second trigger for formal disclosure under the Williams Act. This section applies to anyone (other than the issuer of the stock) making a tender offer for shares of an equity security registered under Section 12 of the Securities Exchange Act (or for certain other specialized types of shares), if, after the transaction (assuming it is successful), the party making the tender offer will own over five percent of the sought after class of stock.[79] Section 14(d) requires the filing of a statement (a Schedule 14D–1) with the Securities Exchange Commission prior to making the tender offer.[80]

Schedule 14D–1 requires disclosing a bit more information than does Schedule 13D. For example, Schedule 14D–1 calls for information about any arrangements between the party making the tender offer and the target corporation or any of its insiders. Schedule 14D–1 also goes beyond Schedule 13D in demanding extensive financial information about the acquirer (assuming the acquirer is not a natural person) if the information would be material to the target's shareholders in deciding what to do with their shares. This, in turn, raises the question of when financial information concerning a party making a tender offer would be material to shareholders in deciding whether to tender their stock. In fact, courts have found such information to be material even if the buyer seeks 100 percent control in exchange for cash.[81] In any event, for public companies, who must report financial information periodically anyway, it is generally easier simply to disclose the financial information in a Schedule 14D–1, rather than worry about whether the information is material.

From the standpoint of a shareholder deciding whether to tender his or her shares, perhaps the most important information would be the plans the prospective acquirer has for the company, and any other facts

78. As would occur, for example, if the acquirer already owned four percent of the outstanding stock and bought two percent more.

79. For Constitutional reasons, Section 14(d) only reaches parties making a tender offer by use of the mail or instrumentalities of interstate commerce. As discussed in other contexts, this jurisdictional limit has little practical impact. After all, it will be extraordinarily difficult, if not impossible, to avoid using instrumentalities of inter-

state commerce (such as the telephone) in making a tender offer for the shares of a public corporation.

80. Securities Exchange Commission rules require the acquirer to send copies of its Schedule 14D–1 to the issuer and to any exchange on which the sought after stock is traded. Exch. Act Rule 14d–3.

81. Prudent Real Estate Trust v. Johncamp Realty, Inc., 599 F.2d 1140 (2d Cir. 1979).

which might give the shareholder an insight into how high a price the prospective acquirer really is prepared to pay. Schedule 14D–1, like Schedule 13D, calls for discussion of the purchaser's plans for the company. Often, however, parties filing a Schedule 14D–1 or 13D will hedge such a discussion by listing various options the acquirer might undertake, rather than setting out any specific plan. Despite undermining the utility of what would seem to be an important item of disclosure, courts have tended to allow this sort of hedged discussion.[82] Courts also have tended not to require disclosure concerning the buyer's valuation of the target's business or assets [83]—despite the fact that such information would seem highly important to a shareholder in deciding whether or not to sell. While the stated rationale for such decisions often is that the buyer's valuation is too speculative or unreliable to be material, this is silly, since, no matter how unreliable the buyer's valuation of the target corporation is from an objective standpoint, such a subjective assessment is still highly relevant for what it shows as to how high a price the buyer is willing to pay. Perhaps the unspoken premise of these decisions is that buyers should not need to disclose their reservation price. Moreover, there is something strange about requiring an outside buyer to tell the shareholders of the target corporation about the value of the shareholders' own company.

Since there is not a huge difference between the information required in a Schedule 14D–1 and the information required in a Schedule 13D, is there any significant practical difference between the two disclosure requirements? In fact, the most critical difference lies in the timing of the two filings: Section 14(d) requires filing *before* making a tender offer, whereas Section 13(d) allows a filing up to 10 days after the acquisition which places one over the five percent threshold. Of course, if the acquisition that will put one over the five percent threshold occurs through a tender offer, then this difference in timing becomes unimportant. Many times, however, an acquirer can gain a significant leg up by purchasing shares through the stock market before making a tender offer. In this event, as noted above, timing of disclosure is important, because the acquirer would like to buy as many shares as it can on the market before the price rises in response to the acquirer's disclosure of its intentions. In fact, during the 10 days acquirers have to file a Schedule 13D after breaking the five percent threshold, acquirers often are able to buy another 10 or 20 percent of the target's outstanding stock through open market purchases.

Section 14(d) excludes from its coverage tender offers by the corporation which issued the stock.[84] Instead, Section 13(e) authorizes the Securities Exchange Commission to promulgate rules covering issuer repurchases—including rules requiring such disclosure as the Commis-

82. *E.g.,* Wellman v. Dickinson, 475 F.Supp. 783 (S.D.N.Y.1979), *aff'd,* 682 F.2d 355 (2d Cir.1982).

83. *E.g.,* Flynn v. Bass Bros. Enterprises, 744 F.2d 978 (3d Cir.1984). *But see* Feit

v. Leasco Data Processing Equip. Corp., 332 F.Supp. 544 (E.D.N.Y.1971).

84. Exch. Act § 14(d)(8)(B).

sion deems appropriate. Pursuant to this authority, the Securities Exchange Commission has adopted rules requiring disclosure by issuers repurchasing stock in various situations. For example, issuers which make tender offers for their own stock must provide their shareholders with disclosure substantially paralleling the disclosure required in a Schedule 14D–1.[85] The Securities Exchange Commission also promulgated rules requiring disclosure by the issuer who seeks to repurchase (even if not through a tender offer) the issuer's outstanding stock during a tender offer by another person,[86] and by the issuer whose repurchases can result in the delisting of the issuer's stock from the stock exchange, or in the issuer otherwise no longer being subject to the registration requirements of the 1934 Securities Exchange Act (so-called going private transactions).[87]

The rules under Section 13(e) only cover the issuer when it is repurchasing stock. Is there any disclosure requirement imposed upon the target's board when faced with a tender offer, regardless of whether the board responds with a stock repurchase? In fact, the Securities Exchange Commission has used its rule-making authority under Sections 14(d) and 14(e) (which we will discuss shortly) to impose such a disclosure requirement. Specifically, if the target's board makes a statement about a third party's tender offer for the target's stock (other than a statement simply saying that the board is considering the offer and will comment shortly), the board must file a Schedule 14D–9.[88] The most significant item on this schedule typically is the requirement to disclose whether any negotiation is underway (for instance, with another buyer) in response to the tender offer—albeit the board need not disclose the specifics of the possible transaction (such as price and the identity of the other party) before reaching an agreement in principle, if more detailed disclosure could upset the negotiations. Suppose the target's board wishes to remain silent. Rule 14e–2 prevents this by requiring a statement by the target's board in response to a tender offer within 10 days of the offer's publication—although the statement can be one of no opinion or neutrality. Even a neutral opinion, however, triggers the 14D–9 disclosure.

In discussing both the federal proxy rules and the general disclosure requirements of the federal securities laws earlier in this book, we saw a pattern under which the law backstops the specific disclosure requirements with a general anti-fraud provision. The Williams Act follows this pattern as well. Section 14(e) prohibits anyone from making false or misleading statements of material fact,[89] or engaging in fraudulent, deceptive or manipulative conduct, in connection with a tender offer.[90]

85. Exch. Act Rule 13e–4.

86. Exch. Act Rule 13e–1.

87. Exch. Act Rule 13e–3.

88. Exch. Act Rule 14d–9.

89. Materiality for purposes of Section 14(e) has the same definition we have seen before in both the proxy and the purchase or sale of a security contexts. *E.g.*, Flynn v. Bass Bros. Enterprises, 744 F.2d 978 (3d Cir.1984).

90. Courts have disagreed on the level of culpability required to violate Section 14(e). *Compare* SEC v. Wills, [1979] Fed. Sec. L. Rep. (CCH) ¶ 96,712 (D.D.C. 1978)

Needless to say, the verbal sparring between the incumbent directors and a party attempting a hostile takeover often gives rise to allegations that each side made false statements, or omitted material facts which made their statements misleading, in making claims in support of, or in opposition to, a tender offer.[91] Indeed, as suggested earlier, the target's directors, simply as a tactical defense, might file a lawsuit challenging the accuracy of a hostile acquirer's statements soliciting the tender of shares. While such a suit, even if successful on the merits, may only require the hostile bidder to issue corrective disclosure,[92] the delay in the tender offer potentially caused by the suit (even if the suit is ultimately not successful on the merits) might be worthwhile to the target's board.[93]

In addition to prohibiting false or misleading statements in connection with a tender offer, Section 14(e) empowers the Securities Exchange Commission to promulgate rules reasonably designed to prevent fraudulent, deceptive or manipulative conduct in connection with tender offers. The Securities Exchange Commission has used this power aggressively to adopt a number of rules regulating the conduct of parties involved with tender offers, including by requiring disclosure. For example, we just saw how the Commission used its authority under Section 14(e) to adopt a rule requiring a response by the target's board within 10 days after learning of a tender offer. Earlier in this book when discussing trading on inside information, we explored how the Commission adopted Rule 14e–3 to prohibit trading on undisclosed inside information concerning tender offers.[94]

Finally, Section 14(f) establishes one fairly narrow additional disclosure requirement. This Section requires that the shareholders receive disclosure equivalent to that called for under the proxy rules, when there will be a change in the composition of a majority of the target's board through the serial resignation and appointment of directors at the behest of a person making a tender offer subject to Section 14(d) or who crossed the five percent threshold under Section 13(d).

b. *Substantive regulation*

As discussed earlier, in passing the Williams Act, Congress was concerned not only with ill-informed decisions, but also with what Congress perceived to be unfair high-pressure tactics used in making tender offers.[95] Hence, in addition to requiring formal disclosure, Section 14(d) imposes substantive rules on tender offers designed to combat such tactics.

(negligence is enough), *with* SEC v. Texas Int'l. Co., 498 F.Supp. 1231 (N.D.Ill.1980) (scienter required).

91. *See, e.g.,* Gulf & Western Indus., Inc. v. Great Atlantic & Pacific Tea Co., 476 F.2d 687 (2d Cir.1973).

92. *See, e.g.,* Dan River, Inc. v. Icahn, 701 F.2d 278 (4th Cir.1983).

93. Of course, filing a meritless lawsuit for purposes of delay raises serious ethical and legal concerns.

94. See § 6.4.2 *supra*.

95. Indeed, disclosure might actually contribute to the coercive effect of a tender offer, as when the acquirer discloses its intention to pay less in the second stage of a two-step acquisition.

The first substantive rule in Section 14(d) borrows an idea found in many consumer protection statutes dealing with door-to-door sales. Such consumer protection statutes often contain a cooling off provision, which allows consumers to change their minds and unwind the sale up to a certain number of days following an at-home purchase. Similarly, Section 14(d)(5) grants tendering shareholders the right to change their minds and get back their stock for up to seven days after publication of the tender offer (and again after 60 days if the offer is still open). Interestingly, the Securities Exchange Commission, pursuant to the Commission's rulemaking authority, expanded the right of shareholders to take back tendered shares. Under the Commission's Rule 14d–7, shareholders can change their minds and withdraw their shares for the entire period the tender offer is open. Moreover, acting under the authority of Section 14(e), the Commission has promulgated a rule requiring that tender offers remain open at least 20 business days.[96]

The next substantive rule found in Section 14(d) concerns what happens if stockholders tender more shares than the acquirer offered to purchase. Acquirers typically would like to use an approach of first-come, first-served, in order to create an incentive to tender. Section 14(d)(6), however, requires a pro-rata acceptance of the tendered shares.[97] While Section 14(d)(6) only grants this treatment for shareholders who tender within the first ten days after the offer (or after an increase in the offered price), again the Commission has expanded this by rule to cover all shareholders who tender during the life of the offer.[98]

Section 14(d)(7) contains a third substantive rule for tender offers. Section 14(d)(7) requires an acquirer who increases the offered price while the tender offer is still open, to give the shareholders who already tendered in response to the offer the benefit of the higher price.[99]

As evident from the discussion thus far, Section 14(d) is not the only source of substantive rules governing tender offers. Other substantive regulation of tender offers comes from rules promulgated by the Securities Exchange Commission. We just saw how the Commission has used its rule-making authority to expand the rights of shareholders to withdraw stock tendered in response to a tender offer, and the requirement for pro-rata acceptance in the case of over-subscribed offers, as well as to create a minimum length for which the offer must be kept open. Indeed, not only does the Commission's Rule 14e–1 require tender offers to be open for at least 20 business days, but the rule also requires the offer to

96. Exch. Act Rule 14e–1.

97. For example, if stockholders have tendered twice as many shares as the acquirer has offered to buy, then the acquirer must purchase half of the shares tendered by each stockholder.

98. Exch. Act Rule 14d–8.

99. Actually, the right of shareholders to withdraw their shares during the life of the offer probably created a self-help equiv-

alent to such price protection anyway. Once again, Securities Exchange Commission rules have expanded the statutory right—in this instance to prevent decreases, as well as increases, in the price paid to just some tendering shareholders during the life of the offer, and to cover the situation in which the acquirer offers to pay different types of consideration to tendering shareholders. Exch. Act Rule 14d–10.

remain open for 10 additional days from any change in the number of shares sought or in the price paid, and requires public announcement of any extension of a tender offer. In addition, the Securities Exchange Commission has adopted a rule (Rule 14d–10) which generally requires that a tender offer be open equally to all holders of the sought after class of shares—in other words, while the acquirer can reserve the right to purchase only a limited number of shares on a pro-rata basis from tendering shareholders, the acquirer cannot exclude any holders of the sought after class of shares from tendering their stock in response to the offer. Yet another rule (Rule 14e–4) prohibits short tendering (tendering shares one does not own) in response to a tender offer for less than all of the target's shares.[100] The Securities Exchange Commission has adopted one rule regulating the conduct of parties involved with tender offers, not pursuant to the Commission's authority under Section 14(d) or (e), but rather pursuant to the Commission's authority under Section 10(b) to combat manipulative practices in connection with the purchase or sale of shares. Rule 10b–13 prohibits a person, who makes a tender offer, from buying or arranging to buy the sought after securities other than through the tender offer, so long as the tender offer remains open.

An important set of substantive rules governing tender offers are the rules which the Securities Exchange Commission promulgated pursuant to the Commission's authority under Section 13(e) to regulate issuer repurchases. The Commission's rules require self-tenders by the issuer to comply with the substantive rules which, with a couple exceptions, parallel the substantive rules governing third party tender offers.[101] Significantly, in light of Delaware's approval of a discriminatory self-tender in *Unocal*, these rules include the requirement that a self-tender be open equally to all holders of the sought after class of stock.[102]

One branch of the federal government which has decided not to get involved in substantive regulation of tender offers pursuant to the Williams Act is the judicial branch. Specifically, in *Schreiber v. Burlington Northern, Inc.*,[103] the Supreme Court rejected the effort of a private litigant to use Section 14(e) as the basis to attack arguably unfair tactics by a party making a tender offer.

Schreiber was a shareholder of El Paso Gas Co. Burlington Northern made a hostile tender offer for 25.1 million El Paso shares at $24 per share. Instead of purchasing the shares tendered in response to this offer, however, Burlington Northern ended up negotiating with El Paso's board a friendly takeover of El Paso. Under this deal, Burlington Northern offered to purchase only 21 million shares from the El Paso shareholders (Burlington Northern purchasing another 4.1 million shares directly from El Paso).[104] Burlington Northern's new offer was

---

100. The concern with short-tendering is that stockholders can use this technique to get more than their pro-rata share of stock purchased in an over-subscribed offer.

101. Exch. Act Rule 13e–4(f).

102. Exch. Act Rule 13e–4(f)(8).

103. 472 U.S. 1, 105 S.Ct. 2458 (1985).

104. The reader might wonder how Burlington Northern could refuse to purchase the shares tendered in response to its

oversubscribed, resulting in a pro-rata purchase from the tendering shareholders. Disappointed at the decrease in the number of shares she could sell, Schreiber sued, claiming that Burlington Northern's change in tender offers constituted a "manipulation" in violation of Section 14(e). The Supreme Court never got into the question of whether there was anything unfair about Burlington Northern's actions. Instead, the court held that Section 14(e) is not violated unless there is some sort of misrepresentation or nondisclosure. Since Schreiber made no claim that Burlington Northern was guilty of lying or nondisclosure, her complaint did not state a cause of action under Section 14(e).

At first glance, the holding in *Schreiber* seems to be an unexceptional adherence to the Supreme Court's earlier holding in *Santa Fe*. As discussed when dealing with Rule 10b–5 in an earlier chapter,[105] in *Santa Fe*, the Supreme Court held that "fraudulent" or "manipulative" conduct within the meaning of Rule 10b–5 and Section 10(b) of the Securities Exchange Act requires some sort of misrepresentation or nondisclosure. Nevertheless, the court in *Schreiber* short-shrifted a number of differences between Section 14(e) and Section 10(b). To begin with, Section 14(e) prohibits making false statements or omitting facts which makes one's statements misleading, *or* engaging in fraudulent, manipulative, or deceptive conduct. Interpreting manipulative conduct to require a false statement or nondisclosure seemingly renders the "fraudulent, manipulative or deceptive" conduct language in Section 14(e) redundant of the prohibition on making false statements or misleading omissions. From a policy standpoint, the Supreme Court in *Santa Fe* was worried that a different interpretation of Rule 10b–5 and Section 10(b) could lead to the development of a federal law of corporate fiduciary duty which would displace much of state corporate law, without any indication that Congress had intended such a result. By contrast, the reach of Section 14(e) is much narrower—being confined to conduct in connection with tender offers—and it is clear from Section 14(d) that Congress did mean to impose substantive rules on tender offers in order to ensure fairness. Finally, if the reach of Section 14(e) only extends to false statements or nondisclosure, how could the Securities Exchange Commission use the Commission's rule-making authority under Section 14(e)

original tender offer without becoming liable for breach of contract to the tendering shareholders. The answer lies in the terms of the tender offer. Often, the acquirer will couch its tender offer as an invitation to shareholders to offer to sell the acquirer their stock, rather than as an offer by the acquirer to purchase stock. Hence, the shareholders' tendering becomes the offer, rather than the acceptance, and there is no contract until the acquirer accepts the shares. Alternately, the terms of the tender offer will allow the acquirer numerous outs under which the acquirer is not obligated to purchase the shares tendered. Occasionally,

however, acquirer's have found themselves subject to breach of contract damages when they failed to purchase tendered shares under circumstances in which the court found the tender offer to constitute an offer to purchase which did not give the acquirer an out covering the circumstances which arose. *E.g.*, Lowenschuss v. Kane, 520 F.2d 255 (2d Cir.1975) (court found breach of contract liability despite the fact that the tender offer had been enjoined on antitrust grounds).

105. See § 6.3.3 *supra*.

to impose substantive rules on tender offers, such as the requirement that tender offers remain open for at least 20 days?

Indeed, the *Schreiber* decision is not the only reason to wonder about the validity of the Securities Exchange Commission's substantive tender offer rules. One also might question how the Commission could create requirements which seem to contradict the specific guidelines contained in Section 14(d). To some extent, Congress itself invited such action. For example, Section 14(d)(5) expressly authorizes the Securities Exchange Commission to create rules altering the withdrawal rights set forth in the section. Moreover, Section 14(e) empowers the Securities Exchange Commission to adopt rules "reasonably designed to prevent" fraudulent, deceptive or manipulative actions—which seemingly contemplates the rules might go beyond simply prohibiting fraudulent, deceptive or manipulative actions, but also could impose requirements or prohibitions whose goal is to make fraudulent, deceptive or manipulative conduct less likely to occur. In any event, no acquirer has yet had the nerve to ignore or challenge the Securities Exchange Commission's tender offer rules—perhaps because the delay entailed in litigating over the validity of the Commission's rules would hamper the takeover attempt.

c. *What transactions fall within the tender offer rules?*

Section 14(d) and Section 14(e) are triggered by the presence of a "tender offer." Unfortunately, no provision either in the Williams Act, or in the rules promulgated by the Securities Exchange Commission pursuant to the Williams Act, defines the term tender offer. Traditionally, one thinks of a tender offer as a general invitation (typically through newspaper advertisements) to the shareholders of a company, proposing to buy some or all of their shares. By contrast, normally, neither open market purchases of shares at prevailing market prices through the stock exchange,[106] nor negotiated purchases with individual shareholders,[107] constitute a tender offer. In some cases, however, whether the transaction constitutes a tender offer is not clear-cut.

The purchases in *Wellman v. Dickinson*,[108] illustrate such a borderline transaction. This case involved purchases by Sun Company of around 34 percent of the stock of Beckton, Dickinson & Company. To obtain these shares, Sun solicited 39 persons and institutions. This included face-to-face dealing with a few insiders over a couple day period, followed by telephone solicitations of some 30 institutional investors. These institutions were called late in the day by persons who followed a written script of what they should say—which included that the buyer (who was not identified) was looking to purchase 20 percent of the outstanding Beckton, Dickinson stock, that no purchases would be final

---

106. *E.g.*, Brascan Ltd. v. Edper Equities Ltd., 477 F.Supp. 773 (S.D.N.Y.1979).

107. *E.g.*, Astronics Corp. v. Protective Closures Co., 561 F.Supp. 329 (W.D.N.Y. 1983).

108. 475 F.Supp. 783 (S.D.N.Y.1979), *aff'd*, 682 F.2d 355 (2d Cir.1982).

until shareholders had agreed to sell the buyer this amount of stock, that the seller could have either $45 per share (which was described as a top final price) or $40 per share with price protection in case the buyer later paid anyone else a higher price, and that the order was filling up fast and a hurried response was essential. The court held this was a tender offer.

In reaching the conclusion that the transaction before it was a tender offer, the court in *Wellman* employed an eight factor test suggested in an amicus brief by the Securities Exchange Commission. Seven of the factors the court felt were present in the case:

> (1) There was active and widespread solicitation of public shareholders for their stock;

> (2) The solicitation was for a substantial percentage of the corporation's stock;

> (3) The offered price represented a substantial premium over the current market price;

> (4) The terms of the offer were firm rather than negotiable;

> (5) Acceptance of the shares was contingent on the tender of a certain number of shares, and subject to a maximum number to be purchased;

> (6) The offer was open only for a limited time; and

> (7) The solicited shareholders were subjected to pressure to sell their stock.

One of the eight factors was not present:

> (8) Publicity about the offer.

The absence of this last factor was not enough, according to the court, to prevent the purchases from being a tender offer.[109]

The eight factor test suggested by the Securities Exchange Commission, and used in *Wellman*, has become a standard in the area.[110] While these factors seem to identify as well as possible the sort of transactions in which shareholders might face structural pressure to sell on an ill-

109. Actually, the court's opinion in *Wellman* is probably both unnecessarily confusing and confused on the question of whether there was a tender offer, because it attacked the same question twice. Specifically, the court engaged in a long preliminary discussion of whether the purchases were a private transaction, and seems to suggest that the Williams Act contains some exemption for private transactions. Unlike the 1933 Securities Act, however, there is no statutory exemption from Section 14(d) of the Williams Act for private transactions. The statutory issue is whether there is a tender offer, and the notion of private transactions is relevant only insofar as a private negotiated sale presumably is not a tender offer.

110. *See, e.g.,* SEC v. Carter Hawley Hale Stores, Inc., 760 F.2d 945 (9th Cir. 1985). *But see* Hanson Trust PLC v. SCM Corp., 774 F.2d 47 (2d Cir.1985) (refusing to treat the eight factor test as decisive, and holding that the existence of a tender offer depends upon whether the solicited shareholders lack information needed to consider the proposal—albeit, the court ended up looking at many of the same factors contained in the eight factor list).

informed basis, applying the list does not always produce an easy answer (especially when courts do not say how many factors must be present).

Not only do the disclosure requirements and substantive rules under Section 14(d) and Section 14(e) make it necessary to determine whether a transaction constitutes a tender offer, but they also make it important to determine when a tender offer begins and when a tender offer ends. Rule 14d–2 provides specific guidelines as to when a tender offer commences. Significantly, this rule considers announcement of an intent to make an offer to constitute the start of a tender offer—thereby triggering the Williams Act disclosure and substantive rules—if the announcement includes sufficient information concerning the offer (such as a price range and what securities the buyer seeks).

The question of when a tender offer ends can become relevant, among other situations, in the context of so-called "street sweeps." In a street sweep, a party makes a tender offer, announces the termination of the offer without accepting the tendered shares, and then is able to purchase a large percentage of the issuer's outstanding stock through open market purchases as disappointed shareholders—who are often arbitragers who bought the stock in order to sell to the party making a tender offer or to any higher bidder—seek to dump their stock. In *Hanson Trust PLC v. SCM Corp.*,[111] the court held that such a sweep, in itself, did not constitute a tender offer. In *Field v. Trump*,[112] however, the court stated that it would not consider a purported termination of a tender offer actually to end the tender offer when the acquirer continued to purchase shares and had not abandoned the goal of the original offer. While *Field* involved an effort to get around the rule requiring all sellers in a tender offer to receive the same price, the judicial flexibility not to recognize a so-called termination of a tender offer by a party still pursuing its acquisition plans could put a crimp on deliberate attempts to buy shares on the cheap through a staged termination of the tender offer followed by a street sweep.

By the section's own terms, some tender offers are beyond the scope of Section 14(d). For instance, as mentioned before, Section 14(d) does not cover self-tenders by the issuer. Section 14(d) also excludes tender offers which would not result in purchasing more than two percent of the outstanding shares of the sought after class of stock in one year (albeit, it hard to imagine such small tender offers often occurring anyway). Moreover, the disclosure requirements and substantive regulations in Section 14(d) only apply to tender offers for shares registered under the 1934 Securities Exchange Act (and a few other types of securities). (Notice this means it is the target, not the acquirer, which must be a 1934 Act reporting company, for Section 14(d) to apply.) By contrast, Section 14(e) applies to any tender offer, even for unregistered shares. Indeed, the Securities Exchange Commission reportedly took into account the broader reach of Section 14(e) in deciding to promulgate

---

111. 774 F.2d 47 (2d Cir.1985).   **112.** 850 F.2d 938 (2d Cir.1988).

certain of its substantive tender offer rules under Section 14(e), rather than under Section 14(d).

d. Private litigation under the Williams Act

The Williams Act contains no express private right of action; the only express enforcement provisions for the Williams Act are the general enforcement provisions of the Securities Exchange Act. Nevertheless, as we have seen in dealing with the proxy rules and with Rule 10b–5, courts have held that there is an implied private cause of action to enforce the Williams Act provisions.[113] One rationale for an implied private right of action under the Williams Act is that Congress patterned the Williams Act upon the proxy rules, where the Supreme Court earlier had recognized a private cause of action.[114] Subsequent Congressional acquiescence after lower courts had recognized an implied private right of action under the Williams Act, despite Congress having amended the Williams Act in other particulars, reinforces the view that an implied private right of action is consistent with Congress' intent.

The existence of an implied private right of action under the Williams Act raises a number of issues we have seen before in dealing with the proxy rules and Rule 10b–5. To begin with, who has standing to sue for violation of the Williams Act? In *Piper v. Chris–Craft Indus., Inc.*,[115] the Supreme Court held that the party who made an unsuccessful tender offer lacked standing to assert a claim for damages based upon a violation of Section 14(e). The court reasoned that the intended beneficiaries of the Williams Act provisions are the shareholders of the target, not the party making a tender offer. Nevertheless, some lower courts have allowed the party making a tender offer to bring an action for injunctive relief—for example, to force a corrective statement by the target's board.[116] In essence, these courts are allowing the party making a tender offer to act as a champion of the shareholders to see that the shareholders receive correct information.

The Supreme Court's reasoning in *Piper* suggests that the shareholders of the target should have standing to sue for damages (or injunctive relief) for violations of the Williams Act.[117] Moreover, because the Williams Act provisions contain no language referring to a purchase or sale of securities, shareholders who did not purchase or sell stock might have standing (unlike the situation with claims under Rule 10b–5 and Section 10(b) of the 1934 Securities Exchange Act).[118] Of course, the

113. *E.g.*, Electronic Specialty Co. v. International Controls Corp., 409 F.2d 937 (2d Cir.1969) (recognizing a private right of action for violation of Section 14(e)).

114. Indiana Nat'l. Corp. v. Rich, 712 F.2d 1180 (7th Cir.1983) (recognizing a private right of action for violations of Section 13(d)).

115. 430 U.S. 1, 97 S.Ct. 926 (1977).

116. *E.g.*, Humana, Inc. v. American Medicorp, Inc., [1977–1978] Fed. Sec. L. Rep. (CCH) ¶ 96,286 (S.D.N.Y. 1978).

117. *See, e.g.*, Electronic Specialty Co. v. International Controls Corp., 409 F.2d 937 (2d Cir.1969).

118. *See, e.g.*, Neuman v. Electronic Specialty Co., [1969–1970] Fed. Sec. L. Rep. (CCH) ¶ 92,591 (N.D. Ill. 1969) (albeit, the court refused to rely on the difference in statutory language between Sections 10(b)

target's shareholders would need to establish reliance in order to recover damages,[119] which presents a problem when the would-be acquirer withdraws its tender offer and so would not have purchased the plaintiff's shares even if the plaintiff had tendered them.[120]

A number of lower courts have held that the target corporation has standing to sue under the Williams Act.[121] Indeed, recovery of damages by the target corporation presumably benefits the non-tendering shareholders, and so this result seems consistent with the *Piper* court's position that the purpose of the Williams Act is to protect the target corporation's shareholders .

Incidentally, a plaintiff seeking injunctive relief for violating Section 13(d) (or presumably any other section of the Williams Act) must establish the traditional grounds for equitable relief, such as the existence of irreparable harm without such a remedy.[122]

7.3.3 *State Takeover Legislation*

State legislatures also have reacted to the hostile takeover phenomenon. We discussed elsewhere one common reaction: the adoption of statutes expressly empowering directors to consider the interests of groups beyond the shareholders in making any decisions for the corporation.[123] State legislatures also have adopted statutory provisions more focused on takeovers.

One common type of state takeover legislation places limits upon the ability of a party, who recently acquired a large percentage of a corporation's outstanding stock, to enter into a merger or other business combination with that corporation. For example, Section 203 of the Delaware General Corporation Law establishes a moratorium period of three years after the acquisition of 15 percent of a corporation's outstanding voting stock during which the buyer cannot complete a merger or other business combination with the corporation unless one of three conditions is met: (1) the board of the target corporation approved either the share acquisition or the combination prior to the share purchase

---

and 14(e) in allowing standing under Section 14(e) for non-tendering shareholders). From a policy standpoint, claims by shareholders, who did not tender their stock purportedly because of a false statement, raise the sort of proof problems which convinced the Supreme Court to limit standing to purchasers or sellers in the Rule 10b–5 context. One difference when dealing with non-tendering shareholders, however, is that there is an inherently limited universe of parties who can make the claim that they would have tendered had they known the truth—which is not the case when dealing with false statements that allegedly led plaintiffs not to buy stock.

119. *E.g.*, Lewis v. McGraw, 619 F.2d 192 (2d Cir.1980).

120. *Id.* An interesting argument in this regard, however, might be to attempt to tie

the withdrawal of the tender offer to the false or misleading statement, and thereby establish a sort of indirect reliance (much like the fraud on the market theory).

121. *E.g.*, Electronic Specialty Co. v. International Controls Corp., 409 F.2d 937 (2d Cir.1969).

122. Rondeau v. Mosinee Paper Corp., 422 U.S. 49, 95 S.Ct. 2069 (1975).

123. Some state legislatures themselves have acted to protect the interests of other constituencies impacted by corporate takeovers—for example, by giving employees terminated following a corporate takeover the right to severance pay. This, however, is more a matter of employment law than it is an issue of corporate law.

taking place; (2) the buyer acquired 85 percent of the target's shares; or (3) two-thirds of the stockholders other than the buyer approved the merger or other combination. A number of other states have added provisions to their corporation statutes which do not contain a moratorium period, but require either a supermajority vote by the target's shareholders (or possibly by disinterested directors), or the shareholders' receipt of at least a certain minimum price, in any merger following the acquisition of a certain percentage of the target's stock by one of the participants in the merger.[124]

What is the rationale behind this type of takeover statute? Notice these provisions make it more difficult to complete the second stage of a two-stage acquisition. As such, these provisions might protect shareholders from coercive tender offers which threaten to freeze-out, on poor terms, a non-tendering minority. Yet, as we shall discuss later in this chapter, the problem of potential prejudice to minority shareholders from freeze-out mergers is not confined to mergers involving a new shareholder, and, accordingly, the law generally provides some protections to minority shareholders facing a freeze-out. Hence, if the law which generally governs freeze-out mergers provides adequate protection to minority shareholders, why was there a need for new statutes to address such mergers after the acquisition of stock? On the other hand, if the law generally governing freeze-out mergers did not provide sufficient protection for minority shareholders, then why did the new statutes not cover mergers or business combinations at the behest of a shareholder who has held his or her shares for an extended period of time?

Another common type of state takeover provision goes beyond protecting shareholders in the second stage of a two-stage acquisition. Instead, these provisions limit the ability of the acquirer to take control of the target corporation. For example, such provisions might require a shareholder vote, either before a party can acquire a so-called controlling amount of voting stock, or to allow the buyer to vote such a controlling block.[125] A controlling amount of voting stock under these statutes is not a majority. Rather, these statutes commonly set a controlling amount at much lower threshold (such as 20 percent), and, indeed, the statutes may have several thresholds (such as 20, 33, and 50 percent) and require a new vote each time a shareholder crosses one threshold. The notion is that with scattered public ownership, a shareholder can have effective control with a large block, even if that block is not a majority. Naturally, the acquirer does not get to vote on approving the transfer or to allow the acquirer to vote his or her shares.

At first glance, statutory provisions requiring a shareholder vote in order for a party to obtain, or to be able to vote, a potentially controlling block of stock seem to represent an extreme and unjustified interference with the ability of shareholders to convey their stock. There is, however,

124. *E.g.*, Ill. Bus. Corp. Act. § 7.85.

125. *E.g.*, Ohio Gen. Corp. Law § 1701.831.

at least some arguable logic behind such provisions. As discussed earlier in this chapter, acquisition of a corporation's business through either a merger or the purchase of substantially all of the target corporation's assets would require a vote by the target corporation's shareholders. By imposing a similar vote requirement in order for a person to obtain control over the target corporation through a purchase of the target's outstanding stock, these provisions establish an approximate parity in the right of the target's shareholders to vote on all three principal ways of structuring the acquisition of a corporation's business. Of course, one might argue that, in selling their shares, stockholders are "voting with their feet." Yet, as discussed before, sometimes shareholders might only tender their stock out of fear of being stuck in a non-tendering minority, but, if able to vote, might vote against the transfer of control.[126]

A third type of state takeover provision gives the stockholders of the target corporation the right to demand the acquirer cash them out at fair value once any person has purchased a so-called controlling percentage (for example, 20 percent) of a corporation's stock.[127] This fair value might be set at not less than the highest price the buyer paid to anyone in order to purchase shares in the target during a specified period of time (for example, 90 days) prior to the buyer reaching the threshold percentage of ownership.

Notice, this third type of takeover provision creates something roughly equivalent to the appraisal rights which corporation statutes commonly grant to shareholders dissenting from mergers. Hence, one might rationalize this sort of takeover provision as simply creating a rough equivalency in shareholder appraisal rights no matter how an acquirer structures its acquisition of a corporation's business.

A fourth type of state takeover provision requires a party, who acquires a controlling percentage (for example, 20 percent) of a corporation's voting stock, and who then sells the stock (presumably following a defeat of this party's efforts to take control), to disgorge to the target corporation any profits made on selling the stock.[128] This sort of statute is somewhat similar to Section 16(b) of the Securities Exchange Act, and one might rationalize this statute as an attempt to prevent the abuse of inside information. On the other hand, the main impact of this provision falls on defeated potential hostile acquirers, who it is unlikely had any inside information. Hence, this provision seems to represent simply a gratuitous slap at parties attempting to undertake hostile takeovers.

Many of the state takeover statutes contain provisions which render them inapplicable to various firms incorporated in the jurisdiction. For example, these statutes normally exclude companies whose shares are not widely traded.[129] Most state takeover statutes allow companies to opt

126. *See, e.g.,* Lucian Bebchuk, *Toward Undistorted Choice and Equal Treatment in Corporate Takeovers*, 98 Harv. L. Rev. 1963 (1985).

127. Penn. Bus. Corp. Law §§ 2542–2547.

128. *Id* at § 2575.

129. *E.g.,* Del. Gen. Corp. Law § 203(b)(4).

out of the statutory rule by a provision in the corporation's articles.[130]

The question of the constitutionality of state takeover legislation has come twice before the United States Supreme Court. In *Edgar v. MITE Corp.*,[131] the Supreme Court dealt with an example of what is now commonly referred to as a "first generation" state takeover statute. These first generation statutes were very different from the state takeover statutes described above.[132] The statute in *MITE* based its essential provisions upon notions employed in state blue sky laws. Specifically, as discussed earlier in this book,[133] many state blue sky laws require a state official to approve the fairness of the transaction before a person can sell securities in the state. Similarly, the Illinois statute involved in *MITE* required a state official to approve the fairness of a tender offer. This imposed two burdens on a tender offer. The obvious burden was the risk that the state official might not approve the tender offer because the official found inadequate disclosure or that the offer's terms were inequitable. More subtly, the process of obtaining state approval delayed the offer, during which time the target's board could undertake defensive steps.

The Supreme Court in *MITE* held that the Illinois statute was unconstitutional. A majority of the court held that the statute was an unconstitutional burden on interstate commerce. At first glance, one might be surprised at this result, since the Illinois statute seemingly followed the model of state blue sky laws, which have not been held to constitute an undue burden on interstate commerce. There is a key difference, however, between the Illinois statute in *MITE* and state blue sky laws. This difference involves the reach of the statutes. Blue sky laws regulate the sale of securities in the state, and so the state can argue that the state has a clear interest in protecting its residents from purchasing unsound investments. By contrast, the Illinois statute in *MITE* did not limit its reach to tender offers only insofar as the offer targeted Illinois residents. Rather, under the statute's terms, one could not make a tender offer anywhere in the country if the target corporation was an Illinois corporation, or if 10 percent of the corporation's shareholders were in Illinois, or if the corporation had its principal office in Illinois. For the Supreme Court, it was a mystery what interest Illinois could have in protecting shareholders who were outside of Illinois—which could be 90 or 100 percent of the targeted shareholders—from an unfair tender offer. Hence, there was no legitimate state interest

---

130. *E.g.*, Del. Gen. Corp. Law § 203(b)(1), (2), (3).

131. 457 U.S. 624, 102 S.Ct. 2629 (1982).

132. In response to the Supreme Court's invalidating the statute in *MITE*, many state legislatures enacted new statutes designed to avoid the constitutional infirmities of the first generation statutes. These later statutes are often referred to as "second generation" state takeover statutes. After the Supreme Court upheld a second generation statute in the *CTS* decision which we will discuss shortly, many states enacted somewhat more expansive (constitutionally speaking) statutes. These post-*CTS* statutes are often referred to as "third generation" state takeover statutes. Hence, the state takeover statutes which are now common are examples of so-called second and third generation state takeover statutes.

133. See § 6.2.1 *supra*.

to offset the obvious burden the statute imposed on interstate commerce by blocking nationwide tender offers.

A plurality of the Supreme Court in *MITE* also found the Illinois statute preempted because of its purported conflicts with the Williams Act. Specifically, the plurality felt that the Illinois statute tilted the playing field in favor of management during a takeover battle—for example, through the greater delay the statute introduced—contrary to the Williams Act's goal of preserving a level field between the contestants in a takeover battle. Moreover, the requirement of state approval of the substantive fairness of a tender offer, conflicted, according to the plurality, with the Williams Act's goal of shareholders making their own decisions about tender offers.

It is not surprising that the Williams Act holding in *MITE* did not receive the support of most of the justices, since the logic of this holding is highly questionable. The fact that Congress did not wish Congress' own legislation (the Williams Act) to tilt the playing field between contestants in a takeover battle does not mean that Congress wished to preempt any state legislation which did. Moreover, the notion behind the Williams Act that investors, armed with full disclosure, should make their own decisions, is the philosophy behind all of the federal securities laws; yet Congress (until recently) expressly disclaimed any intent for the federal securities laws to preempt state blue sky laws which followed a more paternalistic approach of merit review.

Five years after *MITE*, the Supreme Court upheld a second generation state takeover statute in *CTS Corp. v. Dynamics Corp. of America*.[134] The Indiana statute involved in *CTS* was an example of the type of state takeover statute we discussed earlier which requires a shareholder vote in order for the purchaser of a controlling amount of stock to be able to vote the shares. As in *MITE*, the challenges to the Indiana statute in *CTS* involved the statute's burden on interstate commerce, and whether the Williams Act preempted the statute.

After noting that the court was not bound by the plurality opinion on the Williams Act issue in *MITE*, the court in *CTS* dismissed the Williams Act concern by asserting that the Indiana statute did not tilt the field in favor of management in such a way as to conflict with the goals of the Williams Act. Rather, according to the court, by allowing shareholders to vote on the passage of control, the Indiana statute protected the shareholders from the potentially coercive effect of tender offers, which was also a concern of the Williams Act.

The more interesting part of the *CTS* opinion dealt with the commerce clause issue. In fact, the Indiana statute could throw a monkey wrench into a nationwide tender offer, even if almost 90 percent of the offeree shareholders were not Indiana residents.[135] Still, there

---

134. 481 U.S. 69, 107 S.Ct. 1637 (1987).

135. The statute only applied if more than 10 percent of the shareholders of the target corporation were Indiana residents, more than 10 percent of the shares of the target corporation were held by Indiana

were two critical differences between the Indiana statute before the court in *CTS*, and the Illinois statute invalidated in *MITE*. The Indiana statute only covered companies incorporated in Indiana, and the Indiana statute dealt with a subject (shareholder voting rights) traditionally covered by corporation statutes. Hence, had the Supreme Court held the Indiana statute impermissibly burdened interstate commerce, the result would have been to raise serious questions about the long-accepted internal affairs rule, which says that the corporate law of the state of incorporation governs the rights of the shareholders. After all, Delaware corporate law governs numerous nationwide corporate transactions by many of the largest corporations in the United States (if not the world) despite the fact that very few of the shareholders of these companies actually may be Delaware residents.

One common criticism of state takeover statutes is that in many, if not most, cases, their enactment can be traced to a takeover threat confronted by a prominent local corporation. Hence, the suspicion is strong that such statutes reflect parochial concerns with local jobs, or the influence of a local company's board, at the expense of the national interest in facilitating efficient corporate restructurings. Still, if courts hold that noble motives are a prerequisite to constitutional state legislation, then much state legislation might be in question. Indeed, as discussed early in this book, Delaware's corporation statute has emerged as the most influential in the nation precisely as a result of the Delaware legislature's parochial pursuit of the state's interest in corporate franchise fees.

7.3.4 *A Postscript Re Policy*

Writers have spilled considerable ink debating what the law should be in regards to hostile takeovers. Much of this debate has focused on the broad economic impact of corporate takeovers.

As suggested at several points above, some writers—principally associated with the deregulatory "law and economics" philosophy—have applauded the hostile takeover, and have opposed legal rules which hinder such takeovers. The argument in favor of this position often starts with a simple factual observation: the premium price paid by the hostile acquirer in order to purchase the target corporation has made a lot of shareholders a lot of money, which, all other factors being equal, would seem to be a good thing. This, however, leads to the question of where all the money which went to the target corporation's shareholders comes from. The supporters of takeovers assert that this money largely comes from sources which represent the creation of real wealth.[136] For example, combinations of businesses can produce various synergies and efficiencies (such as economies of scale). Of far greater significance for corporate law, the hostile takeover can create real wealth by allowing the

residents, or at least 10,000 shareholders of the target corporation were Indiana residents.

136. *E.g.*, Roberta Romano, *A Guide to Takeovers: Theory, Evidence and Regulation*, 9 Yale J. Reg. 119 (1992).

replacement of poorly performing management with new managers who will do a better job. Indeed, as discussed when dealing with corporate governance earlier in this book, the constant threat of hostile takeovers can serve to discipline corporate managers whose interests otherwise diverge from the interests of the shareholders.[137]

Other writers have been more critical of the hostile takeover. These writers often suggest less benign explanations for the source of the premium paid to the target corporation's shareholders in a takeover.[138] For example, in some instances, perhaps the money ultimately might come from consumers of the goods produced by the target corporation, after the acquisition removes the competition between the target and acquirer which had kept prices lower. Alternately, in some cases, perhaps the money might ultimately come from other taxpayers, after the acquisition lowers the combined taxes paid by the acquirer and the target due to various provisions in the Internal Revenue Code.[139] Still other theories focus on the negative impact of takeovers on the target corporation's creditors and employees. Specifically, if the acquisition involves a significant increase in the target corporation's debt (as in a leveraged buy-out), the result is to increase the riskiness of the target corporation's previously outstanding debt (such as the bonds which the target corporation had issued). This, in turn, decreases the market value of the outstanding bonds, meaning that some of the shareholders' gain in a leveraged buy-out comes at the expense of the bond holders. This might become even more true if, as happened with a number of leveraged buy-outs in the late 1980s, the corporation cannot support the added debt and goes bankrupt.[140] Often, acquisitions lead to layoffs of corporate employees. Of course, one might argue that this result marks an efficiency in that it decreases labor costs to produce the same level of goods and services. A counter argument, however, is that in some circumstances such layoffs might constitute an opportunistic bait and switch pulled off by the shareholders at the expense of the employees. Specifically, the argument is that corporations might be able to obtain employees to work for the

---

137. See § 3.1.5b *supra*. There are a number of variations on this hostile takeover as discipline of inefficient management theme. For example, one area in which managers might place their own interests ahead of their duty to the shareholders involves reinvesting corporate earnings in corporate growth. Corporate growth is in the interest of managers for psychological reasons (a bigger empire) and financial reasons (greater job security in a more diversified company). As a result, managers might expand the corporation through unprofitable, or marginally profitable, growth, rather than distribute earnings to the shareholders (who can diversify their own portfolios). Hence, some hostile takeovers might create wealth by breaking up bloated corporate ventures and selling off the pieces to other businesses which can make more profitable use of the assets. In addi-

tion, borrowing to purchase corporate stock might curb inefficient growth, since service of the debt prevents use of corporate earnings for inefficient expansion.

138. *E.g.*, John Coffee, *Regulating the Market for Corporate Control: A Critical Assessment of the Tender Offer's Role in Corporate Governance*, 84 Colum. L. Rev. 1145, 1221–1294 (1984).

139. For instance, marriage of a corporation generating taxable income, with a corporation generating tax deductions and credits in excess of the company's otherwise taxable income, might save net taxes.

140. An even more extreme prejudice to corporate creditors, as well as non-selling shareholders, occurs if the buyer loots the corporation—a subject addressed earlier in this chapter.

company at a lower salary by developing a reputation of providing more stable employment. After years of gaining the advantage of paying lower wages, shareholders might wiggle out of the implicit deal to provide job security by selling the company to a hostile acquirer who will not keep the unspoken promises made to the employees by the prior management. Finally, the very empire building and management inefficiencies which hostile takeovers are supposed to curb might, in many cases, be at work in the decision-making process of the management of the acquiring corporation. After all, if there were not a fair number of foolish acquisitions, there would not be all of the "bust-up" takeovers based upon the recognition that the target corporations were worth more if one sold off the individual businesses.

While it is fun to debate the overall economic impact of the takeover phenomenon, in fact, these arguments might have only a fairly attenuated impact when it actually comes to assessing the various corporate law rules dealing with tender offers and takeover defenses. For example, it is true that writers, who view takeovers positively, typically oppose allowing the target's directors to employ takeover defenses, as well as the federal and state laws discussed above regulating tender offers and takeovers. Yet, is it doubtful that writers associated with a deregulatory viewpoint would take the position that, because takeovers produce various efficiencies, the law should equip acquirers with a right of eminent domain to force the target's shareholders to sell the company. After all, under a free market philosophy, the best guarantee (if not the very definition) of a transaction' efficiency is that both sides freely entered the transaction believing, ex ante, the transaction to advance their interests.[141] The complication when dealing with the sale of a business conducted by a corporation is that the decision to enter the transaction on the corporate side involves collective action. In other words, the underlying corporate law issue is who decides whether to sell the business: the atomistic response to a tender offer by individual shareholders, a vote by the shareholders as a whole, or a decision by the shareholders' elected representatives (the board of directors). To say that takeovers often produce economically beneficial efficiencies only suggests, at best, an answer to this "who should decide" issue when the particular takeover involves the replacement of inefficient management—in which case, presumably the board is not the best decision maker to pick. Yet, even if one concludes that shareholders, rather than directors, should decide whether to sell to an acquirer purportedly reacting to the inefficiencies of existing management, one still would need to consider whether this decision should be by individual sales or by vote.

141. Moreover, to the extent that a common impact of takeover defenses and the Williams Act is to encourage additional bids for the target corporation, which, in turn, leads to an auction of the company, one might argue that the sale to the highest bidder is the most efficient result. After all, presumably the highest bidder is the party best able to maximize revenues from the corporation's assets.

Similarly, the potentially negative consequences of some takeovers on consumers, taxpayers, creditors, employees, or even the shareholders of the *acquiring* company, also might have only questionable relevance to corporate law rules dealing with takeover defenses by the target corporation's board of directors, or the disclosure or substantive obligations of a person making a tender offer. In other words, it is the task of the antitrust laws to protect consumers potentially injured by anticompetitive mergers and acquisitions, and it is up to Congress, if Congress thinks appropriate, to draft the tax code to limit the ability of corporations to reduce taxes through combinations.[142] Creditors and employees might protect themselves by contract; and, if they need more protection, this is a subject for creditor protection and employment laws.[143] While protection of an acquirer's shareholders is a concern of corporate law, this concern is not addressed by the rules governing takeover defenses or tender offers.

There is, as we discussed earlier, one direct relevance of the consequences of takeovers on creditors, employees, consumers and the like to the corporate law rules governing tender offers and takeover defenses. Many state legislatures and some courts have concluded that the target's board of directors ought to be able to consider the impact of the board's actions, including acquiescence in a takeover, on constituencies of the corporation such as employees, creditors and consumers. We discussed the problems with rules allowing the board to sacrifice shareholder interests for the interests of other corporate constituencies—and particularly the lack of accountability for board actions which could result— earlier in this book. In addition, one might note that this approach to protecting other constituencies from the possibly detrimental effect of corporate takeovers leaves the interests of employees, creditors, consumers and the like to the mercy of the corporation's board. Yet, every day, boards agree to friendly acquisitions, and take other actions, which sacrifice the interests of these other constituencies.

A debate of more immediate relevance to the corporate law rules governing the hostile tender offer involves the impact of such tender offers, and takeover defenses, on the shareholders of the target corporation. After all, the typical rationale of a board employing a takeover defense, the rationale of Congress in passing the Williams Act, and a common express rationale of state legislatures enacting takeover statutes, is to protect the target corporation's shareholders.

To opponents of takeover defenses and of federal and state legislation regulating tender offers and takeovers, the fact that the target's shareholders receive a premium over the market price, in and of itself, suggests that the tender offer is in the interest of the target's shareholders, and should not be hindered. This view reflects not merely the

142. As Congress did in Section 382 of the Internal Revenue Code.

143. Admittedly, as discussed at length at a number of points in this book, corporate law is very concerned with protecting corporate creditors from the possible abuse of limited liability. Nevertheless, such corporate law creditor protection provisions reach well beyond hostile takeovers and tender offers.

opportunity of the shareholders to make a profit, but also a faith in the market price as establishing the value of the shareholders' stock absent the efficiencies promised by the takeover.

Yet, things might not be this simple. Accepting the first tender offer presumably would not be in the interest of the shareholders if a better offer were to come along. Moreover, it is possible that future corporate performance will make the shareholders economically better off holding their stock. Of course, one might ask why, if future corporate performance is likely to make shareholders better off holding their stock than selling at a premium over the current market price, does the current market price not reflect this likelihood. One commonly asserted answer is to argue that the market undervalues long-run corporate prospects in favor of short-term profits. Yet, the performance of many a high technology stock on the NASDAQ seems to contradict this notion. A more sophisticated answer is that the current market price only reflects the prognosis of future corporate performance made by the marginal current shareholder and marginal prospective buyer.[144] In other words, since the future is inherently unknowable, different investors will have different opinions as to the likely future performance of a corporation. Some investors might be very optimistic and hence value a corporation's stock highly. Other investors are more pessimistic, and the value the stock lower. The current price of stock on the stock exchange reflects the point at which enough shareholders find the price over the value they assign to the stock, and so are moved to sell, to meet the demand for stock at this price from prospective buyers. By definition, the shareholders who do not call their brokers to sell at the current price think that the stock is worth more than the current price. Indeed, since those who hold stock in a corporation will be a self-selecting group of those who are the most optimistic about the company's future prospects, many current shareholders might view the value of the stock to be significantly in excess of the current price.

This view of differing individual shareholder valuations of a corporation's stock has several implications for tender offer regulation. To begin with, it suggests that just because an acquirer offers to buy shares at a premium over the market price does not mean that this offer is necessarily in the best interest of the shareholders—different shareholders rationally might reach different conclusions on this question, and, since the future is unknowable, who is to say which shareholders are right. This view also suggests that takeover premiums might not reflect any economic efficiencies at all, but, rather, simply might reflect the fact that, as an acquirer seeks to buy a larger percentage of the outstanding stock, the acquirer must offer a higher price to move the more optimistic shareholders to decide to sell. Finally, this view highlights the fact that one of the principal impacts of the Williams Act is, for better or worse, to prevent tender offerors from taking advantage of the different valuations which different shareholders attach to a corporation's stock. For exam-

---

144. Lynn Stout, *Are Takeover Premiums Really Premiums? Market Price, Fair* *Value, and Corporate Law*, 99 Yale L.J. 1235 (1990).

ple, perhaps the Williams Act disclosure with the most practical significance is the filing under Section 13(d), which, as discussed earlier,
effectively limits how much stock an acquirer can buy from shareholders
who find the current market price to be an attractive point at which to
sell. Moreover, as outlined earlier, the various substantive regulations in
the Williams Act prevent a tender offeror from engaging in price discrimination.

Ultimately, whether takeover defenses, or state or federal takeover
laws, are in the interests of the target's shareholders depends upon
whether they succeed in increasing the shareholders' return on their
investments—either by increasing the price the shareholders receive in a
takeover or because long range corporate profitability made the shareholders better off holding their stock—or whether, instead, takeover
defenses and these laws decrease the shareholders' return by chasing
away profitable opportunities to sell. There have been a number of
efforts to study this question.[145] The results of these studies have been
inconclusive; which means the policy debate about corporate law rules
regulating tender offers and takeover defenses no doubt will continue.

§ 7.4 Freeze–Outs and Recapitalizations

We started this book with a section which discussed, among other
things, the historical development of corporate law in the United States.
One of the features of this historical development was the growth in the
prerogatives of majority stockholders to take actions over the objections
of minority stockholders. We end this book with a look at two of the
most dramatic examples of these majority prerogatives: the ability to
expel minority stockholders from the venture (commonly referred to as a
"freeze-out"), and the ability, short of expulsion, to change the terms of
the minority's interest in the corporation (commonly described as a
"recapitalization").

7.4.1 Freeze-outs

a. Purposes and policy

The desire of majority shareholders to force minority shareholders
out of the corporation can arise in either of two contexts. It can occur in
a situation in which the majority and minority shareholders co-existed
for some time as owners of the corporation, but, for one reason or
another, the majority has become dissatisfied with such co-existence.
Alternately, the majority shareholder might have planned, before becoming the majority shareholder, a two-step acquisition of the corporation—
the first step being to purchase enough stock to become the majority
shareholder, and the second step being to eliminate any minority owner-

---

145. *E.g.*, Gregg Jarrell, *The Wealth Ef-*
fects of Litigation by Targets: Do Interests
Diverge in a Merger?, 28 J.L. & Econ. 151
(1985); Gregg Jarrell & Annette Poulsen,
Shark Repellents and Stock Prices: The Ef-
fects of Antitakeover Amendments Since
1980, 19 J. Fin. Econ. 127 (1987); Michael
Ryngaert, *The Effect of Poison Pill Securi-*
ties on Shareholder Wealth, 20 J. Fin. Econ.
377 (1988).

ship. In either event, it is useful to ask why a majority shareholder (or a majority shareholding group) might wish to force out the minority. While the articulated rationales often vary, when all is said and done, there generally are two broad reasons for this action:[1]

The first motivation for removing minority stockholders is to increase the majority's return by removing other claimants to a share of the corporation's future income. Obtaining this advantage is a function of the price paid to the minority. If the price is low, then the future profits from owning the entire company will make cashing out the minority worthwhile. Moreover, in the context of a two-step acquisition, the threat of freezing out non-selling shareholders at a low price can induce stockholders to accept the original tender offer—thereby lowering the price paid in both steps of acquiring the corporation.[2] On the other hand, if the price paid to remove the minority is high, then there is no gain of profit by removing the minority, since the cost of doing so is to pay out a sum equal to or greater than the present value of owning the entire company.

From a policy prospective, allowing the majority to force out the minority shareholders based upon this first motivation seems to represent an undesirable zero-sum game. After all, the majority is, by definition, forcing the sale because the majority thinks that the stock is worth more than the majority is paying for it. The minority shareholders also think the stock is worth more than they are receiving, or else the minority voluntarily would sell. So what possible justification can there be for the law to facilitate such a transfer of wealth from the minority shareholders to the majority owner(s)?

In fact, there might be some possible justifications for allowing the majority shareholder(s) to force out the minority when the majority's motivation simply is to capture a greater share of the corporation's value. One justification is that the majority is not trying to impose a wealth transfer from the minority to the majority, but, rather, is acting to prevent a wealth transfer in the other direction—from the majority to minority shareholders, who are seeking to free ride on an increase in corporate value resulting from the majority's actions.

Of course, the complaint that minority shareholders are attempting to free ride on the increased value of the corporation resulting from the majority's efforts is a common whine from majority shareholders who decide to kick out the minority. In the context in which majority and minority shareholders have been co-existing for some time, the majority's complaint about the free riding minority might not be that persuasive. If the majority performs services which increase the value of the

§ 7.4

1. Beyond the two broad reasons for a freeze-out, there are potential advantages under tax laws and accounting rules for a parent corporation to own at least 80 or 90 percent of its subsidiary's outstanding stock. Obtaining these advantages, however, does not require the complete elimination of the minority.

2. As discussed earlier in this chapter, this is the theory behind the so-called coercive two-tier tender offer.

corporation, or provides additional capital contributions which achieve the same, the majority presumably should be able to obtain greater compensation in the form of salary, interest on loans, additional stock, or the like.

The free rider argument might be more persuasive in the context of a two-step acquisition. Here, the acquirer might be creating added value for the corporation by virtue of the combination involved (in other words, synergies). The acquirer's compensation for this added value lies in the stock the acquirer obtains, while, either through negotiation, or by market forces, the original shareholders of the acquired corporation will extract some portion of this added value as the price for their cooperation. The problem is, if some of the original shareholders are able to extract greater rewards from this transaction, this might mean that other original shareholders will get less. One possible way to extract greater rewards could be to refuse to sell one's shares, and thereby obtain the full benefit of the added value in the corporation.[3] The power to force out shareholders provides a way to avoid this problem. In fact, this is why merger statutes allow a majority of stockholders to force all stockholders to go along with a transaction in which their company is sold and they all exchange their shares for something else.

The idea of allowing a majority vote to force all shareholders to go along with a deal provokes little controversy in the arms-length situation in which a majority of the stockholders vote for the deal because they find it an attractive opportunity to sell their shares. The problem in the two-step acquisition is that the vote forcing all stockholders to sell does not take place until after the acquirer has become the majority shareholder. This means that a majority of the shares voted in favor of forcing out the minority are not voted by a party who acts based upon his or her personal desire to sell at this price, but rather are voted by a party whose incentive is to force the minority out at as low a price as possible.

Yet, this analysis of the two-step acquisition ignores one fact. The shareholders who sold the majority interest to the acquirer in the first step of a two-step acquisition, in a sense, voted with their feet by selling their shares. This fact does not mean much if the price paid to the forced out shareholders in the second step is less than what the selling

3. To illustrate, assume a corporate acquisition will increase the value of the acquired corporation by $10 per share. Assume also that negotiation or market forces would lead to a division of this increased value 50 percent to the acquirer and 50 percent to the original shareholders. To carry out this agreement, the acquirer could obtain 100 percent of the corporation's stock, and all of the original shareholders could receive cash for their stock at a price $5 per share greater than the current market price for the stock. Suppose, however, almost half of the original shareholders will refuse to go along with the deal by declining to sell their stock to the acquirer. In fact, if they could get away with it, such a refusal makes sense, since, by retaining their stock, each of the holdouts would gain the entire advantage of the $10 per share increase in corporate value. Such a refusal, however, blows the deal, since it means the prospective acquirer only gains around half of the overall increase in corporate value (as the acquirer would end up with only around half the shares). Since, by hypothesis, the agreeable deal was a 50–50 split of the increase in corporate value, if almost half of the shareholders hold out, the acquirer would be unwilling to give anything extra to those shareholders who agree to sell, and, as a result, no shareholder will sell.

shareholders received in the first step. Indeed, as mentioned above, the threat of a low price freeze-out in the second step of a two-step acquisition can coerce shareholders to sell their stock in response to a tender offer at a price less than the tendering shareholders really find attractive. On the other hand, if the price paid to the forced out shareholders in the second step of a two-step acquisition is the same as the price paid to the selling shareholders in the first step, then the positive response of the holders of a majority of the stock to the offer to buy their shares does, in effect, serve as an arms-length vote by a majority in favor of the whole deal.

Some writers have suggested alternate rationales for allowing the majority to force out the minority, even if based solely upon the desire to obtain a greater amount of future corporate income. One such rationale involves treating stock ownership as subject to a sort of option contract allowing the majority to call the interest of the minority.[4] In fact, as discussed in an earlier chapter, corporations commonly issue classes of stock pursuant to article provisions which give the corporation the right to redeem the stock. The purpose of such a redemption right is to allow the corporation to force the holders of this class of stock to sell their shares back to the company when such a freeze-out is in the financial interest of the holders of the other class(es) of stock—in other words, when the price the corporation must pay to redeem the stock is less than the present value of the claims of the holders of this stock to future corporate income. Presumably, the compensation for giving the corporation the option to redeem the stock is a lower price paid initially by persons to buy the shares which are subject to the redemption option.

Yet, when a corporation issues a redeemable class of stock, the right of the corporation to redeem is set out in the articles. By contrast, the holder(s) of a majority of the common shares have no similarly explicit agreement empowering the majority to force out the minority common stockholders. Perhaps, to the extent that courts uphold the use by majority shareholders of the techniques we shall discuss shortly to freeze out the minority, then everyone in the market comes to understand that the majority has this option, and one can say there is an implied agreement. Yet, this analysis makes the existence of the option depend upon a circular argument, since, if courts do not uphold actions by the majority to freeze out minority shareholders, then there is no such implied agreement.

Moreover, there is one other difference between an explicitly redeemable class of stock, and the notion that majority common shareholders have an implied option to force out the minority common stockholders. Article provisions empowering a corporate redemption set the price. By contrast, as we shall see, freeze-outs of minority shareholders take place at a price decided by the majority, subject to judicial remedies under which the minority can seek a so-called fair price. In other words,

---

4. *E.g.*, J.A.C. Hetherington, *Defining the Scope of Controlling Shareholders' Fi-* *duciary Responsibilities*, 22 Wake Forest L. Rev. 9 (1987).

under this option analysis, not only have the minority given an option with an uncertain exercise price (making it rather difficult to figure out how much to discount the stock for the existence of the option), but parties purchasing minority shares are buying, not a conveniently enforceable contract right, but rather an expensive lawsuit if, in fact, the majority exercises the option. It is questionable how many investors would purchase stock subject to such an express option.

Finally, some writers have argued that it does not much matter if parent companies profit by kicking minority shareholders out of subsidiaries, since investors with a diversified portfolio might also own stock in the parent companies.[5] If so, the kicked out stockholders' gain as shareholders in the parent companies can offset their loss as minority stockholders in the subsidiaries. There are, however, a couple problems with this argument. For one thing, the argument only applies if the parent companies are publicly traded rather than closely held, since the subsidiaries' minority shareholders are unlikely to be able to own stock in closely held parent companies. Moreover, it would be an unlikely coincidence if the expelled shareholders' proportionate interest in the parent company exactly matched their proportionate interest in the subsidiary. If the minority shareholders have a larger proportionate interest in the subsidiary, than they have in the parent, then their share of parent's gain will not offset their loss as stockholders kicked out of the subsidiary.[6]

If the only motivation for a freeze-out was the majority's desire to eliminate other claimants to corporate earnings at a price which made this economically attractive, then it would seem that the law should not facilitate such freeze-outs, except as the second step in a two-part acquisition when the price is the same as paid in the first step,[7] or except pursuant to an express provision in the articles. There is, however, another possible motivation for a freeze-out, which complicates the picture. This motivation is to avoid the various costs and inhibitions potentially created by the presence of minority shareholders. Of course, minority stockholders generally are powerless to dictate corporate policies when faced with a cohesive majority block. Nevertheless, various statutory and judicial protections of the minority might limit the majority's freedom of action to do what the majority wishes with the corporation, or, at the very least, impose some expense. For example, a company with over 500 shareholders must make periodic filings under the 1934 Securities Exchange Act, which it can avoid by cashing out the minority.

5. *See, e.g.,* Frank H. Easterbrook & Daniel R. Fischel, *Corporate Control Transactions*, 91 Yale L.J. 698, 711–714 (1982).

6. One might respond to this observation by arguing that the frozen out minority shareholders could be on the profiting end of other freeze-outs in which they own more shares in the parent than in the subsidiary. The logical extension of this sort of argument, however, would be that the law should not prohibit any sort of otherwise tortious activity (such as theft) by one corporation directed at another corporation, because shareholders with a diversified portfolio might be on the benefitting end as often as they are on the losing end.

7. *See, e.g.,* Edward F. Green, *Corporate Freeze-out Mergers: A Proposed Analysis*, 28 Stan. L. Rev. 487 (1976).

(This is often referred to as going private.) In addition, removing the minority can enable majority shareholders to engage in conflict-of-interest transactions with their corporations without concern as to whether minority shareholders might challenge the conduct as unfair.[8]

At first glance, one might not find this motivation to be any more sympathetic than the desire to remove minority shareholders in order to get all of the corporation's future income. After all, why should majority shareholders, who do not plan to abuse their power, fear these protections for minority shareholders? One answer is that formal securities law reporting requirements impose some administrative costs, even if one has nothing to hide–albeit, such costs are fairly minor relative to overall revenues and expenses for most reporting companies. More significantly, the burden of judicial review under the fairness standard might create expense and uncertainty, even for majority shareholders who do not believe that their transactions with the corporation will be unfair.

Indeed, there is an overlap between the problem of proving fairness, and the free rider problem discussed above. Recall that a possible answer to a majority shareholder's complaint that the minority is free riding on the majority's efforts is for the majority to receive added compensation (such as salary, interest, or more stock) from the corporation. Such compensation, however, constitutes a conflict-of-interest transaction, and so faces a potential challenge from the minority. Such challenges might not be that difficult to deal with in the context of normal managerial efforts, but consider the situation in which an acquirer's purchase of a majority interest might increase the value of the corporation due to expected synergies or the like. One way around the problem of hold-out shareholders reducing an acquirer's willingness to pay a premium to the selling shareholders could be to have the corporation issue stock at a bargain price to the acquirer—thereby diluting the interests of the hold-out minority so that they do not capture a disproportionate share of the increase in corporate value. Yet, such a bargain sale designed to dilute the minority's interest could appear, on its face, to be unfair.

b. *Mechanisms*

Several methods exist to force out unwilling minority stockholders. One is to dissolve the corporation, and transfer its operating assets to the majority stockholder(s) (or to a new corporation formed by the majority stockholder(s)), and transfer cash to the minority stockholders, as part of the liquidation. A second method is to undertake a reverse stock split in a sufficiently large ratio so that none of the minority stockholders ends up entitled to more than a fraction of a share.[9] Then, the corporation pays cash to the minority stockholders in lieu of issuing fractional shares under statutory provisions allowing corporations to cash out fractional shares.[10]

---

8. *See, e.g.,* Sinclair Oil Corp. v. Levien, 280 A.2d 717 (Del.1971).

9. *See, e.g.,* Teschner v. Chicago Title & Trust Co., 59 Ill.2d 452, 322 N.E.2d 54 (1974).

10. *E.g.,* M.B.C.A. § 6.04(a)(1).

The most popular freeze-out technique, however, is through a merger in which the plan of merger calls for the minority shareholders to receive cash (or even debt securities) from the surviving corporation in exchange for surrendering their shares. If the majority shareholder is itself a corporation—in order words, we are dealing with a parent corporation which wishes to remove minority interests in its subsidiary—then the freeze-out merger can be between the majority shareholder and its subsidiary. Suppose, however, the majority shareholder is an individual (or there is a cohesive group of individuals holding a majority of the shares). Alternately, suppose a parent corporation does not wish to assume its subsidiary's liabilities, as would occur in a parent-subsidiary merger. In either event, the majority shareholder(s) can set up a new corporation just for the freeze-out merger. The majority shareholder(s) then can transfer the majority of stock in the previously existing corporation to the new corporation in exchange for all of the stock in the new corporation. The new corporation then can merge with the previously existing corporation under a plan in which the shareholder(s) of the new corporation (in other words, the former majority shareholder(s)) end up with all of the stock of the surviving corporation, and the shareholders of the previously existing corporation receive cash or other securities.[11]

A key point to note about these techniques for involuntarily removing minority stockholders is that the statutes employed generally do not expressly state an intent to allow their use by a majority to remove minority stockholders. This fact, in turn, raises the question as to whether these statutes really provide authority for transactions whose purpose is to cash out an unwilling minority. It turns out that courts have had different reactions to this question.

The earliest cases generally involved the use of dissolution as a freeze-out technique. The courts in these cases typically viewed dissolution statutes as not allowing the freeze-out. For example, while corporation statutes typically authorize the dissolved corporation to distribute to its shareholders the assets remaining after payment of creditors, courts have been very reluctant to interpret these provisions as empowering the company to distribute the operating assets to the majority stockholder, and cash (even of proportionate value) to the minority shareholders.[12] Some courts have allowed majority shareholders to avoid this problem by having the corporation first sell all of its assets to the majority shareholder(s) for cash or securities, and then distribute the cash or securities

---

11. Since, going into the merger, the new corporation is a shareholder in the previously existing corporation, the new corporation could be entitled to cash or securities in exchange for the stock it owned in the previously existing corporation. Yet, this simply means having the surviving corporation pay itself. Accordingly, the plan of merger just will cancel the stock in the previously existing corporation owned by the new corporation.

12. *E.g.*, Kellogg v. Georgia–Pacific Paper Corp., 227 F.Supp. 719 (W.D.Ark.1964). The problem is that such a distribution offends the rule that each stockholder is entitled to the same per-share dividend, both in amount and in type, as every other stockholder owning the same class of shares.

to all of the shareholders (including back to the majority).[13] Minority stockholders might be able to frustrate this technique, however, by demanding a public sale of the dissolved corporation's assets, open to the minority or to outside bidders.[14] Moving beyond the asset distribution problem, some courts have gone so far as to hold that a transaction which results in the continuation of the business unchanged except for the elimination of the minority is simply not a dissolution within the meaning of the statutory provisions authorizing corporate dissolution.[15]

By contrast, courts have come to view merger statutes as authorizing freeze-outs. There was a problem with freeze-outs under early merger statutes, because these statutes often provided that the plan of merger only could compel shareholders to take stock in the surviving corporation (as opposed to cash or other securities) in exchange for surrendering stock in the disappearing corporation. Some majority shareholders tried to get around this problem by forcing the minority shareholders to take stock which was redeemable at the option of the corporation, and then having the corporation redeem the stock after the merger. Judicial reactions to this technique were mixed.[16] This problem, however, is largely water under the dam, as most corporation statutes now allow merger plans to force shareholders to surrender their stock for cash or other property.[17] As with dissolution, a broader challenge to the use of freeze-out mergers is to argue that a combination with a shell corporation for the purpose of removing minority stockholders is not a transaction contemplated by merger statutes. While a few courts have accepted this argument,[18] the overwhelming majority of judicial opinions have refused to read merger statutes as so limited.[19]

Judicial acceptance of freeze-outs as being within the scope of the merger statutes raises a couple of policy questions—beyond the broad question explored earlier as to when, if ever, the law should allow freeze-outs. To begin with, this evolution in the cases creates a rather odd premium on the technique used by the majority to freeze out the minority. After all, the economic impact of removing the minority through a dissolution is the same as removal through a merger. Yet, courts seem more receptive to the latter approach than they are to the former.

More significantly, we must ask whether freeze-out mergers really were what state legislatures had in mind when including merger provisions in corporation statutes. In one instance, the answer, to a certain extent, is yes. The purpose of the short-form merger provisions—allow-

---

13.　*E.g.*, Abelow v. Midstates Oil Corp., 41 Del.Ch. 145, 189 A.2d 675 (Del. 1963).

14.　*See, e.g.,* Mason v. Pewabic Mining Co., 133 U.S. 50, 10 S.Ct. 224 (1890). This follows the model of partnership liquidations.

15.　*E.g.*, Theis v. Spokane Falls Gaslight Co., 34 Wash. 23, 74 P. 1004 (1904).

16.　*Compare* Matteson v. Ziebarth, 40 Wash. 2d 286, 242 P.2d 1025 (1952), *with* Outwater v. Public Service Corp., 103 N.J.Eq. 461, 143 A. 729 (Ch. 1928).

17.　*E.g.*, M.B.C.A. § 11.02(c)(3).

18.　*E.g.*, Jutkowitz v. Bourns, No. CA 000268 (Cal. Super.1975).

19.　*E.g.*, Matteson v. Ziebarth, 40 Wash. 2d 286, 242 P.2d 1025 (1952).

ing parent corporations to merge with their 90 percent (or more) owned subsidiaries with only a vote by the parent corporation's board of directors—is to allow transactions which remove small minority ownership in subsidiaries. Note, however, that the original purpose of the short-form merger provisions was to accomplish something more than just the removal of the minority shareholders. Rather, these provisions were an effort to encourage the simplification of corporate structures by the removal of subsidiaries.[20] In other words, the removal of the minority in a short-form merger is only part of a broader impact from such a transaction–which impact includes, among other things, the parent corporation's becoming liable for debts incurred by the subsidiary. By contrast, in a freeze-out merger which involves a shell corporation created just for purpose of the merger, there is no impact to the merger other than the removal of the minority. For the most part, there does not appear to be much legislative history suggesting that, in enacting the general merger provisions, legislatures had such non-merger mergers in mind.

Interestingly, one state (California) has sought to curb the use of merger statutes (as well as other techniques) to freeze out minority shareholders who have a combined ownership of more than 10 percent (and thus would not be subject to removal by a short-form merger). Specifically, Sections 1101 and 1101.1 of the California Corporation Code prevent a cash-out merger by a majority shareholder unless it has the 90 percent ownership necessary for a short form merger, or the merger receives approval by the State Corporations' Commissioner (or other regulatory authority) after a fairness hearing.[21]

In any event, there is one other problem with the use of merger provisions as a tool for freezing out minority shareholders. As suggested above, the result is to create a sort of call option for majority shareholders as a default rule. The difficulty is that this is a hidden default rule, in that the ability to use merger provisions as an expulsion tool is not obvious on the face of the statute. Presumably, if one assumes an efficient stock market, then the price of publicly traded stocks has come to take into account the freeze-out implications of statutory merger provisions. One might not expect, however, this much corporate law sophistication among the owners, or even all of the legal advisors, of closely held corporations—where such hidden default rules could constitute a trap uncompensated for by any market pricing mechanism.

---

20. Historically, the original short-form merger statutes only covered mergers of 100 percent owned subsidiaries, in which case, the only purpose of the merger was to eliminate a subsidiary, rather than minority shareholders.

21. Along the same lines, Section 407 of the California Corporation Code precludes cashing out fractional shares constituting more than 10 percent of any class of outstanding stock, and Section 1001(d) and (e) requires a sale of substantially all of a corporation's assets to the corporation's majority shareholder either (i) to receive approval by a 90 percent vote, (ii) to be in exchange for non-redeemable common shares in the buyer, or (iii) to receive approval by the Corporations' Commissioner after a fairness hearing.

c. *Judicial review based upon fiduciary duty and appraisal rights*

Once courts generally came to decide that mergers provide a mechanism for majority shareholders to force out minority shareholders, minority shareholders were left with two protections under state corporate law against losing their stock in exchange for a pittance: suits for breach of fiduciary duty, and appraisal rights. These two potential protections have a complex interrelationship.

As discussed earlier in this chapter,[22] merger provisions in corporation statutes normally contain sections allowing shareholders, who dissent from a merger, to demand that the corporation cash them out at a "fair price" set by a judicially supervised appraisal. Hence, at first glance, appraisal rights seemingly protect minority shareholders against a freeze-out at an unfairly low price. Minority shareholders, however, often have viewed appraisal rights as not providing an entirely satisfactory remedy against a freeze-out. The earlier discussion of appraisal rights pointed out a couple of the problems: Appraisal provisions commonly contain exacting procedural requirements, the inadvertent noncompliance with which can prevent many a shareholder from being able to assert the rights. More significantly, courts traditionally followed conservative valuation approaches in appraisals, which many times undervalued the dissenters' stock. Besides, in the context of freeze-outs, appraisal rights might not even apply if the majority uses techniques other than a freeze-out merger. Actually, however, appraisal rights have a potentially more fundamental shortcoming specifically in the context of freeze-outs—they do not prevent the removal of minority shareholders who simply do not wish to sell.

Given the weaknesses of appraisal rights from the standpoint of the frozen out minority shareholders, such shareholders commonly bring lawsuits claiming that the majority shareholder(s) and the corporation's directors breached their fiduciary duty in carrying out the freeze-out. In response, majority shareholders often attempt to use appraisal rights provisions as a barrier to, rather than a protection for, complaining minority shareholders. Specifically, proponents of the freeze-out merger will argue that appraisal rights are the exclusive remedy for shareholders who wish to challenge a merger—thereby precluding minority shareholders from challenging the minority's forced removal on the ground that the freeze-out merger constitutes a breach of fiduciary duty.

Both the language of appraisal provisions, and judicial interpretations (which often reach results not expressed by the statute's language), vary between the states as to whether appraisal rights are an exclusive remedy. At one extreme, lie opinions holding that the appraisal provisions preclude any challenge to a merger[23]—except, naturally, for failure to comply with statutory requirements (for example, insufficient votes cast in favor of the merger),[24] or presumably for misrepresentations

---

22. See § 7.2.1a, *supra.*

23. *E.g.*, Yanow v. Teal Indus., Inc., 178 Conn. 262, 422 A.2d 311 (1979).

24. *E.g.*, Johnson v. Spartanburg County Fair Ass'n, 210 S.C. 56, 41 S.E.2d 599 (1947).

inducing the shareholder vote.[25] Short of this extreme lie a host of variations. For example, California's statute draws a distinction depending upon whether the merger involves a conflict-of-interest. Specifically, California's statute makes appraisal the exclusive remedy for a shareholder challenging an arms-length merger, but not for a shareholder challenging a merger with a controlling shareholder[26]—meaning that appraisal rights would not preclude challenges to freeze-out mergers in California. New York courts, by contrast, have developed an approach focusing on the relief requested: the appraisal provision bars an action unless the action seeks primarily an equitable remedy, rather than money damages.[27] Delaware courts—with no particularly relevant language in the appraisal provisions of Delaware's corporation statute— have mixed both New York and California approaches together with a large dollop of judicial discretion. Specifically, in *Weinberger v. UOP, Inc.*,[28] the Delaware Supreme Court stated that any monetary remedy ordinarily should come from an appraisal action, but also expressed the caveat that an appraisal action might not be adequate in cases of "fraud, misrepresentation, self-dealing, deliberate waste of corporate assets, or gross and palpable overreaching." Given the breath and vagueness of this caveat, Delaware's approach seems to be that appraisal rights are the exclusive remedy for those seeking damages, unless the court feels like appraisal rights should not be exclusive. This nebulous approach to the problem is significant, not only because it comes from Delaware, but also because the drafters of the Model Act expressed the intent to have the Model Act's appraisal rights provisions interpreted in the same way.[29]

In light of the problems outlined above with appraisal rights, one's initial conclusion might be that appraisal rights should not constitute the exclusive remedy for frozen out minority shareholders. Yet, perhaps the answer is to fix the problems with appraisal rights, rather than allowing suits for breach of fiduciary duty to become a substitute for such rights. This was the motivation for the Delaware Supreme Court in *Weinberger* to announce that henceforth Delaware courts should not confine themselves to the conservative Delaware block method of valuation in appraisal proceedings.[30]

25. *E.g.*, Victor Broadcasting Co. v. Mahurin, 236 Ark. 196, 365 S.W.2d 265 (1963).

26. *See, e.g.*, Steinberg v. Amplica, Inc., 42 Cal.3d 1198, 233 Cal.Rptr. 249, 729 P.2d 683 (1986).

27. Walter J. Schloss Associates v. Arkwin Indus., 61 N.Y.2d 700, 460 N.E.2d 1090, 472 N.Y.S.2d 605 (1984). The New York statute states that appraisal rights are exclusive except for an action by a shareholder who claims that the merger is "unlawful or fraudulent" as to the shareholder. N.Y. Bus. Corp. Law § 623(k).

28. 457 A.2d 701, 714 (Del.1983).

29. M.B.C.A. § 13.02 Official Comment 2. Interestingly, the actual language of the Model Act provision tracks New York's statute.

30. Courts have less discretion to avoid the problems posed by the various time and procedural limits found in the statutory provisions establishing appraisal rights. Yet, if these limits have some sound policy behind them, then perhaps courts should not allow the circumvention of these limits by use of lawsuits claiming breach of fiduciary duty. The one obvious exception would be when misrepresentations or nondisclosure by the majority lull minority shareholders into failing to meet the procedural requirements for appraisal rights. Of course, if the problem with the appraisal

The real question with respect to whether appraisal rights should be the exclusive remedy for shareholders complaining about a freeze-out merger comes down to whether a suit for breach of fiduciary duty accomplishes something worthwhile from a policy standpoint,[31] which appraisal rights proceedings do not—otherwise why have duplicative remedies? One obvious answer is that a suit for breach of fiduciary duty potentially allows the minority to block their removal from the corporation; whereas appraisal rights allow the minority's removal, but simply seek to ensure a fair price.[32] Yet, this answer, in turn, brings us to a broader policy question as to whether majority shareholders ought to have the ability to kick out the minority, so long as the minority receives a "fair" price.

In addressing this broader question, it is useful to remember that, for the most part, shareholders are investors, not sentimental collectors.[33] Hence, so long as they receive an attractive price for their stock, why should shareholders care about selling?[34] Occasionally, shareholders might have economic reasons for holding their stock, rather than selling even at what a shareholder would concede was a good price. For instance, retaining shares until a stockholder's death can avoid income tax on the pre-death appreciation in the value of the shares.[35] More commonly, however, the reason some stockholders fight a freeze-out is that these shareholders do not believe, even with appraisal rights, they will get a satisfactory price. Indeed, this is not an irrational position.

Keep in mind that valuation of stock is far from an exact science. Hence, even if the court abandons conservative valuation methods, the court ultimately is going to set a so-called fair value for the stock based upon a war of expert witnesses hired to take outlandish positions.[36] What we do know about the value of the stock in question is that one of the two broad motives for a freeze-out is the majority's view that the value of the minority's shares is more than what the majority will need to pay, and also that, if minority shareholders had found the price attractive, they would have sold voluntarily. Ultimately, the argument for exclusivi-

rights remedy in a particular freeze-out is that there are no such rights for the technique used by the majority (say, dissolution), then the majority cannot argue that appraisal rights provide the exclusive remedy, and the whole issue is moot.

31. As opposed just to giving the plaintiff some tactical advantage.

32. This explains why the New York courts focus on the relief demanded, in deciding whether appraisal rights are exclusive.

33. *But see* Coggins v. New England Patriots Football Club, Inc., 397 Mass. 525, 492 N.E.2d 1112 (1986) (minority shareholder complaining about the freeze-out was a fan of the football team owned by the corporation).

34. In this regard, shareholders are much like the recipient of Oscar Wilde's classic rejoinder directed at a woman who said she would sell her virtue for 10,000 £, but took offense at an offer of 100 £: "We have already established what you are madam; now we simply are quibbling over the price."

35. This is due to the impact of Internal Revenue Code Section 1014, and illustrates why tax planners think more favorably of death than do most other mortals.

36. *See, e.g.,* Gilbert v. MPM Enterprises, Inc., 709 A.2d 663 (Del.Ch.1997). *But see* In re Appraisal of Shell Oil Co., 607 A.2d 1213 (Del.1992) (suggesting that the Chancery Court appoint its own experts to aid in appraisal).

ty of appraisal rights is a notion that the law should put its faith in a value set by litigation, rather than a value set by negotiation.

Suppose, however, the minority shares are publicly traded. In this event, one might argue that the market establishes a fair value for the minority shares, and therefore any freeze-out at a price above the market is fair. Yet, then we must ask why the majority finds it (a) desirable, and (b) necessary, to use legal compulsion to freeze-out the minority shareholders, rather than buying the minority's stock on the market—especially if the freeze-out is at a price above the market. Perhaps, this shows that the majority's motive is to avoid challenges to future conflict-of-interest dealings with the corporation, rather than simply to gain a greater share of future corporate earnings at a favorable price. Yet, internal memos in some cases suggest that the majority felt the stock was worth more than the price paid to the minority.[37] Given the majority's access to inside information concerning the corporation, it is certainly not beyond the realm of possibility that the majority knows more about the value of the corporation than the market. Moreover, not only does the majority's willingness to pay more raise questions about the market price, but the minority's unwillingness to sell also makes one wonder.

Perhaps the answer to the conundrum of both why the majority will pay more than, and the minority will not settle for, the market price, is that the market price reflects the valuation placed on stock by the marginal investor. In other words, as discussed earlier in this chapter,[38] since stock valuation is based upon future earnings, and future earnings are unknowable, different investors rationally will attach different values to the same stock. The market price simply reflects the point at which the least optimistic current stockholders decide to sell enough shares to match the demand at this price from the most optimistic potential buyers. The need for legal compulsion therefore might result from the fact that both the majority shareholder(s) and the hold-out minority shareholders are more optimistic about future corporate earnings than are the marginal traders in the market—and who is to say that the majority shareholder(s) and the hold-out minority shareholders are wrong?

There is one other fact which makes reliance on market price questionable particularly in the freeze-out context. Rationally, the market price should reflect the risk that the majority will freeze out the minority.[39] This fact has a couple of policy implications. To begin with, there is a problem of circularity here. Specifically, the less the law protects the frozen out minority (based upon the rationale that any price at or above the market must be fair), the lower (and presumably less

---

37. *E.g.*, Weinberger v. UOP, Inc., 457 A.2d 701 (Del.1983).

38. See § 7.3.4 *supra*.

39. Or, to put the matter in terms of the option analysis we discussed earlier, the market price for minority shares, especially in the situation in which there is a majority shareholder, should reflect a discount for the de facto call option enjoyed by the majority.

fair) will be the market price. One might respond, however, that if the minority stockholders were able to buy their shares at a discount to reflect the danger of a freeze-out, then there is no unfairness. This suggests a second implication from the existence of a market discount for the freeze-out danger: whether the freeze-out is fair arguably might depend, at least in part, on who came first—the majority or the minority. For example, if the existence of a publicly traded minority interest is a carryover from an initial public offering in which the founders retained a majority of the stock, then perhaps the minority paid a discounted price to reflect the freeze-out potential, and the minority should not complain too much. On the other hand, if the majority position is the result of an accumulation of what were originally minority-owned shares, then the non-selling minority stockholders would not have purchased their stock at a discount to reflect the degree of danger in which the minority stockholders now find themselves.[40]

There is, however, a practical problem with the notion that minority shareholders ought to be able to use a suit for breach of fiduciary duty to block their removal, rather than being relegated to appraisal rights. Often, by the time the litigation has wondered its way through the courts, there might be too great a prejudice to third parties if the court unwinds the deal.[41] In this event, about all the court can do is award damages. If this is going to be a common end result, then perhaps it would be better to short-circuit the process by confining the minority shareholders to an appraisal proceeding. Nevertheless, there are a couple of possible reasons why minority shareholders might prefer bringing a fiduciary duty claim, and why the law should allow the minority shareholders to do so, even when it is too late to provide any remedy but damages.

One reason for a fiduciary duty claim would be to allow a more generous measure of damages to reach a larger group of plaintiffs. For example, the Delaware Supreme Court has held that, in the case of breach of fiduciary duty, the Chancery Court might order a "rescissory" measure of damages[42]—in other words, instead of measuring damages based upon the difference between what the minority shareholders received in the merger, and the value of the minority's stock at the time of the merger, the court might award damages based upon the difference between what the minority shareholders received, and the value of the stock at the time of the damage award. If the provable value of the minority's interest increases after the majority forces out the minority, this rescissory measure gives a larger award than would an appraisal.[43]

40. Admittedly, between the time the majority holder reached majority status, and the occurrence of a freeze-out, many of the minority shareholders might have sold to persons who paid a discounted price reflecting the increased danger of a freeze-out. This, however, should not lead to relaxed legal protection, since the greater the protection accorded to new minority shareholders, the less the original minority ownership will suffer because of the market discounting for the freeze-out danger.

41. *E.g.*, Lynch v. Vickers Energy Corp., 429 A.2d 497 (Del.1981).

42. *Id* at 505.

43. If, as one often suspects, the majority is forcing out the minority because the majority expects the corporation's future earnings will more than offset the price

Moreover, if a minority shareholder brings the claim for breach of fiduciary duty as a class action on behalf of all of the kicked out minority shareholders, then all of the minority shareholders will get damages. By contrast, only shareholders who dissent and demand appraisal will be entitled to recover based upon appraisal rights.

While the greater total recovery explains why plaintiffs (or, especially their attorneys[44]) might prefer a suit for breach of fiduciary duty rather than an appraisal proceeding, what is the reason for the law creating this option? Doctrinally, the rescissory measure of damages follows from the notion that the traditional remedy for fraud or breach of fiduciary duty is to void the transaction. Hence, in the case in which voiding the transaction is impractical, the law should measure damages based upon what would happen if each party returned what that party received from the other party in the deal. More fundamentally from a policy standpoint, even with realistic measures of valuation, logic suggests that appraisal rights will fail to deter unfair majority behavior. To see why, consider the incentives facing a majority stockholder who figures that the minority's shares are worth $25 per share, but decides to freeze out the minority at a price of $20 per share. Because asserting appraisal rights can be expensive—with the need to hire an attorney, expert witnesses, and the like—the majority shareholder might calculate that many, if not most, of the minority shareholders with small holdings will forgo the effort, and the majority will profit at their expense. For the minority shareholders who do assert appraisal rights, even if the court discovers that the shares are worth $25 per share, the majority shareholder is no worse off than the majority shareholder would have been if the majority shareholder paid the fair value to start with. Hence, if the appraisal is the only remedy for those dissatisfied with a freeze-out merger, then majority shareholders may as well take a flyer on lowballing the minority.

A second difference between a suit for breach of fiduciary duty, even if the remedy ends up being damages, and appraisal rights, is that a suit for breach of fiduciary duty potentially allows the court to examine a broader range of facts than would be relevant in an appraisal proceeding. Since a freeze-out merger is a conflict-of-interest transaction, the starting point of a fiduciary duty analysis is that majority shareholders, barring some sort of disinterested approval, must show the transaction is fair to the minority.[45] This, however, forces us to ask what courts mean by "fair" in the context of a freeze-out.

Here, one confronts a basic division between those jurisdictions which require a business purpose for removal of the minority as part of the fairness test, and those which do not. The most noted jurisdiction in the latter camp is Delaware, which, after announcing a business purpose

paid to the minority, then the value of the corporation provable in litigation should increase as events after the merger justify the majority's unstated optimism.

44. Who, with a larger total recovery, might obtain a larger fee.

45. *E.g.*, Weinberger v. UOP, Inc., 457 A.2d 701 (Del.1983).

requirement for freeze-out mergers in *Singer v. Magnavox, Co.*,[46] six years later turned around and abandoned the requirement in *Weinberger*. Even after *Weinberger*, however, courts in a number of other states, including the New York Court of Appeals,[47] have insisted on retaining the business purpose requirement.

Actually, there are strong doctrinal and policy arguments for the business purpose requirement. From a doctrinal standpoint, the business purpose requirement is consistent with the general approach to conflict-of-interest transactions. For example, if directors sell some of the directors' property to the corporation, it would not be enough to show that the corporation paid a fair price for the property. Rather, the transaction still would be unfair to the corporation if the corporation had no use for the property, and so the transaction did not serve a business purpose.[48] From a policy standpoint, the business purpose requirement would appear to be a mechanism for screening majority motives in line with the general policy analysis at the beginning of our discussion of freeze-outs. Specifically, we saw earlier that there might be little good reason for courts to allow freeze-outs motivated by the majority's desire simply to capture more of the corporation's earnings—except in the context of a two-step corporate acquisition providing the same price in both steps— while freeze-outs might be legitimate for a majority which believes that conflict-of-interest transactions (such as greater parent-subsidiary dealings) could provide corporate efficiencies, but is deterred from pursuing this goal by fear of litigation under the fairness test.

On the other side, the Delaware Supreme Court also put forward doctrinal and policy arguments for abandoning the business purpose requirement in *Weinberger*. The doctrinal argument was that the court already had interpreted the business purpose requirement virtually out of existence. This is a reference to the Delaware Supreme Court's decision in *Tanzer v. International General Industries, Inc.*[49] In *Tanzer*, the court held that the majority's own business purpose could suffice to meet the business purpose requirement. Yet, seeking to remove the minority simply to gain the minority's share of future corporate earnings at a favorable price literally is a business purpose when looked at from the majority's standpoint. Hence, the result of the holding in *Tanzer* seemingly was to reduce the business purpose requirement to a corporate law equivalent of the prohibition on spite fences.[50] The *Weinberger* opinion's policy argument was that the business purpose requirement was unnecessary in light of the general review of the transaction for fairness and the improved valuation methodologies available in appraisal proceedings.

46. 380 A.2d 969 (Del.1977).

47. *E.g.*, Alpert v. 28 Williams St. Corp., 63 N.Y.2d 557, 483 N.Y.S.2d 667, 473 N.E.2d 19 (1984).

48. See § 4.2.2 *supra*.

49. 379 A.2d 1121 (Del.1977).

50. In other words, freeze-outs motivated solely by the majority's dislike for the minority shareholder(s) would be prohibited, just as many jurisdictions prohibit landowners from putting up fences at the edge of their property solely to spite their neighbors.

Indeed, the *Weinberger* opinion's policy argument goes to the nub of the matter. Assuming that freeze-outs should not be a tool for transferring wealth from minority to majority shareholders, the question becomes how best to achieve this goal. *Weinberger* relies on litigation over the value of stock, coupled with, as we shall see shortly, review of the process leading up the freeze-out. The business purpose requirement outside Delaware adds a demand that the majority show some reason for the freeze-out, other than a desire to profit at the expense of the minority. The lack of such a showing by the majority would seem to speak louder in many cases as to the real economics of the deal than would either the testimony of experts hired to fiddle with the numbers, or the majority's adherence to a scripted process designed to create the appearance, but not the reality, of an arms-length negotiation.

In any event, in those jurisdictions requiring a business purpose for a freeze-out, the question becomes what sort of purposes will suffice. The preceding discussion of the purposes for having a business purpose requirement gives some guidance. As suggested by the discussion of *Tanzer*, courts serious about the business purpose requirement hold that the purpose must be to advance the corporation's interest, not just the financial interest of the majority shareholder(s). Hence, the goal of increasing the majority's profits by removing other claimants, in itself, is the very example used by the New York Court of Appeals of a motive which does not suffice.[51] Things become less clear when the majority claims that the minority is free-riding on actions by the majority which benefit the corporation. As discussed earlier, this argument is persuasive in the context of a two-step acquisition in which the second step is a freeze-out at the same price paid in the first step. Courts sometimes also have accepted a free-riding sort of argument in the context of situations in which the majority and minority shareholders had previously co-existed.[52] Presumably the notion is that allowing the freeze-out is a necessary quid pro quo for the corporation to obtain the benefit provided by the majority shareholder; albeit, perhaps the court should ask why the majority could not have demanded some other compensation. Finally, courts have had conflicting reactions to a business purpose based upon avoiding the disclosure and fairness obligations created by the presence of minority shareholders.[53] This divergence might be justified by the fact that, in some circumstances, the majority is worried about harassing actions challenging what the majority believes are value-enhancing parent-subsidiary dealings, while, in other situations, the majority is planning abusive transactions with the corporation (presumably to the detriment of creditors given the absence of minority shareholders), while, in

51. *E.g.*, Alpert v. 28 Williams St. Corp., 63 N.Y.2d 557, 483 N.Y.S.2d 667, 473 N.E.2d 19 (1984).

52. *See, e.g.*, Cross v. Communication Channels, Inc., 116 Misc.2d 1019, 456 N.Y.S.2d 971 (1982) (allowed a freeze-out by a 53 percent shareholder, who personally guaranteed bank loans for the corporation).

53. *Compare* Tanzer Economic Associates v. Universal Food Specialties, 87 Misc.2d 167, 383 N.Y.S.2d 472 (1976), *with* Coggins v. New England Patriots Football Club, Inc., 397 Mass. 525, 492 N.E.2d 1112 (1986).

yet other cases, the court concluded that the rationale of avoiding fairness obligations to the minority was bogus altogether and the majority simply was trying to capture the minority's portion of future corporate earnings at a favorable price.[54]

After finding a business purpose—or, in jurisdictions like Delaware, which do not require any business purpose—what else do courts review under the fairness test? In *Weinberger*, the Delaware Supreme Court explained that fairness entails "fair dealing and fair price." Fair price gets into stock valuation—a subject discussed earlier in this chapter when we explored appraisal rights. A number of Delaware Supreme Court opinions have explored the parameters of "fair dealing."

In *Weinberger* itself, the Delaware Supreme Court confronted a freeze-out merger which did not meet the test of fair dealing. This was a merger between Signal Oil Company and Signal's 50.5 percent owned subsidiary, UOP, Inc. Several years after acquiring a majority of UOP's shares, Signal decided to cash out the remaining UOP shareholders. Two Signal officers, who were also directors of UOP, prepared a study using UOP data, which concluded that cashing out the remaining UOP shareholders at a price up to $24 per share would be a good investment for Signal. Signal then asked UOP's president for his opinion of Signal's cashing out UOP's minority shareholders at a price of $20 to $21 (not $24) per share. UOP's president thought the price was "generous," but requested some protections for UOP's employees. The easy-going reaction of UOP's president might not be that surprising in light of the fact he had been a long-time Signal employee, who Signal installed as president of UOP a couple years earlier. Ultimately, UOP's president "negotiated" a price of $21 per share for the minority shareholders from Signal. Not satisfied with this price, a minority shareholder (Weinberger) sued to challenge the freeze-out merger.

The Delaware Supreme Court found that Signal had not dealt fairly with UOP's minority shareholders in several particulars. The most critical was Signal's failure to meet Signal's duty of candor. Specifically, Signal did not disclose either to UOP's outside directors, or to UOP's minority shareholders, the study concluding that Signal would obtain a favorable investment at any price up to $24 per share. The materiality of this information seems evident—it shows Signal was prepared to pay a higher price than $21 per share. On the other hand, it is important not to overstate the court's holding on this issue. The court did not create a general obligation for majority shareholders to disclose the highest price it would be worthwhile for the majority to pay the frozen out minority shareholders. The problem in *Weinberger* was that the non-disclosed conclusions came from two persons who were directors of UOP (as well as officers of Signal), and stemmed from the use of data obtained from

---

54. *E.g.*, Young v. Valhi, Inc., 382 A.2d 1372 (Del.Ch.1978). The fact that the courts, in at least some cases, have been able to see past bogus rationales for removing the minority seemingly refutes the notion of some cynics that the business purpose requirement will serve no purpose other than to test the majority's imagination and willingness to lie.

UOP. Non-disclosure of entirely internal evaluations by a majority shareholder would be a different story.[55] Other complaints about the process in *Weinberger* involved the lack of any significant effort by UOP's president to negotiate for a better price than Signal offered, and the need for a rushed fairness study (a valuation of the minority's shares) by UOP's investment banker due to time constraints imposed by Signal.

One question about the *Weinberger* opinion's focus on process is what the court hoped to accomplish. For example, suppose Signal had fully disclosed the $24 per share study, given the investment bankers ample time to prepare a fairness study, and told UOP's president to negotiate aggressively (or, better yet, as the *Weinberger* opinion suggested in a footnote, UOP appointed a committee composed of non-Signal-affiliated UOP directors to conduct the negotiations). Signal still could have refused to pay more than $21 per share, and used Signal's majority of UOP's voting shares and Signal's majority of positions on UOP's board to force through the transaction. In fact, such hardball "negotiations" marked the challenged merger in *Kahn v. Lynch Communication Systems, Inc.*[56]

In *Kahn*, a French company, which owned a controlling (albeit not a majority) position in Lynch Communication Systems, presented a committee of Lynch's independent directors with essentially a "take it or leave it" proposal for a cash-out merger. Feeling they had little choice—because the French company threatened to proceed with the cash-out merger in any event—Lynch's directors accepted the French company's proposal.[57] Given the lack of any give and take negotiation, the Delaware Supreme Court held it was up to the French company to prove the fairness of the merger to the minority. Nevertheless, in a subsequent proceeding, the Delaware Supreme Court refused to treat the French company's use of hardball tactics as, in and of itself, unfair, and thereupon upheld the merger based upon proof that the price was fair.[58]

So, is there any point to inquiring into "fair" process, if, in the end, it all comes down to price?[59] Perhaps yes. This is most evident with

55. Rosenblatt v. Getty Oil Co., 493 A.2d 929 (Del.1985).

56. 638 A.2d 1110 (Del.1994).

57. Given the fact that the French company had neither a majority of the voting stock (it owned 43.3 percent), nor most of the board positions (it designated five of Lynch's eleven directors), one might ask why Lynch's independent directors did not stand up to the French company. Apparently, the directors figured that enough Lynch stockholders would tender their shares in response to the French company's threatened hostile tender offer—after all, it would only take around seven percent more for the French company to obtain a majority—that the directors had no realistic bargain-ing leverage. This was especially true because the French Company (due to a supermajority voting requirement) already had the votes to block any merger with a white knight—albeit, this supermajority voting requirement also could have acted to block the French company's efforts to force through a merger.

58. Kahn v. Lynch Communication Systems, Inc., 669 A.2d 79 (Del.1995).

59. Occasionally, special factors might create obvious significance to the concept of fair process–for example, if a contract commits the majority to pay a greater price if a freeze-out merger takes place within a certain period of time following the acquisition of a majority of the corporation's outstand-

respect to the duty of candor portion of fair process. To see why, consider what the impact of Signal's disclosure of the $24 per share study would be, even given Signal's power to force through director and shareholder approval of a $21 per share cash-out merger. This study provides the minority shareholders ammunition in litigating over the fair price for UOP shares.[60] Hence, enforcing a duty of candor might push majority shareholders into paying a price closer to what they really feel the minority's stock is worth; albeit, cynics might suspect that majority shareholders simply will be more careful about what the majority share-holders say in a writing prepared by any persons who are also officers or directors of the corporation whose minority shareholders the majority plans to freeze-out.

On the other hand, how much can negotiations by so-called independent directors achieve? The problem is more fundamental than the concerns raised in an earlier chapter regarding how independent so-called independent directors really are.[61] Ultimately, even the most fervent negotiator may be only as good as his or her negotiating position. While the French company in *Kahn* may have been more blatant in the use of power than most, the fact is that directors negotiating a freeze-out merger with a majority shareholder do not hold many cards. Indeed, the independent directors' primary card is that, in Delaware, approval by independent directors shifts the burden of proof on the issue of fair price.[62] How much this card is worth depends upon how rigorously the court scrutinizes the fairness of the freeze-out price when the burden of proof is on the majority. Specifically, if the court resolves all doubts against the majority on the price issue, then the independent directors have some bargaining room.[63] In this regard, it is most unfortunate in *Kahn* that the Delaware Supreme Court affirmed a Chancery Court decision which did not resolve all doubts on fair price against the French company.

7.4.2 *Recapitalizations*

Instead of forcing the minority to give up their shares, as in a freeze-out, in a "recapitalization" the majority can change the rights of the minority shareholders. For example, a recapitalization might change the voting rights of shares,[64] change dividend or liquidation preferences,[65] or

---

ing shares, and the court holds that delaying the freeze-out in order to avoid the contractual obligation constitutes unfair process, then fair process has an evident impact. *See* Rabkin v. Philip A. Hunt Chemical Corp., 498 A.2d 1099 (Del.1985).

60. Albeit, on remand, the Chancery Court found a fair price for the UOP stock was only $22 per share. Weinberger v. UOP, Inc., 1985 WL 11546 (Del.Ch.), *aff'd*, 497 A.2d 792 (Del.1985).

61. See § 4.2.3e *supra*.

62. The same is true of an informed vote in favor of the merger by the holders of a majority of the minority-owned shares.

E.g., Rosenblatt v. Getty Oil Co., 493 A.2d 929 (Del.1985).

63. Indeed, recall in discussing the fairness test for conflict-of-interest transactions generally, that we noted how the primary utility of rigorous fairness review may be that it makes the court the unseen negotiating agent curbing the directors' incentive to give full play to their self-interest, even in cases in which the transaction never faces a judicial challenge. See § 4.2.2 *supra*.

64. *E.g.*, Honigman v. Green Giant Co., 208 F.Supp. 754 (D.Minn.1961), *aff'd*, 309 F.2d 667 (8th Cir.1962).

grant the corporation an option to redeem shares (thereby setting up a freeze-out).[66] Historically, recapitalizations frequently involved corporations which had gone through a long period in which the company had not given any dividends to the holders of cumulative preferred shares. As a result, the preferred shareholders were entitled to payment of a considerable arrearage before the corporation could pay dividends to the owners of the common stock. In order to get their hands on distributions without waiting for the corporation to pay all of the skipped dividends to the preferred, the common stockholders often would push through a recapitalization changing the rights of the preferred by wiping out the arrearage.[67]

If the majority has the power to kick out the minority, then, a priori, the majority would seem to have the power to alter the rights of the minority. Indeed, the majority could use the same technique of a merger with a shell corporation as commonly used for freeze-outs.[68] The principal difference would be that the plan of merger requires the minority shareholders to exchange their stock for shares with different rights, rather than for cash or debt securities.

Parties engaged in a recapitalization, however, commonly employ another technique besides a merger. Since the articles of incorporation specify the relative rights of various classes of stock, the majority might amend the articles to change the rights of shares. For example, the majority might amend the corporation's articles to lessen the liquidation preference of a class of preferred shares.[69] Indeed, many statutes expressly or implicitly authorize "amendments" to the articles which require shareholders to exchange their stock for other stock.[70]

What protection does the minority possess against a recapitalization prejudicial to their interest? At one time, dissenting shareholders might have been able to argue successfully that the majority lacked the power to change the minority's rights by amending the corporation's articles. This was because many courts historically refused to interpret ambiguous provisions in corporation statutes as authorizing article amendments which would take away financial rights from an objecting minority.[71] Modern statutes, however, tend to provide broad explicit authority for amendments to corporate articles changing financial and other rights of

65. *E.g.*, Goldman v. Postal Telegraph, Inc., 52 F.Supp. 763 (D.Del.1943).

66. *E.g.*, Cowan v. Salt Lake Hardware Co., 118 Utah 300, 221 P.2d 625 (1950).

67. *E.g.*, Western Foundry Co. v. Wicker, 403 Ill. 260, 85 N.E.2d 722 (1949).

68. *E.g.*, Bove v. Community Hotel Corp., 105 R.I. 36, 249 A.2d 89 (1969). In the case of a recapitalization designed to change the rights of all of the holders of a class of stock (such as preferred), rather than to treat minority holders differently than the majority holders of the same class

of stock, the shell corporation set up for the merger can be a wholly-owned subsidiary of the original corporation.

69. *E.g.*, Goldman v. Postal Telegraph, Inc., 52 F.Supp. 763 (D.Del.1943).

70. *E.g.*, Del. Gen. Corp. Law § 242(a) (allowing amendments to reclassify shares and to include provisions to carry out an exchange of shares).

71. *E.g.*, Consolidated Film Indus., Inc. v. Johnson, 22 Del.Ch. 407, 197 A. 489 (1937).

shares.[72]

The next line of defense is the requirement that shareholders vote to approve the amendment. Critically, corporation statutes typically require that article amendments receive approval from a majority of each separate class of shares potentially affected adversely by the amendment—even if the class is otherwise non-voting.[73] This protection may break down, however, if the holders of a majority of the adversely affected shares also hold shares in classes potentially favored by the change, or if the amendment is packaged in such a way that the shareholders feel coerced into voting for the amendment.[74] Moreover, some corporation statutes do not require a merger (even if used as the tool for a recapitalization) to receive approval by a majority of each class of stock, nor allow shares without voting rights to vote on the merger, even though the merger plan may impact adversely such stock.[75]

Compensating somewhat for not universally requiring approval by a majority of each class of shares, merger provisions, as discussed above, typically extend to dissenting stockholders the right to demand that the company cash the stockholders out at a fair price set by appraisal. Many, but not all, corporation statutes also extend appraisal rights to shareholders dissenting from amendments to corporate articles, when the amendments might adversely impact various rights of the dissenters' stock.[76] As detailed above, the existence of appraisal rights is a two-edged sword, however, in that the existence of such a remedy in some jurisdictions might preclude a suit for breach of breach of fiduciary duty.

This brings us to the possibility of a shareholder challenging a recapitalization, undertaken either through an article amendment or a merger, on the ground that the transaction is unfair, and, hence, a breach of fiduciary duty. Courts differ as to the vigor with which they will review a recapitalization for fairness.[77] Not surprisingly, one of the most critical variables impacting the degree of scrutiny is the extent to which the shareholders who the recapitalization plan arguably disfavors (and presumably who have no offsetting conflict-of-interest) voted to approve the amendment or merger.[78]

---

72. *E.g.*, M.B.C.A. § 10.01. Some courts have held that the owners of stock issued prior to the enactment of a statute authorizing article amendments changing the rights of such stock have "vested rights" which the state cannot constitutionally authorize the corporation to amend away. *E.g.*, Keller v. Wilson & Co., 21 Del.Ch. 391, 190 A. 115 (Del. 1936). *But see* O'Brien v. Socony Mobil Oil Co., 207 Va. 707, 152 S.E.2d 278 (1967). This becomes less relevant over the years as fewer such shares remain extant.

73. *E.g.*, M.B.C.A. § 10.04.

74. *See, e.g.*, Lacos Land Co. v. Arden Group, Inc., 517 A.2d 271 (Del.Ch.1986).

75. *E.g.*, Del. Gen. Corp. Law § 251(c).

76. *E.g.*, M.B.C.A. § 13.02(a)(4).

77. *Compare* Kamena v. Janssen Dairy Corp., 133 N.J.Eq. 214, 31 A.2d 200 (Ch. 1943), *aff'd*, 134 N.J.Eq. 359, 35 A.2d 894 (Err. & App. 1944) (enjoined recapitalization plan as objectively unfair), *with* Barrett v. Denver Tramway Corp. 53 F.Supp. 198 (D.Del.1943), *aff'd*, 146 F.2d 701 (3d Cir. 1944) (refused to enjoin recapitalization plan which the court regarded as unfair because, under Delaware law, unfairness must reach the level of constructive fraud or bad faith before a court will act).

78. *E.g.*, Davis v. Louisville Gas & Electric Co., 16 Del.Ch. 157, 142 A. 654 (1928).

What factors (other than disinterested approval) go into evaluating a recapitalization's fairness? The existence of a legitimate corporate purpose for the plan would seem to be an important criteria.[79] Paralleling our discussion of freeze-outs, fairness also involves comparing the value of the stock the shareholders possessed before the recapitalization, with the value of the stock the shareholders had after the transaction.[80] Notice how much more difficult a task this can present with a recapitalization than with a freeze-out, since now the parties might not only offer conflicting evidence on what the stock was worth to start with, but also the parties might offer conflicting evidence on what the stock is worth after the recapitalization. Moreover, the fairness of a recapitalization can involve a lot of comparing "apples to oranges." For example, a recapitalization might involve the holders of one class of stock agreeing to reduce the voting power of their shares in exchange for an increased equity interest.[81] Historically, many recapitalizations have involved a sacrifice by holders of preferred shares—such as giving up the right to dividends in arrears or lowering a liquidation preference. Proponents of such a plan typically justify the sacrifice as necessary for the corporate welfare. Even if true, the question arises as to what extent it is fair to impose this sacrifice upon preferred shares rather than upon the common. Specifically, taking their cue from bankruptcy law,[82] holders of the preferred often insist that they are entitled to receive stock or securities in the recapitalization with a value at least equal to the preferred's liquidation preference, plus any dividend arrearage, before the holders of the common stock get to retain any continuing interest in the corporation. By and large, however, state courts have not accepted this argument.[83]

79. *E.g.*, Honigman v. Green Giant Co., 208 F.Supp. 754 (D.Minn.1961), *aff'd*, 309 F.2d 667 (8th Cir.1962).

80. *E.g.*, Kamena v. Janssen Dairy Corp., 133 N.J.Eq. 214, 31 A.2d 200 (Ch. 1943), *aff'd*, 134 N.J.Eq. 359, 35 A.2d 894 (Err. & App. 1944).

81. Honigman v. Green Giant Co., 208 F.Supp. 754 (D.Minn.1961), *aff'd*, 309 F.2d 667 (8th Cir.1962).

82. *E.g.*, In re Childs Co., 69 F.Supp. 856 (S.D.N.Y.1946).

83. *E.g.*, Bove v. Community Hotel Corp., 105 R.I. 36, 249 A.2d 89 (1969).

Appendix

RESEARCHING CORPORATION LAW ON WESTLAW®

Analysis

Section 1. Introduction

Corporation Law provides a strong base for analyzing even the most complex problem involving the law of corporations. Whether your research requires examination of case law, statutes, expert commentary or other materials, West books and Westlaw are excellent sources of information.

To keep you abreast of current developments, Westlaw provides frequently updated databases. With Westlaw, you have unparalleled legal research resources at your fingertips.

Additional Resources

If you have not previously used Westlaw or have questions not covered in this appendix, call the West Group Reference Attorneys at 1–800–REF–

ATTY (1–800–733–2889). The West Group Reference Attorneys are trained, licensed attorneys, available 24 hours a day to assist you with your Westlaw search questions. For information on subscribing to Westlaw, call 1–800–762–5272.

Section 2.   Westlaw Databases

Each database on Westlaw is assigned an abbreviation called an *identifier*, which you use to access the database. You can find identifiers for all databases in the online Westlaw Directory and in the printed *Westlaw Database Directory*. When you need to know more detailed information about a database, use Scope. Scope contains coverage information, lists of related databases and valuable search tips. To access Scope, click **Scope** after you access the database.

The following chart lists Westlaw databases that contain information pertaining to business organizations law. On Westlaw, corporation law is categorized under business organizations law. For a complete list of business organizations law databases, see the online Westlaw Directory or the printed *Westlaw Database Directory*. Because new information is continually being added to Westlaw, you should also check Welcome to Westlaw and the Westlaw Directory for new database information.

Selected Business Organizations Law Databases on Westlaw

Database	Identifier	Coverage
Case Law		
Delaware Business Organizations Cases (Delaware & Federal)	DEBUS	Varies by source
Delaware Business Organizations Cases (Federal Courts)	DEBUS–FED	Begins with 1789
Multistate Business Organizations Cases	MBUS–CS	Varies by state
Individual State Business Organizations Cases	XXBUS–CS (where XX is a state's two-letter postal abbreviation, e.g., FLBUS–CS)	Varies by state
Daily Reports and Current Developments		
BNA Corporate Counsel Daily	BNA–CCD	Begins with June 1993
BNA International Business & Finance Daily	BNA–IBFD	Begins with January 1991

CCH Business Franchise Guide	CCH–BFG	Current volumes
Daily Report for Executives	BNA–DER	Begins with January 1986
Westlaw Topical Highlights–Business Organizations	WTH–BUS	Current data

Public Information, Records and Filings

U.S. & Canada Business Finder Records	BUSFIND–ALL	Current data
U.S. Business Finder Records	BUSFIND–US	Current data
Canada Business Finder Records	. BUSFIND–CANADA	Current data
Individual State Business Finder Records	XX–BUSFIND (where XX is a state's two-letter postal abbreviation, e.g., NY–BUSFIND)	Current data
"Doing Business As" Records	. ALL–DBA	Begins with January 1990
Individual State "Doing Business As" Records	XX–DBA (where XX is a state's two-letter postal abbreviation, e.g., MN–DBA)	Begins with January 1990
Corporate & Limited Partnership Records, Combined	CORP–ALL	Current data
Individual State Corporate & Limited Partnership Records	XX–CORP (where XX is a state's two-letter postal abbreviation, e.g., CA–CORP)	Current data
Dun & Bradstreet Business Records Plus	DUNBR	Current data
Individual State Dun & Bradstreet Business Records Plus	XX–DUNBR (where XX is a state's two-letter postal abbreviation, e.g., CA–DUNBR)	Current data
Executive Affiliation Records	EA–ALL	Current data
Litigation Preparation Records	LITPREP–ALL	Current data
Individual State Litigation Preparation Records	XX–LITPREP (where XX is a state's two-letter postal abbreviation, e.g., AK–LITPREP)	Current data

Uniform Commercial Code Records, Combined	UCC–ALL	Varies by state
Individual State Uniform Commercial Code Records	XX–UCC (where XX is a state's two-letter postal abbreviation, e.g., ND–UCC)	Varies by state

Legal Periodicals, Forms and News

Business Organizations–Law Reviews, Texts & Bar Journals	BUS–TP	Varies by publication
Forms–All	FORMS–ALL	Varies by source
Business Organizations News	BUSNEWS	Varies by source

Directories

West Legal Directory®–Corporate Counsel	WLD–CORPCO	. Current data
West Legal Directory–Corporations and Business Organizations	WLD–BUS	Current data

Section 3. Retrieving a Document with a Citation: Find and Hypertext Links

3.1   Find

Find is a Westlaw service that allows you to retrieve a document by entering its citation. Find allows you to retrieve documents from anywhere in Westlaw without accessing or changing databases. Find is available for many documents, including case law (state and federal), the *United States Code Annotated*®, state statutes, administrative materials, and texts and periodicals.

To use Find, simply access the Find service and type the citation. The following list provides some examples:

To Find This Document	Access Find and Type
U.S. v. Bestfoods, 118 S. Ct. 1876 (1998)	**118 sct 1876**
Del. Code Ann. tit. 8, § 106	**8 de st 106**
13 C.F.R. § 102.55	**13 cfr 102.55**
Public Law No. 106–9	**pl 106–9**
Federal Rules of Civil Procedure Rule 23.1	**frcp 23.1**
55 Bus. Law. 625	**55 buslaw 625**

For a complete list of publications that can be retrieved with Find and their abbreviations, consult the Publications List after accessing Find.

3.2 Hypertext Links

Use hypertext links to move from one location to another on Westlaw. For example, use hypertext links to go directly from the statute, case or law review article you are viewing to a cited statute, case or article; from a headnote to the corresponding text in the opinion; or from an entry in a statutes index database to the full text of the statute.

Section 4. Searching with Natural Language

Overview: With Natural Language, you can retrieve documents by simply describing your issue in plain English. If you are a relatively new Westlaw user, Natural Language searching can make it easier for you to retrieve cases that are on point. If you are an experienced Westlaw user, Natural Language gives you a valuable alternative search method.

When you enter a Natural Language description, Westlaw automatically identifies legal phrases, removes common words and generates variations of terms in your description. Westlaw then searches for the concepts in your description. Concepts may include significant terms, phrases, legal citations or topic and key numbers. Westlaw retrieves the 20 documents that most closely match your description, beginning with the document most likely to match.

4.1 Natural Language Search

Access a database, such as Multistate Business Organizations–Cases database (MBUS–CS). In the text box, type a Natural Language description such as the following:

who has the burden of proving director conflicts of interest

4.2 Next Command

Westlaw displays the 20 documents that most closely match your description, beginning with the document most likely to match. If you want to view additional documents, use the Next command or click the **Document** arrow at the bottom of the page.

4.3 Natural Language Browse Commands

Best Mode: To display the best portion (the portion that most closely matches your description) of each document in your search result, choose the **Best Section** or **Best** arrow at the bottom of the window or page.

Standard Browsing Commands: You can also browse your Natural Language search result using Westlaw features such as the citations list, Locate and the term arrows. When you browse your Natural Language search result using the term arrows, the five portions of each document that are most likely to match your description are displayed.

Section 5. Searching with Terms and Connectors

Overview: With Terms and Connectors searching, you enter a query, which consists of key terms from your issue and connectors specifying the relationship between these terms.

Terms and Connectors searching is useful when you want to retrieve a document for which you know specific details, such as the title or the fact situation. Terms and Connectors searching is also useful when you want to retrieve documents relating to a specific issue.

5.1 Terms

Plurals and Possessives: Plurals are automatically retrieved when you enter the singular form of a term. This is true for both regular and irregular plurals (e.g., **child** retrieves *children*). If you enter the plural form of a term, you will not retrieve the singular form.

If you enter the nonpossessive form of a term, Westlaw automatically retrieves the possessive form as well. However, if you enter the possessive form, only the possessive form is retrieved.

Automatic Equivalencies: Some terms have alternative forms or equivalencies; for example, *5* and *five* are equivalent terms. Westlaw automatically retrieves equivalent terms. The *Westlaw Reference Manual* contains a list of equivalent terms.

Compound Words, Abbreviations and Acronyms: When a compound word is one of your search terms, use a hyphen to retrieve all forms of the word. For example, the term **along-side** retrieves *along-side, alongside* and *along side*.

When using an abbreviation or acronym as a search term, place a period after each of the letters to retrieve any of its forms. For example, the term **s.e.c.** retrieves *sec, s.e.c., s e c* and *s. e. c.* Note: The abbreviation does *not* retrieve *securities and exchange commission*, so remember to add additional alternative terms to your query such as **"securities and exchange commission"**.

The Root Expander and the Universal Character: When you use the Terms and Connectors search method, placing the root expander (!) at the end of a root term generates all other terms with that root. For example, adding the ! to the root *corp* in the query

"corp! domicile"

instructs Westlaw to retrieve such terms as *corporate, corporation* and *corporation's*.

The universal character (*) stands for one character and can be inserted in the middle or at the end of a term. For example, the term

withdr*w

will retrieve *withdraw* and *withdrew*. Adding three asterisks to the root *elect*

elect*

instructs Westlaw to retrieve all forms of the root with up to three additional characters. Terms such as *elected* or *election* are retrieved by this query. However, terms with more than three letters following the root, such as *electronic,* are not retrieved. Plurals are always retrieved, even if more than three letters follow the root.

Phrase Searching: To search for an exact phrase, place it within quotation marks. For example, to search for references to *new business rule*, type **"new business rule"**. When you are using the Terms and Connectors search method, you should use phrase searching only if you are certain that the terms in the phrase will not appear in any other order.

5.2 Alternative Terms

After selecting the terms for your query, consider which alternative terms are necessary. For example, if you are searching for the term *admissible*, you might also want to search for the term *inadmissible*. You should consider both synonyms and antonyms as alternative terms. You can also use the Westlaw thesaurus to add alternative terms to your query.

5.3 Connectors

After selecting terms and alternative terms for your query, use connectors to specify the relationship that should exist between search terms in your retrieved documents. The connectors are described below:

Use:	To retrieve documents with:	Example:
& (and)	both terms	**fraud! & fine**
or (space)	either term or both terms	**abstention abstain!**
/p	search terms in the same paragraph	**368(a) /p reorganiz!**
/s	search terms in the same sentence	**disinterested /s director**
+s	the first search term preceding the second within the same sentence	**corp! +s domicile**
/n	search terms within "n" terms of each other (where "n" is a number)	**charitable /3 organization**
+n	the first search term preceding the second by "n" terms (where "n" is a number)	**real +3 property**
" "	search terms appearing in the same order as in the quotation marks	**"net operating loss"**

Use:	To exclude documents with:	Example:
% (but not)	search terms following the %	**r.i.c.o. % puerto porto +3 rico**

5.4 Field Restrictions

Overview: Documents in each Westlaw database consist of several segments, or fields. One field may contain the citation, another the title, another the synopsis and so forth. Not all databases contain the same fields. Also depending on the database, fields with the same name may contain different types of information.

To view a list of fields for a specific database and their contents, see Scope for that database. Note that in some databases not every field is available for every document.

To retrieve only those documents containing your search terms in a specific field, restrict your search to that field. To restrict your search to a specific field, type the field name or abbreviation followed by your search terms enclosed in parentheses. For example, to retrieve a tax case titled *DiGiacobbe v. Sestak,* access the Delaware Business Organizations Cases database (DEBUS–CS) and search for your terms in the title field (ti):

ti(sestak)

The fields discussed below are available in Westlaw databases you might use for researching tax law issues.

Digest and Synopsis Fields: The digest (di) and synopsis (sy) fields, added to case law databases by West's attorney-editors, summarize the main points of a case. The synopsis field contains a brief description of a case. The digest field contains the topic and headnote fields and includes the complete hierarchy of concepts used by West's editors to classify the headnotes to specific West digest topic and key numbers. Restricting your search to the synopsis and digest fields limits your result to cases in which your terms are related to a major issue in the case.

Consider restricting your search to one or both of these fields if

● you are searching for common terms or terms with more than one meaning, and you need to narrow your search; or

● you cannot narrow your search by using a smaller database.

For example, to retrieve New York cases that discuss a loss of corporate opportunity, access the New York Business Organizations Cases database (NYBUS–CS) and type the following query:

sy,di(los! /s "corporate opportunity")

Headnote Field: The headnote field (he) is part of the digest field but does not contain topic numbers, hierarchical classification information or key numbers. The headnote field contains a one-sentence summary for each point of law in a case and any supporting citations given by the author of the opinion. A headnote field restriction is useful when you are searching for specific statutory sections or rule numbers. For example, to retrieve headnotes from Delaware business cases that cite Del. Code Ann. tit. 8, § 101, access the Delaware Business Organizations Cases database (DEBUS–CS) and type the following query:

he(8 +s 101)

Topic Field: The topic field (to) is also part of the digest field. It contains hierarchical classification information, including the West digest topic names and numbers and the key numbers. You should restrict search terms to the topic field in a case law database if

* a digest field search retrieves too many documents; or

* you want to retrieve cases with digest paragraphs classified under more than one topic.

For example, the topic Corporations has the topic number 101. To retrieve state business cases that discuss pre-suit demands of shareholders, access the Multistate Business Organizations Cases database (MBUS–CS) and type a query like the following:

to(101) /p pre-suit /p demand!

To retrieve cases classified under more than one topic and key number, search for your terms in the topic field. For example, to retrieve Texas business cases discussing stockholder liability, which may be classified to Corporations (101) or Limitation of Actions (241), among other topics, access the Texas Business Organizations Cases database (TXBUS–CS) and type a query like the following:

to(stockholder /s liab!)

For a complete list of West digest topics and their corresponding topic numbers, access the Key Number Service or the Key Number Center.

Note: Slip opinions, cases not reported by West and cases from topical services do not contain the digest, headnote and topic fields.

Prelim and Caption Fields: When searching in a database containing statutes, rules or regulations, restrict your search to the prelim (pr) and caption (ca) fields to retrieve documents in which your terms are important enough to appear in a section name or heading. For example, to retrieve Delaware statutes relating to payment of dividends, access the Delaware Statutes–Annotated database (DE–ST–ANN) and type the following:

pr,ca(pay! & dividend)

5.5 Date Restrictions

You can use Westlaw to retrieve documents *decided* or *issued* before, after or on a specified date, as well as within a range of dates. The following sample queries contain date restrictions:

da(2000) & 262

da(aft 1998) & dissol!

da(5/4/2000) & "joint venture" /s "real estate"

You can also search for documents *added to a database* on or after a specified date, as well as within a range of dates. The following sample queries contain added-date restrictions:

ad(aft 1998) & sy("certificate of incorporation")

ad(aft 6/15/1999 & bef 1/15/2000) & sy(dividend)

Section 6. Searching with Topic and Key Numbers

To retrieve cases that address a specific point of law, use topic and key numbers as your search terms. If you have an on-point case, run a search using the topic and key number from the relevant headnote in an appropriate database to find other cases containing headnotes classified to that topic and key number. For example, to search for cases containing headnotes classified under topic 101 (Corporations) and key number 59 (Records), access the Multistate Business Organizations Cases database (MBUS–CS) and enter the following query:

101k59

For a complete list of West digest topic and key numbers, access the Key Number Service or the Key Number Center.

Note: Slip opinions, cases not reported by West and cases from topical services do not contain West topic and key numbers.

Section 7. Verifying Your Research with Citation Research Services

Overview: A citation research service is a tool that helps you ensure that your cases are good law; helps you retrieve cases, legislation or articles that cite a case, rule or statute; and helps you verify that the spelling and format of your citations are correct.

7.1 KeyCite

KeyCite is the citation research service from West Group.

KeyCite for cases covers case law on Westlaw, including unpublished opinions.

KeyCite for statutes covers the *United States Code Annotated* (USCA®), the *Code of Federal Regulations* (CFR) and statutes from all 50 states.

KeyCite Alert monitors the status of your cases or statutes and automatically sends you updates at the frequency you specify when their KeyCite information changes.

KeyCite provides the following:

- Direct appellate history of a case, including related references, which are opinions involving the same parties and facts but resolving different issues

- Negative indirect history of a case, which consists of cases outside the direct appellate line that may have a negative impact on its precedential value

- The title, parallel citations, court of decision, docket number and filing date of a case

- Citations to cases, administrative decisions and secondary sources on Westlaw that have cited a case

- Complete integration with the West Key Number System® so you can track legal issues discussed in a case

- Links to session laws amending or repealing a statute

- Statutory credits and historical notes

- Citations to pending legislation affecting a federal statute

- Citations to cases, administrative decisions and secondary sources that have cited a statute or federal regulation

7.2 Westlaw As a Citator

For citations not covered by KeyCite, including persuasive secondary authority such as restatements and treatises, use Westlaw as a citator to retrieve cases that cite your authority.

For example, to retrieve documents citing the law review article "Juggling Shareholder Rights and Strike Suits in Derivative Litigation: The ALI Drops the Ball," 77 Minn. L. Rev. 1339 (1993), access the Multistate Business Organizations Cases database (MBUS–CS) and type a query like the following:

77 /5 1339

Section 8. Researching with Westlaw—Examples

8.1 Retrieving Law Review Articles

Recent law review articles are often a good place to begin researching a legal issue because law review articles serve 1) as an excellent introduction to a new topic or review for a stale one, providing terminology to help you formulate a query; 2) as a finding tool for pertinent primary authority, such as rules, statutes and cases; and 3) in some instances, as persuasive secondary authority.

Suppose you need to gain background information on the factors the federal courts have considered in determining whether punitive damage awards are taxable.

Solution

- To retrieve recent law review articles relevant to your issue, access the Journals & Law Reviews database (JLR). Using the Natural Language search method, enter a description like the following:

what standard is applied for piercing the corporate veil

- If you have a citation to an article in a specific publication, use Find to retrieve it. For more information on Find, see Section 3.1 of this appendix. For example, to retrieve the article "Shareholder Oppression in Close Corporations: The Unanswered Question of Perspective," found at 53 Vand. L. Rev. 749, access Find and type

53 vnlr 749

- If you know the title of an article but not which journal it appeared in, access the Journals & Law Reviews database (JLR) and search for key terms using the title field. For example, to retrieve the article "The Limited Fiduciary Duties Owed by Corporate Managers to Preferred Shareholders: A Need for Change," type the following Terms and Connectors query:

ti("fiduciary duty" & "preferred shareholder")

8.2 Retrieving Federal Rules

Suppose you've misplaced your rules pamphlet and you need to check the Federal Rules of Civil Procedure.

Solution

- Access the Federal Rules database (US–RULES) and search for key terms in the caption field.

ca(shareholder /s derivative)

To determine the abbreviation for the Federal Rules of Civil Procedure, as well as the Federal Rules of Evidence, Rules of the U.S. Supreme Court, rules of the U.S. courts of appeals and other rules, access Scope.

Note: Local rules of the U.S. district courts and U.S. bankruptcy courts are contained in the state court rules database (XX–RULES, where XX is the state's two-letter postal abbreviation) for the state in which the court sits. Access the appropriate database and search for the rule abbreviation in the citation field (ci), e.g., **ci(usdct)**. To determine the rule abbreviation, access Scope.

- When you know the rule number, use Find to retrieve the rule. (For more information on Find, see Section 3.1 of this appendix.) For example, to retrieve Rule 23.1 of the Federal Rules of Civil Procedure for the United States District Courts, access Find and type

frcp rule 23.1

8.3 Retrieving Statutes and Regulations

Suppose you need to retrieve Delaware statutes specifically addressing issues related to close corporations.

Solution

- Access the Delaware Statutes–Annotated database (DE–ST–ANN). Search for your terms in the prelim and caption fields using the Terms and Connectors search method:

pr,ca("close corporation")

- When you know the citation for a specific statute or regulation, use Find to retrieve it. For example, to retrieve 17 C.F.R. § 240.16a–7, access Find and type

17 cfr 240.16a–7

- To look at surrounding sections, use the Table of Contents service. Click a hypertext link in the prelim or caption field, or click the **TOC** tab in the left frame. You can also use Documents in Sequence to retrieve the section following § 240.16a–7, even if that subsequent section was not retrieved with your search or Find request.

- When you retrieve a statute on Westlaw, it will contain a message if legislation amending or repealing it is available online. To display this legislation, click the hypertext link in the message.

Because slip copy versions of laws are added to Westlaw before they contain full editorial enhancements, they are not retrieved with the update feature. To retrieve slip copy versions of laws, access the United States Public Laws database (US–PL) or a state's legislative service database (XX–LEGIS, where XX is the state's two-letter postal abbreviation). Then type **ci(slip)** and descriptive terms, e.g., **ci(slip) & misdemeanor**. Slip copy documents are replaced by the editorially enhanced versions within a few working days. The update feature also does not retrieve legislation that enacts a new statute or covers a topic that will not be incorporated into the statutes. To retrieve this legislation, access US–PL or a legislative service database and enter a query containing terms that describe the new legislation.

8.4 Using KeyCite

Suppose one of the cases you retrieve in your case law research is *Surowitz v. Hilton Hotels Corporation*, 88 S.Ct. 845 (1966). You want to determine whether this case is good law and to find other cases that have cited this case.

Solution

- Use KeyCite to retrieve direct history and negative indirect history for *Surowitz v. Hilton Hotels Corporation.*

- Use KeyCite to display citing references for *Surowitz v. Hilton Hotels Corporation.*

8.5 Following Recent Developments

As the corporation law specialist in your firm, you are expected to keep up with and summarize recent legal developments in this area of the law. How can you do this efficiently?

Solution

One of the easiest ways to stay abreast of recent developments in corporation law is by accessing the Westlaw Topical Highlights–Business Organizations database (WTH–BUS). The WTH–BUS database contains summaries of recent legal developments, including court decisions, legislation and materials released by administrative agencies in the area of business organization law. Some summaries also contain suggested queries that combine the proven power of West's topic and key numbers and West's case headnotes to retrieve additional pertinent cases. When you access WTH–BUS you will automatically retrieve a list of documents added to the database in the last two weeks.

Table of Cases

A

Aaron v. Securities and Exchange Commission, 446 U.S. 680, 100 S.Ct. 1945, 64 L.Ed.2d 611 (1980)—§ **6.3.1, n. 33.**

Abbey v. Control Data Corp., 603 F.2d 724 (8th Cir.1979)—§ **3.2.2, n. 39.**

Abbott Redmont Thinlite Corp. v. Redmont, 475 F.2d 85 (2nd Cir.1973)—§ **4.2.8, n. 152.**

Abelow v. Midstates Oil Corp., 41 Del.Ch. 145, 189 A.2d 675 (Del.Supr.1963)—§ **7.4.1, n. 13.**

Abercrombie v. Davies, 36 Del.Ch. 371, 130 A.2d 338 (Del.Supr.1957)—§ **5.2.1; § 5.2.1, n. 42.**

Abraham v. Lake Forest, Inc., 377 So.2d 465 (La.App. 4 Cir.1979)—§ **5.2.2, n. 87.**

Abrams v. Allen, 297 N.Y. 52, 74 N.E.2d 305 (N.Y.1947)—§ **4.1.6, n. 99.**

Abreu v. Unica Indus. Sales, Inc., 224 Ill. App.3d 439, 166 Ill.Dec. 703, 586 N.E.2d 661 (Ill.App. 1 Dist.1991)—§ **5.1.2, n. 80.**

Adams v. Smith, 275 Ala. 142, 153 So.2d 221 (Ala.1963)—§ **3.1.4; § 3.1.4, n. 189; § 4.2.6; § 4.2.6, n. 117.**

Adams v. Standard Knitting Mills, Inc., 623 F.2d 422 (6th Cir.1980)—§ **3.2.2, n. 30.**

Adler v. Klawans, 267 F.2d 840 (2nd Cir. 1959)—§ **6.4.1, n. 13.**

Adler v. Svingos, 80 A.D.2d 764, 436 N.Y.S.2d 719 (N.Y.A.D. 1 Dept.1981)—§ **5.2.2, n. 73, 108.**

Affiliated Ute Citizens of Utah v. United States, 406 U.S. 128, 92 S.Ct. 1456, 31 L.Ed.2d 741 (1972)—§ **6.3.2; § 6.3.2, n. 172.**

Alabama Farm Bureau Mut. Cas. Co., Inc. v. American Fidelity Life Ins. Co., 606 F.2d 602 (5th Cir.1979)—§ **6.3.3, n. 201.**

Aladdin Hotel Co. v. Bloom, 200 F.2d 627 (8th Cir.1953)—§ **2.2.2, n. 14.**

Albee v. Lamson & Hubbard Corp., 320 Mass. 421, 69 N.E.2d 811 (Mass.1946)—§ **3.1.3, n. 135, 139.**

Alford v. Shaw, 320 N.C. 465, 358 S.E.2d 323 (N.C.1987)—§ **4.3.4; § 4.3.4, n. 124.**

Alleghany Corp. v. Kirby, 333 F.2d 327 (2nd Cir.1964)—§ **4.3.8, n. 184.**

Allen v. Biltmore Tissue Corp., 161 N.Y.S.2d 418, 141 N.E.2d 812 (N.Y. 1957)—§ **5.3.1; § 5.3.1, n. 18.**

Alley v. Miramon, 614 F.2d 1372 (5th Cir. 1980)—§ **6.3.1, n. 95.**

Allied Freightways v. Cholfin, 325 Mass. 630, 91 N.E.2d 765 (Mass.1950)—§ **4.1.1, n. 3.**

Alpert v. 28 Williams Street Corp., 483 N.Y.S.2d 667, 473 N.E.2d 19 (N.Y. 1984)—§ **7.4.1, n. 47, 51.**

Amalgamated Sugar Co. v. NL Industries, Inc., 644 F.Supp. 1229 (S.D.N.Y.1986)—§ **7.3.1, n. 56.**

American Exp. Co. v. Lopez, 72 Misc.2d 648, 340 N.Y.S.2d 82 (N.Y.City Civ.Ct. 1973)—§ **3.1.1, n. 20.**

American General Ins. Co. v. Equitable General Corp., 493 F.Supp. 721 (E.D.Va. 1980)—§ **2.3.3, n. 62.**

American Timber & Trading Co. v. Niedermeyer, 276 Or. 1135, 558 P.2d 1211 (Or.1976)—§ **4.2.10, n. 192.**

AMP Inc. v. Fleischhacker, 823 F.2d 1199 (7th Cir.1987)—§ **4.2.9, n. 174.**

Anderson v. Campbell, 176 Minn. 411, 223 N.W. 624 (Minn.1929)—§ **3.1.1, n. 23.**

Andrews v. Chase, 89 Utah 51, 49 P.2d 938 (Utah 1935)—§ **2.1.2, n. 29.**

Anixter v. Home–Stake Production Co., 77 F.3d 1215 (10th Cir.1996)—§ **6.3.1, n. 101.**

Applestein v. United Board & Carton Corp., 60 N.J.Super. 333, 159 A.2d 146 (N.J.Super.Ch.1960)—§ **7.2.3, n. 96.**

Application of (see name of party)

A.P. Smith Mfg. Co. v. Barlow, 13 N.J. 145, 98 A.2d 581 (N.J.1953)—§ **3.1.4; § 3.1.4, n. 183.**

Arnesen v. Shawmut County Bank, N. A., 504 F.Supp. 1077 (D.Mass.1980)—§ **6.3.1, n. 96.**

Arnold v. Browne, 27 Cal.App.3d 386, 103 Cal.Rptr. 775 (Cal.App. 1 Dist.1972)—§ **1.5.7, n. 75.**

Arnold v. Society for Sav. Bancorp, Inc., 650 A.2d 1270 (Del.Supr.1994)—§ **4.1.7, n. 101, 102.**

Aron v. Gillman, 309 N.Y. 157, 128 N.E.2d 284 (N.Y.1955)—§ **5.3.2, n. 37.**

Aronoff v. Albanese, 85 A.D.2d 3, 446 N.Y.S.2d 368 (N.Y.A.D. 2 Dept.1982)—§ **4.2.4, n. 67.**

Aronson v. Lewis, 473 A.2d 805 (Del. Supr.1984)—§ **4.1.2; § 4.1.2, n. 17, 19, 26, 27, 36; § 4.2.4; § 4.2.4, n. 77, 79;**

C

D

Dataproducts Corp. Shareholders Litigation, In re, 1991 WL 165301 (Del.Ch. 1991)—§ **3.1.3, n. 171.**

David v. Southern Import Wine Co., 171 So. 180 (La.App.Orleans 1936)—§ **1.3.1, n. 4.**

Davis v. Louisville Gas & Electric Co., 16 Del.Ch. 157, 142 A. 654 (Del.Ch.1928)— § **7.4.2, n. 78.**

Davis v. Sheerin, 754 S.W.2d 375 (Tex.App.-Hous. (1 Dist.) 1988)—§ **5.1.2, n. 77, 84.**

Deal v. Johnson, 362 So.2d 214 (Ala.1978)— § **4.1.2, n. 38.**

Dean v. Kellogg, 294 Mich. 200, 292 N.W. 704 (Mich.1940)—§ **4.3.1, n. 21.**

Debaun v. First Western Bank & Trust Co., 46 Cal.App.3d 686, 120 Cal.Rptr. 354 (Cal.App. 2 Dist.1975)—§ **7.1.1; § 7.1.1, n. 2, 6.**

deHaas v. Empire Petroleum Co., 286 F.Supp. 809 (D.Colo.1968)—§ **4.3.3, n. 81; § 4.3.8, n. 175.**

Denicke v. Anglo California Nat. Bank of San Francisco, 141 F.2d 285 (9th Cir. 1944)—§ **4.3.8, n. 185.**

Derry v. Peek, 14 App.Cas. 337 (H.L. 1889)—§ **6.1.1; § 6.1.1, n. 6.**

Devereux v. Berger, 264 Md. 20, 284 A.2d 605 (Md.1971)—§ **4.3.2, n. 37.**

DeWitt Truck Brokers, Inc. v. W. Ray Flemming Fruit Co., 540 F.2d 681 (4th Cir. 1976)—§ **1.5.1; § 1.5.1, n. 3, 7; § 1.5.4, n. 37; § 1.5.5, n. 46, 50; § 1.5.6, n. 52; § 1.5.7, n. 64, 76.**

Diamond v. Oreamuno, 301 N.Y.S.2d 78, 248 N.E.2d 910 (N.Y.1969)—§ **6.1.2; § 6.1.2, n. 25.**

Diamond v. Parkersburg–Aetna Corp., 146 W.Va. 543, 122 S.E.2d 436 (W.Va. 1961)—§ **5.2.1, n. 63.**

Diamond State Brewery v. De La Rigaudiere, 25 Del.Ch. 257, 17 A.2d 313 (Del.Ch. 1941)—§ **2.1.2, n. 38.**

Diedrick v. Helm, 217 Minn. 483, 14 N.W.2d 913 (Minn.1944)—§ **4.2.8, n. 171.**

Dirks v. S.E.C., 463 U.S. 646, 103 S.Ct. 3255, 77 L.Ed.2d 911 (1983)—§ **6.3.2; § 6.3.2, n. 123.**

Dissolution of Gift Pax, Inc., Matter of, 123 Misc.2d 830, 475 N.Y.S.2d 324 (N.Y.Sup. 1984)—§ **5.1.2, n. 91.**

Dobkin v. Commissioner, 15 T.C. 31 (Tax Ct.1950)—§ **2.2.3, n. 33.**

Dodge v. First Wisconsin Trust Co., 394 F.Supp. 1124 (E.D.Wis.1975)—§ **4.3.2, n. 37.**

Dodge v. Ford Motor Co., 204 Mich. 459, 170 N.W. 668 (Mich.1919)—§ **2.3.1; § 2.3.1, n. 2, 6; § 4.1.5; § 4.1.5, n. 86.**

Dodier Realty & Inv. Co. v. St. Louis Nat. Baseball Club, 361 Mo. 981, 238 S.W.2d 321 (Mo.1951)—§ **7.2.1, n. 43.**

Donahue v. Rodd Electrotype Co. of New England, Inc., 367 Mass. 578, 328

N.E.2d 505 (Mass.1975)—§ **2.3.3; § 2.3.3, n. 58; § 5.1.1; § 5.1.1, n. 9.**

Donald J. Trump Casino Securities Litigation–Taj Mahal Litigation, In re, 7 F.3d 357 (3rd Cir.1993)—§ **6.3.1, n. 14, 22, 24.**

Donovan v. Bierwirth, 680 F.2d 263 (2nd Cir.1982)—§ **7.3.1, n. 11.**

Doran v. Petroleum Management Corp., 545 F.2d 893 (5th Cir.1977)—§ **6.2.2, n. 17.**

Drive–In Development Corp., In re, 371 F.2d 215 (7th Cir.1966)—§ **3.1.1; § 3.1.1, n. 21.**

Dudley v. Southeastern Factor & Finance Corp., 446 F.2d 303 (5th Cir.1971)— § **6.3.1, n. 96.**

Dunlay v. Avenue M Garage & Repair Co., 253 N.Y. 274, 170 N.E. 917 (N.Y.1930)— § **2.1.3, n. 68.**

Dupuy v. Dupuy, 551 F.2d 1005 (5th Cir. 1977)—§ **6.3.1, n. 71.**

Durfee v. Durfee & Canning, 323 Mass. 187, 80 N.E.2d 522 (Mass.1948)—§ **4.2.7, n. 136.**

E

Earthman's, Inc. v. Earthman, 526 S.W.2d 192 (TexCivApp.-Hous (1 Dist.) 1975)— § **5.3.2, n. 24, 28.**

Eckhaus v. Ma, 635 F.Supp. 873 (S.D.N.Y. 1986)—§ **3.1.2, n. 35.**

Edgar v. MITE Corp., 457 U.S. 624, 102 S.Ct. 2629, 73 L.Ed.2d 269 (1982)— § **7.3.3; § 7.3.3, n. 131.**

Eisenberg v. Flying Tiger Line, Inc., 451 F.2d 267 (2nd Cir.1971)—§ **4.3.1; § 4.3.1, n. 10.**

Electronic Specialty Co. v. International Controls Corp., 409 F.2d 937 (2nd Cir. 1969)—§ **7.3.2, n. 113, 117, 121.**

Eli Lilly & Co. v. Sav–On–Drugs, Inc., 366 U.S. 276, 81 S.Ct. 1316, 6 L.Ed.2d 288 (1961)—§ **1.2.1, n. 9.**

Elkind v. Liggett & Myers, Inc., 635 F.2d 156 (2nd Cir.1980)—§ **6.3.2, n. 181, 191.**

Elliott Associates v. J. Henry Schroder Bank & Trust Co., 838 F.2d 66 (2nd Cir.1988)—§ **2.2.2, n. 8.**

Ellis & Marshall Associates, Inc. v. Marshall, 16 Ill.App.3d 398, 306 N.E.2d 712 (Ill.App. 1 Dist.1973)—§ **4.2.9, n. 187.**

Ellzey v. Fyr–Pruf, Inc., 376 So.2d 1328 (Miss.1979)—§ **4.2.8, n. 166.**

Energy Resources Corp., Inc. v. Porter, 14 Mass.App.Ct. 296, 438 N.E.2d 391 (Mass.App.Ct.1982)—§ **4.2.8; § 4.2.8, n. 168.**

Englander v. Osborne, 261 Pa. 366, 104 A. 614 (Pa.1918)—§ **2.1.1, n. 9.**

Epstein v. Schenck, 35 N.Y.S.2d 969 (N.Y.Sup.1939)—§ **4.3.3, n. 96.**

Johnson v. Spartanburg County Fair Ass'n, 210 S.C. 56, 41 S.E.2d 599 (S.C.1947)—**§ 5.2.1, n. 27; § 7.4.1, n. 24.**

Johnson v. Tago, Inc., 188 Cal.App.3d 507, 233 Cal.Rptr. 503 (Cal.App. 1 Dist. 1986)—**§ 3.1.3, n. 125.**

Johnson v. Trueblood, 629 F.2d 287 (3rd Cir.1980)—**§ 7.3.1, n. 15.**

Johnston v. Greene, 35 Del.Ch. 479, 121 A.2d 919 (Del.Supr.1956)—**§ 4.2.7; § 4.2.7, n. 133, 143, 147; § 4.2.8, n. 156.**

Jones v. H.F. Ahmanson & Co., 81 Cal.Rptr. 592, 460 P.2d 464 (Cal.1969)—**§ 7.1.2; § 7.1.2, n. 32.**

Joseph v. Farnsworth Radio & Television Corp., 99 F.Supp. 701 (S.D.N.Y.1951)—**§ 6.1.2, n. 23.**

Joseph Schlitz Brewing Co. v. Missouri Poultry & Game Co., 287 Mo. 400, 229 S.W. 813 (Mo.1921)—**§ 3.1.4, n. 198.**

Joy v. North, 692 F.2d 880 (2nd Cir.1982)—**§ 4.1.3, n. 48; § 4.2.5, n. 95; § 4.3.4; § 4.3.4, n. 106, 122; § 4.3.8, n. 171, 180.**

J.P. Stevens & Co., Inc. Shareholders Litigation, In re, 542 A.2d 770 (Del.Ch. 1988)—**§ 4.1.2, n. 45.**

Juergens v. Venture Capital Corp., 1 Mass. App.Ct. 274, 295 N.E.2d 398 (Mass.App. Ct.1973)—**§ 3.1.2, n. 65.**

Jutkowitz v. Bourns, No. CA 000268 (Cal.Super.1975)—**§ 7.4.1, n. 18.**

K

Kahn v. Lynch Communication Systems, Inc., 669 A.2d 79 (Del.Supr.1995)—**§ 7.4.1, n. 58.**

Kahn v. Lynch Communication Systems, Inc., 638 A.2d 1110 (Del.Supr.1994)—**§ 7.4.1; § 7.4.1, n. 56.**

Kahn v. Roberts, 1994 WL 70118 (Del.Ch. 1994)—**§ 3.1.3, n. 174.**

Kamen v. Kemper Financial Services, Inc., 500 U.S. 90, 111 S.Ct. 1711, 114 L.Ed.2d 152 (1991)—**§ 4.3.3; § 4.3.3, n. 104.**

Kamena v. Janssen Dairy Corporation, 31 A.2d 200 (N.J.Ch.1943)—**§ 7.4.2, n. 77, 80.**

Kamin v. American Exp. Co., 86 Misc.2d 809, 383 N.Y.S.2d 807 (N.Y.Sup.1976)—**§ 4.1.2; § 4.1.2, n. 29.**

Kaplan v. Fenton, 278 A.2d 834 (Del. Supr.1971)—**§ 4.2.8, n. 152.**

Kaplan v. Peat, Marwick, Mitchell & Co., 540 A.2d 726 (Del.Supr.1988)—**§ 4.3.3, n. 67, 72.**

Kaplan v. Wyatt, 499 A.2d 1184 (Del. Supr.1985)—**§ 4.3.4, n. 121.**

Kardon v. National Gypsum Co., 73 F.Supp. 798 (E.D.Pa.1947)—**§ 6.3.1, n. 55.**

Karfunkel v. United StatesLIFE Corp., 116 Misc.2d 841, 455 N.Y.S.2d 937 (N.Y.Sup. 1982)—**§ 2.3.3, n. 57.**

Kartub v. Optical Fashions, Inc., 158 F.Supp. 757 (S.D.N.Y.1958)—**§ 4.3.1, n. 22.**

Katcher v. Ohsman, 26 N.J.Super. 28, 97 A.2d 180 (N.J.Super.Ch.1953)—**§ 5.2.2, n. 100.**

Katz v. Bregman, 431 A.2d 1274 (Del.Ch. 1981)—**§ 7.2.2; § 7.2.2, n. 66.**

Katz v. Oak Industries Inc., 508 A.2d 873 (Del.Ch.1986)—**§ 2.2.2; § 2.2.2, n. 16; § 4.1.5, n. 78.**

Katzowitz v. Sidler, 301 N.Y.S.2d 470, 249 N.E.2d 359 (N.Y.1969)—**§ 2.1.3; § 2.1.3, n. 80.**

Kauffman Mut. Fund Actions, In re, 479 F.2d 257 (1st Cir.1973)—**§ 4.3.3, n. 69.**

K.C. Roofing Center v. On Top Roofing, Inc., 807 S.W.2d 545 (Mo.App. W.D. 1991)—**§ 1.5.3, n. 32; § 1.5.5, n. 49.**

Keenan v. Eshleman, 23 Del.Ch. 234, 2 A.2d 904 (Del.Supr.1938)—**§ 4.3.1, n. 31.**

Keller v. Wilson & Co., 21 Del.Ch. 391, 190 A. 115 (Del.Supr.1936)—**§ 7.4.2, n. 72.**

Kellogg v. Georgia–Pacific Paper Corp., 227 F.Supp. 719 (W.D.Ark.1964)—**§ 7.4.1, n. 12.**

Kemp v. Sloss–Sheffield Steel & Iron Co., 26 A.2d 70 (N.J.Sup.1942)—**§ 3.1.3, n. 166.**

Kemp & Beatley, Inc., Matter of, 484 N.Y.S.2d 799, 473 N.E.2d 1173 (N.Y. 1984)—**§ 5.1.2; § 5.1.2, n. 69.**

Kennedy v. Josephthal & Co., Inc., 814 F.2d 798 (1st Cir.1987)—**§ 6.3.1, n. 72.**

Kennerson v. Burbank Amusement Co., 120 Cal.App.2d 157, 260 P.2d 823 (Cal.App. 1 Dist.1953)—**§ 5.2.2, n. 71, 118.**

Keogh Corp. v. Howard, Weil, Labouisse, Friedrichs Inc., 827 F.Supp. 269 (S.D.N.Y.1993)—**§ 3.1.1, n. 18.**

Kerbs v. California Eastern Airways, 33 Del.Ch. 69, 90 A.2d 652 (Del. Supr.1952)—**§ 4.2.6; § 4.2.6, n. 119.**

Kern County Land Co. v. Occidental Petroleum Corp., 411 U.S. 582, 93 S.Ct. 1736, 36 L.Ed.2d 503 (1973)—**§ 6.4.1; § 6.4.1, n. 19.**

Kessler v. Sinclair, 37 Mass.App.Ct. 573, 641 N.E.2d 135 (Mass.App.Ct.1994)—**§ 4.3.2, n. 43.**

Keypoint Oyster Co., State ex rel. Hayes Oyster Co. v., 64 Wash.2d 375, 391 P.2d 979 (Wash.1964)—**§ 4.2.3, n. 39, 42.**

Keyser v. Commonwealth Nat. Financial Corp., 675 F.Supp. 238 (M.D.Pa.1987)—**§ 4.1.3, n. 69.**

Kidwell ex rel. Penfold v. Meikle, 597 F.2d 1273 (9th Cir.1979)—**§ 6.3.3, n. 201.**

King v. Driscoll, 418 Mass. 576, 638 N.E.2d 488 (Mass.1994)—**§ 5.1.1, n. 30.**

N

O

Obre v. Alban Tractor Co., 228 Md. 291, 179 A.2d 861 (Md.1962)—§ **2.2.3, n. 21.**

O'Brien v. Socony Mobil Oil Co., 207 Va. 707, 152 S.E.2d 278 (Va.1967)—§ **7.4.2, n. 72.**

Oceanic Exploration Co. v. Grynberg, 428 A.2d 1 (Del.Supr.1981)—§ **5.2.1, n. 50.**

O'Hagan, United States v., 521 U.S. 642, 117 S.Ct. 2199, 138 L.Ed.2d 724 (1997)—§ **6.3.2;** § **6.3.2, n. 137;** § **6.4.2;** § **6.4.2, n. 25.**

O'Hazza v. Executive Credit Corp., 246 Va. 111, 431 S.E.2d 318 (Va.1993)—§ **1.5.7, n. 69.**

Old Dominion Copper Mining & Smelting Co. v. Bigelow, 203 Mass. 159, 89 N.E. 193 (Mass.1909)—§ **1.3.3, n. 20.**

Old Dominion Copper Mining & Smelting Co. v. Lewisohn, 210 U.S. 206, 28 S.Ct. 634, 52 L.Ed. 1025 (1908)—§ **1.3.3, n. 20.**

Ollerman v. O'Rourke Co., Inc., 94 Wis.2d 17, 288 N.W.2d 95 (Wis.1980)—§ **6.1.2, n. 16.**

Ortiz v. South Bend Lathe, 46 Cal.App.3d 842, 120 Cal.Rptr. 556 (Cal.App. 2 Dist. 1975)—§ **7.2.2, n. 83.**

Orzeck v. Englehart, 41 Del.Ch. 361, 195 A.2d 375 (Del.Supr.1963)—§ **7.2.3, n. 96.**

Otis & Co. v. Pennsylvania R. Co., 57 F.Supp. 680 (E.D.Pa.1944)—§ **4.3.1, n. 22.**

Ouellette by Ouellette v. Subak, 391 N.W.2d 810 (Minn.1986)—§ **4.1.2, n. 24.**

Outwater v. Public Service Corp. of New Jersey, 143 A. 729 (N.J.Ch.1928)—§ **7.4.1, n. 16.**

P

Pace v. Pace Bros. Co., 91 Utah 132, 59 P.2d 1 (Utah 1936)—§ **2.3.3, n. 54.**

Pace Photographers, Ltd., Matter of, 530 N.Y.S.2d 67, 525 N.E.2d 713 (N.Y. 1988)—§ **5.3.2, n. 35.**

Pacific Scene, Inc. v. Penasquitos, Inc., 250 Cal.Rptr. 651, 758 P.2d 1182 (Cal. 1988)—§ **7.2.2, n. 77.**

Pacific Waxed Paper Co., State ex rel. Everett Trust & Sav. Bank v., 22 Wash.2d 844, 157 P.2d 707 (Wash.1945)—§ **5.2.1, n. 38.**

Page v. Page, 55 Cal.2d 192, 10 Cal.Rptr. 643, 359 P.2d 41 (Cal.1961)—§ **5.1.2, n. 43.**

Palmer v. Morris, 316 F.2d 649 (5th Cir. 1963)—§ **4.3.2, n. 57.**

Palmer v. Scheftel, 194 A.D. 682, 186 N.Y.S. 84 (N.Y.A.D. 1 Dept.1921)—§ **2.1.2, n. 51.**

Papilsky v. Berndt, 59 F.R.D. 95 (S.D.N.Y. 1973)—§ **4.3.3, n. 75.**

Paramount Communications Inc. v. QVC Network Inc., 637 A.2d 34 (Del. Supr.1994)—§ **7.3.1;** § **7.3.1, n. 27.**

Paramount Communications, Inc. v. Time Inc., 571 A.2d 1140 (Del.Supr.1989)— § **7.3.1;** § **7.3.1, n. 12, 20.**

Paramount Publix Corporation, In re, 90 F.2d 441 (2nd Cir.1937)—§ **5.2.2, n. 115.**

Parshalle v. Roy, 567 A.2d 19 (Del.Ch. 1989)—§ **3.1.3, n. 115.**

Parsons v. Jefferson–Pilot Corp., 333 N.C. 420, 426 S.E.2d 685 (N.C.1993)—§ **3.1.3, n. 165.**

Patton v. Nicholas, 154 Tex. 385, 279 S.W.2d 848 (Tex.1955)—§ **5.1.2, n. 79.**

Peek v. Gurney, 6 H.L. 377 (1893)—§ **6.1.1;** § **6.1.1, n. 9.**

Penn–Beaver Oil Co., State ex rel. Cochran v., 34 Del. 81, 143 A. 257 (Del. Supr.1926)—§ **3.1.3, n. 136.**

Penn Central Securities Litigation, In re, 367 F.Supp. 1158 (E.D.Pa.1973)— § **7.2.1, n. 62.**

People v. _____ (see opposing party)

People ex rel. v. _____ (see opposing party and relator)

Pepper v. Litton, 308 U.S. 295, 60 S.Ct. 238, 84 L.Ed. 281 (1939)—§ **2.2.3;** § **2.2.3, n. 28.**

Percy v. Millaudon, 1829 WL 1592 (La. 1829)—§ **4.1.2, n. 13.**

Pergament v. Frazer, 93 F.Supp. 13 (E.D.Mich.1950)—§ **4.3.8, n. 182.**

Perlman v. Feldmann, 219 F.2d 173 (2nd Cir.1955)—§ **4.3.1, n. 32;** § **7.1.1;** § **7.1.1, n. 12.**

Peterson v. Baloun, 715 F.Supp. 212 (N.D.Ill.1989)—§ **1.4.2, n. 18.**

Petition of (see name of party)

Petrishen v. Westmoreland Finance Corp., 394 Pa. 552, 147 A.2d 392 (Pa.1959)— § **2.1.2, n. 25.**

Philadelphia Life Ins. Co. v. Crosland–Cullen Co., 234 F.2d 780 (4th Cir.1956)— § **3.1.3, n. 128.**

Phillips Petroleum Co. v. Rock Creek Min. Co., 449 F.2d 664 (9th Cir.1971)— § **3.1.2, n. 66.**

Piemonte v. New Boston Garden Corp., 377 Mass. 719, 387 N.E.2d 1145 (Mass. 1979)—§ **7.2.1, n. 20, 33.**

Pilat v. Broach Systems, Inc., 108 N.J.Super. 88, 260 A.2d 13 (N.J.Super.L.1969)—§ **3.1.2, n. 33.**

Pillsbury, State ex rel. v. Honeywell, Inc., 291 Minn. 322, 191 N.W.2d 406 (Minn. 1971)—§ **3.1.3;** § **3.1.3, n. 144.**

Pioneer Specialties, Inc. v. Nelson, 161 Tex. 244, 339 S.W.2d 199 (Tex.1960)— § **5.2.2, n. 117.**

S

T

Index

References are to Sections

0–314–21191–8

90000

9 780314 211910